DATABASE SYSTEMS FOR ADVANCED APPLICATIONS '93

Advanced Database Research and Development Series

ADVANCED DATABASE RESEARCH AND DEVELOPMENT SERIES – VOL. 4

DATABASE SYSTEMS FOR ADVANCED APPLICATIONS '93

PROCEEDINGS OF THE THIRD INTERNATIONAL SYMPOSIUM ON DATABASE SYSTEMS FOR ADVANCED APPLICATIONS

TAEJON, KOREA APRIL 6 – 8, 1993

Editors

Songchun Moon

Korea Advanced Institute of Science and Technology, Korea

Hideto Ikeda

Hiroshima University, Japan

World Scientific

Singapore • New Jersey • London • Hong Kong

Published by

World Scientific Publishing Co Pte Ltd
5 Toh Tuck Link, Singapore 596224
USA office: 27 Warren Street, Suite 401-402, Hackensack, NJ 07601
UK office: 57 Shelton Street, Covent Garden, London WC2H 9HE

British Library Cataloguing-in-Publication Data
A catalogue record for this book is available from the British Library.

DATABASE SYSTEMS FOR ADVANCED APPLICATIONS '93
Proceedings of the Third International Symposium on Database Systems for Advanced Applications

ISBN-13 978-981-02-1380-0
ISBN-10 981-02-1380-8

PREFACE

It is our great pleasure to invite you to the third International Symposium on Database Systems for Advanced Applications(DASFAA '93). The last DASFAA '91 that took place in Tokyo, Japan in April 1991 featured 65 papers and over 300 participants from 16 countries. DASFAA is an international symposium which especially focusses on advanced applications of database technologies and/or advanced DBMS technologies. Since the first DASFAA was held in Seoul, Korea in April 1989, it was decided for it to be held biennially. So far, response to DASFAA '93 has been tremendous: 52 high quality papers from 12 countries will be presented at the symposium.

DASFAA aims at bringing together researchers, developers and advanced users from academia, business and industry to exchange information and explore new ideas about advanced applications of databases and advanced database technologies.

The city of Taejon, where DASFAA '93 takes place, will offer you as much excitement as the symposium itself, since EXPO '93 will be held from July near the symposium venue. You will experience more than the world-wide symposium in database.

We are extremely grateful to all the people who have been giving their kind help to organize DASFAA '93: all the organization committee members, all the program committee members. We are sure that many of you were considerate enough to contribute to the success of this symposium in Taejon.

Chan Mo Park
Honorary Chairperson

Sukho Lee
General Chairperson

Program Committee Chairpersons' Message

This publication contains the technical papers selected for presentation at DASFAA'93. There are 52 papers, chosen from a field of 109; 39 technical regular papers, 3 industrial regular papers, and 10 short papers. We had one panel session and four tutorial sessions on topics of timely interest.

Many people helped put together the technical program. The program committee deserves a lot of thanks. Each paper was reviewed three times, and to ensure fair decisions, some papers were reviewed a fourth time. A number of committee members did several last minute reviews before the program meeting. There were also a number of outside reviewers who assisted in processing the large number of submissions. These people also deserve a lot of thanks.

We would like to extend thanks to the Ph. D. students at Korea Advanced Institute of Science and Technology. They managed the massive job of processing about 340 reviews and tabulating the results. Special thanks to Ph. D. students Yoosung Kim, Byung-Yeon Hwang, and Sukhoon Kang at KAIST.

Finally, we would like to thank the authors of the 109 submitted papers. Without their contribution, we would not have been able to make DASFAA'93 a successful one.

Songchun Moon
Program Committee Co-Chair
Computer Science Division
Department of Information and
Communication Engineering
KAIST
207-43, Cheongryangni, Dongdaemun,
Seoul 130-012, Korea
Fax: +82-2-960-6743
Tel: +82-2-958-3315
E-mail: moon@sicom.kaist.ac.kr

Hideto Ikeda
Program Committee Co-Chair
Information Processing Center
Hiroshima University
1-4-2 Kagamiyama,
Higashi-Hiroshima
Hiroshima 724
Japan
Fax: +81-824-22-7045
Tel: +81-824-22-7107
E-mail: hikeda@ue.ipc.hiroshima-u.ac.jp

Organization Committee Chairpersons' Message

Since the First International Symposium on Database Systems for Advanced Applications, DASFAA'89, held in Seoul in 1989, the symposium has been organized biennial. But DASFAA is still at the beginning stage. The tasks involved in the planning and organization of the third DASFAA were not simple, in particular, due to the economic recession in computer industries.

We would like to thank all the committee members of the third DASFAA. In particular, we thank Hae Chul Lim and Kyung Chang Kim for publication, Sang Ho Lee for publicity, Myung Ho Kim for local arrangement, Kyu Chul Lee for treasury, Seog Park and Hyun Chul Kang for coordination with SIGDB of KISS, and all the other organization committee members. We also thank to the supports of a number of industries in Korea, Chung Ho Computer Co., Daou Technology Inc., GoldStar Software, Ltd., IBM Korea, ORACLE Systems Korea, and Samsung Advanced Institute of Technology.

We hope that our symposium offers a meeting place to both theoreticians and practitioners in order to discuss and find their experiences and ideas. Also, we believe that third DASFAA would be an enjoyable and fruitful event for all participants.

Organization Committee Co-Chairs
Yoon-Joon Lee
KAIST, Korea

Yoshifumi Masunaga
Univ. of Library and Information Science, Japan

DASFAA'93

Organization

Honorary Chair

Chan Mo Park (KISS, Korea)

General Chair

Sukho Lee (Seoul National University, Korea)

Steering Committee Chair

Hideko Kunii (Ricoh, Japan)

Steering Committee Vice-Chair

Sukho Lee (Seoul National University, Korea)

Steering Committee

Songchun Moon (KAIST, Korea)
Yoshifumi Masunaga (University of Library and Information Science, Japan)
Myung-Joon Kim (ETRI, Korea)
Rons Sacks-Davis (Royal Melbourne Institute of Technology, Australia)
R. C. T. Lee (National Tsing-Hua University, ROC)
Tok-Wang Ling (National University of Singapore, Singapore)
Yahiko Kambayashi (Kyoto University, Japan)

Program Committee Co-Chairs

Songchun Moon (KAIST, Korea)
Hideto Ikeda (Hiroshima University, Japan)

Program Committee

Hae-Young Bae (Inha University, Korea)
Doo-Kwon Baik (Korea University, Korea)
G.G. Belford (University of Illinois at Urbana-Champaign, USA)
Elisa Bertino (University of Geneva, Italy)

Organization Co-Chairs

Yoon-Joon Lee (KAIST, Korea)

Yoshifumi Masunaga (University of Library and Information Science, Japan)

Treasurer

Kyu Chul Lee (Chungnam National University, Korea)

Publication

Hae Chul Lim (Hong-Ik University, Korea)

Kyung Chang Kim (Hong-Ik University, Korea)

Publicity

Sang Ho Lee (Soongsil University, Korea)

Local Arrangement

Myung Ho Kim (KAIST, Korea)

Coordinators

Hyun Chul Kang (Chungang University, Korea)

Seog Park (Sogang University, Korea)

Organization Committee

Chang-Ho Kim (Goldstar Software Ltd.)

Seungku Yi (Daewoo Telecom Ltd.)

Hong Sik Shinn (KTAI)

Bokgyu Joo (Samsung Advanced Institute of Technology)

Bong Nam Roh (Chonnam Nat'l Univ.)

Soengil Jin (Chungnam Nat'l Univ.)

Hyun Seok Kang (Chonbook Nat'l Univ.)

Lee Nam Cho (KFTC)

Kee-Wook Rim (ETRI)

Jin Pyo Hong (ETRI)

Kun Ho Chun (Ssangyong Computer System Co.)

Jinil Lee (Open Tech Inc.)

Heung Soon Ihm (Hyundai Electronics Industry Co.)

Ki Hoon Baik (Korea Telecom)

Kyu-Soo Kim (KTNET)

In Bok Rhee (Daou Tech Co.)
Youngsil Gimm (Hitech Information Co.)
Choon Bong Lim (DACOM)
Young-Hwa Cho (SERI/KIST)
Joo Hyun Whang (The Chosun Ilbo)
Chin-Chen Chang (National Chung Cheng University, ROC)
Qiming Chen (UCLA, USA)
Dong-Hoon Choi (Dongduck Women's University, Korea)
Yoon Chul Choy (Yonsei University, Korea)
A.K. Elmagarmid (Purdue University, USA)
J.C. Freytag (DEC Munich, Germany)
T. Haerder (University of Kaiserslautern, Germany)
Ki-Joon Han (Kon-Kuk University, Korea)
Bong Hee Hong (Pusan National University, Korea)
Hajime Horiuchi (Hitachi Ltd, Japan)
Tiko Kameda (Simon Fraser University, Canada)
Kyoji Kawagoe (NEC, Japan)
Masaru Kitsuregawa (Tokyo University, Japan)
Yasusi Kiyoki (University of Tsukuba, Japan)
H.F. Korth (Matsushita Information Technology Lab., USA)
J.Y. Lee (Postech, Korea)
Tok-Wang Ling (National University of Singapore, Singapore)
Hongjun Lu (National University of Singapore, Singapore)
Wo-Shun Luk (Simon Fraser University, Canada)
Vincent Lum (Chinese University of Hong Kong, Hong Kong)
Akifumi Makinouchi (Kyushu University, Japan)
Serge Miranda (University of Nice, Sophia Antipolis, France)
Shojiro Nishio (Osaka University, Japan)
Maria Orlowska (University of Queensland, Australia)
Jong-Tae Park (Kyungpook National University, Korea)
Seog Park (Sogang University, Korea)
Calton Pu (Columbia University, USA)
Hans-J. Schek (ETH, Switzerland)
Sang H. Son (University of Virginia, USA)
Kazuo Sugihara (University of Hawaii at Monoa, USA)
Kenji Suzuki (NTT, Japan)

Katsumi Tanaka (Kobe University, Japan)
A. Min Tjoa (University of Vienna, Austria)

Panel and Tutorials Chair
Kyu-Young Whang (KAIST, Korea)

Supporters
Korea Science and Engineering Foundation
Electronic and Telecommunication Research Institute
Korea Telecom Ltd.
Center for Artificial Intelligence Research / KAIST
Chung Ho Computer Co.
Daou Tech. Inc.
Goldstar Software Ltd.
IBM Korea
Oracle Systems Korea
Samsung Advanced Institute of Technology

EXTERNAL REFEREES

Amano, H.
Arikawa, M.
Colomb, R. M.
Deacon, A.
Furukawa, T.
Hac, A.
Harada, L.
Harumoto, K.
Hattori, F.
Houchin, T.
Huang, H.
Hwang, S.
Inoue, U.
Iwaihara, M.
Kataoka, R.
Katsuno, H.
Ke,W.
Ke, X.
Kim, U. M.
Kim, W. S.
Kuroki, S.
Laasch, C.
Lee, J. W.
Lee, M. L.
Lee, S. H.
Lee, S. Y.
Leung, C.
Li, K.-J.
Liu, B.-J.
Liu, X.
Martino, L.
Masunaga, Y.
Montesi, D.
Ogawa, Y.
Ohmori, T.
Ooi, B. C.
Osborn, S.
Park, J. H.
Park, J. S.
Ra, M.
Sakama, C.
Satoh, T.
Schaad, W.
Seung, H.-W.
Shimojo, S.
Shin, D. C.
Suzuki, S.
Suzuki, T.
Tamura, T.
Tresch, M.
Yamamuro, M
Zabback, P.
Zhang, Y.
Zhou, X.

CONTENTS

[†] short paper session

MULTIMEDIA

Towards Dynamics Animation on Object-Oriented Animation Database System "MOVE"

Kunihiko Kaneko, Susumu Kuroki, and Akifumi Makinouchi

Department of Computer Science and Communication Engineering
Kyushu University, 6-10-1 Hakozaki, Higashi-Ku Fukuoka, 812 Japan

ABSTRACT

The authors present why and how to develop three dimensional animation database system MOVE. Three dimensional animation system is an important application of mutilmedia database system, because many animators and engineers want the management facility of animation data.

The authors designed MOVE in object-oriented way. They implemented three dimensional animation database schema on a conventional Object-Oriented Database Management System (OODBMS). The schema contains some basic classes for three dimensional computer graphics such as vector operations, three dimensional object, polygon-meshed curved surface, and local illumination model. They also implemented basic algorithm like the Z-buffer algorithm and scan-line algorithm. Using MOVE, users can combine basic computer graphics objects and can build a scene. They can also extend these classes without knowing the details of MOVE.

And interface between simulation program and computer graphics routines is discussed here from the point of view of kinematic constraint and dynamics simulation.

Keywords : animation database, computer animation, computer graphics, animation data model, object-oriented database, multimedia database system

1 INTRODUCTION

Recently, three-dimensional computer animation became an important research issue and have been worked by many researchers. The application areas of computer animation spread from art and entertainment to CAD, robotics and three-dimensional volumetric simulation. Three dimensional animation is comprehensive enough to show three dimensional mechanical parts, robot manipulators, physical phenomena and so on.

The most important purpose of computer animation systems is to generate a realistic animation automatically. The most attractive way of simulation is to analyze the dynamism of a physical phenomenon by the law of physics and to simulate it automatically by a computer. The animators need not specify the details of motion as long as satisfiable solution is generated by such simulation. At present, many animation systems are being developed based on this idea. For example, hand animation[5], facial animation[20] are produced according to this idea.

Roughly speaking, computer animation involves following three activities: 1) modeling animated entity 2) motion specification and 3) image rendering[14]. In the case of simulation-based animation, animators specify the shape, spatial layout, attributes of the surrounding surfaces (i.e. color, texture, and so on) of three dimensional object, light-sources, and virtual-camera in modeling activity. And they specify how animated entities change their states by implementing simulation routines in motion specification activity. These information about the model and the motion are stored in a computer. And image rendering is performed by a computer automatically. In this activity, the computer calls simulation routines and calculates the states of animated entities at every frame and then generates images from these data.

Thalmann et.al. pointed out that the concept of *state variable* of animated entities is useful to unify various animation algorithms such as keyframe, parametric interpolation, kinematic simulation, dynamics simulation and other simulation-based algorithms[11]. In their idea, the motion of an animated entity is represented by a set of state variables that change by the progress of time. From their points of view, modeling is to determine what kind of state variables the animated entities have and what the initial values of these variables are. Also the motion specification is to specify how the state variables change.

Management of the date of such sets of state variables is one of the main problems of animation systems. So, animation database system is necessary, because it is important to manage the animation data easily. In animation database, state variables are defined as database schema, and each value of state variables is stored as a database record.

Moreover, animation systems should allow the animators and engineers to access these state variables, because many animators and engineers often want to use the animation data which they previously made. So animation data should be stored in such a way that it is easy for them to use the data repeatedly. In addition, it is desirable that the animation systems provide flexible data definition mechanism. For example, the users want to use more flexible data definition mechanism when they design new three dimensional primitive objects, new illumination model, and simulation routines. The solution is to make these model extensible.

Recently, several computer graphics packages are developed such as MIT X-Window[25], PEX[24], and RenderMan[23]. These systems don't have animation data model, and they don't have the management facility of animation data. And they can't store animation data to secondary storage device. For example, Renderman has *current-transform* and *object-handle* mechanism to manipulate animated entities, but it doesn't have animation data model. PEX has *locator* mechanism to manipulate three dimensional objects, but it doesn't mention about data storage to secondary storage device.

That is why computer animation will become an important application of multi-media database systems. KUNII et.al. developed animation their database system based on relational data model[17][27]. They studied about their animation data model[17], management of geometric and motion data[18], and dynamics-based algorithms[26]. And they expressed the data-independence of their system, but they didn't pay much attention to the extensibility.

Among animation systems, some lack the data management mechanism, and others lack the extensibility. This doesn't indicates that an extensible animation model has not been implemented. So the authors propose new extensible animation data model.

Many researchers have pointed out that object-oriented concepts are useful for animation data modeling[12] [13]. So, the authors are now designing and implementing new three dimensional animation database system MOVE in object-oriented way. They are developing MOVE using an Object-Oriented Database System (OODBMS). The purpose of system development is to examine about animation data model and its extensibility. In MOVE, all the state variables of every animated entities are managed by system. And every data is *object*. And the basic unit of data management is also object.

The authors implemented basic classes for three dimensional computer graphics, such as vector operations, three dimensional object, polygon-meshed curved surface, and local illumination model. These classes are implemented as database schema of the conventional OODBMS ONTOS[19] using programming language C++[2]. These basic concepts are introduced in section 2 as well as system architecture of MOVE.

In section 3, the idea of *scene object* of MOVE is discussed. A scene object is a frame of an animation, and the data of the scene object are used to produce the image. The users of MOVE can get an image easily through constructing scene object from basic objects prepared by MOVE.

In section 4, the design and implementation of some classes, such as *solid object*, *surface object*, *surface-shader object*, *light-source object* and *camera object* are explained. System extensibility of MOVE is also discussed, such as user-defined three dimensional primitive object, and extensible illumination model.

In section 5, the authors discuss about the object-orientation and instancing mechanism of MOVE.

Finally, interface between simulation program and computer graphics routines is also discussed from the point of view of kinematic constraint and dynamics in section 6.

2 ANIMATION DATABASE SYSTEM "MOVE"

2.1 General Facilities of MOVE

Animation database systems should have computer graphics facilities, animation facilities and system extensibility. In this subsection, these facilities are introduced briefly.

1. Scene object
   A scene object is a frame of an animation. The users of MOVE can get an image using a scene object in this way: First, the user constructs a scene object with the basic objects of MOVE. After the user completes the scene object, MOVE generates an image from the scene object.
2. Vector operations
   All the geometric data of MOVE are vectors and points in three dimensional world. Mathematically, these data are represented by vectors in affine space[6]. So, MOVE supports affine vectors and their transformations.
3. Three dimensional object
   MOVE manages the data of three dimensional objects with curved-surface. The authors assume that all the objects are solid objects. Modeling the soft-objects is our future works.
4. Virtual camera
   Virtual-camera mechanism transforms three dimensional objects into two dimensional computer screen. This mechanism models perspective transformation and deformation. It is a good approximation of the camera with a simple lens.
5. Light-source
   The environment of a three dimensional world which

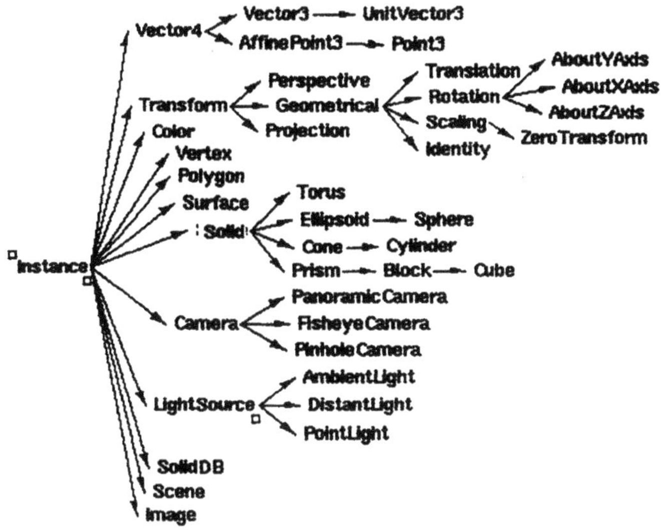

Figure 1: The class hierarchy of MOVE

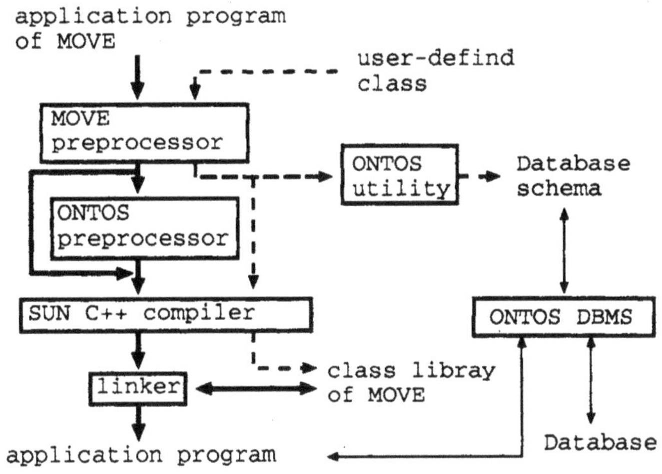

Figure 2: An application development in MOVE

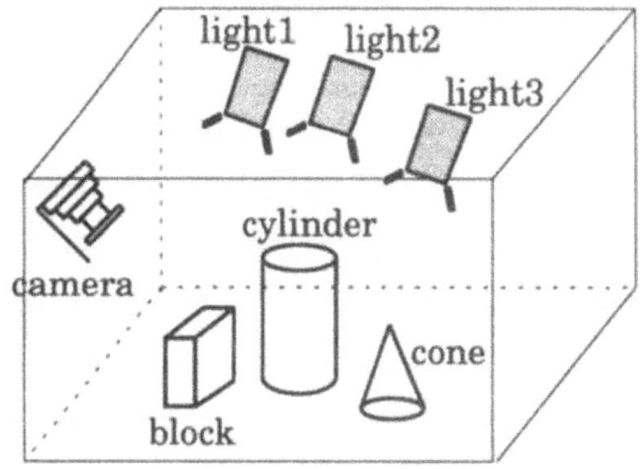

Figure 3: The model of three dimensional world

affects the appearance of animated entities can be represented by a set of light-sources. MOVE has three kinds of light-source models: point light, distant light and ambient light.

6. Local illumination model
To make the computer-generated images realistic, it is important to simulate the illumination and reflection precisely. The color at one pixel of image is calculated from the information about the geometry of three dimensional object, virtual camera, light sources and surface attributes. The equations of the local illumination model are implemented in MOVE.

7. Extensible model
The users of MOVE can define the classes of user-defined three dimensional primitive object, and illumination model (i.e. surface attributes, light-source and virtual camera).

8. Animation support
From the point of simulation-based animation, the interface between a scene objects and their own motion law is necessary. MOVE manages such relationships.

2.2 System Architecture of MOVE

The prototype of MOVE has been implemented on a *SUN SparcStation 2* workstation. The classes of three dimensional computer graphics are developed by SUN C++ ver.2.1. The authors designed classes of MOVE based on object-oriented concepts using Coad-Yordon's *object-oriented analysis*[22]. Figure 1 shows the class hierarchy of MOVE.

The class definition consists of approximately 12,000 lines. The database schema specified by these classes definition is managed by the object-oriented database management system ONTOS. The C++ code are compiled and resulting object files are collected as the library.

Users can create animation data in MOVE. Almost all the animation data are stored in database, and the others are on memory. Users can retrieve animation data which are previously made. And users can invoke the image rendering routines specifying what scene object they want to render. The produced image is also stored in database ONTOS.

MOVE maintains the relationships between 1)three dimensional objects and illumination model data, 2) animated entities and simulation routine and 3) animation data and rendering data.

Figure 2 shows the interfaces between MOVE and users. The user can define a new class which make up for the MOVE's weak points. The user can define the class by C++ and combine the class and MOVE classes. And the user can use the new class as well as MOVE classes. Such extensibility is one of the features of MOVE.

3 SCENE OBJECT

In MOVE, a scene object is a frame of an animation. A scene object contains all the model data that are necessary to generate an image. A scene object contains a pointer

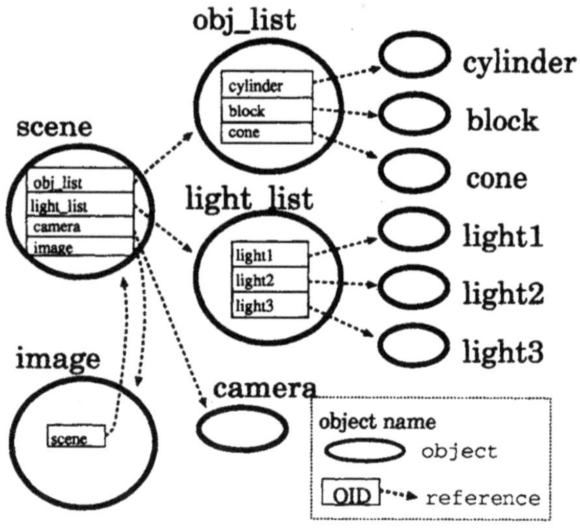

Figure 4: The structure of *scene object*

to the image object, too. The model data is the information about three dimensional world, and it consists of a set of three dimensional object, light-sources and a virtual camera (Figure 3). So, if the user wants to specify a scene object, the user has to specify three dimensional object, light-source objects and a camera object.

The user creates three dimensional objects and light-source objects using instancing mechanism of corresponding classes such as the classes `Cylinder`, `Block`, `Cone` and `PointLightSource`. Then users combine these objects and build a scene object. These basic computer graphics classes are convenient building blocks. The instancing mechanism is described in section 6.

A scene object has a hierarchical structure(Figure 4). A scene object has four pointers as follows, They are: 1) a pointer to a list of three dimensional object, 2) a pointer to a list of light object, 3) a pointer to a camera object, and 4) a pointer to an image object. Here, a list of a three dimensional object is itself an object. And the object has a list of pointers to some three dimensional objects. A list of light object is also an object. And the object has a list of pointers to light objects, too. And the image object has a back pointer to the scene object.

When the user creates a scene object, MOVE initializes these data automatically: 1) List object of three dimensional object, list object of light-sources, camera object and image object are created. 2) The pointers of the scene object are set. 3) The contents of two list objects remain to be empty. 4) The contents of image object is also empty. Now, list object of three dimensional object and list object of light-sources are ready to use. The user can add some corresponding objects to the list objects.

A scene object has two methods. One is the method `render()` and the another is the method `instancing()`. The method `render()` is to render an image, and the method `instancing()` is to create a copy of an object. When the user has defined an object and invokes the method `render()` of the object, the rendering routines are called and the rendering routines store the final image as an image object. And the user updates the scene object and invoke the method `render()`, the contents of image data is substituted by a different image data. When the user wants to avoid such substitution, the user invokes the method `instancing()` to make a copy of the object.

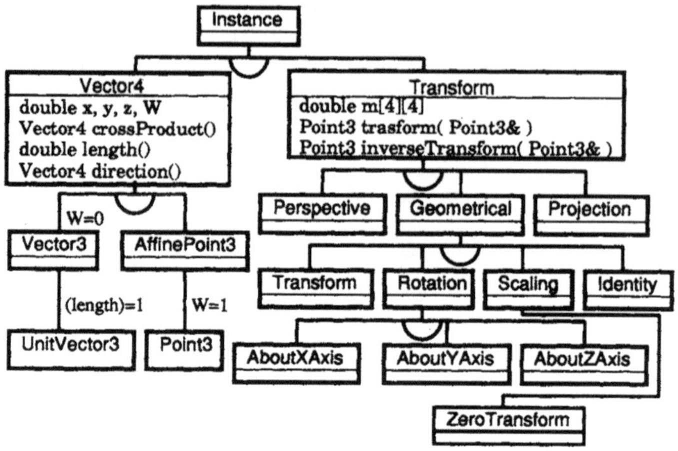

Figure 5: The class design of classes for vector and matrix operations

4 CLASS DESIGN DETAILS

4.1 Vector Operations

class	operations	mathematical expression
Vector3 (x,y,z,0)	addition	$v_1 + v_2$
	subtraction	$v_1 - v_2$
	multiplication	$k \cdot v, v \cdot k$
	division	k/v
	inner product	$v_1 \cdot v_2$
	outer product	$v_1 \times v_2$
Point3 (x,y,z,1)	addition	$p + v,\ v + p$
	subtraction	$p - v$
Transform (4x4matrix)	transformation of a point	$M \cdot a$
	inverted transformation of a point	$M^{-1} \cdot a$
	composed transformation	$M_1 \cdot M_2$

v, v_1, v_2	: vector	k	: floating point number
p	: point	a	: vector in the affine space
M, M_1, M_2	: transformation		

Table 1 : Vector operations

MOVE has classes for representation and transformation of a vector. In a three dimensional world, a vector and a point are quite another, because they have different operators (see Table 5). So, a vector belongs to the class `Vector3` and a point belongs to the class `Point3`.

The vector transformation and the point transformation can be treated similarly using the homogeneous

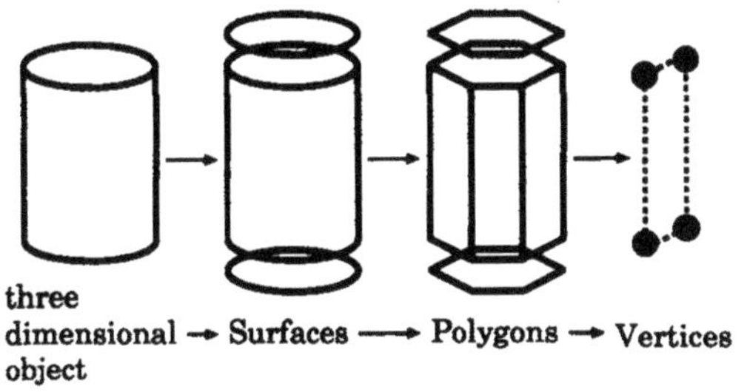

Figure 6: Polygonal approximation of three dimensional object

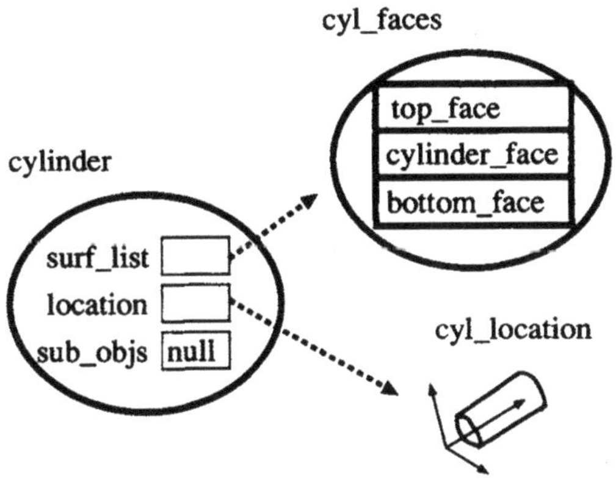

Figure 7: Data structure of three dimensional object in MOVE

co-ordinate system[6]. The class `Vector4` represents a vector in the affine space. The classes `Vector3` and `Point3` are derived from the class `Vector4`. The methods `transform()` and `inverseTransform()` are defined as methods of the class `Transform`. These methods take as an argument an object sometimes in class `Vector4` and sometimes in the derived classes of the class `Vector4`. This is why the class `Transform` represents the both of `Vector3` transformation and `Point3` transformation.

In detail, there twelve kinds of transformation in MOVE (Table 6). The derived classes may have more efficient transformation algorithm than the parent class. For example, the inverted transformation of a vector often needs the inverse matrix. It is time-consuming to calculate the inverse matrix. Besides, if the transformation is orthogonal (i.e. rotation or translation), the inverse matrix is expressed by transposed matrix. It is not time-consuming to calculate the transposed matrix at all. That is why the authors implemented twelve transformation classes.

4.2 The Model of Three Dimensional Object

Three dimensional objects with curved-surfaces are approximated by polygonal facets. For example, a cylinder could be approximated by an octahedron (Figure 6).

There are several researches about the object-oriented representation of three dimensional geometric objects[3][16]. They focused on data representation and query language, but they paid few attention to the hierarchical structure, instancing and user-defined primitive object. That is why the authors designed the class `Solid`.

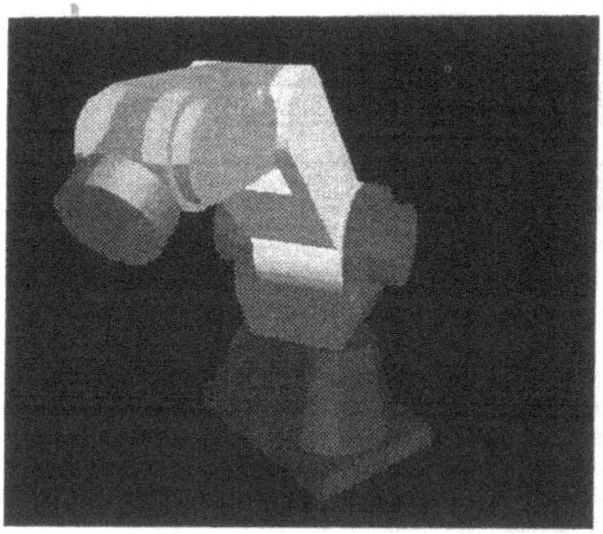

Figure 8: The rendered image of a robot manipulator

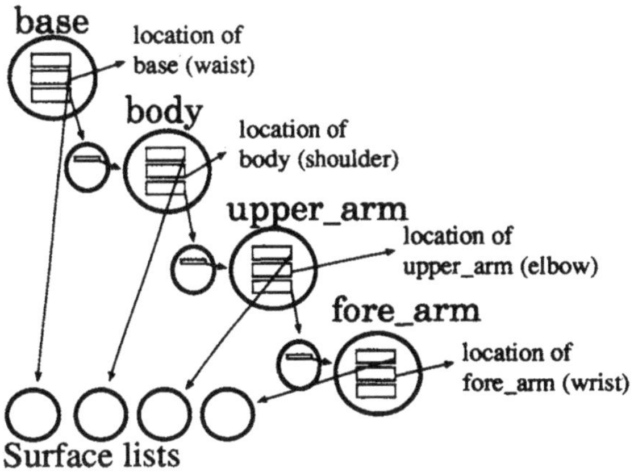

Figure 9: The data structure of the robot manipulator

The data structure are shown in Figure 7. An object `cylinder` contains all the geometric information about itself. An object `cylinder` is defined by a pointer `surf_list` to a list of a surfaces, a pointer `location` to matrix which specifies the cylinder's co-ordinate system, and a pointer `sub_objs` to a list of pointers (in this case, `null`).

MOVE can represent a segmented figure of rigid bodies using `Solid` object. A robot manipulator is a typical example of the segmented figure of rigid bodies (Figure 8). The manipulator is made up of four parts. They are `base`, `body`, `upper_arm` and `fore_arm`. If the `body` moves, `upper_arm` and `fore_arm` also move according to the motion of `body` (Figure 9). But the movement of `base` is not affected by `body`. The location of each part is automatically calculated according to the spatial relationships among the neighbor parts.

Users can combine three dimensional objects to build a structured object. MOVE has seven primitive three dimensional classes – `Block`, `Cube`, `Cone`, `Cylinder`, `Torus`, `Ellipsoid` and `Sphere` (Figure 10). Users can define a

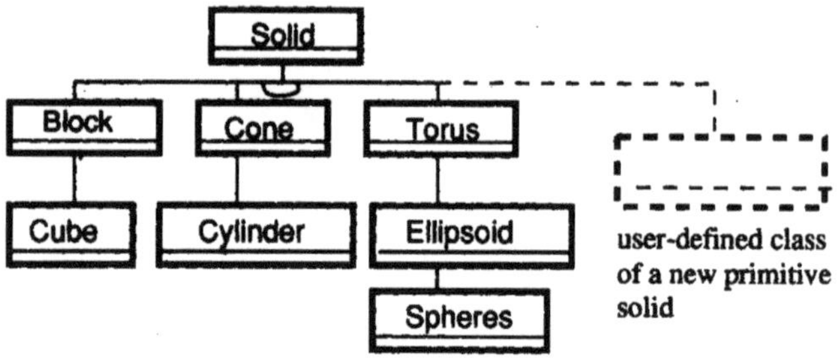

Figure 10: The class hierarchy for representing a solid

new class of three dimensional primitive object: 1) The user defines new class. 2) The user defines the constructor, which is a special method. The constructor is always invoked when a instance is created. 3) The user specifies the shape of the object in constructor. For example, the user specifies the shape of a cylinder as follows:

```
SampleSolid::SampleSolid( int resolution )
{
  ...
 for (i = 0; i <= resolution ; ++i)
   Surface* s->push( x[i],y[i],z[i] );
 this->addSurface(s);
}
```

Finally, the user can define a class of a primitive three dimensional object without knowing the details of the class `Solid` such as geometric modeling and rendering process.

4.3 Illumination Model

Kajiya has pointed out that the illumination process can be formulated as an integral equation[8]. A typical local reflection model is as follows:

$$i(x, x') = \int r(x, x', x'')l(x', x'')dx''$$

Here, $i(x, x')$ is the intensity of light which is incident from the point x' and reaches the point x. The function $r(x, x', x'')$ is the surface bidirectional reflectance function and the function $l(x', x'')$ is the incoming light intensity distribution.

The functions $r(x, x', x'')$ and $l(x', x'')$ is implemented separately.

The routine for the term $r(x, x', x'')$ is called *surface shader*. And the routine for term $l(x', x'')$ is called *light-source shader*.

Light-source shader and surface shader are also objects in MOVE. It is impossible to solve above integral equation and to calculates the solution precisely from two objects, light-source shader and surface shader. So, the authors made one assumption about light shader. The light shaders are approximated by four coefficients, ambient, intensity, direction and color. All the information about light-sources are obtained through these three methods. The assumption is too restrictive to model natural light-source, but the illumination model based on this assumption is good approximation of natural illumination process.

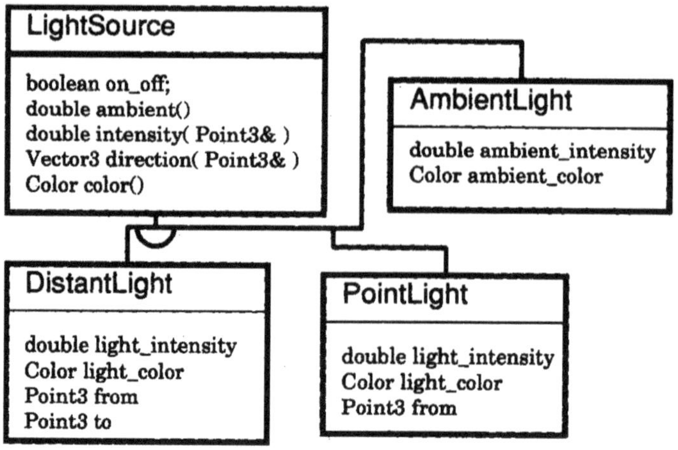

Figure 11: The design of light-source classes

4.3.1 LightSource object

Figure 11 shows the design of the class `LightSource`. The class `LightSource` is a super class for other light-source classes.

- ambient light
  An ambient light is uniformly incident and is reflected equally in all directions by the surface.
- distant light
  All the rays of a distant light come from the same direction. The sun is an example of distant light-source.
- point light
  The rays of a point light-source come from a single point.

The implementation of four methods `ambient()`, `intensity()`, `direction()` and `color()` represent the character of each light-source. For example, in the case of a point light, the intensity of light is:

$$\| l(x', x'') \| = \frac{I}{4\pi \| x' - x'' \|^2}$$

This equation can be implemented as follows:

```
double PointLight::intensity( Point3& p )
{
    return light.intensity /
           4 * pi * ( p-from ) * ( p-from );
};
```

surface material	shading function $r(x, x', x'') =$	what is in DB
constant	K_a	K_a
matte	$K_a + K_d\theta$	K_a, K_d
metal	$K_a + K_s \cos^n \alpha$	K_a, K_s
plastic	$K_a + K_d\theta + K_s \cos^n \alpha$	K_a, K_d, K_s
texture map	$f(x')$	$f(x')$

Table 2 : Five primitive `SurfaceShader` object

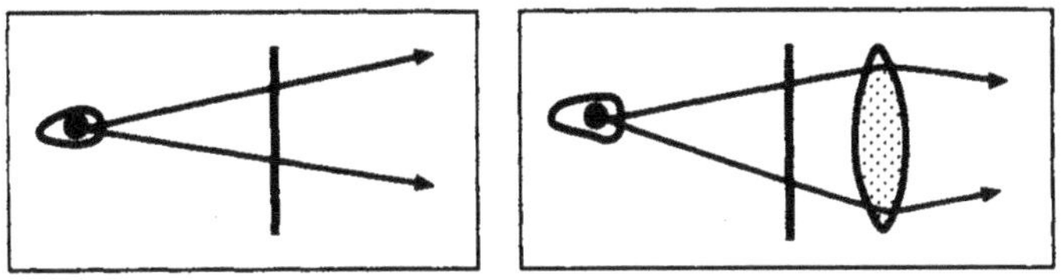

Figure 12: The eyepoint and viewplane camera model. a) without a lens. b) with a simple lens.

4.3.2 SurfaceShader object

The class **SurfaceShader** represents a material of surface. Five typical sub classes of **SurfaceShader**, constant, matte, metal, plastic and texture map are appeared in Table 2. The parameters are stored in the database (in the case of texture map shader, sampled values of $f(x')$ are stored).

Shading classes are defined corresponding to each kind of shading functions. The user can define a new class of surface shader by specifying new shading function.

4.4 Camera object

There are several camera models proposed[4]. Our camera model consists of the eyepoint and viewing transformation A **Camera** object can change the type of the lens (Figure 12).

5 OBJECT INSTANCING

When the user create a new object, instancing mechanism is always used. MOVE has two kinds of instancing mechanisms. One is a class constructor and the other is a virtual constructor.

The class constructor is an ordinal constructor in C++. The *virtual constructor* allows the user to construct a new scene object from other objects already stored in the database. The class constructor requires the name of the class which is to be constructed. So, the user can't use the class constructor to create a new object from other objects in the database, because the user can't know the name of the class until run-time. But, the virtual constructor is implemented as object's method **instancing()**. The users don't have to know the name of class.

In the *virtual constructor* method, the same size of memory as the original object are allocated and the contents are copied. The pointer to the table of method (i.e. *vtbl*) are also copyed.

6 Towards Dynamics Animation

The following procedure generates a series of a hundred of images (i.e. animation). It can be written simply using instancing mechanism.

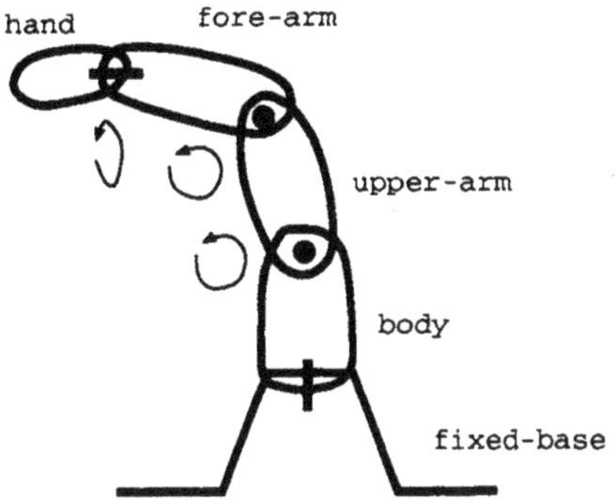

Figure 13: The kinematic structure of the robot

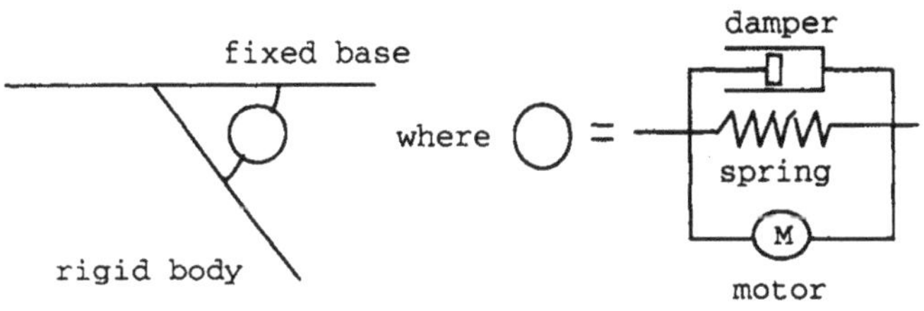

Figure 14: Dynamics elements

```
initialize scene[100] and current_scene;
for ( i = 0; i < 100; ++i )
  scene[i] = current_scene.instancing();
update current_scene;
```

The "*update current scene*" involves kinematic constraints(Figure 13) and Dynamics elements(Figure 14). Arnaldi et al. discussed about the importance of dynamics in animation[1].

Our basic idea is to extend the **Solid** class and to define new classes for kinematic and dynamics simulation. The manipulator has 4 degrees of freedom, then the manipulator can by represented by four variables. The new class maintains the relationships between the four variables and the location of each segment. The relationships between a motor and each segment are also maintained. These are all in object-oriented way.

7 CONCLUSION

In the area of simulation-based computer animation, animation systems manage all the state variables and physical laws of animated entities. To manage animation data easily, animation database is necessary.

The authors designed new animation data model using object-oriented concepts. They authors implemented new animation database system and tested our animation model.

Several interface classes have been defined. Programmers of MOVE can define a new class using programming language C++. If the definition matches the interface class, the users can use the new class as well as pre-defined class.

The authors discussed about the extensibility of MOVE in defining classes of three dimensional primitive objects and illumination models. The next step of MOVE is kinematic constraints and dynamics animation using MOVE's extensibility.

ACKNOWLEDGMENT

The authors would like to thank Yusuke Kondo and Katuhiko Kikkawa Yusuke Kondo converted the classes in C++ into the database classes. Katuhiko Kikkawa tested the rendering routines in the MOVE. This work was partially supported by the Japanese Ministry of Education, Science and Culture under Grant-in-Aid for Scientific Research(B) (Grant-No. 03858007).

REFERENCES

[1] Arnaldi B, Dumont G, Hégron G, Magnenat-Thalmann N, Thalmann D, "*Animation control with dynamics* In:*State-of-the-art in computer animation*", Springer, pp.113-124, 1989.

[2] Bjarne Stroustrup, "*the C++ Programming Language 2nd edition*", Addison-Wesley, 1991.

[3] Eric Grant, Phil Ambum, and Turner Whitted, "*Exploiting Classes in Modeling and Display Software*", IEEE CG & A, November, pp.13-20, 1986.

[4] Geoff Wyvill and Craig McNaughton, "*Optical Models.* In:*CG International '90*", Springer-Verlag, 1990:

[5] Hans Rijpkema and Michael Girard, "*Computer Animation of Knowledge-Based Human Grasping*", ACM Computer Graphics, vol.25, no.4, pp.339-348, July, 1991.

[6] James Foley, Andries van Dam, Steven Feiner, John Hughes, "*Computer Graphics Principles and Practice 2nd edition*", Addison-Wesley, 1990.

[7] James K. Hahn, "*Realistic Animation of Rigid Bodies*", ACM Computer Graphics, vol.22, no.4, pp.299-308, August, 1988.

[8] Kajiya, James T., "*The Rendering Equation*", ACM Computer Graphics 20(4), pp. 143-149, August, 1986.

[9] W. Kim and F. H. Lochovsky, "*Object-Oriented Concepts, Databases, and Applications*", ACM Press, 1988.

[10] Kunihiko Kaneko, Susumu Kuroki, and Akifumi Makinouchi, "*Design of 3D CG Data Model of "MOVE" Animation Database System*", Proc. the 2nd Far-East Workshop on Future Database System, Kyoko, 1992.

[11] D Thalmann, "*Motion Control: From Keyframe to Task-Level Animation* In:*State-of-the-art in computer animation*", Springer, pp.3-18, 1989.

[12] Mangnenat-Thalmann N, Thalmann D, "*The Use of High-Level 3D Graphical Types in the MIRA Animation System*", IEEE CG & A, pp.9-16, 1983.

[13] Magnenat-Thalmann N, Thalmann D, "*CINEMIRA: a 3D computer animation language based on actor and camera data types*", Technical Report, University of Montreal, 1984.

[14] N.Magnenat Thalmann, D.Thalmann, "*Computer Animation. Theory and Practice. Second Revised Edition*", Spring-Verlag, 1990.

[15] Mark Green and Hanqiu Sun, "*A Language and System for Procedural Modeling and Motion*", IEEE CG & A, November, pp.52-64,1988.

[16] Mohammed Mahieddine and Jean Claude Lafon, "*An Object-Oriented Approach for Modeling Animated Entities* In:*Computer Animation'90* ", Springer-Verlag, pp.177-187, 1990.

[17] Myeong W. Lee and Tosiyasu L.Kunii, "*Design Methodology for Computer Animation Database System*", Proc. DASFAA, pp.73-79,1989.

[18] Myeong W. Lee and Tosiyasu L.Kunii, "*Animation Platform: A Data Management System for Modeling Moving Objects* In:*Computer Animation'91*", Springer-Verlag, pp.169-186, 1991.

[19] Ontologic Inc., "*Ontos Object Database version 2.0 Developer's Guide*", Ontologic Inc., Burlingtion Mass, Feb., 1991.

[20] Parke FI, "Parameterized Models for Facial Animation", IEEE Computer Graphics and Applications, vol. 2, no. 9, pp. 61-68, 1982.

[21] Perlin, k., "*An Image Synthesizer*", ACM Computer Graphics, 19(3), pp.287-291, 1985.

[22] Peter Coad, Edward Yourdon, "*Object-Oriented Analysis 2nd edition*", Prentice Hall, 1991.

[23] Pixar Corporation, "*The RenderMan Interface Version 3.0*", Pixar Corporation, San Rafael CA, May, 1988.

[24] R.J.Rost, "*PEX Introduction and Overview, PEX Version 3.20*", MIT X Consortium, 1988.

[25] Scheifler, R.W., J. Gettys, and R. Newman, "*X Window System*", 1988.

[26] Toshiyasu L.Kunii and Linig Sun, "*Dynamic Analysis-Based Human Animation* In:*CG International '90*", Springer-Verlag, pp.3-15, 1990.

[27] Tsukasa Noma and Tosiyasu L. Kunii, "*ANIMENGINE: An Engineering Animation System*", IEEE CG & A, October, pp.24-33, 1985.

RELATIONAL QUERY FORMULATION BY PSEUDONATURAL LANGUAGE TEXT MANIPULATION

Hirofumi Amano

Department of Computer Science and Communication Engineering
Kyushu University
Hakozaki, Higashi, Fukuoka 812, Japan

Yahiko Kambayashi

Integrated Media Environment Experimental Laboratory
Kyoto University
Yoshida-Honmachi, Sakyo, Kyoto 606-01, Japan

ABSTRACT

This paper proposes an approach which allows users to edit natural language fragments given by the system and to obtain a pseudonatural language text describing the meaning of the intended query. Algorithms presented here translate manipulations on the pseudonatural language text being edited into changes on a query hypergraph as its internal representation, calculate possible quantifier scopes on the hypergraph, and translate the interpretation specified by the user into an SQL query.

1 INTRODUCTION

Relational database systems are now considered essential tools to store and process a large amount of data in office works, and widely used by many people including computer-novices. To get necessary information from those systems, however, one must specify to the system exactly what is needed. That request must be given in the way the system can *understand*. For this reason, formal query languages have been used most.

QBE[16] is such a formal query language which is believed easy to learn. In an experiment[13], however, 27% of the QBE queries written by the subjects were semantically incorrect but syntactically correct. As long as a formal query language is used, the system has no way of knowing that a syntactically correct query is different from the user's intention.

To offer users an alternative to formal query languages, many attempts are being made to develop natural language interfaces.[5, 6, 7, 15] Natural language interfaces, however, also have their problems: *natural language processing is not an easy task*. Our everyday language has too many rules and exceptions compared with formal languages.

A more modest approach is to implement a system which can accept only a reasonable variety of queries at the cost of rejecting other questions which are considered rare. Unfortunately, *users must learn the language* of the interface, and must know which sentences are allowed and which are not. This obscures the merit of using *natural* language.

Another problem in this approach is its expressive power. The coverage of queries of such a restricted language has often nothing to do with the coverage desirable to the application, or, is sometimes too small compared to that of formal query languages such as SQL. In most systems, for example, a simple (but also very useful in many applications) sentence like *"Who supplies all the parts with color 'Red'?"* may be rejected just because the interface has not been tuned for this particular usage. This is due to the difficulty in handling *quantifiers* and *aggregation nouns* uniformly within such a simplified natural language translation approach.

In this paper, we present another modest approach, which allows users to edit natural language fragments given by the system and to formulate a *pseudonatural language expression*[8, 1] describing the meaning of the users' intention.

It extensively uses the structural similarity between *hypergraph representations* of relational queries and pseudonatural language expressions in the translation process. Therefore, while users edit a pseudonatural language query by assembling natural language fragments given by the system, the system can modify the internal representation of the query being formulated.

Quantifiers and aggregation nouns are also incorporated in this approach. Since they are formally treated in terms of hypergraphs and their components, the system need not be customized for ordinary expressions like *all*, *only*, *no*, or *at least two*, etc. All the system administrator must do for customization is to prepare a few more natural language fragments for each relation in the database. Pseudonatural language expressions employing quantifiers or aggregation nouns correspond to queries involving set comparisons or aggregation functions. These expressions are translated into various nested SQL queries by the algorithms presented in this paper.

2 BASIC CONCEPTS

2.1 Basic Relational Queries and Hypergraphs

A *conjunctive SPJ query* consists of a finite number of selection, projection, and join operations. Any given conjunctive SPJ query Q_{SPJ} can be transformed into the following style:

$$Q_{SPJ} = \pi_P(\sigma_{C_S}(\sigma_{C_J}(R_1 \times R_2 \times \cdots \times R_n))), \quad (1)$$

where the symbols have the following meaning:

C_S is the conjunction of all the selection conditions;

C_J is the conjunction of all the join conditions;

P is the output attributes;

σ, π, and $\times$ are selection, projection, and Cartesian product operators.

A *hypergraph*[2] is a pair (N, E) where N is a finite set of *nodes*, and E is a set of *hyperedges* which are arbitrary nonempty subsets of N. The union of all the hyperedges is equal to N.

A *Berge cycle* in hypergraph $H(N, E)$ is a sequence $(S_1, x_1, S_2, x_2, \cdots, S_m, x_m, S_{m+1})$ which satisfies the following conditions:

(1) $m \geq 2$;

(2) $x_1, x_2, \ldots, x_m$ are distinct nodes;

(3) $S_1, \ldots, S_m$ are distinct hyperedges, and $S_1 = S_{m+1}$;

(4) $x_i \in S_i$ and $x_i \in S_{i+1}$ for $1 \leq i \leq m$.

A hypergraph is *Berge-cyclic* if it has a Berge cycle. Otherwise, it is *Berge-acyclic*. Figures 1(a) and 1(b) show examples of Berge-cyclic hypergraphs. Examples of Berge-cycles are indicated by dotted lines. A Berge-acyclic hypergraph is shown in Figure 1(c).

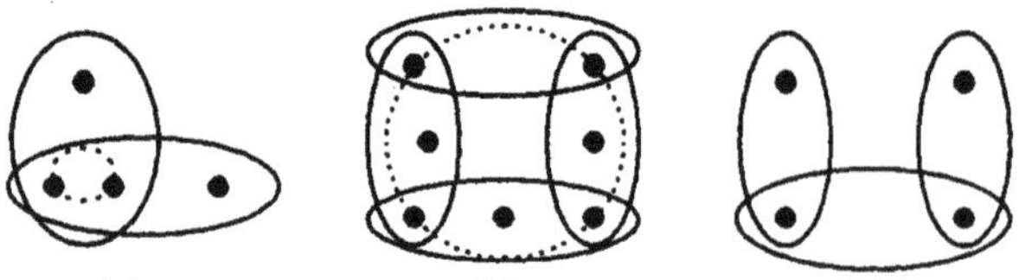

(a) (b) (c)

Figure 1: Examples of Hypergraphs

An *object* is a nonempty subset of a relation schema.*

Suppose that a set of objects is given for each relation, and that the union of each object set is equal to the relation schema. A *query hypergraph* for a given conjunctive SPJ query is a hypergraph such that:

(1) its hyperedges are given by a set of objects which is minimal to cover the union of the selection, projection, and join attributes, where a pair of joined attributes with different names are renamed so that they share the same node;

(2) each node v_A representing an attribute A which appears in a selection condition is labeled with the condition, such as "$A\theta c$";

(3) each node v_B representing an attribute B in P is labeled as "output";

where θ is a scalar comparison operator and c is a constant.

2.2 Query Language SQL

SQL[4] has facilities for querying, data management and data definition. For the rest of this paper, however, we concentrate on its query facility. A typical SQL query construct, called a *query block*, is as follows.

```
  SELECT   ≪ output_specification ≫
  FROM     ≪ relations ≫
[ WHERE    ≪ condition ≫ ]
```

SQL allows a query block to be nested within a predicate in the WHERE clause of another query block. The inner block may contain yet another query block, and so on. In such cases, join predicates may involve attributes of the outer block or a higher block.† A reference by such a join predicate is called an *interblock reference*.

We classify the nested predicates into the following six categories.

(1) **Scalar comparison:** This form of nesting has an effect similar to that of a join operation, but is allowed only when the inner block returns only one value.

$$\ll \mathit{attribute} \gg \ \theta\ (\ll \mathit{query\_block} \gg) \qquad (2)$$

(2) **Quantified scalar comparison:** This form is allowed when the inner block returns a relation with only one attribute.

$$\ll \mathit{attribute} \gg \ \theta\ \{\mathsf{ALL} \mid \mathsf{ANY} \mid \mathsf{SOME}\}\ (\ll \mathit{query\_block} \gg) \qquad (3)$$

(3) **Attribute-aggregation comparison:** This is similar to a selection operation, except that the constant is replaced by an aggregated value returned by the inner query block.

$$\ll \mathit{attribute} \gg \ \theta\ (\ll \mathit{aggregation\_query\_block} \gg) \qquad (4)$$

≪*aggregation_query_block*≫ is as follows.

```
SELECT  {{MAX|MIN|COUNT|SUM|
           AVG}(≪attribute≫)|
          COUNT(*)}
FROM    ≪relations≫
WHERE   ≪conditions≫
```

(4) **Constant-aggregation comparison:** If there is no interblock reference to the outer block or a higher block, the value of this predicate has nothing to do with the result of the query, and the predicate is meaningless.

$$\ll \mathit{constant} \gg \ \theta\ (\ll \mathit{aggregation\_query\_block} \gg) \qquad (5)$$

(5) **Set membership checking:**

$$\ll \mathit{attribute} \gg \ \{\mathsf{IN} \mid \mathsf{NOT\ IN}\}\ (\ll \mathit{query\_block} \gg) \qquad (6)$$

The inner block must return a relation with only one attribute.

(6) **Existential checking:**

$$\{\mathsf{EXISTS} \mid \mathsf{NOT\ EXISTS}\}\ (\ll \mathit{query\_block} \gg) \qquad (7)$$

If the predicate has no interblock reference to any outer block, it is meaningless.

3 PSEUDONATURAL LANGUAGE EXPRESSIONS AND CONJUNCTIVE SPJ QUERIES

This section summarizes the correspondence between conjunctive SPJ queries and pseudonatural language expressions.

Our pseudonatural language text generation strategy[8, 1] is based on a combination of several simple string manipulations, such as insertion of phrases and modifiers. Such natural language fragments are the units of these operation, and must be prepared by hand when the system is customized for a new application. The strategy is summarized as follows:

(1) Determine the attributes which are relevant to a given query;

(2) Assemble prepared natural fragments to form a natural-language-like sentence.

We must determine how to decompose attributes in a relation into several semantic units, and how to attach natural language fragments to those units. Furthermore, we need a set of simple transformation rules to generate natural-language-like sentences.

3.1 Objects and Their Natural Language Fragments

To obtain suitable semantic units for string manipulation, we decompose a relation schema into several attribute sets. We call such an attribute set an *object*. An object is characterized by a simple natural language sentence in which each attribute in the object appears as a noun phrase. The sentence must not contain a noun phrase which refers to any attribute not of the object. If a natural sentence describing an object requires such an "external" attribute noun, the object should include that missing attribute.

Natural language fragments to be prepared are classified into two categories:

*This definition is different from the conventional one.[11] Additional semantic characterization is given in Section 3 of this paper.

†We assume that a join predicate can involve at most one "external" attribute.

Canonical Sentences: Sentences which explicitly contain attribute names, and express the relationships among them;

Canonical Subclauses: Subclauses (relative clauses or prepositional phrases) which can be placed after noun phrases containing attribute names.

A canonical sentence expresses the relationship among the attributes in an object. However, combined descriptions may be necessary to express the meaning of queries, since they are likely to involve several relations and therefore several objects. The easiest way to construct such a combined sentence is to embed a prepared subclause for one object into a prepared sentence for another.

To simplify the transformation process, we introduce some modest restrictions on these natural language fragments. First, for all sentences associated with the objects of a given relation, we insist on a common subject. Second, those attribute names must appear explicitly in the sentences and clauses.

These natural language fragments are concerned only with the attributes of one object. This considerably decreases the customization work compared to the case where we have no localized units.

Example 3.1

Suppose that we have the following database schema:

SUPPLIER(S#, SNAME, ADDRESS);

PART(P#, PNAME, COLOR);

SUPPLY(S#, P#, QTY).

For relation SUPPLIER, we can now make the following sentences which have a noun phrase associated with S# as the common subject:

supplier with supplier-code {*S#*} : *is called* {*SNAME*} ;
: *is located at* {*ADDRESS*} ;

This gives us two objects {S#, SNAME} and {S#, ADDRESS}. The subclauses to be prepared are:

supplier called {*SNAME*} : *which has supplier-code* {*S#*} ;

supplier located at {*ADDRESS*} : *which has supplier-code* {*S#*} ;

Note that the subclauses for S# can be made easily from the sentences above by inserting a relative noun. □

3.2 Translating Conjunctive SPJ Queries into Pseudonatural Language Expressions

Query hypergraphs, defined in Section 2, are intermediate representations for pseudonatural language text generation. We now need procedures to assemble natural language fragments to describe an SPJ query. Let S be the set of selection attributes which appear in the selection condition C_S of Formula (1), and let J be the set of join attributes in C_J.

Algorithm 3.1 (Basic Text Generation)

Input: Attribute sets S, P, J;
Conditions C_S, C_J;
Objects of the database and their canonical expressions.

Output: A pseudonatural language expression describing the query.

Method: (Outline)

(1) **Query Hypergraph Construction:** Find an object set of minimum size which covers $S \cup P \cup J$. Let the object set be $\boldsymbol{O}$. If the hypergraph for $\boldsymbol{O}$ is Berge-cyclic, decompose it into a set of Berge-acyclic hypergraphs. In this case, the next three steps must be repeated for each Berge-acyclic hypergraph.

(2) **Base Sentence Selection:** Of the objects found in the previous step, choose one having the greatest number of attributes to be the generator of the base sentence. Let the object be B.

(3) **Sentence Skeleton Construction:** Find an object in $\boldsymbol{O}$ whose hyperedge is connected to that of B, embed the subclause for the object into the sentence for B. If the object is associated with B by a θ-join (other than '='), insert a phrase corresponding to the scalar comparison (such as *"more than"*, *etc.*). Repeat this until all the subclauses of objects in $\boldsymbol{O} - \{B\}$ are embedded in the sentence.

(4) **Sentence Modification :** Insert a modifier phrase for each selection condition (such as *"more than c"*, *etc.*).

(5) **Formatting:** Emphasize output attributes and format the sentence(s). □

In Step (1), the algorithm decomposes a Berge-cyclic hypergraph into a set of Berge-acyclic ones. In general, the relationships expressed in a sentence cannot be cyclic. Suppose that the hypergraph has a Berge cycle as in Figure 1(b). In such a case, the sentence would be lengthy, and at least one attribute would appear at both the head and the tail of the sequence of words. The decomposition instead makes two or more shorter sentences. Note that this decomposition does not rejects Berge-cyclic queries. It simply treats cyclic queries in a different manner.

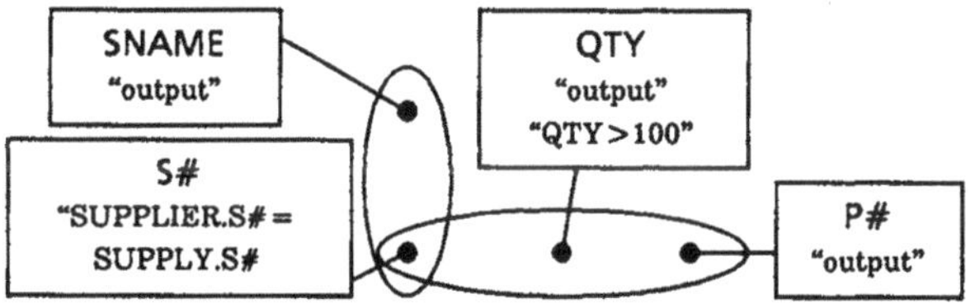

Figure 2: The Query Hypergraph of Query Q_1

Example 3.2

Suppose that we have the following query Q_1:

$$Q_1 = \pi_{\{SNAME, P\#, QTY\}}(\sigma_{QTY>100}(\sigma_{SUPPLIER.S\#=SUPPLY.S\#}(SUPPLIER \times SUPPLY))) \quad (8)$$

The relevant attributes are:

$$S \cup P \cup J = \{SNAME, P\#, QTY, S\#\}. \quad (9)$$

The covering object set $\boldsymbol{O}$ is:

$$\boldsymbol{O} = \{\{SNAME, S\#\}, \{S\#, P\#, QTY\}\}. \quad (10)$$

Q_1 has the hypergraph shown in Figure 2. The base sentence chosen by the algorithm is:

supplier with supplier-code {S#} supplies parts with part-code {P#} in quantity {QTY}.

The sentence skeleton is obtained by inserting the subclause for the object {S#, SNAME}:

supplier with supplier-code {S#} (who is called [SNAME]) supplies parts with part-code {P#} in quantity {QTY}.

Finally, Q_1 is translated into the following pseudonatural language sentence:

List [SNAME], [P#], [QTY] such that:

supplier with supplier-code {S#} (who is called [SNAME]) supplies parts with part-code [P#] in quantity [QTY] (more than 100). □

4 QUERY FORMULATION BY EDITING PSEUDO-NATURAL LANGUAGE EXPRESSIONS

Algorithms presented in the previous section translates conjunctive SPJ queries written in a formal query language into pseudonatural language expressions. These expressions themselves can be used for *query verification* by users.[8, 9, 1]

When a particular query is translated into the corresponding pseudonatural language expression, however, the user may want to modify the query slightly. If a tailored editor can be constructed which guides a user to formulate a legal pseudonatural language expression only and the system can modify the original query following the operations the user performed, it will be useful for: (a) incremental refinement of queries; (b) query formulation on pseudonatural language expressions from scratch.

All that the editor must do is to accept simple manipulations on the pseudonatural language expression displayed on the screen, and to translate them into changes on the internal form without showing them to the user. If quantifiers and aggregation nouns can be used, the user can formulate various patterns of complex queries.

Quantification, however, leads to an important problem: multiple interpretations in quantifier scope. Automatic disambiguation would require situational information or the knowledge about the world, other than the knowledge about the language in use. This is not in the scope of this paper. The basic strategy presented in this section is instead to present those interpretations to the user and to let the user choose the one in his/her mind. After the user chooses the interpretation which fits his/her intention, all that the system must do is to translate it into a query executable on the target database.

4.1 Editing Conjunctive SPJ Queries through Pseudonatural Language Expressions

Suppose that a user is given a pseudonatural language expression displayed on the screen. After moving a cursor to an arbitrary position on the displayed expression, the user may edit it slightly, guided by the system.

Since the structural correspondence between conjunctive SPJ queries and query hypergraphs is obvious, the system can modify the internal query hypergraph automatically.

Let us exhibit the process by an example.

Example 4.1 (Editing Conjunctive SPJ Queries)

Suppose that the user has the pseudonatural language expression in Example 3.2. Now, suppose that the user performs the following edit operations:

(1) locating the cursor at "P#" and inserting a subclause "(called {PNAME})" from the choices the system displays;

(2) locating the cursor at "PNAME" and replacing it with 'Bolts';

These operations gives the following pseudonatural language expression:

List [SNAME], [P#], [QTY] such that:

supplier with supplier-code {S#} (who is called [SNAME]) supplies parts with part-code [P#] (called 'Bolts') in quantity [QTY] (more than 100).

These operations are converted to the following modifications on the hypergraph representation in Figure 2:

(1) adding a hyperedge { P#, PNAME }, and put a label "SUPPLY.P#=PART.P#" to node "P#";

(2) putting the label "PNAME='Bolts'" to node "PNAME".

The modified hypergraph is shown in Figure 3.

With the help of the correspondence between query hypergraphs and conjunctive SPJ queries, this hypergraph can be translated into a new query Q_2 in the form of Formula (1).

$$Q_2 = \pi_{\{SNAME, P\#, QTY\}}(\sigma_{QTY>100 \wedge PNAME='Bolts'}(\sigma_{\substack{SUPPLIER.S\#=SUPPLY.S\# \wedge \\ SUPPLY.P\#=PART.P\#}}(SUPPLIER \times SUPPLY \times PART))). \quad (11)$$

□

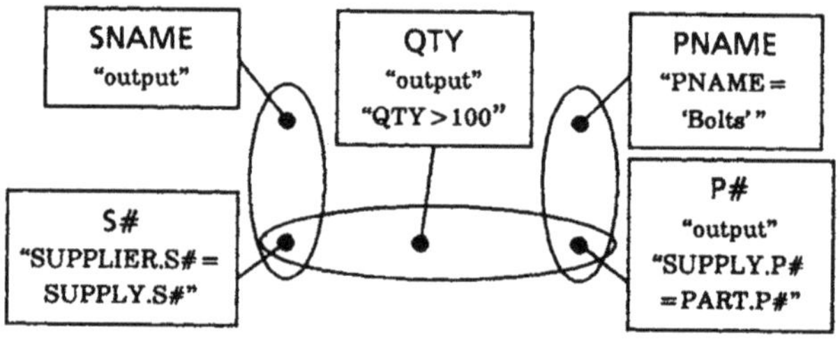

Figure 3: The Query Hypergraph of Query Q_2

4.2 The Scoping Problem of Quantifiers in Pseudonatural Language Expressions

In this paper, a *quantifier* is defined as follows:

a word or phrase which is used with an attribute noun phrase, and which shows either: (a) the cardinality of the set of values for the attribute; or (b) the relative size of the set of values for the attribute with respect to the specified domain.

This is to distinguish quantifiers such as *"all"*, *"only"*, etc. from other descriptions such as *"many"*, *"few"*, etc.‡, or *"three kilograms of"*, etc.§

Suppose that a user inserts a natural quantifier such as "all", "only", "no", or "at least ≪*n*≫". The choices of natural quantifiers should be given by the system. If the system is equipped with plural forms for attribute nouns, it is not difficult to replace a singular form with a plural. If the system can translate the quantified pseudonatural language expression into a formal query, the user can formulate and execute the query without seeing it.

In QBE, queries in this class may involve quantifier "ALL" or aggregation function. An experiment showed that each of these features caused 25% of the errors made by the subjects.[13] McLeod also pointed out that the interpretation of a QBE query is not obvious in cases where it contains multiple set-oriented constructs.[12] Allowing novice users to edit such queries through pseudonatural language expressions thus can be very useful.

Unfortunately, quantified expressions in natural language have ambiguities in quantifier scope. Suppose that we have the following sentence:

Every supplier supplies a red part.

It may mean that every supplier has its own red part to supply. It is, however, logically possible that there exists a red part supplied by all suppliers without exception.

One solution [15] is given by using the following format:

For ≪*natural_quantifier*≫ ≪*variable*≫
which satisfy ≪*domain_specification*≫,
≪*restriction_on_the_domain*≫ . (12)

We adopt this format for displaying the possible interpretations for a given quantified pseudonatural language expressions in an unambiguous way.

The general format of an unambiguously-quantified pseudonatural language expression is:

For ≪*quantifier*≫ ≪*quantified_noun*≫
≪*subclause_for_domain_specification*≫,
≪*restriction_on_the_domain*≫ . (13)

In the rest of this paper, this format is referred to as the *quantification normal form.*

4.3 Disambiguation of Quantifier Scopings

The basic strategy for disambiguation is as follows:

(1) Find all permissible scopings on the hypergraph;

(2) Translate them into pseudonatural language expressions in the quantification normal form, and show them to the user;

(3) Let the user choose the one that he/she has in mind, and translate it into an SQL query.

Assumption 4.1 (Quantifier Scopes)

A *scoping* of a quantified pseudonatural language expression is the classification of the nodes in the query hypergraph such that:

(1) The domain specification part of the hypergraph is:

(i) a single node for the quantified attribute, or

(ii) a connected subhypergraph containing that node;

(2) The restriction part of the hypergraph is a connected, nonempty subhypergraph containing the node for the quantified attribute;

(3) The domain specification part and the restriction part share only the node for the quantified attribute. □

Assumption (1) describes that the domain is either: (i) the set of all possible values for the attribute; or (ii) the values specified by the subhypergraph.

The next assumption just assures that the query has a meaning.

The last assumption assures that a scoping can be described by a plain pseudonatural language expression in the quantification normal form. There is no correlation between the restriction part and the domain specification. The noun phrase for each attribute appears in only one position in the expression. This assumption may eliminate some of the logically possible interpretations. This is, however, necessary to keep its pseudonatural language translation as plain as possible. It is, of course, possible to let the user add a subclause corresponding to correlations between the two parts.

Algorithm 4.1 (Quantifier Scoping)

Input: A query hypergraph containing the label indicating node q for the quantified attribute;
Output: The quantifier scopings on a query hypergraph;
Method: (Outline)

(1) If n distinct connected components shares only q, the scopings are $(2^n - 1)$ combinations indicating which component belongs to which part, except the one with an empty restriction part.

(2) Otherwise, q is the domain specification part, and the restriction is represented by the whole hypergraph. □

Example 4.2

Suppose that the user formulates the following expression:

Supplier with supplier-code [S#] (called [SNAME]) supplies all types of parts (called 'Bolts');

where "types of parts" should be prepared beforehand as a plural. The query hypergraph is shown in Figure 4. For this hypergraph, Algorithm 4.1 generates the three scopings in Figure 5. □

Algorithm 4.2 (Text Generation with a Quantifier)

Input: A query hypergraph and its scoping
Output: A pseudonatural language expression in Format (13);
Method: (Outline)

(1) Put the quantifier and the quantified noun phrase in the template.

(2) If the domain specification part is a single node, Omit "≪*subclause_for_domain_specification*≫".

‡These quantifiers are too vague to use in a database query.
§Such a quantifier should be handled as a selection operation.

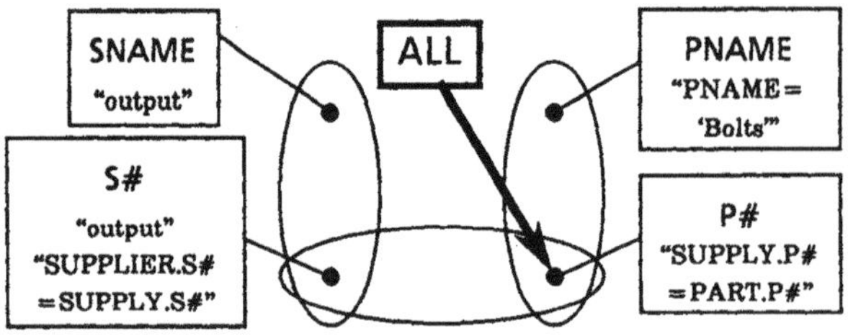

Figure 4: An Example of a Query Hypergraph for a Quantified Pseudonatural Language Expression

(3) If the domain specification part is a nonempty hypergraph, translate this part using Steps (3) and (4) of Algorithm 3.1. Replace "≪*subclause_for_domain_specification*≫" with it.

(4) If the domain specification contains an output attribute, enclose it with "[ ]" instead of { }.

(5) Translate the restriction part by Algorithm 3.1, except that the quantifier must be replaced with "those". □

Example 4.3
For the scopings given in Example 4.2, Algorithm 4.2 generates the following pseudonatural language expression for the scoping in Figure 5(a):

For all types of parts,

supplier with supplier-code [S#] (called [SNAME]) supplies those parts (called 'Bolts').

The scoping in Figure 5(b) has a nonempty hypergraph for the domain specification part. It is translated into the following expression:

For all types of parts (those which are called 'Bolts'),

supplier with supplier-code [S#] (called [SNAME]) supplies those parts .

The scoping in Figure 5(c) is translated into:

For all types of parts (those which are supplied by supplier with supplier-code [S#]),

those parts are called 'Bolts'. □

4.4 Translation of the Chosen Interpretation into SQL

After the user chooses the interpretation which fits his/her intention, all that the system must do is to translate it into a query executable on the target database.

Natural quantifiers introduced in Subsection 4.2 can be expressed by set comparisons or intersection counts involving the set defined by the domain specification part and the set defined by the restriction part.

Example 4.4
When "all" is used in Format (13), this expresses that the set determined by the domain specification is contained in the set determined by the restriction. Let the former set be *Dom*, and the latter be *Res*. Then, this operation is expressed as:

$$Dom \subseteq Res. \tag{14}$$

Some other quantifiers and their set-oriented interpretations are also shown in Table 1. □

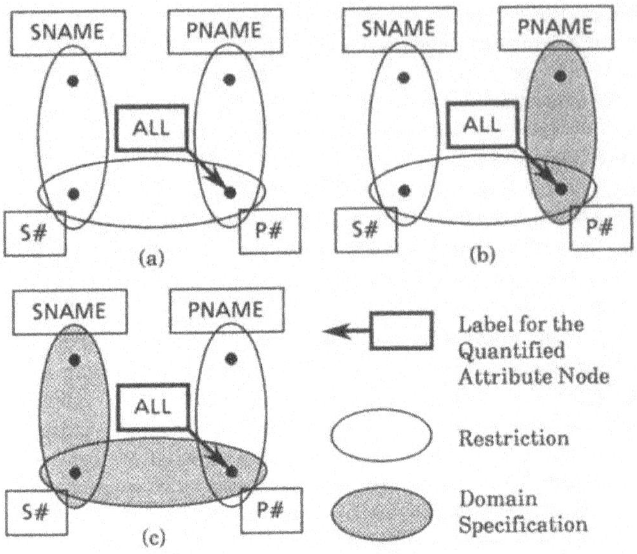

Figure 5: Examples of Scopings

Natural Quantifiers	Operations
"*all* — "	$Dom \subseteq Res$
"*only* — "	$Dom \supseteq Res$
"*no* — "	$\lvert Dom \cap Res \rvert = 0$
"*exactly* ≪n≫ — "	$\lvert Dom \cap Res \rvert = n$
"*more than* ≪n≫ — "	$\lvert Dom \cap Res \rvert > n$
"*at least* ≪n≫ — "	$\lvert Dom \cap Res \rvert \geq n$
"*less than* ≪n≫ — "	$\lvert Dom \cap Res \rvert < n$
"*at most* ≪n≫ — "	$\lvert Dom \cap Res \rvert \leq n$
"*not exactly* ≪n≫ — "	$\lvert Dom \cap Res \rvert \neq n$

Table 1: Quantifiers and Their Set-Oriented Interpretations

When a pseudonatural language expression in the quantification normal form is given, *Dom* and *Res* should be interpreted as the sets of values with respect to a particular tuple fixed on the *residual attributes*, the attributes whose name remains in the expression. These sets can be computed with nested query blocks in SQL.¶ The residual attributes in the pseudonatural language expression participate in the interblock references to the outermost query block.

Thus, the set-oriented interpretations shown in Table 1 can be translated into SQL queries.

An important point is that it can be prepared as a generic query template for each quantifier.

The SQL query templates for "all" is shown in Figure 6. Rectangles illustrate boundaries of query blocks. Dotted lines visualize interblock references.

In Figure 6, the two inner query blocks compute *Res* and *Dom*. Since "all" means that $Res \supseteq Dom$, "CONTAINS" operator is used. Since the set-oriented interpretation of "only" is different from that of "all" just by the order of *Res* and *Dom*, the order of the two inner query blocks is reversed in the template of "only".

This CONTAINS construct, used in the old syntax of SQL[3)] but

¶In this paper, we assume that there is no NULL in the database.

```
SELECT   ≪output_attributes≫
FROM     ≪relations≫
WHERE
  ( SELECT   ≪quantified_attribute≫
    FROM     ≪relations≫
    WHERE    ≪interblock_references≫
    AND      ≪restrictions≫ )
  CONTAINS
  ( SELECT   ≪quantified_attribute≫
    FROM     ≪relations≫
    WHERE    ≪interblock_references≫
    AND      ≪domain_specifications≫ )
```

Figure 6: The Template for Quantifier *"all"*

now abolished[4], tells the semantics of the operation naturally. This can be translated into the current syntax of SQL.[10] The new syntax version employs two-level nesting and double negation.

The FROM clause of the outermost block should contain the relations that contain any output attribute.

The templates for "no" and "at least ≪*cardinal*≫" are given in Figures 7 and 8.

```
SELECT   ≪output_attributes≫
FROM     ≪relations≫
WHERE    ≪quantified_attribute≫ NOT IN
  ( SELECT   ≪quantified_attribute≫
    FROM     ≪relations≫
    WHERE    ≪interblock_references≫
    AND      ≪domain_specifications≫ )
OR   ≪quantified_attribute≫ NOT IN
  ( SELECT   ≪quantified_attribute≫
    FROM     ≪relations≫
    WHERE    ≪interblock_references≫
    AND      ≪restrictions≫ )
```

Figure 7: The Template for Quantifier *"no"*

For other count-oriented quantifiers, the scalar comparison between the cardinal number and the result of COUNT should be modified appropriately.

The following algorithm utilizes the above templates for translating a scoped hypergraph into an SQL query.

Algorithm 4.3 (SQL Query Generation)

Input: A query hypergraph and its scoping;
Output: An SQL query to be executed;
Method: (Outline)

(1) Choose the adequate template for the quantifier.

(2) Decompose the domain specification part into: (a) hyperedges which does not contain residual attribute(s) H_{Dom}; and (b) hyperedges containing residual attribute(s) $H_{residue}$. Decompose the restriction part similarly into H_{Res} and $H'_{residue}$. Add the hyperedges $H'_{residue}$ to $H_{residue}$.

```
SELECT   ≪output_attributes≫
FROM     ≪relations≫
WHERE    n ≤
  ( SELECT   ≪output_attributes≫
    FROM     ≪relation_containing_quantified_attribute≫
    WHERE    ≪quantified_attribute≫ IN
      ( SELECT   ≪quantified_attribute≫
        FROM     ≪relations≫
        WHERE    ≪interblock_references≫
        AND      ≪domain_specifications≫ )
    AND   ≪quantified_attribute≫ IN
      ( SELECT   ≪quantified_attribute≫
        FROM     ≪relations≫
        WHERE    ≪interblock_references≫
        AND      ≪restrictions≫ )         )
```

Figure 8: The Template for Quantifier *"at least ≪n≫"*

(3) Place the relations containing any of $H_{residue}$ in the FROM clause, and the output attributes to the SELECT clause, of the outer most block. If any of the hyperedges are connected, add the join predicates in the WHERE clause of the outermost query block. Add the selection predicates of the hyperedges here, too.

(4) Translate the hypergraph of H_{Dom} into an single query block. Replace the inner block for the domain specification in the template with this actual block. The interblock reference predicates for connections with the hyperedge(s) in $H_{residue}$ should be added to the WHERE clause. The selections in H_{Dom} should be added, too.

(5) Translate the hypergraph of H_{Res} into the inner block for the restriction similarly. □

Example 4.5

When the user makes the pseudonatural language expression in Example 4.2, and chooses the interpretation (b), Algorithm 4.3 generates an SQL query in the old syntax. The result of the translation is shown in Figure 9(a). The current syntax version is given in Figure 9(b). □

5 CONCLUDING REMARKS

In this paper, we presented an approach which allows users to edit natural-language-like fragments given by the system and to obtain a pseudonatural language expression describing the meaning of an intended query.

Its translation algorithms extensively use the structural similarity between hypergraph representations of relational queries and pseudonatural language expressions in the translation process. It does not require sophisticated natural language process-

```
SELECT  S#
FROM    SUPPLY X
WHERE  ( SELECT  P#
           FROM    SUPPLY
           WHERE   S# = X.S# )
        CONTAINS
        ( SELECT  P#
           FROM    PART
           WHERE   PNAME = 'Bolts' )
```

(a)

```
SELECT  S#
FROM    SUPPLY X
WHERE   NOT EXISTS
          ( SELECT  *
            FROM    PART
            WHERE   PNAME = 'Bolts'
            AND     NOT EXISTS
          ( SELECT  *
            FROM    SUPPLY
            WHERE   S# = X.S#
            AND     P# = PART.P# ))
```

(b)

Figure 9: Examples of Final SQL Queries for Execution

ing techniques, and therefore is more feasible than natural language interface approaches.

Quantifiers and aggregation nouns are also incorporated in this approach. These expressions correspond to complex SQL queries employing nested predicates, which are difficult to learn and use for non-expert SQL users. Since they are formally treated in terms of hypergraphs and their components, the system need not be customized for ordinary quantifications such as "all" or "at least n". This means, if the system is properly equipped with a small set of application specific natural language fragments, users can handle a certain set of complex SQL query patterns without seeing the actual SQL source text.

Universal relations are studied as a user interface in which users need not specify relation names.[14)] All that users must do is to state the selection conditions and the output attributes. This facility is achieved at the cost of restricting the possible join paths to those specified in or deduced from the object structure. Intuitively, such queries correspond to single SQL query blocks without nesting.

Instead, our approach makes the user specify the join path step by step. Though it may be slightly inconvenient for users, this scheme works even in the case where the user takes irregular join patterns which are not expected by the database designers. Moreover, quantified expressions can be processed in our approach, and translated into complex nested SQL queries. Such queries cannot be handled in the universal relation interface.

This approach can be useful in a cooperative environment. When non-expert users start working on queries written by other people, the pseudonatural language text generation algorithms[1)] can give easy-to-read paraphrases for those queries. Since the algorithms in this paper allow the new users to modify those queries on the pseudonatural language expressions, the effort required to customize stored queries can be drastically reduced.

REFERENCES

1) Amano, H. and Kambayashi, Y: "Translation of SQL Queries Containing Nested Predicates into Pseudonatural Language," *Proceedings of the Second International Symposium on Database Systems for Advanced Applications*, pp. 116–125, April 1991.

2) Berge, C.: *"Graphs and Hypergraphs,"* North-Holland, 1976.

3) Bradley, J.: *"File and Data Base Techniques,"* Holt, Reinhart & Wilston, 1982.

4) Date, C. J.: *"A Guide to the SQL Standard,"* Addison-Wesley, 1987.

5) Epstein, S. S.: "Transportable Natural Language Processing through Simplicity — The PRE System," *ACM Transactions on Office Information Systems*, Vol. 3, No. 2, pp. 107–120, April 1986.

6) Hafner, C. D. and Godden, K.: "Portability of Syntax and Semantics in Datalog," *ACM Transactions on Office Information Systems*, Vol. 3, No. 2, pp. 141–164, April 1985.

7) Janas, J. M.: "The Semantics-Based Natural Language Interface to Relational Databases," in *Cooperative Interface to Information Systems*, Bolc, L. and Jarke, M. eds., Springer-Verlag, 1986.

8) Kambayashi, Y. and Amano H.: "Transformation of Natural Language Expressions by Basic Relational Database Operations," *Journal of the Information Processing Society*, Vol. 30, No. 10, pp. 1316–1323, October 1989 (in Japanese).

9) Lowden, B. G. T. and De Roeck, A. N.: "The REMIT System for Paraphrasing Relational Query Expressions into Natural Language," *Proceedings of the Twelfth International Conference on Very Large Data Bases*, pp. 365–371, August 1986.

10) Luk, W. S. and Kloster S.: "ELFS: English Language from SQL," *ACM Transactions on Database Systems*, Vol. 11, No. 4, pp. 447–472, December 1986.

11) Maier, D. and Warren, D. S.: "Specifying Connections for a Universal Relation Scheme Database," *Proceedings of the ACM SIGMOD International Conference on Management of Data*, pp. 1–7, June 1982.

12) McLeod, D.: "The Translation and Compatibility of SEQUEL and Query by Example," *Proceedings of the Second International Conference on Software Engineering*, October 1976.

13) Thomas, J. C. and Gould, J. D.: "A Psychological Study of Query by Example," *Proceedings of the AFIPS National Computer Conference*, pp. 439–445, May 1975.

14) Ullman, J. D.: "The U. R. Strikes Back," *Proceedings of the ACM SIGACT-SIGMOD Symposium on Principles of Database Systems*, pp. 10–22, March 1982.

15) Woods, W. A.: "Semantics and Quantification in Natural Language Question Answering," *Advances in Computers*, Vol. 17, pp. 1–87, Academic Press, 1978.

16) Zloof, M. M.: "Query by Example," *Proceedings of the AFIPS National Computer Conference*, pp. 19–22, May 1975.

Similarity Retrieval on Pictorial Databases Based upon Module Operation

J. Liang* and C. C. Chang**

* Institute of Computer Science, National Tsing Hua University, Hsinchu, Taiwan 30043, R.O.C.

** Institute of Computer Science and Information Engineering, National Chung Cheng University, Chiayi, Taiwan 62107, R.O.C.

Abstract

Recently many algorithms have been proposed to solve the similarity retrieval problem within an image database system. Some of these algorithms may utilize schemes like superimposed code, matrix comparison, and hashing, etc.

However, in this paper, we propose an entirely different method based upon module operation to answer a similar query. First, the method transfers each image picture f_i into a positive integer value V_{f_i}. Whenever a similar query q is being issued, the algorithm automatically converts this query pattern into a positive integer value V_q. Then the elements in the answer set will be the pictures f_j's such that the remainder of each V_{f_j} / V_q equals to 0, i.e., V_{f_j} mod $V_q = 0$. The total time we needed for answering a query by our retrieval algorithm is $O(n^2)$, where n is the total number of objects of a query q.

Keywords: prime number, similarity retrieval, module operation, perfect hashing.

1. Introduction

Image database is somewhat different from the conventional database, whose primary work has not only to handle the alphanumerical data but also has to process the object-oriented data associated with their spatial relationship. For example, a query may demand all the pictures associated with a tree to the left of a house or a house above a lake, etc.

Let S be a set of pictures in an image database and q be a query picture. The ***similarity retrieval*** between S and q is to filter out picture subset S' of S such that each picture of S' has some same objects with q and the spatial relationships among these same objects are preserved. In many application fields, suoh as computer-aided design, robotics and remote sensing of earth resources, we can find that the similar retrievals always play as an important role.

In the past few years, with the help of new devised algorithms, the response time of similarity retrieval in an image database has been speeded up, and the implementation efforts based on these algorithms turn more and more convenient.

To simplify the similarity retrieval management, S. K. Chang et al. [4] first introduces the concept of iconic index. An iconic image contains icons whose coordinates are extracted from the feature points of the objects of a real image picture and each icon is assigned an unique symbolic name. Furthermore, the spatial relationships among real objects in a picture are still kept. In other words, an iconic image is a symbolic representation of a real image that can be regarded as this logical view of a physical image. For example, picture f of Fig. 1 stands for a symbolic picture which contains four distinct objects {house, tree, sun, lake}. These four objects can be replaced as four icons A, B, C and D. Note that, in the following, whenever a picture is mentioned, it is regarded as a symbolic icon image implicitly. Besides, we restrict ourselves to images that have at most one icon of each type.

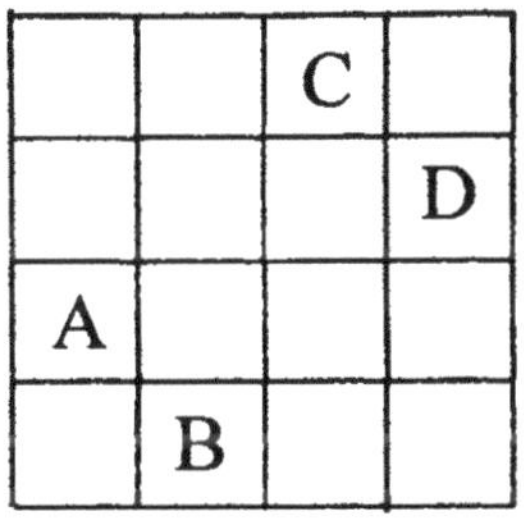

Fig. 1 A symbolic picture instance.

Previous approaches in solving the similarity retrieval problem all use simple table look-up in concept. The Intelligent Image Database System (IIDS) [5] first utilizes the promising ***2D-string data structure*** [4] to decompose a picture P into a set of 2D-string rules that preserve the spatial relationship among objects of original image. Each 2D-string rule involves the use of <, = and > operators to compare the X- and Y-coordinates of the icons. To retrieve the similar pictures, the 2D-string rules matching between S and q have to carried out.

In order to fasten the response time, Lee and Shan [7] tries to combine the ***superimposed coding technique*** with 2D-string which has wildly used among text databases. The basic idea of superimposed code method is to convert image pictures and query picture into binary signatures. Their algorithm first prunes the images whose picture signatures do not contain the same "1"s with the query picture signature. Exhaustive search follows its work along the remaining subset.

To achieve good performance, the superimposed coding technique is applied to represent an image as a binary signature. Better performance can be expected, if distinct '1's of signatures are uniformly distributed. Chang and Lin [3] adopts this concept to develop a more fast superimposed coding technique based upon the ***9DLT*** (9 Direction Low Triangular) ***matrix*** [1]. In [1], C. C. Chang induces that there only exist nine spatial relationships among all possible pairs of icons. And each spatial relationship is characterized by a positive integer value. Since the spatial relation between O_i and O_j can be determined from the spatial relation between O_j and O_i, therefore, only the lower left half of the 9DLT matrix contains integer values. Cluster all iconic pairs that have the same assigned integer value together, then we will have nine groups. Each group then yields their only superimposed codes. Hence, one can get better performance instead of unifying the overall iconic pairs into a unique group [7].

Later, Chang and Lee [2] combines 9DLT matrix and hashing techniques to determine similar matching with less effort. By hashing, we mean a key to address transformation that has desirable retrieval velocity. Given a key *K*, one can calculate the address that accommodates more information associated with the key *K* by a predefined function.

In this paper, we propose an entirely different approach using "***module operation***" to determine the similar pictures satisfying with queries. In our method, each picture f_i is transferred into a positive integer value V_{f_i}, and query picture q is transferred into a positive integer value V_q, too. (Note that integer values appeared in this paper are all restricted to positive integers.) Then the elements in the answering set will be the pictures V_{f_j}'S such that the remainder of $V_{f_j}/V_q = 0$, i.e., $V_{f_j} \bmod V_q = 0$. Further, suppose that there are N pictures in an image database. In order to locate the desired pictures for a given query, we only have to repeat N divide operations at most.

This paper is organized as follows. In Section 2, we introduce the detail of 9DLT matrix. Section 3 explains the concept of our approach. Sections 4 and 5 illustrate the prime numbers assignment and its refinement. The algorithm's layout is represented in Section 6. Finally, the last section states some conclusions.

2. 9DLT (Nine Direction Lower Triangular) Matrix

To transfer each real picture into a symbolic picture, the following procedures should be followed. First, by image processing and pattern recognition techniques, the objects of the original picture are recognized. Next, we enclose each object by a minimum bounding rectangle with boundaries parallel to the X-axis and Y-axis. Afterwards, a symbolic name is substituted for each object. The query picture is also regarded in the similar manner. As we have mentioned, the spatial relationships among real objects can be preserved in symbolic picture.

According to the different levels of demand in checking, *type*-2, *type*-1 and *type*-0 similar matching are defined [4]. Informally, picture f' is said to be a *type*-2 subpicture of picture f if all the objects of f' indeed occur in f, furthermore, the spatial relationship and the distance measure among objects are preserved. f' is said to be *type*-1 subpicture of f if f' is generated by deleting some rows and some columns of the symbolic picture f. f' is said to be *type*-0 subpicture of f if some adjacent rows and columns of f are merged together. In this paper, we only concentrate on *type*-1 and *type*-2 similar matching retrieval, since we believe these two types of matching are more useful than *type*-0 similar matching retrieval. For example, in Fig. 2, f_2, f_3 and f_4 are all *type*-0 subpictures of f_1, f_2 and f_3 are *type*-1 subpictures of f_1, and only f_2 is a *type*-2 subpicture of f_1.

Given a picture, C. C. Chang [1] induced that there totally have nine different spatial relationships among objects (see Fig. 3). In Fig. 3, R denotes the referenced object/icon. Code 0 represents "at the same spatial location as R", code 1 represents "north of R", code 2 represents "north-west of R", code 4 represents "south-west of R", and so on. Let C be the set of nine direction codes, i.e., C={0, 1, 2, 3, 4, 5, 6, 7, 8}. Here each code represents the spatial relationship between two icons. A 9DLT matrix M is an $n \times n$ matrix over C in which t_{ij}, the element of M, is the direction code of icon O_i to the icon O_j for $i > j$ and t_{ij} is undefined if $i \leq j$. Reconsidering Fig. 2, the corresponding 9DLT matrix of f_1, f_2, f_3 and f_4 are depicted in Fig. 4, where matrices M_1, M_2, M_3 and M_4 correspond to pictures f_1, f_2, f_3 and f_4, respectively. Each picture corresponds to a 9DLT matrix.

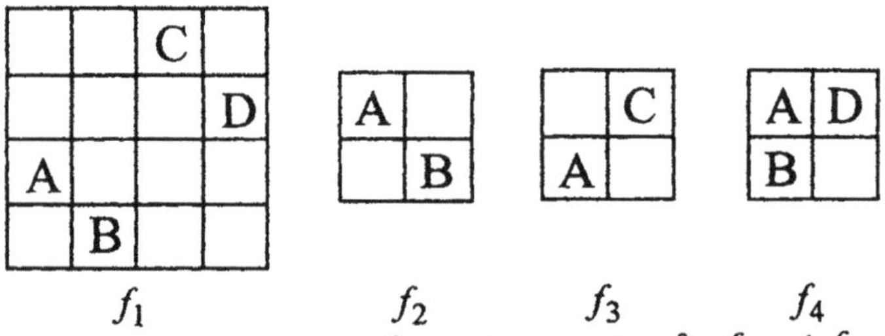

Fig. 2 A symbolic picture f_1 and three queries f_2, f_3 and f_4.

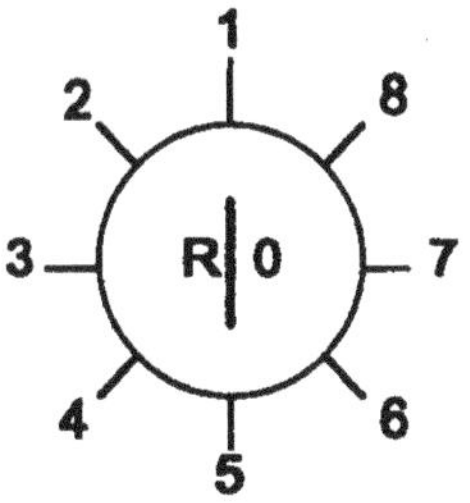

Fig. 3 The direction codes for a 9DLT matrix.

$$M_1 = \begin{array}{c|cccc} & A & B & C & D \\ \hline A & - & - & - & - \\ B & 6 & - & - & - \\ C & 8 & 8 & - & - \\ D & 8 & 8 & 6 & - \end{array} \quad M_2 = \begin{array}{c|cc} & A & B \\ \hline A & - & - \\ B & 6 & - \end{array} \quad M_3 = \begin{array}{c|cc} & A & C \\ \hline A & - & - \\ C & 8 & - \end{array} \quad M_4 = \begin{array}{c|ccc} & A & B & D \\ \hline A & - & - & - \\ B & 5 & - & - \\ D & 7 & 8 & - \end{array}$$

Fig. 4 Four 9DLT matrices of Fig. 2

Let a triple (O_i, O_j, r_{ij}) denote the spatial relationship between objects O_i and O_j, where $0 \le r_{ij} \le 8$. (O_i, O_j, r_{ij}) implies (O_j, O_i, r'_{ij}) where r'_{ij} is the inverse of r_{ij}. In other words, the inverse of "north of" is "south of", the inverse of "south-west of" is "north-east of", and so on. Triple (O_i, O_j, r_{ij}) is said to be an *ordered triple* if $O_i \le O_j$ in lexical ordering. Hence, the 9DLT matrix M_1 of f_1 will correspond to a set {(A, B, 6), (A, C, 8), (A, D, 8), (B, C, 8), (B, D, 8), (C, D, 6)} of ordered triples, and M_4 corresponds to {(A, B, 5), (A, D, 7), (B, D, 8)}. For simplicity, let the set of ordered triples corresponds to the 9DLT matrix M_i be T_i. Since pictures can be expressed as a set of ordered triples, the similarity retrieval problem reduces to check whether the set of ordered triples of a query picture is a subset of the ordered triples of a symbolic picture in an image database. Hence, the similarity retrieval problem can be regarded as the ***triple matching problem***. From Fig. 2, in fact, f_2 is a *type*-1 subpicture of f_1. It can be verified from Fig. 4 that the corresponding elements and their t_{ij}'s are identical between matrices M_2 and M_1. In other words, the ordered triple set T_2 = {(A, B, 6)} of M_2 is the subset of T_1 = {(A, B, 6), (A, C, 8), (A, D, 8), (B, C, 8), (B, D, 8), (C, D, 6)} of M_1. Therefore, f_2 is a *type*-1 subpicture of f_1. Consider the matrices M_1 and M_4, i.e., f_1 and f_4. We find that the corresponding t_{ij}'s are not identical, hence, f_4 is not a similar subpicture of f_1.

3. Basic Concept of Our Scheme

The main concept of this paper is to transfer each image picture f_i into a positive integer value V_{f_i}. Whenever a query picture q is issued, q is transferred into a positive integer value V_q, too. Therewith, employ the module operation between V_{f_i} and V_q, if the remainder of $V_{f_i} / V_q = 0$, i.e., $V_{f_i} \bmod V_q = 0$, then we make sure that q is a *type*-1 subpicture of f_i, in other words, f_i satisfies with q.

For example, four symbolic pictures f_1, f_2, f_3 and f_4 and a query picture q are depicted in Fig. 5. After being processed by a "***black box***", f_1, f_2, f_3 and f_4 become 286, 17, 105 and 2, respectively. At this moment, let us blind and convince ourselves that this black box enables to do this job. Query q is also fed into the black box, and we get one positive integer value 105. Employ the divide operation to calculate the remainders between f_i and V_q, we then obtain

$$V_{f_1} \bmod V_q = 286 \bmod 105 = 72,$$

$$V_{f_2} \bmod V_q = 17 \bmod 105 = 17,$$

$$V_{f_3} \bmod V_q = 105 \bmod 105 = 0,$$

$$V_{f_4} \bmod V_q = 2 \bmod 105 = 2.$$

Because only the third remainder equals to 0, we predicate that the picture f_3 has something to do with q. Examine f_3 and q more carefully, we conclude that f_3 and q are indeed *type*-1 matching.

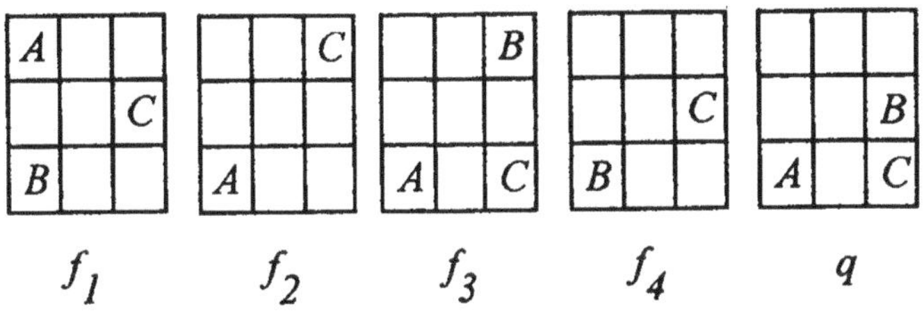

Fig. 5 Four pictures and one query picture.

The readers may wonder what the black box looks like and how does it accomplish to transfer a picture into an integer value. In the following, we will disclose the cover of this black box step by step.

In fact, the major duty of the black box is to transfer all ordered triples that deduced from a 9DLT matrix into a set of ***distinct positive prime numbers***. Since each picture f_i is associated with an ordered triple set T_i, we will get a set of distinct prime numbers by feeding this ordered triple set into black box. Next, let us calculate the ***lowest common multiple*** of these distinct prime numbers, and address this value as the ***standing value*** SV_i of f_i. This gives rise to the standing values 286, 17, 105 and 2. Furthermore, it is easy to verify that 286, 17, 105 and 2 are indeed constituted from the lowest common multiple of a set of distinct prime numbers. Decompose these standing values, we have:

$$286 = 2 * 11 * 13,$$

$$17 = 17,$$

$$105 = 3 * 5 * 7,$$

$$2 = 2.$$

Here 2, 3, 5, 11, 13 and 17 are prime numbers which associate to triples (*B*, *C*, 8), (*A*, *B*, 8), (*A*, *C*, 7), (*A*, *B*, 6), (*A*, *C*, 6) and (*A*, *C*, 8), respectively. This verifies the capability of black box. In the next section, we will introduce how to assign prime number to each ordered triple.

4. A Prime Number Assignment Method

Section 3 illustrates that each picture is transferred into a standing value that resulting from the lowest common multiple of a set prime numbers. And the prime numbers are generated from the corresponding ordered triples of pictures. However, the ordered triples are originated from the 9DLT matrices. Fig. 6 depicts a prime number assignment of the ordered triples of four image pictures of Fig. 5.

f_1	f_2	f_3	f_4
(A, B, 6):11	(A, C, 8):17	(A, B, 8):3	(B, C, 8):2
(A, C, 6):13		(A, C, 7):5	
(B, C, 8):2		(B, C, 5):7	
11*13*2=286	17	3*5*7=105	2

Fig. 6 Prime numbers assignment.

Fig. 6 displays the cross reference table between an ordered triples of a picture and a prime number. However, different assignment will result different standing values. Fig. 7 depicts another assignment. From both assignments, we can induce one common assignment rule, i.e., "*The equivalent ordered triples that belong to different pictures should be assigned the same prime number.*" For example, the ordered triple (*B*, *C*, 8) of Fig. 6 and Fig. 7 that appear in f_1 and f_4 are allocated the prime number 2. Following this assignment rule, we can produce the smaller standing values.

f_1	f_2	f_3	f_4
(A, B, 6):7	(A, C, 8):17	(A, B, 8):3	(B, C, 8):2
(A, C, 6):13		(A, C, 7):5	
(B, C, 8):2		(B,C,5):11	
7*13*2=182	17	3*5*11=165	2

Fig. 7 New prime numbers assignment.

Examining Fig. 6 and Fig. 7, we discover that the maximum standing value in Fig. 6 is 286, however, the maximum standing value in Fig. 7 is 182. From the practical point of view, we would rather have the maximum standing value as small as possible. Thus, the assignment of Fig. 7 is preferable to that of Fig. 6. Since the standing values are generated from the multiplication of prime numbers, without cautious assignment, some standing values may become very large while some others are very small. Furthermore, if the standing values are too large, then we may face integer overflow problem. To avoid this undesirable condition, we should mindfully assign some prime numbers to the ordered triples.

Before going further, let us define some terminologies that will make the representation more clearly. Let $F(O_i,O_j,r_{ij})$ be the frequency of the ordered triple (O_i,O_j,r_{ij}), that indicates the number of occurrences of this triple appears in an image database. Let $PN(O_i,O_j,r_{ij})$ be the prime number being assigned to the ordered triple (O_i,O_j,r_{ij}). The standing value SV_i of a picture f_i is the multiplication of all $PN(O_i,O_j,r_{ij})$s', where (O_i,O_j,r_{ij})s belong to the picture f_i. In the following, we give **Algorithm *PS*** to assign a prime to an ordered triple of image database:

<u>Algorithm PS</u>

Input: A set of ordered triples.

Output: A set of distinct prime numbers associated to the set of ordered triples, respectively.

Step 1: Count the frequencies of ordered triples and sort them on decreasing order. Set all standing values of all pictures to 1.

Step 2: While there are unassigned ordered triples whose frequencies are greater than 1, do Step 3 to Step 6; otherwise, go to Step 7.

Step 3: If there are more than one different ordered triples that have the same largest frequency greater than one, then go to Step 4; otherwise, go to Step 5.

Step 4: Select the ordered triple belonging to one picture with the largest current standing value and assign the candidate prime number to it. Go to Step 6. Here a ***candidate prime number*** means an integer value which has not been assigned to ordered triple but its predecessor has already been assigned to an ordered triple.

Step 5: Assign the candidate prime number to the ordered triple which has the largest frequency value.

Step 6: Calculate the lowest common multiple between this new assigned prime number and the current standing value that is associated to the picture containing this new assigned ordered triple. Go to Step 2

Step 7: While there exists unassigned ordered triple whose corresponding frequency equals to 1, do Step 8 to Step 9. Otherwise, stop executing.

Step 8: If there are more than one picture that have the same largest unassigned ordered triple, select the picture that has the largest standing value up to now, and assign the candidate prime number to the ordered triple; otherwise, assign the candidate prime number to an arbitrarily selected ordered triple of a picture that has the largest number of unassigned ordered triples.

Step 9: Calculate the lowest common multiple between this new assigned prime number and the contemporary standing value associated to the selected picture. Go to Step 7.

For instance, pictures f_1, f_2, f_3 and f_4 of Fig. 5 have eight ordered triples totally, but only triple $(B, C, 8)$ appears in both pictures f_1 and f_4. Therefore, according to the Step 2 of Algorithm **PS**, we assign 2 to $(B, C, 8)$. That is $PN(B, C, 8)=2$. After assigning $(B, C, 8)$, frequencies of the remaining triples are all equal to 1. Hence, according to Step 8, we select an ordered triple of f_3, say $(A, B, 8)$, and set $PN(A, B, 8)=3$. Now, $SV_1 = 2$, $SV_2 = 1$, $SV_3 = 3$ and $SV_4 = 2$. The next candidate prime number is 5, according to Step 8, 5 is assigned to the ordered triple $(A, C, 7)$ of f_3. At this moment, $SV_1 = 2$, $SV_2 = 1$, $SV_3 = 3*5$ and $SV_4 = 2$. Now, prime number 7 is ready, according to Step 8, $(A, B, 6)$ is selected. Since $SV_3 = 3*5$ holds the largest standing value among $SV_1 = 2*7$, $SV_2 = 1$, $SV_3 = 3*5$ and $SV_4 = 2$, next candidate prime number 11 is dedicated to picture f_3. All the ordered triples of f_3 are assigned, thus f_3 is raced out the assignment. Candidate prime number 13 is bounded for $(A, C, 6)$ of f_1 according to Step 8. Afterwards, only the ordered triple $(A, C, 8)$ is left, and candidate prime number 17 is destined to be its associated prime number. At last, we have $SV_1 = 2*7*13$, $SV_2 = 17$, $SV_3 = 3*5*11$ and $SV_4 = 2$.

The spirit of Algorithm **PS** is to reduce the magnitude of the largest standing value. If some ordered triple has largest frequency, it should have the first priority to be assigned candidate prime number. Because this triple has occurred in several pictures, the final standing values associated to these pictures will grow larger if we assign larger prime number to it. Hence, to decrease the standing values, we should give a small prime number to this kind of ordered triples.

5. Refine the Prime Number Assignment

In the last section, we presented a prime number assignment that converts each image picture into a standing value. Each ordered triple is assigned a distinct prime number. Calculate the lowest common multiple of the distinct prime numbers that assigned to ordered triples, the standing value is generated. Since Algorithm **PS** assigns distinct prime number to each distinct ordered triple, the standing value of each picture is equal to the multiplication of these distinct prime numbers.

However, when the total number of objects of an image picture becomes large, the corresponding standing value will grow large, too. In order to reduce the standing values, we inevitably have to lessen the standing value. In this section, we introduce a Canonical Assignment that is distinct from Algorithm **PS** such that the distinct triples of a picture may assign powers of the same prime number. The standing value of an image picture remains the lowest common multiple of the prime numbers associated with the ordered triples belonging to this image picture.

Let there be four pictures whose ordered triple sets are $T_1 = \{(A, B, 8), (A, C, 8), (A, D, 7), (B, C, 8), (B, D, 6), (C, D, 5)\}$, $T_2 = \{(A, B, 6), (A, C, 8), (B, C, 1)\}$, $T_3 = \{(A, B, 4), (A, E, 6), (B, E, 8)\}$ and $T_4 = \{(A, B, 8), (A, C, 6), (A, D, 6), (B, C, 5), (B, D, 6), (C, D, 7)\}$. Among these pictures, triples $(A, B, 8)$, $(A, C, 8)$ and $(B, D, 6)$ appear at more than once. $(A, B, 8)$ and $(B, D, 6)$ occur in both f_1 and f_4, while $(A, C, 8)$ appears in both f_1 and f_2.

According to Algorithm **PS**, we have the standing values $SV_1 = 331890$, $SV_2 = 7285$, $SV_3 = 21199$ and $SV_4 = 359898$ as in Fig. 8.

In Algorithm **PS**, we initially assign a candidate prime number to the ordered triples whose frequencies are greater than 1. In the Canonical Assignment, however, we assign prime numbers to the ordered triples with frequencies greater than 1 later. For all the image pictures f_i's, we temporarily ignore the ordered triples with frequencies greater than 1. Start to assign 2^1, 2^2, ···, 2^{m_1} to the m_1 ordered triples with frequencies equal to 1 in a picture f_i, then powers of 3^1, 3^2, ··· and 3^{m_2} are assigned to the m_2 ordered triples with frequencies equal to 1 of the second selected picture f_j, and etc.

f_1	f_2	f_3	f_4
(A, B, 8):2	(A, B, 6):31	(A, B, 4):17	(A, B, 8):2
(A, C, 8):5	(A, C, 8):5	(A, E, 6):29	(A, C, 6):7
(A, D, 7):13	(B, C, 1):47	(B, E, 8):43	(A, D, 6):11
(B, C, 8):23			(B, C, 5):19
(B, D, 6):3			(B, D, 6):3
(C, D, 5):37			(C, D, 7):41
2*5*13*23*3 *37=33189	31*5*47=7285	17*29*43 =21199	2*7*11*19*3 *41=359898

Fig. 8 Standing values of new image database.

Assume that there are N image pictures and each has at least one ordered triple whose frequency equals to 1. After determining the prime number of ordered triples with frequencies equal to 1, we begin to assign the (N+1)th candidate prime number to the ordered triples with the maximum frequency. Ordered triples with the second largest frequency are allocated with the (N+2)th candidate prime number, and so on. For instance, Fig. 9 illustrates the modified triple assignment based upon the Canonical Assignment.

f_1	f_2	f_3	f_4
(A, B, 8):11	(A, B, 6):5^1	(A, B, 4):7^1	(A, B, 8):11
(A, C, 8):17	(A, C, 8):17	(A, E, 6):7^2	(A, C, 6):3^1
(A, D, 7):2^1	(B, C, 1):5^2	(B, E, 8):7^3	(A, D, 6):3^2
(B, C, 8):2^2			(B, C, 5):3^3
(B, D, 6):13			(B, D, 6):13
(C, D, 5):2^3			(C, D, 7):3^4
$11*13*17*2^3$ =19448	$5^2*17=425$	$7^3=343$	$11*13*3^4$ =11583

Fig. 9 Canonical assignment.

Canonical Assignment initially clusters pictures into several groups, and each group contains those pictures that have the same number of ordered triples. Second, compute two values $e\#_i$ and $G\#_i$ of each picture f_i, where $e\#_i$ is the total number of ordered triples of f_i whose frequencies equal to 1 and $G\#_i$ is the total number of ordered triples of f_i whose frequencies are greater than 1. Pictures f_1 and f_4 that have six ordered triples are clustered into group 1, pictures f_2 and f_3 which have three ordered triples are clustered into group 2. And $e\#_1/G\#_1 = 3/3$, $e\#_2/G\#_2 = 2/1$, $e\#_3/G\#_3 = 3/0$ and $e\#_4/G\#_4 = 4/2$. These values reveal one important fact that smaller powers of prime number should be assigned to the ordered triples of one selected picture with bigger $e\#_i$. According to these values, we determine that f_1 has to be assigned the smaller powers of prime number than f_4, and f_2 has also to be assigned the smaller powers of prime number than f_3. By this way, standing values will become less. In Fig. 9, we assign the powers of 2, 5, 7 and 3 to f_1, f_2, f_3 and f_4.

Subsequently, 11, 13 and 17 become the candidate prime numbers to (A, B, 8), (A, C, 8) and (B, D, 6) after determining the ordered triples with frequencies equal to 1. Following the heuristic criteria, we determine the destination of prime numbers 11, 13 and 17:

(1) Calculate $TN(O_i,O_j,r_{ij})$, where $TN(O_i,O_j,r_{ij})$ is the total number of unassigned ordered triples of a picture f such that f contains (O_i,O_j,r_{ij}).

(2) Sort these summation values in descending order.

(3) Assign candidate prime numbers to ordered triples of this sorted sequence from the beginning to the end.

Since (A, B, 8) and (B, D, 6) appear in f_1 and f_4, (A, C, 8) appears in both f_1 and f_2, we have $TN(A,B,8)$=12 (=6+6), $TN(B,D,6)$=12 (=6+6) and $TN(A,C,8)$=9 (=6+3). Hence, 11, 13 and 17 are assigned to (A, B, 8), (A, C, 8) and (B, D, 6), respectively. Prime number 17 should multiply the other five prime numbers in pictures f_1 and f_4 if (A, B, 8) is assigned with 17. This value will be larger than to multiply another the other five prime numbers with 11 or 13. On the contrary, (A, C, 8) whose corresponding prime number only has to multiply two prime numbers, the standing value will not affect too much if we assign 17 to (A, C, 8). Thus the final standing values of f_1, f_2, f_3 and f_4 are 19448, 425, 343 and 11583.

Comparing Fig. 8 to Fig. 9, we can find that the standing values of Fig. 9 is smaller than those in Fig. 8. Amazing enough that the largest decrease is f_3 that we can reduce about 61 times.

In fact, each ordered triple in Fig. 9 still has distinct values but does not have distinct prime number. If object number increases, then we can use less space to store these standing values and the division operations can be carried more efficiently than Algorithm **PS**. Algorithm of Canonical Assignment is outlined as follows.

Algorithm CA

Input: An image database.

Output: Each ordered triple of image database is associated with a prime number.

Step 1: Compute $e\#_i$ and $G\#_i$ of each image picture.

Step 2: Cluster pictures into groups while each group contains pictures that have the same number of ordered triples.

Step 3: Sort the pictures of each group into an ascending sequence according to $e\#_i$.

Step 4: Select one of the unselected picture f of the sorted ascending sequence of the nonempty group that has the largest $(e\#_i + G\#_i)$ value.

Step 5: Delete this selected picture f from this nonempty group.

Step 6: Assign the powers of candidate prime number to ordered triples of f whose frequencies equal to 1.

Step 7: Repeat Step 4 until there is no nonempty group.

Step 8: Compute the summation values $TN(O_i,O_j,r_{ij})$ of the remaining W ordered triples, where each $F(O_i,O_j,r_{ij})$ is greater than 1.

Step 9: Sort the summation values of Step 8 into descending order. Let $i = 1$

Step 10: Assign the candidate prime number to the i-th ordered triple in the sorted sequence.

Step 11: Let $i = i + 1$.

Step 12: Repeat Step 10 until $i > W$.

Note that the final standing value of each picture is the lowest common multiple of the corresponding prime numbers of ordered triples of this picture.

6. Algorithm

At the last section, we explore the mystery of the black box. In this section, we will examine the black box further and computer the complexity of this algorithm.

Let there be N pictures in the image database and each picture has m_i objects. Let query picture q has n objects and the total ordered triples of these N pictures be SO $(=\sum_{i=1}^{N}[\frac{(m_i-1)*m_i}{2}])$. Sort these SO ordered triples of N pictures, we can create a sorted table in lexical ordering. Each item consists 2 entries, the first entry contains the ordered triple, and the second entry holds the prime number corresponding to the ordered triple of the first entry. Given a query picture, there are $O(n^2)$ ordered triples of query picture. To determine the prime numbers of the ordered triple set of q, we need $O(n^2 \log SO)$ time using binary search to fix the prime number in the predetermined static sorted table. To synthesize the standing value of query picture, we need $O(n^2)$ multiply operations. To determine which picture has the similar matching with query picture, we should need $O(N)$ divide operations. Since each picture has at least one object, $O(N)$ is usually less than $O(n^2 \log SO)$. Thus the overall time complexity of this algorithm is $O(n^2 \log SO)$.

The reader may not be difficult to find the bottle-neck of our algorithm is to determine the corresponding prime number of query's ordered triples. In the following, we will utilize the ***perfect hashing scheme*** to decrease the time complexity from $O(n^2 \log SO)$ down to $O(n^2)$, where n is the number of query objects/icons.

Hashing is a key-to-address transformation that is an useful data structure in determining key's location immediately. The extreme difference between binary search and hashing is that binary search usually takes $O(\log SO)$ time to determine the desired item, but hashing usually renders $O(1)$ retrieval facility. However, if hashing function has not been configured carefully, several keys may map into the same location, i.e., keys collision. In this way, the data structure may grow intricately.

If hashing function is one-to-one mapping from the key space to address space, it is a perfect hashing function. To accommodate perfect hashing scheme into similarity retrieval, each ordered triple (O_i,O_j,r_{ij}) should be hashed into a unique position in address space. In this paper, we utilize the scheme proposed by Cook and Oldehoeft [6] and Chang and Lee [2] to design a perfect hashing scheme. The major idea of this perfect hashing function is $h(O_i,O_j,r_{ij}) = r_{ij}$ + associated value of O_i + associated value of O_j. Let appearance of ordered triple (O_i,O_j,r_{ij}) be the occurrences of (O_i,O_j,r_{ij}) within the image database.

Algorithm Perfect Hashing

Input: A set of ordered triples (O_i,O_j,r_{ij}).

output: Associated values of query's objects.

Step 1: Compute the appearances of the symbolic icons.

Step 2: Sort the objects/icons in decreasing order according to their appearances.

Step 3: For each ordered triple (O_i,O_j,r_{ij}), interchange O_i and O_j if O_j precedes O_i in the sorted sequence of Step 2.

Step 4: Let the second object in each ordered triple be a key, sort the list of the ordered triples generated from Step 3 in descending order.

Step 5: Assign values to objects from the first ordered triple. For each cluster of triples with the same second object, determine a value assigning to the second object. (Note that for this cluster, either the fist object is equal to the

object's appearance after Step 1	object ordering after Step 2	triples after Step 3	triples ordering after Step 4	hashing address after Step 5	object value assignment
A 8	A	(A, B, 4)	(A, B, 4)	7	A 3
B 8	B	(A, B, 6)	(A, B, 6)	9	B 0
C 7	C	(A, B, 8)	(A, B, 8)	11	C 7
D 5	D	(B, C, 1)	(B, C, 1)	8	D 11
E 2	E	(B, C, 5)	(B, C, 5)	12	E 5
		(B, C, 8)	(B, C, 8)	15	
		(B, D, 6)	(A, C, 6)	16	
		(B, E, 8)	(A, C, 8)	18	
		(A, C, 6)	(B, D, 6)	17	
		(A, C, 8)	(A, D, 6)	20	
		(A, D, 6)	(A, D, 7)	21	
		(A, D, 7)	(C, D, 5)	23	
		(A, E, 6)	(C, D, 7)	25	
		(C, D, 5)	(B, E, 8)	13	
		(C, D, 7)	(A, E, 6)	14	

Fig. 10 Perfect hashing scheme.

second object or the first symbol precedes the second object in the object ordering. The first symbol must have been determined, thus we can map triples of group into address space.)

Step 3 forces the objects with larger appearance values be put to front and the objects with smaller appearance values be put to rear. Implicitly, ordered triple will be clustered to several groups such that each group has the same second object. Hence, the value assignment in the Step 5 will assign values to objects with larger appearance values at first. Objects with smaller appearance values may have larger freedom to select a value such that collision can be avoided. Whenever we succeed to find a value assigned to the second object of some group, the addresses of the ordered triples of this group are determined subsequently. If we can not find a value to the second object of some group, we should backup to modify the objects value until one-to-one mapping principle is kept. Fig. 10 illustrates the value assignment using data in Fig. 8.

From Fig. 10, we perceive that Algorithm Perfect Hashing indeed enables to produce a perfect hashing function, four extra spaces are needed to accommodate fifteen ordered triples.

7. Conclusions

In this paper, an entirely new similarity retrieval algorithm is proposed. This algorithm first utilizes perfect hashing scheme to assign prime number to ordered triples. Second, calculate the lowest common multiples to determine the corresponding standing values. Third, execute the module operation to determine the similar matching between query picture q and image picture f_i. The reminder of V_{f_i}/V_q tells us the similarity information between q and f_i, where V_{f_i} is the standing value of the image picture f_i and V_q is the standing value of the query picture q. Whenever the remainder of V_{f_i}/V_q equals to 0, i.e., $V_{f_i} \bmod V_q = 0$, algorithm filters out that query picture q is *type*-1 similar subpicture of image picture f_i. $O(n^2)$ time complexity is binding, where n is the number of query objects. Since the module operation is a common machine instruction, the implementation of our scheme is very simple and efficient.

However, in this paper, the standing value of each picture may not be minimum. Because the optimum algorithm has not been proposed but only heuristic algorithm is offered in this paper. Thus to find an optimum methodology to minimize the standing values still retains open.

References

[1] C. C. Chang, Spatial match retrieval of symbolic pictures, *J. of Information Science and Engineering* 7, 405-422 (1991).

[2] C. C. Chang and S. Y. Lee, Retrieval of similar pictures on pictorial databases, *Pattern Recognition* **24**, 675-680 (1991).

[3] C. C. Chang and J. C. Lin, A fast spatial match accessing scheme for symbolic pictures, *Journal of Electrical Engineering* **33**, 129-137 (1990).

[4] S. K. Chang, Q. Y. Shi and C. W. Yan, Iconic indexing by 2-D strings, *IEEE Trans. Pattern Analysis and Machine Intelligence* **6**, 475-484 (1984).

[5] S. K. Chang, C. W. Yan, D. Dimitrof and T. Arnd, An intelligent image database, *IEEE Trans. Software Eng.* **14**, 681-688 (1988).

[6] C. R. Cook and R. Oldehoeft, A letter-oriented minimal perfect hashing function, *ACM SIGPlan Notices* **17**, 18-27 (Sep. 1982).

[7] S. Y. Lee and M. K. Shan, Access methods of image database, *International J. Pattern Recognition and Artificial Intelligence* **4**, 27-44 (1990).

MULTIDATABASE SYSTEMS

Efficient Global Transaction Management in Multidatabase Systems*

Sharad Mehrotra† Rajeev Rastogi† Yuri Breitbart‡ Henry F. Korth§ Avi Silberschatz†

Abstract

Concurrency control schemes for ensuring global serializability in a *multidatabase system* (MDBS) environment are complicated due to the autonomy of local database management systems (DBMSs). In this paper, we develop concurrency control schemes, for the MDBS environment, that are simple, permit a high degree of concurrency and incur minimal overhead under two different assumptions on the nature of schedules produced by the local DBMSs: (1) each local DBMS produces *rigorous* schedules, (2) each local DBMS produces *strongly recoverable* schedules. Our interest in rigorous schedules stems from the fact that the majority of commercial DBMSs offer a concurrency control protocol that generates rigorous schedules. However, the class of rigorous schedules is quite restrictive in terms of the amount of concurrency permitted. We, therefore, also consider the class of strongly recoverable schedules which permits a higher degree of concurrency. The class of strongly recoverable schedules is the largest class of schedules for which transaction execution order coincides with their commit order. Therefore, the global transaction manager for multidatabase systems with strongly recoverable local DBMSs guarantees global serializability by simple control of global transaction commit execution without infringing on a local DBMS autonomy.

Our proposed schemes exploit the rigorousness and strong recoverability properties of local schedules to ensure global serializability with minimal overhead both, in presence, and absence of failures. Furthermore, our proposed schemes are simple and require only minimal information from the participating local DBMSs.

*This material is based in part upon work supported by NSF grants IRI-8904932, IRI-9003341, IRI-9106450, RRI-8610671 and by grants from the IBM corporation, the HP corporation and the NEC corporation and by the Center for Manufacturing and Robotics of the University of Kentucky and Commonwealth of Kentucky EPSCoR Program.

†Department of Computer Sciences, University of Texas, Austin, TX 78712-1188

‡Department of Computer Sciences, University of Kentucky, Lexington, KY 40506

§Matsushita Information Technology Laboratory, 182 Nassau Street, third floor, Princeton, NJ 08542-7072

1 Introduction

A *multidatabase system* (MDBS) is a facility that allows access to data located in multiple pre-existing and autonomous database management systems (DBMSs). In such a system, a software package built on top of the local DBMSs, referred to as the *global transaction manager* (GTM), coordinates the execution of *global transactions* that execute at multiple sites. Independently, *local transactions* execute at a single site outside the control of the GTM. Each local DBMS is *autonomous* in the sense that no design or internal DBMS structure changes are permitted (*design autonomy*) to the local DBMS. Each local DBMS has complete control over all the transactions executing at its site, including the ability to abort any transaction at any time prior to its commitment (*execution autonomy*). Furthermore, each local DBMS may or may not communicate any information relevant for concurrency control to the GTM or to any others' local DBMS, and may or may not be aware of each others existence (*communication autonomy*).

The concept of *serializability* has been the traditionally accepted notion of correctness for concurrent executions of multiple transactions. In an MDBS environment, however, ensuring global serializability even in a failure-free environment is difficult. This is due to the fact that the local transactions execute outside the control of the GTM, and the local DBMSs may follow different concurrency control schemes. Schemes for ensuring global serializability in a failure-free MDBS environment have been proposed in [5, 2, 6, 7].

In a MDBS, an execution of each global transaction incurs overhead at two levels. First, overhead is incurred by the GTM to ensure global serializability in the presence of local transactions. Second, overhead is incurred by local DBMSs that execute global transactions operations. Therefore, to improve performance, it is highly desirable that the concurrency control scheme used by the GTM result in minimal overhead. In this paper, we develop such GTM schemes under two different assumptions on the nature of schedules produced by the local DBMSs:

- Each local DBMS generates *rigorous* schedules.

- Each local DBMS generates *strongly recoverable* schedules.

Our interest in rigorous schedules stems from the fact that the majority of commercial DBMSs offer a concurrency control protocol that generates rigorous schedules. However, the class of rigorous schedules is quite restrictive in terms of the amount of concurrency permitted. We, therefore, also consider the class of strongly recoverable schedules which permits a higher degree of concurrency. The class of strongly recoverable schedules is the largest class of schedules for which transaction execution order coincides with their commit order. Therefore, the global transaction manager for multidatabase systems in which local DBMSs generate strongly recoverable schedules can guarantee global serializability by simple control of global transactions' commit execution without infringing on a local DBMS autonomy. The class of rigorous and strongly recoverable schedules was originally introduced in [2]. A notion similar to strong recoverability, referred to as *commit order* (CO) was also introduced independently in [10] in which a detailed description of schemes that produce CO schedules was also provided.

Another issue in an MDBS environment is that of making the concurrency control schemes failure-resilient. The problem of developing failure-resilient schemes for MDBS environments has been addressed in [4, 12, 8, 9, 11]. Since global transactions in an MDBS are distributed transactions, that is, they execute at multiple sites, there is a need for a global commit protocol and recovery procedures to ensure the atomicity of such transactions in face of failures. The schemes for fault-tolerance in MDBSs differ widely depending upon whether or not each participating local DBMS supports a *prepared* state for the execution of an *atomic commit protocol*. In case local DBMSs support a prepared state, an atomic commit protocol [1] (e.g. the 2PC protocol) can be used to ensures global transaction atomicity in an MDBS environment. However, if local DBMSs do not support a prepared state, ensuring global transaction atomicity is difficult. In this paper, we concentrate on concurrency control schemes that can be made failure-resilient even if local DBMSs do not support a prepared state.

The remainder of the paper is organized as follows. In the next section, we describe our MDBS model and formally define the notions of rigorousness and strong recoverability. In Section 3, we consider how global serializability can be ensured if the local DBMSs produce rigorous as well as strongly recoverable schedules. In Section 4, we discuss how our GTM scheme can be made failure-resilient in case local DBMSs do not support a prepared state for the execution of an atomic commit protocol. Finally, Section 5 concludes the paper.

2 MDBS Model

An MDBS consists of pre-existing and autonomous local DBMSs located at sites $s_1, s_2, \ldots, s_m$. A transaction T_i is a sequence of **read** (denoted by r_i), and **write** (denoted by w_i) operations followed by either **commit** (denoted by c_i) or **abort** (denoted by a_i) operations, one per site at which T_i executes. The local schedule at site s_k, denoted by S_k, is a sequence of operations belonging to local and global transactions resulting from their concurrent execution at site s_k. We say that transaction T_i is in a *wr* (*rw*, *ww*) conflict with transaction T_j in S_k if and only if S_k contains an operation w_i (r_i, w_i) belonging to T_i, followed by r_j (w_j, w_j) belonging to T_j, such that both w_i (r_i, w_i) and r_j (w_j, w_j) access the same data item x at s_k and T_i does not abort before r_j (w_j, w_j) is executed. If T_i is in a *rw*, *wr*, or *ww* conflict with T_j, then T_i is said to be in conflict with T_j[1]. Transaction T_i is said to be *committed* (*aborted*) in S_k if S_k contains a c_i (a_i) operation. We denote by T_{ik}, the subtransaction of global transaction T_i at site s_k.

We assume that the GTM is centrally located and controls the submission of global transaction operations to the local DBMSs (local transactions submitted to local DBMSs are not subject to central GTM control.). For every global transaction operation, the GTM first selects a local DBMS where the operation should be executed, and then determines whether to submit the operation to the local DBMS, to delay it, or to abort the transaction. At each site, the GTM has an agent (server) that submits global transaction operations to the local DBMS. A local DBMS acknowledges the execution of an operation to the server, which, in turn, passes this information to the GTM. The GTM submits an operation of a transaction for execution to the server after it has received an acknowledgement for the execution of the previous operation of the transaction. Each global transaction thus consists of a set of subtransactions, each of which is executed as a regular local transaction at some local DBMS. Every local DBMS ensures the atomicity of transactions in local schedules and ensures that local schedules are conflict serializable. Furthermore, local DBMSs support mechanisms for detecting and resolving all local deadlocks.

Global serializability in the MDBS is said to be assured if the union of the conflict serialization graphs [1] of all the local schedules is acyclic. We next define the class of *rigorous* schedules and *strongly recoverable* schedules.

Definition 1: A schedule S is said to be *rigorous* if, for all pairs of transactions T_i, T_j in S, if T_i is in conflict with T_j, then T_j does not execute its conflicting operation

[1] Note that conflict is not a symmetric relation, that is, it is possible that T_i is in conflict with T_j, but T_j is not in conflict with T_i.

before T_i commits or aborts. □

Definition 2: A schedule S is said to be *strongly recoverable* if S is recoverable and further for all pairs of transactions T_i, T_j in S, if T_i is in conflict with T_j, then T_j does not commit before T_i commits or aborts. □

Every rigorous schedule is also strongly recoverable. The converse, however, is not true. For example, the local schedule S_1: $r_1(x)\ w_2(x)\ c_1\ c_2$ is strongly recoverable but not rigorous.

3 Ensuring Global Serializability

In this section, we develop concurrency control protocols for ensuring global serializability. We will consider the problem of making our schemes failure-resilient in the next section.

Let us first consider the situation in which each local DBMS produces rigorous schedules. If each local DBMS produces rigorous schedules, then to ensure global serializability, it suffices to ensure that a global transaction T_i does not execute any database operations (that is, read and write operations) after its commit operation has executed at even one site. Since in our model, we have assumed that the local DBMSs acknowledge the execution of each operation, and further, since the commit operations of the transaction execute only after the acknowledgement of each database operation, to ensure global serializability in our system no global scheduling is required. That is, the GTM may submit the operations of the global transaction for execution to the various local DBMSs as soon as they arrive at the GTM. We refer to such a GTM in which the operations of the global transactions are submitted for execution to the various local DBMSs as soon as they arrive as a *trivial* GTM.

Theorem 1: Global serializability is ensured by a trivial GTM if each local DBMS generates rigorous schedules. □

Let us now turn our attention to ensuring global serializability if each local DBMS generates strongly recoverable schedules. First, we note that if each local DBMS only generates strongly recoverable schedules, then global serializability may not be ensured in a trivial MDBS, even if GTM uses the 2PC protocol to execute a commit operation. This is illustrated by the following example.

Example 1: Consider an MDBS consisting of two sites: site s_1 with data item x and site s_2 with data item y. Let T_1 and T_2 be the following global transactions.

$$T_1 : w_1(x)\ w_1(y)$$
$$T_2 : r_2(x)\ r_2(y)$$

Since a trivial GTM does not coordinate the global transaction operations, the following execution may result.

$$S_1 : r_2(x)\ w_1(x)\ c_2\ c_1$$
$$S_2 : w_1(y)\ c_1\ r_2(y)\ c_2$$

Note that even though both schedules S_1 and S_2 are strongly recoverable, global serializability is violated. □

The above example suggests that if each local DBMS generates only strongly recoverable schedules, then to ensure global serializability, the GTM needs to control the order in which operations belonging to the global transactions execute. Before we develop the GTM concurrency control scheme, we examine certain properties of the strongly recoverable schedule which will guide our solution.

We first note that every strongly recoverable local schedule is serializable in an order consistent with the commit order of transactions. This leads us to the following theorem.

Theorem 2: Consider an MDBS where each local DBMS produces strongly recoverable schedules. Global serializability is assured if there exists a total order on global transactions such that at each site s_k, for all pairs of global transactions T_i, T_j executing at s_k, if T_i commits before T_j at s_k, then T_i precedes T_j in the total order. □

A consequence of Theorem 2 is that if the GTM executes global transactions serially and each of the local schedules is strongly recoverable, then global serializability is ensured. Further, in an MDBS where each local DBMS generates strongly recoverable schedules, it is sufficient to synchronize only the commit operations of the global transaction in order to ensure global serializability. Below, we discuss a scheme that utilizes the notion of a *commit graph* introduced in [4] to control the order in which commit operations of the global transactions execute. A commit graph is an undirected bipartite graph consisting of a set of nodes V corresponding to sites (site nodes) and transactions (transaction nodes). Edges in the commit graph are present only between transaction nodes and site nodes. An edge between a transaction node T_i and a site node s_k is present only if transaction T_i executes at site s_k, and T_i's commit operation is submitted to s_k.

Algorithm TM_1

1. When a global transaction T_i submits its commit operation to the GTM, the GTM temporarily adds to the commit graph, edges (T_i, s_k) for each site s_k at which T_i executes.

2. If the augmented commit graph does not contain a cycle, then the global commit operation is submitted by the GTM to local DBMSs for execution and the temporary edges become permanent.

3. If the augmented commit graph does contain a cycle, then the GTM places global transaction T_i on a *waiting queue*, and removes the temporary edges from the commit graph.

4. Upon completion of a global transaction T_i's commit operation at the local DBMSs, the GTM performs the following: if there is no path in the commit graph from T_i to any other transaction T_j that has not completed its commit operation at some local DBMS, then delete from the commit graph T_i and all transactions T_j such that there is a path in the commit graph from T_i to T_j, along with all edges incident on these nodes.

5. If a transaction is deleted from the commit graph, the GTM checks the commit graph (using steps 1 and 2) whether the commit operation of any transaction T_i in the waiting queue can be submitted to the local DBMSs.

The GTM algorithm, TM_1, presented above uses a commit graph in determining if a global commit operation can be submitted for execution to the local DBMSs. The only operations that are potentially delayed are global transaction commit operations. In essence, algorithm TM_1 guarantees global serializability by preventing cycles in the commit graph.

Theorem 3: If each local DBMS generates strongly recoverable schedules, then algorithm TM_1 ensures global serializability. □

4 Dealing with Failures

In this section we consider the problem of making our concurrency control scheme resilient to failures. Since an MDBS is a distributed database system, our scheme must be resilient to various kinds of failures (e.g., site, communication, transaction aborts). Presence of failures complicate the task of ensuring atomicity of transactions. Since, in our model, we assume that each local DBMS has pre-existing recovery procedures that ensure atomicity of local transactions and global subtransactions executing in its control, we can restrict ourselves to ensuring atomicity of global transactions in presence of failures.

It is well known that in homogeneous distributed database systems, the two-phase commit (2PC) protocol [1] can be used to ensure the atomicity of global transactions in the presence of failures. In the 2PC protocol, a coordinator, on completion of a transaction T_i, sends a VOTE-REQ message to all the local sites at which T_i executed (referred to as participants). Upon receipt of a VOTE-REQ message, a local site responds by sending its vote: a YES (commit) or a NO (abort). If the local site at site s_k votes to commit transaction T_i, it forces the log records corresponding to the writes done by subtransaction T_{ik} onto stable storage before responding. If all the participating local sites respond with a YES, then the coordinator decides to commit transaction T_i and sends a COMMIT message to each participating local site. Else, it sends an ABORT message to the local sites. The local site at site s_k upon receiving the coordinator's decision, commits or aborts T_{ik}.

Between the time site s_k responds by sending its YES vote to the coordinator and the time T_{ik} commits or aborts at s_k, T_{ik} is in a special state referred to as the *prepared state*. Local sites cannot unilaterally commit or abort a global subtransaction in the prepared state.

The mechanism of ensuring atomicity of global transactions in MDBSs differs widely, depending upon whether or not each local DBMS supports a prepared state. If each local DBMS supports a prepared state, then atomicity can be ensured in a manner similar to that of homogeneous distributed database systems by employing the above discussed 2PC protocol. However, supporting a prepared state for transactions results in the violation of the execution autonomy of the participating local DBMSs (since the local DBMS cannot unilaterally abort a transaction in the prepared state). Since the preservation of local autonomy is crucial in many applications, some local sites, even if they support a prepared state for transactions, they may be unwilling to participate in an atomic commit protocol to commit global transactions.

If a local DBMS does not participate in an atomic commit protocol to commit a global transaction, it may unilaterally abort a global subtransaction at any time during its execution. Specifically, it may abort a subtransaction of a global transaction even after the GTM has decided to commit the global transaction. Consequently, it is possible that a global transaction is aborted at some local DBMSs and committed at some other DBMSs. In order to ensure global transaction atomicity, in such a case, the only recovery option may be to construct for each aborted subtransaction, a transaction, consisting of the updates made by the aborted subtransaction, and submit it for execution to the local DBMS. We refer to such a transaction as the *redo* transaction and the above approach to recovery from subtransaction aborts as the redo approach. Before we describe a global commit protocol based on the redo approach to recovery, we first note that if the redo approach is used to recover from the subtransaction aborts, then a trivial GTM cannot be used for ensuring global serializability, even if each local DBMS produces rigorous schedules. This is illustrated in the following example.

Example 2: Consider an MDBS consisting of two sites: site s_1 with data item x and site s_2 with data item y. Let T_1 and T_2 be the following global transactions.

$T_1 : w_1(x)\ w_1(y)$

$T_2 : r_2(x)\ r_2(y)$

Suppose that the GTM decides to commit T_1. Further suppose that T_1 successfully commits at s_2, but the local DBMS at s_1 aborts T_1. The server at s_1 constructs the following redo transaction T_3 and submits it for execution to the local DBMS.

$T_3 : w_3(x)$

However, before T_3 is executed, global transaction T_2 executes at both sites s_1 and s_2 and commits at both the sites, following which the redo transaction T_2 executes at s_1 and commits. This results in the following local schedules. In the schedule, the write operation of T_1 that aborted at s_1 is included in angular brackets for clarity and is undone by the local DBMS at s_1.

$S_1 : [w_1(x)]\ a_1\ w_2(x)\ c_2\ w_3(x)\ c_3$
$S_2 : w_1(y)\ c_1\ r_2(y)\ c_2$

Note that since a trivial GTM does not control the order of execution of the global transaction operations, the above schedule would be permitted by a trivial GTM. Further, local schedules S_1 and S_2 are rigorous, illustrating that if the redo approach is combined with the trivial GTM, then even if local DBMSs are rigorous, global serializability may not be ensured. □

In the remainder of the section, we will only consider the problem of how to combine the redo approach to recovery with our concurrency control protocol based on maintaining a commit graph to ensure correctness under the assumption that each local DBMS generates strongly recoverable schedules. Note that since each rigorous schedule is also strongly recoverable, the same solution can be used in case each local DBMS generates rigorous schedules. We begin by first describing a global commit protocol for an MDBS environment where the local DBMSs do not support a prepared state. The protocol, to ensure global transaction atomicity, uses the redo approach to recovery.

Upon the completion of a global transaction, the GTM initiates the 2PC protocol with the servers at sites at which the transaction executed. In this protocol, the GTM plays a role of a coordinator, while each server at sites at which the transaction is executed is considered as a participant. Each server maintains its own *server log* in which it records all changes made by the global transaction to the local database. The server, before responding to the GTM's VOTE_REQ message with a YES vote, forces the log records in the server log corresponding to writes done by the transaction onto stable storage. Note that the servers, and *not* the local DBMSs, participate in the global commit protocol. The server submits a commit operation to the local DBMS only after the GTM has reached a decision to commit the transaction.

We now discuss how recovery from failures is done in a system that uses the above commit protocol. We limit our discussion to recovery from global subtransaction aborts since recovery from other kinds of failures (e.g., local DBMS failure) are simple extensions to recovery from transaction aborts. Global subtransactions may abort for a variety of reasons. A subtransaction may be aborted by the local DBMS due to a logical error, it may be chosen as a *victim* by the local deadlock detection algorithm, or it may be aborted by the local DBMS due to a timeout constraint.

If a failure occurs before the server has voted to commit the transaction, then the commit protocol will result in the decision to abort the global transaction. Since we assume that the local DBMSs undo all the effects of an aborted transaction on local databases, global transaction atomicity will be preserved. If, however, a global subtransaction abort occurs after the server at the site has voted to commit the transaction, and a global decision has been reached to commit the transaction, then the server constructs a *redo transaction* consisting of all the updates performed by a transaction at the site, and submits the redo transaction for execution to the local DBMS. A redo transaction, in case it aborts, is repeatedly submitted to the local DBMSs until it commits. Note that since a redo transaction is a write-only transaction, it cannot fail logically.

Although the above protocol guarantees global transaction atomicity, it nevertheless, suffers from the problem that serializability of even the local schedules is not always maintained. The reason for this is that the redone global subtransaction is considered by the local DBMS as a completely different transaction unrelated to the transaction that has been aborted. However, from the MDBS viewpoint, the redone transaction is part of the same global subtransaction that aborted. To illustrate the difficulty, let us consider an example of a schedule that is not serializable from the MDBS viewpoint but could be generated if the above global commit protocol is used.

Example 3: Consider an MDBS consisting of two sites: site s_1 with data items x, y, and site s_2 with data item z. Let T_1 be the following global transaction.

$T_1 : r_1(y)\ w_1(x)\ w_1(z)$

Suppose that the GTM decides to commit T_1 (using the global commit protocol). Further suppose that T_1 successfully commits at s_2, but the local DBMS at s_1 aborts T_1. The server at s_1 constructs the following redo transaction T_2 from the server log and submits it to the local DBMS.

$T_2 : w_2(x)$

However, before T_2 is executed, a local transaction:

$T_3 : r_3(x)\ w_3(y)$

executes at s_1. This results in the following local schedule at s_1.

$$S_1 : r_1(y)\ [w_1(x)]\ a_1\ r_3(x)\ w_3(y)\ c_3\ w_2(x)\ c_2$$

Since the local DBMS at s_1 considers T_1 and T_2 to be separate transactions, schedule S_1 is serializable in the local view (that is, in the view of the local DBMS). However, from the global MDBS viewpoint, since the read done by T_1 and the write performed by T_2 are part of one transaction, S_1 is not serializable. □

Since our concurrency control protocol ensures global serializability only under the assumption that each local schedule is serializable, we, therefore, must devise means to ensure serializability of each local schedule. Example 3 demonstrates that if the redo approach to recovery is used, it is impossible to recover from global subtransaction aborts without violation of global serializability unless some restrictions are placed on data items accessed by local and global transactions. These restrictions ensure that global and local transactions do not interact in adverse ways as illustrated in Example 3. To identify the required restrictions, as we proposed in [4], we first partition the set of data items at each site into:

- **global data items** - those data items that can only be modified by global transactions.
- **local data items** - all other data items.

An example of global data items are the set of replicated data item (local transactions do not write on replicated data items since that will violate the integrity constraints of the system). On the other hand, the set of data items which pre-existing local applications may modify are local data items. We impose the following restriction on data items accessed by global subtransactions:

> *If a global subtransaction reads a local data item, then it does not write any data item at the site.*

The above restriction is minimal, in the sense that, if a global transaction that reads local data items were to write either local or global data items, then it is possible for schedules to be non-serializable from the MDBS viewpoint. In Example 3, since local transaction T_3 writes data item y, it must be the case that y is a local data item. Thus, since the global subtransaction of T_1 at site s_1 reads local data item y and writes data item x, it violates the above restriction resulting is a loss of serializability in the MDBS viewpoint. Though the above restriction on global transactions is necessary, it is, by itself not sufficient for ensuring serializability of the local schedules. Serializability of the local schedules can, however, be ensured if the MDBS follows the *early commit* (EC) protocol introduced in [8] and further certain modifications are made to the GTM concurrency control protocol. We discuss these in turn.

The EC protocol is similar to the global commit protocol developed earlier, except that the GTM, in the first phase of the protocol, instead of sending a VOTE-REQ message, sends a COMMIT message to the servers at all the sites at which the subtransaction is a read-only transaction. We refer to such servers as *r-servers*. To the remaining servers, referred to as *w-servers*, the GTM sends a VOTE-REQ message. An r-server, on receipt of a COMMIT message from the GTM submits a commit operation for the transaction to the local DBMS. On receipt of an acknowledgement from the local DBMS, the server sends a COMMIT-ACK message to the GTM; if the subtransaction is aborted by the local DBMS, then the server sends a ABORT-ACK message to the GTM. A w-server behaves as in the previous case and sends its vote: YES (commit) or a NO (abort). If the GTM receives a YES from each w-server and a COMMIT-ACK from each r-server, it decides to commit the transaction and sends a COMMIT message to each of the w-servers. If it receives a NO from some w-server or an ABORT-ACK from some r-server, it decides to abort the transaction and sends an ABORT message to each of the w-servers. A w-server, on receipt of a message containing the decision of the GTM, submits either a commit or an abort operation to the local DBMS (depending upon the decision). In the EC protocol, committing the read-only subtransactions of a global transaction early does not result in a violation of its atomicity since the read-only subtransactions do not cause any changes to the database.

We next discuss the modifications needed to the GTM concurrency control protocol such that using the redo approach to recovery does not result in a loss of serializability of the local schedules. To motivate the need for the modification, we first present an example in which loss of serializability of a local schedule results even though each global transaction satisfies the restrictions stated above and the GTM uses the EC protocol to commit global transactions.

Example 4: Consider an MDBS consisting of three sites that produce rigorous local schedules: site s_1 with global data items x, y, site s_2 with global data item u, and s_3 with global data item v. Let T_1 and T_2 be global transactions and T_3 be a local transaction that executes at site s_1.

$$T_1 : r_1(x)\ w_1(y)\ w_1(u)$$
$$T_2 : w_2(x)\ w_2(v)$$
$$T_3 : r_3(x)\ r_3(y)$$

Suppose the GTM decides to commit T_1 (using the EC protocol). Further, suppose that T_1 successfully commits at s_2, but the local DBMS at s_1 aborts T_1. Transaction T_2 then executes at sites s_1 and s_3, and since there are no cycles in the commit graph, the GTM decides to commit T_2. Also, since the GTM considers T_1 to be committed, it executes the following redo transactions T_4 for T_1.

$$T_4 : w_4(y)$$

It is possible for transaction T_3 to execute at site s_1 in such a manner that the local schedule at site s_1 is as follows.

$$S_1 : r_1(x)\ [w_1(y)]\ a_1\ w_2(x)\ c_2\ r_3(x)\ r_3(y)\ c_3\ w_4(y)\ c_4$$

Since T_1 and T_4 are the same transaction in the MDBS viewpoint, global serializability is lost. □

To ensure that each local schedule is serializable and further global serializability is ensured, we need to modify the algorithm TM_1 such that if two global transactions are executing their commit operations concurrently at a site, then they are not in a *rw* or *wr* conflict at the site. The modified algorithm TM_2 is described below.

Algorithm TM_2

1. When a global transaction T_i submits its commit operation to the GTM, the GTM temporarily adds to the commit graph, edges (T_i, s_k) for each site s_k at which T_i executes.

2. If the augmented commit graph does contain a cycle, then the GTM places global transaction T_i on the waiting queue and deletes the temporary edges from the commit graph.

3. If the augmented commit graph does not contain a cycle, the GTM checks whether there is a global transaction T_j that the GTM has not decided to abort, such that at some site s_k,

    - T_{jk} is in a *wr* or *rw* conflict with T_{ik}, and
    - T_{jk} has not yet committed at site s_k.

4. If such a transaction exists, the GTM places T_i on the waiting queue and deletes the temporary edges from the commit graph.

5. If no such transaction exists, then the GTM initiates the EC protocol for T_i, and temporary edges in the commit graph become permanent.

6. If at some site s_k, subtransaction T_{ik} is aborted by the local DBMS, after the GTM has decided to commit global transaction T_i, then every global transaction T_j that reads data items written by T_{ik} is aborted. The server at site s_k then redoes T_{ik}'s write operations at site s_k until the redo transaction commits at s_k. Furthermore, every time the redo transaction is aborted by site s_k, every uncommitted global transaction T_j that reads data items written by T_{ik} is aborted.

7. Upon completion of a global transaction T_i's commit operation at the local DBMSs, the GTM performs the following: if there is no path in the commit graph from T_i to any other transaction T_j that has not completed its commit operation at some local DBMS, then delete from the commit graph T_i and all transactions T_j such that there is a path in the commit graph from T_i to T_j, along with all edges incident on these nodes.

8. If a transaction along with all incidental edges is deleted from the commit graph, the GTM checks the commit graph (using steps 1, 2 and 3) whether the commit operation of any transaction T_i in the waiting queue can be submitted to the local DBMSs.

In a failure-free environment, algorithm TM_2 performs almost identically to algorithm TM_1 with the only difference being that TM_2 keeps track of the *rw* and *wr* conflicts between global transactions, while TM_1 does not[2]. However, if a global subtransaction T_{ik} at site s_k is aborted by a local DBMS after the GTM has decided to commit T_i, then TM_2 aborts all other global transactions T_j such that T_{ik} is in a *wr* conflict with T_{jk}. In addition, any global transaction that submits an operation to read some data item written by the aborted subtransaction (until the redo transaction corresponding to the aborted subtransaction is successfully committed) is also aborted. We could have, instead, resorted to delaying such read operations until the failed subtransaction is redone.

Theorem 4: Consider an MDBS environment where the GTM follows the EC protocol and each local DBMS is strongly recoverable. If the GTM follows algorithm TM_2, then global serializability is assured. □

In algorithm TM_2, the additional checks performed in step 3 are essential, since otherwise, local schedules may not be serializable from the MDBS viewpoint (in the presence of global subtransaction aborts). This is illustrated by schedule S_1 in Example 4, which is non-serializable since the GTM permitted the commit operation of global transaction T_2 to be processed even though T_1 was in a *rw* conflict with T_2. A similar example in which non-serializable executions may result if the GTM permitted the commit operation of a transaction in a *wr* conflict to execute can also be constructed.

In the above discussed algorithm TM_2 the GTM only delays the commit operations of global transactions. In

[2]For this, the GTM would need to submit to the local DBMS, a read (write) operation that conflicts with a previously submitted write (read) operation, only after the acknowledgement for the execution of the previous operation has been received.

contrast, the schemes proposed in [4, 3] require not just the commit but also read and write operations of the global transactions to be delayed. Further, as opposed to TM_2 that only requires each local DBMS to be strongly recoverable, the scheme proposed in [4, 12] assumes that each local DBMS produces rigorous schedules.

5 Conclusions

A multidatabase system (MDBS) is a facility that allows access to data located in multiple pre-existing and autonomous database management systems (DBMSs). In such a system a software package built on top of the autonomous local DBMSs, referred to as the *global transaction manager* (GTM), coordinates the execution of *global transactions* that execute at multiple sites. Independently, *local transactions* execute at a single site outside the control of the GTM.

We studied, in detail, how global serializability can be ensured, both in presence and in the absence of failures, in an MDBS under two different assumptions on the nature of schedules produced by the participating local DBMSs– (1) Each local DBMS generates *rigorous* schedules, (2) Each local DBMS generates *strongly recoverable* schedules. Our interest in the rigorous schedules stems from the fact that the majority of commercial DBMSs offer a concurrency control protocol that generates rigorous schedules. However, the class of rigorous schedules is quite restrictive in terms of the amount of concurrency permitted. We, therefore, also considered the class of strongly recoverable schedules which permit a higher degree of concurrency as compared to the rigorous schedules. We proposed schemes that exploit the rigorousness and strong recoverability properties of the local schedules to ensure global serializability with minimal global overhead. We studied mechanisms to make our concurrency control technique failure-resilient under the scenario that each local DBMS supports a *prepared* state for the execution of the two-phase commit protocol as well as under the scenario that it does not.

References

[1] P. A. Bernstein, V. Hadzilacos, and N. Goodman. *Concurrency Control and Recovery in Database Systems.* Addison-Wesley, Reading, MA, 1987.

[2] Y. Breitbart, D. Georgakopoulos, M. Rusinkiewicz, and A. Silberschatz. On rigorous transaction scheduling. *IEEE Transactions on Software Engineering*, 1991.

[3] Y. Breitbart and A. Silberschatz. Strong recoverability in multidatabase systems. In *Proceedings of the Second International Workshop on Research Issues on Data Engineering: Transaction and Query Processing, Mission Palms, Arizona*, February 1992.

[4] Y. Breitbart, A. Silberschatz, and G. R. Thompson. Reliable transaction management in a multidatabase system. In *Proceedings of ACM-SIGMOD 1990 International Conference on Management of Data, Atlantic City, New Jersey*, pages 215–224, 1990.

[5] A.K. Elmagarmid and W. Du. A paradigm for concurrency control in heterogeneous distributed database systems. In *Proceedings of the Sixth International Conference on Data Engineering*, 1990.

[6] D. Georgakopoulos, M. Rusinkiewicz, and A. Sheth. On serializability of multidatabase transactions through forced local conflicts. In *Proceedings of the Seventh International Conference on Data Engineering, Kobe, Japan*, 1991.

[7] S. Mehrotra, R. Rastogi, Y. Breitbart, H. F. Korth, and A. Silberschatz. The concurrency control problem in multidatabases: Characteristics and solutions. In *Proceedings of ACM-SIGMOD 1992 International Conference on Management of Data, San Diego, California*, 1992.

[8] S. Mehrotra, R. Rastogi, Y. Breitbart, H. F. Korth, and A. Silberschatz. Ensuring transaction atomicity in multidatabase systems. In *Proceedings of the Eleventh ACM SIGACT-SIGMOD-SIGART Symposium on Principles of Database Systems, San Diego*, 1992.

[9] C. Pu. Superdatabases for composition of heterogeneous databases. In *Proceedings of the Fourth International Conference on Data Engineering, Los Angeles*, 1988.

[10] Yoav Raz. The principle of commit ordering. Technical report, Digital Equipment Corporation, 1991.

[11] J. Veijalainen and A. Wolski. Prepare and commit certification for decentralized transaction management in rigorous heterogeneous multidatabases. In *Proceedings of the Eighth International Conference on Data Engineering, Tempe, Arizona*, February 1992.

[12] A. Wolski and J. Veijalainen. 2PC agent method: Achieving serializability in presence of failures in a heterogeneous multidatabase. In *Proceedings of the International conference on databases, parallel architectures and their applications*, pages 321–330, March 1990.

SCHEMA TRANSFORMATION PROCESSORS FOR FEDERATED OBJECTBASES

Markus Tresch **Marc H. Scholl**
Department of Computer Science, Databases and Information Systems
University of Ulm, D-W 7900 Ulm, Germany
{tresch,scholl}@informatik.uni-ulm.de

ABSTRACT

In contrast to three schema levels in centralized objectbases, a reference architecture for federated objectbase systems proposes five levels of schemata. This paper investigates the fundamental mechanisms to be provided by an object model to realize the processors transforming between these levels, namely *schema extension*, *schema filtering*, and *schema composition*. It is shown, how composition and extension are used for stepwise bottom-up integration of existing objectbases into a federation; and how extension and filtering support authorization on different levels in a federation. A powerful View definition mechanism and the possibility to define subschemata (i.e., parts of a schema) are the key mechanisms used in these processes.

1 INTRODUCTION

Federated objectbase (FOB) systems as a collection of cooperating but autonomous local objectbases (LOBs) are getting increasing attention [8]. To clarify the various issues, a first reference architecture for federated database systems was presented by Sheth and Larson [16]. While the ANSI/SPARC three-level schema architecture was adequate for centralized objectbases, they introduced five schema levels for FOBs: (i) the *local schema* as the conceptual schema of a LOB, expressed in the native data model of each LOB; (ii) the *component schema* as the translation of the local schema into a canonical data model, that is, a model common to the federation; (iii) the *export schema* as a subset of the component schema, holding the part that is made available to the federation and its users; (iv) the *federated schema* as the integration of multiple export schemata, forming the global conceptual schema; (v) the *external schema* as a special view of the federated schema, customized for a class of federation users / applications.

A close look at this five-level reference architecture leads to the following observations:

1. Federated schemata are huge. A federated schema, as the global conceptual schema of the FOB, may contain thousands of types and classes. Moreover, due to semantic heterogeneity, a large number of structural conflicts may have to be solved. Thus, static integration of many LOB schemata into one federated schema at one shot is not appropriate, or even not feasible.

2. A view (subschema) mechanism is needed. So far, no widely accepted notion of views and subschemata in object-oriented database systems exists. However, this is essential for support of customization and access control on LOB as well as on FOB level. Within LOBs, views (subschemata) are needed to specify the exported part of the objectbase; within FOBs they are used to define external schemata of the federation.

3. Enforcing fixed schema levels is to restrictive. FOBs are supposed to make existing data repositories dynamically work together. Requiring five specific schema levels maybe too static; in fact, it might even be considered to violate the overall idea. Thus, not predefined schema levels, but types of schema transformation processors should be the main concern.

4. Local objectbases are populated. An FOB is basically developed in a bottom-up process by integrating existing LOBs. Each of these LOBs supposedly comes with already stored objects (type/class instances). Thus, together with schema integration, construction of the FOB must also consider the problem of unifying objects from different LOBs that represent the same real world entity.

This article identifies the fundamental mechanisms that transform between the different levels of schemata in an FOB, while at the same time taking into account the above observations. We thereby restrict our considerations to LOBs with homogeneous data models. That is, we treat the problem of data model transformation as a separate issue. As a representative data model, we use the object-oriented model COCOON, presented together with its algebra in Section 2. However, investigations are not limited to that model, but can similarly be applied to most other object-oriented models/systems. Section 3 introduces three basic schema transformation processors: *schema extension, schema filtering,* and *schema composition*. In Section 4, we describe how to use schema composition together with schema extension for the purpose of integrating multiple LOBs into an FOB. Section 5 shows how to manage authorization and access control in FOBs using schema extension combined with filtering. A comparison to other related work is made in Section 6. Finally, Section 7 shows, how the basic schema transformation processors fit into Sheth/Larson's reference architecture for federated objectbases, and concludes with an outlook on open issues.

2 AN OBJECT MODEL AND ALGEBRA

We briefly review the key concepts of the object model COCOON and its algebra [13], used throughout this paper. The COCOON object-model is an object-function model with the basic constituents *objects, functions, types, classes*, and *views*:

Objects are instances of abstract object types (AOTs), specified by their interface operations. In contrast, **Data** are instances of concrete types (e.g., numbers, strings) or constructed types (e.g., tuple or set).

Functions are the generalized abstraction of attributes (stored or computed), relationships between objects, and update methods (with side-effects). They are described by their name and signature, i.e. domain and range type. Functions can be single- or set-valued. The implementation is given separately, in the object implementation language (OIL), which is not described here any further.

Types describe the common interface to all of its instances. So, a type t is defined by a set of applicable functions *functs(t)*. The subtype (is-a) relationship, which is used for type-checking, corresponds to subset relationship of function sets, such that type t_2 is subtype of t_1 iff $functs(t_2) \supseteq functs(t_1)$. The root of the type lattice is the predefined type **object**. The language is strongly typed, in the sense that it supports full static type checking. Types can be named. However, this is optional because new types can arise dynamically as any set of functions.

Classes are strictly distinguished from types [4]. A class c is a typed collection of objects. It has an associated member type *mtype(c)* and an actual extension *extent(c)*, i.e. the set of objects in the class. We define the extent of a class to include the members of all its subclasses, such that objects can be member of multiple classes at the same time. The subclass relationship is defined on the subset relationship of class extension and subtype relationship. Hence, c_2 is a subclass of c_1 iff $extent(c_2) \subseteq extent(c_1) \wedge functs(mtype(c_2)) \supseteq functs(mtype(c_1))$. The top class of this hierarchy is the class **Objects**.

Views are virtual (derived) classes, that is, classes whose extent and member type are computed by a query expression. We discuss views in more detail in Section 3.1 below.

An objectbase schema is a representation of the structure (syntax), semantics, and constraints on the use of an objectbase in the object model. In the COCOON model, this is given as follows by classes, views, types, and functions:

Definition 1. (Database Schema) A database schema is a four-tuple $S = < C, V, T, F >$, with

- C a set of given classes;
- V a set of views defined on classes C;
- $T = \bigcup_{c \in C} mtype(c) \ \cup \ \bigcup_{v \in V} mtype(v)$ the set of member types of classes C and views V;
- $F = \bigcup_{t \in T} functs(t)$ the set of functions of types T.

Example 1: As a running example throughout this paper, we use the sample scenario shown in Figure 1. It illustrates a situation in a company, using two independent COCOON objectbases: *SalesDB* in the sales department, storing information about articles and customers; and *ProdDB* in the production department, with data on raw materials and their suppliers.

```
define database SalesDB as
    define type article isa object = matn: integer ,
            boughtby: set of customer inv bought ;
    define type screw isa article = thread: string ,
    define type customer isa object =
            name, addr: string ,
            bought: set of article inv boughtby ;
    define class Articles: article ;
    define class Screws: screw some Articles;
    define class Customers: customer ;
end ;

define database ProdDB as
    define type material isa object = mno: integer ,
            weight: kilo ;
            supplby: supplier inv supplies ;
    define type supplier isa object =
            name, street, city: string ,
            supplies: set of materials inv supplby ;
    define class Materials: material ;
    define class Suppliers: supplier ;
end ;
```

The schemata of the two databases *SalesDB* and *ProdDB* are given as:

$$S_{SalesDB} = < \{Articles, Screws, Customers\}, \{\}, \{article, screw, customer\}, \{ano, price, matn, boughtby, thread, name, cstreet, addr, bought\} >$$

$$S_{ProdDB} = < \{Materials, Suppliers\}, \{\}, \{material, supplier\}, \{mno, weight, supplby, name, street, city, supplies\} >$$

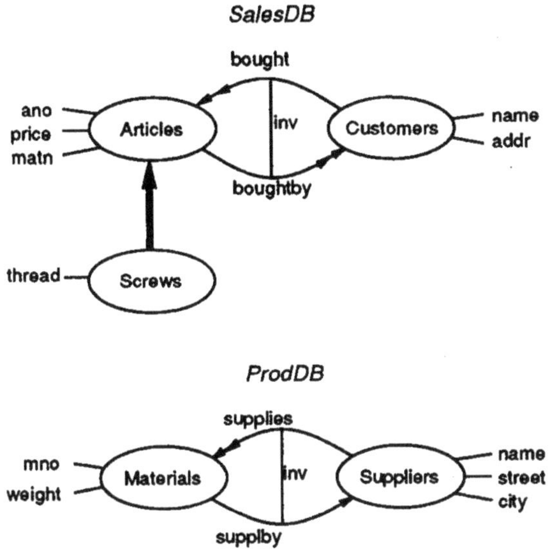

Figure 1: Local objectbases *SalesDB* and *ProdDB*

We use a *set-oriented query language* similar to (nested) relational algebra, where the inputs and outputs of the operations are *sets* of objects. Hence, query operators can be applied to extents of classes, set-valued function results, and query results. The algebra has an object-preserving semantics, in the sense that queries return (some of) the input objects. This semantics for queries allows the application of methods and update operations to results of a query, since these contain base objects. As query operators we provide selection of objects, projection, extension, and the set operations for union, intersection, and difference.

3 BASIC SCHEMA TRANSFORMATION PROCESSORS

In this section we define and analyze three basic schema transformation processors for federated objectbases: (i) *schema extension* to add new derivable information persistently to a schema, (ii) *filtering* to hide schema information from users, and (iii) *composition* to combine several schemata together.

3.1 Schema Extension

It is widely accepted for relational systems that a primary step towards extensibility and flexibility of database schemata is the powerful mechanism of defining *views* (persistent queries). In the COCOON model, views are defined as virtual classes, whose extent and type is derived by a query based on other classes [12]. The main difference to other object-oriented view approaches is that we use the query language (object algebra) and do not introduce special-purpose syntactic constructs for view definition. Hence, views are declared as

define view v **as** e ;

with e an (algebraic) query expression of arbitrary complexity. Another important difference is that views are positioned in the type and class hierarchies according to their computed type and extent.

Notice, that views can also be defined over other views or by composite queries. Below, we describe what the member type and the extent is, and how these are positioned in the type and class hierarchies.

Selection views (**define view** v **as select**$[p](e)$). The extent of the view v is a subset of the base class' members, namely those satisfying the predicate p. The member type remains unchanged, such that there are now two classes, v and c, of that type. Consequently, the view class v is positioned as subclass of the base class c.

Projection views (**define view** v **as project**$[f, \ldots](e)$). The member type of view v is a supertype of the original one, since less functions are defined on it, namely those listed in the projection. However, projection does not manipulate the extent, such that the extent of v is the same as that of e. The view is therefore positioned as a superclass v is a superclass of c.

Extend views (**define view** v **as extend**$[f := expr, \ldots](e)$). While projection eliminates functions, extend defines new derived ones f, by any legal arithmetic, boolean, or set-expression $expr$. So, the type of view v is a subtype of the base class' type, since it has more functions (all the old functions plus the new ones are defined). Like with projection, the extent is unchanged again. The view v is therefore a subclass of c,.

Set-operator views (**define view** v **as** e **union** | **intersect** | **difference** e;). As the extent of classes are sets of objects, we can perform set operations as usual. These views change extents as well as member types. However, in a polymorphic type system, we need no restrictions on operand types of set operations (ultimately, they are all instances of type **object**). A union view creates a common superclass of its bases classes, where the extent is the union of the base class' objects, and the member type is the lowest common supertype (intersection of base class functions) of the input types. An intersection view is common subclass, with the intersection of the input objects and the greatest common supertype (union of base class functions) as member type. Finally, difference views are subclasses of their base classes.

Based on the abstraction of derived classes as views, schema extension is now defined as the processor that enhances a given schema with derived information.

Definition 2. (Schema Extension) Let $S = < C, V, T, F >$ be a database schema. Furthermore, let V_S be a set of views defined on C and V. The extension of S by V_S is a schema $S' = < C', V', T', F' >$ with $C' = C$ and $V' = V \cup V_S$.

Recall from Definition 2, that types (T') and functions (F') are computed from C', V'. Related to federated systems, schema extension is used on two different levels. In LOBs to customize the component schema before it participates the federation, and in FOBs to create external schemata of the global federated system.

Example 2: The following DDL statements define a schema *SalesDB-1* as an extension of *SalesDB*. The **import** clause makes the base schema available, such that additional views can be defined.

```
define schema SalesDB-1 as
    import SalesDB ;
    define view PublArticles as
            project [ ano, matn, boughtby ] ( Articles ) ;
    define view ArticlesUS$ as
            extend [ price$:= price*0.657 ] ( Articles ) ;
    define view UselessCustomers as
            select [ bought = {} ] ( Customers ) ;
end ;
```

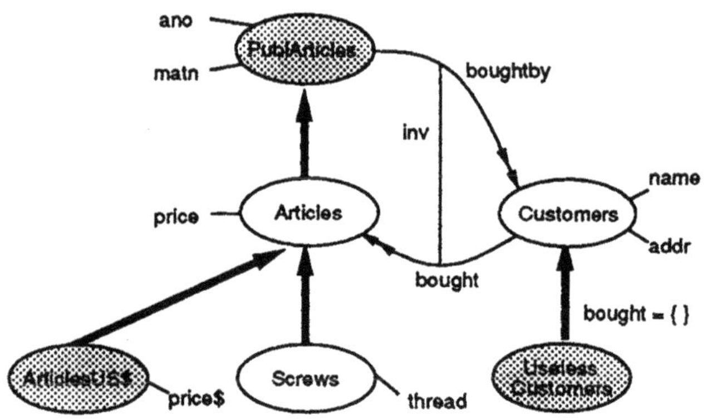

Figure 2: Schema *SalesDB-1* as the extension of *SalesDB* with view classes.

The extended schema *SalesDB-1* is illustrated in Figure 2. Notice, how views are positioned in the class hierarchy. Whereas selection and extend views are subclasses of their base class, the projection view is a superclass.

$$S_{SalesDB-1} = \\ <\{Articles, Screws, Customers\}, \\ \{PublArticles, ArticlesUS\$, UselessCustomers\}, \\ \{article, screw, customer, \\ [ano, matn, boughtby], [ano, matn, price, price\$]\}, \\ \{ano, price, price\$, matn, boughtby, thread, \\ name, addr, bought\} > .$$

Remember that types are sufficiently specified by their applicable set of functions and need not be named. E.g., the projection and the extension view produce new (unnamed) types. For unnamed types we alternatively enumerate its function sets $[ano, matn, boughtby]$ and $[ano, matn, price, price\$]$ in the schema description.

3.2 Schema Filtering

The opposite processor of adding derived information to a schema is filtering, that is, excluding parts of a given schema (e.g., classes and views). After extending a schema with derived information, it is desirable to identify a subset of classes and views in order to build a *subschema*. Only the selected classes and views of a subschema are then exported to foreign services (such as users, applications, or other systems).

Definition 3. (Subschema) Let $S = < C, V, T, F >$ be a schema. Then a subschema of S is a schema $S' = < C', V', T', F' >$ with $C' \subseteq C$ and $V' \subseteq V$.

Schema filtering processors are used in LOBs together with schema extension to define a customized (sub-)schema that does not contain all component classes and views of the LOB. In a FOB, subschemata are similarly used as global external schemata. Below, we give an example on how to use subschemata to hide information from a users.

Example 3: To define a subschema without pricing information, we first extend *SalesDB* with view *PublArticles* projecting out the *price* function from the class *Articles*. Then the **export** clause is used to make visible just the class *Customers*, the view *PublArticles*, and nothing else.

```
define schema SalesDB-2 as
    import SalesDB ;
    define view PublArticles as
            project [ ano, matn, boughtby ] ( Articles ) ;
    export Customers, PublArticles ;
end ;
```

The resulting subschema *SalesDB-2* is illustrated by the dotted area in Figure 3.a below:

$$S_{SalesDB-2} = \\ <\{Customers\}, \{PublArticles\}, \\ \{customer, [ano, matn, boughtby]\}, \\ \{ano, matn, boughtby, name, addr, bought\} > .$$

The major restriction to be imposed on subschemata is (transitive) *closure* of types. This attacks the problem that there must not be a function in a subschema that "leads out of it". More formally, the range type of each function of a subschema has to be part of the subschema itself. "Open schemata" must be omitted, since programs running with them may result in run-time type errors. It is quite intuitive, that an application cannot handle objects whose types are not described in the schema. This restriction leads to the following revised definition:

Definition 4. (Closed Subschema) Let $S = < C, V, T, F >$ be a schema. Then a closed subschema of S is a schema $S' = < C', V', T', F' >$ with $C' \subseteq C$ and $V' \subseteq V$, such that $\forall f \in F'$ with $range(f) \preceq$ **object** : $range(f) \in T'$.

For closure, we consider only object-valued functions, that is, functions returning an instance of an abstract object type. We assume that primitive (value) types (such as integer, boolean, and string) are by definition part of any schema, that is, functions with such range types do not lead out of the schema, even if we did not explicitly include their range.

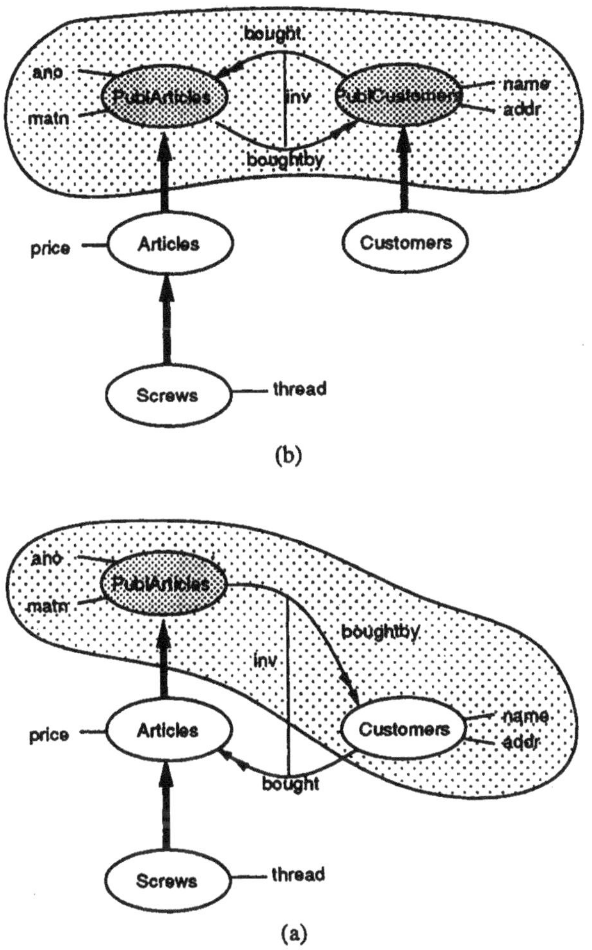

Figure 3: (a) Not closed subschema *SalesDB-2* and (b) closed subschema *SalesDB-3*.

Notice that the subschema of Figure 3.a is NOT closed. This can easily be seen, because the function *bought* leads out of the dotted area. The application of function *bought(c)* to a given customer *c* is a valid expression according to open subschema *SalesDB-2*. The result is a set of articles, though the type *article* is not part of the schema (only a supertype of it, namely [*ano, matn, boughtby*]). To make the schema closed, the transitive closure of all functions' range types must be built (see also [11]), which results in the following closed version of *SalesDB-2*:

$$S_{SalesDB-2*} = \; <\{Customers\}, \{PublArticles\}, \{customer, [ano, matn, boughtby], article\}, \{ano, matn, boughtby, name, addr, bought, price\} > .$$

The schema is now closed again. However, the *price* function was included, which is exactly what we wanted to avoid. The way out from the above dilemma is an enhanced projection operator that allows to redirect function range types. The *redirecting projection* allows to change the range type of a projected function in the projection list:

project [*f::t*, ...] (*e*); with $t \succeq range(f)$.

Redirection must be limited to supertypes in order to stay within the type checking possibilities of a polymorphic type system.

Example 4: The revised attempt to find a closed subschema without pricing information is to define two redirecting projection views as follows:

```
define schema SalesDB-3 as
   import SalesDB ;
   define view PublArticles as
      project [ ano, matn, boughtby::PublCustomers ]
              ( Articles ) ;
   define view PublCustomers as
      project [ name, addr, bought::PublArticles ]
              ( Customers ) ;
   export PublArticles, PublCustomers;
end ;
```

In the final subschema *SalesDB-3*, just these two views are made visible. Figure 3.b shows that *SalesDB-3* is now closed and information about prices are completely hidden.

$$S_{SalesDB-3} = \; <\{\}, \{PublArticles, PublArticles\}, \{[ano, matn, boughtby :: PublCustomers], [name, addr, bought :: PublArticles]\}, \{ano, matn, boughtby :: PublCustomers, name, addr, bought :: PublArticles\} > .$$

An important observation about closure of subschemata is that there is no restriction on the classes, only on types. Obviously the sole purpose of schema filtering is to hide some object collections (i.e., classes) from the export schema, so there should not be a need for inclusion of classes (or views) into an export schema because of closure constraints. Particularly, we do not need to include the base class(es) of a view into the subschema when including the view.

3.3 Schema Composition

Both schema transformations presented so far operate on one single schema. The next processor, called schema composition, is the first step towards interoperability of multiple objectbase systems.

It is the elementary process that combines schemata of multiple LOBs into one *composed schema*. This is the foundation for establishing a federated objectbase system. Schema composition places only minimal requirements on the degree of integration between participating objectbases. In fact, it basically just imports the names of all schema elements (classes, views, types, and functions) from LOBs and makes them globally available [14].

Example 5: Assume we want to create a FOB *FedDB* consisting of the LOBs *SalesDB* and *ProdDB* from Example 1. The very elementary step is to compose the schemata of the participating systems. Figure 4 graphically illustrates how schemata of *SalesDB* and *ProdDB* are put side-by-side by the following **import** clauses.

define schema *FedDB* **as**
  import *SalesDB* ;
  import *ProdDB* ;
end ;

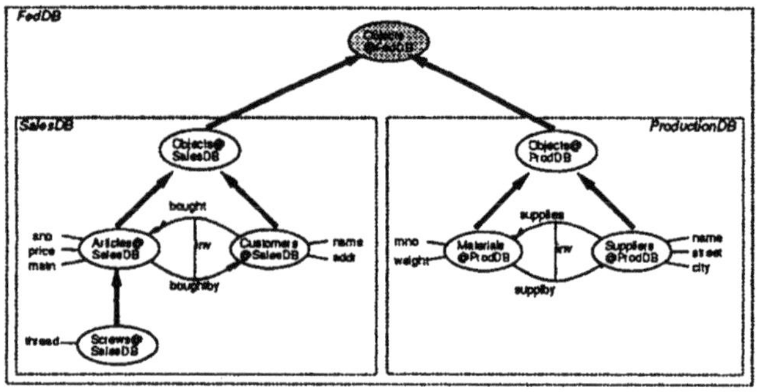

Figure 4: Composition of local schemata *SalesDB* and *ProdDB* into *FedDB*

More precisely, composition of local objectbases LOB_i into a federated system FOB combines the class and type systems of the local objectbases. First, the basic data types (integer, string, ...) of the different systems are unified. Second, the class and type hierarchies of the local objectbases are put together on the schema level AND on the meta-schema level in the following (so far trivial) way:[1]

Schema Level: A global schema is created with a new top type *object@FOB*, a new bottom type *bottom@FOB*, and a new global top class *Objects@FOB*.

The global type hierarchy is established, where all top types of the local objectbases (*object@LOB*$_i$) are made direct subtypes of the new global top element *object@FOB*. The new bottom type *bottom@FOB* is made common subtype of all local bottom types. No further subtype relationships are established.

[1]In the sequel, we use the naming convention that schema components are suffixed by "@" and the name of the local schema. For example, class *Articles* in *SalesDB* has as globally unique name "*Articles@SalesDB*".

Similar, a global subclass hierarchy is composed, with the new top element *Objects@FOB* as common superclass to all local top classes *Objects@LOB*$_i$ (see Figure 4).

Meta-Schema Level: A global meta-schema is created as well. This is the meta schema of the FOB. The meta-schema of each LOB_i contains three meta types *class, type, functions* and three meta classes *Classes, Types, Functions*, respectively (a detailed discussion of the COCOON meta-schema is contained in [20]).

A global meta-schema is created with new types *class@FOB*, *type@FOB*, and *function@FOB*, as well as three new meta classes *Classes@FOB*, *Types@FOB*, and *Functions@FOB*. The FOB meta-schema has therefore exactly the same structure as that of each LOB_i. Then, the local meta classes and meta types are made subclass/subtype of their global counterparts.

Furthermore, meta functions are unified during the composition process, e.g., in each LOB_i there is a meta function *super_types(t)@LOB*$_i$ finding all supertypes of a given type t. These functions are all automatically unified over all objectbases.

Definition 5. (Schema Composition) Let $S_1 = < C_1, V_1, T_1, F_1 >, \ldots, S_n = < C_n, V_n, T_n, F_n >$ be database schemata. Then the composition of $S_1, \ldots, S_n$ is a schema $S' = < C', V', T', F' >$ with $C' = C_0 \cup C_1 \cup \ldots \cup C_n$ and $V' = V_1 \cup \ldots \cup V_n$, where $C_0 = \{$ *Objects*$_0$, *Classes*$_0$, *Types*$_0$, *Functions*$_0$ $\}$ is the set of federated meta classes.

Schema composition is not yet real "objectbase integration". In particular, no instance of *object@FOB* is instance of more than one component type *object@LOB*$_i$. Furthermore, the extent of *Objects@FOB* is partitioned into **disjoint** subsets *Objects@LOB*$_i$. As a consequence, no two objects in *Objects@FOB* can be the same (identical), unless they originate from the same LOB_i and are identical in LOB_i.

4 INTEGRATION OF OBJECTBASES

Real integration of instances and schemata is performed quite easily by applying schema extension processors to formerly composed LOB_i schemata.

Since objectbase integration is not the main topic of this paper, but should just be discussed as an application of schema transformation processors, we refer for more formal details on the mechanism (i.e., *same*-functions, global identity, solving structural and semantic conflicts) to [14]. We recall here some of the results, as far as they are necessary to understand how extension, filtering, and composition processors work on FOBs.

4.1 Unifying Objects

Since LOBs have been used independently of each other, one real world (entity) object may be represented by different database (proxy) objects in different LOBs. The fundamental assumption of object-oriented models, namely that one real world object is represented by exactly one database object, is therefore no longer true in FOBs [9]. We therefore need an additional notion: we say that two local objects are *the same*, iff they represent the same real world (entity) object.

Same objects are identified in FOBs by extending the composed schema using extend views to define so called *same*-functions. Formally, we require that for any two types from different LOBs (T_i from LOB_i and S_j from LOB_j), the instances of which shall be unified, we are giving a query expression that determines, for a given T_i-object, what the corresponding S_j-object is (if any), and vice versa. This query expression is used to define a derived function $same_{T_i,S_j}$ from T_i to S_j and its inverse, $same_{S_j,T_i}$. Obviously, these query expressions are application dependent and can, in general, not be derived automatically.

To state that instances of type *customer* of *SalesDB* are identical with instances of type *supplier* of *ProdDB*, if they have identical names, for example, we have to defined the following *same*-functions:

extend [$same_{\text{customer,supplier}}$:=
    pick(select[*name(c)=name(s)*](*s:Suppliers*))]
    (*c:Customers*) ;
extend [$same_{\text{supplier,customer}}$:=
    pick(select[*name(s)=name(c)*](*c:Customers*))]
    (*s:Suppliers*) ;

Notice, that the **pick** operator does a set collapse, that is, it takes a single object out of a singleton set. This is valid here, since we assume that each object in one objectbase corresponds to at least one object in the other objectbase.

4.2 Schema Integration

After unifying proxy objects in different LOBs, we now focus on schema integration, that is to find out, what the common parts in the local schemata are, and to define a correspondence among them.

In Subsection 3.3, we said that schema composition also constructs a global meta schema. To define correspondences between functions from different LOBs, we make use of the fact, that every function is represented by a meta object. Thus, integrating functions from LOB_i and LOB_j is now straightforward: we unify the objects that represent the functions in the meta-schema by defining a *same*-function from meta type *function@*LOB_i to meta type *function@*LOB_j.

To unify for example the functions *name@SalesDB* and *name@ProdDB*, the following *same*-function is defined on the meta schema of *FOB*:

extend [$same_{\text{function@SalesDB,function@ProdDB}}$:=
    pick(select [*name(f) = 'name'*
        ∧ name(g) = 'name']
        (*g:Functions@SalesDB*))
    ] (*f:Functions@ProdDB*) ;

In contrast to most other schema integration approach that emphasis on solving semantic and structural conflicts among different systems [3, 17], we concentrate here on reducing schema integration to unifying meta objects.

4.3 Objectbase Integration Method

We have now defined all prerequisites for tight objectbase integration: we showed how to find "same" objects over multiple systems and discussed schema integration as unification of meta-objects. As a consequence, we can now come up with a methodology for stepwise integration of populated objectbase systems that uses schema composition together with extension:

Step 1. Use schema composition to put LOB schemata side-by-side and to make types and classes known to each other.

Step 2. Use schema extension to add extend views with *same*-functions to identify proxy objects from different LOBs that represent the same entity object from the real world. Use this mechanism also to integrate corresponding parts of the LOB schemata into an uniform schema element in the FOB, by unifying meta objects representing functions from different LOBs.

Step 3. Use schema extension again to add views that span over several objectbases. They now respect same objects from different LOBs and same properties from different LOB types.

Example 6: Reconsider the schema *FedDB*. Following to the above method, we first compose the local schemata by importing *SalesDB* and *ProdDB*. Then, we extend the classes *Customers* and *Suppliers* with *same*-functions. Finally, the meta class *Functions@SalesDB* is extended to integrate *name@SalesDB* and *name@ProdDB* properties.

define schema *FedDB* **as**
  import *SalesDB ;*
  import *ProdDB ;*
  define view *Customers'@SalesDB* **as**
    extend ...   */* see Subsection 4.1 */ ;*
  define view *Suppliers'@ProdDB* **as**
    extend ...   */* see Subsection 4.1 */ ;*
  define view *Functions'@SalesDB* **as**
    extend ...   */* see Subsection 4.2 */ ;*
  define view *Persons* **as** *Customers'@SalesDB*
    union *Suppliers'@ProdDB ;*
end *;*

Now, we are ready to define views that span multiple objectbases, e.g., a view *Persons* as the union over the extended classes *Customers'@SalesDB* and *Suppliers'@ProdDB*.

One point of interest is the extent and the type of the union view. The extent is defined to be the union of the objects of the base classes. However, if there would be a customer object and a supplier object, having equal names, they are defined through the *same*-function to represent one and the same real world object, and will therefore appear only once in the union view. The type of a union view is defined as intersection of the functions of the base classes. Thus, since the type of *Customer'* is [*name, addr, bought*, $same_{c,s}$] and of *Suppliers* is [*name, street, city, supplies*, $same_{s,c}$], and *name@SalesDB* and *name@ProdDB* functions are defined to be the same, the type of the view is [*name*].

5 ACCESS CONTROL AND AUTHORIZATION

FOBs are supposed to bring together several component systems. Federation users will therefore have possible access to large data repositories. Consequently, access control and authorization is a major problem in the design of federated systems. In this section, we discuss the possibilities there are to permit or deny access to objects in a federation, using schema extension and filtering processors.

5.1 Authorization Possibilities

So far, we introduced two mechanisms of hiding specific information from users: *views* and *subschemata*. Views, as virtual classes, operate on collections of objects. The possibilities of a query language are available to restrict either the set of visible objects, or the applicable functions. Subschemata, as a collection of classes and views, operate on whole schemata. They are used to grant access to a specific user for a defined subset of a given schema.

Selection views are used to hide some of the objects in a class. The hidden objects must be describable by a predicate using information of the database. We can for example hide expensive screws from users of *SalesDB*:

define view *CheapScrews* **as**
  select [*price* < *10*] (*Screws*);

A first idea of how to use projection views in order to hide properties of classes was given in Example 3. Moreover, since functions are abstractions of stored properties as well as of methods, access can be restricted to read, write, or update. Consider in the same example the class *Articles* with an additional method *get_price*. Projecting out the property *price* while keeping *get_price*, has the effect of setting a read-only privilege.

Extend views are thought to keep the result of a query as a new property of objects. As we have seen also in Section 4, this is a very powerful mechanism. For authorization purposes, extend views are adequate to show a new derived property. Assume, users of the *Materials* class are not allowed to see the supplier, but need to know the city where the material is supplied from.

define view *Materials'* **as project** [*mno, weight, city*]
  (**extend** [*scity:= city(supplby(m))*] (*m:Materials*)) ;

Union views make physical distribution transparent. Suppose a union of two classes from different LOBs. If only the union view is visible, a user does not (need to) know in which LOB the objects are physically stored.

Schema extension together with filtering processors are well suited as the basic mechanisms for flexible control of object access in FOBs. In fact, due to object identity, we do not have the problem of view updatability in our model. Furthermore, abstract object types, object encapsulation, and type-specific methods enhance to possibilities of authorization using view classes, compared to relational systems for example. We thereafter propose the following two-step authorization method:

Step 1. Use schema extension to define a view class on those classes where you want to hide some information.

Step 2. Use schema filtering to define a subschema, including your defined views, while filtering out their base classes.

Notice, that filtering out the base class of a view does not restrict updatability. In the example above, we can create a new screw object in the view *CheapScrews* at any time. The update will be propagated to the base class *Screws*, even if it is not part of the subschema. The only side-effect is, that if the newly added object was not a cheap one, it is afterwards not any more visible in the view. Nevertheless, the object is available as an article of course.

5.2 Levels of Access Control

In FOBs, we use schema extension and filtering processors mainly on two different levels: (i) related to LOBs to specify export schemata and therefore to control access to a component system; (ii) related to FOBs to specify global external schemata and therefore to control access to the global federated system. Negotiations between the component DBAs and the federation DBA is necessary to agree who has the control access on which objects.

Example 7: Consider the following scenario: the two LOBs given in Example 1 should be merged into a federated system, such that there will be two new customized databases, a *PersonDB* holding all information about customers and suppliers, and a *ConstructionDB* with all data on articles and materials. To do this, there are mainly two possible alternatives to combine the LOBs *SalesDB* and *ProdDB*, both of which come to the same result.

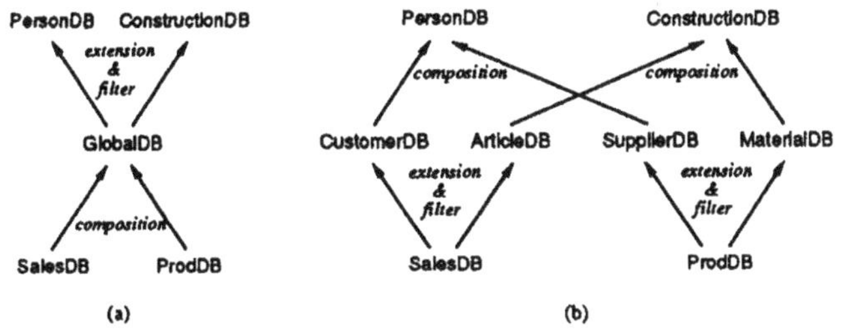

Figure 5: Access control trusted (a) to federation DBAs and (b) to local DBAs

Alternative 1. The federation DBA composes complete LOB schemata into a single schema *GlobalDB*. Based on this global schema, he derives two subschemata by extension and filtering, *PersonDB* including customers and suppliers, and *ConstructionDB* with articles and materials (see Figure 5.a).

In this approach, component DBAs do not make any restriction to the data they export to the federation. Thus, full access control is trusted to the federated DBA, he is responsible to combine the appropriate classes into subschemata of the federation and to make available to the distinct users.

Alternative 2. Each component DBA creates on his LOB site customized subschemata, already splitting the local objectbase into information about persons and construction. To the federation DBA of the *PersonDB* and of the *ConstructionDB*, which may be different, only those subschemata are made accessible, they finally need. So, one will compose *CustomerDB* with *SupplierDB* and the other *ArticleDB* with *MaterialDB* (see Figure 5.b).

In this approach, component DBAs have control on their local data and provide access individually. Federation DBAs may even not know what is the full contents in the LOBs.

6 RELATED WORK

Recently, there has been an increasing number of proposals on how to support views in object-oriented systems. Our approach is fundamentally different in that we make exclusive use of query language expressions (object algebra) to define views. In contrast e.g., O_2 [1] and ORION [5] introduce special purpose view definition features, FUGUE [7] use type hierarchies for information hiding, and POSTGRES [19] uses the rule system for view simulation.

Moreover, most of them do not consider positioning view classes in type and class hierarchies. One exception is a view definition methodology of [11], where one basic step is integration of virtual classes into one consistent global schema. [5] presents a related solution by introducing a new "view derivation hierarchy" that is orthogonal to the type and class hierarchies.

Closure was recognized important for schema correctness in [12, 11]. The latter presents an algorithm making any schema closed by transitively including all range classes. As we discussed in Subsection 3.2, this approach is not satisfactory since it brings in properties of objects through the back door, that we intentionally wanted to filter out.

The approach of database integration by finding corresponding properties and proxy objects was also investigated in [15, 6]. They introduced for each kind of semantic relationship between objects a new special type of generalization class. In contrast, our solution makes exclusive use of an algebraic object view mechanism, using the possibility of the **extend** operator to establish links between LOBs.

The power of views and query languages for access control was discussed very early for relational systems [18]. [10] realized that for databases including richer object-oriented and semantic concepts, an advanced model for authorization is needed. However, they do not investigate the enhanced possibilities of an object-oriented algebra (encapsulation, type-specific methods) for authorization purposes.

7 CONCLUSION

The contribution of this paper is three basic schema transformation processors for federated objectbases: schema *extension* to add views that are computed by an algebraic query language; *filtering* to build a closed subschema, and *composition* to put schemata side-by-side.

FOBs are supposed to follow Sheth/Larson's reference architecture with five schema levels. The three processors are said to be complete in the sense, that every transition between these schema levels can be attained by applying a combination of them as follows:

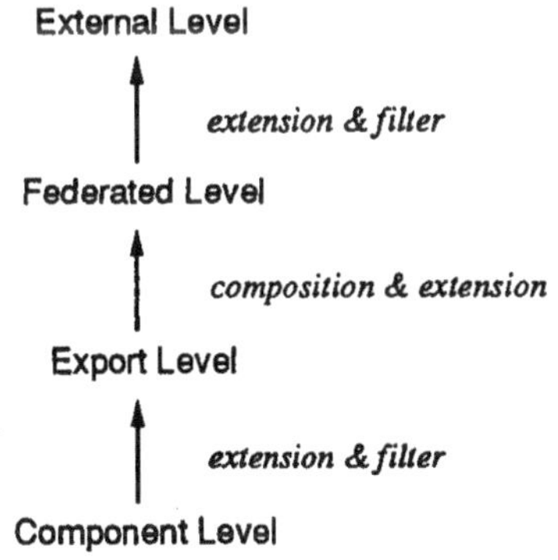

Nevertheless, the processors do not require fixed levels, but support incremental evolution from given LOBs to customized user-oriented FOBs. In fact, one may also see this as a bottom-up development and design methodology for FOBs

Integration of objectbases was introduced as schema composition followed by schema extension. This approach defuses the problem of huge federated schemata, because there is no need to define such a global view, but instead only those parts are to be combined that are really needed. It pays also attention to the fact that LOBs are populated before they come together in a federation.

Access control and authorization in FOBs was shown how to be managed by schema extension together with schema filtering. It was discussed, that access control can be permitted or denied either locally on LOB level, or globally on FOB level.

At the beginning, we mentioned that we are restricted to FOBs with homogeneous data models. Future work will consider a fourth processor: schema *mapping*. This processors is needed to map LOB schemata of different models/languages into a common data model. First results are already available from the FEMUS project [2], where COCOON objectbases and algebra expressions were mapped to an extended entity-relationship model with an ER calculus.

References

[1] S. Abiteboul and A. Bonner. Objects and views. In *Proc. ACM SIGMOD*, Denver, Colorado, June 1991.

[2] M. Andersson, Y. Dupont, S. Spaccapietra, K. Yétongnon, M. Tresch, and H. Ye. The FEMUS experience in building a federated multilingual database. In *Proc. 3st Int'l RIDE-IMS Workshop*, Vienna, Austria, April 1993.

[3] C. Batini, M. Lenzerini, and S.B. Navathe. A comparative analysis of methodologies for database schema integration. *ACM Computing Surveys*, 18(4), December 1986.

[4] C. Beeri. Formal models for object-oriented databases. In *Proc. 1st Int'l Conf. DOOD*, Kyoto, Japan, December 1989.

[5] E. Bertino. A view mechanism for object-oriented databases. In *Proc. 3rd Int'l Conf on EDBT'92*, Vienna, Austria, March 1992.

[6] J. Geller, Y. Perl, and E.J. Neuhold. Structural schema integration in heterogeneous multi-database systems using the dual model. In *Proc. 1st Int'l RIDE-IMS Workshop*, Kyoto, Japan, April 1991.

[7] S. Heiler and S.B. Zdonik. Object views: Extending the vision. In *Proc. 6th Int'l IEEE Data Engineering*, Los Angeles, February 1990.

[8] D. K. Hsiao. Federated databases and systems. *VLDB Journal*, 1(1), 1992.

[9] W. Kent. The breakdown of the information model in multi-database systems. *ACM SIGMOD Record*, 20(4), December 1991.

[10] F. Rabitti, E. Bertino, W. Kim, and D. Woelk. A model for authorization for next-generation database systems. *ACM TODS*, 16(1), March 1991.

[11] E.A. Rundensteiner. MultiView: a methodology for supporting multiple views in object-oriented databases. In *Proc. 18th Int'l Conf. on VLDB*, Vancouver, Canada, August 1992.

[12] M.H. Scholl, C. Laasch, and M. Tresch. Updatable views in object-oriented databases. In *Proc. 2nd Int'l Conf. on DOOD*, Munich, Germany, December 1991.

[13] M.H. Scholl and H.-J. Schek. A relational object model. In *Proc. 3rd Int'l Conf. on ICDT*, Paris, 1990.

[14] M.H. Scholl, H.-J. Schek, and M. Tresch. Object algebra and views for multi-objectbases. In *Proc. Int'l Workshop on Distributed Object Management*, Edmonton, Canada, August 1992.

[15] M. Schrefl. *Object-Oriented Database Integration.* PhD thesis, Technische Universität Wien, Österreich, June 1988.

[16] A.P. Sheth and J.A. Larson. Federated database systems for managing distributed, heterogeneuos, and autonomous databases. *ACM Computing Surveys*, 22(3):183 – 236, September 1990.

[17] S. Spaccapietra, C. Parent, and Y. Dupont. View integration: A step forward in solving structural conflicts. *IEEE Trans. on Knowledge and Data Engineering*, October 1992.

[18] M. Stonebraker and E. Wong. Access control in relational databases management systems by query modification. In *Proc. ACM National Conf.*, 1974.

[19] M.R. Stonebraker, A. Jhingran, J. Goh, and S. Potamianos. On rules, procedures, caching and views in database systems. In *Proc. ACM SIGMOD* , Atlantic City, USA, May 1990.

[20] M. Tresch and M.H. Scholl. Meta object management and its application to database evolution. In *Proc. 11th Int'l Conf. Entity-Relationship Approach*, Karlsruhe, Germany, October 1992.

Determining Schema Interdependencies in Object-Oriented Multidatabase Systems

Jian Yang

Dept of Computer Science
University College, UNSW
Australian Defence Force Academy
Canberra, ACT 2600
Australia

Mike P. Papazoglou

School of Information systems
Queensland University of Technology
GPO Box 2434
Brisbane QLD 4001
Australia

Abstract

Schema analysis is the process of determining and capturing how individual schema items in diverse databases are related to each other. During this process different types of semantic relationships between schema items in different databases are identified and meaningful cross-links are established. The work presented in this paper concentrates on the issue of determining several types of interdependencies among schema items in object-oriented multidatabase systems in terms of their semantic context. A methodology is proposed for semi-automated schema analysis whereby knowledge from schema analysts may be applied in an interactive manner to refine and fully determine potential schema item interdependencies.

keywords: multi-database systems, object-oriented DBs, schema analysis and integration, semantic and structural discrepancies, inter-type assertions, analogical reasoning.

1 INTRODUCTION

A multidatabase system (MDBS) consists of a collection of independently developed and separately administered component database systems (CDBSs). The purpose of an MDBS is to support controlled sharing of system-wide data sources and provide coordinated control among a collection of autonomous and possibly heterogeneous CDBSs. Corporate data may reside anywhere in the CDBS network and can be operated upon transparently by both users and applications. To achieve this functionality an MDBS provides a homogenizing layer on top of the existing CDBSs, thus gives users the illusion of a single unified homogeneous database system.

In order for sharing to take place among heterogeneous CDBSs, some common data model must be used for describing corporate data and for coordinating distributed control. This model must be semantically expressive in order to capture the intended meanings of CDBS schemas which may use different data formats, obey different data modeling conventions and may more importantly model different aspects of the same concepts of some common domain. It is generally accepted that object-oriented models (especially those which include active database capabilities) can be considered as a key core technology for achieving integration and interoperation between multiple autonomous data sources along with providing the capacity to perform distributed object management functions [1], [2], [3], [4].

Successful integration of multiple CDBS schemas requires the identification and subsequent reconciliation of structural and semantic disparities which occur between the individual data elements within the CDBSs. For the purposes of this research it is convenient to distinguish between two complementary sets of such problems: ***structural conflicts and incompatibilities***, and ***semantic inconsistencies and incompleteness*** [6]. By structural conflicts and incompatibilities we mean that the objects, object properties represented in the component databases are either conflicting or they present domain mismatches with respect to one another - even though they may model to the same 'real-world' concepts. Examples include problems in instance matches, units of measurement, contextual and structural mismatches, and so forth.

Semantic inconsistencies involve different interpretations of the meanings of schema entities in the individual CDBSs. For example, consider a CDBS which refers to its students as undergraduate and postgraduate students, whereas a second may choose to refer to them as first, second, third year, Master's and PhD students. The issue of semantic incompleteness relates to the situation where meaningful inter-object and inter-schema relationships, required for the purposes of schema merging and interoperation, are missing from the component schemas. For example, if one data source deals with information regarding commercial enterprises, it is quite unlikely to include all the information relating to a university lecturer with respect to his employment as company consultant. Conversely, a university database may not contain information concerning the consulting record of its lecturers. Only by establishing meaningful inter-schema relationship(s) between `Lecturers` in the university database and `Employees` in the company database and combining information regarding these two views will the corporate information source be able to form an overall picture about employees who are lecturers at the same time.

The issues of structural conflicts and incompatibilities have been extensively researched. There exist various proposals for solving these and related problems [5, 7, 8, 9, 10, 11, 12]. In the area of structural incompatibilities, techniques were proposed for structural and domain mismatches whereby conflicting attributes are mapped to common domains by means of applying extended relational operators [13]. It is only recently that has been realized that tremendous potential lies in the use of sophisticated semi-automated tools for data analysis and integration. Bellcore's Schema Design and Integration Toolkit (BERDI) [14] provides intelligent support to improve the quality and reduce the time required to perform schema analysis and integration of non-trivial schemas in industrial set ups. These capabilities built on and enhance previous attempts to provide interactive support for schema integration purposes [10].

As a general rule most of the above proposals are based on fairly high-level and intuitive understanding rather than a detailed classification scheme. Recently Kim and Seo [15] attempted to resolve this problem in a relational multi-database environment by proposing a systematic classification scheme. However, the issue of a general formal methodology for specifying useful inter-schema relationships and their characteristics during the process of schema analysis has yet to be addressed.

Semantic issues and in particular the problem of semantic incompleteness have either been marginally treated or received no attention thus far. Most notable is the work of Kent [16] where the author describes a great variety of ways to represent a given fact - some of which relate to our perception of semantic inconsistencies. The paper, however, does not propose any solution for resolving semantic inconsistencies. In a more recent paper [17] Kent discusses and proposes solutions to another semantic problem, that of ontological correspondences between entities created in different CDBSs. The author proposes a solution to this problem in terms of spheres of knowledge which act as repositories of abstracted knowledge describing CDB information. Semantic incompleteness has yet to receive appropriate attention, it only received tangential treatment as a by-product of the schema merging activities [18], [19]. The main thrust of these research activities has been towards using a knowledge representation scheme for automating the process of identifying different types of attribute relationships.

The work reported in this paper discusses several fundamental issues which have to be addressed during schema analysis in the context of object-oriented multidatabases and concentrates predominantly on semantic incompleteness issues. Towards this end, we use classification scheme in conjunction with determining inter-schema linkages according to the semantics and structure of analyzed CDBS schema items and a formal methodology for describing inter-schema relationships and their semantics. Research activities described in this paper build upon and partially extend previous research work that we conducted on schema analysis [20], [21], [22]. In [20, 21] we proposed a knowledge-based framework and discussed the basic features of a semi-automated tool for representing the semantics of inter-schema components and for reasoning about them, while in [22] we argued in favor of introducing case-based reasoning techniques for semi-automating the process of discovering structural and semantic relatedness between component schemas in CDBSs.

The remainder of this paper is organized as follows: Section-2 introduces the salient features of an object-oriented model used for discussing our approach to schema analysis. Section-3 outlines our basic approach to schema analysis in object-oriented multidatabases systems and proposes a formal methodology and an algorithm for type comparison in inheritance lattices, i.e., object-oriented schemas. Finally, Section-4 presents our conclusions and discusses future research directions.

2 DATA MODELING

In this paper we assume that the MDBS uses a common object-oriented database model which adapts knowledge representation and reasoning to traditional object-oriented database modeling constructs. To provide a sound basis for discussion we delineate only those object-oriented KOM features which are required for analyzing disparate CDBS schemas. More information about the nature and implementation of this knowledge-oriented model which was developed on the basis of the object-oriented database system ONTOS and the expert system shell CLIPS can be found in [23, 24, 25].

The following discussion will focus on typed objects which have three major characteristics: they are all instantiated from some common *type* description; they each belong to a single type only; and their instances are grouped into *classes*, on the basis of similarity.

The information which we can get from a database system regards its schema and the actual instances of data stored in the database. The former provides us with information on the organization and definitions of data, i.e., intentions, which consist of *types* and *relationships* between types. A type T is a description of the structural and behavioral properties of a set of objects which exhibit the same characteristics and which make up the instances of that type.

In the object model we organize types around a *type* (or *inheritance) lattice* [26], a directed acyclic graph, which supports the notions of generalization and specialization via **is-a** relationships and is used to represent the conceptual schema for an object-base. Different types may be identified with the same set of functions (attributes and methods) and a type T_2 is said to be a *subtype* of type T_1 if T_1 provides a subset of the functions of T_2. Conversely, we also say that T_1 is *supertype* of T_2. Figure 1 illustrates the rudimentary schemas of component databases in terms of types which are organized around inheritance lattices.

The notion of *class* is associated with all instances of a given type [27]. A class is based on the same specification as a type, but it includes the run-time notions of object creation by cloning the prototype for the class, and the *extent*, which is the set of all objects that are instances of the type at any given point in time [27]. Thus objects which correspond to a single type in the inheritance lattice, are grouped together and treated as a single unit, viz. their corresponding class.

Since a class represents only the set of all objects that are instances of a specific type, at any given time, we introduce the concept *Real World Semantic Class* ($\Re$) which will be used later for inter-schema relationship definition. $\Re(T)$ denotes the set of all the possible objects which are instances of type T. Obviously, the class of objects of type T in a database (at a given point in time) is a subset of $\Re(T)$.

In this paper, the term type property is used to refer to attributes, relationships and methods. An attribute may take an instance of a primitive type in ONTOS as its value, such as int, char, float, etc or a non-primitive type such as another object. A relationship relates the current instance of its defining type to other type instance(s). For example, the type `Student` in Figure 2 has the attributes `major, degree, score` and relationship `take_course` which relates an instance of type `Student` to instances of type `Course`.

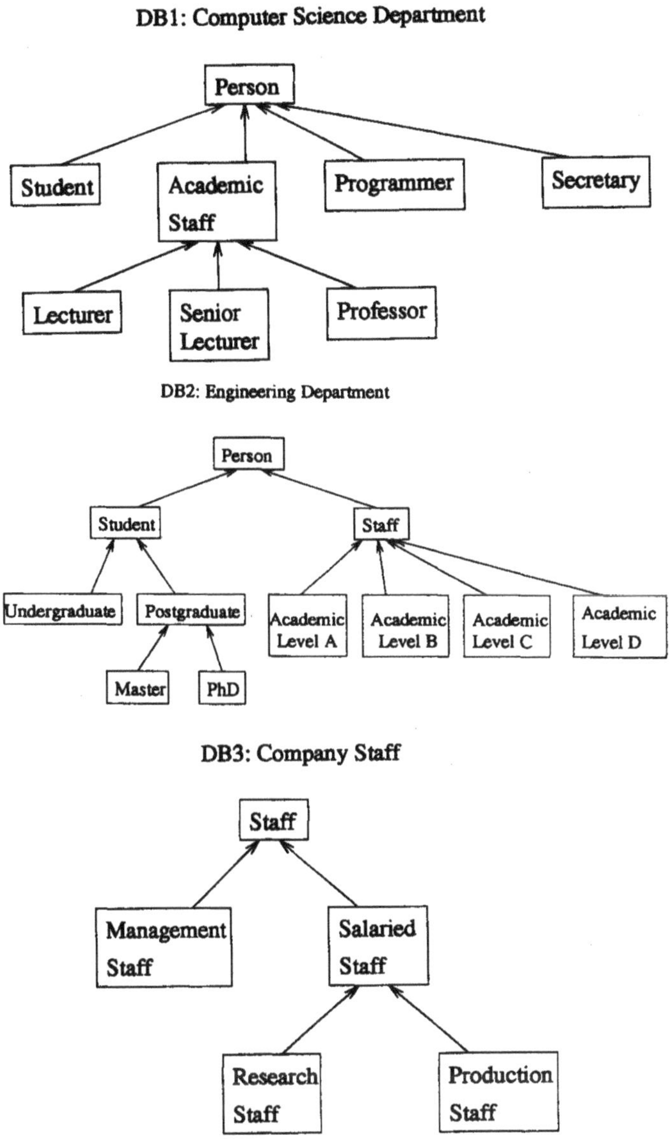

Figure 1: Examples of Component Schemas

```
Type Student
{
        supertype: Person
        attributes:
            major: string
            degree: string
            score: int
        relationship:
            take_course:   Type course
        methods:
            insert_major { }
            insert_degree { }
            calculate_score { }
 } /* Student */
```

Figure 2: Definition of Type Student in Component Database_1

3 A METHODOLOGY FOR OBJECT-ORIENTED SCHEMA ANALYSIS

As a basis for our analysis of and approach to the various types of discrepancies that exist in object-oriented MDBSs we consider developing an application for a collaborative long-term project conducted between three distinct institutions: a university's computer science department, an engineering department and a computer company. Thus the need to integrate at least three distinct but interconnected component databases. Parts of the individual CDBS schemas are shown in Figure 1, where each database carries a tag name of the form $DB_i (1 \leq i \leq 3)$. Figure 3 shows possible properties for the two types `Person` and `Staff`. This figure also indicates which properties these two types share in common and the properties which are private to each of them - referred to as additional properties in the figure.

As with most methodologies, we determine potential relationships between pairs of similarly structured CDBS schema types on the basis of comparison. Currently, a semi-automated knowledge-driven schema analysis tool (SAKSAT) is under development whereby a human-operator is in a position to interact with this relatively sophisticated schema analyzer - which also stores derivation histories and cases of previous findings in a case base - in order to identify potentially related schema types and/or attributes [22]. This approach presents many similarities with BERDI [14]. SAKSAT acts as an "intelligent" assistant and is geared only towards determining the semantic relatedness of schema types, discovering implicit facts about them, reasoning about its findings and classifying the related types with the aid of a human operator whenever it does not have sufficient information. BERDI, on the other hand, addresses the entire schema integration cycle and focuses on the use of graphical user interface facilities to expedite integration. In this sense it uses graphical display facilities for representing extended ER schemas (called source schemas) and graphical query facilities for retrieving model level information (e.g., attributes and relationships with same names) and dictionary information (e.g., aliases, creators, businesses purposes, schemas of origin, entity descriptions and so on).

Following the relevant literature [11] we refer to that part of schema analysis used for determining relationships among different schema types as *type assertions.* Inter-type assertions represent serious sources of problems because they do not exist in the separate schemas, as such and have to be identified during the analysis process. Previous research work for detecting inter-schema relationships either totally relied on attribute equivalence or used heuristics to order pairs of objects for review by the database administrator (DBA) [21]. In fact, two complementary methods were proposed for determining types assertions: *attribute subsumption* [10, 12] and *instance subsumption* [19, 11]. Although these types of approaches present certain similarities and may in fact influence the treatment of type assertions they are rather restrictive in their present form.

Furthermore the proposed methodology a tremendous mental burden on the DBA. The entire process is 'manual' and the DBA acts only as a 'technician' who mechanically encodes the findings regarding type relatedness but cannot interact with the system to help it further refine type/attribute assertions based on previous findings. In order to overcome these limitations it is necessary to examine a variety of existing or implied semantic links between types (and their respective attributes) in the individual CDBSs. Moreover, in order to identify potential type assertions it is imperative that designers rely on the assistance of semi-automated intelligent schema analysis tools whereby the human-operator may be asked to apply his knowledge if additional information is needed to further refine the nature of type assertions.

3.1 A Theoretical Basis for Determining Commonality and Inferring Similarity

We base our discoveries regarding existing commonalities and inferred similarities in CDBS schemas on a sound theoretical foundation. In the following, we provide formal definitions of inter-schema assertions based both on type definitions as well as existing type instances. For this purpose we use two fundamental concepts from the AI areas of Analogy and Induction, namely *existing commonality*, and *inferred similarity* [28]. Subsequently, we classify the various kinds of inter-type assertions and base our findings on these two concepts. In the following we give a list of helpful definitions for this purpose:

T_1/T_2	Person	Staff
Common Attributes	Name	Name
	Id-No	Id-No
	Address	Address
	Tel-No	Tel-No
Additional Attributes	Age	
	Sex	
		Rank
		Salary
		Experience

Figure 3: Common and Additional Attributes

Let $P(T)$ be the set of properties which are defined in a given type T and $Pe(T)$ be the set of all permitted, i.e. conformant, properties of type T which are currently not included in its signature. We refer to such properties as *shareable* properties of the type T.

Since $Pe(T)$ includes the properties which are defined in type T as well as those which are not included in this type's definition but are allowed to be part of it (e.g, attributes like **age** and **sex** in Figure 3 are shareable properties of type $T2$) we then have $P(T) \subseteq Pe(T)$.

Now for any object x, let $Pe(x)$ be the set of all properties which are shareable by that object x, further let $\bar{P}e(x)$ be the set of all those properties not shareable by the object x. Hence:

$Pe(T) = \bigcap_{x \in \Re(T)} Pe(x)$, now we may define

$\bar{P}e(T) = \bigcap_{x \in \Re(T)} \bar{P}e(x)$, and
$Pe'(T) = \bigcup_{x \in \Re(T)} Pe(x) - Pe(T)$

where $Pe(T)$ denotes the set of properties which are shareable by all objects in $\Re(T)$; $\bar{P}e(T)$ denotes the set of properties which are not shareable by all objects in $\Re(T)$; $Pe'(T)$ denotes the set of properties which are shareable by some objects in $\Re(T)$.

If $C(T_1, T_2)$ is the set of common properties between types T_1 and T_2, then we have
$C(T_1, T_2) = C(T_2, T_1) = P(T_1) \cap P(T_2)$. For example from Figure 4, one may observe that $C(T_1, T_2) = C(T_2, T_1) =$ **name, id-no, address, tel-no**.

If $Q(T_1, T_2)$ is the set of properties that a type T_1 includes in addition to its common properties with T_2, we then have $Q(T_1, T_2) = P(T_1) - C(T_1, T_2)$. For example, from Figure 4, one may observe that $Q(T_1, T_2) =$ **age, sex**.

Using the above set definitions we can derive the inferred similarities formula as follows:

$$(C(T_1, T_2) \neq \emptyset) \wedge (q_i \in Q(T_1, T_2)) \xrightarrow{AR} (q_i \in Pe(T_2)).$$

The above formula is used to prescribe the interaction between the schema analysis tool and the DBA. Loosely speaking this formula corresponds to a form of a question that should be answered by the DBA during his interaction with SAKSAT. The interpretation for this formula is as follows: consider the additional properties of type T_1 referred to as $(Q(T_1, T_2))$ and ask the DBA if they can also be shared by type T_2.

Obviously, there are three possible answers to the above question: (1) all the objects of $\Re(T_2)$ can share the additional

T_1/T_2	Person	Staff
$C(T_1, T_2)$	Name	Name
	Id-No	Id-No
	Address	Address
	Tel-No	Tel-No
$Q(T_1, T_2)$	Age	
	Sex	
$Q(T_2, T_1)$		Rank
		Salary
		Experience
Inferred Similarities		?Age
		?Sex
	?Rank	
	?Salary	
	?Experience	

Figure 4: Existing Commonalities and Inferred Similarities

properties of T_1; (2) not all the objects of $\Re(T_2)$ can share these properties; (3) all the objects of $\Re(T_2)$ cannot share these properties. The following formulae correspond to these three types of answers:

1. $C(T_1, T_2) \neq \emptyset) \wedge (q_i \in Q(T_1, T_2)) \longrightarrow (q_i \in Pe(T_2))$.
2. $C(T_1, T_2) \neq \emptyset) \wedge (q_i \in Q(T_1, T_2)) \longrightarrow (q_i \in Pe'(T_2))$.
3. $C(T_1, T_2) \neq \emptyset) \wedge (q_i \in Q(T_1, T_2)) \longrightarrow (q_i \in \bar{P}e(T_2))$.

We exemplify this type of system/DBA interaction in the context of Figure 4. When SAKSAT compares the type `Person` in DB_1 with the type `Staff` in DB_3 it finds that the former type has two additional attributes: **age** and **sex**. Subsequently, it considers these two attributes and asks whether type `Staff` can also share them. The obvious answer is 'Yes, all staff objects can have these two attributes'. Similarly, type **Staff** includes three attributes not contained in type **Person**, namely **rank**, **salary** and **experience**. The same type of question is now asked for **Person**. The obvious answer here is 'Some can, some cannot'. This answer in fact implies that **Staff** is a subtype of **Person**. In this way, the system derives the inferred similarities between related types.

In the following section we use these formal definitions in order to classify type assertions.

3.2 Classifying Inter-Type Assertions

In what follows we give definitions and examples of the most representative classes of type assertions in an object-oriented multidatabase environment. For the classification scheme that follows we assume that the types $T1$ and $T2$ belong to two different schemas in different CDBSs.

Definition 1: T_1 is *Equivalent to (Eq)* T_2 iff $\Re(T_1) = \Re(T_2)$.

Finding 1: If T_1 *Eq* T_2, then either
(1) $(C(T_1, T_2) \neq \emptyset) \wedge (Q(T_1, T_2) = \emptyset) \wedge (Q(T_2, T_1) = \emptyset)$; or
(2) $(C(T_1, T_2) \neq \emptyset) \wedge (q_i \in Q(T_1, T_2)) \wedge (q_j \in Q(T_2, T_1))$
$\longrightarrow (q_i \in Pe(T_2)) \wedge (q_j \in Pe(T_1))$.

Definition 1.1: For case 1.(1) above, we say that T_1 and T_2 are *Identical (Id)*;

Definition 1.2: This case is a subcase of definition 1.1 and corresponds to case 1.(2) above. Here we say that T_1 and T_2 are *Isomorphic (Iso)*.

Description 1: If two types are equivalent, then their real world semantic classes are equal. If two types are equivalent then their definitions are either the same - in which case are identical- or if one type has additional properties, these properties can be shared, i.e, they are permissible, by the other type - in which case the types are isomorphic.

Definition 2: T_1 is a *Generalization (Ge)* of T_2 iff $\Re(T_1) \supset \Re(T_2)$ and T_2 is a *Specialization (Sp)* of T_1.

Finding 2: If T_1 *Ge* T_2, then either
(1) $(C(T_1, T_2)) \neq \emptyset) \wedge (Q(T_1, T_2 = \emptyset) \wedge (q_j \in Q(T_2, T_1))$
$\longrightarrow (q_j \in Pe'(T_1))$; or
(2) $(C(T_1, T_2) \neq \emptyset) \wedge (q_i \in Q(T_1, T_2)) \wedge (q_j \in Q(T_2, T_1))$
$\longrightarrow (q_i \in Pe(T_2)) \wedge (q_j \in Pe'(T_1))$.

Definition 2.1: For case 2.(1) above, we say that T_1 is a *Supertype (Sup)* of T_2.

Definition 2.2: This case is a subcase of definition 2.1 and corresponds to case 2.(2). Here we say that T_1 is a *Conceptual Supertype (Csup)* of T_2.

Description 2: If T_1 is a generalization of T_2 then the real world semantic class of T_2 is a subset of that of T_1. And all the definitions of T_1 are *logically* subsumed by T_2.

Definition 3: T_1 and T_2 are *Category (Ca)* related if $\Re(T_1) \cap \Re(T_2) = \emptyset$, and $C(T_1, T_2) \neq \emptyset$ holds.

Finding 3: If T_1 *Ca* T_2, then
$(C(T_1, T_2) \neq \emptyset) \wedge (q_i \in Q(T_1, T_2)) \wedge (q_j \in Q(T_2, T_1))$
$\longrightarrow (q_i \in \tilde{P}e(T_2)) \wedge (q_j \in \tilde{P}e(T_1))$.

Description 3: The fact that two types are category related implies that although their real world semantic classes are disjoint, they may have some common properties as well as shareable properties. Some of the additional properties of one type cannot be shared by the other type, i.e. they are mutually exclusive.

Types which are inter-related according to one of the above three categories are said to be *overlapping.*

Definition 4: T_1 and T_2 are *Role (Ro)* related if $\Re(T_1) \cap \Re(T_2) \neq \emptyset$ holds.

Finding 4: If T_1 *Ro* T_2, then
$(C(T_1, T_2) \neq \emptyset) \wedge (q_i \in Q(T_1, T_2)) \longrightarrow (q_i \in Pe'(x), x \in \Re(T_2))$;
or
$(C(T_1, T_2) \neq \emptyset) \wedge (q_j \in Q(T_2, T_1)) \longrightarrow (q_j \in Pe'(y), y \in \Re(T_1))$

For the first case above, we say that T_1 and T_2 are role 'T_2' related; whereas for the second case, we say that T_1 and T_2 are role 'T_1' related.

Description 4: If two types are role related, their real world semantic classes are overlapping. All the properties of one type can be shared by some instances of the real world semantic class of another type [29].

Definition 5: T_1 and T_2 are *Disjoint (Dsj)* if the following two conditions $\Re(T_1) \cap \Re(T_2) = \emptyset$ and $C(T_1, T_2) = \emptyset \wedge (Q(T_1, T_2) = \emptyset) \wedge (Q(T_2, T_1) = \emptyset)$ hold.

The above definition implies that two types are disjoint if they have nothing in common.

In the following section we present an algorithm for type comparison and illustrate how this methodology is used to determine the inter-type assertions discussed in this section.

3.3 A Strategy for Type Comparison in Inheritance Lattices

Schemas in object-oriented CDBSs correspond to inheritance lattices. The purpose of the inheritance lattice is to organize types around a rooted and connected directed acyclic graph graph so that each type can be reachable from the root type. From the previous it is obvious that the basic unit in an object-oriented schema is the type. Hence, the primary task of schema analysis in object-oriented databases is concerned with type analysis and comparison, i.e., determining the valid inter-type assertions regarding CDBS schemas.

The fact that types are organized around inheritance lattices facilitates inter-schema type comparison. One can compare types in a systematic way unlike in conventional data models, e.g., relational, ER, etc, where this sort of comparison is intuitive and painstaking since each type (e,.g. relation) in the MDBS must be compared with every other. Moreover, the process of type comparison can be expedited in several occasions by not comparing unrelated sub-lattices. For example, if we ascertain that there is no semantic affinity between two types, $T1$ and $T2$ in two different CDBSs, i.e., they are disjoint, then this can be used as an indication that their descendants are also not related. This reduces the search time since we do not have to compare pairs of types where one type in the pair belongs to schema whereas the other belongs to another schema - which incidentally is common practise for determining attribute relatedness.

The following rules are used to accelerate the process of type comparison:

. Rule 1: If T_2 is a subtype of T_1, then T_2 is disjoint with all the other siblings of T_1 and their descendants.

. Rule 2: If T_1 and T_2 are equivalent, then all the siblings of T_1 and their descendants may be overlapping with all the siblings of T_2 and their descendants.

. Rule 3: If T_1 and T_2 are category related, then all the descendants of T_1 and T_2 are category related to each other.

Using the above rules during the process of type comparison in object-oriented schemas , the search times will be significantly reduced.

In the following we present an algorithm for inter-type comparison in inheritance lattices. We assume that IR is an inter-schema assertions matrix, where an element $IR[T_i, T_j]$ is used to denote the sort of inter-type assertion holding between types T_i and T_j in different CDBs. According to the inter-type assertion definitions in Section 3.2, $IR[T_i, T_j]$ is allowed to assume only one of the following values: $\{Eq, Ge, Sp, Ro, Ca, Un, Dsj\}$. These symbols correspond to assertions of the type *Equivalent, Generalization, Specialization, Role, Category, Unknown, Disjoint*, respectively.

The IR matrix is initialized with Un entries in all its positions. The algorithm which is shown in Figure 5 presents a systematic method for comparing pairs of types in diverse CDBs. This algorithm can be easily generalized and be used for comparison among n-types rather than pairs of types only. In fact in a companion paper we have argued in favor of the use of case-base reasoning techniques for this purpose [22].

```
main
begin
   for all types in two schemas
       IR[Ti, Tj] := Un;
   endfor
   Ti := root of lattice 1; Tj := root of lattice 2;
   compare (Ti, Tj);
end
procedure compare (Ti, Tj)
   if IR[Ti, Tj] ≠ Un then return endif
   result case of
   'Category':
   IR[Ti, Tj] := Ca;
   for each descendant Ti' of Ti do
       for each descendant Tj' of Tj do
           IR[Ti', Tj'] := Ca;
       endfor
   endfor
   return
   'Specialization':
   IR[Ti, Tj] := Sp;
   for each descendant Ti' of Ti do
       IR[Ti', Tj] := Sp;
   endfor
   if there is no overlap between Tj and its sibling Tjb
     for each Tjb and its descendants Tjb' do
         IR[Ti, Tjb*] := Ca;
           * Tjb* can be either Tjb or Tjb'. *
     endfor
   endif
   for each child Tj' of Tj do
       compare (Ti, Tj');
   endfor
   return
   'Generalization':
   IR[Ti, Tj] := Ge;
   for each descendant Tj' of Tj do
       IR[Ti, Tj'] := Ge;
   endfor
   if there is no overlap between Ti and its sibling Tib
     for  each Tib and its descendants Tib' do
         IR[Tj, Tib*] := Ca;
         *Tib* can be either Tib or Tib'. *
     endfor
   endif
   for each child Ti' of Ti do
       compare (Ti', Tj);
   endfor
   return
   'Equivalent':
   IR[Ti, Tj] := Eq;
   if there is no overlap between Ti and its sibling Tib do
     for each Tib and its descendants Tib' do
         IR[Tj, Tib*] := Ca;
     endfor

   endif
   if there is no overlap between Tj and its sibling Tjb do
     for each Tjb and its descendants Tjb' do
         IR[Ti, Tjb*] := Ca;
     endfor
   endif
   for each child Ti' of Ti do
       for each child Tj' of Tj do
           compare (Ti', Tj');
       endfor
   endfor
   return
   'Role':
   IR[Ti, Tj] := Ro;
   for each child Ti' of Ti do
       compare (Ti', Tj);
   endfor
   for each child Tj' of Tj do
       compare (Tj', Ti);
   endfor
   return
   Disjoint 'Disjoint':
           IR[Ti, Tj] := Ro;
           return
   endcase
end compare.
```

Figure 5: An Algorithm for Lattice-based Type Comparison.

4 CONCLUSIONS

Determining the structural and semantic relatedness of types is paramount in our effort to analyze and integrate diverse component database schemas in a multidatabase environment. Unless one understands what the individual object types mean, how they are organized, how they are semantically related to each other, and if there are any conflicts between them, one cannot integrate them effectively. The most critical resource in our effort to resolve these problems is knowledge of the internal structures and semantics of conceptual schemas.

In this paper we identified several fundamental issues which have to be addressed during schema analysis in the context of object-oriented multidatabases. We introduced a formal framework for determining commonalities and inferring similarities between inter-schema types, classified inter-type assertions according to the semantics and structure of analyzed types and proposed an algorithm for type comparison in inheritance lattices. Currently, a case based methodology is being explored to semi-automate the process of discovering structural and semantic conflicts and relatedness of type components from disparate component data sources. As this methodology leans heavily on reasoning, deductive and object-oriented facilities, our implementation vehicle relies on a novel data model based on a merger of the object-oriented database system ONTOS and the expert system shell CLIPS.

Acknowledgments

We gratefully acknowledge the contribution of Brendan McKay for his suggestions and helpful comments regarding an earlier version of this article.

References

[1] F. Manola "Object-Oriented Knowledge Bases", *AI Expert*, vol. 5, no. 3, March 1990.

[2] W. Kim, et. al, "A Distributed Object-Oriented Database System Supporting Shared and Private Databses", ACM trans. on Information Systems, vol. 9, no.1, Jan. 1991.

[3] F. Manola et. al, "Distributed Object Management", Inter'l Journal of Intelligent & Cooperative Information Systems", vol. 1, no. 1, 1992.

[4] M.P.Papazoglou, L.Marinos "An Object Oriented Approach to Distributed Data Management", Journal of Systems & Software, vol. 11, no. 2, 1990.

[5] C. Batini, M. Lenzerini, S. B. Navathe, "A Comparative Analysis of Methodologies for Database Schema Integration", Computing Surveys, vol. 18, no. 4, December 1986.

[6] A. Silberschatz et al., "Database Systems: Achievements and Opportunities", Communications of the ACM, vol. 34, no. 10, October 1991.

[7] B. M. Johansson and C. Sundblad, "View Integration: A Knowledge Problem", SYSLAB Working Paper, no. 15, 1988.

[8] S. Navathe et al., "Integration User Views in Database Design", IEEE Computer, vol. 19, no. 1, January 1986.

[9] M. V. Mannino et al., "A Rule-Based Approach for Merging Generalization Hierarchies", Information Systems, vol. 13, no. 3, 1988.

[10] A. P. Sheth and J. A. Larson, "A Tool for Integration Conceptual Schema And User Views", in Proceedings of 4th Conf. on Data & Knowledge Eng., LA, Feb. 1988.

[11] J. A. Larson et al., "A Theory of Attribute Equivalence in Database with Application to Schema Integration", IEEE Trans. on Software Engineering", vol. 15, no. 4, April 1989.

[12] S. Hayne and S. Ram, "Multi-User View Integration System(MUVIS): An Expert System for View Integration", in Proceedings of 6th Conf. on Data & Knowledge Eng., Feb. 1990.

[13] L. DeMichiel, "Resolving Database Incompatibility: An Approach to Performing Relational Operations over Mismatched Domains", IEEE Trans. on Knowledge & Data Eng., vol.1, no.4, Dec. 1989.

[14] A.P. Sheth, H. Marcus, "Schema Analysis and Integration: Methodology, Techniques and Prototype Toolkit", Bellcore, Techn. DMmemo: TM-STS-019981/1, March 1992.

[15] W. Kim and J. Seo, "Classifying Schematic and Data Heterogeneity in Multidatabase Systems", IEEE Computer, Dec. 1991.

[16] W. Kent, "The Many Forms of a Single Fact", Spring COMPCON89, San Fransisco, March 1989.

[17] W. Kent, "The Breakdown of the Information Model in Multi-Database Systems", SIGMOD Record, vol. 20, no.4, Dec. 1991.

[18] A.P. Sheth, S.K. Gala "Attribute Relationships: An Impediment in Automating Schema Integration", in Proceedings of Workshop on Heterogeneous Databases Systems, Chicago, Dec. 1989.

[19] A. Savasere et al., "On Applying Classification to Schema Integration", in First International Workshop on Interoperability in Multidatabase Systems, Japan April, 1991.

[20] J. Yang and M. P. Papazoglou, "Knowledge-Based Schema Analysis in a Multi-Database Framework", in Procs. Database Expert Systems and Applications (DEXA)-91, Berlin, August 1991.

[21] J. Yang and M. P. Papazoglou, "Schema Analysis Methodology for Distributed Information System Design", in Procs. of the 3rd Australian Database Conference, Melbourne, February 1992.

[22] J. Yang and M. P. Papazoglou, "A Case-Based Reasoning Methodology for Analyzing Multi-Database Schemas", submitted.

[23] M. P. Papazoglou, "Knowledge-Driven Distributed Information Systems", in Proceedings of the 14th Annual International Computer Software & Applications Conference, COMPSAC-90, October 1990.

[24] M.P. Papazoglou, S. Laufmann, T.K. Sellis "An Organizational Framework for Cooperating Intelligent Information Systems", Inter'l Journal of Intelligent & Cooperative Information Systems", vol. 1, no. 1, 1992.

[25] D. Zhou, "The Knowledge-Oriented Data Model and its Language", PhD thesis in preparation, Dept. of Com. Sci., ANU, 1991.

[26] J. Banerjee et al., "Data Model Issues for Object-Oriented Applications", ACM Trsns. on Office Information Systems, vol. 5, no. 1, January 1987.

[27] M. Atkinson, et al, "The Object-Oriented Database System Manifesto", in Procs. 1st Deductive Object-Oriented Database Conf., Kyoto 1989.

[28] S. J. Russell, "The Use of Knowledge in Analogy and Induction", Research Notes in Artificial Intelligence, Morgan Kaufmann Publishers, Inc., San Mateo, CA, 1989.

[29] M.P Papazoglou, "Roles: A Methodology for Representing Multifaceted Objects", in Procs. Database Expert Systems and Applications (DEXA)-91, Berlin, August 1991.

OBJECT-ORIENTED DATABASE SYSTEMS

PINOL: A PERSISTENT INFERENTIAL OBJECT ORIENTED LANGUAGE FOR DATABASES

A HH Ngu* Limsoon Wong†

School of Computer Science & Engineering
University of New South Wales
P.O.Box 1, Kensington 2033 NSW, Australia.
email:anne@cs.unsw.oz.au

ABSTRACT: The Persistent INferential Object oriented Language (PINOL) offers a classification scheme based on canonical and non-canonical perspectives of objects. This supports economical and intuitive modeling of multiple roles of objects. PINOL also has a rule mechanism for establishing relationships between objects located in different classes. This provides a declarative and deductive capability in the framework of an object oriented system.

1 INTRODUCTION

An ability to model and support multiple independent roles of objects is desirable. Consider an example. From the perspective of the income tax department, a taxpayer is an individual person. At the same time, a taxpayer can play the role of an employer if he employs a maid at home. He can also be involved in a partnership while being employed by an organization or a company. In many database programming systems, such as O2[5)], Gemstone[12)], and Orion[3)], it is necessary to artifically create several types to model the different roles played by the taxpayer. How to place a particular taxpayer in these systems can be a problem. In addition, these systems, such as O2, Gemstone, Orion, etc. do not allow objects to change type dynamically. This means that changing roles of an object cannot be modeled.

Inter-object relationships are frequently modeled procedurally as a method or as a an attribute in a class in an object oriented system. This makes understanding and maintaining these relationships and constraints difficult. For example, the relationship between a student and a course can be modeled by including a course-taken method in student. Then only the student knows about this information. In order to get some global information such as "who is taking what courses", it is necessary to iterate over all students. In [9)], it is advocated that object oriented langauge is not declarative enough for querying.

*This work was done when the author was working with Institute of Systems Science, Singapore

†Currently at the University of Pennsylvania.

PINOL is designed to improve the above situations. A prototype version obtained by extending C++ has been successfully implemented. In this Report, some features of PINOL that address the two issues above are presented. More details and earlier thoughts about PINOL can be obtained from our DOOD89 and DOOD91 papers.

This paper is organized as follows. Section 2 describes PINOL canonical and non-canonical classification of objects: `types` and `classes`. It uses special features called `endowed` attribute and method for modeling objects with multiple and independent roles. Section 3 describes the kind of inference rules that PINOL supports. The inferencing mechanism includes a feature called `test predicate` which retain advantages of object orientation such as encapsulation and object identities. This section also contains example declarative specifications of fairly complex recursive relationships. More example PINOL programs are given in Section 4. Finally, in section 5 we present the Summary and related research.

2 PINOL CLASSIFICATION CONSTRUCTS

We differentiate the notions of type and class. A type (PINOL type) is used for providing a basic structure of objects – the *canonical* perspective. A class (PINOL class) is used for collections of objects with structural extension for context sensitive information as well as information common to all the objects in the class. We call the structural extension *endowed* attributes and *class* attributes. *Endowed methods* and *class methods* are supported to manipulate them respectively. This is the *non-canonical* perspective. The canonical perspective of an object is defined by the type of that object. The non-canonical perspective of an object can only be viewed within a particular context, i.e. a class. The non-canonical perspective of an object in a class is defined by the type of that object *and* the structural extension endowed by that class.

We illustrate the modeling of canonical and non-canonical perspectives of persons. The type **person** containing the basic structure of a person, such as name, address, etc. corresponds to the canonical perspective of a person. A non-canonical perspective may be defined by class **employee** of type person with endowed attributes such as department, employer, and address. Another non-canonical perspective is defined by the class **employer** with endowed attributes employee, salary, etc. Yet another non-canonical perspective can be defined as the class **student** with endowed attributes department, courses_taken, etc. There may or may not be an explicit class corresponding to the set of all persons. Endowed attributes may have the same name as class attibutes as well as attributes in the type of the class.

Users may create objects of type person and classify them into different classes. A totally new role of a person can be added to the database by simply creating a new class for the role. This does not affect the existing type or class hierarchy unnecessarily. An object's role can be added or removed by simply classifying or declassifying that object from the associated class. A person gains an additional new role by simply allowing him to be in the new class. A person who ceases being a student is simply deleted from the student class; his or her other roles are unaffected.

The PINOL concepts of canonical and non-canonical classification of objects are described in the following Subsections, especially features of PINOL classes. We describe most of the features through examples. A more extensive description of PINOL classification constructs is reported in[6].

2.1 Types and Classes

PINOL types correspond to types and classes in C++. They form the structural definition of the objects. They can be roughly divided into two kinds: *basic types* and *object types*.

Predefined types available in C++ such as integers, arrays, records, pointers, etc. are basic types of PINOL.

PINOL object types are essentially C++ classes. They provide canonical structure of objects; all objects of the same type have the same canonical structure.

PINOL types are concerned only with the *structure* of objects; *collections* of objects are stored in PINOL *classes*. However, PINOL classes are more than mere collections. They allow context sensitive information to be added to an object to form a *non-canonical* perspective of the object. The syntax and semantics for PINOL class declaration are described in subsequent Subsubsections with the aid of the following examples.

```
class NUS_employees contains objects of type
        employee
    attributes:
        address: add_type ;/* main campus address */
        minimum_salary:float;
        maximum_salary:float;
        increment_level:integer;
    methods:
        integer set_increment_level(inc:integer);
            { return(increment_level = inc) };
            ....
    endowed attributes:
        department: string;
        duties_plan:text;/* teaching duties */
        ....
    endowed methods:
        void display()
            { /*display the teaching duties*/ } ;
        ....
        initialization: NUS_employees()
            { address = prompt_address();
              minimum_salary = 500;
              maximum_salary = 15000;
              increment_levels = 10; } ;
end class ;

class ISS_employees contains objects of type
    employee
    subclass of NUS_employees
    attributes:
        department:string; /* the name of the dept. */
        address:address_type; /* dept. address*/
        director:employee*; /* the director name */
    methods:
        string set_department(dept:string);
            { return( department = dept )};
        employee* set_director(np:employee*);
            { return( director = np )};
        ....
        void display()
            { <body> }; /* print class attributes*/
    endowed attributes:
        address: email_add_type;
        security_card_no:integer;
        ....
    endowed methods:
        void prompt_address() { <body> } ;
        void prompt_sec_card_no() { <body> } ;
        email_type set_address(new_add:email_type)
            { return (address = new_add)};
        ...
    initialization: ISS_employees()
            { address = prompt_string();
              department = prompt_department();
              director = new employee;
              ISS_employees.add(director); } ;
end class ;
```

2.1.1 Members

Objects in a class are called *members* of the class. Members of *ISS_employees* are objects of type *employee* or subtype of *employee*. We call this the *type requirement* of the class *ISS_employees*. The type requirement of a PINOL class should be thought of as the canonical perspective of members of that class. The rest of the PINOL class declaration constitutes the non-canonical perspective.

In figure 1 the object *o1* is a member of *ISS_employees*. The canonical perspective of *o1*, is of type *employee*, the type requirement for *ISS_employees*. The non-canonical perspective of *o1* in class *ISS_employees* is denoted by *o1_ISS_employees*. They refer to the same object, but the non-canonical perspective has extra attributes containing context sensitive information attached to it. It is important to remark here that *o1* and *o1_ISS_employee* have the same object identifiers.

An object's membership of a class extends to all superclasses. Thus members of *ISS_employees* are also members of *NUS_employees*;

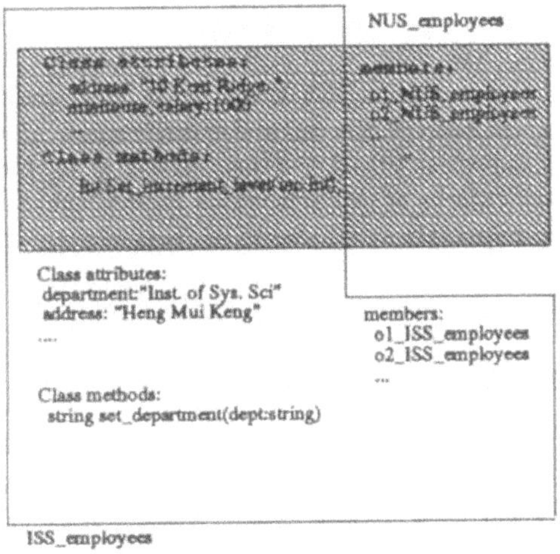

Figure 1: Class and inheritance

2.1.2 Class attributes and methods

Class attributes contain properties of a *class*. They are generic properties of all members of the class, different from attributes of instances of the class. For instance, *ISS_employees* has a class attribute *address* of type *address_type*. This *address* is the same for all members of *ISS_employees*. The type *employee* (type required by *ISS_employees*) may have an attribute whose name is *address*, possibly of the same or different type. This latter attribute may correspond to home addresses of employees, which may differ for each employee.

PINOL class attributes are accessed differently from PINOL type attributes. The syntax for accessing class attributes *s1* in class *C* is *C.s1*, read as "access *s1* in the context of *C*." For instance, to set the *department* of class *ISS_employees* in the above example:

> *ISS_employees.department* = "Institute of Systems Science";

All subclasses inherit class attributes of their superclasses. They inherit both the attributes and the values in the attribute slots, except when the attribute is redefined in the subclass (as depicted in figure 1). We call this inheritance by **value**. In the example, *NUS_employees* contains a class attribute *minimum_salary*, which is also *ISS_employees.minimum_salary*, since it was not redefined. Any changes in the value of *NUS_employees.minimum_salary* is reflected in *ISS_employees.minimum_salary* and vice versa.

Class methods are methods on the class itself; they have access to class attributes. A class method is unrelated to any method of the type requirement of the class. In the example, the PINOL class *ISS_employees* has a class method *set_department*. Any mention of *department* within *set_department* refers to the class attribute *ISS_employees.department*. Also, all references to "self" in *set_department* refers to the class *ISS_employees*. The syntax for invoking class method is of the form *ISS_employees.set_department*(...), read as "invoke *set_department* in the context of *ISS_employees*." Class methods are inherited in a similar way as class attributes.

2.1.3 Endowed attributes and methods

Endowed attributes refer to additional attributes of *each member* of the class. Although all PINOL classes in the same class-subclass hierarchy contain the same type of objects, we may desire that certain objects should have extra information that is applicable only in certain contexts. Endowed attributes and methods are introduced for this reason.

In our example, in addition to attributes and methods defined in *employee*, each member of *ISS_employees* is given *new* local attributes, e.g. *address* of type *email_add_type*. This endowed attribute is unrelated to attributes of type *employee*, or the class attribute *address* in *ISS_employees*. The *employee* attribute *address* contains home addresses of employees and this property is present in all objects of type employee. Whereas the endowed attribute *address* refers *only* to electronic mail addresses of members of *ISS_employees*.

The local nature of endowed attributes must be stressed. Each member of *ISS_employees* has his own endowed attribute *address*, changes in one does not affect others. The syntax for accessing endowed attributes is "*ISS_employees* →ref(*o*)→ *address*," read as "access endowed attribute *address* of object *o* which is a member of *ISS_employees* in the context of *ISS_employees*."

Endowed attributes of members of a class are inherited by members of its subclasses unless they are redefined by the subclasses. Naming conflicts are resolved using standard C++ rules. If *NUS_employees* endows its members with an attribute *bonus*, then all members of *ISS_employees* contain the endowed attribute *bonus* unless *bonus* is redefined in *ISS_employees*. For a given object *o1*, the *bonus* value of *o1* in *ISS_employees* is equal to the *bonus* value of *o1* in *NUS_employees*.

Endowed methods in a class declaration refers to methods endowed by the class on its members. They manipulate endowed attributes. An example of endowed method is *set_address* of *ISS_employees*. It is possible for *employee* to be a PINOL type containing a method whose name is *set_address*. Similarly, it is possible for *ISS_employees* to contain a class method whose name is *set_address*. They are all unrelated.

The syntax to invoke endowed methods is "*ISS_employees* → *ref(o)*→ *set_address(...)*," read as "invoke endowed method *set_address* on *o* which is a member of *ISS_employees* in the context *ISS_employees*." Endowed methods can be inherited.

2.2 Endowed Attributes versus Subtypes

A PINOL class is not a type - members of *ISS_employees* are of type *employee*, not *ISS_employees* (for *ISS_employees* is not a type). In a system with one class per type, this example can be simulated by creating a new subtype for *ISS_employees*. To motivate the PINOL class concept, we compare modeling of information using endowed attributes versus creating new subtypes.

The National University of Singapore has many departments. Each department has its own classifications of people. For example, the two departments, Institute of Systems Science (ISS) and Department of Information Systems and Computer Science (DISCS), classify their employees differently. ISS classifies its staff into software engineer I, software engineer, research associate and research member. DISCS classifies its staff into tutor, lecturer, senior lecturer and professor. These classifications are independent. If a person holds a joint appointment at these two departments, then his/her job title depends on the context. For example, a person may be a research associate from ISS *and* a lecturer from DISCS. To model the above situation using PINOL classification concept, we use only one type, *employee*, which is the type requirement of all the 10 classes. These 10 classes are: *ISS_employee* having four subclasses and *DISCS_employee* having another four subclasses. The endowed attributes are used for the extra fields to support context sensitive information under each classification.

One may combine these independent classifications into a monolithic one by converting endowed attributes in subclasses into subtypes and declaring a class for each of the types. However, this may lead to an explosion of types and classes. For example, given the two PINOL classifications *ISS_employees* and *DISCS_employees* each having four subclasses, and a given object *o* such that *o* is both a member of *research_associate* and *lecturer*; to create a single type hierarchy for the above classifications, it is necessary to declare a mixed type: *lecturer_research_associate*, which is subtype of both *lecturer* and *research_associate* types. We have no means of telling a priori that any combination of other types are not required (since the object *o* could have been a member of research associate and senior lecturer as well). Thus the converted hierarchy needs at least 4^2 classes. In comparison, the classification with endowed attributes requires $2 * 4$ classes. With such a large number of classifications in the former case, it is difficult for anyone to decide where to put a person he is interested in because he has to choose from 16 possible classes compared to looking only at the 4 classes from *ISS_employee* or *DISCS_employee*.

Having independent classifications makes life easier. It also has other uses such as for security or access control. For instance, ISS keeps some sensitive data on projects. So besides the normal classification of projects which is exported to other departments, it may have secret classifications of projects which are not shared. Thus, sensitive information on classified projects can be kept there safely.

3 PINOL RULES

In Ullman's invited talk at DOODS91[9)], he advocated the importance of a declarative language for querying. This is especially true for ad-hoc query such as finding relationship among data in scientific databases. He claimed that it is not possible to take object identity (OID) seriously and still retain the declarativeness enjoyed in a first order logic system. He also believes that declarative languages cannot be object oriented in a non-trival way. We support his claim that an object oriented language is not declarative enough for querying, but do not agree that OID and declarativeness cannot co-exist. We will show in this section how to add logic (Datalog) to our PINOL system to achieve a certain level of declarativeness yet still retain the benefits of an object oriented system. We emphasise the combination of declarativeness and object orientation can be done by choosing object orientation as the base and add logic on top rather than the other way round. An earlier exposition on PINOL rules was given in [11)]. Here we provide only a pragmatic view of PINOL rules with emphasis on how it can be used to define complex (recursive) relationships between objects.

3.1 Syntax and Semantics of Rules

An example of a datalog-like rule *path* has the following syntax:

$path(x, y)$ if given

$path(x,y)$ if $path(x,z)$ and $path(z,y)$
forall $x, y, z : point$

All variables must be listed in the forall part of the rule. This is to indicate that only objects in the correct category can play the roles as stated in the rule. Here *point* may be the name of a type or a PINOL class. If *point* is the name of a type *point* (of course!), then the corresponding variable is considered to have type *point**. Otherwise, *point* is the name of a PINOL class *point* (whatelse?) containing objects of type *t*; then the corresponding variable is consider to have type *t**. Each rule is defined once and is stratified. The keyword *given* is used to stand for extensionally given facts.

Once a rule *R* is defined, all the objects in the system instantly understand it. To reflect this understanding, these objects acquire a set of `foci`. The foci of a rule are the various functions which can be evaluated as methods in the underlying object oriented system[1]. There are basically three kinds of focus for every rule: assert, retract, and query. For instance, with respect to the rule *path* above, the kinds of foci we get are:

assert_1_2_*path*(x:$t*$, y:$t*$) :bool
retract_1_2_*path*(x:$t*$, y:$t*$) :bool
_1_*path*_2(x:$t*$) : set($t*$)
_2_*path*_1(y:$t*$) : set($t*$)
_1_2_*path*(x:$t*$, y:$t*$) : bool
_2_1_*path*(y:$t*$, x:$t*$) : bool
*path*_1_2() : set($t*$)
*path*_2_1() : set($t*$)

assert_1_2_*path*(*a*1, *a*2) establishes a path between point *a*1 and point *a*2. retract_1_2_*path*(*a*1, *a*2) does the opposite thing. The query focus _1_*path*_2(*a*1) is the set { y | *path*(*a*1, y) } provided that *a*1 is of the appropriate type and is in the appropriate PINOL class. The numbers appearing in a query focus (as in _1_*path*_2) explains how input and output are arranged. The digits before the name of the query focus indicate the roles played by the input objects and the digits after the query focus indicate the roles played by the output objects (e.g. the input to _1_*path*_2 plays the role indicated by x in the rule *path*, while the output plays the role of y).

A special form of literal, known as *test predicate*, helps to define a more useful rule in our context. As an example:

rule $grandfather(x,y)$ if
  $\{A\}(!x)$ and
  $parent(x,z)$ and $parent(z,y)$
forall $x, y, z : Person$

[1] by choosing the computation of rules in an object oriented system, there is no conflict between OIDs and logical rules as pointed by Ullman

The literal $\{A\}(!x)$ is a test predicate. A is a block of PINOL codes that does not invoke any other rule focus. In this example it could be a function checking that x is male and over the age of 50. A test predicate must evaluate to a boolean value and is required to terminate. The bang(!) before the x is an annotation to indicate that the test predicate cannot be evaluated until x is instantiated. A bang(!) after a variable annotates that it get instantiated after the evaluation of the test predicate. The only side effect expected in a test predicate is the instantiation of those variables with a bang after them.

Due to the presence of test predicates and negations, not every rule focus can be computed soundly and completely with respect to classical predicate calculus. Therefore, PINOL uses some simple and conservative syntactic criteria to classify foci into legal and illegal foci. Only legal foci may be used in a PINOL program and PINOL guarantees sound and complete evaluation for them. In general, if a rule is quantified over PINOL classes only, all its foci are legal. This is because a PINOL class is finite in size. On the other hand, if one of the variable is quantified over a PINOL type, some foci of the rule may not be legal.

3.2 Inter-object Relationships and Rules

The above description of rules assume that given facts are explicitly stored in tables. Foci are just various smart access routines to this table. In another word, the definition of rules assumes that all the base relationships (given facts) between objects are explicitly specified in somewhere. For example, in order to relate an employee *e* to his/her manager *m*, we create the *employee* object and the *manager* object. When the employee *e* is working for a particular manager *m*, we define the relationship by creating the fact, assert_1_2_*manager*(*e*, *m*). But in an object oriented data model, relationship between two objects is suppose to be modeled as an attribute or as a method in the class. For example, with the *employee* – *manager* problem, the fact that an employee is working for a particular manager can be considered as a property of employee and might be stored in the data structure of the *employee* object. On the other hand, it is also posible to store it as a method in the manager's object.

Modeling relationship as attributes of objects is the philosophy of object oriented paradigm. Here, encapsulation is enforced and data is held by the object. With this approach, however, there is no global view of relationships. For example the *manager* object may not know the relationship with the *employee* object unless the inverse is stored in the *manager* object. If the inverse is being stored, there is no guarantee that the implementation of the inverse relationship is consistent with the implementation of the original relationship. Another problem is that since the relationship is burried somewhere, inference rule such as the *path* which has to depend on the global view of the relationship between the points cannot be supported. On the other hand, specifying relationships using the *assert* focus gives a global view of all relationships between objects. This provides a straight forward method for inferencing. But, as we have pointed out earlier, it violates encapsulation.

We want to keep to the philosophy of modeling relationship as in object oriented paradigm to retain structural object-orientation. But we also wish to be able to specify complex relationship between objects by rules to achieve declarativeness. The key to achieve our goal is to integrate rules with PINOL classes and types in such a way that it is always possible to derive the facts required by the rule through calling the object's methods. In this way encapsulation is respected and inferencing can be supported.

It is found that *test predicate* is a feature adequate for the specification of methods invocation in the rule. So for every rule which requires the base relationships to be extracted from the class, a test predicate specification is used instead of the keyword *given*. So despite storing relationships with objects, the inference engine has a way to access it.

The program transformation technique[11], used to generate the foci for the normal rules is adopted to generate a set of query foci for rules having test predicate specification. We explain the mechanism for deriving the test predicate foci using the following example.

```
object type employee
   attributes are:
      work_for:manager;
      ..
   methods:
      (manager*) get_work_for();
end object type

object type manager
   attributes are:
      ..
      projects_managed: set(project*);
      employee_managed: set(employee*);
methods:
      set(employee*) get_employee_managed();
      ..
end object type

class employee_class contains objects of type
   employee
class manager_class contains objects of type
   manager

/* Querying who is the boss of whom */
rule manager(m, e) if
{ m == employee_class → e → get_work_for() }(!e,!m)
forall m: manager_class, e: employee_class;

rule boss(m, e) if
manager(m, e) or boss(m, x) and boss(x, e)
forall e:employee_class, x,m:manager_class;
```

The relationship between the *manager* and the *employee* is stored with the respective object. When making a query on who is the boss of whom, it would be more declarative to be able to state the query as *boss(x,y)?* This query is really a Datalog rule whose evaluation depends on the *manager* rule. The *manager* rule is defined with the test predicate to access the relationships from the employee's object by the method *get_work_for*. To generate the set of foci for the manager's rule, the test predicate specification is first translated into a function. For the above example, we can introduce a function foo more or less by making a verbatim copy of the test predicate:

```
foo(employee* e, manager* m)
{
   return (m == employee_class -> e ->
      get_work_for())
}
```

A set of foci (functions) is generated for the *manager* rule. Each of the focus will be calling the above test predicate function with the correct mode of input and output. For example, the focus _2_manager_1(m, e), roughly corresponds to the implementation of the following function,

```
set(manager*) _2_manager_1(employee* e)
{
   return{m:manager* | manager_class.contains(m)
      and foo(e, m)}
}
```

The body of this function is expressed using the relative set abstraction, which is another useful feature of PINOL, similar to ML's list comprehension [10] [1]. The other foci associated with *manager* rule are: _1_manager_2(m), _2_1_manager(m,e), _1_2_manager(e,m), manager_1_2(), manager_2_1().

4 EXAMPLES

More examples are given in this Section to illustrate how objects of an employee database of the National University of Singapore (NUS) are created and manipulated. The declaration of the necessary types and classes are assumed.

Creation of objects can be done through the PINOL class operator *new* or the system *new* operator in C++. We first show the creation of employee for ISS using the class operator *new*. This operator is invoked with the name of the class in which the object is to be created. The constructor or initialization procedure for the type requirement of the PINOL class is invoked automatically when the class operator *new* is called. PINOL programs follow as much as possible the syntax of C++. This example shows how objects in the class *ISS_employees* are created. We assume that the class attributes are initialized by the class initialization procedure at compilation time. The object P is initialized by the *employee* object type constructor.

```
/* program to create 10 new iss employees */
void create_10_employee();
{
employee* p;
int i;
for (i=0; i<10; i++)
   { p = ISS_employees.new();
   ISS_employees → p → prompt_sec_card_no();
   ISS_employees → p → add_duties_plan();
   ISS_employees → p → prompt_address();
   ISS_employees → p → prompt_projects();
   }
}
```

Objects can also be created using the system (C++) command *new*. The object accquires default values set up by the constructor of the object type. The following codes illustrate the creation of an employee which we wish to put it in the class *research_associates* which is a subclass of *ISS_employee*.

```
employee* create_a_research_associate();
   {
   employee* p;
   p = new employee;
   research_associates.add(p);
   research_associates → p → prompt_room_no();
   research_associates → p → prompt_projects();
   research_associates → p → prompt_sec_card_no()
   research_associates → p → add_duties_plan();
   research_associates → p → prompt_address();
   return(p)
   }
```

The next example shows how relationship between objects in two different classes are set up.

```
project* pj;
employee* p;
p = create_a_research_associate();
pj = research_projects.new();
research_projects → pj → set_topic();
/* assigning new project leader for the project */
pj → set_proj_leader(p);
```

Information can be retrieved either by writing the imperative C++ codes or using the higher level relative set abstraction. For example,

```
/*retrieve projects whose duration is > 3 years */
set(project*) three_years_proj();
   {
   return({pj:project* |
   research_projects.contains(pj) and
      pj → duration > 3 })
   }
```

Some information is more naturally expressed using rules. We show how some queries from the employee database are expressed using the datalog-like rules.

```
rule same_team(x,y) if common_manager(x,y) and
same_project(x,y).
forall x,y:ISS_employee.

rule works_on(x,y) if
{ s = ISS_employee → y → get_project(); return
true}(!y,s!) and {s→member(x)}(!s,!x)
forall x:research_projects, y:ISS_employee,
s:set(project*).

rule same_project(x,y) if works_on(z,x) and
works_on(z,y)
forall x,y:ISS_employee, z:research_projects.

rule manager(x,y) if { x = ISS_employee→ y →
get_manager(); return true}(!y,x!).
forall x:manager, y:ISS_employee.

/* query whether two ISS employees have the com-
mon manager */
rule common_manager(x,y) if manager(z,x) and
manager(z,y).
forall x,y:ISS_employee, z:manager.
```

5 SUMMARY AND RELATED RESEARCH

In this paper, we have described some features of PINOL as implemented in the prototype. We have highlighted the two unique features of PINOL, its canonical and non-canonical classification constructs and inference capability.

A major advantage of the PINOL class concept is that it provides independent classification of objects without leading to type explosion (2.2) when an object takes on several roles. Furthermore, the behaviour of an object is sensitive to the context in which the object is placed.

Systems such as O2 and Gemstone do not support multiple classifications of an object in a convenient way. In particular, objects cannot dynamically change classes. Iris[2)] do allow an object to gain or lose types throughout its lifetime. However, objects in Iris do not have context dependent behaviours.

Aspects[8)] is a proposal that fully supports independent and dynamic classification of objects. In this system, an object can be given many aspects, which corresponds to gaining memberships in PINOL classes. Object behaviour is also context sensitive. In this system, aspects are first class values and are part of the type system. In addition, it inherited from Emerald[7)] the ability to have several alternative implementations per type. In contrast, PINOL classes are not part of the type system. Furthermore, each PINOL class has exactly one implementation as it is our believe that objects should behave in the same way in the same context. However, Aspects has potential of being a more flexible system.

Rules provide a way of expressing knowledge declaratively in object oriented systems. The inferential strength of our rule is no more than that of Datalog, hence it is too weak for general programming, but it is suitable for expressing static complex relationships between objects in the object oriented system. The test predicate provides a mean to easily extract inter-objects relationships from an object store. Our approach has the benefit that features of object orientation such as object identity and encapsulation can be retained while still achieve a reasonable level of declarativeness. We have shown that by choosing the object oriented system as the base and add logic on top of it, it is possible to get some logic programming into object oriented system. This has the benefit that OIDS and declarativeness can co-exist which has been pointed by Ullman[9] as being one of the open problems in trying to combine deductive database and object oriented paradigm. We don't deny that the introduction of `test predicate` affect the declarativeness of the programming style. But provided it is used in a restricted way, the expressive power that it can bring far outweights this deficiency.

Our design of PINOL is influenced by our goal to simplify the development of object oriented database applications through a closer integration of databases and object oriented programming language constructs. Thus we have emphasised more on the design of high level language constructs as constrasted with E and CO2 which emphasis more on the system level details such as management of persistency and concurrency. A preprocessor for PINOL to C++ which supports PINOL types, class and rules has been implemented[4].

ACKNOWLEDGEMENT

We thank Yan Ling Ling for her contributions to the section on rules. We also want to thank Ho Lye Kuan and Tan Chee Yong for the implementation of PINOL.

References

1) Field A.J., Harrison P.G. Functional Programming. Addison-Wesley Publishing Company, Wokingham, England, 1988.

2) Fishman D., et al. Iris: An object-oriented database management systems. ACM Transcations on Office Information Systems, 5(2):48–69, April 1987.

3) Kim W. Introduction to Object Oriented Databases. MIT Press, Cambridge, Mass., 1990.

4) Hoe L.K., Tan C.Y. "Implementation of PINOL". Technical Report Project no. 945, Department of Information Systems and Computer Science, National University of Singapore, Singapore, 1991.

5) Lecluse C., Richard P., Velez F. "O2, an object oriented data model". In SIGMOD 88, International Conference on the Management of Data, pages 424–433, Chicago, June 1988.

6) Ngu A.HH. ,Wong L.S., Widjojo S. "On canonical and non-canonical classifications". In C. Delobel, M.Kifer, and Y. Masunaga, editors, Proceedings of the 2nd Conference on Deductive and Object Oriented Databases, pages 371–390, Munich, Germany, December 1991.

7) Raj R.K. and el. al. "Emerald: A general purpose programming language". Software - Practice and Experience, 21(1):91–118, January 1991.

8) Richardson J., Schwarz P. "Aspects: Extending objects to support multiple, independent roles". In In SIGMOD 91, International Conference on the Management of Data, pages 298–307, Colorado, May 1991.

9) Ullman J.D. "A comparison between deductive and object-oriented database systems". In C. Delobel, M.Kifer, and Y. Masunaga, editors, Proceedings of the 2nd Conference on Deductive and Object Oriented Databases, pages 263–277, Munich, Germany, December 1991.

10) Wikstrom A. Functional Programming Using ML. Prentice-Hall International, Englewood Cliffs, New Jersey, 1987.

11) Wong L.S. "Inference rules in object oriented programming systems". In W. Kim, J.-M. Nicholas, and S. Nishio, editors, Proceedings of the 1st Conference on Deductive and Object Oriented Databases, pages 459–475, Kyoto, Japan, December 1989.

12) Zdonik S.B., Maier D., editors. Development and Implementation of An Object Oriented DBMS.

Morgan Kaufmann Publishers, Inc., 1990.

Object-Oriented Database with Rule-Based Query Interface for Genomic Computation

Susumu Goto[1] Norihiro Sakamoto[2] Toshihisa Takagi[3]

[1]Department of Computer Science and Communication Engineering, Kyushu University
Hakozaki, Higashi-ku, Fukuoka 812 Japan
[2]Kyushu University Medical School
Maidashi, Higashi-ku, Fukuoka 812 Japan
[3]Human Genome Center, The Institute of Medical Science, The University of Tokyo
Shirokanedai, Minato-ku, Tokyo 108, Japan

ABSTRACT

A large amount of human genome data has been collected and efficient techniques for handling the data and for building and testing biological hypotheses are needed. We developed an object-oriented database system with rule-based query interface for genomic computation. The database is constructed on a commercially available object-oriented database system GemStone and contains GenBank entries as complex objects. To handle complex objects in logical queries, concepts of meta variables and meta atoms are adopted in rule-based query interface. This system is powerful to construct database queries from simple keyword search to various biological hypothesis.

1 INTRODUCTION

The Human Genome Project is directed towards experimentally determining all the sequences of the human genome and acquiring knowledge on the structure, function and evolution of the human genome. The genome of an organism is a set of chromosomes that contains all of its genetic information. The human genome comprises twenty-four chromosomes that consists of about three billion base pairs.

There are various information concerning the genome, which we call the genomic information. For example, DNA sequences consisting of four kinds of bases (adenine, thymine, guanine and cytosine — symbolically represented as A, T, G and C respectively), protein sequences consisting of twenty kinds of amino acids, 3-D structures of proteins and mapping data of a gene to a certain position of the chromosomes are the genomic information. Figure 1 shows relationships between some of the genomic information.

To achieve the goals of the project, a large amount of the genomic information is rapidly increasing. There are several data banks to maintain the genomic information, for example GenBank[1)] for DNA sequences, PIR[2)] for protein sequences, PDB[3)] for 3-D structures of proteins. Some of them support the on-line services for searching based on keywords and homology search (similarity search between sequences such as FASTA[4)]). For more complex searches such as the combination of the above ones, the users have to write programs for their own use.

The project requires not only the accumulation of the genomic information but also the analyses of them. Analysis consists of constructing and testing a hypothesis and additional analyses of the results. We call the iteration of the analyses the genomic computation. For example, the following are genomic computation.

- Searching biologically significant sequences from the data banks.
- Predicting the function or the structure of the experimentally obtained sequences (e.g., by similarity search to the known sequences).
- Getting together the information of a gene usually stored separately in several entries. (An example of GenBank entry is shown in Appendix.)
- Getting together the related information over several data banks.

Most of genomic computation requires the user's program such as SIGNAL SCAN[5)]. Therefore, database systems supporting interfaces to easily construct and test the hypotheses has to be designed.

In 1992, we developed a relational database system ODS that contains GenBank data[6)]. We also integrated deductive functions to it. The system is useful for the signal sequence search or predicting structures of sequences. (Signal sequences are the one of the important ones related to regulatory proteins.) However, the system does not store all of the information in GenBank due to its various and complex structures.

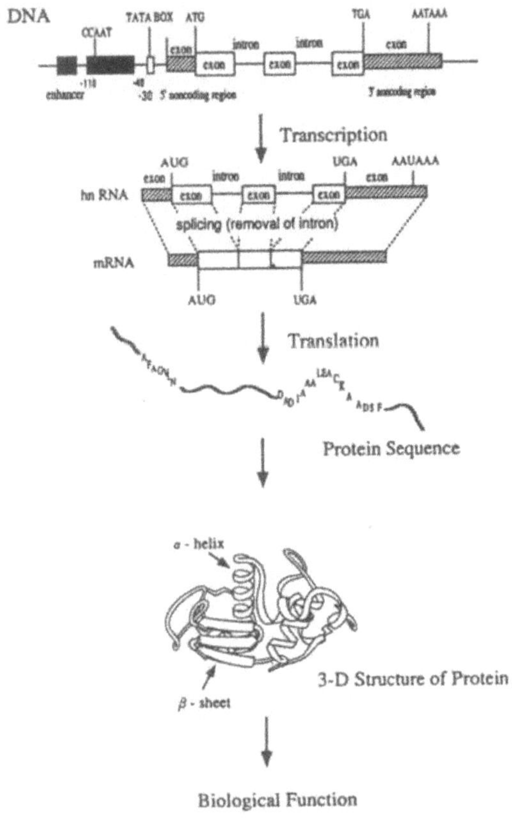

Figure 1: The relationship between the genomic information

GenBank contains keywords for retrieving entries, references in which the sequence is reported, biological features of the sequence, etc., in addition to the sequence data. (An example of GenBank entry is given in Appendix.) The other data banks also contain various kinds of information. The information in the data banks is complex (e.g. biological features and references in GenBank). The object-oriented database (OODB) system is suitable to manage the complex information because it can manage various types of data such as nested relations and long text data like DNA sequences.

We developed an OODB system managing all of the information in GenBank. The system raveled out the inefficiency of ODS, which came from the frequent join operations. We integrated the deductive function for easily constructing and testing hypotheses to the OODB system. Recently, there has been much research in developing logical languages into OODB systems (for example, HiLog[7], LLO[8]). One main topic of the research seems to be the formal discussion of the languages. Our approach is to integrate deductive functions from the practical point of view.

We describe below our OODB system with rule-based query interface for genomic computation. The system contains GenBank data. We show that the OODB systems and their additional deductive function are useful for the genomic computation.

The rest of this paper is organized as follows. Section 2 describes features of genomic information and some classes for them in our OODB system. Section 3 introduces the rule-based query interface of our system. The syntax of the query language is described there. In section 4, we describe the overview of the system. Section 5 concludes this paper.

2 GENOMIC INFORMATION IN OBJECT-ORIENTED DATABASE

Human genome data has been reported (17,752 entries; 18,876,706 bases in GenBank release 73. September. 1992). These data can be obtained in a text file format. GenBank has been internally managed by a relational database (RDB) system[1]. However the services of GenBank are limited to either retrieving sequences based on keywords or homology search. Retrievals of sequences based on biological features requires a new program.

In this section, we describe difficulties in managing the genome data by RDB systems and our approach to managing them by our OODB system.

2.1 Difficulties in Managing Genomic Information by RDB Systems

We developed the system ODS with a high level query processing function[6]. The system integrates information on biological features into the search for signal sequences by using a RDB system and processes rule-based queries by applying a deductive engine to it.

Figure 2 shows an example of genomic information stored in the ODS system. The human DNA sequences kept in GenBank vary from less than 10 base pairs to more than 7 kilobase pairs in length. This variety in length is one of the drawbacks to store and search for signal sequences in a database. The ODS copes with this problem by dividing sequences into the 8 bases long overlapping oligonucleotides (Figure 2: Table Sequences).

It is difficult to store all information of FEATURES TABLE that describes biological features of genes because of complexity of its structure. The ODS stores the biological features in the Table Features (Figure 2: Table Features) and the table is linked to the other tables by the key attribute Locus. Some biological features could not be stored in the table for reasons of complexity. In the research on the genomic information, DNA sequences and their biological features are frequently needed, which results in the frequent join operations of these tables.

There are some interrelated entries, because the relationship between GenBank entries and genes is not one to one. There is the case where several entries belong to one gene. Some DNA entries also have mRNA entries and protein data that originate from them. Hence, the database

Table Keyword

Locus	Keyword
AGMPPINS	preproinsulin
AGMPPINS	preproinsulin
⋮	⋮

Table Features

Locus	Start	End	Signal
AGMPPINS	426	463	5'UTR
AGMPPINS	654	670	5'UTR
⋮	⋮	⋮	⋮
AGMPPINS	426	463	exon
AGMPPINS	654	857	sig_peptide
AGMPPINS	671	742	exon
⋮	⋮	⋮	⋮

Table Sequences

Locus	Start	Sequence
AGMPPINS	1	GGGCCATC
AGMPPINS	2	GGCCATCC
⋮	⋮	⋮

Figure 2: Examples of genome data in relational tables (corresponding to the entry in Appendix)

system for the genomic computation has to provide functions of handling data structure that can store an attribute for the set of entries. And the entries have to be not only the ones in GenBank but also the ones in the other data banks.

2.2 Management of Genomic Information by an OODB System

The OODB consists of objects and linkages between them. An object consists of attributes and methods. Figure 3 shows the classes (represented by rectangles) in the database of genomic information and their linkages. Linkages between attributes and class are represented by arrows and class hierarchy is represented by solid lines. Attribute names are represented in italics.

The references between sequences and their biological features can be easily achieved, because the references from an object to other related objects using pointers are easy in OODB systems. Built-in methods (e.g., for the homology search) reduce the user's burden of programming for a combination of keyword search and homology search.

In the next subsection, we describe data structure for genomic information in detail.

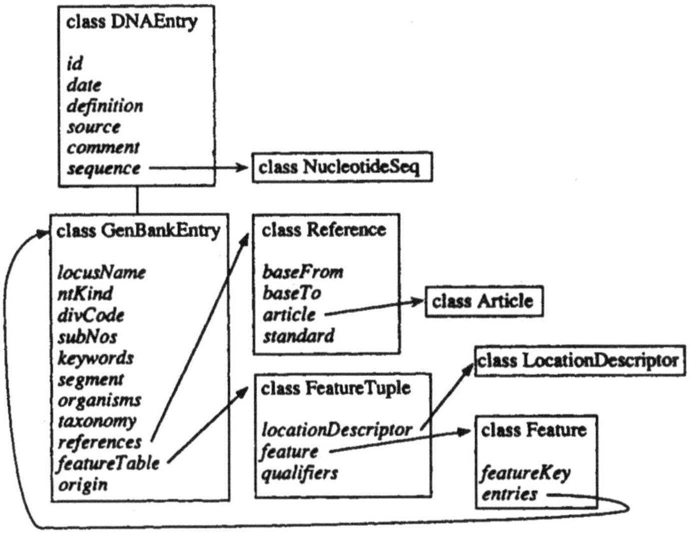

Figure 3: (a) The class GenBankEntry and its related classes

2.3 Classes of Genomic Information in the OODB System

The most important class for GenBank is the class GenBankEntry, which corresponds to the GenBank entry and contains all data fields (LOCUS, DEFINITION, etc., in the example in Appendix) as its attributes. The attributes *id* and *sequence* are necessary for the data not only in GenBank but also in the other data banks. Those attributes are inherited from the class DNAEntry. Classes for the other data banks could be easily designed as the subclasses of the class DNAEntry.

There are attributes defined as complex objects such as *references* and *featureTable* (Figure 3: (a)). The attribute *featureTable* in the class GenBankEntry is defined as a set of instances of the class FeatureTuple. The class FeatureTuple is the one for biological features of the sequences. As described in the previous section, they are important for the researchers and are very complex. It has *locationDescriptor*, *feature* and *qualifiers* as attributes. The value of the attribute *feature* is an instance of the class Feature. The class Feature has *featureKey* for 'exon,' '5'UTR,' etc., and the set of pointers to the GenBankEntry in which the instance of *featureKey* is included. The attribute *featureQualifiers* is a set of instances of the class Qualifier that describes complex objects.

The value of the attribute *locationDescriptor* is the instance of the class LocationDescriptor. This is either the instance of the class SimpleLocation or the instance of the class ComplexLocations such as 'join(426..463,654..670),' as shown in Appendix. The class Location contains the attributes *startPos* and *endPos* representing the regions of biological features in the nucleotide sequence (Figure 3: (b)). These classes have the methods **length** and **toSequence**. The method **length** returns the length of the location and the method **toSequence** returns the corresponding

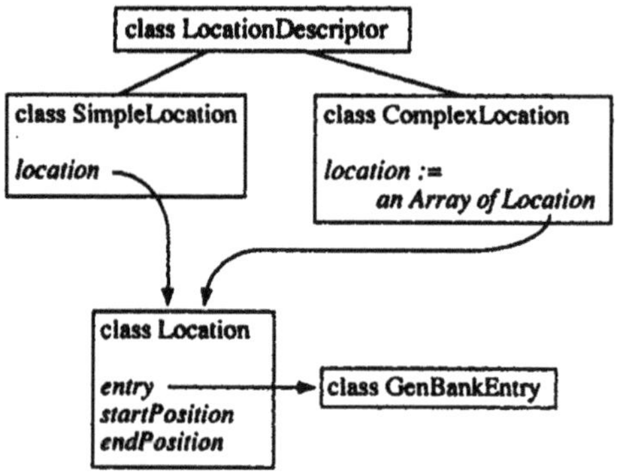

Figure 3: (b) The class LocationDescriptor and its related classes

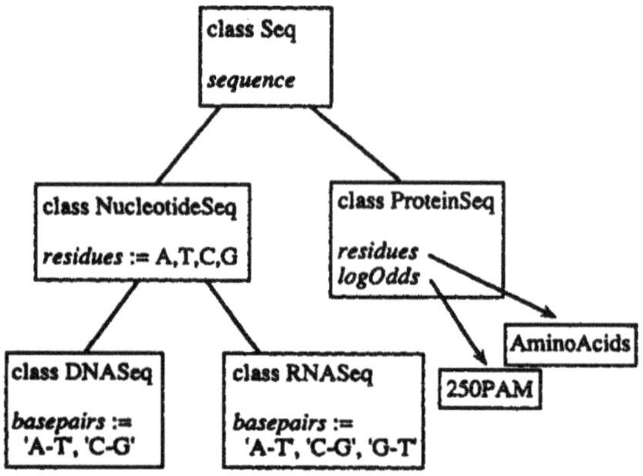

Figure 3: (c) The class Seq and its related classes

sequence to the location.

The attribute *sequence* in the class GenBankEntry is an instance of the class NucleotideSeq. It is a subclass of the class Seq that contains the attribute *sequence* that represents sequence as a string (Figure 3: (c)). The methods **length** and **composition** are defined in the class NucleotideSeq. The method **length** returns the length of the nucleotide sequence and the method **composition** returns the number of each nucleotide (the number of A, C, G, T respectively) in the sequence. Users do not have to distinguish these methods from the attributes, because they can give the query for the computed value in the same form of the query for values stored in attributes.

In the class NucleotideSeq, the method **homology** is defined. It retrieves homology among nucleotide sequences. This ability enables the database to have the same function as homology retrieval programs that are difficult to be implemented to the built-in SQL function in the RDB systems. This method makes the combination of the retrievals easy, such as the retrieval based on keyword and homology search of nucleotide sequences. In the class ProteinSeq, the attribute is defined for storing the information of proteins.

3 RULE-BASED QUERY INTERFACE

In the OODB systems, the users have to program with the procedural language like C++ to describe a complex query. In research on the genomic information, it is necessary to easily construct and test hypotheses and represent a higher structure of DNA or protein. The declarative expression of rule-based queries minimizes the programming effort for constructing hypotheses.

To integrate deductive functions in the OODB systems, we meet the following problems.

- How can complex objects in the forms of facts be managed?
- How can methods be implemented as the deductive functions?

To cope with these problems, logical languages for OODB systems have been proposed (for example, HiLog[7], LLO[8]). Our approach is the one from the practical point of view rather than formal languages discussed in the previous research.

We propose a rule-based query interface for the OODB system. The rules contain the meta variable for a set of objects and can define the methods applied to each instance in the set. Although it is a subset of those languages, it is powerful for the genomic computation. In this section, we introduce the overview of the interface. The proposed query processing function can handle rules in the current fixed class hierarchy, because the database for the genomic information merely requires update for data structure. The update of data is not also considered.

3.1 Examples of Rules in the Interface

We introduce the notion of a meta variable and a meta atom. A meta variable represents an object or a set of objects. A meta atom includes a meta variable in its predicate symbol and plays the role of message passing to each object in the set represented by the meta variable. The syntax of the rules is extended from the first order form in the following constructs.

Meta Variables: Meta variables are terms. Meta variables appear in the meta atoms (described later). A meta variable represents a set of objects and plays a role of extracting elements of the set.

Class Atoms: If A is a class name in which there are n instance variables $i_1, \ldots, i_n$, then $A(i_1, \ldots, i_n)$ is an atom. We call this a class atom. We consider the inheritance of instance variables and method defined in the class. We discuss about them in the end of this section.

Meta Atoms Suppose M is a meta variable that represents a set of objects in the class C, and D is a predicate derived from a class redefinition rule or C itself

(A class redefinition rule is the rule for extracting only required instance variables from a certain class. We describe it later). Then $M/D(i_1, \ldots, i_k)$ is an atom. We call this a meta atom. The intuitive meaning of the meta atom is the message passing to each object in M to obtain the values of instance variables represented by its arguments.

If a rule has only one body literal and the literal is a class atom, then the rule is called a class redefinition rule. This rule redefines the class represented by L_1 to hold only the necessary instance variables.

Example 1: Consider the classes Feature and GenBankEntry as mentioned in the previous section. First, we retrieve the objects in the class Features where *featureKey* is 'CAAT_signal.' Second, we retrieve instances in the class GenBankEntry that contain the objects retrieved from the class Features. Finally, we obtain *locusNo*, *locusName* and *features* of the retrieved objects, and as for *features*, we obtain *location* and *featureKey*.

Although the GenBank on-line service supports entry search based on keywords or locus name, it does not support the one based on the biological features. This search is one of the important tasks in the research on the genomic information (for example, signal sequence search mentioned in Section 1). This example, which is represented by the following rules, shows one of the useful points of the system.

$$
\begin{aligned}
&feature1(Entry, Key) :- \\
&\quad Feature(Entry, Location, Key, Qualifier). \qquad (1) \\
&feature2(Location, Key) :- \\
&\quad Feature(Entry, Location, Key, Qualifier). \qquad (2) \\
&entry(No, Name, Features) :- \\
&\quad GenBankEntry(No, Name, AccNo, Def, \\
&\qquad\qquad Keywords, Ref, Features, Seq). \quad (3) \\
&query(LocusNo, LocusName, Location, Key) :- \\
&\quad feature1(Entries, 'CAAT\_signal'), \\
&\quad Entries/entry(LocusNo, LocusName, Features), \\
&\quad Features/feature2(Location, Key). \qquad (4)
\end{aligned}
$$

The rules (1)~(3) are the class redefinition rules. *Entries* and *Features* in the rule (4) are meta variables, and they represent a set of instances of the classes GenBankEntry and Feature, respectively. The literal $feature1(Entries, 'CAAT\_signal')$ corresponds to the selection operation to the database. The literals *Entries/entry(LocusNo, LocusName, Features*) and *Features/feature2(Location, Key*) correspond to the message passing to the instances of the class GenBankEntry and to the instances of the class Feature, respectively. □

Example 2: In GenBank, there is the case where several entries represent one gene. Thus it is important to investigate the correspondence between entries and genes. This example shows one of such tasks constructing the hypothesis that the entries represent same genes under the following condition.

1. The entries have same keywords. In this example the keyword is 'cystic fibrosis.'
2. The sequences of the entries have similarity over the 95% matches by the homology search such as FASTA.
3. If entry A and entry B, and entry B and entry C represent same gene, respectively, then entry A and entry C also represent same gene.

$$
\begin{aligned}
&cf\_features(Locus, Features) :- \\
&\quad GenBankEntry(Locus, Acc, Def, 'cystic\ fibrosis', \\
&\qquad\qquad Ref, Features, Sequence). \qquad (5) \\
&cf\_sequence(Locus, Sequence) :- \\
&\quad GenBankEntry(Locus, Acc, Def, 'cystic\ fibrosis', \\
&\qquad\qquad Ref, Features, Sequence). \qquad (6) \\
&cf\_exon(Locus, Seq) :- \\
&\quad cf\_features(Locus, Features) \\
&\quad Features/Feature(Entries, Region, 'exon'), \\
&\quad Region/Location(Start, End, Length, Seq). \quad (7) \\
&same\_gene(Locus1, Locus2) :- \\
&\quad cf\_sequence(Locus1, Sequence1), \\
&\quad cf\_sequence(Locus2, Sequence2), \\
&\quad homology(Sequence1, Sequence2, Similarity), \\
&\quad Similarity > 95.0. \qquad (8) \\
&same\_gene(Locus1, Locus2) :- \\
&\quad cf\_exon(Locus1, Sequence1), \\
&\quad cf\_exon(Locus2, Sequence2), \\
&\quad homology(Sequence1, Sequence2, Similarity), \\
&\quad Similarity > 95.0. \qquad (9) \\
&same\_gene(Locus1, Locus2) :- \\
&\quad cf\_sequence(Locus1, Sequence1), \\
&\quad cf\_exon(Locus2, Sequence2), \\
&\quad homology(Sequence1, Sequence2, Similarity), \\
&\quad Similarity > 95.0. \qquad (10) \\
&same\_gene(Locus1, Locus2) :- \\
&\quad same\_gene(Locus2, Locus1). \qquad (11) \\
&same\_gene(Locus1, Locus2) :- \\
&\quad same\_gene(Locus1, Locus), \\
&\quad same\_gene(Locus, Locus2). \qquad (12)
\end{aligned}
$$

The rules (5) and (6) retrieve entries that have the keyword '*cystic fibrosis.*' By using rule (5), the locus names and features of the retrieved entries are obtained. Similarly, sequences of the retrieved entries are obtained using the rule (6). The rule for $cf\_exon(LocusName, Sequence)$ retrieves the exon subsequence of the entry (designated by LocusName). $same\_gene(LocusName1, LocusName2)$ means the entry whose LocusName is *LocusName1* and the entry whose LocusName is *LocusName2* can be the same gene, because similarity of the two sequences exceeds 95% . The predicate *homology* is built-in. This homology search function can be implemented as a built-in method in the OODB system using the FASTA program. □

In the above examples, the class atom has only instance variables in its arguments. The implementation of the class atom uses the message passing to the instance of the class even though the arguments represent only the instance variables. Thus some methods can be also integrated in the arguments. For example, we can extend the class atom *NucleotideSeq* (*Sequences*) to the atom *NucleotideSeq*(*Sequences, Length, Composition*). The meanings of the arguments *Length* and *Composition* are the message passing to the instance of class NucleotideSeq corresponding to the methods length and composition respectively.

4 SYSTEM DESCRIPTION

Figure 4 shows an overview of our system. We use the commercially available object-oriented database system GemStone (version 3.0) and it's Smalltalk Interface. We use the primate data file gbpri.seq (about 50MB) in GenBank release 73. The program that transforms the GenBank file into the data for GemStone is written in ObjectWorks\Smalltalk R4.1.

Users can give either the primitive queries or the rule-based queries. For the primitive queries such as searching based on keywords or/and biological features, the system supports a window interface. For the rule-based queries such as the ones described in the previous section, the rule transformer transforms them into the Smalltalk queries. Both interfaces are written by ObjectWorks\Smalltalk R4.1.

Size of the database (data file and log file) is about 130MB that is about 2.6 times larger than original flat file. It takes about 15 second to retrieve objects in the class GenBankEntry that contains the feature key "CAAT_signal", and then their locus name, feature key, and the location of the key, which is like the one in the example in section 3.

5 CONCLUSION

The database for the genomic information is required to handle various kinds of information obtained by biological experiments. They are not easy to deal with for the relational or deductive database systems. Therefore, we developed the object-oriented database system for the genomic information by using its ability to handle various data types. We integrated the deductive function to the system for the genomic computation. This system is powerful to construct database queries from simple keyword search to various hypotheses.

One of our future work is the integration of the other data banks. For example, it is necessary to classify GenBank entry by using mapping information because there are many cases that GenBank data is not sufficient for clarifying the relationship between entries and genes. For instance, the integration of the information in GDB (mapping information of a gene or locus to a certain position of the chromosomes) is important.

We consider that the OODB system is suitable for this integration because of the following reasons.

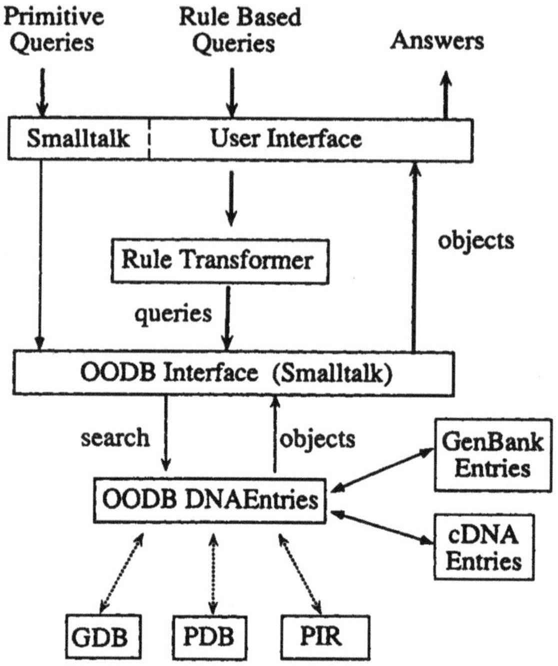

Figure 4: The overview of the system
OODB: GemStone 3.0
Interface: Objectworks\Smalltalk 4.1
Data: GenBank rel.73 Primate (50MB)

- The design and implementation of the new class are relatively easy by using existing class (for example the class DNAEntry or the class Seq)
- The known relationship between the GenBank entry and the information in GDB is easily implemented by linking them using pointers.

We also consider that the deductive function, which enables users to easily construct hypotheses, is powerful to describe the unknown relationship between the information and to test the hypothetical relationship.

We use data from the GenBank flat file. The distribution of GenBank data in ASN.1[9] format (Figure 5) will soon be available and we will use these data.

ACKNOWLEDGEMENTS

We thank Mariko Ohara for reading the manuscript. This work has been supported in part by Grant-in-Aid (04261101) for Scientific Research on Priority Areas from The Ministry of Education, Science and Culture.

REFERENCES

1) Burks,C., Cassidy,M., Cinkosky,M.J., Cumella,K.E., Gilna, Hayden,J.E.-D., Keen,G.M., Kelley,T.A., Kelly,M., Kristofferson,D. and Ryals,J., "Genbank," Nucleic Acids Research, 19, pp.2221–2225(1991).

```
Seq-entry ::= set {
  id {giim {id 340068},
      genbank {name "AGMPPINS", accession "X61092"}},

  descr {title "C.aethiops gene for preproinsulin",
         genbank {source "Cercopithecus aethiops DNA.",
                  keywords {"insulin", "preproinsulin"},
                  date "09-MAR-1992",
                  div "PRI",
                  taxonomy "Eukaryota; ... Cercopithecinae."},
         org {taxname "Cercopithecus aethiops"},
         pub {pub {gen {serial-number 2},
                   gen {cit "Title=""Sequences of ...in  monkeys"",
                             Journal=""Unpublished (1991)""" ,
                   authors {names str {"Seino,S.",..., "Li,W."}}}}},

  inst {repr raw,
       mol dna,
       length 1909,
       strand ds,
       seq-data iupacna "GGGCCATCCATGGGGGCATC...CACGCTCTCT" } ,
  annot {{data ftable {{data imp {key "5'UTR"},
                        location mix {
                           int {from 425, to 462, id genbank {accession "X61092"}},
                           int {from 653, to 669, id genbank {accession "X61092"}}}},...}
```

Figure 5: An example of genome data in ASN.1 format

2) Barker,W.C., George,D.G., Hunt,L.T. and Garavelli,J.S., "The PIR protein sequence database," Nucleic Acids Research, 19, pp.2231–2236(1991).

3) Bernstein,F.C. et al., "The Protein Data Bank: A Computer-based Archival File for Macromolecular," Journal of Molecular Biology, 112, pp.535–542(1977).

4) Pearson,W.R. and Lipman,D.J., "Improved tools for biological sequence comparison," Proc. Natl. Acad. Sci. U.S.A., 85, pp.2444–2448(1988).

5) Prestridge,D.S., "SIGNAL SCAN: a computer program that scans DNA sequences for eukaryotic transcriptional elements," Computer Applications in the Biosciences, Vol.7, No.2, pp.203–206(1991).

6) Sakamoto,N., Takagi,T., Satou,K. and Sakaki,Y., "Development of Overlapping Oligonucleotide Database and its Application to Searching for Signal Sequences over the Human Genome,"(In Japanese) in Proc. Informatics Symposium, 1992, pp.7-46.

7) Chen,W., Kifer,M. and Warren,D.S., "HiLog: A First-Order Semantics for Higher-Order Logic Programming Constructs," in Proc. the North American Conf. on Logic Programming, Vol.2, 1989, pp.1090–1114.

8) Lou,Y. and Ozsoyoglu,Z.M., "LLO: An Object-Oriented Deductive Language with Methods and Methods Inheritance," in Proc. ACM SIGMOD '91, 1991, pp.198–207.

9) National Center for Biotechnology Information, "NCBI Software Development Kit Programmer's Reference," 1992.

Appendix An example of GenBank entry

```
LOCUS       AGMPPINS      1909 bp ds-DNA            PRI       09-MAR-1992
DEFINITION  C.aethiops gene for preproinsulin
ACCESSION   X61092
KEYWORDS    insulin; preproinsulin.
SOURCE      Cercopithecus aethiops DNA.
  ORGANISM  Cercopithecus aethiops
            Eukaryota; Animalia; Chordata; Vertebrata; Mammalia; Theria;
            Eutheria; Primates; Haplorhini; Catarrhini; Cercopithecidae;
            Cercopithecinae.
REFERENCE   1  (bases 1 to 1909)
  AUTHORS   Bell,G.
  JOURNAL   Unpublished (1991)
  STANDARD  full automatic
REFERENCE   2  (bases 1 to 1909)
  AUTHORS   Seino,S., Bell,G.I. and Li,W.
  TITLE     Sequences of primate insulin genes support the hypothesis of a
            slower rate of molecular evolution in human and apes than in
            monkeys
  JOURNAL   Unpublished (1991)
  STANDARD  full automatic
REFERENCE   3  (sites)
  AUTHORS   Seino,S., Bell,G.I. and Li,W.-H.
  TITLE     Sequences of primate insulin genes support the hypothesis of a
            slower rate of molecular evolution in humans and apes than in
            monkeys
  JOURNAL   Mol. Biol. Evol. 9, 193-203 (1992)
  STANDARD  full staff_review
COMMENT     *source: is_macronuclear=N; *source: is_proviral=N; *source:
            is_germline=N;

            From EMBL    entry CEPPINS;  dated 12-NOV-1991.
FEATURES             Location/Qualifiers
     5'UTR           join(426..463,654..670)
     mat_peptide     join(743..857,1607..1749)
                     /product="Insulin"
     mRNA            join(426..463,654..857,1607..1825)
     CDS             join(671..857,1607..1752)
                     /product="Preproinsulin"
                     /codon_start=1
                     /translation="MALWMRLLPLLALLALWGPDPVPAFVNQHLCGSHLVEALYLVCG
                     ERGFFYTPKTRREAEDPQVGQVELGGGPGAGSLQPLALEGSLQKRGIVEQCCTSICSL
                     YQLENYCN"
     exon            426..463
                     /number=1
     intron          464..653
                     /number=1
     exon            654..857
                     /number=2
     sig_peptide     671..742
     intron          858..1606
                     /number=2
     exon            1607..1825
                     /number=3
     3'UTR           1753..1825
BASE COUNT      338 a    612 c    606 g    353 t
ORIGIN
        1 gggccatcca tgggggcatc ttgggcaacc agggactgag aacagggtcc caggacaggg
       61 ggtctgggga ctgtggtgca aagagccctg ccctgcagcc ccagctctcc tggtgtaatg
      121 tggaaagtgg gccggggagg gctttgctct gctggagaca tttcgccccc agctgcgagc
                                       :
     1741 tactgcaact agatccccgg tgaaggccgg cccacaccct ccacctcctg caccaagaga
     1801 gatcgaataa agcccttgaa ctagccctgc tgtgccatct ttttttggcc ctggacaggc
     1861 cgcttccggg cactgttgta agcccctccc agctctctcc acgctctct
//
```

LRU-S: A New Buffer Allocation Approach for OODBMS

Hanxiong Chen
Doctoral Program in Engineering, University of Tsukuba, Japan
Jeffrey Xu Yu
Dept. of Computer Science, the Australian National University
Kazunori Yamaguchi
Dept. of Graphic & Computer Science, The University of Tokyo, Japan
Hiroyuki Kitagawa, Nobuo Ohbo and Yuzuru Fujiwara
Inst. of Information Sciences and Electronics, University of Tsukuba, Japan

ABSTRACT

Composite object reference is supported in most object-oriented database management systems, and object accesses are mainly implemented by the navigation through this reference. In order to support sufficiently the composite object access in the buffer management system of object-oriented database systems, we propose in this paper a new buffer allocation method called *LRU-S* which is to treat a unit of composite objects together by utilizing the composite object references in composite objects. Qualitative analysis is developed to investigate the size of buffer pool at which our proposed method is expected to work better than conventional ones such as LRU and MRU. Simulation results for some access patterns are presented to verify whether or not the proposal will be beneficial.

1 INTRODUCTION

Recently, it has become clear that composite objects play a key role in varieties of advanced database applications [2, 4]. The composite objects mentioned here are nested objects on which the Is-Part-Of relationship implemented by composite references is imposed. As in [11], the composite references are further divided into two categories, the exclusive and shared composite references. The shared composite reference from o1 to o2 means that o1 has o2 as its part and o2 is possibly to be shared by o1 and others. A query on a set of composite objects usually scans a composite object at a time. At a stage of scanning composite objects, composite object references are traversed successively. Consequently, sequences of traversing composite objects within shared objects appear repeatedly in one query.

This situation is quite different from the conventional query processing in relational databases, and the buffer management strategies used in relational databases are less effective in this case. In order to improve the performance of the buffer management system in object-oriented database systems, one of the most important things is to make the reference information available in the buffers [9, 6]. Kemper has mentioned the importance of object accessing along reference chains leading from one object to another in [10]. We have also observed that many applications tend to traverse one composite object continuously before accessing other composite objects, but during traversing one composite object, the number of accesses to other objects is not negligible. These observations encourage us to consider the possibility of utilizing the reference information among components of composite objects in the buffer management system, especially for the buffer allocation. Conventionally, it is not permitted for the buffer management system to see the reference information in composite objects in the buffer, and this has been considered out of the scope of the buffer management system's responsibilities. We however shall adopt the position that making the reference information available to the buffer management system is useful because 1) this enhances the buffer management performance and 2) the implementation is not impossible. For example, we can store the reference information about an object in the header of the storage for the object, and collect such information into a special area of the memory when this object is accessed. Alternatively, we can also collect the reference information of all database objects and store it separately, and read and keep this information in the memory for buffer management.

The related works in relational database management systems are summarized below. LRU (least recently used) and MRU (most recently used) are well-known by their simplicity and effectiveness. LRU and MRU are compared with our proposal in this paper. Effelsberg surveyed some buffer management strategies [7], and Chou investigated the access patterns of queries [5]. The performance of our approach is superior to that of these strategies since it takes the features of queries in object-oriented systems into consideration. For server-client architectures, [13] introduced an approach of page prefetching to reduce the communication between server(s) and clients. This approach differs from ours in that it is not designed for a central database system, and it must recognize a number of patterns, while our approach uses only the "reference" information.

This paper is organized as follow: In section 2, the motivation is detailed using an example. Section 3 simply introduces definition and basic accessing patterns of composite objects. In section 4, a formalization of our new buffer allocation strategy LRU-S, which is a modified LRU utilizing the reference information, is discussed, and some properties of LRU-S are also shown. Section 5 shows the performance evaluation of LRU-S with a number of simulation results. Section 6 concludes this paper.

2 MOTIVATION

In most object-oriented database management systems, two kinds of references, the composite object reference and the object reference, are generally supported. The former is used to construct composite objects, whereas the latter is used to describe relationships between distinct composite objects [11]. In Figure 1, the former and the latter references are illustrated by solid and dotted lines with arrow heads, respectively. Since the two references influence the query processing strategies, the final goal of our research is to support both of them in the buffer management system efficiently. However, at this stage of our research progress, we focus on the management of composite object references in the buffer management system. Note that in the following discussion, we use the term "reference" to mean the composite reference.

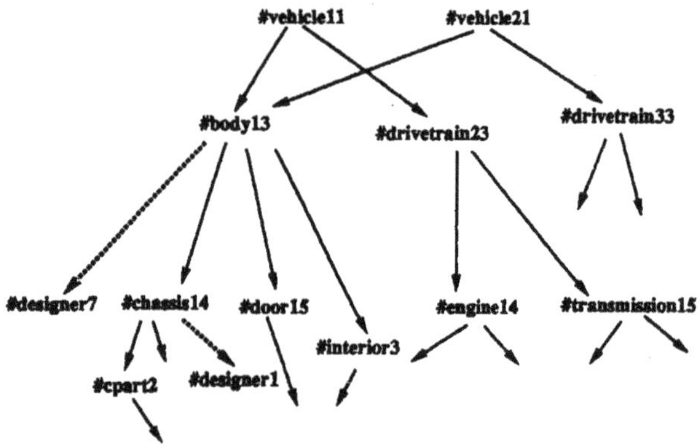

Figure 1: An Example of Composite Object

To informally describe the benefits of our approach, the following example of a composite object access sequence is provided to access two composite objects #vehicle11 and #vehicle21 shown in Figure 1.

```
(#vehicle11 #body13 #chassis14
#cpart2 #designer7 #door15 #vehicle21
#body13 #chassis14 #cpart2 ...)
```

As shown in Figure 1, the two composite objects share the component object #body13. Here, suppose that a buffer can hold up to five objects. The buffer becomes (#vehicle11 #body13 #chassis14 #cpart2 #designer7) after the first five objects are accessed. The leftmost object in the buffer is the bottom object which will be swapped out first under LRU strategy. When object #door15 is accessed, the bottom object #vehicle11 is swapped out, and the buffer becomes (#body13 #chassis14 #designer7 #division7 #door15). For the following access of object #vehicle21, the conventional LRU policy simply swaps out the bottom object #body13. In this way, consecutive object faults will occur when #body13 and #chassis14 are accessed for the second time. And the same phenomenon occurs repeatedly in traversing composite objects. MRU, the optimal replacement policy for looping-references [12], does not work well since it is not a loop access. As mentioned above, since the component objects of a composite object in the buffer will usually be accessed in turn, it is worthy keeping all of the related objects together in the buffer, rather than swapping out some of the objects which are about to be used.

Our approach is described below. When the first five objects are accessed, the buffer content becomes (#vehicle11 #body13 #chassis14 #cpart2 #designer7). When the object #door15 is accessed, #vehicle11 has to be swapped out, since there are no objects directly or indirectly referenced by #door15 in the buffer. When #vehicle21 is accessed, our approach is to swap out the object #designer7 instead of #body13. The rationale is that there exists an object reference between the objects #vehicle21 and #body13. Then, the buffer content becomes (#body13 #chassis14 #cpart2 #door15 #vehicle21). It is easy to see that this policy keeps the objects #body13 and #chassis14 in the buffer when they are accessed for the second time.

It must be noted that we do not combine our LRU-S with the technique of clustering [9, 14, 15] in this paper. As can be seen from the example above, we mentioned nothing about clustering there. The reasons for this are 1) it is often the case that an object is large enough and occupies one or more than one page, and/or 2) if necessary, we can consider the situations after clustering, and substitute "object" with "page" in the discussion above, while not invalidating the consequence.

3 COMPOSITE OBJECT AND ACCESS PATTERN

Before discussing the LRU-S, in this section we explain the composite object model. We also define several basic object access patterns in composite object systems.

3.1 Composite Object

Definition (composite object) A composite object can be described as a DAG $G_{comp} = (N_{comp}, E_{comp})$. N_{comp} is a countable set of objects. $E_{comp} \subseteq N_{comp} \times N_{comp}$ represents the object reference augmented with the Is-Part-Of relationship. We say "o_i is directly referenced by o_j", denoted as $o_i \lhd o_j$, if $(o_i, o_j) \in E_{comp}$. The relation '$\prec$' is defined as follows:

(1) if $o_i \lhd o_j$ then $o_i \prec o_j$,

(2) if $o_i \prec o_j \wedge o_j \prec o_k$ then $o_i \prec o_k$.

$\prec$ is transitive, but is supposed to be asymmetric here; which implies that the structure of a composite object is a DAG.

3.2 Basic Access Patterns

The query algebra of the relational database system is very regular allowing page accessing property to be figured out easily. In [5], [12] and [8], it is shown that *sequential*, *random*, and *looping* accesses cover all the query operations, such as join, index and scan access, and so on. In the following, the basic patterns are introduced for operations in the object-oriented database system. However, it is often the case that an object access in an actual query in object-oriented database systems does not simply correspond to a single pattern, but to a combination of these patterns.

Object Access An "object access" Acs is a sequence of objects $Acs = o_1 o_2 ... o_n$, where o_i's are not necessarily distinct. The subscript 1, ..., n are referred to as "access point".

Sequential Object Access A "sequential object access" is a composite object traversal $TR(o) = TR(o_1)...TR(o_m)$, where $o_i \lhd o$, $i = 1 \ldots m$. We sometimes denote the $TR(o)$ as Acs_s.

Loop Object Access A "loop object access" Acs_l is a sequence $s_1, ..., s_k$, where each s_i is a sequential object access $TR(o)$.

Random Object Access A "random object access" Acs_r is a sequence of objects, in which the ordering of member objects is unrelated to the reference relationship among the objects.

When we search an object without using an index, we must start the traversal at well-known entry objects which are often the roots. Such access comes under the sequential object access. "Backward/forward queries" by [10] are just two of its special cases, and Acs_s covers the "child-depth-first traversal" of [3]. On the other hand, if an index can be used to locate an object directly, we can then access the object directly. In this case, the access comes under the random object access pattern.

4 LRU-S

As mentioned above, in the conventional database system, the basic access patterns are well known. This makes it easy to analyze the effect of buffer management strategies, like LRU, MRU, and so on. Though MRU is known to be efficient for loop access, it collapses when the access is a sequence formed by some random/sequential accesses followed by a loop access. Similarly, LRU loses its efficiency if the access has the form $s_1 s_0 s_2 s_0 ...$, where s_i's are sequences of objects and $s_i \neq s_j$ for $i \neq j$.

This motivates us to consider a buffer management which takes the reference information into account. Suppose that the buffer manager knows the reference information of each object; it is then possible to keep objects, which are going to be accessed, from being swapped out. To implement this idea, a new buffer management strategy LRU-S is proposed here. LRU-S, with S meaning "structure", is LRU with an extension which takes into consideration the structures of data. In the following subsections, a formal definition of LRU-S is given, then, qualitative analysis is developed to identify the situations under which LRU-S is beneficial and when it breaks down.

4.1 Terminology

In order to formalize the movement of objects in the buffer, the DAG defined in section 3.1 is revised here. N stands for a set of nodes of the DAG and the DAG is constructed using the partial order $\prec$. In the object reference interpretation, $o_1 \prec o_2$ means that the node o_2 directly or indirectly refers to the node o_1. For the notational convenience, the reflective extension of $\prec$, denoted as $\preceq$, is defined as $o_1 \preceq o_2 \triangleq (o_1 = o_2) \vee (o_1 \prec o_2)$

A set of sequences whose element is in N is denoted as N^*. The buffer list is a sequence $b = b_1 b_2 \ldots b_m$ where $b_i \in N$ indicates the i'th member of b, b_m is the most recently used node, and $|b| = m$ is the length of b. A k *elements sub-sequence* of a sequence s is denoted as $s^{(k)}$, and ϵ is an empty sequence. The meanings of the following notations are obvious.

$n \in b \triangleq \exists k \; 1 \leq k \leq m, \; n = b_k,$

$n \notin b \triangleq \neg(n \in b),$

$hd(b) = b_1,$

$tl(b) = b_2 \ldots b_m,$

$o_1 \perp o_2 \triangleq \neg(o_1 \prec o_2 \vee o_2 \prec o_1), \; o_1, \; o_2 \in N,$

$n \perp b \triangleq \forall i (n \perp b_i),$

$b \perp n \triangleq \forall i (b_i \perp n),$

$b \perp s \triangleq \forall i (b_i \perp s)$, where $s = s_1 \ldots s_n$.

For example, for a buffer b, $hd(b)$ gives the head element of

b, which is the "most recent used" node in, say, LRU; while $tl(b)$ is the status of b after swapping out $hd(b)$. To utilize the information associated with elements in a sequence,

$$b \downarrow_f \triangleq b_{l_1} b_{l_2} \ldots b_{l_t}, \text{ and } b \uparrow_f \triangleq b \downarrow_{\neg f}$$

are introduced. Here, $b_{l_i} \in b$ satisfies f for $i = 1 \ldots t$, and $l_1 < l_2 < \ldots < l_t$, and for $b_i \notin b_{l_1} b_{l_2} \ldots b_{l_t}$, b_i does not satisfy f. As an example, because $\lambda x.x \prec n$ is a function giving such x that $x \prec n$, recalling the definition of $\prec$ it becomes obvious that $b \downarrow_{\lambda x.x \prec n}$ gives a sequence extracted from the sequence b whose nodes are directly or indirectly referenced by n.

4.2 Definition of LRU-S

Assume that the available buffer size is s_{max}. Starting from a buffer list b, if the buffer reaches a state b' after the reference of an object access n, then the resulting buffer list b' is denoted as $b' = b|_n$. The resulting buffer list $b|_n$ is defined as follows:

Case 1: If there is a k such that $n = b_k$, namely, $n \in b$, then we define

$$b|_n = (b \uparrow_{\lambda x.x \preceq n})(b \downarrow_{\lambda x.x \prec n})n.$$

Case 2: There is no k such that $n = b_k$, namely, $n \notin b$, then

Case 2-1: If the buffer is not full ($|b| < s_{max}$), we define

$$b|_n = (b \uparrow_{\lambda x.x \prec n})(b \downarrow_{\lambda x.x \prec n})n.$$

Case 2-2: If the buffer is full ($|b| = s_{max}$), then we define

$$b|_n = \begin{cases} tl(b)n, & \\ & if \;\; (b \uparrow_{\lambda x.x \prec n}) = \varepsilon \\ (b'' \downarrow_{\lambda x.x \prec n'})(b'' \uparrow_{\lambda x.x \preceq n'})(b \downarrow_{\lambda x.x \prec n})n, & otherwise \end{cases}$$

where $b'' = (b \uparrow_{\lambda x.x \prec n})$ and $n' = hd(b'')$.

For each node n in the access sequence, the algorithm checks the nodes in the buffer to find the reference relationship, based on the reference relationship stored in the database. Accordingly, the complexity of the algorithm, that is, the approximate time of determining the buffer status when an object is accessed, is $O(s_{max})$ in terms of the number of comparisons $\prec$ ($\preceq$).

4.3 Properties of LRU-S

In the following, some properties of LRU-S are given. These properties can be proved straight-forward, by possibly using mathematical induction and checking each case in the algorithm above. The proof is hence omitted due to the limitation of space. Starting from an empty list ε, after accessing an access sequence, the buffer status reaches a resulting buffer list. Let the set of all such resulting buffer lists be B.

The following property shows that LRU-S does not "waste" buffer.

Property 1 Each node appears in a buffer list at most once. That is,
$\forall b \in B \; (n \in b \Rightarrow \exists! j \; b_j = n)$. Here, "$\exists!$" means "uniquely exist".

Property 2 The most recently accessed node is at the tail of the buffer list. That is, for any buffer list b and node n, $b|_n = b'n$ for some b'.

These two properties above are common to LRU, MRU, and LRU-S. Next four properties serve to show the relationship between an access sequence and objects in the buffer.

Property 3 For b, $t \in N^*$, if $t \perp b$ and $s_{max} \geq |t|$, then $t_i \in b|_t$

Since t is irrelevant to b, no elements in b are moved to the right of t. So, after t is accessed, all elements in t are left in $b|_t$. This means that original contents of b are swapped out before t, and guarantees that t_i remains in the buffer. In the other words, LRU-S works for irrelevant objects (say, random accesses) just like LRU does.

Property 4 For b, t, $w_i \in N^*$, if $b \perp t$, $t \perp w_i$, $\forall i \; t_i \preceq t_1$, and
$s_{max} \geq |t| + max_{1 \leq i \leq k-1} |w_i|$, then

$$t_k \in b|_{w_0 t w_1 t w_2 \ldots t w_{k-1}}.$$

Property 5
For b, t, u, $w_i \in N^*$, for $b \perp t$, $b \perp u$, $u \perp w_i$, $b \perp w_i$, and
$s_{max} \geq |t| + |u|$, $s_{max} \geq |u| + \sum_{j=1}^{k-1} |w_j|, \forall \; i \; t_i \preceq t_1$, then

$$t_k \in b|_{t u t_1 w_1 t_2 w_2 \ldots w_{k-1}}.$$

With appropriate size, LRU-S shows a higher possibility of keeping the necessary objects in the buffer than LRU does. This possibility comes from the utilization of the reference information among objects in t. LRU-S increases the chance of keeping t_i in the buffer even if w_j's are accessed between t_{j-1} and t_j.

To explain these properties in detail, we consider a simple ideal example: an access sequence of form $sr_1sr_2 \ldots sr_k$, where s is an Acs_s, and r_i is an Acs_r, and r_1, r_2, ...r_k are different from one another. Suppose that $|s| = x$ and $\forall i$, $|r_i| = y$, and $x > y$. Let the buffer size be $|b| = x + \alpha$, $0 < \alpha < y$. Using the notation of *k elements sub-sequence* of s, $s^{(k)}$ (again, obviously $s^{(x)} = s$, $r_i^{(y)} = r_i$), the behaviors of LRU and LRU-S are compared in the following,

Access point	LRU	LRU-S
1	$s^{(1)}$	$s^{(1)}$
...	...	...
$x+\alpha$	$sr_1^{(\alpha)}$	$sr_1^{(\alpha)}$
...	...	...
$x+y$	$s^{(x+\alpha-y)}r_1$	$s^{(x+\alpha-y)}r_1$
$x+y+1$	$s^{(x+\alpha-y-1)}r_1s^{(1)}$	$r_1^{(y-1)}s^{(x+\alpha-y+1)}$
...	...	...
$x+y+i$	$s^{(x+\alpha-y-i)}r_1s^{(i)}$	$r_1^{(y-i)}s^{(x+\alpha-y+i)}$
...	...	...
$x+y+x$	$r_1s^{(x+\alpha-y)}$	$r_1^{(\alpha)}s$
...	...	...
$x+y+x+y$	$s^{(x+\alpha-y)}r_2$	$s^{(x+\alpha-y)}r_2$
...	...	...

From the assumption that $y < x < |b| = x + \alpha < x + y$, at access point $x + y + i$, the numbers of (possibly to be repeatedly accessed) elements of s remaining in the buffer are $x + \alpha - y$ for LRU and $x + \alpha - y + i$ for LRU-S, respectively. Noting that the above discussion holds true even if we exchange x and y, we are led to the conclusion that LRU-S performs better than LRU for repeats of Acs_s s following a Acs_r r_i, when the buffer size is within the interval $(\max\{|s|, |r_i|\}, |s| + |r_i|)$. More precisely, in the table above, although both LRU and LRU-S raise $x+y$ faults for the first iteration (sr_1), LRU and LRU-S raise $x + y$ and $x + y - (|b| - y)$ faults respectively for each i-th iteration (sr_i, $i > 1$). LRU-S performs better because $|b| > x > y$ hence $x + y - (|b| - y) < x + y$. As an example, we count the number of faults when access s for the second times. In the table above, it can be seen that faults raised at access points $x + y + i$ for $i = 1, ..., y - \alpha$. After access points $x + y + (y - \alpha)$, the whole s is in the buffer and no fault raised. On the other hand, the access of each node of r_2 raises faults. Therefore, the total number of fault for the second iteration is $(y - \alpha) + y = x + y - (|b| - y)$.

Property 6 For b, t, u, $w \in N^*$, $b \perp t$, $b \perp u$, $b \perp w$, $u \perp w$, $t \perp u$, $t \perp w$, $\forall i\ t_i \prec t_1$, and $|t| - 1 + |u| + |w| \geq s_{max}$, then

$$u_1 \notin b|_{tut_1w}$$

Property 6 shows an unfavorable case to LRU-S. In this case the second access of t_1 moves $t_2 \ldots t_m$, which is not accessed follow t_1, to the right of the buffer. This property means that if the shared common sequence $t_1 \ldots t_m$ is not traversed entirely after the root node t_1 is accessed, it is better to avoid accessing the root node t_1 at all.

5 EMPIRICAL RESULTS

In order to evaluate the performance of the LRU-S, experimental results are explained in this section.

5.1 Data Set

The data model used is similar to the one proposed in Anderson's benchmark [1], except that there is no implementation of *refTo/refFrom*. The database is a rooted tree, as shown in Figure 2, where each internal (*non-leaf*) node at level k of the tree has five node of level $k+1$ as its children, and five nodes of level $k+1$ as it parts. On the other hand, any node of level k ($k > 0$) can be a child of only one node of level $k-1$, while it may be a part of more than one node of $k - 1$.

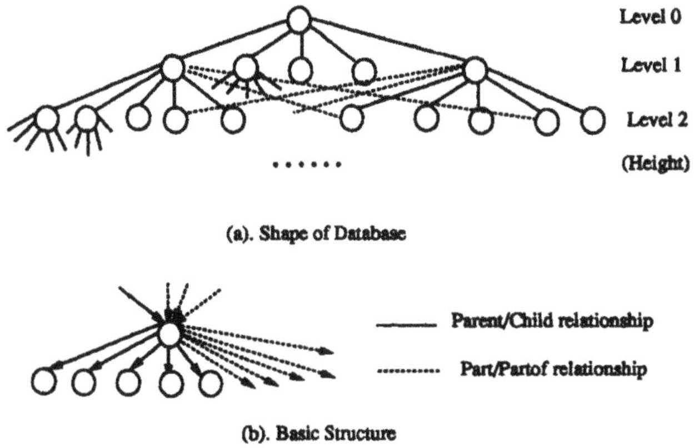

Figure 2: An Example of the Data Set

The parameter considered in the experiments is buffer size. Because I/O plays a predominant role, we measure the performance of buffer management strategies by the rate of object faults, which is the ratio of the number of object faults to the number of object accesses. The following experiments compare LRU-S with both of the well-known LRU and MRU methods. In each figure, the horizontal axis expresses buffer size, while the vertical axis expresses the rate of object faults in percentages.

5.2 Experiment 1: Loop of $Acs_r Acs_s$

A query on a certain part of a composite object, which may involve references to component objects if certain conditions are satisfied, gives an object access which is basically a loop of $Acs_r Acs_s$. In addition to the buffer size, the average length of an iterator $Acs_r Acs_s$ also affects the results. As was pointed out in properties 4 and 5 in the previous section, if the buffer size is within a certain interval, useful objects are kept in the buffer by the LRU-S. By contrast, under LRU or MRU, such useful objects are simply swapped out. We call the interval in which LRU-S performs better the "desired interval". The desired interval of the buffer size in these experiments is (s_1, s_2), where s_1 and s_2 are approximately equal to $\max\{|Acs_s|, |Acs_r|\}$ and $|Acs_r| + |Acs_s|$, respectively. Figure 3 give an extreme

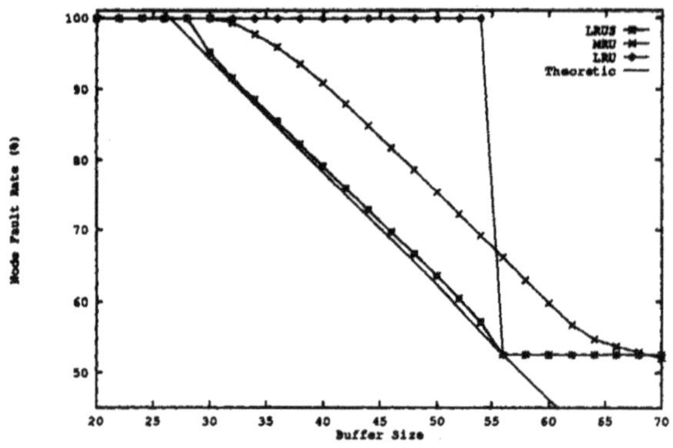

Figure 3: Loop of $Acs_r Acs_s$ ($|Acs_s| = 30, |Acs_r| = 25$)

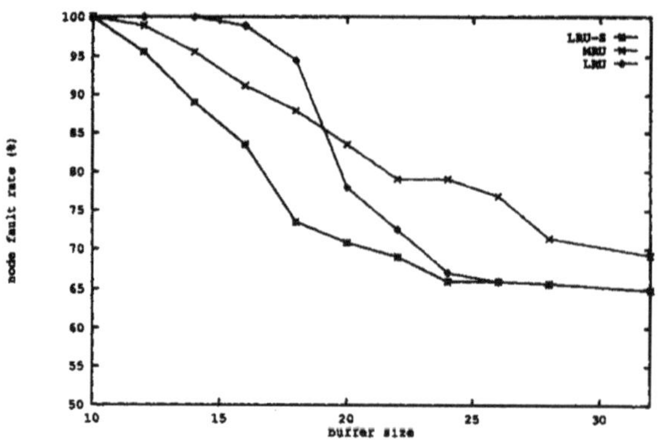

Figure 5: Loop of $Acs_r Acs_s$ ($|Acs_s| \approx 14, |Acs_r| \approx 9$)

result of the typical access pattern: the repeat of an Acs_s following an Acs_{r_i}. This sequence is obtained in the following way: one traversal of a subtree of the database shown in Figure 2 is taken as the Acs_s, and access sequences to some of the other nodes are taken as the sum of all Acs_{r_i}. To make the explanation understandable, the *Part/Partof* relationships are not considered here, and no element of Acs_{r_i} is taken from any ancestor of the subtree being taken as the Acs_s. This guaranteeing that Acs_s and Acs_{r_i} do not intersect or affect one another. According to the formal analysis in Section 4.3, LRU-S performs better than LRU-S when a buffer is of a size within the interval $(\max\{|Acs_s|, |Acs_{r_i}|\}, |Acs_s| + |Acs_{r_i}|)$. From Figure 3, we can readily see that LRU-S performs better than LRU in (30, 55). The "hot point" of LRU clearly appears in both figures. The curve which is the theoretical result of LRU-S based on the analysis given in Section 4.3 is also added to Figure 3. Focusing on the desired interval (30, 55), it can be easily seen that the result of experiment gives good agreement with the theoretical one.

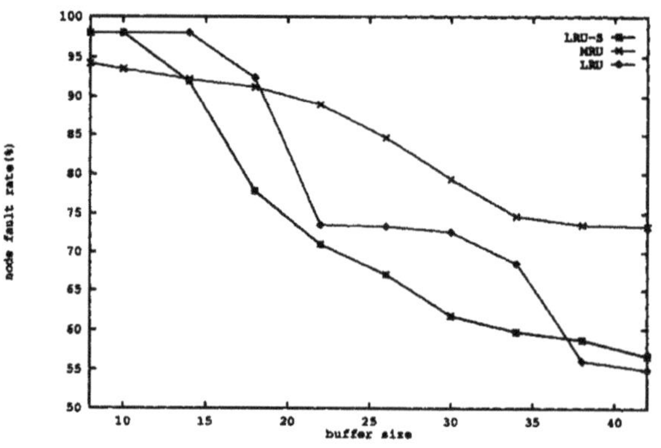

Figure 6: Loop of $Acs_r Acs_s$ ($|Acs_s| \approx |Acs_r| \approx 18$)

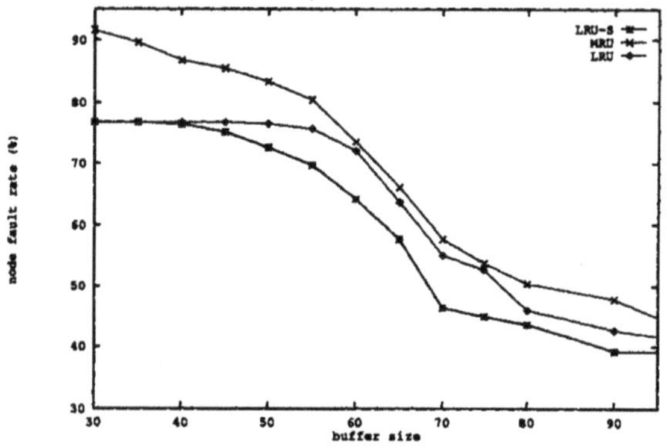

Figure 4: Loop of $Acs_r Acs_s$ ($|Acs_s| \approx 45, |Acs_r| \approx 30$)

Figure 4, 5 and 6 show other results about the desired intervals. For example, in Figure 4, LRU-S behaves better than both LRU and MRU in the interval (45, 80). Here, (45, 80) is approximately equal to the desired interval $(|Acs_s|, |Acs_s|+|Acs_r|)$. Experiments were also conducted for different $|Acs_s|$ and $|Acs_r|$ values, and the results shown in Figure 5 and 6. As predicted, proof that LRU-S behaves better than LRU and MRU in the desired interval can be found in Figure 5 and Figure 6. These figures different from the previous two in that the *Part/Partof* relationships are active here. These relationships affect the performance because the condition "Acs_s and Acs_{r_i} do not intersect one another" is not satisfied. The three strategies behave similarly outside the desired interval. This means that LRU-S is not less effective than LRU or MRU, even outside the desired interval in which it is more effective. Finally, the relationship *Part/Partof* affect the results in that because of sharing, Acs_s and Acs_{r_i} intersect. This in turn affect the desired interval and the shapes of the result curves in the figures. The effect of the relationship *Part/Partof* must be investigated further.

5.3 Experiments 2: Looping Access

Data in these experiments is taken by scanning objects of (say) k'th level of the database shown in Figure 2, and at the same time traversing the subtrees rooted at these k'th objects. In order to tuning the rate of shared, number of *Part/Partof* links in the database are changed. The rate of shared objects and buffer size are considered in this experiment. Using the definition of "reference" in Section 4.3, we calculate the rate of shared objects in the following way: for each component object o_i of a composite object, the number, say d, of direct references to o_i is counted. Then $max\{d-1,\ 0\}$ is named the "referenced degree" of o_i. The average rate of shared objects is calculated by averaging the referenced degrees over all composite and component objects. As mentioned above, composite object traversal is a special case of sequential access. In this case, the desired interval is approximately $(s*\delta,\ s)$, where δ is the rate of shared objects and s is equal to the average number of component objects referenced by a composite object. Figure 7 and 8 illustrates two results: Figure 7 the case for a rate of shared objects of 30% and Figure 8 the case for a rate of shared object of 50%. In Figure 7 LRU-S explicitly behaves better than LRU and MRU. In Figure 8, LRU-S behaves better than LRU in the interval, and is not less effective than MRU. It can be seen that MRU is affected by the location where the common part of the access sequence appears. If the common part appears in the head of the access sequence, then MRU should perform like LRU-S, which is the case of Figure 8. Otherwise, as shown in Figure 7, LRU-S works better than MRU. Changing the average rate of shared objects affects the desired interval. Finally, if the buffer is not initially empty but contains something irrelevant to the access sequence, then LRU and LRU-S will be affected slightly while MRU is seriously degraded. This consequence is confirmed by comparing Figure 7 and Figure 8.

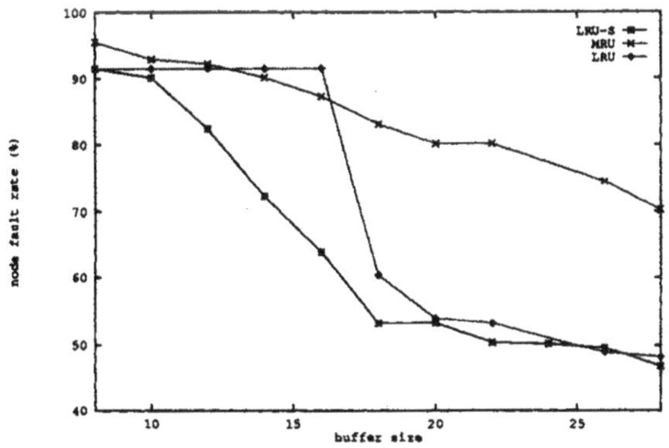

Figure 7: Looping Access (Shared 30%, Number of nodes ≈ 22)

Figure 9 shows a result of an access of another kind of

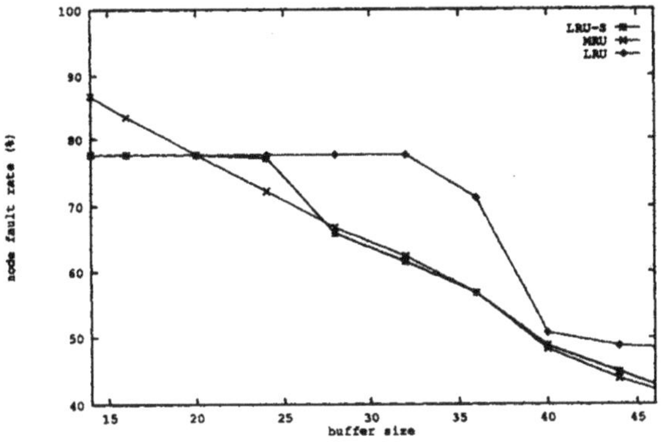

Figure 8: Looping Access (Shared 50%, Number of nodes ≈ 40)

loop. For a tree database of heigh 4 as shown in Figure 2 except the *Part/Partof* references, we repeatedly and randomly access the objects of level 2, and traversal the subtree every time the node of level 2 is touched. It can be seen that LRU-S always performs better than LRU, and almost better than MRU. From this figure, we can see one evident advantages of LRU-S over LRU: LRU-S is not affected by the "hot points," while LRU is affected heavily.

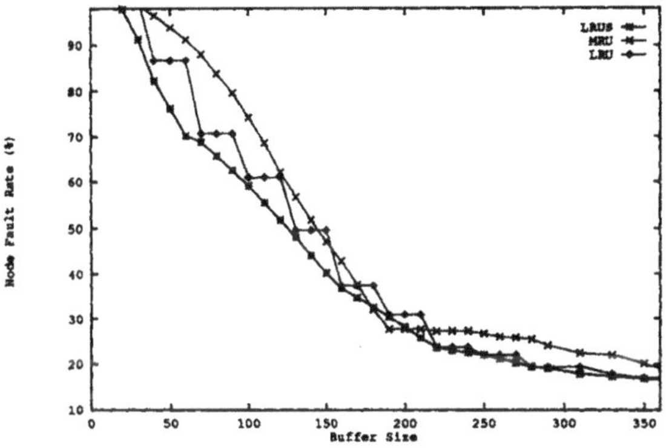

Figure 9: Looping Access: $\{Acs_1|\ldots|Acs_5\}^*$, (No sharing, $|Acs_i| = 30$)

5.4 Experiment 3: Single Sequential Access and Random Access

A single Acs_s behaves like a random access and makes no difference between LRU, MRU or LRU-S. LRU-S is not less effective for Acs_r even if there is no reference information available. Similarly, LRU-S is not less effective even if the paths in Acs_s's are randomly distributed. The reason can be found from property 3 given in the Section 4.3. An result is given in Figure 10. In this experiment, the access sequence is obtained by randomly selecting 2000 nodes from the database shown in Figure 2.

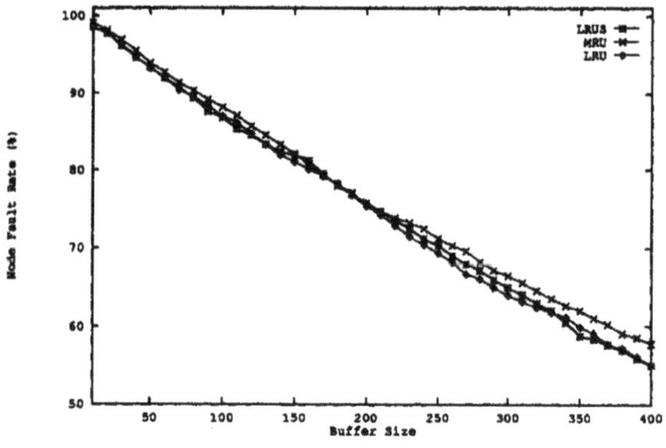

Figure 10: Random Access

6 CONCLUSION

A new policy LRU-S which considers the reference information among objects is proposed for buffer management in the object-oriented database system. The formal definition of the LRU-S makes it possible to explicate some properties of it. Using these properties, we find out the intervals of the buffer size in which LRU-S shows its feature, and discover the situation to which LRU-S is not suitable. The unfavorable situation can be easily avoided by slightly modifying the query pattern. Consequently, LRU-S behaves comparatively to LRU for conventional applications, and works better than both LRU and MRU in many possible cases of composite object queries. Results of the experiments above confirm the conclusion. This approach opens up the new direction for improving the performance of the buffer management system in object-oriented database systems.

We are going to investigate the effect of the rate of shared objects on behaviors of LRU-S. Since the performance of a buffer replacement policy depends heavily on query patterns, possible query patterns should be further investigated. This motivates us to analyze the distribution of query patterns in object-oriented database systems. It is planned to apply LRU-S to some benchmarks like that given in [1].

REFERENCES

[1] T. Lougenia Anderson et al: "The HyperModel Benchmark," in *Proc. of ECOOP'91, European Conference on Object-Oriented Programming*, Geneva, Switzerland, July 15-19, 1991, pp. 317-331.

[2] J. Banerjee, W. Kim & K. Kim: "Queries in Object-Oriented Database," in *Proc. of 4th Data Engineering*, 1988.

[3] Banerjee J., W.Kim, S.J.Kim, J.F.Graza: "Clustering a DAG for CAD Databases," in *IEEE Trans. on Soft. Engineering*, Vol.14(11), Nov. 1988, pp.1684-1699.

[4] M. J. Carey, et al.: "A Data Model and Query Language for EXODUS," in *Porc. of ACM SIGMOD'89*, 1988, pp. 413-423.

[5] H. T. Chou and D. J. DeWitt: "An Evaluation of Buffer Management Strategies for Relational Database System," in *Proc. of VLDB'85*, Stockholm, Aug. 1985, pp.127-141.

[6] D. W. Cornell and P. S. Yu: "Integration of Buffer Management and Query Optimization In Relational Database Environment," in *Proc. of VLDB'89*, Amsterdam, Aug. 1989 pp. 247-256.

[7] Wolfgang Effelsberg & Theo Haerder: "Principles of Database Buffer Management," in *ACM TODS*, Vol. 9, No. 4, December 1984, pp. 560-595.

[8] C. Faloutsos, R. Ng and T. Sellis: "Predictive Load Control for Flexible Buffer Allocation," in *Proc. of VLDB'91*, Barcelona, Sep., 1991, pp. 265-274.

[9] Mark F. Hornick and Stanley B. Zdonik: "A Shared, Segmented Memory System for an Object-Oriented Database," in *ACM Trans. on Office Information Systems*, Vol. 5, No. 1, Jan 1987, pp. 70-95.

[10] A. Kemper & G. Moerkotte: "Access Support in Object Bases," in *Proc. of ACM SIGMOD'90*, 1990, 364-374.

[11] Won Kim, E. Bertino, & J. F. Garza: "Composite Object Revised," in *Proc. of ACM SIGMOD'89*, 1989.

[12] R. Ng, C. Faloutsos and T.Sellis: "Flexible Buffer Allocation based on Marginal Gains," in *Proc. of ACM SIGMOD'91*, 1991, pp. 387-396.

[13] M. Palmer and S. B. Zdonik: "Fido: A Cache That Learns to Fetch," in *Proc. of VLDB'91*, Barcelona, Sep., 1991, pp. 255-264.

[14] H. Schöning & A. Sikeler: "Cluster Mechanisms Supporting the Dynamic Construction of Complex Objects," in *3rd Inte'l Conf. on FDOA*, Paris, France, June 1989, in LNCS 367, pp.31-46.

[15] M. M. Tsangaris and J. F. Naughton: "On the Performance of Object Clustering Techniques," in *Proc. of ACM SIGMOD'92*, 1992. pp. 144-153.

DISTRIBUTED DATABASE

ENHANCED TREE QUORUM ALGORITHM FOR REPLICATED DISTRIBUTED DATABASES

Soon M. Chung †
Department of Computer Science and Engineering
Wright State University
Dayton, Ohio 45435, U.S.A.

Abstract

In this paper, a new replica control algorithm, called the enhanced tree quorum (ETQ) algorithm, is proposed to manage replicated data in a distributed database system. This algorithm provides high availability for read and write operations by imposing a logical structure of modified tree with a backup root on data copies. With ETQ algorithm, a read operation is limited to a data copy in the best case, and a write operation is allowed as long as one of the roots and the majority of the children of each node selected are available in the tree. Compared to other algorithms, ETQ requires lower message cost for an operation, while providing higher availability.

1. Introduction

A distributed system consists of a set of computers (called sites) that communicate through a network. A distributed system differs from a centralized system in the nature of failures. The components of a centralized system typically depend on one another to the extent that the failure of a single component disables the entire system. On the other hand, the components of a distributed system are autonomous computers, and the failure of an individual site does not disable the entire system. The other advantage of distributed systems is that valuable data can be stored redundantly at multiple sites, which is commonly called replication of data.

Replication is a useful technique for distributed database systems where reliability is important, such as banking systems, airline reservation systems, etc. Rather than keeping one copy of important data at a single site, multiple copies of the same data can be maintained at different sites. Replication increases the data's availability: if one copy is temporarily inaccessible, then the transaction can be continued using a different copy. Replication also increases the data's reliability: if one copy is accidentally destroyed, it can be reconstructed from the other copies. The performance of an operation can be enhanced by permitting the authorized user to work on the copy that can be most easily accessed.

In a replicated database, each read and write operation issued by a transaction on some logical data item must be mapped by the database system to the corresponding operation on physical copies. To be correct, the mapping must ensure that the concurrent execution of transactions on replicated data is equivalent to a serial execution on non-replicated data—a property known as one-copy serializability [BER85]. Multiple copies of a data item should appear as a single copy to the transaction. This requirement is enforced by the replica control algorithm.

In order to ensure the requirement of one-copy serializability, a replicated data item x may be read by reading a quorum of copies, and it may be written by writing a quorum of copies. The quorum for an operation is defined as a set of copies whose number is sufficient to execute that operation. The selection of a quorum is restricted by the quorum intersection property: For any two operations $O_i[x]$ and $O_j[x]$ on a data item x, where at least one of them is a write, the quorums must have a non-empty intersection. The correctness of our enhanced tree quorum algorithm will be proved by using this property.

Many replica control algorithms have been proposed: Voting algorithms [GIF79, THO79] become popular because they are flexible and easily implemented. Dynamic replica control methods [BAR86, JAJ87a, JAJ87b, JAJ88, PAR88] are derived from voting to achieve high data availability. Available copies [BER84, LON87] and regeneration methods [PU86] achieve even higher data availability using the same number of copies. They do not have to trade off the read availability with the write availability, but the data consistency is not guaranteed when the network is partitioned. To reduce the storage space for copies, voting with witnesses [PAR86] can be used, but the operation availability will be compromised. The tree quorum algorithm [AGR90a, AGR90b] uses quorums that are obtained from a logical tree structure imposed on data copies, and the multiple tree quorum algorithm [CHU92] is based on multiple logical trees imposed on the data copies. Compared to the tree quorum algorithm, the multiple tree quorum algorithm provides higher availability of the write operation, especially when the network is partitioned. A comprehensive survey of replica control algorithms is presented in [DAV85].

The problem of finding quorums to optimize the performance has been addressed by several researchers. Garcia-Molina and Barbara introduced the method that can be used to generate a subset of the quorums which includes all quorums obtained from vote assignments [GAR85]. In [CHE89], Cheung, Ahamad, and Ammar presented an algorithm for generating all vote and quorum assignments that need to be considered in optimizing the read and the write operations on replicated data. Kumar described a hierarchical quorum consensus algorithm [KUM90], that organizes a group of copies into a multi-level hierarchy and extends the quorum consensus algorithm to such an environment. The algorithm for finding a multi-dimensional vote assignment is proposed by Cheung, Ahamad, and Ammar in [CHE90].

This paper is organized as follows: In Section 2, we review the basic replica control algorithms; read-one/write-all, available copies, voting, and tree quorum algorithms. In Section 3, the enhanced tree quorum algorithm is proposed. In Section 4, the performance of the proposed algorithm is analyzed in terms of message cost and availability, and a comparison with other algorithms is given.

† This research was partially supported by National Science Foundation under grant No. IRI-9008694.

2. Review of Replica Control Algorithms

In this section, we review some of the basic replica control algorithms: read-one/write-all, available copies, voting, and tree quorum algorithms, which will be compared with the proposed enhanced tree quorum algorithm.

2.1. Read-One/Write-All

The simplest technique to maintain replicated data is that a read operation is allowed to read any copy, and a write operation is required to write all copies of the data item, which is called read-one/write-all (ROWA) algorithm. This algorithm works correctly since a transaction processes from one correct state to another correct state. The ROWA has the lowest read cost because only one copy is accessed by a read operation. A weakness of this method is the low write availability because a write operation can not be done at the failure of any copy.

The available copies algorithm [BER84, BER87] is an enhanced version of the ROWA approach in terms of the availability of write operations. Every read is translated into a read of any copy of the data item and every write is translated into writes of all available copies of that data item. This algorithm handles site failures but not communication failures because they assume that each site is either operational or down and that all operational sites can communicate with each other. Therefore, each operational site can independently determine which sites are down, simply by attempting to communicate with them. If a site does not respond to a message within the timeout period, then it is assumed to be down.

2.2. Voting

The first voting algorithm was the majority consensus algorithm proposed in [THO79]. Here, we describe the generalization of the algorithm proposed in [GIF79]. In this approach, every copy of a replicated data item is assigned a certain number of votes, and a transaction has to collect a read quorum of r votes to read a data item, and a write quorum of w votes to write a data item. Quorums must satisfy two constraints: $r+w$ must be larger than the total number of votes v assigned to the copies of the data item, and $w > v/2$.

The first constraint ensures that there is a non-empty intersection between every read quorum and every write quorum. Therefore, each read quorum is guaranteed to have a current copy of the data item. The second constraint ensures that writes can not happen in two different partitions of copies of the same data item. Both constraints together guarantee that each write quorum of a data item has at least one copy in common with every read quorum and every write quorum of the data item.

To help the transaction figure out which copy is up-to-date, we tag each copy with a version number, which is initially 0. When a transaction performs a write, it obtains the current maximum version number of the data, adds one to it, and tags all of the copies that it writes with the new version number. The version number shows how up-to-date each copy is. Each read returns the version number along with the data value, and the transaction selects the copy with the largest version number in the read quorum.

The voting approach ensures the one-copy serializability and works well for the failure caused by the site crash or the network partition. By choosing $r > v/2$, a data item is read accessible in only one partition, where it is write accessible. The read availability is given a higher priority by choosing a small r. A weakness of this scheme is that writing a data item is fairly expensive: A write quorum of copies must be larger than the majority of votes, i.e., $w > v/2$.

2.3. Tree Quorum Algorithm

The tree quorum (TQ) algorithm [AGR90a, AGR90b] imposes a logical tree structure on the set of copies of a data item. One advantage of this algorithm is that a read operation may access only one copy and the number of copies to be accessed by a write operation is always less than the majority of the copies. Thus, the tree quorum algorithm is much better in terms of the write availability than the read-one/write-all algorithm. Since the logical tree structure does not have to correspond to the physical structure of the network, no reconfiguration is required at the failure of sites.

To explain the selection of read and write quorums, a logical tree with 13 copies is shown in Figure 1. For read operations, a read quorum can be formed by the root or the majority of the children of the root. If any node in the majority of the children of the root fails, it can be replaced by the majority of its children, and so on recursively. In the best case, a read quorum contains only the root, {1}. As the root fails, a quorum is formed by the majority of the nodes at level 1, e.g., {2, 3}, {3, 4}, or {2, 4}. Node 2 or node 3 is replaced by the majority of their children, respectively, if no majority at level 1 is accessible and only node 4 is accessible. Such quorums are {5, 6, 4} or {8, 10, 4}. If the nodes at level 0 and level 1 fail, a quorum is formed by the majorities of the children of the selected majority at level 1, e.g., {5, 6, 8, 9} or {8, 9, 11, 13}.

For write operations, a write quorum is formed by the root, and the majority of the children of the root, and the majorities of the children of the selected children of the root, etc. The size of a write quorum for a given tree is fixed, but the members can be different. Possible write quorums are {1, 2, 3, 5, 6, 8, 9}, {1, 2, 4, 6, 7, 12, 13}, etc.

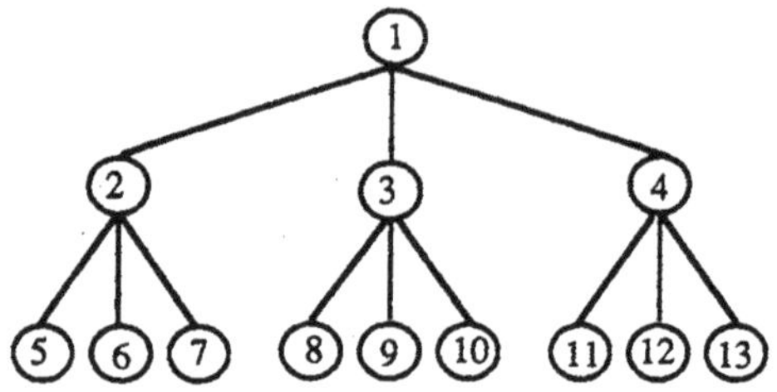

Figure 1. A Tree Imposed on Data Copies

The tree quorum algorithm ensures that each read quorum and write quorum selected by the algorithm have an intersection all the time [AGR90a]. The read cost is low when the root is accessible. The write quorum is usually smaller than the majority of total copies.

A weakness of the tree quorum algorithm is that certain pattern of failures, even if the number of failed copies is small, would reduce the write availability of a data item. For example, when the root fails, a write operation is suspended even if all the other nodes are accessible.

Comparing the replica control algorithms, ROWA is the simplest one. It has low read cost and high write cost, and it can not tolerate any failure for write operation. Voting enhances fault tolerance with two constraints. The read availability can have a higher priority than write availability by choosing a small read quorum and a large write quorum. The tree quorum method relaxes one constraint of voting. It allows a write quorum can be smaller than the majority of all copies. The fault tolerance is increased if the nodes at the low lever of the tree have less failures. In the next section, the enhanced tree quorum algorithm, based on the tree quorum algorithm, is proposed. The new algorithm has higher read and write availabilities because the failure of the root is tolerated.

3. Enhanced Tree Quorum (ETQ) Algorithm

In this section, we propose the enhanced tree quorum (ETQ) algorithm for managing replicated data items in distributed database systems. In this approach, selection of read and write quorums for a data item is based on a logical tree with a backup root imposed on the copies of the data item. Instead of counting votes, a tree-based protocol is used to select quorums.

Here we assume that a distributed system consists of a set of sites that communicate with each other by sending messages over a communication network. No assumptions are made regarding the speed, connectivity, or reliability of the network. We also assume that sites are fail-stop [SCH83] and communication links may fail to deliver messages. Combinations of such failures may lead to partitioning of the network, where sites in one partition may communicate with each other, but no communication can occur between sites in different partitions. A site may become inaccessible due to site failures or network partitioning.

With ETQ algorithm, copies of a data item are logically organized into a modified tree (with a backup root) of height h and degree D, where D is the degree of nodes in the tree. Figure 2 shows a modified tree of height 2 and degree 3 imposed on 14 copies.

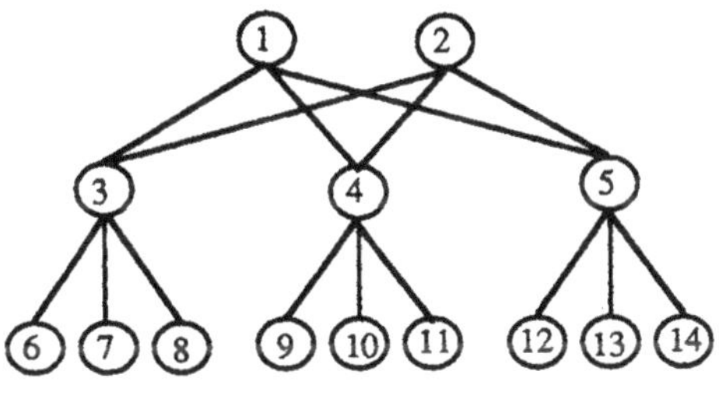

Figure 2. A Tree with a Backup Root Imposed on Data Copies

3.1. Constructing a Read Quorum and a Write Quorum

For a read operation, a read quorum can be formed by one of the roots of the modified tree, or by replacing failed roots with the majority of their children, and so on. In other words, when the two roots fail, a read quorum is obtained for the tree in the same manner as in TQ algorithm. However, the size of the read quorum is one if at least one of the roots is available. For a write operation, a write quorum can be formed by available roots and the majority of children of the roots, and so on. In other words, all the available roots are selected, and the nodes at lower levels of the tree are selected in the same manner as in TQ algorithm. Figures 3 and 4 show the algorithms for constructing the read and the write quorums, respectively.

```
Function ReadQuorum(Tree): QUORUM;
var
   MajorityQuorum, Majority: QUORUM;
begin
   if Empty(Tree) then
      return ({});
   else if one of the roots is accessible then
         return (one available root);
      else
         begin
            MajorityQuorum = {};
            (* replace the failed roots of the tree with the
              majority of its children *)
            for each selected subtree ∈ Majority
            MajorityQuorum = MajorityQuorum ∪
                        ReadQuorum(Subtree);

            if unable to collect Majority then
              return ({});
            else
              return (MajorityQuorum);
         end
end;
```

Figure 3. Read Quorum Construction in ETQ Algorithm.

In Figure 3, the function ReadQuorum first tries to find one of the roots of the modified tree. If successful, one available root forms the read quorum. Otherwise, the algorithm tries to replace the failed roots with the majority of their children. If the majority of the children of the roots are not available, each child of the majority can be replaced by the majority of its children. This process repeats recursively until a set of copies is included in the read quorum, or no such copies are accessible and the empty set is returned.

For the modified tree with 14 copies illustrated in Figure 2, a read quorum can be formed by a root, such as {1} or {2}, in the best case. Or a read quorum can be formed as {3, 4} when roots are inaccessible, by replacing the roots with the majority of the children, 3 and 4. Or a read quorum can be formed as {3, 9, 10} when only node 3 is accessible among the children of the failed roots, by replacing node 4 with the majority of its children, 9 and 10.

In Figure 4, the function WriteQuorum first tries to find all the available roots of the modified tree. If none of the roots is available, a write quorum can not be constructed. Otherwise all the available roots are included in the write quorum. Then, the algorithm tries to include the majority of the children of the root, and the majority of the children of the selected children of the root, and so on recursively, down to the lowest level of the tree.

For the same example illustrated in Figure 2, each write quorum must include at least one of the roots {1, 2} and the majority of the children of the roots, and so on. Therefore, possible write quorums are {1, 2, 3, 4, 7, 8, 10, 11}, {1, 3, 5, 6, 7, 12, 13}, etc.

To satisfy the non-empty intersection between a read quorum and a write quorum, when a root is recovered from failure, it should not be included in a read quorum until it becomes up-to-date. Comparing the possible read quorums and write quorums, we can see that there is always a non-empty intersection between a read quorum and a write quorum.

```
Function WriteQuorum(Tree): QUORUM;
var
   MajorityQuorum, Majority: QUORUM;
begin
   if Empty(Tree) then
      return ({ });
   else if at least one of the roots is accessible then
         begin
            MajorityQuorum = {all the available roots};
            (* collect the majority of subtrees of the roots *)
            for each selected subtree ∈ Majority
            MajorityQuorum = MajorityQuorum ∪
                        WriteQuorum(Subtree);

            if unable to collect Majority then
               return ({ });
            else
               return (MajorityQuorum);
         end
      else return ({ });
end;
```

Figure 4. Write Quorum Construction in ETQ Algorithm.

3.2. Correctness of the Enhanced Quorum Algorithm

The enhanced tree quorum algorithm is based on the tree quorum algorithm. Therefore, the correctness of ETQ can be proved based on the correctness of TQ. With the following theorem proved, we demonstrate that a read quorum and a write quorum constructed by ETQ algorithm always have a non-empty intersection. Note that two write quorums always have a non-empty intersection.

Theorem: The enhanced tree quorum algorithm guarantees a non-empty intersection between a read quorum and a write quorum.

Proof: The proof is by induction on the height of the tree.

Basis: The theorem holds for a tree of height zero since there are only roots in the tree. A read quorum contains an available root and a write quorum contains all the available roots. So both quorums have a non-empty intersection.

Induction Hypothesis: Assume that the theorem holds for a tree of height h.

Induction Step: Consider a tree of height $h+1$. The read and write quorums constructed for this tree have the following form:

1. Read Quorum:

{one of the roots}, or
{read quorums of the majority of the subtrees of height h}.

2. Write Quorum:

{available roots and the write quorums of the majority of the subtrees of height h}.

If a read quorum consists of one of the roots of the tree, it is guaranteed to have a non-empty intersection with any write quorum. If a read quorum consists of the read quorums of the majority of the subtrees of height h, it is guaranteed to have at least one subtree in common with any write quorum. Since the subtrees are of height h, the induction hypothesis guarantees that read and write quorums have a non-empty intersection. Hence, by induction, ETQ algorithm guarantees a non-empty intersection between a read quorum and a write quorum.

The tree quorum and the enhanced tree quorum algorithms use the same principle of imposing a logical structure to improve the write availability over ROWA and to reduce the quorum size compared to voting. In addition, ETQ allows to construct a write quorum on a modified tree even though one root fails, while TQ does not allow to write when the root fails. Thus the proposed ETQ algorithm enhances the fault-tolerance in write operation compared to TQ. For read, the minimum read quorum size of TQ is $\lceil (D+1)/2 \rceil$ when the root fails and the degree of nodes is D. However, it is still one with ETQ if the other root is available.

4. Performance Analysis and Comparison

In this section, we analyze and compare the performance of the enhanced tree quorum algorithm and other replica control algorithms: read-one/write-all, voting, and tree quorum, on the message cost and the operation availability.

4.1. Message Cost Analysis

The message cost of an operation is directly proportional to the size of the quorum required to execute the operation. Therefore, we represent the message cost in terms of the quorum size. In addition, we use C_{XY} to denote the message cost with X algorithm for Y operation, which is R (read) or W (write).

4.1.1. Read-One/Write-All (ROWA)

In ROWA, a read operation needs only one copy, while a write operation needs to access N copies if there are N copies in the system. Thus, the message cost of a read operation is:

$$C_{ROWAR} = 1$$

and the message cost of a write operation is:

$$C_{ROWAW} = N$$

4.1.2. Voting (VT)

In voting, if the majority consensus method is used, the quorum size for both read and write operations can be the same, i.e., the majority of the total number of votes assigned to the copies. Thus, the cost C_{VTR} and C_{VTW} are:

$$C_{VTR} = C_{VTW} = \left\lceil \frac{N+1}{2} \right\rceil$$

where N is the total number of votes assigned to copies.

If the weighted voting method is used, the cost is dependent on the number of votes preselected for read and write operations.

4.1.3. Tree Quorum (TQ)

In estimating the cost of operations with TQ, h denotes the height of the tree, D is the degree of nodes in the tree, and M is the majority of D, i.e.,

$$M = \left\lceil \frac{D+1}{2} \right\rceil$$

In TQ, the cost of a read operation ranges from 1 to M^h [AGR90a]:

$$1 \le C_{TQR} \le M^h$$

When the root is accessible, the read quorum size is 1. As the root fails, the majority of its children replace it, thus the quorum size increases to M. Therefore, for a tree of height h, the maximum quorum size is M^h.

In TQ, all the write quorums have the same size: the root is selected and the majority of the children of each node selected are included, recursively. Thus, the cost of a write operation, C_{TQW}, can be represented as:

$$C_{TQW} = \sum_{i=0}^{h} M^i$$

4.1.4. Enhanced Tree Quorum (ETQ)

The size of a read quorum in ETQ is the same as that of TQ. Thus, it varies from 1 to M^h:

$$1 \le C_{ETQR} \le M^h$$

For a write operation, the two roots are accessed and the majority of the children of each node selected are accessed, recursively. Thus, the cost of a write operation can be represented as:

$$C_{ETQW} = 2 + \sum_{i=1}^{h} M^i$$

4.1.5. Comparison of Costs

Figures 5 and 6 show the read and the write costs of the four algorithms, respectively, for different total number of copies. We plot the maximum read costs for TQ and ETQ in Figure 5, and for voting, we choose the read quorum and the write quorum as the majority of the total copies. ROWA has the lowest cost for a read because only one copy is read. In the best case, TQ and ETQ also have the lowest read cost. In the worst case, the read costs for TQ and ETQ are almost the same. For example, for ETQ with a modified tree of height 2 on 14 copies, the maximum cost is 4, and for TQ with a tree of height 2 on 13 copies, the maximum cost is also 4.

In voting, if we choose the read quorum and the write quorum as the majority of the total copies, then the read cost is always higher than those of ETQ and TQ because $M^h < \lceil (N+1)/2 \rceil$.

For a write operation, ROWA has the highest cost. The write cost of ETQ is almost the same as the cost of TQ: for 14 copies, the write cost of ETQ is 8, whereas for 13 copies, the write cost of TQ is 7. The write costs of TQ and ETQ are always lower than that of voting because the number of nodes selected at each level of the tree is less than the majority of the nodes at the level.

4.2. Availability Analysis

In this section, four replica control algorithms are analyzed and compared in terms of the operation availability. We first introduce the k-out-of-N model which will be used for estimating the operation availability.

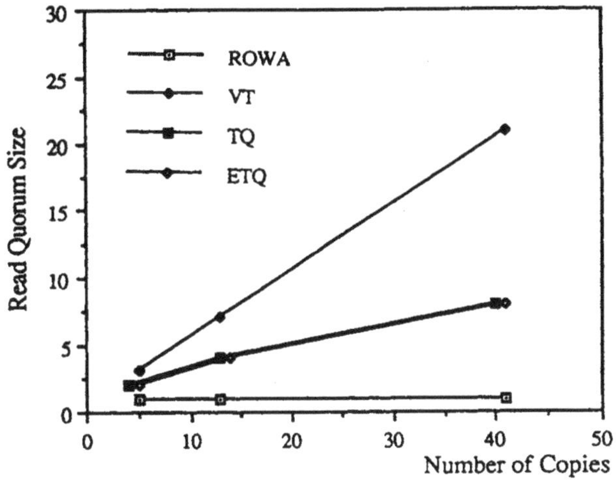

Figure 5. Comparison of the Read Cost

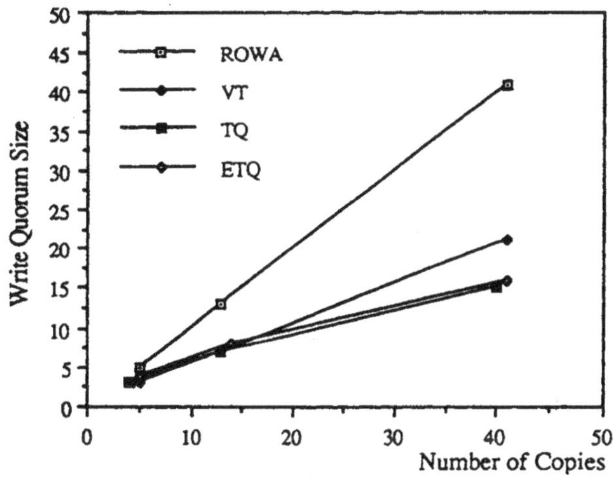

Figure 6. Comparison of the Write Cost

4.2.1. The k-out-of-N Model

We define the availability of a data item as the probability of the data item being accessible for an operation at any given time, which can be represented using the k-out-of-N model [BAR84]. The assumptions of k-out-of-N model are repeated here:

1. The data item and its copies are in one of the two states: accessible or inaccessible.
2. The states of the copies are changed independently.
3. The data item is available for an operation if at least k of its N copies are accessible.

Thus, the k-out-of-N model can be formulated as:

$$k\text{-}out\text{-}of\text{-}N = \sum_{i=k}^{N} \binom{N}{i} p^i (1-p)^{N-i}, \quad k \ge 1$$

where p denotes the availability (accessibility) of a copy.

This formula gives the availability of a data item for an operation if k available copies are needed for the quorum. As k increases, the availability decreases because more accessible copies are required. By using the k-out-of-N model, we can estimate the availability of operations on a data item given the availability of each copy of the data item. In estimating the availability of operations, all copies are assumed to have the same availability p, and A_{XY} will represent the availability of Y operation with X algorithm.

4.2.2. Read-One/Write-All (ROWA)

For a data item replicated, ROWA requires a read on any one of the copies and a write on all copies. Therefore, the availability for a read operation can be represented as 1-out-of-N, and for a write operation as N-out-of-N. Thus, the read availability A_{ROWAR} is:

$$A_{ROWAR} = \sum_{i=1}^{N} \binom{N}{i} p^i (1-p)^{N-i} = 1-(1-p)^N$$

and the write availability A_{ROWAW} is:

$$A_{ROWAW} = \sum_{i=N}^{N} \binom{N}{i} p^i (1-p)^{N-i} = p^N$$

4.2.3. Voting (VT)

For N copies, voting allows N choices for the read and the write quorums from (read 1, write N) to (read N, write 1). If we select a small read quorum, the read availability is high but the write availability becomes low, demonstrating the trade-off between the read and the write availabilities in VT. If we choose the read quorum of k, the read availability A_{VTR} is:

$$A_{VTR} = \sum_{i=k}^{N} \binom{N}{i} p^i (1-p)^{N-i}, \quad k \geq 1$$

and the corresponding write availability A_{VTW} is:

$$A_{VTW} = \sum_{i=N+1-k}^{N} \binom{N}{i} p^i (1-p)^{N-i}$$

4.2.4. Tree Quorum (TQ)

The availability of the read and the write operations in TQ can be estimated by using recurrence equations based on the tree height h. Let R_h and W_h be the availability of the read and the write operations with a tree of height h, respectively, while D denotes the degree of nodes in the tree and M is the majority of D. Then, the availability of a read operation for a tree of height $h+1$ can be represented as:

$$R_{h+1} = p + (1-p) \sum_{i=M}^{D} \binom{D}{i} R_h^i (1-R_h)^{D-i}$$

and the availability of a write operation for a tree of height $h+1$ is given as:

$$W_{h+1} = p \sum_{i=M}^{D} \binom{D}{i} W_h^i (1-W_h)^{D-i}$$

where p is the probability that a copy is available, and R_0 and W_0 are equal to p.

4.2.5. Enhanced Tree Quorum (ETQ)

We can use the equations developed for TQ to estimate the operation availability in ETQ because the read availability and the write availability of a subtree in ETQ are identical to those in TQ for the subtree. Let R_h and W_h denote the read and the write availabilities for a tree of height h, respectively, and let ER_h and EW_h denote the read and the write availabilities in ETQ with a modified tree of height h, respectively. Then, ER_{h+1} can be represented as:

$$ER_{h+1} = [1-(1-p)^2] + (1-p)^2 \sum_{i=M}^{D} \binom{D}{i} R_h^i (1-R_h)^{D-i}$$

The first term corresponds to the case that at least one of the two roots is available, and the second term is for the case that both roots are not available.

The availability of a write operation, EW_{h+1}, is

$$EW_{h+1} = [1-(1-p)^2] \sum_{i=M}^{D} \binom{D}{i} W_h^i (1-W_h)^{D-i}$$

and

$$ER_0 = EW_0 = 1-(1-p)^2$$

where p is the probability that a copy is available.

4.2.6. Comparison of Availabilities

The read and the write availabilities of the four methods, ROWA, VT, TQ, and ETQ, are compared in Figures 7 and 8, respectively. We assume that all data copies have the same availability, and that N is 14 for ROWA, VT, and ETQ, and N is 13 for TQ. Here, we use the same quorum size, $\lceil (N+1)/2 \rceil$, for read and write in VT. The read availabilities of ETQ and TQ are much higher than that of VT because the number of data copies to be read in ETQ and TQ is much smaller than the majority of the copies, required in VT. ETQ has slightly higher read availability than TQ because in ETQ either one of the two roots can be a read quorum, whereas a read quorum in TQ will be the majority of the children of the root when it fails.

The write availability of ETQ is also higher than that of TQ because a write operation is not allowed at the root failure in TQ, whereas a write operation is allowed in ETQ as long as one of the two roots is available. The write availability of VT is lower than those of ETQ and TQ because the write quorum size of VT is selected as $\lceil (N+1)/2 \rceil$, which is larger than the write quorums of ETQ and TQ almost all the cases.

Considering the operation costs and the availabilities, TQ and ETQ are better than ROWA and VT, and ETQ provides higher operation availability than TQ at the same operation cost.

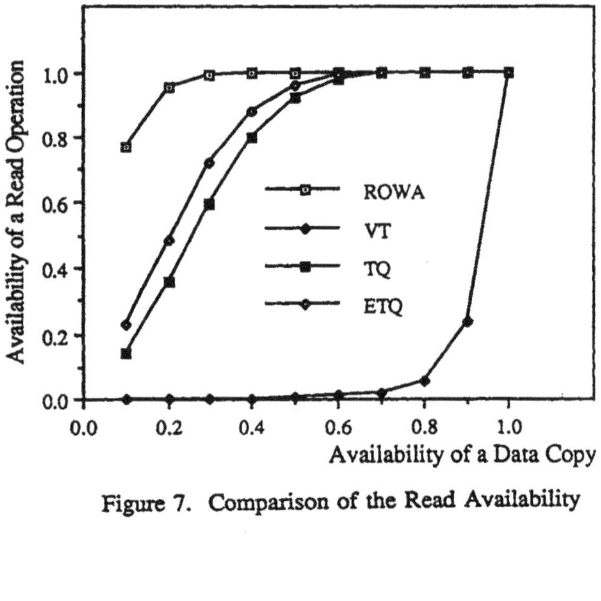

Figure 7. Comparison of the Read Availability

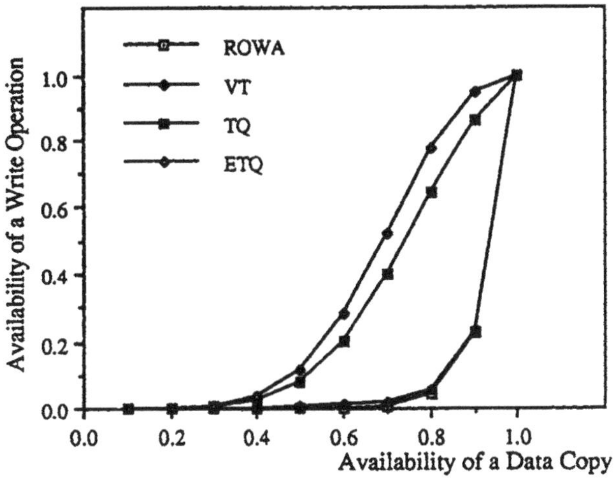

Figure 8. Comparison of the Write Availability

5. Conclusion

In this paper, a new replica control algorithm, called the enhanced tree quorum (ETQ) algorithm, is proposed to manage replicated data in distributed database systems. This algorithm provides high availability for read and write operations by imposing a logical structure of a modified tree on data copies. With ETQ algorithm, a read operation is limited to a data copy in the best case, and a write operation is allowed as long as one of the roots of the modified tree and the majority of the children of each node selected are available. That means, no reconfiguration is required in ETQ for the case of site failures. Compared to other algorithms, ETQ requires lower message cost for an operation, while providing higher availability.

References

[AGR90a] D. Agrawal and A. El Abbadi, "The Tree Quorum Protocol: An Efficient Approach for Managing Replicated Data," Proc. VLDB, 1990, pp.243-254.

[AGR90b] D. Agrawal and A. El Abbadi, "Efficient Techniques for Replicated Data Management," Proc. Workshop on Management of Replicated Data, 1990, pp.48-52.

[BAR84] R. E. Barlow and K. O. Heidtmann, "Computing k-out-of-N Reliability," IEEE Trans. on Reliability, Vol. 33, No. 4, pp.322-323, 1984.

[BAR86] D. Barbara, H. Garcia-Molina, and A. Spauster, "Policies for Dynamic Vote Reassignment," Proc. Int'l Conf. on Distributed Computing Systems, 1986, pp.37-44.

[BER84] P. A. Bernstein and N. Goodman, "An Algorithm for Concurrency Control and Recovery in Replicated Distributed Databases," ACM Trans. on Database Systems, Vol. 9, No. 4, 1984, pp.596-615.

[BER85] P. A. Bernstein and N. Goodman, "Serializability Theory for Replicated Databases," Journal of Computer and System Sciences, Vol. 31, 1985, pp.355-374.

[BER87] P. A. Bernstein, V. Hadzilacos, and N. Goodman, *Concurrency Control and Recovery in Database Systems*, Addison-Wesley Publishing Co., 1987.

[CHE89] S. Cheung, M. Ahamad, and M. Ammar, "Optimizing Vote and Quorum Assignments for Reading and Writing Replicated Data," IEEE Trans. on Knowledge and Data Engineering, Vol. 1, No. 3, 1989, pp.387-397.

[CHE90] S. Cheung, M. Ahamad, and M. Ammar, "Multi-Dimensional Voting: A General Method for Implementing Synchronization in Distributed Systems," Proc. of Int'l Conf. on Distributed Computing Systems, 1990, pp.362-369.

[CHU92] S. M. Chung and C. Cao, "Multiple Tree Quorum Algorithm for Replica Control in Distributed Database Systems," Proc. of IEEE Symp. on Parallel and Distributed Processing, 1992, pp.282-286.

[DAV85] S. B. Davidson, H. Garcia-Molina, and D. Skeen, "Consistency in Partitioned Networks," ACM Computing Surveys, Vol. 17, No. 3, 1985, pp.341-370.

[GAR85] H. Garcia-Molina and D. Barbara, "How to Assign Votes in a Distributed System," Journal of ACM, Vol. 32, No. 4, 1985, pp. 841-860.

[GIF79] D. K. Gifford, "Weighted Voting for Replicated Data," Proc. Symp. on Operating System Principles, 1979, pp.150-162.

[JAJ87a] S. Jajodia and D. Mutchler, "Dynamic Voting," Proc. SIGMOD, 1987, pp.227-238.

[JAJ87b] S. Jajodia and D. Mutchler, "Enhancements of the Voting Algorithm," Proc. VLDB, 1987, pp.399-406.

[JAJ88] S. Jajodia and D. Mutchler, "Integrating Static and Dynamic Voting Protocols to Enhance File Availability," Proc. Int'l Conf. on Data Engineering, 1988, pp.144-153.

[KUM90] A. Kumar, "Performance Analysis of a Hierarchical Quorum Consensus Algorithm for Replicated Objects", Proc. Int'l Conf. on Distributed Computing Systems, 1990, pp.378-385.

[LON87] D. Long and J. F. Paris, "On Improving the Availability of Replicated Files," Proc. Symp. on Reliability in Distributed Software and Database Systems, 1987, pp.77-83.

[PAR86] J. F. Paris, "Voting with Witnesses: A Consistency Scheme for Replicated Files," Proc. Int'l Conf. on Distributed Computing Systems, 1986, pp.606-612.

[PAR88] J. F. Paris and D. Long, "Efficient Dynamic Voting Algorithms," Proc. Int'l Conf. on Data Engineering, 1988, pp.268-275.

[PU86] C. Pu, J. Noe, and A. Proudfoot, "Regeneration of Replicated Objects: A Technique and Its Eden Implementation," Proc. Int'l Conf. on Data Engineering, 1986, pp.175-187.

[SCH83] R. Schlicting and F. B. Schneider, "Fail-Stop Processors: An Approach to Design Fault-Tolerant Computing Systems," ACM Trans. on Computing Systems, Vol. 1, No. 3, 1983, pp. 222-238.

[THO79] R. H. Thomas, "A Majority Consensus Approach to Concurrency Control for Multiple Copy Databases," ACM Trans. on Database Systems, Vol. 4, No. 2, 1979, pp.180-209.

DATA FRAGMENTATION AND ALLOCATION FOR PC-BASED DISTRIBUTED DATABASE DESIGN*

Minyoung Ra, Yang-Sun Park

Computer Science Division
Department of Mathematics
Korea Military Academy
Seoul, KOREA 139-799

ABSTRACT

As the performance of PCs is improved, the need for PC-based distributed database systems has been increased. Data fragmentation and allocation is one of the major design issues for distributed database systems. In this paper, several factors that should be considered in constructing a PC-based distributed database system have been investigated, and a methodology for partitioning and allocating data effectively over a network for PC-based distributed database design is proposed. This methodology is based on the mixed partitioning technique using a grid approach.

1. INTRODUCTION

Recently, the use of Database Systems(DBS) on Personal Computers(PC) has been increased. A database system, which stores and manages data to produce useful information, is a computer oriented system consisting of databases(DB), a database management system (DBMS), data languages, and database administartors (DBAs), [Elma 89]. In the past years, DBS was mainly used on mini computers and mainframes, but now it is widely used on PCs because the performance of PCs has been improved and the cost of PCs came down.

However, most of the DBSs on PCs are for a single-user and thus sharing of resources is not considered. To make up for this weakness PCs are connected into distributed database systems to share resources. Research on distributed database systems (DDBS) has been increased because DDBSs can improve reliability and availability and fit more naturally in the decentralized structures of many organizations [Ceri 84, Oszu 91]. Data fragmentation and allocation called data distribution is the basis for constructing distributed database systems. Since it is possible to construct distributed database systems on PCs, the research on data distribution for PC-based distributed database design should be emphasized. In this paper a distribution scheme for PC based distributed database systems is proposed by using a mixed fragmentation technique. Section 2 deals with some factors that should be considered for data distribution. In Section 3, a methodology for generating distribution scheme by using a mixed partitioning technique is proposed. Section 4 gives the conclusion.

*This research was supported in part by KOSEF (Korea Science & Engineering Foundation) Grant No. 923-1100-088-1.

2. CONSIDERATIONS FOR DATA DISTRIBUTION

There are some factors that should be considered for effective data distribution in constructing PC-based distributed database systems.

2.1 Data Fragmentation

Data fragmentation (or partitioning) is the process that divides a logical object (relation) from the logical schema of the database to several physical objects (files) in a stored database [Nava 84]. There are basically two different ways in data fragmentation: vertical partitioning and horizontal partitioning. Vertical partitioning is the process of dividing attributes into groups. Previous work on vertical partitioning has used objective functions to perform partitioning [Ceri 88, Corn 87, Hamm 79, Nava 84]. Since in these approaches, binary partitioning technique should be applied recursively and objective functions and compliment algorithms such as SHIFT algorithm [Nava 84] are needed, we developed a graph theoretic algorithm that generates all meaningful vertical fragments in one iteration [Nava 89]. Horizontal partitioning is the process of dividing tuples in a relation into groups of tuples. In the most of the previous approaches, the problem is that there may be lots of horizontal partitions since at worst case a horizontal partition can be composed of only one tuple [Ceri 82, Cer 83b, Yu 85]. Because of this reason a new horizontal partitioning technique using predicate clustering is currently being studied to overcome this drawback [Ra 91].

Mixing the two types of partitioning has considered to yield mixed partitioning. The need for mixed partitioning arises in distributed databases because database users usually access data subsets which are both vertical and horizontal fragments of global relations [Elma 89]. The examples of the previous work on mixed partitioning are available in [Aper 88, Nava 90].

2.2 Data Allocation

Data allocation is the process of mapping each logical fragment to one or more sites, and is considered as one of the major design issues for distributed databases [Cer 83a, Cer 83b, Corn 88]. Previous research in this area has been performed in two ways: data allocation by itself for distributed database systems, and extension of the pure data allocation problem by including the network topology and communication channels in the decision variables for distributed computing areas. This paper is concerned with pure data allocation in which the unit of allocation is the mixed fragment which comes from the mixed partitioning procedure in Section 3.2.1. The previous work in this area includes research on the models for data allocation [Cer 83b, Corn 88, Corn 89], and research on allocation heuristics [Aper 88, Ceri 88].

2.3 LAN

When we construct a distributed databases with PCs, the communication among them can usually be performed by using LANs. LANs are particular form of data communications, with hardware and software optimized to support the sharing of devices and information. They offer high degree of autonomy and versatility [Ceri 84, Patt 90]. The technologies related to PC LANs have progressed to replace mini computers, and making it possible to connect with large databases. The two important components comprising a LAN are a network operating system and a server. A network operating system is a system software that provides resource management for services on server machines, and provides the user and application software a window to the LAN environment. The following are key features that a NOS should support [Jord 90]: (1) hardware independence, (2) multiple server support, (3) multi user support, (4) network management, and (5) human engineering reflected user interface. The details are out of the present scope of this paper. Functions of a server are discussed in the next section.

2.4 Database Server

A server refers to a software application that offers a well-defined service to network users. A server application can be run on a special-purpose hardware or an ordinary PC. The most common types of servers are file servers, print servers, and communication servers [Cart 84, Jord 90]. A database server can be considered as a kind of file servers, which is divided into two categories: resource-shared architecture and client-server architecture. In resource-shared architecture, the users mainly work on PCs and send the results to the database server, or the users bring data from the database server and work within the PC. On the other hand, in client-server architecture, a database server processes database access requests from users and sends back the results to users. The criteria for evaluating database servers are (1) SQL-like query support, (2) various data types, (3) data compression, (4) record and database size limits, (5) recovery scheme and failure detection, (6) distributed processing support, and (7) installation and operation, etc. [Rein 89].

3. SCHEME FOR DISTRIBUTION DESIGN

Based on the above considerations, we develop a scheme for PC-based distributed database design.

3.1 Problem Description

Suppose we want to connect databases in PCs using a LAN. There is a database server in the LAN, which supports the distributed database environment. Then the distribution design problem for a PC-based distributed database system on the LAN can be described as follows.

"PCs having data processing facility are interconnected using LANs to form a distributed database system. Data are distributed according to the logical schema of the databases. Using appropriate partitioning techniques relations are partitioned, and the results are allocated to the database server and PCs in order to minimize the total data transmission cost. If replication is needed, we allow replication of data. We, however, do not consider network topology, communication channel, and band width. These factors may be included in the later stage".

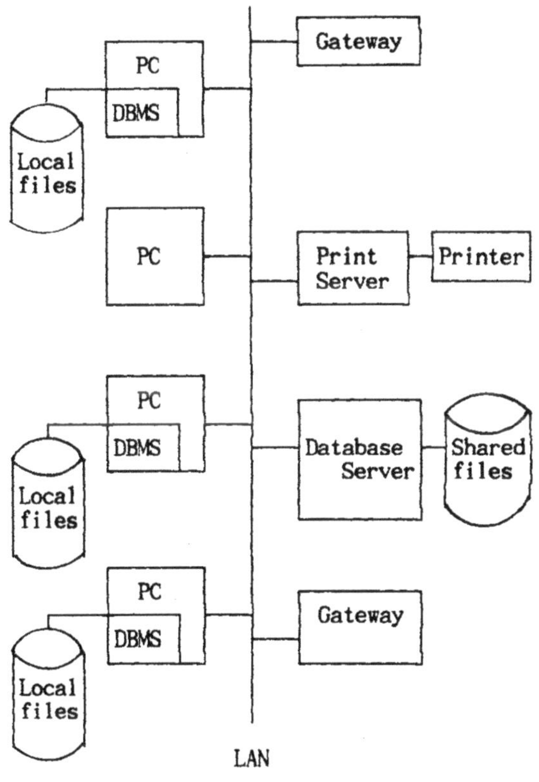

Fig. 1 PC-based distributed database environment

Figure 1 shows our research environment. As shown in Figure 1, we are investigating a server based on the client-server architecture, which processes data access requests from users, sends back the results to the users, maintains data consistency, and protects data collision.

3.2 A Methodology for Distribution Design Scheme

The development of the scheme for distribution design scheme can be done in the following two steps.

(1) mixed partitioning and grid optimization
(2) allocation of mixed fragments

The next sections describes these steps in detail.

3.2.1 Mixed partitioning and grid optimization

A mixed partitioning methodology is a hybrid type of horizontal partitioning technique and vertical partitioning technique. Currently mixed partitioning has not been addressed in the literature. Today's methodology can produce mixed partitioning only in one of the following two ways: by performing horizontal partitioning followed by vertical partitioning or by performing vertical partitioning followed by horizontal partitioning. Obviously, this is not adequate since it potentially leads to different results and leaves out the possibility of combining fragments at a smaller granularity to produce more efficient data distribution. In this paper we adopt a uniform mixed partitioning methodology which generates optimal results called mixed fragments that are formed by merging grid cells to minimize the global transaction processing costs. Grid cells are created by applying independently vertical and horizontal partitioning algorithms to a relation. It should be noted that the mixed fragments cannot be otherwise produced by independent partitioning models. The efficient algorithms for horizontal and vertical partitioning are already presented respectively [Nava 89, Ra 90, Ra 91].

3.2.1.1 Mixed partitioning methodology

In this section we give an overview of the mixed partitioning methodology. It consists of the specification of inputs, vertical partitioning, horizontal partitioning, merging of grid cells, resulting in the generation of the fragmentation scheme.

(1) Specification of inputs: The following set of inputs need to be provided by the user in order to come up with the mixed fragmentation scheme.

(a) schema information : relations, attributes, cardinalities, attribute sizes, etc.

(b) transaction information : name, frequency, attribute usage, etc. The attribute usage matrix is a matrix containing transactions as rows and attributes as columns. Element (i,j)=1 if transaction i uses attribute j, else it is 0.

(c) distribution constarints : any predetermined partitions or fixed allocation of data.

(2) Vertical partitioning for grid
In this step all candidate vertical fragments are determined. We use a graphical algorithm [Nava 89] for generating all fragments in one iteration.

(3) Horizontal partitioning for grid
In this step, all candidate horizontal fragments are determined by using the same graphical technique. Note that the order of this and the above step can be interchanged. Figure 2 shows the transaction specifications for our example both vertical and horizontal partitioning, and an example of grid cells resulting from this specifications is shown in Figure 3.

(4) Grid optimization
In this step, cells are merged so as to minimize the global transaction processing cost. A cost model for evaluating the benefit of merging, and a heuristic greedy procedure to decide if and how the calls are merged, are the major issues that should be attacked.

(5) Generation of fragmentation scheme
The previous step gives us two types of merging options namely: merging of grid cells horizontally or vertically. In this step we map the two merging schemes to generate a set of mixed fragments giving rise to a fragmentation scheme.

Transactions	Attributes	Predicates	Number of accesses per time period
T1	a1,a5,a7	p1,p7	25
T2	a2,a3,a8,a9	p2,p7	50
T3	a4,a6,a10	p3,p7	25
T4	a2,a7,a8	p4,p8	35
T5	a1,a2,a3,a5,a7,a8,a9	p5,p8	25
T6	a1,a5	p6,p8	25
T7	a3,a9	p5,p8	25
T8	a3,a4,a6,a9,a10	p6,p8	15

Fig. 2 Transaction specifications

G_{11}	G_{12}	G_{13}
G_{21}	G_{22}	G_{23}
G_{31}	G_{32}	G_{33}
G_{41}	G_{42}	G_{43}
G_{51}	G_{52}	G_{53}

Fig. 3 Grid creation

3.2.1.2 Grid optimization

The step of grid optimization is the key point among the above steps. This is because the results of mixed partitioning called mixed fragments are generated after grid optimization. There, however, are no cost functions proposed so far, nor merging heuristics. Thus in this paper we propose a feasible solution for this problem.

(a) Transaction mapping

Transaction mapping is done by mapping attributes and the predicates of the transactions with the attributes and the predicates forming the grid cells. Figure 4 shows the mapping of the transactions to grid cells. The transactions here do not mean 100% of expected transactions, but important transactions. Since the 80-20 rule applies to most practical situations, it is adequate to supply information regarding the 20% of the heavily used transactions which account for about 80% of the activity against the database. In this figure H_i represents the results of horizontal partitioning, and V_i represents the results of vertical partitioning. For example, transaction T4 accesses attributes a2, a7 and a8, and is based on predicates p4 and p8, whereas the grid cell G_{11} is formed of attributes a1, a5 and a7, and predicates p3, p4, p6 and p8. Hence transaction T4 access the cell G_{11}. Note that some of the grid cells are not accessed by the most important transactions, but may be accessed by other transactions. Based on this mapping information grid cells are merged to minimize total transaction processing cost.

(b) Cost model

Now we present the cost model that is the basis of grid optimization. To this end, we introduce the following notation.

m : number of horizontal partitions
n : number of vertical partitions
N : number of transactions
G_{ij} : grid cell determined by the i-th horizontal partition and the j-th vertical partition, where $1 \le i \le m$ and $1 \le j \le n$.
R_{ij} : number of tuples in grid cell G_{ij}
L_{ij} : total length of the attribute (in bytes) of a tuple of G_{ij}
c_t : average cost of access of a tuple of the relation
l_t : total length of a tuple in the given relation
α : ratio of the cost of accessing a merged fragment to the cost of accessing its constituent grid cells
C_{ij}: average cost of accessing grid cell G_{ij}

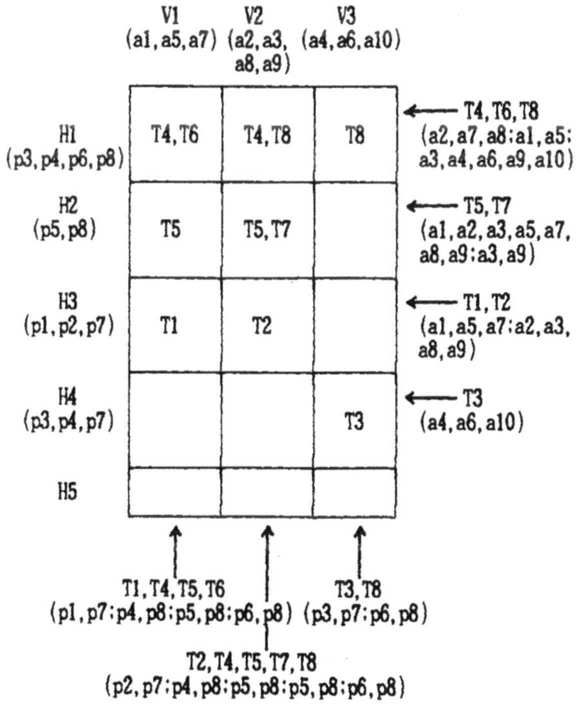

Fig. 4 Transaction mapping

We assume a linear cost access model in that the cost of accessing a grid cell G_{ij} is given by $C_{ij}=R_{ij}*(L_{ij}/l_t)*c_t$. When a transaction needs to access attributes in two horizontal cells that are not merged, there is a need to perform 'matching' of keys in the data obtained from the two cells. This operation is a form of join and we refer to this cost as 'join cost'. Similary, when a transaction needs to access tuples in two vertical cells that are not merged, there is a cost due to the need to perform union of the resultant tuples which we refer to as the 'union cost'. On the other hand, when a transaction needs data from only one of the constituent cells of a fragment, there is an additional cost due to the need to 'project' the attributes and 'select' the tuples of the grid cell from the fragment as needed by a transaction. Specifically, we need the following additional notation.

S(f) : set of constituent grid cells of fragment f
$F_k(f)$: frequency of accessing only fragment f by k-th transaction
C(f) : average cost of accessing fragment f
$F_k(f_1,f_2)$: frequency of accessing both the fragments f_1 and f_2 by the k-th transaction
$J_k(f_1,f_2)$: join cost in processing fragments f_1 and f_2 for k-th transaction
$U_k(f_1,f_2)$: union cost in processing fragments f_1 and f_2 for k-th transaction
$P_k(f)$: projection cost in processing fragment f for k-th transaction
$S_k(f)$: selection cost in processing fragment f for k-th transaction
$TC_k(f_1,f_2)$: total cost or saving for k-th transaction by merging fragments (horizontal or vertical) f_1 and f_2

We use the term "fragment" to denote the result of merging one or more vertical and/or horizontal cells. The two vertical fragments have the same set of attributes (and hence same vertical grid cells) while two horizontal fragments have the same set of tuple ID's (and hence same horizontal grid cells). The average cost of accessing fragment f consisting of two or more grid cells is given by

$$C(f) = \alpha \sum_{G_{ij} \in S(f)} C_{ij}$$

We refer to the combined fragment obtained by merging two fragments f_1 and f_2 as $f_1 \cup f_2$. If V_1 and V_2 are two vertical fragments that can be merged horizontally, then

$$TC_k(V_1,V_2) = F_k(V_1 \cup V_2)(C(V_1 \cup V_2) + P_k(V_1 \cup V_2)) - (F_k(V_1)C(V_1) + F_k(V_2)C(V_2) + F_k(V_1,V_2)J_k(V_1,V_2))$$

Similarly if H_1 and H_2 are two horizontal fragments that can be merged vertically, then

$$TC_k(H_1,H_2) = F_k(H_1 \cup H_2)(C(H_1 \cup H_2) + S_k(H_1 \cup H_2)) - (F_k(H_1)C(H_1) + F_k(H_2)C(H_2) + F_k(H_1,H_2)U_k(H_1,H_2))$$

We note that it is beneficial to merge V_1 and V_2 if

$$\Sigma^{N}_{k=1} TC_k(V_1,V_2) < 0.$$

Similarly it is beneficial to merge H_1 and H_2 if

$$\Sigma^{N}_{k=1} TC_k(H_1,H_2) < 0.$$

There is a trade-off between all these costs. This trade-off determines an optimal merging of grid cells. It is possible to use an integer programming formulation that determines an optimal clustering of grid cells either horizontally or verically. But the formulation will be difficult to solve and the solution procedure lacks intuition. For this reason, we use a heuristic procedure that performs successive merging based on the costs.

(c) Heuristic procedure for merging

Based on the cost functions we want to merge cells as much as possible in order to minimize the transaction processing cost as the given relation is concerned. We perfrom two kinds of merging, namely horizontal merging and vertical merging. Horizontal merging deals with merging of the cells in the same row of the grid.

In horizontal merging, the total number of ways of merging is $\Sigma^{n}_{i=1}\, {}^{n}C_i = 2^n - 1$ where ${}^{n}C_i$ represents combination selecting i form n and n represents the number of horizontal or vertical cells, because the sequence of attributes has no meaning in a relation. In our approach, however, we can minimize the possible ways of combinations of horizontal merging by using the ordered sequence of fragments generated in vertcal partitioning. Thus, given n candidate horizontal fragments, a total of $(n-1) + (n-2) + \cdots + 1 = n(n-1)/2$ merging possibilities are generated. This is because, in the linearly connected spanning tree in vertical partitioning, since a cut edge between two vertical fragments is a bridge that has the maximum affinity value among all connectable edges [Nava 89], we can say that a fragment is more closely related to contiguous fragments compared to noncontiguous fragments.

In vertical merging, cells in the same vertical column of the grid may be merged to produce larger fragments. Since the same graphical partitioning approach is used for horizontal partitioning, the total number of possilble ways of vertical merging can be minimized in the same way as in the horizontal merging.

Thus in our heuristic procedure, only adjacent horizontal or vertical cells or fragments are considered for merging. We use an iterative greedy procedure in which we succesively merge two adjacent fragments either horizontally or vertically until no more saving can be obtained by the merging process. The two adjacent horizontal or vertical fragments that are chosen for merging in each iteration are the pair that yield the maximum savings by merging them together instead of keeping them apart. The heuristic procedure is given as follows:

Procedure MergeCells :

{ Initially each cell by itself is a fragment }

<u>Repeat</u>

1. For each pair of adjacent horizontal or vertical fragments F_1 and F_2, calculate $TC(F_1,F_2) = \Sigma^{N}_{k=1} TC_k(F_1,F_2)$, where $TC_k(F_1,F_2)$ is as defined before.

2. If there exist at least one pair F_1 and F_2 that has $TC(F_1,F_2) < 0$, then find the pair F_1 and F_2 that has the least value of $TC(F_1,F_2)$ and merge them into a horizontal or vertical fragment.

<u>Until</u> No pair (F_1,F_2) exists with $TC(F_1,F_2) < 0$.

End MergeCells.

We note that in step 1, the cost calculation is necessary only for the fragments adjoining the merged fragment of the previous itration. Thus the computation required in each iteration is small.

Example :

Figure 5 shows the costs of accessing each of the horizontal fragments H1, H2, H3, H4 and H5 (i.e. average cost of access of a tuple of the relation times the number of tuples in the grid cell).

They are 100, 150, 200, 75, and 125 (i.e. c_1, c_2, c_3, c_4 and c_5) respectively. The length of the attributes of each of the vertical fragments are 14, 20 and 16 (i.e. l_1, l_2 and l_3) respectively. The cells are denoted by G_{ij}, $1 \le i \le 5$ and $1 \le j \le 3$. Hence the cost of accessing a single grid cell G_{ij} is $C_{ij} = c_i * (l_j / \Sigma^{3}_{j=1} l_j)$. Therefore the cost of accessing grid cell G_{22} is $C_{22} = 150 * (20 / (14+20+16)) = 60$.

Cost \ Attributes length	14	20	16
100	G_{11}	G_{12}	G_{13}
150	G_{21}	G_{22}	G_{23}
200	G_{31}	G_{32}	G_{33}
75	G_{41}	G_{42}	G_{43}
125	G_{51}	G_{52}	G_{53}

$$C_{ij} = \text{cost of accessing the ith horizontal fragment} \times \frac{L(\text{attributes of the jth vertical fragment})}{L(\text{all attributes})}$$

$$\text{i.e)}\ C5 = 150 \times \frac{20}{14 + 20 + 16} = 60$$

Fig. 5 Cost model for merging grid cells

In the following illustration we use the join cost as a variabie to show how merging is dependent upon the join cost. For simplicity in notation we denote grid cell G_{11} as G_1 and grid cell G_{12} as G_2, and cost of accessing them as C_1 and C_2 respectively. The fragment formed by merging cells G_1 and G_2 as G_{12} with the cost of accessing as C_{12}. The frequency of transactions accessing the cells G_1, G_2 and G_{12} is denoted F_{1k}, F_{2k} and F_{12k} respectively. The parameter α is assumed to be 1.2. The projection cost is assumed to be 10.

The cost without merging is:

$$\Sigma^8_{k=1} F_{1k}C_1 = F_{14}*C_1 + F_{16}*C_1 = 35 * 28 + 25 * 28 = 1680$$

$$\Sigma^8_{k=1} F_{2k}C_2 = F_{24}*C_2 + F_{28}*C_2 = 35 * 40 + 15 * 40 = 2000$$

$$\Sigma^8_{k=1} F_{12k}J = F_{124}J = 35 * J$$

Where J is the cost of joining the grid cells G_1 and G_2 and the only transaction T4 accesses the merged fragment with frequency 35.

The cost with the merged cells is:

$$\Sigma^8_{k=1} F_{12k}C_{12} = F_{124}*C_{12} + F_{126}*C_{12} + F_{128}*C_{12} = 35 * 81.6 + 25 * 81.6 + 15 * 81.6 = 6120$$

$$\Sigma^8_{k=1} F_{1k}P_{1/12} + \Sigma^8_{k=1} F_{2K}P_{2/12} = F_{16}*P_{1/12} + F_{28}*P_{2/12} = 25 * 10 + 15 * 10 = 400$$

Where $C_{12} = \alpha * (C_1 + C_2) = 1.2 * (28 + 40) = 81.6$

We shall merge the two cells if:
$1680 + 2000 + 35*J > 6120 + 400$
i.e. if $35 *J > 2840$ or if $J > 81.11$

The objective of above example was to show that the two cells are merged on the basis of the join cost and the frequencies of the transactions accessing the cells. We call the results of the merging "mixed fragments". Figure 6 shows one feasible result of merging.

F1	F2	
F3		X1
F4	F5	X2
X3	X4	F6
X5	X6	X7

Fig. 6 Grid optimization

3.2.2 Allocation of mixed fragments

After merging grid cells, the allocation of the mixed fragments for a PC based distributed databases can easily be performed by using the transaction mapping information. Since the origin sites of each transaction are fixed, the fragments requested from only one site are allocated to the requesting sites. However, the fragments that are not accessed are allocated to a server for future use. For example, fragment F4 in Figure 6 is allocated to site S1 where transaction T1 is originated, F5 to S2, and F6 to S3 (See Figure 7, we assume that transaction T1, T4, and T7 be originated from site S1, etc.). Non-accessed fragments namely X1 to X7 are all allocated to a database server.

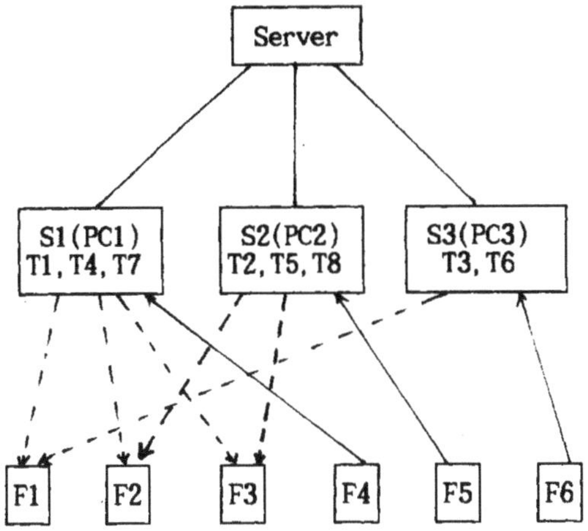

Fig 7. Allocation of the commonly accessed fragments

Now we consider the fragments that are accessed commonly. They can be allocated to a database server or to all the sites requesting them. If the commonly accessed fragments are allocated to a database server, queries are sent to the server and processed there, and then the result of the queries are sent back to the requesting sites. The cost for this scenario depends on the size of results, the frequency of requests, etc. On the other hand, if the commonly accessed fragments are replicated and allocated to all the requesting sites, we should consider the update cost for updating because an update query has effect on all copies of a fragment. Since update cost is determined by the number of replication and the unit cost per update, there is a trade-off between the transmission cost for results and update cost for the allocation of the commonly accessed fragments. For example, Figure 7 shows the environment of the allocation of the commonly accessed fragments in Figure 6. Note that fragment F1 is requested from both site S1 by transaction T4 and site S3 by transaction T6 (See Figure 4). Suppose that F1 be allocated to the server. Then to perform T4 we first send T4 to the server, and send the results of T4 back to S1. Update transaction T6 is performed on the server and no side effect is produced. If, however, we suppose that F1 be allocated to both sites S1 and S3, then T4 is performed at S1 but update transaction T6 gives rise to the updating for both copies of F1 to perform update operations.

4. CONCLUSION

In this paper we investigated several factors that should be considered for the development of effective PC-based distributed database systems. They are data fragmentation, data allocation, LAN, and database server. Then we proposed a methodology for PC-based distributed database design. This methodology, which is based on the mixed partitioning technique using a grid approach, can be done in the following two steps: (1) Grid optimization, (2) Allocation of the mixed fragments. For grid optimization, we developed a cost model and proposed a heuristic procedure for merging grid cells. The results of grid optimization is called "mixed fragments" and are allocated to the PCs on the corresponding sites by analyzing transactions. The proposed distribution scheme can improve the system performance by allowing data sharing among PCs and by optimizing total transaction processing cost.

Our work can be extended by incorporating performance evaluation methods for merging grid cells. We will also continue to study the architecture and functions that a database server should have.

REFERENCES

[Aper 88] Apers, P. M. G., "Data Allocation in Distributed Database Systems," ACM Trans. on Database Systems, Vol. 13, No. 3, pp.263-304, September 1988.

[Cart 84] Carter, G., Local Area Network, ICL, 1984.

[Ceri 82] Ceri, S., Negri, M., and Pelagatti, G., "Horizontal data Partitioning in Database Design," Proc. ACM SIGMOD International Conference on Management of Data, pp.128-136, 1982.

[Cer 83a] Ceri, S., and Navathe, S. B., "A Methodology to the Distribution Design of Databases," Proc. IEEE COMPCON Conference, San Francisco, CA., February 1983.

[Cer 83b] Ceri, S., Navathe, S. B., and Wiederhold, G., "Distribution Design of Logical Database Schemas," IEEE Trans. on Software Engineering, Vol. SE-9, No. 4, pp.487-504, July 1983.

[Ceri 84] Ceri, S., and Pelagatti, G., Distributed Databases : Principles and Systems, McGraw Hill, 1984.

[Ceri 88] Ceri, S., Perinici, B., and Wiederhold, G., "Optimization problems and Solution Methods in the Design of Data Distribution," Working Paper, Stanford University, 1988.

[Corn 87] Cornell, D. W., and Yu, P. S., "A Vertical Partitioning Algorithm for Relational Databases," Proc. Third International Conference on Data Engineering, pp.30-35, February 1987.

[Corn 88] Cornell, D. W., and Yu, P. S., "Site Assignment for Relations and Join Operations in the Distributed Transaction Processing Environment," Proc. Fourth International Conference on Data Engineering, Los Angeles, February 1988.

[Corn 89] Cornell. D. W., and Yu, P. S., "On Optimal Site Assignment for Relations in the Distributed Data Environment," IEEE Trans. on Software Engineering, Vol. 15, No. 8, pp.1004-1009, August 1989.

[Elma 89] Elmasri, R., and Navathe, S. B., Fundamentals of Database Systems, Benjamin /Cummings Publishing, 1989.

[Hamm 79] Hammer, M., and Niamir, B., "A Heuristic Approach to Attribute Partitioning," Proc. ACM SIGMOD International Conference on Management of Data, May 1979.

[Jord 90] Jordan, L., and Churchill, B., Communication and Networking for the IBM PC and Compatibles, Third Edition, Brady Books, New York, 1990.

[Nava 84] Navathe, S. B., Ceri, S., Wiederhold, G., and Dou, J., "Vertical Partitioning Algorithms for Database Design," ACM Trans. on Database Systems, Vol.9, No.4, pp.690-710, December 1984.

[Nava 89] Navathe, S. B., and Ra, M., "Vertical Partitioning for Database Design: A Graphical Algorithm," Proc. ACM SIGMOD International Conference on Management of Data, pp.440-450, May 1989.

[Nava 90] Navathe, S. B., Ra, M., Varadarajan, R., Karlapalem, K., and Streewastav, K., "A Mixed Partitioning Methodology for Distributed Database Design," UF-CIS TR 90-17, University of Florida, 1990.

[Ozsu 91] Ozsu, M. T., and Valduriez, P., Principles of Distributed Database Systems, Prentice Hall, 1991.

[Patt 90] Pattipatti, K. R., "A File Assignment Problem Model for Extended Local Area network Environments," The 10th International Conference on Distributed Computing Systems, Paris, France, May 1990.

[Ra 90] Ra, M., "Data Fragmentation and Allocation Algorithms for Distributed Database Design," Doctoral Dissertation, University of Florida, 1990.

[Ra 91] Ra, M., "A Graph-based Horizontal Partitioning Algorithm for Distributed Database Design," Journal of the Korea Information Science Society, Vol. 19, No. 1, 1992.

[Rein 89] Reiner, D. S., "PC-based Database Management System," ACM SIGMOD Tutorial, May 1989.

[Yu 85] Yu, C. T., Suen, C., Lam, K., and Siu, M. K., "Adaptive Record Clustering," ACM Trans. on Database Systems, Vol. 10, No. 2, pp.180-204, June 1985.

STRATEGIES FOR SELECTION FROM HETEROGENEOUS RELATIONS

Chiang Lee
Cheng-Lun Tsai

Institute of Information Engineering
National Cheng-Kung University
Tainan, Taiwan
Republic of China

leec@dblab.iie.ncku.edu.tw

ABSTRACT

In this paper, we propose solutions to resolving the domain mismatch problem. Processing data of mismatched domains in multiple databases will in general result in a very large amount of uncertain data. In the past, these data are considered in the same level of uncertainty. We modified the past model and classify the data uncertainty into multiple levels in accordance with the so-called mismatch hierarchy. Our solutions enhance the previously proposed approaches in the literature by allowing the user to specify the way the uncertain information is extracted. In this manner, the amount of uncertain information derived from the mismatched domains can be limited to those with lower uncertainty so as to improve the reliability of the answer. Also, a probability-based approach is proposed which can utilize the domain knowledge to find an optimal set of data in which the size of these data is the smallest but the degree of certainty (to be defined) is the highest.

KEYWORDS Heterogeneous databases, domain mismatch problems, maybe tuples.

1. INTRODUCTION

Due to the fast growth of communication speed and communication territory, there is an increasing need to share information among existing autonomous databases. This desire requires multidatabases to be interoperable [Lit86a&90, Car80, Dem89a&89b, Hsi89, She90, Tho90]. However, since these databases are established independently, various types of mismatch exist among them [Kim91]. One of the often seen mismatch is that the representations of the same information are in a similar but non-equivalent manner. This seemingly incompatible data representation causes the so-called domain mismatch problem in executing a multidatabase query.

1.1 The Domain Mismatch Problem

We use a simple example to illustrate the problem. Assume that there are two restaurant relations, R1 and R2, existed in two independent databases. Each of the relations has NAME, LOCATION, and CUISINE attributes. Assume that the domain of R1.CUISINE is {French, Italian, Chinese, Mexican} and the domain of R2.CUISINE is {Cantonese, Hunan, Szechuan, Taiwanese}. In other words, R2 only records Chinese restaurants. As we can see, there exists mismatch between the values of the two relations. If a simple selection query is to find all restaurants that serve Hunan food, the result obtained by traditional value matching method will include only tuples from R2, but none from R1. However, this is not a complete answer. In an environment of interoperable databases, it is required that the mismatch be resolved in order to access all relevant information from multidatabases. In the following, we give a brief survey on past solutions to the problem. Note that in this paper, we ignore the part of the data that can be processed in a traditional sense (e.g., the way to process R2). Only the part that cannot be processed in a traditional manner (e.g., R1) is the focus of the paper.

1.2 Past Solutions

The domain mismatch problems in interoperable databases are rather new. There are not many papers proposed a viable solution yet. Extensive research on this issue is still needed. Among the published works, Litwin and Vigier [Lit86b] proposed a solution using *dynamic attributes*, which allows the user to explicitly specify in a query the discrepancy between attributes. To achieve this, the query language is enhanced with new features such as the define_by clause. An example is as follows.

define_by R(QUALITY) = (***,20/20), (***,19/20), (**,18/20), (**,17/20)

It indicates that the QUALITY of '***' is equal to the score range from 19 to 20, etc. In this approach, it is the user's responsibility to resolve the mismatch. Although this may not be impossible for a knowledgeable and experienced user, it is rather difficult for a novice or occasional user.

Czejdo, Rusinkiewicz, and Embley [Cze87] proposed a different approach to resolving the similar problem by using the concept of *extended abstract data type*. An extended abstract type for an elementary data item is a representation of knowledge about a domain of data values and includes all necessary procedural and descriptive information needed in a particular context. The extended abstract data types of all items are grouped as a domain knowledge base. Heterogeneity is resolved by referring to the information in the domain knowledge base.

The characteristic of the above two approaches is that they resolve the mismatch between data by using an exact value mapping mechanism. More specifically, in [Lit86a, Lit86b, Cze87] one value in a domain corresponds (or is semantically equivalent) either to another value or to a set of values in another domain.

However, there are cases that exact mapping can not be found. DeMichiel [Dem89a&89b] relaxed the requirement of exact mapping between domains by allowing the mapping to be uncertain. This concept is supported by using the mechanisms of *virtual attributes* and *partial values*. In other words, a value in one domain may correspond to a set of "maybe" values in another domain in which only one of maybe values is correct. In this manner, the result of a query will contain uncertain (maybe) tuples.

Although the last approach avoided the need of specifying the resolution of mismatch in a query, it is not without problems. Some of the major ones are first, mismatch can exist in between more than one attributes of the relations. For example, besides the mismatch on CUISINE of two relations, the domain of LOCATION of R2 is {San Francisco, San Jose, Oakland} and that of R1 is {Richmond, North Beach, Chinatown}. Note that the values in the latter domain are the areas of San Francisco in the former domain. For a query like "Find a restaurant that serves Hunan food and resides in Richmond area", maybe tuples will be resulted from both relations. To the user, there is a need to distinguish the maybe tuples that are caused by different reasons. This distinction is even more important when more mismatched domains of attributes are involved. Secondly, maybe tuples can be resulted in evaluating each selection predicate. Intuitively, the number of maybe tuples can be much larger than the number of true tuples obtained in processing a multidatabase query. The more predicates in the selection condition, the more maybe tuples will be obtained. However, to the user the maybe tuples are not very useful information and the number is desired to be limited. How to select the more useful ones from a vast number of maybe tuples becomes an important issue. Thirdly, a query normally contains some selection conditions. To the user, the importance of the conditions can be different. For example, the location of the restaurant (in Richmond) is more important than the cuisine, if the user decides to have meal in Richmond no matter whether a restaurant serving Hunan food is found. To allow the user to have preference on the selection conditions, the query language must provide such capability that the user can specify his/her needs in the query.

1.3 Our Solutions and Paper Outline

In this paper, we propose several methods to improve the effectiveness of the previous approaches. The methods include a priority-based approach, a precision-based approach, a weight-based approach, and a probability-based approach. Each of the approaches can be used when mismatch exists in between multiple pairs of attribute. The first three approaches allow the user to specify in a query the preferred answer if there are maybe tuples resulted in the query processing. So the way that the query is processed is fixed. The system can not have an input to the optimization in selecting maybe tuples. The last approach utilizes the degree of certainty of the maybe tuples. We design an algorithm which can find an optimal answer that contains the least number of maybe tuples whose degree of certainty in total is the greatest.

Our focus in the paper is on selection query processing. Since the selection operation is one of the most fundamental DB operations, our result is extensible to the processing of other complex DB operations. The remaining sections of this paper are as follow. In Section 2, Section 3, and Section 4, we present a priority-based approach, a precision-based approach, and a weight-based approach, respectively. The probability-based approach is presented in Section 5. Finally in Section 6, a brief conclusion is presented.

2. A PRIORITY-BASED APPROACH

By enhancing the capability of a query language, this method allows the user to specify his/her requirement in a query. Note that the language used here (and in the next two approaches) is modified from SQL. We use it only for the purpose of easily presenting the key concepts of our idea. The detailed or formal definition of the language is not of our concern in the paper and omitted here for the continuation in presentation.

In general, a selection query has some selection predicates specifying the conditions that a qualifying tuple must satisfy. A predicate is normally a complex one (named **composite predicate**) which is a conjunction or disjunction of some **simple predicates**. A simple predicate is defined as a predicate involving only one attribute. For example, the simple predicate LOCATION="Tainan" involves the attribute LOCATION. For simplicity in presenting our methodologies, we will mean simple predicate whenever we mention predicate in the rest of the paper.

The key feature of this approach is to distinguish the importance of the predicates and to allow the user to specify the priorities of the predicates in a query. In the following, we show an extended SQL with a new statement called "PRIORITY" which allows the user to define the priority order of attributes in the simple predicates of the WHERE clause.

```
SELECT     attributes
FROM       multidatabase relations
WHERE      predicates containing attributes A1, A2,...,An
PRIORITY   A1,A2,...,An
```

In this informal SQL expression, the PRIORITY statement states that the attribute on the left has a higher priority than the attribute on the right (e.g., A_1 is the most important attribute and A_n the least important one). We notice that if only selection predicates appear in WHERE clause, the PRIORITY statement is in fact not necessary. The default priority of attributes can be defined in the same order as the attributes of the simple predicates appeared in the WHERE clause. The PRIORITY clause is needed when predicates such as joins (e.g., $A_1=A_3$ and $A_2=A_4$) inevitably disrupt their priority order of attributes which may be defined as $A_1 \succ A_2 \succ A_3 \succ A_4$, where "$\succ$" symbol indicates that the attribute on its left is higher in priority than the attribute on its right.

In query evaluation, the tuples satisfying all predicates (defined as **true tuples**) will certainly be selected. For those maybe tuples, since their maybe status can be caused in evaluating different predicates, we select as the result the tuple(s) whose maybe status is caused by the predicate ranked in the lowest position in PRIORITY. We use the following example to illustrate the idea. Assume that there are three simple predicates represented by using attributes A_1, A_2, and A_3, respectively. Their priority order is assigned as $A_1 \succ A_2 \succ A_3$. Suppose there are four maybe tuples obtained in the query processing as follows.

	A_1	A_2	A_3
tuple_1	T	M	T
tuple_2	M	M	T
tuple_3	T	T	M
tuple_4	M	M	M

where T stands for "true" and M for "maybe" in predicate evaluation. In this case, tuple_3 will be selected as the final result since its maybe status is resulted from evaluating predicate containing A_3, which is of the least concern to the user. The maybe status of tuple_1 and tuple_2 are caused by predicates contain A_2 and A_1, which are of higher priority than A_3 as defined in the query. tuple_4 is the worst choice due to an obvious reason.

From the above description, we can see that the user should give a higher priority to the attribute(s) whose evaluation is strongly desired to be true. This approach has the advantage that it provides the user a choice to obtain result that is truly demanded. For example, a user in San Jose will pass by San Francisco and would like to have Cantonese food there. To the user, LOCATION = "San Francisco" is the most important predicate since the user will not drive a long distance to another city for a meal. Thus, the user should give the LOCATION attribute a higher priority than the CUISINE attribute.

3. A PRECISION-BASED APPROACH

Besides listing the priority order of attributes, the user may wish to acquire the tuples that are more "correct" than the others. For example, the following shows the evaluation result of simple predicates containing attributes $A_1,\ldots,A_6$.

	A_1	A_2	A_3	A_4	A_5	A_6
tuple_1	T	M	T	T	T	T
tuple_2	T	T	T	M	M	M

If the priority of attributes is assigned as $A_1 \succ A_2 \succ A_3 \succ A_4 \succ A_5 \succ A_6$, then according to the first approach tuple_2 should be selected. However, from the view point of correctness, tuple_1 is more reliable since only one of the predicates is evaluated as maybe. This situation can occur when the user feels that the importances of attributes are about the same. In that case, the one(s) with most predicates evaluated to be true is (are) selected.

To provide the user with such a choice, the SQL is extended with another clause, called PRECISION. The PRECISION clause does not have any parameters. All attributes are considered as of equal importance. As an example, tuple_1 will be selected from the above two tuples if the PRECISION requirement is asked by the user. In this case, the priority of attributes is not a concern to the user. Note that the number of resultant maybe tuples obtained in this case can be much more than those obtained using the first approach.

4. A WEIGHT-BASED APPROACH

This approach is used to improve the flexibility of the above two approaches. A WEIGHT clause in place of PRIORITY and PRECISION is designed for this purpose. The SQL can be like

```
SELECT   attributes
FROM     multidatabase relations
WHERE    predicates containing attributes A1, ...,An
WEIGHT   A1 w1, A2 w2, ...,An wn, θ
```

where $A_1,\ldots,A_n$ are attributes appeared in the predicates in WHERE clause and $w_1,\ldots,w_n$ are weights associated with those attributes. The values of weight are given by the user. A high weight assigned to an attribute means that the user would prefer the evaluation of the corresponding simple predicate to be true. θ is a threshold that only the tuples whose weights are <u>greater</u> than this value will be selected. The total weight of a tuple is calculated as follows:

$$Total\ weight=\sum_{i=1}^{n}\delta_i * w_i$$

where δ_i is defined as

$\delta_i =$ 1, if the tuple is evaluated to be true using the predicate containing A_i,
0, if the tuple is evaluated as maybe.

Note that we did not consider the "false" case in δ_i since if a predicate evaluation is false for a certain tuple and the tuple still satisfies the conditions in WHERE, then the predicate must be OR-ed with other predicates in the selection condition. For this reason, we need not consider the weight caused by this predicate. In another case, the tuple is evaluated as a false tuple. Then, the tuple is discarded and the weight of its attribute need not be counted either.

Here we use a simple example to illustrate the method. Assume that in a selection query there are four simple predicates containing attributes A_1, A_2, A_3, and A_4, and their weights are assigned as 4, 1, 3, and 1, respectively. Consider tuple_1 and tuple_2 shown below.

	A_1	A_2	A_3	A_4	Total weight
tuple_1	T	M	T	M	4+3=7
tuple_2	M	T	T	M	1+3=4

If the θ value is 5, then only tuple_1 is selected. Note that when all weights are equal, this approach is the same as the Precision-Based Approach. Also, by assigning weights from large to small values in order, this method mimics the Priority-Based Approach.

Up to now, we have presented three approaches that allow the user to specify his/her need in a query. Note that there can be other ways to achieve this goal. We only present those that are more likely to be required by the user.

5. A PROBABILITY-BASED APPROACH

There are cases that the user does not give a specification in a query but wishes the multidatabase system to find from the set of maybe tuples those most likely to be correct. In this section, we present such an approach which is probability-based. In the method, since a new concept, called *mismatch hierarchy*, will be used, we first present the concept. Following that, the method is presented.

5.1 Mismatch Hierarchy

In studying the past approaches we found that in their solutions, when there is mismatch between two domains of values, only these two mismatched sets of values are dealt with in processing a query. The fact that

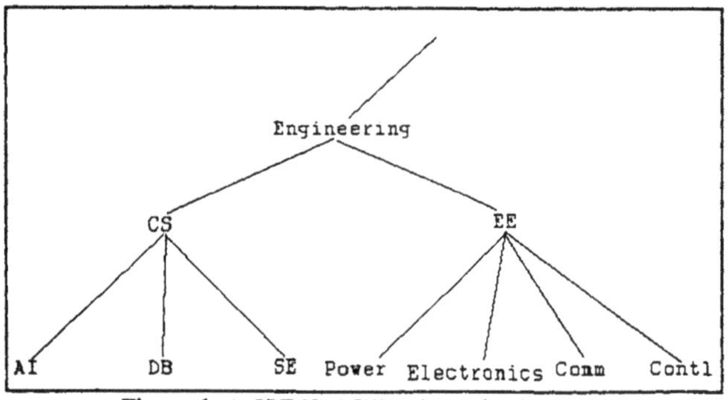

Figure 1. A SPECIALTY mismatch hierarchy.

the extent of mismatch can be different for different attributes is not considered. We distinguish mismatches between attributes, organize them in a structured manner, and utilize the information in query processing.

An example shown in Figure 1 illustrates the concept. The SPECIALTY attribute of faculty relations in multidatabases may contain data that are represented at so many levels. Each level of values corresponds to a domain that mismatches with the values in another level, which corresponds to another domain of attribute in a different relation. The integrated levels of mismatches that are within the same hierarchy reflect various possible mismatches among the relations that have a SPECIALTY (or semantically equivalent) attribute. For this reason, we call it the mismatch hierarchy. The past definitions on domain mismatch concept are considered as a special case of the proposed concept.

The mismatch hierarchy concept entails improvements in the execution of selection, join, and update operations. Since the issues with join and update operations are not the focus of the paper, we will only present the result relevant to selection operation. Readers may refer to [Lee92] for details on other operations.

In performing a selection operation, if the selection condition is issued at a certain level (say, the i-th level) of the mismatch hierarchy and the tuples of a relation are represented at any of the levels higher than the i-th level, where i<j (i.e., closer to the root of the hierarchy than level i), then in processing a query these tuples can be distinguished into two sets. One of the sets contains tuples that may satisfy the condition (i.e., those having an attribute value which in the hierarchy is a direct ancestor of the value in selection condition), and another contains tuples that are definitely undesirable (i.e., those having an attribute value that is not a direct ancestor of the value in selection condition). The second set of tuples can be discarded, since it is certain that they do not satisfy the selection condition. In the first set, each of the maybe tuples has a *degree of certainty* (to be defined). The degree of certainty of a maybe tuple can be different from that of another maybe tuple, if their values are represented at different levels in the mismatch hierarchy. From this, it is apparent that simply a "maybe" status assigned to each resultant tuple as indicated in past approaches is not precise enough. Instead, the "maybe" value should be split into multiple levels, each corresponding to a certain degree of certainty. If each of these maybe tuples (represented at level i of the mismatch hierarchy) is associated with a degree of certainty and the selection predicate is represented at level j (where i<j), we can envision a fact that the greater the distance between i and j, the less precise is the tuple representation with respect to that of the selection predicate, resulting in more qualifying maybe tuples, each with a lower degree of certainty. Thus, there is a need to limit the number of those tuples so as to improve the accuracy of the final result.

5.2 The Method

5.2.1 The Basic Concept

Let us illustrate the concept of our method by using an example. Assume that there are some multidatabase restaurant relations containing a LOCATION attribute whose mismatch hierarchy is shown in Figure 2. A query is to search for one restaurant located in Tainan:

$$\sigma_{LOCATION="Tainan"}R$$

where we have used a R to stand for all restaurant relations in the multidatabases. Note that the query is issued at level 2 of the mismatch hierarchy. If no tuples can satisfy the condition, the predicate will be modified to re-evaluate the tuples. The modification is made by moving its content value up along the path of its direct ancestors in the mismatch hierarchy. Note that we do not

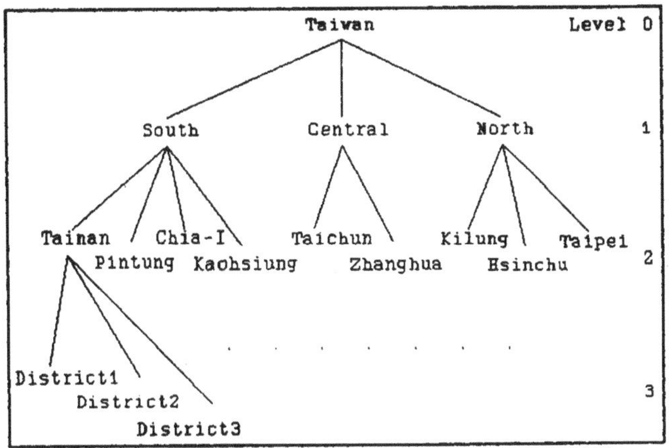

Figure 2. An example mismatch hierarchy of LOCATION.

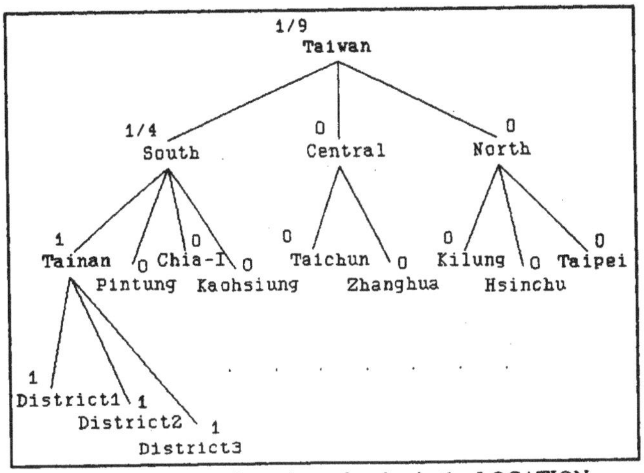

Figure 3. Degree of certainty of nodes in the LOCATION mismatch hierarchy.

move the predicate down the hierarchy because in that case, the selection condition becomes more rigorous such that still no qualifying tuples will be found. If the predicate is moved up one level, the selection predicate is modified as follows:

LOCATION = "South Taiwan"

The qualifying tuples obtained by using the modified predicate are maybe tuples. The higher level to which a predicate moves, the lower is an obtained maybe tuple's certainty. Let

$T^M(i)$ = the number of resultant maybe tuples when the predicate moves up to level i of the mismatch hierarchy during query processing

If there are n predicates in a query, then representation of the above parameter can be generalized as $T^M(i_1,\ldots,i_n)$, where i_j is the level that the j-th predicate moves to. Since maybe tuples can be obtained in evaluating each predicate and the numbers of maybe tuples corresponding to predicates can be different, it is possible that by adjusting each predicate level in their mismatch hierarchies, we can find the <u>least</u> number of maybe tuples that will <u>most</u> likely contain a correct one (i.e., one that truly desired by the user). Details of the method are presented in the following.

5.2.2 Degree of Certainty Represented by Probability

In this approach, each node in a mismatch hierarchy has a probability which is used to represent the degree of certainty of a maybe tuple. For a given query, the probability of each node in a mismatch hierarchy is created as follows. Let n_{ij} denote the j-th node in the level i of the hierarchy and m_i denote the number of nodes in level i. Assume that the value of a predicate (i.e., "Tainan") is equal to the value at node n_{ij}. The probability of node n_{ij} is assigned to 1 as shown in Figure 3, since node n_{ij}'s value (being "Tainan") is identical to the given value in the selection query. The probabilities of n_{ij}'s descendents (containing more specific domain information than "Tainan") are all assigned to 1, since tuples having those values will also satisfy the selection query. The probabilities of those nodes at level i but other than n_{ij} are all assigned to 0, since values of those nodes do not satisfy the query. The probabilities of the descendents of nodes n_{ik}, where $1 \le k \le m_i$ and $k \ne j$, are also assigned to 0 due to the same reason. The probability of node n_{ij}'s ancestors, say n_{pq} where $0 \le p \le i-1$, is assigned to

1/(the number of descendents of node n_{pq} at level i)

This means that if the predicate LOCATION = "Tainan" moves up to LOCATION = "South Taiwan" and then matches with a relation tuple, then there is a probability of 1/4 that its value indeed means "Tainan". The reason is that there are four values, {Tainan, Ping-Tung, Kao-Hsiung, Cha-I}, corresponding to "South Taiwan". A tuple of LOCATION's value being "South Taiwan" can really mean any of the cities within South Taiwan. Their probabilities are equivalent. In other words, when a predicate promotes from "Tainan" to "South Taiwan" and a tuple's LOCATION value matches with this value, then the probability of the maybe tuple which is correct (i.e., the degree of certainty) is 1/4. If the predicate promotes to LOCATION = "Taiwan", then the degree of certainty of a tuple which satisfies this predicate will be 1/9.

Note that in the above we only discuss the case that one attribute is involved in a query. Generally speaking, there may be more than one attributes in a query and each of their corresponding predicates can cause the evaluation of a tuple to become a maybe tuple. Assuming that there are n selection predicates in a query. The degree of certainty of a tuple in this situation is

$$T^P(j_1,j_2,\ldots,j_n) = Prob(i_1,j_1)*Prob(i_2,j_2)*\ldots*Prob(i_n,j_n)$$

where i_k is the level of the node that the k-th predicate promotes to and j_k is the j-th node in level i_k. $Prob(i_k,j_k)$ is the certainty degree of the j-th node in the i-th level for the k-th predicate.

Next we need to consider in what order the multiple predicates are promoted in their mismatch hierarchies, since this order will significantly affect the accuracy and the size of the result. This issue is answered in the algorithm of the next subsection.

5.2.3 The Algorithm

The goal of our method is to minimize the number of maybe tuples and at the same time to maximize the total certainty degree of maybe tuples. To achieve this, the query processing should start from moving the predicate among others that gives the highest chance in gaining a true tuple. Calculation details are as follows. (Another similar, but suboptimal, algorithm is given in Appendix for reference.)

ALGORITHM

/* In general, a query contains n predicates. Each predicate has a corresponding mismatch hierarchy and the k-th predicate is at the i_k-th level of the hierarchy. */

Initially, n predicates are at level $i_1, i_2, \ldots,$ and i_n of their corresponding mismatch hierarchies.
A state can be represented by a n-tuple $s(i_1,\ldots,i_n)$ or simply an s.
Define $s_k = s(i_1, \ldots, i_{k-1}, i_k-1, i_{k+1}, \ldots, i_n)$.
    /* This state indicates that the k-th predicate moves up one level. */
Define the energy of a state as $E(s) = T^M(s)*T^P(s)$.
Define the expected number of true tuples in the set of resultant maybe tuples as ET^h.
Initially, $ET^h=0$.

REPEAT
    Current state $= s(i_1,\ldots,i_n)$;
    $E(s) = T^M(s)*T^P(s)$ is the current energy;
    Find from $\{s_1, s_2, \ldots, s_n\}$ such that $T^P(s) = MAX_{1\le k\le n}T^P(s_k)$;
    Let $S=\{s_1, s_2, \ldots, s_m\}$ be the set whose elements satisfy the MAX condition;
    Find from $\{s_1, s_2, \ldots, s_m\}$ such that $T^M(s) = MIN_{1\le k\le m}T^M(s_k)$;
    Let $S'=\{s_1, s_2, \ldots, s_p)$ be the set whose elements satisfy the MIN condition;
    k=0;
    WHILE (NOT $ET^h \ge 1$) AND $k \le p$ DO
        k = k+1;
        IF $i_k \neq 0$
            THEN $ET^h = ET^h + E(s_k)$;
                $i_k = i_k-1$;
    END;
UNTIL $ET^h \ge 1$ OR $i_1=i_2=\ldots=i_n=0$.
END.

In this algorithm, we presented the calculation of ET^h, the expected number of true tuples, based on the $T^M(i_1,\ldots,i_n)$ and the $T^P(i_1,\ldots,i_n)$ proposed in the previous subsections. The value "1" in the inequality criterion $ET^h \ge 1$ indicates that only one true tuple is expected from the set of resultant maybe tuples. The value can be replaced by a N ($\in$ positive integer), if more true tuples are expected. The second termination condition of this algorithm is $i_1=i_2=\ldots=i_n=0$. This occurs when all the predicates have moved up to the root of their corresponding mismatch hierarchies and still the system has not find enough high probability tuples to satisfy the criterion $ET^h \ge 1$. In this situation, the algorithm is forced to terminate while the result is unsatisfactory.

Definition 1:

M^N-set is a set of maybe tuples whose degree of certainty in total is at least N.

Definition 2:

A M^N-set is *optimal* if it contains the least number of elements (i.e., maybe tuples) for a given N.

THEOREM 1

The result obtained by using the above algorithm is an optimal M^I-set if the algorithm terminates at the condition $ET^h \ge 1$.

Proof: The set of resultant maybe tuples is an M^I-set due to the condition $ET^h \ge 1$. Next, since the algorithm finds in each iteration the maximum $T^P(\cdot)$ values for all s_k, the sequence of the obtained $T^P(\cdot)$ values is non-increasing. For a similar reason, the sequence of obtained $T^M(\cdot)$ values is non-decreasing. Since the $T^P(\cdot)$ values are non-increasing, the algorithm ended with the fewest number of larger $T^P(\cdot)$ values. Since non-decreasing, the $T^M(\cdot)$ values multiplied by these $T^P(\cdot)$ values form the smallest set of maybe tuples. ∎

Corollary 1:

If the algorithm terminates at $i_1=i_2=\ldots=i_n=0$, then the result is not an M^I-set. Also, the result is irrelevant to the order on which the promotion of the predicates are based.

Proof: If any two algorithms start with the same initial condition (i.e., the same initial state s and the same set of mismatch hierarchies) and both ended at this termination condition, then the $T^P(\cdot)$ and the $T^M(\cdot)$ values for all states are identical. In other words, the result sets obtained by using these two algorithms are the same. ∎

Corollary 2:

Theorem 1 and Corollary 1 are still true for an M^N-set.

Proof: It is quite self-evident. ∎

Note that the theorem states that the result is optimal in the sense that it contains the minimum set of maybe tuples with each of them having the highest probability to be true. Certainly, we note that there is no guarantee that this optimal set of maybe tuples will indeed contain a true tuple. We only claim that in searching for a true tuple from a vast space of maybe tuples, our solution provides a heuristically optimal answer to the user.

Finally, before we leave this section, we take a final look at the approaches presented in this and the previous sections. The main advantage of the three approaches proposed in Section 2, Section 3, and Section 4 is to limit the number of resultant maybe tuples so that the user will not receive too many of them from the system with each of the tuples having only a slim chance to be correct. However, these methods are still improvable in the sense that they did not well utilize all the mismatch information existed in multidatabases. Also, they are not flexible enough to optimize the number of useful maybe tuples, because once a method is selected (fixed in processing one query), the system can not contribute to optimize the number of output tuples. In the approach presented in this section, however, the system utilizes the degree of certainty of a tuple and optimizes the answer for the user.

6. CONCLUSIONS AND FUTURE WORK

We have presented several solutions to the domain mismatch problems in a heterogeneous databases environment. These solutions combines some of the features in previous approaches in the sense that maybe results are allowed to exist in query processing (as in [Dem89b]), and that the user can give specification on the selection predicates in the WHERE clause (as in [Lit86b]).

Also, a probablistic approach to the same problem was proposed. The advantage of this approach is to utilize in query processing the abundant domain knowledge contained in multiple databases so as to select a minimum set of maybe tuples whose degree of certainty in total is the maximum.

Besides the difficulties in executing a selection query, the multi-level mismatched domains in heterogeneous databases also cause troubles in performing join as well as update queries. From the view point of mismatch hierarchy, these problems are more complex than those presented in previous proposals. They are discussed in the following.

(i) *Difficulties in Executing a Join Query*

In performing a join operation, if the join attribute values are represented at different levels of the mismatch hierarchy, the result will be a null set since none of the identical value pairs can be found. However, it is possible that some of the tuples in two database relations indeed represent the same entity and are therefore joinable. To resolve this mismatch problem, we need to define a non-traditional join operation which can be performed over attributes of mismatched domains. Note that this problem is different from the join problem proposed in [Dem89b]. From our point of view, their mismatch only occurs between domains of two different levels. However, there was no discussion on the situation when there are more than two relations to be joined and mismatch exists among join domains of those relations. In this case, the mismatch hierarchy formed by the join domains is expected to be used in the operation.

(ii) *Difficulties in Executing an Update Query:*

As for update in heterogeneous databases, the operation is normally not allowed. The reason is similar to the above ones that the update condition can be given at level j of the domain hierarchy and the relation tuples are represented at level i where $i<j$. In this circumstance, we can only find tuples that may satisfy the update condition. This is not strong enough in order to update the tuple since there is still a chance that the tuple is not what the user desired. Update on these data can cause inconsistency. More importantly, even if there is another relation whose tuples happen to be represented at the same level as the update condition is (i.e., there is no mismatch problem for this relation), its tuples are still not allowed to be updated since the update may cause data inconsistency between this and other relations . Note that a value of some attribute can be updated only if the update condition does not result in any maybe tuples in processing all the other attributes of domains semantically similar to the domain of that attribute. The exceptionally difficult part to do is that the relations containing these semantically similar attributes may not all be given in the update request. Due to these difficulties, the update issue is seldom discussed in the literature. It is still a hard problem yet to be solved.

Currently, we are looking into the issues presented above. Also, we are considering the problem that two mismatch hierarchies may overlap. In this case, some more involved issues are to be studied. Some preliminary result for join and update operation has been obtained [Lee92] and a solid solution is under development.

REFERENCES

[Ahm91] Ahmed, R., P.D. Smedt, W. Du, W. Kent, M.A. Ketabchi, W.A. Litwin, A. Rafii, and M.C. Shan, "The Pegasus Heterogeneous Multidatabase System", IEEE Computer, Vol. 24, No. 12, December 1991.

[Bat86] Batini, C., M. Lenzerini, and S.B. Navathe, "A Comparative of Methodologies for Database Schema Integration", ACM Computing Surveys, Vol. 18, No. 4, December 1986.

[Car80a] Cardenas, A. F., "Heterogeneous Distributed Database Management: The HD-DBMS", Proceeding of The IEEE, Vol. 75, No. 5, May 1987.

[Car80b] Cardenas, A. F., M.H. Pirahesh, "Data Base Communication in A Heterogeneous Data Base Management System Network", Information Systems, Vol. 5, 1980.

[Cze87] Czejdo, B., M. Rusinkiewicz, and D.W. Embley, "An Approach to Schema Integration and Query Formulation in Federated Database Systems", Proceedings of Third International Conference on Data Engineering.

[Day84] Dayal, U., and H.Y. Hwang, "View Definition and Generalization for Database Integration in a Multidatabase System", IEEE Transactions on Software Engineering, Vol. SE-10, No. 6, November 1984.

[Dem89a] Demichiel, L. G., "Performing Operations over Mismatched Domain.", IEEE Proceedings of the Fifth

International Conference on Data Engineering, 1989.

[Dem89b] Demichiel, L. G., "Resolving Database Incompatibility", IEEE Transactions on Knowledge and Data Engineering, 1:4 (Dec. 1989).

[Elm90] Elmagarmid, A. K., Y. Leu, W. Litwin, Rusinkiewicz, M., "A Multidatabase Transaction Model for InterBase", Proceedings of the 16th VLDB Conference, Brisbane, Australia, 1990.

[Gra91] Grant, J., W. Litwin, N. Roussopoulos, and T. Sellis, "An Algebra and Calculus for Relational Multidatabase Systems", Proceedings of First International Workshop on Interoperability in Multidatabase Systems, April 1991.

[Hsi89] Hsiao, David K. and Magdi N. Kamel, "Heterogeneous Databases: Proliferations, Issues, and Solutions", IEEE Transactions on Knowledge and Data Engineering, Vol. 1, No. 1, Mar. 1989.

[Hsi90] Hsiao, David K., Tutorial notes on Federated Databases and Systems, in the VLDB Conference, Australia, August 1990.

[IMS91] The Proceedings of the First International Workshop on Interoperability in Multidatabase Systems, Ed. Y. Kambayashi, M. Rusinkiewicz, and A. Sheth, Kyoto, Japan, 1991.

[Kim91] Kim, Won, Jungyun Seo, "Classifying Schematic and Data Heterogeneity in Multidatabase systems", IEEE Computer, Vol. 24, No. 12, December 1991.

[Kri91] Krishnamurthy, Ravi, Witold Litwin, and, William Kent, "Language Features for Interoperability of Databases with Schematic Discrepancies" ACM SIGMOD Conference on Management of Data, 1991.

[Kri91] Krishnamurthy, Ravi, Witold Litwin, and William Kent, "Interoperability of Heterogeneous Databases with Schematic Discrepancies", Proceedings of First International Workshop on Interoperability in Multidatabase Systems, April 1991.

[Lee92] Lee, C. and Tsai C.-L., "Executing Join and Update Operations in Heterogeneous Databases," Technical Report #81-415, 1992.

[Lit86a] Litwin, W., A. Abdellatif, "Multidatabase Interoperability", IEEE Computer (Dec. 1986)

[Lit86b] Litwin. W., P. Vigier, "Dynamic Attributes on the Multidatabase system MRDSM", IEEE International Conference on Data Engineering, 1986.

[Lit87] Litwin, W., A. Abdellatif, "An Overview of the Multi-Database Manipulation Language MDSL", Proceeding of The IEEE, Vol. 75, No. 5, May 1987.

[Lit90] Litwin, W., Leo Mark, Roussopoulos, Nick, "Interoperability of Multiple Autonomous Databases", ACM Computering Surveys, Vol 22, Number 3, September 1990.

[Raf91] Rafii, A., R. Ahmed, P. DeSmedt, B. Kent, M. Ketabchi, W. Litwin, and M.-C. Shan, "Multidatabase Management in Pegasus", Proceedings of First International Workshop on Interoperability in Multidatabase Systems, April 1991

[She90] Sheth, Amit p., James A. Larson, "Federated Database Systems for Managing Distributed, Heterogeneous, and Autonomous Databases", ACM Computering Surveys, Vol. 22, Number 3, September 1990.

[Tho90] Thomas, G., G.R. Thompson, C.W. Chung, E. Barkmeyer, F. Carter, M. Templeton, S. Fox, and B. Hartman, "Heterogeneous Distributed Database Systems for Production Use", ACM Computering Surveys, Vol. 22, Number 3, September 1990.

APPENDIX

A suboptimal algorithm for obtaining maybe tuples that satisfy the $ET^{\wedge} \geq 1$ condition is given in the following. This algorithm retrieves the maybe tuples from the energy point of view.

ALGORITHM

A state s in the process of the query execution is represented by a n-tuple $(i_1,\ldots,i_n)$.
Define the energy of a state as $E(s) = T^M(s)*T^P(s)$.
Define the expected number of true tuples in the set of resultant maybe tuples as $ET^{\wedge}$.

```
REPEAT
    The current state s is (i_1,...,i_n);
    E(s) = T^M(s)*T^P(s) is the current energy;
    Find Cont = MAX_{1≤k≤n}(E(s')-E(s)), where s' is
    (i_1,..,i_{k-1},i_k-1,i_{k+1},..,i_n);
        /* The k-th predicate moves up one level;
        "Cont" stands for the contribution due to a
        predicate's move in the hierarchy. */
    ET^ = ET^ + Cont;
    s = s';
UNTIL ET^ ≥ 1 or i_1=i_2=...=i_n=0.
END.
```

Industrial Database Applications

Information Integration through Contract

Toncan Duong, John Hiller, Anne Ngu
School of Computer Science & Engineering,
University of New South Wales
Kensington, Australia

ABSTRACT

We propose a new architecture to integrate information for a multi-databases environment. It can be used in a wide range of configurations and has advantages over other approaches when the connections between databases are dynamic and numerous. The proposal emphasizes the autonomy in each system and includes a flexible negotiation processor to import/export data. Its main features are:

i) Explicit specification of How, When and What to integrate,
ii) Support for re-using of established integrations,
iii) Support for different ways to integrate data, and
iv) Conceptual simplicity.

1. INTRODUCTION

Data integration has evolved from a globally centralized approach to an autonomous federation of information systems. There remain some unsolved problems, such as how to identify the same object irrespective of its forms [EK91, KE91a, KE91b], how to interrelate different data models [SM81, BO86, CH90, KR91, PE91a, PE91b], how to resolve heterogeneities in structure and semantics [KE91b, SL90], and how to effectively model the integrating systems [SL90]. This paper concentrates on the last issue and proposes a *Contracting Mechanism* that can be used in a static environment where the integrating data is specific, as well as in a dynamic environment where the data needs to be negotiated and clarified.

There are different ways in which two systems come to data integration. Some integrations are specific and have a nominated provider and receiver as well as the set of data involved. Other integrations are task oriented and initially do not have a particular provider. Here the receiving system needs to negotiate with other systems for its requirements; the system that is selected to supply the data then becomes the provider. Also, if the task has not detailed exactly the data required, the actual data used in the integration may only become clear during the negotiation. Also, integration can be ad-hoc or permanent, the former has only a short life-span and tends to be numerous. Our proposal can support these different configurations by a suitable data structure—*contract*, and a flexible *negotiation* mechanism.

Each *contract* specifies an integration task; besides nominating the data from the provider and the data that is expected from the receiver; it also specifies how and when the integration is effected. Contracts are stored and maintained locally and only at the relevant systems; we argue that this provides a robust and efficient integration environment because multiple contracts can get executed simultaneously and the failure of a system affects only the systems that it is contracting with.

To integrate data from different databases, it needs to accommodate the structural as well as semantic differences. While there are already some useful tools to translate between different data structures [SP91], the semantic differences like synonyms, homonyms, classification and descriptive differences[1], are much harder to resolve because the description may be deficient. Often the user-experience is needed to resolve these difficulties before data correspondence can be established; we look to extensively using the DBA to clarify 'impasses' in negotiation.

[SL90] suggested a reference model for multi-databases. It consists of five layers, namely local schema, component schema, export schema, federated schema and external schema (fig.1a). With the exception of local schema, all layers are expressible in a canonical data model. The reference model requires the whole local schema to get translated to the component schema but often only a subset needs to be exported for a particular integration. Federated schema is the integrated view of a number of these exported schemas and above this, is the external schema. Note that there may be many federated schemas contributing to one external schema.

Our proposal reflects the top four layers by a Contracting Mechanism (fig.1b). We will show that this architecture is expressive and sufficiently flexible to cover a wide range of integration needs, in particular, it emphasizes the 'openness' in that the needed information may be acquired elsewhere on the network by negotiation.

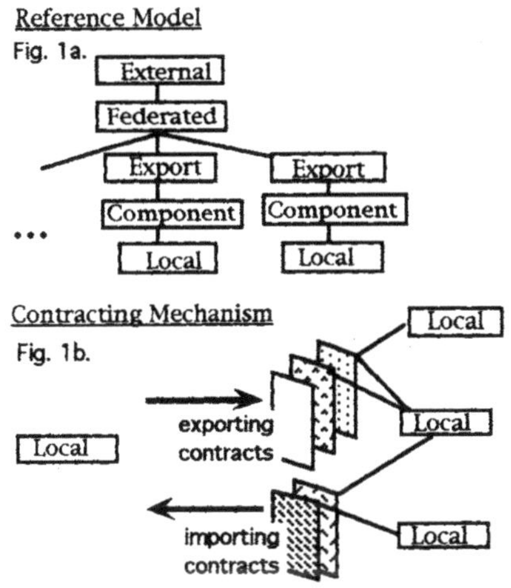

Fig 1. Reference model (1a) as reproduced from [SL90] and 'Contracting Mechanism' (1b). In the 'contracting mechanism', each system may have series of exporting and importing contracts that it has engaged, the arrow denotes the data flow from a provider to a receiver.

The remainder of this paper is organized as follows. In section 2 we discuss the various aspects of the 'Contracting Mechanism'. This includes a detailed description of the 'contract', the hierarchic organization of contracts within each system, the issue of reusability and a brief introduction to various processors. In section 3 we discuss linguistic indices and their use to correlate contracts names across the systems. In section 4 we discuss the negotiation process, section 5 discusses and compares the proposed with other approaches. Lastly, section 6 summarizes and expands issues that need further research and development.

[1] Classification difference occurs when the same entity is classified differently, for example, "Gone with the Wind" may be classified as "novel" or "oeuvre" . Whereas Descriptive difference occurs when the same class like "Car", is described differently in different databases. For example, the attributes of "Car" are (registration#, year, make) in database-A, but in database-B, the same concept "Car" may have different set of attributes as (owner, engine#, year, model) .

2. CONTRACTING MECHANISM

Contracting Mechanism is a framework for data integration using the concepts of *'contract'* and *'negotiation'*. It forms an interconnecting network (fig.2a) of which each node is an autonomous database and each link represents a data interchange; the link is directional and joins the providing system to the receiving system. The mechanism proposed supports 'dynamic' integration in the sense that the total data available to a particular database is not bound by a pre-defined export schema but depends only on the response of the network at the time. It should be noted that there is no explicit 'joining' or 'quitting' of the network; every system on the network has a 'contracting module' (fig.2b) and can integrate with other systems without the need to register on a 'federated' or 'global' schema. Actually, we argue that it is not feasible to completely define every possible need by an 'overall schema' and look to model the integration environment on a 'needs basis'. Also as the specification for integration is stored locally and only at the systems which are involved, it is intrinsically secure and robust.

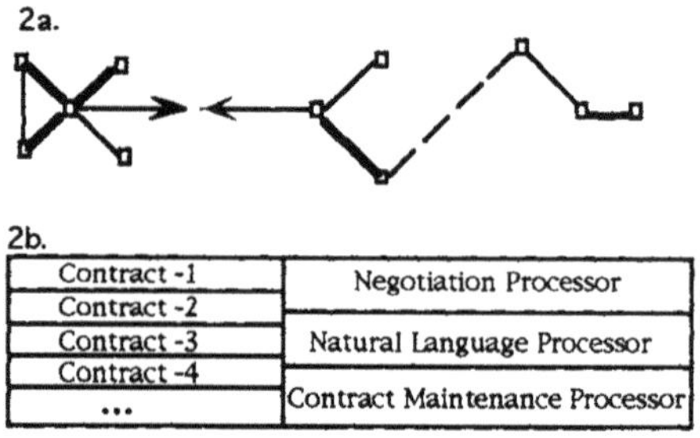

Fig.2. a) Integration network: each o represents an autonomous database and each link represents a contract, — represents a one-off contract, — represents a permanent contract, - - - represents an ad-hoc contract (short life-span) and the arrow pair represents the negotiation of a new contract. (The link is directional but for clarity purpose, the arrow is omitted). b) Contracting Module: each system has a set of contracts managed by three processors of Negotiation, Natural Language and Maintenance.

Each 'contracting module' has three processors. The Negotiation Processor (NP) is used to negotiate a new contract when external data is required and to respond to requests from other NP's (see section 4). The Natural Language Processor (NLP) is used to linguistically index the contract names and to match the name supplied by the NP with the ones registered in the export list[2] (see section 3). The Contract Maintenance Processor (MP) is used to maintain the contract hierarchy (see 2.1.2), its functions include adding a new contract after successful negotiation or subtracting an existing contract when it is terminated; when a contract lapses, the MP needs to notify its provider and receivers and delete the relevant entries in the hierarchy.

2.1. Contracts

[BR90] commented on the limitations of the global schema approach as being single semantic and redundant in nature. Federated systems [HM85] adopts a more flexible technique; for each application that may access external data, the local database needs to establish a schema for only the data required. The Contracting Mechanism corresponds to the federated approach but it models each integration as a named task or contract, that includes not only the data specification but also its execution conditions.

Autonomous systems may differ in their data models, data semantics and design assumptions [SC91]. The data translation between these systems may be direct or via a canonical data structure (CDS). The direct technique incurs N(N-1) possible mappings between N systems whereas the use of a canonical data structure reduces to 2N mappings. We choose to use the CDS approach but the choice of a particular CDS is an issue of expressiveness and semantic relativism, this will not be discussed further.

Each contract is uniquely identified by its header—*<Name_of_Contract,Provider,Receiver>*, and may have aliases. A contract name needs to meaningfully denoting the integration task because it will be indexed and subsequently used by the NLP for negotiation. The contract body contains clauses expressing the data required in the form of a CDS, comments, a conditional block and protocol statements. The protocol statements has two parts: one specifies the mapping from the provider to the CDS and the other specifies the mapping from the CDS to the receiver. The mapping needs not be simple, it can include the code to merge conflicting data; but for clarity, we will use a simple example to illustrate the concepts.

```
Contract Header
Contract Body
  Comment
  Clauses of contract
  { Conditional block }
  Protocol statements
    {Protocol (Provider) statements }
    { Protocol (Receiver) statements }
End
```

Example :

Alpha is a relational database of a financial company and has the following relations :

- Staff(name, address, tel#, staff#, salary)
- Customer(name, address, tel#, contact_name, position)

Beta is an Object-Oriented database of a mail-order house and has the class hierarchy as follows :

```
Object
  Person(name, address, age, tel#)
    Employee(employer, addr, work_tel#)
```

The following is a contract named *Contact (Mail-Order)* provided by Alpha to Beta :

```
<Contact (Mail-Order), Alpha, Beta>
 Comment =
  - Alpha is the database of a financial company and Beta is the database
    of a mail-order company.
  - A list of contacts is provided by Alpha to Beta for all its staff who are
    earning more than 5K.
 Clauses = {name, telephone#, address, company="Alpha" }
 Conditions =
  Time = [01/01/91 .. ∞]
  Termination = unilateral
  Binding = one-off
  Controller = {Alpha}
  Sub-contractible = no
 Protocol =
  // Provider
  Alpha is RDBMS
   name=Alpha .Staff.name where salary > 5K
   telephone# = Alpha .Staff.tel# where salary > 5K
   address = Alpha .Staff.address where salary > 5K
  // Receiver
  Beta is OODBMS
   name=Beta .Object.Employee.name
   telephone# = Beta .Object.Employee.work_tel#
   address = Beta .Object.Employee.addr
   company=Beta.Object.Employee.employer
```

[2] Each database has an export list containing all the contract names that it is a provider

2.2. Contract Specifications

A contract has two parts; the conditions under which it will be executed and the terms that it needs to fulfil. The former control the invocation of a query processor when external data is needed. The latter are used by the query processor to retrieve data and transform it to a useful format required by the receiver.

Conditions

Time : Each contract has a life-time. For example, [01/01/92 .. ∞] specifies that the contract starts from 01-Jan-91 and lasts forever. Time specification can be qualified by a periodic term like ∀[9:00-17:00] to restrict the access from 9 a.m. to 5 p.m. each day.

Termination : A contract may get terminated uni- or bi-laterally. Unilateral termination means that the provider can stop sending out data of its own will whereas bilateral termination requires the approval from the receiver. When a request for external data fails, the system should be able to distinguish the causes being lapsed contract, or system failure.

Binding : There may be two modes, 'one-off' corresponds to a 'snap-shot' being sent to the receiver; the later changes by the provider are not propagated. 'Permanent' corresponds to the up-to-date data, the receiver gets the current version and any change to the data at the provider gets reflected automatically.

Controller : This contains a list of systems that may assume control to the integrating data. It defaults to the provider and barring the receiver from re-exporting the provided data. To be able to re-export the data, the receiver has to be on the controller list, and such a contract is called a 'transferable contract' (see 2.1.3).

Sub-contractible : This condition mainly applies to the receiver. If a contract is specified as sub-contractible, the information provided can be indirectly obtained. In the example, "Contact (Mail-Order)" is not sub-contractible, it means that Alpha may only export to Beta its local data.

The following table summarizes the impact of different conditions on the provider and receiver :

Conditions	Provider	Receiver
Time	√	√
Termination	(Bi-lateral) √	√
	(Uni-lateral) √	
Binding	√	
Controller	√	√
Sub-contractible		√

Terms

A contract binds the provider to supply a certain amount of data and this data is delivered to the receiver in the expected format. As discussed before, we need to use a CDS as the intermediary. Assuming the CDS and other necessary functions[3] are available, we will illustrate the concept by correspondence assertion [SP91].

A contract has two parts, the first part specifies the data needed from the provider, the second part specifies the data expected by the receiver. For example, in the "Contact (Mail-Order)"; **name, address, telephone#** are exported from the **Staff** relation at Alpha database for those who earn more than 5K. At the Beta database, it is expected that **telephone#** is mapped to the **Employee.work_tel#**, **address** to **Employee.addr**, and **name** to **Employee.name** (Fig.3).

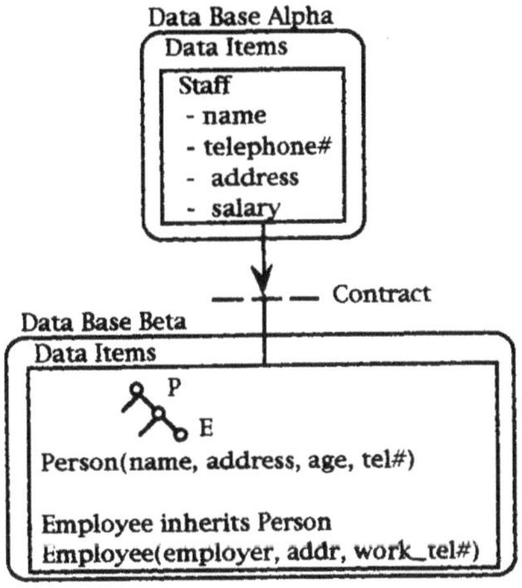

Fig.3. Schematic illustration of "Contact (mail-order)" between Alpha and Beta databases

The correspondence assertions for this contract are:

Alpha.Staff ↔ Beta.Object.Person.Employee
Staff.salary > 5k
Staff.telephone# ↔ telephone# ↔ Object.Person.Employee.work_tel#
Staff.address ↔ address ↔ Object.Person.Employee.addr
Staff.name ↔ name ↔ Object.Person.Employee.name
"Alpha" ↔ company ↔ Object.Person.Employee.employer

2.3. Organization of contracts within each system.

Types of contracts

Contracts may be classified into *bound* or *pending* (fig.4). A contract is bound when it has both the provider and receiver. When either party is not yet filled, it is called a pending contract; a pending contract is further specialized into receiver-pending and provider-pending. The pending party is denoted by a wild-character * as in **<Contact,Alpha,*>**.

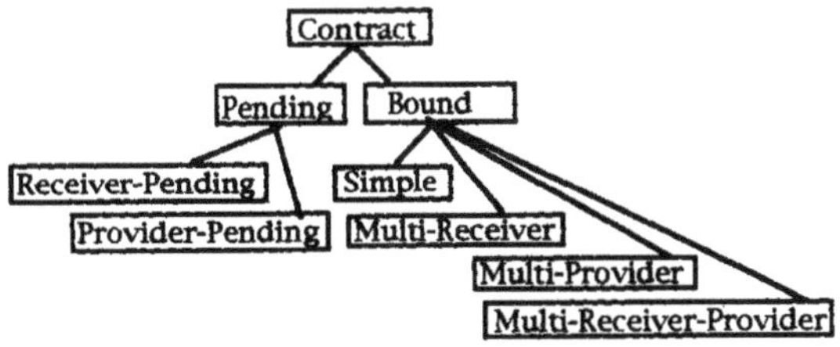

Fig.4. Taxonomy of contracts.

[3][SL90] describes four types of functions that are essential in the databases integration. *Transforming* is used to translate a source language to a target language and it requires schema and command translations. *Filtering* is used to check the commands and associated data of its access, syntax and semantic integrity. *Constructing* is for merging or splitting the data to other processors. *Accessing* executes the task with local database commands.

There are four types of bound-contracts (fig.5) corresponding to one-to-one, one-to-many, many-to-one and many-to-many relationships between provider(s) and receiver(s). A contract is 'simple' if there is only one provider and one receiver, it is 'multi-receiver' if the contract has one provider but applies to many receivers, it is 'multi-provider' if the contract has many providers but only one receiver, and it is 'multi-provider-receiver' if the contract has many providers and many receivers.

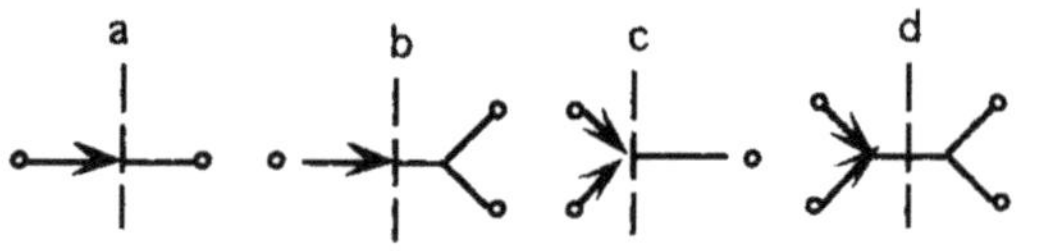

Fig.5. a) Simple, b) Multi-Receiver, c) Multi-Provider and d) Multi-Provider-Receiver contracts : the dashed line represents a contract, the circle represents a provider or a receiver, and the line represents the data integration with the provider at the origin of the arrow.

A contract is *complete* when it has all its terms and conditions agreed. When either the terms or the conditions are not yet set, the contract is called *incomplete*. An incomplete contract can be bound meaning that it has a provider and a receiver but the terms and conditions need to be worked out. But a pending contract is always not complete because it is impossible to know the final set of terms and conditions without both the receiver and provider.

Hierarchy of contracts

Each system has a hierarchic structure of contracts (fig.6). The export list is an aggregate of all the contracts for which the particular database is the provider, and the import list is an aggregate of all the contracts for which the database is the receiver. For example, Alpha database may have its export list as { <Contact,Alpha,*>,<Co-Report,Alpha,*>,<Cust-Info,Alpha,Omni> }. The export list is the first interface for any negotiation.

The export and import lists may be partitioned by each of their respective receivers and providers. It should be noted that the top three levels —Contract, Export/Import lists, Receiver/Provider partitions, are solely for system maintenance. The actual working contracts are under the providers and receivers.

Not all the contracts are negotiated successfully as the terms and conditions may not be agreeable at the time of negotiation, the receiver may choose to suspend the negotiation and asks the provider to store the incomplete contract in a 'waiting list'. Depending on the terms and conditions, the DBA of the system may choose to set up a new contract that can meet the requirements. That incomplete contract is then removed from the list and the receiver is notified.

A contract may relate to a generalized contract by specialization when the data needed is in a more restricted form, it follows that a generalized contract automatically accepts its specialized contracts with the same or more restricted conditions.

To illustrate the point, we need to expand the example to include a generalized contract :

<Contact(Customer & Employee),Alpha,Beta>
Comment =
- Alpha is the database of a financial company and Beta is the database of a mail-order company.
- A list of contacts is provided by Alpha to Beta for all its staff ar customers

...
Protocol =
// Provider
Alpha is RDBMS

< name=Alpha.Staff.name, telephone#=Alpha.Staff.tel#, address=Alpha.Staff.address, type="Staff" >
union
< name=Alpha.Customer.name, telephone#=Alpha.Customer.tel#, address=Alpha.Customer.address, type="Customer" >

constraints :
salary=Alpha.Staff.salary //this variable is only for applying constraints
...

By the restriction of type = "Staff", <Contact(Customer&Employee),Alpha,Beta> is specialized to <Contact(Employee),Alpha,Beta> and to <Contact(Mail-Order),Alpha,Beta> by selecting salary > 5K; "salary" is provided as an attribute to constrain the selection and is not included in the exporting data. As Beta already has the contract <Contact(Employee),Alpha,Beta>, the more specific contracts like Contact(Mail-Order) do not need to be negotiated, Beta may establish the contract and only needs to notify Alpha.

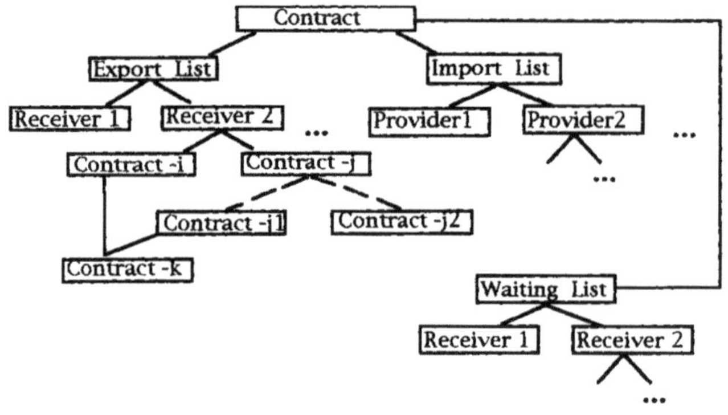

Fig.6. Contract structure is hierarchic and may contain two types of relationship; specialization is represented by a dashed line --- and the aggregate relationship is represented by a —. The Export list is sub-classified by its receivers and the Import List is subclassified by its providers. Each provider-partition contains the set of contracts that can be imported from that provider and each receiver-partition contains the set of contracts that need to export to that receiver. Working contracts may be related by spcialization or aggregation relationships. In the diagram, contract-j is specialized to j1 and j2, whereas contract -j1 and contract -i forms an aggregate contract -k. The waiting list is at the far right hand side, it holds the incomplete contracts that have the system as their provider.

Comparing with a specialized contract, the aggregate contract represents new information, consequently the receiver needs to negotiate with the provider before it may be used. For example, assuming there are two contracts established between Alpha and Beta, <Dept,Alpha,Beta> and <Emp,Alpha,Beta>. The aggregate contract <Dept-Emp,Alpha,Beta> represents the information relating individual employee to his/her department. The provision of this relationship has not been previously agreed, Beta needs to negotiate with Alpha for its access.

The Specialization and Aggregation relationships facilitate the maintenance and negotiation of contracts. Once a generalized contract is agreed, its more specialized forms are automatically accepted by the provider, this contributes to the name space that can be referred in future negotiation. Specialization also helps in information retrieval because it defines the specific task and can be used directly in a query. When a generalized contract gets deleted, the deletion propagates to all its specialized contracts. However, aggregate contracts behave differently, if the contract is specified as independent, then the deletion is isolated. For example, the deletion of <Dept-Emp,Alpha,Beta> is independent of the deletion of <Dept,Alpha,Beta> or <Emp,Alpha,Beta>.

2.4. Contract Reusability

A contract may be re-used in various ways. The provider of an existing contract may include an additional receiver if the information sought by this receiver can be provided by the same contract; however, the data gets sent only to the requesting receiver. Similarly, the receiver of a contract may use the imported data to create a new contract with other systems. The re-exportation needs to satisfy two conditions: the external data has to come from a transferable contract and the new contract has to be subcontractible.

Transferability

When a contract has the receiver included in its controller list, the receiver may re-export part or whole of the information that it imports. This is the receiver's version of information which may have been filtered and transformed; the query processor needs to map each contract in the sequence. For example, assuming <Contract(Mail-Order),Alpha, Beta> is transferable, Beta may re-export 50% of the imported data to another organization Gamma via <Contact(Donation),Beta,Gamma>.

Sub-contractibility

When a contract is sub-contractible, the information provided to the receiver may be indirectly obtained. For example, assuming <Contact(Donation),Beta,Gamma> is subcontractible, Beta may supply Gamma with its own data or from the imported data.

3. NATURAL LANGUAGE PROCESSOR (NLP) AND THE INDEXING OF CONTRACTS.

The traditional data integration techniques including federated databases, incur overhead in setting up an 'overall' schema, and limits what the schema may hold. We look to supporting a more dynamic kind of integration that allows any system on the network to **negotiate** for its data; but an explicit federated schema is not required.

The first step in a negotiation is to match one contract name with another (section 4). However, as the systems are autonomous, they may use different ways to assign contract names. Unlike other approaches, the 'contracting mechanism' has neither a federal dictionary [HM85], nor a federated schema [SL90], to enable one system knowing where and what contract is available, we propose to linguistically index the contracts of each system, these indices are stored and maintained locally but can be correlated with the help of the NLPs. We explore using the linguistic knowledge in two perspectives: 1) system-wise, NLP compares favorably with the traditional key-word technique that may not work efficiently in an autonomous environment. 2) user-wise, NLP provides a natural interface that the user may express an expression in English but still be able to match to an appropriate heading by semantic correlation.

3.1. Natural Language Processor

[CL88] has studied the matching of a customer's query and the headings provided in the French Yellow Page, the same observations may apply to the matching of contract names. A key-word match usually performs poorly in the autonomous environment, for example, the word "contact" may be used as a noun in "Contact of Employee" at system-A but as an adjective in "Contact Lens" at system-B. Another disadvantage of key-word matching is its syntactic nature, the "Contact (Employee)" may match to "Contact (Extraterrestrial)" if a less constrained form needs to be used.

It will not be possible to describe the whole NLP and its knowledge base in this length of paper, but we will use the methodology in [CL88] to illustrate how to build indices for the examples that we have been using.

3.2. Indexing the contract

Each contract has a meaningful name and is uniquely identified by a code. [CL88] distinguished three classes of words, namely Predicate[4]-, Object[5]- and Empty[6]-words. After the NLP parses the name to these classes, indices are extracted either from the O-words or the combination of O- and E-words. There may be many indices relating to the same name but the ordered-pair <code,index> is unique. These indices are then grouped into categories or domains of activities indicated by the P-words; an index may belong to more than one category (fig. 7). A reproduction of thirteen categories from [CL88] is:

1. Retail	7. Design and Fitting
2. Wholesale	8. Medical care
3. Manufacturing	9. Reservation/Order
4. Repairs	10. Lessons
5. Renting	11. Practice/Training
6. Transport	12. Custom-made Contracts
13. When none of the above applies.	

The categories are useful to limit the search of indices by the domain of a task. As in the following example, if the requesting data is about *"personal contacts to sale merchandise"*, the NLP will identifies the domains being Retail, Wholesale and Reservation/Order, and matches with "Contact(Mail-Order)". 'Noises' like "Contact(Extraterrestrial)" or "Mail-Contractor" will not be selected because they are of different categories—Miscellaneous and Transport.

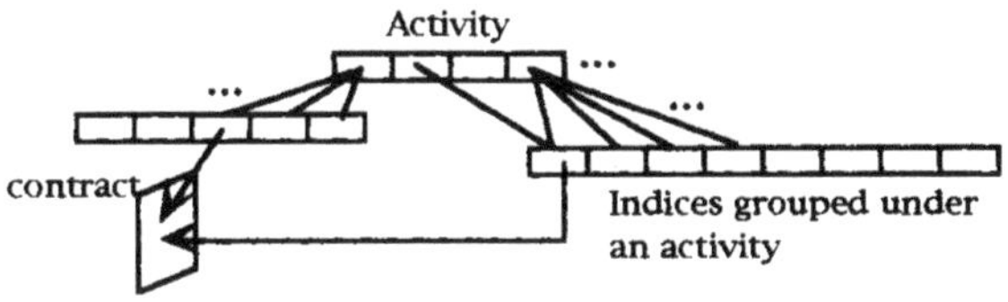

Fig.7. Within each contract directory, there are indices grouped by activities. an index may belong to more than one activity and there may be many indices relating to one contract.

Example:

Assuming the contract "Contact (Mail-Order)" has the code of 001, its name is parsed to words of different classes; P-class = {retail,sales,order}, O-class = {contact}, E-class = {mail-order}. Then a set of possible indices is formed—{contact(mail-order), contact, ...etc}. Finally, because the contract relates to retail, sales and order, the indices are grouped under the categories of Retail and Reservation/Order.

Retail : <001,Contact (Mail-Order)>, <001,Contact>
Reservation/Order : <001,Contact (Mail-Order)>

[4][CL88] defines Predicate-words as those words that are central and relate to other words like to sale, to repair, to order.

[5][CL88] defines Object-words as those words that directly refer to an object like furniture, car, contact.

[6][CL88] defines Empty-words as those words that are semantically poor but are used to strengthen the Object-words— we bracket these words. For example, mail-order by itself has little meaning but it is used to strengthen the object-word in "contact (mail-order)".

4. NEGOTIATION

Negotiation is defined as a two-way communication to complete a contract between the provider and the receiver. When a system needs to negotiate for a contract, it nominates a set of terms and conditions. The contract in this stage is incomplete and needs to be negotiated and agreed by a provider. If the contract has its provider specified (provider-bound but incomplete), the negotiation processor (NP) initiates a direct negotiation with the nominated provider. If the contract needs to search for a provider (provider-pending and incomplete), the NP broadcasts a request to the network and proceeds to negotiation only when there is a responding system. It should be noted that during the negotiation, the contract can evolve and its final terms and conditions may get modified by the negotiating systems.

The first step in negotiation is to correspond the contract names of the receiver and provider. When there is a request to negotiate on the network and it is a provider-pending contract, each system responds by using its NLP to linguistically match the name to its exporting list. To the case of provider-bound contract, only the nominated provider needs to respond. As contracts support aliases, the receiver can be sure of the matching by using the same contract name as the provider. So there are two corresponding contracts in a negotiation, each from the receiver and the provider; the receiver is holding an incomplete contract waiting to be negotiated and the provider is holding a contract that it refers to during negotiation. Note that there may be one to many correspondences, then it is up to the user to chooses a particular one to be negotiated.

The functions performed by the NP of a receiving system are :

- to initiate a negotiation
- to propose a contract for data integration by direct negotiation or by broadcasting to the network.
- to modify the original terms and conditions suggested by the provider's NP, this step sometimes needs the clarification of the system DBA. If there is no response from the network to the request of negotiation, it is probably due to the contract name not corresponding to any of the existing contracts on the network, a new name may be substituted and the negotiation process re-starts.
- to complete negotiation and append to import list if the negotiation is successful.

OR

- to ask the provider to keep the failed contract in its 'waiting list'.

The functions performed by the NP of a providing system are :

- to respond to a request for negotiation
- to match the proposed contract name with the ones in the export list.
- to suggest modification based on existing contracts.
- to complete negotiation and append to export list.

OR

- to append the failed contract to the waiting list.

In general, negotiation consists of a sequence of specific steps, each of which gets executed only when its predecessor succeeds. A negotiation fails when it can't progress to the final state. Each negotiation step (fig.8) can be described by a Data Flow Diagram that has a starting event (R) and a final event. There are two decisions made in each negotiation step; P decides whether to accept R or suggest a R', and R decides whether to accept R' or reject R'. The step is successful if its final event is of (R-OK) or (R'-OK).

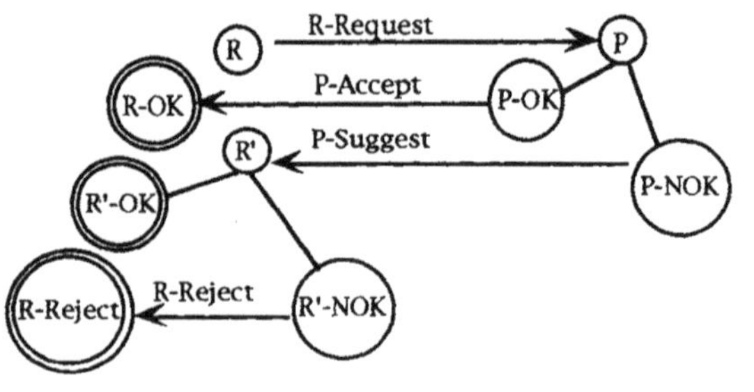

Fig.8. A negotiation step between a Receiver and Provider of data consists of events (circle), messages (arrow), decision (line) and final events (double circle).

The contract negotiation—represented by <T,C> where T stands for terms and C stands for conditions, consists of two steps (fig.9). The first step is terms-negotiation, its outcome can be <T,C>, <T'C> or <T-Reject>; T' and C' stand for the modified versions of terms and conditions. If it is not T-Reject, it proceeds to the conditions-negotiation, there are five possibilities: <T,C>, <T'C>, <T,C'>, <T',C'> and <C-Reject>, the negotiation succeeds if the outcome is not <C-Reject>. Both the terms- and conditions-negotiation need to make decisions based on system rules or the clarification by a DBA, the general algorithm is as follows :

```
T-NOK -> exit:=1 // T-NOK denotes the state of failure on terms-negotiation
C-NOK -> exit:=2
// C-NOK denotes the state of failure on conditions-negotiation
T-OK ∧ C-OK -> exit:=0   // successful negotiation
TR=Tp -> T-OK
// TR and Tp stand for the terms specified by the Receiver and Provider
TR ⊂ Tp -> T-OK //  "⊂" stands for subset relationship
TR ⊃ Tp -> (TR :=Tp) ∧ T-Clarify
// R needs to clarify P's suggestion in changing TR to Tp
CR=Cp -> C-OK
// CR and Cp stand for the conditions specified by the Receiver and Provider
CR ⊂ Cp -> (CR :=Cp) ∧ C-Clarify
// CR ⊂ Cp means that R has less restrictive conditions than P, R needs to
clarify P's suggestion to change from CR to Cp.
CR ⊃ Cp -> (CR :=Cp) ∧ C-OK
// P allows R to relax the condition.
T-Clarify-OK -> T-OK              // R accepts P's suggestion in terms.
C-Clarify-OK -> C-OK              // R accepts P's suggestion in condition.
T-OK ∧ (TR ⊂ Tp) -> create P<TR,Cp>
// a specialized contract is created in P
```

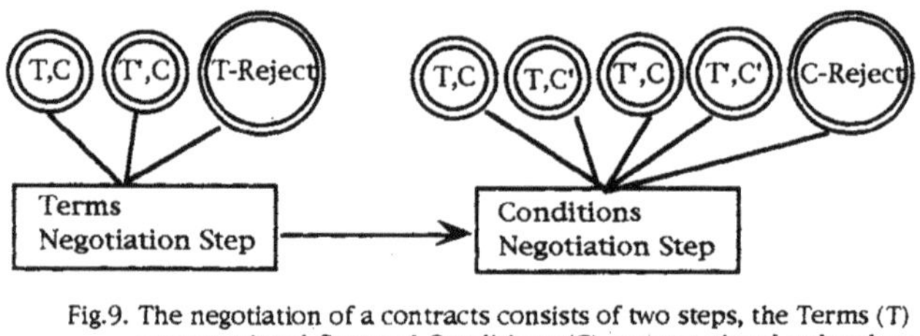

Fig.9. The negotiation of a contracts consists of two steps, the Terms (T) are negotiated first and Conditions (C) get negotiated only when the outcome of the terms-negotiation is not <T-Reject>. The final acceptable states of the negotiation are <T,C>,<T',C>,<T,C'>, and <T',C'>.

Negotiation needs to be flexible and cater for various configuration. Our proposal allows direct negotiation between two systems and broadcast negotiation between the initiator and the respondent. Also, if the two systems are managed by the same DBA, a direct contract may be drawn without the negotiation steps (fig.10). Not all negotiations are successful; the NLP may not be able to match the contract name, the negotiating systems do not agree on the terms and conditions,... etc. These may require the clarification from a knowledgeable user like DBA. The mechanism proposed supports both interactive and non-interactive clarifications; the latter is effected by suspending the negotiation and storing the incomplete contract in the provider's 'waiting list'. Later, if the clarification by the system DBA is successful and the receiver still needs the information, a new contract is established.

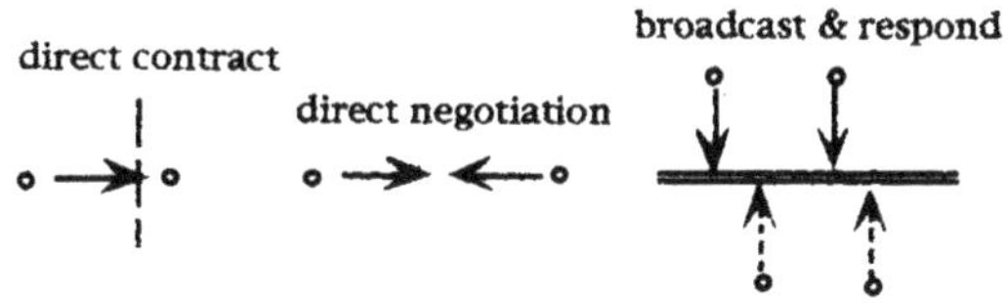

Fig.10. There are three ways to establish a contract : direct contract, direct negotiation and broadcast & respond.

Example :

Beta requests Alpha to supply a list of contacts for its mailing list. Beta does not know exactly what data structure is used in Alpha, so a preliminary contract is drawn up as :

```
<Contact (Mail-Order), Alpha, Beta>
 Comment =
  - Alpha is the database of a financial company and Beta is the database
    of a mail-order company.
  - A list of contacts is requested by Beta to Alpha for all its staff .
 Clauses = {name, telephone#, address, salary}
 Conditions =
  Time = [01/01/91 .. ∞]
  Termination = unilateral
  Binding = Permanent
  Controller = {Alpha,Beta}
  Sub-contractible = no
 Protocol =
  // Provider completes here ...
  // Receiver
     Beta is OODBMS
      name=Beta .Object.Employee.name
      telephone# = Beta .Object.Employee.work_tel#
      address = Beta .Object.Employee.addr
      salary = Beta.Object.Employee.salary
```

There are 2 possibilities:

a. The proposed contract matches with the name of a contract in Alpha's exporting list; for example, <Address(Employee),Alpha,*>.

   Negotiation starts and

   - if the outcome is <T,C>, then Alpha will include Beta at the header, the contract becomes <Address(Employee),Alpha,{Beta}>, it is the alias for <Contact(Mail-Order),Alpha,Beta> at Beta.
   - if the outcome is <T,C'>, Beta has to modify its original condition C to C'; for example, Binding is modified from Permanent to One-Off.
   - if the outcome is <T',C>, Beta has to modify its original terms T to T'; for example, the terms need to exclude salary.
   - if the outcome is <T',C'>, Beta has to modify both its original T to T' and C to C'; for example, the terms need to exclude salary and condition of binding needs to change from Permanent to One-Off, the final contract at Beta becomes :

```
<Contact (Mail-Order), Alpha, Beta>
 Comment =
  - Alpha is the database of a financial company and Beta is the
database of a mail-order company.
  - A list of contacts is provided by Alpha to Beta for all its staff
 Clauses = {name, telephone#, address }
 Conditions =
  ...
  Binding = one-off
 Protocol =
  // Provider
   Alpha is RDBMS
   ...
  // Receiver
   Beta is OODBMS
   ...
```

b. The proposed contract does not match with any of the existing contracts in Alpha's exporting list, Beta may choose to suspend the negotiation and requests Alpha to store the incomplete contract in its waiting list. It should be noted that Beta may also try to change the contract name to "Address(Mail-Order)" to enhance the chance of negotiation.

5. DISCUSSION AND COMPARISON WITH OTHER APPROACHES.

A contract is similar to a view in the sense that they both contain a view-specification and a data-specification, for example, the protocol of <Contact(Mail-Order),Alpha,Beta> can be expressed by view as:

```
range Beta is Beta.Object.Employee;
create view Beta(name, telephone#, address) as
  select name,tel#,address from Alpha.Staff where salary > 5K;
```

Note : a view has the form of, < Create view *view-spec* as select *data-spec*. from *{database.data_object}* where *qualification* >

But contract is more expressive and contains more semantics, it models each integration as a task object including the execution conditions like time constraint, data version, ... etc, also the same contract may applies to more than one receiver. For example, to add Gamma as a new receiver, the contract <Contact(Mail-Order),Alpha,Beta> only needs to change its header to <Contact(Mail-Order),Alpha,{Beta,Gamma}> and includes Gamma in its protocol :

```
// Receiver
 Beta is OODBMS
  name=Beta.Object.Employee.name
  telephone#=Beta.Object.Employee.work_tel#
  address=Beta.Object.Employee.addr
 Gamma is RDBMS
  name=Gamma.Customer.name
  telephone#=Gamma.Customer.tel#
  // address is not needed by Gamma
```

Compared with the reference model [SL90], we don't have a component schema in strict sense. Each contract contains the data mapping specification, to and from the canonical data structure. The export list contains all the contracts that being exported, so it corresponds to the export schema of the reference model, and the federated schema can be seen as a union of all the export lists in the network. A view to the federated schema is called an external schema in the reference model, this corresponds to the individual contract in our proposal.

The 'Contracting Mechanism' shares the same goals as other federated databases to provide autonomy and cooperation between systems, but our proposal has the following characteristics:

- A federated schema defines the integrated data for the whole federation. It is advantageous only when its component databases have similar data requirements and the number of databases in the federation is small. If the number is large and the data requirement is not uniform, then the federated approach performs poorly mainly due to the difficulties in managing the federated schema, and coordinating different integrating activities. Our approach does not pre-suppose the existence of such a federation and does not require an 'overall' schema—federated or global. The integration is defined for, and only on the participating systems, hence it is secure and robust. When a system is down, it can affect only the systems that it is contracting with. Every system on the network can be integrated with other systems by a flexible negotiation process, both directly and by broadcasting. As the contracts are linguistically indexed, 'browsing' is another possible extension that would require only a small change to the current framework.

- Our proposal modularizes each integration as a re-usable task. Besides the data definition, the contract includes also the execution conditions. The provider of information may specify how the data gets re-used (in the controller list), and the receiver may specify how the data is obtained (in the condition of sub-contractibility). The modularization is essential for the negotiation process because it provides the necessary abstraction (name space) that different systems may understand before the sorting out of actual details of data. We believe that some semantic conflict cannot be resolved mechanically and look to supporting the clarification by system DBA.

- Our proposal can support the static environment as well as by federated systems albeit it is arguable when the network is fully connected and uniform in data requirement. But in an autonomous environment, this is a rare situation rather than norm On the other hand, it is well-suited to ad-hoc integration where the data required is of short life-span and dynamic.

[HM85] proposed a federated architecture with a federal dictionary registering what is available on the network. A system wanting to import data from other systems needs to look at this dictionary to see where to negotiate and what can be negotiated. The contracting mechanism uses another approach. A system wanting to import data poses a data specification to the network and it is up to the other systems to respond to the request. This approach avoids the problems of keeping a centralized registry up-to-date at all time. Most importantly, it achieves a true 'openness' in information. There are no pre-defined boundaries and the success of information acquisition depends only on the systems in the network and the knowledge of how to negotiate with other systems. Also, the negotiation process supported by our proposal is more flexible.

[LI90] described the multidatabase structure called MRDSM. Here the data integration is effected by an interoperable query language—MSQL that extends to multi-databases. MRDSM does not need an 'overall' schema but it does not include the negotiation process and requires the user to understand different available schemas. The query is reasonably complicated as it needs to specify not only the data to be retrieved but also it must indicate how to resolve data conflict. There is also no concept of re-using any existing integration in this mode.

6. SUMMARY

To summarize, we have described an effective and flexible way to integrate different information systems. The Contracting Mechanism can support different integration needs, including ad-hoc (short life-span), one-off (providing a fixed version of data), and permanent (always providing the current version of data). It can model not only the static integrations as in other federated systems but also the dynamic integrations of data. The user may access the local data plus the external data that have been contracted; new data may be imported directly or via negotiation.

By abstracting each integration task to a contract and providing a flexible negotiation mechanism, we achieve the following goals :

1. *An integration task can be re-used, its definition and the knowledge in data mapping can be shared by other systems.*
2. *There is support for various integration needs. A contract can be as large as the whole schema of a system or as small as several data items. The integration may be established as one-off, ad-hoc or permanent. Also the sub-contractible and transferable contracts form the basis for a robust and dynamic way of integration.*
3. *Each integration is secure because all the integrated information are locally managed, an exclusively bound contract may be known only to the participating systems and not seen by other negotiators. It is effective because each integration task may be carried out independently and the integration network is established naturally without the constrain of 'overall' schema.*

Contracting Mechanism discussed in this paper is one of the constructs of the Multi-World data model that we are developing. The data model supports public/private data management and dynamic data integration, it also supports multiple viewpoints and data conflict resolution. There are various areas that we currently research and develop, the ones related to the contracting mechanism include:

- Incorporating negotiation to query processing.
- Expanding the negotiation processor to support 'browsing' and 'natural language'.
- Expanding the mechanism to support updating of data.
- Formalizing the guidelines in establishing a contract, especially the choice of its name.

Acknowledgments

The authors thank Goretti Chao, Warren McPherson for their useful discussions and insightful comments. Thanks are given especially to Warren McPherson, Kathy Thanh for helpful suggestions to improve the presentation.

7. REFERENCES.

[BO86] Y.Breitbart, P.Olson & G.Thompson, *Database Integration in a Distributed Heterogeneous Database System*, (Proc. Data Eng. Conf., IEEE, Los Alamitos, Calif., 1986, p.301-310).

[BR90] Y.Breitbart, *Multidatabase Interoperability*, (SIGMOD RECORD, Vol.19, No.3, Sep-90, p.53-60).

[CH90] C.Chung, *Dataplex : An Access to Heterogeneous Distributed Databases*, (Comm. ACM, Vol. 33, No.1, Jan-90, p.70-80).

[CL88] G.Clemencin, *Querying The Frecnch Yellow Pages : Natural Language Access To The Directory*, (Information Processing & Management, Vol.24, No.6, 1988, p.633-649)

[EK91] F.Eliassen, & R.Karlsen, *Interoperability and Object Identity*, (SIGMOD RECORD, Vol.20, No.4, Dec-91, p.25-29)

[HM85] Dennis Heimigner & Dennis McLeod, *A Federated Architecture for Information Management*, (ACM Transactions on Office Information Systems, Vol.3, No.3, Jul-85, p. 253-278)

[KE91a] W.Kent, *A rigorous model of object reference, identity, and existence*, (Journals of Object-Oriented Programming, Vol 4, Jun-91, p.28-36).

[KE91b] W.Kent, *The Breakdown of the Information Model in Multi-Database Systems*, (SIGMOD RECORD, Vol.20. No.4, Dec-91, p.10-15).

[KR91] Ravi Krishnamurthy, W. Litwin & W.Kent, *Language Features for Interoperability of Databases with Schematic Discrepancies*. (Proc. ACM SIGMOD Int'l Conf on Mgmt of Data, Denver, Colorado, May-92, p.40-49).

[LI90] W.litwin, L.mark & N.Roussopoulos, *Interoperability of multiple Autonomous Databases"*, (ACM Computing Surveys, Vol.22, No.3, Sep-90, p. 267-293).

[PE91a] R.Ahmed, P.DeSmedt, W.Kent, M.Ketabchi, W.Litwin, A.Rafii & M.Shan, *Pegasus : A System for Seamless Integration of Heterogeneous Information Sources* (Proc. IEEE COMPCON, Mar-91, p.128-136).

[PE91b] R.Ahmed & P.DeSmedt & W.Du & W.Kent & M.Ketabchi & W.Litwin & A.Rafii & M.Shan, *The Pegasus Heterogeneous Multidatabase System*, (IEEE Computer, Dec-91, p.19-27).

[SC91] F.Saltor, M.Castellanos & M.Garcia-Solaco, *Suitability of data models as canonical models for federated databases*, (SIGMOD RECORD, Vol.20, No.4, Dec-91, p.45-49)

[SH91] Amit P.Sheth, *Semantic Issues in Multidatabase Systems*, (SIGMOD RECORD, Vol.20, No.4, Dec-91, p.5-9)

[SL90] Amit Sheth & J.Larson, Federated Database Systems for Managing Distributed, Heterogeneous, and Autonomous Databases, (ACM Computing Surveys, Vol.22, No.3, Sep-90, p.183-236).

[SM81] J.Smith, P.Bernstein, U.Dayal, N.Goodman, T.Landers, K.Lin & E.Wong, *Multibase - integrating heterogeneous distributed database systems*. (Proc. of AFIPS, 1981, p.487-499).

[SP91] S.Spaccapietra & C.Parent, *Conflicts and Correspondence Assertions in Interoperable Databases*, (SIGMOD RECORD, Vol.20, No.4, Dec-91, p.49-54)

[TH90] G.Thomas et al., *Heterogeneous Distributed Database Systems for Production Use*, (ACM Computing Surveys, Vol.22, No.3, Sep-90, p.237-266).

THE DiNG - A PARALLEL MULTIATTRIBUTE FILE SYSTEM FOR DEDUCTIVE DATABASE MACHINES

T.A. Mueck

Dept. of Information Systems
University of Vienna
Liebigg. 4/3-4
1010 Vienna, Austria
mueck@ifs.univie.ac.at

ABSTRACT

We investigate the main requirements for mass storage subsystems with regard to the needs of deductive database machines. In particular, we focus in this paper

- on fully integrated index data structures, namely a multiattribute search structure based on a grid file derivate and
- on certain hardware requirements, i.e., redundant arrays of inexpensive disks in order to avoid a disk I/O bottleneck during rule processing.

The former requirement is motivated by an example, in particular by a closer look at the execution of Datalog¬* rule sets. As a solution, we propose the DiNG file system as specialised mass storage subsystem for high performance deductive database machines. The DiNG file system is a highly parallel file system which supports symmetric multiattribute queries against fact- and rulebases. At the moment, the DiNG file system is operational on an experimental shared nothing MIMD machine, namely an eight-processor/eight-disk intel iPSC/2.

1. INTRODUCTION

During the last decade, considerable research effort has been invested into parallel rule base processing in deductive databases (see [WDSY91] and [GaST90] for recent results) and in deductive database machines (DDBM) based on parallel hardware platforms in general (see [MKMK88] and [GRBB88]). Until now, not so much attention has been paid to questions regarding the *mass storage components* of such systems. In most cases, standard mass storage subsystems commercial relational DBMS have been used. However, due to the fact- and rulebase size of large scale practical applications and to the recent advent of real-time expert systems, the special requirements for mass storage subsystems (MSSS) used by DDBM have to be investigated. In other words, specialised high performance MSSS have to be designed and implemented according to the particular needs of DDBM. The main design goal has to be best possible mass storage support for upper layer components like inference engines.

In this paper, we give an outline of MSSS requirements as far as DDBM are concerned, motivate these requirements by means of an example, namely the execution of Datalog¬* rule sets, and propose the DiNG file system as an appropriate MSSS for high performance DDBM. The DiNG file system is the first operational component of a new federated DBMS system, namely the **PARABASE** architecture as described in [Muec92] and in [KoMV92]. The PARABASE research effort focuses on shared nothing MIMD machines used as high performance DBMS servers participating in distributed workstation environments, in particular on a prototype designed and implemented for an iPSC/2 hypercube machine linked into an TCP/IP based network. Our intention in this paper is to show that the highly parallel file system of the PARABASE project is an efficient choice for a MSSS in deductive database environments. In particular, we argue that a specialised parallel file system is needed to process exact match, partial match and range queries against fact sets as low level file system operations instead of conventional low level read/write operations against flat files (see [Witz91] for an outline of the file system and [MuSc91] for a description of the data structure).

After a brief requirement specification and an additional motivation for multiattribute search structures in Sections 2 and 3, the current hardware platform and the corresponding system software environment is described in Section 4. A sketchy description of the underlying index data structure is given in Section 5. This section might be skipped if the reader is not interested in the details of multiattribute search structures, since the following section does not rely on this material. Section 6 deals with a number of technical issues regarding the parallel file system. In particular, the basic structure, the data distribution policy and interprocess communication pattern are addressed. Section 7 provides conclusions and a short outlook at work in progress.

2. REQUIREMENTS FOR THE MASS STORAGE SUBSYSTEMS OF DDBM

From out point of view, there are two main requirements for a mass storage subsystem (MSSS) to be used in the context of a deductive database machine. Both requirements are equally important with respect to the overall usability and performance of the MSSS although they are quite different with respect to the architectural layers of a DDBM (the first is somewhat hardware-oriented whereas the second leads to search structure considerations).

At first, a MSSS to be used in a DDBM should be able to operate disk arrays in an application-transparent fashion. The reason is very simple and refers to the increasing discrepancy between enhancements in CPU power and disk

I/O bandwidth. The former are impressing both with respect to functionality and speed whereas the latter are rather modest. Conseqently, RAID technologies (see [WeZS91] for an example) can be used to achieve a better balance between CPU power and I/O bandwidth. However, the existence of disk arrays has to be application-transparent, since an application designer is usually not interested in the hardware-technical details of the underlying MSSS. This is certainly not a *specific* requirement for DDBM (it could be stated as well for any MSSS to be used by data intensive applications), nevertheless, a reasonable combined disk I/O bandwidth is a crucial point for real-life sized fact bases including several billions of tuples, i.e., several gigabytes of data.

Secondly, an appropriate MSSS has to support symmetric multiattribute search operations, i.e., queries which are specified with respect to several key attributes. In the following section, an example is used to provide additional motivation for this requirement. Basically, any inference process issues a considerable number of queries to be executed in large fact sets which are usually represented by k-tuples. Most of these queries refer either to all or at least to several values of the k-tuples. In other words, a distinction between primary and secondary keys in the context of query execution (like for example in commercial database environments) is not meaningful. Consequently, the MSSS has to be build upon a multikey index data structure which yields an efficient multiattribute clustering and allows therefore fast multiattribute search operations (we elaborate on this issue in the next section).

With respect to these requirements, we use

- a shared nothing MIMD hardware platform with multiple disk arrays (i.e., the possibility to access one SCSI disk array per computing node) in order to provide sufficient disk I/O bandwidth for the handling of large deductive databases and
- a state-of-the-art multikey index data structure based on a grid file derivate as basic file structure which is intended to speed up symmetric multiattribute search operations.

In an overall DDBM architecture, the hardware platform together with the MSSS can be used either as high performance fact- and rulebase server to be accessed via TCP/IP or directly as a low-level retrieval machine for a parallel inference engine running on the same hardware platform. Neither of these architectural alternatives yields a significant change in the requirements stated above.

3. MULTIATTRIBUTE SEARCH OPERATIONS IN FACT- AND RULEBASES - AN EXAMPLE

From several alternatives, a recent Datalog variant has been chosen as demonstration example in favour of multiattribute query support to be offered to inference engines running on top of the MSSS. In particular, the evaluation of Datalog¬* rule sets (see [AbSi91]) is investigated. The choice is nearly arbitrary, since all inference schemes lead to similar query request patterns. Informally, Datalog¬* allows negative literals both in the head and in the body of a rule. Consequently, a rule contains several literals of the form $f(arg_1, ..)$ or $\neg f(arg_1, ..)$ and has therefore the general structure

$$[\neg]f_h(arg_{h1}, ..) \Leftarrow [\neg]f_{b1}(arg_{b1.1}, ..), .. [\neg]f_{bn}(arg_{bn.1}, ..)$$

As usual, any argument might be either a variable (denoted by a capital letter) or a constant (denoted by an integer). The semantics of rule instantiations are straightforward. Each variable has to be bound in such a way that

- positive literals in the body correspond to facts stored in the factbase and
- negative literals in the body correspond to facts *not* stored in the factbase.

Additionally, for each rule instantiation, a positive literal in the head means a fact insertion upon rule execution whereas a negative literal corresponds to a fact deletion. This rather informal description can be illustrated by the following program fragment representing an operational semantics specification for Datalog¬* rulebase execution. The comments used to indentify execution phases are subsequently referenced in an example.

```
rb_exec(IN rs: rulebase, IN-OUT fb: factbase)
{  inst: set of instantiated rule heads;
   i: instantiated rule head;
   LOOP
   {  // instantiation
      inst ⇐ all heads of rule instantiations
                with respect to rs and fb
      // check if fixpoint
      FOREACH i IN inst
         IF ((i is positive) AND (i IN fb)) OR
            ((i is negative) AND (i NOT IN fb))
            inst ⇐ inst \ {i}
      IF inst = {} EXIT;
      // remove pairwise inverse heads
      FOREACH i IN inst
         IF ¬i IN inst
            inst ⇐ inst \ {i ¬i}
      // execute heads
      FOREACH i IN inst
         IF i is positive
            fb ⇐ fb ∪ {i}
         ELSE
            fb ⇐ fb \ {i}
   }
}
```

Figure 1: *Datalog¬* operational semantics*

The following example of a rulebase execution is rather simple, since all rules contain only positive literals. However, using negative literals in the example would only increase the complexity without any additional contribution to the requirement motivation. In other words, a need for multiattribute search operation support can be demonstrated even by such a simple rulebase. In particular, we consider the following input to rb_exec():

RULEBASE	FACTBASE				
a(X,Y,Z) ⇐ b(X,Y), c(Y,Z).	b(1,2)	c(2,4)	d(1)	e(1)	f(2)
c(3,X) ⇐ d(X), e(X).	b(2,3)		d(2)		
c(3,X) ⇐ f(X).					

Figure 2: *rulebase and factbase example*

to be launched during rule instantiation and execution. The instantiation process is admittedly naive, i.e., non-optimised, but illustrative as far as multiattribute query requests are concerned.

Phase I: rule instantiation
  a(X,Y,Z) ⇐ b(X,Y), c(Y,Z).
    query1 b(*,*) ⇒ { b(1,2), b(2,3) }; take b(1,2)
  a(1,2,Z) ⇐ b(1,2), c(2,Z).
    query2 c(2,*) ⇒ { c(2,4) }; take c(2,4),
    query2 exhausted, terminate
  a(1,2,4) ⇐ b(1,2), c(2,4).
    insert into inst values (+,a,1,2,4)
    resume query1; take b(2,3),
    query1 exhausted, terminate
  a(2,3,Z) ⇐ b(2,3), c(3,Z).
    query3 c(3,*) ⇒ { };
    query3 exhausted, terminate
  a(2,3,Z) ⇐ fail.
    no query open for a(X,Y,Z)
  c(3,X) ⇐ d(X), e(x).
    query4 d(*) ⇒ { d(1), d(2) }; take d(1)
  c(3,1) ⇐ d(1), e(x).
    query5 e(1) ⇒ { e(1) }; take e(1),
    query5 exhausted, terminate
  c(3,1) ⇐ d(1), e(1).
    insert into inst values (+,c,3,1,-)
    resume query4; take d(2),
    query4 exhausted, terminate
  c(3,2) ⇐ d(2), e(x).
    query6 e(2) ⇒ { };
    query6 exhausted, terminate
  c(3,2) ⇐ fail.
    no query open for c(3,X)
  c(3,X) ⇐ f(X).
    query7 f(*) ⇒ { f(2) }; take f(2),
    query7 exhausted, terminate
  c(3,2) ⇐ f(2).
    insert into inst values (+,c,3,2,-)
    no query open for c(3,X)
  inst = { a(1,2,4), c(3,1), c(3,2) }

Phase II: checking if a fixpoint has been reached
  query8 a(1,2,4) ⇒ { };
  query9 c(3,1 ⇒ { };
  query10 c(3,2) ⇒ { };
  inst = { a(1,2,4), c(3,1), c(3,2) }

Phase III: checking for pairwise inverse heads
  query11 inst(-,a,1,2,4) ⇒ { };
  query12 inst(-,c,3,1,-) ⇒ { };
  query13 inst(-,c,3,2,-) ⇒ { };
  inst = { a(1,2,4), c(3,1), c(3,2) }

Phase IV: factbase update
  insert into a values (1,2,4)
  insert into c values (3,1)
  insert into c values (3,2)

Figure 3: *execution trace with respect to MSSS requests*

Although this execution trace is significantly abridged (it represents only the first interation of the LOOP-processing), it contains a considerable number of mass storage requests even for a very small fact- and rulebase. Considering the number of query/update requests in real-life deductive database processing within gigabyte fact- and rulebases, the performance of the underlying MSSS becomes a crucial issue for the overall performance of a DDBM.

4. HARDWARE ENVIRONMENT, SYSTEM SOFTWARE AND OVERALL ARCHITECTURE

Currently, an eight processor intel iPSC/2 hypercube machine is used as shared nothing MIMD platform. The iPSC/2 is mainly intended as MSSS server to be accessed via standard TCP/IP connections. In a normal scenario, several workstations running local applications are allowed to access shared data sets (relational databases, fact- and rulebases, object collections ..) maintained by the mass storage server. This is related to the so called federated DBMS paradigm. In such architectures, several clients use their private databases (PDB) on local machines and a number of shared databases (SDB) on one or more host machines. The high-level data exchange protocol is simple. Data sets (tuple sets, fact- and rule sets, object sets, ...) can be transferred to or from a shared database employing a simple yet elegant exchange mechanism, namely the CHECK-IN and CHECK-OUT protocol known from [Kim91]. This concept is based on a data set transfer from a shared database to a private database (CHECK-OUT), an eventually long lasting data manipulation phase and a final retransmission of the data set to the shared database (CHECK-IN).

System software includes UNIX System V at the "system resource manager" (SRM), an i386 based workstation which serves as a front end system to the actual hypercube, a UNIX derivate called NX/2 as symmetric node operating system and the intel supplied "concurrent file system" (CFS, see [Pier89] for details) used to operate the disk array. The DiNG file system is meant to replace the CFS in all cases. However, the current file system prototype is still using low-level disk access functionality (basically raw device handling) provided by the CFS.

In contrast to ordinary iPSC/2 or iPSC/860 platforms, all processors of this configuration serve both as computing nodes and as I/O nodes. Each node is equipped with a standard SCSI controller and, at least at the present moment, with one 650MB SCSI disk. The next hardware extension should include several disks per controller device in order to take full advantage of the SCSI bus bandwidth. The architectural distinction between computing nodes accessible for application processes and mass storage nodes (so called I/O nodes) only accessible via file system calls (as used by intel for NIC applications) would be counterproductive for a mass storage oriented project and has been omitted for that reason.

Consequently, the current hardware configuration looks like this:

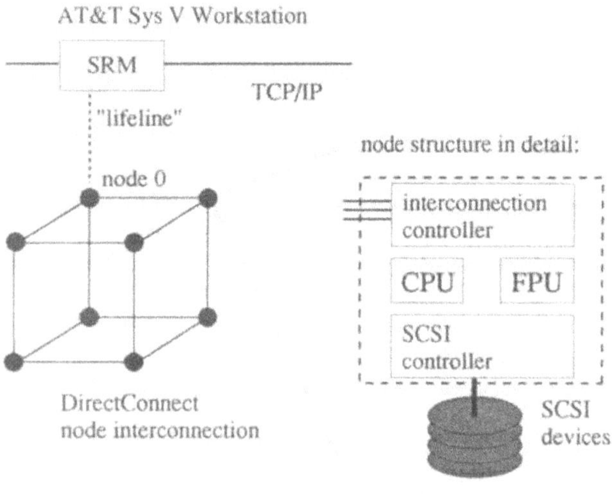

Figure 4: *iPSC/2 hardware configuration*

The different communication hardware technologies depicted in Figure 4, namely standard Ethernet for client-server communication, intel proprietary DirectConnect for node-node communication and SCSI for node-controller communication, yield to challenging problems with respect to bandwidth balancing. Additionally, considering the rapid change in communication hardware and the resulting rapid change of bandwidth ratios between the communication layers (client-server, node-to-node, node-controller), any parallel DBMS architecture has to provide means for optimisations in case of changing bandwidth ratios.

The important point with respect to this hardware and system software configuration is obviously **not** performance. In fact, it is the possibility to design, implement and evaluate different parallelisation concepts in a common framework, namely a shared nothing MIMD machine running a symmetric node operating system based on well-known architectural concepts.

5. A PARALLEL NON-STANDARD FILE SYSTEM FOR LARGE FACT- AND RULEBASES

Replacing stable and well-known standard MSSS, like for example the UNIX file system, by novel MSSS prototypes is a resource-consuming process which has to be motivated. Consequently, this section contains a short rationale for non-standard file systems to be used by data intensive clients. This rationale is given prior to the description of the DiNG internal data structures. The presentation of several technical core issues like data distribution and communication structure in a parallel environment is delayed to the next section.

5.1. Non-standard file systems for data intensive applications - a rationale

Standard UNIX file systems as well as state-of-the-art parallel file systems (see [Pier89]) maintain *flat files*, i.e., unstructured byte strings held on mass storage devices. Common access primitives on such files are *read*, *write* and *seek*. The operating system supports atomic data transfer actions for continuous byte segments belonging to files. In other words, each file system read or write call issued by an application is intended to transfer a certain amount of uninterpreted data from a mass storage device into the application address space or vice versa. In most cases, the continuous byte segments to be transferred are specified as a number of bytes relative to a so called *file pointer*. The crucial point is that all the data have to be uninterpreted, i.e., without any structure or semantics, as far as the file system itself is concerned. In any other case, the flexibility of the data type *file* and the general usability for all kinds of applications would vanish.

This type of mass storage subsystem is well established and absolutely sufficient for non-database environments, especially for numerical computing. However, data intensive applications which have to rely on high-performance persistent storage management subunits (e.g. all kinds of database management systems and all kinds of software database machines) reveal the inherent weaknesses of flat file systems very quickly. Recalling the example contained in the previous section, we already motivated a strong need for access operations which act directly on sets of facts and/or rules. In case of performance critical data intensive applications, a set of specialised query/update operations have to be implemented in order to replace the standard access operations acting on continuous byte segments. In Section 4, we showed that the inference engine of a DDBM issues a large number of mass storage requests for fact and/or rule sets fulfilling certain logical conditions defined over certain attributes of the data.

From our point of view, a file system designed to process such requests with reasonable performance has to include two key features, namely internal (in the sense of tightly integrated) multikey indices and parallel request processing. The former supports fast symmetric multiattribute search operations whereas the latter helps to bypass the ever present disk I/O bottleneck. Additionally, the design of a non-standard MSSS requires a decision whether the persistent storage management system should use internal index structures *on top of the common flat file system* or *instead of the flat file system.* The second alternative implies a complete logical bypass of the original file system which actually ends up in a physical replacement in most cases since the partitioning of mass storage devices for different file systems seems to be rather unattractive for various reasons. Some basic performance considerations favour the second alternative, even in spite of the need for additional development work. Intuitively, each additional layer in a persistent storage management system consumes a certain fraction of the overall system power, therefore the integration of the basic data storage functionality and of the index maintenance functionality yields significant performance improvements.

Consequently, the new DiNG file system is meant to replace the current flat file system (in particular the CFS) in case of data intensive applications. It has to provide flat file system capabilities as well as the tuple set capabilities outlined above. Fortunately, CFS source code has been already supplied by intel, therefore an integration of DiNG file and flat file functionality does not end up in too much additional effort at the moment.

5.2. Distributed and nested grid files as internal data structure

Following from the above, a file system prototype based on distributed and nested grid files (called DiNG files in the sequel, see [Witz91] or [MuSc91] for details) has been implemented. It supports fact and/or rule insert and delete operations as well as parallel exact match, partial match and range queries quasi at system call level.

Distributed and nested grid files are a multikey index structure designed for MSSS on shared nothing MIMD machines, i.e., an index structure which allows for parallel queries against key attribute sets. Prior to the description of the DiNG file system, a few words about the underlying basic data structure, i.e., nested grid files as presented in [Free87] or [Free89], seem to be appropriate.

The key idea common to all grid file design approaches is the interpretation of n-tuples as elements of an n-dimensional space. This space, called data space in the sequel, has to be successively partitioned into smaller subspaces as the number of tuples increases. The resulting set of smaller subspaces used to give a partitioning of the initial data space has to be mapped to a totally ordered set, namely the disk block address space. This is to ensure that each relevant subspace of the n-dimensional data space corresponds to one physically transferable storage unit, i.e., a disk block, since any possible n-tuple has to be stored in one of the allocated disk blocks if passed to the mass storage subsystem for insertion. In the original grid file design (see [NiHS84]), the geometric contents of any two subspaces have to be disjoint. With respect to a reasonable directory expansion behaviour in case of non-uniformly distributed or correlated raw data, the nested grid file approach relaxes this condition to some extent. The relaxed partitioning condition reads as follows: if any two hyperrectangles intersect, one has to enclose the other. The resulting partitioning schema, which in turn determines the geometric shape of the subspaces, is conceptually simple. Basically, it is a buddy system with subsequent *binary* partitioning of the initial data space. All hyperrectangles are created as a result of alternating and cyclic binary domain splitting as depicted for the 2-dimensional case in Figure 5(a) below. Region numbers are created by successive bit interleaving of the domain subinterval bit signatures. The interleaving sequence is given by the cyclic domain split sequence, i.e., 1.bit of $domain_1$, 1.bit of $domain_2$ .. 1.bit of $domain_n$, 2.bit of $domain_1$, 2.bit of $domain_2$ .. 2.bit of $domain_n$ and so on. Figure 5(b) illustrates the bit interleaving concept.

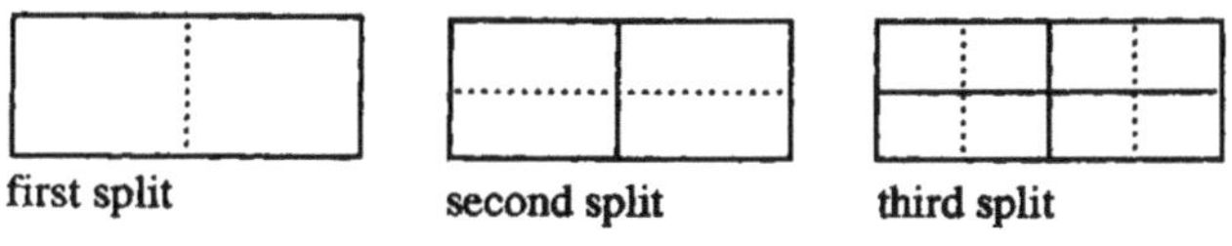

(a) successive data space partitioning

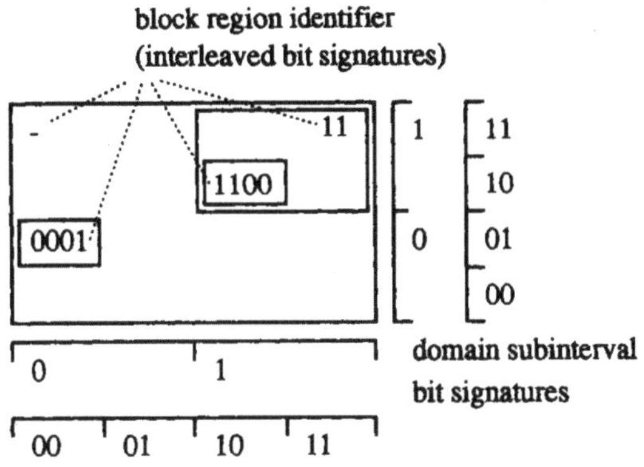

(b) hyperrectangle identification

Figure 5: *Partitioning and subspace identification*

The physical directory structure is implemented as height-balanced multiway tree. Figure 6 shows a small file (very much resembling the example of Figure 5a), both in its geometrical and in its data structure oriented representation. As depicted, the file consists of one directory bucket and four data buckets.

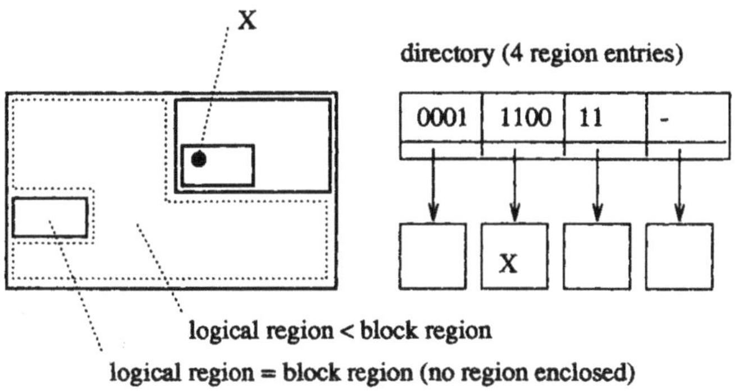

Figure 6: *Nested grid file example*

A search for tuple X in Figure 6 includes a directory traversal to find the subspace identifier corresponding to the enclosing block region. The data bucket reference attached to the region identifier provides access to the data bucket in which X is actually stored. However, a closer look at the search process reveals that the *smallest* enclosing subspace has to be found. Tuple X is contained in three subspaces (-, 11 and 1100) but actually stored in the data bucket referenced by the smallest enclosing region (1100 in this case). A detailed discussion of the reasons for this kind of data space organisation is beyond the scope of this paper. Basically, the region nesting is motivated by a graceful performance degradation in case of non-uniformly distributed raw data. Standard grid file organisations exhibit an unacceptable (i.e., exponential) worst case behavior with respect to directory expansion.

This symmetric multikey approach is in strong contrast to B^+-tree approaches, which either favour certain attributes or attribute combinations or force a database administrator to use an unacceptably large number of index structures for one single file. In particular, 2^n-1 B^+-trees would be needed for a file with **n** key attributes. Additionally, the attribute *sequence* in a compound single-key index is not even considered in this figure although it is of prime relevance for any query optimiser.

6. THE DiNG FILE SYSTEM - STRUCTURE, DATA DISTRIBUTION AND COMMUNICATION

After the motivation for the design and implementation of a non-standard file system and the brief outline of the underlying basic data structure, the technical characteristics of the resulting parallel file system can be described. In particular, we elaborate on the actual file system structures, i.e., on superblock and i-node maintenance, on the current data distribution policies and on the inter-node communication structure of the MSSS processes with regard to client applications.

6.1. The client-server structure of the file system

The basic mass storage block allocation, handling and administration schema of the DiNG file system is conceptually simple and similar to the UNIX mass storage block administration. At that level, the main differences between a standard parallel file system and the DiNG file system stem from the separate handling of data blocks and index block. Free space administration is done with bit map structures, i.e., the MSSS control process maintains a super block, an i-node bit map, a bit map for data and index block, a list of i-nodes and a list of block containing data blocks as well as index blocks. Since data blocks and index blocks are handled by different subprocesses of the file system, a differentiation between the two block classes is necessary even at this lowest level of block administration. At the moment, the block buffer cache employs a standard hash table based LRU displacement strategy (see [Tane92] for example). Other displacement strategies are currently considered, however, a detailed discussion of buffer cache considerations would be beyond the scope of this report. Readers interested in this topic may refer to [MuSc91].

At this point, the internal process structure of one of the parallel MSSS processes (depicted in Figure 7 below) has to be described. However, the discussion of the control flow and the data flow between the subprocesses and the client processes in case of fact- and/or rule insert requests or query requests is delayed to Subsection 6.2.

Each DiNG file system client has to use a *client library* which is responsible for correct protocol handling and appropriate message formats. This library provides access to the local file system server, i.e., the MSSS process located on the same node as the client process. In other words, all MSSS requests issued by any client process are initially handled by the local MSSS process. Subsequent parallel processing is transparent to the client, since requests are passed to and results are obtained from the local server.

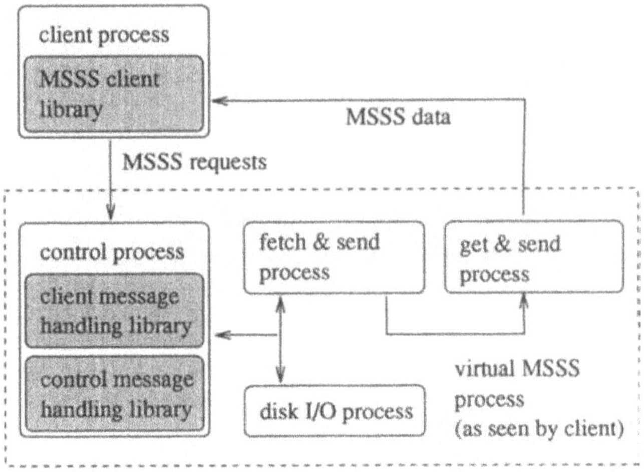

Figure 7: *MSSS process subcomponents*

The client library has a counterpart in the MSSS process, namely the *client message handling library* used by the MSSS *control process.* The control process uses a second message handling module, namely the control message handling library for all internal communications with other control processes on different nodes. Besides all coordination and control tasks in the context of insert, delete and query request handling, the control process manipulates directly all index blocks. In other words, the control process executes all index searches and passes the resulting data block numbers subsequently to the *fetch & send process*, which is responsible for data block handling. A third process, the so called *get & send* process is responsible for all query result deliveries. It collects all query subresults from all fetch & send processes, i.e., from the local as well as from all other fetch & send processes on different nodes and passes the collected data to the client process.

The data distribution policy can be described as round robin distribution. Each insert request

INSERT <fact or rule> INTO <file>

is passed to the local control process and triggers a lookup operation in the corresponding i-node which yields the appropriate node number for the next insert into <file>. In particular, if *last_P*(<file>) denotes the number of the MSSS process which received the last tuple previously inserted into <file> and if **p** denotes the number of operational server processes, the expression (*last_P*(<file>)+1 modulo **p**) yields the number of the MSSS process which is going to receive the fact or rule for insertion. If the calculated process number refers to the local node, the correct data block number is determined, the fact or rule together with the data block number is passed to the fetch & send process and finally inserted by this process. If the calculated process number refers to a different node, the control process passes the data item to the corresponding control process which takes the appropriate steps for local insertion. All further implementation details of the distribution process (e.g. the node counter update per file) are omitted in here. In fact, their contribution would be rather limited in the context of this paper.

As a result of this distribution schema, each DiNG file is spread over all available nodes. In other words, each logical DiNG file as seen from a client's point of view consists of a number of physical DiNG files. The contents, i.e., the tuple set of one logical file equals the union of all corresponding physical files.

6.2. Control and data flow during query execution

Control flow and data flow in the context of query executions represent probably the most interesting parts of the interprocess communication in the file system.
The following description refers to the process structure discussed in Subsection 6.1 and to Figure 8 below, which depicts the situation in case of a query execution.

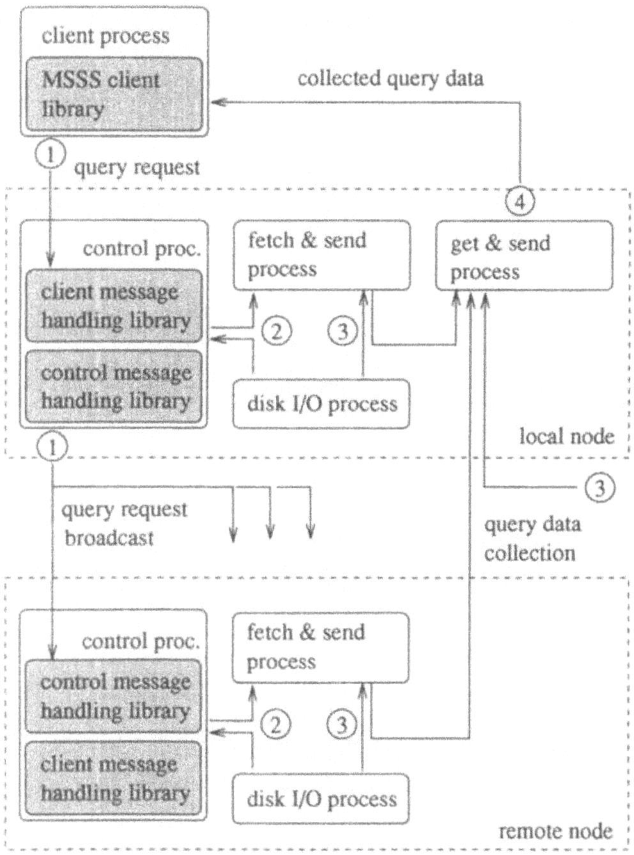

Figure 8: *Query execution*

A particular query request on node **i** is launched via an appropriate library call, received by a client message handling function and passed to the local control process on node **i**. This responsible control process sends the query request to all other control processes (phase 1). All control processes perform an index search on their local part of the DiNG file (see above) in parallel and extract all relevant data block numbers from the index (phase 2) and pass these numbers to the corresponding fetch & send processes. All fetch & send processes fetch the appropriate data blocks in parallel and send the retrieved data to the get & send process on node **i** (phase 3). As soon as the get & send buffer area on node **i** is filled, the get & send process broadcasts some kind of <stop_transmission> signal to all fetch & sendf&s processes. Subsequently, it engages in the data delivery to the client process (phase 4). As soon as the get & send buffer contents has been delivered, a <restart_transmission> signal is broadcasted by the get & send process and the receiving fetch & send processes restart their delivery operations. This protocol iterates in phase 3 and phase 4, until all the data qualified by the query request has been delivered.

7. CONCLUSIONS

A non-standard parallel file system, namely the DiNG file system, is proposed as mass storage subsystem for deductive database machines. We argue that the DiNG file system meets two crucial performance requirements for specialised MSSS to be used as part of deductive database environments. In particular, the DiNG file system takes advantage of disk arrays in shared nothing MIMD configurations and uses multikey indices as internal search structure. The need for high-performance MSSS is demonstrated by an example, namely the inference procedure for Datalog¬* rulebases. The DiNG file system adheres to a strict client-server architecture and is structurally tailored for recent microkernel approaches on highly parallel platforms (like for example the MACH kernel).

References

[AbSi91] S. Abiteboul and E. Simon, "Fundamental properties of deterministic and nondeterministic extensions of Datalog*," *Journal of Theoretical Computer Science*, vol. 7, no. 4 (1991).

[Free87] M.W. Freeston, "The BANG file: A new kind of grid file," in *Proc. ACM SIGMOD Conf.*, ACM Press, San Francisco (1987).

[Free89] M.W. Freeston, "Advances in the design of the BANG file," 3rd Int. Conf. on Foundations of Data Organisation and Algorithms, Paris (1989).

[GaST90] S. Ganguly, A. Silberschatz, and S. Tsur, "A Framework for the Parallel Processing of Datalog Queries," in *Proc. ACM SIGMOD Conf. on Mangement of Data*, ACM Press, Atlantic City (1990).

[GRBB88] R. Gonzalez-Rubio, J. Rohmer, A. Bradier, and B. Bergsten, "DDC: A Deductive Database Machine," in *Database Machines and Knowledge Base Machines*, ed. H. Tanaka, Kluwer Academic Publishers (1988).

[Kim91] W. Kim, "A Distributed Object-Oriented Database System Supporting Shared and Private Databases," *ACM TOIS*, vol. 9, no. 1 (1991).

[KoMV92] M. Kollingbaum, T.A. Mueck, and G. Vinek, "PARABASE - A federated DBMS architecture supported by a shared nothing database server," in *Proc. of the OpenForum92 Technical Conference*, EurOpen, Utrecht (1992).

[MKMK88] H. Matsuda, M. Kohata, T. Masuo, Y. Kaneda, and S. Maekawa, "Implementing Parallel Prolog System on Multiprocessor System PARK," in *Database Machines and Knowledge Base Machines*, ed. H. Tanaka, Kluwer Academic Publishers (1988).

[MuSc91] T.A. Mueck and M. Schauer, "Sorting in the BANG file," Tech.Rep. #109, Dept. of Information Systems, University of Vienna (1991).

[Muec92] T.A. Mueck, "Using a shared nothing MIMD machine as high performance database server," in *4th GI-Workshop on Foundations of DB Systems, ECRC-92-13*, ed. U. Lipeck, European Computer-Industry Research Centre (1992).

[NiHS84] J. Nievergelt, H. Hinterberger, and K.C. Sevcik, "The Grid File: An Adaptable, Symmetric Multikey File Structure," *ACM-TODS*, vol. 9, no. 1, pp. 38-71 (1984).

[Pier89] P.A. Pierce, "A Concurrent File System for a Highly Parallel Mass Storage Subsystem," in *Proc. of the 4th Conf. on Hypercubes, Concurrent Computers and Applications*, Pasadena (1989).

[Tane92] A.S. Tanenbaum, *Modern Operating Systems*, Prentice Hall, Englewood Cliffs (1992).

[WeZS91] G. Weikum, P. Zabback, and P. Scheuermann, "Dynamic File Allocation in Disk Arrays," in *Proc. ACM SIGMOD Conf. on Mangement of Data*, ACM Press, Denver (1991).

[Witz91] J. Witzmann, "The DING file system," Master Thesis, Dept. of Information Systems, University of Vienna (1991).

[WDSY91] O. Wolfson, H.M. Dewan, S.J. Stolfo, and Y. Yemini, "Incremental Evaluation of Rules and its Relationship to Parallelism," in *Proc. ACM SIGMOD Conf. on Mangement of Data*, ACM Press, Denver (1991).

DATABASE USER INTERFACE DESIGN EDITOR

Cuie Zhao Ging Yang Choo Kia Chek Phua Robin C. G. Seow

Dept. of Information Systems and Computer Science
National University of Singapore
Lower Kent Ridge Road
Singapore 0511
{zhaocuie@iscs.nus.sg}

Abstract

In this paper, we present the design and implementation of Database User Interface Design Editor which employs the WYSIWYG approach for users to interactively access and manipulate user interface widgets and database widgets to build database interfaces. By binding UIMS techniques with the database primitives, the editor provides a platform to fast prototype UIs and rapidly create reusable graphical constructs for representing database objects. It makes design-test-modify cycle which is universally recognized as the only efficient way to successful UI design an easier task by supporting two design modes – development mode and simulation mode. The simulation mode allows users to visualize the actual behaviour of the interface under development at any time without having to compile and run the interface codes created. Users can switch between these two modes.

Keywords: User Interfaces, Databases, Applications

1. INTRODUCTION

Due to the fact that traditional DBMSs are application oriented systems and targeted at novice users, most of the past efforts on database user interface (UI) have been either centered on the design of end user interface tools like graphical query language, data browser and schema editor (eg. [Mot89]), and targeted at a specific application area. Very few UI systems meet or even consider the needs for DBMS application programmers to interactively develop database application systems and DBAs to interactively manage and administrate database application systems. The lack of supports for DBAs and application developers further makes both end-users and developers very system oriented specialists. The recent emergence of new application areas for DBMSs such as geographic information systems, the management of systems with large scientific experiments and data, and design databases has engendered new challenges to database researchers.

While many aspects of DBMS have been re-examined, the user interface issue has been largely ignored. The trend towards the implementation of extensible database systems as a fast implementation platform for application specific database systems further increases the amount of database applications. For each application, the user interface is individually designed and implemented. With conventional coding, the process is tedious and time consuming. At the same time, the community of potential users of database systems has grown well beyond the traditional administrative business professionals, and now involves people from outside of database area, who are not comfortable with textual based interface. Most of them are unwilling to spend too much time to learn and use a complex system.

These collectively leads to the consideration of designing a more general user interface management system which can be customized fairly easily for different applications. Recently, the achievement in UIMS techniques has motivated the database researchers to the UIMS techniques to develop higher level graphical interfaces for new generation DBMSs to support graphical toolkits for UI construction for DBMSs. DUET [OZL92] is in such an effort that aims to integrate UIMS techniques with graphics and database interface tools to support the selection of database objects as part of the UIMS presentation component. To better support database needs, DUET directly supports basic and common complex database object types and operations. In this paper, we present the design and implementation of DUET user interface editor which is a major component of DUET system. The Editor handles the interaction between the UI designer and DUET; it also supports facilities to design UI using WYSIWYG approach.

The rest of the paper is organized as follows. In the next section, we give the outline of DUET system. Section 3 and section 4 describe the design, implementation and functionality of DUET user interface design editor. We illustrate the working of the system through the design of a database front-end and a database schema browser in section 5. Finally, we conclude in section 6

2. THE ARCHITECTURE AND FEATURES OF DUET

The fact that new generation database systems are targeted at wider range of applications signifies the toolkit approach to design highly interactive and consistent UIs for matching various DBMS applications. DUET is an effort towards bridging the UIMS, UI toolkits and database primitives to provide sufficient functionalities and facilities required by database UI designers. With UIMS capability, user gets the feeling of directly manipulating the application objects, rather than ask the interface to manipulate the objects. The user is free to click on push buttons, operate scroll bars and make menu selections. The user is thus free to select graphical objects representing the application data. This is by means of click and drag of widgets on the user interface design editor through the control of mouse. In short, DUET is a UIMS coupled with database application primitives and knowledge about DBMS. It is an integrated graphical user interface development environment for the development of end-user database applications with GUI facilities.

As illustrated in Figure 1, DUET system consists of five main components: (1) UI design editor, (2) Object display editor, (3) Database application support subsystem, (4) Demo GUI (which is not shown in Figure 1), (5) Help subsystem.

The *UI design editor* can be seen as a UIMS with extended tools on database applications. It takes the main role of a common WYSIWYG interface builder and as such, it is responsible for creating the presentation component of a user interface. The *database display method editor* is used to specify the behaviour of a database user interface and to check the syntax of a user actions sequence. The *database*

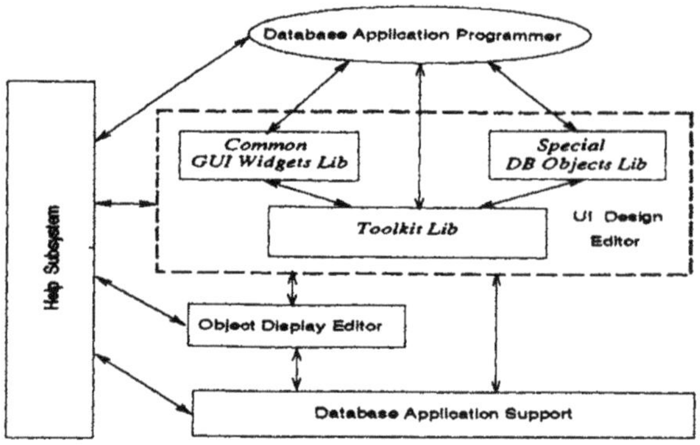

Figure 1: Structure of DUET system.

application support subsystem handles the communication between UI and the database backend. It provides an interface layer that maps the database objects into UI objects and translates graphical manipulation commands into what can be understood by the backend. The *demo GUI* part simulates a running graphical database user interface created by other components of DUET for demonstration purposes and also acts as a testing of DUET. The *help-subsystem* provides a help manual for using the system to create UI and facilities to write help information for the applications.

User communicates with DUET UI design editor and the help subsystem directly. The display method editor provides the mechanism for editing and controlling the widgets through the interface design editor. The database application support contains information about the backend and provides interface layer between the backend and UI. This is unique to our system. The help subsystem is accessible through all the other components. It provides help information of each component and supports facilities to create user application help information.

DUET is not a translator in that it does not have to reside on top of a DBMS. Using direct manipulation techniques, the user specifies high-level design specifications, such as which widgets to use, as well as low-level details of an interface, such as the size and layout of widgets. It then generates User Interface Language (UIL) or C codes which can be readily integrated into the DBMS by linking the two together, making UI appear to be a part of DBMS. The power of the interfaces generated matches those that can be produced by conventional coding. If not, the UI designer would have to fall back to conventional coding. Further, the codes generated are ensured to be error-free and to support user interface presentation independence. User interface presentation independence characteristic separates the design of an interface from the design of the computational application program so that modifications in either do not require changes in the other. This separation simplifies the task of DBMS application customization.

3. DUET USER INTERFACE DESIGN EDITOR

To support the DBMS application programmers in developing the style of interface, we have included a common graphical user interface widgets library, a special database widgets library and a toolkit library in the WYSIWYG *user interface design editor* of DUET. The tools in the toolkit library, which provide the interactive techniques to access and manipulate user interface widgets and database widgets, are employed to fast prototype UIs based on X Window System and OSF/Motif toolkit. While these tools can be used independently, DUET integrates them into a comprehensive interface development environment.

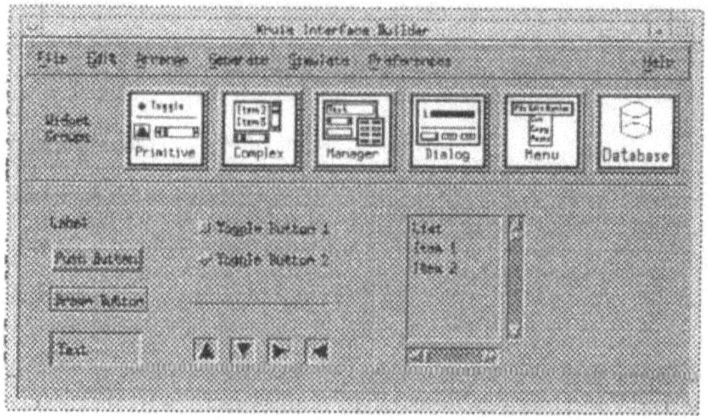

Figure 2: Screen dump of DUET UI design editor.

Figure 2 is a screen dump of DUET user interface design editor. The interface editor has a menu bar with several cascade buttons. The pulldown menu cascaded on the cascade button provides a variety of operations for the interface designer to design his/her user interface. Below the menu bar is an icon palette. Each icon on the palette represents a subgroup of widgets under a particular class. Click on one of the icons, the widgets grouped under such a class will be displayed at the widget palette at the bottom half of the window. The UI designer is free to click, drag and edit the widgets displayed on the widget palette to design his/her user interface.

This interface design editor aims to help create, manage and modify interactive, graphical, direct-manipulation user interfaces using graphical specification and direct manipulation methods. This is in line with the approaches of some recent UIMSs, such as Peridot [Mye88] and Druid [SKN90], that replace the traditional text-based user interface specification.

The iterative development is almost universally recognized as the only efficient way to successful UI design. The interface design editor facilitates rapid prototyping by significantly reducing the time needed to develop a user interface. The ease and efficiency of creating prototypes encourages experimentation, and may therefore result in better user interfaces. DUET interface design editor makes design-test-modify cycle an easier task by supporting two design modes, namely *development mode* and *simulation mode*. The simulation mode is activated by the interface simulator. Such feature allows the user to visualize the actual behaviour of the interface under development instead of requiring the designer to compile and run the user interface code created each time he/she wants to check the interface behaviours. The designer can continue constructing his/her UI by switching back to the development mode.

A UI design can be saved after a session and resumed in the next session. By enabling cut and paste process, a UI can be merged with various interfaces that were created at different time.

Figure 3 illustrates the architecture of DUET UI design editor. The UI design editor consists of the following eight components: (1) Widget Library, (2) Resource Database, (3) Code generator, (4) File Manager, (5) Presentation Editor, (6) Resource Processor, (7) Error Handler, (8) Interface Simulator.

UI designers are able to manipulate the Presentation Editor, File Manager, Code Generator, Resource Editor and Error handler directly to design and customize their UIs. Error Handler handles all the errors encountered during the design of a UI. File Manager provides a means by which the UI designer can store his/her work so that it can be retrieved for modification and enhancement at a later time. It stores user

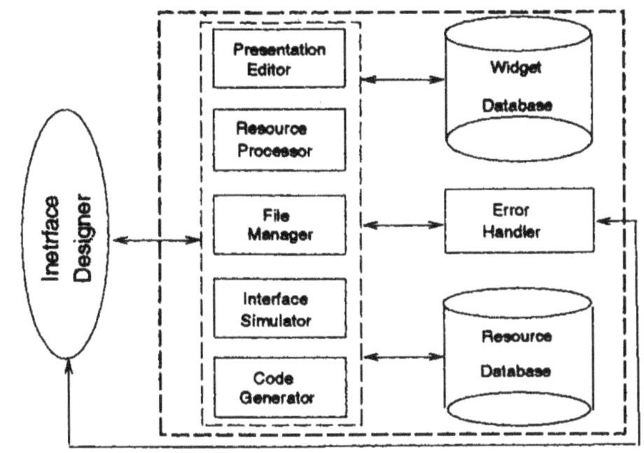

Figure 3: Structure of DUET user interface editor.

interface components and/or customized widgets into a file in UIF file format which can be used by many UI designers. This would save time and design effort for the UI designer and ensures high consistency of user interfaces. Code Generator can generate UIL/C codes for the user interface created so that it can be linked with application programs. Resource Processor supports facilities for user to edit and customize customizable widget resources to meet his/her preference. The Interface Simulator allows user to visualize the actual behaviour of the interface and/or interface component under development at any time instead of requiring the user to compile and run every time he/she wants to see how his/her interface behaves. Widget Library includes all the widgets and techniques of DUET. It has three sub-libraries, namely, commonly used UI widgets library, special database widgets library, and toolkit library which stores all the techniques for widget components. Resource Database saves all the widget resources used by DUET user interface design editor.

In the following sections, we will discuss these components in detail.

4. DUET SYSTEM COMPONENTS

4.1. Widget Library

The Widget Library has three sub-libraries namely: common user interface widget library, special database widget library, and the toolkit library. Common user interface widget library and special database widget library are tightly coupled with the toolkit library which provides class inheritance techniques for widgets stored in these two libraries. Figure 4 shows the class hierarchy of widgets in the common user interface widget library.

Motif produces a large number of widgets for conventional applications, but not for most database applications. Special purpose widgets which are not provided by Motif widget set are needed for database applications. Consider relational DBMS as an example, table (relation) is the basic structure and for a database UIMS designed for relational DBMS, it must handle column oriented data and present them in a table form. Using the Motif widget set, this requires N x M text widgets for the construction of a N x M table. Clearly, specialised table widget is more appropriate. DUET provides additional widgets that are common to the applications supported by the underlying DBMS. Some common widgets include date, time, image, chart and graphics widgets and gadgets. Figure 5 shows the class hierarchy of widgets in the special database widget library which includes all the special database widgets supported by DUET. There is a rich set of public functions attached to the respective database widgets which we will present in the next subsection.

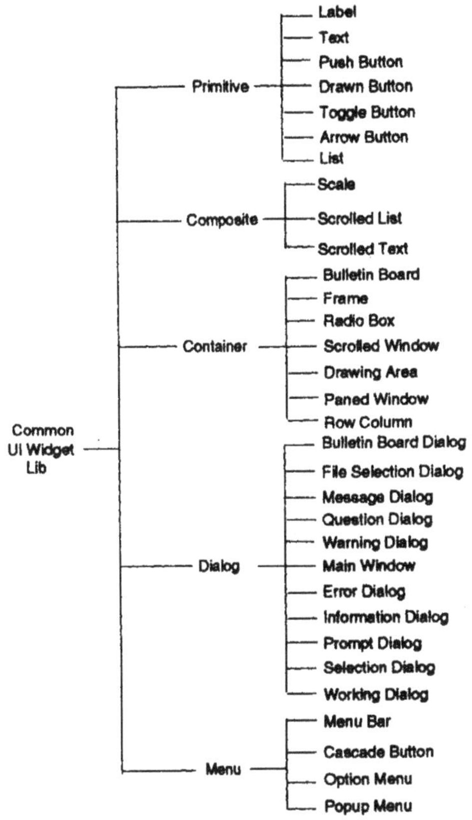

Figure 4: Class hierarchy of common widget library.

The class inheritance hierarchy of the toolkit library is given in Figure 6. DUET does not provide undo function for the following facilities: (i). No undo for File Manager to input/output file; (ii). No undo for the Interface Simulator; (iii). No undo for the Code Generator.

As shown in Figure 6, all the classes which implement File Manager, Code Generator and Interface Simulator are direct or indirect subclasses of the NoUndoCmd class. Derived classes of the EditCmd and ArrangeCmd are classes which provide methods to implement the Presentation Editor. Users can undo the last operation on these methods. The QuitCmd is derived from the WarnNoUndoCmd which itself again is a derived class from the AskFirstCmd. As one can guess from the class names, before a user quit an operation or quit the design of UI, he will be asked to confirm his operation and a warning message will be given. All the UI widgets and default callbacks associated with widgets are implemented by those subclasses derived from the UIComponent class.

4.2. Database Widgets and Functions

While it is the database UI designers' job to provide application functions to access a specified DBMS, a UI design editor should provide ways to change, modify and display user interface representations so that whenever a database objects changes, its respective UI representation will be changed accordingly. For each database widget, DUET provides a set of functions to do this.

The *table widget* provided by DUET is implemented on top of Motif widget set and is used to display an editable array of string data in a scrollable table in a similar manner to a spreadsheet. The number of rows is dynamic and determined during display. During creation of a table, the

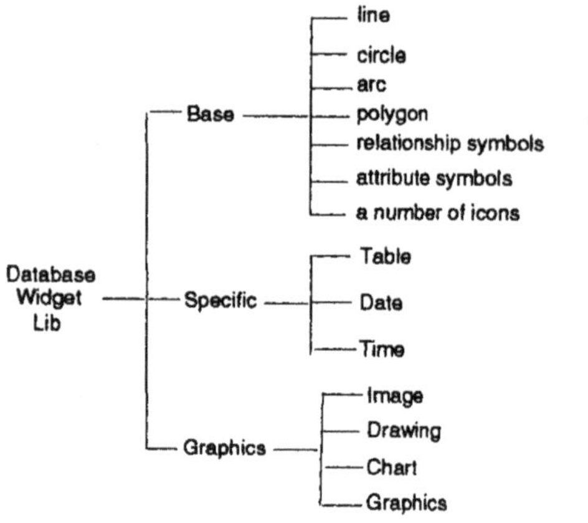

Figure 5: Class hierarchy of database widget library.

number of columns can be set by specifying a number or by dynamically adding a new column at a user specified position. Once it is created, the user may enter data into a new row, which is created by appending a row at the bottom of the table or inserting a row at a user specified position. Each cell of the table may be edited. It has callback functions for doing database objects and database object attributes validating and customizing. It allows rows (database objects), columns (database attributes), and cells (specified attributes of specified object) to be selected (highlighted). A set of alignment rules for rows, columns, and cells are selectable. The callback function list forces a certain table widget to match user's action and display the result required by the user. And, a number of fixed leading rows and columns may be specified to act as labels of database objects and database object attributes. Other functions include a set of type converters to convert one data type to another and functions to get information from a table widget and save to a database.

The *graphics widget* has a viewing widget pad acting like a row-column widget. It can hold several viewing ports which provide users a facility to display different views of the same object or view different objects at the same time. Each viewing port is a drawing area that users can focus on by selecting it and edit the object view. The selected viewing port is highlighted and may be browsed. Two default push buttons are provided: zoom-in and zoom-out. Focus on a viewing port, and push any of these two buttons, the object on this viewing port will be zoomed in or out.

The *rectangle gadget* and *circle gadget* need a graphics widget or a Motif DrawingArea widget as their parent widget. They provide different outlook for the viewing port in a graphics widget.

The *drawing widget* permits user to draw a figure, to modify and display a figure in its drawing area. There are some default pushbuttons: save, commit, quit etc. When the commit button is clicked, the modified figure is saved.

The *chart widget* provides a convenient way to display a database chart object. Ticks, titles of the X/Y axes etc. can be set according to a specified database chart object.Functions are attached to get, modify, or add a point from or to the chart widget, to set chart title, and so on.

A number of drawing tools are provided for these graphical widgets, such as draw/get/edit a line/point/arc/box, save a graphical object to a database file in Postscript format or print a graphical object to a printer in Postscript format.

The *image widget* is to support the display of database bitmap objects. With the increased disk storage capacity, images have become common database objects, and thus such display capability is important. The functions provided

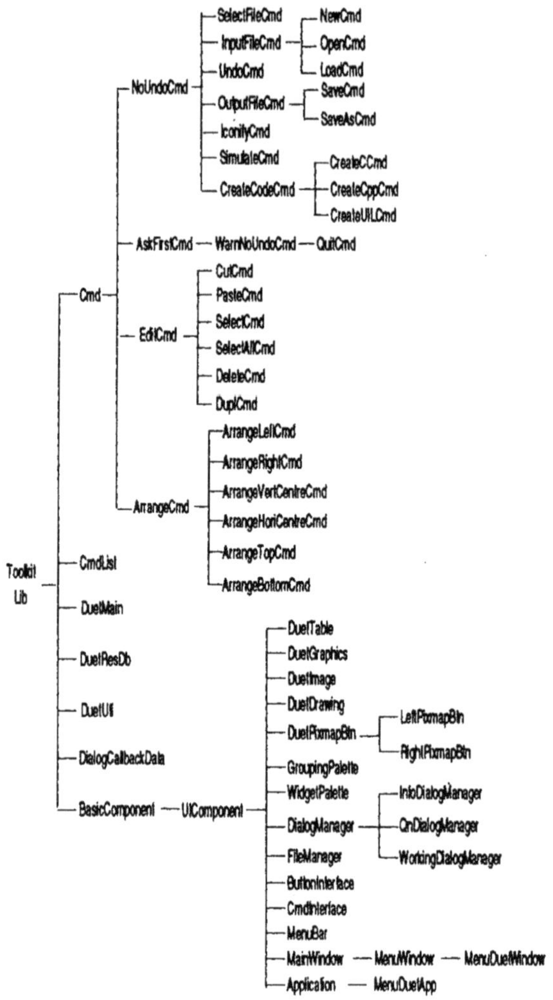

Figure 6: Class inheritance hierarchy of toolkit library.

include zoom-in, zoom-out and scrolling. A more sophisticated function such as edit can be added when the need arises.

The *date widget* is a database time widget with the form of MM/DD/YY, where MM represents the month, DD the date, and YY the year. The three fields: MM, DD, YY are actually three text cells. When a cell is filled, the cursor moves to the next cell automatically.

The *digital time widget* has the similar structure to that of date widget, but has the form of HH:MM:SS, where HH represents the hour, and MM the minutes, SS the seconds.

We have so far described the common database widgets and functions provided by DUET. Those widgets common to interface builders such as form, text, pushbutton, toggle button, etc., are no longer new and hence have not been discussed.

4.3. Resource Database

A resource is any user-customizable data such as colors, fonts, names of windows. It consists of three elements, namely, *resource name, resource type* and *default value*. The resource type indicates the general category to which each of these resource entities belongs, while the resource name identifies the specific resource entity. The default value is a reasonable default provided by the application programmer for a resource required by the program. A *resource set* is a set of resources. In Motif toolkit, each widget class owns a specific set of resources and inherits all resource sets of its superclasses. These resources are referenced by the Resource Processor, the Code Generator, the File Manager, the Presentation Editor, and the Interface Simulator. Thus, we need a resource database whereby we can access the resources of a widget class using the resource name as key. In addition, the Presentation Editor and Resource Processor require additional information such as access right and resource class of each resource.

Hardcoding the information of all resources supported by the widgets in the program is considered not feasible because of the large number of resources and non-extensible to include new resources. Thus, we use a widget resource database description file, in which, new resources for existing classes can be added easily, and default values can be modified without changing the program source codes.

4.4. Presentation Editor

The Presentation Editor is the module that facilitates the construction of user interface using direct manipulation techniques. To facilitate this interactive editing operations, the default behaviours of the widget are overridden by adding new event handlers to handle events. Some of the widget resource values are inherited from and maintained by the X window system. These resources can be accessed through the library functions. Some other resource types like pixmap and XtCallbackList require us to maintain special data structures. In our Presentation editor, we view the user interface as a collection of widgets being glued together. A *widget segment list* is used to store the widgets created. A segment representing a widget is inserted to the segment list automatically when it is created by user. Routines are provided for inserting, deleting, freeing, destroying, duplicating segment list, and to initialize and destroy a segment list.

Following facilities are supported by the Presentation Editor for UI designers to create and edit their UIs interactively.

Select. It is used to select a widget or a collection of widgets which will be edited. The selected widgets are highlighted to distinguish them from the unselected widgets. This highlighting is however made difficult by the need to handle exposure and resize events. It is not enough to re-highlight the selected widgets as the highlighting is done with XOR display function. Our solution is to redraw the background of the selected parent's background and then highlight the selected widgets.

Alignment. A collection of selected widgets can be aligned by left, right, top and bottom.

Clear. When a widget is cleared, it is destroyed and its associated segment is removed from the widget segment list. All its children is then destroyed recursively.

Duplicate. This operation is to duplicate the selected widget or widgets.

Cut and *Paste.* To support these operations, a clipboard and the associated data structure is maintained.

Moving. Widget movement is accomplished by changing the x and y resources of the widget to be moved.

Reparenting. Motif does not provide routines to perform reparenting of widget. Our solution is to create a new widget with the destination parenting widget as parent and copy all information and resources of the original widget to the new widget. After that the original widget is destroyed. Note that the original widget may contain children widgets. All these children's information and resources must be duplicated in the widget and this action is performed recursively.

Sizing. We select a model widget by comparing the location of all selected widgets. After that, the width/height of the model widget is determined. Depending on the particular sizing operation, the width/height of the other widgets are set to that of the model widget.

Undo. We undo only the last reversible action by performing the corresponding ***anti-action***. For different operations, different information must be recorded so that we can undo the operation. When the Undo operation is being activated, the undo record is being retrieved to examine the last reversible operation and the necessary operation to be performed.

4.5. Resource Processor

For each widget supported by DUET, there is an associated popup resource edit option menu. The interface designer can edit the widget resources according to his/her preference interactively by popping up the associated resource edit window through clicking the respective button on the resource edit option menu. Figure 7 shows the color resource edit window popped up when we click the background color button on the resource edit option menu.

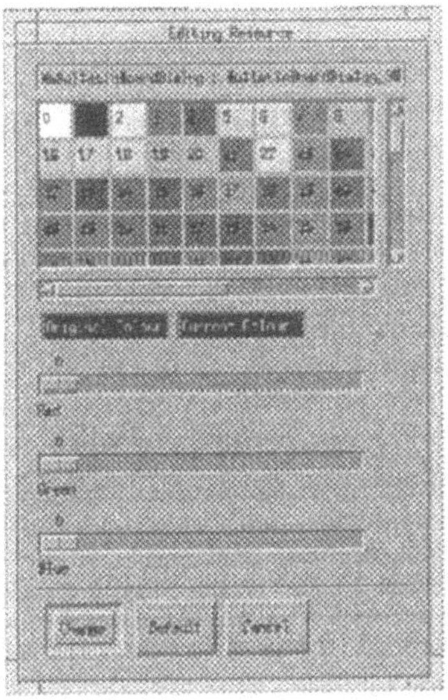

Figure 7: Color resource edit window.

The edited resources are stored and interpreted by DUET. The presentation constrained by the edited resources is then displayed on the user interface which is being designed.

4.6. File Manager

File Manager provides a means by which the UI Designer can store his work so that it can be retrieved, modified and enhanced at a later time. It helps to save time and effort for UI designers and ensures high consistency in the user interfaces of a system.

The File Manager consists of a File Input and Output subsystem. File Input Subsystem reads UIF (user interface file) file and restores the original work of the UI Designer. It also verifies the contents of the UIF file and performs the necessary house-keeping tasks if any error occurs. File Output Subsystem stores the work of the UI Designer in the UIF file format. Just like the Code Generator, it attempts to minimize the size of the UIF file by generating the least number of lines of codes possible. Figure 8 illustrates message passing between the File Manager and other components.

4.7. Code Generator, Interface Simulator and Error Handler

Code Generator can generate UIL, and C codes for the UI created. The generated codes can be linked with application

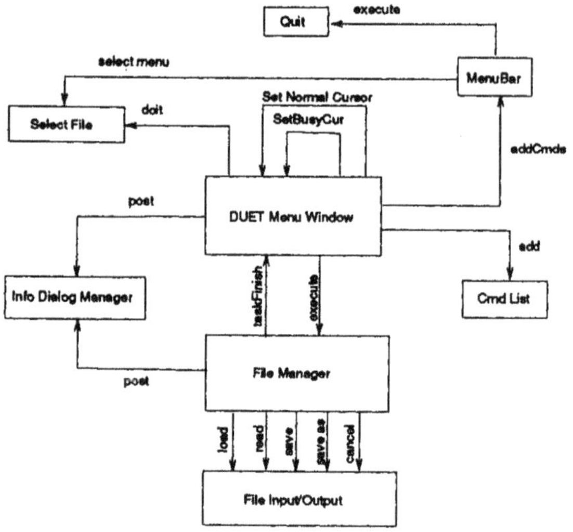

Figure 8: A message passing diagram for File Manager.

program and run with application program without having to run DUET concurrently with the application program. Thus it supports user interface presentation independence which separates the design of an interface from the design of the computational program so that modifications in either do not require changes in the other. This separation simplifies the task of DBMS application customization.

Interface Simulator provides a facility for UI designer to dynamically check the UI behaviour at any time during his design. It provides instant feedback as to how the newly designed interface will behave without having to exit DUET. The designer can continue constructing his/her UI by switching back to the development mode. The simulation feature is important since the design of a user interface needs to go through many refinement cycles before it is finalised.

Error Handler handles all errors encountered during the design of UIs. It provides feed back information to both UI designers and DUET user interface editor and provides methods to process these errors according to the response from UI designers and other components of DUET user interface design editor.

5. EXAMPLES

In this section, we illustrate two examples built by DUET in order to show users how DUET works.

5.1. Xmonitor: A Demo GUI for POSTGRES

In this subsection, we will take a short browse on the interface designed by DUET on top of POSTGRES[StR86] Database Management System. POSTGRES is an object-oriented database system. It leverages four constructs: Classes, inheritance, types, and functions. The fundamental notion of POSTGRES is that of a class, which is a named collection of instances of objects. Each instance has the same collection of named attributes, and each attribute is of a specific data type. Furthermore, each instance has a unique (never changing) identifier (OID). A subclass may inherit all attributes from its parent class, and a class can inherit from zero or more other classes. POSTGRES also supports composite types, user defined types and user defined operations and functions.

Xmonitor has the knowledge about the data model and the database management tools provided by POSTGRES for data manipulation. It is a graphical interactive frontend of POSTGRES constructed by DUET. It enables one to interactively formulate, edit and view queries and query result. As the first element of the database application's purpose is to create, update, delete, and display objects, It requires the interface be able to communicate with the application, be able to manage the visual representations, and also be able to coordinate interface tasks. Thus, we have to define the representations for each object class and the operations on the object to accomplish this task while we construct Xmonitor for POSTGRES. In the next subsection, we define the presentations of Xmonitor and we identify the operations of Xmonitor in the following subsection.

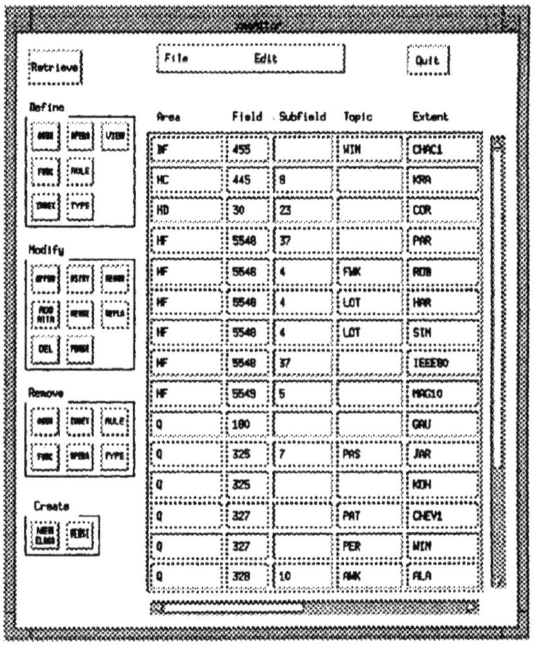

Figure 9: Main window of Xmonitor

5.1.1. Defining object representations

The basic responsibility of the object representational component is to manage the visual appearance of database objects. The representational component is also responsible for the input and output associated with the interface. Whenever an object is called, it should produce the proper visual representations for the object. For example, when an object whose type is defined as pixmap is called, the pixmap image should be displayed in the right position at the correct time. An object may have many different apperances that mean different representations in the same interface.

A table widget provided by DUET is an input/output control abstraction that implements a major application operation or mode of POSTGRES DBMS corresponds to a spreadsheet. It contains records and fields through which very large data can be displayed in the text cells in different fonts.

In the DUET main window, drag the Bulletin Board widget from the dialog widget group and release on any place on the screen you like. The Bulletin Board will act as the parent window of Xmonitor. Users can edit the representations via poping up the respective resource edit dialog and specifying the resources. Now press down mouse button 3 with the mouse arrow point to the bulletin board and a resource edit option menu is poped up. Move the mouse till the arrow point to "Value/Label" and release the mouse button 3 on the "Title" attribute of the popup submenu. Then a Dialog Title resource editor is poped up. Change the Dialog Title as "Xmonitor". Similarly, we change the background and foreground of Xmonitor to white and black respectively.

Now click and drag other widgets from DUET main window and land on Xmonitor bulletin board. The interface changes to look like Figure 9. For the table widget, users can specify rows, columns,visible rows, visible columns, fixed rows, fixed columns, etc. as needed. For the "Retrieve" push button, when it is pushed by the end user, a retrieve specification window is supposed to be popped up. So we have to drag another bulletin board from the DUET main window and design the retrieve specification window as figure 10. As the details of changing widget resources are very similar to the examples above, we will not repeat this part. Instead, we will give some examples of defining operations, i.e., widget functionality in the next subsection.

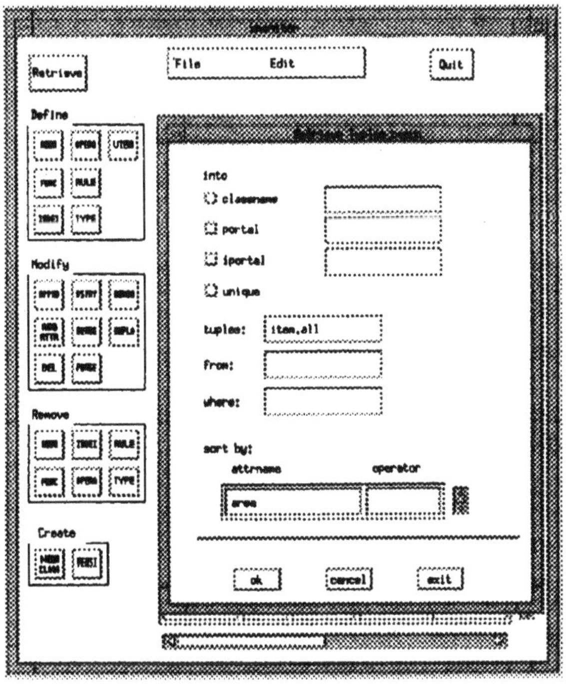

Figure 10: Retrieve tuples window of Xmonitor

5.1.2. Defining operations on objects

The operational component has access to the POSTGRES management tools and POSTQUEL interface. POSTQUEL is the POSTGRES query language interface. It is responsible for processing user queries and passing the results to the presentational component so that the correct object display can be produced or updated at the correct time and in the right order.

X window system provides three separate machnisms that can be used to link widgets and applications. One of them is callbacks. A widget interacts with an application via declaring one or more callback lists as resources; the application adds functions to these callback lists, which will be invoked whenever the predefined callback conditions are met. Callback lists are resources, so that the application can set or change the function that will be invoked.

Press down mouse button 3 on the "ok" button and pop up the callback resource editor window to add the predefined functions as XmNactivateCallback callbacks of the "ok" button. After adding these callbacks, push the "ok" button, the user specified retrieve restrictions are parsed and binded by Xmonitor as a query string.If without error, the query string is sent to the postgres backend to fetch the required tuples and displayed the result on the Xmonitor main window. After defining all the operations of retrieve tuples window, we add the retrieve tuples window as a pop up window of the "Retrieve" push button of the Xmonitor main window, by specifying it as a callback resource of the "Retrieve" push button and specifying the "Retrieve" button as the parent widget of the retrieve tuple window. After this, the retrieve tuple window can be popped up as and when the end user pushes the "Retrieve" button to specify the query.

In Xmonitor interface, the pull down menus and popup windows hold all the operations supported by POSTGRES which can perform computations, change values displayed through the table, and call dialog windows or other interfaces. A dialog window is a control abstraction that requires an immediate response from the user. It requests additional information needed from the user to complete a task, or it notifies the user error. By clicking on the ok button, an operation is commited. Xmonitor then parses this action sequence, and communicate with POSTQUEL parser to check and make sure that the semantics of the action sequences is legal, and the object type is of the class constructed. If not, an error dialog will pop up with error message. Otherwise, the specified operation and operation result is bound to the specified database object, and the transaction is processed by postgres backend.

However, both the presentation part and the operation part need to be refined. After the refinement, we turn to test the behaviour of Xmonitor. Click the "Retrieve" button on Xmonitor main window and specify the query as shown in Figure 10. The query is constructed as "retrieve (item.all) sort by area using <" by Xmonitor and is sent to the POSTGRES backend to parse and execute the constructed query string once the "ok" button is clicked. The query result is displayed on the main window (see Figure 9). As the book item with call no. 5548.4.Lot.Sim is no longer available, we need to delete it from the book item database (where the call no. is combined by "area.field.subfield.topic.extent"). Highlight the tuple that matches the call no. and click the delete icon on the modify pane, a warning dialog window pops up to warn the user that the hightlighted tuple or tuples will be deleted from the database once the user confirms this deletion action with clicking "ok" button on the warning dialog window. Since the book is no longer available, we confirm the deletion. At the mean time, several new books have been received, and we have to add them to the database to make them available to the readers. We add all the new arrived items to the blank entries of the table at the end. After we have checked that there is no typing error, we click the append icon on the modify pane to append all the added items to the database. These items are now available to readers for reading and borrowing.

5.2. Another Example

DUET can construct various GUIs for various DBMS applications. Figure 11 shows a schema browser interface for an automobile database. The interface aims to allow users to examine classes and the attributes associated with each class through selecting and clicking the push button on the top left corner in the schema browser.

To create this interface by DUET, firstly, drag out a Bulletin Board from the widget palette of DUET UI Design Editor under the "Dialog" widget group. As each of the icons in Figure 11 is actually a push button loaded with a pixmap, the user has to place in the necessary number of push buttons into the Bulletin Board. Push buttons can be chosen from the primitive widget group via clicking the "Primitive" icon in the Top right palette of DUET interface builder.

To load a pixmap into each desired push button, the user will click on the third button of the mouse. This will allow

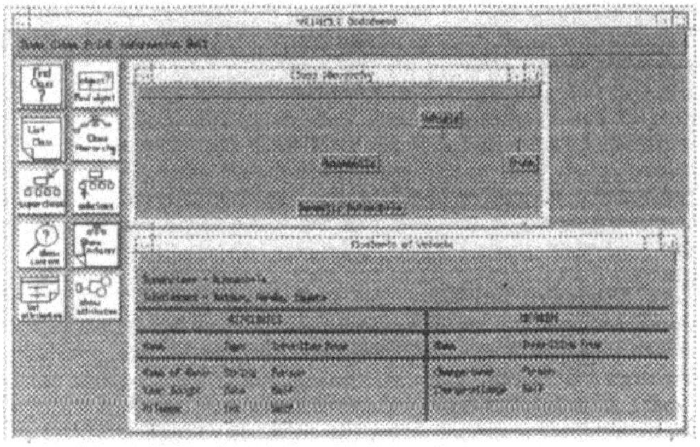

Figure 11: A database schema browser.

the choosing of a "string type" for the loading of the pixmap. The pixmap has to be created in the first place.

Upon loading the pixmaps on the desired push buttons, the user can then position them at the appropriate positions on the Bulletin Board.

Next, the user creates the interface associated with the "Find Class" icon and other icons. Bulletin Board is used as the parent in many cases. Also, through the clicking of the third button of the mouse, the user is allowed to add and associate callbacks to the push button. Vertical and horizontal lines can be drawn by clicking *line* under the database "base" group. In the near future, automatic line drawing will be supported for class relationships.

The UI designed allows end users to click on "show attributes" icon to display related attributes of a class. Note that DUET only supports UI building; at the moment, it does not support database functions like data/schema retrieval. These are database functions and they can be easily coupled with certain widgets via widget callback resources.

6. CONCLUSION

The integrating of UIMS techniques and graphics tools as a database UIMS is an essential component of new generation DBMSs to cater for a wider range of applications. DUET is an effort towards bridging the UIMS, UI toolkits and database primitives to provide sufficient functionalities and facilities required by database UI designers. In this paper, we have briefly reviewed the design and features of DUET and mainly discussed the design and implementation of DUET User Interface Design Editor, which is a major component of DUET system.

The Presentation Editor of DUET User Interface Design Editor aims to help UI designers to fast prototype database UIs and rapidly create graphical constructs for representing database objects with minimal programming effort. Its Interface Simulator provides a facility for UI designer to dynamically check the UI behaviour at any time during his/her design without having to exit DUET. The designer can switch back to the development mode from the simulator mode to continue his/her interface design. Its Code Generator can generate UIL/C codes, which can readily be compiled with application program or database backend. The File Manager helps to save time and effort for UI designers and ensures high consistency of UIs as it provides facilities for UI designers to store and retrieve their works.

More functionalities and facilities for database user interface design are currently being implemented and some will be incorporated into the system in the near future.

Acknowledgement We would like to thank our supervisor, Dr. Beng Chin Ooi, for reviewing and giving useful comments on the paper, who has also advised on the design and implementation of the system. The first author, Cuie, would like to thank her supervisor, Dr. Hongjun Lu, for his supervision, suggestion and help during the project. We would also like to thank Chin Hui Ong for his implementation effort on the first version of the system.

References

[BMP92] P. Borras, J. C. Mamou, D. Plateau, B. Poyet and D. Tallot: Building user interface for database applications: The O2 experience. *SIGMOD RECORD, 21*, 1, 32-38 (1992)

[DEU91] O. Deux et al. The O2 System. *Communications of the ACM, 34*, 10 34-48 (1992)

[KKS88] H.-J. Kim, H. F. Korth, A. Silberschatz: PICASSO: A graphical query language. Software *Practice and Experience 183*, 169-203 (1988).

[KiN89] R. King, M. Novak: FaceKit: A Database Interface Design Toolkit. *Proceedings of the Fifteenth International Conference on Very Large Data Base.* 115-123 (1989).

[KiN92] . King, M. Novak: Building Resuable Data Representations with FaceKit. *SIGMOD RECORD, Vol. 21, No. 1*, 11-17 (1992).

[Mot89] A. Motro: The design of KIVIEW: an object-oriented browser. *Proc. 2nd Int'l. Conf. on Expert Database Systems.* 107-131 (1989).

[Mye88] B. Myers: *Creating User Interfaces by Demonstration.* Academic Press, Boston, (1988).

[Ols87] D. R. Olsen: Larger issues in user interface management. *Computer Graphics, 2*, 134-136 (1987).

[OZL92] B. C. Ooi, C. Zhao, H. Lu: DUET: A Database User Interface Management System. Technical Report TRP3/92, Department of Inf. Sys. and Computer Sc., NUS, (1992).

[PCL89] D. Plateau, R. Cazalens, D. Leveque, J.-L. Mamou, B. Poyet: *Building user interfaces with LOOKS hyper-object system,* Altair Technical Report 18p (1989).

[Row92] L. A. Rowe: A Retrospective on Database Application Development Frameworks. *SIGMOD RECORD, 21*, 1, 5-10, (1992).

[RKS91] L. A. Rowe, J. A. Konstan, B. C. Smith, S. Seitz, C. Liu: The Picasso application framework. *ACM Symposium on User Interface Software and Technology,* South Carolina, 95-105 (1991).

[Shu88] N. C. Shu: *Visual Programming.* Van Nostrand Reinhold Company, New York (1988).

[Sin89] G. Singh: Automating the lexical and syntactic design of graphical user interfaces. Ph. D. Thesis, The University of Alberta (1989).

[SKN90] G. Singh, C. H. Kok, T. Y. Ngan: Druid: A system for demonstrational rapid user interface development. *Proc. ACM Siggraph Symposium on User Interface Development,* 167-177 (1990).

[StR86] M. Stonebraker, L. A. Rowe: The design of POSTGRES. *Proc. ACM Sigmod Int'l. Conf. on Management of Data,* 340-355 (1986).

[ThH83] J. J. Thomas, G. Hamlin (eds): Graphics input interaction technique (GIIT) workshop summary. *Computer Graphics, 1*, 5-66 (1983).

Object-Oriented Data Models

AN OBJECT-CENTERED DATA MODEL FOR ENGINEERING DESIGN DATABASES

Huibin Zhao
Boston University
Boston, MA 02215
zhaohb@cs.bu.edu

Alexandros Biliris
AT&T Bell Laboratories
Murray Hill, NJ 07974
biliris@research.att.com

ABSTRACT: Entities in engineering design databases reveal a need for dynamic evolution in both structure and behavior. Such a need, however, is not addressed by object-oriented data models that are heavily based on the class concept. On the contrary, models that are based on the prototype concept fully allow dynamic object evolution. However, they do not have the abilities for object classification and strong typing supported by models that have classes. In this paper we present a new object-oriented model that properly consolidates those two modeling approaches to achieve dynamic object evolution, flexible object classification, and strong typing, of all the benefits in each approach.

1. INTRODUCTION

In the past few years, the advancement of database technologies has led the research and development of database systems to more advanced engineering design applications encompassing computer-aided design (CAD), computer-aided manufacturing (CAM), computer-aided engineering (CAE). and computer-aided software engineering (CASE). Unlike entities in traditional business applications, design entities usually are complex-structured and related by complicated relationships. Moreover, design entities reveal an evolutionary characteristic; from time to time, they may need to change their structure and behavior due to the iterative and exploratory nature of the engineering design process.

With the rapid development and acceptance of the object-oriented methodology in different fields of computer science, there is an ever-growing consensus in the database community that the object-oriented methodology provides a suitable paradigm for the design of advanced engineering design database systems.[1)] A major reason for this is that object-oriented data models provide suitable modeling constructs for direct representation and efficient manipulation of design entities. Despite their large number and variety, existing object-oriented data models can be classified into two broad categories: class-based and prototype-based.

Class-based models focus heavily on classes.[2, 6)] Classes that represent the structure and behavior of entity sets in the real world are defined first; instances that represent individual entities are instantiated from classes. Instances are permanently bound to their instantiating class from which they inherit both structure (attribute) and behavior (method) definitions. Consequently, all instances of a class must have a uniform structure and behavior that cannot be changed independently of the class. Although this property allows efficient representation and access of instances of a class, it inhibits instances from changing their structure or behavior on individual basis.[7, 8)]

Prototype-based models focus on objects instead.[5, 9)] In prototype-based models, classes do not exist at all; each object exists by itself and defines its own structure and behavior. An object can also have some other objects as its *prototypes* from which it inherits either definitions or states. Clearly, all forms of structural and behavioral evolution of objects can be achieved in this approach. However, by totally discarding classes, this approach loses both the object classification and strong typing capabilities supported by the class concept.

In this paper we present a new object-oriented data model, called *object-centered*, that consolidates the above two conventional approaches. As in prototype-based models, objects in our model exist by themselves and carry their own structural definitions. However, our model introduces a novel object classification mechanism which defines classes as structural constraints enforced for class membership, instead of as structural template of their instances as in class-based models. Objects can be dynamically associated with classes to inherit their behavioral definitions. Such a loose and non-permanent binding between objects and classes allows objects to change their structure and behavior dynamically in their lifetime. Still, by enforcing all its instances to have a mandatory set of attributes, a class provides a uniform and strongly-typed view of its instances in spite of the dissimilarities in their structures and behaviors. As a result, our model achieves dynamic object evolutions, flexible object classification, and strong typing, of all the benefits in either the class-based or the prototype-based modeling approach.

The rest of the paper is organized as follows. Section 2 defines the basic notions of the model, such as objects, classes, schema and database. Section 3 discusses the typing behavior of the model, in particular, the class instanceship condition and the typing semantics of classes. Section 4 discusses the object evolution mechanism of the model in details. In Section 5, we briefly describe the object versioning constructs of the model. Section 6 reviews other related work. Finally, Section 7 concludes the paper.

2. BASICS OF THE OBJECT-CENTERED DATA MODEL

2.1. Objects: Independent Entities

This subsection defines the notation of objects. All definitions are based on the existence of the following disjoint sets:

- A finite set of *basic domains* $D_1, \cdots, D_n$ for $n \geq 1$. For instance, the set of integers, the set of reals, and the set of strings.

- A finite set of *basic types* $T_1, \cdots, T_n$, one for each basic domain, i.e., the domain of T_i is D_i for $1 \le i \le n$.
- A countable infinite set A of symbols called *attribute names*.
- A countable infinite set ID of symbols called *object identifiers*.
- A finite set CN of symbols called *class names*
- A finite set MN of symbols called *method names*

Definition *Values*: There are four types of values:

1. Every $d \in \bigcup_{i=1}^{n} D_i$ is a *basic value*.
2. Every $id \in$ ID is an *object reference value*.
3. If $v_1, \cdots, v_n$ are values, then $\{v_1, \cdots, v_n\}$ is a *set value*.
4. If $a_1, \cdots, a_n$ are attribute names in A and $v_1, \cdots, v_n$ are values, then $[a_1: v_1, \cdots, a_n: v_n]$ is a *tuple value*.

The symbol V denotes the set of all values. □

An *object* in the object-centered model represents an entity in the real world. An object has a unique and immutable identifier and a collection of attributes.

Definition *Objects*: An *object* is a triple $o = (id, pro, A)$ where

- $id \in$ ID is the identifier of o.
- $pro \in$ ID is the identifier of the *prototype* object of o.
- $A = \{<a_i: v_i> \mid 1 \le i \le n\}$ is the set of (locally defined) *attributes* of o, each being a pair $<a_i: v_i>$ where $a_i \in$ A is its name and $v_i \in$ V is its value.

We use $o.id$, $o.pro$, and $o.A$ to denote the identifier, the prototype, and the set of attributes of object o. Also, we use symbol O to denote the set of all objects. □

As in prototype-based models, objects exist independently of any class and carry their own structural definitions and attribute values. In addition to changing their attribute values, objects can add or drop attributes from time to time.

An object may also have some other object as its *prototype*,[1] and itself is called an *extension* of its prototype. The association between a prototype and an extension defines an inheritance relationship as stated by the following delegation axiom:

> **Axiom of Delegation:** For every $o \in$ O, $a \in$ A and $v \in$ V, $<a: v>$ is *defined* on o iff:
>
> 1. $<a: v> \in o.A$; or
> 2. Case 1 fails and $<a: v>$ is defined on $o.pro$.

Namely, all attributes of a prototype will be inherited by its extensions unless they have been redefined in the extensions. The above delegation mechanism can be realized by forwarding all messages that access inherited attributes of an extension to its prototype. We use $o.EA$ to denote the set of *all* attributes defined on object o, either locally defined or inherited.

[1] For simplicity of discussion, only single inheritance will be considered in this paper.

We now give some examples of objects. For clarity, all entities will be denoted directly using their identifiers or names in all examples of the paper.

```
V6Engine =        ( V6Engine,
                    nil,
                    { num_cylinders:     4,
                      compression_ratio: 7.6,
                      min_octane_num:    89 } )
ToyotaStdTrans =  ( ToyotaStdTrans,
                    nil,
                    { num_gears:         5,
                      final_gear_ratio:  4.2 } )
Camry =           ( Camry,
                    nil,
                    { engine:            V6Engine,
                      transmission:      ToyotaStdTrans,
                      chief_designer:    [last: "Major", first: "John"]} )
WhiteCamry =      ( WhiteCamry,
                    Camry,
                    { chief_designer:    [last: "Smith", first: "Mark"],
                      color:             "White" } )
```

In object *Camry*, the values of attributes *engine* and *transmission* are object references to object *V6Engine* and *ToyotaStdTrans* respectively. The value of *chief_designer* is a tuple attribute consisting of two sub-attributes *last* and *first*. Object *WhiteCamry* inherits *engine* and *transmission* attributes from its prototype *Camry*, redefines the *chief_designer* attribute, and adds a new *color* attribute.

2.2. Classes: Classification by Constraints

In this subsection, we define the notion of classes.

Definition *Types*: A *type* can be one of the following:

1. A basic type T_i.
2. A class name $cn \in$ CN called a *class type*.
3. If t is a type, then $\{t\}$ is a type called a *set type*.
4. If $a_1, \cdots, a_n$ are attribute names in A, and $t_1, \cdots, t_n$ are types, then $[a_1: t_1, \cdots, a_n: t_n]$ is a type called a *tuple type*.

We denote by T the set of all types. □

Definition *Method Specifications*: A *method specification*, or simply a *method*, is a pair $m = (mn, s)$ where

- $mn \in$ MN is the name of m.
- $s = t_1 \times t_2 \times \cdots \times t_n \rightarrow t$, where $t_1, t_2, \cdots, t_n$ and t are types in T, is the *signature* of m.

M is used to denote the set of all methods. □

Classes model the roles that entities play in the real world. A class definition consists of a set of attribute specifications and a set of method specifications.

Definition *Classes*: A *class* is a tuple $c = (cn, sup, AS, MS)$ where

- $cn \in$ CN is the name of the class.
- $sup \in$ CN is the name of its (immediate) superclass.
- $AS = \{<a_i: t_i> \mid 1 \le i \le n\}$ is the set of (locally specified) *attribute specifications* of c, each being a pair $<a_i: t_i>$ where $a_i \in$

A is its name and $t_i \in$ T is its type.

- $MS = \{m_i \mid 1 \le i \le k\}$ is the set of (locally specified) method specifications of c.

We use C to denote the set of all classes. □

A class also has a set of member objects called its *instances* associated with it. All instances of a class inherit the behavior specifications – but not the structure specifications – of the class. Classes can be related by the *specialization* or *subclassing* relationship, denoted as $IS\text{-}A(c, c')$. This *IS-A* relationship between a *subclass* c and its *superclass* c' is also an inheritance relationship, as stated by the following inheritance axiom:

> **Axiom of Inheritance:** For every $c \in$ C, $a \in$ A, $t \in$ T and $m \in$ M, $<a : t>$ (or m) is *specified* on c iff:
> 1. $<a : t> \in c.AS$ (or $m \in c.MS$); or
> 2. Case 1 fails and $<a : t>$ (or m) is specified on $c.sup$.

Namely, all attribute and method specifications of a superclass will be inherited by its subclasses, unless they have been re-specified in the subclasses. In the later case, the re-specified attributes or methods in a subclass must be a refinement of their corresponding ones in the superclass. Similar to the delegation mechanism, the inheritance mechanism can be realized by dynamically forwarding messages that cannot be responded locally by a subclass to its superclass. Alternatively, it can be realized by copying all inherited attribute and method specifications to the subclass to speed up schema access. Likewise, we use $c.EAS$ and $c.EMS$ to denote the set of *all* attribute specifications and the set of *all* method specifications of class c, either locally specified or inherited.

Following are some examples of classes:

```
VehicleEngine =    ( VehicleEngine,
                     Class,
                     { num_cylinders:       int,
                       compression_ratio:   real }
                     { horse_power:         VehicleEngine → int } )
GasolineEngine =   ( GasolineEngine,
                     VehicleEngine,
                     { min_octane_num:      int }
                     { ...                      } )
VehicleTransmission = ( VehicleTransmission,
                     Class,
                     { num_gears:           int },
                     { ...                      } )
Vehicle =          ( Vehicle,
                     Class,
                     { engine:              VehicleEngine,
                       transmission:        VehicleTransmission }
                     { ...
                       max_speed:           Vehicle → real } )
```

The *engine* attribute specification in the *Vehicle* class specifies that all instances of *Vehicle* must have an *engine* attribute with its value being a reference to some instance of the *VehicleEngine* class; similarly for its *transmission* attribute specification. The *GasolineEngine* class is defined as a subclass of *VehicleEngine*, from which it inherits *num_cylinders* and *compression_ratio* attributes and *horse_power* method specifications. Other three classes are defined as subclasses of the system-defined root class *Class*.

2.3. Schema and Database

A database in our model can be considered as consisting of two layers: an object layer and a classification layer, see Figure 1. The *object layer* maintains the set of objects in the database and controls their creation and manipulation. The *classification layer* maintains the set of classes in the database that are used to classify objects in the object layer. The classification layer provides a uniform and strongly-typed view of objects in the database.

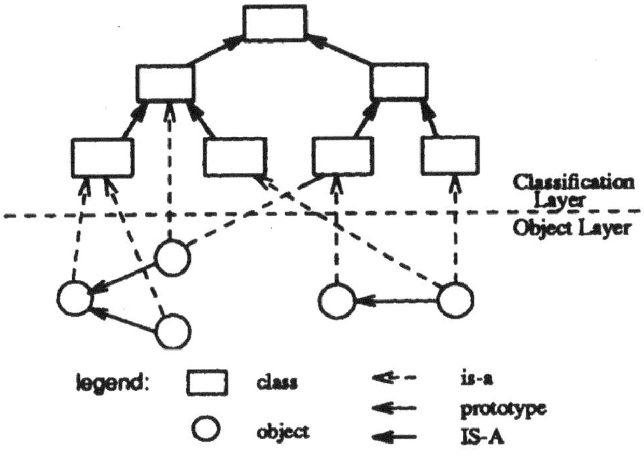

Figure 1. Two-layered database structure

Classes in the classification layer and their specialization relationships form a hierarchical structure called *class hierarchy*. The class hierarchy defines the schema of the database:

Definition *Schema*: A *schema* is a set of classes C satisfying the following constraints:

1. For all $c, c' \in C$, $c.cn \neq c'.cn$. (No two classes in the schema have the same name.)
2. For every $c \in C$, $ref(c) \subseteq C$ where $ref(c)$ denotes the set of classes referenced by class c in its definition. (All classes referenced by c are also defined in the schema.)
3. For all $c \in C$ other than *Class*, $c.sup \neq$ nil. (Every class other than *Class* has a superclass.) □

Thus a class hierarchy must be a connected tree with the system-defined class *Class* as the root.

Definition *Database*: A *database* is a pair $DB = (C, O)$ where C is a schema and O is a set of objects satisfying the following constraints:

1. For all $o, o' \in O$, $o.id \neq o'.id$.
2. For every $o \in O$, $ref(o) \subseteq O$.

Objects in O may be assigned to none, one or many classes in C at any moment. □

An imaginary vehicle design database can be defined as

VehicleDB = (O = { *V6Engine*, *ToyotaStdTrans*, *Camry*, *WhiteCamry* },
C = { *VehicleEngine*, *GasolineEngine*, *VehicleTransmission*, *Vehicle* })

where the objects and classes of *VehicleDB* were defined in the previous subsections.

3. CLASS INSTANCESHIPS AND TYPING RULES

This section discusses the typing behavior of our model. We first present the type inference rules of the model. Then we formally define the condition for an object to become an instance of a class. We also show that classes provide a uniform and strongly-typed view of their instances.

In our model, a type represents a set of values. The semantic assertion "value v having a type t", denoted as $v:t$, is then interpreted as v being a member of the set defined by t, and assertion "t_1 *being a subtype of* t_2", denoted as $t_1 \leq t_2$, corresponds to the mathematical set inclusion condition $t_1 \subseteq t_2$.

In the following, the *type inference rules* of the model are presented. Those rules are in the form of $\frac{X}{Y}$ where the horizontal line denotes a logical implication, i.e., if we can infer X, then we can infer Y. In those rules, a denotes an attribute name variable, v a value variable, t a type variable, o an object variable, and c a class variable. The following five rules are used to deduce the subtyping relationships among types:

(Basic) $$\frac{D_i \subseteq D_j}{T_i \leq T_j}$$

This rule states that the subtyping relationships on basic types are determined by the set inclusion relationships on their corresponding domains.

(Set) $$\frac{t_1 \leq t_2}{\{t_1\} \leq \{t_2\}}$$

This rule says that the subtyping relationships on set types are determined by the subtyping relationships on their element types.

(Tuple) $$\frac{t_1 \leq t'_1, \ldots, t_n \leq t'_n}{[a_1:t_1, \ldots, a_n:t_n, a_{n+1}:t_{n+1}, \ldots, a_{n+k}:t_{n+k}] \leq [a_1:t'_1, \ldots, a_n:t'_n]}$$

This rule states that a tuple type is a subtype of another only when it has at least those attributes of the supertype and with more restrictive domains.

(Class) $$\frac{IS\text{-}A(c_1, c_2)}{c_1.cn \leq c_2.cn}$$

This rule states that a subclass is also a subtype of its superclass.

(Transition) $$\frac{t_1 \leq t_2, t_2 \leq t_3}{t_1 \leq t_3}$$

This rule says that the subtyping relationship is transitive.

The next five rules are used to deduce the type(s) that a value has:

(Basic) $$\frac{v \in D_i}{v:T_i}$$

This rule states that all values in the domain of a basic type have this basic type.

(Set) $$\frac{v_1:t, \ldots, v_n:t}{\{v_1, \ldots, v_n\}:\{t\}}$$

This rule states that a set value has a set type $\{t\}$ if all its elements have type t.

(Tuple) $$\frac{v_1:t_1, \ldots, v_n:t_n}{[a_1:v_1, \ldots, a_n:v_n]:[a_1:t_1, \ldots, a_n:t_n]}$$

This rule states that a value of a tuple type must have at least of those attributes in the tuple type with values of corresponding types.

(Object) $$\frac{is\text{-}a(o, c)}{o.id:c.cn}$$

Here $is\text{-}a(o, c)$ denotes that object o is an instance of class c. This rules states that all instances of a class have this class type.

(Subtype) $$\frac{v:t_1, t_1 \leq t_2}{v:t_2}$$

This rule says that all values of a subtype is also values of its supertypes.

In our model, classification of objects is achieved by associating objects with certain classes. A *class assignment* operation is provided for assigning an object o to a class c. The operation will check o to see whether it satisfies the instanceship condition of c according to the following axiom:

> **Axiom of is-a:** An instance $o = (id, pro, A)$ of a class $c = (cn, sup, AS, MS)$ must satisfy the *instanceship condition* of c, formally defined as:
>
> For every $<a: t> \in c.EAS$, there exists a $<a: v> \in o.EA$ such that $v:t$.

Namely, for o to become an instance of c, it must have at least of those attributes specified in c with values of required types. Otherwise, the assignment is rejected. In *VehicleDB*, objects *V6Engine* and *ToyotaStdTrans* can be assigned to classes *GasolineEngine* and *VehicleTransmission* respectively. Afterwards, objects *Camry* and *WhiteCamry* can be assigned to class *Vehicle*.

As we can see, instances are allowed to have more attributes than those required by their class. For instance, object *Camry* has an additional *chief_designer* attribute than those required by its *Vehicle* class. Therefore, the attribute specifications of a class actually define the minimum structural requirements or constraints that instances of the class must satisfy, in contrast to serving as the structural template of its instances in class-based models. Classes thus can be used to classify objects of heterogeneous structures. Such a classification mechanism also has two other benefits.

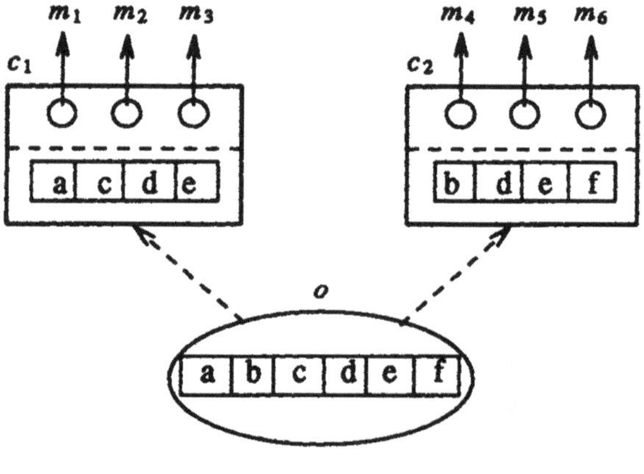

Figure 2. Multiple views of object

One benefit is that an object can be assigned to multiple classes concurrently when it satisfies instanceship conditions of all those classes. This essentially gives the capability to support multiple views of the same entity observed from different perspectives, as shown in Figure 2. In the figure, object o is assigned to both class c_1 and c_2, each defining a different view of the object: in the view defined by c_1, attributes a, c, d and e of o are visible and methods m_1, m_2 and m_3 are applicable; in the other view defined by c_2, attributes b, d, e and f of o are visible and other three different methods m_4, m_5 and m_6 are applicable instead. As in the relational system, such a view mechanism can be used to support multiple levels of abstraction, authorization, and interoperability in heterogeneous environment.

Another benefit is that the association between an object and a class can be changed dynamically. A *class de-assignment* operation is provided for removing an object from a class. Thus it is possible for an object to be assigned to a class at time $t1$, then removed from the class at $t2$, and finally assigned to a different class at $t3$. The dynamic nature of the *is-a* relationship allows an object to play a different role at different time or play multiple roles at the same time. As a result, objects can also change their behavior dynamically.

Besides for classification of objects, classes are also used for typing of objects. According to the *object* typing rule, a class c is a type with its domain being the set of all its instances. The significance of a class type is that, as speculated by the next two typing rules, it provides a uniform view of its instances which may actually have different structures and behaviors:

(Attr. Sele.) $$\frac{is\text{-}a(o,c),\ \langle a:t\rangle \in c.EAS}{o.a:t}$$

This rule states that for an instance o of a class c, if c has an attribute specification named as a and typed as t, then the value of attribute a of object o must be of type t.

(Meth. Appl.)

$$\frac{is\text{-}a(o,c),\ v_2{:}t_2,\ldots,v_n{:}t_n,\ (mn,\ c\times t_2\times\cdots\times t_n\rightarrow t)\in c.EMS}{mn(o,\ v_2,\ \ldots,\ v_n):t}$$

This rule states that for an instance o of a class c, if c has a method specification with its name being mn and the types of arguments being $t_2, \cdots, t_n$ and the result type being t, then an invocation of method mn on object o with arguments of required types must return a result of type t. The above two rules provide the basis for strong typing of objects as in class-based models.

4. OBJECT EVOLUTION

4.1. Object Evolution Invariants

As mentioned in previous sections, the object-centered model allows object to evolve in both their structure and behavior. In addition to changing their attribute values, objects can also add or drop attributes from time to time, or change their classes to obtain different behavior. However, if not controlled properly, such dynamic evolution of objects may result in unexpected invalidation of their instanceships. For example, for the *ToyotaStdTrans* object in the *VehicleDB* database, if it drops its *num_gears* attribute, then its previous instanceship to the *VehicleTransmission* class will be invalidated as a result of the update because *VehicleTransmission* requires all its instances to have a *num_gears* attribute. More seriously, an update to an object not only may invalidate instanceships of this updated object itself, but it may further trigger the invalidation of the instanceships of its referencing objects. Continuing the above example, for the *Camry* complex object in *VehicleDB* which refers to the *ToyotaStdTrans* object, once the instanceship of *ToyotaStdTrans* to class *VehicleTransmission* is invalidated after the update, the previous instanceship of *Camry* to the *Vehicle* class will also be invalidated consequently because the *Vehicle* class requires all its instances to have a *transmission* attribute of *VehicleTransmission* type.

The above unexpected invalidation of objects' instanceships caused by dynamic object evolution is problematic for the following two reasons. First, to maintain the type consistency of class types according to the *Axiom of is-a*, all objects whose instanceships have been invalidated must be promptly removed from corresponding classes. However, determining those invalidated objects may require substantial amount of execution time due to the cascading effect of instanceship invalidation. Second, cascading invalidation of instanceships creates a severe difficulty for static type checking of objects, because it makes practically impossible to determine the types of objects at compile time. Those reasons suggest that appropriate control should be applied to dynamic evolution of objects so that unexpected instanceship invalidation can be totally prevented.

Below we identify two *object evolution invariants* that define the necessary and sufficient condition for preventing any unexpected instanceship invalidation. The invariants are presented in the form of "$\{P\}u_o\{Q\}$" which states that if a precondition P holds before an update operation u is applied to an object o then a postcondition Q must become true after the update:

is-a Object Evolution Invariant:

For any object o, any class c, and any object update operation u other than the class de-assignment operation:

$$\{is\text{-}a(o,c)\}u_o\{is\text{-}a(o,c)\}$$

This invariant says that all object update operations except the class de-assignment must not invalidate any instanceship of the object they update.

as-a Object Evolution Invariant:

For any object o, any class c, and any object update operation u:

$$\{as\text{-}a(o,c)\}u_o\{as\text{-}a(o,c)\}$$

This invariant says that all object update operations, including the class de-assignment operation, must not invalidate any *as-a* relationship of the object they update. Here relation $as\text{-}a(o,c)$ denotes that object o is referenced by some other object(s) *as* an instance of class c, formally defined as (see Figure 3): there exist at least a complex object o_x and a complex class c_x such that: (1) c_x has an attribute specification, say $\langle a: c\rangle \in c_x.EAS$, whose type is a reference to class c; and (2) o_x has a same named attribute $<a:o> \in o_x.EA$ whose value is a reference to object o; and (3) o_x is an instance of class c_x (this implies that o must be an instance of c).

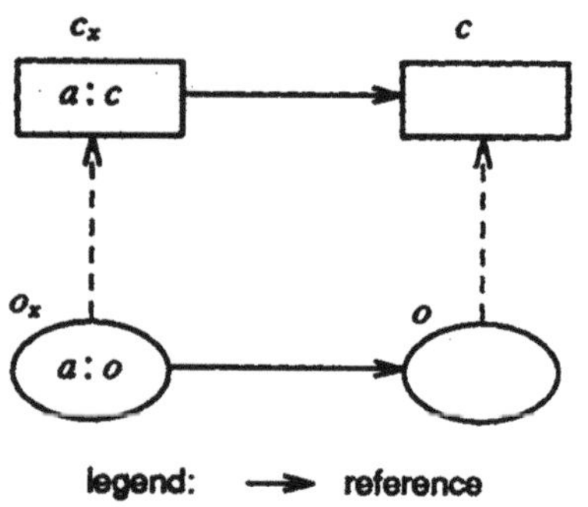

Figure 3. *as-a*(o, c) **relation**

The *is-a* invariant assures that, from the time when an object o is explicitly assigned to a class c and until it has been explicitly de-assigned from c with a class de-assignment operation, all object update operations applied to o during this period will not affect the instanceship of o to c. Furthermore, the *as-a* invariant assures that, from the time when the first reference to object o as an instance of c is made and until all such references have been removed, object o cannot be de-assigned from class c. Consequently, the instanceships of objects that refer to o will also be unaffected at any time by updates to o. Together the above two invariants guarantee that under no circumstance will the instanceships of objects be affected by object evolution operations.

4.2. Object Evolution Rules

In the previous subsection, we identified two invariants that must be preserved by object evolution operations in order to avoid unexpected instanceship invalidation. In this subsection, we present a set of *object evolution rules* that represent the strategies adopted by the model in maintaining those object evolution invariants.

Class Assignment Rule:

> If an object o belongs to more than one class, then for any two classes c and c' that o belongs to, i.e., $is\text{-}a(o, c)$ and $is\text{-}a(o, c')$, if $min\_type(o, a, c) \neq$ nil and $min\_type(o, a, c') \neq$ nil then $min\_type(o, a, c) = min\_type(o, a, c')$ must hold.

Here function $min\_type(o, a, c)$ denotes the minimum type that the value of attribute a of object o has to obtain in order to preserve its instanceship to class c, formally defined as:

$$min\_type(o, a, c) = \begin{cases} t & \text{if } is\text{-}a(o, c) \text{ and } <a:t> \in c.EAS \\ \text{nil} & \text{otherwise} \end{cases}$$

This rule says that for all classes which an object belongs to and require an attribute a, they must require the same type for a. This rule ensures that objects can be updated independently by each of those classes that they belong to without affecting their instanceships to other classes.

Class De-Assignment Rule:

> For an object o and a class c to which o belongs, if $as\text{-}a(o, c)$, then o cannot be de-assigned from c.

This rule ensures that the removal of an object's instanceship will not affect the instanceships of its referencing objects.

Attribute Deletion Rule:

> For an object o and an attribute a, if there exists a class c such that $min\_type(o, a, c) \neq$ nil, then a cannot be deleted from o.

This rule says that if an attribute of an object is still required by some class to which the object belongs, then the attribute cannot be dropped from the object.

Attribute Update Rule:

> For any new value v to be assigned to an attribute a of an object o, if there exists a class c such that $min\_type(o, a, c) \neq$ nil, then $v : min\_type(o, a, c)$ must hold.

This rule says that all attribute values assigned to an object must fall into the minimum types required by those classes that the object belongs to.

It is not hard to see intuitively that above object evolution rules maintain the two object evolution invariants of the last subsection. By enforcing those rules, the model allows objects to evolve without sacrificing its strong-typing capability.

5. OBJECT VERSIONING

In design systems, changes to design entities usually need to be versioned for various purposes such as documenting their evolution process or representing different design alternatives and revisions. Current object-oriented version models use *generic objects* as an abstraction to represent the version sets of versioned entities. Generic objects also support *dynamic references* used to dynamically configure complex designs. However, the typing rules for dynamic references require that a generic object must be bound to some type t all the time. As a result, in current version models versions of a generic object can only model incremental changes on a versioned entity.[4, 10]

In this section, we describe a generalized object versioning scheme that is fully integrated with the object-centered data model. We show that our versioning scheme can capture a broader spectrum of the evolution process of versioned entities than existing version models.

5.1. Generic Objects

A version of a design entity is a semantically meaningful snapshot of the entity at a point of time. For each versioned entity, a *generic object* is defined, which represents all versions – each being an object by itself – of this versioned entity. A derivation relationship, *derived-from*, is also defined among the set of versions of a generic object to capture the evolution history of the versioned entity. A generic object does not have any user-defined attribute and is not assigned to any user-defined class (though they can be assigned to some system-defined class such as *Generic* to inherit version-related operations defined on the class).

Definition *Object Versions*: An object version is a tuple $o_v = (id, pro, A, gen)$ where id, pro, and A are the identifier, prototype identifier, and attributes of o_v, and $gen \in$ **ID** is the identifier of the generic object to which o_v belongs. □

Definition *Generic Objects*: A generic object is a triple $o_g = (id, VS, VG)$ where

- $id \in$ ID is the identifier of the generic object.
- $VS \in 2^{O}$ is a set of object versions called the *version set* of the generic object. For every $o_v \in VS$, $(o_v).gen = id$.
- $VG = (VS, E)$ is a DAG (Directed Acyclic Graph) called *version graph* of the generic object, in which nodes represent versions in VS and edges represent the *derived-from* derivation relationships among those versions. □

From now on, the set of all objects **O** will be partitioned into three subsets, $\mathbf{O} = \mathbf{O}_u \cup \mathbf{O}_v \cup \mathbf{O}_g$, where $\mathbf{O}_u$ denotes the set of all unversioned objects, $\mathbf{O}_v$ the set of all object versions, and $\mathbf{O}_g$ the set of all generic objects.

A new object version can be created from scratch or derived from some existing one. In the later case, a new copy of the *predecessor* object version is made as the initial state of the newly derived *successor* version and a derived-from relationship is established between the two versions. After the creation of an object version, its structure and behavior as well as its attribute values can still be changed. These general forms of changes, though not allowed in current version models, are possible in our model for two reasons. First, they are allowed by the host object-centered data model, as we have described in the previous sections. Second, they are also allowed by the object versioning mechanism, because generic objects are not associated to any class type and thus do not enforce any typing constraint on their versions. Therefore, different versions of a generic object may belong to different classes and have different structures and behaviors. As a result, versions of a generic object in our model are able to capture the complete evolution process of a versioned entity.

For example, assume that the *VehicleDB* database has evolved substantially since its creation, see Figure 4. In particular, additional subclasses have been added under *VehicleEngine*, and more versions of $V6Engine_g$ have been derived.[2] Those versions of $V6Engine_g$ belong to different classes (except $V6Engine_v^2$ which does not belong to any class) and have different structures and behaviors.

5.2. Version References

Versions of a generic object can be referenced either statically or dynamically:

Definition *Static vs. Dynamic References*: A *static reference* is an object reference value $v = o_v.id$ where $o_v \in \mathbf{O}_v$, and a *dynamic reference* is an object reference value $v = o_g.id$ where $o_g \in \mathbf{O}_g$. □

Both static and dynamic version references can be used to configure complex objects, as shown in the following example:

[2] Here $V6Engine_g$ is used to denote the generic object for *V6Engine* designs and $V6Engine_v^i$ is used to denote its i th version.

```
Lexus = ( Lexus,
          nil,
          { engine:          V6Engine_g,
            transmission:    ToyotaStdTrans_v^k } )
```

Here the value of the *engine* attribute of complex object *Lexus* is a dynamic reference to generic object $V6Engine_g$, and the value of its *transmission* attribute is a static reference to object version $ToyotaStdTrans_v^k$.

Dynamic references to generic objects are resolved into static ones at run time by *context functions*. A context function takes a generic object as the argument and returns a version of the generic object as the result. Accordingly, all dynamic references to the argument generic object are mapped into static references to the result object version. In this way, up-to-date versions of component designs can be dynamically incorporated to configure complex designs using different context functions.

An unconventional feature of dynamic references in our model is that they can also have a *selection condition* associated with them. The selection condition restricts the versions that can be mapped to by the dynamic references.

Definition *Conditioned Dynamic References*: A *conditioned dynamic reference* is a dynamic reference argumented by a class parameter: $o_g.id(c.cn)$ where $o_g \in \mathbf{O}_g$ and $c.cn \in$ CN, which enforces the following constraint on any context function π:

$$\pi(o_g.id(c.cn)) \in \{\, o_v^i.id \mid o_v^i \in o_g.VS \text{ and } is\text{-}a(o_v^i, c)\}$$

The class argument $c.cn$ is called the *selection condition* of the conditioned dynamic reference. □

Namely, unlike a normal dynamic reference which can select any version of the referenced generic object to map to, a conditioned dynamic reference will select only among those versions that belong to the class specified by its selection condition for subsequent mapping.

Conditioned dynamic references allow complex designs to dynamically select qualified component design versions according to their configuration requirements. For instance, assume that the previous *Lexus* complex object must use a *GasolineEngine* type of engine in its design as determined by certain design rules. Then a selection condition can be added to its dynamic reference to the $V6Engine_g$ generic object, as shown below, so that it will select only those versions of $V6Engine_g$ that are of *GasolineEngine* type:

```
Lexus = ( Lexus,
          nil,
          { engine:          V6Engine_g(GasolineEngine),
            transmission:    ToyotaStdTrans_v^k } )
```

Thus only version $V6Engine_v^1$ or $V6Engine_v^5$ of $VehicleEngine_g$ can be selected in a configuration of *Lexus* (see Figure 4).

Conditioned dynamic references are also beneficial for typing of dynamic references. In contrast to an ordinary dynamic reference $o_g.id$ that cannot be statically type-checked because it can be mapped to any version of o_g which belong may belong to any type, a conditioned dynamic reference $o_g.id(c.cn)$ is strongly

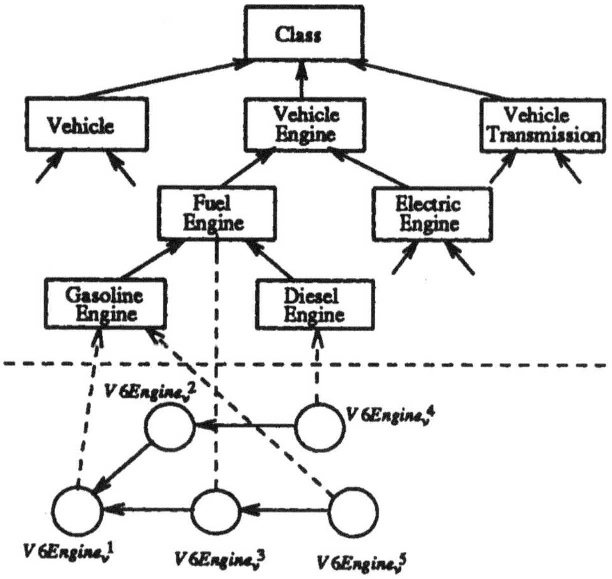

Figure 4. Versions of $V6Engine_g$

typed with type c as it can only be mapped to a version of o_g which belongs to type c. Therefore, the selection condition in conditioned dynamic references supplements generic objects with the typing information required for static type-checking of dynamic references.

6. Related Work

The object-centered model is not the first attempt on consolidating both the class-based and the prototype-based modeling approaches. There exist also other models that combine features of both types of models.

One such a model is Pegasus, an extension of the EXTRA class-based model.[3] In addition to the specialization inheritance relationship among types, a new kind of inheritance relationship, called *extension*, is added which specifies that an instance of an extension subtype must have a prototype in its extension supertype. Such an extension relationship improves the inheritance flexibility of class-based model by supporting a limited form of object-level inheritance among certain types of objects. Still, no improvement for object evolution has been achieved since all instances of a type have a uniform structure as in class-based models.

In another model Vision,[8] a real-world entity is modeled as an *object hierarchy* wherein objects represent different roles of the entity and are related by the prototyping inheritance relationships. In addition, *template hierarchies* can be defined as prototype hierarchies used for cloning instances. Although template hierarchies provide an elegant way of ensuring uniformity of newly cloned objects, their use is purely advisory and one may arbitrarily change the structure and behavior of an object after its has been cloned from a template no matter whether it is sill being referenced or not. The model, however, is not strongly-typed due to its heavy basis on the prototype-based approach.

By contrast, our model provides a more balanced combination of the two modeling approaches. Following the prototype-based approach, our model defines objects as independent structural entities that can share among them both definitions and states through the prototyping relationship. Following the class-based approach, our model uses classes to classify objects and to ensure uniformity on their instances. But by substituting the intimate and permanent binding between objects and classes with a loose and non-permanent one, our model overcomes the limitation of class-based models in allowing objects to evolve in their structure and behavior. Furthermore, by enforcing a small number of object evolution rules, our model still preserves the strong typing capability that can not be achieved in prototype-based models.

7. Conclusions

In this paper we have presented a new object-oriented data model that consolidates features of both class-based and prototype-based models. The model extends the prototype-based modeling approach with a novel classification mechanism which enables objects to be loosely and temporally associated to classes to inherit their behavioral definitions. We showed that the model not only allows object to evolve in both structure and behavior, but also supports flexible object classification and strong typing as required by advanced engineering design databases. We also showed that the model provides the basis for a generalized object versioning scheme that can capture the complete evolution process of versioned entities.

References

1) Atkinson, M., *et al*, "The object-Oriented Database System Manifesto," in Proc. of 1st DOOD, 1989, pp. 40-57.

2) Banerjee, J., *et al*, "Data Model Issues for Object-Oriented Applications," *ACM Trans. on Office Info. Systems*, Vol. 5, No. 1 (Jan. 1987), pp. 3-26.

3) Biliris, A., "Modeling Design Object Relationships in PEGASUS," in IEEE Proc. of Int. Conf. on Data Engineering, 1990, pp. 228-237.

4) Katz, R.H, "Toward a Unified Framework for Version Modeling in Engineering Databases," ACM Computing Surveys, Vol. 22, No. 4 (Dec. 1990), pp. 375-408.

5) Lieberman, H., "Using Prototypical Objects to Implement Shared Behavior in Object Oriented Systems," in ACM Proc. of OOPSLA '86, 1986, pp. 214-223.

6) Maier, D, J. Stein, A. Otis, and A. Purdy, "Development of an Object Oriented DBMS," in ACM Proc. of OOPSLA '86, 1986, pp. 472-482.

7) Richardson, J.E., and P. Schwarz, "Aspects: Extending Objects to Support Multiple, Independent Roles," in ACM Proc. of SIGMOD, 1991, pp. 298-307.

8) Sciore, E., "Object Specialization," ACM Transaction on Information Systems, Vol. 7, No. 2 (April 1989), pp. 103-122.

9) Stein, L.A., "Delegation is Inheritance," in ACM Proc. of OOPSLA '87, 1987, pp. 138-146.

10) Zhao, H., Biliris, A., "Integrating Object and Schema Versioning in an Object-Centered Data Model," submitted for publication, 1992.

CONCEPTUAL LAYERS IN AN OBJECT ORIENTED DATABASE. AN UNIFIED MODEL

Prof. Gabriel Baum   Prof. Silvia Gordillo
Lic. Claudia Pons   Clara Smith
Carlos Tau

LIFIA. Departamento de Informática, Facultad de Ciencias Exactas,
Universidad Nacional de La Plata. Calle 50 esq. 115. 1er piso.
Tel:(54)(21)4-2738. E-mail: lifia1@cespivm2.unlp.edu.ar
Fax:(54)(21)25-6607, (54)(21)24-4330.
(1900) La Plata, Bs.As., Argentina.

ABSTRACT

When the programming languages for database applications emerged, a greater abstraction for representing knowledge was reached. Rapidly, specific application areas needed a precise conceptual modelling of the data.

As object oriented paradigm allows modelling real world situations in a clear and natural way, it seems interesting to combine its principles with those of database development.

The sound and reusable development of Object Oriented Databases (OODB) should be possible only on the top of a strong theoretical basis. This work presents an object oriented approach to the specification and design of an OODB, based on the following key concepts: objects, abstraction mechanisms for defining object types, relationships among objects, object composition and multiple implementations. It also researchs sound theoretical foundations for building OODB in a correct, verifiable and reusable way. The proposal includes: a) a conceptual model of an OODB, b) an algebraic specification language for defining OODB elements.

INTRODUCTION

An object is a dynamic entity: it has an internal state that may be modified in response to certain events, and can only be partially observed through its features. An object has also the power of performing certain activities (its behavior).

Far from being isolated entities, objects organize themselves in different ways, and coexist in a complex and dynamic society, acting one on each other.

When the programming languages for database applications emerged, a greater abstraction for representing knowledge was reached.

The OODBs provide facilities for manipulating abstraction mechanisms (such as classification, generalization-specialization, composition and parameterization) and for capturing connections and restrictions among objects.

The OODMBSs ORION [4] and IRIS [3], the O2 language and its extensions for database management [6], and the extensible system for databases EXODUS [2] were studied.

O2 proposes a separation between a type specification and its corresponding implementation. It distinguishes private from public methods, and allows the creation of exceptional objects. EXODUS separates the type definition from the instances declaration, and allows the manipulation of several sets of objects belonging to the same type. Also it offers an interesting definition of component objects. IRIS introduces the possibility of defining disjoint types. ORION supports the management of invariant rules for schema manipulation and presents the notion of composite object through the ''is_part_of'' relationship.

These four systems constitute the incentive for working on a unified model for OODBs.

This paper is organized as follows: section 1 presents a model for OODBs, consisting in three conceptual layers. Section 2 describes formal syntax and semantics for the elements belonging to each layer. Finally, a case of study is encountered in section 3.

1. STRUCTURE OF AN OODB

In an OODB three different planes, layers or levels can be identified: the definition layer, the schema construction layer and the implementation layer (Fig.1).

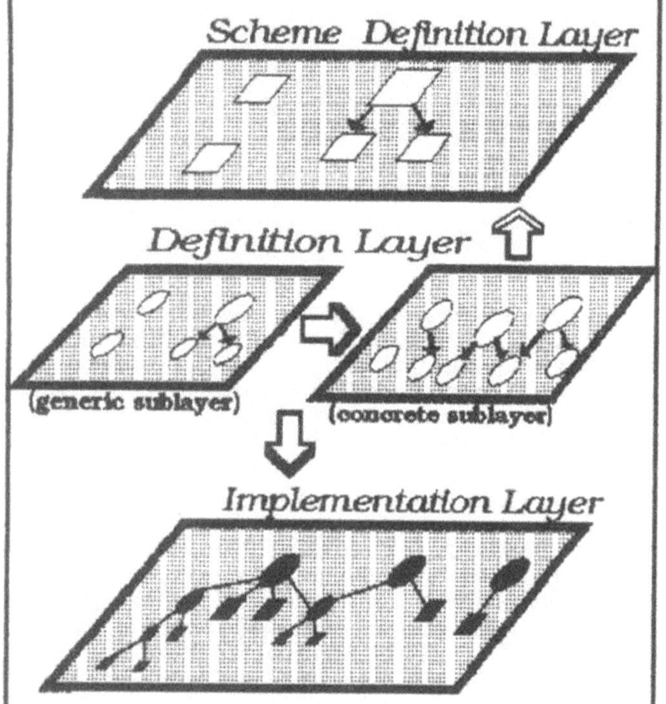

Figura 1: Conceptual Layers in an OODB

The definition layer consists in specifiying object types. This process originates a type universe, with types organized in a hierarchy and with eventual composite references between them.

In the schema construction layer, those types of interest (for the application) are selected. These types are well fitted for the application needs. Also relationships between the selected types are defined in this layer.

The third layer reflects the construction of implementations for the types in the universe. It is possible to define multiple implementations for each type, building a hierarchy with them.

Extra details on this layer are not found in this paper.

1.1 Definition Layer

1.1.1 Abstraction mechanisms for building the universe.

An important concept in object orientation is abstraction, as a powerful tool for managing complexity. On constructing the universe, three useful abstraction mechanisms are provided: classification, composition and parameterization.

a- To classify consists in grouping similar objects in object types. A type specifies the common properties of its instances.

Also, types can be organized hierarchically (according to their abstraction levels) in such a way that a type in the hierarchy is an abstraction of all its descendent types (''is_a'' relationship), providing the generalization-specialization mechanism.

b- Composing means clustering objects in another object, frecuently named composite object, associating properties that govern the interaction and behave as a whole. The typical relationship that occurs in a composite object is the ''is_part_of'' relationship [5].

c- Parameterization is a mechanism that gives the possibility of defining generic types. Generic types play the role of patterns, receiving types as arguments and generating new types.

According to the abstraction mechanisms presented, a type can be:

- a basic type,
- an extension of an existent type (''is_a'' relationship),
- a composition of existent types (''is_part_of'' relationship).

Inside the definition layer, two parallel sub-layers can be distinguished:

- the ''concrete'' sub-layer, which contains type specifications, and
- the ''generic'' sub-layer, formed by parameterized type definitions that can be considered functions ranging over the concrete sub-layer.

1.1.2 Features and behavior.

Type operations can be classified in two well differenciated groups: features and behavior.

Features define characteristic and descriptive parts of the objects of a specified type; the features are the operations that permit the observation of the object's state. Each feature recovers some descriptive attribute (either showing the contents of some structure used to represent the type, or evaluating some function whose domain is the object itself).

The behavior is the set of activities that objects belonging to the specified type are capable of performing.

1.2 Schema Construction Layer

When defining the schema for the database, those types (specified in the definition layer) which reflect the real world entities features are selected from the universe.

Relationships among the selected types are defined. Some ''is_part_of'' relationships in composite objects may be fitted, as well.

Application restrictions are established in this layer as schema axioms.

Every definition made during the schema construction is valid only in the current schema; changes and adjustments have no effect upon the definition layer.

1.2.1 Relationships among types

Although relationships are elevated to the same abstraction level as types (instead of being stated inside of them), a relationship is modeled in a different way from a type: the former describes a set of groups of associated objects (the object oriented view of a table), while the latter defines characteristic features of an entity.

Relationships can be derived from existing generic specifications (which belong to the generic sub-layer), such as Binary Relation, Partial Order Relation, and so on.

Defining features and behavior when setting up a relationship among types, allows representing its descriptive attributes.

1.2.2 Structured objects

Four kinds of composite links among objects are presented, each with two versions. These links represent different ''is_part_of'' references between objects:

i- Exclusive component of a type: an object o of type O is a component part of another object t of type T, and cannot be (at the same time) a component part of any other object of any other type. This reference shows some kind of ''physical component''.

Version a) o can exist in the database, no matter t exists or not. i.e. an engine is considered part of a single car, but is possible to take it off from the ''owner'' car in order to repair it.

Version b) o's existence depends on the existence of t. i.e. a chip is part of a motherboard, and has no sense to keep the chip if the motherboard no longer exists.

ii- Homogeneously shared component: an object o of type O is a component part of various objects, say t1, ..., tn of type T, but cannot be (at the same time) a component part of any other object with type different from T. This kind of reference reflects a ''logical component''.

Version a) o can exist in the database, no matter t1, ..., tn exist or not.

Version b) o's existence is conditioned to the existence of at least one ti in the database.

iii- Heterogeneously shared component: an object o of type O is a component part of an object t of type T, and may also be a component part of various objects (say a, b, c,...) of any type different from T.

Version a) o can exist in the database, no matter r, s, t,... exist or not.

Version b) o's existence depends on the existence of at least one of the objects r, s, t....

iv- Freely shared component: an object o of type O is a component part of various objects, say r, s, t, u,... , no matter what type they belong to.

Version a) o can exist in the database, no matter r, s, t, u,... exist or not.

Version b) o's existence is conditioned to the existence of at least one of r, s, t, u,...

This classification is quite wide to cover a large set of object composition alternatives. In addition to these references, weak (standard) references between objects should be supported.

Restrictions imposed to a type T, when composing objects, are suitable for the subtypes of T, preserving the ''is_a'' relationship semantics.

1.3 Implementation Layer

It is widely accepted that separating the specification from the implementation is a good design mechanism. On the one hand, specification establishes features and behavior, as well as classification and composition of types. On the other hand, a type implementation provides representation an methods associated with features and behavior specified.

In the implementation layer, implementations for the types conforming the universe are build. Multiple implementations of a type are supported. A multiple implementation is a tree, where each node is an implementation of its parent. Nodes in the tree represent different levels of abstraction, begining with the root (which is the most abstract level) and ending in the leaves, which are the concrete implementations [8].

The fact of dealing with several implementation alternatives for a type, allows the selection of the best choice for a particular situation, increasing in this sense eficiency and reusability.

2. THE SIGMA DEFINITION LANGUAGE

The design of suitable data structures is one of the crucial points in the construction of large software systems. Inner composition, properties and available operations of these data structures determine questions of simple realizability on concrete systems, provability of correctness and simple handling by users. One of the most important developments in the area of software technology are the ''Abstract Data Types'', where data structures are characterized by the sorts (names of their carrier sets), the names of the operations and their properties; most of the concrete implementation details, which may cause problems for the understanding and the portability, can be omitted that way.

An abstract data type can be seen as a class of total heterogeneous algebras. That type can be specified by a signature (a collection of sorts and operators) together with a set of axioms [7].

ASL is a well-typed higher order language for algebraic specifications. It contains constructions for building signatures, sets of terms, and sets of formulas as well as constructs embodying primitive operations on algebraic specifications. It also allows the construction of parameterized specifications [7].

In this work is presented an algebraic specification language for defining OODBs, called SIGMA. This language is based on the ASL language.

SIGMA provides constructors for formally specifying the elements (eventually generic) belonging to each conceptual layer in an OODB:

i- Definition layer:

- Basic type constructor:
  Takes a signature and a set of axioms, and creates a type specification.

- Subtype constructor:
  Enriches (or extends) an existent type specification, forming a type specification.

- Composite type constructor:
  Makes a type specification composing existent type specifications (the constituent parts), allowing the association of properties in order to define the whole.

ii- Schema construction layer:

- Relationship constructor:
  Permits the establishment of a relation among two or more types (the components).

- Constructor for fitting composite relationships:
  Sets up the kind of composition reference (exclusive, shared, dependent, independent) in an established ''is_part_of'' relationship between objects.

- Schema constructor:
  The schema definition includes: the relevant types selection, the definition of relationships among the selected types, and the establishment of application-sensitive restrictions.

2.1 Syntax

i) SIGMA expressions belonging to the definition layer:

```
<def_expr>::= <basic_spec> | <subtype_spec>
              |<comp_spec>

<basic_spec>  ::=  Btype  <expr>
                    Features:  <expr>
                    Behavior:  <expr>
                    Axioms:  <expr>
                   endtype

<subtype_spec>  ::=  Stype  <expr>
                      Supertypes:  <expr>
                      Features:  <expr>
                      Behavior:  <expr>
                      Axioms:  <expr>
                     endtype

<comp_spec>    ::=  Ctype  <expr>
                     Uses:  <expr>
                     Features:  <expr>
                     Behavior:  <expr>
                     Axioms:  <expr>
                    endtype
```

ii) SIGMA expressions belonging to the schema construction layer:

```
<schema_const_expr>  ::=  <rel_spec>  |
          <fitting_spec>  |  <schema_spec>

<rel_spec>  ::=
    Relation  <expr>
        Components:  <expr>
        Features:  <expr>
        Behavior:  <expr>
        Axioms:  <expr>
    endrel
```

```
<fitting_spec> ::=
    customize  type  <expr>
        with
         (<expr>  :  <kind_link>)*
    endcustom

    <kind_link>  ::=  <dep_indep>  <link>
    <dep_indep>  ::=  dependent  |
                       independent
    <link>  ::=  exclusive  |
                 homogeneously shared  |
                 heterogeneously shared|
                 freely shared
<schema_spec>  ::=
    Schema  <expr>
        with
        Types:  <expr>
        Relations:  <expr>
        Axioms:  <expr>
    endschema
```

2.2 Semantics

For the understanding of the semantic of ASL-specifications, every specification can be seen as a pseudo-axiomatic class of algebras, that is, a class of algebras which can be axiomatized using hidden sorts operators; and every parameterized specification can be seen as a function from specification to specification [7].

Every SIGMA expression can be translated into an equivalent ASL expression. This means SIGMA¦s semantics can be expressed in terms of ASL¦s semantics.

In order to simplify the translation of SIGMA expressions, the following abbreviation is used:

```
enrich  T  by  sorts  S  opns F  axioms  E
    = T + (signature <(sorts sig T) U S,
                      (opns  sig  T)  U  F>
          axioms  E)
```

Let spec be a function that associates a specification name with its corresponding text.

i) SIGMA expressions belonging to the definition layer:

a) A <basic_spec> expression is directly translated into a <basic spec> ASL expression.

```
  Btype  T
    Features:  F
    Behavior:  B
    Axioms:  E
  endtype   =
        signature <T,  F  U  B>   axioms  E
```

b) A <subtype_spec> expression involves the renaming of the sort of interest (inheritance) and an eventual enrichment with operations and axioms.

```
Stype  T
    Supertypes:  S
    Features:  F
    Behavior:  B
    Axioms:  E
endtype=

 enrich (derive from spec S by [S -> T])
       by opns  F  U  B
           axioms  E
```

This notion of subtype settles an inclusion relationship between the models for the types of interest. Given a type T, T subtype of S, every model for T, restricted to S's signature, is also a model for S.

c) A <comp_spec> expression can be translated as the sum of all the component sorts, subsequently enriched with new sorts, operations and axioms.

```
Ctype  T
    Uses:  T1,  ...,  Tn
    Features:  F
    Behavior:  B
    Axioms:  E
endtype=
            enrich(spec  T1+...+spec  Tn)
               by  sorts  T
                   opns  F  U  B
                   axioms  E
```

ii) SIGMA expressions belonging to the schema construction layer:

The central concept in this layer is the definition of relationships among types.

a) Semantically speaking, relations behave the same way as types.

```
  Relation  L
    Components:  T1,  ...,  Tn
    Features:  F
    Behavior:  B
    Axioms:  E
  endrel          =

            enrich(spec  T1+...+spec  Tn)
               by  sorts  L
                   opns  F  U  B
                   axioms  E
```

b) The BDOO schema specification is build up from the sum of its components' specifications and from the attachment of application-specific axioms. The BDOO schema semantics can be understood as the set of all the valid BDOO instances of that schema.

```
Schema  S
   with
        Types:  T1,..,Tn
         Relations:  R1,..,Rk
        Axioms:  E
endschema  =

        enrich(spec  T1+...+spec  Tn  +
               spec  R1  +...+  spec  Rk  )
          by  axioms  E
```

3. A CASE OF STUDY

3.1 A Type Universe Construction.

Considering a situation where a Football Association organizes an annual Championship, in wich several teams take part, the following are types representing persons and football players. Both types belong to the type universe:

```
Ctype  Person
   Uses:  Integer,  String,  Boolean
   Features:
       name:  String
       age:  Integer
   Behavior:
       birthday:  Person  ->  Person
       ...
   Axioms:
              age(birthday(P))=age(P)+1
       ...
endtype.
```

```
Stype  Football_Player
   Supertypes:  Person
   Features:
       position:  Integer
         goals:  Integer
             ...
   Behavior:
       make_goal:  Football_Player  ->
                        Football_Player
       ...
   Axioms:
       goals(make_goal(J))=goals(J)+1
               ...
endtype.
```

A football team will be modeled as a set of football players. The generic specification of a Set type will be used to generate the concrete type Footballers_Set.

```
Footballers_Set  =  Set(Football_player)
```

Football players, together with their coach, form a Football Team. The strategy used by the coach to train the footballers is a private feature, and cannot be observed from outside a football team object.

```
Ctype  Football_Team
  Uses:
    Footballers_Set,   Person
  Features:
    name:  String
    coach:  Person
    football_players:  Footballers_Set
    strategy:  String          Private
  Behavior:
    replace_coach:  Football_Team,Person
                             ->Football_Team
    replace_strategy:  Football_Team,String
                             -> Football_Team
               ...
  Axioms:
    coach(replace_coach(T,P))=P
       ...
endtype.
```

3.2 Relationship Specification.

A match could be modeled as a pair of football teams. A championship could be though as several match-days. During each match-day, every team disputes a match with another team.

The following is a specification for the relationship Match-date:

```
relation    Match-date
  Components:Football_Team,  Football_Team
  Features:
    score:  Integer
    referee:  Person
               ...
  Behavior
    addMatch:  Match-date,  Football_Team,
               Football_Team  ->  Match-date
   asignReferee:  Match-date,Football_Team,
     Football_Team,  Person  ->  Match-date
               ...
  Axioms:
          ...
endrelation.
```

Relationship definitions are also suitable for the subtypes of the types related. For example, if the type Boy belongs to the universe, a boy can be a member of a football team. But some axioms may restrict the possibility of conforming a football team to persons over 18 years. Relation domains may be reduced in this way.

3.3 Fitting Composite References.

If there's a need for reflecting any object composition alternative (presented in section I), a ''customization'' of types should be performed. To customize means to adequate a pure type (selected from the universe) to the requirements specification.

For the Football Association schema, this is a Football_Team type fit:

```
customize type Football_Team

  with
  football_players: independent exclusive
  coach:independent heterogeneously shared

endcustom
```

The exclusive clause states that the football players are a component part of a Football Team, and cannot be (at the same time) a component part of any other object. The independent clause means that the football players could exist in the database, no matter the team they belong to exists or not.

The fact of the coach being heterogeneously shared means that he can be a component part of other entities (of different type from Football_Team) i.e. his family, a Football Association Comitee, and others; but he cannot be another football team's trainer.

3.4 Schema Definition.

When defining the schema for the Football Association, the relevant types Person, Football_Player, Footballers_Set and Football_team are selected from the universe. Also the Supervisor and the Goaler are included in the schema. Should be noticed that several instances of the relationship Match-date constitute the championship. Each instance of this relationship is a relation containing pairs of football teams (which represent the matches for that date).

```
Schema Football_Association with
    types: Person, Football_Player,
       Footballers_Set, Football_team, ...
    relations: Match-date, ...
    axioms: ...
endschema.
```

3.5 Multiple Implementations

The generic type Set, may have the following associated implementation hierarchy:

```
                     SET
              /                \

     LIST-BASED_SET        TREE-BASED_SET
        /         \

ARRAY-BASED       POINTER-BASED
LIST-BASED_SET      LIST-BASED_SET
```

4. CONCLUSIONS

Differing from several existing OODB models, this proposal presents the database schema building in a separate layer from the type universe construction. An additional step of first selection and later adequation and inclusion of types in the schema is provided. This distinction of layers allows reusability and abstraction. Generic or concrete existing types and relationships are highly reusable.

Schema construction and implementation layers are independent one from the other. A type implementation does not depend on the adjustments made to the type for a special application, and vice versa. Implementations present then the same degree of reusability as types belonging to the definition layer does.

REFERENCES

[1] - A. Albano, G,. Ghell,''A Strongly Typed, Interactive Object Oriented Database Programing Language'',IEEE, pgs 94 to 102, 1986.

[2] - M. Carey, D. DeWitt and S. Vandemberg,''A Data Model and Query Language for EXODUS.'', SIGMOD 88, pgs 413 to 423, 1988.

[3] - D. Fishman, J. Annevelink,''Overview of the IRIS DBMS'', Object Oriented Concepts, Databases and Applications, W. Kim and F. Lochovsky eds, Addison Wesley, 1989.

[4] - W. Kim, N. Ballou,''Features ofthe ORION OODBS'', Object Oriented Concepts, Databases and Applications, W. Kim and F. Lochovsky, eds, Addison Wesley, 1989.

[5] - W.Kim, E. Bertino, J. Garza, ''Composite Objects Revisted'', SIGMOD 89, pgs 337 to 347, 1989.

[6] - C. Lecluse, P. Richard and others, ''O2, an Object-Oriented Data Model'', SIGMOD '88, pgs 424 to 433, 1988.

[7] - M. Wirsing,''Structured Algebraic Specifications: a Kernel Language'', Theoretical Computer Science, 42, 1986.

[8] - M. Wirsin, R. Hennicker, R. Stabl, ''MENU - An Example for the Systematic Reuse of Specifications'', Techinsche Berichte der Facultat fur Mathematik und Informatik, Universitat Passau, MIP-8930, 1989.

GENERATING OBJECT-ORIENTED VIEWS FROM AN ER-BASED CONCEPTUAL SCHEMA

Tok-Wang LING
Department of Information Systems
and Computer Science
National University of Singapore

Pit-Koon TEO
Data Resources
DBS Bank

Ling-Ling YAN
Institute of Systems Science
National University of Singapore

ABSTRACT

A 3-level schema architecture is proposed to address some inadequacies in recent object-oriented data models. The conceptual schema is based on a normal form object-oriented entity relationship (OOER) diagram. A set of mapping rules is defined that allows OO external schemas, based on the O2 data model, to be generated from the conceptual schema. Similar mapping rules can be defined to generate external schemas for other OO data models. Other features of this model include the incorporation of derived attributes, deductive rules, triggers and methods.

1 INTRODUCTION

There exist many inadequacies[16] in the object-oriented (OO) paradigm, eg. lack of a formal foundation, general disagreement about OO concepts, a navigational, as opposed to a declarative, interface, lack of a standard declarative query language etc. Some of these inadequacies have been addressed but many issues remain unresolved. In this paper, a three-level schema architecture, comprising an external schema level, a conceptual schema level and an internal schema level, is proposed to address a set of OO data modelling issues, viz. (1) the problematic way in which m-n, n-ary and recursive relationships are handled in the OO approach, (2) the lack of general and flexible support for external schemas or views, and (3) the inability to differentiate good OO schema design from bad. Our approach leverages research efforts in Entity Relationship (ER) data modelling [5].

The OO data modelling issues are resolved at the conceptual schema level. To represent the conceptual schema, the notion of a ***normal form OOER diagram*** is introduced. A normal form OOER diagram has all the structural features of a classic ER diagram[5,14]. It goes beyond the classic ER diagram in two areas. First, a behavioural dimension is included that incorporates the notions of methods, derived attributes, deductive rules and triggers. This yields an OOER diagram. Second, the structural quality of the OOER diagram is improved by applying the techniques of [14] to convert the OOER diagram into a normal form OOER diagram. Informally, a normal form OOER diagram is a normal form ER diagram [14] extended with the notions of methods, derived attributes, deductive rules and triggers.

Each OO database schema (based on any of the proposed OO data models [3,6,7,17 etc]) is treated as an external schema that is generated from the conceptual schema by applying a set of mapping rules. Distinct sets of mapping rules are needed to handle different OO data models. Each OO database schema is, therefore, a view of the conceptual schema. User applications (OO or otherwise) can then be written based on the OO external schemas that are generated from the conceptual schema. The advantages of the OO approach are therefore preserved at the external schema level. To illustrate our approach, a set of mapping rules is defined in this paper to generate, as examples, O2 class definitions from a normal form OOER diagram. Similar mapping rules can be defined for other OO data models.

Section 2 provides some background information. Section 3 compares the OO and ER data models. Section 4 presents some salient features of our approach. In Section 5, a set of mapping rules for deriving O2 external schemas from a normal form OOER diagram is given. Section 6 discusses some related work. Section 7 concludes.

2 BACKGROUND

The OO concepts presented in this section are based primarily on the O2[6] data model, supplemented with examples from ORION[3] and POSTGRES[17].

A ***conceptual entity*** is anything that exists and can be distinctly identified. For example, a person, an employee, a student etc are conceptual entities. In an OO system, all conceptual entities are modelled as ***objects.*** An object has structural properties defined by a finite set of attributes and behavioural properties defined by a finite set of methods. Each object is associated with a logical non-reusable and unique ***object identifier*** (OID) [11]. The OID of an object is independent of the values of its attributes.

All objects with the same set of attributes and methods are grouped into a ***class,*** and form instances of that class. We distinguish between a lexical class and a non-lexical class. A ***lexical class*** contains objects that can be directly represented by their values, eg. integer, string etc. A ***non-lexical class*** contains objects, each of which is represented by a set of attributes and methods. Instances of a non-lexical class are referred to by their OIDs. Examples of non-lexical classes include PERSON, EMPLOYEE, SUPPLIER etc.

The domain of an attribute of a non-lexical class A can be one of the following:

(Case a) a lexical class such as integer, string etc. An attribute with this domain is called a ***data-valued*** attribute[8].

(Case b) a non-lexical class B. An attribute with this domain is called an ***entity-valued*** attribute [8].

Note the recursive nature of this definition. There is an implicit ***binary relationship*** between A and B. The value of the attribute is the OID of an instance of B, which must exist before it can be assigned to the attribute. This provides ***referential integrity.*** A special case exists in which the class B is, in fact, A. This represents a ***cyclic definition*** in the OO model. Cyclic definitions are used to specify recursive relationships such as a part and its subparts, a course and its prerequisite courses etc. A cyclic definition needs not be direct; for instance, a class A may reference a class B1 which in turn reference class B2 and so on until class Bn is referenced by class Bn-1 for some n. Then Bn can reference A, thus completing the cycle. In some OO systems, eg. ORION, the relationship between A and B can be given semantics such as IS-PART-OF, in which case A is a composite object [12] comprising B. Orion also supports the concept of an ***existentially-dependent object,*** in which the existence of the object depends on the existence of its parent object. The deletion of an object triggers a cascading delete of all objects that are existentially dependent on the deleted object. This adds to the integrity features of ORION.

(Case c) a set, set(E) where E is either a lexical class or a non-lexical class. An attribute with this domain is called a ***set-valued*** attribute.

If E is lexical, values from E are stored in the set. If E is a non-lexical class, members of the set can either be an instance of E or its subclasses. In this case, the set comprises instances from possibly heterogeneous classes. Only the OID of each instance is stored in the set. In some systems, eg. O2, both sets and lists are supported. While it is correct to differentiate between a list and a set, this paper treats a set and a list as equivalent.

(Case d) a query type whose values range over the set of possible queries coded in a query language. An attribute with this domain is called a ***query-valued*** attribute.

The value of a query-valued attribute is the result of the query, which is a set of objects satisfying the query condition. An example of a system that allows attributes of type query is POSTGRES.

(Case e) a tuple type. An attribute with this domain is called a ***tuple-valued*** attribute.

This represents an aggregation of attributes of the tuple type, which is treated as a composite attribute of A. An attribute of the tuple type can be a data-valued, entity-valued, set-valued, query-valued or tuple-valued attribute.

A ***type constructor*** is a mechanism for building new domains. For example, the set and tuple constructs described above are used to create domains for set-valued and tuple-valued attributes respectively. A ***complex object*** is built using type constructors such as sets, tuples, lists and nested combinations of these. The structure of objects (complex or otherwise) is hierarchical.

The **class hierarchy** is one of the most important features of the OO paradigm. It provides a taxonomy of classes that are related through the ISA relationship. Given two classes X and Y, X ISA Y implies that each instance of X is also an instance of Y. This has a ***set inclusion*** semantics. We call X a ***subclass*** of Y and we call Y a ***superclass*** of X. A class hierarchy provides an inheritance mechanism which allows a class to inherit properties (attributes/methods) from its superclass(es), if any.

3 COMPARISON BETWEEN OO AND ER MODELS

The ER model was first introduced in [5]. It incorporates the concepts of entities, relationships and attributes and allows the structural representation of a database to be captured in an ER diagram. The ER diagram has proven to be a useful database design tool. Good normal form relations can be generated from a normal form ER diagram [14] and directly implemented on any relational DBMS. Figure 1 shows an ER diagram which will be used to illustrate the various concepts of this paper.

We believe that all the structural properties of the OO approach can be derived (generated) from the ER model. For instance, an OO class hierarchy can be directly represented using the ER relationship type 'ISA'. Figure 1 shows a representation of a class hierarchy rooted at the PART entity type. The composite entity type VEHICLE with component parts ENGINE and DRIVETRAIN is represented using the IS-PART-OF relationship type. Weak entities (eg. DEPENDENTS) correspond to existentially dependent objects [12] which cannot exist independently of their parent objects. Table 1 provides a summary of the comparison between these two models. Note that there is no equivalent concept of methods in the ER model.

The ER model supports functional dependencies, multi-valued dependencies and cardinality constraints among entities, relationships and attributes. These concepts are not inherent in the OO approach and have to be explicitly enforced using, for example, programming. Each regular entity or relationship type is associated with an identifier which is dependent on the values of the primary key attributes. This is different from the OID of an object. The OO approach provides only one type of ISA relationship. In contrast, the ER approach provides special ISA relationship types[14] such as UNION, INTERSECTION, DECOMPOSE etc. which consider the set properties between entity types.

4 RESOLVING OO DATA MODELLING ISSUES

The OO approach suffers from a number of OO data modelling inadequacies, viz. (1) the problematic way in which m-n, n-ary and recursive relationships are handled in the OO approach, (2) the lack of general and flexible support for external schemas or views, and (3) the inability to judge the quality of an OO database schema. We address these issues by adopting the following steps:

(1) Represent a database schema by an ER diagram.

(2) Imbue the ER diagram of Step(1) with methods, derived attributes, deductive rules and triggers to obtain an OOER diagram.

(3) Convert the OOER diagram of Step(2) into a normal form OOER diagram, using the techniques introduced in [14]. The normal form OOER diagram is used as the conceptual schema.

(4) Apply a set of mapping rules to generate OO external schemas from the normal form OOER diagram.

Step 1 ensures that relationships such as m-n, n-ary, recursive, ISA, IS-PART-OF etc are ***explicitly*** represented. In the OO approach, to represent m-n, n-ary and recursive relationship types, or to answer symmetric queries, some data redundancy may need to be introduced, eg. through the use of inverse pointers. This redundancy is not controlled and introduces problems similar to those of the hierarchical model. By providing strong support for association among entity types, it eliminates the need to maintain inverse pointers among related entities, because their semantic association is now conceptually represented by a relationship. Another advantage of supporting relationships directly is that the cardinalities of entity types participating in a relationship type are displayable on the ER diagram. This is a cardinality constraint which is absent from most OO data models.

Step 2 provides a behavioural dimension to an ER diagram to obtain an OOER diagram. (See later subsections)

Step 3 converts an OOER diagram into a normal form OOER diagram, using the techniques of [14]. A normal form OOER diagram is considered 'good' structurally since it satisfies the criteria for a normal form ER diagram[14]. Note that a normal form ER diagram is based on a firm theoretical foundation provided by normalisation/dependency theories.

Step 4 allows the generation of OO external schemas from the conceptual schema. This addresses the problem of a lack of general and flexible support for views or external schemas in the OO approach. In Section 5, a set of mapping rules is provided to generate O2 external schemas. Similar mapping rules can be defined for other OO data models.

The rest of this section describes the behavioural component of our model, viz. methods, triggers, derived

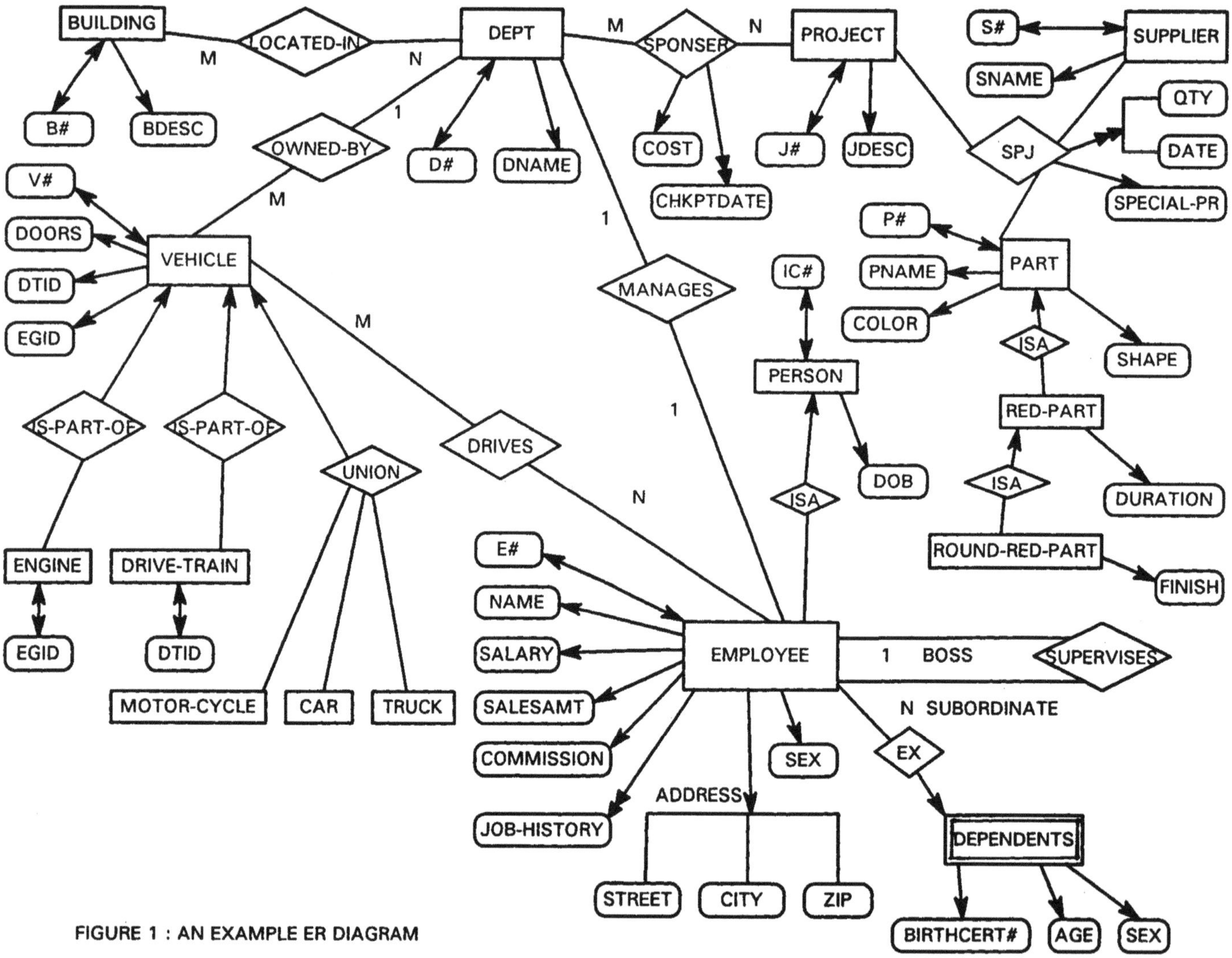

FIGURE 1 : AN EXAMPLE ER DIAGRAM

Object-Oriented Data Model	Entity Relationship Model
Class	Entity Type or Relationship Type or Domain of attributes
An instance of a class	Entity or relationship or attribute value
Class has attributes describing its structural properties	Attributes
Domain of an attribute of a class can itself be a class. Implicitly, a binary relationship exists between these two classes.	The relationship type between two or more entity types is made explicit.
Existentially Dependent object	Weak Entity (with associated EX or ID relationship)
Methods	No equivalent concept
Composite object	Entity types connected by IS-PART-OF relationship type
Use of cyclic definition (see text) to represent recursive relationships (eg. part-subpart, course-prerequisites etc)	Natural way of representing recursive relationships. Role names are used to distinguish entity types participating in recursive relationships.
Class hierarchy	ISA, INTERSECTION constructs
Set-valued attributes	Multi-valued attributes
Tuple-valued attributes	Composite attributes

Table 1: Comparison of ER and OO Data Models

attributes and deductive rules.

4.1 Adding Methods to the OOER Model

Methods are categorized into ***system generated methods, database administrator (DBA) definable methods*** and ***programmer-definable methods.*** System generated methods exist in both the conceptual and external schema levels and include code to browse instances of a class, or to retrieve or update an object's attribute values. These methods are more efficiently optimised and they free programmers from writing trivial code. Updates to identifiers of entity types are handled independently of system generated methods. A DBA must treat these updates as special one-time operation and ensure that database consistency is maintained after the updates are done. DBA-definable methods are accessible by all authorised users of the database and can be defined at both the conceptual and external schema levels. For instance, the DBA can define methods to provide generic computations such as calculation of interest, commission based on generic formulas, etc. Programmer-definable methods, eg. hire an employee, print an entity etc are application specific and not generally accessible. The proper place for programmer-definable methods is at the external, rather than conceptual, schema level. This is no different from conventional practice, in which a database programmer writes application programs based on an external schema available to him.

4.2 Triggers.

Triggers can be system generated to enforce simple integrity constraints, or explicitly coded by DBA and programmers at both the conceptual and external schema levels. For example, consider Figure 1, in which projects sponsered by departments are shown by the relationship SPONSER. A simple trigger to enforce the referential constraint that exists between PROJECT and SPONSER is:

AFTER DELETE ON PROJECT
REFERENCING OLD AS OLD_PROJECT
DELETE FROM SPONSER S WHERE S.P# = OLD_PROJECT.P#.

Note that it is difficult to enforce more complicated constraints using triggers, eg. suppliers who do not supply all red parts must supply a blue part or a green part with quantity greater than 100.

4.3 Derived Attributes

Derived attributes can be obtained from other attributes, based on some derivation rules. For example, in Figure 1, the 'Commission' attribute of the EMPLOYEE entity type is derivable from the 'Salary' and 'SalesAmt' attributes by some computation rule. Derived attributes can be treated as being computed by a method in the OO sense. Derived attributes are explicitly coded by either the DBA (conceptual and external schema levels) or programmers (at external schema level).

4.4 Deductive Rules

Simple deductive rules can be defined for classes by predicating on attributes of a class. For example, a RED_PART deductive rule can be defined as:

RED_PART(P#, Pname, Price) :- PART(P#, Pname, 'red', Price).

The RED_PART deductive rule is characterised by the fact that the positions of the variables (ie P#, Pname, Price) in each clause are important. However, the positions of attributes in an ER diagram representation of an entity are immaterial. In [19], we propose a notation to address this difference. Example 4.4.1 illustrates this notation.

Example 4.4.1 : The above RED_PART deductive rule can be either be rewritten as:

RED_PART(X:P#, Y:Pname, Z:Price) :-
PART(X:P#, Y:Pname, 'red':Color, Z:Price).

OR

RED_PART(Z:Price, X:P#, Y:Pname) :-
PART(Y:Pname,X:P#,'red':Color,Z:Price).

In the above representations, a variable is placed to the left of ':' and a corresponding attribute name or role name is placed to the right of ':'. This notation provides for more expressive power in the sense that each variable in a predicate is tagged with an attribute or role name. It ensures that the positions of variables in a predicate no longer matter; two attributes can be interchanged without affecting the meaning of the rule. Another advantage of this notation is that it reduces the need for anonymous variables.

5 MAPPING RULES

In this section, a set of mapping rules which allows O2 external schemas to be constructed from a normal form OOER diagram is provided. The justifications and motivations for these rules are given through several examples. Mapping rules for other OO data models can be similarly obtained. Appendix I gives an example O2 schema which will be used to illustrate the mapping rules.

5.1 Generic Rules

(Rule 1) Each (regular or weak) entity type can be mapped to an external class. Only regular relationship types can be mapped to an external class.

Two points are to be noted: (1) It is possible to have class specifications for regular relationship types (eg. SPJ_VIEW1 in Appendix I is based on the SPJ relationship type in Figure 1). As noted in [4], it is necessary to provide class specifications for ternary and higher degree relationship types if it is required to model such relationship types in an external schema. (2) A weak entity type A may be mapped to an external class A' without also mapping the entity type on whose existence A depends. See Rule 6 for a mapping rule that applies to weak entity types.

(Rule 2) Not all entity/relationship types have a corresponding external class in the external schema.

This satisfies the maxim that an external schema is an abstraction of the conceptual schema which emphasises relevant details while suppressing unwanted details.

(Rule 3) An entity/relationship type of the conceptual schema may have more than one corresponding external class specification.

An entity/relationship type can therefore be viewed in different ways. In Appendix I, external classes EMPVIEW1 and EMPVIEW2 have the same underlying entity type EMPLOYEE. Classes SPJ_VIEW1 and SPJ_VIEW2 are different views of the same underlying relationship type SPJ.

(Rule 4) An external class A' whose underlying entity type is A must include at least one key of A as its attribute. This is an *entity-preserving* condition, which ensures the updatability of A'. However, an external class A' generated from a relationship type may not possess a key of the underlying relationship type as its attribute.

This rule ensures that apparently frivolous and meaningless views (eg. a class comprising only attributes sex and salary generated from the entity type EMPLOYEE in Appendix I) cannot be generated from any entity type. There is no equivalent 'relationship-preserving' condition because, in some cases, it may be semantically meaningful to generate an external class from a relationship set without retaining the key of the relationship set. For instance, given the SPJ relationship set, it is meaningful to generate a view SP which contains information about the parts supplied by suppliers.

In Appendix I, key attributes of external classes based on entity types are indicated using comments. Both SPJ_VIEW1 and SPJ_VIEW2 are created from the relationship set SPJ but SPJ_VIEW1 retains the key attributes of SPJ while SPJ_VIEW2 does not.

(Rule 5) Consider a regular entity type A of the conceptual schema. An external class A' whose underlying entity type is A can base its data-valued attributes on some or all the single-valued attributes of A, or from a single component of a composite attribute of A. A' can construct each of its tuple-valued attributes, if any, from some single-valued attributes of A, or from a composite attribute, or part of a composite attribute, of A. Each multi-valued attribute of A is mapped, if needed, to a set-valued attribute of A'.

In Appendix I, EMPVIEW1 is derived using Rule 5.

(Rule 6) Consider a regular entity type B connected to a weak entity type A by an existence dependent or an identifier dependent relationship type R. B can easily be mapped to an external class, say, B' by using Rule 5. The mapping of A to an external class, say A', depends on R. If R is an existence dependent relationship type, then A' can be derived from A in exactly the same manner as any regular entity type by applying Rule 5. If R is an identifier dependent relationship type, then A' must include the identifier of B as one of its attributes. In each of these cases, if it is desired to impose the existence dependency constraint of A' on B', then B' can specify either an entity-valued attribute whose domain is A' (if the cardinality of A in R is 1) or a set-valued attribute whose domain is set(A') (if the cardinality of A in R is n, n>1). The attribute is given a name which reflects the role of A' in B'.

In Appendix I, classes EMPVIEW1 and DEPENDENTS_VIEW are defined from the regular entity type EMPLOYEE and weak entity type DEPENDENTS respectively. If DEPENDENTS does not have any identifier attribute (thereby changing the relationship type into an identifier dependent relationship type), then DEPENDENTS_VIEW must include E# (the identifier of EMPLOYEE) as an attribute. In this case, inserts to DEPENDENTS_VIEW are possible provided that the EMPLOYEE entity identified by E# already exists. Other updating constraints exist. For example, when an instance of EMPVIEW1 is deleted, the underlying EMPLOYEE tuple will be deleted. This triggers a corresponding deletion of all DEPENDENTS tuples whose existence depends on the deleted EMPLOYEE tuple. The set of instances of DEPENDENTS_VIEW that forms the value of the attribute 'Support' of the deleted EMPVIEW1 instance automatically disappears.

(Rule 7) Recursive relationships are mapped to a cyclic definition (Section 2) in the external schema. Cycles in the conceptual OOER diagram (eg. the cycle involving

VEHICLE, EMPLOYEE and DEPARTMENT of Figure 1) can also be mapped to a cyclic definition.

In Appendix I, VEHICLE_VIEW, EMPVIEW2 and DEPTVIEW1 represent a cyclic definition based on the cycle involving VEHICLE, EMPLOYEE and DEPARTMENT. Further, EMPVIEW2 represents a view of the EMPLOYEE entity type that considers the recursive relationship SUPERVISES in the conceptual schema. A cyclic definition enables the computation of the transitive closure of a class. For example, from EMPVIEW2, it is possible to compute all the bosses (supervisors) of a particular employee.

(Rule 8) Consider an n-ary relationship type R involving n entity types E1,..,En, which have external classes $E'_1,..,E'_n$ derived using Rule 5 respectively. R has associated single valued attributes $Y_1,.., Y_m$ (m>0) of respective domains $D_1,..,D_m$ (not necessarily distinct) and multivalued attributes $Z_1,..,Z_p$ (p>0) of respective domains $F_1,..,F_p$ (not necessarily distinct). An external class E'_i ($0<i\leq n$) can have a set-valued attribute named Rext with domain constructed using the set and tuple constructors on different permutations of $E'_1,.., E'_n$, except E'_i and the attributes of R. The domain of Rext is therefore a nested set (of tuples) construct. Each entity type $E'_1.. E'_n$, except E'_i, is the domain of one, and only one, component of a tuple in the nested set construct. The deepest set includes the attributes of R. Further, to allow for different restructuring, any two entity types E'_u and E'_v (u<>i, v<>i) can be interchanged positionally. Formally, Rext has a domain :

$$\begin{aligned}&\text{set(tuple(}Q_{(L0)1}:E'_{(L0)1},..,Q_{(L0)q0}:E'_{(L0)q0},\\&\quad P_1:\text{set(tuple(}Q_{(L1)1}:E'_{(L1)1},..,Q_{(L1)q1}:E'_{(L1)q1},..,\\&\quad P_k:\text{set(tuple(}Q_{(Lk)1}:E'_{(Lk)1},..,Q_{(Lk)qk}:E'_{(Lk)qk},\\&\quad Y_{i1}:D_{i1},..,Y_{im}:D_{im},Z_{j1}:\text{set}(F_{j1}),..,Z_{jp}:\text{set}(F_{jp})))..)))),\end{aligned}$$

where

(1) the domain is a set of sets nested k times, q0+q1+..+qk = n-1

(2) $(L0)_1,..,(L0)_{q0},(L1)_1,..,(L1)_{q1},..,(Lk)_1,..,(Lk)_{qk}$ are different permutations of 1,..,n, except i, i1,..,im and j1,..,jp are different permutations of 1,..,m, and 1,..,p respectively,

(3) $Q_{(L0)q0'},Q_{(L1)q1'},..,Q_{(Lk)qk'}$, $P_1,..,P_k$ are attribute names,

(4) $E'_{(L0)q0'},E'_{(L1)q1'},..,E'_{(Lk)qk'}$ are external classes whose underlying entity types are $E_{(L0)q0'},E_{(L1)q1'},..,E_{(Lk)qk'}$ respectively, and

(5) for all qi, i=0,..,k, qi > 0, ie at each level of nesting, there must be at least one entity-valued attribute.

(6) when n=2 (ie a binary relationship), k = 0 and therefore Rext has a domain set(tuple($Q_{(L0)1}:E'_{(L0)1},Y_{i1}:D_{i1},..,Y_{im}:D_{im},Z_{j1}:\text{set}(F_{j1}),..,Z_{jp}:\text{set}(F_{jp})$)). If the cardinality of the link between R and $E_{(L0)1}$ is 1 (ie R is m-1), then Rext is a tuple-valued attribute; if R is m-1 and all attributes of R are discarded, then Rext is an entity-valued attribute.

In Appendix I, SUPPLIER_VIEW1, SUPPLIER_VIEW2 and SUPPLIER_VIEW3 represent three views created from the ternary relationship set SPJ. DEPTVIEW1 is an external class, based on DEPT in Figure 1, that considers the binary relationship sets SPONSERS and MANAGES. If the cardinalities of the links between R and its entity types are equal to 1, then external schemas can be generated in some preferred ways. For example, if the cardinality of the link from SPJ to PROJECT in Figure 1 is 1, then SUPPLIER_VIEW1 is preferred over SUPPLIER_VIEW2 and SUPPLIER_VIEW3, because it is semantically more correct. As another example, the attribute 'Manager' of DEPTVIEW1 is an entity-valued attribute of domain EMPVIEW2. This is because the cardinality of the link between EMPLOYEE and MANAGES in Figure 1 is 1, and no attributes are associated with MANAGES. If MANAGES has associated attributes, then the attribute 'Manager' of DEPTVIEW1 is tuple-valued.

(Rule 9) Given a relationship type R, we can construct a new relationship type from R by :

(a) projecting out some of the associated attributes of R,
(b) projecting out part of a composite attribute of R,
(c) restricting the values of some attribute of R, and/or
(d) removing the participation of some entity types of R.

The previous mapping rules can then be applied to the constructed relationship type to derive external classes.

Note that the cardinalities of attributes of the constructed relationship type may not be the same as their original cardinalities. For example, SPJ_VIEW2 is derived from a relationship type constructed from SPJ by removing the participation of PROJECT. Because the cardinality of the link from SPJ to PROJECT is m, the cardinality of the attribute 'SpecialPrice' of SPJ is changed from single-valued to multi-valued when PROJECT is removed. However, if the cardinality of the link from SPJ to PROJECT is 1, then the cardinality of 'SpecialPrice' will not be changed.

5.2 Rules Arising From The Inheritance Lattice

(Rule 10) Given an external class specification A with an attribute A' of domain B, the value of the attribute A' can be drawn from B or any of the subclasses of B.

(Rule 11) The structure of an inheritance lattice can be viewed in different ways, as long as the inclusion dependency between a class and its subclasses is maintained.

In Appendix I, ROUND_RED_PART_VIEW is a direct subclass of PART_VIEW. This is a consequence of the fact that the ISA relationship type is transitive.

(Rule 12) If two entity types A and B are connected by an ISA relationship such that A ISA B, then A inherits and may possibly override attributes/methods of B. An external entity type A' can then be derived from A using the relevant mapping rules, eg. rule 5.

EMPVIEW1 shows a view of EMPLOYEE in which the attribute DOB is inherited from PERSON entity type.

(Rule 13) Given two entity types A and B such that A ISA B, and B is participating in a relationship type R, we can construct a virtual relationship type R' from R in the ER diagram by replacing the participant B in R by A. We can then use R' for constructing external classes.

Rules 12 and 13 apply to special relationships such as

UNION, INTERSECT, DECOMPOSE. For example, if entity types A, B1,..,Bn are connected by the special relationship UNION such that A = UNION (B1,B2,..,Bn), then Bi ISA A for all i=1,2,..,n. External class specifications can then be constructed using rules 12 and 13.

(Rule 14) We may specify the value range of any attribute of an external class. This derives a subclass of the external class based on attribute values.

For example, a class PART with attribute colour can have a subclass RED-PART which is the set of parts with colour='red'. By predicating on the values of other attributes, other subclasses can be defined, eg. in Figure 1, ROUND_RED_PART is predicated on the 'shape' attribute in RED_PART.

5.3 Rules Arising From The Reachability Principle.

An entity type is ***reachable*** from another entity type if both entity types are connected, directly or indirectly, by some relationship type(s) and/or entity type(s). For example, in Figure 1, the entity type PROJECT is reachable from the entity type BUILDING through the relationship types LOCATED_IN and SPONSER and the entity type DEPT.

(Rule 15) An external entity type may include attributes from a reachable entity type. The cardinalities of such attributes in the external entity type may not be the same as their original cardinalities in the conceptual schema.

In general, an external entity type may not include attributes of entity types which are not related according to the reachability principle. The rules of Sections 5.1 and 5.2 can then be applied to derive external class specifications from the external entity type obtained. In Appendix I, DEPTVIEW2 is an example class, based on DEPT, that includes attributes from the reachable entity types BUILDING and PROJECT.

5.4 Rules Relating To Methods

(Rule 16) An external class can contain programmer-defined methods which derive new attributes (properties) for the class.

For example, in Appendix I, a method can be defined for EMPVIEW1 that computes the age of an instance of EMPVIEW1, based on the attribute DOB. Another method can be defined for EMPVIEW2 that allows all the superiors of an instance of EMPVIEW2 to be computed.

(Rule 17) A method defined at the conceptual schema level can be used at the external schema level if it does not refer to resources which are not present at the external schema level or which are protected from access.

For example, EMPVIEW1 can include a method (defined at the conceptual schema level) that derives a count of the number of children for an employee instance, if the execution right on that method has been granted by the DBA to users.

6 RELATED WORK

Most OO database systems (DBMSs) do not fit into the three level schema architecture as spelled out in the ANSI/X3/SPARC[2] proposal for DBMSs. These OODBMSs typically provide a large grained conceptual schema with minimum or no facility for defining views or external schemas. Several proposals have been made to incorporate some view mechanisms in OODBMSs [1,9,13,18]. The works of [9,18] focussed on defining multiple interfaces (views) to an object class. Each interface or views defines a set of methods and different views of an object class may share methods. Generally, these proposals do not sufficiently address the need for a flexible and declarative view mechanism such as that found in relational DBMSs. In [1,13], a query based view mechanism is used to derive subclasses from superclasses. [1] treats views as queries and uses the view mechanism to define virtual classes, which are structured into inheritance lattice. The behavioural aspects of the views defined are generated automatically by the system. Furthermore, such views are not updatable. In [13], updates apply only to views that are based on a join of the primary keys of the base tables. The views are non-recursive. Many of the view mechanisms proposed are defined on OO schemas which themselves suffer from several limitations (eg. problematic way of representing m-n, n-ary (n>2), recursive relationships, presence of redundancy etc). This seriously hampers the usefulness of these view mechanisms.

7 CONCLUSION

The OO paradigm is not a panacea that will address all the data modelling problems of complex applications. This paper has proposed a framework to address several OO data modelling issues, viz. (1) the problematic way in which m-n, n-ary and recursive relationships are handled in the OO approach, (2) the lack of general and flexible support for external schemas or views, and (3) the inability to differentiate good OO schema design from bad. Our approach allows OO external schemas to be generated from a conceptual schema which is represented by a normal form OOER diagram. A set of mapping rules is defined to derive O2 external schemas from the conceptual schema. A normal form OOER diagram incorporates several OO concepts, eg. methods, inheritance, existentially dependent objects etc. The model also include triggers for simple constraint enforcements, derived attributes and deductive rules.

As future work, we are currently investigating the updatability of the external schemas.

REFERENCES

[1] S. Abiteboul, A. Bonner, Objects and Views, Proc ACM SIGMOD Int'l Conf. on Mgmt of Data, Denver, Colorado, 1991.

[2] ANSI/X3/SPARC Study Group on Data Base Management Systems, Interim Report, FDT (ACM Sigmod bulletin) Vol 7 No 2,1975.

[3] J. Banerjee et al, Data Model Issues for Object-Oriented Applications, ACM Trans. Office Information Syst., Vol 5 No 1, Jan 87, pp. 3-26.

[4] R. Cattell, Object Data Management: Object-Oriented and Extended Relational Database Systems, Addison Wesley, 1991.

[5] P.P. Chen, The Entity-Relationship Model: Toward a Unified View of Data, ACM Trans. on Database Systems, Vol 1, No 1, 1976.

[6] O. Deux et al, The Story of O2, IEEE Trans. on Knowledge and Data Engineering, Vol 2, No 1, Mar 1990, pp. 91-108.

[7] D. Fishman et al, IRIS: An object oriented database management system, ACM Trans. Office Information Syst., Vol 5 No 1, Jan 87, pp. 48-69.

[8] B. Fritchman, R. Guck, D. Jogannathan, J. Thompson, D. Tolbert, SIM : Design and Implementation of a Semantic Database System, Proc ACM Sigmod Conf. 1989, pp 46-55.

[9] B.Hailpern, H.Ossher, Extending Objects to Support Multiple Interfaces and Access Controls, IEEE Trans. Software Engineering,Vol 16,No 11,Nov 1990.

[10] A. Keller, Choosing a View Update Translator by Dialog at View Definition Time, Computer, Jan 1986.

[11] S. Khoshafian, G. Copeland, Object Identity, Proc OOPSLA, 86, Portland, Oregon, 1986.

[12] W. Kim, An Introduction to Object-Oriented Databases, MIT Press, 1990.

[13] ChenHo Kung, Object Subclass Hierarchy in SQL: A Simple Approach, CACM 33, 7, 1990.

[14] T.W. Ling, A Normal Form for Entity-Relationship Diagrams, Proc. 4th Int'l Conf. on Entity-Relationship Approach, 1985, pg 24-35.

[15] T.W. Ling, A Three Level Schema Architecture ER-Based Data Base Management System, Proc. 6th Int'l Conf. on Entity Relationship Approach, 1987, pp 181-196.

[16] T.W. Ling, P.K. Teo, Towards Resolving Inadequacies in Object-Oriented Data Models, Submitted for Publication, 1992.

[17] L. Rowe and M. Stonebraker, The Postgres Data Model, in The Postgres Papers, Memo No UCB/ERL M86/85 Jun 87 (Revised), U.C.(Berkeley).

[18] J. Shilling, P. Sweeney, Three Steps to Views: Extending the Object-Oriented Paradigm, Proc OOPSLA 89.

[19] P.K. Teo, An Object-Oriented Entity Relationship Data Model, MSc Thesis, National University of Singapore, 1992.

Appendix I : Example O2 Schema Based on Figure 1

```
add Class EMPVIEW1 type tuple (
        E#              : string;          /* key */
        Name            : string;
        Address         : tuple(street:string, Zip:string);
        Job_History     : set (string);
        Support         : set(DEPENDENTS_VIEW);
        DOB             : string;)         /* from PERSON */
add Class EMPVIEW2 type tuple (
        E#              : string;          /* key */
        Name            : string;
        Boss            : EMPVIEW2;        /* cyclic definition */
        Subordinate     : set(EMPVIEW2);
        Drives          : VEHICLE_VIEW;)   /* defined below */
add Class DEPENDENTS_VIEW type tuple (
        BirthCert#      : string;          /* key */
        Sex             : char;
        Age             : integer;)
add Class DEPTVIEW1 type tuple (
        D#              : string;          /* key */
        Dname           : string;
        Manager         : EMPVIEW2;
        Sponser         : set(tuple(J:PROJECTVIEW,
                                Cost:float, ChkPtDte:set(string))))
add Class DEPTVIEW2 type tuple (
        D#              : string;          /* key */
        Dname           : string;
        Projects        : set(string);     /* project descriptions */
        Location        : string;)         /* from Bdesc attribute */
add Class VEHICLE_VIEW type tuple (
        V#              : string;          /* key */
        OwnedBy         : DEPTVIEW1;)
add Class SUPPLIER_VIEW1 type tuple (
        S#              : string;          /* key */
        Sname           : string;
        PJ : set(tuple(P:PARTVIEW, J:PROJECTVIEW,
                  QtyDate:set(tuple(Qty:integer,date:string)))))
add Class SUPPLIER_VIEW2 type tuple (
        S#              : string;          /* key */
        Sname           : string;
        PJ : set(tuple(P:PARTVIEW, ProjQtyDate:set(tuple
                (J:PROJECTVIEW, Qty:integer, date:string)))))
add Class SUPPLIER_VIEW3 type tuple (
        S#              : string;          /* key */
        Sname           : string;
        JP  :  set(tuple(J:PROJECTVIEW,  PartQtyDate:set(tuple
                (P:PARTVIEW, Qty:integer, date:string)))))
add Class PARTVIEW type tuple (
        P#              : string;          /* key */
        Pname           : string;
        Color           : string;
        Shape           : string;)
Class ROUND_RED_PART_VIEW inherits PARTVIEW
        type finish:string;
add Class PROJECTVIEW type tuple (
        J#              : string;          /* key */
        Jdesc           : string;)
add Class SPJ_VIEW1 type tuple (
        /* key is composite comprising S, P and J */
        S               : SUPPLIER_VIEW1;
        P               : PARTVIEW;
        J               : PROJECT_VIEW;
        QtyDate         : set(tuple (Qty:integer, Date:string));
        SpecialPrice    : integer;)
add Class SPJ_VIEW2 type tuple (
        S         : SUPPLIER_VIEW1;   /* no underlying key */
        P         : PARTVIEW;
        SpecialPrice : set(integer));
```

PARALLEL DATABASE

A Parallel Pattern Search Algorithm for Processing Object-Oriented Databases in a Cellular Array Architecture*

Stanley Y.W. Su, Soon J. Hyun, Rahul B. Patel

Database Systems Research & Development Center
Department of Computer and Information Sciences
Department of Electrical Engineering
University of Florida

Abstract

This paper presents a parallel association-pattern search scheme useful for object retrieval and manipulation of object-oriented databases in a cellular array architecture. The search scheme exploits intra-object parallelism and high granularity of computation by directly mapping data objects to the processing nodes of the architecture. It also utilizes both the broadcasting feature of SIMD architecture and the message-passing feature of MIMD architecture for performing pattern identification and result collection operations. A set of primitive functions has been defined based on the proposed scheme. These primitive functions are microprogrammed into all the processing elements and executed simultaneously. Some performance evaluation results are presented in this paper.

1 Introduction

Many advanced database applications have ever increasing demands for manipulating large quantities of complex data. The traditional data models are known to be inappropriate for capturing the complex semantic association structure and the behavioral properties of objects in more advanced applications such as CAD/CAM, CASE, office information systems, and command control systems. [BAT85, HUL87]. As potential alternatives to existing record-oriented data models, several object-oriented models have been developed based on different features of the object-oriented programming paradigm [CAR86, AGR89, HAR89, HUD89, DEU90, SU89, KIMW90, STO90, WIL90]. These models provide a variety of constructs to efficiently model complex domain knowledge. In an object-oriented database the domain knowledge can be represented by objects and their associations. The query languages used for querying the database can be pattern-based as opposed to the attribute-based relational languages. Pattern-based languages allow the user to express the query as complex patterns (linear patterns, trees, and network structures) which specify object classes and their associations with other object classes, data conditions desired, and operations to be performed on the selected objects [ALA89].
The use of conventional query processing approaches in a centralized computer system has been shown to be unsuitable for manipulating large database applications [SU88a] and for dealing with the complexity of knowledge processing [UHR87]. The architectures and the algorithms vary from system to system according to different application requirements and data characteristics. In an effort to achieve faster and more efficient knowledge processing, various parallel processing architectures and algorithms have been proposed [FAH83, HILR84, HILW85, MOL85, BIC89]. In general, they exploit specialized, massively parallel architectures suitable for knowledge representation and processing by directly mapping a graph-structured semantic network into a fine-grained network of a large number of processing elements. The main advantage of these parallel processing strategies is that the processing speed is dependent on the complexity of the pattern matching algorithms but independent of the amount of data to be searched. The problem of finding interrelated objects in an object-oriented database can be regarded as a semantic pattern search problem [WOO75, ALA89, MOL90]. An association pattern specified in a query may involve an arbitrary number of classes and different types of associations among them. Searching for a set of objects and their associations according to the query specification is a non-trivial task. It involves time-consuming navigational operations from the objects of one class to the objects of other class(es). Moreover, these navigational operations often need to be repeated many times depending on the complexity of the query expression. Therefore, the efficiency of the pattern search mechanism is the key to supporting the processing of large object-oriented databases.
In this paper, we present a parallel association-pattern search algorithm, called *path mechanism*, for processing an object-oriented database stored in a *cellular array* architecture. The proposed scheme takes advantage of the modeling capability of a graph-structured *Object-oriented Semantic Association Model* (OSAM*) [SU89]. Section 2 briefly describes the object-oriented view of the database

*Acknowledgment: This research was supported by the National Science Foundation Grant MIP-8822328. The continuation work of this project is supported by Fujitsu Limited.

and the structure of a pattern-based query language. Section 3 presents the processing details of the proposed pattern search scheme as well as a parallel architecture and a set of primitive operations that support the proposed scheme. The efficiency of the proposed pattern search scheme is verified in comparison with the algorithm used in SNAP [MOL85] in Section 4. In Section 5, some performance evaluation results over various operational parameters are provided. Conclusions follow in Section 6.

2 O-O View of Databases and Pattern Specification

The object-oriented view of a database consists of a set of object classes, their associations with other object classes, object properties represented by instance variables, and system and user-defined operations. The main features of object-oriented systems are: (1) object *identification* by a system-assigned unique object identifier(OID), (2) *encapsulation* of data and operations upon the data, (3) abstract *data typing* and representation of complex data in the form of aggregation hierarchies, and (4) *generalization hierarchy* (or lattice) and *inheritance* of structural and behavioral properties among object classes.

2.1 O-O Data Model

The object-oriented data model referenced here is OSAM* [SU89]. In this model, a database is represented graphically by a *schema graph* and an *object graph* representing the *intension* and *extension* of the database, respectively. In a schema graph, the database is viewed as a collection of object classes interrelated through various types of semantic associations. Two general types of object classes are distinguished: *entity class* (E-class) and *domain class* (D-class). An E-class represents a collection of objects having the same structural and behavioral properties which occur in an application world. Each object of an E-class is assigned by the system a unique object identifier(OID). A D-class, on the other hand, represents a collection of possible values that can be drawn for descriptive properties of other E-class or D-class objects. Association types or abstractions used to relate object classes vary from one model to another. There are five types of system-predefined associations in OSAM*. Two fairly common association types also used in other models are *Generalization* (IS-A relationship) and *Aggregation* (IS-A-PART-OF or IS-A-PROPERTY-OF relationship). The former denotes super-subclass relationships between two classes, and the latter denotes descriptive attributes. An association between two object classes is represented by a bi-directional edge between the classes in the schema graph. An example schema graph is shown in Figure 1(a), in which the association types *G* for generalization and *A* for aggregation are explicitly labeled beside the E-classes in which the associations are defined.

An object graph represents an extensional database, in which the database is viewed as a collection of interconnected object instances. An example object graph is shown in Figure 1(b), in which vertices such as *si* represent *object instances* (or instances) in the STUDENT class, and each edge represents the association between two object instances. An object instance is uniquely identified by an instance identifier(IID), which is the concatenation of a class ID and an OID, and contains descriptive data and references to other object instances.

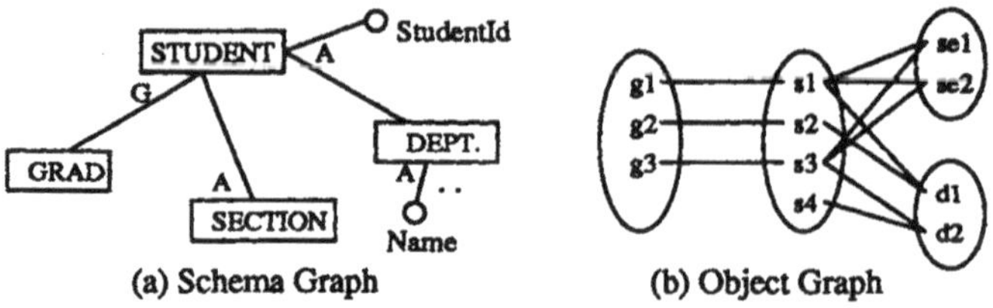

Figure 1: Schema Graph and Object Graph

2.2 Pattern-based O-O Query Language

Accompanying an object-oriented data model, a query language which possesses the essential properties of the object-oriented paradigm such as data abstraction, property inheritance, object identity, and object association, is necessary for manipulating object-oriented databases. The query language used in this work is the *Object-oriented Query Language* (OQL) developed for OSAM* [ALA89]. Using OQL and its underlying association algebra [GUO91], an object-oriented database can be accessed and manipulated by pattern specifications and verifications. An association expression in OQL using appropriate association operators specifies a certain semantic pattern. A pattern specification using OQL results in a *subdatabase* which contains two components of pattern representation: *intensional* pattern and *extensional* pattern. The intensional pattern specifies a set of classes and their associations specified in an OQL query, and the extensional pattern is the object instances and their associations which satisfy the pattern specification. The general syntax of an OQL query block is as follows:

```
CONTEXT association pattern expression
   [WHERE conditions]
   [SELECT object class(es) and/or attribute(s)]
OPERATION(s) parameter list
   [Operation parameter list] ...
```

The CONTEXT clause and its optional subclauses (WHERE and SELECT) are used to unambiguously specify the extensional pattern types which are relevant to a query. The OQL query processor will produce a *subdatabase* containing only the extensional association patterns which belong to those pattern types. In other words, only the objects and their associations which are relevant to the query are identified and retained in the subdatabase.

The OPERATION clause is used to specify the message to be sent to the identified objects in the subdatabase. The operation can be a system-defined operation (e.g., Display, Update, Delete, etc.) or a user-defined operation (e.g., Rotate, AssignAdvisor, etc.). Multiple operations can be specified to perform different operations on different object classes in a subdatabase. An example illustrates some of the key OQL constructs:

Query: "Display the StudentIds of all the students who are not in the graduate program of the Electrical Engineering Department."

```
CONTEXT Grad ! Student *
        Dept[Name = 'EE']
    SELECT Student[StudentId.]
DISPLAY Student
```

The query will result in a subdatabase which contains only the association patterns containing Student objects that are associated with Dept objects whose Name='EE' but not associated with any Grad object. As shown, *operators* relate two E-classes in the schema. *Associate* operator is denoted by an asterisk (*) and *non-associate* operator is denoted by an exclamation(!). When "*" is applied between two classes A and B (i.e., $A * B$), it returns a subdatabase whose intensional pattern consists of two classes A and B, and whose extensional patterns are the object instances of A and B that are associated with each other. When "!" is applied between two classes A and B (i.e., $A\,!\,B$), it returns all the A instances which are not associated with any B instance, and all the B instances which are not associated with any A instance. It is to be noted here that when both operators are applied to classes A, B and C such that $(A\,!\,B*C)$; $(B*C)$ is first processed and then $(A\,!\,B)$ is processed over those B object instances which have satisfied the $(B * C)$ specification. They can also be used in tree-structured or network-structured expressions that contain AND and OR branches among object classes [ALA89]. Figure 2 illustrates these operations on the example database shown in Figure 1. Here, we assume that the name of department $d2$ is 'EE'.

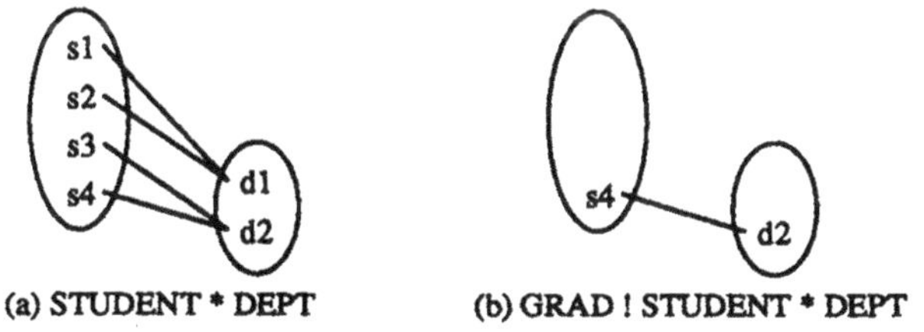

Figure 2: Associate(*) and Non-associate(!) Operations

3 Pattern Search in O-O Databases

The problem of finding a context (as defined in OQL) in an object-oriented database can be regarded as a *semantic pattern search* problem. An association-pattern search by navigating through a large complex database is a non-trivial task. The time required for a pattern search operation mainly depends on the control strategy, algorithms, and data structure used for storing and processing object instances. If all the semantic links emanating from all the object instances are stored explicitly and all the possible patterns formed from those are generated and stored, then it is possible to apply *text pattern matching* algorithms to search for the specified patterns [TAK84, SU88]. However, a large number of object instances and associations among them make it impractical to generate and store all the possible patterns in a database. On the other hand, if object instances and links (or storage representations of associations) are represented in $a1$-*link*-$b2$ structure, where $a1$ and $b2$ are object instances that are related via a semantic link, then the operation to search for the specified association pattern is to navigate from one object to the other by traversing the links between them. For example, if $(A * B * C)$ is a specified pattern, the search engine in this case will first find all *A-link-B* and then, for those B object instances that are linked to A object instances, it will identify all *B-link-C*. If, however, the number of object instances present in each object class is large and there are a lot of association links among them as shown in Figure 3, then searching for each instance and/or each link between two instances one by one will take a tremendous amount of time. This is known as the *multiple pattern search* problem.

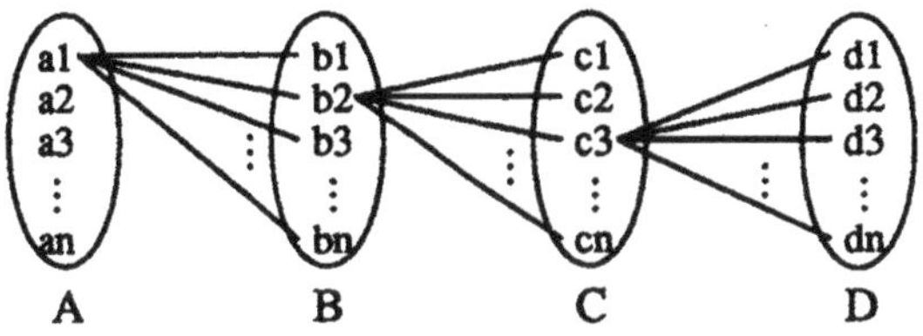

Figure 3: Multiple Pattern Search

Often, after a long traversal, a long string of associated object instances has to be disqualified because it failed to satisfy the next operator or condition specified in the pattern expression. Thus, a pattern search system has to keep track of the interrelationships among object instances during the search process in order to reflect the effect of the navigational operation by propagating the intermediate results back to all the participating classes. This problem is known as the *ripple-back* problem [THA90]. This kind of search requires much time and memory space. Therefore, a parallel processing scheme would be a highly desirable alternative, in that time-consuming multiple pattern searches and ripple-back operations are carried out in parallel.

3.1 A Parallel Pattern Search Algorithm: Path Mechanism

The basic idea of the proposed parallel pattern search scheme, called ***path mechanism***, is to identify association links that satisfy the query and assign them ***path identifiers*** (PIDs). In this scheme, during the traversal of semantic association links, the identity of a traversal path represented by a PID is to be preserved as long as participating object instances and their interconnections satisfy the query specification. When a traversal path with a PID is found to have no further links and thus no longer satisfy the query, the path is regarded as an *incomplete pattern* and is subject to deletion. The scheme, therefore, results in sets of object instances each with a unique path identification of correlated PIDs at the end of a pattern search operation. A simple example database is given in Figure 4 to illustrate the proposed pattern search scheme.

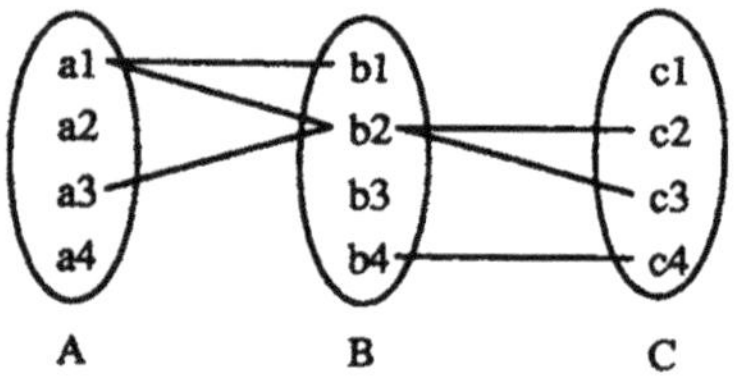

Figure 4: Example Database

Obviously, $a1$-$b2$-$c2$, $a1$-$b2$-$c3$, $a3$-$b2$-$c2$, and $a3$-$b2$-$c3$ are four qualified association patterns which satisfy the query $(A * B * C)$. The proposed pattern search operation for $(A * B * C)$ starts with searching for the links between all the A and B instances that have been qualified by their respective data condition(s). There are three semantic links between class A and B. As a result of the $(A*B)$ operation, the link $a1$-$b1$ is assigned with $PID1$, $a1$-$b2$ with $PID2$, and $a3$-$b2$ with $PID3$. This beginning step of the search operation is called the *initial PID assignment procedure.* In the next step, path traversal goes on from all the qualified B instances to C instances that corresponds to the $(B * C)$ operation. As shown, instance $b2$ has interconnections with both $c2$ and $c3$, and thus two different traversal links $b2$-$c2$ and $b2$-$c3$ are assigned with new PIDs, each preserving the identity of its preceding path. However, $b1$ has no further link and thus the previously established link (i.e, $a1$-$b1$ with $PID1$) is regarded as an incomplete path (or pattern). Consequently, it can be noted that the performance of an association pattern search algorithm depends on the efficiency of both link identification and incomplete pattern elimination operations. Two different approaches are proposed to efficiently deal with path traversals under different data conditions i.e., *path versioning* and *path duplication.* Each approach is described in the subsequent sections using an example database (given in Figure 4) and an operation table in which each column illustrates the progress of the search operation.

3.1.1 Parallel Pattern Search Using the Path Versioning Approach

The main idea of this approach is to assign *versions* of the PID of the preceding link to the multiple links fanning out from an object instance to the instances of another class according to the query specification. For a single link situation, the PID(s) of the preceding link(s) is(are) simply copied to preserve path identification(s). During the traversal, if no further link from an object is found and thus the query is not satisfied, then the PID(s) which has(have) been identified is(are) regarded as incomplete and thus deleted. Also, the same PID is sent back to the source object(s) for deletion. During the elimination of those incomplete PID(s), any PID whose versions have been deleted is also deleted wherever they are present in the system in a recursive manner. As a result, the complex object associations represented as a complex network are reduced to a strict representation of *tree-structured* PIDs. This provides a very efficient means for the result collection operation as well as the backtracking operation to eliminate unmatched object instances. Figure 5 illustrates how the versions of association patterns for multiple links are generated and maintained in the corresponding object instance.

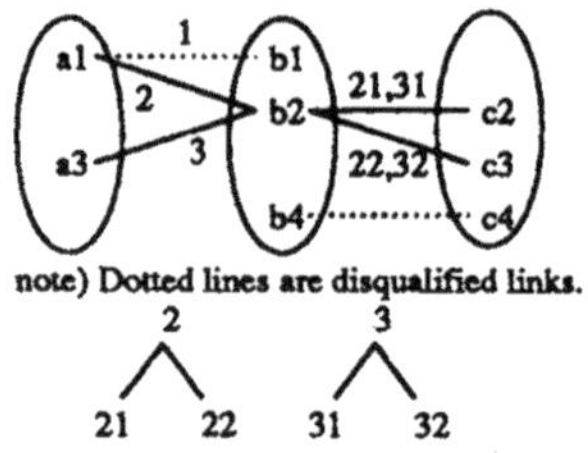

(a) Result of A * B * C

Object		Link	A * B		A * B * C	
			Path	Flag	Path	Flag
A	a1	b1, b2	1, 2	s	--, 2	s
	a3	b2	3	s	3	s
B	b1	--	1	s	--	
	b2	c2, c3	2, 3	s	21,31,22,32	s
	b4	c4	--	-	--	-
C	c2	--			21,31	s
	c3	--			22,32	s
	c4	--			--	-

note) Only forward links are shown.

Figure 5: Pattern Search by Path Versioning Approach

Instance $b2$ has two identified incoming links($PID2$ and 3) from $a1$ and $a3$, and also has two outgoing links to $c2$ and $c3$. Hence, $b2$ generates versions of $PID2$ and 3 i.e., (21, 31) and (22, 32) for the links $b2$-$c2$ and $b2$-$c3$ respectively, and stores in both $b2$ and the respective C instances (i.e., $c2$ and $c3$) as shown in the table. Selection flags are set in $c2$ and $c3$. On the other hand, since $b1$ has no link to any C instance, its PID (i.e., 1) assigned during the previous step of search operation is now deleted and the same PIDs are sent to $a1$ for deletion. The <s> flags set in $b1$ is reset. However, the <s> flag set in $a1$ still remains set due to another active link $a1$-$b2$ with $PID2$. Therefore, two active PIDs(i.e., 2 and 3) have been identified for four different patterns: 2-21, 2-22, 3-31, and 3-32 in two tree-structured PIDs as shown in Figure 5. The subsequent result collection operation is carried out by broadcasting each active PID registered in the control computer. In the first step, those object instances which have matched PIDs and the specified flag are identified. In the second step, the versions of the PID are searched in a recursive fashion until no more versions are found. All the matched object instances(IIDs) and their descriptive data (if requested) are collected by the control computer. The overall result collection operation terminates when all the active PIDs registered in the control computer have been traversed so that sets of matched object instances and their interconn-

-ections have been collected to form a subdatabase. The detailed algorithm of this approach is provided in 3.3.

3.1.2 Parallel Pattern Search Using the Path Duplication Approach

The design of the path duplication approach was motivated by observing that pattern identification and some of the result collection operations in the path versioning approach relied on inter-cell communications by message-passing. Thus, path deletion operations (i.e., traversing object connections backwards to eliminate disqualified objects) can be intensive thus degrading overall performance. This is possible in some situations where (1) objects are wide-spread over a large number of cells and (2) patterns requested are complex involving a large number of object classes.

To efficiently cope with these situations, the path duplication approach has been designed to fully exploit the broadcasting capability of the architecture. The basic concept of this approach is that, instead of versioning PIDs for multiple outgoing links, it generates buddy PID(s) from the original one(s) and then duplicates it(them) back to all the preceding association links along the path. As a result, all the association patterns can be represented in a *normalized* set of PIDs as opposed to the tree-structured representation of PIDs in the previous approach. Figure 6 illustrates this operation.

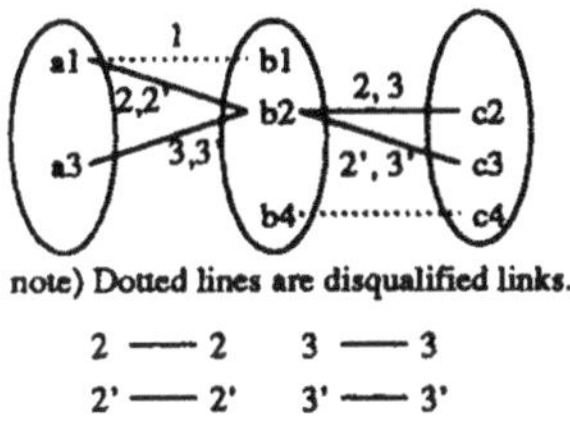

(a) Result of A * B * C

Object		Link	A * B		A * B * C	
			Path	Flag	Path	Flag
A	a1	b1, b2	1, 2	s	2, 2'	s
	a3	b2	3	s	3, 3'	s
B	b1	--	1	s	--	-
	b2	c2, c3	2, 3	s	2, 3, 2', 3'	s
	b4	c4	--	-	--	-
C	c2	--			2, 3	s
	c3	--			2', 3'	s
	c4	--			--	-

note) Only forward links are shown.

Figure 6: Pattern Search by Path Duplication Approach

$PID2$ and 3 of link $a1$-$b2$ and $a3$-$b2$ are copied to the first link $b2$-$c2$, from which the buddy PIDs(say, $2'$ and $3'$) are generated for the next link $b2$-$c3$. The newly generated PIDs($2'$ and $3'$) are then broadcast back to the preceding links $a1$-$b2$, $a3$-$b2$ for path duplication, respectively. The elimination operation for the incomplete patterns can be accomplished similarly using the broadcast feature of the parallel architecture. The table in Figure 6 illustrates the procedure. The operation results in four different association patterns which have been identified with four active PIDs in a normalized representation such as 2-2, $2'$-$2'$, 3-3, and $3'$-$3'$.

The subsequent result collection operation can be quite simple in this approach using a set of normalized PIDs. Instead of traversing versions of PIDs recursively, all the matched objects can be collected through a single broadcast of an active PID. The detailed algorithm of this approach is provided in 3.3.

3.1.3 Comparison Between the Two Approaches

We have identified three important performance parameters in comparing the relative efficiencies of these two approaches: (1) the number of objects in a database, (2) the complexity of search pattern, and (3) the degree of object-level parallelism.

On the first parameter, since the global broadcast operations are strictly sequential, the path duplication approach can be very expensive where a query requires a large number of such operations. This is possible in a case where the number of object instances (or associations) is so large that the average number of broadcast operations to eliminate unmatched instances tends to be large also. The path versioning approach, although it involves time-consuming recursive path deletion operations, can be efficient because the path deletions are performed in parallel using a highly parallel architecture to be described in the following section. On the second parameter regarding the complexity of search patterns (i.e., number of classes involved), the path duplication approach outperforms the path versioning approach since it can take advantage of its normalized representation of patterns(i.e., PIDs) and broadcast operations. With a single broadcast of an incomplete PID, all the preceding unmatched instances having the same PID can be eliminated. The third parameter is the degree of object parallelism in mapping between object instances and physical cells (to be described in 3.2). As the instance/cell ratio increases, the efficiency of broadcast operations used in the path versioning approach is decreased due to the serial processing of the broadcast instructions within a cell against a large number of instances in it. The path versioning approach, on the other hand, is insensitive to the instance/cell ratio. A performance evaluation over the amount of parallelism is provided in Section 5.

3.2 A Cellular Array Architecture

A parallel processing architecture, called a *cellular array architecture*, has been designed to support the proposed parallel pattern search algorithm. The main design considerations are as follows:

1. The semantic structure in which the domain knowledge is represented is rather complex and often changing. Consequently, memory access is frequent, and thus a high degree of memory parallelism is essential.

2. Associations among objects can be specified in different forms of semantic patterns. The association pattern search operation is therefore one of the most important and often used operations in the knowledge processing.

3. The problem size can grow to such an extent that scalability is of great importance.

4. High speed processing is essential in knowledge processing applications. Thus, the semantic gaps between high-level query constructs and low-level hardware functions, and between high-level data representation and low-level storage representation need to be minimized.

Several parallel processing schemes have been proposed exploiting the intra-object parallelism and fine granularity of their architectures in meeting the above requirements [FAH83, HILR84, MOL85, BIC89]. The prototype architecture we use here is a SNAP-like two dimensional cellular array [MOL85, MOL90]. The architecture provides both the broadcasting feature of SIMD and the message-passing feature of MIMD architectures for supporting pattern identification and result collection operations. An outside control computer presides over the cellular array in addressing instructions, supervising pattern search processes, and receiving the result of queries. The cellular array architecture consists of an array of identical cells each containing functional units for executing microprogrammed instructions, storing various object and association information, and inter-cell communications. Cells are globally connected through a common bus to an outside control computer, and also interconnected via local buses. Figure 7 shows the overall structure of the cellular array architecture and its simplified cell structure.

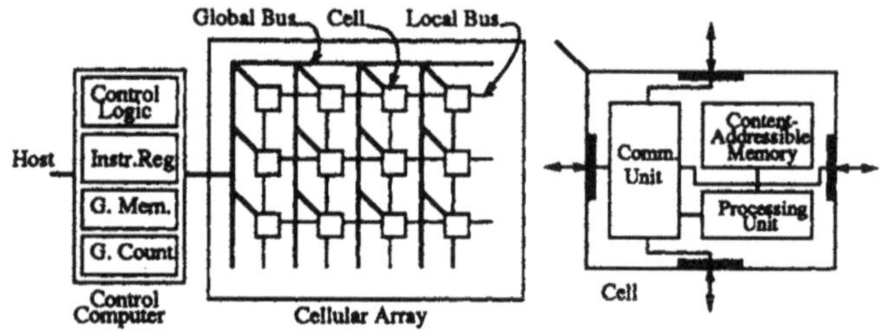

Figure 7: Cellular Array and Cell Architecture

This type of massively parallel architecture is suitable for representing object-oriented semantic networks. Since complex graph-structured semantic networks can be directly mapped into its fine-grained interconnection network of processing nodes, the gap between high-level data representation and low-level storage representation is significantly narrowed. Another advantage is that high-level query constructs can be directly mapped into a limited set of primitive instructions microprogrammed at all the cells so that the role of the global functions is minimized. The underlying functional concepts of the prototype architecture are associative processing and intra-object parallelism. We outline the functions of each component of the cellular array architecture.

A *control computer* (CC) provides an interface between the host computer and the cellular array network. A *global bus* gives an overall connection between the CC and all the cells in the network. The CC also plays a central role in the pattern identification procedure with its *global counter* and *global memory* to keep tract of unique PID assignments and to store active PIDs during the course of pattern search. The CC, upon receiving an OQL query from the host computer, decomposes it into a sequence of predefined *primitive instructions* or *functions* (to be described in 3.3), and broadcasts them to the network of cells through the global bus. The instructions are thus executed simultaneously at all the cells which hold those object classes specified in the instructions (SIMD). Each cell consists of a *processing unit* (PU), *communication unit* (CU), and *content-addressable memory* (CAM). The PU executes microprogrammed sequences of instructions. The CU provides the inter-cell communication facility that maintains an input message queue and an output packet register. Instructions for communications between cells have several cycles. Each cycle has two phases: processing phase and sending phase. In the processing phase, the PU takes the top packet of its input queue (if any), processes it, and puts it into a packet register if it is bound for another cell. In the sending phase, the CU checks the packet register and determines the next immediate destination according to a routing algorithm. The CU also provides the cell's access to the global bus which consists of two parts: a global instruction bus and a data bus transferring instructions and data, respectively.

Pattern identification operations are performed based on the proposed scheme and, as a result, a set of extensional patterns is identified, each of which has a unique system-defined identifier. These patterns are collected by the CC. The primitive functions which represent a translated query are broadcast one by one to all the cells. The cells that hold the relevant data execute each function and signal the completion of it by setting their local control lines which, in turn, are logically ANDed to produce the global completion signal to the CC. Thus, the synchronization of a function execution is aided by hardware.

In order to support the pattern search scheme proposed here, the cell's memory organization is partitioned into four parts. Figure 8, as an example, depicts the memory structure of node $s3$ of class STUDENT in Figure 1.

Class	OID	Link	Path	Flags
S	s3	g3	3	s
		se1	31	s
		se2	32	s
		d2	33	s

note) Path and flags are specified based on G * S * SE.

Figure 8: Node Structure of Object Instance s3

1. A *cell memory* stores class name, OID and descriptive properties of the object.
2. A *link memory* stores the link information to the objects of other classes. Thus, the data structure is basically a two-way linked list.
3. A *path memory* stores information about association pattern identifiers indicating different extensional patterns corresponding to an intensional pattern while a search is in progress.
4. A set of *flags* are used to identify the selection of a particular object in the course of various operations.

3.3 Primitive Functions

A set of *primitive functions* has been defined to support the proposed parallel pattern search operation. All the primitive functions are microprogrammed at each cell, activated by the control computer, and executed against the cell's data associated with object(s). One or more objects and their associated data can be mapped into a single cell (i.e., physical node). The primitive instructions are in a general format:

```
function <arg1> <arg2> <arg3> <arg4>
```

The first field is the function name, and the argument fields are the conditions to be matched. The conditions can be class names, flags, predicates, OIDs, or nulls depending on the function. If the flags are provided as arguments, only those objects with the specified flags set are involved in the operation. The primitive functions we have defined are SELECT, SEARCH1, SEARCH, SET-FLAG, AND, OR, NOT, COLLECT, INSERT, and DELETE.

1. SELECT *A* <flag><intra-class conditions>: This function is applied at the onset of the pattern search operation in order to set the flags in all the object nodes of class *A*. Flag and intra-class conditions (if any) can be specified optionally. The default flag is named *selection* and denoted as <*s*>. The <intra-class conditions> field specifies descriptive properties of those objects that are to be selected.
2. SEARCH1 *A*<flag1> B<flag2>: This function initiates pattern identification process from all the *A* instances which have been selected by SELECT function and performs initial PID assignment procedure as discussed in 3.1. Each instance of class *A* is checked for links to the instances of class *B*. For each link found, a unique identifier (PID) is assigned and stored in the path memory of *ai*. At the same time, <*s*> flag is set. Also the same PID is sent to the corresponding *bj* and <*s*> flag of *bj* is set. Flag1 and flag2 are optional. When given, the search is carried out on *A* instances whose <flag1> were set and *B* instances whose <flag2> were set. Otherwise, the default flag is <*s*>. The PID is fetched from the global path counter of the control computer which, after each fetch, is incremented automatically for the next link to be found. The same PID is registered in the global path memory of the control computer which keeps track of all the active paths.
3. SEARCH *B*<flag1> C<flag2>: This function is used for all the subsequent associative searches after SEARCH1, if the association pattern involves more than two object classes. This operation plays a main role in parallel pattern search operation. Two different approaches i.e., path versioning and path duplication have been discussed in detail in Section 3.1.
4. SET-FLAG *A* <flag1><flag2>: This function sets <flag2> of all the *A* instances with <flag1> set and deletes (or resets) <flag1>. This function is used to have a variety of flags set in the instances of the specified class during a complicated pattern search operation. If the class name is not specified, then all the object nodes are involved.
5. AND, OR, and NOT: The AND/OR functions are mainly used for searching non-linear patterns that contain AND and/or OR branches, and are performed at the branching object classes [ALA89]. (AND/OR *A* <flag1> <flag2> <flag3>) will set <flag3> by taking the logical AND or OR operation between the settings of <flag1> and <flag2>. NOT function will perform a logical inversion operation and is used for identifying object instances in two classes that are not associated (i.e., the implementation of the non-associate operator "!"). (NOT *A* <flag1><flag2>) will set <flag2> in all the *A* instances which do not have their <flag1> set.
6. COLLECT *A* <flag><class.attribute-list>: This function returns all the values of the specified attributes of those object instances that satisfy the query (i.e., those *A* instances whose <flag> are set). If a class name is not specified, then all the nodes are examined. To collect the result of a pattern search operation, the global path memory of the CC is first looked up for the active PIDs that have been identified during the pattern search operation. For each active PID, those matched object instances storing the same PID or its version will be collected by the CC, in which a subdatabase is to be formed.
7. INSERT <*ai*><*bj*>: This function inserts a new link between two object nodes *ai* and *bj*. If *ai* or *bj* or both are new, then the control computer will assign some new node(s) to the object instance(s).
8. DELETE <*ai*><*bj*>: Similarly, this function deletes a link between two existing object nodes *ai* and *bj*. The isolated object node(s) can be permanently deleted from the array network during a garbage collection operation.

Of those primitive functions described above, SEARCH and COLLECT functions behave differently for the two pattern searching approaches described in 3.1.

(1) Path Duplication algorithm:

```
SEARCH B C:           /*Path Versioning*/
for each bi {
  if <s>flag is set{    /*assuming default flags*/
    check for link to cj;
    if not empty{   /*pattern search begins*/
      if only one link   /*simple pattern*/
        copy PID(s) in bi to cj;
      else          /*multiple patterns*/
        for each link to cj
          generate version(s) of PID(s) in bi;
    }
    else{ /*eliminate incomplete ones*/
      delete PID(s) in bi;
      reset flags when no PID left;
      send PID(s) in bi to their source(s)
              for deletion;
    }
  }
}
```

```
COLLECT <flag>:
for each active PID {     /*broadcast from CC*/
  if PID and <flag> match {    /*step-1*/
    send OIDs and data(if requested);
    find linked object;
    if version exists           /*step-2*/
      for each version {
        repeat above two steps recursively;
      }              /*until no version left*/
  }
}
```

(2) Path Versioning algorithm:

```
SEARCH B C:            /*Path Duplication*/
for each bi {
  if <s>flag is set { /*assuming default flags*/
    check for link to cj;
    if not empty {  /*pattern search begins*/
      if only one link      /*simple pattern*/
        copy PID(s) in bi to cj;
      else     /*path duplication*/
        copy PID(s) in bi to the first link to cj;
        for each next link {
          generate new PID(s) from previous link;
          broadcast for duplicating the previous
                    link(s);
        }
    }
    else {      /*eliminate incomplete patterns*/
      broadcast PID(s) of bi for deletion;
      reset flags of bi when no PID left;
    }
  }
}
```

```
COLLECT <flag>:
for each active PID {    /*broadcast from CC*/
  if PID and <flag> match
    send OIDs and descriptive data(if requested);
}
```

4 Comparison with the SNAP Algorithm

In this section, we verify the efficiency of the path mechanism in comparison with the SNAP algorithm [MOL85]. For the comparison purpose, the same example schema and query pattern used in [MOL85] have been employed here. The schema graph and object graph are shown in Figure 9.

Pattern Searching Using Path Mechanism:
Query: $A * B * C * D$

1. SELECT A: selects all the A instances and sets <s> flags.
2. SEARCH1 A B: assigns PIDs for links between A and B instances and sets <s> flags.

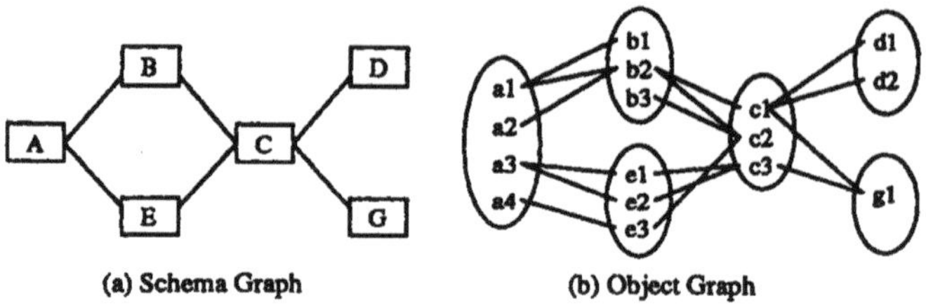

(a) Schema Graph (b) Object Graph

Figure 9: Example Database

3. SEARCH B C: identifies further association links from B instances to C instances.
4. SEARCH C D: identifies further association links from C instances to D instances based on path versioning.
5. COLLECT <s>: collects sets of matched object instances using the identified PIDs with <s> flag set.

The result of the pattern search using path versioning approach is shown in Figure 10(a) where four different association patterns have been searched under the following PIDs: 2-21-211, 2-21-212, 3-31-311 and 3-31- 312, each of which involves a set of matched object instances.

Pattern Searching Using SNAP Algorithm:
Query: $A * B * C * D$

1. Select all the A instances and set flag <f1>.
2. From instances with <f1>, trace down the links to B instances and set flag <f2> in B instances.
3. From instances with <f2>, trace down the links to C instances and set flag <f3> in C instances.
4. From instances with <f3>, trace down the links to D instances and set flag <f4> in D instances.
5. Select all the D instances and set flag <f5>.
6. AND flag <f5> with flag <f4> and put the result back to flag <f4>. If there are cells with flag <f4> after this operation, then the query pattern(specification) exists.
7. From D instances with flag <f4>, trace back the links to C instances to eliminate unmatched instances, and set flag <f6> in C instances.
8. At C instances, take the intersection of flag <f6> and flag <f3>, and set flag <f3>.
9. From C instances with flag <f3>, trace back the links to B instances to eliminate unmatched instances, and set flag <f7> in B instances.
10. At B instances, take the intersection of flag <f7> and flag <f2>, and set flag <f2>.
11. From B instances with flag <f2>, trace back the links to A instances to eliminate unmatched nodes, and set flag <f8> in A instances.
12. At A instances, take the intersection of flag <f8> and flag <f1>, and set flag <f1>.
13. Collect instances with flag <f4>.
14. Collect instances with flag <f3>.
15. Collect instances with flag <f2>.
16. Collect instances with flag <f1>.

As seen, ripple-back operations (instructions 7 to 12) to eliminate unmatched instances are intensive in the SNAP algorithm. The result is shown in Figure 10(b).

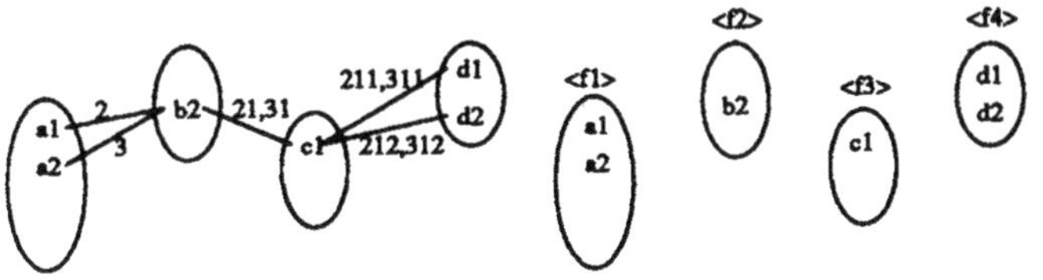

(a) (A * B * C * D) using Path Mechanism (b) (A * B * C * D) using SNAP Algorithm

Figure 10: Results of Example Operations

It is to be noted that the association patterns among objects are not explicitly identified by the SNAP algorithm. Therefore, additional result collection operations for finding association patterns among matched object instances are necessary. The performance comparison between SNAP algorithm and the proposed scheme is provided in the following section.

5 Performance Evaluation

In this section, we present the result of performance evaluation of the proposed association pattern search scheme. An analytical model and evaluation factors are described in Section 5.1. In Section 5.2, performance variations are observed by varying the size of database (i.e., the number of objects) and the number of object instances per cell (i.e., the degree of parallelism). The performance behaviors of two different approaches over the degree of intra-object parallelism are demonstrated. Also, a performance comparison between the proposed scheme and the SNAP algorithm is provided. We employed path versioning approach in this analysis.

5.1 Analytical Model

The analytical model used in this performance analysis is shown in Figure 11, where O[i] is an object class, n[i] is the number of objects contained in O[i], and link[i] is the number of association links between O[i] and O[i+1].

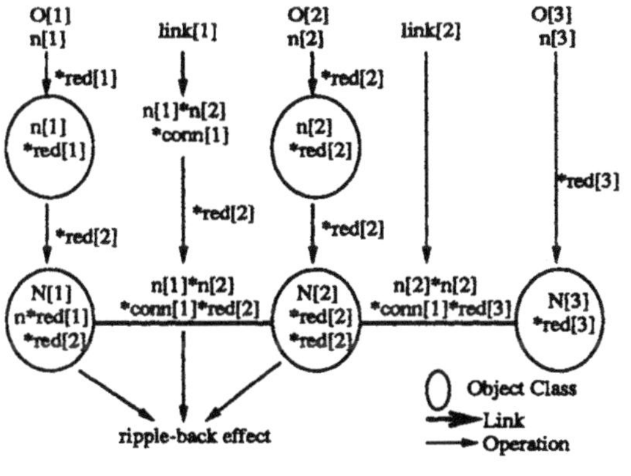

Figure 11: Analytical Model

The sel[j] is the selectivity factor of j-th object of a specified object class resulting from some intra-class comparison conditions. If no condition is given, then all the objects are selected and hence the selectivity factor is 1.0. The red[i] is defined as a reduction factor of O[i]. The reduction corresponds to the decrease in the number of selected objects as a result of an association search operation. The conn[i] is a connectivity factor resulting in a reduction of the number of association links between two object classes, O[i] and O[i+1].
Using the above modeling parameters, different types of associations can be modeled. For example, for an associate(*) operation denoted by (O[1]*O[2]), the following modeling parameters can be generated:

```
n[1]=1000, n[2]=200, sel[1]=sel[2]=1.0(default),
red[1]=200/1000=0.2, link[1]=n[1]*n[2]*conn[1]=200,
red[2]=200/200=1.0, conn[1]=0.001
```

Analysis has been performed on a Sun Workstation using the discrete event simulation technique by varying the size of database, query patterns, and modeling parameters, etc. The analysis of a context search operation contains three major components: (1) forward path identification, (2) ripple-back operations, and (3) result processing. Thus the total processing time is as follows:

```
T[total] = t[forward] + t[ripple-back] + t[result]
```

Each primitive function defined in the earlier section may correspond to one or more of the three components. Accordingly, equations can be modeled in terms of the predefined number of machine cycles(steps) required to perform each function. Once the total number of steps is found, it is multiplied by the clock speed to obtain the actual performance.
In this analysis, we assume that the cell memory is large enough to store the descriptive data of an object instance. We also adopt the *two-phase* query processing strategy [LAM89], in that the object instances which satisfy the association pattern specification are identified in the first phase and then, in the second phase, retrieve, update or other system-defined or user-defined operations are carried out over those object instances. The main advantage of this strategy is to avoid unnecessary data accesses and transfers over a large number of object instances of different classes during the complex pattern identification phase.

5.2 Analysis

Plot-1 shows the performance variation against the size of database. The computational complexity reflected here can be represented as $O((l+S)*L)$, where L is the length of pattern, l is the average number of links associated with an object instance, and S is the number of steps to search for an associated instance. The number of object instances mapped into each cell is assumed to be one("1"). Plot-2, on the other hand, shows the performance variation against the number of instances mapped into a single cell.

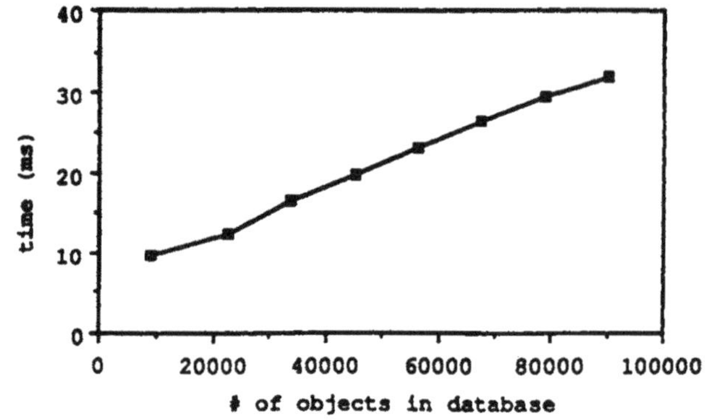

Plot - 1

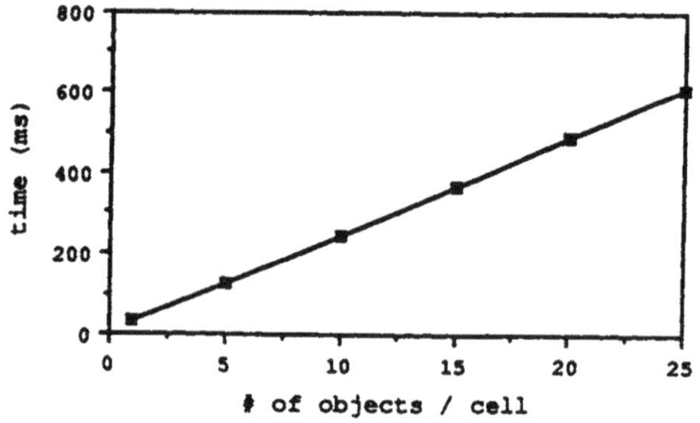

Plot-2

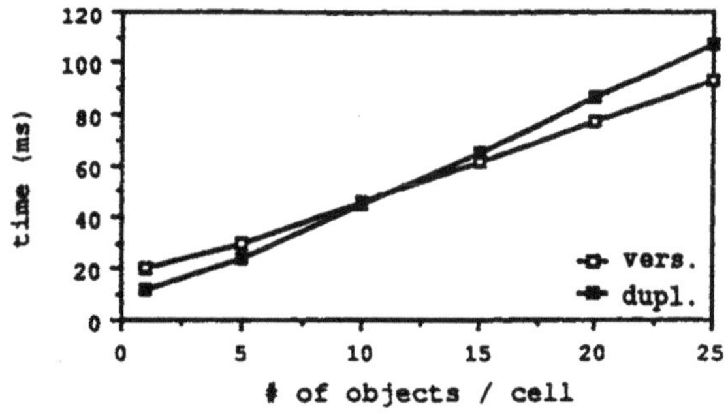

Plot-3

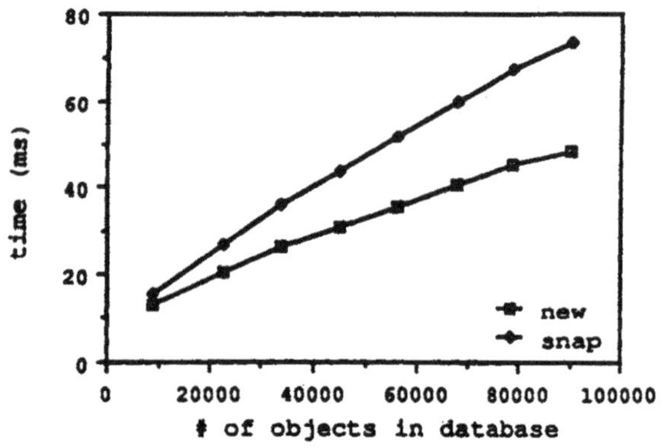

Plot-4

It reflects that the complexity of computation becomes O(NL * object/cell) as the value of instance/cell ratio changes. Plot-3 shows the performances of two different approaches in comparison with each other. The path versioning approach shows relatively better performance at higher instance/cell ratio. This is because path identification and path deletion operations in the path versioning approach mainly relies on inter-cell communications and are relatively insensitive to object level parallelism. On the other hand, the path duplication approach behaves relatively better at a lower instance/cell ratio because the efficiency of broadcast operations depends on the degree of node parallelism. An apparent trade-off is shown between the two approaches in the plot. In Plot-4, the performance of the SNAP's pattern search algorithm and that of the proposed scheme are compared. It is apparent from the earlier discussion that, among the three processing time components described in 5.1, the SNAP algorithm shows considerably lower performance than the proposed scheme in the time components of t[ripple-back] and t[result].

6 Conclusions

In this report, we have presented a parallel pattern search algorithm, called path mechanism, using a highly parallel architecture. In order to make this type of architecture useful for processing large O-O databases, we need to consider the issues of database size and the support for multiple query execution. Designers are often tempted to expand the number of processing elements to increase the processing speed as well as the memory size. However, this approach can hardly be justified due to the tremendous amount of overhead for synchronizing the huge network and the high probability of system failure which is proportional to the amount of circuitry and the number of processing elements. A more realistic way is to map data objects into a corresponding number of *logical nodes* which are in turn mapped to a smaller number of *physical nodes* (i.e., processing elements) and store the large amount of data in their secondary storage devices.

In order to support concurrent execution of multiple user's queries, the control computer needs to provide multi-server capability by adding multiple number of processors. For these queries to traverse the cellular array network concurrently, a possible strategy is to explicitly specify different query identifiers in the instruction sequences, message tokens, and node memories. The completion of an instruction sequence can thus be detected by checking the query id in all the message queues of the network. For supporting multiple query execution, parallel algorithms also need to be developed for concurrency control and recovery management.

References

[AGR89] Agrawal, R. and Gehani, N., "ODE: The Language and the Data Model," *Proc. of the ACM SIGMOD Int'l Conf. on Management of Data*, 1989, pp.36-45.

[ALA89] Alashqur, A.M., Su, S.Y.W., and Lam, H., "OQL: A Query Language for Manipulating Object- oriented Databases," *15th Int'l Conf. on VLDB*, Aug. 1989, pp.433-442.

[BAT85] Batory, D. and Kim, W., "Modeling Concepts for VLSI CAD Objects," *ACM Trans. on Database Systems*, Vol.10, No.3, Sept. 1985, pp.322-346.

[BIC89] Bic, L. and Hartmann, R.L., "AGM: A Dataflow Database Machine," *ACM Trans. on Database Systems*, Vol.14, No.1, March 1989, pp.114-146.

[CAR86] Carey, M.J., DeWitt, D.J., Richardson, J.E. and Shekita, E.J., "The Architecture of the Exodus Extensible DBMS," *Proc. of the Int'l Workshop on Object-Oriented Database Systems*, Sep. 1986.

[DEU90] Deux, O., et al., "The Story of O2," *IEEE Trans. on Knowledge and Data Engineering*, Vol.2, No.1, March 1990, pp.91-108.

[FAH83] Fahlman, S.E., Hinton, G.E. and Sejnowski, T.J., "Massively Parallel Architectures for AI: NETL, Thistle, and Boltzman Machines," *Proc. of the Annual National Conf. on Artificial Intelligence*, Aug. 1983, pp.109-113.

[GUO91] Guo, M., Su, S.Y.W. and Lam, H., "An Association Algebra for Processing Object-Oriented Databases," *7th Int'l Conf. on Data Engineering*, April 1991, pp.23-32.

[HAR89] Hardwick, M., and Spooner, D., "The ROSE Data Manager: Using Object Technology to Support Interactive Engineering Applications," *IEEE Trans. on Knowledge and Data Engineering*, Vol.1, No.2, June 1989, pp.285-289.

[HILR84] Hillman, R., "The Connection Machine: A Computer based on Cellular Automata," *Physica*, 1984, North-Holland Physics Publishing.

[HILW85] Hillis, W.D., "The Connection Machine," *MIT Press Series in Artificial Intelligence*, 1985.

[HUD89] Hudson, S.E., and King, R., "Cactis: A Self-Adaptive, Concurrent Implementation of an Object-Oriented Database Management System," *ACM Trans. on Database Systems*, Vol.14, No.3, Sept. 1989, pp.291-321.

[HUL87] Hull, R. and King, R., "Semantic database Modeling, Survey, Applications, and Research Issues," ACM Computing Surveys, Vol.19, No.3, 1987, pp.201-260.

[KIMW90] Kim, W., et al., "Architecture of the ORION Next-Generation Database System," *IEEE Trans. on Knowledge and Data Engineering*, Vol.2, No.1, March 1990, pp.109-124.

[LAM89] Lam, H., Lee, C. and Su, S.Y.W., "An Object Flow Computer for Database Applications," *Proc. of the Int'l Workshop on Database Machines*, Deauville, France, June 1989.

[MOL85] Moldovan, D., and Tung, Y.W., "SNAP: A VLSI Architecture for Artificial Intelligence Processing," *JPDC*, Vol.2, 1985, pp.109-131.

[MOL90] Moldovan, D., Lee, W. and Lin, C., "Parallel Knowledge Processing on SNAP," *Proc. of Int'l Conf. on Parallel Processing*, 1990.

[STO90] Stonebraker, M., Rowe, L.A. and Hirohama, L., "The implementation of POSTGRES," *IEEE Trans. on Knowledge and Data Engineering*, Vol.2, No.1, March 1990, pp.125-142.

[SU88a] Su, S.Y.W., "Multiprocessor Database Computers," In *Database computers: Principles, Architectures and Techniques*, McGraw-Hill, New York, 1988, pp.226-411.

[SU88] Su, S.Y.W., "Text Processors," In *Database computers: Principles, Architectures and Techniques*, McGraw-Hill, New York, 1988, pp.412-456.

[SU89] Su, S.Y.W., Krishnamurthy, V. and Lam, H., "An Object-Oriented Semantic Association Model(OSAM*) in *A.I. in Industrial Engineering and Manufacturing: Theoretical Issues and Applications*, S. Kumara, A.L. Soyster, and R.L. Kashyap(eds), American Institute of Industrial Engineering, 1989.

[TAK84] Takahashi, K. et al., "A New String Search Hardware Architecture for VLSI," *13th Annual Symposium on Computer Architecture*, Tokyo, Japan, pp.20-27.

[THA90] Thakore, A.K., Su, S.Y.W., Lam, H., and Shea, D.G., "Asynchronous Parallel Processing of Object Bases Using Multiple Wavefronts," *Proc. of the Int'l Conf. on Parallel Processing*, Chicago, Aug.1990, pp.127-135.

[UHR87] Uhr, L., "Multi-computer Architectures for Artificial Intelligence," *Wiley-Interscience Publication*, New York, 1987.

[WIL90] Wilkinson, K. et al., "The Iris Architecture and Implementation," *IEEE Trans. on Knowledge and Data Eng.*, Vol.2, No.1, Mar. 1990, pp.63-75.

[WOO75] Woods, W.A., "What's in a link: Foundation for Semantic Networks," In Bobrow, D.G., and Collins, A.M.(Eds.), *Representation and Understanding*, Academic Press, NY, 1975, pp.35-82.

Evaluation of a Parallel Database Machine for Caller Dependent Routing

Ilsoo Ahn
AT&T Bell Laboratories
Columbus, Ohio 43213, U.S.A.

Abstract

Caller dependent routing is a feature to route a phone call to a destination based on the phone number of the caller. It requires a high performance database, somewhere in the telecommunications network, to maintain information on all the phone subscribers. There are several relational database machines with a highly parallel architecture utilizing multiple processors. We have evaluated such a machine in terms of performance and related issues to see if it can support the database needs of the caller dependent routing in the telecommunications environment. This paper summarizes the results with an emphasis on the performance implications of the parallel architecture.

1. Introduction

Telecommunications services are becoming ever more sophisticated to support competitive activities of the modern business environment. For example, the *800* service in the U.S.A. charges the cost of phone calls to the callees rather than the callers. Similar services are available elsewhere in different names. Such a service allows people to make long distance calls for free without worrying about phone bills, and to enjoy convenience, savings, and choices beyond the geographic boundaries. For many companies, it widens the market to do business with customers from all across the country at the cost of phone calls. Another benefit is the flexibility in routing those calls as needed. When customers dial a single number for a company, the service can control the routing of the calls based on many factors such as time of day, day of week, area code of the caller, amount of traffic, and user inputs through computerized voice interactions. By changing the destinations of phone calls properly depending on situations, companies can serve customers better at a lower cost.

In addition, there is a demand to route a call based on the phone number of the individual caller, which can indicate the location where the call is coming from and the identity of the person who is making the call. Based on the information, the call may be routed to an appropriate office, department, or agent who can handle the needs of the caller best. Such a service, *caller dependent routing*, takes advantage of *automatic number identification* currently available on the telephone network, and can be offered as an extension of the 800 service on the platform of the *intelligent network* [1] [2] shown in Figure 1.

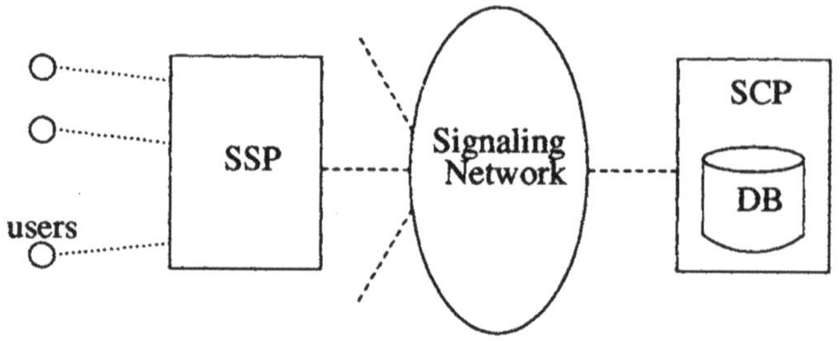

Figure 1. Intelligent Network

When a user dials a number that requires a special service of the intelligent network, *e.g.* an 800 number, the service switching point (SSP) that handles the phone line of the user passes the request to a service control point (SCP) through the signaling network. The SCP gets the request, executes service instructions as specified in the customer database (DB), and returns the destination of the call to the SSP which finally completes a connection. Note that there are many SSPs spread throughout the country, each covering a small geographic area, while each SCP can provide specific services for a large number of SSPs over a wide area. Therefore the intelligent network allows service providers to offer new features rather quickly by implementing the necessary changes on a small number of SCPs rather than modifying the hardware or the software on many SSPs at the same time. SCPs are built on general purpose computers, not special telephone switches, so they are usually cheaper, faster and easier to program. By changing the SCP software, the intelligent network can provide other advanced features such as *private virtual networks*, *calling card verification*, *tele-voting*, and caller dependent routing too.

For the 800 service, the database of customer records is usually small enough to fit in the main memory of the SCP, and the real-time delay in setting up the calls can be minimized. Caller dependent routing, however, requires a database of all the phone subscribers in the U.S.A., amounting to over 100 million people. The database has to store a record of two phone numbers at least, one for each subscriber and the other for the corresponding destination. There is also a need or incentive to collect additional information on calling patterns and various statistics for business and marketing purposes. This suggests that the database is expected to serve as a repository for personal information on each customer and to provide capabilities for analyzing such data for future applications. Furthermore, the database must be able to support multiple customers with different sets of customer records on the same platform.

These requirements call for a very large database, and present interesting challenges to a database management system in several aspects.

- Size : The data volume, on the order of several gigabytes at the minimum, is too big to be stored in the main memory, requiring a disk-based database.
- Query throughput : The DB must sustain a high throughput of queries to handle the load from all parts of the network.
- Query delay : The real-time delay for queries must be minimized to reduce the call set-up time.
- Update throughput : The DB must handle a certain rate of updates without degrading the query throughput or delays.
- Analysis capability : The DB must support analytic processing of data in both pre-planned and ad-hoc manners.
- Availability : The DB must not disrupt the service even if the hardware or the software fails.
- Miscellaneous issues : The DB must provide convenient facilities for application development, operation, administration, and maintenance (OA&M).

To study the feasibility of supporting such an application as a feature of the intelligent network, we evaluated a parallel database machine in terms of performance, availability, and miscellaneous issues. This paper describes the architecture of the machine, the test environment, and the benchmark queries used to test the performance of insertions and retrievals on various hardware configurations. It then discusses the results of the evaluation with an emphasis on the performance implications of the parallel architecture.

2. *A Parallel Database Computer*

As the microprocessors become cheaper and more powerful, it becomes feasible and attractive to build a high performance machine by combining many of those processors in parallel. Such a machine may equal or exceed the power of a large mainframe or even a supercomputer at a much lower cost, though it is difficult to exploit full parallelism for general purpose applications.

The most popular database management systems these days, and will be in the foreseeable future, are based on the relational model [3]. The relational model offers conceptual simplicity and flexible versatility through the standard interface of Structured Query Language (SQL). Yet supporting relational database capabilities is expensive in terms of CPU capacity, and performance is still *the* major concern in most on-line or real-time applications using the relational database. Since relational database operations are based on a set of well-defined primitives, processing those operations seems to be amenable to parallelism. Hence several parallel machines have been specially designed to support relational database management [4] [5] [6] [7].

Figure 2 shows a relational database machine with a highly parallel architecture utilizing multiple processors [8] [9]. The machine works as a backend database server supporting the SQL interface for one or more general purpose host machines. It consists of multiple processors, which are of three types: Interface Processors (IFPs), Communications Processors (COPs), and Access Module Processors (AMPs). The IFP and the COP handle communications with other hosts, either through an I/O channel of an IBM compatible mainframe or through the local area network, respectively. They also parse SQL requests received from host applications, divides them into a series of primitive operations, and dispatch those to one or more AMPs depending on the nature of the request.

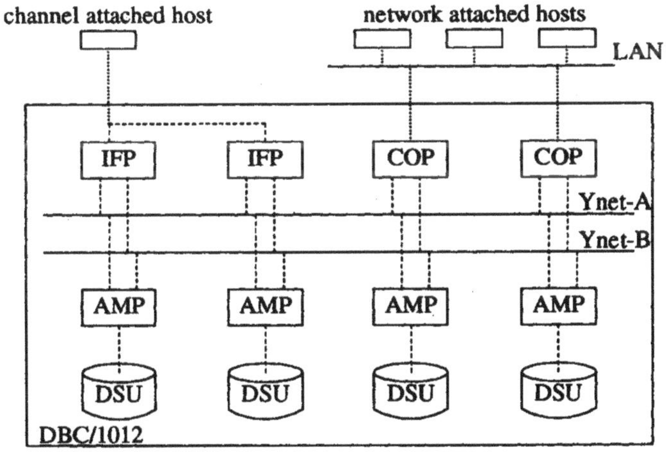

Figure 2. Architecture of a Parallel Database Machine

Each AMP executes the primitives against the data stored on one or more Data Storage Units (DSUs) attached to it, and sends the result to the IFPs or COPs that returns the answer to the host applications. Note that the machine distributes data across multiple DSUs by hashing on the primary key of each record. Hence accessing a record through a complete key is very fast involving only a single AMP, but other types of accesses are more expensive as will be described in Sections 3.6 and 3.7.2.

There are two types of processors currently available for the COPs and AMPs: the Model-3 processors built with the 80386 chips and the Model-4 processors built with the 80486 chips. As the test results in later sections indicate, Model-4 processors are about twice faster than Model-3 processors.

Communications among the processors go through the *Ynet* that serves as a high speed bus and also provides routing and sorting functions. The Ynet is duplicated for load sharing and redundancy, and can be expanded to support a very large number, hundreds or even thousands, of processors. The main use for a database machine like this is in the area of business data processing where large and expensive mainframes are burdened by a heavy load of database applications, but we evaluated it for a telecommunications application which demands a real-time performance.

There are three approaches to develop applications for the machine on the host machines, all of which use the SQL interface [10]. One is through an interactive command processor that is convenient for simple ad-hoc uses. The second is through a preprocessor for embedded SQL statements in a host programming language, which is relatively easy to use but can handle only one session in an application process. The third is to program with the call level interface (CLI) library routines, which offers the most flexibility including the ability to handle multiple sessions in a process. We used the third approach for our evaluation.

3. *Performance Evaluation*

We evaluated a parallel database machine with 4 COPs, 4 AMPs, and 4 DSUs connected to several host machines through one ethernet. All the AMPs were of Model-4, but the COPs we got initially were of Model 3. We later replaced three of the COPs with Model-4s. All the results reported in this paper are those for the Model-4 COPs, unless specified otherwise. We designed a set of benchmark queries, created a test database, and ran the tests for various configurations. We measured the performance and studied the results, analyzing the effects of the parallel architecture with a varying number of processors.

3.1 Test Database

We created a test database with 3 tables, `Tdirectory`, `Tcaller`, and `Toffice`. Table `Tdirectory` contains a pair of phone numbers, each with an area code (NPA) and a 7-digit number (NXX), for a caller and a corresponding office. Each of tables `Tcaller` and `Toffice` has a phone number and an office code, but may be expanded to include additional information in the future if necessary.

```
create table Tdirectory, fallback-or-not,
  no before journal, no after journal
 (npa_i smallint format '9(3)'
    between 1 and 999 not null,
  npa_o smallint format '9(3)'
    between 1 and 999,
  nxx_i integer format '9999999'
    between 0 and 9999999 not null,
  nxx_o integer format '9999999'
    between 0 and 9999999)
  unique primary index (npa_i, nxx_i);

create table Tcaller, fallback-or-not,
  no before journal, no after journal
 (ofc_id smallint format '9(4)'
    between 0 and 9999,
  npa_i smallint format '9(3)'
    between 1 and 999 not null,
  nxx_i integer format '9999999'
    between 0 and 9999999 not null)
  unique primary index (npa_i, nxx_i);

create table Toffice, fallback-or-not,
  no before journal, no after journal
 (ofc_id smallint format '9(4)'
    between 0 and 9999 not null,
  npa_o smallint format '9(3)'
    between 1 and 999,
  nxx_o integer format '9999999'
    between 0 and 9999999)
  unique primary index (ofc_id);
```

When the *fallback-or-not* option is specified as `fallback`, two copies of data are maintained for the table. This option allows the table available even when an AMP or a DSU fails, but costs about twice the disk space. We tried both the `fallback` and the `no fallback` options, and evaluated the space usages, update performance, and availability issues. We did not use transaction journaling to avoid any performance overhead.

3.2 Benchmark Queries

We designed a set of benchmark statements to insert test data into the tables and to run three types of queries, *point*, *range*, and *join*. Though these queries are rather simple, they could demonstrate interesting performance characteristics of the machine with multiple processors.

```
Q_i1:
using n_i(smallint), n_o(smallint),
  x_i(integer), x_o(integer)
insert Tdirectory
  (:n_i, :n_o, :x_i, :x_o);
Q_i2:
```

```
using o_id(smallint),
  n_i(smallint), x_i(integer)
insert Tcaller (:o_id, :n_i, :x_i);
Q_i3:
using o_id(smallint),
  n_o(smallint), x_o(integer)
insert Toffice (:o_id, :n_o, :x_o);

Q_p1:
using n_i(smallint), x_i(integer)
select npa_o, nxx_o from Tdirectory
  where npa_i = :n_i and nxx_i = :x_i;
Q_r1:
select * from Tdirectory
  where npa_i = 123;
Q_r2:
select count(nxx_i) from Tdirectory
  where npa_i = 123;

Q_j1:
using n_i(smallint), x_i(integer)
select npa_o, nxx_o
    from Tcaller, Toffice
  where npa_i = :n_i and nxx_i = :x_i
  and Tcaller.ofc_id = Toffice.ofc_id;
Q_j2:
using n_i(smallint), x_i(integer)
select npa_o, nxx_o
    from Tcaller, Toffice
  where npa_i = :n_i and nxx_i = :x_i
    and Tcaller.nxx_i + 1000000 =
        Toffice.nxx_o;
```

Q_i1 through Q_i3 are used to insert data into three tables with and without the `fallback` option. Since data records are spread evenly across all the DSUs through hashing on the key values, all the AMPs participate in the update operations. Q_p1 is a point query to retrieve the phone number of an office corresponding to a caller. Table `Tdirectory` is accessed through hashing on the primary key values, which is a single AMP operation.

Q_r1 and Q_r2 are range queries that retrieve a set of records based on the initial portion of the primary key. As it turns out, these queries need to scan the whole table, involving all the AMPs. Q_j1 and Q_j2 involve a join operation of two tables. Q_j1, functionally equivalent to Q_p1, selects a record from table `Tcaller` on a single AMP, and then joins the result with a record from table `Toffice` on another AMP. Q_j2 also selects a record from table `Tcaller` on a single AMP, but the result is joined with data selected by scanning table `Toffice` on all the AMPs.

We created test programs that run on the host machines as database clients and open a number of simultaneous sessions, ranging from one to twenty, to the database server. The programs randomly generate the input parameters such as the NPA (`n_i`) and the NXX (`x_i`) of a caller, send one of the above queries to the database server, and process the results from the server. We measured the throughputs and the delays as we ran varying (one to seven) copies of the test program on various configurations with the Model-3 and Model-4 COPs.

3.3 Insertions

We used Q_i1 through Q_i3 to populate three tables, and measured the throughput and resource usages for inserting records into table `Tdirectory` with and without using the `fallback` option. Figure 3 shows the insertion rate as the number of records per second. The rate with the `fallback` option is significantly lower than that without the option.

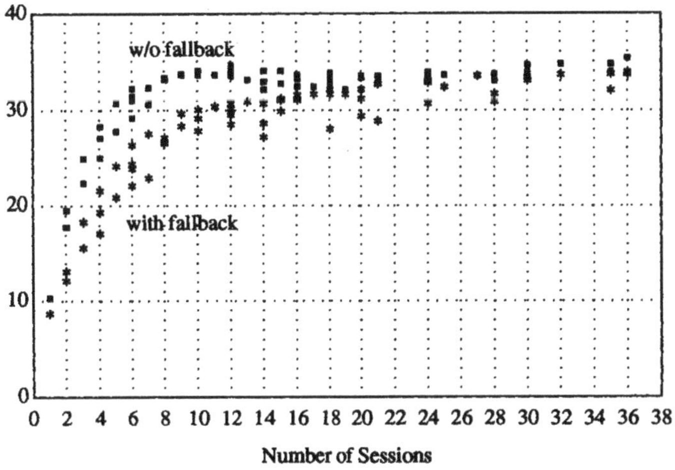

Figure 3. Throughput for Insertions with 1 Model-4 COP

We also tried to bundle multiple, up to 10, insertions into each request. The throughput increased significantly with bundling, which was more so when the `fallback` option was not used, as shown in Figure 4. But we found that deadlocks could occur in some cases (denoted by —) when we bundled multiple queries using two or more COPs. This problem deserves further investigation to achieve a higher throughput for update intensive applications.

Queries/Request		1	2	4	6
with Fallback	1 COP	29.2	31.4	39.0	41.7
	2 COPs	34.4	34.0	40.1	—
without Fallback	1 COP	34.3	47.3	63.5	68.0
	2 COPs	62.1	68.1	75.1	74.6

Figure 4. Throughput for Bundled Insertions

Measurement results of resource usages, omitted due to space limitation, show that insertions with the `fallback` option puts almost twice as much load on the AMPs and DSUs as those without it, though there is not much difference in the COPs usages. For insertions with the `fallback` option, adding a COP did not make much difference because the capacity of the AMPs was the bottleneck.

3.4 Space Usage

While populating tables with and without the `fallback` option as above, we measured the disk spaces used to store such data. The raw size of each record in table `Tdirectory`, with two 2-byte integers and two 4-byte integers, is 12 bytes. But there are additional overheads of 13 bytes for each record, which is significant for short records, and miscellaneous system information takes up additional space. The following table shows that the `fallback` case requires about twice the space of the `no fallback` case which stores only one copy of the table. The size indicates the number of records in the table, 1, 10, and 80 million records, respectively.

Size	Fallback	Disk(MB)	Time
1,000,000	no	26	15min
	yes	52	15min
10,000,000	no	261	2hour 39min
	yes	522	2hour 36min
80,000,000	no	2087	21hour 15min

Figure 5. Space Usage and Time for *fastload*

To generate tables with up to 80 million records, we used the *fastload* feature which can populate empty tables much more quickly than insertions like Q_i1 through Q_i3. Note that it would take over a month to store 80 million records if we used *insertions* at the rate of about 30 records per second as shown in Figure 3. We measured the elapsed times to load 1, 10, and 80 million records into table `Tdirectory` using 2 COPs. The results in Figure 5 show that there is not much difference in the elapsed time for *fastload* between the `fallback` and the `no fallback` case.

3.5 Point Query

We ran query `Q_p1` on a table with 80 million records. The machine we first received contained only the Model-3 COPs. We ran query Q_p1 and measured the throughputs with one and two Model-3 COPs, respectively. We later repeated the test after replacing three COPs with Model-4s.

3.5.1 Model-3 COPs

We found that one Model-3 COP supported about 16 queries per second, while two Model-3 COPs supported about twice as many. We could see that the throughput for Q_p1 is heavily dependent on the capacity of the COPs. In both cases, the throughput increased up to a certain limit as the number of sessions increased. We also measured the average delay as the time elapsed to receive an answer after sending a request. The result showed that using two COPs, instead of one, increased the throughput and reduced the delays at the same time. Note that the delay increases significantly without improving the throughput if the number of sessions increases over a limit.

3.5.2 Model-4 COPs

We replaced three Model-3 COPs by the same number of Model-4 COPs, and repeated similar tests for running query Q_p1. Figure 6 shows that each Model-4 COP supports about 30 queries per second, which is about twice the performance of a Model-3 COP, and that the throughput increases almost linearly as the number of COPs increases.

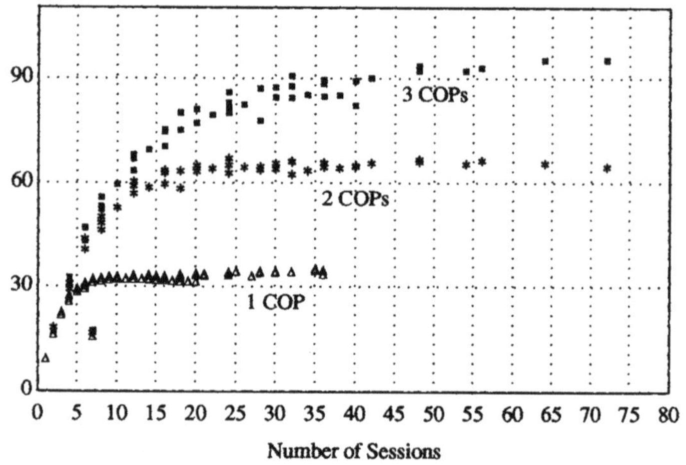

Figure 6. Query Throughput on Model-4 COPs

Figure 7 shows that the delay increased significantly for a throughput over a limit, and that a machine with more COPs supported higher throughputs with lower delays.

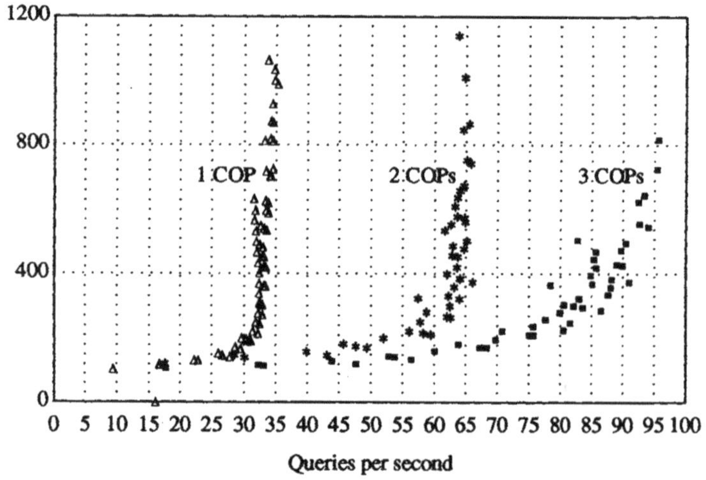

Figure 7. Delays (in *msec*)

We also measured the resource usages of COPs, AMPs, and DSUs for various combinations of process and session counts, where the number of COPs varies from one to three respectively. In each case, the number of processes varied from 1 to 14, where each process handled from 1 to 20 sessions. These showed that the COPs were over 95% busy in most cases, while the AMPs and DSUs had more spare capacities. The usages of AMPs and DSUs went higher as the throughput increased with more COPs, but the AMPs still remained under 50% busy. We concluded that the capacity of the COPs was the bottleneck for query Q_p1.

3.5.3 Bundled Queries

To enhance the throughput further, we tried to bundle several queries in each request instead of one query per request. We measured the throughputs, delays, and resource usages, while running 2 processes on each COPs with each process handling 6 sessions. Figure 8 shows the query throughput with the X axis representing the bundling factor which is defined as the number of SQL queries in each request. The throughput goes over 150 queries per second with 3 COPs for the bundling factor of 3 or higher, but becomes rather erratic for the factor of 5 or more.

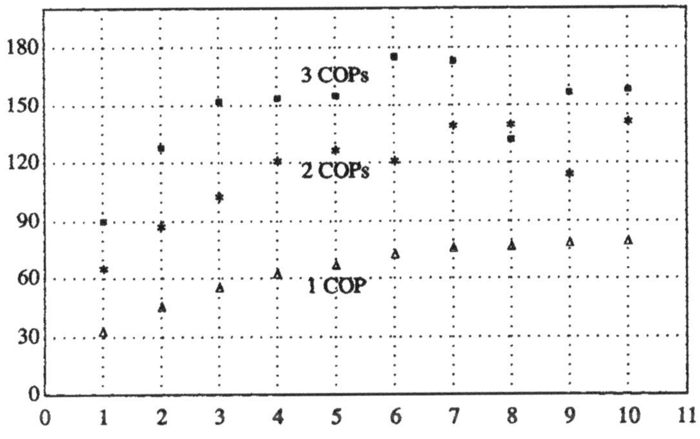

Figure 8. Throughput for Bundled Queries

Figure 9 shows the resource usages of the COPs, AMPs, and DSUs for various counts of the COPs and bundling factors. Compared with the results for non-bundling, bundling multiple queries in each request has the effect of reducing the load on the COPs and hence improving the throughput. When we bundle multiple queries on 2 or 3 COPs, the bottleneck moves from the COPs to the DSUs which become busy over 100%. On the other hand, the delays for each request increased almost linearly with bundling. For example, the delay was about 400 *msec* when 3 COPs were used with no bundling. The delay increased to 1160 and to 2270 *msec*, respectively, as the bundling factor changed to 5 and to 10.

We also repeated some of the above tests on a table with different sizes, and got similar measurement results showing that hashing works well regradless of the file size.

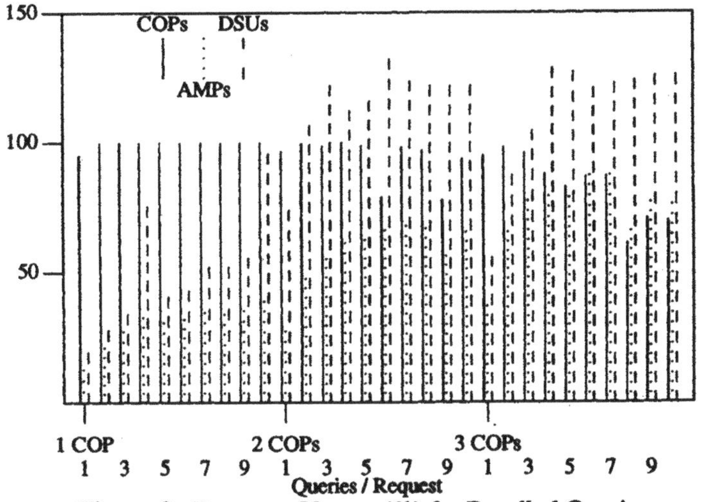

Figure 9. Resource Usages (%) for Bundled Queries

3.5.4 Performance with 3 AMPs

So far, all the tests were run on the machine with 4 AMPs. To evaluate the effects of the AMPs on the performance, we turned one AMP offline and repeated some of the Q_p1 tests. We ran tests bundling between 1 and 8 queries per request with 3 AMPs, while varying the number of COPs from 1 to 3. For each COP, we ran 2 processes with each process handling 6 sessions.

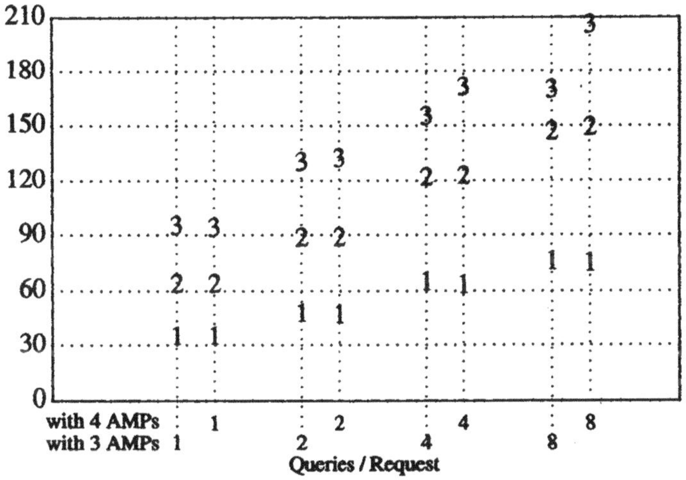

Figure 10. Throughput: 3 AMPs *vs.* 4 AMPs

Figure 10 compares the throughputs with 3 AMPs *vs.* 4 AMPs side by side, while the number of COPs varies from 1 to 3 as indicated by symbols 1, 2, and 3 in the graph. The X axis represents the number of queries per request executed on the configurations of 3 AMPs and 4 AMPs, respectively. The graph shows that the throughputs with 3 AMPs and 4 AMPs are virtually the same when the number of COPs is either 1 or 2 and when the bundling factor is 2 or less for 3 COPs, because the bottleneck is at the COPs as discussed in Section 3.5.2. The throughput of 4 AMPs gets better than that of 3 AMPs when the bundling factor becomes 4 or higher with 3 COPs, because the bottleneck moves from the COPs to the DSUs.

3.6 Range Queries

We ran queries Q_r1 and Q_r2 on the machine with combinations of 1 or 2 COPs and 3 or 4 AMPs. These queries have a selection clause specifying the initial portion of the primary key, `npa_i`. But it is still necessary to scan the whole table, because the primary access mechanism in the machine is based on hashing of the complete key and a partial key is of no use. For Q_r1, each AMP scans the portion of the table stored on its DSUs in parallel, and the results from all the AMPs are returned as the answer. For Q_r2, each AMP runs an aggregate operation while scanning its DSUs, then the results from all the AMPs are combined to generate the final answer. Thus these queries are expected to put a heavy load on the AMPs, which was confirmed by the measurement of resource usages not shown here. Figure 11 shows that the throughputs for both queries are quite dependent on the number of AMPs and not much on the number of COPs. It also shows that the growth in throughput from 3 AMPs to 4 AMPs is bigger for Q_r1 than Q_r2, because Q_r1 involves less communications among the AMPs than Q_r2. Need for more communications reduces the parallel effects of multiple processors. Note that the throughput is one to two queries per minute, not per second, and that range queries are expensive on the machine.

Query	# of COPs	with 3 AMPs	with 4 AMPs
Q_r1	1 COP	1.53 q/min	2.03 q/min
	2 COPs	1.46 q/min	2.02 q/min
Q_r2	1 COP	1.04 q/min	1.27 q/min
	2 COPs	1.04 q/min	1.39 q/min

Figure 11. Throughput for range queries

3.7 Join Queries

We ran queries Q_j1 and Q_j2 on the machine configured similarly to the one described in Section 3.5.4. Both Q_j1 and Q_j2 involve a join operation of two tables, but they behave differently in terms of performance. Q_j1 is processed by two single-AMP operations, while Q_j2 involves all AMPs scanning a whole table [9] [11].

3.7.1 Single-AMP Join

Query Q_j1, as described in Section 3.2, is functionally equivalent to query Q_p1, but exhibits different performance characteristics. Figure 12, compared with Figure 10, shows that the throughput of Q_j1 is much lower than that of Q_p1. It also shows that the number of AMPs does not make any difference in the throughput for 1 COP or for 2 COPs without bundling, because the capacity of the COPs is the bottleneck. For 2 COPs with bundling or for 3 COPs, the throughput improves significantly when there are 4 AMPs instead of 3 AMPs. It is because the bottleneck has moved from the COPs to the AMPs in those cases. On the other hand, there is no difference in performance between two and three COPs, except for the case of 4 AMPs without bundling. This fact is consistent with the above reasoning that the capacity of the AMPs is the bottleneck in those cases.

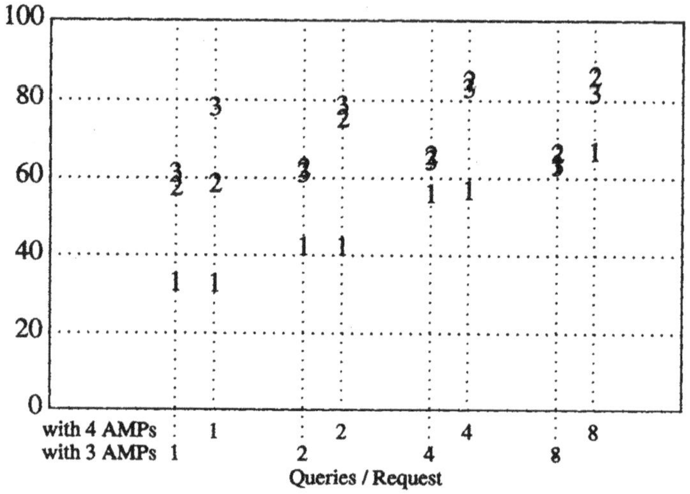

Figure 12. Throughput for a single-AMP join

3.7.2 All-AMPs Join

To process query Q_j2, a record is selected from table `Tcaller` through hashing on the the primary key values. Then the record is sent to all the AMPs, each of which scans table `Toffice` on the corresponding DSUs to find the records that satisfy the join condition. This suggests that query Q_j2 puts a heavy load on the AMPs, and the results in Figure 12 confirm that the capacity of the AMPs is indeed the bottleneck. The throughput remains the same for varying number of COPs, but differs significantly between the cases of 3 AMPs and 4 AMPs. Note also that the throughput is much lower than other types of queries, because scanning a table is a time consuming operation.

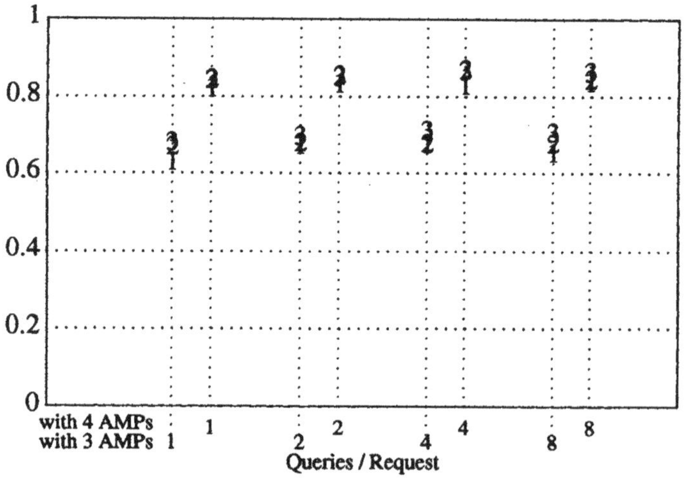

Figure 13. Throughput for an all-AMPs join

3.8 Availability

As shown in Figure 2, there is a high degree of redundancy built into the architecture of the machine with two independent Ynets, multiple COPs, AMPs and DSUs. The system is supposed to operate as usual, though at a reduced capacity, even when a Ynet, some processors or DSUs fail. To observe the behavior of the system under abnormal situations, we simulated component failures by switching them offline or turning their power off. If a COP, an AMP, or a DSU failed, the system went down first, then got restarted automatically without the affected component in about 4 minutes. Sessions that set the `wait_across_crash` option on and accessed the tables with the `fallback` option could continue to run without an AMP or a DSU. But the system could not come up if two or more AMPs were down. To provide a truly fault tolerant service without any interruption, not even a few minutes, we need to use two or more machines together so that the rest can handle all the load even when a machine fails.

3.9 Miscellaneous Issues

Since the parallel database machine is different from ordinary general purpose computers, it takes special training for operations, administrations, and maintenance (OA&M). It also requires a learning period to become familiar with the programming interfaces, though based on the SQL standard, of the machine. Some utilities, *e.g.* the *archive and recovery* program for making dump, restore, and checkpoint, are available only for the IBM mainframes, and not for the UNIX® environment yet. These issues require further studies depending on the specific environment under which the machine is used.

4. Conclusions

We have evaluated a parallel database machine for a telecommunications application, caller dependent routing, with an emphasis on the performance implications of the parallel architecture. We found that the performance improved almost linearly for some queries as more processors were added. For queries that involved heavier communications among processors, the improvement was not quite linear, though still significant. But such improvements occurred only when no other performance bottleneck existed in the system. For example, adding more AMPs or COPs did not help when there was a bottleneck at the DSUs. These results suggest that it is important to identify the performance characteristics of the applications correctly and provide a balanced system with the right amount of resources to meet the needs.

The machine we tested is a relatively small configuration for the machine. Utilization of the Ynet was found to be less than 4.5% in all of our tests. When the machine gets bigger, the Ynet utilization may become a factor in the performance of queries that require heavy inter-processor communications. It would be interesting to repeat some of the tests on a much larger configuration, evaluate the effects of more processors on the performance, and identify the limiting factors of the parallel architecture. We still conclude, based on the test results so far, that the machine offers the flexibility and expandability for a heavy load, and that it can be effective for caller dependent routing as well as for other types of telecommunications applications demanding a high performance database.

ACKNOWLEDGEMENT

The author thanks John Jagoe of AT&T Bell Laboratories for valuable discussions and comments.

REFERENCES

1. W. D. Ambrosch, A. Maher, B.Sasscer: *The Intelligent Network*, Springer-Verlag, 1989.
2. H. W. Kettler, E.G. Sable: *Intelligent Network Directions*, AT&T Technical Journal, Vol. 70, No.3-4, 1991.
3. E. F. Codd: *A relational model of data for large shared databanks*, Communications of the ACM, June 1970.
4. D. DeWitt, J. Gray Maher: *Parallel database systems: the future of high performance database systems*, Communications of the ACM, June 1992.
5. Tandem Performance Group: *A Benchmark of NonStop SQL on the Debit Credit Transaction*, ACM SIGMOD Record, Vol. 17, No. 3, Sep. 1988, pp. 337-341.
6. D. DeWitt, S. Ghandeharizadeh, D. Schneider: *A Performance Analysis of the Gamma Database Machine*, ACM SIGMOD Record, Vol. 17, No. 3, Sep. 1988, pp. 350-360.
7. H. Boral et al.: *Prototyping Bubba: A highly parallel database system.* IEEE Knowledge and Data Engineering, Vol. 2, No. 1, Mar. 1990.
8. Teradata Corporation: *DBC/1012 Data Base Computer Concepts & Facilities*, 1990.
9. Teradata Corporation: *DBC/1012 Data Base Computer System Manual*, 1991.
10. Teradata Corporation: *DBC/1012 DBC/SQL Reference Manual*, 1991.
11. D. Schneider, D. DeWitt: *A Performance Evaluation of Four Parallel Join Algorithms in a Shared-Nothing Multiprocessor Environment*, ACM SIGMOD Record, Vol. 18, No. 2, Jun. 1989, pp. 110-121.

A Design of a Transparent Backup System Using a Main Memory Database

Hiroki TAKAKURA Yahiko KAMBAYASHI

Integrated Media Environment Experimental Lab.,
Faculty of Engineering, Kyoto University
Sakyo, Kyoto 606-01 JAPAN

Abstract

In this paper, we mainly focus on a problem to realize high-performance systems without sacrificing system reliability. One solution for high-performance is to use main memory as a database storage. Since main memory cannot be free from software bug or electricity hazard, we cannot avoid archive storages such as disks. To reduce the time of checkpoint and recovery for a main memory database, some mechanism is required. For this purpose we have developed continuous backup RAMs which can store their contents periodically to an archive storage while they are used for usual process. By extending this concept continuous backup disks are also designed. A transparent backup system is organized using such RAMs and disks. As a backup process is performed by hardware mechanism during the execution of usual database operations, a backup process does not require to stop a system or to keep transactions waiting to record system status at each checkpoint and thus, users are not aware of the existence of a backup process. Furthermore, an interval between two adjacent checkpoints can be shortened, since hardware control does not require much computation overhead. This short interval contributes to reduce recovery time.

1 Introduction

Recently, databases have been widely used in systems of various fields such as online process control. This kind of systems must have the property of a real-time system, i.e. all processes can be finished before predefined deadline, and also must have the property of a fault-tolerant system where control operations should not stop even if a system fails, since the process of a plant cannot be stopped instantaneously. If a system cannot decide an appropriate action to prevent a plant from being runaway within predetermined time or if a system stops for even a very short period, then it may become unable to control a whole plant and we may suffer a great loss. For such applications, a high performance and highly reliable system must be realized.

To achieve high performance, a lot of papers have been published on query processing, concurrency control, database machines and main memory databases. One should notice, however, that even if high speed database operations are realized we must still stop a system for recovery when some serious failure occurs.

To realize high reliance a fault-tolerant system employs a dual system approach which avoids time-consuming recovery process[CER85][KIM84]. In that system data are available regardless of any single failure of a system. Repairs can be done without affecting availability of data and it is assumed that repairs can be completed before next failure. It is required, however, to record system status for multiple failure cases.

A fault-tolerant system is designed to be based on the disk resident database, since main memory in general does not have enough reliability compared with a disk, even if it is nonvolatile. The disk resident system has a serious drawback due to disk I/O bottleneck to realize a high performance system.

A highly reliable main memory database system which has both properties of high performance and high reliance should be developed to solve these problems. In order to realize such systems continuous backup RAMs are designed by the authors[KAM91]. These RAMs can store their contents to archive storage while they are used for usual process.

In this paper, continuous backup disks are introduced which are extensions of continuous backup RAMs. A system architecture to reduce overhead for recovery using such RAMs and disks is discussed.

We supposed only the case where current data are lost by some failure such as system failure and media failure, and at least one checkpoint data can be available. Transaction failure is not considered here, since it does not make data lost and should be recovered by database management system.

Conventional checkpoint and recovery processes are as follows.

A) At each checkpoint, dirty pages or whole database pages are dumped to an archive storage, such as tapes or disks.

B) While database operations are performed, log records are stored in a stable storage (tapes or disks).

C) In case of system failure, the status at the latest checkpoint is transferred to a system from its archive storage and a system can restart from this checkpoint. In case of media failure, a system must be repaired at first.

D) Using log records after this checkpoint, the status of a system can be recovered just before the point when failure happened.

Overhead at each step is as follows.

a) A system have to be stopped while dumping checkpoint data or transactions which require to write dumping pages must wait until dump of these pages completes.

b) To take log records requires CPU consumption and results in system overhead.

c) After failure the checkpoint status needs to be reloaded to a system. The reloading usually takes time.

d) In addition to the reloading time, the computation time is also required for D).

Use of reliable main memory which consists of the battery backed-up RAM or electrically erasable ROM (Flash Memory) can avoid the dumping operation. Combined with battery operated disks[COP89] a reliable storage system may be able to be organized. Even if such a system is used, recovery process cannot be avoided. Examples are failures caused by memory peripheral circuit failure and by software bugs

In order to reduce the time required for c) and d), incremental reloading[LEH87] can be used, where data are recovered only when they are required for the first time. Even in such a system the time to load essential data such as database management system, operating system, etc., is needed before restarting a system.

Our system reduces these overheads as follows.

a′) A continuous backup RAM and a continuous backup disk are used to get the status of each checkpoint without stopping a system or keeping transactions waiting, since they are controlled by simple hardware mechanism which works independently of database process.

b′) Although details are not discussed in this paper, we are currently designing hardware mechanism to get log records efficiently, which will contribute to reduce software overhead. The outline of log record structure will be mentioned in Section 2.

c′) Our system has redundant main memory and disk which store the status at the latest checkpoint. By connecting these main memory and disk, the status of a system at this checkpoint can be recovered. The reloading time is unnecessary.

d′) As a system is not required much overhead to take checkpoint data, the interval between two consecutive checkpoints, which contributes to reducing the average time required for D), can be reduced.

The organization of this paper as follows. In Section 2 basic concepts required to describe our system are given. Organization of continuous backup memories and that of continuous backup disks, which are the major components of our system, are discussed in Sections 3 and 4, respectively. The overall system architecture and the recovery process are discussed in Section 5. Performance evaluation is carried out in Section 6.

2 Basic Concepts

In this section necessary basic terms and a problem are discussed.

Hot Spot Data(80/20-Rule)

The access of database may concentrate in very small part of database. In typical database systems, it is known that about 80 percent of access concentrates in about 20 percent of database (80/20-Rule)[GAW85]. Such data are called hotspot data.

A Partial Main Memory Database

A main memory database originally means that whole database is resided in main memory[EIC86][EIC87]. Although a main memory database is one effective solution to realize high performance database systems, it is not currently realistic because of cost and capacity limitation.

In such a case, we propose a partial main memory database where hotspot data are resided in main memory and another data are read from a disk on demand. To use a partial main memory database may be one answer to solve these limitations and it can realize high performance without using the very large memory required for a main memory database. We expect, however, that a main memory database can be realized in the near future.

Write-Ahead Logging(WAL)

Some systems such as IBM ARIES[MOH89] are based on the write-ahead logging (WAL) protocol where a log record must save in a stable storage before a dirty page is reflected to database. In the system where physical log records are used, in-place updating that a dirty page is written back to the same nonvolatile storage location from where it was read must be performed[MOH89].

Checkpoint and Recovery

At recovery possible latest contents of main memory and a disk should be calculated using checkpoint data and log records. Although to reduce this calculation overhead checkpoint should be taken as frequently as possible, frequent checkpoint operations cause more overhead to a system, since in the conventional database system these operations are controlled by software and, thus, require CPU which is also used for database operations.

A Problem between Backup and Logging

Some papers on backup of a main memory database claim that they can be used in both original and partial main memory database systems. Most of them use physical logs and suppose that whole or a part of main memory is nonvolatile. The physical log can be used in a main memory database system because this system can guarantee in-place updating, but a partial main memory database system, like our system, cannot use such a physical log, since hotspot pages are removed from main memory when they become non-hotspot and, thus, in-place updating cannot be guaranteed.

Although logical log can be avoid this problem, since it can indicate data object by their logical name, this log causes an another problem when a backup operation is performed asynchronous with database operations. In case that a page is backed up during it is being updated by one logical operation, a system cannot recover from failure using a logical log,

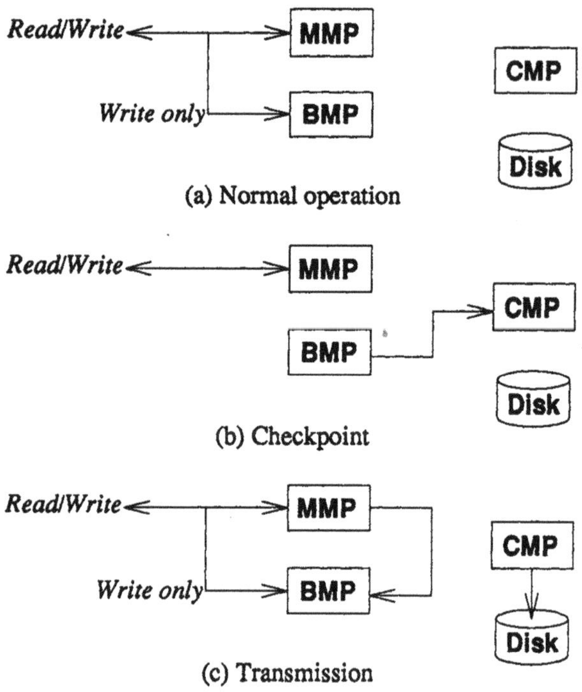

Figure 1: Two-Plane Backup System

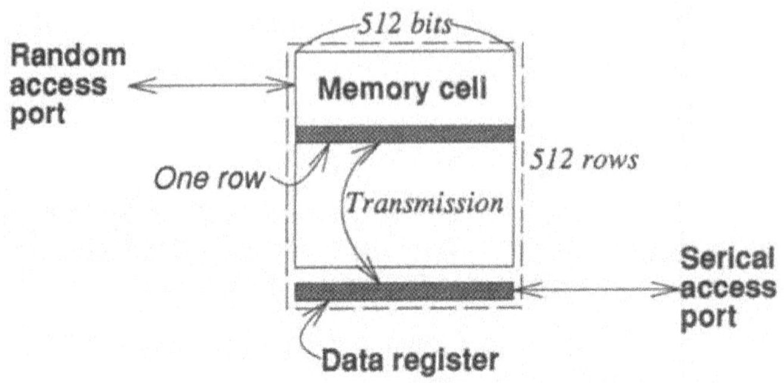

Figure 2: The Structure of Dual-Port RAM

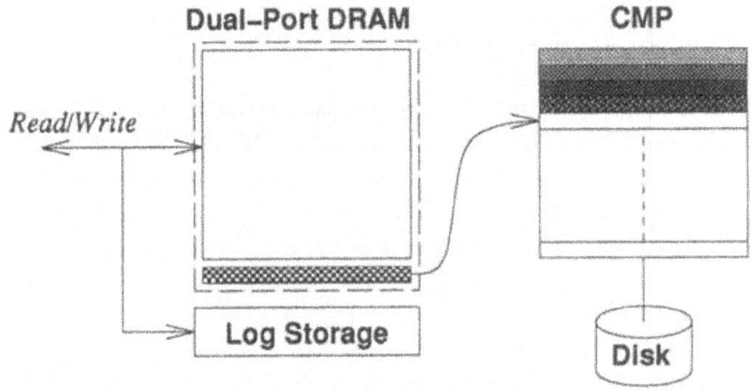

Figure 3: Organization of Continuous Backup RAMs Using Dual-Port RAMs

since already reflected part cannot be distinguished from not reflected part.

To avoid these problem, we have been studying a new log management system. The outline of this system is as follows. To manage a log record of non-hotspot data, our system uses conventional log management method, like ARIES, except that only a physical log record is used. Every log record is assigned unique log sequence number (LSN) and every data page has page_LSN field which contains LSN that describe the latest update log record to the page[MOH89].

To manage the log record of hotspot data, our system uses a new log management system which is controlled by hardware to reduce the overhead. The log record has similar format as that of non-hotspot data. Each transaction produces at most a 256byte log record which contains transaction's ID, address of a main memory page, and after and before images of the record.

Our system needs log records describing data replacement between new hotspot page and non-hotspot page which were hotspot and resided in main memory. This log record contains disk address of the new hotspot page.

3 Continuous Backup RAM

In this section three methods to realize continuous backup RAMs are summarized[KAM91]. The first one is shown in Figure 1.

3.1 Two-Plane Backup System

A system consists of three memory planes, main memory plane (MMP), backup memory plane (BMP) and checkpoint memory plane (CMP). A disks is attached to CMP which is used to store main memory contents. Figure 1(a) shows the situation for normal access. At a checkpoint, BMP is disconnected from CPU which works for database process and starts to transmit its contents to CMP (Figure 1(b)). After transmission, BMP is again connected to CPU and CMP stores its contents in a disk (Figure 1(c)). The system performs write operations to both MMP and BMP, and read operations to MMP. Contents of MMP are transmitted to BMP by DMA (direct memory access) control concurrently with these read and write operations in a time-shared manner. After transmission contents of MMP and BMP become identical, since write operations during transmission are also applied to BMP. As the DMA transmission is performed simultaneously with database operations, database operation becomes slower when it competes with the DMA operation for the same memory module.

3.2 Continuous Backup by Dual-Port DRAMs

Figure 2 shows a structure of dual-port DRAM, which is developed for display memory. Memory contents can be modified through a random access port while a serial access port is used to display its contents. One row data of a memory cell are transmitted to a data register when row address is given to random access port . As this mechanism is realized by hardware, it is very much efficient. The organization of a continuous backup system using dual-port DRAM as MMP is shown in Figure 3. At one access only one row's data can be transmitted to CMP. Thus a row's data will be stored at different time . Let T_{Trans} be the time required to transmit all contents to CMP. The data transmission for t_i, ith checkpoint time, must be started before $t_i - T_{Trans}$. Write operations after $t_i - T_{Trans}$ are stored in

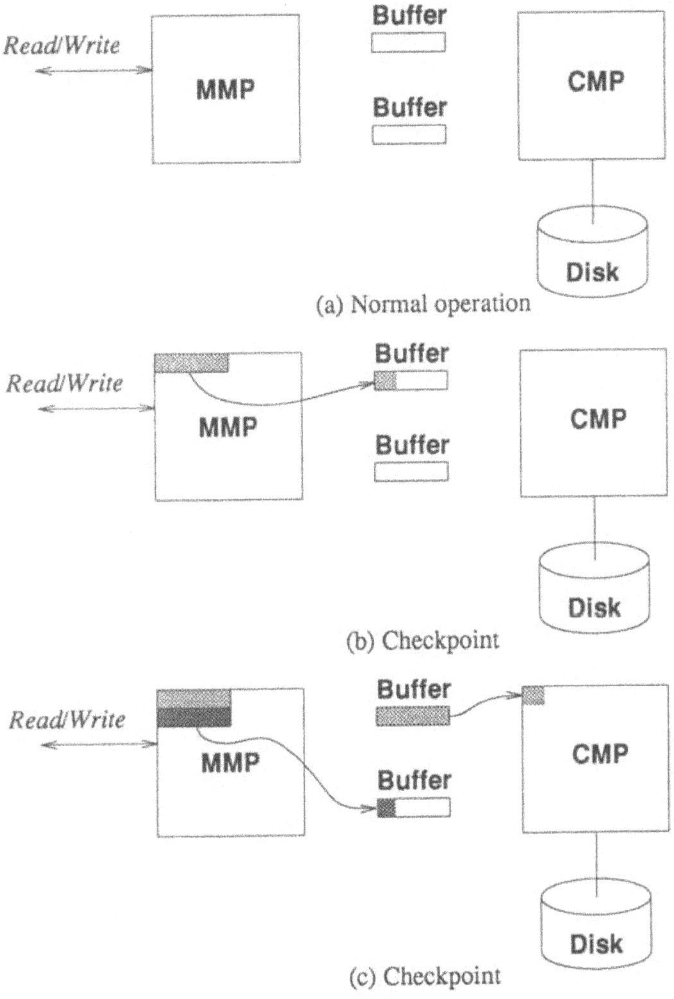

Figure 4: Double Buffer Backup System

Log Memory. At t_i, all write operations performed between $t_i - T_{Trans}$ and t_i are stored in Log Memory. Using contents of Log Memory, contents of CMP must be modified and then memory contents at t_i are obtained. After this operation CMP stores the data at the checkpoint t_i. During this modification process failure of dual-port DRAM may occur. In such a case both CMP and Log Storage must be used in order to get correct data values for recovery.

3.3 Double Buffer Backup Method

A problem of using currently available dual-port DRAMs is that access speed is slow, since it is designed for conventional TV systems such as NTSC. The access cycle for random access port is about 200[ns]. For HDTV (High Definition Television) random access port would become faster. We expect such dual-port RAMs will be available in the near future.

Double buffer backup is developed to simulate the operation of dual-port DRAM, in order to realize the high-speed operation. The architecture is shown in Figure 4(a). This is a hardware version of the double buffer algorithm. A part of MMP's contents is transmitted to one buffer and at the same time contents of the other are sent out to CMP. Two buffers are alternatively used (Figure 4(c)). Compared with a two-plane backup system, hardware cost can be reduced, although modification by Log Memory is a little bit complicated.

4 Continuous Backup for Disk

We can design continuous backup disk similar to memories discussed in previous section when a partial main memory system is used. One typical characteristics of disk should be considered; one sequential access is much faster then a number of direct random access to retrieve the same amount of data.

4.1 Two-Disk Backup System

The organization is similar to the system shown in Figure 1. Here, MMP, BMP and CMP are disks and Log Memory discussed in Section 3.2 is required. After transmission, BMP catches MMP up using Log Memory data, since transmission from MMP to BMP competes usual data access and causes MMP many random accesses. As the sequential access is preferred, contents of Log Memory must be sorted in order to reduce the time required for catching up.

4.2 Simulation of Dual-Port DRAM

A dual-port disk can be developed, if it has one extra read head. One head is used for usual read/write purpose, while other head is used for sequential access to read backup data. One cylinder is considered to correspond to one row of dual-port DRAM. Differently from dual-port DRAMs, while sequential access port is used to read backup data, write operations using usual port must be prohibited and stored in main memory, since the magnetic field generated by usual port's head may affect data read from the sequential access port. Stored write operations are not lost by failure, since backup operations perform for both main memory and a disk at a checkpoint and thus they are also stored as checkpoint data of main memory. Read operations through both ports can be performed simultaneously.

Since to develop a new hardware is not the cost effective, currently available disk using disk cache can be used. Figure 5 shows an organization of such a system, here cache is assumed to have its own backup disk. During the sequential read to cylinders, all requests for the read and the write are stored in cache. Only data existing in cache can be read. Sequential

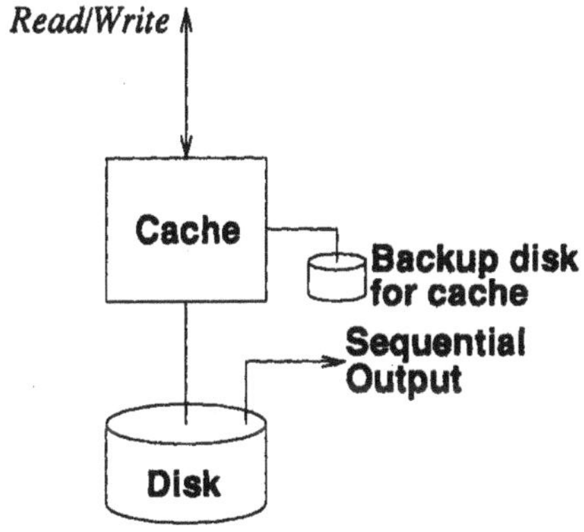

Figure 5: Simulation of Dual-Port RAMs by a Disk

access are done continuously and after sequential access completes all the requests in cache must be applied.

5 Organization of a Transparent Backup Database System

By combining previous discussion we will discuss how to organize a transparent backup database system in this section.

It is assumed that checkpoints are denoted by $t_1, t_2, \cdots, t_i$. For simplicity it is assumed that the system status can be completely described by (1) contents of CPU registers, (2) contents of main memory, and (3) contents of disk. Let R_t, M_t, and D_t are these contents at time t.

Figure 6 shows basic organization of a transparent backup database system and its recovery process. The effective connection is shown by bold lines. Let us assume that the current time t satisfies $t_i \leq t < t_{i+1}$ (i.e., the latest checkpoint is t_i).

In Figure 6(a) the current contents are stored in disk and main memory shown in the left side. Right side disk and main memory store the data at the checkpoint t_i. The small disk attached to right main memory holds memory image of M_{t_i}, which will be used for recovery process of main memory. After system failure, main memory and disk storing checkpoint data are used as shown in Figure 6(b). Thus reloading is not required. Disk and main memory in the left side can be used to store the next checkpoint data. The status of CPU registers is assumed to be also stored in main memory as a part of checkpoint data, since only several steps of instructions are required to store them.

Since a system is not safe if the crash occurs while taking the next checkpoint, an additional set of main memory and disk is needed. There are two cases, i) the additional set also stores D_{t_i} and M_{t_i} (duplicated backup) or ii) $D_{t_{i-1}}$ and $M_{t_{i-1}}$.

The whole system organization is outlined in Figure 7. Memories in Systems II and III are alternatively used to store memory data at checkpoint (CMP), so that data at the two consecutive checkpoints can be stored. A memory in System I are used to store the current state of main memory (MMP and BMP). Log Storage stores all log records for main memory and disk after t_{i-1}. Since transmission of contents of System I is controlled by DMACs (Direct Memory Access Controller) which are connected with sub buses shown in Figure 7, this transmission does not cause any contention with main bus access.

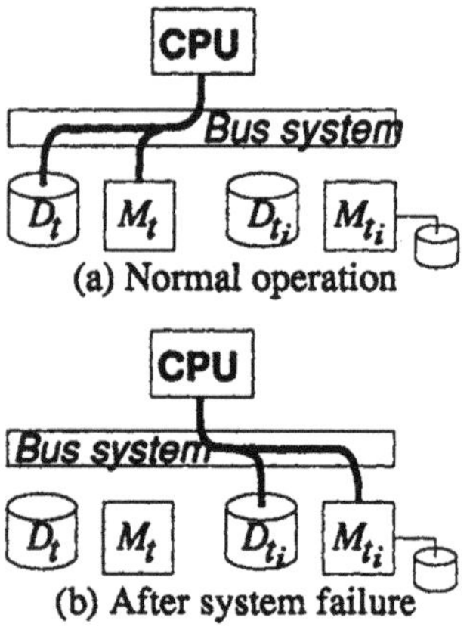

Figure 6: Basic Organization of a Transparent Backup Database System

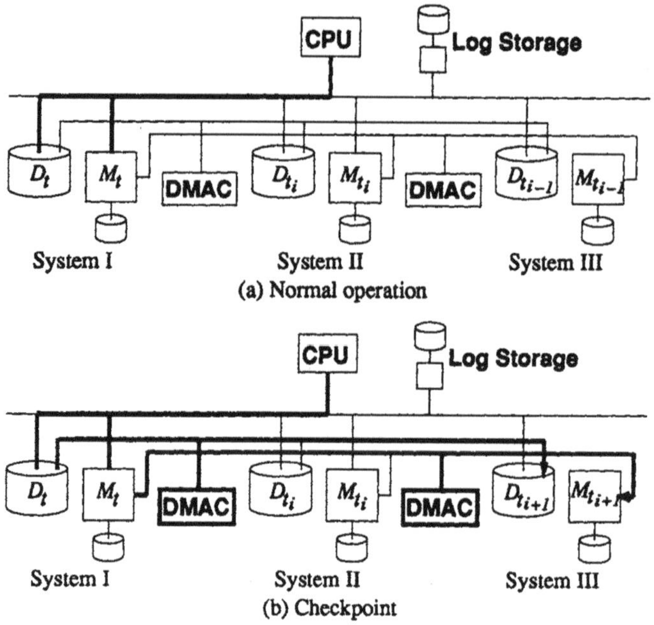

Figure 7: Organization of a Transparent Backup Database System

If some crash occurs System II is used and system can restart from the checkpoint t_i. If another crash occurs before t_{i+1} System III has to be used. Using Log Storage contents of System III can be modified to very close to the crash time. If further crash occurs before t_{i+1}, a system must reload from an archive storage, which stores sampled checkpoint data. In such a case recovery becomes slow, but we believe that such a case rarely happens.

6 Evaluations of a Transparent Backup Database System

In this section we discuss performance evaluation of our system on the time to take checkpoint data and to recover from failure. The evaluation is based on TPC benchmark B[GRA91].

6.1 Outline of TPC Benchmark B

In TPC benchmark B each transaction updates four databases; Account, Branch, Teller and History. Basically, the size of databases, except for History, is in proportion to the number of transaction throughput(tps). History disk must be large enough to store records which are produced for the eight hour running. The profile of a transaction is as follows.

Begin transaction.
  Update a record of Account.
  Update a record of Teller.
  Update a record of Branch.
  Insert a record into History.
Commit transaction.

The definition of databases is shown in Table 1.

Database	Record length	Number of record/tps
Account	100B	100000
Branch	100B	1
Teller	100B	10
History	50B	

Table 1: Definition of Databases

	Current	A few years later
Bit per inch	50000	70000
Track per inch	2000	3000
Rotation [rpm]	3600	5000
Serial data transfer rate	15Mb/s	35Mb/s

Table 2: Disk Technology

Number of tracks	Number of sector	Capacity per a surface
2000	108	100MB

Table 3: 3.5 Inch Disk Drive Specification

6.2 Specification of Disks

The current and near future disk technology are shown in Table 2. The future 3.5-inch disk specification expected form Table 2 is shown in Table 3. The seek time is supposed to be calculated with a following formula[STR83],

$$T_{Seek} = a + b\sqrt{i}$$

Here, $a = 5$[ms], $b = 0.5$[ms] and i denotes distance from starting cylinder to destination cylinder.

6.3 Performance of Checkpoint Operations

In this section, the time to take checkpoint is estimated. Main memory (disk) is supposed to be divided into several blocks (drives) and backup operation of each main memory block (drive) is also supposed to be performed parallel.

At first, the time to back up disk contents is estimated. It is supposed that contents stored in a track can be read while a disk makes one rotation. Time to transfer data between disks is,

$$N_{Cylinder} \cdot (T_{Seek} + T_{Rotation}) \cdot N_{Surface}$$

Here, $N_{Cylinder}$ denotes the number of cylinders and $N_{Surface}$ denotes the number of disk surfaces of a drive. T_{Seek} represents seek time calculated using the formula discussed section 6.2 where $i = 1$ and $T_{Rotation}$ represents rotation time. From Table 2, the expression above becomes,

$$35 \cdot N_{Surface}[\mathrm{s}]$$

The result is shown in Figure 8.

Our checkpointing method need not to optimize disk access scheduling, since only sequential access is performed by hardware control.

Next, the time to back up main memory contents is estimated. Here, a dual-port DRAM backup system is supposed to be used. The size of a main memory block is denoted by S_{Block}. The access cycle of serial access port is denoted by T_{Serial} and the bus size of each block is denoted by S_{Bus}. When $Serial\_Cycle = 40$[ns] and $Bus\_Size = 4$[byte], the time to take checkpoint is,

$$\frac{S_{Block}}{S_{Bus}} \cdot T_{Serial} \simeq 10 \cdot S_{Block}[\mathrm{ns}]$$

The result is shown in Figure 9.

6.4 Performance of Recovery Operations

Considering the characteristic of the TPC benchmark, all records of Branch and Teller are hotspot and should be resided in main memory. In this paper 80 percent of transactions is supposed to access the hotspot records of Account. In respect to the TPC benchmark, the access pattern of Account is uniform, i.e. there is no hotspot record in Account, but when it is supposed, large main memory on which 20 percent of databases can be resided is needed. The evaluation of recovery under this supposition shows temperate results. Each record of History is produced and stored in the database only once, so History has no hotspot record.

The interval of two adjacent checkpoints is denoted by T[s]. During T, at most $tps \cdot T$ transactions commit. In our log management system, each transaction produces at most four 256-byte log records.

In our system, the incremental recovery where only hotspot data are recovered immediately is performed. In this paper, the time to recover hotspot data is discussed. The recovery is supposed to be the time to read log records from Log Storage (disk), because our system need not to reload hotspot data and this time is the most part of recovery procedure. Then, the recovery time becomes maximum when a failure occurs just before the checkpoint and its time is,

$$\frac{tps \cdot T \cdot (1 + 1 + 0.8) \cdot S_{Log}}{R_{Serial}} \simeq 156 \cdot tps \cdot T[\mu\mathrm{s}]$$

Here, R_{Serial} represents the access rate to read disk data serially and S_{Log} represents the size of a log record.

The result from this expression is shown in Figure 10. The minimum recovery time is 0[s] when the latest checkpoint data can be used immediately (a failure occurs just after the checkpoint).

This result shows that if the system cannot stop even for a few seconds the incremental recovery where most needed hotspot data are recovered immediately must be performed, or the system must restart using only contents of the checkpoint abandoning log utilization. We cannot think, however, that such a system is reliable.

7 Concluding Remarks

In this paper a new approach to reduce the overhead of a recovery process is introduced. Since a highly available system is essential for various applications, we can design a super highly available system by combining the currently available technologies, for example a fault-tolerant system and a disk array technology. Using a disk array total time for backup can be reduced due to their parallel processing property. Although a triple redundant system is expensive, we expect this technology will be practically used, since the annual reduction of cost of the disk for one bit is said to be about 40% and that of the memory chip is about 25%.

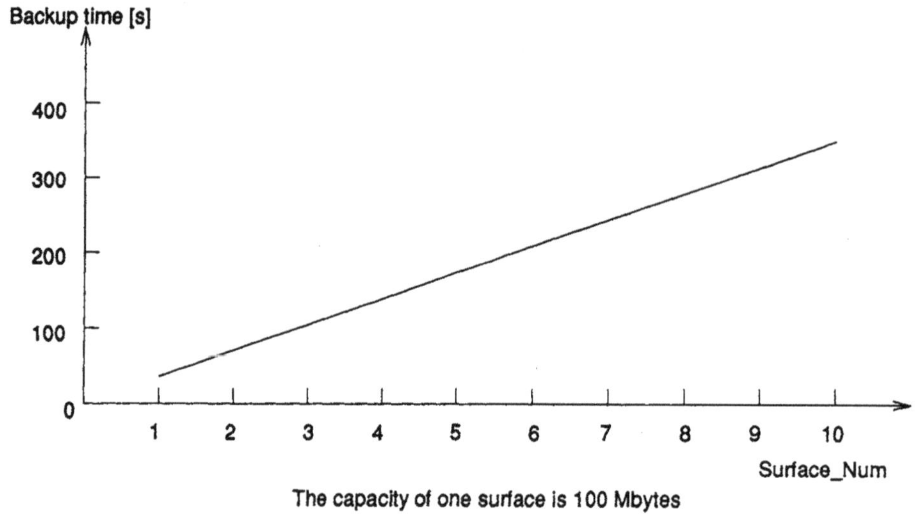

Figure 8: Surface Number vs Backup Time (Disk)

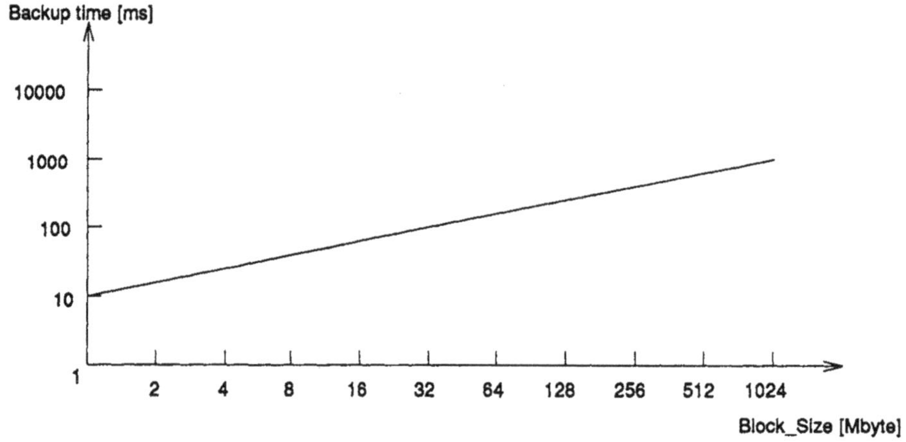

Figure 9: Block Size vs Backup Time (Main Memory)

The authors have been discussing on the use of flush memory which is a kind of EEPROM as an archive storage. This approach is expected to realize efficient checkpoint and recovery procedures[TAK93].

Acknowledgment

We would like to express our sincere appreciation to Professor Kazuo Iwama of Kyushu University for his constructive criticism and valuable insight.

References

[BAR91] N.S. Barghouti, G.E. Kaiser, "Concurrency Control for Advanced Database Applications," ACM Computing Surveys, Vol.23, No.3, 1991, pp.269-317.

[BER87] P.A. Bernstein, V. Hadzilacos, N. Goodman, "Concurrency Control and Recovery in Database Systems," Addison Wesley, 1987.

[CER85] S. Ceri, G. Pelagatti, "Distributed Databases Principles and Systems," McGraw-Hill Book Company, 1985, pp.292-298.

[COP89] G.Copeland, T.Keller, R.Krishnamurthy, M.Smith, "The Case For Safe RAM," Proc. of the 15th International Conf. on VLDB, 1989, pp.327-335.

[DEW84] D. DeWitt, et al, "Implementation Techniques for Main Memory Database Systems," Proc. of ACM SIGMOD Conf., 1984, pp.1-8.

[EIC86] M.H. Eich, "Main Memory Database Recovery," ACM FJCC, 1986, pp.1226-1232.

[EIC87] M.H. Eich, "A Classification and Comparison of Main Memory Database Recovery Techniques," Proc. IEEE 3rd Conf. on Data Engineering, 1987, pp.332-339.

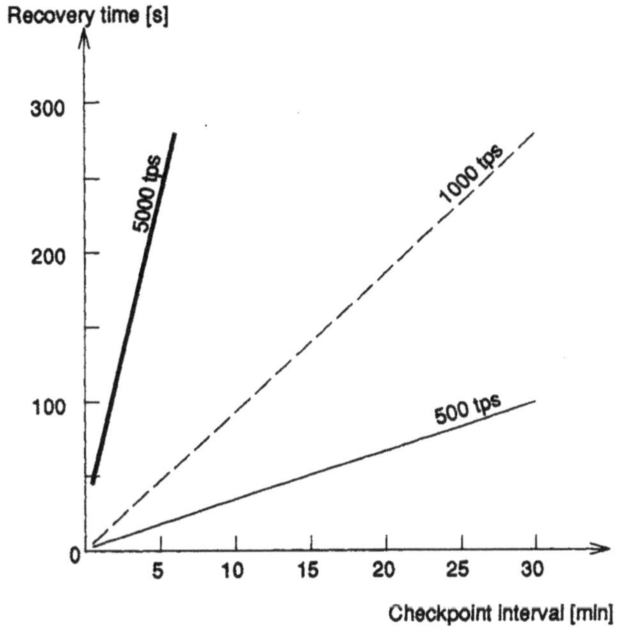

Figure 10: Checkpoint Interval vs Recovery Time
(Worst Case)

[EIC88] M.H. Eich, "MARS : The Design of a Main Memory Database Machine," Database Machines and Knowledge Base Machines, Kluwer Academic Publishers, 1988, pp.325-338.

[EIC89] M.H. Eich, "Main Memory Database Research Directions," Proc. 6th International Workshop, IWDM'89, 1989, pp.251-268.

[GAW85] D. Gawlick, "Processing Hot Spots' in High Performance Systems," Proc. of IEEE Spring Computer Conference, 1985, pp.249-251.

[GRA91] Jim Gray, "The Benchmark Handbook," Morgan Kaufmann Publishers, 1991, pp.19-117.

[GRU91] L. Gruenwalld, M.H. Eich, "MMDB Reload Algorithms," Proc. of ACM SIGMOD International Conf. on Management of Data, 1991, pp.397-405.

[HAG86] R.B.Hagmann, "A Crash Recovery Scheme for a Memory-Resident Database System," IEEE Trans. on Computers, Vol. C-35, No.9, September, 1986, pp.839-843.

[KAM91] Y. Kambayashi, H. Takakura, "Realization of Continuously Backed-up RAMs for High-Speed Database Recovery," Database Systems for Advanced Applications '91, World Scientific, 1992, pp.236-242.

[KIM84] W. Kim, "High Available Systems for Database Application," ACM Computing Surveys, Vol.16, No.1, 1984, pp.71-98.

[KUM91] V. Kumar, A. Burger, "Performace Measurement of Some Main Memory Database Recovery Algorithms," Proc. 7th Int. Conf. Data Engineering, 1991, pp.436-443.

[LEH87] T.J. Lehman, M.J. Carey "A Recovery Algorithm for A High-Performance Memory-Resident Database System," Proc. ACM SIGMOD Conf., 1987, pp104-117.

[LEH89] T.J. Lehman, M.J. Carey "A Concurrency Control Algorithm for Memory-Resident Database Systems," Proc. 3rd International Conf, FODO, 1989, pp.490-504.

[MOH89] C. Mohan, D. Haderle, B. Lindsay, H. Piahesh, P. Schwarz, "ARIES: A Transaction Recovery Method Supporting Fine-Granularity Locking and Partial Rollbacks Using Write-Ahead Logging," IBM Research Report RJ6649, IBM Almaden Research Center, January 1989; Revised April 1991.

[MOH90] C. Mohan, K. Treiber, R. Obermarck, "Algorithms for the Management Remote Backup Data Base for Disaster Recovery," IBM Research Report RJ7885R, IBM Almaden Research Center, December 1990; Revised June 1991.

[STR83] R.A. Scranton, D.A. Thompson, D.W. Hunter, "The Access Time Myth," IBM Technology Report, RC10197, September, 1983.

[TAK93] H. Takakura, Y. Kambayashi, "Continuous Backup Systems Utilizing Flash Memory, " Conf. on Data Engineering, 1993 (to appear).

ACCESS METHODS

ABSTRACT INDEXING MECHANISM OF THE EXTENSIBLE DBMS MODUS

Kazutaka Furuse
Doctoral Program in Engineering, University of Tsukuba

Kazunori Yamaguchi
Department of Graphic and Computer Science, University of Tokyo

Hiroyuki Kitagawa and Nobuo Ohbo
Institute of Information Sciences and Electronics, University of Tsukuba

ABSTRACT

To meet the requirements from non-standard database application areas such as engineering design, DBMS is required to be able to introduce application-specific data types and access methods a posteriori. The extensible DBMS MODUS is designed to cope with these requirements. MODUS consists of the *kernel* and several *managers*, and is able to include new data types and access methods by putting user defined *modules* under the control of managers.

This paper describes the indexing mechanism of MODUS. In MODUS, the access method manager controls the user defined access method modules and provides the kernel with indexing facility. The major advantage of MODUS is that the mechanism of the data type extension and the mechanism of the access method extension are *orthogonal*. Therefore, in MODUS, it is possible to use an access method module for indexing data objects of more than one data types without any modification.

1. INTRODUCTION

It is well understood that the conventional database management systems (DBMSs) are lacking in capability to support non-standard database applications, such as engineering design, image/voice applications, and scientific/statistical applications[1,22]. The conventional DBMSs are monolithic, that is, support only a fixed set of predefined (i.e., system defined) data types and a fixed set of access methods. In the non-standard application areas, it is inherently required for DBMSs to support application specific data types and new access methods to improve expressive power and efficiency. For example, in case of spatial (or multi-dimensional) databases, it is known that R-tree[9,16], which is a hierarchical file structure similar to B-tree, is a useful and effective access method for storing and retrieving spatial objects.

Recently, there are some research projects on DBMSs coping with these requirements by introducing the concept of *extensibility*. These systems are called *extensible DBMSs*[6]. In these systems, users[†] are allowed to construct DBMSs customized to particular database applications (i.e., the *application-specific DBMSs*) by embedding *user defined modules* into the DBMSs.

However, in the extensible DBMSs currently proposed, writing user defined modules is not an easy task. Especially, implementing new access method modules is rather heavy task. For example, in EXODUS[3,4,5] and POSTGRES[15,17,18,19,20,23], users can write and embed new access method modules written in E (persistent C++) and C, respectively. In these systems, users are required to be highly skilled. If a user wants to describe a new access method for extension, he has to know the details of the DBMSs including page buffering, locking protocol, logging mechanism, etc. To make the extensible DBMSs be more practical, task for implementing access methods should be minimized.

Major objective of the research project on MODUS[7,24] is to design and implement a practical, easy-to-use extensible DBMS. MODUS is composed of *kernel* and some components called *managers*. Each manager implements each DBMS facility. The kernel coordinates the managers and provides database applications with services such as data retrieval and data manipulation. In MODUS, users are allowed to extend the DBMS by implementing *modules* and embedding them into the system. For example, users are possible to embed new access methods by implementing *access method modules*.

It is one of advantages of MODUS in comparison with other extensible DBMSs that the mechanism of the data type extension and the mechanism of the access method extension are *orthogonal*. That is, it is desired that these mechanisms are independent of each other. This independency makes users' work to implement access method modules smaller. If the two mechanisms of extension are orthogonal, users do not have to write codes sensitive to each data type in access method modules. Furthermore, independency of data types and access methods improves the reusability of user defined modules. For example, if an R-tree access method module is implemented independently of data types, this module can be used for indexing both two-dimensional data objects and three-dimensional data objects (and even objects of other data types) without any modification.

In this paper, we describe the abstract mechanism of indexing in MODUS. The reminder of this paper is composed as follows. Section 2 presents design philosophy and the architecture of MODUS. Section 3 describes the mechanism of indexing with some simple examples. In Section 4, the mechanism of query processing in MODUS is described. Finally, in Section 5, we summarize this paper and discuss remaining problems of our project.

[†]In the extensible DBMSs, users who construct application-specific DBMSs are called as *database implementors* (DBIs) or *database designers*. Note that role of DBIs and that of DBAs (database administrators) are quite different. The former is to construct DBMSs, and the latter is to administrate the DBMSs constructed by DBIs.

2. OVERVIEW OF MODUS

2.1. Design Goals

Followings are the major design goals of MODUS.

- Extensible system
  - New data types should be able to be embedded into the system.
  - New access methods should be able to be embedded into the system.
- Easy-to-use system
  - Work required for extension should be minimized.
  - Skills required for extension should be minimized.

First two design goals are to make the system sufficiently extensible and efficient. To meet the requirements from the non-standard applications, data types should be extensible. Although there are some monolithic DBMSs that support the user defined data types (e.g., object-oriented DBMSs), we think it is not enough. To provide sufficiently efficient service for applications, user defined data types should be handled just same as system defined data types in DBMS. In other words, any user defined data types must be *basic*. There should not be any difference between implementation of system defined data types and that of user defined data types. In MODUS, all (both system defined and user defined) data types handled in the DBMS are uniformly implemented as *data type modules*. Each module implements each data type and is managed by the *data type manager*. Some modules of primitive data types (such as `Integer` and `Boolean`) are provided a priori. Using these modules, users can construct their own data type hierarchies.

In addition, mechanism of access methods should be extensible. As stated above, it is well known that there are some special access methods which are effective for particular application areas (e.g., R-tree). To construct efficient application specific DBMS, it is required not only that new access methods can be introduced, but also that each access method implementation can be replaced and modified by users with small labor. In MODUS, access methods are also implemented as modules. These modules are managed by *access method manager*. Some modules including B-tree and hash file are provided in advance.

Next two design goals of MODUS are quite different ones from other extensible DBMSs. They are important to make MODUS be an easy-to-use (or easy-to-extend) system. In the extensible DBMS, procedures needed for extension should not require any special knowledge on the DBMS. We must not assume that every user is *super programmer*. Moreover, the extension procedures should be done in a short term. For users, main purpose is not to construct a DBMS, but to build applications using the DBMS. Time needed for constructing the DBMS must be much shorter than time needed for building applications.

To meet these requirements, in MODUS, functionalities of DBMS are decomposed and let each functionality be implemented by a component called *manager*. In MODUS, each user extension is implemented as a *user defined modules*. The modules are embedded into the system, and used in the course of data manipulation or query processing. Embedded modules are managed by some of managers. For example, as described earlier, data type modules are managed by the data type manager.

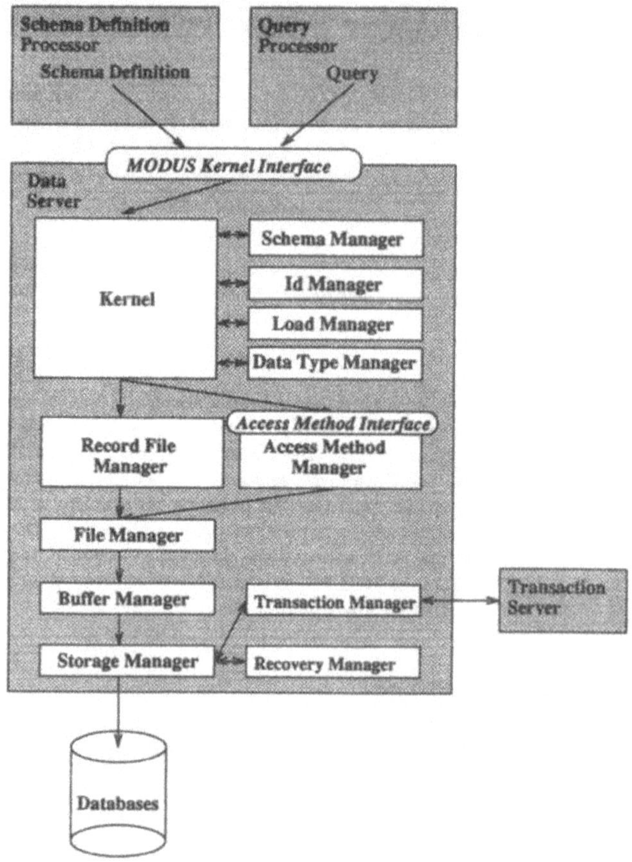

Figure 1: The architecture of MODUS

Since each manager encapsulates each DBMS facility into itself, users are not required to have knowledge on details of MODUS. For example, as the recovery manager implements and encapsulates the recovery facility of MODUS, users do not have to pay attention to recovery of index files when writing their own access method modules.

Further more, followings are desirable.

- Dependency among user defined modules should be minimized.
- Dependency among user defined modules should be explicitly described.

Implementing independency between user defined modules is important for making MODUS be a practical system. If two modules are completely independent of each other, these two modules can be implemented and modified without concerning the influence between them. This is especially desirable when two modules are implemented by different users.

Compared with the other extensible DBMSs, in MODUS, dependency among modules is rather small. Especially, independency between data type modules and access method modules is completely implemented. The mechanism of this independency is described in detail in Subsection 3.2.

2.2. Architecture

Figure 1 shows the architecture of MODUS. MODUS is composed of four processes: *data server*, *transaction server*, *schema definition processor*, and *query processor*. The transaction server implements the atomicity of transactions handled by the data server. The schema definition processor translates schema definitions to expressions in a form of *schema definition plans* (SDPs), and sends requests of data definition to the data server. Same way, the query processor translates queries to expressions in a form of *query evaluation plans* (QEPs), and sends requests of data manipulation to the data server.

Main part of MODUS is the data server. The data server provides services for manipulating databases to the schema definition processor and the query processor. The data server is constructed by three types of components: *kernel*, *managers*, and *modules*. The kernel is responsible for answering the requests received from the query processor. Functionalities of DBMS are decomposed and the managers which implement each functionality. The kernel coordinates the behavior of the managers. User extensions are implemented as modules and they are embedded into the system. Embedded modules are placed under the control of the managers. The data type modules and the access method modules are managed by the data type manager and the access method manager, respectively.

Data type manager manages all data types introduced into MODUS. Each data type is defined in a *data type module*. Users can introduce new *basic* data types into MODUS by writing data type modules. As system defined data types are also introduced by modules and any modules are handled in a uniform way, there is no difference between system defined data types and user defined data types in MODUS.

Figure 2 shows an example of a data type module defining the data type `Rectangle2` (a two dimensional data type). Each data type module is composed of three parts: interface part, representation part, and implementation part. In the interface part, imported and exported operators as well as referred data types are declared by the compiler directives. The imported operators and the exported operators are explicitly declared with `#import` and `#export` compiler directives, respectively. From the outside of the data type modules, only the exported operators are allowed to call. In the representation part, the structure of the data type is described. This is done by using `define-type` programming construct. The implementation part describes the operators related to the data type of the module by `define-operator`.

Each data type module must contain a pair of exported conversion operators called `Dump` and `Undump`. In MODUS, a data type named `Bytes` are provided for special purpose. Instances of the data type `Bytes` are used to store the data objects in the secondary storage. Users can specify structures of the data objects in the secondary storage by defining these conversion operators so that it is suited to the applications. The operators `Dump` converts the data objects of a certain data type (in main memory format) to those of data type `Bytes` (in secondary storage format). `Undump` is a reverse function of `Dump`.

The access method manager provides indexing mechanism. In MODUS, each access method is defined in an *access method module*. The access method modules are controlled by the access method manager. We will discuss details of the mechanism of access methods in MODUS in the next section.

Coordinating the managers, the kernel processes queries served through MODUS kernel interface. When the kernel receives a query, it consults the schema manager to find out whether the query is valid. It also checks which files are needed to process the query and which data types of objects are stored in the files by consulting the schema manager. Next, the kernel obtains record identifiers in the files from the access method

```
%% interface

#refer Integer
#refer Boolean
#refer Point

#import Equal(Integer, Integer) \
        returns Boolean
#import Equal(Boolean, Boolean) \
        returns Boolean
#import True() returns Boolean
#import False() returns Boolean
#import And(Boolean, Boolean) returns Boolean
#import Equal(Point, Point) returns Boolean

#export Equal(Rectangle2, Rectangle2) \
        returns Boolean
#export Overlap(Rectangle2, Rectangle2) \
        returns Boolean
#export Union(Rectangle2, Rectangle2) \
        returns Rectangle2
#export Volume(Rectangle2) returns Integer
#export Dump(Rectangle2) returns Bytes
#export Undump(Bytes) returns Rectangle2

%% representation

define-type Rectangle2
{
    Point origin;
    int width;
    int height;
}

%% implementation

define-operator Equal(Rectangle2 r1, Rectangle2 r2)\
        returns Boolean
{
    if (And(Equal(r1.origin, r2.origin),
            And(Equal(r1.width, r2.width),
                Equal(r1.height, r2.height))))
        return True();
    else
        return False();
}

...
```

Figure 2: Definition of Two Dimensional Rectangle Data Type

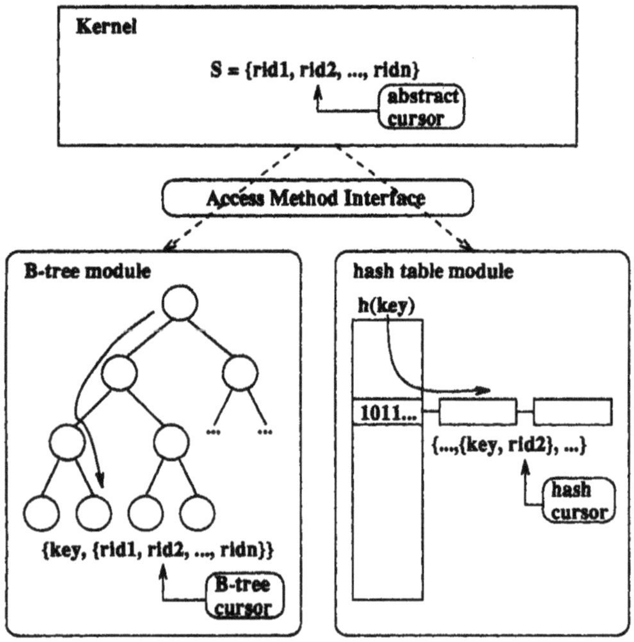

Figure 3: Abstract Concept of Cursors

manager through AMI. Record themselves are received from the record file manager by sending the obtained record identifiers to the manager. Type information is served by the data type manager. Using this information, the kernel evaluates expressions included in the query. Results are sent back to the query processor. Details of the mechanism of query processing are described in Section 4.

3. INDEXING MECHANISM OF MODUS

3.1. Access Method Module

As described in the previous section, the access method manager implements the indexing mechanism of MODUS. The role of the access method manager is to provide kernel with indexing service by controlling access method modules written by users. Here, the point is, from the kernel's point of view, that there must not be any difference among access method modules to implement the extensibility. In other words, to be extensible, it is necessary for the kernel to control all access methods embedded into the system in a uniform way. To achieve this goal, we set an interface between the kernel and the access method manager. This is called *access method interface* (AMI). AMI is a fixed set of abstract functions.

The specification of major functions of AMI is defined based on the concept of *cursors* (or *iterators*). A cursor is an abstract structure which moves on a set of record identifiers. Each cursor has its own context, and always points to one entry of the set on which the cursor moves. This entry is called *current position.*

The concept of the cursors is a basis of abstraction of the indexing mechanism. As described above, to implement the indexing mechanism to be extensible, it is necessary to provide

```
%% interface

#require Equal(Object, Object) returns Boolean
#require Overlap(Object, Object) Boolean
#require Area(Object) returns Integer
#require Union(Object, Object) returns Object

#support Overlap(key, data)
#support Overlap(data, key)

%% representation

...

define-descriptor Rtree {
    file     rtrfile;
    int      max;
    int      min;
    rtrflg   status;
    type     keytype;
    page     root;
}

define-cursor Rtree {
    rtrpos   current;
    int      slot;
}
...

%% implementation

define-ami create(filename, type, rops)
{
    ...
}
...
```

Figure 4: Definition of R-tree Access Method

a uniform way to access index files. However, the implementation of AMI functions depends on organization of index files of each access method. For example, consider cases of retrieving all record identifiers which are associated with a specified key value. In the case of a B-tree module, it follows tree structure. On the other hand, in the case of a hash table module, it calculates a hash value followed by looking into table entries (Figure 3). For making it invisible such difference among modules from the kernel, at AMI level, the abstract concept of cursors is useful. The implementation which depends on each access method such as tree traverse and table lookup is encapsulated into the cursors, and is hidden from the kernel. With the cursors, the kernel can access entries in index files in a uniform way.

In each access method module, users must give a concrete implementation of AMI functions and cursors. When the kernel sends requests using the cursor through AMI, then the access method module acts to answer the requests using the definition of the AMI functions and the cursor in the access method module.

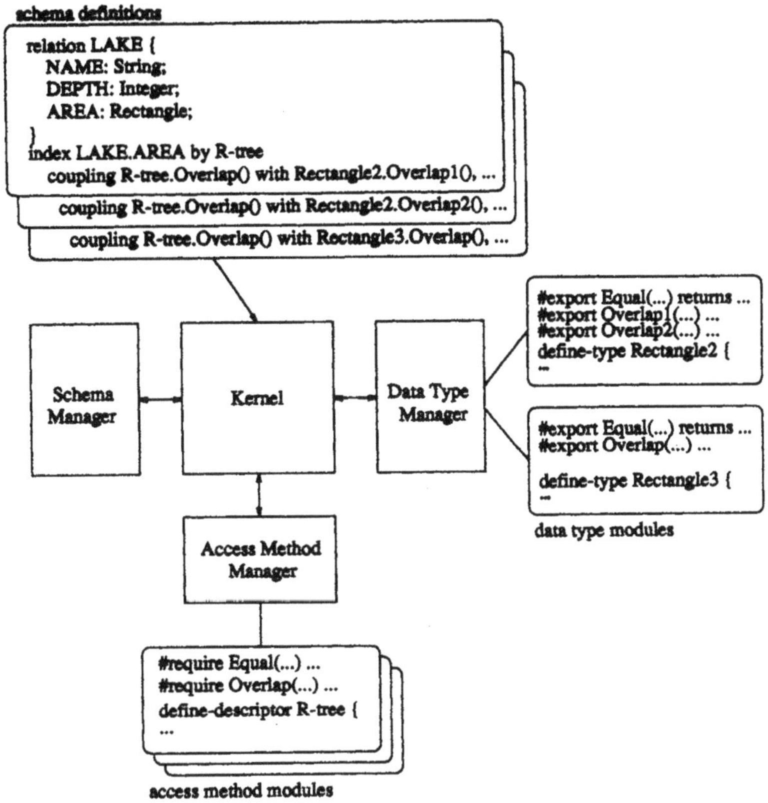

Figure 5: Coupling Data Types and Access Methods

3.2. Achieving Orthogonality of Data Type Extension and Access Method Extension

For practical use, it is desirable that the mechanism of the data type extension and the mechanism of the access method extension are *orthogonal*. In other words, these mechanisms should be independent of each other. This independency makes users' work to implement access method modules smaller. If the two mechanisms of extension are orthogonal, users do not have to write codes sensitive to each data type in access method modules.

Moreover, the independency of data types and access methods improves the reusability of user defined modules. For example, if an R-tree access method module is implemented independently of data types, this module can be used for indexing objects of `Rectangle2` (a two-dimensional data type), for indexing objects of `Rectangle3` (a three-dimensional data type), and even for indexing objects of other data types, without making any modification on the access method module.

There are few systems in which data type independency is mentioned in literature. That is, in most extensible DBMSs, the access method modules are dependent on data types. In such systems, an access method can be used to index objects of only one or a few data types. If a user wants to use an access method embedded into the DBMS earlier for indexing objects of a data type which is defined later on, he or she has to modify the access method module so that it can be used for the data type. This is undesirable.

To the best of the authors' knowledge, EXODUS is the only exception. In EXODUS, a concept called *generic classes* is introduced to implementing data type independent access method modules. It can be said that the generic classes are *parameterized* classes. By using generic classes, it is possible to describe access method modules independently of data types. However, they are not operator independent. As described earlier, each implementation of data type is composed of the structure of objects of that data type and a set of related operators. Thus, to implement orthogonality between data types and access methods, the access method modules must be not only data type independent but also operator independent.

For implementing access methods, some operators are used for constructing, managing, and accessing index files. For example, in R-tree, some operators including the operator which checks if two data objects are equal and the operator which checks if two data objects have shared area. In this paper, we call these operators *required operators* (ROPs). In MODUS, since access method modules are parameterized by ROPs, they are not only data type independent, but also operator independent.

Figure 4 is an examples of an R-tree access method module. Similar to data type modules, each access method module is composed of three parts: interface part, representation part, and implementation part. In the interface part, ROPs are declared with the compiler directives `#require`.

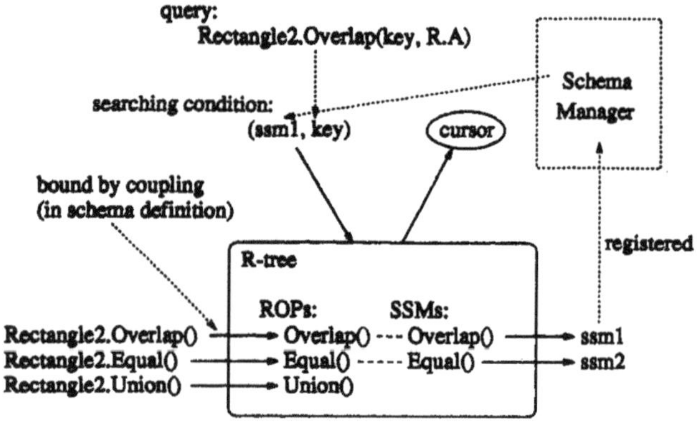

Figure 6: Mechanism of ROPs and SSMs

In MODUS, orthogonality between data types and access methods is implemented by introducing the concept *coupling*. When an access method module is used for indexing objects of a certain data type, in MODUS, it is necessary to specify operators required for that access method modules by coupling the required operators with exported operators defined in the module of the data type. Coupling of operators of data types and operators of access methods is determined in the schema definition for each database (Figure 5). By coupling with types and operators, in MODUS, users can use each access method module for indexing objects of various data types.

3.3. Supported Searching Methods

In general, each access method can support more than one methods for searching data objects in the index file. For example, the R-tree access method can support a searching method to find out data objects in the index file which overlaps with a specified key value. Also, the R-tree can support another searching method to find out data objects in the index file which is equal to a specified key value. In this paper, we call such methods *supported searching methods* (SSMs). In MODUS, each access method module is parameterized by SSMs as well as ROPs (Figure 6).

When ROPs of an access method module are bound with operators by coupling, one or more SSMs are provided by the module. These SSMs are registered in the system catalogs in the schema manager, and are used in the course of query processing to search data objects stored in the index files. When a searching condition which is composed of an SSM and key values is issued, the access method module creates a cursor for the searching condition and returns it to the kernel. The kernel can use this cursor for accessing the data objects which satisfy the searching condition in the index file.

4. QUERY PROCESSING IN MODUS

With the examples of modules shown in the previous sections, we can construct a simple application-specific DBMS that can handle two-dimensional spatial data objects. In this subsection, we describe the mechanism of query processing with this spatial DBMS. Suppose that there is a database which includes following relations in the DBMS.

```
COUNTRY(name, population, area)
LAKE(name, depth, area)
```

We assume that data types of the attributes named **area** are both **Rectangle2**. The attribute **area** of the relation **LAKE** is assumed to be indexed by the R-tree access method which is implemented by the access method module described in the previous section.

Consider that the following query is issued.

```
retrieve (LAKE.name)
where Overlap(LAKE.area, COUNTRY.area)
    and COUNTRY.name = "Japan"
```

This query is to retrieve names of all lakes located in Japan. The function **Overlap** is defined in the data type module of **Rectangle2** shown in Subsection 2.2. This query is parsed by the query processor and is translated into *query evaluation plans* (QEPs). The query of our example will be translated to the following QEPs.

```
(set xact (start-transaction))
(for-each country (scan-relation xact db-example
                                 rel-country)
    (if (string-equal
            (get-attribute xact db-example
                           rel-country
                           attr-country-name
                           country)
            "Japan")
        (for-each lake
                  (scan-index
                      xact db-example
                      rel-lake
                      idx-lake-area
                      (get-attribute
                          xact db-example
                          rel-country
                          attr-country-area
                          country))
            (get-attribute xact db-example
                           rel-lake
                           attr-lake-name
                           lake))))
(commit-transaction xact)
```

According to the QEPs, the kernel decides its action by evaluating each expression in the QEPs. First of all, the kernel consults the schema manger and checks whether the QEPs are suited to the system catalogs of the database. Then, the kernel calls functions in the access method modules through AMI to get record identifiers. The AMI functions are then send requests the file manager to read some pages of the index file in the secondary storage.

For each record identifier obtained from the index file, the kernel sends request to the record file manager to get records in the database. At this stage, the operator **Undump** in the data type module **Rectangle2** is used to convert sequence of bytes obtained from the storage manager to objects of type **Rectangle2**.

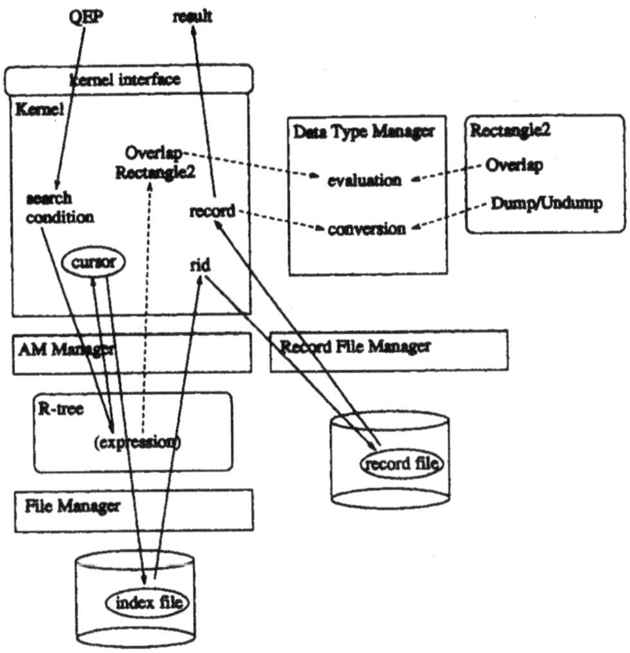

Figure 7: Mechanism of Query Processing in MODUS

Other functions in the data type module such as `Overlap` are also used in the course of query processing. These functions are provided by the data type manager.

Results of evaluation of the QEPs (i.e., results of the query) are sent back to the query processor. The mechanism of the query processing is illustrated in Figure 7.

5. SUMMARY AND FUTURE WORK

In this paper, we described the architecture and the indexing mechanism of MODUS. MODUS is composed of the kernel and some managers. Each manager is highly modular, and coordinated by the kernel to provide database applications with DBMS services.

The indexing mechanism in MODUS is based on two abstract concepts: AMI and the cursors. By AMI, the kernel can access any index files in a uniform way. In other words, it can be said that the kernel does not have to know inside of the access method modules. The cursors are the abstract structures for handling index files. As with AMI, the concept of cursors encapsulates difference between access method modules and provides a uniform way to access entries in index files.

Major advantage of MODUS in comparison with the other extensible DBMS is that the orthogonality between the mechanism of data type extension and the mechanism of access method extension is implemented. The access method modules in MODUS are not only data type independent, but also operator independent. Specification of data types and operators used in the access method modules is defined in each schema definition by coupling. This independency makes users' work to implement access method modules smaller. In MODUS, since each access method module has nothing to do with any specific data types and operators, users do not have to write codes sensitive to each data type. Furthermore, when some new data types are introduced in future, users do not have to modify previously written access method modules.

Part of prototype system of MODUS have been implemented on SPARCstation workstations running under SunOS 4.1 (an extended version of UNIX 4.3BSD). So far, prototypes of most managers as well as the kernel have been implemented. Also, some access method modules including B-tree and R-tree have been implemented.

There are still some works remaining. Design of another record file manager which implements richer data model such as nested relational model[10,14] and object-oriented data model[2,11,13] is one of major future works. When the record file manager is replaced, the mechanism of concurrency control and recovery may have to be modified so that it is suited for the new data model. The mechanism of another managers including the access method manager and the schema manager as well as the kernel will be also modified.

Design and implementation of query optimizer is another future work. When system is extended by user defined modules, the policy of query optimization should be modified so that it exploits the extensions. In other words, the query optimizer should be also extensible. The rule based optimizer will be desirable for coping with this difficulty. The query optimizer generator[8] will be another candidate for the solution.

ACKNOWLEDGEMENTS

The authors are grateful to Prof. Yuzuru Fujiwara of Institute of Information Sciences and Electronics, University of Tsukuba for his helpful comments and encouragement to this research.

REFERENCES

1) Atkinson, M., Bancilhon, F., DeWitt, D., Dittrich, K. R., Maier, D., and Zdonik, S., "The Object-Oriented Database System Manifesto," Altaïr Technical Report 30-89, Altaïr, Sep. 1989 (also in *Proc. of 1st Int'l. Conf. on Deductive and Object-Oriented Databases*, Kyoto, Japan, Dec. 1989).

2) Banerjee, J., Chou, H.-T., Garza, J. F., Kim, W., Woelk, D., Bllou, N., and Kim, H.-J., "Data Model Issues for Object-Oriented Applications," *ACM Trans. on Office Information Systems*, Vol. 5, No. 1, Jan 1987.

3) Carey, M. J. and DeWitt, D. J., "The Architecture of the EXODUS Extensible DBMS," in *Proc. of the Int'l. Workshop on Object-Oriented Database Systems*, Asilomar, California, pp. 52–65, Sep. 1986.

4) Carey, M. J., DeWitt, D. J., Richardson, J. E., and Shekita, E. J., "Object and File Management in the EXODUS Extensible Database System," in *Proc. of the 12th Int'l. Conf. on Very Large Data Bases*, Kyoto, Japan, pp. 91–100, Aug. 1986.

5) Carey, M. J. and DeWitt, D. J., "An Overview of the EXODUS Project," *IEEE Database Engineering*, Vol. 6, NO. 2, pp.107–114, June 1987.

6) Carey, M. J. and Haas, L., "Extensible Database Management Systems," *ACM SIGMOD Record*, Vol. 19, No. 4, pp.54–60, Dec. 1990.

7) Furuse, K., Ishikawa, Y., Yamaguchi, K., Kitagawa, H., and Ohbo, N., "Design and Implementation Technique of the Extensible DBMS MODUS," in *Proc. of Advanced Database System Symp.*, Tokyo, Japan IPSJ, Dec. 1990 (in Japanese).

8) Graefe, G. and DeWitt, D. J., "The EXODUS Optimizer Generator," in *Proc. of ACM SIGMOD 1987 Annual Conf.*, San Francisco, pp. 160–172, May 1987.

9) Guttman, A., "R-trees: A Dynamic Index Structure for Spatial Searching," in *Proc. of Annual Meeting SIGMOD '84*, Boston, Massachusetts, pp. 47–57, June 1984.

10) Jaeschke, G. and Schek, H. J., "Remarks on the Algebra of Non First Normal Form Relations," in *Proc. of 1st ACM SIGACT-SIGMOD-SIGART Symposium on Principles of Database Systems*, Los Angeles, California, pp. 124–138, Mar. 1982.

11) Kim, W. and Lochovsky, F. H. (eds.), *Object-Oriented Concepts, Databases, and Applications*, Addison-Wesley, 1989.

12) Kim, W., Garza, J. F., Ballou, N., and Woelk, D., "Architecture of the ORION Next-Generation Database System," *IEEE Trans. on Knowledge and Data Engineering*, Vol. 2, No. 1, Mar. 1990.

13) Lécluse, C., Richard, P., and Velez, F., "O_2, an Object-Oriented Data Model," in *Proc. of SIGMOD Int'l. Conf. on Management of Data*, Chicago, Illinois, June 1988.

14) Makinouchi, A., "A Consideration on Normal Form of Not-Necessarily-Normalized Relation in the Relational Data Model," in *Proc. of the 3rd Int'l. Conf. on Very Large Data Bases*, Tokyo, Japan, pp. 447–453, Oct. 1977.

15) Rowe, L. A. and Stonebraker, M. R., "The POSTGRES Data Model," in *Proc. of the 13th Int'l. Conf. on Very Large Data Bases*, Brighton, England, pp. 83–96, Sep. 1987.

16) Sellis, T., Roussopoulos, N., and Faloutsos, C., "The R^+-tree: A Dynamic Index for Multi-Dimensional Objects," in *Proc. of the 13th Int'l. Conf. on Very Large Data Bases*, Brighton, England, pp. 507–518, Sep. 1987.

17) Stonebraker, M. and Rowe, L. A., "The Design of POSTGRES," in *Proc. of ACM SIGMOD '86 Int'l. Conf. on Management of Data*, Washington, D. C., pp. 340–355, June 1986.

18) Stonebraker, M., Anton, J., and Hanson, E., "Extending a Database System with Procedures," *ACM Trans. on Database Systems*, Vol. 12, No. 3, pp.350–376, Sep. 1987.

19) Stonebraker, M., Anton, J., and Hirohama, M., "Extendability in POSTGRES," *IEEE Database Engineering*, Vol. 10, No. 2, pp.76–83, June 1987.

20) Stonebraker, M., Hanson, E., and Hong, C., "The Design of the POSTGRES Rules System," in *Proc. of 3rd Int'l. Conf. on Data Engineering*, Los Angeles, California, IEEE, Feb. 1987.

21) Stonebraker, M., Jhingran, A., Goh, J., and Potamianos, S., "On Rules, Procedures Caching and Views in Data Base Systems," in *Proc. of the 1990 ACM SIGMOD Int'l. Conf. on Management of Data*, Atlantic City, NJ, pp. 281–290, May 1990.

22) Stonebraker, M., Rowe, L. A., Lindsay, B., Gray, J., Carey, M. J., Brodie, M., Bernstein, P., and Beech, D., "Third-Generation Database System Manifesto," *ACM SIGMOD Record*, Vol. 19, No. 3, pp.31–44, Sep. 1990.

23) Stonebraker, M. and Kermnitz, G., "The POSTGRES Next-Generation Database Management System," *Communications of the ACM*, Vol. 34, No. 10, pp.78–92, Oct. 1991.

24) Yu, X., *Supporting Surnctured Objects in MODUS*, PhD thesis, University of Tsukuba, 1990.

A NEW INDEXING AND TEXT RANKING METHOD FOR JAPANESE TEXT DATABASES USING SIMPLE-WORD COMPOUNDS AS KEYWORDS

Yasushi OGAWA Ayako BESSHO Masajirou IWASAKI
Mina NISHIMURA Masako HIROSE
Research & Development Center, RICOH Co., Ltd.

Abstract

This paper describes a new indexing method for Japanese text databases using the *simple keyword string*. A compound word is treated as a string of simple words, which are the smallest units in Japanese grammar which still maintain their meanings. As a result, retrieved texts can be ranked, according to the similarity of their meaning and the query, without using a control vocabulary or thesaurus. For automatic indexing, the newly introduced *keyword feature*, which describes the syntactic and semantic characteristics of a word, enables a precise keyword assignment and simplifies dictionary maintenance.

1 INTRODUCTION

Conventional DBMSs are in wide use for managing well-defined or structured data, however, their use for unstructured data, such as free text, is limited [8][16]. At the same time, there is an explosion in the volume of text in offices, and companies must now face the problem of dealing with them. In response, we are developing a database management system for Japanese free texts.

Full-text search, as a means for managing texts, is becoming popular [5][17], however, there are still substantial problems with these methods: full-text systems generally utilize special hardware, and do not include intelligent search functions such as retrieval of synonyms or text ranking. Our solution is to adopt a keyword-based method, using keywords as indices. We considered two indexing methods[15], *controlled vocabulary* and *uncontrolled vocabulary* or *free term*, and chose the latter. This is due to the fact that a controlled vocabulary requires the the creation and maintenance of large dictionaries, and restricts the user to a strictly designated set of words.

In a keyword based system, keywords actually express the contents of the texts and queries, so they should be compared not as literal strings but as meanings. Especially in Japanese where words are easily compounded to express complicated objects, it's important to include a mechanism for handling compound words in their meanings. In addition, because meanings often are inherently ambiguous and vague, a meaning based matching should be gradationally valued rather than binary. Retrieved texts should also be ranked by grade according to the similarity, or relevance, between the query and the text. As methods for ranking texts based on their content, there are several methods including the vector-space and thesaurus-based methods[15]. The vector space method expresses texts and queries as points in a keyword space[14][15]. The similarity between a text and a query is defined, for example, by the inner-product of these vectors. However, the method uses select keywords as the axes for the keyword space, and is thus only useful with a controlled vocabulary. Thesaurus based methods enhance a conventional thesaurus by grading relationships among terms, and use these grades to compute the similarity between texts and queries. Fuzzy logic and probabilistic models are used to infer the similarity between texts[7][10][13]. However, all of these methods utilize a thesaurus with only predefined keywords and thus used with a controlled vocabulary.

To match meanings, we propose using a method based on the *simple keyword string*. A simple word is the smallest unit in Japanese grammar which still maintains its meaning[9][12]. The most basic system using this would manage each simple word within a word independently. However, since this method ignores the relationships among simple words constituting a compound, it tends to miss necessary texts or to retrieve unnecessary ones. Thus, we treat a compound as a string of simple words and maintain the order of the simple words. The concept of a string of simple words as a keyword is described in Section 2.

The automatic indexing method is described in Section 3. Indexing extracts the important words from a text, and assigns them as keywords for the text. Our method is based on a conventional keyword assignment methods for Japanese text [4][6][11], and modifies it for simple word strings. In conventional methods, nouns or noun phrases are extracted from the target text and unsuitable words are eliminated using a stop word list[4][6]. However, because creation and maintenance of the list is difficult and a list must be prepared for each application, this method is not practical in a real environment. To solve this, we introduce the concept of the *keyword feature*, which shows the syntactic and semantic characteristics of a simple word. It is used to evaluate whether a keyword candidate is actually a keyword, so that our method can be expected to attain high precision without a stop word list.

The ranking of retrieved texts is explained in Section 4. Basically, simple words are matched as being either equal or unequal. Compound words are matched using grades which are computed from the matches of the included simple words. Thus, based on these grades, the similarity of a text is computed according to the proximity of its meaning to that of the query. In this way, the retrieved texts can be ranked without a controlled vocabulary or thesauri.

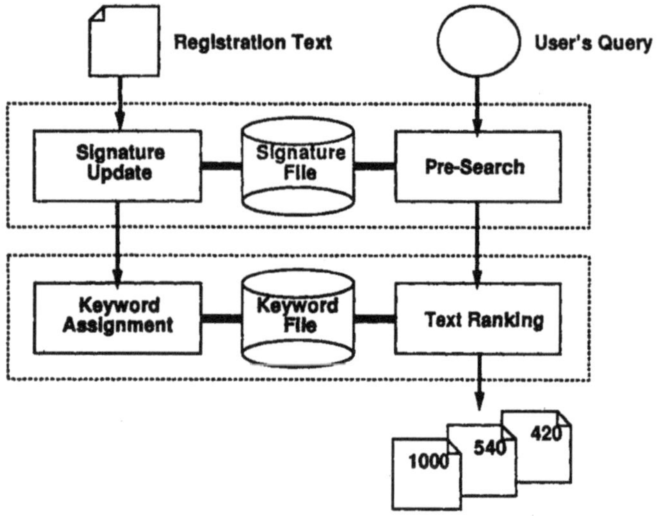

Figure 1: Text Registration and Retrieval Flow

Since the system has to maintain the order of the simple words within the indexed keywords, a conventional inverted file architecture is not suitable. Instead, we adopt a signature file based method to pre-search the texts to be ranked, while a separate keyword file is used to store the order of the simple words which is used to rank texts. That is, as shown in Figure 1, the signature file is first updated and then automatic indexing is performed during text registration. Text retrieval procedure first pre-searches texts to be ranked using the signature file, and then computes the similarities for those texts using the keywords file. The signature file method adopted here is character-based [5][18], but we modified for Japanese text. This signature file method is explained in Section 5.

Evaluation results are given in Section 6.

2 SIMPLE WORD STRING KEYWORD

A *simple word* is the smallest unit in Japanese text which maintains its meaning, and is equivalent to the β-unit as used by The National Language Research Institute (NLRI) [12]. A *word* contains one or more simple words, and a word with more than two simple words are referred to as a *compound word*. For example, the Japanese word 物体認識装置 (object recognition device) has three simple words: 物体 (object), 認識 (recognition), 装置 (device). In our system, it is treated as a string of simple words, expressed as /物体/認識/装置/.

The component simple words can be easily dealt with independently: during text registration, each simple word is assigned as an independent keyword. During text retrieval, the user's request can also be segmented into simple words and the final result is generated from retrieved texts of component words (intermediate results). There are two methods to generate the final result; one is to AND the intermediate results, and the other is, to OR the results. In the case of AND, the final result is the set of texts which contain all of the component words in the query. Thus texts which are assigned only a part of query simple words cannot be retrieved. In the case of OR, the final result is the set of texts which contain at least one of the components in the query. Therefore, the result usually contains so many undesirable texts. However, since a simple word string holds its containing simple words, a retrieval based on this string can exclude the falsely matched texts from the above naive method. In addition, retrieved texts can be graded as we explain in Section 4.

Another important advantage in using simple words as the unit is that, during automatic indexing as described in the next section, a lexical parser is used to divide text into words. This requires only a relatively small dictionary containing only simple words. Based on a word count of newspaper articles by the NLRI[12], the simple word count was approximately 47,000 while the compound word counting was nearly 101,000. Furthermore, the most frequent 10,000 (compound/simple) words only accounted for 79.5 % of the compound words, whereas there was 92.6 % coverage by the simple words. This makes simple words very favorable for system applications.

3 AUTOMATIC INDEXING METHOD

To simplify the text registration procedure for the users, the system must provide automatic indexing. Conventionally, free term indexing methods for Japanese texts parse texts lexically (and syntactically) and extract nouns or nouns phrase from the target text [4][6][11].We have modified this method to be applicable for simple word strings. The overall flow of the indexing is as follows:

1. Lexical and Syntactic Parsing:
   Since Japanese text contains no obvious space between (simple) words, the text must be lexically and syntactically parsed to identify simple words. Our system utilizes the Japanese parser developed at our Research Center[3]. A part of speech and keyword features, which are explained later, are also assigned to each simple word.
2. Keyword Candidate Extraction:
   Based on the part of speech, simple words are extracted from the parsed text as keyword candidates.
3. Keyword Candidate Evaluation:
   Unnecessary simple words are deleted from the candidate, resulting in the actual keywords.

3.1 Keyword Candidate Extraction

Simple words are selected from the parsed text based on their parts of speech. A keyword candidate is formed by successive simple words whose parts of speech are one of the followings:

- nouns

  Japanese includes four kinds of nouns: common nouns, proper nouns, verbal nouns and copular nouns [9]. The latter two are unique to Japanese. A *verbal noun* is a noun which constitutes the stem of a compound verb when followed by する (*suru*) or one of its conjugative forms. A *copular noun* (adjectival noun) is a noun which constitutes the stem of a compound adjective when followed by な (*na*) or one of its conjugative forms.

- prefixes
- suffixes
- the particle の (*no*; "of" or "'s")
- numerals
- numeratives
- unregistered

  A string of characters which cannot be identified during parsing is treated as *unregistered*.

3.2 Keyword Candidate Evaluation

Keyword candidates may include unsuitable simple words; whether a word is a keyword or not is determined not only by its part of speech but also by its syntactic and semantic characteristics. However, candidates are extracted only based on simple word's part of speech. Therefore, we have to evaluate keyword candidates and eliminate unnecessary simple words from them.

3.2.1 Keyword Features

To address the above problem, we introduce *keyword features* which describe the characteristics of each word more precisely than part of speech. They are used in the mark-up rules of the elimination process and also in text ranking.

Currently, we use the following four features:

1. Modifier:

   This feature is attached to nouns and prefixes.

   It is assigned to nouns where the word seldom appears as an isolated noun and is commonly used as the modifier within a compound noun. For example, 国際 (international) is a common noun with the modifier feature. This word is usually found in compound words such as /国際/関係/(international relationship) and /国際/会議/(international conference).

   This feature is also assigned to prefixes which commonly, strongly modify the succeeding words and serve to discriminate the meaning of the compound word.

2. Compound Noun Base (CNB):

   This feature is assigned to nouns with rather broad meanings which commonly serve as the base or stem of compound words. For example, a common noun システム (system) has this feature. It is usually found in compound words such as /データベース/システム/(database system), /画像/処理/システム/(image processing system).

3. Less-Discriminating Place name (LDP):

   This feature is attached to copular nouns or place name which discriminate to a lesser degree. This feature is attached to Japanese prefectures, large cities, etc.

4. Electronics Field (ELF):

   This feature is assigned to numeratives found in documents particular to electronics field. This includes terms such as ビット (bit), バイト (byte).

A keyword feature can be assigned to a simple word, and is managed in a separate file from the parsing dictionary. The feature makes it much easier to modify or tune the automatic indexing to specific applications since the indexing criteria can be easily modified by changing the indexing rules.

3.2.2 Elimination Algorithm

Unnecessary simple words in a keyword candidate are eliminated based on their keyword feature as well as parts of speech. Relationships among successive simple words are also used to evaluate a keyword candidate[1].

We, first, classify simple words into three classes:

TYPE1 : the particle の, and prefixes without any features,

TYPE2 : common and proper nouns with modifier, CNB or LDP feature, verbal and copular nouns, prefixes with modifier feature, suffixes, and numeratives without any features,

TYPE3 : common and proper nouns without any features, numeratives with ELF feature, and unregistered.

Numeral parts are combined into one unit and classified according to the following simple word: When a numeral part is followed by a ELF numerative, the part is categorized as TYPE3. If the following word is a numerative without ELF or a non-numerative, the part is recognized as TYPE1.

Each keyword candidate is processed as follows:

1. Mark-up simple words with TYPE1, TYPE2 or TYPE3,
2. Eliminate TYPE1 simple words,
3. Eliminate TYPE2 simple words:

   A TYPE2 word is removed only when the length of the candidate string is 1 after all TYPE1 words are deleted.

Note that a TYPE3 word is never eliminated.

3.3 Example

Consider the following sample text: リコーの研究開発所は超音波センサを使った３次元物体識別装置を開発した。(Ricoh's Research and Development Center has developed a 3-dimensional object recognition device using ultra-sonic sensors.)

The parsing result and its word-by-word translation[1] is shown in Table 1. The "mark" column shows the intermediate results:

[1] Grammar, word segmentation, word order and parts of speech differ greatly between Japanese and English.

Table 1: Result from Parsing and Mark

simple word		part of speech	feature	mark
リコー	(Ricoh)	proper noun		3
の	('s)	particle		1
研究	(Research)	verbal noun		2
開発	(Development)	verbal noun	CNB	2
所	(Center)	suffix		2
は		particle		
超	(ultra)	prefix	modifier	2
音波	(sonic)	common noun		3
センサ	(sensors)	common noun		3
を		particle		
使っ	(using)	verb		
た		aux. verb		
3	(3)	numeral		1
次元	(dimensional)	numerative		1
物体	(object)	common noun		3
識別	(recognition)	verbal noun		2
装置	(device)	common noun	CNB	2
を		particle		
開発	(developed)	verbal noun	CNB	2
し		aux. verb		
た	(has)	aux. verb		

a black entry indicates the corresponding word is not extracted as keyword candidate, and "1", "2" and "3" stand for marks TYPE1, TYPE2 and TYPE3.

For instance, in the candidate string /3/次元/物体/識別/装置/, where a numeral 3 is followed by a numerative 次元 which has no feature, both 3 and 次元 are marked as TYPE1 and eliminated from the final keyword. Even 識別 and 装置 are marked as TYPE2, the string length is 3 even after deleting 3 and 次元, and these words are included in the result. On the other hand, the candidate 開発 (developed), marked as TYPE2, is eliminated because its length is 1. The final result contain the three keywords: (1) /リコー/研究/開発/所/(Ricoh research development center), (2) /超/音波/センサ/(ultra sonic sensor) and (3) /物体/識別/装置/(object recognition device).

4 TEXT RANKING METHOD

As explained in Section 1, since it is difficult to simply evaluate a text as either matching the query or not, our system grades and ranks retrieved texts. Our ranking method differs, however, from those using the vector space model or thesauri[15]. The method does not require a controlled vocabulary or a large thesaurus, and relevance values for texts can be determined from simple rules.

The ranking is performed as follows:

1. Extracts simple word strings from the query:

   The users can input any noun phrase. The system parses the input and extracts a simple word string keyword using the method described in Section 3.

2. Assigns a weight to each simple word in the query:

   The *weight* shows the relative importance of each simple word within the query word string.

3. Compute text relevance value for all pre-searched texts:

   The *text relevance value* (TRV) grades the similarity between a query and a text and is calculated from the *keyword relevance values* (KRVs) for keywords in the text. KRV is a grade of similarity of an indexed keyword to the query keyword.

   To compute the TRV, indexed keywords are read from the keyword file. To reduce the amount of I/O operations to speed up the retrieval process, our system introduce a pre-search, finding texts which are likely to have non-zero TRV. The pre-search method is explained later.

4. Sort texts in descending order of TRVs.

   After computing TRVs for all pre-searched texts, texts are sorted in order of TRVs.

In the rest of this section, we detail the methods for weight assignment, KRV and TRV computations.

4.1 Weight Assignment

At this stage, the user's input has been parsed and recognized as a simple word string. The importance of each simple word in the query string differs from others because each word has distinct syntactic and semantic meanings. Thus, we assign to each simple word a weight to represent its relative importance.

We classified simple words into three categories on their parts of speech and features. We introduce two pre-determined values, *initial value* η and *increasing value* δ, then weights are assigned in the following order:

CLASS1 : Prefixes and suffixes

For prefixes, the weight is set to η if the prefix has the modifier feature, or to 0, otherwise. All suffixes are weighted by η.

CLASS2 : Common and proper nouns with features, verbal nouns, copular nouns, numerals and numeratives

We introduce a variable called *point*, initially set to η. The simple word string is inspected from its tail to its head. If a simple word of this class is found, its weight is set to *point*, and *point* is increased by δ for the next simple word.

CLASS3 : Common and proper nouns without features

We again use a variable *point*. First, *point* is set to the sum of assigned weights of CLASS1 and CLASS2, and increased by δ. Then, words belonging to this class are processed from the tail to the head. If one finds a word of the class, *point* is assigned to it and $point = 2 \times point + \delta$.

4.2 Keyword Relevance Value Computation

As explained before, keyword relevance values (KRV) grades the similarity between two keyword strings. A larger KRV means that two keywords are more similar to each other. It is used to compute text relevance value (TRV).

In the following, the query keyword Q consisting of m simple words will be expressed as $q_i \cdots q_m$, and the indexed keyword K of n words, as $k_i \cdots k_n$. Then, we introduce a following values, $krv_Q(K)$, to express the similarities of K to Q:

$$krv_Q(K) = \prod_{i=1}^{n} w(k_i) \times \alpha^{v(Q,K)}$$

where $w(q)$ is a weight of the simple word q, and yields 1 when q is not included in the query. α is the pre-determined *adjacent value*. $v(Q, K)$ gives the number of adjacences of query's simple words which coincide with keyword's ones. For example, $v(Q, K) = 1$ when Q = /A/B/C/ and K = /C/A/B/D/, because the adjacence /A/B/ is found both Q and K.

In the formula above, the first term, *word point*, reflects the importance of words which are common in the query and indexed keywords. The second term, *adjacent point*, is to distinguish the order of two simple words which are found both in the query and indexed keywords. That is, because the order of simple words is ignored in computation of the first term, there is no way to distinguish two compound words such as /A/B/ and /B/A/.

Assume that we define KRV by the above value, comparing KRVs for different queries has no meaning because weight assignment results vary according to the queries. This means such KRVs are not useful as absolute measurements of the similarity of each text visa-vis the queries. Thus, the final KRV is defined as the above value divided by a *query point*, $krv_Q(Q)$:

$$KRV_Q(K) = krv_Q(K)/krv_Q(Q)$$

4.3 Text Relevance Value Computation

A text relevance value (TRV) grades the similarity between a query and a text, and is computed from the KRVs for the keywords indexed to the text. TRV is defined as the maximum of the KRVs:

$$TRV_Q(T) = \max_{K \in T} KRV_Q(K)$$

4.4 Example

We illustrate how the TRV is computed. First, we set parameters used in the computation: the initial value $\eta = 2$, the increasing value $\delta = 1$, the adjacent value $\alpha = 2$.

We choose /物体/認識/装置/(object recognition device) as an example query keyword, and the result is shown in Table 2. 認識 and 装置, belonging to CLASS2, are processed first; since 認識 precedes 装置, w(認識) becomes w(装置) $+ 1 = 3$. 物体 is the only word of CLASS3, its weight is set to $(3+2)+1 = 6$ (the sum of weights of 認識 and 装置, increased by 1). The query point for this keyword is given by $(6 \times 3 \times 2) \times 2^2 = 72$.

Table 2: Weight Assignment Result

simple word	part of speech	feature	weight
物体 (object)	common noun		6
認識 (recognition)	verbal noun		3
装置 (device)	common noun	CNB	2

Then the TRV is computed. We assume a text which has two indexed keywords: /物体/表面/(object surface) and /文字/認識/装置/(character recognition device). Firstly, the KRV for 物体表面 is computed as follows: Only a simple word 物体 is in common between the query and this word, so the word point is w(物体) $= 6$ and the adjacent point is 1. Thus, the KRV becomes $6/72 = 0.083$. Next, for 文字認識装置, because words 認識 and 装置 are matched the word point is w(認識) $\times$ w(装置) $= 6$. Since a word adjacency between 認識 and 装置 is also matched, the adjacent point is 2. Thus, the KRV is $(6 \times 2)/72 = 0.167$. As a result, the TRV for the text becomes 0.167.

5 PRE-SEARCH METHOD USING CHARACTER-BASED SIGNATURE METHOD

Usually an inverted file is used for text management using keywords. However, the naive inverted file method cannot be used here because the order of the simple words in a keyword must be maintained. However, some access method is still needed to achieve high performance. we have adopted another indexing method based on the signature method [2].

5.1 Character-based Superimposed Signature Method and Its Problem

Usually, a text signature is computed from words in the text [2]. Since there is no obvious separation between the words in Japanese text, we adopt the signature method based on characters [5][18]. More precisely, the method is as follows:

- Each character is treated as one word, that is, a character is the unit of computing signature,
- The bit width of a signature is set to the size of alphabet,
- A hash function is selected so that it yields a signature where only one bit corresponding to a character is set,
- A text signature is a superimposed or ORed result of all characters' signatures of a text.

We call this method the Character-based Superimposed Signature (CSS) Method.

One of the drawbacks of signature methods, including CSS, is false drop, which retrieves some texts which do not actually qualify the query condition. This problem is usually solved by expanding the signature size. For CSS, it is solved by generating the signature from two adjacent characters, as is done in the Map Array Signature (MAS) [18]. However,

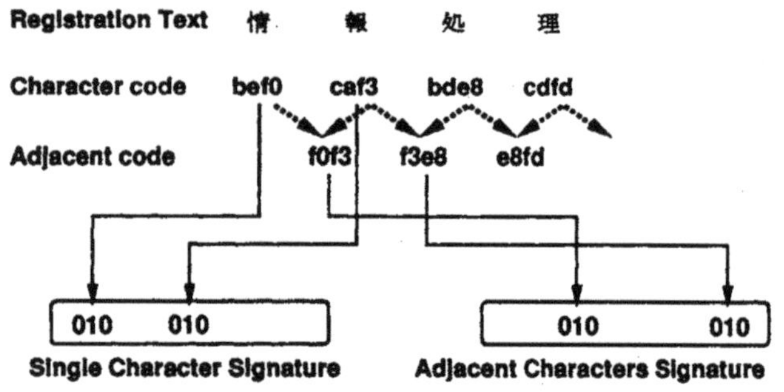

Figure 2: SCS and ACS Configuration

Japanese alphabet is so large (about 7,000) that the resulting signature size becomes huge ($7,000^2 = 49 \times 10^6$). Thus we cannot directly use the MAS method for Japanese texts.

5.2 Extended CSS Method

To lower false drop while keeping the signature size small, we propose an extended CSS method. In this method, we use two signatures:

- Adjacent character signature (ACS):

  A newly introduced signature is made using an adjacent code. An *adjacent code is* the concatenation of the lower bytes [2] of adjacent characters. The signature is made in the same way to generate SCS.

- Single character signature (SCS):

  This is the same as the conventional character signature. Since the ACS signature uses only the lower byte, false drops increase compared to MAS. Thus we use SCS at the same time.

Figure 2 illustrates the configuration of these signatures. The total size of the signatures becomes $7,000 + 2^{7+7} = 23 \times 10^3$, and is much smaller than MAS. In addition, these signature files are compressed using the Exp-Golomb algorithm[19]

When a text is registered, the signatures for the text are generated as described below, and added to the corresponding files. In the following, the text is represented by $T = t_1, \cdots, t_l$, where t stands for a character. For the SCS, $S_{single}(c, T)$, a bit corresponding to character c for T, is set by:

$$S_{single}(c, T) = \begin{cases} 1 & : \exists t_j, c = t_j \\ 0 & : otherwise \end{cases}$$

Let $F(c_1, c_2)$ represent a function which concatenates lower bytes of characters c_1 and c_1. For the ACS, $S_{adjacent}(d, T)$, a bit corresponding to adjacent code d for T, is set by:

$$S_{adjacent}(d, T) = \begin{cases} 1 & : \exists t_j, d = F(t_j, t_{j+1}) \\ 0 & : otherwise \end{cases}$$

During text retrieval, the result is obtained in the same way as the conventional method. Let $Q = q_1, \cdots, q_m$ be the query consisting of m characters, $L_{single}(c) = \{T_i | S_{single}(c, T_i) = 1\}$ be the set of texts which include character c, and $L_{adjacent}(d) = \{T_i | S_{adjacent}(d, T_i) = 1\}$ be the set of texts which include adjacent code d. The result is given by:

$$\{\bigcap_{i=1}^{m} L_{single}(q_i)\} \bigcap \{\bigcap_{j=1}^{m-1} L_{adjacent}(F(q_j, q_{j+1}))\}$$

6 EVALUATION

We have implemented the described automatic indexing method, text ranking method and pre-search method on UNIX workstations [3]. Then, we have evaluated these methods.

We prepared 20,000 news articles, and selected 200 articles (50 electronics related articles and 150 others) randomly for detailed evaluation. The electronics articles were separated from others because some keyword features are assigned simple words which are found mainly in this field. The average length of the articles is 650 Japanese characters (that is, 1.3 K bytes).

6.1 Effectiveness Measurement

Usually the effectiveness of automatic indexing or information retrieval is measured by the recall and precision rates[15]. While the recall shows the ability of the method to present all relevant keywords or texts, the precision, the ability to present only the relevant keywords or texts. The recall R and the precision P are defined by:

$$R(\%) = \frac{\#(\text{Relevant selected keywords/documents})}{\#(\text{All relevant keywords/documents})} \times 100$$

$$P(\%) = \frac{\#(\text{Relevant selected keywords/documents})}{\#(\text{Selected keywords/documents})} \times 100$$

where $\#(X)$ is the number of X.

6.1.1 Automatic Indexing

We compute recalls and precisions individually for each of the 200 articles, then take the average. Extracted keywords are manually evaluated as either relevant or not.

Because the system assigns a keyword as a simple word string, we judge automatically indexed keywords in two ways: a *partial match* indicates that an extracted keyword is judged as relevant when at least one component simple word in the keyword is found in the manually assigned keyword, and a *complete match* indicates the word strings are completely the same as the corresponding keyword manually assigned.

To evaluate the effectiveness of keyword features (KFs), we compared R/P for indexing results using KF and not. The results are shown in Table 3. Comparing both methods, although Rs are slightly decreased ($(96.8-94.5)/96.8 = 2.3\%$ for average in complete match), Ps are greatly improved

[2] Actually, we only use the lower seven bits, because the MSB of the lower byte is not used in EUC (Extended Unix Code).

[3] Sun SPARCstation 2; equips a 40M Hz SPARC chip and 32M Byte main memory, and runs on SunOS 4.1.1.

Table 3: Automatic Indexing Evaluation Results

	Electronics		Others		Average	
	R	P	R	P	R	P
Par. (no KF)	97.6	48.1	96.5	45.6	96.8	47.5
(KF)	95.3	58.2	94.2	54.3	94.5	55.1
Com. (no KF)	68.8	17.4	67.2	19.2	67.5	17.8
(KF)	64.3	26.5	60.8	26.0	61.4	26.1

Table 4: Text Ranking Evaluation Results

	Electronics		Others		Average	
	R	P	R	P	R	P
Simple AND	57.1	82.5	45.8	70.6	52.4	76.2
Simple OR	100	60.0	100	57.6	100	58.8
Top 10	82.4	86.0	88.6	64.0	86.0	75.0

$((55.1 - 47.5)/47.5 = 16.0\%)$. Thus, the effectiveness of the keyword features is confirmed. When the electronics field results are compared with the others, both rates are higher for electronics. This result shows the importance of assigning keyword features carefully, as we did for the electronics. As might be expected, the partial match attains much higher recall/precision rates than the complete match.

6.1.2 Text Ranking

We first evaluated a naive method which handles a compound word as independent simple words. We examined two cases in which the final retrieval result is given by AND/OR of intermediate results for component simple words. These methods are named as Simple AND and Simple OR. A Simple OR result corresponds to the pre-searched texts which are ranked in our method. Then, we evaluated ranking method; R/P were computed using only the top 10 texts[4].

We issued 10 queries, 5 electronics related queries and 5 others. The results are shown in Table 4. Naive methods cannot attain high R/P at the same time: Simple AND yields low R while P is high. On the other hand, R for Simple OR is high, but P becomes low. However, R/P are both high for Top 10 texts. Compared with Simple AND, Top 10 attains much higher R while keeps P. Compared with Simple OR, although R is slightly decreased $((100 - 86.0)/100 = 14.0\%)$, P is greatly increased $((75.0 - 58.8)/58.8 = 27.6\%)$. This means, as we expected, relevant texts tend to be ranked in higher position, and irrelevant texts, lower. Thus we can conclude that our method is quite effective in text ranking.

Comparing electronics and other fields, the former attained higher values for both R/P as the same in keyword extraction.

6.2 Performance Measurement

6.2.1 Text Registration

Text registration consists of an update of the signature files and the keyword assignment. We measure registration time, and there is liner relationship between the text length and response time. Table 5 gives registration speed calculated using the relationship.

[4] We set ranking parameters as follows: $\eta = 2$, $\delta = 1$, and $\alpha = 2$.

Table 5: Registration Speed

	Speed (chr/sec)[5]
Signature File Update	135.1
Keyword Assignment	140.9
Total	69.0

Table 6: Pre-search Speed

Length of Character String	Speed (text/sec)	
	cold start	warm start
1	69100	10200000
2	15800	92900
3	8970	36900
4	6610	28300
5	5310	24700

6.2.2 Text Retrieval

We measure response time for a *cold start*, which runs the sample query with a empty cache, and a *warm start*, which runs with the cache filled with the necessary data.

Text retrieval also consists of two phases, pre-search and ranking. First, the measurement of pre-search is summarized in Table 6. We can see that the speed is fast enough, especially with a warm start. In a real environment, because we might expect a warm cache, the pre-search method is suitable for our system.

Then we show the total performance including text ranking. As a result of measuring the response time for 200 queries, we find a relationship between the number of pre-searched texts and the response time. Using this relationship, we compute the retrieval performance (Table 7). As the pre-searched texts increase, the speed decreases, because the more indexed keywords have to be accessed to compute TRV for the pre-searched texts.

7 CONCLUSION

We proposed the new indexing and text ranking methods for Japanese text database using the simple keyword string. Conventional keyword-based text management systems require a controlled vocabulary or a thesaurus for retrieving texts in their meanings. However, since our method uses simple words, the smallest units in Japanese grammar which still maintain their meanings, as the unit of text management, the method can retrieve texts in order of their similarity to the query. In order to describe the syntactic and semantic nature of each simple word more specifically than part of speech, we introduced the keyword feature. It is used to evaluate keyword candidates so

[5] Because, since the length of one Japanese character is 2 Byte, the speed should be doubled for byte/sec.

Table 7: Text Ranking Speed

Pre-searched Texts	Speed (text/sec)	
	cold start	warm start
1000	1180	5000
2000	1000	2500
4000	830	1250
6000	690	833
8000	588	625

that our keyword extraction method can eliminate unsuitable simple words in the candidates without a stop word list. It's also utilized in computing relevance value of two keywords during text ranking.

The method was confirmed to be effective by measurement results of recall and precision rates. In automatic indexing, the keyword evaluation process based on the keyword features effectively eliminated unsuitable simple words in keyword candidate; compared with keyword candidates, the final keywords attained much higher precision while recalls were slightly decreased. In addition, the nearly perfect recall rate means the method extracted almost all of the necessary keywords from the text. The evaluation results confirmed our retrieval method ranked relevant texts in higher position than irrelevant ones. Precisions were greatly improved for Top 10 texts from all pre-searched texts.

To speed up retrieval, we utilized the pre-search procedure using the character-based signature (CSS) method. Because our method introduces the adjacent character signature, the method achieves lower false drop rate than the conventional CSS, and keeps the signature size much smaller than the MAS.

References

[1] J. Fagan. Automatic phrase indexing for document retrieval: An examination of syntactic and non-syntactic methods. In *Proc. of 10th ACM SIGIR Conf.*, pp. 91–101, 1987.

[2] C. Faloutsos and S. Christodoulakis. Signature files: An access method for documents and its analytical performance evaluation. *ACM Trans. on Office Information Systems*, Vol. 2, No. 4, pp. 267–288, 1984.

[3] A. Itoh, M. Mochinushi, and Y. Kojima. A method of morphological analysis using features (*in japanese*). In *Proc. of the 43th Conf. of Info. Proc. Society of Japan*, pp. 3– 113–114, 1991.

[4] T. Kamio. Automated indexing for making of a newspaper article database (*in japanese*). *Journal of Information Processing and Management*, Vol. 32, No. 4, pp. 283–293, 1989.

[5] K. Kato, H. Fujisawa, and H. Kawaguchi. An index-free full-text search machine for large Japanese text bases. In *Proc. of Advanced Database System Symposium '89*, pp. 75–82, 1989.

[6] H. Kimoto, N. Nagata, and A. Kawai. Automatic indexing system for Japanese text. *Review of Elec. Comm. Laboratories of NTT*, Vol. 37, No. 1, pp. 51–56, 1989.

[7] J. J. Lee and Kantor P. A study of probabilistic information retrieval systems in the case inconsistent expert judgement. *Journal of the American Society of Information Sciences*, Vol. 42, No. 3,, 1990.

[8] C. Lynch and M. Stonebraker. Extended user-defined indexing with application to textual databases. In *Proc. of '88 Very Large Data Bases Conf.*, 1988.

[9] Y. M. McClain. *Handbook of Modern Japanese Grammar*. Hokuseido Press, 1981.

[10] S. Miyamoto and K. Nakayama. Fuzzy information retrieval based on a fuzzy pseudothesaurus. *IEEE Trans. on Systems, Man and Cybernetics*, Vol. SMC-16, No. 2, pp. 278–282, 1986.

[11] M. Morohashi. Automatic indexing survey (*in japanese*). *Journal of Information Processing Society of Japan*, Vol. 25, No. 9, pp. 918–925, 1984.

[12] The National Language Research Institute of Japan. Studies on the vocabulary of modern newspapers. Report 37, 1970.

[13] Y. Ogawa, T. Morita, and K. Kobayashi. A fuzzy document retrieval system using the keyword connection matrix and its learning method. *Fuzzy Sets and Systems*, Vol. 38, pp. 17–41, 1991.

[14] V. V. Raghavan and S. K. M. Wong. A critical analysis of verctor space model in information retrieval. *Journal of the American Society for Information Science*, Vol. 37, pp. 279–287, 1986.

[15] G. Salton and M. J. McGill. *Introduction to Modern Information Retrieval*. McGraw-Hill, 1983.

[16] E. Shapiro. Text databases. *Byte*, Vol. 13, No. 10, pp. 147–150, 1984.

[17] K. Takahashi, H. Yamada, and M. Hirata. A string search processor LSI. *Journal of Information Procesing*, Vol. 13, No. 2, pp. 153–163, 1990.

[18] N. Tavakoli and A. Ray. A new signature approach for retrieval of documents from free-text databases. *Information Procesing & Management*, Vol. 28, No. 2, pp. 153–163, 1992.

[19] J. Teuhola. A compression method for clustered bitvectors. *Information Processing Letters*, Vol. 7, No. 6, pp. 147–150, 1978.

B-TREE CONCURRENCY CONTROL ALGORITHM FOR NESTED TRANSACTION SYSTEMS

John Kyu Lee
School of Information Systems,
Queensland University of Technology
Brisbane, Qld 4000, Australia

ABSTRACT: This paper presents a concurrency control algorithm for a B-tree in a nested transaction system. The algorithm is based on some useful ideas such as a new way to perform page split and page merge, a new link structure to reduce backtracking during search, and the use of different lock modes for successful and unsuccessful operations.

1 INTRODUCTION

Many database management systems use some variant of the B-tree data structure in order to provide fast random access to records in relations that may grow and shrink a lot. Since a B-tree index may be used by many accesses, it is important for performance to develop algorithms for manipulating the index concurrently, while preserving the integrity of the information. Many algorithms have been proposed for this; some of these are [6, 12, 13, 1, 3, 4].

The transaction has long been accepted as a central abstraction for applications, and more recently, systems like Argus [9] and Camelot have been extended the programming model to include nesting of transactions within other transactions. A useful B-tree algorithm must not only allow individual operations such as read, insert, or delete, to run concurrently, but it must also preserve the correctness (serializability) of transactions that can contain multiple operations. This issue has not been addressed by many algorithms proposed so far, such as [6, 12, 13]. A system using these algorithms may experience the "phantom problem" [2]. This paper presents an algorithm that provides concurrency control so that serializability is maintained.

The algorithm suggested is based on existing algorithms for B-link trees, combined with some new ideas (summarized in Section 2) that help eliminate recursive backtracking, reduce the number of locks being held simultaneously by the transaction (in particular, for page splits and merges), reduce the number of page splits and merges, and prevent the phantom problem. However, we do not deal with a nonunique keys, variable length keys and range scans, although we do not see great difficulty to extend this algorithm to support these features. We do not consider liveness [12] since we assume that all the operations have reasonably similar processing time. We also do not consider the case where the root page is a leaf.

The rest of paper is as follows: Section 2 describes the ideas that are newly suggested in this paper and also the useful concepts taken from other research. Section 3 describes the concept of nested transaction. Section 4 describes the tree structure that this paper uses, Section 5 describes the latches and locks used, Section 6 details the search logic with different operations, Section 7 describes how Structure Modification Operations (such as page split and merge) are done, Section 8 details the delete operation logic with page merge and page redistribution, Section 9 details the insert operation logic with page split, Section 10 details the read operation logic and Section 11 describes transaction commit and abort.

2 PRINCIPAL IDEAS

This section summarizes the main ideas suggested in our algorithm and also some useful concepts taken from other research in the subject. We believe that the new ideas will be useful not only for nested transactions but also for ordinary transaction processing systems.

2-1 A New Tree Structure

Pages in each level are backward and forward chained using link information (i.e., prevpage and nextpage) in each page. This is similar to the concept of [1] but the links are used in different ways. In particular, multiple Structure Modification Operations (i.e., page deletes and page splits) and read, insert and delete operations can run concurrently without causing restart of operations. The tree structure also help minimize recursive backtracking.

A nonleaf page of this tree consists of lowkey,pointer pairs instead highkey,pointer pairs as in [7]. This helps reduce the propagation efforts of SMOs.[1] More details are in Section 4.

2-2 A New Way To Perform SMOs Such As Page Split And Page Merge

[1]For a tree structure whose nonleaf page consists of highkey,pointer pairs, some propagation efforts can be saved by splitting a page RIGHT to LEFT instead of LEFT to RIGHT. Notice that if splits are done to the RIGHT as in [7] then two pairs in the parent page are affected: the highkey of the existing page is changed, and a new pair is inserted for the new page. However, if splits are done to the LEFT then the highkey and pointer of the split page remains intact since the lower valued keys are moved into the new page. Only one thing that has to be done: to insert a new highkey and pointer of the new page. Thereby, unnecessary modification can be avoided. A similar concept can be applied to the merge.

This allows more concurrency by eliminating the need for a tree latch; it also reduces the number of page latches held at any time.

2-3 A New Merge Criterion

When a key,pointer pair is deleted from a page, it may become less than half full. In this situation conventional algorithms redistribute or merge the page with a neighbor. Our algorithm delays merging until the page becomes more empty. This helps avoid the problem where the merged page has to split soon after. Thus, it eventually results in less SMOs.

2-4 Merge Of Nonsibling Pages

Conventional algorithms allow merging only between pages with the same parent. Our algorithm allows the merge of any consecutive pages.

2-5 A Way Of Preventing The Phantom Problem [2, 11]

Our algorithm guarantees repeatable read[2] (i.e., it solves the phantom problem) by using commit duration locks on the target key, as in [7].

2-6 Distinguishing Locks For Successful And Unsuccessful Operations

Our algorithm increases the degree of concurrency by distinguishing the locks obtained for unsuccessful operations from those for successful ones. See the discussion in Section 5.

Our algorithm also adopts some useful ideas from other researches such as the concept of semaphores called latches for ensuring the physical consistency of pages, the method of splitting the root without altering its location (these are from [7]), and the concept of page redistribution from [13].

3 NESTED TRANSACTION

In order for transactions to be useful for general distributed programming, the notion needs to be extended to include nesting. Thus, in addition to accesses to data objects, a transaction can also contain subtransactions. The transaction nesting structure can be expressed as a tree such that the top level transaction at roots and the accesses to data at the leaves. However, the distance from the root transaction to each leaf transaction need not be same. Each set of sibling transactions or subtransactions is supposed to execute serializably. As with top-level transactions, subtransactions can commit or abort. Each set of sibling transactions runs as if all the transactions that committed ran in a serial order, and all the transactions that aborted did not run at all. An external consistency property is also required for each set of siblings, ensuring that if a transaction waits for one child T to complete before invoking another child T′,

[2]A query within a transaction must be able to get the same response at any time unless the transaction has changed the data base.

then T is before T′ in the apparent serial order.

When a subtransaction commits or aborts, the commit or abort is reported to its parent transaction. The parent can then decide on its next actions based on the reported results. For example, if a subtransaction aborts, its parent can use the reported abort to trigger another subtransaction, one that implements some alternative action. This flexible mechanism for handling failures is especially useful in distributed systems.

4 TREE STRUCTURE

All the leaf pages are the same distance from the root, and the height of the tree is expressed by the number of levels in the tree such that a leaf page is at level 0, and the pages immediately above the leaf pages for level 1, and so on.

A nonleaf page has two main components: the header and elements. The page header of a nonleaf page maintains the pagelevel that shows the level of the page in the tree, the prevpage field that is the pointer to the immediate left neighbor at the same level, and the nextpage field that is the pointer to the immediate right neighbor at the same level. This enables a backward or forward scan at a level. The elements of a nonleaf consist of pairs, thus the contents have the form of $(v_0 p_0 v_1 p_1 .... v_n p_n)$, such that v_i is a value (called lowkey) that is lower than or equal to all the keys of the page pointed by p_i, and higher than all the keys in the page pointed to by p_{i-1}.

The pointers in a nonleaf page point to subtrees, where p_i points to the subtree whose leaves have all key values v, such that $v_i \leq \mathrm{v} < v_{i+1}$ or $v_i \leq \mathrm{v} < v_0$ of the immediate right neighbor at the same level if v_{i+1} does not exist in the nonleaf page or $v_i \leq \mathrm{v} < +\infty$ if the nonleaf page is a rightmost. As a special case, v_0 is the lowkey of a page (note that v_0 in a leftmost page is $-\infty$ and prevpage in a leftmost page is nil).

The lowkey in each page[3] is useful to find out the range of values reachable from a page, so that an unnecessary search within a page can be avoided. It also allows us to cope with a scenario at the leaf level such that: 1) a transaction wants to insert a pair such as key,pointer into a leaf page; 2) it meets a wrong leaf page; 3) it travels to the left or the right neighbor until it reaches a correct page. However, there is a problem when the target key lies on between two pages, such that if the target key is larger than the last key of the previous page but smaller than the first key of the current page, then there is no way to determine which page must contain the pair. Unless each page stores its key range to determine the correct page, the insertion of the pair into one of those pages may upset the lowkey (or highkey) that represents the page in the upper level so may cause additional changes, for example, (a) if the target key is inserted into the previous page but the target key is

[3]In [4], the structure does not include a highkey associated to the last pointer in a nonleaf page, in order to support suffix suppression. The tree structure (i.e., lowkey,pointer pairs) suggested here satisfies this rationale.

greater than (or equal to) the lowkey of the current page (greater than or equal to the highkey[4] of the previous page) or (b) if the target key is inserted into the current page but the target key is less than the lowkey of the current page (less than the highkey of the previous page). Thus, since our algorithm is such that concurrent SMOs occur (without being serialized using tree latches), each leaf page needs to maintain either its lowkey or highkey to show its range.

A leaf page also has two main components as a nonleaf page, its header contains the same properties as a nonleaf page's and plus the lowkey. The elements of a leaf page is $(v_0 p_0 v_1 p_1 ... v_n p_n)$ and p_i in a leaf page points to the record with key value v_i (note that v_0 in a leaf page may not be the lowkey of the leaf page).

A leaf and a nonleaf page both can have up to 2k pairs for some fixed $k \geq 1$ [6, 15].
2k is used as the maximum number of pairs. Usually k is the minimum number of pairs in each page. Therefore, if the situation that the number of pairs in a page equal to 2k or less than k then SMOs could be initiated. However, the lower bound, k, on the number of pairs may be violated: for the root page, a leftmost page (see Section 8) and occasionally for nonroot pages to be explained later in Section 7.

Keys (or lowkeys) in a page are kept in ascending order together with their pointers. For variable length keys, one must keep these indirectly, using a key map as described in [7].

[4]We assume that the highkey of a page is the possible lowest key of the next page of the page as in [7].

5 PAGE LATCHES AND KEY LOCKS

In our algorithm, the concept of semaphore or latch (as in [5, 7, 8]) is used to guarantee physical consistency of pages; while locks are used to control access to keys in leaf pages. Acquiring a latch is cheaper than acquiring a lock and latches are usually held for a short time, unlike locks that are held till transaction commit. (For nested transactions, they are then passed on to the parent, and so released only when the top level transaction completes.)

Different types of locks are kept on the target keys, such as 'write' locks for inserts or deletes, 'read' locks for reads, 'key-not-found' locks for unsuccessful deletes and reads, 'key-already-exists' locks for unsuccessful inserts. In detail, 'key-not-found' locks are obtained by the transaction whose *kind* = "read" or "delete", when the target key does not exist in the correct leaf page, and 'key-already-exists' locks are obtained by the transaction whose *kind* = "insert" when the target key already exists in the leaf page, where *kind* is a function that produces a kind of operation such as "read", "insert" or "delete". The purpose of these locks (i.e., key-not-found and key-already-exists locks) is to guarantee serializability (see [2, 11]). In contrast there is only one type of latch, called X-latch for exclusive mode.

A transaction that holds a X-latch on a page conflicts with any other transactions that seeks to obtain a X-latch on the same page.

In order for a transaction to obtain a lock, it is required that all conflicting locks on the same key must be held by its ancestor transactions. In brief, two locks on the same key conflict when at least one is a write lock. If a transaction commits then all locks being held by the transaction are inherited by its parent transaction, however, if a transaction aborts then all locks being held by the transaction and its descendant transactions are discarded. However, latches are not inherited by parent transaction but discarded.

6 SEARCH ALGORITHM

This section discusses in detail the search algorithm, used as a routine within read, insert and delete operations.

Before searching commences, a transaction tries to obtain the appropriate lock (i.e., a read lock for a read operation, a write lock for an insert or a delete operation) on the key involved. If a lock on the target key (let us write key(T) as the target key of transaction T) is not available, then there exists some uncommitted transaction affecting on key(T) and so the search must wait until the lock becomes available.

Once an appropriate lock on the target key is obtained, the search starts from the root of the tree (which is accessible in a fixed place). The search traverses the tree from one page to its child page using a pointer p_i in the current page such that $v_i \leq$ target key $< v_{i+1}$ (or $v_i \leq$ target key $< v_0$ of the immediate right neighbor page of the current nonleaf page if v_i is the last lowkey in the page, or if the current nonleaf page is a rightmost and v_i is the last lowkey in the rightmost page, $v_i \leq$ target key $< +\infty$). If there is no such p_i (that is, the current page is not correct, due to concurrent SMOs), then the search travels to the previous page using prevpage of the current page or the next page using nextpage. During a search traversal, no latch on pages is required at all as in [13]. The search logic for transaction T (described in Section 6) is same regardless of the operation involved except for the type of lock acquired initially, and the action taken once the appropriate leaf is found (notice that a search for an insert or delete must X-latches the correct leaf page, but a search for a read does not do this).

To latch a page, if the page is not in a buffer pool then it must be read into the buffer pool and then it can be latched. As in [4] the latch is actually associated with the corresponding buffer slot. We skip the details of the search login due to the space limit.

7 STRUCTURE MODIFICATION OPERATION

Operations such as page splits and page deletions that modify the structure of the tree are referred to as Structure Modification Operations.

In our algorithm, SMOs are basically performed under the responsibility of the transaction that actually causes those SMOs except of the aborted transaction (Refer to Section 11). Since SMOs in our algorithm do not require a tree latch (in contrast to [7]), so multiple SMOs can be concurrently processed. The effects of SMOs are propagated in the tree from the leaves to the nonleaves in a bottom-up manner.

7-1 A New Merge Criterion

When a key,pointer pair is deleted from a page, the number of elements is reduced. In [13], if the number of pairs in two consecutive sibling pages such as A and B (where B is the right sibling neighbor of A) is no more than 2k then all the pairs in B are shifted into A (that is, A and B are merged), but if it is more than 2k then pairs are shifted from one to the other so that each one will have at least k pairs. This means that the merged page has 2k pairs. Since in the typical environment the number of insert operations far exceeds the number of delete operations [13], the page may have to be split soon after. By contrast, in [7], merging is not done; instead each page is allowed to shrink until it becomes empty (when it is simply deleted). This avoids these redundant merges, but can lead to trees that are deeper than necessary. Here we suggest an flexible intermediate policy.

Our algorithm focuses on maintaining the size of each page so as to have reasonable space for insertions so that the number of page split can be reduced. In our algorithm, when a delete operation removes a pair (i.e., key and pointer) from a page, if the size of the page affected by the delete operation becomes less than k, we act on the page and its left neighbor, based on a number m such that $k \leq m < 2k$. That is, if the combined size of the consecutive pages is less than m then they are merged, but if is greater than (or equal to) m and less than 2k then the delete operation is terminated without further action. However, if their size is larger than 2k then they are redistributed evenly as in [13]. Therefore, it is possible that some pages could have less pairs than k, but the redistribution eliminates the possibility of an empty nonleaf page that is not a leftmost one. We feel that this is a valid approach, in anticipation of more insertions than deletions.

Note that a leftmost page is never merged since it does not have a left neighbor but instead it is deleted when it becomes empty (In fact, a nonleaf leftmost page never becomes empty once it has been created - refer to Section 8).

Later, the merge operation is described along with a delete operation in Section 8.

8 DELETE OPERATION WITH PAGE MERGE AND REDISTRIBUTION

When a delete operation for transaction T is initiated at the end of the search, a X-latch is already held on a correct leaf page and a write lock on key(T). Then T deletes a pair (i.e., key(T) and the pointer associated with key(T)) from the leaf page, and unlatches the leaf page and terminates if a merge is not necessary.

However, after the deletion, the number of pairs of the leaf page may become less than k. Then as described previously, the leaf page could be merged into its immediate left neighbor (i.e., the page pointed by prevpage in the current page) only if the total number of pairs the current leaf page and its left neighbor is less than m. Otherwise pairs are redistributed between the two pages (if the total pairs is greater than 2k) or T just terminates without further actions.

After a merge has been performed, some changes in the upper level are required to reflect the changes (i.e., to delete a lowkey,pointer pair for the deleted page from its parent). This may itself cause changes in the parent's level. Thus, the merge will be propagated up on the tree recursively until a safe page[5] [6] is met. However, if the number of pairs in the current page after the merge is greater than k (or else if the current page and its left neighbor combined have between m and 2k pairs) then the delete operation is terminated without initiating further actions.

The sibling merge three different cases depending on the page involved must be considered such as (1) neither a leftmost nor a rightmost page, 4(2) a leftmost page and (3) a rightmost page. We skip the details of each case due to the space limit. Notice that the propagation of a nonsibling merge is a bit different and that it is also possible that the propagation of a sibling merge can also cause a nonsibling merge.

[5]One which need not be modified by SMOs.

9 INSERT OPERATION WITH PAGE SPLIT

When an insert operation for transaction T is initiated at the end of the search, a X-latch on the correct leaf page has been obtained as well as a write lock on key(T). Then T inserts a pair such as (key(T),pointer(T)), where pointer(T) is the pointer to the new record containing key(T) which T wants to insert, into the correct leaf page. If there is room for the insertion then it finally unlatches the correct leaf page and terminates. However, there may not be room for the insertion (i.e., when the number of pairs in the leaf page is already 2k).

Then the leaf page must be split into a new page (which becomes its immediate right neighbor). Some changes in the upper levels are required to reflect the results of the split. So, the split will be propagated up on the tree recursively until a safe page is found.

It is sometimes possible that the page in the upper level (which was stacked during the search) can not be found. In this case the same logic as in Section 8 is applied by popping out another page from the stack.

10 READ OPERATION

When a read operation for transaction T is initiated at the end of the search a read lock on key(T) are already obtained. Then T returns a pointer associated with key(T). No propagation is necessary for a read operation.

11 COMMIT AND ABORT

If a transaction commits then its effects become visible to its parent transaction, it passes all its key locks up to the parent and releases all its latches immediately.

The abort of a transaction is a bit tricky. We consider the cases for the abort of Transaction T. We write descendant(T) for any descendant of T (including T itself) that ran at the given object.

11-1 Descendant(T) Has Already Committed

parent(T) triggers a compensation transaction to undo the effects done by descendant(T). The compensation transaction inherits a lock on the target key of descendant(T) from T and starts searching from the root page as an ordinary transaction does.

11-2 Descendant(T) Has Not Yet Committed

Descendant(T) has inserted or deleted a pair and no SMO caused by descendant(T) is in process parent(T) triggers a compensation transaction, which inherits a lock being held by descendant(T) on the target key of descendant(T) and starts undoing (i.e., an insert for a delete or a delete for an insert) the effects done by descendant(T) by searching from the root page as an ordinary transaction does. After the compensation is successfully initiated, descendant(T) aborts by releasing all latches that it holds.

Descendant(T) has inserted or deleted a pair and a SMO caused by descendant(T) is in process parent(T) triggers two compensation transactions, one of which inherits a lock being held by descendant(T) on the target key of descendant(T) and starts undoing the effects done by descendant(T), the other inherits all latches being held by descendant(T) and continues the SMO caused by descendant(T). After the compensation transactions are successfully initiated, descendant(T) then aborts.

Descendant(T) has neither inserted nor deleted a pair but a SMO caused by descendant(T) is in process parent(T) triggers a compensation transaction to continue the SMO caused by descendant(T).

The compensation transaction inherits all latches being held by descendant(T). After the compensation transaction is successfully initiated, descendant(T) releases the lock it holds and then aborts.

Descendant(T) has neither inserted not deleted a pair and no SMOs are in process descendant(T) immediately aborts by releasing all latches and a lock on the target key. No compensation activities are required.

In fact, T can not abort until all descendant(T) have been aborted and undone.

12 FURTHER WORK

This paper aims to provide an efficient algorithm for nested transactions. For simplicity, we do not deal directly with some important facts such as flexible length keys, range scans, nonunique keys. However, we plan to extend this work to support them. We also plan to allow more overtakings amongst different operations to increase concurrency.

References

[1] A. Biliris. *"Operation Specific Locking in B-Trees"*. In *Proceedings of 6th ACM SIGACT-SIGMOD-SIGART Symposium on Principles of Database Systems*, pages 159–169, August 1987.

[2] K. P. Eswaren, J. Gray, R. Lorie, and I. Traiger. *"The Notion of Consistency and Predicate Locks in a Database System"*. Communications of the ACM, Vol. 19, No. 11, November 1976.

[3] A. Fu and T. Kameda. "Concurrency Control of Nested Transactions Accessing B-Trees*". In *Proceedings of 8th ACM SIGACT-SIGMOD-SIGART Symposium on Principles of Database Systems*, pages 270–284, March 1989.

[4] C. Mohan and F. Levine. "An Efficient and High Concurrency Index Management Method Using Write-Ahead Logging". IBM Research Report RJ6846, IBM Almaden Research Center, 1989.

[5] C. Mohan, D. Haderle, B. Lindsay, H. Pirahesh, and P. Schwarz, "A Transaction Recovery Method Supporting Fine-Granularity Locking and Partial Rollbacks Using Write-Ahead Logging"., IBM Research Report RJ-6649R, IBM Research Division, 1989.

[6] R. Bayer and M. Schkolnick. "Concurrency of Operations on B-Trees". In Readings in Database Systems, (ed: Stonebraker) p129-139. Morgan Kaufmann 1988.

[7] C. Mohan. "A Key-Value Locking Method for Concurrency Control of Multiaction Transactions Operating on B-Tree Indexes". IBM Research Report RJ7008A, IBM Almaden Research Center, 1990.

[8] C. Mohan, "A Novel and Simple Method for Reducing Locking and Latching in Transaction Processing Systems"., IBM Research Report RJ7344, IBM Almaden Research Center, 1990.

[9] B. Liskov. "Distributed computing in Argus". *Communications of the ACM*, 31(3):300–312, March 1988.

[10] J. K. Lee, and A. Fekete. "Multi-Granularity Locking For Nested Transaction Systems" In *Proceedings of MFDBS-91 International Conference*, pp 160-172, Lecture Notes in Computer Science 495, Springer Verlag, May 1991.

[11] J. K. Lee, and A. Fekete. "Predicate Locking For Nested Transaction Systems" In Proceedings of Australian Database Research Conference, pages 217-331, February 1992.

[12] P. L. Lehman and S. B. Yao. "Efficient Locking for Concurrent Operations on B-Trees" ACM Transactions on Database Systems, Vol. 6, No. 4, December 1981.

[13] Y. Sagiv. *"Concurrent Operations on B^*-Trees with Overtaking"*. Journal of Computer System Sciences 33, pages 275–296, 1986.

[14] D. Shasha and N. Goodman. *"Concurrent Search Structure Algorithms"*. ACM Transactions on Database Systems, Vol. 13, No. 1, pages 53–90, March 1988.

[15] V. Srinivasan, and M. J.Carey, "Performance of B-Tree Concurrency Control Algorithms"., In Proceedings of the ACM Symposium on Management of Data, pages 416–425, May 1991.

REAL-TIME DATABASE

Scheduling and Concurrency Control for Real-Time Database Systems

Sang H. Son and Seog Park†

Department of Computer Science, University of Virginia, Charlottesville, VA 22903, USA

† Department of Computer Science, Sogang University, Seoul, Korea

Abstract

The design and implementation of real-time database systems presents many new and challenging problems. Compared with traditional databases, real-time database systems have a distinct feature: they must satisfy timing constraints associated with transactions. Transactions in real-time database systems should be scheduled considering both data consistency and timing constraints. In this paper we describe characteristics and requirements of real-time database systems such as timing constraints, correctness criteria and predictability. Also we address the issues associated with transaction scheduling and concurrency control and present a scheduling algorithm for distributed real-time database systems. The protocol does not assume any knowledge about the data requirements or the execution time of each transaction. This makes the protocol widely applicable, since in many actual environments such information may not be readily avaiable.

1. Introduction

A real-time database system (RTDBS) has (at least some) transactions with explicit timing constraints such as deadlines. The correctness of the system depends not only on the logical results but also on the time within which the results are produced. In RTDBS, transactions must be scheduled in such a way that they can be completed before their corresponding deadlines expire. For example, both the update and query on the tracking data for a missile must be processed within given deadlines.

Real-time database systems are becoming increasingly important in a wide range of applications, such as aerospace and weapon systems, computer integrated manufacturing, robotics, nuclear power plants, network management, and traffic control systems. Unfortunately, conventional database systems are not designed for time-critical applications and they lack features required for supporting real-time transactions. They are designed to provide good average performance, while possibly yielding unacceptable worst-case response times. It has been generally recognized that there is a lack of basic theory for RTDBS since the traditional models are not adequate for time-critical applications. Researchers pointed to the need for basic research in database systems that satisfy timing constraints in collecting, updating, and retrieving shared data [Abb92, Buc89, Gra92, Har90, Hua91, Kor90, Lin89, Sha91, Son88, Son90, Son91].

Transactions in real-time database systems can be categorized as *hard* and *soft* transactions. We define hard real-time transactions as those transactions whose timing constraints must be guaranteed. Missing deadlines of this type of transaction may result in catastrophic consequences. In contrast, soft real-time transactions have timing constraints, but there may still be some justification in completing the transactions after deadline. Catastrophic consequences do not result if soft real-time transactions miss their deadlines. Soft real-time transactions are scheduled taking into account their timing requirements, but they are not guaranteed to make their deadlines. There are many real-time systems that need database support for both types of transactions.

The reasons why conventional database systems are not used in real-time applications include their poor performance and lack of predictability. In conventional database systems, transaction processing requires access to a database stored on secondary storage; thus transaction response time is limited by disk access delays, which can be in the order of milliseconds. Still these databases are fast enough for traditional applications in which a response time of a few seconds is often acceptable. However, those systems may not be able to provide a response fast enough for high-performance real-time applications. One approach to achieve high performance is to replace slow devices (e.g., a disk) by a high speed version (e.g., a large RAM). Another alternative is to use application-specific knowledge (e.g., semantic information associated with transactions and data) to increase the degree of concurrency.

Since an RTDBS is often used in safety-critical applications, it must provide predictable performance. An unpredictable system can do more harm than good under abnormal conditions. There are many reasons why traditional database systems show unpredictable

This work was supported in part by ONR, by DOE, by IBM, and by CIT.

performance. For example, to ensure the data consistency, traditional database systems often block certain transactions from reading or updating certain data if these data are locked by other transactions. Blocking will cause transactions to be delayed. Even worse, it is often difficult for a transaction to predict how long the delay will be since the blocking transactions themselves in turn may be blocked by other transactions. Consequently, the response time for a transaction in conventional database systems is often unpredictable.

Hard real-time transactions must be guaranteed that their deadlines are always met. To make such a strong guarantee, we cannot simply use the *best-effort* scheduling protocols. We must have scheduling protocols which can control the locking behaviors to guarantee the locking delays. To do this, RTDBS must have advance knowledge of the resource and data requirements of transactions. The priority ceiling protocols may reject the locking requests of transactions if doing so may cause more urgent transactions to have uncontrollable locking delays [Sha91, Son90b]. Using priority-based scheduling algorithms with predefined resource usage patterns, these protocols can guarantee that all transactions with shared resources can always meet their deadlines as long as some well-defined schedulability conditions are satisfied. A drawback of the priority ceiling protocols is that they require knowledge of all transactions that will be executed in the future. This is too harsh a condition for most database systems to satisfy.

In addition to timing constraints of transactions such as deadlines, criticalness which represents the importance of transactions should be considered in computing the priority of transactions. Therefore, proper management of priorities and conflict resolution in real-time transaction processing are essential for predictability and responsiveness of RTDBS.

One of the challenges of RTDBS is the creation of a theory for real-time scheduling and concurrency control protocols that maximizes both concurrency and resource utilization subject to three constraints: data consistency, transaction correctness, and transaction deadlines [Stan88]. Several recent projects have investigated the issue of adding real-time constraints into database systems to facilitate efficient and correct management of timing constraints in RTDBS [Buc89, Gra92, Son88, Son91, Son92c]. There are several difficulties in achieving this goal. A database access operation, for example, takes a highly variable amount of time depending on whether disk I/O, logging, buffering, etc. are required. Furthermore, concurrency control may cause aborts or delays of indeterminate length. In this paper we address the issues associated with transaction scheduling and concurrency control, and present a scheduling algorithm for distributed real-time database systems.

2. Scheduling and Concurrency Control

Conventional real-time systems take into account timing constraints of individual tasks, but ignore data consistency problems. Also, they typically deal with simple tasks that have predictable data requirements. In real-time task scheduling, it is usually assumed that all tasks are preemptable. But preempting a task that uses a file resource in exclusive mode of writing may result in subsequent tasks reading inconsistent information.

In contrast to real-time systems, conventional database systems do not emphasize the notion of timing constraints or deadlines for transactions. The performance goal is to reduce response times of transactions by using a serialization order among conflicting transactions. Thus, when a decision of database scheduling is made, individual timing constraints are ignored. For example, most commonly used two-phase locking (2PL) protocol [Bern87] synchronizes concurrent data access of transactions by blocking and roll-back, and might violate timing constraints of transactions.

The goal of scheduling in RTDBS is twofold: to meet timing constraints and to enforce data consistency. Real-time task scheduling methods can be extended for real-time transaction scheduling, yet concurrency control protocols are still needed for operation scheduling to maintain data consistency. However, the integration of the two mechanisms in RTDBS is not straightforward. The general approach is to utilize existing concurrency control protocols, especially 2PL, and to apply time-critical transaction scheduling methods that favor more urgent transactions [Abb92, Gra92, Sha91, Son90]. Such approaches have the inherent disadvantage of being limited by the concurrency control protocol upon which they depend, since all existing concurrency control methods synchronize concurrent data access of transactions by the combination of two measures: blocking and roll-backs of transactions. Both are barriers to meeting time-critical schedules.

Concurrency control protocols induce a serialization order among conflicting transactions. For a concurrency control protocol to accommodate timing constraints of transactions, the serialization order it produces should reflect the priority of transactions. However, this is often hindered by the past execution history of transactions. A higher priority transaction may have no way to precede a lower priority transaction in the serialization order due to previous conflicts. For example, let T_H and T_L be two transactions with T_H having a higher priority. If T_L writes a data object x before T_H reads it, then the serialization order between T_H and T_L is determined as $T_L \rightarrow T_H$. T_H can never precede T_L in the serialization order as long as both reside in the execution history. Most of the current (real-time) concurrency control protocols resolve this conflict either by blocking T_H until T_L releases the writelock or by aborting T_L in favor of the higher priority transaction T_H. Blocking a transaction may cause *priority inversion*. Priority inversion is said to occur when a high priority transaction is blocked by lower priority transactions [Sha91]. Priority inversion is contrary to the requirement of real-time scheduling. Aborting is also not desirable because it degrades the system performance and may lead to violations of timing constraints. Furthermore, some aborts can be wasteful when the transaction which caused the abort is also aborted due to another conflict.

Abbott and Garcia-Molina have proposed a restart-based 2PL [Abb92]. It incorporates priority information in lock setting so that transactions with higher priority will be given a preference. Whenever a higher priority transaction is in conflict with a lower priority transaction, the lower priority transaction will be aborted and restarted later on. One of the weaknesses of this scheme is the impact of restarts on scheduling other transactions to meet their timing constraints. Restarting a transaction could be very costly in terms of wasted resources, and a large number of restarts will increase the workload of the system and may cause other transactions to miss their deadlines. To reduce the number of restarts, the conditional restart protocol is proposed, in which the lower priority transaction will have to be restarted only if the slack time of the higher priority transaction is smaller than the remaining execution time of the lower priority transaction that holds the lock [Abb92]. There are few problems with this protocol. First, the effectiveness of this checking is greatly affected by the probability of blocking of the lower priority transaction. Second, the scheduler should have the information such as the execution time and slack time. In real-time database systems, such information is hard to get due to the dynamic nature of resource demands and data-dependent execution path of transactions. Furthermore, priority inversion and deadlock is still possible, although they have a lesser degree of impact.

For conventional database systems, it has been shown that optimal performance may be achieved by compromising blocking and roll-back [Yu90]. For RTDBS, we may expect similar results. Aborting a few low priority transactions and restarting them later may allow high priority transactions to meet their deadlines, resulting in improved system performance.

To improve the timeliness of RTDBS, it is highly desirable to take timing requirements of transactions into consideration for scheduling decisions. An optimistic approach [Kung81] is a possible way to achieve this goal. Due to its *validation phase* conflict resolution, it can be ensured that eventually discarded transactions do not abort other transactions and timing requirements of transaction are considered.

The key component of optimistic concurrency control protocols is the *validation phase* where a transaction's destiny is determined. In the optimistic approach, write requests issued by transactions are not immediately processed on data objects but are deferred until the transaction submits a commit request, at which time the transaction must go through the validation phase. Because write operations effectively occur at commit time, the serialization order selected by an optimistic concurrency control protocol is the order in which the transactions actually commit through validation phase. Transaction validation can be performed in one of the two ways: *forward validation* and *backward validation*.

In optimistic concurrency control protocols that perform backward validation, the validating transaction either commits or aborts depending on whether it has conflicts with transactions that have already committed. Thus, this validation scheme does not allow us to take transaction characteristics into account. In forward validation, however, either the validating transaction or conflicting ongoing transactions can be aborted to resolve conflicts. This validation scheme is advantageous in RTDBS, because it may be preferable not to commit the validating transaction, depending on the timing characteristics of the validating transaction and the conflicting ongoing transactions. A number of real-time concurrency control methods based on the optimistic approach using forward validation have been studied [Har90, Hua91, Son92]. Few of them (e.g., OPT-WAIT protocol in [Har90]) incorporate priority-based conflict resolution mechanisms, such as *priority wait*, that make low priority transactions wait for conflicting high priority transactions to complete. However, this approach of detecting conflicts during validation phase degrades system predictability, since it may be too late to restart the transaction and meet the deadline.

A scheduling algorithm can solve this problem if a lock-based concurrency control protocol supports a mechanism to adjust dynamically the serialization order of active transactions. The integrated scheduler presented in the next section integrates a priority-based locking with an optimistic approach.

Another important issue that needs further study is a notion of "correct execution" in transaction processing, different from *serializability*. As observed by Bernstein [Bern87], serializability may be too strong as a correctness criterion for concurrency control in database systems with timing constraints, because of the limitation on concurrency.

Based on the argument that timing constraints may be more important than data consistency in RTDBS, attempts have been made to satisfy timing constraints by sacrificing database consistency temporarily to some degree [Lin89, Vrb88]. It is based on a new consistency model of real-time databases, in which maintaining *external data consistency* (values of data objects represent correct values of external world outside the database) has priority over maintaining *internal data consistency* (no data that violates consistency constraints). Although in some applications weaker consistency is acceptable, a general-purpose consistency criterion that is less stringent than serializability has not yet been proposed. The problem is that temporary inconsistencies may affect active transactions and so the commitment of these transactions may still need to be delayed until the inconsistencies are removed; otherwise even committed transactions may need to be rolled back. However, in real-time systems, some actions are irreversible.

The use of semantic information in transaction scheduling and multiversion data is often proposed for RTDBS applications [Lin89, Son88, Song90]. Multiple versions are useful in situations that require the monitoring of data as values are changing with time. In such situations, the trends exhibited by the values of the data can be used to initiate proper actions [Kor90]. Examples include falling values in stock-market trading and rising temperature of a furnace in a nuclear reactor. Another objective of using multiple versions is to increase the degree of concurrency and to reduce the possibility of transaction rejection by providing a succession of views of data. There are several problems that must be solved in order to use multiple versions effectively. For example, the selection of old versions for a transaction must ensure the required consistency of the state seen by the transaction.

3. The Integrated Real-Time Locking Protocol

3.1. Basic Concepts

An RTDBS is often used by applications such as tracking. Since we cannot predict how many objects need to be tracked and when they appear, we assume randomly arriving transactions. Each transaction is assigned an *initial priority* and a *start-timestamp* when it is submitted to the system. The initial priority can be based on the deadline and the criticalness of the transaction. The start-timestamp is appended to the initial priority to form the *actual priority* that is used in scheduling. When we refer to the priority of a transaction, we always mean the actual priority with the start-timestamp appended. Since the start-timestamp is unique, so is the priority of each transaction. The priority of transactions with the same initial priority is distinguished by their start-timestamps.

With two-phase locking and priority assignment, we can encounter the problem of priority inversion. What we need is a concurrency control algorithm that allows transactions to meet the timing constraints as much as possible without reducing the concurrency level of the system in the absence of any *a priori* information. The integrated real-time locking protocol presented in this paper meets these goals. It has the flavor of both locking and optimistic methods.

Transactions write into the database only after they are committed. By using a priority-dependent locking protocol, the serialization order of active transactions is adjusted dynamically, making it possible for transactions with higher priorities to be executed first so that higher priority transactions are not blocked by uncommitted lower priority transactions, while lower priority transactions may not have to be aborted even in face of conflicting operations. The adjustment of the serialization order can be viewed as a mechanism to support time-critical scheduling.

All transactions that can be scheduled are placed in a ready queue, *R_Q*. Only transactions in *R_Q* are scheduled for execution. When a transaction is *blocked*, it is removed from *R_Q*. When a transaction is *unblocked*, it is inserted into *R_Q* again, but may still be waiting to be assigned the CPU. A transaction is said to be *suspended* when it is not executing, but still in *R_Q*. When a transaction is doing I/O operations, it is blocked. Once it completes, it is usually unblocked.

The execution of each transaction is divided into three phases: the read phase, the wait phase and the write phase. During the read phase, a transaction reads from the database and writes to its local workspace. After it completes, it waits for its chance to commit in the wait phase. If it is committed, it switches into the write phase during which all its updates are made permanent in the database. A transaction in any of the three phases is called *active*. We take an approach of integrated schedulers in that it uses 2PL for read-write conflicts and the Thomas' Write Rule (TWR) for write-write conflicts. The TWR *ignores* a write request that has arrived late, rather than *rejects* it [Bern87].

In the protocol, there are various data structures that need to be read and updated in a consistent manner. Therefore we assume the existence of critical sections to guarantee that only one process at a time updates these data structures. We assume critical sections of various classes to group the various data structures and allow maximum concurrency. We also assume that each assignment statement of global data is executed atomically.

3.2. Read Phase

The read phase is the normal execution of a transaction except that write operations are performed on private data copies in the local workspace of the transaction instead of on data objects in the database. We call such write operations *prewrites*, denoted by $pw_T[x]$. A write request from a transaction is performed by a prewrite operation. Since each transaction has its own local workspace, a prewrite operation does not write into the database, and if a transaction previously wrote a data object, subsequent read operations to the same data object retrieve the value from the local workspace.

The read-prewrite or prewrite-read conflicts between active transactions are synchronized during this phase by a *priority-based locking protocol.* Before a transaction can perform a read (resp. prewrite) operation on a data object, it must obtain the read (resp. write) lock on that data object first. A read (resp. write) lock on x by transaction T is denoted by $rlock(T,x)$ (resp. $wlock(T,x)$). If a transaction reads a data object that has been written by itself, it gets the private copy in its own workspace and no read lock is needed. In the rest of the paper, when we refer to read operations, we exclude such read operations because they do not induce any dependencies among transactions.

The locking protocol is based on the principle that higher priority transactions should complete before lower priority transactions. That is, if two transactions conflict, the higher priority transaction should precede the lower priority transaction in the serialization order. Using an appropriate CPU scheduling policy for RTDBS, a high priority transaction can be scheduled to commit before a low priority transaction in most cases. If a low priority transaction does complete before a high priority transaction, it is required to wait until it is sure that its commitment will not lead to the higher priority transaction being aborted.

Suppose active transaction T_1 has higher priority than active transaction T_2. We have four possible conflicts and the transaction dependencies they require in the serialization order as follows:

(1) $r_{T_1}[x]$, $pw_{T_2}[x]$

The resulting serialization order is $T_1 \rightarrow T_2$, which satisfies the priority order, and hence it is not necessary to adjust the serialization order.

(2) $pw_{T_1}[x]$, $r_{T_2}[x]$

Two different serialization orders can be induced with this conflict; $T_2 \rightarrow T_1$ with immediate reading, and $T_1 \rightarrow T_2$ with delayed reading. Certainly, the latter should be chosen for priority scheduling. The delayed reading means that $r_{T_2}[x]$ is blocked by the write lock of T_1 on x.

(3) $r_{T_2}[x]$, $pw_{T_1}[x]$

The resulting serialization order is $T_2 \rightarrow T_1$, which violates the priority order. If T_2 is in the read phase, it is aborted because otherwise T_2 must commit before T_1 and thus block T_1. If T_2 is in its wait phase, avoid aborting T_2 until T_1 commits, in the hope that T_2 gets a chance to commit before T_1 commits. If T_1 commits, T_2 is aborted. But if T_1 is aborted by some other conflicting transaction, then T_2 is committed. With this policy, we can avoid unnecessary and useless aborts, while satisfying priority scheduling.

(4) $pw_{T_2}[x]$, $r_{T_1}[x]$

Two different serialization orders can be induced with this conflict; $T_1 \rightarrow T_2$ with immediate reading, and $T_2 \rightarrow T_1$ with delayed reading. If T_2 is in its write phase, delaying T_1 is the only choice. This blocking is not a serious problem for T_1 because T_2 is expected to finish writing x soon. T_1 can read x as soon as T_2 finishes writing x in the database, not necessarily after T_2 completes the whole write phase. If T_2 is in its read or wait phase, choose immediate reading.

As transactions are being executed and conflicting operations occur, all the information about the induced dependencies in the serialization order needs to be retained. To do this, we retain two sets for each transaction, *before-trans-set* and *after-trans-set*, and a count, *before-count*. The set *before-trans-set* (resp. *after-trans-set*) contains all the active lower priority transactions that must precede (resp. follow) this transaction in the serialization order. The *before-count* is the number of the higher priority transactions that precede this transaction in the serialization order. When a conflict occurs between two transactions, their dependency is set and their values of before-trans-set, after-trans-set, and before-count will be changed accordingly.

By summarizing what we discussed above, we define the real-time locking protocol as follows:

LP1. Transaction T requests a read lock on data object x.

```
for all transactions t with wlock(t,x) do
   if (priority (t) > priority (T)
        or t is in write phase)
                /* Case 2, 4 */
   then deny the lock and exit;
   endif
enddo
for all transactions t with wlock(t,x) do
                /* Case 4 */
  if t is in before-trans-set_T then abort t;
  else if (t is not in after-trans-set_T)
       then
         include t in after-trans-set_T;
         before-count_t := before-count_t + 1;
       endif
  endif
enddo
grant the lock;
```

LP2. Transaction T requests a write lock on data object x.

```
for all transactions t with rlock(t,x) do
   if priority (t) > priority (T)
   then /* Case 1 */
```

```
            if (T is not in after-trans-set_t)
            then
              include t in after-trans-set_t;
              before-count_T := before-count_T + 1;
            endif
      else
        if t is in wait phase  /* Case 3 */
          then
            if (t is in after-trans-set_T)
                then abort t;
            else
              include t in before-trans-set_T;
            endif
            else if t is in read phase
                then abort t;
                endif
            endif
      endif
    enddo
    grant the lock;
```

LP1 and LP2 are actually two procedures of the lock manager that are executed when a lock is requested. When a lock is denied due to a conflicting lock, the request is suspended until that conflicting lock is released. Then the locking protocol is invoked once again from the very beginning to decided whether the lock can be granted now. With our locking protocol, a data object may be both read locked and write locked by several transactions simultaneously.

3.3. Wait and Write Phases

The wait phase allows a transaction to wait until it can commit. A transaction can commit only if all transactions with higher priorities that must precede it in the serialization order are either committed or aborted. Since before-count is the number of such transactions, the transaction can commit only if its before-count becomes zero. A transaction in the wait phase may be aborted due to two reasons; if a higher priority transaction requests a conflicting lock, or if a higher priority transaction that must follow this transaction in the serialization order commits first. Once a transaction in the wait phase gets its chance to commit, i.e. its before-count goes to zero, it switches to the write phase and release all its read locks. The transaction is assigned a final-timestamp, which is the absolute serialization order.

Once a transaction is in the write phase, it is considered to be committed. All committed transactions are serialized by the final-timestamp order. Updates are made permanent to the database while applying Thomas' Write Rule (TWR) for write-write conflicts [Bern87]. After each operation the corresponding write lock is released.

4. Extension for Distributed Systems

In this section, we extend the integrated scheduler for distributed database systems. We do not consider recovery protocols for site or communication link failures in this paper. We assume that the execution of a distributed transaction T involves several sites and there is an agent (process) for T at all sites where T accesses data items. Each agent receives read and write requests from the home site of T, performs the operations and sends the results back to the home site. For a write request, the agent writes to the local workspace as in a centralized system. Similar to a centralized system, each agent maintains its local before-trans-set, after-trans-set and before-count for the transaction T it represents. Each site maintains its local read phase, wait phase, and write phase. Suppose each site has a unique site number. To produce unique priority for transactions originating at different sites, the home site number is appended as well as the start-timestamp to the initial priority of a transaction.

When a site receives the first read or write request of a transaction from its home site, a new agent is created for its execution. The locking protocol works in the same way as a centralized system using the local information at the site. To detect transactions that are doomed to be aborted, local before-trans-set and after-trans-set of each agent are sent back to the home agent when they are changed. Such information can be sent with the reply messages for read or write requests to reduce the communication overhead. The home agent of each transaction changes its before-trans-set and after-trans-set according to its local information and information sent back from other sites. In this way, transactions that are in both before-trans-set and after-trans-set of a transaction can be detected and aborted. The home agents of these aborted transactions may be at different sites. The common sites of two transactions are the sites at which both access some data. For one transaction to send an abort command to another transaction, it only has to send the command to one of their common sites. A common site must know the home site of the aborted transaction. Each agent can also send its local before-trans-set and after-trans-set after a certain number of changes in order to reduce the number of messages. There is a trade-off between communication cost and resource contention because it is desirable to abort a failed transaction as soon as possible without much overhead.

A transaction in a distributed database system is a logically atomic operation: it must be processed at all sites or none of them. Thus a commit or abort operation of a transaction must be processed at all sites where the transaction is executed to ensure a consistent termination. In a centralized system, a transaction in the wait phase is committed when its before-count becomes zero. In a distributed system, a transaction can be committed if before-count goes to zero at all sites where it has an agent. This is not simple because local before-count of a transaction can be incremented by other high priority transactions at any time. If we freeze before-count for transactions in the wait phase, high priority transactions may be blocked by low priority transactions that are in the wait phase. This is obviously undesirable. Also, if we allow before-count to be changed all the time, a transaction can never be committed because the home agent may never be certain that the local before-counts of the transaction at all sites are zero. Our solution to this problem is a compromise – a short term freeze. A transaction in the wait phase can be switched into the *semicommitted* state, in which its before-count is frozen for a short period of time so that its before-count can only be decreased but not increased. High priority transactions may have to be blocked during this short period.

When a transaction has finished its read phase, the home agent sends a read phase termination message to all participating agents. This message also contains the site addresses of all agents who will participate in the termination protocol. Upon receiving this message, each agent switches into the wait phase and sends back an acknowledgment along with the local before-count. After receiving acknowledgments from all agents, the home agent then waits until the before-count of all agents becomes zero in order to initiate an attempt to commit. During this waiting period, each agent reports to the home site whenever its before-count switches from one to zero or from zero to one.

Each *commit attempt* is a variant of the two-phase commit (2PC) protocol. If before-counts of all agents including the home agent are zero, then the home agent initiates a commit attempt by sending a TRY-COMMIT message to all agents. If an agent finds its before-count to be zero, it switches into the semicommitted state and sends back a reply to the home agent. Only when all agents are in the semicommitted state, can the home agent decide to commit the transaction. Then the home agent sends a COMMIT message to all agents. The commit attempt will fail if at least one agent finds its before-count greater than zero. If it fails, then the failed agent sends an ATTEMPT-FAIL message to all other agents, which takes them back to the wait phase. Then the home agent has to wait for the next chance to initiate another commit attempt. This process goes on until either a commit attempt succeeds or the transaction is aborted by a high priority transaction.

Only the transactions in the wait phase can be switched into the semicommitted state. A transaction in the semicommitted state is different from one that is in the wait phase in two aspects. First, when an agent is in the semicommitted state, agents in the read phase for other transactions cannot increase its before-count. If the commit attempt fails, then this agent is changed back from the semicommitted state to the wait phase, and the higher priority transaction is unblocked and the locking protocol is invoked again to decide if the lock is available now. In this way, high priority transactions may be blocked by uncommitted low priority transactions only for their commit attempt periods. Second, a transaction in the semicommitted state cannot be aborted. This may require high priority transactions to delay commit operations. The only reason to cause a transaction to be aborted in the semicommitted state is the commitment of another higher priority transaction whose before-trans-set contains this transaction.

To commit a transaction, the home agent sends the commit command and a final-timestamp to all agents. With serial commitment of conflicting transactions, a correct timestamp assignment policy only has to ensure that at each site, if transaction T_1 commits and is assigned a final-timestamp before another transaction T_2, the final-timestamp of T_2 will be greater than that of T_1. Each site should maintain the largest final-timestamp, *max_ts*, ever assigned to a committed transaction on that site. When an agent switches into the semicommitted state, it sends this *max_ts* to the home agent. The home agent assigns a final-timestamp that is greater than any *max_ts* of the agents. This timestamp can always be made unique by appending either the transaction identifier or home site number to it.

5. Conclusions

In this paper, we have discussed characteristics and requirements of RTDBS such as correctness criteria, predictability, and timing constraints. We also addressed the issues associated with transaction scheduling and concurrency control for RTDBS. We focused on the operation scheduling aspect of time-critical scheduling, and introduced an integrated scheduler for conflict resolution, which integrates a priority-based locking with an optimistic approach.

In the integrated scheduler, the execution of a transaction is divided into read, wait, and write phases, in a way similar to optimistic concurrency control mechanisms. By delaying write operations of transactions, the restrictions imposed by past execution history on the serialization order can be relaxed. We introduced the priority-dependent locking protocol, which dynamically adjusts the serialization order of active transactions. We assume the priority of a transaction reflects its timing constraints such as deadline and criticalness.

This integrated scheduler incurs less blocking and aborts than the 2PL protocol with high priority scheme [Son92b]. Also it can reduce the number of late restarts and the number of conflicting transactions over that of the Wait-50 protocol [Har90], since it analyzes read-write conflicts among transactions as early as possible, and resolves them by giving preference to higher priority transactions without unnecessarily delaying conflict resolution. It features the ability to allow transactions to meet their timing constraints as much as possible without reducing the concurrency level of the system. It works in applications that require handling of unpredictable data. The scheduler has been extended for distributed database systems. We are currently working on the implementation details of the distributed version of the scheduler. Other issues that need further investigation include scheme for efficient dynamic priority assignment, extensions to periodic transaction model, and methods to combine it with time-critical CPU scheduling.

REFERENCES

[Abb92] Abbott, R. and H. Garcia-Molina, "Scheduling Real-Time Transactions: A Performance Evaluation," ACM Trans. on Database Systems, vol. 17, no. 3, pp 513-560, Sept. 1992.

[Bern87] Bernstein, P., V. Hadzilacos, and N. Goodman, *Concurrency Control and Recovery in Database Systems,* Addison-Wesley, 1987.

[Buc89] Buchmann, A. et al., "Time-Critical Database Scheduling: A Framework for Integrating Real-Time Scheduling and Concurrency Control," *5th Data Engineering Conference,* Feb. 1989.

[Gra92] Graham, M., "Issues in Real-Time Data Management," *Journal of Real-Time Systems,* vol. 4, Sept. 1992, pp 185-202.

[Har90] Haritsa, J., M. Carey, and M. Livny, "Dynamic Real-Time Optimistic Concurrency Control," *Real-Time Systems Symposium,* Orlando, Florida, Dec. 1990.

[Hua91] Huang, J., J. Stankovic, K. Ramamritham, and D. Towsley, "Experimental Evaluation of Real-Time Optimistic Concurrency Control Schemes," *VLDB Conference,* Sept. 1991.

[Kung81] Kung, H. and J. Robinson, "On Optimistic Methods for Concurrency Control," *ACM Trans. on Database Syst.,* vol. 6, no. 2, pp 213-226, June 1981.

[Kor90] Korth, H., "Triggered Real-Time Databases with Consistency Constraints," *16th VLDB Conference,* Brisbane, Australia, Aug. 1990.

[Lin89] Lin, K., "Consistency issues in real-time database systems," *Proc. 22nd Hawaii Intl. Conf. System Sciences,* Hawaii, Jan. 1989.

[Sha91] Sha, L., R. Rajkumar, S. H. Son, and C. Chang, "A Real-Time Locking Protocol," *IEEE Transactions on Computers,* vol. 40, no. 7, July 1991, pp 793-800.

[Son88] Son, S. H., guest editor, *ACM SIGMOD Record 17,* 1, Special Issue on Real-Time Database Systems, March 1988.

[Son90] Son, S. H. and J. Lee, "Scheduling Real-Time Transactions in Distributed Database Systems," *7th IEEE Workshop on Real-Time Operating Systems and Software,* Charlottesville, Virginia, May 1990, pp 39-43.

[Son90b] Son, S. H. and C. Chang, "Performance Evaluation of Real-Time Locking Protocols using a Distributed Software Prototyping Environment," *10th International Conference on Distributed Computing Systems,* Paris, France, June 1990, pp 124-131.

[Son91] Son, S. H., C. Iannacone, and M. Poris, "RTDB: A Real-Time Database Manager for Time-Critical Applications," *Euromicro Workshop on Real-Time Systems,* Paris, France, June 1991, pp 207-214.

[Son92] Son, S. H., J. Lee, and Y. Lin, "Hybrid Protocols using Dynamic Adjustment of Serialization Order for Real-Time Concurrency Control," *Journal of Real-Time Systems,* vol. 4, Sept. 1992, pp 269-276.

[Son92b] Son, S. H., S. Park, and Y. Lin, "An Integrated Real-Time Locking Protocol," *Eighth IEEE International Conference on Data Engineering,* Phoenix, Arizona, February 1992, pp 527-534.

[Son92c] Son, S. H., R. Cook, J. Lee, and H. Oh, "New Paradigms for Real-Time Database Systems," in *Real-Time Programming,* K. Ramamritham and W. Halang (Editors), Pergamon Press, 1992.

[Song90] Song, X. and J. Liu, "Performance of Multiversion Concurrency Control Algorithms in Maintaining Temporal Consistency", *COMPSAC '90,* pp 132-139, October 1990.

[Stan88] Stankovic, J., "Misconceptions about Real-Time Computing," *IEEE Computer 21,* 10, October 1988, pp 10-19.

[Vrb88] Vrbsky, S. and K. J. Lin, "Recovering Imprecise Transactions with Real-Time Constraints," *Symp. Reliable Distributed Systems,* Oct. 1988, pp 185-193.

[Yu90] Yu, P. and D. Dias, "Concurrency Control using Locking with Deferred Blocking," *6th Intl. Conf. Data Engineering.,* Los Angeles, Feb. 1990, pp 30-36.

A PROTOCOL FOR CONSISTENT CHECKPOINTING RECOVERY FOR TIME-CRITICAL DISTRIBUTED DATABASE SYSTEMS

Junguk L. Kim, Taesoon Park, Prabaharan I. Swarnam
Department of Computer Science
Texas A&M University
and
Myung-Joon Kim
Electronics and Telecommunications Research Institute

ABSTRACT

This paper presents a checkpointing scheme which effectively copes with media failures for a distributed database system (DDBS), which employs the timestamp ordering scheme for concurrency control. In our scheme, normal transactions are executed during the checkpointing process without any interruption. The state of the database taken as a checkpoint by all sites in the system is consistent, so that fast recovery from media failures can be performed. Since our scheme does not interfere with the normal transaction processing, the scheme is essential for time-critical distributed database systems. Simulation results show that our scheme outperforms the existing schemes.

Index Terms — Distributed Databases, Checkpointing, Media Failure, Recovery, Consistency.

1 INTRODUCTION

In a database system, failures in the system might leave the database in an inconsistent state due to abnormal termination of transactions. Three types of failures cause this inconsistency; *transaction failure*, which is the abnormal termination of the transactions, *system failure*, which causes the loss of the contents in volatile storage, such as cache or main memory, and *media failure*, which causes the loss of non-volatile storage, such as the contents of database state stored in a secondary storage.

To restore the database to a correct state after such failures, recovery techniques are used as described in [1] and [2]. The most widely used recovery technique for failures is to reconstruct the correct database state by using the information of the database operations executed by the transactions, which is usually saved in a specified secondary storage space, called a *log*. Using the log information, the transaction operations are undone and/or redone to bring the database up to the most recent consistent state. However, in case of a media failure, both the database and the log in the secondary storage are lost. To recover from this type of failure, the database state is periodically copied into a secure storage, which is assumed not to be affected by any type of failure; we call this copy a *checkpoint*. For the system to resume its computation correctly, the correct and consistent state of the database must be checkpointed.

The data items of a database in a distributed database system (DDBS), are replicated and located over the different sites and a global transaction may access the data items in several sites and update them. Hence, the checkpointing in a distributed database system is quite complicated since the atomicity of the global transaction must be reflected in the checkpoint. That is, if a site S_i takes a checkpoint after a global transaction $T(a)$ has updated the database at S_i, while another site S_j takes the checkpoint before $T(a)$ has updated the database at S_j, then the global checkpoint produced is inconsistent and a recovery with this checkpoint may produce another inconsistent state. Moreover, if $T(a)$ reads one or more data items modified by another transaction, say $T(b)$, then the effects of $T(b)$ at all sites must also be reflected in the checkpoint for the checkpoints taken to be consistent. Hence, to avoid these inconsistencies, a system–wide coordination for checkpointing is required.

The checkpointing for DDBS has been extensively studied and various methods have been proposed and are classified, based on how the coordination among the sites are performed, into non-synchronized and synchronized [3]. In the non-synchronized schemes, each site takes a checkpoint when it finds its local database to be consistent, without respect to the global state of the distributed database. The globally consistent state of the DDB is then constructed during the recovery process by finding the consistent set of checkpoints among the saved ones [4]. In [5] and [6] the checkpointing is performed as part of the transaction-commit process and the recovery is performed by finding the set of transactions and their dependents whose operations have to be discarded and the respective sites, at which these transactions operated on, are informed to discard the effects of these transactions. Possible drawbacks of the above methods are that each site should maintain more than one checkpoint and may take a longer time to recover due to information exchange for finding a globally consistent point.

The checkpointing in the synchronized schemes is performed in coordination between the sites to result in a single checkpoint which is globally consistent. [7] and [8] suggested schemes which produces globally consistent checkpoints, but the initiation of transactions during the checkpointing process at the sites are delayed until the checkpointing process has been completed. A site initialization method adopted to take checkpoints was proposed in [9], where taking of globally consistent checkpoints may delay transaction processing and may cause unnecessary aborts due to deadlocks. In another synchronized scheme, proposed in [3], the transactions to be included in the checkpoint are identified and the transactions that arrived after the checkpoint initiation at some sites but which should have been included in the checkpoint, are aborted. To avoid this delay and abortion of transactions, the idea to deviate the database during the checkpointing process was proposed by *Fischer, et. al.*, which would minimize interruption of transaction processing [10]. This idea was used by two schemes which tried to minimize the transaction processing interruption [11] and [12].

[11, 13] suggested a scheme where the largest timestamp of the transactions ongoing at the time of checkpoint initiation is found and the updates of transactions which have a lower timestamp than this selected value are included in the checkpoint. However, the transactions which should have been included in the checkpoint but arrive at a site after it takes a checkpoint, are aborted. In the scheme proposed in [14], the transactions carry the last checkpoint number of the originating site and the data items carry the last checkpoint number of the transaction which updated it, to detect consistency among checkpoints and to avoid interruption of transaction processing. However, it is possible that a few transactions may be aborted if they were initiated before the checkpointing process and their subtransactions arrived at sites after the data items at those sites had been checkpointed.

In this paper, we suggest a synchronized scheme for taking globally consistent checkpoints. Our scheme has been designed for a system employing the timestamp ordering policy for concurrency control. Our scheme uniformly identifies, using the largest timestamp value among active transactions, the transactions which are active at the time of checkpointing initiation at all sites, as well as all the transactions on which such active transactions depend identified. After all these identified transactions complete their execution at all sites, the checkpoints are taken including the effects of only the identified transactions [1]. As a result, the global consistency among the checkpoints taken at each site is maintained. Moreover, our checkpointing scheme does not interfere with the normal transaction execution by using the database deviation concept suggested in [10]; that is, no transactions are aborted or interrupted due to the checkpointing process. Our scheme is particularly essential for the systems which executes the time critical transactions. Extensive simulation was performed to compare our scheme with the scheme proposed in [11] and the scheme proposed in [7]. The simulation results show that our scheme outperforms both these scheme in all the cases where the simulation parameters were varied.

The rest of this paper is organized as follows: In Section 2, we explain the system model; The notion of globally consistent checkpointing and the problems in achieving a globally consistent checkpoint are identified in Section 3; We then present our globally consistent and non-intrusive checkpointing scheme in Section 4; In Section 5 we present the simulation results of our scheme and two other existing schemes and we conclude the paper in Section 6.

2 SYSTEM MODEL

We consider a database system whose data items, the smallest accessible units by transactions, are physically distributed among N sites in the system and are replicated if necessary. The sites are connected through a communication network and the message exchange between the processes residing on different sites are assumed to be reliable, *i.e.*, the message which is sent by a site is delivered uncorrupted to the destined site within an arbitrary but finite time period. However, the message delivery order need not be maintained.

A transaction is the basic consistent unit of user activity to access the data items and consists of a set of subtransactions, which may be executed at several different sites. The site which is responsible for initiation and termination of a transaction is called the *coordinator* and the participating sites are called *cohorts*. For the termination of a transaction, we assume the two-phase commit protocol; that is, at the time of transaction completion, the coordinator asks the intention of commit or abort of each cohort and based on the intentions collected from all cohorts, the coordinator makes a decision and then all the cohorts follow the decision [15].

In our system model, we do not impose any restriction on when to flush the updates of transactions in the cache or main memory into the database state in the secondary storage. Hence, a recovery from a transaction failure or a site failure (not a media failure) may have to undo and/or redo the log [16].

A set of transactions can be executed concurrently at a site, and for these concurrent transactions to be executed serializably, the basic timestamp ordering concurrency control policy is assumed to be employed at each site [17]. For this, each transaction initiated at a site carries the logical clock value at the time of initiation of that site as its timestamp and all its subtransactions carry the same timestamp. The logical clock value at each site is maintained by the clock rule proposed in [18].

Each transaction can be uniquely identified by its timestamp concatenated with the identifier of its initiating site and all of its subtransactions carry the same identifier. For convenience, we use the following notations in this paper; a transaction with identifier a is denoted by $T(a)$, and a subtransaction of $T(a)$, which is executed at a site S_i, is denoted by $T_i(a)$. Similarly, a set of data items updated by $T(a)$ is denoted by $D(a)$, and a set of data items updated by $T_i(a)$ is denoted by $D_i(a)$. Note that $D_i(a) \subseteq D(a)$.

At site S_k, $T_k(a)$ is said to be *directly dependent on* $T_k(b)$, if $T_k(a)$ reads a data item updated by $T_k(b)$, and this dependency relation is denoted by $T_k(b) \rightarrow T_k(a)$. Similarly, the *transitive dependency*, which is the transitive closure of the direct dependency, is defined as follows: if $T_k(c) \rightarrow T_k(b)$ and $T_k(b) \rightarrow T_k(a)$, then $T_k(a)$ is said to be *transitively dependent on* $T_k(c)$ and this dependency relation is denoted by $T_k(c) \rightarrow^* T_k(a)$. Moreover, if for any k, $T_k(b) \rightarrow T_k(a)$, then $T(b) \rightarrow T(a)$; and if for any k, $T_k(c) \rightarrow^* T_k(a)$, then $T(c) \rightarrow^* T(a)$.

[1] We reasonably assume no long-lived transactions in the system, which is not quite suitable for the timestamp ordering concurrency control policy

3 CONSISTENT GLOBAL CHECKPOINT

A *global checkpoint* of the system is defined as a collection of local checkpoints, one from each site; that is, $GCP(t) = (L_1(t), L_2(t), ..., L_N(t))$, where $GCP(t)$ is a global checkpoint having a unique identifier t and $L_i(t)$ is a local checkpoint at site S_i. $GCP(t)$ must be consistent in order for the system to restore the correct database state on recovery from a media failure.

One of the conditions for a $GCP(t)$ to be consistent is that the atomicity of each transaction (subtransaction) at a site S_i must be reflected in $L_i(t)$, because a transaction is a basic consistent unit of the database operation. That is, if any update of a transaction is included in $L_i(t)$, then all the updates by that transaction must be included in $L_i(t)$. Similarly, a transaction must also be globally atomic, *i.e.*, if any updates by a subtransaction $T_i(a)$ at site S_i are reflected in $L_i(t)$, then the updates of all other subtransactions of $T(a)$ must also be reflected in the corresponding local checkpoint of $GCP(t)$.

Another consistency constraint is that if the updates of a transaction, say $T_i(a)$, is reflected in $L_i(t)$, then every transaction on which $T_i(a)$ depends at site S_i, say $T_i(b)$, must reflect its updates in $L_i(t)$. This constraint is quite necessary because, by reflecting the updates of $T_i(a)$ in $L_i(t)$, the partial effect of $T_i(b)$ is implicitly reflected on $L_i(t)$. Then, for preserving the atomicity of the transaction $T(b)$, all effects of $T_i(b)$ must be included in $L_i(t)$.

More formally, the consistent global checkpoint can be defined as follows:

Definition 1: A global checkpoint $GCP(t)$ is said to be *consistent* if and only if the following conditions are satisfied :

C1: For any data item $x \in D_i(a)$, if the update of x is reflected in $L_i(t)$, then for every data item $y \in D_i(a)$, the update of y must be reflected in $L_i(t)$.

C2: For any data item $x \in D_i(a)$, if the update of x is reflected in $L_i(t)$, then for every data item $y \in D(a)$, the update of y must must be reflected in $GCP(t)$ at the corresponding sites.

C3: If the updates of $D_i(a)$ are reflected in $L_i(t)$, then for every $T_i(b)$, for which $T_i(b) \rightarrow^* T_i(a)$, the updates of $D_i(b)$ must be reflected in $L_i(t)$. □

The partial state of the database in the cache or main memory is assumed to be flushed into the secondary memory at any time, hence, it is not straightforward to catch the locally consistent state of the database instantly, as required in Condition C1. To cope with this problem, the concept of *database deviation* was introduced in [10], [11] and [12]. That is, after a checkpointing is initiated at S_i, the values of updated data items at the site are recorded in a separate data area with the timestamp of the transactions which updated that data item. We call this data area to store the data items to be deviated at S_i, the *Deviated Database Area* of S_i (DDA_i), which can be in the main and/or secondary memory. Moreover, all read operations must be consistently performed with the data items recorded in DDA_i. Hence, when the transactions to be included in $GCP(t)$ are consistently identified, only the updates made by

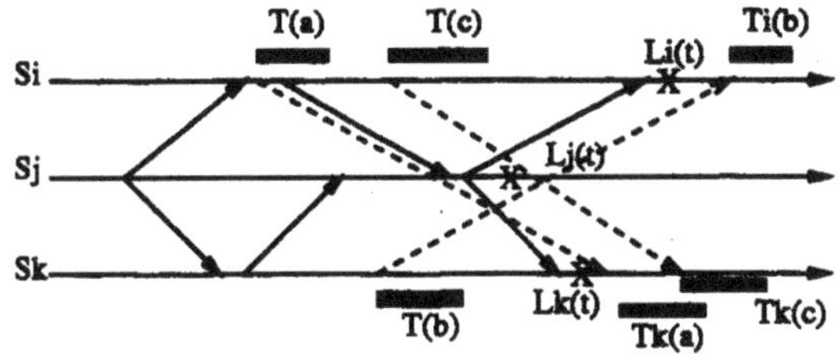

Figure 1: Inconsistent Checkpoint

those transactions can be separated and reflected in $GCP(t)$.

Let OTL_i be the set of transactions which are on-going at site S_i when a global checkpointing for $GCP(t)$ is initiated. Then, every $T_i(a)$ in OTL_i must be included in $GCP(t)$, since their partial effect might already have been reflected in the database state, and to satisfy the condition C2, every subtransaction of $T(a)$ must also be included in $GCP(t)$. Those transactions are uniformly identified by the largest timestamp among the on-going transactions of all sites in the system, in [11]. To collect the largest timestamp, two phases are used: the first phase to collect the largest timestamp among the transactions in OTL_i for every S_i in the system and the second phase to inform the largest timestamp among the collected ones. Then, by including all the transactions having the timestamp lower than the selected one into $GCP(t)$, the condition C2 and also the condition C3 can be satisfied at all sites, because all transactions on which the transactions in OTL_i depend must have lower timestamps than the selected one.

However, there is still some possibility of inconsistency, since some subtransactions of a transaction $T(a) \in OTL_i$ may arrive at another site, S_j, after all the transactions to be included in $L_j(t)$ are already identified, as shown in Figure 1. Then, $T(a)$ can result in an inconsistent $GCP(t)$ since its updates are included in $L_i(t)$ but not in $L_k(t)$. To cope with this possible inconsistency problem, such transactions are identified and aborted in [11], hence this checkpointing scheme does not satisfy the non-intrusive property as claimed. Moreover, to identify such transactions before their executions begin, two-phase initiations are used for each transaction initiation, hence, the initiation of normal transactions are delayed and the response time must be higher.

Hence, we introduce our non-intrusive and globally consistent checkpointing scheme, which consists of three phases: in the first phase, the transactions to be included in $GCP(t)$ are identified, any subtransactions which might cause the inconsistency problem are identified in the second phase, and finally in the third phase, each site actually takes its checkpoint. The detailed description of our checkpointing scheme is shown in the next section.

4 CHECKPOINTING RECOVERY

4.1 Checkpointing Scheme

In this section, we present our non-intrusive checkpointing scheme, in which a designated site, called *checkpointing coordinator*, initiates a checkpointing periodically and all other sites in the system, called *checkpointing cohorts*, participate in the checkpointing process to produce a consistent global checkpoint.

Our scheme consists of three major phases: In the first phase, the transactions in OTL are identified at all sites in the system, by using the timestamp values of the on-going transactions at each site when the global checkpointing is initiated, and the timestamp value is informed to the coordinator. In the second phase, the coordinator after collecting the timestamp values from all the sites, selects the largest value among them, and forces every site to include the updates of transactions having a lower timestamp value than the selected one in the $GCP(t)$. Since we assume the timestamp ordering concurrency control policy, the dependency happens according to the timestamp order. That is, the transactions on which $T_i(a)$ depends must have a lower timestamp value than $T_i(a)$. Hence, when the largest timestamp value is selected, every site updates its local clock value to the one higher than the selected one. By doing so, we can guarantee that the transactions in OTL cannot be dependent on the transactions initiated after this point of time, since the former transactions have a timestamp value lower than the latter ones. However, there are still some active transactions, having a lower timestamp than the selected one, which is spawning the new subtransactions during the checkpointing coordination, and hence, we have to wait until all these transactions complete, for consistent checkpointing. Finally, in the third phase, each site then takes the checkpoint which forms a consistent $GCP(t)$.

For simplicity, we assume page level concurrency control, that is, a data item corresponds to a data page, and we also assume no site failures during the checkpointing coordination process in this section. Our algorithm, however, can be easily extended to handle other levels of concurrency control with slight modification in DDA space management. Handling of site failures will be discussed in the subsection 4.3. We now describe the tasks in the checkpointing process in detail by explaining each checkpointing phase:

Phase I:

(1) The checkpointing coordinator sends the *checkpointing initiation* message, $CHCK_{INIT}$, to all the sites in the system.

(2) Upon receipt of $CHCK_{INIT}$, each of the cohorts, say S_j, sets the value of CLT_j as the current local clock value and responds to the coordinator with CLT_j. Note that all the active transactions at site S_j have timestamps lower than or equal to the value of CLT_j.

(3) Each site S_i then creates OTL_i, which is the set of identifiers of the transactions which are on-going at that time.

(4) Each site S_i begins to deviate its database. DDA_i is implemented as a set of linked lists of data pages updated by the transactions with higher timestamps than CLT_i (one list per each data item), and maintained in the main memory until it reaches a certain limit. That is, the deviated data pages in the buffer space are marked and the buffer manager does not select those pages for replacement, unless the buffer space allocated for the DDA_i space reaches a limit. If the limit is reached, those data pages are flushed into the DDA_i residing on disk. For efficient access to the data pages in DDA_i in the disk, *DDA page map table* is maintained in the main memory. The detailed description of database deviation managed by the buffer manager are as follows:

- When a transaction $T_i(a)$ with a higher timestamp than CLT_i wants to update a data page containing x:
  - If that page is not found in the buffer, the DDA page map table is first checked. If an entry for any updated version of x is found in DDA page map table, then the most recent version of x in DDA_i is fetched. Otherwise, the data page in normal database area is fetched. Once the page is updated, it is marked as *Deviated Data Pages*(DDP).
  - If the page is found in the buffer, $T_i(a)$ cannot directly update the page due to the database deviation, unless the page has not been updated yet. If that page has been read only, then $T_i(a)$ updates that page and marked as DDP. Otherwise, the page is copied into another data page in the main memory and the updates is made on the new page, and the link between two pages are maintained if old page has been updated by a transaction with higher timestamp than CLT_i.
- When a transaction $T_i(a)$ with a higher timestamp than CLT_i wants to read a data page containing x:
  - If that page is not found in the buffer, the DDA page map table is first checked. If an entry for any updated version of x is found in DDA page map table, then the most recent version of x in DDA_i is fetched for read. Otherwise, the data page in normal database area is fetched. This fetched page need not to be marked as DDP, because it is read only.
  - If the page is found in the buffer, $T_i(a)$ read from the most recent version of the page.
- When a transaction $T_i(a)$ with a lower timestamp than CLT_i wants to read or update a data page containing x, the operation is performed on the pages in the normal database area.

  Note that if the requesting transaction $T_i(a)$ has timestamp lower than CLT_i and there is any version of x found in DDA_i in the main memory or in the disk, then $T_i(a)$ must be aborted due to the concurrency control.

Phase II:

(1) After receiving CLT_j from every site S_j, the coordinator selects the largest value among CLT_js and CLT_i, and assigns the value as the *globally largest timestamp* (GLT).

(2) It then adjusts its local clock with the value of GLT, and broadcasts GLT to all the checkpoint cohorts.

(3) Upon receipt of GLT, each cohort adjusts its current local clocks with the value of GLT, if its current local clock value is lower than GLT. Note that all the transactions initiated after this point have a larger timestamp than GLT.

(4) Each site S_i then adjusts its OTL_i to include the identifiers of the transactions which are on-going at this time and have a lower timestamp value than GLT. Note that these

transactions are finally included in $GCP(t)$.

(5) For each data item in DDA_i, if the timestamp of an updating transaction is smaller than GLT, the updates are reflected in the normal database space and deleted from DDA_i by unmarking the data page if it is in the main memory, or by discarding the space if it is in the disk. That is, the DDA_i now maintains only the updated versions of data items which are not included in $GCP(t)$. Moreover, for the updated versions of data items remaining in DDA_i, only the most recent version of the data items are maintained from this phase, by deleting the older versions.

(6) S_i then waits until all transactions in OTL complete their execution and then sends a $CHCK_{OK}$ message to the coordinator.

Phase III:

(1) After the checkpoint coordinator receives the $CHCK_{OK}$ from all the cohorts, it broadcasts a $CHCK_{COMMIT}$ message, which informs the sites to begin taking the actual checkpoint.

(2) Upon receiving the $CHCK_{COMMIT}$ message, each site S_i begins taking the checkpoint using the following procedure :

- A new checkpoint is taken at the site by copying the database state in the secondary memory into a secure storage, and associates a new identifier for the global checkpoint. This copying operation is performed concurrently with the normal data base execution not to interfere with the normal transaction processing.
- The current state of the database in the main memory is reflected into the database residing in the secondary memory or into the checkpointed database in the secure storage, according to the timestamp of the transaction which updates the data page most recently, when the page has to be flushed out for the replacement.

4.2 Correctness

We first show that our checkpointing scheme produces a globally consistent checkpoint.

Theorem 1: A global checkpoint $GCP(t)$ created under our scheme is consistent.

Proof : Assume that $GCP(t)$ is not consistent. It then should have violated at least one of the conditions C1, C2 and C3.

Case 1) Suppose that condition C2 is violated. In this case, without loss of generality, we can assume that $T_i(a)$ was included in $L_i(t)$ and $T_j(a)$ was not included in $L_j(t)$, for $T(a)$. Since both of the transactions have the same timestamp, they must be included in $GCP(t)$ in both sites, unless $T_j(a)$ arrives at a site S_j after the checkpointing is terminated. In order for $T_i(a)$ to be included in $L_i(t)$, it should have been in adjusted OTL_i. Since all the transactions in OTL_i complete their execution when informing the $CHCK_{OK}$, $T_i(a)$ should have already completed its execution, before the transmission of $CHCK_{OK}$. Then, under our assumption of two-phase commit protocol, it is not possible for $T_j(a)$ to arrive at site S_j after the termination of the checkpointing. A contradiction.

Case 2) Suppose that C3 is violated. There should have been transactions $T_i(a)$ not included at $L_i(t)$ and $T_i(b)$ included at $L_i(t)$, such that $T_i(a) \rightarrow^* T_i(b)$ and timestamp of $T_i(b)$ is lower than GLT. Since we assume the timestamp ordering concurrency control policy, the timestamp of $T_i(a)$ must be less than $T_i(b)$. Hence, the timestamp of $T_i(a)$ is less than GLT, and it must have been decided that $T_i(a)$ should be in $GCP(t)$. Moreover, the checkpointing is actually taken when all the transactions, having smaller timestamp than GLT, have completed, hence, $T_i(a)$ should have been committed. Then, $T_i(a)$ should have been included in $L_i(t)$. A contradiction.

Case 3) Suppose that condition C1 is violated by $T_i(a)$. The updated versions of the data items accessed by $T_i(a)$ are made in DDA_i, after a checkpointing is initiated. Hence, if $T_i(a)$ is decided to be in $GCP(t)$, all updated version in DDA_i of $T_i(a)$ should have been transferred to the normal database area before $L_i(t)$ was taken. A contradiction.

Therefore, our checkpointing scheme produces a consistent global checkpoint. □

We now show that our checkpointing scheme terminates within a finite period of time.

Theorem 2: A global checkpointing coordination under our scheme will terminate within a finite period of time.

Proof : The first phase of our checkpointing scheme consists of collecting the current local clock values from all sites. Since no site failures are assumed during the checkpointing and the message delay is also assumed to be finite, the clock value can be collected within a finite time. The second phase can finish when all the transactions having a smaller timestamp than GLT are completed at all sites. Since every site changes its clock value, when it receives GLT from the coordinator, with the value larger than GLT, the transactions having a lower timestamp value than GLT can be initiated only before this point of time. Hence, each site can have a finite number of such transactions and the execution time for these transactions is finite. Hence, the second phase can also be completed within a finite time. When the third phase begins, all transactions to be included in the checkpoint should have already committed. The time to deliver the $CHCK_{COMMIT}$ messages and the checkpoint saving time at each site in the third phase are also finite. Therefore, our global checkpointing coordination process can be completed within a finite period of time. □

4.3 Recovery and Failure Handling

When a site S_i recovers from a media failure, it first restores its recent checkpoint, $L_i(t)$, and forces all other sites to restore their checkpoints corresponding to $GCP(t)$. For the consistent recovery from a media failure, it is necessary for any $GCP(t)$ to be consistent. However, if any of the sites fail during the global checkpointing and cannot take a checkpoint, then the global checkpoint produced cannot be used for the recovery since some committed transactions which are included in a $L_i(t)$ are not included in the most recent checkpoint of that failed site (*i.e.* violation of C2 of the definition of consistency).

We here assume that the failure of a site can be detected by other sites within a finite time. Hence, in our scheme, the failures during the global checkpointing are handled as follows:

- If a checkpointing cohort fails during the first or second phase of the checkpointing: Then, the checkpointing coordinator broadcasts the *checkpointing abort* message instead of GLT or $CHCK_{COMMIT}$

- If a checkpointing cohort fails during the third phase of the checkpointing: To handle this problem, we can introduce one more phase in our checkpointing scheme to ensure the completion of the checkpointing. After each site actually saves its checkpoint on a stable storage, it sends the *checkpointing complete* message to the coordinator. The coordinator after collecting this message from all the sites in the system sends the *final checkpointing commit* message to all of them. Upon the receipt of the *final checkpoint commit*, each site discards the old checkpoint and mark the new checkpoint as a globally consistent checkpoint. Hence, each site in the system need to maintain only one checkpoint which is globally consistent.
- If a checkpointing coordinator fails during the checkpointing: Then, all the checkpointing cohorts decide to abort the on-going checkpointing process.

5 DISCUSSION

Extensive simulation was performed to compare the performance of our scheme with two other schemes proposed in [7] and [11]. For simplicity, we denote the scheme suggested in [11] as scheme S, the scheme mentioned in [7] as scheme I and our scheme as scheme K. Scheme I blocks the initiation of new transactions, once the checkpointing is initiated at each site. After the transactions which are active at the time of checkpointing initiation have completed their execution, the checkpoint is taken and the transactions which have arrived during the checkpointing can get serviced. Scheme S uses a two-phase checkpointing mechanism, where it collects the largest timestamp of the ongoing transactions in the system and all updates by transactions with a timestamp lower than this largest value is included in the checkpoint. However, in this scheme, some transactions which initiated before the checkpointing may get aborted if its subtransactions arrive at some remote sites after their checkpointings are completed.

5.1 Simulation Model

A distributed database system with 10 sites connected through a general network was simulated. Each site consists of a CPU, a main memory, a disk, and a secure storage device for the checkpoint, each of which is managed by a scheduler, buffer manager, disk manager, and recovery manager, respectively. In our simulation, it is assumed that CPU and disk processing time for data item is 5 milliseconds and 24 milliseconds respectively. It is also assumed that 128 pages of buffer space is available in the main memory for data caching, and the buffer management policy is LRU. The granularity of the data items accessed by the transactions is assumed to be pages. The database residing at each site is assumed to have 5000 data items.

A global transaction is initiated at each site with an interarrival time which follows an exponential distribution with a rate λ_t and spawns subtransactions at other sites. The number of sites for subtransactions and to which the subtransactions are sent are randomly selected for each transaction. Each subtransaction consists of a sequence of write requests for data items. A normal distribution with a mean N_d and standard deviation

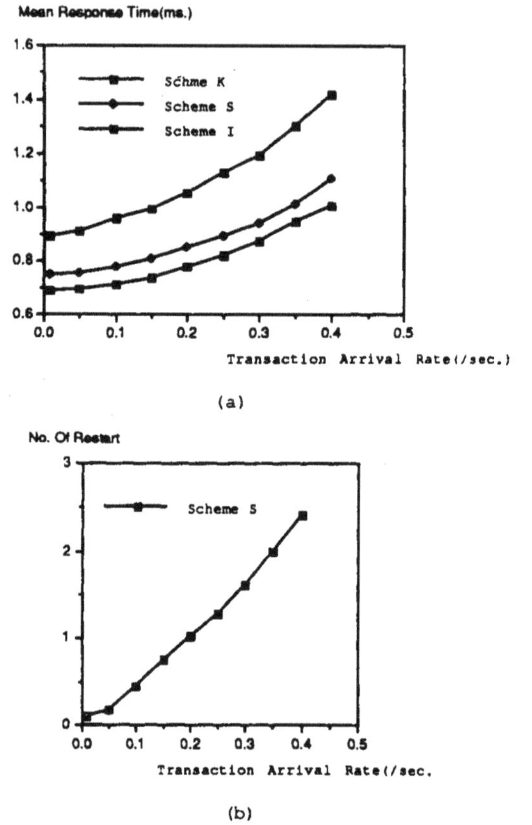

Figure 2: Mean Transaction Response Time and Number of Transaction Restart Vs. Transaction Arrival Rate

δ_d is used to choose the number of data items that a transaction accesses. We assume the two-phase commit procedure for each global transaction, for all schemes. In scheme S, the two-phase initiation mechanism is also used for transactions during the checkpointing process. However, there is no restriction for initiation of subtransactions in scheme K and scheme I.

Message transmission delay of a link in the network follows an exponential distribution with a rate λ_c, and to be more realistic, the delay is bounded by a certain minimum and maximum values.

The checkpointing process is initiated by one designated site with a fixed time interval. The DDA space management during the checkpointing coordination exactly follows the algorithm described in section 4, and the same management scheme is also simulated for scheme K and scheme S. No site failure is assumed in the current simulation. The simulation program is written in C language and was executed on Sun Sparc stations under Sun OS 4.1.1.

5.2 Simulation Results

The main performance index used in our simulation is the *mean response time* of the transactions executed during the checkpointing coordination process. This performance index of the three schemes is compared through simulation by varying the parameters, such as transaction arrival rate at each site(λ_t), the

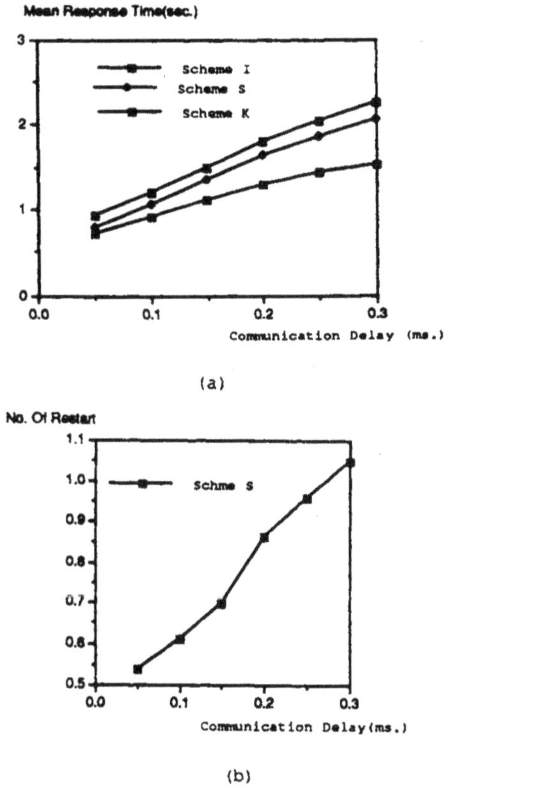

Figure 3: Mean Transaction Response Time and Number Of Transaction Restart Vs. Communication Delay

mean communication delay of the network($\frac{1}{\lambda_c}$) and the mean number of data items accessed by each subtransaction at a site(N_d). In our simulation, the effect of the actual checkpoint saving time is not considered, since all three schemes have the same overhead for saving the checkpoint.

We first compare the mean response time of the schemes by varying the value of λ_t, from 0.01 transactions/second to 0.4 transactions/second. Figure 2.a shows the mean response times of the schemes where $\frac{1}{\lambda_c}$ is 50 millisecond, N_d is 6 and δ_d is 2. It can be seen that scheme K outperforms the other schemes throughout the variation in λ_t. The relatively poor performance of scheme I is due to the fact that the initiations of new transactions are blocked during the checkpointing coordination. Since the waiting time for the transaction to be initiated is considered in the response time, the transactions under the scheme I experienced the longest response time in all cases. We can also notice that the performance difference becomes larger for scheme I as the transaction arrival rate increases. As the transaction arrival rate becomes higher, there can be more active transactions at the time of checkpointing initiation, which has to complete their execution to take a checkpoint, and hence, the checkpointing coordination time becomes longer, which in turn cause longer delay for the newly arrived transactions.

The performance difference between scheme K and scheme S is mainly due to the communication delay experienced for two-phase initiation in scheme S. Another factor affecting the performance difference between scheme K and scheme S is the restart during the checkpointing coordination in scheme S, because the response time of those transactions includes the time spent for two-phase initiation before its abort. Figure 2.b shows the number of restarts in scheme S for each site per checkpoint against the transaction arrival rate. Since the number of restarts increase according to the the transaction arrival rate, the performance difference between scheme K and scheme S widens slightly, as the transaction arrival rate increases.

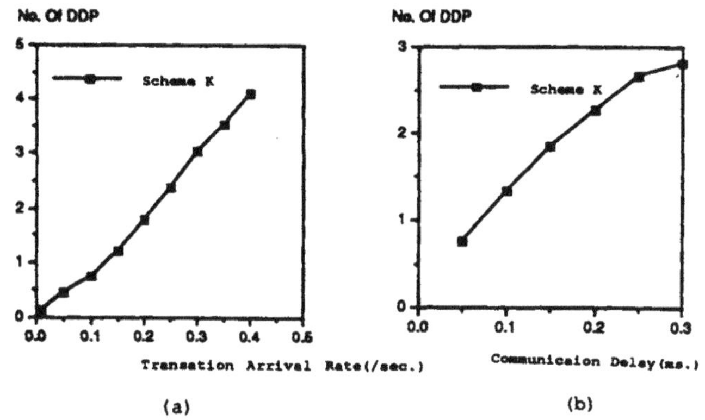

Figure 4: Number Of Deviated Data Pages Vs. Transaction Arrival Rate and Communication Delay

In Figure 3.a the response time is compared with different communication delay time, when λ_t is 0.1 transactions/second, N_d is 6 and δ_d is 2. Communication delay affects the response time of the transaction because of the two-phase commit, which is common for all three scheme, hence, the increase in communication delay causes the longer response time. In scheme S, the communication delay also affects the time for two-phase initiation, and hence, the performance difference between scheme K and scheme S become larger as the communication delay increases. Moreover, as the communication delay increases, the possibility that subtransaction initiation requests sent by the global transactions arrive at the remote sites after their checkpointings is increased. This increase in the number of transaction restarts per checkpoint at each site can be seen in Figure 3.b. This steep increase in the transaction restarts explains the rapidly widening gap between scheme K and scheme S in Figure 3.a.

From the simulation results, our scheme is found to outperform the other schemes in terms of response time, and the performance difference becomes larger as the transaction arrival rate and the communication delay increases. Such performance difference exists mainly because our scheme never blocks/aborts the transactions and does not requires the two-phase initiation to achieve a consistent checkpoint, thus providing a non-intrusive checkpointing.

Another factors to be considered for performance of the system is the storage overhead and the number of messages exchanged during the checkpointing. Since our checkpointing coordination requires one more phase compared with the scheme S, extra space and messages are required during that phase. To validate our scheme, we also count the average number of deviated data pages maintained for phase III of our scheme throughout the simulation. Figure 4.a shows the number of deviated data pages per each site and each checkpointing against the transaction arrival rate, and Figure 4.b shows the same performance indices against the communication delay. As shown in both figures, the space overhead is not that severe in our simulation environment. Moreover, the number of messages required for phase III of our checkpointing process is $2*N$, where N is the number of sites in the system, and hence the total number of messages exchanged during our checkpointing process is still $O(N)$.

6 CONCLUSIONS

In this paper, we presented a checkpointing scheme for media failure in a distributed database system with timestamp ordering concurrency control, which can be executed concurrently with normal transaction processing, that is, no transactions are aborted or no transaction initiations are delayed due to the checkpointing process. Our scheme always produces a globally consistent checkpoint, so that it can be used for recovery from media failures, where all sites are forced to start from the consistent checkpoints.

Our scheme identifies, in three phases, completion of the transactions active at the time of checkpointing initiation and the transactions on which the active transactions depend, and hence the checkpoints can be safely taken including only the effects of those transactions. For this, the transactions executing during the checkpointing period are provided with a deviated database area, so that each update of newly initiated transactions, after the initiation of checkpointing, are saved separately and only the updates of necessary transactions can be appropriately included in the checkpoint. The overhead involved in providing this service is some space requirement to retain each value of a data item updated by the active transactions, during the first two phases of the checkpointing scheme. As shown in simulation results, the space required in our scheme during the first phase of the checkpointing coordination is almost equal to the scheme proposed in [11]. Moreover, the maximum difference in space required by our scheme over [11] during the second phase and third phase is not great.

In summary, our scheme does not impose any restriction in initiating subtransactions through a two-phase initiation mechanism, which is required for the scheme in [11]. The global transaction in our scheme is not forced to send the subtransactions to the sites at the start of the transactions, but the scheme in [11] requires that the global transactions send the subtransactions at the beginning of its execution.

References

[1] Verhofstad, J.S.M., "Recovery Techniques for Database Systems," *ACM Computing Surveys* Vol.10, No.2, pp. 167–195, June 1978.

[2] Haerder, T. and Reuter, A., "Principles of Transaction-Oriented Database Recovery," *ACM Computing Surveys*, Vol.15 No.4, pp. 287–317, December 1983.

[3] Dadam, P. and Schlageter, G., "Reconstruction of Consistent Global States in Distributed Databases," *Information Processing, North-Holland Publishing Company, Amsterdam*, pp. 191–201, 1980.

[4] Dadam, P. and Schlageter, G., "Recovery In Distributed Databases Basaed On Non-synchronized Local Checkpoints," *Information Processing, North-Holland Publishing Company, Amsterdam*, pp. 457–462, 1980.

[5] McDermid, J., "Checkpointing and Error Recovery in Distributed Systems," *in Proceedings of the 2nd International Conference on Distributed Computing Systems*, pp. 271–282, April 1981.

[6] Kuss, H., "On Totally Ordering Checkpoints in Distributed Databases," *in Proceedings of the ACM SIGMOD*, pp. 293–302, 1982.

[7] Jouve, M., "Reliability Aspects in a Distributed Database Management System," *in Proceedings of AICA*, pp. 199–209, 1977.

[8] Moss, J., "Checkpoint and Restart in Distributed Transaction Systems," *in Proceedings of the 3rd Symposium on Reliability in Distributed Software and Database Systems*, pp. 85–89, 1983.

[9] Attar, R., Bernstein, P., and Goodman, N., "Site Initialization, Recovery, and Backup in a Distributed Database System," *IEEE Transactions on Software Engineering*, Vol.SE-10, No.6, pp. 625–650, November. 1984.

[10] Fischer, M., Griffeth, N., and Lynch, N., "Global States of a Distributed System," *IEEE Transactions on Software Engineering*, Vol. SE-8, No.3, pp. 198–202, May. 1982.

[11] Son, S. and Agrawala, A., "Distributed Checkpointing for Globally Consistent States of Databases," *IEEE Transactions on Software Engineering*, Vol.15, No.10, pp. 1157–1167, October. 1989.

[12] Lim, J. and Moon, S., "A Checkpointing Scheme for Heterogeneous Distributed Database Systems," *in proceedings of the 11th International Conference on Distributed Computing Systems*, pp. 608–615, May 1991.

[13] Son, S. and Agrawala, A., "A Non-Intrusive Checkpointing Scheme in Distributed Database Systems," *in Proceedings of the 15th International Symposium on Fault Tolerant Computing*, pp. 99–104, 1985.

[14] Pilarski, S. and Kameda, T., "A Novel Checkpointing Scheme for Distributed Database Systems," *in ACM Proceedings of the 9th Principles of Database Systems*, pp. 368–378, 1990.

[15] Gray, J., "Notes on data base operating systems. in: Operating systems," *Lecture Notes in Computer Science 60*, pp. 393–481, 1978.

[16] Bernstein, P., Goodman, N., and Hadzilacos, V., "Recovery Algorithms For Database Systems," *Information Processing, North-Holland Publishing Company, Amsterdam*, 1983.

[17] Eswaran, K., "The Notion of Consistency and Predicate Locks in a Database System," *Communications of the ACM*, pp. 624–633, November 1976.

[18] Lamport, L., "Time, Clocks and the Ordering of Events in a Distributed System," *Communications of the ACM 21(7)*, pp. 558–565, July 1978.

A Token-Based Synchronization Scheme using Epsilon-Serializability and Its Performance for Real-Time Distributed Database Systems

Sang H. Son and Spiros Kouloumbis

Computer Science Department
University of Virginia
Charlottesville, VA 22903, USA

ABSTRACT

Schedulers for real-time distributed replicated databases must satisfy timing constraints of transactions and preserve data consistency. In this paper, we present a replication control algorithm, which integrates real-time scheduling and replication control. The algorithm adopts a token-based scheme for replication control and attempts to incorporate the urgency of real-time transactions into the conflict resolution policies. The algorithm employs epsilon-serializability, new correctness criterion which is less stringent than conventional one-copy-serializability. The performance of the algorithm is evaluated using a simulation environment.

1. Introduction

In real-time distributed database systems, transactions must be scheduled to meet the *timing constraints* and to ensure *data consistency* [Son90]. Real-time task scheduling can be used to enforce timing constraints, while concurrency control is employed to maintain data consistency. Unfortunately, the integration of the two mechanisms is non trivial because of the trade-offs involved. Serializability may be too strong as a correctness criterion for concurrency control in database systems with timing constraints, for serializability limits concurrency. As a consequence, data consistency might be compromised to satisfy timing constraints.

In real-time scheduling, tasks are assumed to be independent, and the time spent synchronizing their access to shared data is assumed to be negligible compared with execution time. Knowledge of resource and data requirements of tasks is also assumed to be available in advance.

In replication control methods, on the other hand, the objective is to provide a high degree of concurrency and thus faster average response time without violating data consistency [Son87]. Two different policies can be employed in order to synchronize concurrent data access of transactions: *blocking* and *aborting*. However, blocking may cause priority inversion in which a high priority transaction is blocked by lower priority transactions. Aborting lower priority transactions wastes the work done by them. Thus, both policies have negative effects on time-critical scheduling.

Conventional replication control algorithms are synchronous, in the sense that they require the atomic updating of some number of copies. This leads to reduced system availability and decreased throughput as the size of the system increases. On the other hand, asynchronous replication control methods that would allow more transactions to meet their deadlines suffer from a basic problem: the system enters an inconsistent state in which replicated copies may not share the same value. Standard correctness criteria such as the *1-copy serializability* (1SR) [Ber87] are thus hard to attain with asynchronous consistency control.

A less stringent, general-purpose consistency criterion is necessary. The new criterion should allow more real-time transactions to satisfy their timing constraints by temporarily sacrificing database consistency to some small degree. *Epsilon-serializability* (ESR) is such a correctness criterion, offering the possibility of maintaining mutual consistency of replicated data asynchronously [Pu91]. Inconsistent data may be seen by certain query transactions, but data will eventually converge to a consistent (1SR) state. Additionally, the degree of inconsistency can be controlled within a specified threshold.

The goal of our work is to design a replication control algorithm that supports transactions to meet their deadlines and at the same time maintains data consistency in the absence of any *a priori* information. Our algorithm is based on a token-based synchronization scheme for replicated data. Real-time scheduling features are developed on top of this platform and epsilon-serializability is employed as the correctness criterion.

2. Transactions and Tokens

The smallest unit of data accessible to the user is called *data object*. A data object is an abstraction that does not correspond directly to a real database item. In distributed database systems with replicated data objects,

This work was supported in part by ONR, DOE, and IBM.

a logical data object is represented by a set of one or more replicated physical data objects.A *transaction* is a sequence of operations that takes the database from a consistent state to another consistent state. Two types of transactions are allowed in our environment: *query* transactions and *update* transactions. Query transactions consist only of read operations that access data objects and return their values to the user. Update transactions consist of both read and write operations.

Transactions arriving at the system are assumed to be non-periodic. A globally *unique timestamp* is generated for each transaction [Lam78]. Each time a transaction is aborted and resubmitted, a new timestamp value is assigned to it. If a transaction T_1 has a smaller timestamp than another transaction T_2, we say that T_1 is the *older* transaction and T_2 is the *younger* one.

A *token* designates a read-write copy. Each logical data object has a predetermined number of tokens, and each token copy is the latest version of the data object. The site which has a token-copy of a logical data object is called a *token site*, with respect to the logical data object. In order to control the access to data objects, the system uses timestamps. When a write operation is successfully performed and the transaction is committed, a new version is created which replaces the previous version of the token copy.

When a transaction performs a write operation to a physical data object, there are two values that are associated with the data object: the *after-value* (the new version) and the *before-value* (the old version). Because the before-value is available during the transaction processing, it is natural to ask if concurrency can be improved by giving out this value [Bay80].

Let T_1 be the transaction which already issued an access request, and T_2 cause the conflict. For each token copy of X, conflicts are resolved as the following [Son89]:

(1) RW conflict: If T_2 is younger than T_1, then it waits for the termination of T_1. If T_2 is older than T_1, then it reads before-value of X.

(2) WR conflict: If T_2 is younger than T_1, then its write request is granted with the condition that T_2 cannot commit before the termination of T_1. If T_2 is older than T_1, then T_2 is rejected.

(3) WW conflict: If T_2 is younger than T_1, then it waits for the termination of T_1. If T_2 is older than T_1, then T_2 is rejected.

The coordinator of an update transaction maintains the *before-list* (BL), a list of transactions which read the before-value of any data object in its write set, and the *after-list* (AL), a list of transactions which write the after-value of any data object in its read set. The BL and AL are used during the commitment phase of every update transaction.

When a transaction T_2 reads the before-value of a data object locked by T_1, the token-site which gives the before-value, conveys the identifier of T_2 to the coordinator of T_1. Hence, the identifier of T_2 is inserted in the before-list of T_1, which stores all the transactions that read the before-values of any data object in T_1's write-set. The transaction manager at the read-only site of T_2 also conveys the identifier of T_1 to the coordinator of T_2. Actually, the identifier of T_1 is inserted in the after-list of T_2, which stores all the transactions that write the after-value of any data object in T_2's read-set.

When a transaction terminates (either commits or aborts), the coordinator of the terminating transaction must inform the coordinator of each transaction in its AL about the termination by sending Termination Messages (TM). On receiving a TM from the coordinator of a transaction in its BL, the coordinator of the active transaction removes the identifier of the terminating transaction (sender of the TM) from the BL. A transaction can commit only when its BL is empty. By this way, we prevent non-serializable execution sequences to occur.

Update transactions have their own *private workspace* where they initially apply their write operations. Update transactions commit by employing a two-phase protocol. In the first phase (*vote-phase*), an update transaction sends an update message to each token-site of every data object in its write-set. The transaction waits until it gets a response from all the token-sites for each data object. If all token-sites vote YES, then the transaction enters the second phase (*commit phase*). It sends the actual value of each data object to be written to the respective token-sites. Update messages to non token-sites can be scheduled after commitment. Therefore, a temporary and limited difference among object replicas is permitted; these replicas are required to converge to the standard 1SR consistency as soon as all the update messages arrive and are processed. An update transaction that executes its commit phase can never be aborted, even if it potentially conflicts with another transaction.

Query transactions fall into three different categories as far as the correctness of their response is concerned:

• *Required consistent queries*. Queries are specified as such when they are first submitted by the user, and they are always guaranteed to return consistent data;

• *Consistent queries*. Their final output is correct regardless of any requirement by the user;

• *Possibly inconsistent queries*. In case of such a

query, there exists a small possibility that returned values of a replicated data object might reflect an inconsistent state of the database.

3. Epsilon-Serializability

Epsilon-serializability (ESR) is a correctness criterion that enables asynchronous maintenance of mutual consistency of replicated data [Pu91]. A transaction with ESR as its correctness criterion is called an *epsilon-transaction* (ET). An ET is a query ET if it consists of only reads. An ET containing at least one write is an update ET. Query ETs may see an inconsistent data state produced by update ETs. The metric to control the level of inconsistency a query may return is called the *overlap*. It is defined as the set of all update ETs that are active and affecting data objects that the query seeks to access. If a query ET's overlap is empty, then the query is serializable.The overlap of an active query transaction Q can be used as an *upper bound of error* on the degree of inconsistency that Q may accumulate. Given that we are interested in how many update transactions overlap with Q more than which transactions those are, the term overlap, in its further usage, will reflect the cardinality of the set of update transactions that conflict with the query ET Q.

Among several replica control methods based on ESR, we have chosen the ordered updates approach [Pu91]. The ordered updates approach allows more concurrency than 1SR in two ways. First, query ETs can be processed in any order because they are allowed to see intermediate, inconsistent results. Second, update ETs may update different replicas of the same object asynchronously, but in the same order. In this way, update ETs produce results equivalent to a serial schedule; these results are therefore consistent.

There are two categories of transaction conflicts that we examine: conflicts between update transactions and conflicts between update and query transactions.

Conflicts between update transactions can be either *RW* conflicts or *WW* conflicts. Both types must be strictly resolved. No correctness criteria can be relaxed here, since execution of update transactions must remain 1SR in order for replicas of data objects to remain identical.

Conflicts between update and query transactions are of *RW* type. Each time a query conflicts with an update, we say that the query overlaps with this update, and the overlap counter is incremented by one. If the counter is still less than a specified upper bound, then both operation requests are processed normally, the conflict is ignored, and no transaction is aborted. Otherwise, RW conflict must be resolved by using the conventional 1SR correctness criteria of the accommodating algorithm.

The performance gains of the above conflict resolution policies are numerous. Update transactions are rarely blocked or aborted in favor of query transactions. They may be delayed on behalf of other update transactions in order to preserve internal database consistency. On the other hand, query transactions are almost never blocked provided that their overlap upper bound is not exceeded. Finally, update transactions attain the flexibility to write replicas in an asynchronous manner.

4. Real-Time Issues

In real-time databases, transactions are characterized by their timing constraints and their data and computation requirements. Timing constraints are expressed through the *release time* and the *deadline*. Computation requirements for transactions are unknown, and no run-time estimate is available for every transaction that enters the system. Our goal is to minimize the number of transactions that miss their deadlines.

The real-time scheduling part of our scheme has three components: a policy to determine which transactions are eligible for service, a policy for assigning priorities to transactions, and a policy for resolving conflicts between two transactions that want to lock the same data object. None of these policies needs any more information about transactions than the deadline and the name of the data object currently being accessed.

All transactions which are currently *not tardy* are eligible for service. Transactions that have already missed their deadlines are immediately aborted. When a transaction is accepted for service at the local site where it was originally submitted, it is assigned a priority according to its deadline. The transaction with the *earliest deadline* has the highest priority. This policy meshes efficiently with the "not tardy" eligibility policy adopted above, so that transactions that have already missed their deadlines are automatically screened out before any priority is assigned to them. *High priority* is the policy that is employed for resolving transaction conflicts. Transactions with the highest priorities are always favored. The favored transaction, i.e. the winner of the conflict, gets the resources that it needs to proceed. The loser relinquishes control of any resources that are needed by the winner. The loser transaction will either be aborted or blocked depending on the relative age of the two conflicting transactions and the special provisions made by the replication control scheme.

5. Replication Control Scheme

In this section, we present the token-based replication control scheme in detail, along with the embedded ESR correctness criteria and real-time constraints.

5.1 Controlling Inconsistency of Queries

Queries are only involved in RW/WR conflicts. When a query transaction is submitted to the system, the user may quantify it with the restriction "*required to be consistent.*" Such a characterization means that all possible future RW/WR conflicts between this query and update transactions will have to be resolved in a strict (1SR) way. In other words, *consistent queries* (*CQ*s) are treated in the same fashion as update transactions. Values returned by *CQ*s are always correct, reflecting the up-to-date state of the respective data objects.

If no consistency constraints are specified explicitly by the user on a submitted query, then the *ESR correctness criterion* is employed to maintain the query's consistency. The overlap upper bound is computed, and an overlap counter is initialized to zero. Each time the query conflicts with an update transaction over the same data object and the counter is less than the overlap upper bound, the conflict is ignored, the counter is incremented, the query reads the value of the data object in question and proceeds to read the next object. When the overlap counter is found to be equal to the upper bound, current and all subsequent conflicts must be resolved in a strict manner, so that no more inconsistency will be accumulated on the query.

When a query transaction eventually commits, the user is able to determine the degree of correctness of the data values returned. If the query was qualified as a *CQ*, then the user can be confident that the values returned are consistent. For regular query transactions, the private overlap counter is checked. If the counter is still zero, this means that no conflict has occurred throughout the entire execution of the query and the results must again be perfectly accurate. Such a query falls into the *CQ* class. An overlap counter greater than zero indicates that a certain number of conflicts with update transactions remained unresolved; the query had seen some possibly inconsistent states, and might yield some inaccurate data. This last type of query falls into the "*possibly inconsistent*" queries class.

Since arbitrary queries may produce results beyond allowed inconsistency even within its overlap limit, it is important to restrict ET queries to have certain properties that permit tight inconsistency bounds. A first attempt in this approach is proposed in [Ram91]. It is beyond the scope of this paper to deal with such strategies. In the remainder of the paper, we assume that inconsistency bounds can be enforced by the system if necessary.

5.2 Conflict Resolution

Mechanisms for conflict resolution between update transactions comprise the core of our scheme. Query transactions need not be considered separately because queries that are forced to resolve their RW conflicts with update transactions can be treated as update transactions.

We examine three separate categories of conflicts, and for each category we present a table of all possible conflicts between younger and older transactions, and between higher priority and lower priority transactions.

Before we get into the detailed discussion of conflict resolution in each case, we must clarify what we mean by "conditional abort." Let T_1 be an accepted and successfully processed transaction issuing a write request on data object X. Let T_2 be another transaction attempting to read or write X. In the case that T_1 has to be aborted (possibly for real-time priority reasons or to preserve database consistency), T_1's phase of commitment must first be checked. If T_1 is in the vote-phase, it can be aborted normally. All writes on T_1's private workspace will be discarded, and T_1 will be resubmitted, provided that it has not already missed its deadline. However, if T_1 is in the commit-phase and update messages have already been sent to token-sites, then T_1 cannot be aborted. Consequently, "conditional abort" refers to the action of aborting an update transaction T only in the case where T is still in the vote-phase. If T_1 and T_2 are in conflict and T_1 has entered the second phase of commitment, then T_2 must be aborted in order for the database to remain consistent.

(1) R - W Conflict.

Transaction T_2 requests to read a data object X for which transaction T_1 has already issued a write request.

If T_2 is younger than T_1, then the original token-based scheme (Section 2) requires that T_2 must wait for the termination of T_1 before it reads the value of X. In case T_2 has lower priority than the priority of T_1, this requirement does not contradict with the priority status and T_2 can wait for T_1 to terminate. On the other hand, if T_2 has higher priority than T_1, we cannot apply this rule and force T_2 to wait. Instead, T_2 must read the data object and proceed whereas T_1 has to be conditionally aborted in order for the consistency of data read by T_2 to be preserved.

If T_2 is older than T_1, then T_2 should be allowed to read the before-value of X and proceed. T_2 is then inserted in the before-list (BL) of T_1, and T_1 is inserted in the after list of T_2. According to the commitment criteria of the token-based scheme, T_1 has to wait for T_2 to terminate before it can commit. Such resolution is acceptable when T_2 has higher priority than T_1. However, in the case that T_2 has lower priority than T_1, we conditionally abort T_2 when T_1 requests to commit in order to maintain the consistency of data written by T_1.

(2) W - R Conflict.

Transaction T_2 requests to write data object X for which transaction T_1 has already issued a read request.

If T_2 is younger than T_1, then T_1 should be allowed to read the before-value of X and T_2 write an after-value of X. Moreover, T_1 is inserted in the BL of T_2, and T_2 is inserted in the AL of T_1. In this way, T_2 has to wait for the termination of T_1 before it can commit. In the case that T_2 has lower priority than T_1, there is no contradiction between its priority status and its obligation to be blocked. In the case that T_2 has a higher priority than T_1, T_1 is conditionally aborted when T_2 requests to commit.

If T_2 is older than T_1, then T_2 should be conditionally aborted and T_1 reads the correct, up-to-date value of X. Aborting T_2 is perfectly justified in the case T_2 has a lower priority. In the case that T_2 has a higher priority, aborting T_2 would violate the real-time constraints. Therefore, we let T_2 proceed and write a new value for X while T_1 is aborted, since it has seen a value of X that has already become obsolete.

(3) W - W Conflict.

Transaction T_2 requests to write data object X for which transaction T_1 has already issued a write request.

If T_2 is younger than T_1, then T_2 should wait for the termination of T_1 before it writes a new value for data object X. Such conflict resolution favors T_1 and is compatible with the situation where T_2 has lower priority than T_1. However, when T_2 has a higher priority, it is not required to wait for the lower priority transaction T_1. Hence, T_2 will proceed, and T_1 will be conditionally aborted in order for the database to remain internally consistent.

If T_2 is older than T_1, then T_2 should be aborted. Note that we are interested only in the most recent value of X, i.e. the value written by the younger T_1 transaction. In the case that T_2 has a lower priority, the above resolution is acceptable, since the higher priority T_1 is favored to proceed. On the contrary, when T_2 has the higher priority, T_2 must be allowed to write its own new value of X, and T_1 must be conditionally aborted for the database to remain consistent with respect to the data object X.

5.3. Transaction Commit

The coordinator of a transaction decides to commit when the following conditions are satisfied:

- The transaction must not have missed its deadline;
- All the token-sites of each data object in the write-set of the transaction have precommitted (this only applies to update transactions);
- There is no active transaction that has seen before-value of any data object in the transaction's write-set. In other words, the *before-list* of the transaction must be empty (this only applies to update transactions).

6. Performance Results

In this section we compare the above real-time replication control scheme (RTS) with the respective conventional non real-time scheme (NRTS) on which our algorithm is based. We present a number of performance experiments for the two approaches under various assumptions about the transaction load, the percentage of update transactions, and the database size.

A real-time distributed database prototyping environment was used to build the simulation program [Son92b]. The environment provides the user with multiple threads of execution and guarantees the consistency of concurrently executing processes. Several requests can be submitted at the same time, and many read/write operations take place simultaneously at different sites.

The performance metric employed is the percentage of transactions that missed their deadlines (% missed) [Abb92] in the total number of transactions that were submitted to the system during the simulation period.

Certain parameters that determine system configuration and transaction characteristics remain fixed throughout the experiments: the database size (1000 data objects), the transaction size (12 data objects), the computation cost per update (8 msec), the I/O cost (20 msec), the percentage of operations that are updates in each transaction (40%), the abort cost for each transaction (19 msec), and the overlap factor (0.03, i.e. 3% of the queries return possibly incorrect data). These values are not meant to model a specific distributed database application, but were chosen as reasonable values within a wide range of possible values. In particular, we want transactions to access a relatively large fraction of the database (1.2%) so that conflicts occur more frequently.

Parameters used as independent variables in one-variable functions describing the % missed deadlines performance metric are the mean inter-arrival time of transactions (varying between 10msec and 80msec), the database size (varying from 200 to 1,000 data objects), and the percentage of read-only transactions submitted to the system (varying from 10% up to 90%). We assume that the database is fully replicated at all sites. A standard, modulo-based formula is used to assign token-sites to a data object.

6.1. Transaction Inter-arrival Time

In this experiment we vary the inter-arrival time of transactions from 10msec (for a heavily loaded system), to 80msec (for a non saturated system state). The database has a size of 1,000 data objects and 40% of the transactions submitted to the system are read only.

Figures 1 and 2 show that curves start from a high percentage of missed deadlines and descend until a minimum percentage is reached at the vicinity of 80msec. When the inter-arrival time is 10msec, the system is overloaded by a huge number of transactions striving to access a limited number of data objects (hot spots). Consequently, the number of conflicts becomes so large that transactions will be blocked and eventually miss their deadlines. As the inter-arrival time increases, the number of active transactions per second in the system decreases. Fewer transactions conflict with each other and need to be blocked and, as the graphs show, the vast majority of the transactions meet their deadlines.

RTS performs better than NRTS in all cases. When we have a small number of token-sites (i.e. 1 token-site out of 5 sites, or 3 token-sites out of 10 sites), the RTS and the NRTS curves are relatively close to each other. The greater the number of token-sites becomes, the further the respective RTS and NRTS curves veer away from each other. Finally, when all sites are token-sites for each data object, we observe the maximum distance between the curves for the "% missed deadlines" of the two schemes.

The results shown in Figures 1 and 2 clearly favor RTS. This was expected, since in the majority of the cases RTS schedules the most urgent transactions first, while NRTS is not at all sensitive to how close a transaction is to missing its deadline. The difference in performance of the two algorithms becomes even greater when the number of token-sites increases. A large number of token-sites means that each update transaction T must request consent for commitment from a large number of sites. Therefore, T must remain pending for a longer period of time, and consequently T will be exposed to more conflicts with other transactions. The increased number of conflicts that must be resolved, combined with the fact that conventional NRTS does not incorporate any intelligent real-time conflict resolution policy, makes the inferiority of NRTS even more apparent.

6.2. Read Only Transactions

We vary the percentage of read-only transactions submitted to the system from 10%, where the majority of the transactions are updates, to 90%, in which case the system behaves almost like a static database, where very few values of data objects change. We assume an average inter-arrival time of 30msec, and a database size of 1,000 data objects.

Figures 3 and 4 show that both RTS and NRTS behave similarly. The respective "% missed deadlines" curves start from a very high missed-deadline percentage, in the neighborhood of 10% (which is reasonable given that 90% of the transactions are update ones) and descend very steeply as the percentage of read only transactions increases. In the vicinity of 90%, almost all transactions are queries, very few conflicts occur, and the two approaches perform identically with each other.

When the percentage of read only transactions is near 10%, then the conflict rate between update transactions is very high, and RTS clearly exhibits lower miss rates than NRTS. When the percentage of read only transactions is 10%, the whole burden of scheduling is shifted onto the conflicting-updates resolution policy. NRTS allows time-critical updates to be aborted and restarted in order for less critical transactions to proceed, provided that the database remains consistent. On the contrary, RTS adopts the time criticality of a transaction as the first criterion for resolving conflicts with other transactions: less critical transactions are blocked or even aborted whenever necessary in order for transactions closer to their deadlines to proceed freely. An increased number of token-sites makes the difference in performance even greater for the same reasons as mentioned in the previous section.

The smaller the percentage of read-only transactions becomes, the fewer conflicts occur and the less important role the conflict resolution mechanism plays. Therefore, the two approaches behave almost identically near the 90% point.

6.3. Database Size

We assume an average inter-arrival time of 30msec, and 40% read only transactions. We vary the database size from 200 data objects to 1,000 data objects. Figures 5 and 6 show that RTS performs much better than NRTS. The distance between the curves is great throughout the spectrum of possible database sizes. When the database size is very small, in the vicinity of 200 data objects, the possibility that two transactions might conflict is very high given that the transaction size remains constant at 12 data objects. As a result, more conflicts between update transactions will have to be resolved. More conflicts means that more sophisticated real-time scheduling is necessary to meet the maximum possible number of deadlines. Moreover, a small-size database causes more queries to conflict with pending updates. In such case, ESR comes into play; queries in RTS are allowed to overlap freely with a limited number of updates, and neither of them need to be blocked or aborted as the strict 1SR criteria would require in NRTS. Controlled query inconsistency is a feature that works for the benefit of RTS and leads to further decrease of the missed deadlines percentage.

7. Concluding Remarks

In this paper we have presented a synchronization scheme for real-time distributed database systems. The algorithm is based on a *token-based approach*, in which two additional components are built. The first is a set of *real-time constraints* that each transaction has to meet. A separate priority scheme is employed to reflect the demand of a transaction to finish before its deadline. The second component is the ESR correctness criterion with which query transactions have to comply. Instead of applying 1SR to all transactions, 1SR is applied only to updates, and queries are left free to be interleaved with updates in a more flexible way.

By relaxing the consistency criteria for query transactions, queries and updates hardly ever have to abort or block each other due to conflicts between them. As an immediate consequence of this, more transactions may terminate successfully before their deadlines expire. Additionally, the ESR further improves performance; updating the different replicas of the same data object is done asynchronously, but in the same order. Thus, logical write operations become disjoint from the corresponding physical write operations, and update transactions are free to proceed to the next step of their execution or even to commit. Internal database consistency is preserved strictly. Data returned by certain queries are allowed to exhibit limited inconsistency, under user control.

Another advantage of our scheme lies in the fact that there is very little information the user has to provide to achieve efficient system operation. No *a priori* knowledge of the kind or the number of the data objects that are included in the read-set or the write-set of a transaction is needed. The only information required is the kind of each submitted transaction (query or update). Moreover, no execution time estimate is required for each submitted transaction. It would be extremely difficult to compute a run-time estimate, especially in the distributed environments for which our scheme is designed.

There is a price to pay for relaxing correctness criteria and meeting more deadlines. Although the user can control the maximum permissible inconsistency of queries, one cannot know exactly which one transaction out of the set of all possibly inconsistent queries will return incorrect data, unless a tight inconsistency bound is provided. Note that an overlap counter greater than zero does not necessarily mean that the respective query transaction is inconsistent. It simply indicates that certain RW/WR conflicts were passed unresolved, and inconsistency might be present among the data values returned.

REFERENCES

[Abb92] R.Abbott, and H.Garcia-Molina, "Scheduling Real-time Transactions: a Performance Evaluation," ACM Trans. on Database Systems, vol. 17, no. 3, pp. 513-560, Sept. 1992

[Bay80] R. Bayer, H. Heller, and A. Reiser, "Parallelism and Recovery in Database Systems," ACM Trans. Database Syst. 5, 2, June 1980.

[Ber87] P.A.Bernstein, V.Hadzilacos, and N.Goodman, "Concurrency Control and Recovery in Database Systems," Addison-Wesley Publishing,,1987.

[Lam78] L.Lamport, "Time, Clocks, and the Ordering of Events in a Distributed System," Comm. ACM, vol. 21, no. 7, pp. 558 - 565, July 1978.

[Pu91] C.Pu, and A.Leff, "Replica Control in Distributed Systems: An Asynchronous Approach," ACM SIGMOD Conference, May 1991.

[Ram91] K. Ramamritham and C. Pu, "A Formal Characterization of Epsilon Serializability," Tech. Rep. 91-91, Dept. of Computer Science, Univ. of Massachusetts, Dec. 1991.

[Son87] S.H.Son, "Synchronization of Replicated Data in Distributed Systems," Information Systems, vol. 12, no. 2, pp. 191 - 202, 1987.

[Son89] S.H.Son, "A Resilient Replication Method in Distributed Database Systems," Proceedings of IEEE INFOCOM '89, Ottawa, Canada, April 1989.

[Son90] S.H.Son, "Real-Time Database Systems: A New Challenge," Data Engineering, vol. 13, no. 4, Special Issue on Future Directions on Database Research, December 1990.

[Son92] S.H.Son, J. Lee, and Y. LIn, "Hybrid Protocols using Dynamic Adjustment of Serialization Order for Real-Time Concurrency Control," Journal of Real-Time Systems, vol. 4, pp. 269-276, Sept. 1992.

[Son92b] S.H.Son, "An Environment for Integrated Development and Evaluation of Real-Time Distributed Database Systems," Journal of Systems Integration, vol. 2, no. 1, pp. 67-90, February 1992.

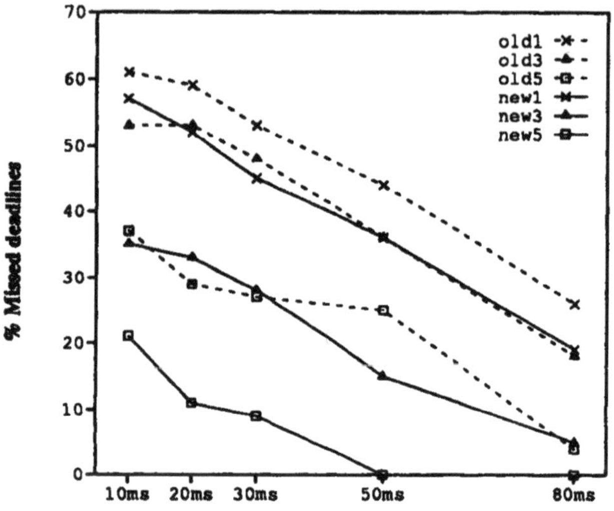

Figure 1: SITES=5, Interarrival time.

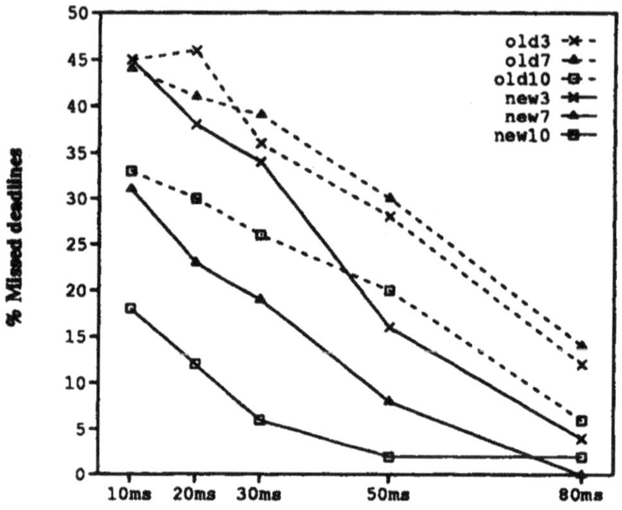

Figure 2: SITES=10, Interarrival time.

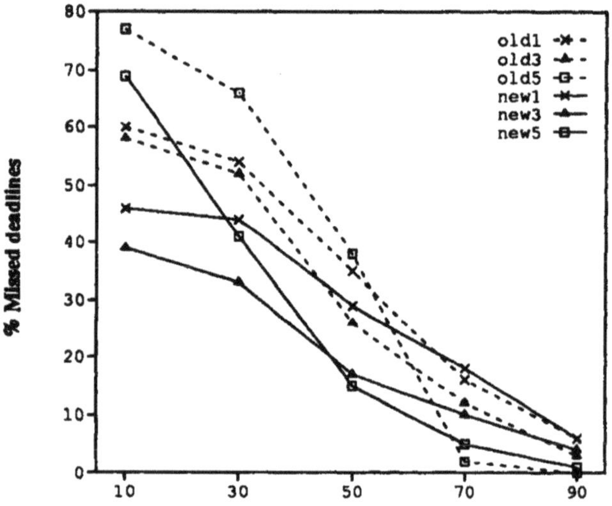

Figure 3: SITES=5, Read only trx.

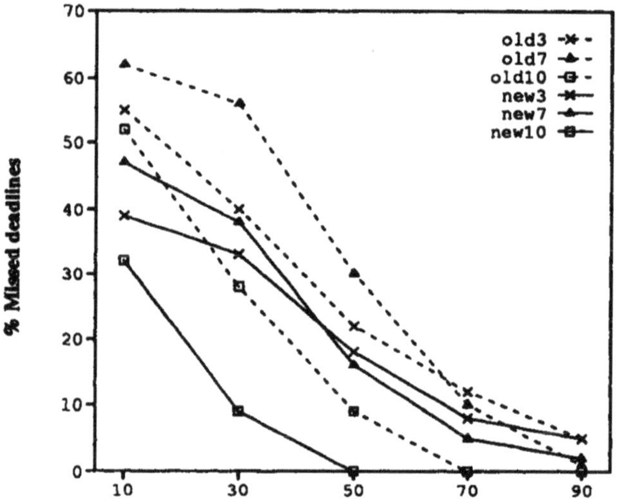

Figure 4: SITES=10, Read only trx.

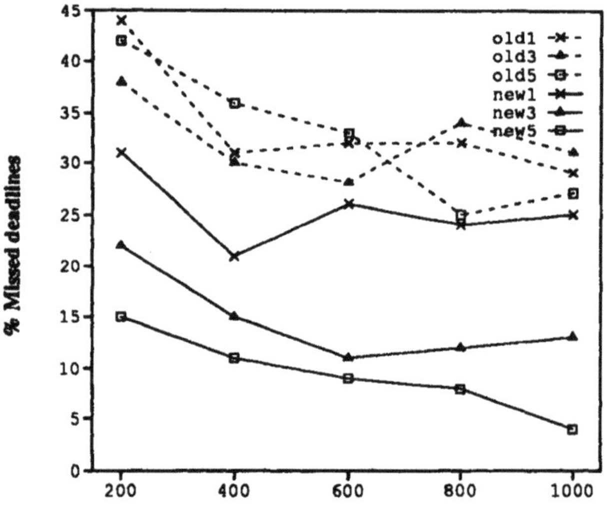

Figure 5: SITES=5, Database size.

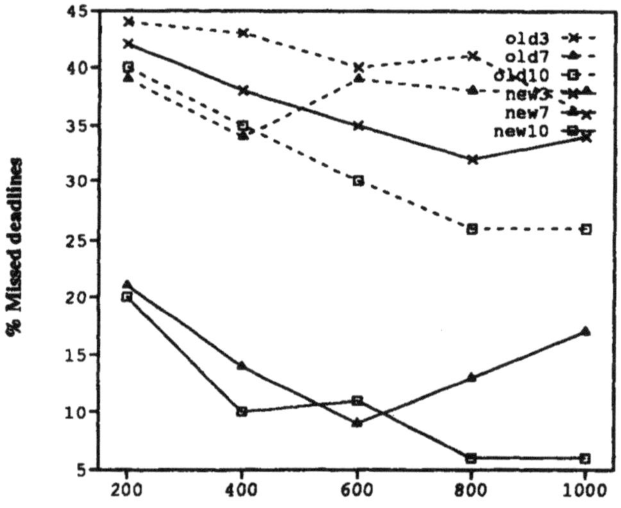

Figure 6: SITES=10, Database size.

QUERY PROCESSING (I)

QUERY PROCESSING TECHNIQUES IN THE TEAM-ORIENTED DATABASE QUERY LANGUAGE

Jorng-Tzong Horng*, Gwo-Dong Chen**, Baw-Jhiune Liu**

*Department of Computer Science & Information Engineering, National Taiwan University, Taipei, Taiwan
**Department of Electrical Engineering, National Central University, Chungli, Taiwan
bjliu@ncuee.ncu.edu.tw

ABSTRACT

In this paper, we introduce the concept "team" and incorporate the team query into data language SQL. Existing relational query languages use tuple variables of tables to specify required data. Queries that are expressed by these languages are used to get all the data which satisfy the specified conditions. While a team variable represents a subset of a table, a team query is to retrieve all the teams that meet certain constraints.

We introduce team qualifications and discuss their implementations. The search space of a team query may be very large. Therefore, instead of using conventional breadth-first search method, we adopt a depth-first search method for query processing. Thus, users can always get results, if one exists.

In decision support environments the selection of teams with extreme values like maximum or minimum is frequented needed. In some cases, finding such teams is NP-complete or NP-hard. Genetic algorithms are proposed and computational results are presented. We incorporate genetic algorithms in the query optimization algorithm. The approach makes it possible for a DBMS to respond to team queries in a predicate restricted amount of time.

1 INTRODUCTION

Relational database systems are being used in data processing community. Relational database systems (DBMSs) provide nonprocedural query languages such as SQL[7, 8, 20] and set-at-a-time operators. Thus, the application programmers or users need only specify what he wants without regarding how the results are retrieved. This greatly reduce application development time.

However, relational query languages can not be used to express *teams* that meet certain team constraints. Let us take a simple team example, a baseball team coach is looking for a team of nine players from the database of a baseball team to play a baseball game. The constraints of this team are (1) there are nine players in each team, (2) there should be exactly one player for each defense position. The result of this query may have many teams. This query is different from the queries like "get all the players who can play the pitcher position." Each player in the result of the query meets the constraint "the player who can play the pitcher position." An application programmer or user needs to write procedural programs to solve such team problems.

Obviously, a team query is different from a query of relational database query languages such as SQL. SQL finds a set of individuals and all individuals in the set satisfy the condition which is specified in the query. An element of a set meets all the constraints, while an element of a team may only meet some constraint(s) of the team constraints.

A SQL query and a team query have two different aspects. The first difference is the number of results. The result of a SQL query is a set of tuples, if one exists. However, the result of a team query is a set of teams. The second difference is in the team constraints. A SQL query does not specify the set of team constraints while a team query must specify the set of team constraints. Conditions that are used in SQL are not enough to express team criteria.

Teams are common and well understood in modern society. For example, in a company, a manager needs to organize teams to perform certain jobs; in an exercise, a coach has to assign a team of players to play games; a foreign needs to assign a team to negotiate with other countries; and so on. Teams exist everywhere in the real-world. However, so far we did not find any relational database languages that address the team query in the research literature. We extend SQL to be able to express and process teams that meet certain constraints. Hence, users with knowledge of SQL can easily take advantage of the team retrieval capabilities without learning a new language.

Team queries have two categories: (1) to select an optimal team, (2) to select all possible teams. The selection of a project team with minimal cost is of the first category. Queries of this category wish to find a team which has a maximum or minimum value of a given expression such as the sum of the salaries in the whole prospective teams. The selection of all possible teams of nine players from a baseball team is of the second category.

In some cases, finding teams with extreme values like minimum or maximum is NP-complete or NP-hard. It may take a very long time to find an optimum solution. Genetic algorithms discussed in this paper are designed to find near-optimal solutions. We found they performed well, both on the computational effort and the quality of the solutions via a variety of test problems.

The processing of team queries is quite different from that of the conventional database queries. Conventional database query processing uses a tuple-by-tuple evaluation strategy, while team query processing uses a set-by-set evaluation strategy. The search space of a team query is all subsets of the set of tuples of a relation. The search space of a team query may be large. Therefore, instead of using conventional breadth-first search method, we adopt a depth-first search method for query processing. Thus, users can always get results, if one exists.

1.1 Related Research

Sets and set manipulation occur naturally in many applications. Database query languages that attempt to incorporate sets and set operators have been defined in recent years by Abiteboul and Gramback[2], Kuper[17], Berri et al.[3, 4], Chen[6], and Gavish and Segev[10].

COL[2] is a logic-based language for complex objects. In addition to tuple and set constructs, the language also provides so called "data functions". LDL[3, 4] is an attempt to combine the benefits of logic programming with those of relational query languages. In LDL[3, 4], sets and set operators are introduced into this language. In HiLog[6], sets can be represented naturally by parameterized predicates. The work[10] addresses the problem of optimizing queries that involve set operations (set queries) in a distributed relational database system. A set query is defined to be any query that can be represented as a sequence of relational operations followed by set operations between one set of tuples and a group of sets of tuples.

Although, the above languages support sets and set manipulation, however, they did not identify the concepts of team.

Genetic algorithms[11, 12] are general purpose optimization algorithms (somewhat akin to simulated annealing in that sense). They were developed by Holland[12] to search irregular, poorly characterized spaces. The genetic algorithm does not necessarily find an optimal to any one problem, but does find good solutions to problems that are resistant to most other known techniques. Holland was inspired by the example of population genetics and used crossover rather than mutation as the primary genetic operator. Thus, genetic search proceeds over a number of generations, with each generation represented by a population of current chromosomes. "Survival of the fittest" provides the pressure for populations to develop increasingly fit individuals. Genetic algorithms have been successfully applied to various combinatorial optimization problems. Algorithms have been proposed for optimizing complex queries in the past[5, 14, 15, 16].

1.2 Overview of This Paper

This paper is organized as follows. In Section 2 the language is briefly described and a number of motivating examples are given. Section 3 defined basic and special team qualifications. In Section 4, we present the query processing techniques of basic and special team qualifications. Transformation rules for team qualifications and operations are stated in Section 5. Analysis of query processing techniques is presented in Section 6. The last section is the conclusion.

2 TEAM-ORIENTED QUERIES

In this section we first briefly describe the syntax of team-oriented queries and then present a number of motivating examples. For a detailed description of the language, one is referred to the work[13].

2.1 Query Specification in Team-Oriented Query Language

Let U = { $R_1, R_2, \ldots, R_p$} be the universal set of relations, and W = {$A_1, A_2, \ldots, A_n$} be the universal set of attributes. A team is a subset of the set of tuples over the specified attributes of a relation that satisfies a set of qualifications and a set of team qualifications. More formally, a team can be defined as a 4-tuple:

$$TEAM = (R, A', \Theta s, s\Theta s),$$

where $R \in U$, $A' \subseteq W$, Θs is a set of qualifications, and sΘs is a set of team qualifications. The set of tuples over the set of attributes A' of relation R constructs the domain of a team.

A qualification Θs is made up of a number of clauses of the form:

Attr **rel-op** const-value

where Attr ∈ W, rel-op is normally one of the operators {=, ≥, ≤, ≠, <, >}, and const-value is a constant value. Clauses can be arbitrarily connected by the Boolean operators AND, OR, and NOT to form a general qualification. A qualification here corresponds to a selection condition of the SELECT operation.

A team qualification sΘs is any qualification that involves set operations between two sets. A team qualification may be of the form :

tuple-set($Attr_1$, $Attr_2$, ..., $Attr_n$) **set-op** tuple-set($Attr_1$, $Attr_2$, ..., $Attr_n$), or

tuple-set($Attr_1$, $Attr_2$, ..., $Attr_n$) **set-op** set-tuple-const-value, or

aggregate-fun(tuple-set($Attr_1$, $Attr_2$, ..., $Attr_n$)) rel-opconst-value

where $Attr_1, Attr_2, \ldots, Attr_n \in W$, $n \geq 1$, tuple-set($Attr_1$, $Attr_2$, ..., $Attr_n$) is a set of tuples over the specified attributes $Attr_1$, $Attr_2$, ..., $Attr_n$, set-op is normally one of the set operators { ≡, ==, ⊂, ⊆, ⊃, ⊇}, set-tuple-const-value is a set of n-tuple constant values, and aggregate-fun is normally one of the aggregate functions {SUM, AVG, COUNT, MIN, MAX}. An n-tuple constant value is a tuple which is composed of n constant values. The semantics of the well-known set operations such as ⊂, ⊆, ⊃, ⊇, are the same in our definition. A bag is like a set except that its elements can be duplicate. In our definition, We particularly distinguish the difference between the definitions of the set equality (≡) and bag equality (==). Set A is equal to set B if they both have the same members. Bag A is equal to bag B if they both have the same members and the numbers of the same member in these two sets are equal.

2. 2 Example Team Queries

We present two queries to illustrate various features of the language. In the following queries, underlined attributes are keys.

Query 1. The query uses a Baseball Database with two relations, which are given below.

PLAYERS(<u>player</u>, year-of-birth, year-joined, batting-avg, team-name)

PLAYER-POSITION(<u>player</u>, <u>position</u>, #-of-times)

The relation PLAYERS gives the number, year-of-birth, year-joined, batting average, team-name of each player. The relation PLAYER-POSITION gives each player that plays certain positions. The #-of-times is the number of times of a position that a player had been played. Find a team of nine players and their corresponding positions that satisfies the following conditions.

(a). They were born after 1960 and joined before 1990.

(b). The number of a position which was played by a player must be greater than 50 times.

(c). One player plays only one position and one position is played by only one player.

(d). The nine players are composed of 3 players, 2 players, 2 players, and 2 players. They belong to teams Elephant, Dragon, Lion, and Tiger respectively.

(e). The total batting average of the team is greater than 0.28.

The team query can be expressed as follows:

```
SELECT <TP.player, TP.position> IN TEAM <PP.player,
          PP.position> TEAM-PLAYERS TP
FROM  PLAYERS P, PLAYER-POSITION PP
```

WHERE P.player = PP.player and P.year-of-birth > 1960 and P.year-joined < 1990 and PP.#-of-times > 50
and (SELECT position FROM TP) == { pitcher, catcher, 1st, 2nd, 3rd, short, left, center, right}
and (SELECT TP.player, COUNT(TP.position) FROM TP GROUP BY TP.player) ≡ {(*, 1)}
and (SELECT P.team-name, COUNT(P.player) FROM P, TP WHERE P.player=TP.player GROUP BY P.team-name) == {(Elephant, 3), (Dragon, 2), (Lion, 2), (Tiger, 2)}
and AVG (SELECT P.batting-avg FROM P, TP WHERE P.player=TP.player) > 0.28

Query 2. The query uses a Orchestra Database with six relations which are given below.

INSTRUMENT(<u>iname</u>, first-player)
MUSICIAN(<u>mname</u>, sex)
SYMPHONY(<u>sname</u>, time)
ORCHESTRA(<u>sname</u>, <u>iname</u>, <u>mname</u>)
TOUR(<u>city</u>, <u>sname</u>)
PLAYS(<u>mname</u>, <u>iname</u>, #-of-times)

The relation INSTRUMENT gives the name of the first player of each instrument. MUSICIAN contains information about players. The relation SYMPHONY gives the duration in minutes of each symphony. The relation ORCHESTRA gives the set of players that execute each instrument in each symphony. TOURS contains the set of symphony names to be played in each city. The relation PLAYS gives each player that plays certain instruments. The #-of-times is the number of times of an instrument that a player had been played. Now we want to find a group of ten players to play symphonies. It satisfies the following conditions.

(a). The ten players consist of 3 players for violin, 1 player for conductor, 2 players for cello, 2 players for vola, and 2 players for bass drum.
(b). Each player in the group must have been acted the first player of some instrument.
(c). The ten players are composed of 6 male musicians and 4 female musicians.
(d). The #-of-times of an instrument which was played by a musician must be greater than 300 times.
(e). Each player must have been played the symphony "Tchaikovsky" in the city New York.

The team query can be expressed as follows:

SELECT <OT.mname, OT.iname> IN TEAM <PL.mname, PL.iname> ORCH-TEAM OT
FROM INSTRUMENT IN, MUSICIAN MU, ORCHESTRA ORCH, TOUR, PLAYS PL
WHERE PL.mname = ORCH.mname and TOUR.sname = ORCH.sname and PL.#-of-times > 300 and TOUR.city = "New York" and TOUR.sname = "Tchaikovsky" and PL.mname = IN.first-player
and (SELECT iname, COUNT(mname) FROM OT GROUP BY iname) == { (conductor, 1), (violin, 3), (cello, 2), (viola, 2), (bass drum, 2)}
and (SELECT mname, COUNT(iname) FROM OT GROUP BY mname) ≡ {(*, 1)}
and (SELECT MU.sex, COUNT(MU.mname) FROM MU, OT WHERE OT.mname = MU.mname GROUP BY MU.sex) == {(F, 4), (M, 6)}

3. BASIC TEAM QUALIFICATIONS

In this section, we turn our attention to a collection of team qualifications. The team qualifications are usually divided into two groups. One group includes team qualifications from mathematical theory, which are applicable because each operand is defined to be a set of tuples. These team qualifications include BTQ1, BTQ2, BTQ3, and BTQ4. The other group consists of special team operations which are specifically defined for query optimization. These operations include STO1 and STO2, STO3, STO4, STO5, and STO6. Before starting our definition, we use the following notations:

(a) sf($\hat{t}$) = SELECT <attribute-list> FROM $\hat{t}$ {WHERE <search-condition>};
(b) sqlf($\hat{t}$, $t_1, \ldots, t_n$) = SELECT <attribute-list> FROM $\hat{t}$, $t_1, \ldots, t_n$ WHERE <search-condition>;
(c) sgf($\hat{t}$) = SELECT <attribute-list> FROM $\hat{t}$ WHERE <search-condition> GROUP BY<attribute-name>{,<attribute-name>};
(d) bsqlf(t) = SELECT <attribute-list> FROM t { WHERE <search-condition> };
(e) agf1($\hat{t}$, $t_1, \ldots, t_n$) = Aggregate-fun(sqlf($\hat{t}$, $t_1, \ldots, t_n$) or $\hat{t}$) IS MAXIMUM;
(f) agf2($\hat{t}$, $t_1, \ldots, t_n$) = Aggregate-fun(sqlf($\hat{t}$, $t_1, \ldots, t_n$)) IS MINIMUM;
(g) agf3($\hat{t}$, $t_1, \ldots, t_n$) = Aggregate-fun(sqlf($\hat{t}$, $t_1, \ldots, t_n$)) < constant-value
(h) constant-set = $\{c_1, \ldots, c_m\}$;
(i) tuple-constant-set = $\{(s_i, n_i), i=1, \ldots, p\}$.

Where $\hat{t}$ is a team name; t and t_i, $i=1, \ldots, n$, are general table names; s_i, $i=1, \ldots, p$ are instances of some attribute of a relation; n_i, $i=1, \ldots, p$ are positive integers. A <search-condition> is a boolean expression. A <attribute-list> is a list of attributes. Aggregate-fun is normally one of the aggregate functions {SUM, AVG, COUNT, MIN, MAX}. A constant-value is a constant value. A constant-set is a set of constant values. A tuple-constant-set is a set of 2-tuple constant values.

Basic Team Qualifications

(BTQ1) sf($\hat{t}$) ≡ constant-set or bsqlf(t)
(BTQ2) sf($\hat{t}$) == constant-set or bsqlf(t)
(BTQ3) sqlf($\hat{t}$, $t_1, \ldots, t_n$) θ constant-set or bsqlf(t), $\theta \in \{\equiv, ==, \subset, \subseteq, \supset, \supseteq\}$
(BTQ4) sgf($\hat{t}$) θ tuple-constant-set , $\theta \in \{\equiv, \geq\}$

Special Team Operations

(STO1) (constant-set or bsqlf(t)) **match** (constant-set or bsqlf(t))
(STO2) (constant-set or bsqlf(t)) **maxmatch$_A$** (constant-set or bsqlf(t))
(STO3) (bsqlf(t)) **mincover$_A$** (constant-set or bsqlf(t))
(STO4) (bsqlf(t)) **cover$_C$** (constant-set or bsqlf(t))
(STO5) (bsqlf(t)) **minpart$_A$** (constant-set or bsqlf(t))
(STO6) (bsqlf(t)) **part$_C$** (constant-set or bsqlf(t))

Aggregate Function

(AGF1) agf1($\hat{t}$, $t_1, \ldots, t_n$)
(AGF2) agf2($\hat{t}$, $t_1, \ldots, t_n$)
(AGF3) agf3($\hat{t}$, $t_1, \ldots, t_n$)

For more detailed description about basic team qualifications and special team operations, one is referred to the contents of[13].

4. QUERY PROCESSING

In this section we describe query processing techniques of each team qualification.

Two important things must be considered in processing a team query. One is the choice of a team candidate, and the other is the evaluation of team qualifications. In this paper, we focus on the former, that is , how to reduce the search space. In fact, many team candidates can be avoided generating in query processing. For example, consider the following team query :

SELECT <TEAM-SP.s#, TEAM-SP.p#> IN TEAM
<SP.s#, SP.p#> TEAM-SP
FROM SP
WHERE (SELECT s# FROM TEAM-SP) == {s1, s2, s3, s4}
and (SELECT p#, COUNT(s#) FROM TEAM-SP GROUP BY p#) ≡ {(*, 1)}

If the first team qualification is evaluated to **True**, then the set of tuples over s# in TEAM-SP must contain one s1, one s2, one s3, and one s4. If the set of tuples over s# contain other values then the team qualification will be evaluated to **False**. Thus we only have to consider the team candidates that contain one s1, one s2, one s3, and one s4 and ignore other candidates when we choose team candidates. The technique of choosing team candidates can greatly reduce the search space. In this case, the first team qualification plays an important role in generating team candidates. A team query is specified by giving a set of team qualifications. We choose the first team qualification in a sequence of team qualifications as a team generator (TG), and other team qualifications as team qualifications (TΘs). A team generator uses the information which is specified in the team qualification to generate team candidates. The team candidate is then evaluated by team qualifications. If the team candidate is evaluate to **True**, the team candidate becomes a team and is returned.

In Section 3, we introduce four basic team qualifications BTQ1, BTQ2, BTQ3, and BTQ4. Each can be used as a team generator. Different team generators use different algorithms to generate team candidates. We also define six special team operations for query optimization. In this section, we implement these algorithms.

4.1 The Algorithm for BTQ1 and BTQ2

(**BTQ1**) SELECT < Attrl > FROM T {<search condition>} ≡ constant-set

(**BTQ2**) SELECT < Attrl > FROM T {<search condition>} = = constant-set

Suppose team T is composed of a set of tuples over attribute Attrl and other attributes of R. Let constant-set ={ $c_1, c_2, ..., c_n$ } be the set of constant values. If BTQ1 or BTQ2 is used as a team generator, then the generator uses the following algorithm to generate team candidates. Some of these steps are valid for the BTQ1, some for the BTQ2, and some for both. The default is valid for both.

Algorithm 1

Step 1. PROJECT (R.Attrl, ...) Giving S /* Constructs the domain of a team. */
Step 2. SELECT (S.1 = c_i), i = 1, ..., n, Giving S* /* Selects those tuples over Attrl that are in the set *constant-set*. */
Step 3. Sort the tuples in S* on attribute Attrl.
Step 4a. (BTQ1) Select one tuple or more tuples for each distinct instance of the attribute Attrl in S* and give T. /* Generates a team candidate */
Step 4b. (BTQ2) Select certain tuples for each distinct instance of the attribute Attrl in S* and give T. /* Generates a team candidate */

Step 1 projects R over the specified attributes. This step is used to construct the domain of a team. Step 2 selects those tuples over the specified attribute that are in the given set. This step also excludes those tuples over the specified attribute that are not in the given set. The search space can be greatly reduced in this step. In Step 4b, owing to the operation is a bag equality, thus certain tuples for each distinct instance over the specified attribute are chosen according to the number of the value in the given set. In Step 4a, one tuple or more tuples for each distinct instance is/are chosen. A team candidate is generated in this step. The team candidateis then evaluated. If all team qualifications return True, T is returned and the algorithm terminated. Otherwise goto Step 4a or Step 4b depending on BTQ1 or BTQ2. The algorithm terminates when either a team is found, or no such team exists. If all teams are required to generate, then the process is repeated until all teams are generated.

4.2 The Algorithm for BTQ4

(**BTQ4**) (SELECT Attrl, COUNT (Attr2) FROM T GROUP BY Attrl) ≡ tuple-constant-set

Let tuple-constant-set = $\{(s_1, n_1), (s_2, n_2), ..., (s_p, n_p)\}$ be a set of 2-tuple constant values, where s_i, i = 1, ..., p are instances of some attribute of a relation, and $n_i > 0$, i = 1, ..., p. If BTQ4 is used as a team generator, then the generator uses the following algorithm to generate team candidates.

Algorithm 2

Step 1. PROJECT (R.Attrl, R.Attr2, ...) Giving S
Step 2. SELECT (S.1 = s_i), i = 1, ..., p Giving S*
Step 3. Sort the tuples in S* on attribute Attrl
Step 4. Select n_1 tuples for the instance s_1, n_2 tuples for the instance s_2, ..., n_p tuples for the instance s_p in S* and give T.

4.3 The Algorithm for BTQ3

(**BTQ3**) (SELECT Attr2 FROM R, T WHERE R.Attrl = T.Attrl) θ constant-set, where θ ∈ { ≡, ==, ⊃ }

The algorithm for BTQ3 is similar to that of BTQ1 and BTQ2.

4.4 The Algorithm for STO1 and STO2

The general form of the match and maxmatch operations is as follows:

(constant-set-1) **match** (constant-set-2),
(constant-set-1) **maxmatch**$_A$ (constant-set-2).

Let constant-set-1, constant-set-2, and W be three sets of tuples over attributes Attrl, Attr2, and A of relation R respectively. Let constant-set-1=$\{c_{11}, c_{12}, ..., c_{1n}\}$, constant-set-2 =$\{c_{21}, c_{22}, ..., c_{2n}\}$, and W=$\{w_1, ..., w_p\}$. The match and maxmatch team operations are implemented by the following algorithm.

Algorithm 3

Step 1a. (match) PROJECT(R.Attrl, R.Attr2) Giving S
Step 1b. (maxmatch) PROJECT(R.Attrl, R.Attr2, R.W) Giving S
Step 2. SELECT ((S.1=c_{1i}), (S.2=c_{2i})), i=1, 2,..., n. Giving T /* Selects those tuples of R that satisfy the Boolean condition. */
Step 3a. (match) Relation-to-Graph(T) Giving G(V1, V2, E)
Step 3b. (maxmatch) Relation-to-WeightGraph(T) Giving G(V1, V2, E)

Step 4a. (match) Applying bipartite graph matching algorithm Giving S'
Step 4b. (maxmatch) Applying maximum-weight bipartite graph matching algorithm Giving S'
Step 5. Set-to-relation(S') Giving T.

Relation-to-Graph is used to transform relation T with two attributes into a bipartite graph G, where V1={c_{11}, c_{12}, ..., c_{1n}} and V2={c_{21}, c_{22}, ..., c_{2n}}, and E={(c_{1i}, c_{2j}), ...}, $1 \le i, j \le n$, and (c_{1i}, c_{2j}) is a tuple over attributes Attr1 and Attr2. Similarly, Relation-to-WeightGraph transforms relation T with three attributes Attr1, Attr2, and A into a weighted bipartite graph G. A tuple <c_{1i}, c_{2j}, w_k>, $1 \le i, j \le n$, $1 \le k \le p$, over the attributes Attr1, Attr2, and A constructs an edge (c_{1i}, c_{2j}) which has a weight w_k. Step 4a applies a matching algorithm. Step 4b applies a maximum-weight matching algorithm. The result of this step is a set of ordered pairs. Step 5 transforms a set of ordered pairs into a relation.

4.5 The Algorithms for STO3 and STO4

The general form of the **mincover** and **cover** operations is as follows:

(bsqlf(t)) **mincover**$_A$ (constant-set or bsqlf(t))
(bsqlf(t)) **cover**$_C$ (constant-set or bsqlf(t))

The mincover$_A$ operation is to find teams with minimum total value of attribute *A*. It may take a very long time to find a team with minimum value. The cover$_C$ operation is to find feasible teams whose cost satisfies certain constraint *C*. These two operators can be modeled as set covering problems. We describe genetic algorithms to implement these operations.

Formally, let *E* be an *m* x *n* binary matrix, *w* an n-dimensional nonnegative vector, and *x* an n-dimensional binary vector, with *wx* the inner product of the two, and $\underline{1}$ an m-dimensional column vector of ones. Then the set covering problem[9] can be formulated as

minimize (over x) wx		(1)
subject to	$Ex \ge \underline{1}$	(2)
$x_i = 0, 1$	for $i = 1, ..., n$	(3)

Any x satisfying (2) and (3) is called a cover solution.

The genetic algorithm deals with a population of chromosomes, each of which can be decoded into a solution of the problem. For each chromosome in the population, a fitness function is calculated. Chromosomes are selected from the population to become parents, based on a fitness function. Then, reproduction occurs between pairs of chromosomes to produce the offspring. The newly created population becomes the next generation and the process is repeated.

The structure of a simple algorithm is as follows:

```
GENETIC ALGORITHM
procedure genetic algorithm
begin
  t = 0
  initialize P(t)
  evaluate P(t)
  while (not termination-condition) do
        begin
           t = t + 1
           select P(t) from P(t-1)
           recombine P(t)
           evaluate P(t)
        end
end
```

During iteration t, the genetic algorithm maintains a population P(t) of solutions x_1^t, ..., x_n^t (the population size n remains fixed). Each solution, x_i^t, is evaluated by computing f(x_i^t), a measure of fitness of the solution. A new population, P(t + 1), is then formed: we select solutions to reproduce on the basis of their relative fitness, and the selected solutions are recombined by use of genetic operators (such as mutation and crossover) to form the new population.

A solution of the set covering problem can be easily encoded as a binary chromosome (0, 1, 1, 0, ...) which would be interpreted as the second and third columns are included in the solution, but the first and fourth are not. The fitness function *F(x)* is a large number MAX minus the sum of the cost of the columns used (i.e., the original objective function value) and a penalty for a failure to cover. Therefore, the fitness function is

$$F(x) = MAX - \sum_{i=1}^{n} w_i x_i - P(x)\eta(x)$$

where x_i and are binary with $\eta(x) = 0$ if the solution x is a cover and $\eta(x) = 1$ otherwise. *P(x)* is the penalty function procedure for the covering. The latter term

$$\sum_{i=1}^{n} w_i x_i + P(x)\eta(x)$$

will be referred to as "cost."

For these two operations, we adopted the greedy crossover and *P3* in[18]. To find a cover with lower cost, we modified the penalty function *P3* in[18]. The greedy crossover and the penalty function *P3* will be explained later. We use the natural encoding/decoding of chromosomes that represent solutions of the problems together with associated greedy crossover and new penalty function to implement the cover and mincover (sumcover) operations.

The *penalty function procedure* P3 of[18] is stated as follows:

P3: If S is a cover, cost = $\sum_{i \in S} W_i$

If S fails to be a cover, let R be the rows that remain uncovered. For each $i \in R$, let S_i be the columns that cover i. Let $w^*_i = \min \{w_j\}$ for $j \in S_i$. Then cost = $\sum_{i \in S} W_i + \sum_{i \in R} W^*_i$

In order to find a cover with lower cost, the above penalty function procedure P3 is simply modified to become P3' as follows:

P3': If S is a cover, cost = $\sum_{i \in S} W_i$

If S fails to be a cover, let R be the rows that remain uncovered. For each $j \in S$, strike column j and the rows covered by j. For some $i \in R$, let S_i be the unused columns that cover i. For each $j \in S_i$, calculate the cost-ratio(j)(w_j / number-of-1's-uncovered in j). Let j* = min { cost-ratio(j) } for $j \in S_i$. Append to S the column j*. The process is repeated until S becomes a cover.

Where cost-ratio(j) is the cost of column j over the number of 1's in the column j.

The *greedy crossover*[18] is described as follows:

For every pair of parent genes:

Step 1. Initialize the set *S* to be empty and the matrix *A* to be the original set covering matrix with column costs (w_j).

Step 2. For the unused columns and uncovered rows, calculate the cost-ratio (w_j / number-of-1's-uncovered).

Step 3. Append to S the column (say column c) with the least cost-ratio that is included in one of the parents. (Break ties randomly.)

Step 4. Strike column c and the rows covered by c from A and let this new matrix be A'.

Step 5. If S is a cover or if no other columns are represented in the parents, stop. Otherwise, set A to A' and go to Step 2.

We use simple genetic algorithm with random initial population, proportional selection, generational replacement, greedy crossover and no mutation for these two operations. In the calculation of fitness penalty function procedure P3 is used for $cover_C$ operations, while P3' is used for $mincover_A$ operation.

4.6 The Algorithms for STO5 and STO6

The $minpart_A$ and $part_C$ operations can be modeled as set partitioning problems. Similarly, a solution of the set partitioning problem can be easily encoded as a chromosome. In this subsection we use the greedy crossover of[18] and penalty function procedure PP to implement the operations.

The genetic algorithm starts by checking whether an individual violates the definition of partition. That is to say, no element is covered by more than one set. If an individual violates the definition of set partitioning problem, then a mutation operator is repeatedly applied until no individual violates the definition of set partitioning problem. Then the algorithm computes the fitness of all valid individuals by using the given penalty function procdure PP and uses the greedy crossover of[18] to generate the offspring. Finally, the algorithm examines whether the partition solution covers all elements. If the partition solution does not cover all elements, then it attempts to improve the partition solution obtained. The penalty function procedure PP is described below:

PP: if S is a partition, cost = $\sum_{i\in S} Wi$

If S fails to be a partition, let R be the rows that remain uncovered. For each $j \in S$, strike column j and the rows covered by j. In addition, for each $j \in S$, every column $k \neq j$ such that $a_{ij}=a_{ik}=1$ (i=1, ..., m) must be deleted. For some $i \in R$, let S_i be the unused column that cover i. If S_i is an empty set, let cost=∞. Otherwise, for each $j \in S_i$, calculate the cost-ratio(j)(w_j / number-of-1's-uncovered in j). Let $j^* = \min$ { cost-ratio(j) } for $j \in S_i$. Append to S the column j^*. The process is repeated until S is a partition or the cost is ∞.

The algorithm for $minpart_A$ and $part_C$ is described below.

Step 1. If any row r of A has all 0's, there is no solution since constraint r cannot be satisfied.

Step 2. Choose a desired population size n and initialize the starting population P randomly.

Step 3. Check whether a chromosome of the population P violates the definition of set partitioning problem. If any chromosome violates the definition, mutate a randomly chosen bit of 1's of this chromosome. The step is repeated until no chromosomes of population P violate the definition of set partitioning problem.

Step 4. Evaluate fitness of each individual according to the penalty function procedure PP.

Step 5. If the fitness of all individuals is equal to 0, there is no partition solution. The algorithm returns "No Partition.Solution" and terminates.

Step 6. If termination-condition held, go to Step 7; else probabilistically select a pair of individuals (according to their fitness determined by the penalty function procedure PP) to generate the offspring using greedy crossover. The step is repeated until n offspring are generated. Return to step 3.

Step 7. If the resultant solution, say S, contains a partition solution, the algorithm terminates. If S fails to be a partition, let R be the rows that remain uncovered. For each $j \in S$, strike column j and the rows covered by j. In addition, for each $j \in S$, every column $k \neq j$ such that $a_{ij}=a_{ik}=1$ (i=1, ..., m) must be deleted. For some $i \in R$, let S_i be the unused columns that cover i. If S_i contains only one column, append to S the column (say column c). Strike column c and the rows covered by c. Otherwise, for each $j \in S_i$, calculate the cost-ratio(j) (w_j / number-of-1's-uncovered in j). Let $j^* = \min\{\text{cost-ratio}(j)\}$ for $j \in S_i$. Append to S the column j^*. The step is repeated until S is a partition.

The reason why we need Step 7 is that the genetic algorithm sometimes found partial solutions with few elements not covered. Therefore, Step 7 in the algorithm attempts to improve the partition solution obtained in Step 6 by applying the procedure like the penalty function procedure. After applying this local fix-up procedure of Step 7, feasible solutions have been always produced.

5 PROPERTIES

There are many properties that can be used for transforming a sequence of team qualifications into equivalent ones. Then an optimization algorithm can utilize some of these properties to transform an initial query into an optimized form that is more efficient to execute (in most case). In this section, we state some important properties without proving them. The following notation is used in their description: the symbol $BTQi_j$, i=1, 2, 3, 4, j=1, 2, represents the jth team qualification of BTQi. For example, $BTQ2_1$ represents the first team qualification of BTQ2.

Definition. Two team expressions are equivalent if the sets of all the possible teams of those expressions are identical.

Property 1. Commutativity of BTQ1:

($BTQ1_1$ and $BTQ1_2$) = ($BTQ1_2$ and $BTQ1_1$)

Property 2. Commutativity of BTQ2:

($BTQ2_1$ and $BTQ2_2$) = ($BTQ2_2$ and $BTQ2_1$)

Property 3. Suppose a team is composed by a set of tuples over attributes A_1 and A_2 in relation R. Let BTQ_1 be a team generator and BTQ4 be one of other team qualifications. The expression (BTQ_1 and BTQ_4) can be transformed into a BTQ_2 if they satisfy certain constraints.

(BTQ_1 and BTQ_4) $\Rightarrow$ BTQ_2

Property 4. Suppose a team is composed by a set of tuples over attributes A_1 and A_2 of relation R. Let BTQ2 be a team generator, and BTQ4 be one of other team qualifications. The expression (BTQ2 and BTQ4) can be transformed into a special team operation STO1 if they satisfy certain constraints. That is,

(BTQ2 and BTQ4) $\Rightarrow$ STO1

Property 5. (i) Assume that the <attribute-list> of $BTQ2_1$ involves only one attribute, and also that the <attribute-list> of $BTQ2_2$ involves only the other attribute. Two BTQ2's can be transformed into a STO1. That is,

($BTQ2_1$ and $BTQ2_2$) ⇒ STO1

(ii) Assume that the <attribute-list> of $BTQ4_1$ involves an attribute, say A_1, which is also used by the GROUP BY clause, and also that the <attribute-list> of $BTQ4_2$ involves the other attribute, say A_2, which is also used by the GROUP BY clause. If the tuple-constant-set of two BTQ4 is of the form (*, 1), then

($BTQ4_1$ and $BTQ4_2$) ⇒ STO1.

Property 6. Suppose attributes X, Y, and Z are defined on relation R and attributes X and Y uniquely identify attribute Z. Suppose a team is composed by a set of tuples over attributes A_1 and A_2 of relation R and the <attribute-list> of AGF1 involves only Z. If we add the aggregate function AGF1 to the expressions of Properties 4 and 5, then these expressions can be combined into a special team operation STO2. That is,

($BTQ2_1$ and $BTQ2_2$ and AGF1) ⇒ STO2

(BTQ2 and BTQ4 and AGF1) ⇒ STO2

($BTQ4_1$ and $BTQ4_2$ and AGF1) ⇒ STO2

Property 7. Suppose a team consists of a set of tuples over attribute A_1 of R2. Suppose the <attribute-list> of BTQ3 involves only attribute A_2 of R2 and the operator between two sets is a **set equality**. A BTQ3 is followed by a AGF2 and a BTQ3 is followed by a AGF3 can be transformed into a STO3 and STO4 respectively. That is,

(i) (BTQ3 and AGF2) ⇒ STO3

(i) (BTQ3 and AGF3) ⇒ STO4

Property 8. All assumptions are the same as those of Property 7 except the operator between two sets in BTQ3 is a **bag equality**. A BTQ3 is followed by a AGF2 and a BTQ3 is followed by a AGF3 can be transformed into a STO5 and STO6 respectively. That is,

(i) (BTQ3 and AGF2) ⇒ STO5

(i) (BTQ3 and AGF3) ⇒ STO6

6 ANALYSIS OF EVALUATION OF TEAM QUERIES

6.1 Genetic Algorithms for mincover, cover, minpart, and part Operations

Simulations have been performed for the set covering problem on 12 test problems, and for the set partitioning problem on 10 test problems. The problem size of set covering problems was obtained from the work[1]. The problem size of set partitioning problems 1-5 was obtained from[1]. The reamining problem sizes were designed by the authors. The examined instances have been generated as follows. The *A* matrix for all set covering and set partitioning problems was obtained from a matrix generator. All the test problems have coefficient matrices whose density varies from 1% to 20%. If a row or a column of *A* does not contain 1 in the row or the column then one 1 is added in any entry of the row or column. That is, each row or column must at least contain one 1. Following the work of[1], the coefficient of the objective function was equal to the number of ones in the corresponding column plus a random variable between 0 and 1. Information on these test problems, as well as on the computational results, is presented in Tables I and II. The genetic algorithms were programmed in C and run on a DEC station 5000/200.

TABLE I

Computational Results for mincover and cover

No. of test	m	n	Popsize*	cpu time**	cost
1	15	32	12	0.060	22.132
2	30	90	16	0.437	40.984
3	200	300	64	17.281	375.320
4	200	413	72	24.580	367.645
5	50	450	60	4.402	66.269
6	36	455	60	3.706	41.410
7	104	498	64	10.731	161.914
8	200	500	80	23.350	396.976
9	46	683	60	7.921	54.867
10	26	777	64	4.890	28.910
11	50	905	64	12.041	58.920
12	134	1642	120	62.554	211.726

Note:
m=Number of constraints, n=Number of variables
*Population Size, **(seconds) DEC station 5000/200

TABLE II

Computational Results for minpart and part

No. of test	m	n	Popsize*	cpu time**	cost
1	13	87	16	0.269	15.854
2	13	63	16	0.191	16.755
3	14	71	16	0.246	17.848
4	12	75	16	0.292	15.894
5	13	88	16	0.312	15.879
6	50	200	48	20.049	62.940
7	100	600	80	159.875	129.429
8	150	700	80	696.775	183.920
9	100	1000	120	476.942	113.852
10	200	1000	150	1996.273	242.022

Note:
m=Number of constraints, n=Number of variables
*, ** have the same meaning as in Table I

The results of these tests are very interesting. For all these test problems, feasible solutions have been always produced. The results show that the CPU time is nearly proportional to the product of the number of constraints and the number of variables for the set covering problems. The CPU time for set partitioning problems is larger than that for the set covering problems. This is to be expected since the penalty function of set partitioning problems is much more complicated than that of set covering problems. Also, the CPU time for set partitioning problems is not linear to the product of the number of constraints and the number of variables. We are currently working on the problem of reducing the processing time of the set partitioning problems, possibly by adopting the Annealing Genetic algorithm of Lin, Kao, and Hsu[19].

6.2 Comparisons of Different Processing Algorithms

In this subsection, we use an example to illustrate the importance of a transformation from an expression to a special operation. Consider the following team query:

```
SELECT   <T'.player, T'.position> IN TEAM <player,
position> TEAM-PLAYERS T'
FROM        PLAYERS
WHERE (SELECT position FROM T') == { pitcher,
        catcher, 1st, 2nd, 3rd, short, left, center, right}
  and       (SELECT player, COUNT(position) FROM T'
        GROUP BY player) ≡ {(*, 1)}
```

Two team qualifications in a query can be transformed into a special team operation STO1 if they satisfy certain constraints. The corresponding team query is shown below.

SELECT <T'.player, T'.position> IN TEAM <player, position> TEAM-PLAYERS T'
FROM PLAYERS
WHERE ({pitcher, catcher, 1st, 2nd, 3rd, short, left, center, right} **match** (SELECT player FROM PLAYERS))

TABLE III

# of test / position	A	B	C	D
pitcher	2	3	4	5
catcher	3	2	5	6
1st	1	3	3	5
2nd	2	3	3	5
short	1	2	6	7
3rd	2	2	4	5
left	2	5	3	4
center	1	4	5	6
right	1	3	6	7
# of distinct instances of player	12	15	20	25
# of tuples in PLAYERS	15	27	40	50

TAB:LE IV

Alg. / # of tuples in PLAYERS	Alg. 1	Alg. 2	STO1
15	25,321	24	315
27	2,379,378	6,480	648
40	236,866,163	259,200	1,160
50	1,156,110,375	2,205,000	1,700

Information about the number of tuples in relation PLAYERS, the number of distinct instances of the attribute player in PLAYERS, and the number for each instance of the attribute position appears in relation PLAYERS is shown in Table III. The average of the number of tests to generate a team for different algorithms is shown in Table IV. It can directly be seen that STO1 is highly efficient than other two algorithms. All algorithms were programmed in C and run on a 80486-based PC.

7. CONCLUSIONS

Team query processing uses a set-by-set evaluation strategy. The search space is all subsets of the set of tuples of a relation. The search space of a team query may be very large. Therefore, instead of using conventional breadth-first search method, we adopt a depth-first search method for query processing. Thus, users can always get results, if one exists, in a predicate restricted amount of time. In the selection of teams with extreme values, a team query perhaps can not find such teams in a small amount of time, however a team query can generate teams with near-optimal values by incorporating genetic algorithms or simulated annealing algorithms into query optimization algorithms.

The genetic algorithms described in this paper are designed to implement special team operations. The genetic algorithms for STO3, STO4, STO5, and STO6 always produce feasible solutions.

Further research includes improving the implementation of the evaluation algorithm and the incorporation of further optimization techniques.

REFERENCES

[1] Balas, E. and Martin, C.H., "Pivot and Complement - A Heuristic for 0-1 Programming," Management Science 26(1), pp. 86-96, January 1980.

[2] Abiteboul, S. and Grumbach, S., "A Rule-Based Language with Functions and Sets," ACM Transaction on Database Systems, March 1991.

[3] Beeri, C., Naqvi, S., Ramakrishnan, R., Shmueli, O., and Tsur, S., "Sets and Negation in a Logic Programs," Proceedings of 6th Principle of Database Systems, 1987.

[4] Beeri, C., Naqvi, S., Ramakrishnan, R., Shmueli, O., and Tsur, S., "Set Constructors in a Logic Database Languages," MCC Technique Report.

[5] Bennett, K., Ferris, M.C., and Ioannidis, Y.E., "A Genetic Algorithm for Database Query Optimization," Proceedings of the Fifth International Conference on Genetic Algorithms, 1991.

[6] Chen, W.D., Kifer, M., and Warren, S., "Hilog: A foundation for Higher-Order Logic Programming," SUNY at Stony Brook Technical Report also in Proceedings of Logic Programming 1989.

[7] Codd, E.F., The Relational Model for Database Management, Version 2. Reading, MA: Addison-Wesley, 1990.

[8] Date, C.J., A. Guide to the SQL Standard,. Addison-Wesley, Reading, Mass. (1987).

[9] Garfinkel, R.S. and Nemhauser, G.L., Integer Programming, John Wiley & Sons, 1972.

[10] Gavish B. and Segev, A., "Set Query Optimization in Distributed Database Systems," ACM Transaction on Database Systems, Sept. 1986.

[11] Goldberg, D.E., Genetic Algorithms in Search, Optimization, and Machine Learning, Addison-Wesley, 1989.

[12] Holland, J.H., Adaption in Natural and Artificial Systems, Ann Arbor: The University of Michigan Press, 1975.

[13] Horng, J.T., Chen, G.D., and Liu, B.J., "A Team-Oriented Query Language," Department of Computer Science & Information Engineering Technical Report, National Taiwan University, Taiwan, 1992.

[14] Ioannidis Y.E. and Wong, E., "Query Optimization by Simulated Annealing," in Proc. of the 1987 ACM-SIGMOD Conference on the Management of Data, San Francisco, CA, May 1987, pp. 9-22.

[15] Ioannidis, Y.E. and Kang, Y.C., "Randomized Algorithms for Optimizing large Join Queries," in Proc. of the 1987 ACM-SIGMOD Conference on the Management of Data, Allantic City, NJ, May 1990, pp. 312-321.

[16] Kirkpatrick, S., Gelatt, Jr. C.D., and Vecchi, M.P., "Optimization by Simulated Annealing," Science 220, 4598 (May 1983), pp. 671-680.

[17] Kuper, G., "Logic Programming with Sets," Proceedings of 6th Principle of Database Systems, 1987.

[18] Liepins, G.E., Hilliard, M.R., Richardson, J., and Palmer, M., "Genetic Algorithms Applications to Set Covering and Traveling Salesman Problems," in Operations Research and Artificial Intelligence: The Integration of Problem-Solving Strategies, edited by D.E. Brown, C. White, III, Kluwer Academic Publishers, 1990.

[19] Lin, F.T., Kao, C.Y., and Hsu, C.C., "Applying the Genetic Approach to Simulated Annealing in Solving Some NP-Hard Problems," To Appear in IEEE Trans. on Systems, Man, Cybernetics, 23(3), May 1993.

[20] Database Language SQL, Document ANSI X3.135-1986. Also: ISO/TC97/SC21/WG3 N143.

DISTRIBUTIVE JOIN ALGORITHM FOR CUBE-CONNECTED MULTIPROCESSORS

Soon M. Chung † and Jaerheen Yang
Department of Computer Science and Engineering
Wright State University
Dayton, Ohio 45435, U.S.A.

Abstract

This paper presents a parallel distributive join algorithm for cube-connected multiprocessors. The performance analysis shows that the proposed algorithm has an almost linear speedup over the sequential distributive join algorithm [NEG91] as the number of processors increases, and its performance is comparable to that of the parallel hybrid-hash join algorithm [OMI89]. A big advantage of the proposed algorithm over the hash-based join algorithms is that it does not have the bucket-overflow problem caused by the nonuniform hashing. Moreover, the proposed algorithm can easily support the non-equijoin operation, which is very hard to be implemented by the hash-based join algorithms.

1 Introduction

In the context of very large relational databases, a major problem is how to process the relational operations on databases in a minimum amount of time to satisfy user queries. To speed up the relational operations on very large databases, parallel processing is essential [CHU90, CHU91, CHU92] and many special hardware units have been proposed for parallel database operations [OZK86, SU88]. However, most of them are not cost-effective as noted in [BOR83, STO88], and the current trend is to use general-purpose multiprocessor architectures, such as cube-connected processors [FRI90, OMI89], to reduce the design cost of the machine.

One of the important relational operations is the join operation because it is executed frequently and also time-consuming. There are three major join algorithms: nested-loop, hash-partition, and sort-merge join algorithms. With the nested-loop join algorithm, each tuple of one operand relation is compared with all the tuples of the other operand relation. It has been shown that the nested-loop join algorithm is acceptable when the operand relations are small because the processing time is inversely proportional to the number of processors [BRA84, VAL84].

In sort-merge join, both operand relations are sorted based on the join attribute values, then the merging step performs the pairwise comparison of the sorted tuples to test the join condition. The performance of the sort-merge join algorithm for the non-equijoin is as good as that for the equijoin because, once the two operand relations are sorted, the merging step handles the equijoin and the non-equijoin in the same way by performing the corresponding comparison. The database machine DELTA [ITO87] has multiple relational database engines composed of sort-merge units and performs the sort-merge join algorithm. In the case of the sort-merge algorithm, increasing the number of processors beyond a certain number causes very little decrease in the processing time. The reason is that the degree of parallelism is divided by b at each merge pass, after a certain number of passes, if b-way merge is used for sorting [VAL84].

The hash-partition join algorithm is adopted by the database machine GRACE [KIT84]. Each operand relation is partitioned into a number of buckets depending on the hash value of the join attribute, then matching is performed within each bucket by a processor assigned to that bucket. Usually the hash-partition join algorithm is better than the sort-merge join algorithm in the case of the equijoin operation, because sorting creates a total ordering of the tuples in both relations whereas the hashing simply groups related tuples together in the same bucket [DEW85]. However, in the case of the non-equijoin, the operation of each processor is not limited to a single bucket, and the workloads of the processors may not be uniform. Another problem of the hash-partition join algorithm is the bucket-overflow caused by the nonuniform distribution of the join attribute value. In this case, rehashing of the overflow bucket is necessary.

In this paper, we propose a parallel distributive join algorithm for cube-connected multiprocessors. The proposed algorithm is based on the sequential distributive join algorithm [NEG91], where the smaller relation is sorted completely while the larger relation is only partially sorted. Thus, it requires much less processing time than the sort-merge join. It is comparable to parallel hash-based join algorithms in terms of performance, without having the buck-overflow problem. Moreover, the proposed algorithm can easily support the non-equijoin, which is quite difficult for hash-based join algorithms.

Section 2 describes the sequential distributive join algorithm. In Section 3, a cube-connected architecture model is described briefly, and the parallel distributive join algorithm for both equijoin and non-equijoin operations are presented. The performance modeling of the proposed algorithm is in Section 4, and in Section 5, we analyze the performance of the proposed algorithm and compare it with those of sequential algorithm and the parallel hybrid-hash join algorithm [OMI89].

2 The Distributive Join Algorithm

In this section, the sequential distributive join algorithm [NEG91] is described. The size of relation **R** is assumed to be smaller than or equal to the size of relation **S** throughout this paper.

The distributive join is based on the idea that it is sufficient to sort the smaller relation completely and the larger one partially to perform the join efficiently. As a result, we can save the processing time compared to the sort-merge join algorithm.

The difference of the distributive join from the sort-merge join is illustrated in Figure 1, where relation **R** is completely sorted while the other relation **S** is decomposed into m subrelations (m = 4, in this example). Note that each subrelation is not sorted. However, the maximum join

†This research was partially supported by National Science Foundation under grant No. IRI-9008694.

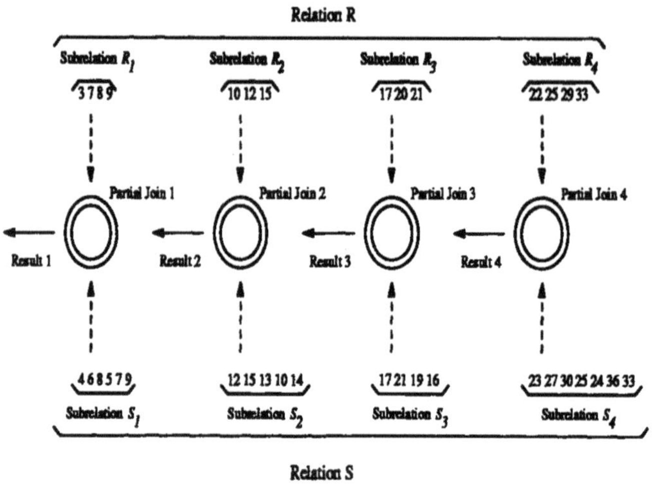

Figure 1: Last Pass in Distributive Join Algorithm

attribute value contained in subrelation S_i is less than the minimum join attribute value contained in subrelation S_{i+1}. The final join consists of m partial joins between each subrelation S_i and R_i, for $1 \leq i \leq m$.

The distributive join algorithm consists of three phases:

1. Sort the smaller relation **R** and partition it into m subrelations, $R_1, R_2, ..., R_m$, such that their sizes $|R_i|$, $1 \leq i \leq m$, expressed in pages satisfy the following constraints:

   $|R_1| = |R_2| = \cdots = |R_{m-1}| = M - 1$

   $|R_m| \leq M - 1$

   where $M + 1$ is the size of the available main memory expressed in pages and m is the number of subrelations. The value of m is obtained by the following formula:

   $$m = \left\lceil \frac{|\mathbf{R}|}{M - 1} \right\rceil$$

   where $|\mathbf{R}|$ is the size of relation **R** expressed in pages. Thus, each $|R_i|$, for $1 \leq i \leq m$, can fit into $M - 1$ pages of the memory.

   Then, the distribution table containing $m - 1$ sorted values, $v_1, v_2, \ldots, v_{m-1}$, of the join attribute is constructed, such that

   (a) the values of the join attribute of subrelation R_1 are less than or equal to v_1;

   (b) the values of the join attribute of subrelation R_i, for $2 \leq i \leq m - 1$, are between v_{i-1} and v_i (i.e., $v_{i-1} <$ join attribute value $\leq v_i$);

   (c) the values of the join attribute of subrelation R_m are greater than v_{m-1}.

2. Distribute the larger relation **S** into subrelations using the distribution table to determine the boundaries of subrelations.

   Having sorted relation **R** and built the distribution table, a partial distributive sort is now applied to relation **S** using the distribution table, so that relation **S** is decomposed into m subrelations, $S_1, S_2, \ldots, S_m$, satisfying the conditions (a), (b), and (c) above. However, note that the size of different subrelations of **S** may not be the same, and that each subrelation is not sorted internally.

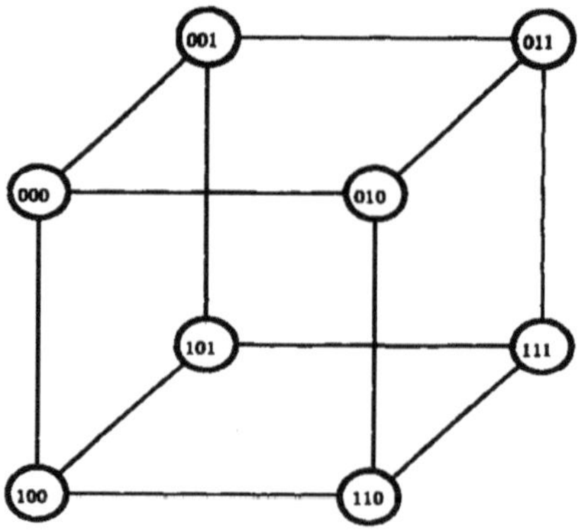

Figure 2: Structure of 3-cube with 8 nodes

3. The result of the actual join $\mathbf{R} \bowtie \mathbf{S}$ is the union of the results of the m partial joins; $R_1 \bowtie S_1, R_2 \bowtie S_2, \ldots, R_m \bowtie S_m$. To perform $R_i \bowtie S_i$,

   (a) Read R_i into the memory completely, which is possible since $|R_i| = M - 1$.

   (b) Repeat Step (c) until S_i has been completely scanned.

   (c) Fetch one page of S_i into one of the two free pages of the memory and perform the join of this page with R_i. This operation is performed in main memory and can take advantage of the fact that subrelation R_i is completely sorted. For example, R_i can be binary searched for each tuple of S_i to find matching tuples.

3 The Parallel Distributive Join Algorithm

This section describes the hardware model assumed and the parallel distributive join algorithm for both equijoin and non-equijoin operations.

3.1 Hardware Model

The hypercube model used here is identical to the one in [OMI89]. Each node consists of a processor, main memory, and secondary storage. However, note that the terms "node" and "processor" are used interchangeably in this paper. Each node is assumed to have two independent communication processors capable of simultaneously receiving and transmitting packets along two separate links. Nodes exchange tuples via variable-size packets with an upper bound imposed on the packet size.

Figure 2 shows a 3-cube with 8 nodes. Each node has $n = \log_2 N$ neighbors where n and N denote the dimension of the system and the total number of nodes, respectively. In this figure, $n = 3$ and $N = 8$. There are n bits in the address of a node and the bits are numbered 0 to $n - 1$ from the right to the left. The address of each neighbor of node i differs in one bit from the address of node i. For example, the node 110 in this figure has three neighbors with addresses 111, 100, and 010, respectively.

Each node allocates one output buffer for each neighbor. Output buffers are numbered 0 through $n - 1$, where output buffer i is associated with the neighbor whose address differs in bit i. Output buffer i of a node contains the tuples whose destined locations (node addresses) have bits i to $n-1$ identical to the address of its associated neighbor.

3.2 Equi-join Algorithm

Here we assume that tuples from each operand relation are evenly distributed among the nodes initially. Even though this uniform data distribution may not be realistic, the dynamic tuple balancing phase proposed in [FRI90] can handle the nonuniform data distribution so that the number of tuples per node becomes approximately the same across the system [OMI89].

With n-cube architecture with $N = 2^n$ nodes, the actual join $\mathbf{R} \bowtie \mathbf{S}$ is performed by executing N partial joins; $R_1 \bowtie S_1, R_2 \bowtie S_2, \ldots, R_N \bowtie S_N$. First, the smaller relation $\mathbf{R}$ is sorted in parallel and the divided into N subrelations, $R_0, R_1, \ldots, R_{N-1}$, where R_i is allocated to node i, for $0 \leq i \leq N-1$. The distribution table is constructed using the maximum join attribute value of each R_i and the address of the node to which it is allocated. Therefore, the i-th entry in the distribution is the maximum join attribute value in subrelation R_i and its corresponding location, i.e., node i, for $0 \leq i \leq N-1$.

Using the distribution table, relation $\mathbf{S}$ can be divided into subrelations, $S_0, S_1, \ldots, S_{N-1}$, which are partially sorted. Here, "partially sorted" means that the value of a join attribute in S_i is always less than the value of a join attribute in S_j for $i < j$. But inside the subrelation S_i, the tuples need not be sorted according to the join attribute values. The basic idea in parallel distributive join is to allocate R_i and S_i to node i for $0 \leq i \leq N-1$, so that all the N partial joins can be processed in parallel.

Suppose that the subrelation R_i allocated to node i is too large to be resident in the main memory of node i. In this case, node i can use the sequential distributive join algorithm described in Section 2 to perform the partial join $R_i \bowtie S_i$ by dividing R_i further according to the memory size M. If R_i can be resident in the memory of node i, the sorted R_i is binary searched for each tuple of S_i to perform the partial join.

The parallel distributive join algorithm for equijoin is described below in pseudo codes. In this algorithm, "neighbor i" of a node denotes the neighbor node whose address differs in bit i; "*location*" is the address of a node obtained from the distribution table; "$S_{location}$" indicates the subrelation of $\mathbf{S}$ allocated to the node with address *location*.

```
<Relation R processing>
Each of N processors sorts its local partition of R;
Merge the results into node 0; /* log_2 N steps are required
with 2-way merge */
/* In node 0 */
Divide the sorted relation R into N subrelations
R_0, R_1, ..., R_{N-1}, such that
|R_0| = |R_1| = ... = |R_{N-2}| >= |R_{N-1}|;
For i := 0 to N - 1 Do
    Build the distribution table using the maximum join
    attribute value of R_i and i;
End_For
Broadcast the distribution table to N - 1 nodes;
Transfer the relations R_i to node i for 1 <= i <= N - 1;

<Relation S processing>
Each processor reads the local partition of S, page by page;
For every tuple t in the input buffer Do
    location := corresponding node address from the
    distribution table for t;
    If location is this node Then
        Insert the tuple t into S_location;
    Else
        Store t and its location in the corresponding output
        buffer;
    End_If
End_For
For i := n - 1 downto 0 Do
    /* following two operations are executed in parallel */
    Send output buffer i to neighbor i;
    Receive tuples from neighbor i;
    For every(t, location) in the input buffer Do
        If location is this node Then
            Insert the tuple into S_location;
        Else
            Store(t, location) in the corresponding output
            buffer;
        End_If
    End_For
End_For

<Partial join operation in node i >
If |R_i| <= M - 1 or |S_i| <= M - 1 Then
    Choose the smaller relation as external and load it
    into the memory;
    Do the join operation;
Else
    m := ceil(|R_i| / (M-1));
    Divide the sorted relation R_i into R_{i_0}, R_{i_1}, ..., R_{i_{m-1}},
    such that |R_{i_0}| = |R_{i_1}| = ... = |R_{i_{m-2}}| = M - 1
    and |R_{i_{m-1}}| <= M - 1;
    For j := 0 to m - 1 Do
        Build the local distribution table using the
        maximum join attribute value of R_{i_j} and j;
    End_For
    Partition S_i into S_{i_0}, S_{i_1}, ..., S_{i_{m-1}} using the local
    distribution table;
    For j := 0 to m - 1 Do
        Join R_{i_j} and S_{i_j}
    End_For
End_If

<Get the final result>
Merge the partial join output in each node into node 0;
```

3.3 Non-equijoin Algorithm

Non-equijoin operations can be easily implemented with a small change in the parallel distributive join algorithm for the equijoin. For non-equijoin, relation $\mathbf{R}$ is handled by the same procedure of the equijoin. In the case of equijoin, only one *location* is allocated for a $\mathbf{S}$ tuple by the corresponding entry in the distribution table. For non-equijoin, more than one *location* can be allocated for a $\mathbf{S}$ tuple due to the join condition and the distribution of $\mathbf{R}$ tuples over multiple nodes. Since the distribution table entries are ordered based on the join attribute values of $\mathbf{R}$, all the *locations* relevant to a given $\mathbf{S}$ tuple can be determined easily. In this case, the **S** tuple is copied into the corresponding output buffers to be transferred to the *locations*. The number of copies of the **S** tuple is the same as the number of the *locations* selected for the tuple – one for each *location*, and each copy is associated with the corresponding *location*. After the **S** tuples are distributed, the partial join operation is performed at each node. If the join attribute value of a **S** tuple falls between the boundary join attribute values of node i, the non-equijoin operation is performed by comparing the R_i tuples with the **S** tuple. Otherwise, every tuple of R_i should be joined with that **S** tuple.

4 Performance Modeling

In this section, we develop a deterministic modeling to evaluate the processing time of the parallel distributive equijoin operation in various cases.

4.1 Notation

Following is the list of notations used for the modeling:

$\|\|R\|\|$	Number of tuples in relation **R**
$\|R\|$	Size of relation **R** (pages)
JS	Join selectivity of $R \bowtie S$, i.e., $\|\|R \bowtie S\|\|/(\|\|R\|\| \times \|\|S\|\|)$
P	Size of a page (bytes)
N	Total number of processors in the cube
n	Dimension of the cube, i.e., $\log_2 N$
PR	Size of a node address (bytes)
TS_R	Size of a tuple in **R** (bytes)
TS_{DT}	Size of an entry in the distribution table (bytes)
TP_R	Number of tuples in a page for **R** (tuples)
PS	Maximum packet size (bytes)
$comm$	Communication rate (bits/sec)
$comp$	Time for comparing two values (sec)
$move$	Time for moving one tuple within main memory (sec)
P_{ovhd}	Overhead time for a packet (sec)
IO_{read}	Time for reading a page from the disk (sec)
IO_{write}	Time for writing a page to the disk (sec)
$M+1$	Size of memory in each processor (pages)
A	Size of a join attribute value (bytes)

4.2 Relation R Processing

4.2.1 Reading the relation R

Assuming a uniform distribution of **R** tupleas over N nodes, the access time is

$$tr\_read = \frac{|R|}{N} \times IO_{read}$$

4.2.2 Local sort of a partition of R

Each processor sorts its partition of **R**, which requires the sorting of each page and the merging of the sorted pages:

$$tr\_local\_sort = \frac{|R|}{N} \times (comp + move) \times TP_R \log_2 TP_R$$

$$tr\_local\_merge = (\frac{|R|}{N} - 1) \times comp \times \frac{||R||}{N} + move \times \frac{||R||}{N}$$

$$tr\_local\_merge\_sort = tr\_local\_sort + tr\_local\_merge$$

4.2.3 Global merging into node 0

1) Merging:
It requires n steps and for step i, the time needed for merging is $|R|/N \times TP_R \times 2^i \times (comp + move)$. Therefore, the total time for merging relation **R** into node 0 is

$$tr\_global\_merge = \sum_{i=1}^{n} \left(\frac{||R||}{N} \times 2^i \times (comp + move) \right)$$

2) Communication:
The cost includes the transmission of **R** tuples in n steps.

$$tr\_global\_merge\_comm = \sum_{i=1}^{n} \left(2^{i-1} \times \frac{||R||}{N} \times TS_R \times \frac{8}{comm} \right) + \sum_{i=1}^{n} \left(\left\lceil 2^{i-1} \times \frac{||R||}{N} \times TS_R \times \frac{1}{PS} \right\rceil \times P_{ovhd} \right)$$

4.2.4 Distributing R to $N-1$ nodes

The time for distributing **R** tuples to $N-1$ nodes is the same as the $tr\_global\_merge\_comm$:

$$tr\_dist = tr\_global\_merge\_comm$$

Therefore, the total time required for the processing of relation **R** is

$$tr = tr\_read + tr\_local\_merge\_sort + tr\_global\_merge + tr\_global\_merge\_comm + tr\_dist$$

4.3 Distribution Table Processing

4.3.1 Building the distribution table

The size of an entry in the distribution table is obtained by adding the size of a node address and the size of a join attribute value:

$$TS_{DT} = PR + A$$

Since the number of entries in the distribution table is N, the cost to build the distribution table is

$$tdt\_build = N \times move'$$

where $move'$ denotes the time for moving an entry of the distribution table, and it can be represented as

$$move' = move \times \frac{TS_{DT}}{TS_R}$$

4.3.2 Copying the distribution table

To broadcast the distribution table to all the N nodes, it is required to copy the distribution table certain number of times to the output buffers at each of n steps:

$$tdt\_dist = N \times move' \times \sum_{i=1}^{n} \left(\frac{N}{2^{i-1}} - 1 \right)$$

4.3.3 Communication

The time for distributing the distribution table to $N-1$ nodes is

$$tdt\_comm = \sum_{i=1}^{n} \left(\frac{N}{2^i} \times N \times TS_{DT} \times \frac{8}{comm} \right) + \sum_{i=1}^{n} \left(\left\lceil \frac{N}{2^i} \times N \times TS_{DT} \times \frac{1}{PS} \right\rceil \times P_{ovhd} \right)$$

Therefore, the total time required for the processing of the distribution table is

$$tdt = tdt\_build + tdt\_dist + tdt\_comm$$

4.4 Relation S Processing

4.4.1 Reading the local partition of S page by page

Assuming a uniform distribution of S tuples over N nodes, the access time is

$$ts\_read = \frac{|S|}{N} \times IO_{read}$$

4.4.2 Handling the tuples of S before the exchange

This includes the time for looking up the distribution table to check the location, moving $1/N$ of the tuples into $S_{location}$, and moving the rest of tuples into the output buffers.

$$ts\_before\_exchange = \frac{\|S\|}{N} \times (comp \times \log_2 N + \frac{1}{N} \times move + \frac{N-1}{N} \times move)$$

4.4.3 Handling the tuples of S after the exchange

Assuming the uniform distribution of tuples over N nodes, the number of tuples sent out by a node to the neighbors at each step is $\|S\|/(2 \times N)$ [OMI89], and each tuple requires one comparison and one movement:

$$ts\_after\_exchange = n \times \frac{\|S\|}{2 \times N} \times (comp + move)$$

4.4.4 Communication

The time for the transmission of **S** tuples between nodes over n steps is

$$ts\_comm = n \times \left(\frac{\|S\|}{2 \times N} \times (TS_S + PR)\right) \times \frac{8}{comm} + n \times \left\lceil \frac{\|S\|}{2 \times N} \times (TS_S + PR) \times \frac{1}{PS} \right\rceil \times P_{ovhd}$$

Therefore, the total processing time required for the processing of **S** tuples is

$$ts = ts\_read + ts\_before\_exchange + ts\_after\_exchange + ts\_comm$$

4.5 Local Distributive Join Processing

4.5.1 Disk I/O

The total disk I/O time required for the local distributive join at node i includes the I/O time for partial sort of S_i, join operation, and the result writing. The I/O time for partial sort of S_i is

$$tj\_IO\_sort\_S = \frac{|S|}{N} \times (IO_{read} + IO_{write})$$

To perform the join operation, $|R|/N$ and $|S|/N$ pages are required to be read by each processor:

$$tj\_IO\_join = (\frac{|R|}{N} + \frac{|S|}{N}) \times IO_{read}$$

The I/O time for writing the result is

$$tj\_IO\_result = \frac{\|R\|}{N} \times \frac{\|S\|}{N} \times (JS \times N) \times \frac{1}{TP_O} \times IO_{write}$$

where TP_O is the number of tuples per page of the output relation. Thus, the total I/O time required for the local distributive join is

$$tj\_IO = tj\_IO\_sort\_S + tj\_IO\_join + tj\_IO\_result$$

4.5.2 Partitioning of S_i using the local distribution table

At node i, the number of partitions, denoted by m, for R_i and S_i is

$$m = \left\lceil \frac{|R|/N}{M-1} \right\rceil$$

Since the number of entries in the local distribution table is m, $\log_2 m$ comparisons are needed on the average to look up the local distribution table, and a movement is required for each tuple of S_i.

$$tj\_partition\_S = \frac{\|S\|}{N} \times (comp \times \log_2 m + move)$$

4.5.3 Building the local distribution table

Since the number of entries in the local distribution table is m, the time required to build the local distribution table is

$$tj\_dt\_build = m \times move'$$

4.5.4 Join R_i and S_i

The number of tuples in R_{i_j}, for $0 \leq j \leq m-1$, is equal to $(M-1) \times TP_R$, and since they are sorted, $\log_2((M-1) \times TP_R)$ comparisons are needed for each tuple of S_i to find a matching tuple. Considering the multiple tuples with the same join attribute value, $(M-1) \times TP_R \times (JS \times N) + 1$ comparisons are needed additionally to locate all the remaining matching tuples. Here, the probability that a R_i tuple and a S_i tuple is to be joined at each node is $JS \times N$ since we assume that **R** and **S** tuples are uniformly distributed over N nodes. Also, the joined tuples are needed to be moved. Thus, the time required for the in-memory join between R_i and S_i is

$$\begin{aligned} tj\_join = & \frac{\|S\|}{N} \times (comp \times \log_2((M-1) \times TP_R) \\ & + comp \times ((M-1) \times TP_R \times (JS \times N) + 1)) \\ & + \frac{\|R\|}{N} \times \frac{\|S\|}{N} \times (JS \times N) \times move \end{aligned}$$

Therefore, the total time required for the partial join operation is

$$tj = tj\_IO + tj\_partition\_S + tj\_join + tj\_dt\_build$$

4.6 Total Distributive Join Time on n-Cube

By adding all the component times, the total processing time for a parallel distributive join on a n-cube machine is:

$$T = tr + tdt + ts + tj$$

5 Performance Analysis and Comparison

In this section, we analyze the performance of the parallel distributive join algorithm using the following parameter values:

P	: 4K bytes
$M+1$	: 4096 pages
TS_R, TS_S	: 128 bytes
PS	: 64K bytes
$comm$	: 8M bits/sec
$comp$	: 3 μsec
$move$	: 20 μsec
P_{ovhd}	: 5 msec
IO_{read}, IO_{write}	: 25 msec
A	: 13 bytes

Based on the equations developed in Section 4, the parallel distributive join on a cube-connected machine is evaluated and analyzed for different cases in terms of the total number of processors, size of the relations, and the join selectivity. We also evaluate the speedup of the parallel algorithm over the sequential distributive algorithm executed by a uniprocessor system. Comparison with the parallel hybrid-hash join algorithm proposed in [OMI89] is also given in this section.

Figure 3 shows the total processing time of the parallel distributive join when the number of processors and the size of **S** change. As the number of processors increases, the total processing time decreases due to the higher degree of parallelism. The processing time increases as the size of **S** increases because each node has more **S** tuples to process and there are more joined tuples to be stored for the same join selectivity assumed.

Figure 4 illustrates the relationship between the components of the total processing time and the number of processors. When the number of processors is small, the time for writing the join result to the disk is the dominant time component because there is not enough main memory available for the join result. However, as the number of processors increases, the time for writing the join result is not dominant anymore because more join output tuples can be stored in the main memory. The time for the distribution table increases as the number of processors increases. This is due to the fact that the size of the distribution table becomes larger, which requires more time to build and distribute, as the number of processors increases. If the number of processors doubles, it takes one more step to broadcast the distribution table.

The effect of relation **S** size on the time components can be observed in Figure 5. When the size of relation **S** becomes larger than certain value, the total execution time begins to increase rapidly. It is when the size of join result is so big that it cannot fit into the main memory of the processors, so the join result should be written to the disk which becomes the dominant time component. The time for handling relation **S**, which includes the initial read and the exchange of the tuples between processors, increases as the size of relation **S** increases. But it does not increases as fast as the join result writing time.

Figure 6 shows the effect of the size of the relations **R** and **S**. For a fixed value of relation **S** size, the total processing time increases as relation **R** becomes larger because it takes more time to sort and distribute relation **R**.

The effect of join selectivity on the total processing time can be observed in Figure 7. As the join selectivity increases, the size of the join result also increases and the time for writing it on the disk contributes to the increase of the total processing time.

Figure 8 shows the speedup of the parallel distributive join over the sequential distributive join by a uniprocessor system. We measured the speedup for different memory size in the uniprocessor system. As the size of the memory in the uniprocessor increases, the speedup decreases because less number of joined tuples are written to the disk. The speedup is saturated when there are more than certain number of processors in the cube. The reason is that increased overhead for merging and distributing **R** and for building and broadcasting the distribution table compensates the decreases in other time components.

The effect of relation **S** size on the speedup can be observed in Figure 9. As the size of relation **S** increases, the size of joined result is increased with the same join selectivity and the same size of relation **R**. For the uniprocessor system, writing the result to disk becomes the dominant

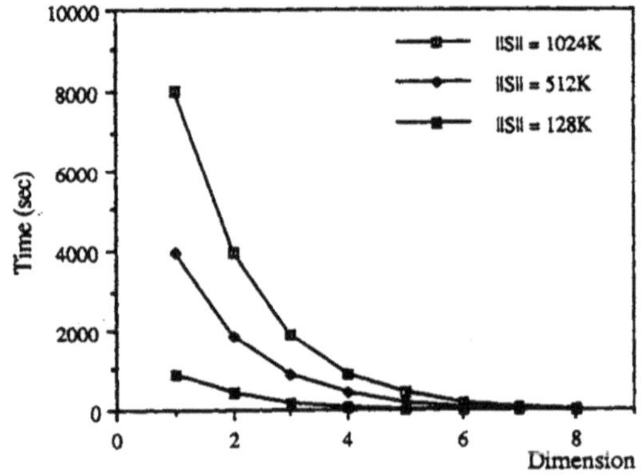

Figure 3: Effect of the Number of Processors (||R||=16K, JS=0.001)

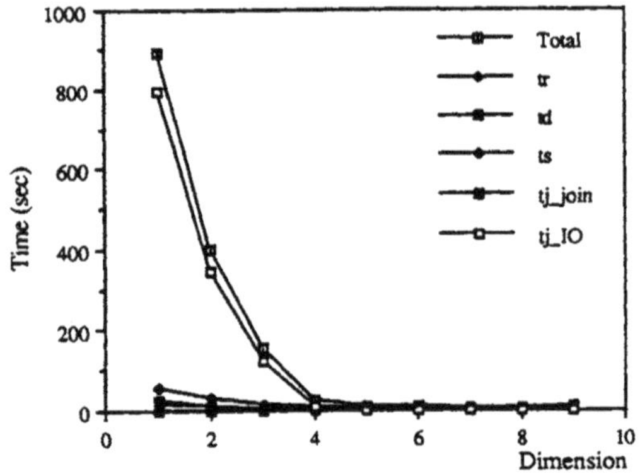

Figure 4: Time Components of the Total Processing Time (||R||=16K, ||S||=128K, JS=0.001)

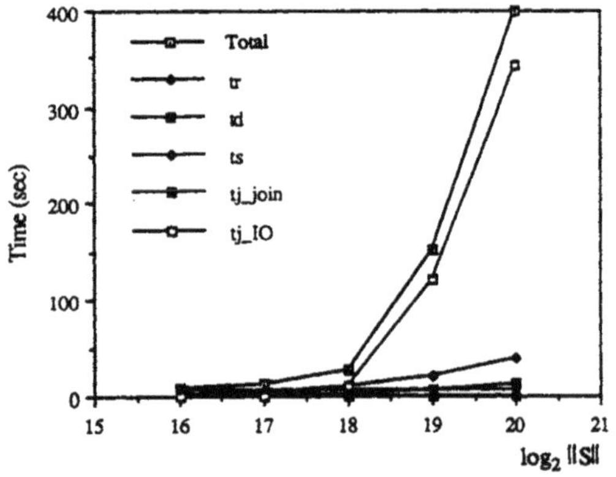

Figure 5: Effect of the Size of Relation S (||R||=16K, JS=0.001, N=32)

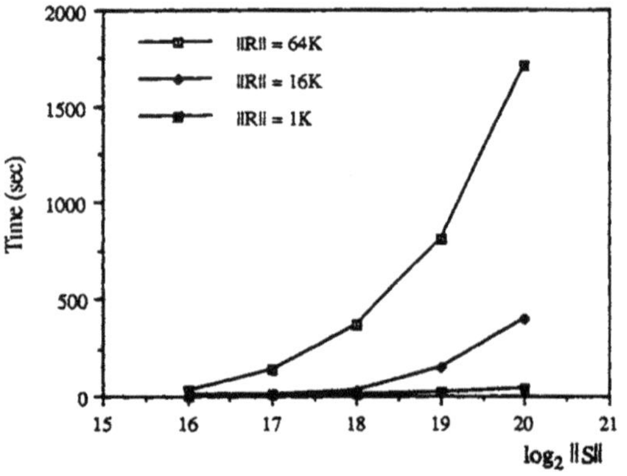

Figure 6: Effect of the Size of Relations R and S (JS=0.001, N=32)

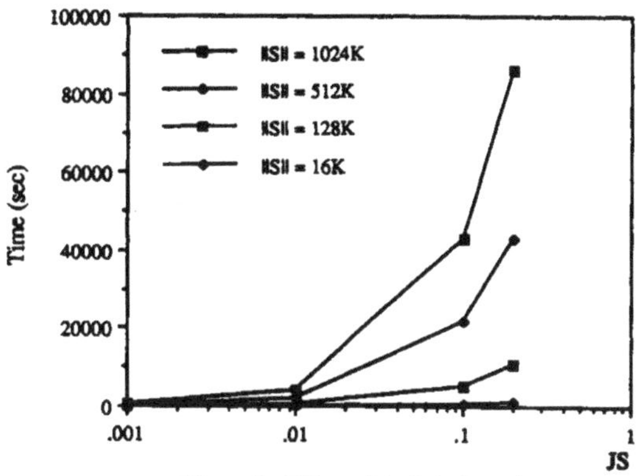

Figure 7: Effect of the Join Selectivity
(‖R‖=16K, N=32)

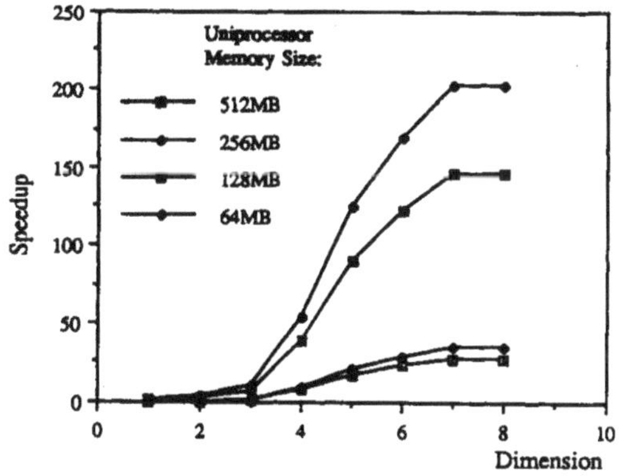

Figure 8: Speedup vs. the Number of Processors
(‖R‖=16K, ‖S‖=128K, JS=0.001)

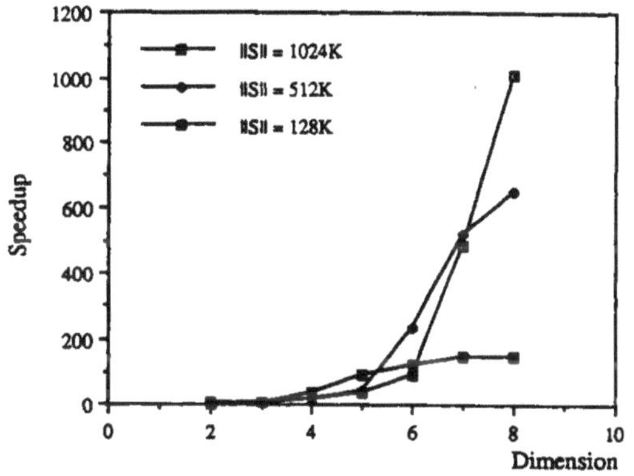

Figure 9: Speedup vs. the Number of Processors
(‖R‖=16K, JS=0.001, Uniprocessor Memory Size = 128MB)

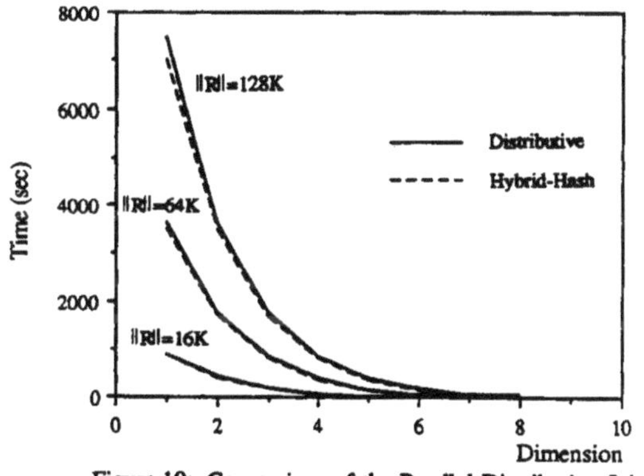

Figure 10: Comparison of the Parallel Distributive Join and the Parallel Hybrid-Hash Join
(‖S‖=128K, JS=0.001)

factor in total processing time as the size of join result increases. But in the parallel system, since the workload of writing the result is distributed to N processors, the portion of writing the result in total execution time decreases as the number of processors increases. Consequently, the speedup increases rapidly up to certain number of processors.

The performance of the parallel distributive join algorithm and that of the parallel hybrid-hash join algorithm [OMI89] for n-cube machines are compared in Figure 10. In [OMI89], the time for writing join result to disk was not considered since they assumed that there is an infinite amount of main memory in each processor. For fair comparison, the time for writing the join result to disk is considered in Figure 14. We can see that the parallel distributive join is comparable to the parallel hybrid-hash join in terms of processing time. While having a comparable processing time, the parallel distributive join algorithm has the following advantages over the parallel hybrid-hash join algorithm:

- Since the smaller relation **R** is completely sorted in parallel and the larger relation **S** is partially sorted in the parallel distributive join, non-equijoin operations can be implemented easily as described in Section 3.3. On the other hand, it is hard to be implemented by the parallel hybrid-hash join algorithm because it requires an order-preserving hash function [GAR86]. Since different attributes may have different data types, formats, and value distributions, we have to select a specific order-preserving hash function for each join attribute. Moreover, the value distribution of the join attribute can change if the relation is updated frequently.

- The parallel hybrid-hash join could have a bucket-overflow problem which is not critical in the parallel distributive join. A bucket-overflow occurs when the tuples are not uniformly hashed to the buckets so that a bucket is too big to fit in the main memory of a processor. In the parallel distributive join algorithm, distribution of the smaller relation into subrelations is based on the distribution of the join attribute values. Thus, we can easily balance the size of the subrelations (partitions) to balance the workloads of the processors. If the size of a subrelation is bigger than the size of the available main memory of a processor, the sequential distributive join algorithm is applied in that processor to solve the problem without degrading the performance.

6 Conclusion

In this paper, the parallel distributive join algorithm for the cube-connected architecture is proposed, analyzed, and compared with the sequential distributive join algorithm [NEG91] and the parallel hybrid-hash join algorithm [OMI89].

The speedup of the parallel distributive join algorithm over the sequential distributive join algorithm is based on the followings:

- Disk I/O time for each input and output relation is reduced.

- Sorting, merging, and distribution of the smaller operand relation are performed in parallel.

- Partitioning of the larger operand relation is performed in parallel.

- Partial joins are performed in parallel.

The additional cost needed to achieve the parallelism is the cost for broadcasting the distribution table and for the data communication, which is negligible compared to the effect of the high degree of parallelism.

The performance of the parallel distributive join algorithm is comparable to that of the parallel hybrid-hash join algorithm [OMI89] proposed for the same processing environment. A big advantage of the proposed algorithm over the hash-based join algorithms is that it does not have the bucket-overflow problem caused by the nonuniform hashing of the operand relations. Moreover, the proposed algorithm can easily support the non-equijoin operation, which is very hard to be implemented by the hash-based join algorithms.

References

[BOR83] H. Boral and D. J. DeWitt, "Database Machines: An Idea Whose Time Has Passed?," Proc. of Int'l Workshop on Database Machines, 1983, pp. 166-187.

[BRA84] K. Bratbergsengen, "Hashing Methods and Relational Algebra Operations," Proc. VLDB, 1984, pp. 323-333.

[CHU90] S. M. Chung and P. B. Berra, "A Database Machine Based on Concatenated Code Words for Very large Databases," *Computers for Artificial Intelligence Processing*, eds: B. W. Wah and C. V. Ramamoorthy, John Wiley and Sons, 1990. pp.352-375.

[CHU91] S. M. Chung, "Optical Database Machine Using Spatial Light Rebroadcasters," Proc. of Int'l Parallel Processing Symposium, 1991, pp.265-268.

[CHU92] S. M. Chung, "Parallel Main Memory Database System" Proc. of ACM Symposium on Applied Computing - SAC'92, 1992, pp.273-282.

[DEW85] D. J. Dewitt, R. Gerber, "Multiprocessor Hash-based Join Algorithms," Proc. VLDB, 1985, pp. 151-164.

[FOX88] G. Fox, M. Johnson, G. Lyzenga, S. Otto, J. Salmon, and D. Walker, *Solving Problems on Concurrent Processors, Vol. 1: General Techniques and Regular Problems*, Prentice-Hall, 1988.

[FRI90] O. Frieder, "Multiprocessor Algorithms for Relational-Database Operators on Hypercube Systems", IEEE Computer, Vol. 23, No. 11, 1990, pp. 13-28.

[GAR86] A. K. Garg and C. C. Gotlieb, "Order-preserving key transformations," ACM Trans. on Database Systems. Vol. 11, No. 2, 1986, pp. 213-234.

[ITO87] H. Itoh, M. Abe, et al., "Parallel Control Techniques for Dedicated Relational Database Engines," Proc. Int'l Conf. on Data Engineering, 1987, pp. 208-215.

[KIT84] M. Kitsuregawa, H. Tanaka, T. Moto-Oka, "Architecture and Performance of Relational Database Machine Grace," Proc. of Int'l Conf. on Parallel Processing, 1984, pp. 241-250.

[NEG91] M. Negri, and G. Pelagatti, "Distributive Join: A New Algorithm for Joining Relations," ACM Trans. on Database Systems, Vol. 16, No. 4, 1991, pp. 655-669.

[OMI89] E. R. Omiecinski, and E. T. Lin, "Hash-Based and Index-Based Join Algorithms for Cube and Ring Connected Multicomputers," IEEE Trans. on Knowledge and Data Engineering, Vol. 1, No. 3, 1989, pp. 329-343.

[OZK86] E. Ozkarahan, *Database Machines and Database Management*, Prentice-Hall, 1986.

[STO88] M. Stonebraker, "Future Trends in Data Base Systems," Proc. of Int'l Conf. on Data Engineering, 1988, pp. 222-231.

[SU88] S. Y. W. Su, *Database Computers*, McGraw-Hill, 1988.

[VAL84] P. Valduriez, and G. Gardarin, "Join and Semi-join Algorithms for a Multiprocessor Database Machine," ACM Trans. on Database Systems, Vol. 9, No. 1, 1984, pp. 133-161.

OPTIMIZATION OF CHAIN QUERIES

Sergio Greco
DEIS
Università della Calabria
87030 Rende, Italy
greco@ccusc1.unical.it

Abstract

Simple chain logic programs contains exactly one single recursive rule and this rule is a *chain rule*, i.e., the goals are structured in such a way that a binding on the first argument of the head predicate is propagated to the second argument. This structure gives the opportunity to exploit possibly bindings while answering queries. Indeed many methods have been proposed in the literature to devise efficient execution of bound queries on particular simple chain logic programs, e.g., linear programs. In this paper we present a general method, called the *cons-method*, which is applicable to any simple chain logic program. The method is based on the analogies of chain programs with the context free languages that are recognized by a particular scheme of pushdown automaton; indeed, the method implements this automaton as a factorized left-linear logic program. The cons-method represents a uniform generalization of previous methods such as the 'counting' and 'right-, left-, mixed-linear' methods.

1 Introduction

Recently, there has been a growing interest in the efficient bottom-up execution of logic programs with bound queries and a number of optimizations techniques, based on the rewriting of a program into an equivalent one, have been developed [3,4,6,9,13,14,18]. The presence of bindings in the query permits us to generate a new program equivalent, with respect to the query, to the original one. The new program is obtained by application of some rewriting technique and it is much more efficient under a bottom-up model computation. Rewriting techniques make the bottom-up computation preferable to the top-down computation typical of Prolog. All deductive database systems and prototypes developed exploit such techniques.

The most general rewriting technique is the *magic-set* method which can be applied to all programs. However, in many cases it is possible to optimize programs in a better way than the magic-set method does. This is the case of linear programs, that is, the class of programs whose rules contain at most one subgoal mutually recursive with the head. Many optimization techniques have been defined for subclasses of linear programs; these include the optimizations for *left-linear*, *right-linear*, *counting linear* and others. The computation of linear programs can be done efficiently also because the semi-naive evaluation considers only the incremental parts of the relations associated with the recursive predicates contrary to non-linear programs where the complete relations are also to be considered [18].

The above considerations lead to the conclusion that linear programs can be computed efficiently while non-linear do not. In [4] it has been shown that there is an order of magnitude between the performances of the linear and the non-linear versions of the program computing the transitive closure of a graph. Therefore, an interesting topic is to determine when a given non-linear program can be rewritten into a query equivalent linear program. Consider the non-linear transitive closure logic program P

```
p(X,Y) ←  b(X,Y).
p(X,Y) ←  p(X,Z),p(Z,Y).
```

It is well known that such a program is equivalent to the ('right') linear program P_1 defined as follows:

```
p(X,Y) ←  b(X,Y).
p(X,Y) ←  b(X,Z),p(Z,Y).
```

or to the following ('left') linear program P_2

```
p(X,Y) ←  b(X,Y).
p(X,Y) ←  p(X,Z),b(Z,Y).
```

However, if the query on the predicate p has one argument bound, the predicate p can be rewritten into a unary predicate. For instance, if the query is $p(a, Y)$ the above program can be rewritten as follows:

```
p(Y) ← b(a, Y).
p(Y) ← p(Z), b(Z, Y).
```

Unfortunately, there is no method that guarantees that, for a given non-linear program, it is possible to generate an equivalent linear program [1,7]. Sufficient conditions, to generate linear query equivalent programs, have been defined for restricted classes of programs [10,20,13,14,17,19]

In this paper we investigate the class of simple chain programs (chain programs with only one recursive rule) with acyclic databases, for which it is possible to generate a new equivalent linear program. The new program is equivalent to the original one with respect to the query, that is it gives the same answers for each instance of the database. We present a general method, called the *cons-method*, which is applicable to any simple chain logic program; moreover, it can be easily extended to all logic programs which contain more than one recursive chain rule. The method is based on the analogies of chain programs with the context free languages [5,2,7,8] that are recognized by a particular scheme of pushdown automaton; indeed, the method implements this automaton as a factorized left-linear logic program.

The following examples show how our method works.

Example 1 Consider the following program with the query **path(b, Y)**:

```
path(X, Y) ← X = Y.
path(X, Y) ← red(X, U), path(U, V),
             blue(V, W), path(W, Y).
```

This program defines paths from X to Y, consisting of red and blue arcs starting from the node b. The number of red arcs must be equal to the number of blue and, the number of blue arcs in each subpath starting from the node b must be less or equal than the number of red arcs in the subpaths. This program can be rewritten as a linear program where the predicate *path* contains an argument which works as a counter. This counter is incremented when a red arc is used and is decremented when is used a blue arc. The resulting program is as follows:

```
path(b, 0).
path(U, I) ← path(X, J), red(X, U),
             I = J + 1.
path(U, I) ← path(V, J), J > 0,
             blue(X, U), I = J - 1.
```

The correct answers can be obtained as answers of the query **path(Y, 0)**. □

The remainder of this paper is organized as follows In Section 3 we present the class of simple chain programs analyzing the connections with the context-free grammars and we present the rewriting method which gives a linear program equivalent, with respect to the original query, to the source program. In section 4 we informally present a reduction technique which permits to eliminates redundant rules and arguments. This technique permits to apply a counting-like technique also to non-linear programs. For space limitations the formal proofs are omitted.

2 Basic definitions

We shall assume that the reader is familiar with basic definitions and concepts of the logic programming [11] and of the DATALOG language [18]. In this section we shall only present ad-hoc definitions and notations that will be used throughout the paper.

A *cons-DATALOG program* P consists of a finite set of Horn clauses (*rules*) whose predicate symbols are classified into:

1. *base* predicate symbols, that are function-free and do not occur in any rule head of P, or

2. *derived* predicate symbols, that either are function-free or at most contain the *cons* function symbol in their arguments.

It turns out that classical DATALOG programs are a subclass of cons-DATALOG.

Following the analogy with DATALOG, base predicate symbols are defined by a set of ground facts that are stored into a database so that a cons-DATALOG program P is actually a parametric logic program which must be instantiated on some database D of facts.

A *query* Q is a pair $< G, P >$ where G is an atom, called *query-goal*, and P is a cons-DATALOG (possibly DATALOG) program. The *answer* to the query Q on a database D, denoted by $Q(D)$, is the set of substitutions for the variables in G such that G is derived from the rules in P and the facts in D. Two queries $Q =< G, P >$ and $Q' =< G', P' >$ are *equivalent* if for each database D, $Q(D) = Q'(D)$.

A *chain conjunction* is a conjunction of the form

$$p^1(X_1, X_2), p^2(X_2, X_3), ..., p^n(X_n, X_{n+1})$$

where $n \geq 0$, the predicate symbols p^i, $0 \leq i \leq n$, are not necessarily distinct, all variables X_i, $1 \leq i \leq n+1$, are distinct, and for each i, $0 \leq i < n$, the second argument of p^i is equal to the first argument of p^{i+1}. A chain conjunction will be denoted by $\mathbf{p}(X_1, X_n)$, where $\mathbf{p}$ is the string $p^1p^2 \cdots p^n$. If the conjunction is empty then $\mathbf{p}$ is the empty string ϵ and $X_1 = X_{n+1}$.

A *chain rule* is a rule of the form

$$p_0(X_1, X_n) \leftarrow \mathbf{p}(X_1, X_n).$$

We use the following general format to represent any chain rule r:

$$\begin{array}{lcl} q_0(X_1, Y_n) & \leftarrow & \mathbf{a}_1(X_1, Y_1),\ q_1(Y_1, X_2), \\ & & \mathbf{a}_2(X_2, Y_2),\ q_2(Y_2, X_3), \\ & & \ldots, \\ & & \mathbf{a}_{n-1}(X_{n-1}, Y_{n-1}), \\ & & q_{n-1}(Y_{n-1}, X_n), \\ & & \mathbf{a}_n(X_n, Y_n). \end{array}$$

where $n \geq 1$, each $\mathbf{a}_i(X_i, Y_i)$, $1 \leq i \leq n$, is a (possibly empty) chain conjunction of base predicates, each q_i, $0 \leq i \leq n-1$, is a (not necessarily distinct) derived predicate symbol.

If $n = 1$ (thus r reduces to $q(X, Y) \leftarrow \mathbf{a}(X, Y)$.) then r is called an *exit rule*. Moreover if $\mathbf{a}(X, Y)$ is the empty conjunction (thus r reduces to $q(X, X)$.) then r is called an *elementary* exit rule.

A *chain program* is a set of chain rules. A chain program is a *simple chain program* if it consists of two rules of the form:

$$\begin{array}{lcl} q(X, Y) & \leftarrow & \mathbf{a}(X, Y) \\ q(X_1, Y_n) & \leftarrow & \mathbf{a}_1(X_1, Y_1), q(Y_1, X_2), \\ & & \mathbf{a}_2(X_2, Y_2), q(Y_2, X_3), \\ & & \ldots, \\ & & \mathbf{a}_{n-1}(X_{n-1}, Y_{n-1}), \\ & & q(Y_{n-1}, X_n), \\ & & \mathbf{a}_n(X_n, Y_n) \end{array}$$

where $n \geq 1$. Thus a simple chain program is a DATALOG program with one exit rule and one recursive rule where only one derived predicate symbol occurs.

A simple chain program P is

1. *linear* if the derived predicate symbol occurs once in the body of the recursive rule, i.e., the recursive rule is

$$\begin{array}{lcl} q(X_1, Y_2) & \leftarrow & \mathbf{a}_1(X_1, Y_1),\ q(Y_1, X_2), \\ & & \mathbf{a}_2(X_2, Y_2); \end{array}$$

2. *left-recursive* if $\mathbf{a}_1(X_1, Y_1)$ is the empty conjunction, i.e., the recursive rule is

$$\begin{array}{lcl} q(Y_1, Y_n) & \leftarrow & q(Y_1, X_2),\ \mathbf{a}_2(X_2, Y_2), \\ & & q(Y_2, X_3), \\ & & \ldots, \\ & & \mathbf{a}_{n-1}(X_{n-1}, Y_{n-1}), \\ & & q(Y_{n-1}, X_n), \\ & & \mathbf{a}_n(X_n, Y_n); \end{array}$$

3. *right-recursive* if $\mathbf{a}_n(X_n, Y_n)$ is the empty conjunction, i.e., the recursive rule is

$$\begin{array}{lcl} q(X_1, X_n) & \leftarrow & \mathbf{a}_1(X_1, Y_1),\ q(Y_1, X_2), \\ & & \mathbf{a}_2(X_2, Y_2),\ q(Y_2, X_3), \\ & & \ldots, \\ & & \mathbf{a}_{n-1}(X_{n-1}, Y_{n-1}), \\ & & q(Y_{n-1}, X_n).; \end{array}$$

4. *elementary* if the exit rule is elementary, i.e., it is $q(X, X).$;

5. *trivial* if it is elementary and all conjunctions $\mathbf{a}_i(X_i, Y_i)$, $1 \leq i \leq n$, are empty.

As common in the literature, the terms left-recursive linear (resp., right-recursive linear) will be abbreviated to *left-linear* (resp., *right-linear*).

A *1-bound simple chain query* Q, is a query $< q(b, Y), P >$, where P is a simple chain program with q as derived predicate symbol, and b is a bound argument.

Observe that the recursive rule of a trivial simple chain program can be removed so that the program collapses into the single exit rule and any 1-bound query on it has only b as answer. Therefore, from now on, we shall assume that all simple chain queries are not trivial.

In the next section we present a method which, given any 1-bound simple chain query Q, constructs an equivalent query on a left-linear cons-DATALOG programs.

3 Simple Chain Programs

Consider a 1-bound simple chain query $Q =< q(b, Y), P)$ where P is:

$$\begin{array}{lcl} q(X, Y) & \leftarrow & \mathbf{a}(X, Y) \\ q(X_1, Y_n) & \leftarrow & \mathbf{a}_1(X_1, Y_1),\ q(Y_1, X_2), \\ & & \mathbf{a}_2(X_2, Y_2),\ q(Y_2, X_3), \\ & & \ldots, \\ & & \mathbf{a}_{n-1}(X_{n-1}, Y_{n-1}),\ q(Y_{n-1}, X_n), \\ & & \mathbf{a}_n(X_n, Y_n) \end{array}$$

	$\mathtt{a}_1$	$\mathtt{a}_2$	..	$\mathtt{a}_{n-1}$	$\mathtt{a}_n$	$\mathtt{a}$	ϵ
(q_1', Z_0)	$(q_1', A_1 Z_0)$					(q_{n-1}'', Z_0)	
(q_1', A_1)	$(q_1', A_1 A_1)$					(q_1'', A_1)	
(q_1'', A_1)		(q_2', A_2)					
(q_2', A_2)	$(q_1', A_1 A_2)$					(q_2'', A_2)	
(q_2'', A_2)							
.....							
(q_{n-2}', A_{n-2})	$(q_1', A_1 A_{n-2})$					(q_{n-2}'', A_{n-2})	
(q_{n-2}'', A_{n-2})				(q_{n-1}', A_{n-1})			
(q_{n-1}', A_{n-1})	$(q_1', A_1 A_{n-1})$					(q_{n-1}'', A_{n-1})	
(q_{n-1}'', A_{n-1})					(q_{n-1}'', ϵ)		
(q_{n-1}'', A_{n-2})							(q_{n-2}'', A_{n-2})
.....							
(q_{n-1}'', A_2)							(q_2'', A_2)
(q_{n-1}'', A_1)							(q_1'', A_1)

Figure 1: *Pushdown Automaton recognizing L_Q*

where $n > 1$.

We now assume that the base predicate symbols of P form an alphabet Σ, i.e., $\Sigma = \{x | x \in \mathtt{a} \vee x \in \mathtt{a}_i, 1 \leq i \leq n\}$. We associate to the query Q the context-free language $L_Q \subseteq \Sigma^*$ that is defined by the following grammar:

$$Q \rightarrow \mathtt{a}$$
$$Q \rightarrow \mathtt{a}_1\ Q\ \mathtt{a}_2\ \cdots\ \mathtt{a}_{n-1}\ Q\ \mathtt{a}_n$$

The language L_Q is recognized by the pushdown automaton shown in Figure 1 [15].

The initial state is q_1', the final state is q_{n-1}'', the start pushdown symbol is Z_0, the other pushdown symbols are $A_1, ..., A_{n-1}$ and the recognition of L_Q is by empty store. The first column of the figure contain pairs whose first element is a state e the second element is the top symbol of the pushdown store. As for the input symbols on the first row, we have used strings rather than single elements of the input alphabet Σ for the sake of presentation. As these strings are not necessarily distinct (and, besides, may coincide with the empty string and, then, with the ϵ input symbol), some columns may overlap and, then, the automaton becomes non-deterministic.

Given a database D and a string $\alpha = a_{i_1} a_{i_2} ... a_{i_m}$ in Σ^*, a *path spelling α on D* is a sequence of $m+1$ (not necessarily distinct) constants $b_0, b_1, b_2, ..., b_m$ such that for each j, $1 \leq j \leq m$, $a_{i_j}(b_{j-1}, b_j)$ is in D; if $m = 0$ then the path spells the empty string ϵ.

It is well known that, given a database D, c belongs to $Q(D)$ if and only if there exists a path from b to c, spelling a string α of L_Q on D. Therefore, in order to compute $Q(D)$, it is sufficient to use the automaton of Figure 1 to recognize all paths leaving from b and spelling a string α of L_Q on D. This can be easily done by a cons-DATALOG program P' which implements the automaton. The program P' can be directly constructed using all production rules of Figure 1. In particular, we use two predicate symbols, q' and q'', corresponding to the two types of states. Each predicate symbol has three arguments: the first stores a node of the path that is being generated, the second identifies the state, and the third is for the pushdown store. Every production rule $\delta(q, A, a) = (\hat{q}, \hat{A})$ is implemented as a cons-DATALOG rule where the

$$\begin{array}{llll}
(a): & q'(b, 1, [\,]). & & \\
(b): & q'(Y, 1, [1|T]) & \leftarrow\ q'(X, i, T),\ \mathtt{a}_1(X, Y). & \forall i: 1 \leq i \leq n-1 \\
(c): & q'(Y, i, [i|T]) & \leftarrow\ q''(X, i-1, [(i-1)|T]),\ \mathtt{a}_i(X, Y). & \forall i: 2 \leq i \leq n-1 \\
(d): & q''(Y, (n-1), [\,]) & \leftarrow\ q'(X, 1, [\,]),\ \mathtt{a}(X, Y). & \\
(e): & q''(Y, i, [i|T]) & \leftarrow\ q'(X, i, [i|T]),\ \mathtt{a}(X, Y). & \forall i: 1 \leq i \leq n-1 \\
(f): & q''(Y, (n-1), T) & \leftarrow\ q''(Y, (n-1), [(n-1)|T]),\ \mathtt{a}_n(X, Y). & \\
(g): & q''(Y, i, [i|T]) & \leftarrow\ q''(Y, (n-1), [i|T]). & \forall i: 1 \leq i \leq n-2
\end{array}$$

Figure 2: *Rewritten Program*

domain of the production occurs in the body and the range occurs in the head. The start-up of the automaton is simulated by a fact which sets both the initial state and initial path node. The resulting program is shown in Figure 2.

The rule (a) is the start-up fact; the rules of type (b) correspond to the production entries on the column $\mathbf{a}_1$; the rules of type (c) correspond to the production entries on the columns from $\mathbf{a}_2$ to $\mathbf{a}_{n-1}$; the rule (d) corresponds to the first production entry of the column $\mathbf{a}$ and the rules of type (e) correspond to the other production entries of the column; the rule (f) corresponds to the production entry of the column $\mathbf{a}_n$; finally, the rules of type (g) correspond to the production entries of the column ϵ. By using a generic index to identify a state, the rules of types (c), (e) and (g) can be actually written as three single rules as follows:

$$
\begin{array}{lll}
(b): q'(Y,1,[1|T]) & \leftarrow & q'(X,I,T), \mathbf{a}_1(X,Y). \\
(e): q''(Y,I,[I|T]) & \leftarrow & q'(X,I,[I|T]), \mathbf{a}(X,Y). \\
(g): q''(Y,I,[i|T]) & \leftarrow & q''(Y,(n-1),[I|T]).
\end{array}
$$

The above cons-DATALOG program P' is called the *cons-program* of the query Q and the query $Q' =< q''(Y,n,[\,]), P' >$ is called the *cons-query* of Q. The technique for constructing cons-queries is called the *cons-method.*

Example 2 Consider the 1-bound simple chain query $Q =< \mathtt{sg(b,Y)}, P >$, where P is the following non-linear same generation program:

$$
\begin{array}{ll}
\mathtt{sg(X,Y)} \leftarrow & \mathtt{a(X,Y)}. \\
\mathtt{sg(X_1,Y_3)} \leftarrow & \mathtt{a_1(X_1,Y_1)},\ \mathtt{sg(Y_1,X_2)}, \\
 & \mathtt{a_2(X_2,Y_2)},\ \mathtt{sg(Y_2,X_3)}, \\
 & \mathtt{a_3(X_3,Y_3)}.
\end{array}
$$

The language L_Q is generated by the following grammar:

$$
\begin{array}{lll}
S & \rightarrow & a \\
S & \rightarrow & a_1\ S\ a_2\ S\ a_3
\end{array}
$$

The automaton is shown in Figure 3.

The cons-program of Q is the following cons-DATALOG program P':

$$
\begin{array}{lll}
(a): q'(b,1,[\,]). & & \\
(b): q'(Y,1,[1|T]) & \leftarrow & q'(X,I,T), \mathbf{a}_1(X,Y). \\
(c): q'(Y,2,[2|T]) & \leftarrow & q''(X,1,[1|T]), \mathbf{a}_2(X,Y). \\
(d): q''(Y,2,[\,]) & \leftarrow & q'(X,1,[\,]), \mathbf{a}(X,Y). \\
(e): q''(Y,I,[I|T]) & \leftarrow & q'(X,I,[I|T]), \mathbf{a}(X,Y). \\
(f): q''(Y,2,T) & \leftarrow & q''(Y,2,[2|T]), \mathbf{a}_3(X,Y). \\
(g): q''(Y,I,[I|T]) & \leftarrow & q''(Y,2,[I|T]).
\end{array}
$$

Note that there is only one rule for each group (b)-(c)-(e)-(g). The query $< \mathtt{sg}''(\mathtt{Y},2,[\,]), P' >$ is the cons-query of Q. □

Theorem 1 *Let Q be a 1-bound simple chain query. Then the cons-query of Q is equivalent to Q.*

Proof (sketch): Let P be a simple chain program. Let $G(P)$ be the grammar associated with P and let $L(P)$ be the language generated by $G(P)$. Let $L_b(P)$ be the set of strings spelled (on the database D) by a path with initial node b. A constant c belongs to $Q(D)$ if and only if there exists a path from b to c spelling a string of $L(P)$ on D. Clearly the set of strings recognized by the pushdown automaton of Figure 1 is equal to $L_b(P)$. Then we conclude that a constant c belongs to $Q(D)$ if and only if it belongs to $Q'(D)$. □

3.1 Linear Programs

Consider now the case that the query Q is linear, i.e., P is

$$
\begin{array}{lll}
q(X,Y) & \leftarrow & \mathbf{a}(X,Y) \\
q(X_1,Y_2) & \leftarrow & \mathbf{a}_1(X_1,Y_1),\ q(Y_1,X_2),\ \mathbf{a}_2(X_2,Y_2)
\end{array}
$$

In this case, since $n = 2$, the cons-program of Q is

$$
\begin{array}{lll}
(a): q'(b,1,[\,]). & & \\
(b): q'(Y,1,[1|T]) & \leftarrow & q'(X,1,T), \mathbf{a}_1(X,Y). \\
(d): q''(Y,1,[\,]) & \leftarrow & q'(X,1,[\,]), \mathbf{a}(X,Y) \\
(e): q''(Y,1,[1|T]) & \leftarrow & q'(X,1,[1|T]), \mathbf{a}(X,Y). \\
(f): q''(Y,1,T) & \leftarrow & q''(Y,1,[1|T]), \mathbf{a}_2(X,Y).
\end{array}
$$

	$\mathbf{a}_1$	$\mathbf{a}_2$	$\mathbf{a}_3$	$\mathbf{e}$	ϵ
(q'_1, Z_0)	$(q'_1, A_1 Z_0)$			(q''_2, Z_0)	
(q'_1, A_1)	$(q'_1, A_1 A_1)$			(q''_1, A_1)	
(q''_1, A_1)		(q'_2, A_2)			
(q'_2, A_2)	$(q'_1, A_1 A_2)$			(q''_2, A_2)	
(q''_2, A_2)			(q''_2, ϵ)		
(q''_2, A_1)					(q''_1, A_1)

Figure 3: *Pushdown Automaton for non-linear same generation query*

No rule of types (c) and (g) exists because $n = 2$. Moreover, the two rules (d) and (e) can be merged in the following rule:

$$(d/e) : q''(Y,1,T) \leftarrow q'(X,1,T), \mathrm{a}(X,Y).$$

Moreover, since there is a single store symbol, the pushdown store can be realized through a counter which keeps the current number of elements in the store. Finally, the second argument of the state predicates can be removed as it always holds 1. Therefore the above rules can be rewritten in the following way:

$$\begin{array}{llll} (a): & q'(b,0). & & \\ (b): & q'(Y,J') & \leftarrow & q'(X,J),\ \mathrm{a}_1(X,Y), \\ & & & J' = J+1. \\ (d/e): & q''(Y,J) & \leftarrow & q'(X,J),\ \mathrm{a}(X,Y). \\ (f): & q''(Y,J') & \leftarrow & q''(Y,J),\ \mathrm{a}_2(X,Y), \\ & & & J' = J-1. \end{array}$$

Proposition 1 *The query $Q' =< q''(Y,0), P' >$ is equivalent to Q.* □

The above results is known as the counting method that turns to be a special case of the pushdown method.

The cons-method further simplifies in the case of a 1-bound elementary right-linear simple chain query $Q =< q(b,Y), P)$, where P is:

$$\begin{array}{lll} q(X,X). & & \\ q(X_1,X_2) & \leftarrow & \mathrm{a}(X_1,Y_1),\ q(Y_1,X_2). \end{array}$$

In this case the language L_Q is regular as it is defined by the following grammar:

$$\begin{array}{lll} Q & \rightarrow & \epsilon \\ Q & \rightarrow & \mathrm{a}\,Q \end{array}$$

The pushdown automaton of Figure 1 reduces to a finite state automaton with exactly one state and the following production rule: $\delta(q'',\mathrm{a}) = q''$. Hence the cons-program P' becomes to the following DATALOG program:

$$\begin{array}{lll} q''(b). & & \\ q''(Y) & \leftarrow & q''(X),\ \mathrm{a}(X,Y). \end{array}$$

Again we obtain a known result as a special case of the cons-method.

Proposition 2 *The query $Q' =< q'(Y), P' >$ is equivalent to Q.* □

The analogy with the counting method points out that the cons-method has a severe drawback: in general, as for counting method, termination for cons-queries is not guaranteed. In fact there can be infinite paths leaving b and spelling an infinite string of L_Q. On the other side, a counting query always terminates on acyclic databases. As shown below, this is also the case for cons-queries.

A 1-bound simple chain query $Q =< q(b,Y), P >$ is *acyclic* w.r.t. a database D if there exists $m \geq 0$ such that for each string $\alpha = a_{i_1} a_{i_2} \ldots a_{i_k}$ in Σ^* for which $k > m$ and $\alpha \cdot \beta \in L_Q$ for some β in Σ^*, there exists no path spelling α on D.

Proposition 3 *The cons-query of an acyclic 1-bound query is safe.*

It is easy to see that 1-bound left-recursive simple chain queries are cyclic for any database D. Thus the cons-method cannot be actually applied to such queries. Nevertheless, in the next section, we shall adapt the cons-method so that this anomaly is removed.

4 Programs Reduction

We have seen in the previous section that we can not apply the cons-method to programs which are left recursive since we push into the pushdown store an infinite number of symbols. The modification of the method consists to insert a symbol only if the corresponding conjunction is not empty. Moreover, we insert a symbol into the pushdown when the first non empty conjunction is used and we extract (resp. modify) the symbol on the top of the pushdown store when the last (resp. an intermediate) non empty conjunction is used. Therefore, if the recursive rule contains at most one non-empty conjunction the pushdown store is not updated, whereas, if the recursive rule contains exactly two non-empty conjunctions then it is sufficient to use a counter instead of the pushdown store.

Example 3 Consider the query `path(b,Y)` on the following red-blue path program.

```
path(X,Y) ← red(X,Y).
path(X,Y) ← path(X,U), blue(U,V), path(V,Y).
```

By applying the cons-rewriting method we obtain the following program P':

(a) path'(b, [ ]).
(b) path"(Y, L) ← path'(X, L), red(X, Y).
(c) path'(X, L) ← path'(X, L).
(d) path"(U, L) ← path'(X, L), red(X, U).
(e) path'(V, L) ← path"(U, L), blue(U, V).
(f) path"(Y, L) ← path'(V, L), red(V, Y).
(g) path"(Y, L) ← path"(Y, L).

□

Fact 1 *Given a program P and a rule r of the form $p(X) \leftarrow p(X)$ in P. Then, P and $P - \{r\}$ are equivalent.* □

The rules (c) and (g) of the above example can be deleted. Further, the rules (d) and (f) can be deleted since they are equivalent to the rule (b). The resulting program P" is as follows:

(a) path'(b, [ ]).
(b) path"(Y, L) ← path'(X, L), red(X, Y).
(e) path'(V, L) ← path"(U, L), blue(U, V).

Fact 2 *Given a set of mutually recursive predicates $p_1, p_2, \ldots, p_n$ then the pushdown store argument can be deleted if there is no ground rule of the form $p_i(X_i, L_i) \leftarrow p_j(X_j, L_j), \ldots$ $(1 \le i, j \le n)$ such that $L_i \ne L_j$.* □

By Fact 2 , the pushdown store argument of the program of Example ?? can be deleted. The resulting program is as follows:

(a) path'(b).
(b) path"(Y) ← path'(X), red(X, Y).
(e) path'(V) ← path"(U), blue(U, V).

Again, we have obtained the specialized optimization technique as a special case of the pushdowd method.

The next Example presents a detailed transformation of the red/blue-path program of Example 1.

Example 4 Consider the following program with the query path(b, Y):

path(X, Y) ← X = Y.
path(X, Y) ← red(X, U), path(U, V), blue(V, W), path(W, Y).

Since there are only two non-empty conjunctions in the recursive rule, the pushdown store argument reduces to a counter giving the program:

(a) path'(b, 0).
(b) path"(Y, 0) ← path'(X, 0), X = Y.
(c) path'(U, I) ← path'(X, J), red(X, U), I = J + 1.
(d) path"(V, I) ← path'(U, I), U = V.
(e) path'(W, I) ← path"(V, J), blue(V, W), I = J − 1.
(f) path"(Y, I) ← path"(W, I), W = Y.
(g) path"(Y, I) ← path"(Y, I).

The rules (d), (f) and (g), after the deletion of the equality conditions, can be deleted, giving the program:

(a) path'(b, 0).
(b) path"(Y, 0) ← path'(Y, 0).
(c) path'(U, I) ← path'(X, J), red(X, U), I = J + 1.
(e) path'(W, I) ← path"(V, J), blue(V, W), I = J − 1.

Further, by substituting the predicate path" with the predicate path' and by deleting the rule (b) we obtain the optimization presented in the introduction. □

In the previous Example we have a case where the cons-method reduces to the counting-like thechnique. We conclude this section by applying the cons-method to the non-linear transitive closure program. The reduction of the rewritten program gives a program expressing the left-linear transitive closure .

Example 5 Consider the non-linear transitive closure with the query-goal path(b, Y).

path(X, Y) ← arc(X, Y).
path(X, Y) ← path(X, Z), path(Z, Y).

The cons-method generates the following seven rules, where the pushdown store argument has been omitted because it is never updated (Fact 2):

(a) path'(b).
(b) path"(Y) ← path'(X), arc(X, Y).
(c) path'(X) ← path'(X).
(d) path"(Z) ← path'(X), arc(X, Z).
(e) path'(Z) ← path"(Z).
(f) path"(Y) ← path'(Z), arc(Z, Y).
(g) path"(Y) ← path"(Y).

The correct rewritten query-goal is path"(Y). The rules (c) and (g) can be deleted since they are of the form $p(X) \leftarrow p(X)$ (Fact 1). The rules (b), (d) and (f) coincide and then two of them can be deleted. Assume that the rules (d) and (f) are deleted. The resulting program (assuming to delete the rules (d) and (f)) contains the rules (a), (b) and (e) and is as follows:

(a) path'(b).
(b) path"(Y) ← path'(X), arc(X, Y).
(e) path'(Z) ← path"(Z).

□

5 Conclusions

In this paper we have presented a method, called *cons-method*, which transform simple chain DATALOG programs into linear cons-DATALOG programs. The method is based on the analogy of chain programs with context free languages that are recognized by a particular scheme of pushdown automaton; indeed, the method implements this automaton as a factorized left-linear logic program. The cons-method represents a uniform generalization of previous methods such as the 'counting' and 'right-, left-, mixed-linear' methods.

References

[1] F. Afrati, S. Cosmadakis. Expressiveness of Restricted Recursive Queries. In *Proc. ACM SIGACT Symp. on Theory of Computing*, 1989, pages 113–126.

[2] F. Afrati, C.H.. Papadrimitriou. The parallel complexity of simple chain queries. In *Proceedings of the Sixth ACM Symposyum on Principles of Database Systems*, 1987, pages 210–213.

[3] F. Bancilhon, D. Mayer, Y. Sagiv, and J.F. Ullman. Magic sets and other strange ways to implement logic programs. In *Proceedings of the Fifth ACM Symposyum on Principles of Database Systems*, 1986, pages 1–15.

[4] F. Bancilhon and R. Ramakrisnhan. Performance evaluation of data intensive logic programs. In J. Minker, editor, *Foundations of Deductive Databases and Logic Programming*, Morgan-Kaufman, Los altos, CA, 1988, pages 439-518.

[5] C. Beeri, P. Kanellakis, F. Bancilhon, and R. Ramakrisnhan. Bounds on the Propagation of Selection into Logic Programs, *Journal of Computer and System Science*, Vol. 41, No. 2, Oct. 1990, pages 157-180.

[6] C. Beeri and R. Ramakrisnhan. On the power of magic. *Journal of Logic Programming*, 10 (3 & 4), 1991, pages 255-299.

[7] G. Dong, On Datalog Linearization of Chain Queries. In J.D. Ullman, editor, *Theoretical Studies in Computer Science*, Academic Press, 1991, pages 181–206.

[8] G. Dong, Datalog Expressiveness of Chain Queries: Grammar Tools and Characterization. In *Proc. of the Eleventh ACM Symp. on Principles of Database Systems*, 1992, pages 81–90.

[9] S. Greco and C. Zaniolo, Optimization of linear logic programs using counting methods. In *Proceedings of the Extending Database Technology*, 1992, pages 187–200.

[10] Y.E. Ioannidis and E. Wong. Transforming non linear recursion to linear recursion. In *Proceedings Second Int. Conf. on Expert Database systems* (L. Kerschberg ed.), pages 187–207, 1988.

[11] J.W. Lloyd. *Foundations of Logic Programming*. Springer-Verlag, New York, 2nd edition, 1987.

[12] A. Marchetti-Spaccamela, A. pelaggi, and D. Saccà. Comparison of methods for logic query implementation. *Journal of Logic Programming*, 10 (3 & 4):333-361, 1991.

[13] J. Naughton, R. Ramakrisnhan, Y. Sagiv, and J.F. Ullman. Argument Reduction by Factoring. In *Proc. of the 15th Conf. on Very Large data Bases*, pages 173-182, 1989.

[14] J. Naughton, R. Ramakrisnhan, Y. Sagiv, and J.F. Ullman. Efficient evaluation of right-, left-, and multi-linear rules. In *Proceedings of the 1988 ACM SIGMOD Int. Conf. on Management of Data*, pages 235–242, 1989.

[15] J.E. Hopcroft, and J.F. Ullmann. *Introduction to Automata Theory, Languages and Computation*. Addison-Wesley, 1979.

[16] D. Saccà and C. Zaniolo, The generalized counting method of recursive logic queries for databases. *Theoretical Computer Science*, Vol. 4, No. 4, 1988, pages 187–220.

[17] Y.P. Saraiya. Linearizing nonlinear recursions in polynomial time In *Proceedings of the Eighth ACM Symposyum on Principles of Database Systems*, 1989, pages 182–189.

[18] J.F. Ullmann. *Principles of Data and Knowledge-Base Systems*. Volule 1 & 2, Computer Science Press, New York, 1989.

[19] P.T. Wood. Factoring Augmented Regular Chain Programs. *Proc. of the 16th VLDB Conference*. Brisbane, Australia, 1990, pages 225–263.

[20] W. Zang, C.T. Yu and D. Troy. Linearization of Nonlinear Recursive Rules. *IEEE Transaction on Software Engineering*, Vol. 15, No. 9, September 1989, pages 1109–1119.

RULE MANAGEMENT

DATABASE UPDATES USING ACTIVE RULES: A UNIFIED APPROACH FOR CONSISTENCY MAINTENANCE

Jong P. Yoon

School of Information Technology and Engineering
George Mason University, Fairfax, VA 22030-4444
jyoon@gmuvax2.gmu.edu

Abstract

Database operations specify the *scopes* that ensure database states and/or the *assertions* that generate database states. A query specifies the scope only, while an update specifies both the scope and the assertion. This paper describes a scheme for formulating a sequence of database updates which are constituted with appropriate constraints and rules. Constraints and rules are associated with an update (1) to ensure both an old and a new database states, (2) to correct the constraint violations, and (3) to propagate the update effects. This research contributes to a developing attack on the problem of heterogeneous processing (database update, constraint enforcement, and rule execution), by formulating a unified calculus. A semantically rich sequence of updates is then generated in a set-oriented manner.

1 Introduction

Database states are changed by means of a user's update. For the user's update posed in a knowledge and database, one or more constraints and rules are activated. As in active databases[1], an update activates constraints and rules without user's intervention. Therefore, the knowledge and database needs ***heterogeneous processes***. An update operation is to set values for attributes in a set-oriented manner. Update execution leads to new database states. Constraints are enforced to ensure database states. The predicates of a constraint are evaluated by database states. Constraint enforcement leads to a decision either to commit or abort the update. Active database systems monitor database states and activate applicable rules. Among these rules reasoning proceeds through repetitive sequences of search for selection, match, and execution of a rule at a time.

The problems of having these heterogeneous processes include first so called *impedance mismatch*. Because an update is executed based on set-oriented manner, rules and constraints are based on tuple-oriented manipulation. Although some researchers have reduced this impedance mismatch problem as in [GP91, WF90], the following second and third problems still remain. Second, an overhead control mechanism is required to switch among these heterogeneous processes for update execution, constraint enforcement, and rule deduction. To lessen this problem, active rules are specified by an IF-THEN-ON pattern, where ON clause specifies a database operation to determine when to activate the IF-THEN rule. An issue is to determine when to execute IF-THEN rules as the ON-clause is satisfied. An IF-THEN rule can be executed when either each tuple or all the tuples satisfy the ON-clause. Third, because of these heterogeneous processes, more than one processor are required and thus expensive. Although parallel processing is known to be a solution for this problem, the heterogeneous processes can not be always decomposed and so parallelized efficiently for parallelization. Update execution, constraint enforcement, and rule deduction are by nature sequential many times, for example, constraints and rules are activated in response to an update in active databases. These problems are explained using the following equation: *Database update = Logic + Control* [CCC*90]. A database update consists of a logic part that describes the semantics of the update and of a control part that determines its strategic efficiency. In connection with this equation, heterogeneous operational calculi discussed above requires three different logical expressions and correspondingly three different control mechanisms.

[1] Active rules are formed by a procedural language: IF-THEN-ON pattern [DBB*88], functioning as either constraints or rules. The semantics will be discussed in great detail in Section 2.

To overcome these problems, we propose a unified update calculus, by which updates, constraints, and rules are uniformly specified and controlled by a single control mechanism. The issues described in this paper includes the following:

- Unified Operational Calculus. Database operations specify the *scopes* that ensure database states and/or the *assertions* that generate database states. A query or a constraint specifies the scope only, while an update or a rule specifies both the scope and the assertion. Using these two underlying specification parts (i.e., scopes and assertions), updates, constraints, and rules are represented in a unified update calculus.

- Database Consistency. We develop a novel concept not only for checking database state consistencies but also for correcting constraint violations. It is quite possible that the "correction" of one violation may violate another, so does a consistent update.

The contribution of our research is a unified representation of heterogeneous operational calculi which fits the manipulation of knowledge and databases. The database updates, constraints, and rules can be specified by the *single logical* expression, and update execution, constraint enforcement, and rule deduction can be manipulated by the *single control* mechanism.

The paper is organized as follows: The remainder of this section states a motivating example to examine the problems and investigates the related work. Section 2 models constraints and rules in a model-theoretic interpretation. Section 3, Section 4, and Section 5 address a notion of consistent database update by enforcing constraints and by deducing rules for constraint violation corrections, and by deducing rules for update effect propagation, respectively. A unified framework for sequential view modification is discussed in Section 6. Finally, the summary and our future work are described in Section 7.

1.1 Motivating Example

Suppose the following update is presented to increase employee's salary by ten percent if he or she has worked over two years:

```
UPDATE      Payroll
SET         salary = salary * 1.1
WHERE ssn IN
            (SELECT  ssn
             FROM    Employee
             WHERE   years_of_expr > 2)
```

By the changes from this (SQL) update, a number of rules can be activated in an active database without user's intervention. Suppose the following rule is activated:

```
IF      salary is greater than $80000
THEN    insert into the list of high payee
ON      Update
```

The increment of salary causes the activation of the above rule, which treats the employee as a high payee if his or her salary is over $80,000. This "active" rule processing possesses the problems as follows: (1) Two heterogeneous operational calculi, update execution and rule execution, requires two processors, for example, a database management processor and a rule engine. Use of more than one processor is expensive. Moreover, an overhead control mechanism is needed to switch update execution to rule deduction, because update execution modifies database states and in turn the database state changes activate rule execution. (2) The typical SQL update language specifies only the condition (i.e., a WHERE clause) which tests for the old database not for a new database. The above update expression does not ensure whether salary is increased correctly.

1.2 Related Work

In this section, we investigate literature on constraint management, active databases, update reformulation, view update, and inconsistent states correction.

Many researchers have developed ways of specifying constraints [Kow78, Mor86, SK86], enforcing constraints [CGM90, DBB*88, SK86]. Moreover, the research of Hecht and Kerschberg [HK81], of Morgenstern [Mor84] and of Abiteboul and Hull [AH85] addresses the need for update propagation in maintaining the overall database consistency.

Active databases monitor the database states as shown in [AWH92, DBB*88] and hence appropriate rules are activated to trigger additional actions if the database states change. A declarative update specification can be transformed to a procedural specification of database updates. Manchanda in [Man89] has developed a declarative expression in which an update procedure is expressed as a sequence of primitive updates. As a special case of update, queries are reformulated in the Starburst system [PHH92]. Rules are used to transform queries into equivalent queries for a better performance. Rules are reasoned about to guide query optimization, rather than they themselves are optimized with query optimization (so called *semantic* query optimization). This idea works well if those rules are precisely designed in advance.

View update problems have been dealt with by many researchers. Kakas and Mancarella in [KM90] have used abductive approach in a way that constraint checking associated with an update is incorporated into the update to reject the generation of inconsistent states. Gottlob, Paolini, and Zicari have described in [GPZ88] how primitive update operators can be rewritten into complex updates and how view updates are translated into database updates. Our approach is similar to this approach in a way that an update is performed in a view, which may be called *view*. This consistent view update problem is generalized in our research by remodeling constraints and rules so that a user-issued update as well as relevant constraints and rules are treated as *view modifiers*.

Ceri and Widom in [CW90] have used production rules to repair inconsistent states. A method of translating constraints, which are used to detect inconsistent states, into constraint maintaining production rules, which now are used to both detect inconsistent states and initiate database operations that restore consistency. The translation requires mainly user's intervention, and it is static and manual. However, the framework for correcting constraint violations being described in our approach fits active databases. In particular, the translation in our paper is automatic, by not depending on user's interventions.

2 Modeling the Behavior of Constraints and Rules

In order to make use of constraints and rules over the course of database updates, we analyze constraints and rules in this section. Active rules are of the form IF p THEN q ON r, where p is a condition, q is an action, and r is a database operation[2], as used in [DBB*88]. These active rules are interpreted as either constraints or rules, meaning that if the condition p is satisfied then either the condition q is checked (for *constraints*) or action q is taken (for *rules*) when an UPDATE r is presented to a database.

2.1 Definition of Constraints and Rules

We define constraints or rules are defined as a pair $\mathcal{K} = \langle \mathcal{D}, \mathcal{F} \rangle$, with the following elements:

- $d \in \mathcal{D}$ is the set of predicates which characterize a subset of a database. Note that $d \in \mathcal{D}$ is a so called *view*.
- $f \in \mathcal{F}$ is a mapping of type $\mathcal{D} \longrightarrow$ T/F, where f is called a *constraint*. The constraint specifies testing one or more database states. E.g., *integrity constraints* (or simply constraints), or *functional dependencies* (in [Cod72]), etc. Note $\mathcal{D}$ denotes view and T/F denotes a truth value.
- $f \in \mathcal{F}$ is a mapping of type $\mathcal{D} \longrightarrow \mathcal{D}$, where f is called a *rule*. The rule specifies both testing one or more database states and generating one or more corresponding database states. E.g., *production rules* (or simply rules), or *triggers* etc.

[2]Since a query, an insertion, or deletion is a special case of an update, we consider only update cases in this paper.

As defined above, constraints specify the scopes of a database to restrict the view similar to queries, and rules specify the scope and then assert a new view from the specified scope similar to updates. Constraints can be rewritten in a SELECT-FROM-WHERE pattern and rules are in an UPDATE-SET-WHERE pattern.

2.2 Update Language

As stated in Section 1.1, a typical update expression, an UPDATE-SET-WHERE pattern, does not ensure both pre- and post-database states of the execution. Since update modifies from an old database to a new database, it specifies both conditions to ensure the old database and to ensure the new database. We propose the *update calculus* as follows.

```
UPDATE     relation
SET        assignment
PRECOND    condition
POSTCOND   condition
```

This update is to perform (or SET) the designated assignment on a relation if the condition in PRECOND is satisfied. It is committed (disk-updated) if the condition in POSTCOND is satisfied. Otherwise, this update is rejected unless correction process is activated. Note that "condition" in PRECOND and POSTCOND clauses can be specified by an SQL query language as described in the following sections.

2.3 Semantics of Constraints

Constraints are interpreted by using a model-theoretic approach. Both the interpretations satisfying constraints (we call it the *constraint models*, which is so called *views*) and the interpretations not satisfying (we call it the *constraint violations*) are determined. Consider constraint IF p THEN q ON r. Note that q in the THEN clause can be the value "false" (F) such that IF p THEN F ON r, meaning that there is not such case of p. In model-theoretic interpretation, constraint models are the case if p is false or if both p and q are true, while constraint violations are the case if p is true and q is false as follows.

	p	q	
case 1:	T	T	constraint model
case 2:	F	T	constraint model
case 3:	F	F	constraint model
case 4:	T	F	constraint violation

Because a constraint is a mapping $\mathcal{D} \longrightarrow$ T/F as shown in Section 2.1, the constraint ensures the view of the constraint. The view of constraint model ($\mathcal{D}$) is mapped to true (T) and the one of constraint violation is mapped to false (F). That is, constraint models represent a set of tuples satisfying the constraint, called *constraint modeling views*. Cases 1 through 3 are denoted by a mapping $\mathcal{D} \longrightarrow$ T. The constraint modeling view is for (1) both p and q hold or (2) p does not hold. On the other hand, the case 4 is denoted by a mapping $\mathcal{D} \longrightarrow$ F. The tuples corresponding to constraint violations are called the *constraint violating views*.

Consider the constraint: any employee who has over three years of work experience earns over $35,000.

```
IF      Employee.years_of_expr is greater than 3
THEN    Payroll.salary is greater than $35,000
ON      Update
```

The constraint holds if either (1) both the years of experience is over 3 and his salary is greater than $35000, or (2) the years of experience is not greater than 3. Therefore, the constraint modeling view is formed:

```
SELECT  salary
FROM    Payroll, Employee
WHERE   years_of_expr > 3 AND salary > 35000
OR      ¬(years_of_expr > 3)
```

On the other hand, the constraint violating view specifies the case such that the years of whose experience is not over three years and his or her salary is over 35,000 dollars.

```
SELECT  salary
FROM    Payroll, Employee
WHERE   years_of_expr > 3 AND ¬(salary > 35000)
```

The later section will describe that an update is performed on the constraint modeling view and the correction process is performed on the constraint violating view.

2.4 Semantics of Rules

Consider rule IF p THEN q ON r. Because a rule is defined as a mapping $\mathcal{D} \longrightarrow \mathcal{D}$, the views about the rule are divided into two views, the one before the action of the rule, which is called the *pre-execution view*, and the one after, which is called the *post-execution view*. A pre-execution view specifies the old database, and a post-execution view specifies a subset of the new database. A rule is executed on a pre-execution view, leading to a post-execution view.

Consider the rule: the salary for those who has the evaluation of "A" and the grade of 10 is $40,000.

```
IF      evaluation is "A" AND grade is 10
THEN    salary is set to be $40,000
ON      Update
```

A pre-execution view is obtained from the IF clause. The pre-execution view for the above rule is specified as follows.

```
SELECT  *
FROM    Payroll, Evaluation
WHERE   evaluation = A AND grade = 10
```

A post-execution view is obtained from the THEN clause.

```
SELECT  ssn
FROM    Payroll
WHERE   evaluation = A AND grade = 10
AND     salary = 40000
```

These rules may be used to correct constraint violating views or to propagate the effects of an update.

3 Database Update Using Constraints

This section describes that database state consistencies can be maintained by means of ordinary database updates. It is well known that constraint checking aims to determine constraint violations and to prevent them from the update execution. That is, consistent updates are guaranteed within the constraint modeling views, which are the interpretations satisfying the constraint. Notice that for notational convenience the condition $p_<$ is used in the constraints checking an old database, and the condition $p_>$ is used in the ones checking a new database. Consider the following update and constraints.

```
IF      p<          //* constraint *//
THEN    q<

UPDATE  relation
SET     assignment
WHERE   po

IF      p>          //* constraint *//
THEN    q>
```

The constraint modeling view of the first constraint is used to specifying the pre-condition of the update and the one of the second constraint is used to specifying the post-condition. The pre-condition is:

```
SELECT  *
FROM    relation
WHERE   p< AND q< AND ¬p<
```

and the post-condition is:

```
SELECT  *
FROM    relation
WHERE   p> AND q> AND ¬p>
```

This constraints - an update - constraints pattern is rewritten as:

```
UPDATE      relation
SET         assignment
PRECOND     (SELECT *
            FROM relation
            WHERE p0 AND p< AND q< OR ¬p<)

POSTCOND    (SELECT *
            FROM relation
            WHERE p> AND q> OR ¬p>)
```

An update associates "constraint checking" in this simple database update calculus.

Example: Consider the following database schema and constraints.

Employee(name, ssn, years_of_expr, dependent)
Payroll(ssn, salary)
Evaluation(ssn, job_category, evaluation, grade)
Tax_table(ssn, taxRate)

```
IF      years_of_expr is greater than 20
THEN    F
ON      Update
```

```
IF      years_of_expr is less than 5
THEN    salary is less than $50,000
ON      Update
```

Suppose that once again the update example is posed to increment of employee's salary by ten percent. Consistent update is ensured by using the above two constraints. The first constraint serves as the pre-condition, while the second constraint serves as the post-condition. The constraint modeling view of the first constraint is

```
SELECT  ssn
FROM    Employee
WHERE   ¬(years_of_expr > 20)
```

Likely, the POSTCOND is also obtained:

```
SELECT  ssn
FROM    Payroll, Employee
WHERE   years_of_expr < 5
AND     salary < 50000
OR      ¬(years_of_expr < 5)
```

Therefore, an update and two constraints are rewritten in an update calculus as follows:

```
UPDATE      Payroll
SET         salary = salary * 1.1
PRECOND ssn IN
            (SELECT   ssn
             FROM     Employee
             WHERE    ¬(years_of_expr > 20))
POSTCOND ssn IN
            (SELECT   ssn
             FROM     Payroll, Employee
             WHERE    years_of_expr < 5
             AND      salary < 50000
             OR       ¬(years_of_expr < 5))
```

4 Database Update Using Rules Toward Constraint Violations Correction

The constraint violations can be warned to users and/or be corrected (or suggested). Correction of the constraint violations is suggested by user's direct interventions [CW90] or by the consequences of rule deduction. This section describes how the constraint violations can be corrected by reasoning about the rules. These appropriate rules are also associated with an update. Consider the following update, constraint and rule. Notice that the first active rule functions as a constraint and the second functions as a rule.

```
UPDATE      relation
SET         assignment
WHERE       p0

IF      p>          //* constraint *//
THEN    q>
ON      UPDATE

IF      p           //* rule *//
THEN    q
ON      UPDATE
```

As discussed in Section 2, the constraint violating view is obtained:

```
SELECT  *
FROM    relation
WHERE   p> AND ¬q>
```

The pre-execution view of rule deduction is obtained as follows:

```
SELECT  *
FROM    relation
WHERE   p
```

The above update, constraint, and rule are rewritten by a sequence of simple database update operations. The new database resulted from the update execution is checked by constraints. The tuples satisfying this constraint now may be corrected by rule deduction. This rule deduction is performed on the intersection between the constraint violating view of constraints and the pre-execution view of a rule. Therefore, a constraint and a rule can be rewritten as follows:

```
UPDATE      relation
SET         q
PRECOND     (SELECT *
            FROM relation
            WHERE p AND p> AND ¬q>)
POSTCOND    (SELECT *
            FROM relation
            WHERE p> AND q> OR ¬p>)
```

Example: Suppose there exist the following constraint and rule:

IF	*years_of_expr* is less than 5
AND	*salary* is more than \$50,000
THEN	*taxRate* ≥ %15
ON	Update

IF	*dependent* is greater than 4
THEN	*salary* is set by *withholding_rate*(*salary*, *dependent*)
ON	Update

Consider one more time the previous update, increasing employee's salary by ten percent. The constraint violations can be specified for someone whose years of experience is less than five and salary is more than \$50,000, but tax rate is not over 15 percent, after his or her salary increment. That is, the tax table for those employees does not satisfy the constraint. These constraint violations can be corrected by rule deduction. To correct constraint violations by an update, the rule is executed on the intersection of the pre-execution view and the constraint violating view:

```
SELECT  ssn
FROM    Payroll, Employee
WHERE   salary > 50000
AND     years_of_expr < 5
AND     ¬(taxRate ≥ 0.15)
AND     dependent > 4
```

The result of the correction is ensured by using the constraint which was once violated and is now to be satisfied. The reason of specifying the post-condition is to ensure whether the correction does not lead to any other inconsistencies. The result of the correction must be in the constraint modeling view. The update associates constraints and rules to be an update as follows:

```
UPDATE   Tax_table
SET      taxRate = withholding_rate(salary, dependent)
PRECOND ssn IN
         (SELECT  ssn
          FROM    Payroll, Employee
          WHERE   salary > 50000
          AND     years_of_expr < 5
          AND     ¬(taxRate ≥ 0.15)
          AND     dependent > 4)
POSTCOND ssn IN
         (SELECT  ssn
          FROM    Payroll, Employee
          WHERE   years_of_expr < 5
          AND     taxRate ≥ 0.15
          AND     salary > 50000
          OR      ¬(taxRate ≥ 0.15))
```

This approach fits the efforts on available resources reuse in active databases.

5 Database Update Using Rules Toward Update Effects Propagation

In active databases, database state changes lead to further rule execution. Rule execution for correcting the constraint violations has been discussed in Section 4. This section describes rule execution for propagating the update effects. Very similar to the notion in the previous section, we consider an update and a rule.

```
UPDATE   relation
SET      assignment
WHERE    p0

IF    p        //* rule *//
THEN  q
ON    UPDATE
```

Update effect propagation is performed based on the intersection between the post-execution view of the update and the pre-execution view of the rules. Notice that since the new database contains the tuples satisfying the WHERE clause, the pre-execution view is used for propagation. The given rule can be rewritten as:

```
UPDATE   relation
SET      q
PRECOND  (SELECT *
          FROM relation
          WHERE p AND p0)
```

<u>**Example:**</u> Suppose the following update which is to increase employee's salary by ten percent where *years_of_expr* is over 2 years.

```
UPDATE   Payroll
SET      salary = salary * 1.1
WHERE ssn IN
         (SELECT  ssn
          FROM    Employee
          WHERE   years_of_expr > 2)
```

IF	*dependent* is greater than 4
THEN	*salary* is set by *withholding_rate*(*salary*, *dependent*)
ON	Update

The rule is rewritten by an update calculus and so are used to update effect propagation.

```
UPDATE   Tax_table
SET      taxRate = withholding_rate(salary, dependent)
PRECOND ssn IN (SELECT  ssn
                FROM    Employee
                WHERE   dependent > 4
                AND     years_of_expr > 2)
```

6 Discussion

The update calculus we developed in this paper can be used to allow an expressive power update sequence. An update associates constraints and rules in the update calculus as the following paradigm:

```
//* (1) Update with constraint checking *//
UPDATE     relation
PRECOND    constraint modeling views
POSTCOND   constraint modeling views
//* (2) Correction with rule deduction *//
UPDATE     relation
SET        assignment
PRECOND    constraint violating views
           AND pre-execution views
POSTCOND   constraint modeling views
//* (3) Propagation with rule deduction *//
UPDATE     relation
SET        assignment
PRECOND    pre-execution views
POSTCOND   post-execution views
```

This update sequence consists of only update execution with constraint checking (labeled (1) above), and at least update execution with rule deductions (labeled (2) or (3)). The difference between the updates (1), (2) and (3) is based on the view description. The condition clause in (1) is about constraint models, while the the one in (2) is about constraint violations and the one in (3) is about an inquired view. (3) is processed by forward chaining with a view materialization technique. Using this update calculus, rules and constraints can be rewritten in the update calculus and therefore, set-oriented manipulation becomes realistic.

The issues left undeveloped in this paper include first update optimization. What appropriate constraints and rules are selected and associated with an update in what order. Conflict resolution is another big research issue. During update optimization, secondly, an update algebra is necessary. The semantically rich sequence of updates described in this paper is to be compiled for primitive database algebraic expression.

7 Summary and Future Work

We have presented a unified approach for consistent update management using constraints and rules in active databases. The summary of our work is as follows.

- A unified database update calculus has been developed. A single database update issued by a user can be transformed as a semantically rich update expression by associating with constraints and rules.
- Since a system-constituted update associates with constraints and rules, database consistencies are maintained efficiently. This notion has been implemented in object-oriented databases [YK92].
- Tolerant database updates are performed. Updates are performed on the only valid tuples and the update effects are propagated for those valid tuples. However, invalid tuples can be corrected by rule deduction as well under system administrators.

The update calculus described in this paper expresses a negation. An implementation issue about the negation in an update calculus, however, is a determination between the closed world assumption or the open world assumption.

The benefits described in this paper include the following:

- The update calculus makes it easy to express update execution with constraint enforcement and rule deduction in a unified set-manipulation.
- Semantic query optimization is a particular case of semantic update optimization stated in this paper. Therefore, the semantic update reformulation framework can be used to optimize queries semantically [LHQ91].
- Updating on views is useful for software engineers to check out a portion (a view) of the design from the software repository, to move the view to a local view and to work on it.

Let us conclude this paper by giving some outlines of the research we plan to carry out in the future. Because many rules and constraints are related to an update, it is necessary to take account of a small number of those rules and constraints if applicable. We may reduce this number of rules and constraints with which the largest inquired view can be preserved.

As seen earlier, a database can be divided into constraint modeling view and constraint violating view. These two divided views may activate rules for propagation and rules for correction in parallel. This idea is similar to the concept of *incremental join* developed to enable a parallel process of *Rete network* in [For82]. We believe that this notion may lead to parallel activation of constraints and rules for an update.

References

[AH85] S. Abiteboul and R. Hull. Update propagation in the IFO database model. In *Proceedings of the International Conf. on Foundations of Data Organization*, pages 243–251, Kyoto, 1985.

[AWH92] Alexander Aiken, Jennifer Widom, and Jeseph M. Hellerstein. Behavior of database production rules: termination, confluence, and observable determinism. In Michael Stonebraker, editor, *Proc. ACM SIGMOD Intl. Conf. on Management of Data*, pages 59–68, San Diego, 1992.

[CCC*90] F. Cacace, S. Ceri, S. Crespi-Reghizzi, L. Tanca, and R. Zicari. Integrating object-oriented data modeling with a rule-based programming paradigm. In Hector Garcia-Molina and H.V. Jagadish, editors, *Proc. ACM SIGMOD Intl. Conf. on Management of Data*, pages 225–236, Atlantic City, NJ, 1990.

[CGM90] Upen S. Chakravarthy, John Grant, and Jack Minker. Logic-based approach to semantic query optimization. *ACM Transactions on Database Systems*, 15(2):163–207, June 1990.

[Cod72] E. F. Codd. Relational completeness of data base sublanguages. In R. Rustin, editor, *Data Base Systems*, pages 65–98, Prentice-Hall, Englewood Cliffs, N.J., 1972.

[CW90] S. Ceri and J. Widom. Deriving production rules for constraint maintenance. In *Proc. Intl. Conf. on Very Large Data Bases*, pages 650–661, Brisbane, Australia, 1990.

[DBB*88] U. Dayal, B. Blaustein, A. Buchmann, U. Chakravarthy, R. Ledin M. Hsu, D. McCarthy, A. Rosentha., S. Sarin, M. J. Carey, M. Livny, and R. Jauhari. The HiPAC project: combining active databases and timing constraints. *ACM SIGMOD Record*, 17(1):51–70, March 1988.

[For82] C. L. Forgy. Rete: a fast algorithm for the many pattern/many object match problem. *Artificial Intelligence*, 19:17–37, 1982.

[GP91] Douglas N. Gordin and Alexander J. Pasik. Set-oriented constructs: from rete rule bases to database systems. In J. Clifford and R. King, editors, *Proc. ACM SIGMOD Intl. Conf. on Management of Data*, pages 60–67, Denver, 1991.

[GPZ88] G. Gottlob, P. Paolini, and R. Zicari. Properties and update semantics of consistent views. *ACM Transactions on Database Systems*, 13(4):486–524, 1988.

[HK81] Matthew S. Hecht and Larry Kerschberg. *Update Semantics for the Functional Data Model.* Technical Report Database Research Report No. 4, Bell Laboratories, Holmdel, New Jersey, January 1981.

[KM90] A. C. Kakas and P. Mancarella. Database updates through abduction. In *Proc. Intl. Conf. on Very Large Data Bases*, pages 650–661, Austrailia, 1990.

[Kow78] R. Kowalski. Logic for data description. In H. Gallaire and J. Minker, editors, *Logic and Data Bases*, pages 77–103, Plenum Press, New York, 1978.

[LHQ91] Sang-goo Lee, Lawrence J. Henschen, and Ghassan Z. Qadah. Semantic query reformulation in deductive databases. In *Intl. Conf. on Data Engineering*, pages 232–239, 1991.

[Man89] Sanjay Manchanda. Declarative expression of deductive database updates. In *Proceedings of the ACM Symposium on Principles of Database Systems*, pages 93–100, Philadelphia, 1989.

[Mor84] M. Morgenstern. Constraint equations: declarative expression of constraints with automatic enforcement. In *Proc of VLDB*, pages 111–125, 1984.

[Mor86] M. Morgenstern. The role of constraints in databases. In Larry Kerschberg, editor, *Expert Database Systems*, pages 351–368, Morgan Kaufmann, 1986.

[PHH92] Hamid Pirahesh, Joseph M. Hellerstein, and Waqar Hasan. Extensible/rule based query rewrite optimization in starburst. In *Proc. ACM SIGMOD Intl. Conf. on Management of Data*, pages 39–48, 1992.

[SK86] A. Shepherd and L. Kerschberg. Constraint management in expert database systems. In Larry Kerschberg, editor, *Expert Database Systems*, pages 309–368, Morgan Kaufmann, 1986.

[WF90] Jennifer Widom and Sheldon J. Finkelstein. Set-oriented production rules in relational database systems. In Hector Garcia-Molina and H. V. Jagadish, editors, *Proc. ACM SIGMOD Intl. Conf. on Management of Data*, pages 259–270, Atlantic City, NJ, 1990.

[YK92] Jong P. Yoon and Larry Kerschberg. A framework for constraint management in object-oriented databases. In *Proc. of the First International Conference on Information and Knowledge Management*, pages 292–299, Baltimore, MD, 1992.

A Database Rule Language Compiler Supporting Parallelism

J.-P. Cheiney
ENST , 46 rue Barrault
Paris , France
cheiney@inf.enst.fr

G. Kiernan
INRIA Rocquencourt
78153 Le Chesnay, France
kiernan@rodin.inria.fr

C.de Maindreville
Alcatel-Alsthom Recherche
91460 Marcoussis, France
maindrev@aar.alcatel-alsthom.fr

Abstract
This paper presents an extension to a database rule language compiler to support parallelism. The rule language is called RDL//C and is based on an extended version of tuple relational calculus. The grain of parallelism introduced into RDL//C is the production rule. The user is made aware of parallel processing by having to specify in a sub-language of control which sets of rules are to run in parallel and in which order. From the user view point, the parallelism is managed as a partial order over a set of rules. The compiler translates rule programs into C based applications which run over the DBMS. Our implementation is over a set of UNIX workstations which corresponds to a MIMD shared-nothing architecture. Parallelism is achieved by having the application connect to different DBMS servers residing on workstations on a local network. Initial performance results are presented. They show the advantages and limitations of parallel execution in this architecture. The main contributions of the paper are (i) the definition of a sub-language of control to specify a parallel execution of a rule program and (ii) to show how parallel extensions can be brought to a rule language compiler using a standard distributed environment with a relational DBMS.

***Key words** : Production Rules, Parallelism, Language of Control, Compilation, RDBMS, Implementation.*

1. Introduction

Rule languages have long been recognized as candidates for parallel languages [Almasi89, Ganguly90, Wolfson90]. Parallel evaluation of Datalog programs has been studied in [Ganguly90, Wolfson90]. These papers introduce the notion of *discriminating predicate* which allows the instanciations of rules to be partitioned among different processors. Both papers are concerned with the reduction of communication overhead and load balancing between the processors and discuss the trade-off between non-redundancy and communication costs. One important result stated in [Wolfson90] is the undecidability of the decomposition problem. The parallel evaluation of Datalog-neg programs is discussed in [Wolfson90]. For such programs, in general, the processors have to be synchronized at each stratum. This means that each processor has to wait until all the processors have completed their computation before proceeding to the next stratum.

Experiments with parallelism in production systems such as OPS5 [Brownston85] have been presented in [Gupta89]. In such environments, it is up to the system to detect the possible sources of parallelism in a rule program. It is also the system's job to guarantee that the parallel execution of a rule program is equivalent to the sequential one. Different sources of parallelism have been identified [Almasi89]. The most obvious one is the production rule as the unit of parallelism. Production rules which can run independently are detected and each group is assigned a processor. Three other sources of parallelism are AND-parallelism, OR-parallelism, and Parallel pattern matching. These last three sources of parallelism concern intra-rule parallelism. A single production rule is decomposed into sub-parts which can run independently. The first two types of parallelism come from AND/OR graphs which represent the connection between the predicates and rules which comprise a production system. In the case of Horn clauses, for example, the ANDs are the conjunction of expressions which form the body of a rule; and the ORs are rules with identical heads. Parallel pattern matching is the implementation of a parallel version of the inference engine.

In [Almasi89], the authors report the claim that a production rule application which is written with parallel processing in mind yields a higher degree of useful parallelism than one which is written with a serial machine in mind. Moreover, the performance gained is proportional to the number of rules in the system; and of course to the number of processing elements. They also claim that the useful parallelism and the speed-up from the "rule-per-processor-approach" is yet to be fully established. This indicates that while it is up to the system to detect and implement parallelism, the user must know how the system achieves this parallelism in order to exploit it fully. In [Srivastava89], two types of parallelism are proposed for database production systems. These are user-visible and user-transparent categories. It is the user's responsibility to divide a task into non-interacting subtasks and it is the system's responsibility to execute each element of a subtask in parallel.

The approach presented in this paper supports parallelism at the rule level. The user is made aware of parallel processing by having to specify which sets of rules are to run in parallel and in which order. A control sub-language is used for this purpose. We propose that a parallel algorithm is better than a sequential one on which a certain degree of parallelism might be automatically extracted. We do not address in this paper the automatic detection of parallelism in rule programs.

This paper presents an extension to a rule language compiler to support parallelism. A prototype of the RDL//C compiler is operational on a network of UNIX workstations [Unix84]. Since RDL/C [Kiernan90b, Kiernan91] production rules are based on relational calculus, they can be solved by a relational DBMS without having to extract data during the inference cycle. The inference is driven from the application (generated by the compiler) through a series of calls to the DBMS using an SQL interface. The compiler manages parallelism in production rules by generating a program which connects to several DBMS over a network of workstations. In this framework, each DBMS is a parallel processing unit. The application communicates with each DBMS using standard UNIX interprocess communication facilities called sockets. To run a set of rules in parallel, the application process forks (fork is a UNIX system call which creates a new process from a current process) a number of times equal to the number of sets of rules which are to be run in parallel. The system architecture is an MIMD share-nothing architecture. Intra-rule parallelism cannot be supported without modification of the underlying DBMS, it is therefore not discussed in this paper.

The main contribution of the paper is to show how a parallel production system can be implemented over a network of workstations. Initial performance results indicate the advantages of this approach for high performance production rule systems. Section 2 presents an overview of the production rule language which is used throughout this paper. Production Compilation Networks (PCN) [Maindreville88] as a model of parallelism are introduced in Section 3. PCN are the computational model for the RDL//C production rule system. Section 4 describes the syntactic extensions that were brought to the serial version of the compiler to support parallelism. Section 5 concerns the architecture. The compiler and the run-time support are presented. Section 6 details the implementation and Section 7 gives performance results and discuss the advantages and limitations of this approach.

2. Overview of the Language

RDL//C is derived from RDL1 [Maindreville88, Kiernan90a], a production rule language which has been integrated in the Sabrina RDBMS [Gardarin89]. The RDL//C language supports declarative programming based on RDL1 and procedural programming based on C code. In this section, we present an overview of the language through some examples. The syntax and semantics of RDL//C are given in [Kiernan90b, Kiernan91].

2.1. Illustrative Example

Consider the base relation Parent having the schema Parent (asc integer, desc integer). The following rule program computes the transitive closure of the Parent relation :

```
MODULE ancestor ;
BASE
        Parent (asc int, desc int);
DEDUCED
        Ancestor LIKE Parent;

RULES
r1 is
   IF Parent (x)
        THEN + Ancestor (x) ;
r2 is
   IF Parent (x) and Ancestor(y) (x.desc = y.asc)
        THEN + Ancestor (asc = x.asc, desc = y.desc);
END MODULE
```

A parallel version of this program will be presented in Section 7, when performance issues are discussed.

2.2. The Kernel Language

2.2.1. The Syntax

The rule part of an RDL//C program is composed of a set of if-then rules. The IF part of a rule is a tuple relational calculus expression. Its syntax is very close to the syntax of a WHERE clause in the SQL language. The THEN part of a rule is a set of *actions* that are insertions, deletions of tuples in relations, procedural side-effects and variable assignments. A discussion of the latter two types of actions are beyond the scope of this paper. However, they are described in [Kiernan90b]. The action part is very close to the SELECT clause of an SQL statement.

Let Person and Worker, be two relations having the same schema (id integer, name char, age integer).

The following expressions are valid Left-Hand-Sides (LHS) of rules :

```
Person(x) and Worker(y) (x.id = y.id)
Foreach x in Person (x.age + 1 > 20)
Person(x) (x.age > 20)
```

The Right-Hand Side (RHS) of a production rule supports two elementary actions, denoted "+" and "-". The update action "+" takes a set of facts and maps a database state into another state which contains these facts. On the contrary, the action "-" takes a set of facts and deletes it from a relation. A *multiple action* consists in a sequence of actions.

The following expressions are valid RHS of rules :

```
+Person(x)
-Person(x)    +Person(id = x.number, name =
x.name, age = x.age + 1)
+Person(x) + Person(y) - Worker(x)
```

Following is a set of valid rules :

```
If Person(x) then + Worker(x) ;
If Person(x) ( x.id = 4) then - Worker(x) ;
If Person(x) then + Person(x)   -Person(id= x.id,
name= x.name, age= x.age +1);
```

2.2.2. The Semantics

The semantics adopted for the RDL//C language is a set oriented one. When a condition is evaluated against the database, it returns the set of instances which make the condition valid. When an action is executed against the database, it is executed for all the values which appear as arguments in the action. In the following, we present examples of rule execution.

Let us consider the following rules :

Firing the following rule causes the insertion into the Worker relation of the contents of the Person relation .

```
if Person(x) then + Worker(x) ;
```

Firing the following rule causes the deletion from the R1 relation of the contents of the Person relation.

```
if Person(x)  then - R1(x) ;
```

Firing the following rule leads to a null action.

```
if Person(x)  then - R1(x)  + R1(x) ;
```

Firing the following rule

```
if Person(x) and R1(y) and x.att1 = 10 and
x.att2 = y.att2
then +Q1(att1 = x.att1, att2 = y.att1) - R1(y) ;
```

causes the insertion into the Q1 relation the set of tuples :

```
I = {x.att1, y.att2/Person(x) and R1(y) and
x.att1 = 10 and x.att2 = y.att2 }
```

and the deletion from R1 the set

```
D = {x | Person(x) and R1(y) and x.att1 = 10 and
x.att2 = y.att2}
```

2.3. Partial Ordering of Rules

The mixing of declarative reasoning and imperative control has been shown necessary for many applications. A control language has been designed to specify an application mode over the rules. It induces a partial ordering over the rules. Each expression of the sub-language is declared in the module. The basic terms of control language are rule names. A general expression exp in the control language is :

```
block (exp) means that exp has to be fired until
a fixpoint is reached.
seq (exp1,exp2 ) means that exp1 is fired once
and then exp2 is fired once.
```

If a rule name does not appear in the control part of the program, its firing is chosen at random by the inference engine. If there is no CONTROL section, the rule interpreter applies a default strategy. The priority of rules is according to the order of their appearance in the module.

Let us consider a rule program {r1, r2, r3, r4, r5}.

seq (r1, block (r2, r3, r4), r5) is a possible expression. It enforces a computation of the form : $(r1)^a \; ((r2)^*(r3)^*(r4)^*)^\sigma (r5)^a$ using standard notation for context-free grammars. The notation $()^\sigma$ stands for "fire up to saturation", * is equal to N or 0 and a is equal to 1 or 0.

3. The PCN Model of Parallelism

The PCN is used as an execution model for the RDL//C language. It provides the inference engine with a graphical representation of a rule program. The PCN model has been introduced in [Maindreville88]. The PCN model is a Petri Net based model and derived from Predicate Transition Nets (PrTN). A formal definition of PrTN can be found in [Genrich86]. The structure of a PCN represents the relationships between rules and relational predicates which occur in a rule program. We represent each rule by a transition and each relational predicate involved in the rule by a place. The relational predicates that occur in the condition part of a rule are input places to the transition representing the rule and the relational predicates that occur in the action part of the rule are the output places of the transition. The condition of a rule is represented in the transition's condition. Figure 3.1 represents the PCN associated to the rule program which computes the transitive closure of the Parent relation. The initializing rule is modelled by the transition T1. The recursive rule is modelled by the transition T2. Place P corresponds to the Parent relation and Place A corresponds to the Ancestor relation.

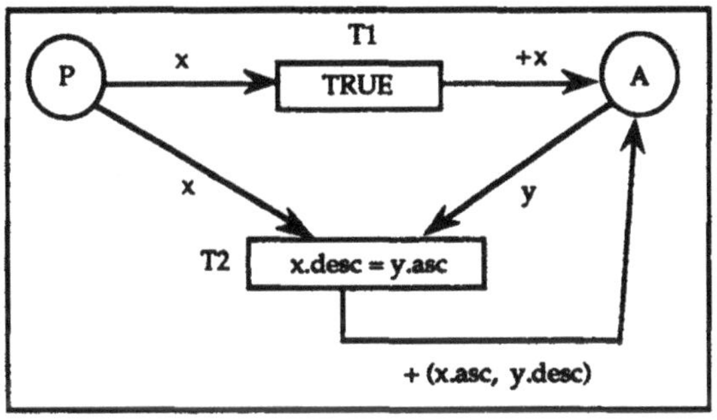

Figure 3.1: *PCN for the Ancestor rules*

A *marking* is a distribution of tokens over the places of a PCN. The token is a basic concept in the PCN model, and represents a database tuple. Traditionally, a Petri Net based model proceeds by firing transitions. A transition can be fired if it is enabled. A transition firing produces tokens according to the labels of the output edges. For a given initial marking, a place P has a *stable marking* iff none of its input transitions is enabled. A transition T is said to be *stable* for a given initial marking iff all its output places have a stable marking. When the PCN reaches a stable marking, no transition can be enabled and the PCN evaluator procedure halts. This corresponds to a fixpoint for the set of rules modelled by the net.

The control language defined in the previous section can be mapped onto a PCN [Maindreville88]. Rule names are then replaced by transition names. A sequence of the control language is called annotation. A PCN and its annotation constitutes an *annotated PCN*.

The PCN model supports parallelism at the rule level as it is shown in the following example : consider the PCN,

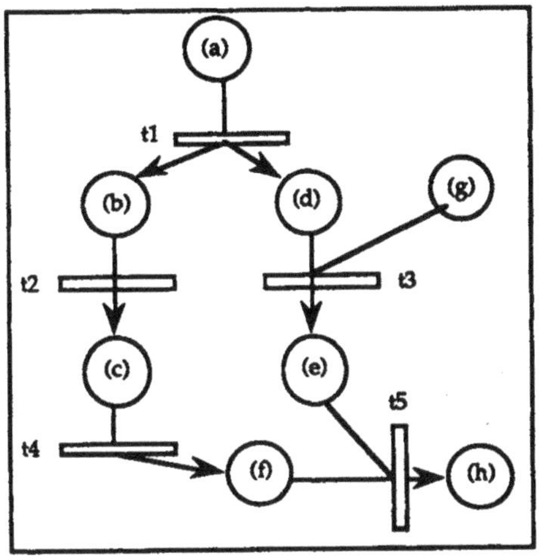

Figure 3.2 : *PCN*

The firing of the transitions t2 and t3 is easily parallelized since they do not share any post places in the PCN structure. On the contrary, the transitions t4 and t5 are not easily parallelized since the firing of t5 needs the contents of the place named f which is given by the firing of t4. Such a restriction is due to the set oriented computation of each transition (rule). A dataflow execution would have allowed the relaxation of this kind of limitation.

We now give syntactic restrictions over the PCN structure that allow the parallelization of a rule program. The limitations are of two different kinds. The first one is due to the parallel granularity we chose, i.e. the rule. The second one is for semantic considerations. As discussed in [Wolfson90], for non deterministic languages such as Datalog-neg, the processors have to be synchronized at each stratum. As RDL//C is an extension of Datalog-neg, the same limitation applies : a non recursive transition is fired iff its input places have reached a stable marking. As shown in [Maindreville88], this induces a partial ordering on the rule program and, for instance, implements the notion of stratification. This limitation synchronizes read/write operations between rules. That is, a rule is not allowed to write data in a relation which is read by another rule in parallel (see rules t4 and t5 in the previous section).

These limitations are expressed over the PCN model as follows:

Let us consider {ti} a set of transitions, and Pre(ti) and Post(ti) the input and output places of ti. Then tl and tk can be parallelized (noted by tl // tk), iff:

- $Post(tl) \supset Pre(tk)$ or $Post(tk) \supset Pre(tl)$
- $Post(tl) \neq Post(tk)$ for each l, k

These two conditions allow only independent rules to be fired in parallel. They ensure that the semantics of the rule program are preserved by the parallel processing. On the PCN displayed in figure 3.2, only transitions (rules) t2, t4 and t3 can be run in parallel.

4. Extending the Language to Support Parallelism

The RDL/C language has been extended to support inter rule parallelism. The parallelism is specified in the control language as an explicit partial ordering over the set of rules. The language extension used to specify parallelism among the rules is the PAR structure, found in the control string. Each argument is itself a control argument. PAR can be nested. Semantic checks are done over the arguments to ensure that the rules to be run in parallel are independent as defined in the previous section. Consider the following example:

```
SEQ (r0, PAR (SEQ (r1, BLOCK (r2)), SEQ (r1B,
BLOCK (r2B))), r3)
```

This control structure specifies two sets of rules to be run in parallel. The first set contains rules r1 and r2; the second set contains rules r1B and r2B. The control structure of the first set states that rule r1 fires once and that rule r2 fires up to saturation. Rules r1 and r2 will run on the server servA and rules r1B and r2B will run on the server servB. When a set of rules has been fired according to the control structure given in the control string, the process controlling it attempts to synchronize with other processes running other sets in parallel. All rules in the PAR control structure must have fired according to the control string before the engine attempts to fire rule r3. Consider the following control string.

```
SEQ (r0, PAR (r1, r2), r3, PAR (r4, r5), r6)
```

In the above example, the engine will attempt to fire rule r0, and then fire rules r1 and r2 in parallel. When r1 and r2 are no longer firable, the engine will move on to rule r3 and then, attempt to fire rules r4 and r5 in parallel before firing r6. The following control structure is equivalent to the previous one.

```
SEQ (r0, PAR (BLOCK (r1), BLOCK (r2)), r3, PAR
(BLOCK (r4), BLOCK (r5)), r6)
```

A rule which is run in parallel can also be run sequentially in the same module. This is the case for rule r2 in the following example.

```
SEQ (r0, r1, PAR (r2, r3), r4, r2, r5)
```

The inference engine will attempt to fire rules r2 and r3 in parallel. It will then attempt to fire rule r4 before attempting to fire rule r2 again.

5. Architecture

5.1. Overview of the Compiler

The general architecture of the RDL//C compiler is portrayed in Figure 5.1.

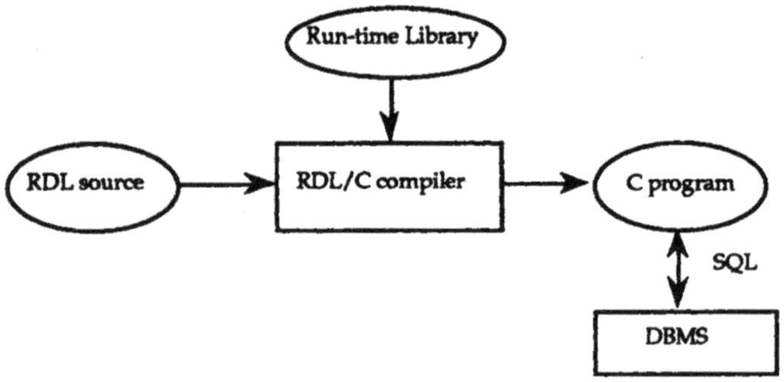

Figure 5.1 : *Sketch of the RDL//C compilation environment.*

The compiler accepts a source program and produces, as output, a C program which implements the rule program. The C program contains code to implement each rule and includes the inference engine which fires rules until a fixpoint is reached. The DBMS does not require any inferencing capabilities to process the program. The extraction of the data from the DBMS to the application is not required during the inference process. This is because rules are based on relational calculus and can thus be solved by the DBMS.

The compiler generates an SQL connection statement for each server specified in the ON statement in the module. The PAR structure is compiled from the control string in basically the same way as are the other two structures SEQ and BLOCK. The run-time library which is linked with the C program produced by the compiler manipulates parallelism. These procedures are the topic of the next section.

5.2. Run-time Environment

The run-time environment is a set of workstations linked to one another through a network. Each workstation has similar computational power. The application resides on one workstation while each workstation is assigned one DBMS process. Each DBMS has its local database. Each relation referenced in a module must be found in at least one site. This allows a horizontal and vertical partitioning of relations in so long as each partition is a named relation existing on a site. The DBMS is a standard relational DBMS. Although the one that we are using supports Abstract Data Types [Gardarin89], this is not relevant for parallel processing. Parallelism is achieved by having the application access each DBMS concurrently.

5.2.1. UNIX System Tools

This architecture is supported by the UNIX operating system. The key facilities used to support parallelism are the process control facilities and network facilities. The UNIX *fork* statement creates a duplicate process from a running process. Running concurrent processes communicate using sockets and pipes. Sockets and pipes are similar structures used to support interprocess communication. The Network File System (NFS) allows users on different machines to share files.

5.2.2. Schema of the Run-Time Environment

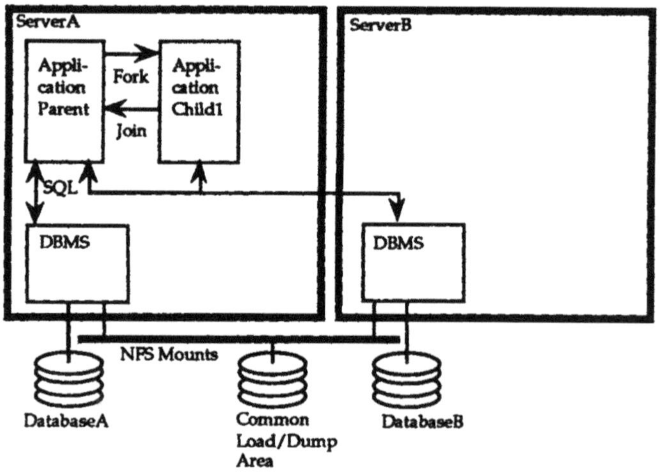

Figure 5.2 : *The Run-Time Environment.*

5.2.3. The Application and the DBMSs

An application requiring access to the database issues an SQL *connect* statement to establish a connection to the DBMS. The application and the DBMS then communicate through sockets. The application issues SQL commands to the DBMS and the DBMS returns its results after each command. There is normally one such connection between an application and the DBMS. However, to exploit the power of parallel processing, the compiler generates an application which establishes a connection with DBMS residing on different machines. The application can thus communicate with each DBMS by using the communication link that is assigned to it.

5.2.4. The Parent Application and its Children

Although the application can access each DBMS independently, it cannot do so in parallel without creating extra processes. To run a set of rules in parallel, the parent (or main) process creates a child process for each set of rules which are to be run in parallel. This is achieved with the UNIX fork system call. Each child is assigned a particular DBMS. All application processes reside on the same machine regardless of the fact that they access DBMS which are on different machines. Before creating a child, the parent dumps all the relations which are referenced in the set of rules managed by the child. The child loads the relations before starting to process the rules. Running parallel processes synchronize when they have finished running the set of rules they have been assigned. Each child must return information on the rules that it fired; this communication is done through pipes. One such pipe is created per child process. Relations which were created by a child process must be made available to the parent. This is achieved by having the child dump these relations on a common file system and the parent load them from this same file system. The restrictions over the PCN avoid any collisions between relations being dumped. Two rules running in parallel can not reference a same relation in the RHS. After having done this, the child process exits. The parent process synchronizes with the child processes once it has finished running the set of rules that were assigned to it. The parent synchronizes with each child, one after the other. Once it has finished, the parent process can resume firing rules in sequence or in parallel.

6. Implementation

Processing a PAR in the Control String

The algorithm used to process PAR in the control string is the following one. It is given in pseudo C language notation.

The control string is the support for parallelism in the language. The control string is mapped to an in-memory data structure which is used by the inference engine. While processing the control string, if the inference engine encounters a Par control structure, the engine tries to fork child processes to run rules in parallel. To do this, it goes through the following steps. First, it determines, for a set of rules, if there are pertinent rules in the set. If there are no pertinent rules, it marks the fact that no child process has been created to run the rules. Otherwise, it scans the rules in a set to determine which relations are manipulated by the rules. Each non-empty relation that has not been dumped is unloaded into the common load/dump area. Then, a pipe is created to communicate between the parent and the child and the fork system call is issued. The child sets a number of variables to identify and to communicate with the DBMS on which it will run its set of rules. It attempts to load the relations which have been dumped by the parent process. It will then run independently from the parent until it has fired all the rules in its set. At this point, it will synchronize with the parent.

Version numbers are used to determine if a relation has been dumped. Each time a relation is modified by the RHS of a rule, its version number is incremented. When scanning relations to unload them into the common area, the version number is compared to the dump number of the relation. If it is less, the relation is unloaded and the dump number is set to the version number. The unload is realized by the SQL-like Copy command.

```
function processControlString (*cl : controlString) -> rule ;
    controlString *c2;
begin
    while (cl <> NULL) do
    begin
        switch (cl->type) /*on the type of control structure being processes*/
        ..
        case PAR:
            /* process each par parameter */
            /* the first parameter is handled by the parent */
            /* each remaining parameter is handled by a child process */
            c2 = cl->parameterList;
            c2 = c2->next;
            i=0;
            while (c2 <> NULL) do
                begin
                    i++;
                    if (c2 has no pertinent rules) then
                        begin
                            idChild[i] = 0;
                            c2 = c2->next;
                        end
                    else
                        begin
                            dumpRelations (c2);
                            pipe (pipes[i]);
                            pid = fork();
                            if (pid is the parent) then
                                begin
                                    idChild[i] = pid;
                                    c2 = c2->next;
                                end
                            else
                                begin
                                    /* prepare the child */
                                    serverId = i;
                                    fp = fdopen (pipe in write mode);

                                    /* eliminate all other PAR parameters*/
                                    c2->next = NULL;

                                    /* set DBMS communication link */
                                    /* for child */
                                    fdr = fdw = fdrw[serverId];

                                    loadRelations();
                                    cl = c2;
                                end
                        end
                end
            processControlString (cl->parameterList);
        end

        case RULE:
                if (the rule pointed to by cl
                    ISIN the list of pertinent rules) then
                    return (the rule pointed to by cl);
        end;

        cl = cl->next;
    end
    return(NULL); /* no pertinent rule can be found in this parameter list */
end
```

The child process scans all relations which are referenced in its set of relations and loads those relations which are not empty and have not yet been loaded. Again, version numbers are used to determine if the DBMS process associated to the child already has a relation in it memory. If the version number of the child process is less than the parent's, the relation is loaded.

7. Performance Analysis

7.1. The Environment

The objective of this section is to measure the performances of the execution of a RDL//C program. The Sabrina DBMS [Gardarin89] we used, implements all the standard features of commercial relational DBMS. The system architecture is a network of Sun SPARK workstations, each one having disk capabilities to store the database. This environment is somewhat different from bus-based backend database processing. Particularly, workstations are not designed for stand-alone processing (as dedicated database servers). Rather, they offer resource sharing to obtain load balancing through a local area network. However, such an environment can provide a larger memory space and faster computation in many cases. Moreover, a network of workstations constitutes a very common environment which has the advantages of parallel processing but without the specialized or dedicated hardware.

7.2. The Application

The application used to measure performance is based on a typical transitive closure operation to solve the ancestor problem. A sequential version of the rule module which calculates ancestors has been given in Section 2. We give a parallel program for the same problem. Parallelization of transitive closure has been widely studied [Valduriez88, Agrawal88, Cheiney90]. Within proposed algorithms, parallelism is included in the operator itself. In our approach, we express the parallelism within the rule language by adding localization predicate to rules [Wolson90] and using the PAR structure within the control string.

The relation Parent is duplicated on n nodes. The processing task is divided into n parts: a first station computes the ancestors of desc value whose (value MOD2) = 0 ; a second station computes the ancestors of desc value whose (value MOD2) = 1; and so on, for n workstations. In the case of total replication of the relation Parent, the ancestors problem can be partitioned among n workstations without intermediate transfer. Only the building of the complete Ancestor relation implies transfers.

We give the RDL//C program for two nodes :

```
MODULE ancestor;

BASE
    Parent (asc int, desc int) ;

DEDUCED
    Anc[] LIKE Parent ;
    Ancestor LIKE Parent ;

RULES

r1 IS
    IF Parent (x) (x.desc MOD 2 = 0)
    THEN +Anc[0] (x) ;
r1bis IS
    IF Parent (x) (x.desc MOD 2 = 1)
    THEN +Anc[1](x) ;

r2[] IS
    IF Parent (x) Anc[] (y) (x.desc = y.asc)
    THEN +Anc[] (asc = x.asc, desc = y.desc) ;

r3 []IS
    IF Anc[] (x) THEN +Ancestor(x) ;

CONTROL

    SEQ (PAR (SEQ (r1, BLOCK (r2[0])), SEQ (r1bis, BLOCK (r2[1]))), r3[0],
r3[1]) ;

END MODULE
```

We will compare the performances of the system varying the load and the number of processors available. The load will vary according to the number of tuples in the Parent relation. Measurements are done with different loads. These loads are generated as a tree of ancestors, which has h levels (Figure 7.1). h is also the number of firings of the recursive rule (i.e. the depth of the induced join loop in our implementation). There are no indexes on the relations. The number of tuples vary in each set by having the number of descendants at each node vary by one. In the first set of tuples each node has three descendants; in the second set, each node has four; and in the last set, each node has seven descendants. With h=4, we obtain the five following loads: 363 tuples, 1364 tuples, 3905 tuples, 9330 tuples, 19607 tuples. The number of processors varies from one to five.

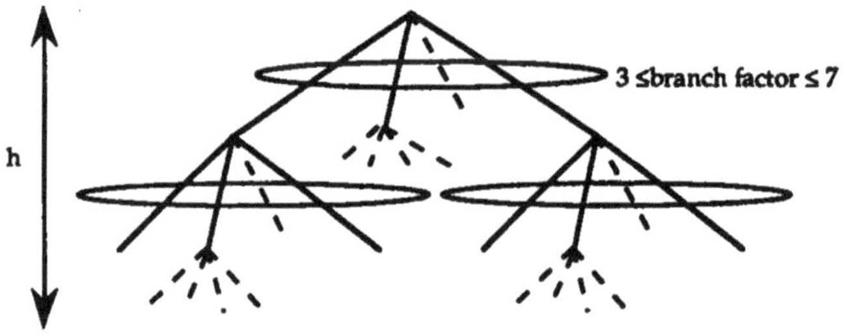

Figure 7.1: *Tuples generation tree*

7.3. Performance Results

To obtain performance results, we use some system time routines provided by the UNIX System. Eight time measurements are investigated, that are :

(1) Sql_connection. The time measured includes starting up a DBMS process on each remote station. This time is *a priori* proportional to the number of stations ;

(2) Validation of the schema of base relations at run-time ;

(3) Synchronization. Using the NFS, passing relations consists in loading and dumping relations in files ; running parallel processes are synchronized by waiting for each one to have finished running the assigned set of rules. This time measures transfer and synchronization tasks (i.e. the parallelism overhead) ;

(4) Left Hand Side (LHS) of rule processing. This time measures select/join processing time ;

(5) Sql_get_schema. The schema is obtained at run-time ;

(6) Validation of the schema of the deduced relations at the run-time ;

(7) Right Hand Side (RHS) of rule processing. This measures the computation time of the union ;

(8) Sql_disconnect measures the time to disconnect the applications from the DBMS.

The first results have shown that only three of these measurements are significant within the overall time : synchronization, LHS and RHS rule processing. The sum of the other five components represents always less than 3% of the overall time (except for a few tuple -363 tuples- and a single processor where the overhead time -connection, deconnection, validation of schema- reaches to 5%). For this reason, the main point of discussion will be the three main time-consuming actions.

7.3.1. Sequential Time

The first measurements are the times with a single workstation. The aim was to reveal the behavior of the rule program and the relative amount of execution time spent in each part of the program. Particularly, the time spent to evaluate the *condition part* of the rules (the LHS processing corresponds to a selection and a join) and the time spent to process the *action part* (the RHS processing corresponds to an union). Right and Left parts of rules compose the computation time. An external time, obtained as the sum of the connections, disconnections, validations of schema, is also calculated. Table 1 gives the measurements of the three main components of the elapsed time.

	363 tuples	1364 tuples	3905 tuples	9330 tuples	19607 tuples
connection, disconnection and schema control	3s	7s	8s	10s	12s
Left Hand Side processing (Select/Join)	12s	339s	923s	2309s	4490s
Right Hand Side processing (Union)	41s	451s	1553s	4601s	9571s

Table 1: *Time spent in part for sequential processing*

Table 1 shows the importance of union processing time. Moreover, these measurements make clear that the external time is very limited and can be neglected when processing large sets of tuples (from 5% of the overall time for a load of 323 tuples to less than 1% for a load of 19,607 tuples). The overhead time due to rule program connection and controls, is very small ; the computational power is almost completely used to process the rules.

7.3.2. Parallel Time

Neglecting the connection time, the components of the total time are the join computation, the union computation and the parallelism overhead including the dumps, the loads and the waiting. We measured the overall and the partial times for five sets of basic tuples : the first one (363 tuples) produced 1641 ancestors, the second one (1,364 tuples) produced 6,372 ancestors, the third one (3,905 tuples) produced 18,555 ancestors, the fourth one (9,330) produced 44,790 ancestors and the fifth one (19,607) produced 94,773 ancestors. The number of workstations ranged from one to five.

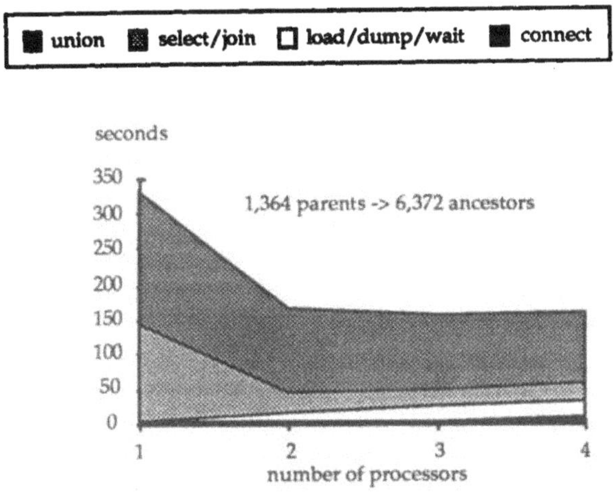

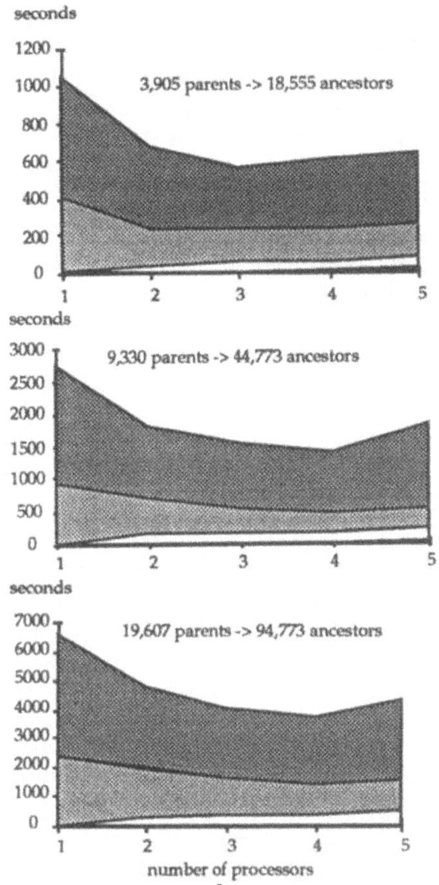

Figure 7.2 : *Evolution of overall and partial times in parallel processing*

Figure 7.2 presents a summary of these results. The times spent within the union and the select/join processing are represented by the grey areas. The black areas concern the time used to connect and disconnect the application and the DBMS processes. They can be neglected for a large amount of tuples. Last, the white areas summarize the overhead introduced by the parallelism, i.e. the time spent loading and dumping relations and files, and synchronizing. These times are cumulated to illustrate the overall response time.

7.3.3. Discussion

Figure 7.2 shows the benefits and limitations of parallelism in our experiment. Two points have to be discussed.

The first one concerns the application. The curves show that the join and the union processing times are not divided by the number of processors. For LHS processing, the partition of the processing does not divide the work into the number of processor. The complete Parent relation has indeed to be read at each iteration *on each server*. The corresponding amount of time increases with the number of processor. The benefit is concentrated in the parallel generation of new tuples, without redundant production, which allows the response time to decrease with an increase in the number of processors. The RHS or the cost of the UNION operation is expensive. Intuitively, we would have expected better performances since no duplicate computation is done on individual nodes. Rebuilding the full ancestor relation from the individual partitions is responsible for these results. In fact, the UNION operation is used in the last rule, to merge an individual result to those already merged in the ancestor relation. In our example, this is done by rule r3. Better results should be obtained by using a relational MERGE operation instead of the UNION operation to obtain the final result. This is possible knowing that there are no duplicates among nodes.

The second remark concerns the overhead induced by the parallelism. This overhead is represented on Figure 7.2 by the white area. Our experiments show that its augmentation, as a function of the number of processors, is limited. The parallelism is thus a good solution in our case. However, it is necessary to note that the transfers in our program are reduced to computation of the final result. In the case of more sophisticated algorithms, transfers are necessary during the ancestors generation ; the overhead due to these transfers would increase, especially in our configuration (a network of workstations) which is not an ideal hardware to reach high performances of parallelism.

Efficiency of the parallelism with a grain of a rule, is largely influenced by the user's choices in his RDL//C program. There is a traditional tradeoff between a good partition of computation tasks and a limitation of the transfers.

We have also tried to evaluate the influence of the number of tuples on the benefit provided by using multiple workstations. Figure 7.3 draws the overall time as function of the number of basic tuples. The maximum benefit is achieved for three or four stations for any number of tuples.

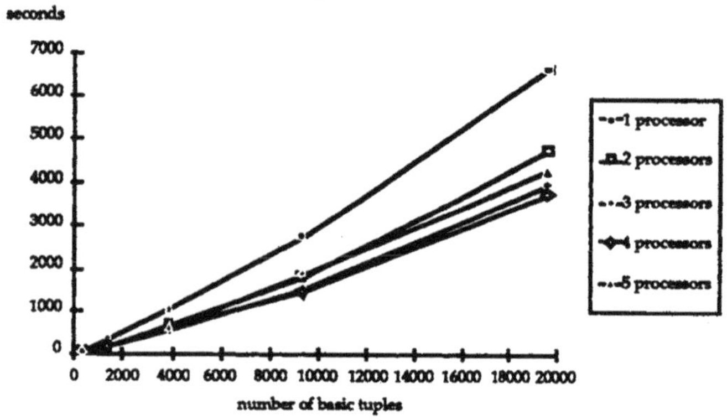

Figure 7.3: *Overall time as a function of the number of basic tuples*

During the measurements, the database was duplicated on each station's disk. We have also experimented the storage of all the databases on a single disk; because a large main memory was available within each station, the results were rather identical.

8. Conclusion and Future Work

This paper presented a database rule language compiler which supports parallelism among rules. The type of parallelism supported by the language is user-specified, as opposed to user-transparent parallelism. The user partitions his application into independent tasks, which are scheduled to run in parallel. The compiler checks that the sets of rules to be run in parallel are independent and that the number of sets does not exceed the number of servers available.

The run-time framework for the parallel execution of database rule based applications is a set of UNIX workstations connected on a network. While the application process resides on one workstation, it drives DBMS processes which are on different workstations, each with its own database. Parallelism is achieved by having the application process fork into N processes, each one assigned a set of rules to be processed on one DBMS. Relations are transferred among the different DBMS by dumping relations onto files and loading relations from files using a common file sub-system managed by the network.

The main contribution of the paper are (i) the definition of a sub-language of control to specify a parallel execution of a rule program and (ii) the support of parallelism without specialized hardware and with standard relational technology. A prototype of RDL//C is operational over a set of UNIX workstations. Future works will study an automatic generation of the control structure which specifies the parallelism and the use of the RDL//C system to prototype parallel database algorithms that have been developed.

9. References

[Agrawal88] R. AGRAWAL, HV. JAGADISH: "Multiprocessor Transitive Closure Algorithms", In *Proceedings International Symposium on Databases in Parallel and Distributed Systems,* Austin, Texas, USA, December 1988.

[Almasi89] G. ALMASI, A. GOTTLIEB: *"Highly Parallel Computing"*, Redwood City, CA The Benjamin/Cummings Publishing Company, Inc., 1989

[Brownston85] L. BRONSTON, R. FARRELL, E. KANT, M. MARTIN: "Programming Expert Systems in OPS5 : An Introduction to Rule-Based Programming", Book, Addison-Wesley, 1985.

[Cheiney90] J.-P. CHEINEY, C. de MAINDREVILLE: "A Parallel Strategy for Transitive Closure Using Double Hash-based Clustering" In *Proceedings 16th International Conference on Very Large Data Bases,* Brisbane, Australia, August 1990.

[Ganguly90] S. GANGULY, A. SILBERSCHATZ, S. TSUR: "A Framework for the Parallel Processing of Datalog Queries", In *Proceedings of ACM SIGMOD 1990 International Conference on Management of Data,* Atlantic City NJ, USA, June 1990.

[Gardarin89] G. GARDARIN, J.-P. CHEINEY, G. KIERNAN, D. PASTRE, H. STORA: "Managing Complex Objects in an Extendible Relational DBMS", In *Proceedings 15th International Conference on Very Large Databases,* Amsterdam, The Nederlands, August 1989.

[Genrich86] H. J. GENRICH: "Predicate / Transition Nets ", In *Advances in Petri Nets' 86*. Springer Verlag, 1987.

[Gupta89] A. GUPTA. et al.: " High-Speed Implementations of Rule-Based Systems", In *ACM Transactions on Computer Systems,* Vol 7, N° 2, May 1989.

[Kiernan90a] G. KIERNAN, C. de MAINDREVILLE , E. SIMON: "Making Deductive Database a Practical Technology: a step forward", In *Proceedings of SIGMOD 1990 International Conference on Management of Data,* Atlantic City NJ, USA, June 1990.

[Kiernan90b] G. KIERNAN, C. de MAINDREVILLE: "The RDL/C Language Reference Manual", INRIA Technical Report N° 123, October 1990.

[Kiernan91] G. KIERNAN, C. de MAINDREVILLE: "Compiling a Rule Database Program into a C-SQL Application", to appear in *Proceedings IEEE 7th International Conference on Data Engineering,* Kyoto, Japan, April 1991.

[Maindreville88] C. de MAINDREVILLE , E. SIMON: "Modelling Non-deterministic Queries and Updates in Deductive Databases", In *Proceedings 14th International Conference on Very Large Data Bases,* Los Angeles, USA, 1988.

[Srivastava89] J. SRIVASTAVA et al.: "Parallelism in Database Production Systems", In *Proceedings IEEE 6th International Conference on Data Engineering,* Los Angeles, USA, February 1990.

[Unix 84] Unix System V. User Reference Manual

[Valduriez88] P. VALDURIEZ, S. KHOSAFIAN: "Parallel Evaluation of the Transitive Closure of a Database Relation", In *International Journal of Parallel Programming,* Vol 17, N°1, February 1988.

[Wolfson90] O. WOLSON, A. OZERI: "A New Paradigm for Parallel and Distributed Rule Processing", In *Proceedings of ACM SIGMOD 1990 International Conference on Management of Data,* Atlantic City NJ, USA, June 1990.

A Knowledge Based System Converting ER Model into an Object-Oriented Database Schema

Il-Yeol Song and Heather M. Godsey
College of Information Studies
Drexel University
Philadelphia, PA 19104

Abstract

In this paper, we discuss a knowledge based system, KERO, which implements a methodology converting an entity-relationship (ER) model into a structurally object-oriented database schema. A set of rules that can convert most semantic constructs of ER models into an OODB schema is discussed. Our method is an improved one which can properly convert many-to-many relationships with non-key attributes and aggregation in ER model. The ideas which can further enhance the converted OODB schema are also presented. We think that the translation methodologies from semantic data models into OODB schema are important since most existing relational database design methodologies are based on the semantic approach and OODB systems must subsume existing relational database systems. The KERO system has been implemented in MIKE, which is a meta-interpreter written in Prolog.

Keywords: Entity-Relationship, Object-oriented databases, database schema, database design, knowledge based system

1 Introduction

The purpose of this paper is to present the design and implementation of a knowledgebased system, KERO, that converts an entity-relationship (ER) model into a structurally object-oriented (OO) database schema.

Our work is a continued effort in developing an easy to use OODB design methodology which could prove to be useful independent of database application domains. We have done a comprehensive survey of object-oriented database design methodologies [Song 1992]. We think that the translation methodologies from semantic data models are important for the following main reasons: Most existing relational database design methodologies are based on the semantic approach. By utilizing existing methodologies, we will not lose the valuable knowledge of many information engineers, obtained throughout the design and use of relational database systems. So the transition from existing systems to OODB systems can be smooth once a set of guidelines is provided. This is particularly true since OODB systems must subsume relational database systems and open to other subsystems [Stonebreaker+ 1990, Kim 1990].

Based on these observations, we have developed a knowledgebased system, KERO, that converts ERDs into OO database schema. We define a meta ER model to keep the input ER model structure, and a meta OO model for an output OODB schema. We present a set of rules converting each of ER model constructs defined in the input ER model into a corresponding OO schema component. Cattell [1991] and Hughes [1991] both have examples converting ERD into OODB schema. Cattell does not show how to deal with aggregation, and Cattell and Hughes do not handle many-to-many relationships with non-key attributes properly. Our work is an enhanced version of the previous work in this area in that we solve some problems of handling many-to-many relationships in [Cattell 1991, Hughes 1991] and discuss aggregation in more detail than [Hughes 1991, Song and Godsey 1993]. The converted OO schema can serve as an initial conceptual schema which can be further enhanced depending on the target OODBMS. We also suggest several ideas about how the converted schema can be semantically further improved. The KERO system has been implemented in MIKE [Eisenstadt+ 1990], which is a public-domain meta-level interpreter of Prolog.

Other approaches using ER-like models for OODB schema design include Gorman and Choobinch [1991], Nachouki, et al. [1991]. Gorman and Choobinch propose OOERM by extending ERD to include methods and message passing structures. However, the diagram becomes very messy, loses intuitiveness, and poses difficulty in representing all messages for most real-world applications. Nachouki, et al. discus how to integrate logical data access in the definition of an OODB schema from an ERD.

The rest of this paper is organized as follows: Section 2 discusses the conceptual design and implementation of our knowledge based system, and Section 3 presents an example of schema translation. Section 4 concludes the paper.

2. Methodology

In this section, we present the design and implementation aspects of our knowledge based system, KERO, which converts ERDs into OODB schema. The design of KERO can be broken down in three main segments: ERD representation, OODB representation, and translation rule development. The ER model which will be converted into an OO model is represented in a meta ER model understood by KERO (see Section 2.1). KERO converts the ER model into a meta OO model for OODB schema (see Section 2.2). The conversion rules are discussed in Section 2.3, the architecture of KERO in Section 2.4, and semantic enhancement to the converted OO model is discussed in Section 2.5.

2.1 ERD Representation

ER model and its variations [Chen 1976, Teorey+ 1986, Batini+ 1991] are the most popular approach for relational database design, and have been widely adopted in CASE tools. As such it is natural to consider the ER model as a starting point of designing an

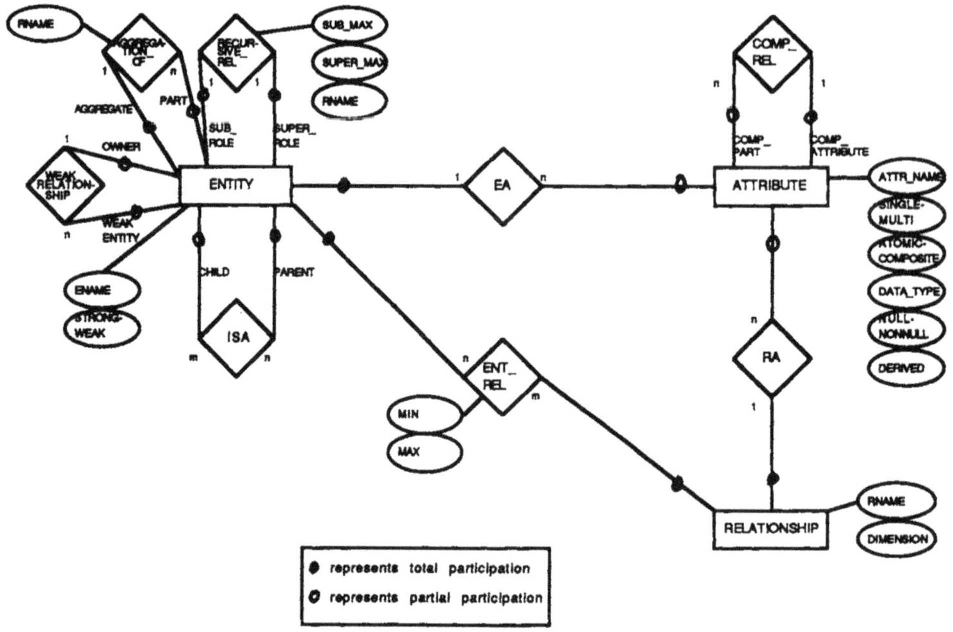

Figure 1 Meta ER Model

OODB schema. There are many complex semantics which may be modeled by the entity relationship diagram. The semantic constructs of the EER (ER henceforth) model which we have chosen for the KERO system include entities, relationships, recursive relationships, ternary relationships, generalization/specialization, inheritance, set-valued attributes, and composite attributes as discussed in Elmasri and Navathe [1989].

The ERD for the representation of the meta-model for the ER model (called *meta ER* model) is shown in Figure 1, and its important semantics are explained below.

- ENTITY represents either a regular (strong) entity or a weak entity.
- ENTITY can have weak entities (WEAK_RELATIONSHIP), and they have an owner entity.
- ENTITY can have recursive relationships (RECURSIVE_REL).
- ENTITY can have many children (sub) entities and many parent (super) entities.
- ENTITY participates in (ENT_REL) relationships, and has (min, max) cardinality constraints.
- ENTITY can have many attributes.
- ATTRIBUTE belongs to either an ENTITY via EA relationship or a RELATIONSHIP via RA.
- ATTRIBUTE can be either a single,multi-valued, or composite attribute.
- A composite ATTRIBUTE consists of several simple attributes.

What is shown in Figure 2 is a relational representation of the above meta ER model.

ENTITY(ENAME, WEAK/STRONG, OWNER)
ATTRIBUTE(ENAME, ATTR_NAME, NULL/NON-NULL, SINGLE/MULTI_VALUED, ATOMIC/COMPOSITE, DATATYPE)
RELATIONSHIP(RNAME, DIMENSION)
ENTITY_RELATIONSHIP(ENAME, RNAME, MIN, MAX)
RELATIONSHIP_ATTR(RNAME, ATTR_NAME, SINGLE/MULTI, ATOMIC/COMPOSITE, DATATYPE)
RECURSIVE(ENAME, SUBROLE, SUPERROLE, SUB_MAX, SUPER_MAX, RNAME)
ISA(PARENT, CHILD)
COMPOSITE_ATTR_PARTS(COMP_ATTR, PART, SINGLE/MULTI, ATOMIC/COMPOSITE, DATATYPE)

Figure 2. Relational Schema for meta ER model

For efficiency of implementation, the following was added for ternary relationships and 1:1 and M:N binary relationships.

```
/* for binary: */
MEMBER(RNAME, MEMBER1, MEMBER2)
/* for ternary */
MEMBER(RNAME, MEMBER1, MEMBER2,
       MEMBER3)
```

Note that a ternary relationship can also be represented using the above meta model. The maximum cardinality (MAX attribute in ENT_REL relationship) of a binary relationship is represented using the typical "Look Across" notation (i.e., look across the relationship to find the cardinality, the cardinality is written in the other side of the entity), while that of a ternary relationship is represented using the "Look Here" notation (cardinality is written near the entity side). For example, the CONTROLS and SUPPLY relationships in the ERD of Figure 3 can be represented as in Figure 4 below:

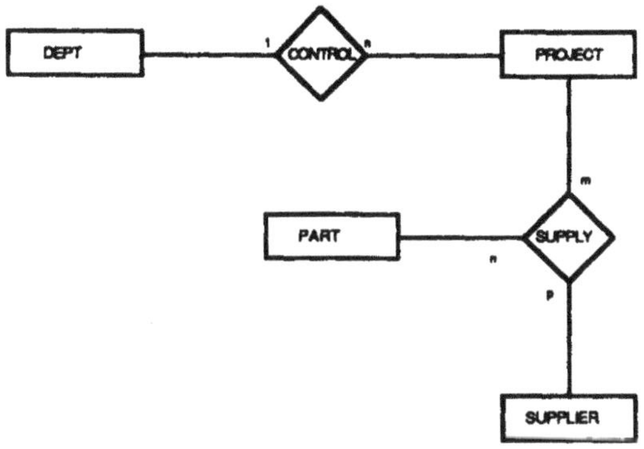

Figure 3. ERD with a Ternary Relationship

relationship(control, 2)
relationship(supply, 3)
ent_rel(department, control, 0, n)
ent_rel(project, control, 1, 1)
ent_rel(project, supply, 1, n)
ent_rel(part, supply, 1, n)
ent_rel(supplier, 0, n)
member(control, department, project)
member(supply, project, part, supplier)

Figure 4. Meta ER Representation of CONTROLS and SUPPLY in Figure 5

An example of a complete ERD is shown in Section 3. It should be pointed out that the ER design approach to OODB schema does not produce operations. Other methodologies should be used to come up with and represent them, but these are beyond the scope of this paper.

2.2 OODB Representation

An OODB schema consists of a collection of *classes*. Each class has a set of *instances*, which are the objects belonging to that class. Each class is an abstract data type which has a group of *attributes* (called instance variables in some OO systems) and a set of operations (or methods) defined on them (classification). These attributes describe properties of instances of a class. Each object has an object identity independent of the values that it contains (identification). Classes form a set of class hierarchies, forming superclass and subclass relationships (generalization). Subclass objects inherit the attributes and operations of superclasses. The class hierarchy becomes a class lattice in the form of directed acyclic graph (DAG) when a class can have more than one parent class (multiple inheritance). It is common practice to refer to a class lattice, as a class hierarchy. Attributes in OODB could be simple attributes, collection attributes (set values, lists, arrays), derived attributes (whose value are computed by procedures or methods), class attributes (whose value represent properties of the class as a whole or summary values, rather than each individual object instance) or *reference attributes* (which point to other object(s)). Simple attributes are atomic attributes which do not have their own components. Examples of the simple attributes are integers, numbers, strings, and other simple values. Set attributes are those which have a set of simple values or other objects. Examples of class attributes are average number of players or uniform color of a baseball team. Reference attributes are used to represent relationships between objects (association). A reference attribute can represent either a single object or a set of objects (*reference-set attribute*). These attributes may be aggregated to form an object, and objects may be aggregated to form composite objects (aggregation).

Our target OO model, currently implemented in KERO, has classification, generalization, and aggregation abstractions. Identification is automatically supported by the target OODBMS in the form of an object identifier. Associations are implemented as a pair of reference attributes and their associated inverse attributes (See Section 2.3 for more on this).

The template class definition used for output from KERO is similar to the syntax used in Hughes [1991], and is shown in Figure 5 as follows:

```
Class <class_name>
        Inherit <other_class>
        Properties
                /* simple attribute: */
                <attribute_name>: <simple data type> ;
                /*set-valued attribute:*/
                <attribute_name>: set (<simple data type>);
                /* reference attribute: */
                <attribute_name>: (other_class_name);
                /* reference-set attribute:*/
                <attribute_name>: set (<other_class_name>);
                  inverse is <other_class_name>.
                        <attribute_name>;
                ...
        Operations
                <operation_name>;
                ....
End.
```

Figure 5. Template for Class Definition

The "Inherit" clause defines the superclass, "Properties" clause defines attributes of the class, and "Operations" clause defines operations which will be added later using other methods. The "Properties" clause shows four different types of attributes.

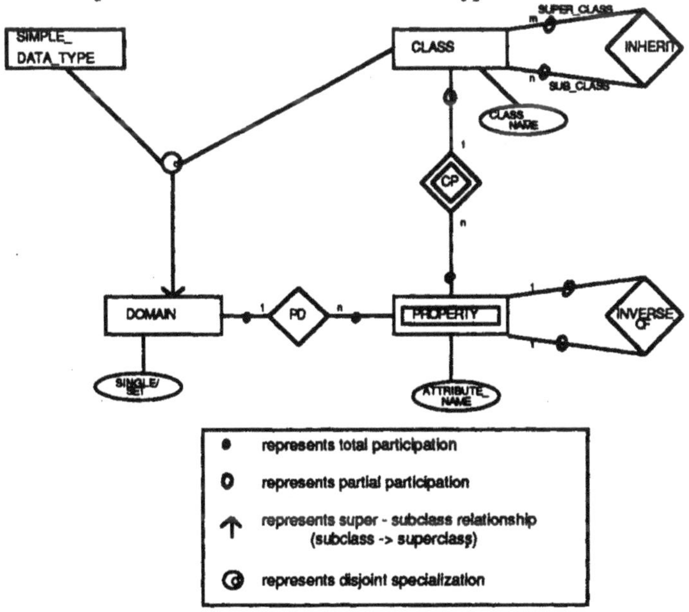

Figure 6 Meta OO model

The ERD representation of meta OO model in Figure 6 can be explained as follows:

- A CLASS has attributes.
- A PROPERTY (Attribute) has a domain.
- A DOMAIN is either a simple data type or a CLASS type.
- Generalization/specialization is handled through INHERIT relationship. Since the SUPER_CLASS has many cardinality, it supports multiple inheritance.
- Aggregation is handled via the recursive application of CP relationship and PD relationship from CLASS via ATTRIBUTE through DOMAIN. An aggregated class has a set of attributes via CP relationship, which some of them are again defined by DOMAIN class via PD relationship. This process can be recursively applied until each attribute is broken down to simple attributes.

The relational representation of meta OO model is shown below in Figure 8.

```
CLASS(CNAME)
SUPER(CNAME, SUPER_CNAME)
PROPERTY(ATTRIBUTE_NAME, CNAME, DATATYPE,
    SINGLE/SET)
  /* Variations of PROPERTY are: */

  /* Handles recursive relationships between CNAME */
  PROPERTY(SUBROLE/SUPERROLE, CNAME,
      CNAME, SINGLE/SET)

  /*Handles relationships REL_NAME between CNAME
      and OTHER_CLASS */
  PROPERTY(REL_NAME, CNAME, OTHER_CLASS,
      SINGLE/SET)

  /* Handles aggregation with an INVERSE clause below*/
  PROPERTY(HAS_PARTS, CNAME, OTHER_CLASS,
      SINGLE/SET)

INVERSE(ATTRIBUTE, CNAME, OTHER_CLASS,
    OTHER_ATTRIBUTE)
  /* Variation of INVERSE is:*/

  /* Handles aggregation with a PROPERTY clause */
  INVERSE(HAS_PARTS, CNAME, OTHER_CLASS,
      IS_A_PART_OF)
```

Figure 7. Relational Schema for meta OO model

2.3 Translation Rules from EER Model to OO Model

The representation of relationships is one of the most fundamental ways in which data models differ. As there are several translation techniques in converting an ERD into a relational model structure depending on how relationships are handled [Song 1992], there could be at least two translation paradigms in translating an ERD into an OODB schema. The first approach is to convert each entity and each relationship into one object. The relationship object is called a link object in Rumbaugh et al. [1991]. Thus, the resulting schema will keep the structure of the original ER model. We will call this approach *stable translation,* as we did for the relational model [Song 1992]. There are two approaches using this idea [Navathe+ 1988, Ku+ 1991], and both are called the OOER model. Another approach is to combine certain relationships (1:1 and 1:N) into object classes using a pair of a reference attribute and its inverse attribute. For example, if there is a WORK_ON relationship between EMP and DEPT with many to one cardinality, then the EMP object has a reference attribute DEPT and the DEPT object has an inverse attribute EMP as a reference-set attribute (see Rule 2.2 below). These inverse relationships are necessary for the maintenance of relationship integrity and for two ways of accessing related objects. However, many-to-many and ternary relationships are created as separate object classes, called *link object classes.* And thus in this approach the original structure of the ER model is not kept in the target OODB schema. We call this approach *mapped translation,* as the original structure of the ERD is mapped away. This method is more complex than stable translation, but will result in a more compact OODB schema.

The stable translation method is advantageous since it can be easily converted from the EER diagram and the structure of the original ER model remains within the target model such as the relational, network model, and OO model. Also the maintenance of OODB schema in this structure is easier than in other structures because of its explicit relationship representation. However, this does not allow us to take full advantage of OO concepts where composite objects are allowed. This also results in a proliferation of objects as compared with other methodologies for OODB schema design. Whereas the stable translation can still explicitly show the ER's cardinality constraints in the OO diagram, the mapped translation only implicitly shows the cardinality by single-valued and set-valued attributes, unless otherwise defined by integrity constraints. Another advantage of mapped translation is that it can enforce one property of encapsulation by incorporating all the relevant concepts under one definition. However, it violates another property of encapsulation in that whenever a reference attribute in one class is modified, there is a need to modify its associated inverse attribute defined in another class. As shown in Rumbaugh et al. [1991], however, the link object in a stable translation schema can be physically implemented as a pointer at the implementation stage.

In KERO, the mapped translation approach was used instead of a stable one since the mapped translation takes advantage of the OODB quality of encapsulation using the inverse clause and can be directly implemented by most commercial OODBMSs. The shear number of classes is also reduced, and the connections between two objects are more direct without accessing the third object to link them (except in many-to-many relationships).

<u>Converting Rules from ER model to object-oriented schema</u>

(1) Entity type:
  - Each entity type becomes an object class.

(2) Binary relationships (from entity type A to another entity type B)

  (2.1) 1:1: Object class A has a reference attribute B, and object class B has a reference attribute A.

  (2.2) 1:N: Object class A has a reference-set attribute B and object class B has a reference attribute A.

  (2.3) M:N: Create a link object class L for the M:N relationship. Add a reference attribute A and B within the link object class L. The non-key attributes of the relationship then become properties of L. Object class A and object class B have a reference-set attribute of type L, respectively.

(3) "isa" relationship between A isa B
  Declare as super class B in object class A.

(4) Attributes

(4.1) Single-valued attributes: They become simple attributes of the object class with atomic data types.

(4.2) Multi-valued attributes: If the order of values is important, they become list attributes. Otherwise they become set-valued attributes.

(4.3) Derived attributes: They become derived attributes whose values are computed by operations.

(4.4) Composite attributes: They become a reference attribute whose domain is an object class which consists of attributes making up the composite attribute in ERD.

(4.5) Attribute of 1:1 relationship: The attribute can be an attribute of a more permanent object (e.g., Department is more permanent than manager).

(4.6) Attribute of 1:N relationship: The attribute becomes an attribute of the N-side object.

(4.7) Attribute of M:N relationship: The attribute becomes an attribute of the link object class created in Rule 2.3.

(5) Weak entity type

Weak entity type becomes a set-valued attribute of the owner object, where the domain of the set-valued attribute is the weak entity type.

(6) Ternary relationship

Create an object class corresponding to the ternary relationship.

(7) Recursive relationship with entity type A with roles of Sub-Role and Super-Role.

(7.1) 1:1: Object class A has a reference attribute Sub-Role and Super-Role.

(7.2) 1:N (Super-Role: Sub-Role): Object class A has a reference-set attribute Sub-Role and a reference attribute Super-Role.

(7.3) N:1 (Super-Role: Sub-Role): Object class A has a reference-set attribute Super-Role and a reference attribute Sub-Role.

(7.4) M:N: Create a link object class L for the recursive relationship. Add a reference attribute Super-Role and Sub-Role within the link object class L. The non-key attributes of the relationship then become properties of L. Object class A have reference-set attributes Super-Role and Sub-Role of type L, respectively.

(8) Aggregation in ER model

(8.1) Create an aggregated object class G from the relationship enclosed in the aggregation entity.

(8.2) Add two participating entity types within G as a reference attribute.

(8.3) Add non-key attribute of the relationship as simple attributes of G.

(8.4) Each participating entity type has either reference attribute or reference-set attribute of type G, depending on the cardinality of relationship between them as in Rules (2.1), (2.2), and (2.3).

This approach is similar to Hughes [1991], Cattell [1991]. However, our approach is different from them by the way we handle many-to-many relationships and aggregation. Cattell does not show how to deal with aggregation; Hughes explain the ideas of the aggregation, but does not show explicit rules for the conversion to OO schema. Cattell and Hughes do not properly handle many-to-many relationships with non-key attributes. Cattell and Hughes represent a many-to-many relationship between A and B using the following rule, instead of our Rule 2.3 above:

> Object class A has a reference-set attribute B, and object class B has a reference-set attribute A.

In this case, if the relationship does not have its own attribute (non-key attribute in ER model, such as HOURS attribute in WORKS_FOR relationship in Figure 11), then this method is usable. However, if it does have its own attribute, then the attribute becomes awkward to handle. Furthermore, if the relationship has some constraints, then these may be specified redundantly and distributed to participating objects rather than encapsulating them into a single object class [Rumbaugh 1988]. Many real-world applications have many-to-many relationships with non-key attributes. Note that this problem can be easily handled in a one-to-many relationship, since any attribute or constraint imposed on the one-to-many relationship can be imposed on many-side object class.

We illustrate a simple example in this section. The ERD with an aggregation is shown in Figure 8 and derived OO schema is shown in Figure 9.

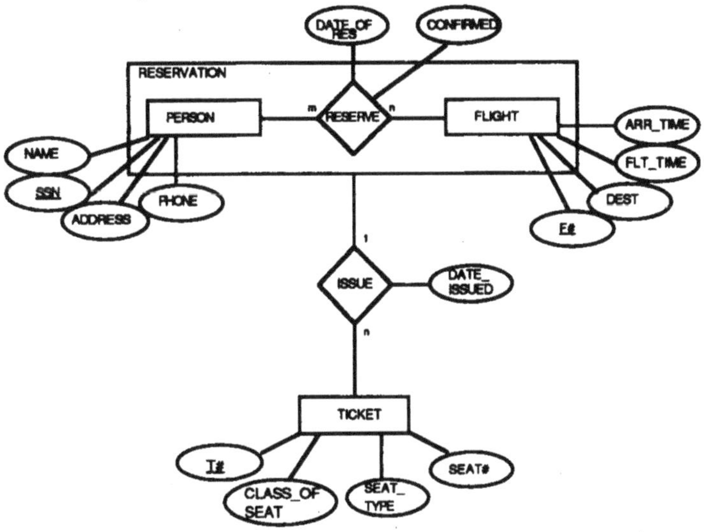

Figure 8 ERD with Aggregation

```
class Reservation
        Properties
                date_of_res: Date;
                confirmed: Boolean;
                issues: set(Ticket)
                        inverse is Ticket.issued_by;
                made_by: Person
                        inverse is Person.reserves;
                made_for: Flight
                        inverse is Flight.reserved_by;
end.

class Person
        Properties
                name, address, phone, SSN: String;
                reserves: Set(Reservation)
                        inverse is Reservation.made_by;
end.

class Flight
        Properties
                flight#: Integer;
                destination: CityCode;
                flight_time, arrival_time: Time;
                reserved_by: Set (Reservation)
                        inverse is Reservation.made_for;
end.
```

```
class Ticket

        Properties
                ticket#, seat#: Integer;
                class_of_seat: (Business, Fst_class, Economic);
                seat_type: (Window, Aisle, Middle);
                date_issued: Date;
                issued_by: Reservation
                        inverse is Reservation.issues;
end.
```

Figure 9. Derived OO Schema from Figure 8

None of the literature we surveyed explicitly spelled out the translation rules as we have done in this paper. A more complete example is illustrated in Section 3.

The process of converting an ERD into an OO schema is not deterministic. For example, relationships in an ERD can be mapped into either an attribute, an operation, or an object class. Relationships with non-key attributes can become a separate object class. In addition, handling participation constraints, ternary relationships, and other constraints in OO databases are not clearly analyzed yet.

2.4 Architecture and Implementation of KERO

KERO is classified as a *design* expert system. The design system needs iteration for refinements until certain conditions are satisfied or all the rules have been exhaustively applied and no more changes to the working memory can be made. These iterations are typically implemented as a forward chaining system. The overall flow diagram of KERO is shown in Figure 10.

We have implemented KERO using MIKE, which is a meta-interpreter of Prolog based on a public domain Prolog. KERO has a total of 58 rules in MIKE syntax. MIKE was quite slow because of the nature of meta-interpreter and the looping of the forward chaining. Currently, we are reimplementing KERO using KnowledgePro for Windows for a faster performance and better user interface.

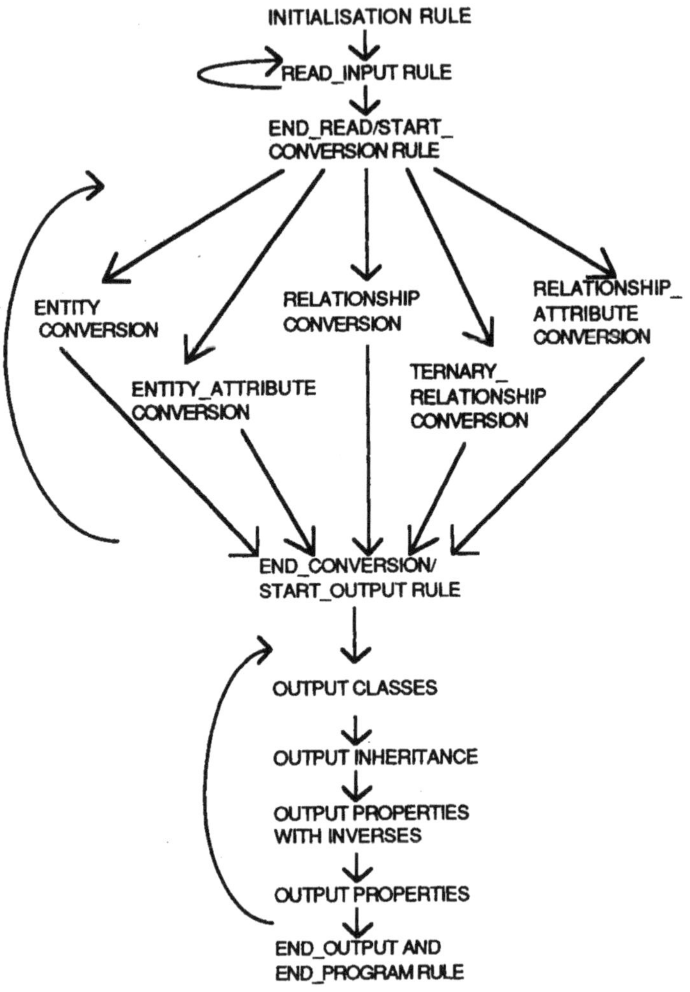

Figure 10 Flow Diagram of KERO System

2.5 Enhancing Converted OO Schema

We think that the OODB schema converted from the ERD can serve as a conceptual model which is a result of a conceptual *analysis*. This analysis can be further semantically enhanced for the *design* as discussed in this section. By design, we mean to add more implementation-oriented aspects to the conceptual model to create a logical model, which is ready to be implemented.

(1) Abstract class

The notion of entity in ER model is not exactly the same as the class in OO model. Every entity in the ER model can be a class in OO model, but not every class in OO model will be an entity in ER model. An entity in ER modeling is a real-world object which will store meaningful data. Thus, an entity type without any significant attributes in the ER model may exist at the analysis stage, but can be deleted at the logical design stage. However in the OO model, a class even without any significant attributes may exist to support the inheritance of operations. This kind of class is called the abstract class. The abstract class is a class which is declared as a class, but which will not have any instantiated objects. C++ supports the abstract class via the pure virtual function.

(2) Type class and object class

Type class is a data type used as a domain of an attribute, while an object class is a meaningful class modeled for the semantics of application. Even though both of them can be implemented as classes in OO system, they are semantically different. For example, composite attributes ADDRESS (COUNTRY, CITY, NUMBER, STREET and NAME (LAST, FIRST) could be a class type in OO system, but they are not very meaningful in OODB unless they are related to meaningful classes such as person and employee. Programming convenience may introduce this kind of class in OO system.

(3) Class attribute (method)

A class attribute is one which has only one value for all the objects of a class. They typically represents a summary or a collective value for a class (such as the total number of instantiated objects in the class). The ER model does not capture the semantics of the class attribute (and, of course, class method, also). So identify them and add to the OO model.

(4) Constraint modeling

We can impose some constraints on the OODB schema depending on the attribute type and relationship as follows:

- If an attribute has an enumerated data type, then that can be specified as a constraint.
- If an attribute has a range of values, then that can be specified as a constraint.

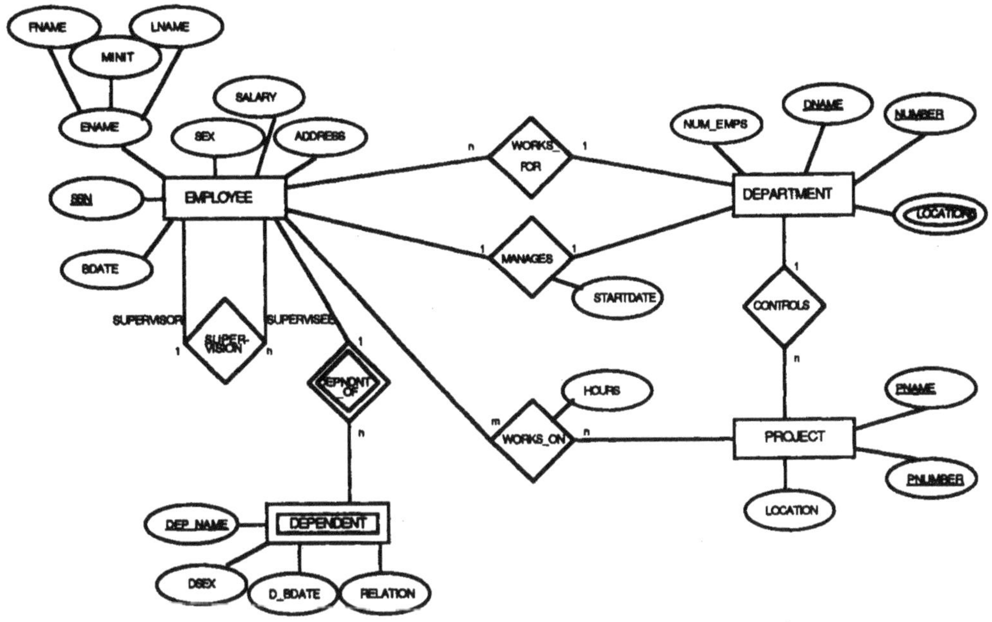

Figure 11. Company ER Model (taken from Elmasri & Navathe1989)

- For each set-valued attribute or reference-set attribute
  - if they require a sequence, declare as a list data type
  - if it allows a redundant value, declare as a bag data type
- For each relationship in ER model
  - if it has a specific maximum cardinality such as 1:6, then specify as a constraint
  - if it needs to specify the participation constraint, then specify as a constraint methods and message introduction (they are application specific)

(5) Operations

Attribute methods can be automatically generated. Typical operations such as constructor, destructor, accessor operations can be generated as a form of attribute methods. However, operations are application-specific, and thus other methodologies must be used to generate a more complete list of operations, such as transformer and interface operations with external systems.

3. Example

In this section, we illustrate our methodology using an example taken from Elmasri and Navathe [1989]. The ERD is shown in Figure 11 and output OODB schema is shown in Section 3.2.

3.1 Input ER Model

3.2 Output OODB Schema

```
class(works_on)
  properties
    participant: employee
      inverse of employee.participates;
    object: project
      inverse of project.done_by;
    hours: integer;
end.
```

```
class(employee)
  properties
    manages: department
      inverse of department.manages;
    works_for: department
      inverse of department.works_for;
    has_property: ename
      inverse of ename.is_property_of;
    participates: set(works_on)
      inverse of works_on.participant;
    has_parts: set(dependent)
      inverse of dependent.is_part_of;
    supervisor: employee;
    ssn: string;
    bdate: date;
    sex: m/f;
    address: string;
    salary: integer;
    supervisee: set(employee);
end.
```

```
class(department)
  properties
    manages: employee
      inverse of employee.manages;
    works_for: set(employee)
      inverse of employee.works_for;
    controls: set(project)
      inverse of project.controls;
    startdate: date;
    dname: string;
    number: integer;
    num_emps: integer;
    locations: set(string);
end.
```

```
class(project)
  properties
    controls: department
      inverse of department.controls;
    done_by: set(works_on)
      inverse of works_on.object;
    pname: string;
    pnumber: integer;
    location: string;
end.

class(dependent)
  properties
    is_part_of: employee
      inverse of employee.has_parts;
    dep_name: string;
    dsex: m/f;
    relation: string;
end.

class(ename)
  properties
    is_property_of: employee
      inverse of employee.has_property;
    fname: string;
    minit: character;
    lname: string;
end.
```

4. Summary and Conclusion

Our research focuses on advancing methodologies for object-oriented database (OODB) schema design. While OO database systems themselves have been widely researched and regarded as next generation database systems, there is no well accepted methodology for OODB schema design. We think that as a short term solution the translation methodologies from semantic data models are important for the following main reason: Most existing relational database design methodologies are based on the semantic approach. By utilizing existing methodologies for OODB design, we will not lose the valuable knowledge of many information engineers, obtained throughout the design and use of relational database systems. So the transition from existing systems to OODB systems can be smooth once a set of guidelines is provided, as done in this paper. The complexities of the OODB design process make an automated design assistance extremely desirable, as well. For the long term, we need to develop direct object modeling approaches, for both structure and behavior, which may prove to be useful independent of database application domains.

Based on these, we have presented the design and implementation of KERO, a knowledge based system that converts an ER model into a OODB schema. Our translation scheme, called mapped translation, can convert various semantic constructs of the ER model such as entity, relationship, ternary, recursive, weak entity, generalization/specialization, inheritance, and aggregation. We have spelled out the step-by-step transformation rules for each construct of the ER model. We have presented in detail how to properly convert many-to-many relationships with non-key attributes and discussed the translation of the aggregation in ER model into OODB schema with examples. We have also suggested ideas about how the converted schema may be further semantically enhanced. The output from KERO can be directly implemented in most commercial OODBMSs. We will add to KERO increased interaction with designers to facilitate customized OODB output. The KERO system has been implemented in MIKE, a public domain meta interpreter of Prolog.

References

Batini, C., Ceri, S. & Navathe, S.B. (1991). *Conceptual Database Design: An Entity-Relationship Approach.* The Benjamin Cummings.

Cattell, R.G.G. (1991). *Object Data Management: Object-Oriented and Extended Relational Database Systems*, Addison-Wesley, Reading, MA.

Chen, P.P. (1976). "The Entity Relationship Model - Toward a Unified View of Data," *ACM TODS*, 1:1, pp. 9-36.

Eisenstadt, M. and Brayshaw, M. (1990). "A Knowledge Engineering Toolkit," *BYTE*, October 1990, pp. 268-282.

Elmasri, R. and Navathe, S.B. (1989). *Fundamentals of Database Systems*, The Benjamin/Cummings.

Gorman, K. and Choobineh, J. (1991). "An Overview of of the Object-Oriented Entity-Relationship Model (OOERM), in *Proc. of the Twenty-Third Annual Hawaii Int'l Conf. on System Sciences*, Hawaii.

Hughes, J.G. (1991). *Object-Oriented Databases*. Prentice Hall.

Kim, W. (1990). "Object-Oriented Databases: Definition and Research Directions," *IEEE Transaction on Knowledge and Data Engineering*. 2(3), pp. 327-341.

Ku, C.S., Youn, C. & Kim, H.-J. (1991). "An Object-Oriented Entity-Relationship Model," 1991 ISMM International Conference on *Computer Applications in Design, Simulation and Analysis*," Las Vegas, Nevada, March 19-21, 1991, PP. 55-58.

Nachouki, J., Chastang, M.P. and Briand, H. (1991). "From Entity-Relationship Diagram to An Object Oriented Database," in *Proc. of 10th Int'l Conf. on Entity-Relationship Approach*, pp. 459-481.

Navathe, S.B. & Pillalamarri (1988). "OOER: Toward Making the E-R Approach Object-Oriented," in *Proc. of 8th Int'l Conf. on Entity-Relationship Approach*, pp.55-76.

Rumbaugh, J. , Blaha, M., et al. (1991). *Object-Oriented Modeling and Design*, Prentice-Hall.

Song, I.-Y. (1992). "Translation Techniques from ERD to Relational Model," Submitted for publication.

Song, I.-Y. (1992b). "A Survey of Object-Oriented Database Design Methodologies," in Proc. of *First Int'l Conf. on Information and Knowledge Management*, Baltimore, MD, Nov. 9-11, 1992, pp. 52-59.

Song, I.-Y. (1993). "A Knowledge Based Object-Oriented Database Schema Generator," To appear in Proc. of *1993 IEEE/ACM Int'l Conf. on Developing & Managing Intelligent System Projects*," Washington, D.C, March 29-31, 1993.

Stonebraker, M., Rowe, L.A., etc. (1990). Third-Generation Database System Manifesto," *SIGMOD Record*, 19(3), pp.31-44.

Teorey, T.J., Yang, D., and Fry, J.P. (1986). "A Logical Design Methodology for Relational Databases Using the Extended Entity-Relationship Model," *Computing Surveys*, 18:12, June, pp. 197-222.

TEMPORAL DATABASE

DESIGN OF HISTORICAL DATABASES USING THE 3-D RELATIONAL DATA MODEL

TaeNam Cho
Dept. of Computer Science,
Kwan-Dong University
Kangneung, Korea

KyungChang Kim
Dept. of Computer Science,
Hong-Ik University
Seoul, Korea

ABSTRACT

In search of appropriate semantics for the inclusion of structures and operations that meet the needs of a wide class of users interested in a database system supporting temporal views of their data, this paper includes a discussion of many problems that must be addressed, and a proposal for a 3-D relational data model and relational historical operations within the model. The discussion of issues motivates the proposal to keep time characteristics in the 3-D cell, rather than in the attributes of a relation or in tuples. The proposed operations incorporates this view with a general treatment of non-first normal form relation.

Keywords : historical database, non-first normal form relation, 3-D relational model, time attribute, historical relational operators

1. INTRODUCTION

Temporal information are basically different in concept from the informations handled by traditonal databases because the contents of temporal information must be managed with the time concept when they are inserted, deleted or updated. Therefore, the attributes of temporal information are complex objects keeping the time and their values.[8]

R.Snodgrass and I.Ahn divide the time concept which should be maintained in temporal database systems into three kinds: valid time, transaction time, and user defined time.[5,6]

The transaction time is not discussed in this paper because it is used in systems when DBs or files are deleted or updated. Since user defined time is the same concept as the valid time in theory, this paper aims at designing historical databases which controls and maintains valid time only.

To design relational historical database systems, a data model and operations suitable for historical database systems should first be considered.

The structure of the historical database is cubic. Hence, in this paper, we propose a 3-D relational data model to capture the semantics and structure of historical databases. The rest of the paper is as follows. The proposed 3-D relational data model is introducted in Chapter 2 and operators within the 3-D relational data model is described in Chapter 3. Conclusion and further works are discussed in Chapter 4.

2. DATA MODEL FOR HISTORICAL DATABASES

Historical databases are considered within the framework of relational databases. We define a relational historical database as a collection of historical relations. In formalizing the historical database, we distinguish the time-invariant description of a historical relation vsrsus its contents for the historical relations life span. The description of historical relation is called a relational historical schema and consists of a set of historical attributes.

The historical attribute is classified into two kinds; constant attribute [consA] and time-varying attribute[tivaA]. ConsA is time-invariant and has simple domains; but it can keep the value of time optionally. For example, the historical relation Employee's attribute Eno(see figure 2.2) is a consA and we keep in there the Employee's date of entering the company. In this case, the domain of the attribute is a function which is the same as for tivaA. TivaA vary potentially over time; the domain of this attribute is a function of time to some simple domains.[2]

2.1. 3-D Relational Data Model

We define the 3-D relational data model (abbr. 3-D RDM) for the relational historical database as a triple which is given in expression (2.1).

expression (2.1) : 3-D RDM = (hisR, Ω, C)

hisR is a set of historical relations, Ω is a set of relational algebra operators, and C is a set of constraints which the system should maintain.

2.2. Relational Historical Scheme

The scheme of historical relation in the 3-D RDM is represented as given in expression (2.2) if it has relation name hisR-name, m constant attributes, and n time-varying attributes.

expression (2.2) : hisR-name (consA(1), consA(2), ..., consA(M), tivaA(1), tivaA(2), ..., tivaA(N))

Expression (2.2) is made more concise as given in the expression (2.3) using FORTRAN subscription.

expression (2.3) : hisR-name (consA((i), i=1,m), tivaA((j), j=1,n))

The primary key of historical relation is in the consAs, and if the number of attributes in historical relation is (m+n) it is called (m+n)ary relation scheme. The domain of historical attribute is a function having the pair (T,V) in which T is the value of valid time and its domain is either an integer or an integer of type YYMMDD, and V is the value of an attribute having simple domains. Figure 2.1 shows an example of a relational historical scheme.

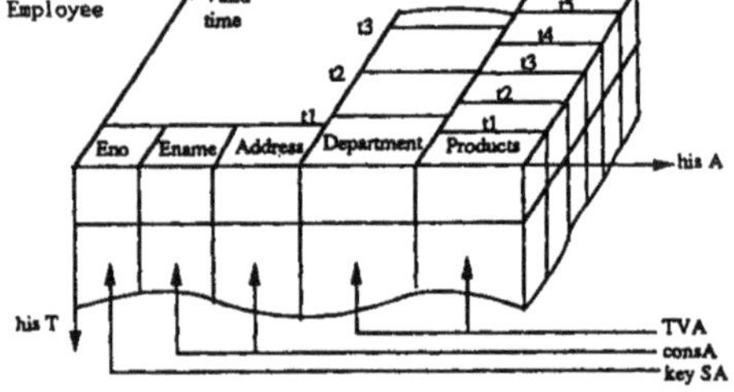

Figure 2.1 : An example of relational historical scheme

In the scheme of historical relation Employee as shown below ;

Employee (Eno, Ename, Address, Department, Products)

Attributes Eno, Ename, Address are the employee's number, name, and address respectively and since they are consA they keep only one valid time optionally.

Attributes Department, Products are the employee's department and daily products of employee respectively and they are tivaA. Hence they keep many valid times according to their properties. For example, the interval of attribute department may be in unit of years, the Products may be in unit of days. It is especially noteworthy that the set of Eno=100's valid times are usually different from the set of Eno=101's valid times in the case of tivaA. In figure 2.1 the value of valid time t1, t2, ..., are always t1> t2> ....

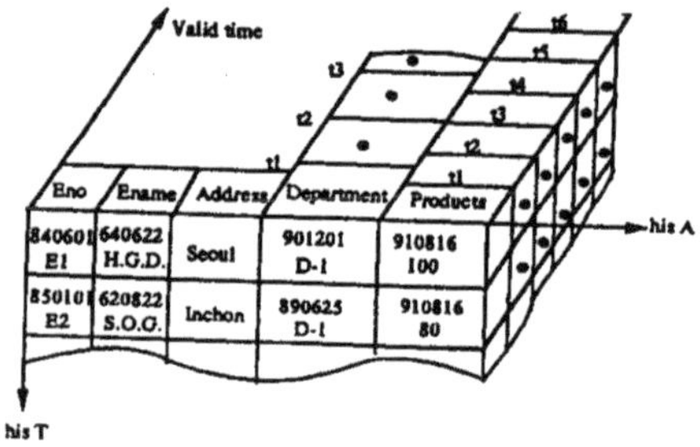

Figure 2.2 : Some instances of Employee

Figure 2.2 show some instances of Employee. As shown in figure 2.2, constant attribute Eno has two values: Start date of an employee(i.e.YYMMDD:840601) and the employee number. Attribute Ename has values for date of birth and his name, but attribute Address do not keep valid time. Time-varying attribute Department has date of an employee's move into a department and department name and attribute Products has date and quantity of goods that an employee produces in a day.

There are two types in time-varying attributes: Step-Wise Constant [abbr. SWC] and Discrete Type [abbr. DT]. Step-wise constant type have in general a triplet valid time value (start time, end time, duration). In this paper only the start times are kept in memory. The end time or duration is searched by " valid time search algorithm".[1] For example, in figure 2.4 the employee number E1's history of department are (D-1, 901201), (D-3, 880601), · · · . If we wish to know the end time or duration of employee E1's working in department D-3, the answers are obtained by searhing the cell created just after the cell. If we wish to know where E1 worked at a time t_i, the answer is obtained by searching the cell where value of valid time t_j is

$$t_h > t_i \geq t_j \text{ , where } t_h \text{ is the value of valid time of cell created just after the cell.}$$

Discrete type have only one valid time value which is a data point, and hence the mapping of valid time is simple.

2.3. Implementation Techniques of 3-D RDM

The historical relation in 3-D RDM can be expressed by three dimensional coordinates as follows :

a axis ; position of historical attributes
t axis ; position of valid time's values
s axis ; position of tuples (or surrogates)

Figure 2.3 shows those three axis and a system variable cell (i,j,k).

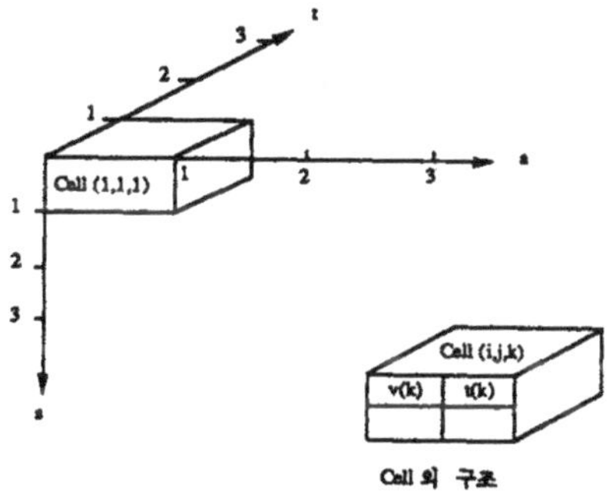

Figure 2.3 : Three axis and cell structures

The system variable cell(i,j,k) keeps a pair of values (V(k), T(k)); T(k) is value of Kth valid time within jth attribute and ith surrogate, and V(k) is value of jth attribute within ith surrogate and kth valid time.

The subscripts i,j,k are automatically created or deleted by the system when data are inserted or deleted and invoked when a query enters the system.[1]

2.4. Formal Definition of a Historical Relation

As in relational databases, historical tuples in relational historical databases are elements of the historical relation.[3] If a historical tuple consists of m number of constant attributes and n number of time-varying attributes, the ith tuple of the historical relation, hisT(i), is expressed as shown in the expression (2.4).

expression (2.4) :
his T(i) = (ConsA-cell((i,j,1),j=1,m), tivaA-cell((i,j,k),k=1,*),j=m+1,m+n))
where * means its value are varying according to the number of surrogate's valid time.

An instance of a historical tuple from the schema given in figure 2.2 is shown in figure 2.4.

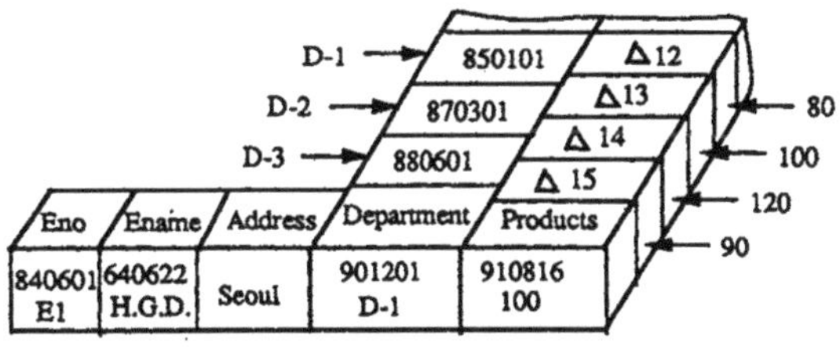

Figure 2.4 : Instances of historical tuple

Special properties of historical tuple are :

1. In the time-varying attribute each surrogate has a different number of subscript k according to their history.
2. All of the constant attributes have only one number of subscript k, but it is the designer's option.
3. Long period attributes (i.e. Department) have a small number of subscript k, but short period attributes (i.e.Products) have a large number of k.

Historical columns of a historical relation are vertical partitions of the historical relation. Instances of a historical column are shown in figure 2.5.

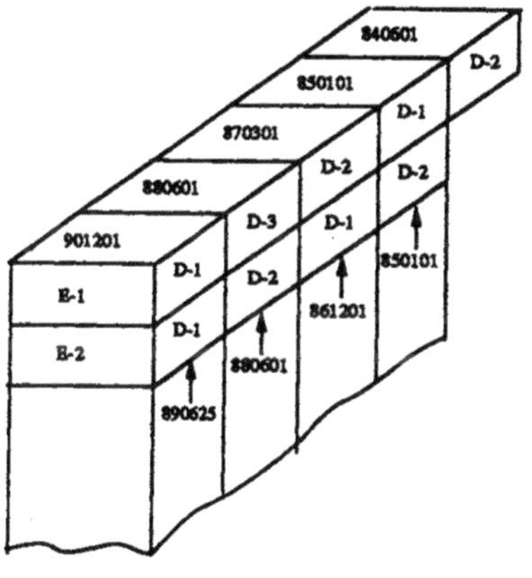

Figure 2.5 : Instance of a historical column

Using the historical tuple definition, the formal expression of historical relation [hisR] with the numbers of tuple L is given in expression (2.5).

$$\text{expression (2.5)} : hisR = (\, hisT(i), i=1,l) = ((\, consA\text{-}cell\,((i,j,1), j=1,m), tivaA\text{-}cell(((i,j,k), k=1,*), j=1,m)), i=1,l)$$

Formal expression of jth column of historical relation is given in expression (2.6).

expression (2.6) :

$$A: consA : hisC(j) = (consA\text{-}cell((i,j,1), i=1,l))$$

$$B: tivaA : hisC(j) = (tivaA\text{-}cell(((i,j,k), k=1,*), i=1,l))$$

2.5. Constraints

In the 3-D relational historical database system two constraints are added to traditional relational database systems : one is primary key, the other is operation.

Constraint for the primary key is "time-varying attributes could not be a primary key". For example, in the table of figure 2.2, the attribute Department is time-varying attribute and foreign key in other table(See figure 3.8), but it can not be primary key in the relation Employee.

Constraints for the operation is "Operate on historical tuples or historical relation with unit of tuple, not with unit of cell". This constraint is described in detail in Chapter 3.

2.6. Operations

Operations in the 3-D relational historical database systems are divided into two classes: one is traditional set operations and the other is special relational historical operations.These are described in Chapter 3.

3. RELATIONAL HISTORICAL OPERATIONS

The operations in the relational historical database must involve predicate of valid time. The first predicate group are used when the query on the historical database are at time point as given in the expression (3.1).

$$\text{Expression (3.1)} : t = \{\, a, present \,\}$$

"t = a" means valid time's value t is constant, and

"t = present" means valid time's value t is present time.

The second predicates group are used when the query on the historical database are duration as given in the expression (3.2).

$$\text{Expression (3.2)} : t = \{(*), (t1,*), (*,t1), (t1,t2)\}$$

"t = *" means all valid time values,

"t = (t1,*)" means valid time's start time is t1 and all the rest valid time values.

"t = (*,t1)" means all the valid time values until t1,

"t = (t1,t2)" means all the valid time values from t1 to t2.

In the discrete type of tivaA, the subscript k is binding directly when a query occurs, but in the step-wise constant type of tivaA, the subscript k does not. "The valid time mapping algorithm"[1] is used in the step-wise constant type of tivaA to access the suitable cell.

In this paper, traditional set operators: union, intersection, difference, cartesian product are used without time concept. And special relational operators: projection, selection, join, division are extended to involve time concept and are called his-projection, his-selection, his-join and his-division respectively.

3.1. Traditional Set Operators

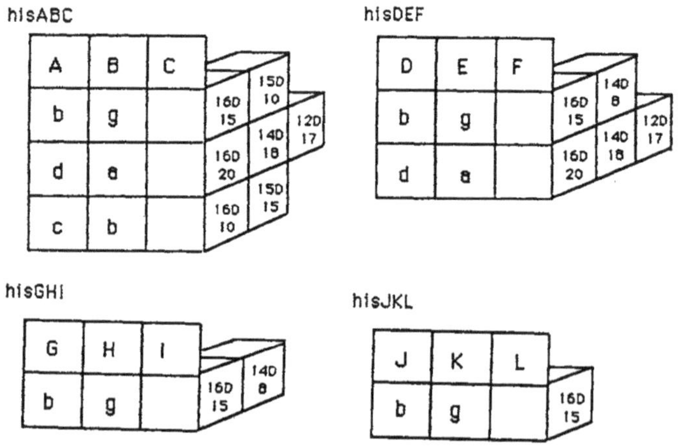

Figure 3.1 : sample historical relations for operation

Traditional set operators can be used without time concepts in the relational historical database. But the operators must operate on unit of historical tuple or historical relation. It is the first constraint on operation in relational historical database. The second constraint in relational historical database on operation is "to operate on the same type of tivaA".

For example, historical relations: hisABC, hisDEF, hisGHI, hisJKL are shown as in figure 3.1.

example 1 ; hisDEF ∪ hisGHI = hisDEF

example 2 ; hisDEF ∪ hisJKL ¬= hisDEF,
because the first tuple of hisDEF is not same as that of hisJKL.

If the second example is permitted, the completeness of the operation is not guaranted.[4,7]

If hisDEF ∪ hisJKL = hisDEF, the difference (hisDEF - hisJKL) is shown as follows in figure 3.2.

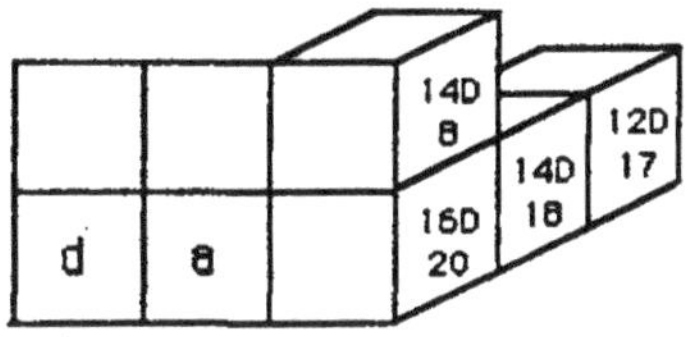

Figure 3.2 : Result of (hisDEF - hisJKL)

The cartesian product of hisABC and (hisDEF - JKL) is also shown as follows in figure 3.3.

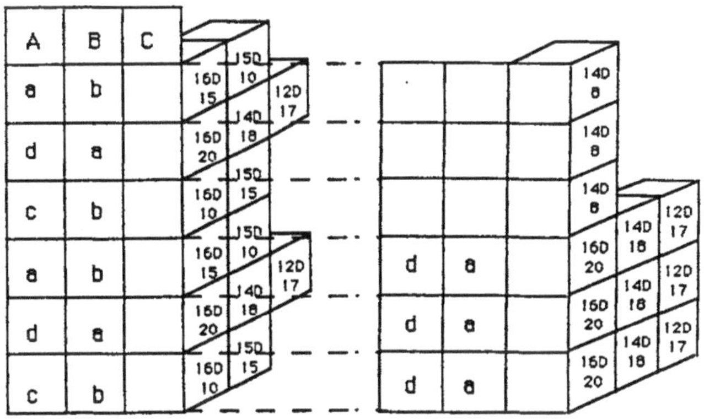

Figure 3.3 : Result of hisABC and (hisDEF - hisJKL)

The cartesian product of hisABC and hisDEF is shown as follows in figure 3.4.

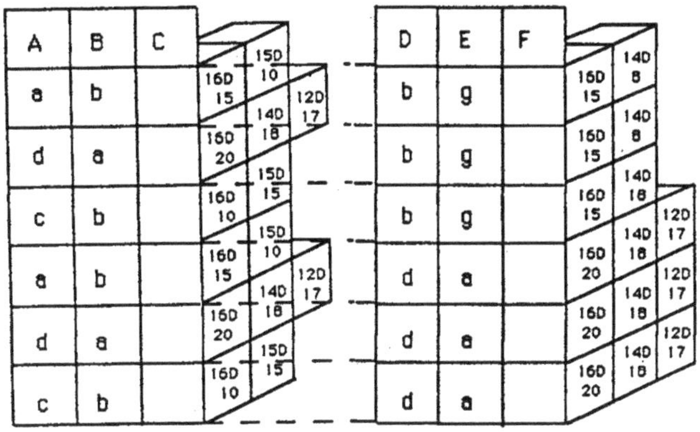

Figure 3.4 : The result of cartesian product hisABC and hisDEF

The cartesian product of hisABC and hisJKL is shown as follows in figure 3.5.

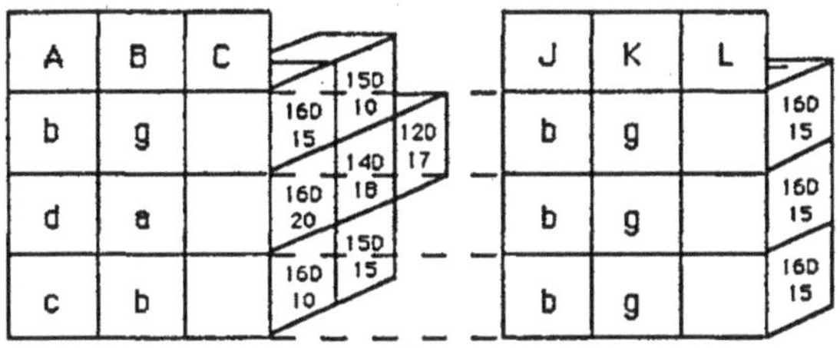

Figure 3.5 : The result of cartesian product hisABC and hisJKL

The difference (hisABC * hisDEF - hisABC * hisJKL) is shown as follows in figure 3.6.

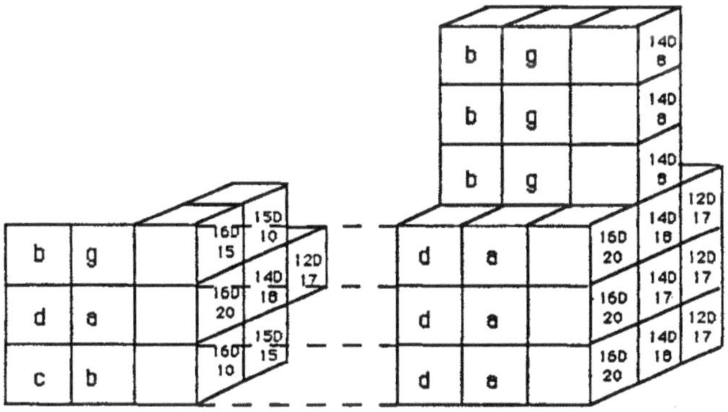

Figure 3.6 : The result of (hisABC * hisDEF - hisABC * hisJKL)

Comparing figure 3.6 to figure 3.3, hisABC * (hisDEF - hisJKL) ¬= hisABC * hisDEF - hisABC * hisJKL.

If we use relation hisGHI, the result of hisABC * (hisDEF - hisGHI) is

hisABC * (hisDEF - hisGHI) = hisABC * hisDEF - hisABC * hisGHI.

The operations in relational historical database must satisfy the following conditions;

1. The degree of two relations is the same as in the relational operation.
2. The domains of corresponding attribute is the same as in the relational operation.
3. The type of tivaA (discrete, step-wise constant) corresponding attribute is the same.
4. The unit of operation is historical tuple or historical relation.

3.2 Special Relational Historical Operators

Special relational operators were called special relational historical operators in relational historical database which were extended to involve time concept. The algorithm of special relational historical operator to involve time concept is described in paper.[1] In this paper, we describe the algorithm narratively.

The operators in 3-D RDM create two dimensional view for the query of time point but for the query of duration a three dimensional view is created. The query language must be extended to predicate the valid time. The query language SQL was extended, called XSQL, to involve predicate of valid time. The Where clause of XSQL has the predicate of valid time "t = ".

3.2.1. His-projection operator : His-projection operator create historical columns which are the vertical subset of the given historical relation. For example, some instances of historical relation Employee is shown in figure 3.7.

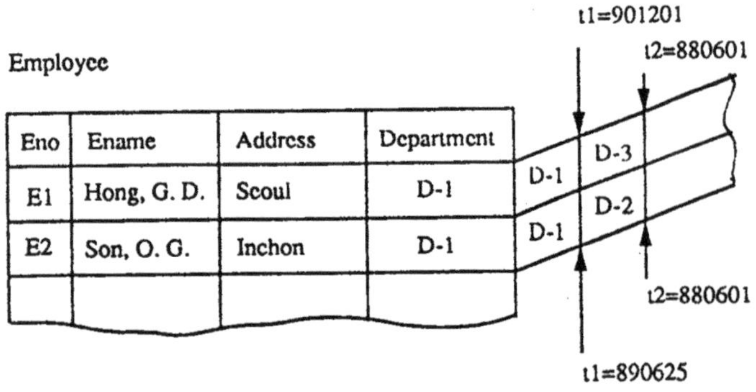

Figure 3.7 : Some instances of Employee

Examples of his-projection over figure 3.7 are given in following query 1 and query 2.

Query 1 : Get employer's Ename and Department who work there on June 01, '88.

o XSQL expression :

```
SELECT  Ename, Department
FROM    Employee
WHERE   t = 880601
```

o Result of query 1 :

Ename	Department
Hong. G. D	D-3
Son. O. G	D-2

o Explanation of query 1 evaluation :

1. Binding subscript i,j,k in cell(i,j,k).
   when query is input, subscript i,j,k in cell(i,j,k) bind as follows :
   (1) J=4, because tivaA department is the 4th attribute of Employee
   (2) K=2, because t=880601 is true in the second valid time
   (3) I=1, because the first surrogate of Department is true

By (1) (2) (3), cell(1,4,2) is accessed and cell(1,2,1) is also accessed for the consA Ename wanted in the query. Cell(2,2,1) and cell(2,4,2) can also be accessed by the same method.

2. Constructing results of query.
   (1) cell(1,2,1) organize a CELL(1,1)
   (2) cell(1,4,2) organize a CELL(1,2)
   (3) cell(2,2,1) organize a CELL(2,1)
   (4) cell(2,4,2) organize a CELL(2,2)

* CELL(x,y,z) is temporal system variable to be used to construct the result of query.

Query 2 : Get Employer's Ename and Department who work there from June 1, '88 to present.

o XSQL expression :

```
SELECT  Ename, Department
FROM    Employee
WHERE   t = (880601, * )
```

o Result of query 2 :

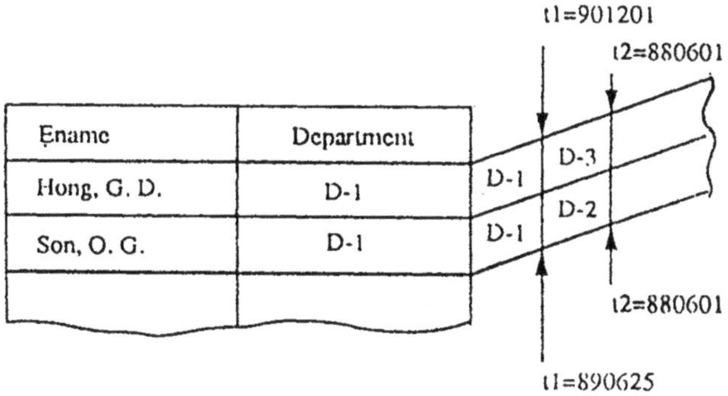

o Explanation of query 2 evaluation :

This query is that valid time is duration. Evaluation of query is the same as that of query 1 except that the result is 3 - D view.

The formal notation of his-projection operation is given in expression (3.1).

expression (3.1) : π { A } tc (R)

where tc : predicate of valid time.
R : relation name.
A : set of attributes to project
π : projection operator

<u>3.2.2. His-selection operator</u> : His-selection operator create historical tuples which are horizontal subset of given historical relation. Examples of his-selection over the schema of figure 3.7 are given in the following queries 3 and 4.

Query 3 : Get all attributes for department "D-3" on June 25, '90.

o XSQL expression :

```
SELECT  *
FROM    Employee
WHERE   Department = "D-3" and
        t = 900625
```

o Result of query 3 :

Eno	Ename	Address	Department
E1	Hong.G.D	Seoul	D-3

Query 4 : Get all attributes for employer " Son.O.G ".

o XSQL expression :

```
SELECT  *
FROM    Employee
WHERE   Ename = "Son.O.G" and
        t = *
```

o Result of query 4 :

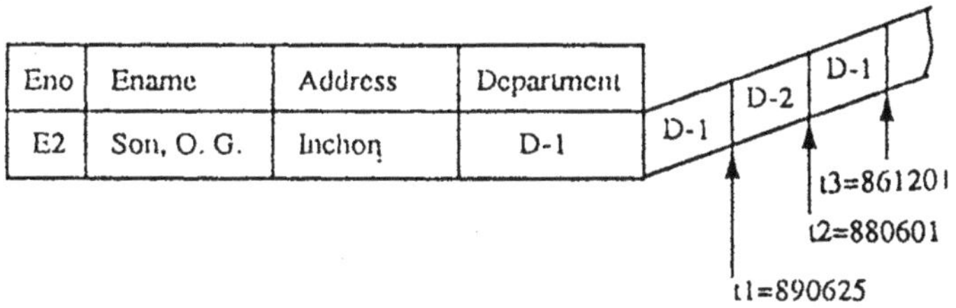

The formal notation of his-selection operation is given in expression (3.2).

expression (3.2) : $\sigma(A\ \theta\ \alpha)tc$ (R)

where tc : predicate of valid time
R : relation name
A : attribute to select
α : subset of domain in A
θ : sets of comparison operators.

<u>3.2.3. His-join operator</u> : The his-join operation of historical relation R1 on attribute A with historical relation R2 on attribute B is the set of all historical tuples t such that t is the concatenation of a historical tuple 'a' belong to R1 and a historical tuple 'b' belonging to R2 and the prediate "a.R1 θ b.R2"evaluate to true. (attribute a.R1 and b.R2 should be defined on the same domain, and the operation θ must make sense for that domain.)

The his-join operator must do join at the any time point and duration and create cubic view as the same in projection and selection operation. Examples of the his-join over figure 3.7 and figure 3.8 are given in the following query 5.

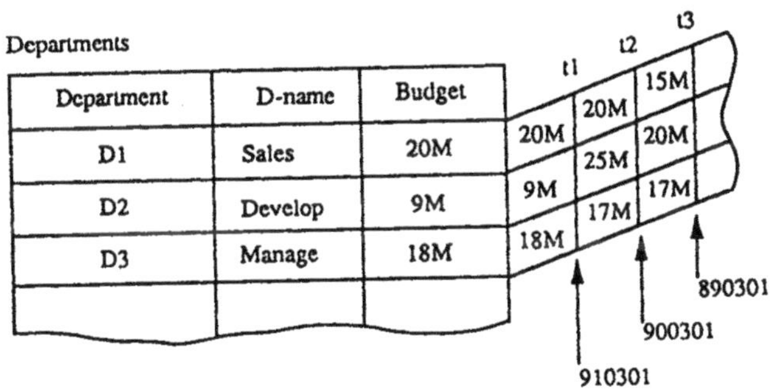

Figure 3.8 : Some instrances of Departments

Query 5 : Get a list of join for Employee and Departments on May, '90.

o XSQL expression : SELECT *
FROM Employee, Departments
WHERE Employee . Department = departments . Department
and t = (9005*)

but, t = (9005*) means t = (900501 ~ 900531)

o Result of query 5 ;

Eno	Ename	Adress	Department	D-name	Budget
E1	Hong, G. D.	Seoul	D-3	Manage	17M
E2	Son, O. G.	Inchon	D-1	Sales	20M
E3	Lee, S. S	soowon	D-1	Sales	20M

o Explanation of query 5 evaluation ;
the predicate of valid time constraint on both two relations R1 and R2, and the values of Budget are on May, '90.

The formal notation of his-join is given in expression (3.3).

Expression (3.3) : $R1 \ [\ ai \triangleright\triangleleft_{tc} bi\ ]\ R2$

where tc : predicate of valid time.
R1, R2 : two historical relation.
ai : attribute name from R1.
bi : attribute name from R2.
but, ai, bi must be in same domain.

<u>3.2.4. His-division operator</u> : The his-division operator divides a dividend historical relation R1 of degree (m + n) by a divisor historical relation R2 of degree n, and produces a quotient historical relation of degree m. The (m + i)th attribute of R1 and the ith attribute of B (i= 1, 2, . . . , n) should be defined on the same domain. Consider the first m attribute of R1 as a single composite attribute X, and the last n as another, Y ; relation R1 can then be thought of as a set of pairs of values (x , y). Similarily, relation R2 can be thought of as a set of single values (y). Then the result of dividing R1 by R2, that is, the result of evauluating the expression;

R1 hisDIVIDE BY R2

is the historical relation R3, with sole(composite) attribute X, such that every value x of R3.X appears as a value of R1.X, and the pair of values (x , y) appears in R1 for all values y appearing in R2. The m attributes of the quotient have the same qualified names as the first m attribute of relation R1. Some examples of division are given in example 1 and example 2 over figure 3.9.

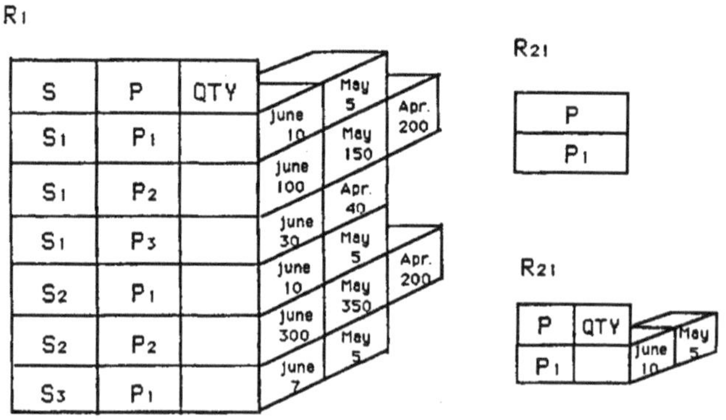

Figure 3.9 : Sample relations for division

Example 1 : R1 divide by R21 are R31

R31

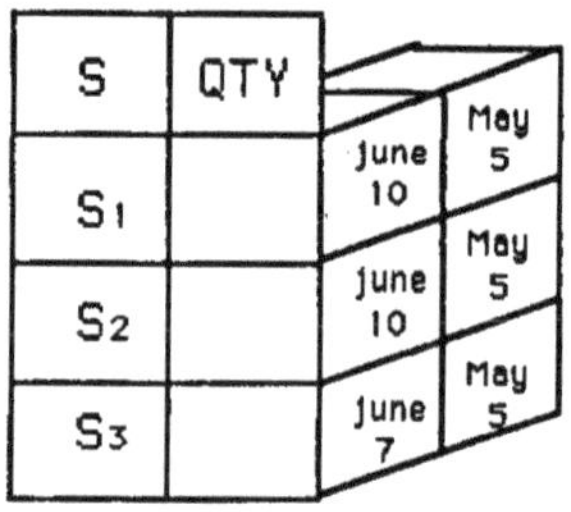

Example 2 : R1 divide by R21 are R32

R32.

S
S1
S2

4. CONCLUSION AND FURTHER RESEARCH

In this paper we introduced a methodology for incorporating time dimension into the relational model. We propose a system variable cell(i, j, k) in 3-D to implement the 3-D RDM. Each cell value is stored along with a start time which is valid. Non-first normal form relations are used for this purpose. The attribute in historical relation is divided into constant attribute and time-varying attributes. The two types of attributes preserve time (history), but constant attribute is optional.

To extract information from historical relations, time concept is preserved in special relational historical operators.

The proposed approach has several advantages. First, it is a closer abstraction of the real world. Second, it eliminates data redundancy resulting from duplication of unchanged attributes which is inherent in the case of tuple time-stamping . Third, it is possible to obtain past relation instances which allow a user to extract information for any time point or time interval since the begining of the database by the valid time mapping algorithm. Fourth, by using extended SQL, i.e. XSQL, to preserve time, all the operations can be performed. Furthermore, the proposed methodology is flexible and provides convenience to the user since it allows different types of attributes to coexist in the same relation.

Further research is needed in several directions. First, more detail is needed in functions in the predicates of valid time. Second, designing a graphical query language for 3-D RDM is needed for better user interface. Third, efficient method for secondary memory storage are needed for a historical databases which demands massive storage. Currently we are planning to explore the strategies for a prototype implementation of the proposed model and language.

REFERENCES

1). Cho T. N., "Design for Historical Database System", PhD. Diss., Hong-Ik University, Seoul, Korea, December 1991.

2). Clifford J. and Tansel A.,"On an Algebra for Historical Relational Database:Two views", Proc. of ACM SIGMOD, May 1985.

3). Gadia,S.K., and Yeung,C.S., "A Generalized Model for a Relational Temporal Database", ACM TODS, 1988.

4). Mckenzie E, and Snodgrass R.,"An Evaluation of Historical Algebras", Technical Report TR87-020, Univ. of North Carolina, Chapel Hill, October 1987.

5). Segev A. and shoshani A.,"Logical Modeling of Temporal Data, Proc. of the ACM SIGMOD, May 1987.

6). Snodgrass R. and Ahn I., "A Taxonomy of Time in Databases", Proceedings of the ACM SIGMOD, May 1985.

7). Tuzhilin A.and Clifford J., "A Temporal Relational Algebra as a Basis for Temporal Relational Completeness", Proc. of the 16th Int'l Conf. on VLDB, 1990.

8). Käfer W., Rittler N., and Shöning H., "Support for Temporal Data by Complex Object", Proc. of the 16th. Int'l Conf. on VLDB, 1990.

Offstage Objects and their Renovations in the Temporal Object System TOS

Abad A. Shah[1], *F. Fotouhi*[2], *W. Grosky*[2], *S.P. Rana*[2], and *A. Vashishta*[2]

[1]Department of Computer Science, King Saud University, Riyadh, Saudi Arabia
[2]Department of Computer Science, Wayne State University, Detroit, Michigan 48202, U.S.A.

email: fotouhi@cs.wayne.edu

ABSTRACT

TOS, the temporal object system proposed in[4,5] maintains changes to both the structure and state of an object. Objects in TOS are referred to as temporal objects. In this paper we show how the aggregation of temporal objects in a family, i.e., collection of temporal objects with the same common knowledge, allows the construction of an offstage object. During its life-span, an offstage object may go through changes due to the changes in its participant temporal objects. We refer to this as the renovation of an offstage object. Here, we discuss two types of renovations for such an object.

1. INTRODUCTION

Relational databases and their temporal extensions are suitable for simple record-based applications, but are not suitable for engineering and other complex database applications due to their limitations in defining a complex object directly and at one place[8]. Several types of object-oriented databases have been proposed to support the development of these application systems. In the object-oriented paradigm, an object is defined by the two parameters *structure* and *state*. The *structure* (SR) of an object provides the structural and behavioral capabilities of that object, which is defined by a set of instance variables, methods, and rules (or integrity constraints). The *state* (ST) of an object assigns data values to the instance variables of the objects and methods which operate on them. A set of objects sharing the same structure is referred to as a *class*. An object-oriented database is a collection of classes which are organized as a DAG. Figure 1 shows the schema of an Automobile Manufacturing Database. In this figure bold lines represent *part-of* relationships.

In the existing object-oriented database systems, changes in the state of an object are maintained via *version management* [1,6]. Also, structural changes are supported in most object-oriented database systems. Such changes to a class are referred to as *schema evolution* in the literature[10]. There are three possible scenarios for a class to change its structure. These are:

Type I) Adding new instance variables, methods, and/or rules
Type II) Deleting instance variables, methods, and/or rules
Type III) Changes to instance variables, methods, and/or rules

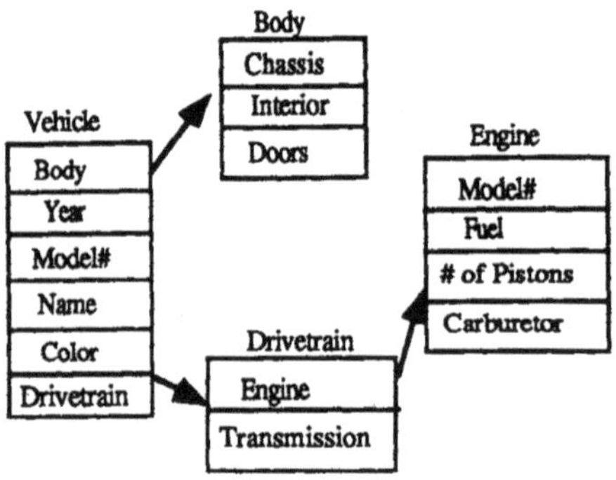

Figure 1. Schema of the class Vehicle

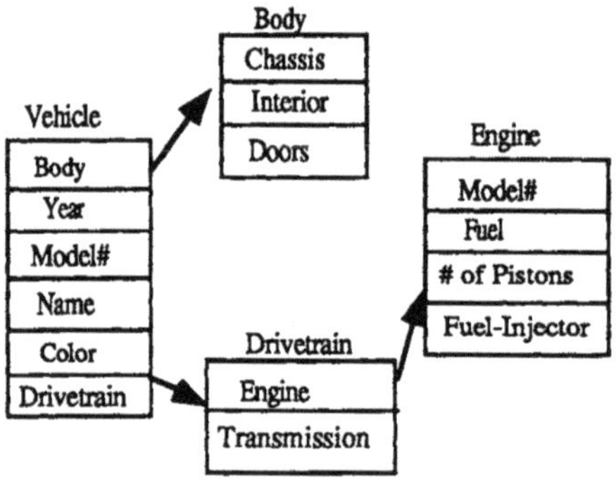

Figure 2. Type II change for the class Vehicle

For type I changes, there is no loss of knowledge of a class because the previous knowledge of the class structure is also retained along with the new one. On the other hand, for type II and type III changes, the history of changes in a class structure is not readily available, as it is overwritten or deleted in the latest version of the class structure. Current object-oriented database systems keep only the current version of each class structure. *After* any one of the type II or type III changes, it is necessary to reload a previous version of the database to retrieve any information from a previous version of a class structure. For example, Figure 1 and Figure 2 are two snapshots of the class structure for the class Vehicle at time instances t_1 and t_2 where $t_1 \leq t_2$, respectively. In Figure 2, instance variable Carburetor in the class Engine is replaced by a new instance variable Fuel-Injector. After this change, all queries about the class Engine can be answered from its current version of the class structure (Figure 2) unless the user explicitly asks for the previous version of class Engine.

In[4,5], we introduced a temporal object-oriented system (TOS) which maintains the history of changes to both the structure and the state of an object in a consolidated and elegant manner. We associated time (point model) to both structure and state of an object. Such an object is referred to as a *temporal object*. A temporal object evolves over time by changing its state or structure. A set of temporal objects which share a common knowledge (i.e., structure and state) is referred to as a *family*. The TOS also facilitates the construction of a *complex family* which is an aggregation of temporal objects from various families. The objects in a complex family are referred to as *temporal complex objects*. A complex family increases the knowledge sharing of non-homogeneous temporal objects and the transportability of them. A temporal object system (TOS) is then a collection of families which are defined at different time instances.

In this paper we briefly discuss TOS, simple and complex families, temporal objects, temporal complex objects, and offstage objects. We also describe renovation of offstage objects. The remainder of this paper is organized as follows: In Section 2, we describe the TOS and its objects. In Section 3, we discuss renovation of the offstage objects and define two types of renovations. Finally, in Section 4 we give concluding remarks and future research directions.

2. TEMPORAL OBJECT SYSTEM

As mentioned in the previous section Temporal Object System (TOS) is a collection of simple and complex families which are defined at different time instances. A family is a collection of temporal objects and a temporal object is a collection of stages. Figure 3 shows a schema of TOS, where *RTOS* represents the root node of the system with n families, i.e., F_1, F_2, . . ., F_n as its children. The figurative notations which are used in Figure 3 and in other figures are give in the appendix.

Now we first give a brief overview of the temporal objects which are building blocks of the family, and then we discuss the concept of families.

2.1 Temporal Objects

As mentioned in the previous section, an object is represented by its structure and state. With the passage of time an object may change its structure and/or its state. By associating time to both the structure and the state of an object, we can keep the history of changes to that object. Therefore, we define a temporal object (TO) to be an ordered set of objects which is constructed at different time instances. A temporal object is represented as TO = $<(SRt_1, STt_1), (SRt_2, STt_2), \ldots, (SRt_n, STt_n)>$ where $t_i \leq t_{i+1}$ for all $1 \leq i < n$, where the ordered pair (SRt_i, STt_i) is the i-th object of the temporal object which is constructed at the time instance t_i with structure SRt_i and state STt_i. An i-th object of the temporal object is referred to as its i-th *stage*[4,5].

A stage is maintained in a prototypical form, i.e., a structure, a state, or a combination of the two[3]. For example, if a temporal object suffers a structural change, then new stage of the temporal object captures only the structure change. We are using time instance as a physical time and time point. A temporal object may also be referred to as an ordered set of stages. For example, in Figure 4 the temporal object TO_a of the family F_i has n stages. The first and last stages of a temporal object are significant because they hold the initial and current knowledge of the temporal object. We refer to these stages as the *birth stage* (stage $S_{1,a}$ in Figure 4) and the *current stage* (stage $S_{n,a}$ in Figure 4) of the temporal object. The time from the birth stage of a temporal object to the time of its current stage is referred to as the *life-span* of the temporal object. The set of temporally ordered stages of a temporal object is refereed to as the *life-sequence* of the object. A new stage is appended to a temporal object if the structure and/or state associated with its stage changes (see [4,5,11] for more details).

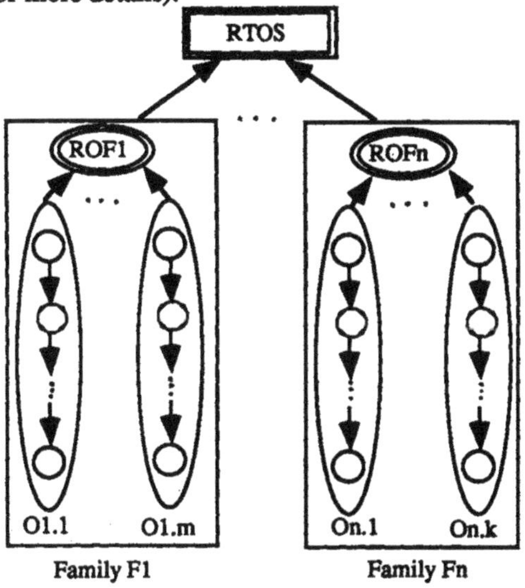

Figure 3. Schema of the Temporal Object System (TOS)

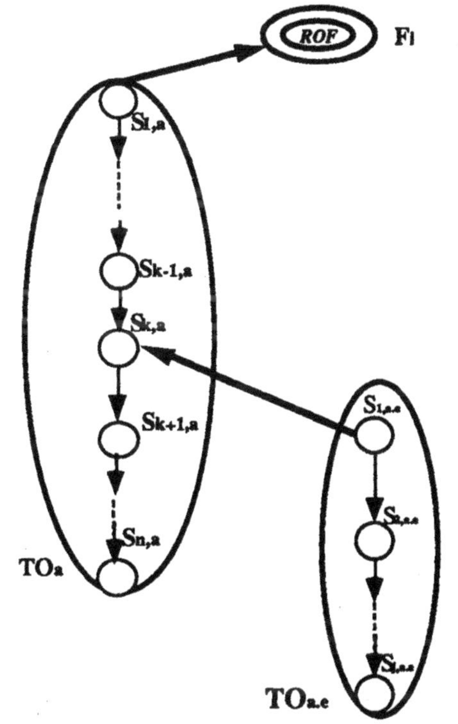

Figure 4. A participant object TO_a and an offstage object $TO_{a.e}$

2.1.1 Offstage objects

Within a family TOS allows the creation of a new temporal object from a set of existing temporal objects. We refer to such a new temporal object as *offstage object* and the existing objects as *participant objects*. In Figure 4 the temporal object $TO_{a.e}$ is an offstage object and the stage $S_{k,a}$ of the temporal object TO_a is referred to as an *offstage*. The temporal object TO_a is the participant object of the offstage object $TO_{a.e}$. The offstage $S_{k,a}$ is the stage from where the offstage object $TO_{a.e}$ starts sharing the knowledge of the participant object TO_a. In other words, the offstage object $TO_{a.e}$ has taken its birth at time instance $t_{1,a.e}$ by sharing the set of stages $\{S_{k,a}, S_{k-1,a}, \ldots, S_{1,a}\}$ of the participant object TO_a. Note that the temporal object TO_a and offstage object $TO_{a.e}$ have different object identities.

The set of time-spans of stages and life-span of the offstage object $TO_{a.e}$ are as follows:

$T_{a.e} = \{[t_{1,a.e}, t_{2,a.e}), [t_{2,a.e}, t_{3,a.e}), \ldots, [t_{j,a.e}, now]\}$

life-span$_{a.e} = [t_{1,a.e}, now]$

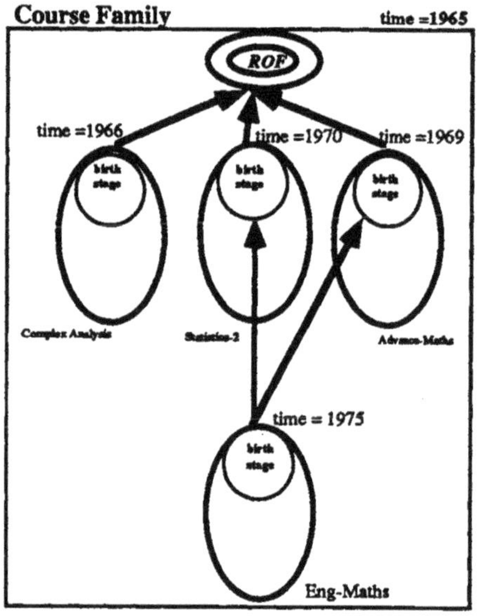

Figure 5. An example of offstage object "Eng-Maths" in the "Course" Family

Figure 5 and Figure 6 exhibit an offstage object "Eng-Maths" which is constructed in the "Course" Family. The offstage object "Eng-Maths" is defined at the time instance 1975 by sharing knowledge of two participant objects "Statistics-2" and "Advance-Math" through the offstages $S_{1,Statistics-2}$ and $S_{1,Advance-Maths}$, respectively. Note that these offstages are also birth stages of the participant objects. Each participant objects has one stage (see Figure 5) at the time instance when the offstage object is defined. Figure 6(a) shows the *ROF* of the family "Course". The stages $S_{1,Statistics-2}$ and $S_{1,Advance-Maths}$ of the participant objects are shown in Figure 6(b) and Figure 6(c), respectively. Figure 6(d) shows the birth stage of the offstage object "Eng-Maths". A temporal condition (Eng-Maths.1975 ≥ Statistics-2.1970) and (Eng-Maths.1975 ≥ Advance-Maths.1969) must hold *before* defining the offstage object, where 1970 and 1969 are the time instances when the offstages of the participant objects are defined.

If an offstage object shares knowledge of only one participant object, then this is analogous to simple inheritance in the class-based approach, and if it shares knowledge from more than one participant objects, then this is similar to the concept of multiple inheritance in the class-based approach. An offstage object has some similarities and differences with an object which is defined by using the class-based approach. For example, an offstage object of family and an object of a class both share the same common knowledge *ROF* and class structure respectively. In a family, state of a temporal object can also be shared by an offstage object but, in the class-based approach all objects of a class usually share only class structure. The concept of an offstage enhances the reusability of knowledge (both structure and state) within a family, whereas the class-based approach does not allow the sharing of the both structure and state.

2.2 Families of the TOS

The concept of a family is used to assemble a group of temporal objects sharing a common context. For example, various Engine temporal objects form an Engine family. All temporal objects within a family can be handled in a similar fashion by responding uniformly to a set of messages. A set of similar structures and/or states defines a *common context* of a family. The common context of a family is referred to as the *root-of-family* (*ROF*) where *common knowledge* about all its temporal objects is maintained (see[4,5] for more details). Temporal objects of a family can be defined only *after* the construction of the *ROF* of the family.

In the class-based object-oriented systems class is used to assemble a set of objects which share some common assets as it is with the definition of family in TOS. However, a family encapsulates more features than a class. For example, in a class, the structure of the class is *always* shared by all its states (or instances), and a change in its structure affects all states, subclass structures and their corresponding states. Also, if one deletes Color instance variable from the class Vehicle of Figure 1, then all its instances are going to delete data value of the instance variable Color. In a family, however, the structure or state of each temporal object of the family shares the *ROF* only at the time instance of its birth. After that each temporal object is independent and a change in a particular temporal object does not effect the *ROF* or any other objects of the family. In other words, the *ROF* of a family is *read-only*, it does not change with passage of time. Time is associated with a temporal object and *ROF* of family.

In TOS two types of families, *simple families* and *complex families*, can be defined. They are described in the next two sections.

2.2.1. Simple families

A *simple family* represents an independent object development environment in which temporal objects can be constructed without sharing any knowledge of other families. For example, in Figure 5, the family "Course" is a simple family. Two simple families do not share any knowledge, and in term of knowledge sharing they are mutually disjoint. A simple family is analogous to a class in the class-based approach, which has no super-class (expect *system class* or *root class*).

ROF (Course)

Instance-variables
{ time:1965,
course-code,
prereq,
outlines
}

Methods
{update}

(a) The *ROF* the family "Course"

(b) The participant object "Statistics-2"

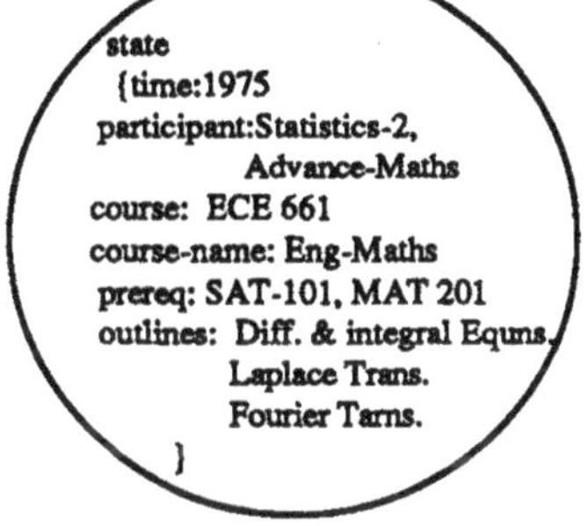

(c) The offstage object "Eng-Maths"

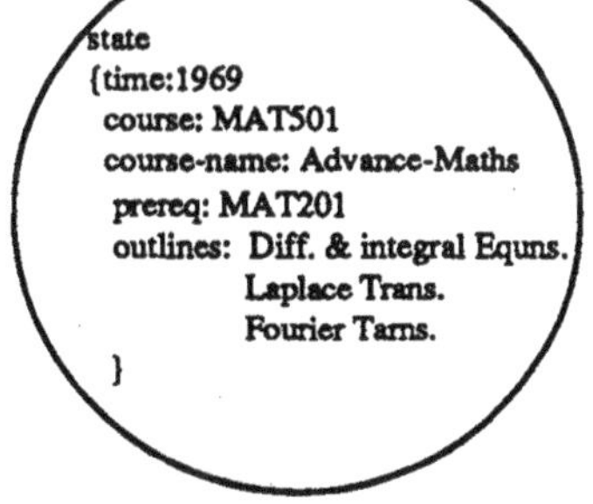

(d) The participant object "Advance-Maths"

Figure 6. The details of the offstage objects and it's participant objects

2.2.2. Complex families

In existing class-based object-oriented systems, a complex object is defined as an object which can have another object as the value of a particular instance variable[7]. For example, Figure 7 shows the structure of complex object Vehicle. Here, we extend our definition of family to *complex family* which provides a facility for the integration of nonhomogeneous temporal objects of different families in order to build another temporal object which is referred to as *temporal complex object* (TCO). The components of a TCO are temporal objects of nonhomogeneous families (or independent families), and the temporal objects which take part in the construction of a TCO are called *subobjects* (or *components*) of the TCO.

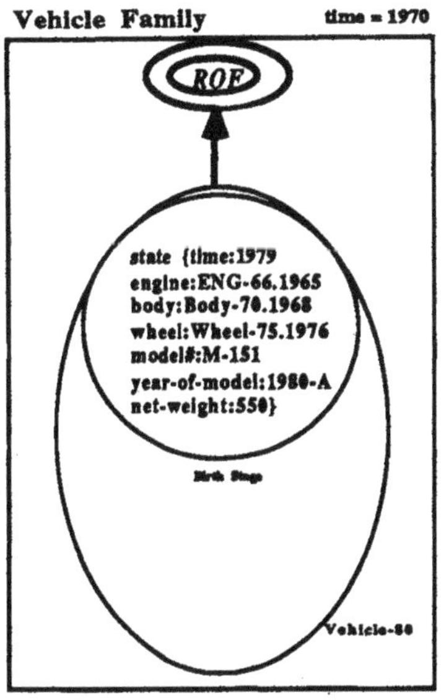

Figure 7. The TCO Vehicle-80 and its subobjects

A new TCO, TCO_c, can be defined in a family F_c at a given time instance $t_{1,c}$ with r subobjects from r different simple families. The birth stage of TCO, TCO_c, may be created at time instance $t_{1,c}$ if the temporal condition $(t_{1,k} \leq t_{1,c}) \wedge (t_{Fc} \leq t_{1,c})$ is true for all k such that $1 \leq k \leq r$, where t_{Fc} is the time instance when the complex family F_c was created, and $t_{1,k}$ is the time instance when birth stage of the k-th subobject was created. This temporal condition ensures that all temporal subobjects and the complex family exist *before* the existence of TCO. Figure 7 shows the birth stage of the complex family Vehicle which is an aggregation of three simple families Engine, Body and Wheel. In this figure the TCO Vehicle-80 is created at time instance 1979 (denoted by Vehicle-80.1979) if the temporal condition, (ENG-66.1965 ≤ Vehicle-80.1979) ∧ (Body-70.1968 ≤ Vehicle-80.1979) ∧ (Wheel-75.1976 ≤ Vehicle-80.1979) ∧ (Vehicle-Family.1970 ≤ Vehicle-80.1979) is true, where ENG-66.1965, Body-70.1968 and Wheel-75.1976 are the time instances when the subobjects ENG-66, Body-70 and Wheel-75 are created respectively, and Vehicle.1970 is the time instance when the family Vehicle is created. A TCO has all temporal parameters, time-span, life-span, and life-sequence, like the temporal objects of the simple family. *ROF* of the family Vehicle at a

time instance 1970 can be defined as follows:
ROF(Vehicle)
Aggregation-of: {Engine, Body, Wheel}
Instance-variables: {time=1970, model#, year-of-model, net-weight}
Methods: {assemble, test-it}
Note that the concept of an offstage object enhances reusability within a family, and the concept of a TCO enhances reusability within a TOS.

Within the boundary of a simple family, we use the *offspring* technique and among the families we prefer the *copying* technique for knowledge sharing[2]. The aggregation and integration of temporal objects into a TCO can generate certain conflicts and compatibility problems such as naming and scaling between a TCO and its subobjects. For example, Naming conflicts occur when two or more subobjects of a TCO contain instance variables or methods with the same name such as the instance variable "weight" which has been defined in subobjects Engine and Body as well as the TCO Vehicle. We are currently investigating these issues.

2.3 Time Dimension in TOS

A time dimension is associated with the creation of a stage, a temporal object, and a family in TOS. The time is explicitly defined by user as an instance variable. While introducing a new family, data type of the time is defined and it is followed in creation of a temporal object and its stages. The granularity of time depends on the application domain. In TOS, we use time point model for creation of families, temporal objects and stages. A time point is referred to as a *time instance*. A time instance is a distinct and discrete point on the time-line and a dimension less entity. Time interval is also used in TOS to represent time duration between two time instances, for example, time-span of a stage and life-span of a temporal object. In this paper we use an abstract time "year" in each stage, temporal object and family for the sake of simplicity.

2.4 TO²L: A Query Language for TOS

In[11,12] we proposed a temporal object-oriented query language (TO²L) for the TOS. The query Language TO²L is a superset of SQL. The proposed language can answer the temporal queries on families (simple and complex). The TO²L uses a set of logical operators {=,<,>,≤,≥,<>} and a set of temporal operators {Before, After, During, Equivalent, Adjacent, Overlap, Follows, Precedes} of the SQL and TSQL, respectively[9]. The TSQL also adds a new clause WHEN. This clause evaluates temporal predicates by checking relative chronological ordering of timings in a relation. We also using this clause but in our case it works on families and temporal objects. We introduce a parameter *Time* which is time instance variable in *ROF* of family and each stage of temporal object. When we mention in a query Time During $[t_1, t_2]$, it means that value of instance variable Time lies in the time interval $[t_1, t_2]$.

The TO²L can answer both temporal and non-temporal queries for TOS. A temporal query has a WHEN clause which contains time, whereas, a non-temporal query does not include this clause. Non-temporally TOS gives a latest and aggregated view of the objects and families. As a temporal query includes a time parameter in WHEN clause, therefore its search space for temporal object and family is time dependent. On the other hand a non-temporal query does not include any time parameter, therefore its search space is complete life-spans of temporal object and family. In general, we can say that search space for a non-temporal query is greater than search space for a temporal query.

The following is an example of a query on simple family Engine.
Q1: 'List all 6 cylinder Engines from 1965 to 1980'.
SELECT Engine
FROM Engine Family
WHERE # of pistons = 6
WHEN Time During [1965, 1980]

The following is an example of a query on an offstage object.
Q_2: 'List the most recent outline of the course Eng-Maths'.
SELECT outline
FROM Course Family
WHERE Course=Eng-Maths

3. RENOVATION OF OFFSTAGE OBJECTS

During its life-span, an offstage object may go through changes. These changes may occur to its participant objects. For example, in the offstage object "Eng-Maths" the course "Advance-Maths" at time instance 1969 was used as the participant object at a time instance 1975 when the offstage object was originally designed. At some later time instance, "Advance-Maths" at time instance 1969 may be replaced by an updated version, say course "Advance-Maths" at time instance 1977 (see Figure 8 and Figure 9), or added another course "Complex Analysis" (see Figure 10) in the offstage object "Eng-Maths". This replacement or addition in the offstage object is referred to as the *renovation* of the offstage object. In this paper we consider two types of renovations, and refer to them as Type-I and Type-II renovations. These two types of renovations are described in the next two sections.

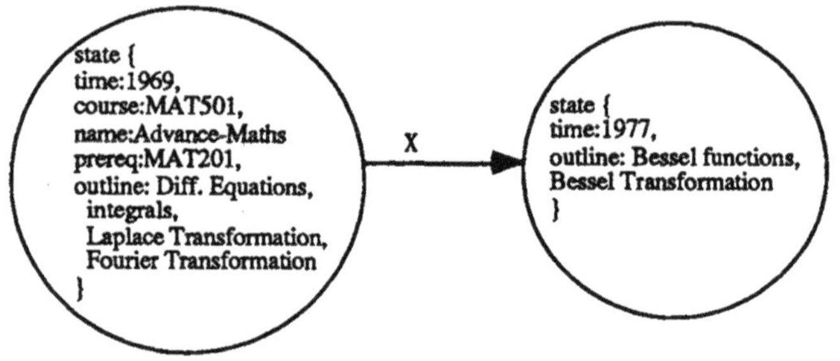

Figure 8. The participant object "Advance-Maths" *after* the stature change

3.1 Type I Renovation

In the first type of renovation, an offstage object is updated automatically if it goes through changes. For example, in the offstage object "Eng-Maths" one stage (only birth stage) of the participant object "Advance-Maths" was shared while defining the offstage object. At some later time when the object "Advance-Maths" goes through a stature change, then this change (i.e., Bessel Functions and Bessel Trans. are added in the instance variable outlines at time instance 1977 as shown in Figure 8) is also needed to be recorded in the offstage object "Eng-Maths". This renovation of the offstage object "Eng-Maths" is performed at the time instance 1988 by defining a new stage at that time instance as shown in Figure 9. The renovation will occur if the temporal condition (Advance-Maths.1977 ≤ 1988)∧ (Eng-Maths.1975 ≤ 1988) is true, where Advance-Maths.1977 is the time instance when the current stage of the participant object "Advance-Maths" is defined and 1988 is the time instance when the offstage object is renovated. If more than one participant object participates in renovation of an offstage object, then all participant objects must satisfy the temporal condition. The double arrow shows *re-sharing* (or renovated) from the participant object "Advance-Maths" to the offstage object at the time instance 1988. Also, the offstage object must satisfy a temporal condition which ensures the existence of the new participant object or new version of the participant object (or participant objects) *before* renovation of the offstage object.

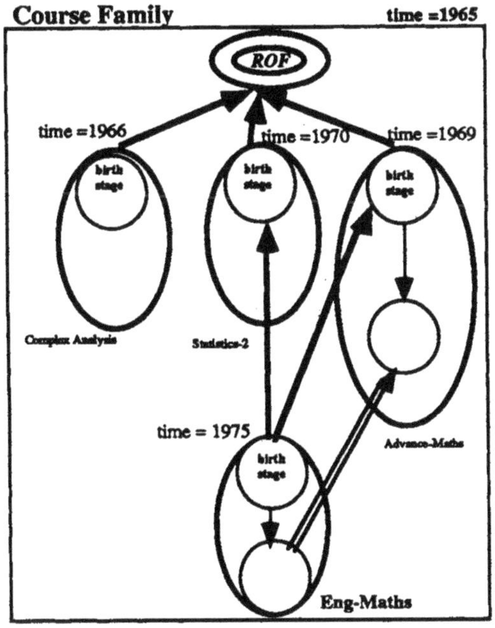

Figure 9. Renovation of Type I of the offstage object "Eng-Maths"

Before (*Before* ≤ 1988) renovation the offstage object "Eng-Maths" was sharing only one stage (birth stage) of the participant object "Advance-Maths" (see Figure 9), and it is shown by a single dark arrow in Figure 5. *After* (*After* ≤ 1988) the renovation, the offstage object is sharing two stages of the participant object (see Figure 9). The participant object "Advance-Maths" is shared two times in the offstage object at the time instances 1969 and 1988. The life-sequence of the participant object was different at different time instances. The life-sequence of the participant object "Advance-Maths' is $\{S_{1,\text{Advance-Maths}}\}$ and $\{S_{1,\text{Advance-Maths}}, S_{2,\text{Advance-Maths}}\}$ at time instances 1969 and 1988, respectively. In type I of renovation, object identities of the participant objects remain the same.

3.2 Type II Renovation

In type-II renovation, a participant object of an offstage object is replaced by a new participant object of the family at the same time instance. The new participant object will be completely compatible with the old participant object, that is, the new participant and old participant object perform the same function. For example, if a new participant object, "Complex Analysis", is added to the offstage object (see Figure 10) then both participant objects ("Advance-Maths" and "Complex Analysis") will have different object identities as they are two different temporal objects of the family "Course".

The type-II renovation can be performed on an offstage object when an existing participant object of the offspring object is replaced by a new and different participant object of the same family. Note that the temporal condition should hold before the renovation can take place.

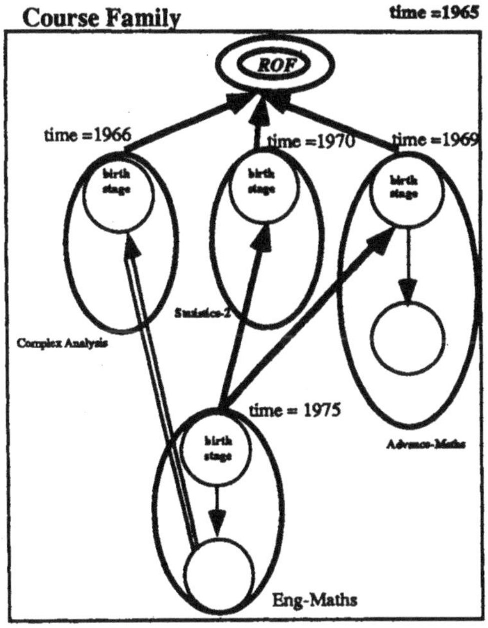

Figure 10. Renovation of Type II of the offstage object "Eng-Maths"

4. CONCLUSIONS

In this paper we discussed the Temporal Object System (TOS) which maintains changes in both the structure and the state of an object. An object in a TOS is referred to as a temporal object which evolves over time. Changes to both the structure and the state of the object are maintained throughout its various stages. In this paper we showed how the aggregation of temporal objects (participant objects) in a family allows the construction of an offstage object. Renovation of an object improve reusability in a family. We discussed two types of renovations for offstage objects. In the first type of renovation an offstage object changes when one or more of its participant objects change. For the second type of renovation, an offstage object changes when it tries to use a different participant object from the same family. Currently we are working on implementation of such a system and also improving on its query language.

REFERENCES

1) R. Agrawal et al,"Object Versioning in Ode," *Proc. of Data Eng.*, 1991.

2) A.M. Alashqur,S.Y.W. Su, and H. Lam,"OQL: A Query Language for Manipulating Object-Oriented Databases", *Proc. of 15th Intl. Conf. on VLDB*, 1989.

3) A.H. Borning,"Classes Versus Prototypes in Object-Oriented Languages," *ACM/IEEE Fall Joint Conf.*, November, 1986.

4) F. Fotouhi, A. Shah and W. Grosky, "TOS:A Temporal Object System,"*the 4th Intl. Conf. on Computing. & Info.*, Toronto, Canada, 1992.

5) F. Fotouhi, A. Shah and W. Grosky,"Complex Objects in the Temporal Object System," *IEEE Post-Proceeding of the 4-th International Conference on Computing & Information*, 1992.

6) R.H. Katz, E. Chang, and R. Bhateja,"Version Modeling Concepts for Computer-Aided Design Databases," *Proc. of ACM SIGMOD Conf.*, 1986.

7) Won Kim, J.Banerjee et al, "Composite Object Support in an Object-Oriented Database System," *Proc. of Data Eng.* 1989.

8) David Maier,"Why Object-Oriented Database Can Succeed Where Others Have Failed," *Proc.of Intl. Workshop on Object-Oriented Database Systems,* September, 1986.

9) S. B. Navathe and R. Ahmed,"TSQL: A language Interface for History Databases *Temporal Aspects in Information Systems,*" Edited by C. Rolland, F. Bodart, and M. Leonard, North-Holland, 1988.

10) G.T. Nguyen and D. Rieu,"Schema Evolution in Object-Oriented Database Systems,"*Data & Knowledge Engineering Journal, North-Holland,* No.4, 1989.

11) Abad A. Shah,"TOS:A Temporal Object System,"*Ph.D. Dissertation*, Wayne State University, Detroit, Michigan, 1992.

12) A. Shah, F. Fotouhi, and W. I. Grosky, "Renovation of Complex Objects in the Temporal Object System," to appear in the Proc. of the IEEE Phoenix Conf., 1993.

APPENDIX

The following set of figurative notations are used to represent different entities of the TOS.

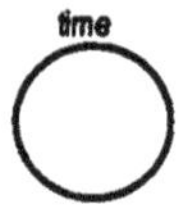

A stage of a temporal object

A temporal object

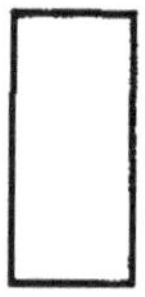

A family

A root-of-family (ROF)

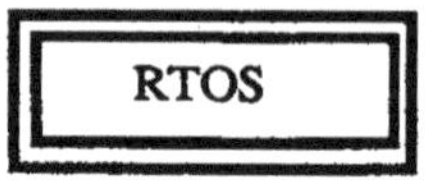

Root of the TOS (RTOS)

Transition to the next stage

Temporal inheritance

Renovation

Logical Data Independence Via Views: A Misapprehension?

J.M. de Graaff, R.J. Veldwijk and M. Boogaard

Vrije Universiteit
FEWEC/BIK
De Boelelaan 1105, 1081 HV Amsterdam, The Netherlands
E-mail: v67cmb01@hasara11.bitnet

Abstract

Most information systems are subject to changing requirements that can lead to alterations of the underlying database schema. Part of these alterations are information-preserving and can be regarded as schema restructuring. One of the objectives of the relational model is to provide logical data independence, i.e. to insulate application programs from the effects of information-preserving changes to the database schema. It is claimed that the relational view mechanism is sufficiently powerful to achieve logical data independence. This paper argues that the relational view mechanism fails to fulfil these claims in both a theoretical and a practical sense.

Key Words

Relational Model, Data Independence, View Mechanism, Maintenance

1. INTRODUCTION

In designing and building information systems it is necessary to design database schemata that are adequate representations of some Universe of Discourse (UoD). These schemata should capture the relevant rules, objects and object structure that apply to the environment to be modelled. For most, if not for all information systems, the UoD represented by the information system changes over time. Since the database schema has to remain an adequate representation of the UoD, changes in the UoD have to result in modifications of the database schema. However, schema modifications require time and money consuming changes to application programs that run against the schema. In order to avoid this application programs and terminal users should be independent of changes in the way data is structured and stored in the database. This quality is known as *data independence*.

One of the main objectives claimed by the relational model is to offer this independence (see, e.g. Codd 1970, 1990). Within this model physical and logical data independence are distinguished. According to Codd (1990, p. 345) *physical* data independence means that "... application programs and terminal activities remain logically unimpaired when changes are made in storage representation, access method or both". Again according to Codd (1990, p. 346), *logical* data independence means that "... application programs and terminal activities remain logically unimpaired when information-preserving changes are made to the base tables ...". This type of independence deals with changes at the relational level instead of changes below this level. We can define information-preserving changes as modifications of the database structure with no information explicitly supplied to or deleted from the database extension. In other words, information-preserving changes do not affect the information content of the database. Making information-preserving changes can be regarded as *restructuring* the database schema.

Returning to our discussion of schema changes induced by changes in the UoD rules, we contend that these never lead to changes at the physical level directly. Modifications at the physical level are typically induced by changes in the hardware configuration, in the cardinality of the base tables, or by changing priorities assigned to application programs. Adjustability below the relational level, i.e. physical data independence, is obviously very important with respect to the efficient allocation of scarce machine resources, but has no direct relationship with the state of the UoD.

A similar look at the adjustability *at* the relational level, i.e. logical data independence, results in a picture that is not so clear. It is possible to conceive alterations of the database structure that do not reflect changes in the rules the database enforces. An example of such an alteration would be the partitioning of a table into two or more tables by rows using row content. Such an alteration would typically be effected for technical reasons. The really interesting aspect of logical data independence concerns support for schema changes that reflect changes in the rules pertinent to the UoD. An example of such a change would be the alteration of a one-to-many relationship between two tables into a many-to-many relationship.

The claim of the relational model and relational DBMS products to provide physical data independence is largely achieved. In relational DBMS environments application programs are independent of many changes at the implementation level. With respect to logical data independence the relational model offers the view mechanism as a vehicle to make application programs immune to schema changes. Because implementation of the view mechanism in relational DBMS products is still very limited (see Date 1990, p. 383) these products do not offer any practical form of logical data independence.

The question addressed by the present paper is whether the relational view mechanism is sufficiently powerful to offer logical data independence, especially with respect to information-preserving schema alterations induced by changes in the UoD (the interesting kind). With respect to this kind of changes we take the position that *the view mechanism provided by the relational model does not provide the user with logical data independence at all.* The paper attempts to show the validity of this position by means of both theoretical and pragmatic arguments. These arguments are applied to the latest version of the relational model as published by Codd (1990), rather than against some implementation of the model.

The structure of this paper is as follows. Section 2 discusses some examples of information-preserving changes as given by Codd (1990) and shows that these examples have little or nothing to do with changes in the state of the UoD. Section 3 examines the view mechanism with respect to a basic UoD-induced information-preserving change to a database schema and shows that it does not work on both practical and theoretical grounds. Section 4 confronts the ambitious claim that the view mechanism provides logical data independence with our equally strong claim that it does not. The paper ends with some suggestions aimed at developing a mechanism that does provide some form of logical data independence.

2. EXEMPLARY APPLICATIONS OF THE VIEW MECHANISM

Views can be defined as virtual relations represented by their names and definitions only. By using views the users are insulated from the base relations. Some of the advantages of using views are that they allow the same data to be seen by different users in different ways and that they provide a powerful authorization mechanism. However, the most important feature of views is to provide logical data independence. To quote Codd (1990, p.322): "... *application programs and terminal users should always use views as the means of interacting with a relational database - the only way now known for application programs and end users to be able to cope with many kinds of changes in the logical database design without the need for reprogramming and retraining. This is also known as logical data independence*".

In discussing the subject of logical data independence Codd (1990, ch. 20) provides three examples of information-preserving changes in which views should be used to provide logical data independence. These examples are listed below.

1. Partitioning a table into two or more tables by rows using row content.
2. Splitting a table into two or more tables by columns using column names, provided the original primary key is preserved in each result.
3. Combining two tables into one by meaning of a non-loss join.

Although Codd does not give a detailed description of the application of the view mechanism with respect to these examples, it is easy to conceive the view definitions necessary to represent the situation as it was before the information-preserving change. The question is, however, whether these changes are reflections of changes in the UoD.

Looking at the first example in which a table is partitioned horizontally, we find that the obvious reason to make this change is a physical one, e.g. to store the different parts of the table on different devices or different locations. In this example the UNION operator makes it possible to combine the two new tables into one view that represents the situation before the change to the database schema. Of course it is essential that the view is updatable. Because Codd's new specification of the relational model provides a feature that determines in which base relation an insertion of a new tuple should be made (1990, p. 313), the UNION-view is indeed updatable.

Although the view mechanism provides logical data independence according the definition given by Codd, the example does not represent a case in which any change in UoD-rules has occurred. Instead it demonstrates the applicability of the view mechanism to insulate the application programs from changes induced by physical considerations.

To end our discussion of Codd's first example, it should be noted that this information-preserving change (and the one described in Codd's second example) allow the database to contain data that the original database structure prohibited. Specifically, it is possible that tuples with the same values for the primary key columns occur in more than one of the partitioned relations. Therefore, constraints need to be defined to restrict the allowed content of the database in accordance with the constraints implicitly enforced by the original schema[1] (see Veldwijk et al, 1991b).

Codd's second example concerns the replacement of an table by two or more projections that all inherit the primary key of the original relation but are otherwise disjunct. Provided no changes are made to the primary keys of the new tables, these alterations will be effected for the same kind of technical reasons mentioned in our discussion of Codd's first example. Thus, the same considerations as mentioned for this example are valid.

Codd's third example deals with combining two tables into one by means of a non-loss join. Because several kinds of non-loss joins are feasible it is unfortunate that Codd is not any more specific. Although in certain situations this alteration could represent a changing rule in the UoD, in practice the most obvious reason for this non-loss join would be to reverse the alteration as described in the second example or to denormalize a relation for performance reasons. It is clear that these reasons are also of a technical nature and are not induced by UoD changes.

---

[1] Theoretically, the information-preserving change could be induced by the wish to drop these constraints. If so, the example would indeed reflect a change in the UoD.

In conclusion, the examples given by Codd do not represent information-preserving changes due to alterations in the UoD. They only demonstrate the fact that views provide a kind of extended physical data independence.

3. THE VIEW MECHANISM AND CHANGES IN THE UOD

This section deals with an information-preserving schema change that is unmistakably caused by a change in the rules of the UoD the database schema reflects. The example is a very basic one which has been discussed before by Date (1986, ch. 19). It concerns a database containing information on employees and the departments they work for. Every employee works for exactly one department (one-to-many relationship) and each attribute is mandatory (not null). The normalized database schema is displayed in Figure 1.

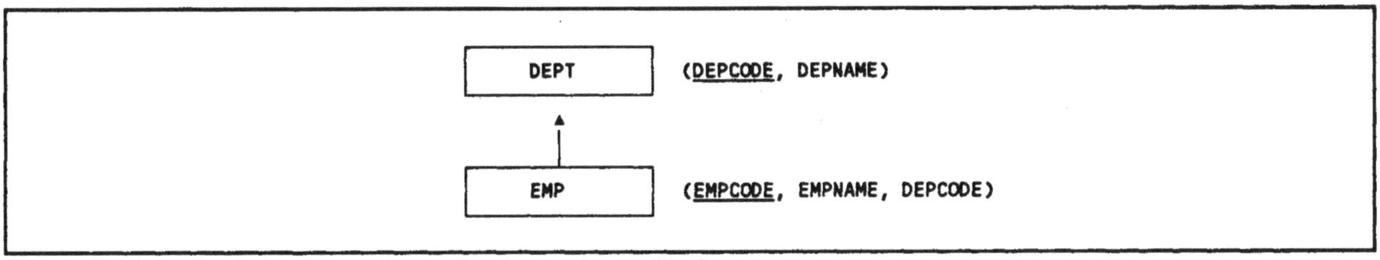

Figure 1. Normalized database schema for the employee database

In this figure, the primary key of each relation is underlined. The arrows represent foreign key to primary key references between the relations. During the design process the database designer could pay attention to the eventuality of changing requirements in time. For instance, the constraint that any employee must work for exactly one department might be relaxed. Because this constraint is enforced by the schema of Figure 1 such a constraint relaxation leads to a different database schema in which a many-to-many relationship between employees and departments occurs.

In order to prepare for the structural rearrangements, the database designer is supposed to apply the view mechanism. In theory there are two possible approaches to use views in this situation. One is to have the views reflect the situation of Figure 1 while the base tables reflect the many-to-many database structure. In the second approach the situation is reversed: the base tables reflect the situation of Figure 1 while the views reflect the many-to-many database structure. We shall describe both approaches and we shall demonstrate that both fail to provide immunity from changes to the schema.

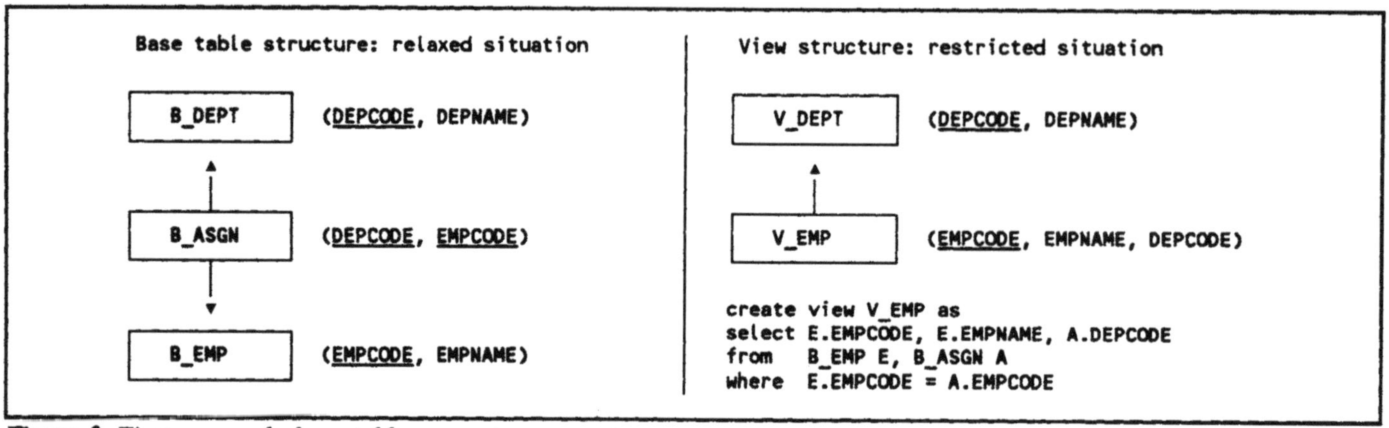

Figure 2. First approach: base tables many-to-many, views one-to-many

Figure 2 depicts the first approach in which the views reflect the restricted (one-to-many) state of the UoD. The view V_DEPT is a one-to-one representation of the base table B_DEPT. As will be obvious, this application of the view mechanism solves nothing because the application programs that run against the two views must be rewritten if the state of the UoD represented by the base-table structure ever becomes real. Because the application programs are not immune to information-preserving schema changes logical data independence is not achieved. This observation lends itself to generalization too: every application of the view mechanism that is more restrictive than the base table structure on which the views are defined fails to provide immunity from certain information-preserving schema changes.

The second design option, depicted in Figure 3 (overleaf), seems much more promising at first. Here the views reflect the relaxed (many-to-many) situation, while the base tables reflect the restricted (one-to-many) situation. In this approach the schema alterations that are foreseen do not affect the application programs since these were designed to operate on a database structure reflecting a many-to-many relationship. Changes occur only in the structure of the base tables and in the view definitions. To be specific: the base table B_EMP is replaced by two projections that conform fully to the definitions of the projection views V_EMP and V_ASGN. These views V_EMP and V_ASGN become copies of the new base tables B_EMP and B_ASGN, just like V_DEPT is a copy of B_DEPT.

Unfortunately there are certain problems attached to this approach. First, it leads to an increase in programming effort because extra joins are necessary. The programmers find themselves in a situation in which they have to create complex DML-statements that the view translation algorithm has to translate into simpler ones. Second, information-preserving changes like the one in the example are often accompanied by changes in the user-interface. If screen and print lay outs have to be adjusted anyway, the view mechanism alone cannot provide full immunity from application program changes. Third, the database structure quickly becomes unintelligible for all those who have knowledge about the real state of the UoD, because the UoD suggested by the schema does not correspond to the UoD as it is known. Both these

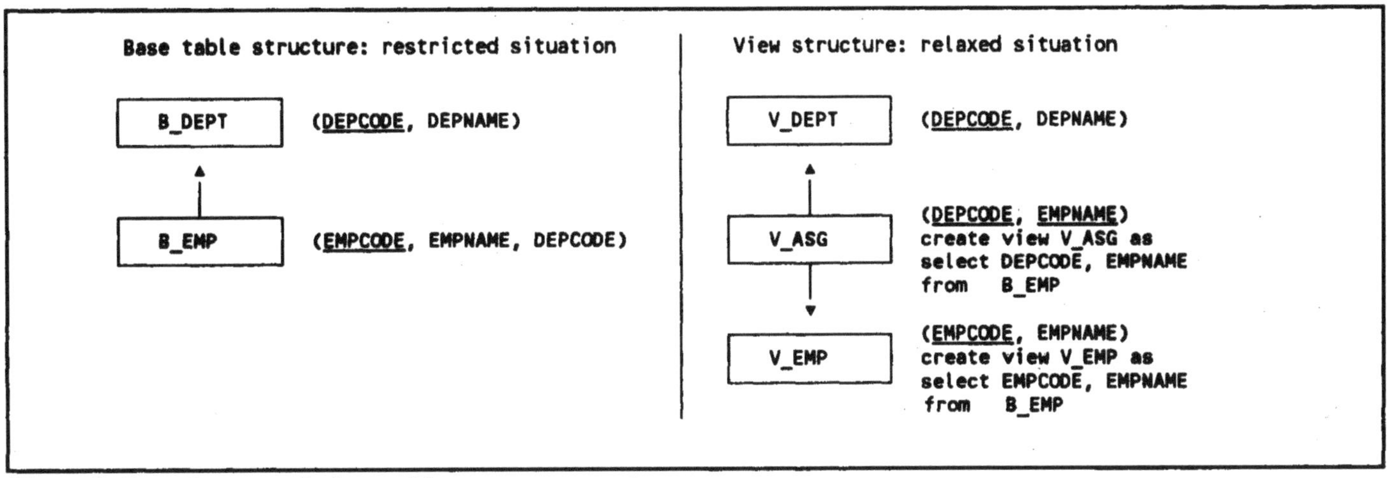

Figure 3. Second approach: base tables one-to-many, views many-to-many

observations lead to the conclusion that application of the view mechanism to obtain logical data independence is not without a price.

Third, and all important is the fact that the views V_EMP and V_ASGN are non-updatable according to the powerful view updating algorithm developed by Codd (1990, ch. 17). To demonstrate this we must first examine how the addition of a new employee must be translated from the view level to the base table level.

Suppose employee 'Smith' with code 'E4' working for the existing department 'D2' is inserted into the database. At the view level this requires a transaction consisting of two insert operations:

1) insert into V_EMP (EMPCODE, EMPNAME) values ('E4', 'Smith')
2) insert into V_ASGN (DEPCODE, EMPCODE) values ('D2', 'E4')

The view updatability mechanism must translate these statements into equivalent statements on the base table B_EMP:

1) insert into B_EMP (EMPCODE, EMPNAME) values ('E4', 'Smith')
2) update B_EMP set DEPCODE = 'D2' where EMPCODE = 'E4'

Although both single operations temporarily violate the integrity constraint that each property of B_EMP is mandatory, the transaction as a whole does not. However, the second insert must be translated into an update operation on the underlying base table B_EMP (irrespective of sequence).

If we apply Codd's powerful view updatability (VU) algorithm[2] to the example, we instantly run into difficulties because transformations of relational operators (like 'insert') into different relational operators (like 'update') are categorically forbidden by one of the basic assumptions underlying Codd's VU algorithm (1990, p. 298). Provided the VU-algorithm determines the views V_EMP and V_ASGN to be updatable[3], the two insert operations on the views will both be translated into insert operations on the base table B_EMP. Because both inserted tuples have the same value 'E4' for their primary key attribute EMPCODE the transaction will fail. To conclude, the views V_EMP and V_ASGN are not fully updatable and support for logical data independence, if practical, is found to be very problematic if judged by the VU-algorithm.

4. CONFRONTING THE CLAIMS

It is possible to raise objections against our claim that the view mechanism does not support logical data independence. One objection could be that our criticism is only directed against Codd's present VU-algorithm, which could someday be sufficiently enhanced. Another objection could be that we have given only one example of a situation in which the view mechanism fails to provide logical data independence, which is far from proving that the view mechanism does not provide *any* support for logical data independence.

Our answer to the first objection is that Codd has specified the assumption that relational operations on views may not be translated into different operations on base tables for a good reason, i.e. to make the updating of views comprehensible for the users (1990, p.298). If the assumption were dropped and the VU-algorithm were made sufficiently powerful to overcome its present limitations, the effects of view updating would quickly become unpredictable by database administrators. As a consequence the view mechanism would only be applied reluctantly for fear of unexpected consequences. A second answer to the objection is that it will probably prove to be very hard or even impossible to come up with a sufficiently powerful extended VU-algorithm. For one thing, the algorithm should be able to evaluate any number of view update statements in one transaction and translate these into a number of different update statements on the underlying base tables. As a third and final answer, we feel that whoever makes a claim should

[2] Although Codd (1990) discusses two view updatability algorithms, namely VU-1 and VU-2, the differences between these algorithms are not relevant to the discussion in this paper. Therefore, the term *VU-algorithm* is used without qualification.

[3] In fact, the VU-algorithm will determine that insert operations are not allowed on the views because both lack a column that is mandatory in the underlying base table. The update and delete operators can be applied to the views. If the columns EMPNAME and DEPCODE were not mandatory the views would accept the insert operator.

either fully prove it or make clear to what extent the claim holds. To be specific, any partial refutation of the claim that views provide logical data independence should either lead to a stronger VU-algorithm or to a clear and reliable redefinition of the concept of logical data independence[4].

The objection that we have only given one example of the failure of views to provide immunity to information-preserving changes can be answered in several ways. First of all, our last answer to the preceding objection is also an answer to this one. A second answer would be that failure to support the common information-preserving schema alteration we have discussed would severely limit the practical applicability of the view mechanism. As a third answer we can observe that limited view updatability reduces the understandability and reliability of the view mechanism. This argument reflects the same philosophy lying behind Codd's assumption that update operations on views may not be translated into different update operations on base tables. As a fourth and final answer, we have found it very hard to find non-trivial information-preserving schema alterations that do not offer the kind of view update problems described in the previous section.

5. ALTERNATIVES FOR THE VIEW MECHANISM

The discussion of the preceding section shows that the fundamental question is whether or not it is possible to offer logical data independence without limitations, i.e. to find some mechanism that makes it possible to accept any kind of information-preserving change to a database schema without requiring changes to application programs. Such a facility would remain extremely desirable, even considering the observation of section 3 that information-preserving changes are often accompanied by changes in the information system's user interface.

Without pretending that we can offer anything like the ultimate solution we can distinguish two alternative approaches that can lead to a level of logical data independence that is at least practical in the sense that it supports the most common schema changes.

The least ambitious approach would be to enumerate a limited number of commonly occurring information-preserving schema alterations. For each kind of alteration an algorithm would have to be developed that makes it possible to modify both data structures and application

[4] In fact, Codd provides a more precise definition of the term 'logical data independence' (1990, p. 346) by restricting it to information-preserving changes supported by his algorithm VU-1 *or by a stronger algorithm.* This definition of the term only specifies a lower limit of logical data independence. Moreover, if the added restriction were to rule out the vast majority of information-preserving schema changes, the definition itself would become questionable.

programs. This implies that the application programs would have to be changed but these changes would be executed automatically. This would amount to a kind of surrogate logical data independence. View updating problems do not occur because no views are involved. The main limitation is that solutions like this, which have been described by Shneiderman and Thomas (1982) and by Veldwijk et al (1991a), provide at best a pragmatic solution but never one that is applicable to all relevant schema changes.

A very ambitious approach would be to develop a data model on top of the relational model which would deal with information-preserving schema changes in the same way in which the relational model deals with alterations at the physical level (see Boogaard et al, 1991). Such a model should offer even higher level data structures to its users. What such model should look like is hard to tell, although it is obvious that its highest level data structures may not reflect any UoD rule that is liable to change. The development of such a model may very well prove to be a mirage, if only because the number of conceivable information-preserving schema alterations is huge, unlike the number of possible alterations at the physical level. Nevertheless, it may be possible to develop a model in which a limited number of commonly occurring information-preserving schema alterations is made transparent. With respect to logical data independence, however, this would greatly reduce the ambition level of the approach.

In conclusion, we would like to draw attention to the fact that over twenty years after the introduction of the relational model, adequate support for logical data independence is still not in sight. Because of the huge beneficial effects this support would have on the maintenance costs of today's many relational information systems, relational DBMS vendors and users have every incentive to be interested in the outcome of any research in this area.

ACKNOWLEDGEMENT

The authors would like to thank dr. Edu Spoor for his comments on earlier versions of this paper.

REFERENCES

Boogaard, M., Dijk, van M.V., Spoor, E.R.K., and Veldwijk, R.J. (1991), "Inherently Flexible Information Systems," *Proceedings of the first STINFON Conference*, Nijmegen, The Netherlands, December 1991.

Codd, E.F. (1970), "A Relational Model of Data for Large Shared Data Banks," *Communications of the ACM*, 13, 6, pp. 377-387.

Codd, E.F. (1990), *The Relational Model for Database Management, Version 2*, Reading, Massachusetts: Addison-Wesley Publishing Company.

Date, C.J. (1986), "Updating Views," *Relational Database, Selected Writings*, Reading, Massachusetts: Addison-Wesley Publishing Company.

Date, C.J. (1990), *An Introduction to Database Systems: Volume 1*, 5th edition, Reading, Massachusetts: Addison-Wesley Publishing Company.

Shneiderman, B., and Thomas, G. (1982), "An Architecture for Automatic Relational Database System Conversion," *ACM Transactions on Database Systems*, 7, 2, pp. 235-257.

Veldwijk, R.J., Boogaard, M., Dijk, van M.V., and Spoor, E.R.K. (1991a), "EDSOs, Implosion and Explosion: Concepts to Automate Part of Application Maintenance of Relational Databases," *Information and Software Technology*, 33, 5, pp. 343-350.

Veldwijk, R.J., Spoor, E.R.K., Boogaard, M., and Dijk, van M.V. (1991b), "On the Expressive Power of the Relational Model, a Database Designers Point of View," *Proceedings of the 12th International Conference on Information Systems*, New York, December 1991, pp. 65-73.

INTEGRITY

OPTIMIZING DISTRIBUTED INTEGRITY CONSTRAINTS

Subhasish Mazumdar

Mathematics, Computer Science, and Statistics,
University of Texas at San Antonio,
San Antonio, TX 78249, U.S.A.
EMail: mazumdar@ringer.cs.utsa.edu

ABSTRACT

Database integrity constraints can be extremely expensive to maintain unless attention is paid to the problem during the design of the database. In the case of distributed databases, and particularly in the case of heterogeneous databases, the problems associated with constraint maintenance are even more acute. We lay the basis for an design-time tool that derives sufficient conditions from the original constraints as well as those derived after transaction analysis with the aim of reduction in non-locality of the constraints.

INTRODUCTION

Database integrity* is a guarantee of protection provided by a Database Management System against misuse, more specifically, against nonmalicious errors [34].

Integrity is specified through a set of integrity constraints, which are assertions that each *legal* or *consistent* database state is supposed to respect, *i. e.*, the assertions can be expressed as predicates on database states [6]. In practice, however, the database designer finds the guarantee of integrity to be limited mainly because integrity checking generally consumes excessive computing resources. Indeed, commercial relational database systems of today support few integrity constraints — at best, one can hope for the (often indirect) support of *key* and *referential integrity* [13]. Turning to the research community, we find that in exploring the process of design of relational databases, the choice of good relation forms has been examined in depth, but the problem of choosing a *good* set of integrity constraints [19] has been largely neglected [21, 30]. The neglect is even more dramatic in the case of distributed databases.

The simplest way of assuring integrity is of course to include the constraint as a test at the end of every transaction. But the integrity constraint is usually a non-trivial boolean query whose evaluation may necessitate the scanning of whole relations, or worse, joins of two or more relations. Such queries are costly in terms of execution time, and repeating these queries after every transaction implies a gigantic overhead for transaction processing. It is easy to see that this method can be impractically expensive.

For centralized databases, researchers have suggested that this check be optimized by exploiting the fact (first noted by Stonebraker [32]) that the constraints need only to be *preserved*, *i. e.*, the query representing the integrity constraints is *repeated* at every state and the result of the query was **true** in the state prior to the update. The advantage of using precondition checks instead of backing out a transaction after failure was also suggested by Buneman and Clemons [4].

Nicolas [19] examined the syntactic structure of the constraints written in prenex normal form and showed how checking could be improved for constraint preservation after a simple update.

Bernstein and Blaustein [2] first showed how redundant data (that is kept up-to-date) could help in the evaluation of such repeated queries. The idea was well known: the computation of the average of a growing numeric sequence, for example, can make good use of the current sum and sequence length.

Henschen *et al.* first suggested the use of theorem proving at compile time in order to find run-time tests that would ensure the preservation of constraints and also show that tests that are only sufficient can be found.

Sufficient tests are especially useful in cases where the necessary and sufficient tests are all expensive; cheaper sufficient tests help conserve resources.

Distributed databases exacerbate the problem of constraint maintenance [21]. Owing to horizontal and vertical fragmentation of relations with the fragments stored at different locations, the integrity constraints must be translated into constraints on the fragments. Thus there are a lot more constraints to maintain when databases get distributed. In addition, replication of data imposes a constraint that the replicas have equal values at all times.

The naive method of checking constraints after each transaction is worse in the distributed case since the checking would typically require data transfer as well as computation. Further, the penalty for allowing a transaction to execute with the intention of aborting it at commit time in the event of violation of constraints is more severe since rollback and recovery must occur at all the sites in which the transaction participated.

Simon and Valduriez [28] extends the above methods of centralized databases to the case of distributed databases.

The basic question to be addressed is not merely how distributed constraints can be simplified but how they can be reformulated into constraints that are more local, and at best are entirely local?

One approach to this question is taken by Qian [21] who translates a distributed constraint into a constraint over the

*Some [10] would prefer the term *semantic integrity* here, leaving *integrity* to comprise semantic integrity, concurrency control, and recovery from failures. Others [34] use our term. Since we are not concerned with concurrency control and recovery, our use of the term *integrity* should cause no confusion.

fragments and then detects a situation where more than one site contains replicas of a fragment involved in a constraint, and removes that redundancy by assigning the job of checking that part of the constraint to the site containing the maximal number of relevant fragments. A general framework is suggested for finding sufficient conditions.

An old common-sense idea is relevant to the question at hand: when a number of people co-operate to sell raffle tickets, they do not need to make a conference call every time any individual seller encounters a prospective buyer. The solution is to divide the tickets among the sellers so that they may proceed independently for the most part, that is, until some sellers have exhausted their supply at which time a redistribution of unsold tickets takes place. Garcia-Molina [9] has clearly been thinking along these lines. He has suggested that numeric constraints† on heterogeneous distributed databases be broken up so that they become entirely local constraints. He gives the example of an airline which wants to sell tickets for one of its flights, but also wants other airlines to sell for that flight. This implies a global constraint that the sum of the number of tickets sold by the two airlines should be less than some maximum number. In practice, airlines give each other blocks of seats to sell and thus convert a distributed constraint into a local one. He suggests the desirability of tools to break up distributed constraints into local ones.

This paper addresses the last suggestion. With the aim of reducing the non-locality of a constraint, *i. e.*, the number of sites involved, this paper generalizes the above common-sense idea beyond numeric constraints. It describes the basis for a tool that uses the standard method of backchaining for finding sufficient conditions, and thus can easily be integrated with a design-time theorem proving approach. Like Qian, this approach aims at the reformulation of constraints, but it uses a standard approach to finding sufficient conditions. Further, the optimizations do not require replicated data. Like Bernstein and Blaustein we suggest that in some cases redundant data be stored, but our use of that data and method of its computation are different. The approach is especially fruitful because it addresses the needs of multi-databases which offer the advantages of distributed database in spite of accepting full site autonomy.

Another advantage of our approach is that we can find sufficient conditions not only for the distributed integrity constraints given but also those arising as tests for particular transactions. Often these tests are simpler.

Finally, our approach conforms with the admonition of Nicolas to concentrate on the problem of finding *good* constraints.

This paper is structured as follows. The next section reviews related work. The subsequent section introduces a metric on constraints called **scatter**. Next we introduce our theorem proving approach. In the following section, we discuss the constraint reformulation approach and in the penultimate section deal with the application of that approach on binary relation constraints. We use the last section for making concluding remarks.

†He claims elsewhere [1] that most distributed database constraints involve arithmetic relations.

RELATED WORK

Stonebraker [32] first showed that a query modification technique exploiting the fact that the database is initially consistent (prior to the update) leads to simplification of constraint checking. For constraints expressed in the relational language QUEL, Stonebraker gives efficient and straightforward algorithms for obtaining tests that must be added as conjunctions to the precondition of the update. However, INGRES [33] offers the support of key and domain constraints only. Simon and Valduriez [27] have improved on the technique for enforcement of domain constraints.

Sarin [24] concentrated on transactions that allow at most one update on any relation. He did a perturbation analysis of the effect of the transaction on the constraint, converting perturbations that falsify the constraint into run-time tests. Although he offered compelling examples, he did not present an algorithm.

Nicolas [19] also studied the same class of transactions; his constraints could be *range-restricted* well-formed formulas of first-order predicate calculus. He showed how to instantiate variable expressions in constraints so as to obtain simplified constraints that could be evaluated on the database after the transaction (*i. e.*, post-tests; the method could be used to obtain pre-tests as well). However, the substitutions would not work for certain patterns of quantifiers.

Bernstein and Blaustein [2] worked on transactions that could be single tuple *insert* and *delete* statements. Constraints could be relational calculus formulas expressed in prenex normal form with the restriction that the variables in the prefix must range over *distinct* relations. A well formed formula is in *prenex normal form* iff it consists of a prefix of quantifiers (universal or existential or both) followed by a *matrix* of quantifier-free formula which is either in conjunctive normal form or is an implication with both antecedent and consequent in conjunctive normal form. Examining only the *pattern* of the quantifiers in the prefix (and thereby neglecting the semantics of the predicates in the matrix) and the updates, they determined how the constraint could be simplified into a simpler but equivalent one. Kobayashi [15] extended this work of Bernstein and Blaustein by including prefixes in which the same relation could appear more than once, *i. e.*, more than one variable could be quantified over the same relation.

Hsu and Imielinski [14] further generalized (and corrected) the algorithms of Bernstein and Blaustein allowing multiple quantifiers and multiple tuple updates for the same relation. They too examine only the quantifier prefix during the analysis.

It is well known that redundant data improves the performance of certain queries. Integrity constraints are special cases of (boolean) queries. The fact that the database is consistent prior to the update indicates that the result of the last boolean integrity constraint query is known to be **true**.

Thus it is clear that the combination of this fact and the use of redundant data, provided it is kept up to date cheaply, can be exploited for better test generation. Bernstein *et al.* [3] introduced this scheme for a small class of integrity constraints. Hsu and Imielinski [14] also take advantage of this idea through their use of system-maintained sets called effective ranges. Koenig and Paige [16] generalized the idea with their technique of *finite differencing*. Their method can deal with aggregate constraints directly. Paige [20] also introduced rudimentary complexity measures for the predicates in the constraints and associated the goal of simplification with the reduction in the complexity of the evaluation of the constraints.

The above approaches can be thought of as syntactic ones because they exploit the pattern of the quantifiers ignoring the matrix.

Qian suggests [22] the Floyd-Hoare-Dijkstra approach [7, 12] for test generation. However, the weakest precondition so obtained may not be in simplified form.

All the above approaches are deficient in that they cannot generate tests that are sufficient (*i. e.*, tests that would guarantee the preservation of the constraints, but are not always necessary for their preservation). As we have mentioned before, sufficient tests are often cheaper. This deficiency was rectified by Henschen, McCune, and Naqvi [11] who first suggested the use of a theorem prover for test generation. They prove a theorem at compile time stating that the integrity constraints are preserved by transactions that are single updates. Converting constraints into clausal form (*i. e.*, prefix of universal quantifiers only and a matrix in conjunctive normal form), they used a resolution theorem prover and showed how sufficient tests could be generated from the failure to prove that the update maintained the constraint. Recently their work has been extended by McCune and Henschen [18] to produce necessary and sufficient tests as well.

Sheard and Stemple [26] also use a theorem-proving approach but they focus on transactions written in a rich high level language called ADABTPL. Transactions are programs that change the database state atomically‡, and so the integrity assertions need to be invariants of all transactions whereas updates within transactions may legally violate the constraints. They use an extension of a Boyer-Moore theorem-prover in order to show at the time of compilation that transactions will preserve constraints with the knowledge of the types of their inputs but not their actual values. The feasibility of this approach has been demonstrated [25]. The preservation of constraints may well depend on data values input to the transaction and thus the designer must code correct but inexpensive run-time tests within the transaction programs. Since it is not realistic to expect database designers to write correct and optimal database specifications all at once, automated help is necessary in identifying relatively inexpensive run-time tests. Mazumdar [17] extends the ADABTPL approach and shows how run-time tests (both necessary and sufficient and only sufficient) can be generated and other useful mechanical feedback offered to the designer [31].

The approach of Henschen *et al.* [11] is similar to the ADABTPL approach in that both make use of theorem proving, but the latter uses a very powerful theorem prover and a richer transaction language with sophisticated update functions. The syntactic approaches, on the other hand, use a very simple update language.

In the case of distributed databases, there are much fewer results.

Simon and Valduriez [28] argue that the methods of test generation suggested for centralized databases outlined earlier can be extended to the fragments of distributed relations. They make use of finite differencing and the storage of redundant data in the manner of Bernstein and Blaustein.

Qian [21] shows that distributed constraints can be translated into constraints on the fragments given the definition of the fragmentation, and offers a framework for constraint reformulation [23]. Initially a site s is allowed to participate in the computation of a constraint C if s contains a fragment involved in C. The next improvement detects a redundancy in that assignment: for a constraint C, if sites s_1 and s_2 both contain replicas of some of the fragments involved in C, but all of the s_2 fragments of C are also contained in s_1, then s_2 is relieved from the computation of C. Sufficient conditions are also recommended by an algorithm that performs an unbounded search over all possible constraints attempting to minimize a generalized cost function; the effectiveness of the suggested heuristics in helping that search is not reported.

SCATTERING METRIC

Our aim in this section is to define a metric on constraints that captures the amount of their non-locality.

To capture the amount of non-local access necessary to evaluate a constraint, we define a metric on constraints. We will call it the the *scatter* of a constraint and denote it by σ. Let $\mathcal{R}$ be the set of all relation fragments. We assume that each relation fragment is located in exactly one§ of a set of sites $\mathcal{S}$; hence we define a function $site{:}\mathcal{R}\rightarrow\mathcal{S}$, i.e, $site(r)$ denotes the location of a relation fragment r.

We assume that integrity constraints are conjunctions of simpler constraints, the latter being safe [34] first-order formulas. A simple constraint C is given by:

$$(Q_1x_1 \in r_1)(Q_2x_2 \in r_2)\ldots(Q_nx_n \in r_n)\ p(x_1, x_2, \ldots, x_n),$$

where $Q_i \in \{\exists, \forall\}, 1 \leq i \leq n$, and p is a computable predicate¶. We define the *site-set* of the constraint C as the set of sites of the relations that its bound variables range

‡A transaction is a sequence of *deferred updates* in Date's terminology [5].

§More correctly, a relation fragment is stored in one *primary* site: we do not rule out replication of fragments.

¶By *computable*, we mean that taking a database snapshot as the model [8], the constraint can be evaluated to **true** or **false**. This must be so even if some of the relations r_i are not stored in the database but are derived.

over; and we define the scatter of C as the cardinality of its *site-set*, *i. e.*,

$$site\text{-}set(C) = \{site(r_1), site(r_2), \ldots, site(r_k)\},$$
$$\text{and } \sigma(C) = |site\text{-}set(C)|$$

For a compound constraint $C = \bigwedge_{i=1}^{i=m} C_i$, where C_i $(1 \le i \le m)$ are simple constraints, we define its scatter as:

$$\sigma(C) = \max(\sigma(C_1), \sigma(C_2), \ldots, \sigma(C_m)).$$

The intuition is that the scatter of a compound constraint is determined by the worst scatter of the conjuncts; the basis for this intuition is that we are interested primarily in data transmission and the conjuncts can be evaluated in parallel. For a centralized database, all constraints have $\sigma = 1$. Hence a constraint with a value of 1 for σ is the best we can hope for in the distributed case.

By abuse of notation, we will refer to the site of a bound variable and mean the site of the relation over which that bound variable ranges. For the above formula, the site of variable x_2 would mean $site(r_2)$.

Constraints that assure the preservation of integrity after the execution of a transaction would typically involve the transaction inputs. For such constraints (and others we will encounter shortly), we need to extend the definition of σ to take care of free variables.

Given a formula with free variables, we must first associate with each free variable a set over which its values may range. For example, in the case of transaction inputs, this would be a singleton set. Next, we find the sites at which that set can be located, and call it *possible-sites* for that free variable. This set is obtained from the meaning of the free variable. For transaction inputs, for example, *possible-sites* would include the site of *every* relation that is updated by the transaction through this input.

Let C be a simple constraint:

$$(Q_1 x_1 \in r_1)(Q_2 x_2 \in r_2)\ldots(Q_n x_n \in r_n)\; p(a, x_1, x_2, \ldots, x_n),$$

C has a free variable a, and bound variables $x_1, \ldots, x_n$; its scatter σ can be found by the following rule:

if $(possible\text{-}sites(a) \cap site\text{-}set(C)) = \emptyset$
  then $1 + cardinality(site\text{-}set(C))$
  else $cardinality(site\text{-}set(C))$

The case of more than one free variable is an extension of the above. For each free variable, we intersect the *possible-site* set with $site\text{-}set(C)$. If the intersection is non-empty, we ignore that variable. The other sets are all disjoint with $site\text{-}set(C)$; these are intersected with each other and the minimum number of sites necessary to cover them is added to the cardinality of $site\text{-}set(C)$. Although this sounds complex, it is rarely important because we do not often encounter more than two variables with overlapping *possible-site* sets.

A THEOREM PROVING APPROACH

Mechanical theorem proving is a method of symbolic manipulation employing rules and techniques that respect logical inference; an element of heuristic-based search is usually involved in the selection of these rules and techniques, and thus the time required to come to a conclusion cannot be predicted in advance. A test generation approach based on theorem proving is feasible since the designer deals with transactions at the time of their *compilation* (as contrasted with their execution), when considerable computing resources can be invested at ease, with enormous potential savings during execution.

The ADABTPL environment offers a design-time tool for database designers. Although the tool uses a theorem prover, the database designer need not be concerned with its internal working. The prover has at its disposal a set of rewrite rules (a *lemma base* or *rule base*), each rule having been mechanically validated. The set of rewrite rules may also be viewed as an algebraic *theory* [29] capturing the interaction among the data structures in the schema, the predicates in the integrity constraints, and the update functions that occur in the transactions. By describing the effect of a transaction on a database predicate through an algebraic expression, the rewrite rules of the theory can be used to transform the expression or parts thereof: thus one can *reason* about a transaction.

Given a transaction and a set of constraints, the prover attempts to establish that the transaction will preserve all the constraints. If it fails, it computes tests which need be added to the transaction as pre-conditions. These tests are necessary and sufficient for the preservation of the constraints.

We have also demonstrated [17, 31] that tests that are only sufficient can also be found by adapting the operational semantics of PROLOG (which uses backtracking with unification on Horn clauses). We find sufficient conditions by back-chaining from a necessary and sufficient test. Back-chaining is an automated procedure of rewriting an expression of the form‖ $p(\overline{x}, \overline{y})$ that unifies with the consequent of a rule, which is an implication $p(\overline{u}, \overline{v}) \leftarrow p_1(\overline{u}) \wedge p_2(\overline{v})$ (written in PROLOG style; it reads *p if p_1 and p_2*) by another expression of the form $p_1(\overline{x}) \wedge p_2(\overline{y})$. Note that variables in the left hand side of rules, *i. e.*, the consequent of the implication, are universally quantified whereas variables occurring only in the right hand side are existentially quantified.

We are extending the above tool in order to deal with distributed constraints. The extension involves an additional module which, while backchaining, attempts to reduce scatter.

Example: Consider, for example, a referential integrity expressed** by the following constraint††:

‖$\overline{x}$ stands for a vector of variables of unspecified size.

**The constraint as it is expressed here is more general than that required by referential integrity. The missed key constraint is irrelevant for this discussion.

††We use the notation *t.fld* to mean the *fld* component of tuple *t*.

C_1: $(\forall x_1 \in r_1)(\exists x_2 \in r_2)\, x_1.frnkey = x_2.key$,

where $site(r_1) = s_1$, $site(r_2) = s_2$, and $s_1 \neq s_2$.

If a transaction inserts a tuple a into the relation r_1, the *necessary and sufficient* condition for the preservation of the referential integrity constraint is the simpler constraint††

$$C_2:\ a.frnkey \in \Pi_{key} r_2,$$
$$i.\ e.,\ (\exists x_2 \in r_2)\ a.frnkey = x_2.key.$$

Since $possible\text{-}site(a) = \{s_1\}$, we have $\sigma(C_1) = \sigma(C_2)$, *i. e.*, C_2 is no worse than C_1 in terms of scatter, but not any better either.

However, if we consider the *sufficient* condition C_3 for the preservation of C_1 for the above transaction:

$$C_3:\ a.frnkey \in \Pi_{frnkey} r_1,$$
$$i.\ e.,\ (\exists x_1 \in r_1)\ a.frnkey = x_1.frnkey,$$

we see that $\sigma(C_3) < \sigma(C_1)$, *i. e.*, there is a definite reduction in scatter.

C_3 is obtained by the prover using backchaining.

CONSTRAINT REFORMULATION

In this section, we look at the basis for reformulation of constraints through sufficient conditions. Note that reformulation is not restricted to logically equivalent formulas.

In general, we look at the given integrity constraints and attempt to reformulate them without regard to the transactions. However, the transaction-specific tests (such as the one in the example at the end of the last section) are also amenable to this method; often such tests are simpler and lead to simple sufficient tests. This is an advantage of our method.

Basis for Reformulation

Here we examine the basis for our belief that the standard backchaining approach to finding sufficient conditions, can lead to new constraints that are less distributed.

Typically, the rule that computes a sufficient condition either introduces new variables or drops some. The following two lemmas explore these two cases.

The first lemma says that if a backchaining rule drops some variables, then it can be used without worsening scatter and in certain cases, scatter can improve as well.

Lemma 1: If there is a rule $p(x_1, \ldots, x_{n-1}, x_n) \leftarrow p_1(x_1, \ldots, x_{n-1})$ and a constraint C given by

$$(Q_1 x_1 \in r_1) \ldots (Q_n x_n \in r_n)\ p(x_1, x_2, \ldots, x_{n-1}, x_n),$$

then C has a sufficient condition C_s:

$$(Q_1 x_1 \in r_1) \ldots (Q_{n-1} x_{n-1} \in r_{n-1})\ p_1(x_1, x_2, \ldots, x_{n-1}),$$

Corollary 1: $\sigma(C_s) \leq \sigma(C)$.

Corollary 2: If $site(r_n) \notin site\text{-}set(C_s)$, then $\sigma(C_s) < \sigma(C)$.

The first corollary says that the application of this lemma during backchaining does not worsen the scatter. Thus the process of can continue if p_1 unifies with any other rule.

The second corollary identifies a condition (in fact *the* condition) when the scatter will definitely reduce.

The second lemma says that if there is a backchaining rule that adds variables, then also, it can be used to reduce scatter in some conditions, and at worst, does not reduce scatter.

Lemma 2: If there is a rule $p(x_1, \ldots, x_n) \leftarrow p_1(x_1, \ldots, x_j, z) \wedge p_2(z, x_{j+1}, \ldots, x_n)$, where $n > 1$ and $j < n$, and a constraint C given by

$$(Q_1 x_1 \in r_1) \ldots (Q_n x_n \in r_n)\ p(x_1, \ldots, x_n),$$

then C has a sufficient condition $C_s = C_1 \wedge C_2$, where C_1 is given by

$$(Q_1 x_1 \in r_1) \ldots (Q_j x_j \in r_j)(\exists z \in r')\ p_1(x_1, \ldots, x_j, z),$$

and C_2 is given by:

$$(\forall z \in r')(Q_{j+1} x_{j+1} \in r_{j+1}) \ldots$$
$$(Q_n x_n \in r_n)\ p_2(z, x_{j+1}, \ldots, x_n)$$

Proof: Let $\mathcal{M}$ be a model for C_s. We will show that $\mathcal{M}$ must also be a model for C.
Since $\mathcal{M} \models C_s$, it follows that $\mathcal{M} \models C_1$ and $\mathcal{M} \models C_2$.
Choose x_1 from $r_1, \ldots x_j$ from r_j as many times as dictated by the quantifiers $Q_1, \ldots, Q_j$. For each such choice, since C_1 holds in $\mathcal{M}$, an assignment can be made for the variable z such that p_1 holds with $x_1, \ldots x_j, z$ as input. Similarly choose x_{j+1} through x_n as per the quantifiers of C_2 and with any of the z values found from C_1, p_2 will hold.
In that case, a choice of $x_1, \ldots x_j, z$ and a choice of x_{j+1} through x_n satisfies the right hand side of our rule. Hence for the given choice of $x_1, \ldots, x_n$, by the given rule, p holds. But the quantifiers of C are exactly those of C_1 and C_2. Hence $\mathcal{M} \models C$. ∎

Corollary 3: $\sigma(C_s) \leq \sigma(C)$.

Corollary 4: Let $site\text{-}set(C) = S$, $site\text{-}set(C_1) = S_1$, and $site\text{-}set(C_2) = S_2$. Then if $S - S_1 \neq \emptyset$ and $S - S_2 \neq \emptyset$, then $\sigma(C_s) < \sigma(C)$.

The last corollary gives us a condition about the distribution of the relations that yields a reduction in scatter.

For example, consider a rule

$$p(x_1, x_2) \leftarrow p_1(x_1, z) \wedge p_2(z, x_2),$$

and a constraint:

$$(\forall x_1 \in r_1)(\exists x_2 \in r_2)\ p(x_1, x_2)$$

we get the sufficient condition:

$$[(\forall x_1 \in r_1)(\exists z \in r')\ p_1(x_1, z)] \wedge [(\forall z \in r')(\exists x_2 \in r_2)\ p_2(z, y)]$$

The sufficient condition has introduced a new bound variable z, but the set r' that it ranges over must be computed for the constraint to be useful. The above proofs indicate that the set is to be computed by evaluating the sufficient condition in a model, *i. e.*, a database instance. Furthermore, it can always be done since the rules always involved computable predicates.

Next, we examine specific classes of constraints.

BINARY RELATION CONSTRAINTS

In this section, we focus on what we believe is the most important form of integrity constraints — binary relations and examine cases of total ordering, partial orderings, and equivalence relations.

Total Orderings

The first lemma gives us the important result that it is enough to store a singleton set as redundant data and get a reduction in scatter for certain constraints.

Lemma 3: Let C be given by

$$(Q_1x_1 \in r_1)(Q_2x_2 \in r_2)\ldots(Q_nx_n \in r_n)\ f(x_1,\ldots,x_j) > g(x_{j+1},\ldots,n),$$

where $>$ is a total ordering. Then a sufficient condition C_s can be found for C, where $C_s = C_1 \wedge C_2$, and C_1 is given by:

$$[(Q_1x_1 \in r_1)\ldots(Q_jx_j \in r_j)(\exists z \in r')\ f(x_1,\ldots,x_j) > z],$$

and C_2 is given by:

$$[(\forall z \in r')(Q_{j+1}x_{j+1} \in r_{j+1})\ldots(Q_nx_n \in r_n)\ z > g(x_{j+1},\ldots,x_n)],$$

and r' is a singleton set.

Proof: We use the transitivity rule for $>$ to get C_s through the lemma 2.

Now no matter what the choice of $x_1,\ldots,x_j$, we can take the minimum of the set r' (well defined since since $>$ is a total order and the set is finite) and let that element constitute a singleton set r'.

Each previous choice of $x_1,\ldots,x_j$ remains a choice that satisfies C_1 and each choice of $x_{j+1},\ldots,x_n$ still satisfy C_2. ∎

Corollary 5: $\sigma(C_s) \leq \sigma(C)$.

Now it is clear that the constraint with the $>$ predicate has a f-term and g-germ on its two sides. For certain functions f,g, it is possible to switch them around the $>$ predicates. For such functions, it will be possible to rewrite the constraint so that the resulting rewritten constraint has less scatter. Let us illustrate this observation with an example.

Example: Consider the following constraint:

$$(\forall x_1 \in r_1)(\exists x_2 \in r_2)(\forall x_3 \in r_3)\ x_2.fld_2 + x_3.fld_3 > x_1.fld_1$$

Let $site(r_1) = s_1$, $site(r_2) = s_2$, and $site(r_3) = s_3$, with $s_1 \neq s_2 \neq s_3$. The constraint has a scatter value of 3.

Here f is the $+$ function and g is the identity function. Applying the above lemma, we get the following conjunct as the sufficient condition:

$$(\exists x_2 \in r_2)(\forall x_3 \in r_3)\ x_2.fld_2 + x_3.fld_3 > k_1,$$
$$(\forall x_1 \in r_1)\ k_1 > x_1.fld_1$$

where k_1 is a constant. Clearly the conjunct has a scatter value of 2.

It should be possible to go further as the transitive rule for $>$ yields formulas with $>$ predicates. Clearly it is possible to move the additive terms on the other side of the $>$ predicate (the switching-around property we were alluding to). Hence exploiting that characteristic of f and g, with respect to $>$, this process can finally result in unit scatter constraints.

The second conjunct already has unit scatter, so we can focus on the first and using the fact that additive terms can be switched around the $>$ predicate, we get the following condition equivalent to the first conjunct:

$$(\exists x_2 \in r_2)(\forall x_3 \in r_3)\ x_2.fld_2 - k_1 > -x_3.fld_3$$

Now we apply Lemma 2 to get its sufficient condition as the conjunct:

$$(\exists x_2 \in r_2)\ x_2.fld_2 - k_1 > k_2$$
$$(\forall x_3 \in r_3)\ k_2 > -x_3.fld_3,$$

where k_2 is a constant. Clearly, now we have unit scatter for the first conjunct as well as the second conjunct.

Partial Orderings

In the case of partial orders, we need to store at most m elements, where m is the maximum number of incomparable elements in the partial order. But note that the actual size of the storage need be the number of incomparable elements in any snapshot of the database.

Lemma 4: Let C be given by

$$(Q_1x_1 \in r_1)(Q_2x_2 \in r_2)\ldots(Q_nx_n \in r_n)\ f(x_1,\ldots,x_j) > g(x_{j+1},\ldots,n),$$

where $>$ is a partial ordering with at most m incomparable elements. Then a sufficient condition C_s can be found for C, where $C_s = C_1 \wedge C_2$, and C_1 is given by:

$$[(Q_1x_1 \in r_1)\ldots(Q_jx_j \in r_j)(\exists z \in r')\ f(x_1,\ldots,x_j) > z],$$

and C_2 is given by

$$[(\forall z \in r')(Q_{j+1}x_{j+1} \in r_{j+1})\ldots(Q_nx_n \in r_n)\ z > g(x_{j+1},\ldots,x_n)],$$

and r' has at most m elements.

Proof: As in the previous lemma, we choose $x_1,\ldots,x_j$ and find values of z that satisfy p. We make all the choices dictated by the quantifiers $Q_1, \ldots, Q_j$ and from the set of z values so generated, we find the minimum of all comparable elements. The resulting set cannot contain more than m elements. ∎

Equivalence Relations

In the case of equivalence relation, it is enough to store the number of partitions in the equivalence relation.

Lemma 5: Let C be given by

$$(Q_1x_1 \in r_1)\ldots(Q_nx_n \in r_n)f(x_1,\ldots,x_j) \equiv g(x_{j+1},\ldots,n),$$

where $\equiv$ is an equivalence relation with m partitions. Then a sufficient condition C_s can be found for C, where $C_s = C_1 \wedge C_2$, and C_1 is given by:

$$(Q_1x_1 \in r_1)\ldots(Q_jx_j \in r_j)(\exists z \in r')\ f(x_1,\ldots,x_j) \equiv z,$$

and C_2 is given by

$$(\forall z \in r')(Q_{j+1}x_{j+1} \in r_{j+1})\ldots(Q_nx_n \in r_n)\ z \equiv g(x_{j+1},\ldots,x_n),$$

and r' contains at most m elements. ∎

For example, consider the constraint:

$$(\forall x)(\exists y)x = y \pmod 5$$

It generates the following conjunct as sufficient condition:

$$(\forall x)(\exists z)x = z \pmod 5,$$
$$(\forall z)(\exists y)z = y \pmod 5$$

CONCLUSION

In this paper, we have described the basis for a design-time tool that analyzes integrity constraints as well as transactions, and derives sufficient conditions with reduced scatter, a metric we have introduced for the amount of non-locality of a constraint. We plan to implement these ideas as an extension of our earlier work with centralized databases, and we have argued that they can be integrated.

This approach is especially relevant in the context of heterogeneous distributed databases where not only is the reduction of scatter useful, but reduction to unit scatter is extremely useful owing to site autonomy.

We are working on a precise description of a class of constraints for which it is possible to get unit scatter in reformulated constraints.

Future work involves the inclusion of aggregate constraints and an evaluation of the advantages (if any) of using a first-order formula representation of constraints as against a functional format. In the latter, referential integrity, for example, would be encapsulated as a single function taking both relations as arguments instead of a formula with two quantifiers. Also we are working on protocols for heterogeneous databases to follow when a violation of a sufficient condition occurs. Relaxation of the notion of constraint violation — making it permissible for a constraint to be violated for a period of time or number of updates — is another idea that we would like to explore.

ACKNOWLEDGEMENTS

The author is grateful to the anonymous referees for their helpful comments and suggestions.

REFERNCES

1) Barbara, D. and Garcia-Molina, H. The Case for Controlled Inconsistency in Replicated Data. In *Proceedings of the Workshop on Management of Replicated Data*, pages 35–38, 1990.

2) Bernstein, P. A. and Blaustein, B. T. A Simplification Algorithm for Integrity Assertions and Concrete Views. In *Proceedings of the Fifth International Computer Software and Applications Conference (COMPSAC-81)*, pages 90–99, 1981.

3) Bernstein, P. A. , Blaustein, B. T. , and Clarke, E. M. Fast Maintenance of Semantic Integrity Assertions Using Redundant Aggregate Data. In *Proceedings of the Sixth International Conference on Very Large Databases*, pages 126–136, 1980.

4) Buneman, O. P. and Clemons, E. K. Efficiently Monitoring Relational Databases. *ACM Transactions on Database Systems*, 4(3):368–382, September 1979.

5) Date, C. J. *An Introduction to Database Systems*, volume 2. Addison-Wesley, 1983.

6) Eswaran, K. and Chamberlain, D. Functional Specification of a Subsystem for Data Base Integrity. In *Proceedings of the First International Conference on Very Large Databases*, pages 48–68, 1975.

7) Floyd, R. Assigning Meanings to Programs. In *Proceedings of the Symposium on Applied Mathematics, AMS, Providence, Rhode Island*, pages 19–32, 1967.

8) Gallaire, H., Minker, J., and Nicolas, J. Logic and Databases: A Deductive Approach. *ACM Computing Surveys*, 16(2):153–185, June 1984.

9) Garcia-Molina, H. Global Consistency Constraints Considered Harmful. In *Proceedings of the First International Workshop on Interoperability in Multidatabase Systems (IMS 91)*, pages 248–250, 1991.

10) Gardarin, G. and Valduriez, P. *Relational Databases and Knowledge Bases.* Addison-Wesley, 1989.

11) Henschen, L., McCune, W., and Naqvi, S. Compiling Constraint Checking Programs from First-Order Formulas. In Gallaire, H., Minker, J., and Nicolas, J., editors, *Advances in Database Theory*, volume 2, pages 145–169. Plenum Press, New York, 1984.

12) Hoare, C. A. R. An Axiomatic Basis for Computer Programming. *Communications of the ACM*, 12(10), October 1969.

13) Honkanen, P. The Integrity Problem, and What Can Be Done About It Using Today's DBMSs. *Data Base*, 20(3):21–27, Fall 1989.

14) Hsu, T. and Imielinski, T. Integrity Checking for Multiple Updates. In *Proceedings of the ACM-SIGMOD International Conference on Management of Data*, pages 152–168, 1985.

15) Kobayashi, I. Validating Database Updates. *Information Systems*, 9(1):1–17, 1984.

16) Koenig, S. and Paige, R. A Transformational Framework for the Automatic Control of Derived Data. In *Proceedings of the Seventh International Conference on Very Large Databases*, pages 306–318, 1981.

17) Mazumdar, S. *Enhancing Database Integrity and Security through Feedback to Designers.* PhD thesis, University of Massachusetts at Amherst, 1991.

18) McCune, W. and Henschen, L. Maintaining State Constraints in Relational Databases. *Journal of the ACM*, 36(1):46–68, Jan 1989.

19) Nicolas, J. M. Logic for Improving Integrity Checking in Relational Databases. *Acta Informatica*, 18(3):227–254, December 1982.

20) Paige, R. Applications of Finite Differencing to Database Integrity Control and Query/Transaction Optimization. In Gallaire, H., Minker, J., and Nicolas, J., editors, *Advances in Database Theory*, pages 171–209. Plenum Press, New York., 1984.

21) Qian, X. Distribution Design of Integrity Constraints. In Kerschberg, L., editor, *Proceedings of the Second International Conference on Expert Database Systems*, pages 205–226. Benjamin Cummings, Redwood City, California, 1989.

22) Qian, X. An Axiom System for Database Transactions. *Information Processing Letters*, 36(4):183–190, November 1990.

23) Qian, X. and Smith, D. Constraint Reformulation for Efficient Validation. In *Proceedings of the Thirteenth International Conference on Very Large Databases*, pages 417–425, 1987.

24) Sarin, S. Automatic Synthesis of Efficient Procedures for Database Integrity Checking. Master's thesis, Massachusetts Institute of Technology, 1977.

25) Sheard, T. *Proving the Consistency of Database Transactions.* PhD thesis, University of Massachusetts at Amherst, 1985.

26) Sheard, T. and Stemple, D. Automatic Verification of Database Transaction Safety. *ACM Transactions on Database Systems*, 12(3):322–368, September 1989.

27) Simon, E. and Valduriez, P. Design and Implementation of an Extendible Integrity Subsystem. In *Proceedings of the ACM-SIGMOD International Conference on Management of Data, Boston, Massachusetts*, pages 9–17, 1984.

28) Simon, E. and Valduriez, P. Integrity Control in Distributed Database Systems. In *Proceedings of the Nineteenth Hawaii International Conference on System Sciences*, pages 622–632, 1986.

29) Stemple, D. and Sheard, T. Specification and Verification of Abstract Database Types. In *Proceedings of the Third ACM SIGACT-SIGMOD-SIGART Symposium on Principles of Database Systems, Waterloo, Ontario*, pages 248–257, 1984.

30) Stemple, D., Simon, E., Mazumdar, S., and Jarke, M. Assuring Database Integrity. *Journal of Database Administration*, 1(1):12–26, Summer 1990.

31) Stemple, D., Mazumdar, S., and Sheard, T. On the Modes and Meaning of Feedback to Transaction Designers. In *Proceedings of the ACM-SIGMOD International Conference on Management of Data, San Francisco, California*, pages 374–386, 1987.

32) Stonebraker, M. Implementation of Integrity Constraints and Views by Query Modification. In *Proceedings of the ACM-SIGMOD International Conference on Management of Data, San Jose, CA*, pages 65–78, 1975.

33) Stonebraker, M., Wong, E., Kreps, P., and Held, G. The Design and Implementation of INGRES. *ACM Transactions on Database Systems*, 1(3):189–222, 1976.

34) Ullman, J. D. *Principles of Database and Knowledge-Base Systems*, volume 1. Computer Science Press, 1988.

On Deriving Specialization Constraints over Complex Objects

Minoru Ito Michio Nakanishi
ito@ics.osaka-u.ac.jp naka@ics.osaka-u.ac.jp

Department of Information and Computer Sciences
Faculty of Engineering Science, Osaka University
Toyonaka, Osaka 560, Japan

Abstract

For a complex object model, a form of range restriction, called *specialization constraint* (SC), has been proposed, which is associated not only with the properties themselves but also with property value paths. The domain and range of an SC, however, were limited to single classes. In this paper, SCs are generalized to have sets of classes as their domains and ranges. It is proved that an SC is a logical consequence of a set of SCs if and only if it is a *finite* logical consequence of the set. Then a sound and complete axiomatization for SCs is presented. Finally, a polynomial time algorithm is given, which decides whether or not an SC is a logical consequence of a set of SCs.

1. Introduction

In most object-oriented data models, complex objects can be defined in which property value may be any other object. In addition, range restrictions (or property typing) may be specified, not only on properties associated with a given class, but also on properties inherited from superclasses.

A general form of restriction called *specialization constraints* (SCs) was first presented in [5], in which only *unary* SCs were treated. A unary SC is an SC whose domain and range are limited to single classes, respectively. It was novel that range restrictions of unary SCs are associated with *path descriptions* in stead of single properties. Unary SCs can be used to assert property typing, since an individual property name is one kind of path description. In addition, unary SCs also abstract superclass relationship by using another kind of path description, denoted Id (short for *identity*), which allows one to refer to property value paths of zero length.

In this paper, we consider a class of SCs, in which each SC has sets of classes as its domain and range. To concentrate on the essential ideas, we illustrate a simple complex object model. An example database schema characterizing information about student, staff and course for a hypothetical UNIVERSITY application in terms of our model appears in Figure 1. Our diagrammatic convention is to represent each class by a labeled rectangular box of solid line, where the label denotes the class name together with a set of immediate properties. We also represent a set of classes by a non-labeled rectangular box of dotted line.

We represent SCs as directed arcs between sets of classes. The path description associated with an unlabeled arc is assumed to correspond to Id, and asserts that the 'to' class is a superclass of the 'from' class. In other words, 'from' class object *isa* 'to' class object. Thus, the unlabeled arc from Undergraduate to Student implies that each Undergraduate object is also in the Student class, and must therefore also have takes and owns property values (although it is more common to say that Undergraduate *inherits* these properties from Student). The arc labeled cnum, from Course to Int[1-300], represents a property typing constraint which restricts the values of the cnum property for Course objects to the set of integers.

It was unable to express a constraint using unary SCs such that every staff owns Internet-address and/or BITNET-address. Defining a new superclass of two classes (Internet-address and BITNET-address) might be needed to express the constraint. Since we allow an SC to have a set of classes as its domain and range, we can write the constraint without defining a superclass, as shown in Table 1 of the next section.

By specifying Id, we can also write a restriction called *cover constraint*, such that a person in Student class must be in one of the three classes, Graduate, MC-student and DC-student, as shown by an unlabeled arc from Student to the set of Undergraduate, MC-student and DC-student. This type of constraint cannot be expressed by unary SCs, but may be expressed using *union extended generalizations* (UXG) as defined in [1].

To see how such constraints can be beneficial, consider the following query to the hypothetical UNIVERSITY database.

> *Retrieve the BITNET or Internet addresses which are owned by students who take the course numbered 100 and belong to the department that offers the course.*

This query can also be expressed in terms of complex object algebra [4], as follows :

$$\mathtt{T1} := (\sigma_{cnum=100}\ \mathtt{Course}) \bowtie_{offered\_by=belongs\_to} (\sigma_{takes.cnum=100}\ \mathtt{Student})$$
$$\mathtt{T2} := \pi_{owns}\ \mathtt{T1}$$

It is possible to use the SC represented by the arc labeled takes.cnum for type checking of this query, since the SC limits property values to Integer[1-300], the course numbers of courses that students are taking. In

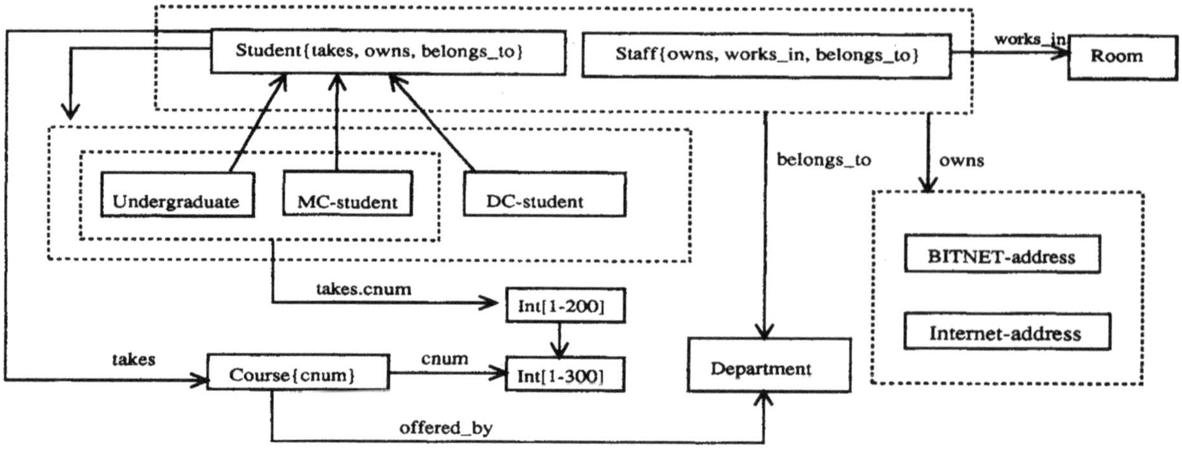

Figure 1: A UNIVERSITY Schema Diagram.

addition, SCs also support a form of *molecular abstraction* [2].

In [3], unary SCs were considered for two models. The first model imposes no constraints on class membership for an object beyond those implied by subclassing constraints, thus an object may be a member of any set of classes as long as the superclass-subclass relationships are maintained. For this case, a sound and complete axiomatization for arbitrary unary SCs was presented, and polynomial time decision procedures for the corresponding membership problems was given. The second model requires that each object is created with respect to at most one class. Membership problems for this model were shown to be NP-hard, and NP-complete if the class schema include a "bottom" class, denoted $\perp$. (A bottom class is a class which is a subclass of any other class.) Polynomial time procedures were given when $\perp$ does exist and the length of any path descriptions mentioned in antecedent unary SCs is bounded by some constant. Another special case was studied in which class schema also satisfy a lower semi-lattice condition and a sound and complete axiomatization was presented for well-formed unary SCs together with efficient decision procedures for the membership problem for well-formed constraints and for determining if an arbitrary constraint is well-formed. Then it was proved that the membership problem for arbitrary unary SCs remains NP-complete, even for class schema satisfying the lower semi-lattice condition.

In this paper, we consider only the first model for our extended SCs, that is, an object may be created as a member of any set of classes. We also consider another kind of restriction called *property functionality* constraint (FUNC) which characterizes a property that is single-valued and total on its class. The major contribution of this paper is threefold. First, we prove that an SC is a logical consequence of a set of SCs and FUNCs *iff* it is a *finite* logical consequence of the set. Second, we present a sound and complete axiomatization for SCs. Finally, we show a polynomial time algorithm for deciding whether or not an SC is a logical consequence of a set of SCs and FUNCs.

2. Definitions

A *database schema* is an ordered pair $\langle \mathbf{S}, \Sigma \rangle$, where $\mathbf{S}$ is a *class schema* and Σ is a finite set of *constraints*. The class schema $\mathbf{S}$ is a finite set of declarations of the form

$$C\{P_1, \ldots, P_n\},$$

where C is a *class* and each P_i is an *immediate property* of C. The set of classes in $\mathbf{S}$ is denoted *Classes*($\mathbf{S}$), and the set of immediate properties of C is denoted *Props*(C). The *domain* of a property P, written *Dom*(P), is defined as $\{C \in Classes(\mathbf{S}) \mid P \in Props(C)\}$. The set of properties in $\mathbf{S}$ is denoted *Props*($\mathbf{S}$); that is, $Props(\mathbf{S}) = \bigcup_{C \in Classes(\mathbf{S})} Props(C)$.

For convention, we use C (with a possible subscript) for a class in *Classes*($\mathbf{S}$), and $\ldots, X, Y, Z$ (with possible subscripts) for subsets of *Classes*($\mathbf{S}$). Furthermore, we write C for a singleton set $\{C\}$, if no confusion occurs.

A *database* over $\mathbf{S}$ is a (possibly infinite) labeled directed graph $G(V, A)$. The label for a vertex $v \in V$ is denoted $Cl(v)$, and corresponds to a subset of *Classes*($\mathbf{S}$). The label for an arc in A corresponds to a property. The database G must also satisfy the following condition.

A property value integrity condition: If $u \xrightarrow{P} v \in A$, then $Cl(u) \cap Dom(P) \neq \emptyset$.

The condition requires any object with one or more values for the property P to be in at least one class for which P is an immediate property. For example, the declaration over the UNIVERSITY database schema is listed in Table 1. An example database for the UNIVERSITY schema appears in Figure 2. Clearly, this database satisfies a property value integrity condition. For example, vertex u has an out-arc labeled owns in Figure 2. For the

Table 1: A UNIVERSITY database schema.

S (Class Schema)	Σ (Constraints)
`Student{takes,owns,belongs_to}`	`Student(takes:Course)`
`DC-student{}`	`DC-student(Id:Student)`
`MC-student{}`	`MC-student(Id:Student)`
`Undergraduate{}`	`Undergraduate(Id:Student)`
	`Student(Id:{Undergraduate, MC-student, DC-student})`
	`{Undergraduate,MC-student}(takes.cnum:Int[1-200])`
`Course{cnum,offered_by}`	`Course(cnum:Int[1-300])`
`Int[1-300]{}`	`Course(offered_by:Department)`
`Int[1-200]{}`	`Int[1-200](Id:Int[1-300])`
`Staff{owns,works_in,belongs_to}`	`{Student,Staff}(owns:{BITNET-address, Internet-address})`
`BITNET-address{}`	`FUNC(works_in)`
`Internet-address{}`	`FUNC(belongs_to)`
`Room{}`	
`Department{}`	

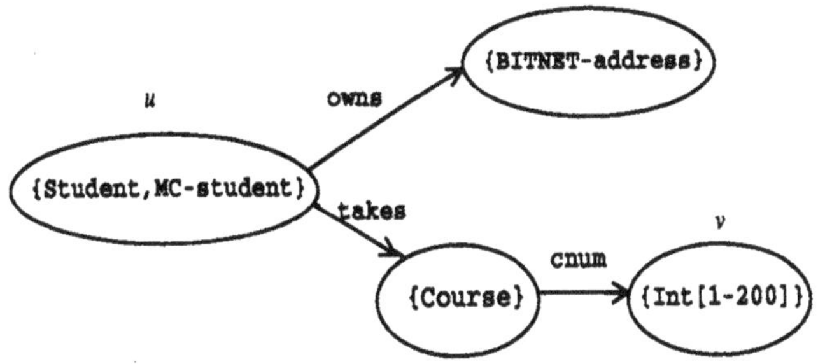

Figure 2: A database of the UNIVERSITY schema.

arc, $Cl(u)$ = {`Student`,`MC-student`} and Dom(`owns`) = {`Student`, `Staff`}, thus $Cl(u) \cap Dom(\texttt{owns}) \neq \emptyset$.

A *path description*, *pd*, is either `Id` (short for *identity*), or a sequence of properties separated by *dots*. Their composition and length are defined as follows:

$$pd_1 \circ pd_2 \equiv \begin{cases} pd_1 & \text{if } pd_2 \text{ is Id,} \\ pd_2 & \text{if } pd_1 \text{ is Id,} \\ pd_1.pd_2 & \text{otherwise.} \end{cases}$$

$$len(pd) \equiv \begin{cases} 0 & \text{if } pd \text{ is Id,} \\ 1 + len(pd_1) & \text{if } pd \text{ has the form } P \circ pd_1, \\ & \text{where } P \text{ is a property.} \end{cases}$$

Note that composition is associative; that is, $pd_1 \circ (pd_2 \circ pd_3) = (pd_1 \circ pd_2) \circ pd_3$. The following is also a straightforward consequence of our definitions.

$$len(pd_1 \circ pd_2) = len(pd_1) + len(pd_2)$$

A path in a database $G(V, A)$ over S is *described* by a path description *pd* *iff* (1) the path is of zero length (that is, consists of a single vertex) and *pd* is `Id`, or (2) *pd* corresponds to the sequence of property labels on the path. By $u \rightsquigarrow_{pd} v \in G$, we mean that there is a path in G from a vertex u to a vertex v described by *pd*. Note that $u \rightsquigarrow_{\texttt{Id}} u \in G$ for any $u \in V$ and that $u \rightsquigarrow_P v \in G$ *iff* $u \xrightarrow{P} v \in A$, where P is a property. For example, in Figure 2, the path from vertex u to vertex v is denoted $u \rightsquigarrow_{\texttt{takes.cnum}} v$.

We consider two kinds of constraints in Σ. The first, *property functionality constraint* (FUNC), allows us to characterize a property that is single-valued and total on its domain classes, and is declared with the form `FUNC`(P). A declaration `FUNC`(P) is *satisfied* by a database $G(V, A)$ over S *iff* G satisfies the following two conditions.

1. (*property functionality*) If $u \xrightarrow{P} v$ and $u \xrightarrow{P} w$ are in A, then $v = w$.

2. (*property value completeness*) If $Cl(u) \cap Dom(P) \neq \emptyset$, then there is an arc $u \xrightarrow{P} v \in A$.

In the UNIVERSITY schema, `FUNC(works_in)` states that every staff must have his/her room.

The second kind of constraint is a *specialization constraint* (SC), and is our main concern in this paper. An SC is used to assert a *type* condition on a path description, and has the form $X(pd : Y)$. In particular, a *unary* SC is an SC of the form $C(pd : C')$. A database $G(V, A)$ over S satisfies an SC $X(pd : Y)$ *iff* whenever there are vertices $u, v \in V$ such that $u \rightsquigarrow_{pd} v \in G$, then $X \cap Cl(u) \neq \emptyset$ implies $Y \cap Cl(v) \neq \emptyset$.[1] If $X = \emptyset$, then $X(pd : Y)$ is *trivial* in the sense that any database over S must satisfy the SC. As noted in the introduction, SCs can be used to specify *isa* relationship and cover constraint. For example, `Undergraduate (Id:Student)` denotes that every undergraduate *isa* student. A set of four SCs, `DC-student(Id:Student)`, `MC-student(Id:Student)`, `Undergraduate(Id:Student)`, and `Student (Id: {Undergraduate, MC-student, DC-student})` denotes that every student must be in

[1]Note that G satisfies a unary SC $C(pd : C')$ *iff* whenever there are vertices $u, v \in V$ such that $u \rightsquigarrow_{pd} v \in G$, then $C \in Cl(u)$ implies $C' \in Cl(v)$.

one of the three classes, Graduate, MC-student and DC-student.

Let Σ be a finite set of constraints (SCs and FUNCs). By Σ_{FUNC} and Σ_{SC}, we mean the sets of FUNCs and SCs in Σ, respectively. An instance of either kind of constraint σ is a *logical consequence* of Σ, written $\Sigma \models \sigma$, *iff* any database over S satisfying Σ must also satisfy σ, where the database schema $\langle \mathbf{S}, \Sigma \rangle$ is understood from context.

3. On Finite Implication

Let Σ be a finite set of constraints and let σ be an additional SC. In this section, it will be shown that σ is a logical consequence of Σ *iff* σ is a *finite* logical consequence of Σ. Formally, σ is a finite logical consequence of Σ, written $\Sigma \models_{\text{finite}} \sigma$, if any *finite* database over S satisfying Σ must also satisfy σ. By definition, $\Sigma \models \sigma$ implies $\Sigma \models_{\text{finite}} \sigma$. We will prove its opposite direction; that is, $\Sigma \not\models \sigma$ implies $\Sigma \not\models_{\text{finite}} \sigma$. Let us denote σ by $X(pd : Y)$.

For a path description pd $(= P_n.P_{n-1}. \cdots .P_1)$, a *pd-List* over S is a directed graph $G(V, A)$ of the form

$$v_n \xrightarrow{P_n} v_{n-1} \xrightarrow{P_{n-1}} \cdots \xrightarrow{P_1} v_0,$$

where each v_i has a label $Cl(v_i)$ that is a subset of $Classes(\mathbf{S})$. If $pd = \mathtt{Id}$, then G consists of a single vertex v_0 with no arcs. Note that G is not necessarily a database over S, since it may not satisfy a property value integrity condition. If a pd-List over S satisfies a property value integrity condition, then it is called a *pd-List database* over S.

Theorem 1: The following three statements are equivalent.

1. $\Sigma \not\models X(pd : Y)$.
2. $\Sigma \not\models_{\text{finite}} X(pd : Y)$.
3. There is a pd-List database over S that satisfies Σ_{SC} but violates $X(pd : Y)$.

Proof. By definition, (2) implies (1). In the following we will prove that (1) implies (3) and that (3) implies (2).

Proof that (1) implies (3). Assume that $\Sigma \not\models X(pd : Y)$. Then there is a (possibly infinite) database $G(V, A)$ over S that satisfies Σ but violates $X(pd : Y)$. That is, there is a path $u \rightsquigarrow_{pd} v \in G$ such that $X \cap Cl(u) \neq \emptyset$ but $Y \cap Cl(v) = \emptyset$. Let $pd = P_n.P_{n-1}. \cdots .P_1$. The path $u \rightsquigarrow_{pd} v$ can be denoted $u_n \xrightarrow{P_n} u_{n-1} \xrightarrow{P_{n-1}} \cdots \xrightarrow{P_1} u_0$, where $u_n = u$ and $u_0 = v$.[2] Let $G_{pd}(V_{pd}, A_{pd})$ be a pd-List $v_n \xrightarrow{P_n} v_{n-1} \xrightarrow{P_{n-1}} \cdots \xrightarrow{P_1} v_0$ over S such that $Cl(v_i) = Cl(u_i)$ for $0 \leq i \leq n$. We will prove that G_{pd} is a pd-List database over S that satisfies Σ_{SC} but violates $X(pd : Y)$. (Hence (1) implies (3).)

Since G satisfies Σ_{SC} $(\subseteq \Sigma)$ and the path $u \rightsquigarrow_{pd} v$ is a subgraph of G, the path $u \rightsquigarrow_{pd} v$ must also satisfy Σ_{SC}. Furthermore, since $Cl(v_i) = Cl(u_i)$ by definition, G_{pd} also satisfies Σ_{SC}. On the other hand, since (1) $X \cap Cl(u) \neq \emptyset$, (2) $Y \cap Cl(v) = \emptyset$, (3) $Cl(u) = Cl(u_n) = Cl(v_n)$, and (4) $Cl(v) = Cl(u_0) = Cl(v_0)$, it holds that $X \cap Cl(v_n) \neq \emptyset$ and $Y \cap Cl(v_0) = \emptyset$; that is, G_{pd} violates $X(pd : Y)$. It remains to show that G_{pd} is a pd-List database over S. Since G is a database over S, it satisfies a property value integrity condition. Thus $Cl(u_i) \cap Dom(P_i) \neq \emptyset$ for $1 \leq i \leq n$. Since $Cl(v_i) = Cl(u_i)$, it holds that $Cl(v_i) \cap Dom(P_i) \neq \emptyset$ for $1 \leq i \leq n$; that is, G_{pd} also satisfies a property value integrity condition. Hence G_{pd} is a pd-List database over S.

Proof that (3) implies (2). Assume that there is a pd-List database $G_{pd}(V_{pd}, A_{pd})$ over S that satisfies Σ_{SC} but violates $X(pd : Y)$. Let us denote G_{pd} by $v_n \xrightarrow{P_n} v_{n-1} \xrightarrow{P_{n-1}} \cdots \xrightarrow{P_1} v_0$. In order to prove that $\Sigma \not\models_{\text{finite}} X(pd : Y)$, it suffices to show that there is a *finite* database over S which satisfies Σ but violates $X(pd : Y)$.

If G_{pd} satisfies Σ_{FUNC}, then G_{pd} is itself a finite database over S that satisfies Σ but violates $X(pd : Y)$, since $\Sigma = \Sigma_{SC} \cup \Sigma_{FUNC}$. Thus there is nothing to prove.

Assume that G_{pd} does not satisfy Σ_{FUNC}; that is, that G_{pd} violates a FUNC constraint $\mathtt{FUNC}(P) \in \Sigma_{FUNC}$. Since each vertex in V_{pd} has at most one out-arc, G_{pd} satisfies property functionality for $\mathtt{FUNC}(P)$. Thus G_{pd} must violate property value completeness for $\mathtt{FUNC}(P)$; that is, there is a vertex $v_i \in V_{pd}$ such that $Cl(v_i) \cap Dom(P) \neq \emptyset$, but which has no out-arc labeled P. By adding one vertex and a number of arcs to G_{pd}, however, we can construct a database $G(V, A)$ over S that satisfies Σ_{FUNC} as well as Σ_{SC}. Let us consider how to construct such a database G.

Initially, let $V = V_{pd} \cup \{u\}$, where $Cl(u) = Classes(\mathbf{S})$, and let $A = A_{pd}$. Then add a number of arcs to A as follows.

1. For each $\mathtt{FUNC}(P) \in \Sigma_{FUNC}$, add an arc $u \xrightarrow{P} u$ to A.
2. For each $\mathtt{FUNC}(P) \in \Sigma_{FUNC}$ and each v_i with $0 \leq i \leq n$, if $Cl(v_i) \cap Dom(P) \neq \emptyset$ and v_i has no out-arc labeled P, then add an arc $v_i \xrightarrow{P} u$ to A.

We will prove that $G(V, A)$ constructed as above is a finite database over S which satisfies Σ but violates $X(pd : Y)$. Clearly, G is finite. Since (1) $v_n \rightsquigarrow_{pd} v_0 \in G_{pd}$ and (2) G_{pd} is a subgraph of G by construction, there is a path $v_n \rightsquigarrow_{pd} v_0 \in G$. Furthermore, $X \cap Cl(v_n) \neq \emptyset$ and $Y \cap Cl(v_0) = \emptyset$, since G_{pd} violates $X(pd : Y)$. Thus G must also violate $X(pd : Y)$. It remains to prove that G is a database over S and satisfies Σ.

Let us prove that G is a database over S; that is, that G satisfies a property value integrity condition. Since G_{pd} is a pd-List database over S, G_{pd} satisfies a property value integrity condition; that is, $Cl(v_i) \cap Dom(P_i) \neq \emptyset$ for each $v_i \xrightarrow{P_i} v_{i-1} \in A_{pd}$. For each arc $u \xrightarrow{P} u$ added to A in Step 1, it follows that $Cl(u) \cap Dom(P) \neq \emptyset$, since $Cl(u) = Classes(\mathbf{S})$. Furthermore, for each arc $v_i \xrightarrow{P} u$ added to A in Step 2, it follows from the precondition in Step 2 that $Cl(v_i) \cap Dom(P) \neq \emptyset$. That is, for every arc $w \xrightarrow{P} w' \in A$, it holds that $Cl(w) \cap Dom(P) \neq \emptyset$. Thus G satisfies a property value integrity condition, and hence is a database over S.

[2]A vertex u_i may coincide with another u_j, since G may contain cycles.

Let us next prove that G satisfies Σ. Let $\texttt{FUNC}(P) \in \Sigma_{\texttt{FUNC}}$. Since every vertex in V has at most one out-arc labeled P by construction, G satisfies property functionality for $\texttt{FUNC}(P)$. On the other hand, by Steps 1 and 2 above, for every $w \in V$, if $Cl(w) \cap Dom(P) \neq \emptyset$, then w must have an out-arc labeled P. Thus G satisfies property value completeness for $\texttt{FUNC}(P)$. Hence G satisfies $\Sigma_{\texttt{FUNC}}$. We finally prove that G satisfies Σ_{SC}. Let $Z(pd' : W) \in \Sigma_{\text{SC}}$, and assume that there is a path $w \rightsquigarrow_{pd'} w' \in G$ such that $Z \cap Cl(w) \neq \emptyset$. In order to prove that G satisfies Σ_{SC}, it suffices to show that $W \cap Cl(w') \neq \emptyset$. If $w' = u$, then this is true, since $Cl(u) = Classes(\mathbf{S})$. Assume that $w' \neq u$. Since the destination of every arc added in Steps 1 and 2 is the new vertex u, the assumption $w' \neq u$ implies that the path $w \rightsquigarrow_{pd'} w'$ must be on G_{pd}; that is, that $w \rightsquigarrow_{pd'} w'$ is a subgraph of G_{pd}. Since G_{pd} satisfies Σ_{SC} (in particular, $Z(pd' : W)$) by assumption, $Z \cap Cl(w) \neq \emptyset$ implies $W \cap Cl(w') \neq \emptyset$. Hence G satisfies Σ_{SC}. Consequently, (3) implies (2). This completes proving Theorem 1. □

Example 1: Let $\mathbf{S}$ be a class schema defined as follows: $\texttt{A}_1\{\texttt{c}\}$, $\texttt{A}_2\{\}$, $\texttt{A}_3\{\texttt{b}\}$, $\texttt{B}\{\texttt{a,d}\}$, $\texttt{C}_1\{\}$, $\texttt{C}_2\{\}$, $\texttt{D}\{\texttt{b}\}$, $\texttt{E}\{\texttt{c}\}$, $\texttt{F}\{\}$, $\texttt{G}\{\texttt{c}\}$, where $Dom(\texttt{a})=\{\texttt{B}\}$, $Dom(\texttt{b})=\{\texttt{A}_3,\texttt{D}\}$, $Dom(\texttt{c}) = \{\texttt{A}_1,\texttt{E},\texttt{G}\}$, $Dom(\texttt{d})=\{\texttt{B}\}$.
Let Σ_{SC} consists of the following seven SCs:
$\texttt{A}_1(\texttt{Id:A}_2)$, $\texttt{A}_1(\texttt{c:C}_2)$, $\texttt{A}_2(\texttt{Id:A}_3)$, $\{\texttt{A}_3,\texttt{D}\}(\texttt{b:B})$, $\texttt{B}(\texttt{a:A}_1)$, $\texttt{C}_1(\texttt{Id:C}_2)$, $\texttt{E}(\texttt{c:}\{\texttt{C}_2,\texttt{F}\})$, $\texttt{G}(\texttt{c:A}_2)$.
Let $\Sigma_{\texttt{FUNC}} = \emptyset$. The database schema $\langle \mathbf{S}, \Sigma \rangle$ is illustrated in Figure 3. Let us consider whether or not $\Sigma \models \{\texttt{A}_2,\texttt{A}_3\}(\texttt{b.a.c:}\{\texttt{C}_1,\texttt{F}\})$. Since there is a 'b.a.c'-List database $v_3 \xrightarrow{\texttt{b}} v_2 \xrightarrow{\texttt{a}} v_1 \xrightarrow{\texttt{c}} v_0$ that satisfies Σ_{SC} but violates $\{\texttt{A}_2,\texttt{A}_3\}(\texttt{b.a.c:}\{\texttt{C}_1,\texttt{F}\})$, as in Figure 4, it follows from Theorem 1 that $\Sigma \not\models \{\texttt{A}_2,\texttt{A}_3\}(\texttt{b.a.c:}\{\texttt{C}_1,\texttt{F}\})$. □

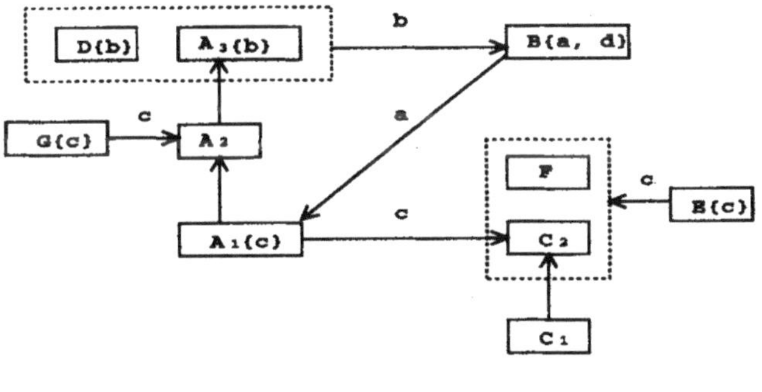

Figure 3: A database schema $\langle \mathbf{S}, \Sigma \rangle$.

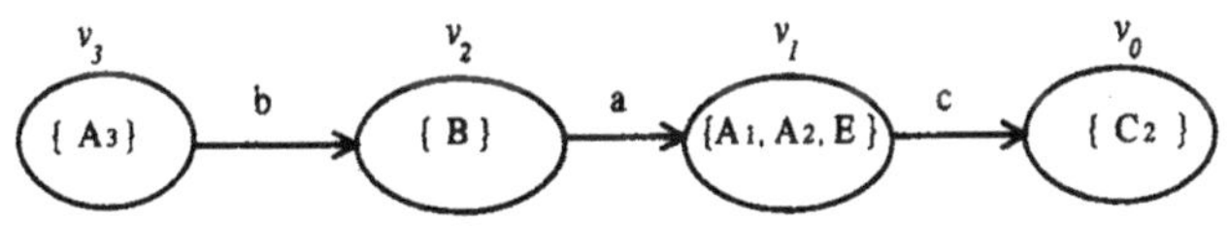

Figure 4: A 'b.a.c'-List.

4. Complete Axiomatization

Let Σ be a finite set of constraints and let σ be an SC. There is a *derivation* of σ from Σ, written $\Sigma \vdash \sigma$, *iff* σ is a member of Σ, or is derivable from Σ with the use of any inference axioms A1 to A5 in Table 2. In this section, it will be shown that axioms A1 to A5 are sound and complete for deciding whether or not $\Sigma \models \sigma$; that is, $\Sigma \models \sigma$ *iff* $\Sigma \vdash \sigma$.

Lemma 1: Axioms A1 to A5 are sound; that is, $\Sigma \vdash \sigma$ implies $\Sigma \models \sigma$.

Proof. Let $G(V, A)$ be a database over $\mathbf{S}$ satisfying Σ and let $u \in V$. We will prove soundness for each axiom.

A1: If $X \subseteq Y$, then $X \cap Cl(u) \neq \emptyset$ implies $Y \cap Cl(u) \neq \emptyset$. Thus G satisfies $X(\texttt{Id} : Y)$.

A2: Assume that G satisfies $X(pd : Y)$ and $Y(pd' : Z)$. Further, assume that $X \cap Cl(u) \neq \emptyset$ and $u \rightsquigarrow_{pd \circ pd'} v \in G$ for some $v \in V$. Clearly, $u \rightsquigarrow_{pd \circ pd'} v \in G$ implies $u \rightsquigarrow_{pd} w \in G$ and $w \rightsquigarrow_{pd'} v \in G$ for some $w \in V$. Then $X \cap Cl(u) \neq \emptyset$ implies $Y \cap Cl(w) \neq \emptyset$ by $X(pd : Y)$. Furthermore, $Y \cap Cl(w) \neq \emptyset$ implies $Z \cap Cl(v) \neq \emptyset$ by $Y(pd' : Z)$. That is, $X \cap Cl(u) \neq \emptyset$ implies $Z \cap Cl(v) \neq \emptyset$, and thus G satisfies $X(pd \circ pd' : Z)$.

A3: Assume that G satisfies $X(pd : Z)$ and $Y(pd : Z)$. Further, assume that $(X \cup Y) \cap Cl(u) \neq \emptyset$ and $u \rightsquigarrow_{pd} v \in G$ for some $v \in V$. Then $X \cap Cl(u) \neq \emptyset$ or $Y \cap Cl(u) \neq \emptyset$. In either case, $Z \cap Cl(v) \neq \emptyset$ by $X(pd : Z)$ and $Y(pd : Z)$. Thus G satisfies $(X \cup Y)(pd : Z)$.

A4: If $X = \emptyset$, then every database over $\mathbf{S}$ satisfies $X(pd : Y)$ *trivially* by definition.

A5: Assume that G satisfies $Dom(P)(P \circ pd : Y)$. Further, assume that $u \rightsquigarrow_{pd' \circ P \circ pd} v \in G$ for some $v \in V$. It suffices to show that $Y \cap Cl(v) \neq \emptyset$. Clearly, $u \rightsquigarrow_{pd' \circ P \circ pd} v \in G$ implies $u \rightsquigarrow_{pd'} w \in G$ and $w \rightsquigarrow_{P \circ pd} v \in G$ for some $w \in V$. Since (1) G satisfies a property value integrity condition and (2) w has an out-arc labeled P, it holds that $Dom(P) \cap Cl(w) \neq \emptyset$. Since G satisfies $Dom(P)(P \circ pd : Y)$ by assumption, $w \rightsquigarrow_{P \circ pd} v \in G$ and $Dom(P) \cap Cl(w) \neq \emptyset$ imply $Y \cap Cl(v) \neq \emptyset$. □

Table 2 also has another axiom A6 which is derivable using axioms A1 and A2. In fact, since $Z \subseteq X$ implies $Z(\texttt{Id} : X)$ by axiom A1, $Z(\texttt{Id} : X)$ and $X(pd : Y)$ imply $Z(pd : Y)$ by axiom A2, where $\texttt{Id} \circ pd = pd$. Thus axiom A6 is redundant from the view of completeness, but is useful for deriving SCs.

Example 2: Consider whether or not an SC $\texttt{A}_3(\texttt{b.a.c} : \{\texttt{C}_2,\texttt{F}\})$ is derivable from the database schema $\langle \mathbf{S}, \Sigma \rangle$ of Example 1. For property 'a', where $Dom(\texttt{a}) = \{\texttt{B}\}$, $\texttt{B}(\texttt{a} : \texttt{A}_1)$ is in Σ. Thus by axiom A5, $\texttt{A}_3(\texttt{b.a} : \texttt{A}_1)$ is derived. By axiom A2, $\texttt{A}_3(\texttt{b.a.c} : \texttt{C}_2)$ is also derived from $\texttt{A}_3(\texttt{b.a} : \texttt{A}_1)$ and $\texttt{A}_1(\texttt{c:C}_2)$. Since $\texttt{C}_2(\texttt{Id:}\{\texttt{C}_2,\texttt{F}\})$ holds by axiom A1, $\texttt{A}_3(\texttt{b.a.c} : \{\texttt{C}_2,\texttt{F}\})$ is derived from Σ. □

In the following we will prove completeness of axioms A1 to A5; that is, $\Sigma \not\vdash \sigma$ implies $\Sigma \not\models \sigma$. Let us denote σ by $X(pd : Y)$. The proof will be done by showing

Table 2: Axioms for SCs.

A1:	(*reflexivity*)	If $X \subseteq Y$, then $X(\mathtt{Id} : Y)$.
A2:	(*composition*)	If $X(pd : Y)$ and $Y(pd' : Z)$, then $X(pd \circ pd' : Z)$.
A3:	(*additivity*)	If $X(pd : Z)$ and $Y(pd : Z)$, then $(X \cup Y)(pd : Z)$.
A4:	(*triviality*)	If $X = \emptyset$, then $X(pd : Y)$ for any path description pd and any $Y \subseteq Classes(\mathbf{S})$.
A5:	(*prefix extension*)	For a property $P \in Props(\mathbf{S})$, if $Dom(P)(P \circ pd : Y)$, then $X(pd' \circ P \circ pd : Y)$ for any $X \subseteq Classes(\mathbf{S})$ and any path description pd'.
A6:	(*restriction*)	If $X(pd : Y)$ and $Z \subseteq X$, then $Z(pd : Y)$.

that if $\Sigma \not\vdash X(pd : Y)$, then there is a pd-List database over $\mathbf{S}$ that satisfies Σ_{SC} but violates $X(pd : Y)$. (Hence $\Sigma \not\models X(pd : Y)$ by Theorem 1.) In order to construct such a pd-List database, we introduce the concept of *SC base*.

Let $pd = P_n.P_{n-1}.\cdots.P_1$. For $0 \leq i \leq n$, let us denote $pd_i = P_i.P_{i-1}.\cdots.P_1$.[3] The *SC base* of a subset Y of $Classes(\mathbf{S})$ and a path description pd under $\langle \mathbf{S}, \Sigma \rangle$, written $SCbase(Y, pd)$, is a sequence $\langle S_n, S_{n-1}, \cdots, S_0 \rangle$ such that $S_i = \{C \in Classes(\mathbf{S}) \mid \Sigma_{SC} \vdash C(pd_i : Y)\}$ for $0 \leq i \leq n$.

Lemma 2: Let $SCbase(Y, pd) = \langle S_n, S_{n-1}, \cdots, S_0 \rangle$. If $\Sigma_{SC} \vdash Z(pd_i : Y)$, then $Z \subseteq S_i$, where $0 \leq i \leq n$.

Proof. Assume that $\Sigma_{SC} \vdash Z(pd_i : Y)$. Let $C \in Z$. By axiom A6, $Z(pd_i : Y)$ implies $C(pd_i : Y)$ for each $C \in Z$; that is, $\Sigma_{SC} \vdash C(pd_i : Y)$. By definition, $C \in S_i$, and thus $Z \subseteq S_i$. Hence Lemma 2 holds. □

Lemma 3: If $SCbase(Y, pd) = \langle S_n, S_{n-1}, \cdots, S_0 \rangle$, then the following four conditions hold.

SCB1: If $Z \subseteq S_i$, then $\Sigma_{SC} \vdash Z(pd_i : Y)$, where $0 \leq i \leq n$.

SCB2: $Y \subseteq S_0$.

SCB3: For an SC $Z(pd' : W) \in \Sigma_{SC}$, if $pd' = P_i.P_{i-1}.\cdots.P_{j+1}$ and $W \subseteq S_j$, then $Z \subseteq S_i$.[4]

SCB4: If $Dom(P_i) \subseteq S_i$, then $S_j = Classes(\mathbf{S})$ for $i \leq j \leq n$.

Proof. SCB1: Assume that $Z \subseteq S_i$. If $Z = \emptyset$, then $\Sigma_{SC} \vdash Z(pd_i : Y)$ by axiom A4. If $Z \neq \emptyset$, then $\Sigma_{SC} \vdash C(pd_i : Y)$ for every $C \in Z$ by definition. Then $\{C(pd_i : Y) \mid C \in Z\}$ implies $Z(pd_i : Y)$ by axiom A3, and thus $\Sigma_{SC} \vdash Z(pd_i : Y)$. Hence SCB1 holds.

SCB2: Since (1) $\Sigma_{SC} \vdash Y(\mathtt{Id} : Y)$ by axiom A1 and (2) $pd_0 = \mathtt{Id}$ by definition, $Y \subseteq S_0$ by Lemma 2. Hence SCB2 holds.

SCB3: Assume that there is an SC $Z(pd' : W) \in \Sigma_{SC}$ such that $pd' = P_i.P_{i-1}.\cdots.P_{j+1}$ and $W \subseteq S_j$. By SCB1, $W \subseteq S_j$ implies $\Sigma_{SC} \vdash W(pd_j : Y)$. Thus $Z(pd' : W)$ and $W(pd_j : Y)$ imply $Z(pd' \circ pd_j : Y)$ by axiom A2. Since $pd' \circ pd_j = pd_i$, $\Sigma_{SC} \vdash Z(pd_i : Y)$. Thus $Z \subseteq S_i$ by Lemma 2. Hence SCB3 holds.

SCB4: Assume that $Dom(P_i) \subseteq S_i$. By SCB1, $\Sigma_{SC} \vdash Dom(P_i)(pd_i : Y)$. Note that $pd_i = P_i \circ pd_{i-1}$. Thus by axiom A5, $\Sigma_{SC} \vdash Z(pd' \circ pd_i : Y)$ for any $Z \subseteq Classes(\mathbf{S})$ and any path description pd'. In particular, by letting $Z = Classes(\mathbf{S})$ and $pd' = P_j.P_{j-1}.\cdots.P_{i+1}$, $\Sigma_{SC} \vdash Classes(\mathbf{S})(pd_j : Y)$, where $i \leq j \leq n$. Thus $Classes(\mathbf{S}) \subseteq S_j$ by Lemma 2. Clearly, $S_j \subseteq Classes(\mathbf{S})$. Hence SCB4 holds. □

[3]Note that $pd_n = pd$ and $pd_0 = \mathtt{Id}$.

[4]If $pd' = \mathtt{Id}$, then $i = j$.

Using the following lemma, we will prove in Section 5 that conditions SCB1 to SCB4 are necessary and sufficient for a sequence $\langle S_n, S_{n-1}, \cdots, S_0 \rangle$ to coincide with $SCbase(Y, pd)$.

Lemma 4: Assume that a sequence $\langle S_n, S_{n-1}, \cdots, S_0 \rangle$ satisfies SCB2 to SCB4.[5] If $X \not\subseteq S_n$, then $\Sigma \not\models X(pd : Y)$.

Proof. Assume that $X \not\subseteq S_n$. For $0 \leq i \leq n$, let $\overline{S_i}$ denote the complement of S_i under $Classes(\mathbf{S})$; that is, $\overline{S_i} = Classes(\mathbf{S}) - S_i$. Let $v_n \xrightarrow{P_n} v_{n-1} \xrightarrow{P_{n-1}} \cdots \xrightarrow{P_1} v_0$ be a pd-List over $\mathbf{S}$ such that $Cl(v_i) = \overline{S_i}$ for $0 \leq i \leq n$. We will prove that the pd-List is a pd-List database over $\mathbf{S}$ that satisfies Σ_{SC} but violates $X(pd : Y)$. (Hence $\Sigma \not\models X(pd : Y)$ by Theorem 1.)

Let us first prove that the pd-List is a pd-List database over $\mathbf{S}$. Assume conversely that the pd-List is not a pd-List database over $\mathbf{S}$. Then the pd-List does not satisfy a property value integrity condition; that is, $Cl(v_i) \cap Dom(P_i) = \emptyset$ for some i with $1 \leq i \leq n$. Then $Dom(P_i) \subseteq S_i$, since $Cl(v_i) = \overline{S_i}$. Thus it follows from SCB4 that $S_j = Classes(\mathbf{S})$ for $i \leq j \leq n$. In particular, $S_n = Classes(\mathbf{S})$. This, however, contradicts that $X \not\subseteq S_n$. Hence the pd-List is a pd-List database over $\mathbf{S}$.

Let us next prove that the pd-List violates $X(pd : Y)$. Since $Cl(v_n) = \overline{S_n}$, $X \not\subseteq S_n$ implies $X \cap Cl(v_n) \neq \emptyset$. On the other hand, $Y \cap Cl(v_0) = \emptyset$, since (1) $Y \subseteq S_0$ by SCB2 and (2) $Cl(v_0) = \overline{S_0}$. Thus the pd-List violates $X(pd : Y)$.

Let us finally prove that the pd-List satisfies Σ_{SC}. Assume conversely that the pd-List does not satisfy Σ_{SC}. Then for an SC $Z(pd' : W) \in \Sigma_{SC}$, there are two vertices v_i, v_j such that $Z \cap Cl(v_i) \neq \emptyset$, $W \cap Cl(v_j) = \emptyset$, and $pd' = P_i.P_{i-1}.\cdots.P_{j+1}$. Since $W \cap Cl(v_j) = \emptyset$ and $Cl(v_j) = \overline{S_j}$ imply $W \subseteq S_j$, it follows from SCB 3 that $Z \subseteq S_i$. Thus $Z \cap Cl(v_i) = \emptyset$ by $Cl(v_i) = \overline{S_i}$ — a contradiction. Hence the pd-List satisfies Σ_{SC}. This completes proving Lemma 4. □

[5]The sequence may not necessarily coincide with $SCbase(Y, pd)$.

We are now ready to prove the following theorem.

Theorem 2: The following three statements are equivalent.

1. $\Sigma \models X(pd : Y)$.
2. $\Sigma \vdash X(pd : Y)$.
3. $X \subseteq S_n$ for $SCbase(Y, pd) = \langle S_n, S_{n-1}, \cdots, S_0 \rangle$.

Proof. By Lemma 1, (2) implies (1). Since $SCbase(Y, pd)$ satisfies SCB1 by Lemma 3, (3) implies (2). Since $SCbase(Y, pd)$ satisfies SCB2 to SCB4 by Lemma 3, it follows from Lemma 4 that $X \not\subseteq S_n$ implies $\Sigma \not\models X(pd : Y)$. That is, (1) implies (3). □

5. Implication Problem

In this section, it will be shown that $SCbase(Y, pd)$ can be computed in polynomial time. Thus it can also be decided in polynomial time whether or not $\Sigma \models X(pd : Y)$. Computing $SCbase(Y, pd)$ is based on the following lemma.

Lemma 5: $SCbase(Y, pd) = \langle S_n, S_{n-1}, \cdots, S_0 \rangle$ *iff* $\langle S_n, S_{n-1}, \cdots, S_0 \rangle$ satisfies SCB1 to SCB4 of Lemma 3.

Proof. Let $SCbase(Y, pd) = \langle T_n, T_{n-1}, \cdots, T_0 \rangle$. Assume that $\langle S_n, S_{n-1}, \cdots, S_0 \rangle$ satisfies SCB1 to SCB4. It suffices to show that $S_i = T_i$ for $0 \leq i \leq n$.

Proof of "$\subseteq$": Since $\Sigma_{SC} \vdash S_i(pd_i : Y)$ by SCB1, it follows from Lemma 2 that $S_i \subseteq T_i$.

Proof of "$\supseteq$": Assume that $C \notin S_i$ for some $C \in Classes(\mathbf{S})$. Then $\Sigma \not\models C(pd_i : Y)$ by Lemma 4. Thus $\Sigma \not\vdash C(pd_i : Y)$ by Theorem 2. Since $T_i = \{C \in Classes(\mathbf{S}) \mid \Sigma \vdash C(pd_i : Y)\}$ by definition, $\Sigma \not\vdash C(pd_i : Y)$ implies $C \notin T_i$. Hence $T_i \subseteq S_i$. □

The following procedure will compute $SCbase(Y, pd)$.

Procedure 1: (Computing $SCbase(Y, pd)$.)
input: a database schema $\langle \mathbf{S}, \Sigma \rangle$, a subset Y of $Classes(\mathbf{S})$, and a path description pd $(= P_n.P_{n-1}. \cdots .P_1)$.
output: $SCbase(Y, pd) = \langle S_n, S_{n-1}, \cdots, S_0 \rangle$.
method:

1. Divide Σ_{SC} into two sets: $\Sigma_{Id} = \{Z(pd' : W) \in \Sigma_{SC} \mid pd' = \mathrm{Id}\}$ and $\Sigma_{\neg Id} = \Sigma_{SC} - \Sigma_{Id}$.
2. $S_0 \leftarrow Y$ and $S_i \leftarrow \emptyset$ for $1 \leq i \leq n$.
3. **for** $i \leftarrow 0$ **to** n **do begin**
4. **for** each $Z(pd' : W) \in \Sigma_{\neg Id}$ **do**
   if $pd' = P_i.P_{i-1}. \cdots .P_{j+1}$ and $W \subseteq S_j$ for some j
   then $S_i \leftarrow S_i \cup Z$.
5. **while** there is an SC $Z(\mathrm{Id} : W) \in \Sigma_{Id}$ such that $Z \not\subseteq S_i$ and $W \subseteq S_i$ **do** $S_i \leftarrow S_i \cup Z$.
   end
6. **if** $Dom(P_i) \subseteq S_i$ for some i
   then $S_j \leftarrow Classes(\mathbf{S})$ for $i \leq j \leq n$. □

We will prove the correctness of Procedure 1. Clearly, Procedure 1 always terminates for any input. Let $\langle S_n, S_{n-1}, \cdots, S_0 \rangle$ be the output of Procedure 1. By Lemma 5, it suffices to show that the output satisfies SCB1 to SCB4. Note that Procedure 1 does not make S_i small for any i with $0 \leq i \leq n$. Thus the output satisfies SCB2, since the initial value of S_0 is Y. By Step 6, SCB4 also holds.

As for SCB3, assume conversely that there is an SC $Z(pd' : W) \in \Sigma_{SC}$ such that $Z \not\subseteq S_i$, $W \subseteq S_j$, and $pd' = P_i.P_{i-1}. \cdots .P_{j+1}$.[6] Then it must hold that $Dom(P_j) \not\subseteq S_j$, since otherwise, $j \leq i$ implies $S_i = Classes(\mathbf{S})$ by Step 6, which contradicts $Z \not\subseteq S_i$. Similarly, $Dom(P_i) \not\subseteq S_i$. Thus both S_i and S_j remain unchanged by Step 6. There are two cases to be considered.

Case 1: where $pd' = \mathrm{Id}$. Then $i = j$ and $Z(pd' : W) \in \Sigma_{Id}$ by definition. Since $Z \not\subseteq S_i$ and $W \subseteq S_j$ by assumption, the precondition of Step 5 would be satisfied. Thus $Z \subseteq S_i$ by the assignment "$S_i \leftarrow S_i \cup Z$" in Step 5 — a contradiction.

Case 2: where $pd' \neq \mathrm{Id}$. Then $j < i$ and $Z(pd' : W) \in \Sigma_{\neg Id}$ by definition. Since $W \subseteq S_j$ by assumption, the precondition of Step 4 would be satisfied. Thus $Z \subseteq S_i$ by the assignment "$S_i \leftarrow S_i \cup Z$" in Step 4 — a contradiction. That is, in either case, there is a contradiction. Hence the output must satisfy SCB3.

As for SCB1, we first prove that $\Sigma \vdash S_i(pd_i : Y)$ at the beginning of Step 6, by induction on the number of executing the assignment "$S_i \leftarrow S_i \cup Z$" in Steps 4 and 5.

Basis. Initially, $S_0 = Y$ and $S_i = \emptyset$ for $1 \leq i \leq n$ by Step 2. Thus if $i \neq 0$, then $\Sigma_{SC} \vdash S_i(pd_i : Y)$ by axiom A4. If $i = 0$, then $pd_0 = \mathrm{Id}$, and thus $\Sigma_{SC} \vdash S_i(pd_i : Y)$ by axiom A1. Hence the basis case holds.

Induction. As an induction hypothesis, assume during an execution of Step 3 to 5 that $\Sigma_{SC} \vdash S_j(pd_j : Y)$ for $0 \leq j \leq n$. Assume that S_i is changed to $S_i \cup Z$ by one assignment in Step 4 or 5. Then there is an SC $Z(pd' : W) \in \Sigma_{SC}$ such that $pd' = P_i.P_{i-1}. \cdots .P_{j+1}$ and $W \subseteq S_j$. It suffices to show that $\Sigma_{SC} \vdash (S_i \cup Z)(pd_i : Y)$. Since $\Sigma_{SC} \vdash S_j(pd_j : Y)$ by the induction hypothesis, $W(\mathrm{Id} : S_j)$ implies $\Sigma_{SC} \vdash W(pd_j : Y)$ by axiom A6. Thus $Z(pd' : W)$ and $W(pd_j : Y)$ imply $Z(pd' \circ pd_j : Y)$ by axiom A2. Since $pd' \circ pd_j = pd_i$, $\Sigma_{SC} \vdash Z(pd_i : Y)$. Furthermore, since $\Sigma_{SC} \vdash S_i(pd_i : Y)$ by the induction hypothesis, $S_i(pd_i : Y)$ and $Z(pd_i : Y)$ imply $(S_i \cup Z)(pd_i : Y)$ by axiom A3. This completes the induction proof.

By the induction proof above, $\Sigma_{SC} \vdash S_i(pd_i : Y)$ at the beginning of Step 6. Assume that $Dom(P_i) \subseteq S_i$ for some i at Step 6. Then S_j is changed into $Classes(\mathbf{S})$ for $i \leq j \leq n$ by Step 6. Since $\Sigma_{SC} \vdash S_i(pd_i : Y)$, $Dom(P_i) \subseteq S_i$ implies $\Sigma_{SC} \vdash Dom(P_i)(pd_i : Y)$ by axiom A6. Since $pd_i = P_i \circ pd_{i-1}$, by axiom A5, $\Sigma_{SC} \vdash Z(pd' \circ pd_i : Y)$ for any $Z \subseteq Classes(\mathbf{S})$ and any path description pd'. By letting $Z = Classes(\mathbf{S})$ and $pd' = P_j.P_{j-1}. \cdots .P_{i+1}$, $\Sigma_{SC} \vdash Classes(\mathbf{S})(pd_j : Y)$ for $i \leq j \leq n$. Hence, at the end of Step 6, it will continue to hold that $\Sigma_{SC} \vdash S_i(pd_i : Y)$ for $0 \leq i \leq n$. Therefore, by axiom A6, if $Z \subseteq S_i$, then $\Sigma_{SC} \vdash Z(pd_i : Y)$. That is, $SCbase(Y, pd)$ satisfies SCB1. This completes proving the correctness of Procedure 1.

[6] If $pd' = \mathrm{Id}$, then $i = j$; otherwise, $j < i$.

Example 3: Consider the database schema $\langle \mathbf{S}, \Sigma \rangle$ in Example 1. Let us execute Procedure 1 for a set of classes {C$_2$,F} and a path description 'b.a.c'. In Step 1, Σ_{SC} is divided as follows:

$$\Sigma_{\mathtt{Id}} = \{ \mathtt{A_1(Id:A_2), A_2(Id:A_3), C_1(Id:C_2)} \}$$
$$\Sigma_{\neg\mathtt{Id}} = \{ \mathtt{A_1(c:C_2), \{A_3,D\}(b:B), B(a:A_1), E(c:\{C_2,F\}), G(c:A_2)} \}$$

In Step 2, $S_0 = \{\mathtt{C_2,F}\}$ and $S_1 = S_2 = S_3 = \emptyset$. Consider the for loop in Step 3. Let $i = 0$. In Step 4, no applicable SC exists in Σ_{SC}. In Step 5, since $\mathtt{C_1(Id:C_2)} \in \Sigma_{\mathtt{Id}}$ and $\{\mathtt{C_2}\} \subseteq S_0$, $\mathtt{C_1}$ is added to S_0 and we have $S_0 = \{\mathtt{C_1,C_2,F}\}$. For $i = 1$, $\mathtt{A_1(c:C_2)}$ and $\mathtt{E(c:\{C_2,F\})}$ are applicable in Step 4, thus $S_1 = \{\mathtt{A_1,E}\}$. There is no SC in $\Sigma_{\mathtt{Id}}$ that satisfies the while condition in Step 5. For $i = 2$, since $\mathtt{B(a:A_1)}$ is applicable in Step 4, $S_2 = \{\mathtt{B}\}$. There is no SC in $\Sigma_{\mathtt{Id}}$ that satisfies the while condition in Step 5. For $i = 3$, since there is no applicable SC in Σ_{SC}, S_3 remains unchanged. Thus, $S_3 = \emptyset$. In Step 6, S_2 and S_3 are set to *Classes*(**S**), since *Dom*(a) $= \{\mathtt{B}\} \subseteq S_2$ for $i = 2$. Now, we have obtained *SCbase*({C$_2$,F},b.a.c); $S_3 = S_2 =$ *Classes*(**S**), $S_1 = \{\mathtt{A_1,E}\}$, $S_0 = \{\mathtt{C_1,C_2,F}\}$.

Let us consider whether or not $\Sigma \models \{\mathtt{A_2,A_3}\}$ (b.a.c:{C$_2$,F}). Since $\{\mathtt{A_2,A_3}\} \subseteq S_3 =$ *Classes*(**S**), it follows from Theorem 2 that $\Sigma \models \{\mathtt{A_2,A_3}\}$ (b.a.c:{C$_2$,F}). □

Now consider the time complexity of Procedure 1. Let D denote the size of $\langle \mathbf{S}, \Sigma \rangle$ and let *Classes*(**S**) consist of K classes. Note that $K \le D$. We use bit arrays of size K to represent arbitrary subsets of *Classes*(**S**), such as those denoted by the variables S_i which are used in the procedure. Then for two sets S and T, testing for set containment "$S \subseteq T$" or assignment "$S \leftarrow S \cup T$" can be executed in $O(|T|)$ time, where $|T|$ is the cardinality of T.

Clearly, Step 1 runs in $O(\|\Sigma_{SC}\|)$ time, where $\|\Sigma_{SC}\|$ is the size of Σ_{SC}, and Step 2 requires $O(K \cdot (n+1))$ time to initialize each S_i.[7]

In Step 4, for each $Z(pd' : W) \in \Sigma_{\neg\mathtt{Id}}$, testing the precondition requires $O(len(pd') + |W|)$ time and the assignment "$S_i \leftarrow S_i \cup Z$" requires $O(|Z|)$ time; that is, these require $O(\|Z(pd' : W)\|)$ time. Thus one execution of Step 4 requires $O(\|\Sigma_{\neg\mathtt{Id}}\|)$ time, that is, $O(D)$ time.

In Step 5, finding an SC $Z(\mathtt{Id} : W) \in \Sigma_{\mathtt{Id}}$ such that $Z \not\subseteq S_i$ and $W \subseteq S_i$ requires $O(\|\Sigma_{\mathtt{Id}}\|)$ time, that is, $O(D)$ time. After that, the assignment "$S_i \leftarrow S_i \cup Z$" requires $O(|Z|)$ time, where $|Z| \le D$. Furthermore, once the assignment is executed for an SC, we do not need to test the precondition of Step 5 for the same SC any more. Thus Step 5 requires $O(|\Sigma_{\mathtt{Id}}| \cdot D)$ time, where $|\Sigma_{\mathtt{Id}}|$ is the cardinality of $\Sigma_{\mathtt{Id}}$. Hence the for loop of Step 3 to 5 requires, as a whole, $O((1 + |\Sigma_{\mathtt{Id}}|) \cdot D \cdot (n+1))$ time, that is, $O(D^2 \cdot (n+1))$ time. It is easy to see that Step 6 requires $O(K \cdot (n+1))$ time.

By the discussions above, the dominant factor of Procedure 1 is $O(D^2 \cdot (n+1))$. Hence we have the following lemma.

[7] We use $n+1$ instead of n, since $n = 0$ if $pd = \mathtt{Id}$.

Lemma 6: For a subset Y of *Classes*(**S**) and a path description *pd*, *SCbase*(Y, *pd*) can be computed in $O(D^2 \cdot (len(pd) + 1))$ time, where D is the size of $\langle \mathbf{S}, \Sigma \rangle$. □

By Theorem 2 and Lemma 6, we have the following theorem.

Theorem 3: Given an SC $X(pd : Y)$, it can be decided in $O(D^2 \cdot (len(pd) + 1))$ time whether or not $\Sigma \models X(pd : Y)$. □

6. Conclusion

In this paper, we showed that as SC is a logical consequence of a set of contraints *iff* it is a finite logical consequence of the set, then presented a sound and complete axiomatization for SCs. Finally, we gave a polynomial time algorithm for deciding whether or not an SC is a logical consequence of a set of constraints.

It can be decided in a similar way discussed in [3] [5] whether or not a FUNC is a logical consequence of a set of constraints.

There may exist a need to distinguish pathological cases, such as the following SC over the UNIVERSITY schema: `Student(cnum:Int[1-200])`. This is "meaningless", since it suggests that `Student` should have `cnum` property — an impossibility according to the schema in Figure 1. This was discussed in [3] [5], however, we have omitted the discussion here because of space limitation.

Acknowledgments

We would like to thank Prof. Grant E. Weddell for his helpful discussion of this paper.

References

[1] H. Arisawa and T. Miura. On the properties of extended inclusion dependencies. *Proc. 12th VLDB*, pp.449–456, Aug. 1986.

[2] D. S. Batory and W. Kim. Modeling concepts for VLSI CAD objects. *ACM TODS*, **10**(3), pp.322–346, Sep. 1985.

[3] M. Ito, G. E. Weddell, and N. Coburn. On specialization constraints over complex objects. *Technical Report, University of Waterloo*, CS91-62, 1991.

[4] S. L. Vandenberg and D. J. DeWitt. Algebraic support for complex objects with arrays, identity, and inheritance. *SIGMOD*, pp.158–167, May 1991.

[5] G. E. Weddell and N. Coburn. A theory of specialization constraints for complex objects. *Proc. 3rd Int. Conf. on Database Theory*, pp.229–244, Dec. 1990.

IMPROVING INTEGRITY CHECKING FOR ∃-CONSTRAINTS

Tok Wang LING and Sin Yeung LEE
Department of Information Systems and Computer Science
National University of Singapore
Lower Kent Ridge Road, Singapore 0511, Singapore.
email : lingtw@iscs.nus.sg, jlee@iscs.nus.sg

Abstract Efficient methods to enforce integrity constraints have been studied by many researchers. However, most of these methods can only provide efficient constraint enforcement for some particular types of constraints. In particular, one type of constraints called ∃-constraints, of which specification starts with "There exists ...", is not well solved. Few methods such as the finite differencing method have been targeted to solve this type of constraints, but the performance of the overall constraint enforcement is degraded by the heavy overhead incurred. In this paper, we propose a new technique which makes use of the result of previous evaluation of the ∃-constraint to supplement the constraint checking process so that the ∃-constraint can be validated more efficiently. This technique can be easily incorporated into existing integrity checking methods to improve their performance on validating ∃-constraints. We analyse the improvement with our method. Finally, we show that this method can be easily extended to enforce integrity constraints in deductive databases.

1.0 INTRODUCTION

[Nico82] made use of the assumption that database is consistent prior updates to simplify the constraint checking process. While his method works fine for constraints in the form of $\forall x\ W(x)$, it is incapable of simplifying the checking for constraints which are in the form of $\exists x\ W(x)$. We shall define this class of constraints as ∃-constraints. This type of constraints can be expressed by a well-formed formula in prenex conjunctive normal form such that at least one ∃ quantifier in the expression is not governed by any ∀ quantifier. If we use the famous supplier-part database in [Date86], the constraint "There is a red part which is supplied by every NY supplier." is a ∃-constraint and is expressed as

$$\exists p\#\forall s\#\exists q\left[p(p\#,\text{RED})\wedge(\neg s(s\#,\text{NY})\vee sp(s\#,p\#,q))\right]$$

Other research works [Bry88,Kowa87,Ling87,Llyod87, Qian87] improved on [Nico82]. However, they still cannot provide any significant improvement on checking of ∃-constraints. The reason why ∃-constraints are more difficult to be simplified is obvious. Given a constraint of the form $\exists x\ W(x)$, to validate this constraint after a transaction, we are required to find a value for the variable x, say c, such that $W(c)$ is true. Without any extra information to guide the search for c, such process incurs essentially the same cost as the direct evaluation. Hence, unless extra information is given, it is impossible to produce a general simplification algorithm for ∃-constraints.

By making use of extra information, [Hsu85] presents a method to simplify ∃-constraints. His method makes use of some summarizations of the database knowledge. For example, given the constraint "There is a red part which is supplied by every NY supplier", when a deletion of a red parts occurs, [Hsu85] states that we can optimize the constraint checking process if we know the collection of red parts, V_{red}, which are supplied by every NY supplier. In particular, [Hsu85] needs to check only if the deleting red part is found in V_{red}. If it is not, then no checking is necessary. Otherwise, the constraint remains valid if and only if V_{red} contains another red part other than the deleting red part. In this example, [Hsu85] provides a very efficient constraint validation method. We don't even need to access the relations s and sp.

The most important condition which establishes such good performance is the assumption that we know exactly all the red parts which are supplied by every NY supplier.

However, in actual implementation, how such an assumption can be realized determines the success of Hsu's method. If we need to re-calculate V_{red} every time the constraint is evaluated, then the computation effort to obtain V_{red} is essentially no better than the effort incurred in a direct evaluation. On the other hand, we may adopt an incremental approach to update V_{red} incrementally. For example, when a red part is deleted, V_{red} can be maintained by deleting the corresponding part in V_{red}.

However, there are updates which even the incremental approach fails to cut down the maintenance cost. For instance, when a supplier is deleted, the maintenance of V_{red} will be activated to find out all the red parts which are supplied by all suppliers except the deleting supplier. The computation effort is at least the same as a direct evaluation of the constraint itself. Worse still, this cost does not exist in other validation methods such as [Ling87, Nico82] since the deletion of any supplier can never falsify the constraint.

The second draw back of [Hsu85] is that it cannot simplify constraint which has more than one existential-quantifier such as $\exists x_{\in D_1} \exists y_{\in D_2} W(x,y)$ because of the combination problem.

Such inferiority of heavy overhead is also found in [Paig84]. His method maintains several different concrete views and reference counts. It transforms the constraint into set operations which involve those auxiliary informations. For example, the constraint "There is a red part" is translated into "Given a concrete view, *View*1, of parts which are red, the size of *View*1 is always greater than or equal to one.". Though this method is beneficial in some cases, however, the number of intermediate concrete views that have to be maintained is quite enormous. For example, in order to validate constraint $\exists x\ W_1(x) \wedge \cdots \wedge W_n(x)$ where $W_i(x)$ is a well-formed formula, it is required to maintain n intermediate concrete views. Similar to [Hsu85], unnecessary evaluation of constraint is needed even when the update will not violate the constraint. As mentioned in [Qian87], blindly applying this method can lead to more costly operations.

The failure of all these previous methods lies in the fact that a complete summarization of the current database is required. This requirement imposes a very heavy overhead on maintenance. Even for those database updates which cannot falsify a given constraint, the maintenance is still unavoidable. Hence, we are motivated to investigate the situation where we do not need to keep the complete summarization. In contrast, we only remember the last instance when the constraint is evaluated to be valid. Due to this incompleteness of knowledge, our method will not always reduce the effort in validating $\exists$-constraints. However, as shown in the later section, we can greatly reduce the average cost incurred in the validation process.

2.0 MOST RECENT UNIFICATION

In this section, we will establish our method. We begin with a lemma on which our method is based and then state the complete algorithm which improves any existing integrity constraint checking method for $\exists$-constraints. We then present examples of how our method can be used to improve [Nico82] in constraints checking.

Lemma 1 Let $W(c_1, \ldots, c_n)$ be a well-formed formula which is not necessary quantifier free and $c_1, \ldots, c_n$ be constants. If $W(c_1, \ldots, c_n)$ is satisfiable in the current database, then so is $\exists x_1 \cdots \exists x_n\ W(x_1, \ldots, x_n)$ where x_i are distinct variables which do not appear in $W(c_1, \ldots, c_n)$. Furthermore, if $W(c_1, \ldots, c_n)$ remains consistent after a transaction *TR*, so does $\exists x_1 \cdots \exists x_n\ W(x_1, \ldots, x_n)$. □

The following is our algorithm which improves an integrity checking method *M* for a $\exists$-constraint *IC*.

Algorithm 1 Given an integrity checking method *M* and a constraint *IC* of the form of $IC_1 \vee \cdots \vee IC_N$ where N is a positive integer and each IC_i is in the form $\exists x_{i,1} \cdots \exists x_{i,n}\ W_i(x_{i,1}, \ldots, x_{i,n})$. The well-formed formula $W_i(x_{i,1}, \ldots, x_{i,n})$ is not necessarily quantifier-free. Let $\sigma = \{x_{K,1}/c_1, \ldots, x_{K,n}/c_n\}$ be a substitution (of constants for variables) and K be an integer such that $IC_K\sigma$ is satisfiable in the current database *DB* and *TR* be a transaction. We validate *IC* against *TR* by the following steps.

1. Treat $IC_K\sigma$ as a constraint. Use method *M* to find out if $IC_K\sigma$ remains satisfiable after *TR*. In this process, *M* can make use of the assumption that $IC_K\sigma$ is satisfiable prior *TR* to perform optimization.
2. If $IC_K\sigma$ remains satisfiable after *TR*, then no checking is required. Exit the algorithm.
3. Otherwise, use *M* to find out if *IC* remains satisfiable after *TR*. If there is a substitution $\sigma' = \{x_{K',1}/c'_1, \ldots, x_{K',n}/c'_n\}$ and an integer K' such that $IC_{K'}\sigma'$ is satisfiable in the database after *TR*, replace σ by σ' and K by K'. We conclude that the constraint is valid.

4. If such σ' and K' do not exist, then the constraint is violated. Abort the transaction and the values of σ and K remain unchanged. □

Note that the σ' obtained after the evaluation of IC will be used as the input σ for the subsequence calls of the algorithm until IC is re-evaluated again in step 3. We shall call the value of σ as the **most recent unification.**

Example 2.1 We will show an example how Algorithm 1 can improve [Nico82] to handle $\exists$-constraint more efficiently. Consider the constraint IC "There is a red or blue part which is supplied by every NY supplier", it can be expressed in well-formed formula in prenex conjunctive normal form as,

$$\exists p\#\exists c\forall s\#\exists qty\left[p(p\#,c)\wedge(c=\text{RED}\vee c=\text{BLUE})\wedge(\neg s(s\#,\text{NY})\vee sp(s\#,p\#,qty))\right]$$

which can be rewritten as $IC_1 \vee IC_2$, where IC_1 is

$$\exists p\#\forall s\#\exists q\left[p(p\#,\text{RED})\wedge(\neg s(s\#,\text{NY})\vee sp(s\#,p\#,q))\right]$$

and IC_2 is

$$\exists p\#\forall s\#\exists q\left[p(p\#,\text{BLUE})\wedge(\neg s(s\#,\text{NY})\vee sp(s\#,p\#,q))\right]$$

Assume the most recent unification σ is $\{p\#/\text{P1}\}$ and K is 1, i.e., the following formula, $IC_1\sigma$, is true in the current database,

$$\forall s\#\exists q\left[p(\text{P1},\text{RED})\wedge(\neg s(s\#,\text{NY})\vee sp(s\#,\text{P1},q))\right]$$

Now we will consider three different updates and show how our method can be incorporated with [Nico82] to make constraint validation more efficient.

Update 1 : delete the red part P2 and all the dependent tuples which reference P2 in relation sp. (Cascade deletion)

According to Algorithm 1, we will first apply [Nico82] to find out if $IC_1\sigma$ remains satisfiable after the deletion. Since there is no positive predicate in $IC_1\sigma$ which can unify with either $p(\text{P2},\text{RED})$ or any of the deleting sp tuples $sp(s_i,\text{P2},q_i)$, [Nico82] concludes without any database access that $IC_1\sigma$ remains satisfiable after the transaction. By Algorithm 1, no checking is required. Note that without making use of $IC_1\sigma$, direct application of [Nico82] requires the evaluation of the entire constraint.

Update 2 : insertion of a new supplier $s(\text{S1},\text{NY})$.

According to Algorithm 1, we will first apply [Nico82] to test for $IC_1\sigma$. There is only one negated occurrence $s(s\#,\text{NY})$ in $IC_1\sigma$ which can unify with $s(\text{S1},\text{NY})$, [Nico82] will simplify the formula $IC_1\sigma$ to be

$$\exists q\ [\ p(\text{P1},\text{RED})\wedge sp(\text{S1},\text{P1},q)\ ]$$

Therefore, if the new supplier S1 supplies part P1, then the constraint is still valid. No further checking is required. On the other hand, if the new supplier S1 does not supply part P1 in the updated database, then Algorithm 1 requires us to find another red or blue part which is supplied by all NY suppliers. In this case, no saving is achieved. Take note that without using most recent unification, we need full checking for all times.

Update 3 : cascade deletion of part P1.

Clearly $IC_1\sigma$ will be evaluated to be false because $p(\text{P1},\text{RED})$ no longer exists in the current database. By Algorithm 1, we will need to find another red or blue part which is supplied by all NY suppliers. In this case, we have incur an extra cost of evaluating $IC_1\sigma$ than direct checking.

In the previous example, it does not clear that our method can greatly improve the performance because definite saving can only be found in the first update example. However, consider the cascade deletion of any part p, as long as $p \neq \text{P1}$, no database access is required for the validation process, as shown in the first update example. The only case where no saving is achieved is when $p = \text{P1}$. Hence, if the database contains a large number of parts, then for almost every cascade deletion of a part, the constraint can be validated without any database access. Note that without using our method, every deletion of a part incurs a heavy direct checking cost. In the next section, we will give a more formal presentation on how much our method can improve the performance of integrity constraint checking by reducing database accesses.

The most recent unification technique can be applied not only to the Nicolas's method but to other general integrity constraint methods for relational databases as well. For example, [Hsu85] expresses integrity constraint in tuple calculus. Hence variables which are quantified by $\exists$ quantifier are tuples variables instead of domain variables. We can easily incorporate our method with [Hus85] by remembering the tuples' instance instead of just set of constants which satisfies a given constraint.

Example 2.2 "There is a red part which is supplied by every NY supplier." is expressed in tuple calculus as,

$$\exists_{t_1 \in p} \forall_{t_2 \in s} \left[\left[(t_1.color = \text{RED}) \wedge (t_2.loc = \text{NY}) \right] \rightarrow \left[\exists_{t_3 \in sp} ((t_1.pno = t_3.pno) \wedge (t_2.sno = t_3.sno)) \right] \right]$$

Our method will remember the last tuple instance, say, $\{t_1/p(\text{P1},\text{RED})\}$, which satisfies the constraint.

3.0 PERFORMANCE ANALYSIS

As mentioned in the previous section, our method does not guarantee that the cost of every validation is reduced. It will, however, improve the overall performance of a constraint checking system. In this section, we will first show that the extra storage cost incurred in our method is insignificant. We will then compare our performance with [Nico82] by looking at four different cases of updates, and for each cases, we will show how much our method improves [Nico82].

The storage overhead of our method involves only the storage of variables which are $\exists$ quantified but not governed by any $\forall$ quantifier. They are few and fixed for every constraint. Hence, the storage overhead is almost negligible.

To estimate the expected improvement of the performance in terms of database access, we define the improvement factor η as *the ratio of database access cost incurred without using the most recent unification over that using the most recent unification.* When $\eta = 1$, it represents in terms of database accesses, our method is as good as the convention method. If $\eta > 1$, then our method will require less database accesses. For example, when $\eta = 5$, our method will have a five-fold improvement and only requires 1/5 of the tuple accesses required by the conventional method. If $\eta < 1$, then our method is worse. In the following, we will therefore investigate under which situation will η become less than unity.

Let $cost1$ be the cost to validate IC in terms of database accesses, and $cost2$ be the cost to verify $IC_K\sigma$. Let p be the probability that $IC_K\sigma$ is falsified after a given transaction, and $q = 1-p$. With probability p, both IC and $IC_K\sigma$ need to be evaluated and both $cost1$ and $cost2$ are incurred. Otherwise, with probability q, $IC_K\sigma$ is not violated, we do not need to evaluate IC and only $cost2$ is incurred. In this way, the improvement factor η can be written as,

$$\eta = \frac{cost1}{p \times (cost1 + cost2) + q \times cost2}$$

or, after simplification,

$$\eta = \frac{cost1}{p \times cost1 + cost2}$$

To simplify the analysis, we assume N in Algorithm 1 is one, and we shall drop the K subscript in the expression $IC_K\sigma$. For those constraints with N greater than one, it is easily seen that $cost2$ remains the same while $cost1$ increases. Hence, the improvement factor will become even larger if $N > 1$, i.e., IC is a disjunction of more than one independent constraints.

Now assume a given constraint is expressed in prenex conjunctive normal form [Nico82] and is of the form

$$\exists x_1 \cdots \exists x_m \forall y_1 \cdots \forall y_n \left[r_1(x_{11}, \ldots, x_{1m_1}) \wedge \cdots \wedge r_M(x_{M1}, \ldots, x_{Mm_M}) \wedge (\neg s_1(y_{11}, \ldots, y_{1n_1}) \vee \cdots \vee \neg s_N(y_{N1}, \ldots, y_{Nn_N}) \vee W) \right]$$

where W is a well-formed formula which is not necessarily quantifier-free. $r_1, \ldots, r_M, s_1, \ldots, s_N$ are relational and/or evaluable predicates. Each x_{ij}, which are not necessary distincted, is either one of the x_k or a constant. But for each x_k, there are i and j such that x_{ij} is x_k. Similarly for each y_{ij}. M is a positive integer, and N is a non-negative integer.

We will analyse the value of η for the following four different types of transactions.

Case 1 : When transactions cannot falsify the constraint.

If a transaction contains only insertions which unify only with some predicates $r_i(x_{i1}, \ldots, x_{im_i})$, or deletions which unify only with some of the $s_j(y_{j1}, \ldots, y_{jn_j})$, then [Nico82] concludes that those updates cannot falsify the constraint. It is easily shown that [Nico82] can arrive the same conclusion if the method is to check $IC\sigma$ instead of IC. In this case, with or without most recent unification, both conclude that no checking is necessary without any database access. Thus, the improvement factor η in this case is 1.

Case 2 : $\exists$-updates.

Given a transaction of insertions or deletions which can unify only some predicates $r_i(x_{i1}, \ldots, x_{im_i})$, but not any predicate $s_j(y_{j1}, \ldots, y_{jn_j})$, nor any predicate of W in IC, since $IC\sigma$ is in the form of

$$\forall y_1 \cdots \forall y_n \left[r_1(c_{11}, \ldots, c_{1m_1}) \wedge \cdots \wedge r_M(c_{M,1}, \ldots, c_{M,m_M}) \wedge (\neg s_1(y_{11}, \ldots, y_{1n_1}) \vee \cdots \vee \neg s_N(y_{N1}, \ldots, y_{Nn_N}) \vee W)\sigma \right]$$

where c_{ij} are constants. If none of the tuple $r_i(c_{i1}, \ldots, c_{im_i})$ is deleted, then [Bry88, Ling87, Llyod87, Nico82] conclude that $IC\sigma$ remains satisfied after the transaction. Otherwise, we need to evaluate the original constraint. As $IC\sigma$ will be falsified if and only if some of the tuples $r_i(c_{i1}, \ldots, c_{im_i})$ are deleted, we can decide the satisfibility of $IC\sigma$ without any database access. Hence $cost2$ is virtually zero. In this case,

$$\eta = \frac{cost1}{p \times cost1 + 0} = \frac{1}{p}$$

In other words, η is always greater than one and improvement is always possible. We can further analysis the value of p. Recall that $IC\sigma$ will not be violated if and only if none of the tuple $r_i(c_{i1}, \ldots, c_{im_i})$ is deleted. Now, assume in a given transaction, for each $i = 1, \ldots, M$, there are d_i deletions which unifies with $r_i(c_{i1}, \ldots, c_{im_i})$ in $IC\sigma$. Now if the size of relation r_i is D_i, then $\left(1 - \frac{d_i}{D_i}\right)$ represents the probability that the tuple $r_i(c_{i1}, \ldots, c_{im_i})$ is not deleted by the transaction. The probability that $IC\sigma$ remains satisfiable, q, is estimated to be,

$$q = \prod_{i=1}^{M} \left(1 - \frac{d_i}{D_i}\right) > 1 - \sum_{i=1}^{M} \frac{d_i}{D_i}$$

Hence, $\eta = \frac{1}{p} > \frac{1}{\sum_{i=1}^{M} \frac{d_i}{D_i}}$

Hence, a large improvement is easily achieved for a transaction which updates a small portion of a database for this type of updates. For instance, if we insert 100 red parts, then validation of the constraint given in Example 2.1 against a database with 10,000 parts (M is here equal to 1), can be improved by at least 100 times.

Case 3 : $\exists\forall$-updates.

If a transaction contains both deletions which can unify with some predicates $r_i(x_{i1}, \ldots, x_{im_i})$ and also insertions which can unify with some predicates $s_j(y_{j1}, \ldots, y_{jn_j})$ in IC, but not any other predicate in W, then $cost2$ is no longer zero. However, $cost2$ is still very low as compared to $cost1$. To justify this, we can compare $cost1$ with $cost2$ in the following two aspects:

1. To validate IC, we need to find some values $c_1, \ldots, c_n$ to form the substitution $\tau = \{x_i/c_i\}$ such that the following formula F_1

$$\exists x_1 \cdots \exists x_m \left[r_1(x_{11}, \ldots, x_{1m_1}) \wedge \cdots \wedge r_M(x_{M1}, \ldots, x_{Mm_M})\right]$$

is satisfied. Then we validate $F_2\tau$ where F_2 is

$$\forall y_1 \cdots \forall y_n \left[\neg s_1(y_{11}, \ldots, y_{1n_1}) \vee \cdots \vee \neg s_N(y_{N1}, \ldots, y_{Nn_N}) \vee W\right]$$

to find out if IC is satisfiable. If it fails, then another set of $c_1, \ldots, c_n$ is searched until either F_2 is satisfied or we cannot find any other set $\{c_i\}$ to satisfy F_1. However, validating $IC\sigma$ requires only the validation of $F_2\sigma$ and it is done once instead of trying each possible τ one after another. Now assume N_{search} is the expected number of the sets $\{c_i\}$ to be found out during the validation process of IC, it is easily seen that $\frac{cost1}{cost2}$ will at least be N_{search}.

2. There is another reduction of $cost2$. As $F_2\sigma$ is a typical $\forall$-constraint which has been successfully simplified by many researches [Hsu85, Ling87, Nico82]. By making use of the assumption that $IC\sigma$ is satisfied prior updates, we only need to check for those inserted tuples to test if they will obey the constraint, hence the saving is that we need not check for every tuple in the entire updated relation but only the inserted tuples. This is not so for IC where some of the y_i is governed by some $\exists$ quantifiers. Hence, assume there are e_i insertions which can unify with some of the s_j, the evaluation of $IC\sigma$ needs only to check for all the e_i inserted tuples while the evaluation of IC needs to check all the tuples unifiable in each s_j union with the inserted tuples. If we assume E_i be the number of tuples in the database which can unify with the predicate s_i, $cost2$ and $cost1$ differs by another factor of

$$\prod_{i=1}^{N}(E_i + e_i) \Big/ \left(\prod_{i=1}^{N}(E_i + e_i) - \prod_{i=1}^{N} E_i\right)$$

which is greater than

$$1 \Big/ \sum_{i=1}^{N} \frac{e_i}{E_i + e_i}$$

Therefore, the relationship between $cost1$ and $cost2$ can be expressed as,

$$\frac{cost2}{cost1} < \frac{1}{N_{search}} \times \sum_{i=1}^{N} \frac{e_i}{E_i + e_i}$$

Recall that η is greater than unity if and only if $q \times cost1 > cost2$. In other word, if

$$q > \frac{1}{N_{search}} \times \sum_{i=1}^{N} \frac{e_i}{E_i + e_i}$$

then $q > \frac{cost2}{cost1}$ and saving can be achieved. In general, q, the probability that $IC\sigma$ is not violated, is not easily quantified. Due to the presence of insertions on relation s_i, $IC\sigma$ is not necessary true even none of the deletions unify with $IC\sigma$. On the other hand, the right hand side of the inequality usually has a small value. Although the value of N_{search} can be as small as one, but in normal case, it is usually a large number. Hence $\frac{1}{N_{search}}$ is expected to be quite small. Furthermore, the second factor $\sum_{i=1}^{N} \frac{e_i}{E_i + e_i}$ diminishes as the database size increases, hence, the larger the size of the database, the more likely that there is an improvement.

Case 4 : ∃∀∃-updates.

If a transaction contains not only updates which unify with some r_i and s_j in IC, but also contains updates which unify with some of the predicates in W, then in such case, as no significant simplification methods currently known can simplify $IC\sigma$ (an ∀∃-constraint with the ∃-domain being updated) as in case 3, the further simplification for ∀-constraints, is no longer valid to reduce $cost2$. However, N_{search} can still reduce $cost2$. In this case, improvement can still be achieved if

$$q > \frac{cost2}{cost1} = \frac{1}{N_{search}}$$

However, as N_{search} does not depend on the size of a transaction, but the probability q decreases as the size of a given transaction increases, hence, for a large enough transaction it may come to a point that

$$q < \frac{1}{N_{search}}$$

and our method may turn out to become more costly. However, as the cost of evaluation $IC\sigma$ is at most as that of evaluating IC, i.e., $cost2 \leq cost1$. Hence, the value of the improvement factor, η, has a worst minimum of ½, but it can be arbitrary large. In another word, the improvement can be arbitrary large, while the unlikely worst case only doubles the effort.

4.0 EXPERIMENT RESULT

The following experiment shows quantitatively how the most recent unification improves integrity checking for ∃-constraints under a well-mixed of different types of transaction. The experimental database contained three relations : supplier, part and supply. The database contained 100 suppliers distributed equally into five locations : London, NewYork, Tokyo, Paris and HongKong. The database had 100 parts of four different colors : red, blue, green and yellow. There were 1,200 tuples simulated in the supply relation. We had two ∃-constraints in this experiment. They are,

IC1 There is a NY supplier who supplies some red parts.
$\exists s\#\exists p\#\exists q\ [s(s\#,\text{NY}) \wedge p(p\#,\text{RED}) \wedge sp(s\#,p\#,q)]$

IC2 There is a HK supplier who supplies all green parts.
$\exists s\#\forall p\#\exists q\ [s(s\#,\text{HK}) \wedge (\neg p(p\#,\text{RED}) \vee sp(s\#,p\#,q))]$

The transactions are classified into following types :

1. Insert a new supplier of randomized location and some corresponding supply tuples, and
2. cascade delete an existing supplier tuple, and
3. insert a new part of randomized color with some corresponding supply tuples, and
4. cascade delete an existing part tuple, and
5. insert/delete/modify a set of supply tuples.

500 such transactions had been simulated. The method M we used is [Nico82]. If [Nico82] cannot simplify certain checkings, we assume that a direct checking is used. The following table summarizes the experiment result,

Transaction Type	Improvement over [Nico82] IC1	IC2
1	1.0	1.0
2	99.3	97.5
3	1.0	23.9
4	101.1	99.8
5	1192.4	49.7
Overall	100.2	28.7

The three occurrences of 1.0 in the table is due to the fact that the specified transaction will not falsify the corresponding constraint. For example, transaction type 1, which inserts tuples into supplier and supply relations, will never falsify IC2 and both methods conclude no checking is needed. The large improvement of transaction type 5 on IC1 agrees with the theoretical estimation as the chance that the corresponding most recent unification being deleted is very little. From the table, it is easily seen that when the most recent unification is incorporated with [Nico82], the overall performance of [Nico82] is much improved. For example, for transaction type 2, we can improve the validation of IC1 by 99.3 times, and IC2 by 97.5 times.

5.0 COMPARISON WITH OTHER EXISTING METHODS

In the previous section, we have shown that in most cases, our method can improve the integrity constraint checking method described in [Nico82]. In this section, we will further compare our method with other existing integrity checking methods which solve ∃-constraints in some other way.

[Hsu85] reduces the database accesses of validating ∃-constraints by remembering every instances of successful unification. While the method sounds promising especially when only the leading ∃-domain is updated, however, the following illustrates why the overall performance of [Hsu85] is not as good as our method.

Firstly, [Hsu85] in general cannot simplify constraints with more than one leading ∃-quantifiers. This implies that [Hsu85] can only apply to some limited types of ∃-constraints. Hence, his method does not provide a general constraint validation system. On the other hand, our method can handle any number of leading ∃-quantifiers.

Secondly, [Hus85] relies on the complete set of values V_D of the domain D which is ∃-quantified but not governed by any ∀ quantifier. However, the maintenance of such set is very costly. Even for some transactions which do not falsify a given ∃-constraint, [Hsu85] requires to find out those instances which are no longer violated the constraint after the update and add them into V_D. In most case it is more costly than the direct validation of the constraint itself. However, methods such as [Bry88, Ling87, Nico82] can easily conclude that no checking is required. For example, for constraint "There is a red part which is supplied by every london supplier", deleting of a london supplier may need to add some new red parts to the set V_{red}. Hence, the overall performance of [Hsu85] is worse than even [Nico82] for such transactions. Our method, however, does not incur such maintenance cost and thus immune from such problem and can perform better than [Hus]'s AND-OR decomposition method.

Similar comment can be applied to [Paig84]. The method maintains other form of complete information which requires update even the given transaction is not going to violate the constraint.

6.0 APPLICATION IN DEDUCTIVE DATABASES

The most recent unification method can also be applied to deductive databases. For example, if we define the predicate "supervise" as the transitive closure of manager-subordinate relation, then the constraint "There is a person who supervises every employee working in the personnel department" can be validated more efficiently by remember the person p who supervises every employee from the personnel department.

Example 6.1 Given a deductive database containing the following relations :

employee (emp-id, department)
manage (supervisor-id, emp-id)

and deductive rules :

(Rule1) $supervise(X,Y) :- manage(X,Y)$
(Rule2) $supervise(X,Y) :- manage(X,Z), supervise(Z,Y)$

The constraint "There is a person who supervises every employee in the personnel department" is expressed as :

$$\exists X\ \forall Y\ [\ supervise(X,Y) \vee \neg emp(Y, personnel)\ ]$$

Our method requires us to remember a value α of the variable X such that it represents the emp-id of a supervisor who supervies all the employees of the personnel department. To validate the constraint after some transactions, we will first evaluate $IC\sigma$, which is expressed as,

$$\forall Y\ [\ supervise(\alpha,Y) \vee \neg emp(Y, personnel)\ ]$$

Methods such as [Asir85, Bry88, Koba87, Lloy87] can be applied to validate $IC\sigma$. If $IC\sigma$ remains valid in the updated database, then the constraint IC is not violated. Otherwise, a complete evaluation is required.

7.0 CONCLUSION

We have presented the basic idea of most recent unification. This idea can be incorporated with other constraint checking methods to improve the average performance of validation of ∃-constraints. We have compared our method with few major existing checking methods and proved that our method has reduced database accesses for checking of ∃-constraints. Contrast to other existing methods, we incur only an insignificant overhead to achieve such saving.

Application of this idea does not only limit to relational databases, we have shown that similar idea can be easily extended for deductive databases. Beside storing the instance of the successful unification, further research can be investigate if similar idea can be used to store the successful path of a SLD-tree during the refutation process. Extension from single instance of most recent unification to multiple instances can be another research direction. There is another type of constraints known as ∀∃-constraint. Currently there is no general simplification method can handle it if the update is performed on the variables which are existentially quantified. For example, constraints such as "Every red parts must be supplied by some NY suppliers" requires full checking if some NY suppliers are deleted. Further research can be done on this area.

REFERENCE

[Asir85] D. Asirelli, M.D. Santis and M.Martelli, "Integrity constraints in logic databases", *Journal in Logic Programming*, Vol 3, 1985, 221-232.

[Bry88] F.Bry, H.Decker and R.Manthey, "A Uniform Approach to Constraint Satisfaction and Constraint Satisfiability in Deductive Databases", *EDBT*, 1988.

[Date86] C.J. Date, *An introduction to database systems, Vol. 1* 4th edition Addison Wesley 1986.

[Hsu85] A. Hsu and T. Imielinski, "Integrity Checking for Multiple updates", *Proceedings of ACM-SIGMOD*, May 1985, 152-168.

[Kowa87] R. Kowalski, F. Sadri, and P. Soper, "Integrity Checking in Deductive Databases", *Proceedings of 13th VLDB 1987*, Brighton, England.

[Lloy87] J.W. Lloyd, E.A. Sonenberg and R.W. Topor, "Integrity Constraint Checking in Stratified Databases", Journal of Logic Programming, Vol 4, No 4, 1987.

[Ling87] T.W. Ling, "Integrity constraint checking in deductive database using Prolog not-predicate", *Data and Knowledge Engineering* Vol 2, 1987, 145-168.

[Nico82] J.M. Nicolas, "Logic for improving integrity checking in relational databases", *Acta Informatica* 18,(3), 1982, 227-253.

[Paig84] R. Paige, "Application of finite differencing to database integrity control and query/transaction optimization", *Advances in database theory*, Vol. 2, ed. H. Gallaire, J.Minker and J.M.Nicolas, Plenum Press, N.Y. 1984, 171-210.

[Qian87] X. Qian and D.R. Smith, "Integrity constraint reformulation for efficient validation", *Proceedings of 13th VLDB Conference*, Brighton, UK, Sept 1987, 417-425.

DEDUCTIVE AND FUZZY DATABASE

ON EXCLUSIVE DISJUNCTIONS IN DEDUCTIVE DATABASE

Dong-Hoon Choi
Department of Computer Science
Dongduck Women's University, Seoul, Korea

Lawrence J. Henschen
Department of Electrical Engineering and Computer Science
Northwestern University, Evanston, Illinois, U.S.A.

Abstract

In modeling the real world, disjunctive information is useful to represent incomplete and uncertain facts. According to the real situation, disjunctions in the information can be interpreted either inclusively or exclusively to capture the natural meaning of the real world. Our attention is paid on the exclusive disjunction which has never been explored in the deductive database (DDB) studies so far.

We observe that the disjunctive clause with exclusive disjunctions is expressed by a set of negative clauses and a disjunctive clause with inclusive disjunctions. The set of negative clauses may derive the provably false facts which should be propagated to get correct answers to a query.

In this paper, we propose a representation of disjunctive information with exclusive disjunctions and a compiled approach to evaluating queries in DDB. Including disjunctive information in the extensional database (EDB) poses a problem that the relational model cannot give us all of the definite answers. We extend the relational model to accommodate two types of disjunctive information and to derive all of the definite answers from the EDB. We also develop a query processing procedure to meet our goal.

1. Introduction

In modeling the real world, disjunctive information is useful to represent incomplete and uncertain facts. Many researchers[CH88, HP88, LS90, Re86, RT88, Sa91, YC88] have studied disjunctive and indefinite information in relational databases and in deductive databases (DDB's). Disjunctive information consists of more than a literal and disjunctions. According to the semantics of the real situation, disjunctions in the information have different interpretations. For example, in *Bloodtype(john, A)* v *Bloodtype(john, O)* only one of the two atoms should be true because nobody can have two bloodtypes simultaneously. On the other hand, in *Bloodtype(john, A)* v *Bloodtype(tom, B)* both of the two atoms may be true simultaneously. Based on this point, we can classify disjunctions into inclusive disjunctions and exclusive disjunctions so as to capture the natural meaning of the real world.

Reiter's compiled approach to processing queries in DDB's [Re78] separates the deduction process from the retrieval process. The deduction process is accomplished during the compile time by applying resolution to the intentional database (IDB) which is a set of the deductive laws. During the query time, the relational system retrieves extensional database (EDB) which consists of the ground clauses (or facts). Including disjunctive information in the EDB poses a problem that the relational model cannot give us all of the definite answers. Thus, this approach is incomplete for a DDB with disjunctive information.

Our attention is paid on the exclusive disjunction which has never been explored in the compiled approach to processing queries in the DDB studies so far. A disjunctive clause with exclusive disjunctions is expressed by a set of negative clauses and a disjunctive clause with inclusive disjunctions[RT88]. The set of explicit negative clauses do not allow any pair of atoms in the original disjunctive clause to be true simultaneously. The explicit negative clauses, however, cause some additional efforts to process queries in DDB. Because their ground instances combined with other positive clauses may derive new negative unit ground clauses, that is, provably false facts. And the new negative unit clauses should be propagated to get correct answers to a query.

In this paper, we propose a representation of exclusive disjunction and a compiled approach to evaluating queries in DDB. EDB includes ground disjunctive and definite facts. IDB consists of definite and disjunctive clauses (rules) and does not include recursive clauses. We extend the relational model to accommodate two types of disjunctive clauses. We also develop procedures for propagating the provably false facts and deriving all of the definite answers from the EDB with disjunctive information. We do not need any meta rule such as the generalized closed world assumption [Mi82] and the disjunctive database rule [RT88] because we do not deal with inferring negative information here.

In sections 2 and 3, we introduce disjunctive information with exclusive disjunctions and describe the problems due to the exclusive disjunctions. The extended relational model is proposed to store and manipulate them in section 4. In section 5, we develop a query processing procedure to derive definite answers from disjunctive information to make our approach complete.

2. Representing Exclusive Disjunctions in DDB's

In this section, we present how a clause with exclusive disjunctions is expressed by a set of negative clauses and a clause with inclusive disjunctions. We first define the clausal form of DDB's and new terminologies to make it easy to explain the representation.

Definition A clause is of the form A_1 v...vA_m v -B_1 v ... v -B_n where A_i's and -B_j's are positive and negative literal, respectively. A_i's and B_j's arguments are universally quantified variables or constants. A clause in which arguments are constants is ground.
If m=1, the clause is definite i.e. Horn clause.
If m=0 and n > 0, the clause is negative.
If m>1, the clause is disjunctive, i.e. non-Horn.

A DDB consists of intentional database (IDB) and extensional database (EDB) where IDB is a set of deductive laws and EDB is a set of ground clauses. A DDB is non-Horn if it contains at least one non-Horn clause. We do not consider any recursive clause in DDB.

A disjunctive clause can be classified into two ways according to the number of positive literal in the clause. To make our discussion simple, we introduce new terms, IN-D, EX-D and NEG-SET. A clause is IN-D if its disjunctions are interpreted as inclusive one. That is, more than one positive literal in the clause may be true simultaneously. A clause is EX-D if only one positive literal is true. NEG-SET is a set of negative clauses which represent that any pair of positive literal in an EX-D clause cannot be true simultaneously.

We denote v as an inclusive disjunction and v' as an exclusive disjunction for a moment. The connective v is the same as the inclusive OR. v', however, is not the same as the exclusive OR. Although the exclusive OR becomes true when the odd number of literal is true, the connective v' becomes true for an expression with only one true literal.

Lemma 1 P_1 v' P_2 v'...v' P_n is expressed by P_1 v P_2 v...v P_n and a NEG-SET of -P_i v -P_j where i and j are in [1, m] and n > 1.
proof) To express v' by v, any combination of P_1 ... P_n should not be true simultaneously. -P_i v -P_j represents P_i and P_j cannot be true simultaneously. All the other negative clauses composed of more than three literal are subsumed by the negative clauses composed of two literal.

example 1) P v' Q v' R = (P v Q v R) & (-P v -Q) & (-P v -R) & (-Q v -R).
Because -P v -Q v -R is subsumed by -P v -Q, -P v -R and -Q v -R. NEG-SET is { -P v -Q, -P v -R, -Q v -R } and IN-D clause is P v Q v R.

From lemma 1 we can define IN-D and EX-D.

Definition A clause P_1 v...v P_m v -B_1 v...v -B_n is IN-D if P_1 v... v P_m v -B_1 v...v -B_n is in a DDB but -P_i v -P_j is not in the DDB where i and j are in [1,m], i not= j and n > 1. A clause is EX-D if P_1 v...v P_m v -B_1 v...v -B_n is in the DDB and for all i and j -P_i v -P_j is in the DDB.

Since every EX-D can be expressed by an IN-D and NEG-SET, the actual formulas in our DDB will have IN-D clauses and NEG-SET.

3. Problems in Manipulating EX-D and IN-D clauses in DDB's

An exclusive disjunction poses some problems for updating clauses in the EDB and evaluating queries according to the deductive laws in the IDB because it requires to consider NEG-SET. In this section, we describe the problems introduced by the NEG-SET. We will solve them in section 4.

A. New Provably False Facts From EX-D Clauses

If a clause subsumes an EX-D clause, new negative unit clauses may be derived from the EX-D clause. The derived negative unit clauses, provably false facts, may be resolved further with other clauses in the DDB. In other words, further resolution or processing may be required to get correct answers to some query.

example 2) D = { p v q, -p v -q, q v r, -q v -r, s v t, -s v -t}. If p is inserted, then
D' = { p, p v q, -p v -q, q v r, -q v -r, s v t, -s v -t}. D' is further resolvable.
Thus, D' = {p, -q, r, s v t, -s v -t }. We can observe that -q is derived and thereby r is true in D' while r is in disjunctive clause in D.

Lemma 2 C= P_1 v' P_2 v'...v' P_k v' P_{k+1} v'...v' P_n and D= P_{k+1} v'...v' P_n produce -P_1, -P_2,...,-P_k. That is, if we know that exactly one of P_1,..., P_n is true and we also know that exactly one of P_{k+1}, ..., P_n is true, then all of P_1,..., P_k must be false.
proof) From lemma 1 we get P_1 v P_2 v....v P_k, P_{k+1} v ...v P_n and NEG-SET { -P_1 v -P_2, -P_1 v -P_3,..., -P_1 v -P_n, -P_2 v -P_3,..., -P_2 v -P_n,..., -P_{n-1} v -P_n }. Resolving P_{k+1} v P_{k+2} v ...v P_n with NEG-SET, we get -P_1, -P_2, -P_3,... and -P_k.

In Horn DB, the negative clauses are categorized into integrity constraints which are checked in update time because they do not have an effect on query processing[Re78]. In non-Horn DB, however, they derive new negative facts which should be propagated to get correct answers. Thus, they would be handled as a part of DB in our approach.

The lemma 2 is the basis of a procedure for propagating provably false facts. Although subsumption occurs in both EDB and IDB, we do not deal with subsumption in IDB. We denote a provably false fact derived from EDB as EPF. Propagation of EPF's is explained in section 4.

B. Incompleteness of Reiter's Compiled Approach in DDB's with Disjunctive Information

The compiled approach which has been introduced in [Re78] separates deduction of IDB and retrieval of EDB. However, it cannot be applied to a DDB with disjunctive information because it can lead to incorrect answers to some queries.

example 3) D = {P(x) v -A(x) v -B(x), P(x) v -C(x), A(a) v C(a), B(a) v C(a)} and a query P(a).
Accessing EDB gives {P(a) v C(a), P(a) v B(a), P(a) v A(a)} where P(a) is in disjunctive information. However, resolving P(a) v C(a) and P(a) v - C(a) leads to P(a). Thus, P is true.

From the viewpoint of the theorem proving, accessing the EDB may be regarded as only one time positive hyperresolution [CL73] in which the nucleus is a compiled

IDB clause and the electrons are EDB clauses. It prohibits further resolution of a compiled IDB clause and ancestry resolvents. This problem can be remedied by further resolution [CH88] after accessing EDB or by compiling disjunctive clauses with IDB during the compile time[HP88]. In section 5, we will give an efficient procedure to derive all of the definite answers.

4. Extended Relational Model with IN-D and EX-D clauses

Extended relational models to support IN-D clauses in EDB have been studied in [Ki88], [Re86], [YC88] and [LS90]. Their models do not concern EX-D clauses and propagation of EPF. And they commonly fail to notice the possibility that a definite clause can be derived from a set of IDB clauses and EDB disjunctive clauses.

Since any EX-D clause is replaced by an IN-D and NEG-SET by lemma 1, actual EDB includes only IN-D clauses and NEG-SET. In this section, we define an extended relational model to store and manipulate IN-D clauses and NEG-SET and to propagate EPF's during union and projection. To retrieve the proper answers to a query, the extended model maintains the additional information on IN-D and EX-D clauses that may contribute to deriving a definite clause. The semantics of the extended model is based on the fixpoint model discussed in [RT88].

Definition Extended Relation Scheme
An extended relation scheme R_E is (A_1, ... , A_n, t-type, trigger) where A_j is an attribute for j = 1, ... , n. The t-type represents a type of a tuple. The trigger is the special attribute which will be defined below.

A tuple of an extended relation r_E over R_E is an element of $D(A_1)$ X ... X $D(A_n)$ X D(t-type) X D(trigger). $D(A_j)$ is a domain of the attribute A_j. D(t-type), a domain of the tuple type, is {0, 1} in which 0 denotes a definite tuple and 1 denotes a disjunctive tuple. A tuple in an extended relation represents a literal of a clause. A definite clause is stored as a tuple whose type is definite. An IN-D (or EX-D) clause, however, occupies several tuples whose types are all disjunctive. Because an IN-D clause consists of a disjunction of several literal.

To check definiteness of a tuple which is explained in section 3, we should maintain definite and disjunctive clauses which are used to produce the tuple. For this purpose, we define new terms, PI-SET and trigger.

Definition Positive IN-D Clause Set (PI-SET)
PI-SET is a set of positive IN-D clauses in the EDB. Each PI-SET element has the form $relation_1$(tuple) v.... v $relation_k$(tuple) where $relation_i$(tuple) is a literal of the IN-D clause. During the extended relational operations, the PI-SET is searched to find out which tuples are disjunctive with some tuples.

Definition Trigger
Trigger of a disjunctive tuple is the numbers of PI-SET elements and the $relation_i$(tuple) where $relation_i$(tuple) is a definite clause. The trigger is a set of clauses which produce the disjunctive tuple during the extended relational operations. A definite tuple has no trigger.

A ground IN-D clause is stored in PI-SET and extended relations with a t-type and trigger.

example 4) A(a,b) v' A(a,c) B(i,j) v B(j,c) A(c,d) B(c,b)

A

A1	A2	t-type	trigger
a	b	1	PI-SET(1)
a	c	1	PI-SET(1)
c	d	0	

B

B1	B2	t-type	trigger
i	j	1	PI-SET(2)
j	c	1	PI-SET(2)
c	b	0	

PI-SET = { 1. A(a,b) v A(a,c), 2. B(i,j) v B(j,c) }
NEG-SET = { -A(a,b) v -A(a,c) }

A. Propagation of EPF
EPF is produced during union and projection. Forming the union of two extended relations means adding them, deleting the tuples in duplicate or subsumed clauses and propagating EPF. The EPF's are derived from NEG-SET and EX-D clauses (see lemma 2). Let's see a motivating example.

example 5)
S = { a, b v c, c v e, -b v -c }
T = { a v d, b }.
S U T = { a, a v d, b, -c, -b v -c }.

S

A1	t-type	trigger
a	0	
b	1	PI-SET(1)
c	1	PI-SET(1,2)
e	1	PI-SET(2)

T

A1	t-type	trigger
a	1	PI-SET(3)
b	0	
d	1	PI-SET(3)

PI-SET = { 1. S(b) v S(c), 2. S(c) v S(e), 3. T(a) v T(d) }
NEG-SET = { -S(b) v -S(c) }

ST

A1	t-type	trigger
a	0	
e	0	
b	0	
d	1	PI-SET(1)

Since b v c is subsumed by b and is EX-D clause, -c is derivable from { b, -b v -c }. -c is propagated to produce e.

Projecting out the unnecessary attributes may produce a clause subsuming another EX-D clause. Here is an example for projection.

example 6) A = {(a,b,c) v (a,c,c), (a,d,c) v (b,d,e), (b,d,e) v (a,f,g), -(a,d,c) v -(b,d,e) }

A	A1	A2	A3	t-type
	a	b	c	1
	a	c	c	1
	a	d	c	1
	b	d	e	1
	a	f	g	1

$\Pi_{1,3}$ (A) = { (a,c) } whose tuples are definite. The projection on the clause (a,b,c)v(a,c,c) results (a,c) which is definite. From -(a,c)v -(b,e) and (a,c), -(b,e) is provable. -(b,e) should be propagated to produce (a,g) from (a,g)v(b,e). PI-SET and trigger are abbreviated.

From lemma 2, we can devise a procedure to propagate EPF.

```
procedure PROPAGATE(PFLIST, DONE)
/* PFLIST is a list of EPF which should be propagated */
/* DONE is a list of EPF which have already been propagated
*/
    while (PFLIST is not empty) do
        get a tuple, ln, from PFLIST
        find a set, PS, of clauses including ln as a literal
        for each clause e in PS
            delete e from PI-SET
            if (e-ln) is not definite clause, insert (e-ln)
                into PI-SET
            call MAKE_EPF (e-ln)
            /* (e-ln) may derive new provably false facts */
        end
        delete ln from PFLIST
        insert ln into DONE
    end
end PROPAGATE
```

```
procedure MAKE_EPF(d)
    find a set, S, of EX-D clauses subsumed by d
    for each clause f in S
        delete the tuples in (f-d) from extended relation
        /* tuples in (f-d) are those which are in f but not in d */
        if the tuples are not in DONE, put them into PFLIST
        delete f from PI-SET
    end
end MAKE_EPF
```

B. Extended Operations

Definition Union

S U T = { t | t is a tuple in S or T.
If a clause e in S (or T) is subsumed by a clause d in T (or S), the types of tuples in (e - d) are disjunctive.
Otherwise, the types of tuples are inherited from S or T. }

```
procedure UNION (S, T) /* union of S and T */
    add two extended relation S and T
        /* call the result UST */
    delete duplicate tuples from UST
    for subsuming clause d in UST
        call MAKE_EPF(d)
    end
    clear DONE
    call PROPAGATE (PFLIST, DONE)
end UNION
```

Definition Cartesian product

S x T = { st | S and T are extended relations of arity k1 and k2, respectively.
st is a (k1 + k2)-tuple where first k1 components form a tuple in S and whose last k2 components form a tuple in T.
If s and t have triggers, append them.
If both s and t are definite, type of st is definite. }

The procedure for Cartesian product is obvious.

example 7) S = {(a,1), (b,1) v (c,1)} T = { (1,t), (1,r) v (1,s)}

S

A1	A2	t-type	trigger
a	1	0	
b	1	1	PI-SET(1)
c	1	1	PI-SET(1)

T

A2	A3	t-type	trigger
1	t	0	
1	r	1	PI-SET(2)
1	s	1	PI-SET(2)

PI-SET = { 1. S(b,1) v S(c,1), 2. T(1,r) v T(1,s)}
NEG-SET = { T(1,r) v T(1,s) }

ST

A1	A2	A2	A3	t-type	trigger
a	1	1	t	0	
a	1	1	r	1	PI-SET(1),S(a,1)
a	1	1	s	1	PI-SET(1),S(a,1)
b	1	1	t	1	PI-SET(2),T(1,t)
c	1	1	t	1	PI-SET(2),T(1,t)
b	1	1	r	1	PI-SET(1),PI-SET(2)
b	1	1	s	1	PI-SET(1),PI-SET(2)
c	1	1	r	1	PI-SET(1),PI-SET(2)
c	1	1	s	1	PI-SET(1),PI-SET(2)

PI-SET =
{1.ST(a,1,1,r) v ST(a,1,1,s),
2.ST(b,1,1,t) v ST(c,1,1,t),
3.ST(b,1,1,r) v ST(b,1,1,s) v ST(c,1,1,r) v ST(c,1,1,s) }

Definition Projection

$\Pi_{i_1,i_2,\ldots,i_m}(S)$ = { t | t is an m-tuple $a_1a_2...a_m$ such that there is some k-tuple $b_1b_2...b_k$ in S, $a_j = b_{i_j}$ for j = 1,2,...,m and -t is not derivable. If t already has triggers, append them. }.

```
procedure PROJECTION (S, n1, n2,..., nk)
    project out the columns of n1,..., nk from S
    eliminate duplicate tuples
    for each subsuming clause d
        call MAKE_EPF(d)
        clear DONE
        call PROPAGATE (PFLIST, DONE)
        /* propagate provably false facts */
    end
end PROJECTION
```

Definition Selection

$\sigma_F(S)$ = { t | t satisfies F. If t already has triggers, append them. }

example 8)

A

A1	A2	A3	t-type	trigger
b	c	d	1	PI-SET(1)
b	d	e	1	PI-SET(1)
c	f	g	1	PI-SET(2)
c	d	g	1	PI-SET(2)
c	e	h	1	PI-SET(2)

PI-SET = { 1.A(b,c,d) v A(b,d,e),
2.A(c,f,g) v A(c,d,g) v A(c,e,h) }
NEG-SET = { A(b,c,d) v A(b,d,e) }
$\sigma_{A2='d'}$(A) = { A(b,d,e, 1, PI-SET(1)), A(c,d,g, 1, PI-SET(2)) }.

The procedure SELECTION is obvious.

Definition Join.

$R \bowtie S = \Pi_{i1,i2,\ldots,im}\, S_{R.A=S.A}\,(R \times S)$.

During the EDB access, the extended relational operators generate disjunctive tuples resulting from those types of tuples in the base relations. Their triggers represent the EDB clauses which derive those tuples through the extended relational algebra.

example 9)

D is { 1. Q(x,z) v -A(x,y) v -B(y,z),
2. Q(x,z) v -C(x,y) v -F(y,z),
3. Q(x,y) v -D(x,y),
4. Q(x,y) v -G(x,y),
5. A(a,b) v C(a,b) v D(a,c),
6. B(b,c) v G(a,c),
7. F(b,c),
8. B(c,d) v D(c,d) },

and the query is Q(a,c)?

A

A1	A2	t-type
a	b	1

B

B1	B2	t-type
b	c	1
c	d	1

C

C1	C2	t-type
a	b	1

D

D1	D2	t-type
a	c	1
c	d	1

F

F1	F2	t-type
b	c	0

G

G1	G2	t-type
a	c	1

PI-SET = {5. A(a,b) v C(a,b) v D(a,c), 6. B(b,c) v G(a,c),
8. B(c,d) v D(c,d) }

$A \bowtie B$:

A1	A2	B3	t-type	trigger
a	b	c	1	PI-SET(5,6)

$C \bowtie F$:

C1	C2	F2	t-type	trigger
a	b	c	1	PI-SET(5),F(b,c)

From D:

D1	D2	t-type	trigger
a	c	1	PI-SET(5)

From G :

G1	G2	t-type	trigger
a	c	1	PI-SET(6)

Unioning the results from the above four IDB clauses gives the following answer:

Q(a, c, 1, (PI-SET(5, 6), F(b,c)))

To prove the correctness of the extended relational operations, fixpoint semantics is introduced. While different kinds [RT88, MR87] of fixpoint semantics can be defined for a database with disjunctive clauses, we adopt the definition of fixpoint from [RT88].

Definition Fixpoint Operator T_D [RT88]

$T_D(I)$ = { A in B_D | A v K v -A1 v -A2 v ... v -An is a ground instance of a clause in D and { A1,..., An } in I }. I is a Herbrand interpretation, B_D is a Herbrand base of a database D and K is a positive clause.

Definition Least Fixpoint of T_D : $T_D \uparrow w$. [L184]

$T_D \uparrow w = T_D(T_D \uparrow (w-1)) = \ldots = T_D(T_D(\ldots(T_D \uparrow (0))\ldots))$.

$T_D \uparrow (0) = \phi$ and $w = B_D$.

example 10) D = { P(a), P(b) v P(c), P(d) v -P(a) v -P(c), P(e) v -P(f) }

T_D (ϕ) = {P(a), P(b), P(c)} = T1, T_D (T1) = {P(a), P(b), P(c), P(d)} = T2, T_D (T2) = T2 . Thus, T2 is the least fixpoint of T_D.

In example 9, $T_D \uparrow w$ = { A(a,b), C(a,b), D(a,c), B(b,c), G(a,c), F(b,c), B(c,d), D(c,d), Q(a,c), Q(c,d) }. Obviously, the results from accessing the EDB, i.e. Q(a,c) and Q(c,d), are in T_D|w.

Theorem 3 For each compiled IDB clause, accessing the EDB through the extended relational operators produces the tuples in {$T_D \uparrow$ w-EPF} where D is the compiled IDB and the EDB.

proof) Let's consider a compiled IDB clause C: IP1 v IP2 v ...v IPn v -EP1 v -EP2 v...v -EPm where EPi's are the EDB predicates and IPi's are the IDB predicates. Let CI be all possible ground instances of C. Suppose D = CI+EDB. $T_D \uparrow (0) = \phi$. Then, $T_D(\phi)$ = EDB and T_D(EDB) = EDB+NEWATOM where NEWATOM is a set of all the possible ground literal of IPi's such that negative literal of some element in CI is satisfied by the EDB. T_D(EDB+NEWATOM) = EDB+NEWATOM because literal in NEWATOM is all IDB literal and no compiled rule has a negative IDB literal. Thus, $T_D \uparrow$ w = EDB+NEWATOM. We can get NEWATOM by joining EPi's. The extended Cartesian product during the extended join does not produce any new EPF because no clause subsumes EX-D clauses in the same extended relation. New EPF may be derived by the extended projection because new clauses subsuming EX-D clauses may be produced. The EPF's are propagated during the extended projection. Thus, database access through the extended relational model produces the tuples in { $T_D \uparrow$ w - EPF }.

5. Compiled Approach to Query Processing

A. Classification of Answers in DDB's

Let Q denote a query, K be a disjunction of K_1, ..., K_n where K_i's are positive literals. Answers to a query in DDB fall into the following cases;

Definition For an open query Q(c,x) and a tuple A,
1. A is definite answer if D derives Q(c,A).
2. A is disjunctive answer if D derives Q(c,A) v K and D does not derive Q(c,A).

B. Checking Definiteness of Disjunctive Tuple

In this section, we solve the problem described in section 3 to ensure our compiled approach to derive all the definite tuples by using the trigger defined in section 4 instead of further resolution.

Lemma 4 Let IDB(Q) be { Q(x) v -B1(x,y), Q(x) v -B2(x,y), ... , Q(x) v -Bk(x,y) } where Bi is a conjunction of EDB literals and x and y are vectors of variables. Let EDB(Q) be a set of EDB clauses which contain predicates in the Bi's, and let c be a vector of constants. Then IDB(Q) + EDB(Q) derive Q(c) iff B1(c,y) v B2(c,y) v .... v Bk(c,y) is valid in EDB(Q).

proof)
IDB(Q)+EDB(Q) derive Q(c) iff Q(x) v -(B1(x,y) v B2(x,y) v...v Bk(x,y))+EDB(Q) derive Q(c)
iff -(B1(c,y) v ... v Bk(c,y)) + EDB(Q) derive null clause
iff EDB(Q) derive B1(c,y) v ... v Bk(c,y)

We observe that EDB(Q) in lemma 4 can be replaced with the trigger of disjunctive tuples in Q because the trigger represents the clauses which are used to derive them during the extended relational operations. Note that EDB(Q) is not equal to the trigger because accessing the EDB produces definite answers as well as disjunctive answers and definite answers have no trigger.

Lemma 5 compiled IDB(Q)+triggers derives Q(c) iff B1(x,y) v ... v Bk(x,y) is valid for the triggers.
proof) By lemma 4, trivial.

Lemma 5 gives us a procedure DERIVE_DEF to derive definite answers from definite and disjunctive clauses by using trigger. To efficiently check if the trigger satisfies B1(x,y) v...v Bk(x,y), we can use the conjunctive normal form (CNF) of B1(x,y) v...v Bk(x,y) where Bi is a conjunction of the EDB predicates. The CNF is a conjunction of disjunctive clauses. Each of the clauses in the CNF repesents a possible form of disjunctive EDB clauses that will make the CNF valid.

```
procedure DERIVE_DEF (Q(d), trigger)
   find CNF for Q(d)
   for each clause c in trigger
      if c subsumes any of disjunctive clauses in CNF,
            then delete it from CNF
   end
   /* Q(d) is satisfied and definite */
   if CNF is empty,    return 'yes'
          else,    return 'no'
end DERIVE_DEF
```

example 11) D is the same as in the last example 9.

The disjunction of the IDB clauses for Q(a,c) is:

Q(a,c) v - ([A(a,y) & B(y, c)] v [C(a,y) & F(y,c)] v H(a,c) v G(a,c))

The conjunctive normal form(CNF) of the body in the above disjunction is

[A(a,y) v C(a,y) v H(a,c) v G(a,c)] c1
& [A(a,y) v H(a,c) v F(y,c) v G(a,c)] c2
& [B(y,c) v C(a,y) v H(a,c) v G(a,c)] c3
& [B(y,c) v H(a,c) v F(y,c) v G(a,c)] c4

To see whether Q(a, c, 1, (PI-SET(5,6),F(b,c))) is definite, we should check if the trigger satisfies c1, c2, c3 and c4. PI-SET(5) satisfies c1, F(b,c) satisfies c2, PI-SET(6) satisfies c3, and PI-SET(6) and F(b,c) satisfy c4. Thus, Q(a,c) is definite.

Theorem 6 The procedure DERIVE_DEF generates all the definite answers.

proof) The conjunctive normal form (CNF) of B1(d,y) v ... v Bk(d,y) is a set S of clauses which is equivalent to B1(d,y) v ... v Bk(d,y). In order for the set of clauses, trigger, to imply S, it is necessary and sufficient for the trigger to subsume S. From lemma 5, the theorem is proved.

C. Query Evaluation Procedure

The procedure QUERY_EVAL generates definite and disjunctive answers to a given query P(c, X).

```
procedure QUERY_EVAL
   /* query is P(c,X) */
   select a set, SP, of compiled IDB clauses which has
         a positive P literal
   for each clause in SP
   access EDB /* each IDB clause generate a partial view */
   end
   union the results from accessing EDB and call it UV
   /* c' is one of constants for X */
   for each disjunctive tuple P(c, c') in UV
   call DERIVE_DEF(P(c,c'), trigger)
   for clause d in UV subsumed by P
      call MAKE_PF(d)
      clear DONE
   end
   output P
end QUERY_EVAL
```

Theorem 7 QUERY_EVAL correctly answers a given query.

proof) By theorem 3, lemma5 and theorem 6, obvious.

6. Conclusion and Future Research

We proposed an extended relational model to accommodate ground IN-D and EX-D clauses. The extended relational model produces tuples in { $T_D \uparrow w$ - EPF } where EPF is a set of all provably false facts from EDB. A procedure to derive definite clauses from EX-D and IN-D clauses was developed. Query evaluation procedure also was presented to cover EX-D and IN-D clauses which are included in EDB.

Further refinement should be done to get more efficient DERIVE_DEF algorithm for processing queries. Updating disjunctive information introduces *maybe* information which complicates formal extension of relational model. Although we do not consider this kind of information in this paper, it also would be solved later on. The problems caused by subsuming EX-D clauses in IDB would be solved. It can be done by the procedure based on expanding and labeling an AND-OR tree.

References

[CH88] Chi, S. and Henschen, L. J. "A Three-phase Query Processing Technique for Indefinite Databases", Proceedings of Conference on Automated Deduction, 1988.

[CL73] Chang C.-L. and Lee, R. C.-T. *Symbolic Logic and Mechanical Theorem Proving*, Academic Press, N.Y. and London, 1973.

[GM86] Grant, J., and Minker, J. "Answering Queries in Indefinite Database and the Null Value Problem", *Advances in Computing Research* (P. Kanellakis, Ed.), JAI Press, London, 1986, pp.247-267.

[HP88] Henschen, L.J. and Park, H "Compiling GCWA in Indefinite Deductive Databases", *Foundations of Deductive Databases and Logic Programming* (J. Minker, Ed.), Morgan Kaufmann Publishers, Los Altos, CA, 1988, pp395-438.

[Ki88] Kim, H. "A Storage Scheme for Efficient Processing of Queries in Indefinite Deductive Databases", Ph.D thesis, Northwestern University, Evanston, 1988.

[Ll84] Lloyd, J. W. *Foundations of Logic Programming*, Springer-Verlag, Berlin, 1984.

[LS90] Liu, K. and Sunderraman, R. "Indefinite and Maybe Information in Relational Databases", ACM TODS, Vol.15, No.1, March 1990, pp1-39.

[Mi82] Minker, J "On Indefinite Databases and The Closed World Assumption", Proceedings of Conference on Automated Deduction, 1982, pp.292-308.

[MR87] Minker, J. and Rajasekar,A. "Fixpoint Semantics for non-Horn Logic Programs", Technical Report, University of Maryland, 1987.

[Re78] Reiter, R. "Deductive Question-Answering on Relational Databases", *Logic and Data Bases* (H. Gallaire and J. Minker, Eds.), Plenum Press, New York, N.Y., 1978, pp.149-177.

[Re86] Reiter, R. "A Sound and Sometimes Complete Query Evaluation Algorithm for Relational Databases with Null Values", JACM, Vol.33, No.2, April 1986, pp.349-370.

[RT88] Ross, K. and Topor, R. "Inferring Negative Information from Disjunctive Databases", *Journal of Automated Reasoning*, 1988.

[Sa91] Sadri, F "Modeling Uncertainty in Databases", Proceedings of IEEE International Conference on Data Engineering, 1991.

[YC88] Yuan, L. and Chiang, D. "A Sound and Complete Query Evaluation Algorithm for Relational Databases with Null Values", Proceeding of the ACM-SIGMOD International Conference on the Management of Data, Chicago, IL, June 1988, pp. 74-81.

A Fuzzification of the Relational Data Model

Doheon Lee, Myoung Ho Kim, Hyung Lee-Kwang and Yoon-Joon Lee

Dept. of Computer Science,
Korea Advanced Institute of Science and Technology,
373-1, Kuseong-dong, Yuseong-gu,
Taejon, 305-701, South Korea
Tel: +82-42-869-3563
Fax: +82-42-869-3510
E-mail : doheony@dbserver.kaist.ac.kr

Abstract

Expression and processing of vagueness, which has many real world applications, is not handled effectively in the conventional relational model. In this paper we investigate a fuzzy extension to the relational data model and propose three fuzzy relational query languages. Two of them are the *Level-1 Fuzzy Relational Algebra* and *Level-1 Fuzzy Relational Calculus*. They are fundamental query languages and serve as a theoretical framework for the fuzzy relational database. Based on them, the *Fuzzy Selective Relational Algebra* is presented to express fuzzy constants and fuzzy comparators, which are more effective to represent vagueness in user queries. We show that the three proposed query languages have the same expressive powers.

Keywords: fuzzy database, relational algebra, relational calculus, relational data model

1. Introduction

The relational data model proposed by E.F.Codd has been widely used due to its effective data independency and its simple mathematical structure[COD70]. However, the relational data model has several limitations. One of them is lack of dealing with subjective vagueness in user's data retrieval requests. Many efforts to introduce vagueness into the theory of the relational data model have been made in the past. They can be classified into two major categories, i.e. Crisp Data and Fuzzy Query(CDFQ) and Fuzzy Data and Fuzzy Query(FDFQ) categories. In the CDFQ category, queries with fuzzy concepts can be processed for database storing only crisp values[LEE92, ICH86, KAC86, MOT88, WON90]. In the FDFQ category, queries with fuzzy concepts can be processed for database which can store fuzzy values[BUC82A, BUC82B, PRA84, UMA91, ZEM85, ZEM89].

To be accepted by most database users, fuzzy database systems need to have sufficient compatibilities with conventional database systems[MOT90]. Even though the FDFQ approaches can greatly enhance database functionalities, they are too far from conventional database systems yet. On the other hand, the CDFQ approaches are more compatible with conventional database systems. They can also enhance database functionalities significantly.

Among the CDFQ approaches, ARES[ICH86] and VAGUE [MOT88] are worthy of notice. ARES and VAGUE introduced the 'similar-to' comparator into the relational algebra. They can deal with vagueness to some extent but cannot deal with fuzzy concepts such as "big", "about-5", etc. In this paper we propose a fuzzified relational data model to accomodate vagueness using the CDFQ approach.

The remainder of this paper is organized as follows. In section 2, we present the Level-1 Fuzzy Relational Algebra(FRA-1) and Level-1 Fuzzy Relational Calculus(FRC-1). They are fundamental query languages of the proposed model. In section 3, we define the Fuzzy Selective Relational Algebra(FSRA) to express fuzzy constants and fuzzy comparators. It is a query language which is more effective to represent vagueness in user queries. We also show that FRA-1, FRC-1 and FSRA have the same expressve powers. Section 4 analyses various aspects of the proposed model. Finally we give concluding remarks in section 5.

2. The Level-1 Fuzzy Relational Data Model

In this section we define two fundamental query languages in the proposed level-1 fuzzy relational data model. They are Level-1 Fuzzy Relational Algebra(FRA-1) which is a fuzzy extension of the relational algebra, and Level-1 Fuzzy Relational Calculus(FRC-1)

which is a fuzzy extension of the relational calculus. As the relational algebra and the relational calculus are defined on relations, FRA-1 and FRC-1 are defined on level-1 fuzzy relations. A level-1 fuzzy relation is a subset of cartesian product of level-1 fuzzy sets[KLI88].

DEFINITION 1

Suppose that $D_1, D_2, \ldots, D_k$ are domains. Then a *level-1 fuzzy relation* R is defined as

$R = \{ (t, \mu_R(t)) \mid t = \langle x_1, x_2, \ldots, x_k \rangle, 0 < \mu_R(t) \leq 1, x_1 \in D_1, x_2 \in D_2, \ldots, x_k \in D_k \}$,

where $\mu_R(t)$ denotes the degree to which tuple t belongs to the level-1 fuzzy relation R.

For simplicity, we will use the term "fuzzy relation" to refer to *level-1 fuzzy relation* .

2.1. The Level-1 Fuzzy Relational Algebra

The Level-1 Fuzzy Relational Algebra(FRA-1) is a collection of formal operators acting on fuzzy relations and producing fuzzy relations as results. It is an extension of the conventional relational algebra by using the extension principle[KLI88].

DEFINITION 2

The *Level-1 fuzzy relational algebra* has six basic operators i.e. σ, Π, $\cup$, $\cap$, $\times$, $-$. Suppose that there are two fuzzy relations R_1 and R_2 .

(1) Selection : σ

$\sigma_{X \Theta Y}(R_1) = \{ (t, \mu_{\sigma X \Theta Y(R_1)}(t)) \mid X \Theta Y$ with respect to t is true, $\mu_{\sigma X \Theta Y(R_1)}(t) = \mu_{R_1}(t) \}$,

where X is an attribute name, Y is either an attribute name or a crisp constant and Θ is a comparator among $=, \neq, \leq, \geq, >$ and $<$.

(2) Projection : Π

$\Pi_S(R_1) = \{ (t, \mu_{\Pi S(R_1)}(t)) \mid \mu_{R_1}(t') > 0,\ t = \text{sub-list}(t' \mid S),$
$\mu_{\Pi S(R_1)}(t) = \text{MAX}[\mu_{R_1}(t_i)],\ t_i = \text{same-project-set}(t' \mid S) \}$,

where sub-list(t' | S) is a projected tuple of t' with respect to the attribute list S and same-project-set(t' | S) denotes $\{ t^* \mid \text{sub-list}(t^* \mid S) = \text{sub-list}(t' \mid S) \}$

(3) Union : $\cup$

$R_1 \cup R_2 = \{ (t, \mu_{R_1 \cup R_2}(t)) \mid \mu_{R_1 \cup R_2}(t) = \text{MAX}(\mu_{R_1}(t), \mu_{R_2}(t)) \}$

(4) Intersection : $\cap$

$R_1 \cap R_2 = \{ (t, \mu_{R_1 \cap R_2}(t)) \mid \mu_{R_1 \cap R_2}(t) = \text{MIN}(\mu_{R_1}(t), \mu_{R_2}(t)) \}$

(5) Cartesian Product : $\times$

$R_1 \times R_2 = \{ (t, \mu_{R_1 \times R_2}(t)) \mid \mu_{R_1}(t_1) > 0, \mu_{R_2}(t_2) > 0, t = \text{concatenate}(t_1, t_2). \mu_{R_1 \times R_2}(t) = \text{MIN}(\mu_{R_1}(t_1), \mu_{R_2}(t_2)) \}$

Here, if $t_1 = \langle x_1, x_2, \ldots, x_p \rangle$ and $t_2 = \langle y_1, y_2, \ldots, y_q \rangle$, then $\text{concatenate}(t_1, t_2) = \langle x_1, x_2, \ldots, x_p, y_1, y_2, \ldots, y_q \rangle$.

(6) Difference : $-$

$R_1 - R_2 = \{ (t, \mu_{R_1 - R_2}(t)) \mid \mu_{R_1 - R_2}(t) = \text{MIN}(\mu_{R_1}(t), 1 - \mu_{R_2}(t)) \}$

When we restrict the value in μ attribute to be either 0 or 1, it is easy to see that FRA-1 is reduced to the relational algebra. Though we use MIN and MAX operators to represent AND and OR semantics, respectively, they were just for illustrations. Depending on the circumstances, we may use any t-norm, t-conorm operators[KLI88] instead of MIN and MAX. Note that unlikely to the relational algebra, the intersection operator cannot be represented by the combination of the other five operators.

2.2. The Level-1 Fuzzy Relational Calculus

We define Level-1 Fuzzy Relational Calculus(FRC-1) by applying the extension principle to the relational calculus. In fact, formulas in FRC-1 are syntactically equivalent to those in the domain relational calculus. Their interpretations are extended to handle fuzzy truth values.

DEFINITION 3

A *Formula in FRC-1* is either an atomic formula or compound formula.

(1) Atomic formula

- Every literal $p(X_1, X_2, \ldots, X_k)$ is an atomic formula, where p is a fuzzy predicate symbol[KLI88] and $X_1, X_2, \ldots, X_k$ are attribute names.
- Every arithmetic comparison $X \Theta Y$ is an atomic formula, where X is an attribure name, Y is either a constant or an attribute name and Θ is a comparator among $=, \neq, \leq, \geq, >$ and $<$.

(2) Compound formula

Compound formulas are defined recursively. If f_1 and f_2 are formulas and X is an attribute name, the followings are also formulas.

$f_1 \wedge f_2$, $f_1 \vee f_2$, $\sim f_1$, $(\exists X) f_1(X)$, $(\forall X) f_1(X)$.

As in the relational calculus, each formula in FRC-1 represents a fuzzy relation i.e. *interpretation*. To make domain independent interpretations, we adopt the same safety criteria[ULL88] in FRC-1. From now on, we will use the term "FRC-1 formula" to refer to the safe FRC-1 formula because unsafe formula is beyond the scope of this paper.

DEFINITION 4

The followings are *interpretations of FRC-1 formulas*. We use lower-case letters to denote the formulas and upper-case letters to denote the corresponding fuzzy relations. v(f) denotes the (fuzzy) truth value of the formula f.

(1) When the formula f is $p(X_1, X_2, \dots, X_k)$,

$F = \{ (t, \mu_F(t)) \mid t = <X_1, X_2, \dots, X_k>, \mu_F(t) = v(p(X_1, X_2, \dots, X_k)) > 0 \}$.

(2) When the formula f is $X \Theta Y \wedge f_2 (X_1, \dots, X_k)$,

$F = \{ (t, \mu_F(t)) \mid t =$ a list of free variables of f, $\mu_F(t) = v(f) > 0 \}$,

where $v(f) = v(X \Theta Y \wedge f_2) = MIN (v(X \Theta Y), v(f_2))$.

(3) When the formula f is $f_1 \wedge f_2$,

$F = \{ (t, \mu_F(t)) \mid t =$ a list of free variables of f, $\mu_F(t) = v(f) > 0 \}$,

where $v(f) = v(f_1 \wedge f_2) = MIN (v(f_1), v(f_2))$.

(4) When the formula f is $f_1 \vee f_2$,

$F = \{ (t, \mu_F(t)) \mid t =$ a list of free variables of f, $\mu_F(t) = v(f) > 0 \}$,

where $v(f) = v(f_1 \vee f_2) = MAX (v(f_1), v(f_2))$.

(5) When the formula f is $\sim f_1 \wedge f_2$,

$F = \{ (t, \mu_F(t)) \mid t =$ a list of free variables of f, $\mu_F(t) = v(f) > 0 \}$,

where $v(f) = v(\sim f_1 \wedge f_2) = MIN (1 - v(f_1), v(f_2))$.

(6) When the formula f is $(\exists X) f_1(Y_1, \dots, Y_p, X, Z_1, \dots, Z_q)$,

$F = \{ (t, \mu_F(t)) \mid t = < Y_1, \dots, Y_p, Z_1, \dots, Z_q >, \mu_F(t) = v(f) > 0 \}$,

where $v(f) = v((\exists X) f_1(Y_1, \dots, Y_p, X, Z_1, \dots, Z_q))$

$= MAX_X (v(f_1(Y_1, \dots, Y_p, X, Z_1, \dots, Z_q)))$.

(7) When the formula f is $(\forall X) f_1(Y_1, \dots, Y_p, X, Z_1, \dots, Z_q)$,

$F = \{ (t, \mu_F(t)) \mid t = < Y_1, \dots, Y_p, Z_1, \dots, Z_q >, \mu_F(t) = v(f) > 0 \}$,

where $v(f) = v((\forall X) f_1(Y_1, \dots, Y_p, X, Z_1, \dots, Z_q))$

$= MIN_X (v(f_1(Y_1, \dots, Y_p, X, Z_1, \dots, Z_q)))$.

In (2) and (5) of Defintion 4, we ANDed secondary formula f_2 with the original single formula in Definition 3. In any safe formula, such a single formula cannot exist alone. It has to be ANDed with another safe formula. As in FRA-1, when we restrict the truth value of each formula to be either 0 or 1, FRC-1 can be easily shown to be reduced to the relational calculus.

2.3. The Relationship between FRA-1 and FRC-1

We show that the expressive power of FRA-1 and FRC-1 is equivalent to each other. First, we show that the expressive power of FRC-1 is greater than or equal to that of FRA-1.

THEOREM 1

Every query expressible in FRA-1 is expressible in FRC-1.

Proof:

We show by induction that for every expression e of FRA-1 defining a k-ary fuzzy relation, there is a formula $f(X_1, X_2, \dots, X_k)$ of FRC-1 defining the same relation. We use E, E_1 and E_2 to denote the fuzzy relations of FRA-1 expressions e, e_1 and e_2, respectively. We also use F, F_1 and F_2 to denote the fuzzy relations corresponding to the FRC-1 formulas f, f_1 and f_2, respectively.

The basis covers the case where e is a single fuzzy relation R. If we use a fuzzy predicate r to represent a fuzzy relation R in FRC-1 formula, the corresponding formula to e is trivially $r(X_1, X_2, \dots, X_k)$.

For the induction, we consider six cases corresponding to the six basic operators of FRA-1.

Case 1: $e = e_1 \cup e_2$

We show that the FRC-1 formula, $f = f_1 \vee f_2$ represents the same fuzzy relation as E. By defintions,

$E = \{ (t, \mu_E(t)) \mid \mu_E(t) = MAX(\mu_{E_1}(t), \mu_{E_2}(t)) \}$ .... < 1.1 >

$F = \{ (t, \mu_F(t)) \mid \mu_F(t) = v(f) = v(f_1 \vee f_2) \}$

$= \{ (t, \mu_F(t)) \mid \mu_F(t) = MAX(v(f_1(t)), v(f_2(t))) \}$. ... < 1.2 >

By the induction hypothesis, we already know that E_1 and E_2 are the same fuzzy relations as F_1 and F_2, respectively. So,

$\mu_{F_1}(t) = \mu_{E_1}(t)$ and $\mu_{F_2}(t) = \mu_{E_2}(t)$ .... < 1.3 >

Now, by the interpretation of FRC-1,

$\mu_{F_1}(t) = v(f_1(t))$ and $\mu_{F_2}(t) = v(f_2(t))$ .... < 1.4>

From equations <1.1>, <1.2>, <1.3> and <1.4>

$\mu_E(t) = MAX(\mu_{E_1}(t), \mu_{E_2}(t)) = MAX(\mu_{F_1}(t), \mu_{F_2}(t)) = MAX(v(f_1(t)), v(f_2(t))) = \mu_F(t)$.

Thus, E is equal to F.

Case 2: $e = e_1 \cap e_2$

By the similar procedure to Case 1 except substituting $\cup$ and MAX with $\cap$ and MIN, respectively, we can easily show that the formula, $f_1 \wedge f_2$ represents the same fuzzy relation as E.

Case 3: $e = e_1 - e_2$

In the same manner as Case 1, we can easily show that the formula, $f_1 \wedge \sim f_2$ represents the same fuzzy relation as E.

Case 4: $e = e_1 \times e_2$

In the same manner as Case 1, we can easily show that the formula, $f_1(X_1, \dots, X_p) \wedge f_2(Y_1, \dots, Y_p)$ represents the same fuzzy relation as E when $E_1 = \{ (t_1, \mu_{E_1}(t_1)) \mid t_1 = <x_1, \dots, x_p> \}$ and $E_2 = \{ (t_2, \mu_{E_1}(t_2)) \mid t_2 = <y_1, \dots, y_q> \}$.

Case 5: $e = \sigma_{X\Theta Y}(e_1)$

In the same manner as Case 1, we can easily show that the formula, $f_1 \wedge X \Theta Y$ represents the same fuzzy relation as E.

Case 6: $e = \Pi_{X_1, X_2, \dots, X_p}(e_1)$

Suppose that attribute list of E_1 is $(X_1, X_2, \dots, X_p, Z_1, Z_2, \dots, Z_q)$. In the same manner as Case 1, we can easily show that the formula, $f(X_1, X_2, \dots, X_p) = (\exists Z_1)(\exists Z_2)\dots(\exists Z_q)f_1(X_1, X_2, \dots, X_p, Z_1, Z_2, \dots, Z_q)$ represents the same fuzzy relation as E.

Q. E. D.

The next theorem shows that the expressive power of FRA-1 is greater than or equal to that of FRC-1. Then by Theorem 1, we can conclude that FRA-1 and FRC-1 have equivalent expressive powers.

THEOREM 2

Every query expressible in safe FRC-1 is expressible in FRA- 1.

Proof:

We show that for every query f of FRC-1 representing a k-ary fuzzy relation, there is an expression e of FRA-1 defining the same relation by using induction. In addition to the same notational conventions as those in Theorem 1, we use $Z'_1, Z'_2, \dots,$ and Z'_r to denote the same attribute names $Z_1, Z_2, \dots$, and Z_r, respectively.

The basis covers the case where f is an atomic formula $r(X_1, X_2, \dots, X_k)$. If we use fuzzy predicate r to represent the fuzzy relation R in FRC-1 formula, the corresponding FRA-1 expression is trivially $R(X_1, X_2, \dots, X_k)$.

For the induction, we consider six cases corresponding to the six basic connectives and quantifiers of FRC-1.

Case 1 : $f = X \Theta Y \wedge f_1(X_1, \dots, X_p)$ **and** FV **is a list of free variables.**

According to the FV, we can consider three sub-cases. The other possibilities are excluded due to the safety criteria.

If $FV = (X_1, \dots, X_p)$,

We've already prove that the above formula and the expression $e = \sigma_{X\Theta Y}(e_1)$ of FRA-1 represent the same fuzzy relations in Case 5 of Theorem 1.

If $FV = (X_1, \dots, X_p, X)$, Y is a constant α and $\Theta = "="$,

We show that FRA-1 expression, $e = e_1 \times \{ (\alpha, 1.0) \}$ generates the same fuzzy relation as F. By definitions,

$$F = \{ (t, \mu_F(t)) \mid \mu_F(t) = v(f) = v(X = \alpha \wedge f_1) \}$$
$$= \{ (t, \mu_F(t)) \mid \mu_F(t) = MIN(v (X = \alpha), v(f_1)) \}$$
$$= \{ (t, \mu_F(t)) \mid \mu_F(t) = v(f_1) \} \quad \text{......................<2.1>}$$
$$E = \{ (t, \mu_E(t)) \mid \mu_E(t) = \mu_{E_1}(t_1)) \quad \text{....................<2.2>}$$

By the induction hypothesis, we already know that E_1 is the same fuzzy relations as F_1. So,

$$\mu_{F_1}(t_1) = \mu_{E_1}(t_1) \quad \text{..<2.3>}$$

Now, by the interpretation of FRC-1,

$$\mu_{F_1}(t_1) = v(f_1(t_1)) \quad \text{...<2.4>}$$

From equations <2.1>, <2.2>, <2.3>, and <2.4>

$$\mu_E(t) = \mu_{E_1}(t_1) = \mu_{F_1}(t_1) = v(f_1(t_1)) = \mu_F(t).$$

Thus F is equal to E.

If $FV = (X_1, \dots, X_p, X)$, $Y \in \{ X_1, \dots, X_p \}$ and $\Theta = "="$,

By th similar manner, we can easily show that FRA-1 expression, $e = \sigma_{Y'=Y}(e_1 \times \Pi_Y(e_1))$ generates the same fuzzy relation as F.

Case 2 : $f = f_1(X_1, X_2, \dots, X_p, Z_1, Z_2, \dots, Z_r) \wedge f_2 (Y_1, Y_2, \dots, Y_q, Z'_1, Z'_2, \dots, Z'_r)$,

We show that the FRA-1 expression $e = \Pi_{X_1, \dots, X_p, Y_1, \dots, Y_q, Z_1, \dots, Z_r} (\sigma_{Z_1 = Z_1'} (\dots (\sigma_{Z_r = Z_r'}(e_1 \times e_2)) \dots))$, represents the same fuzzy relation as F. By defintions,

$$F = \{ (t, \mu_F(t)) \mid \mu_F(t) = v(f) = v(f_1 \wedge f_2) \}$$
$$= \{ (t, \mu_F(t)) \mid \mu_F(t) = MIN(v(f_1(t)), v(f_2(t))) \}. \quad \text{...<2.5>}$$
$$E = \{ (t, \mu_E(t)) \mid \mu_E(t) = MIN(\mu_{E_1}(t_1), \mu_{E_2}(t_2)) \} \quad \text{......<2.6>}$$

By the induction hypothesis, we already know that E_1 and E_2 are the same fuzzy relations to F_1 and F_2, respectively. So,

$$\mu_{F_1}(t) = \mu_{E_1}(t) \text{ and } \mu_{F_2}(t) = \mu_{E_2}(t) \quad \text{..........<2.7>}$$

And by the interpretation of FRC-1,

$$\mu_{F_1}(t) = v(f_1(t)) \text{ and } \mu_{F_2}(t) = v(f_2(t)) \quad \text{.........<2.8>}$$

From the equations <2.5>, <2.6>, <2.7>, and <2.8>

$$\mu_E(t) = MAX(\mu_{E_1}(t), \mu_{E_2}(t)) = MAX(\mu_{F_1}(t), \mu_{F_2}(t))$$
$$= MAX(v(f_1(t)), v(f_2(t))) = \mu_F(t).$$

Thus F is equal to E.

Case 3 : $f = f_1(X_1, X_2, \dots, X_k) \vee f_2(X_1, X_2, \dots, X_k)$,

We've already prove the above formula and the expression $e_1 \cup e_2$ of FRA-1 represent the same fuzzy relations in the Case 1 of Theorem 1.

Case 4 : $f = \sim f_1(Z_1, Z_2, \dots, Z_r) \wedge f_2 (Y_1, Y_2, \dots, Y_q, Z'_1, Z'_2, \dots, Z'_r)$,

By the induction hypothesis, we already know that E_1 and E_2 are the same fuzzy relations to F_1 and F_2, respectively. We denote $DOM(f_1)$ to refer to the set of all values that appear in the formula f_1 itself and the corresponding fuzzy relation F_1, except the rational numbers for the degrees of memberships[Ul188]. Under the domain independency, the corresponding fuzzy relation to $\sim f_1$ is $DOM(f_1)^r - E_1$. So, this is a special case of the Case 1.

Case 5 : $f = (\exists X) f_1(Y_1, \dots, Y_p, X, Z_1, \dots, Z_q)$,

We have already proved the above formula and the

expression $\Pi_{Y_1, \dots, Y_p, Z_1, \dots, Z_q}(e_1)$ of FRA-1 represent the same fuzzy relation at the Case 3 of Theorem 1.

Case 6 : $f = (\forall X) f_1(Y_1, \dots, Y_p, X, Z_1, \dots, Z_q)$,

It is easy to see that $(\forall X) f_1(Y_1, \dots, Y_p, X, Z_1, \dots, Z_q) = \sim(\exists X) \sim f_1(Y_1, \dots, Y_p, X, Z_1, \dots, Z_q)$. So, this case is already covered in Case 4 and Case 5.

Q. E. D.

COROLLARY 1

FRA-1 and FRC-1 have the same expressive powers

Proof:

From Theorem 1 and Theorem 2, the collorary immediately follows.

Q. E. D.

In the conventional relational model, if a query language can express all of the basic operators of the relational algebra, we call them relationally complete. For the case of the fuzzy relational model, we extend the notion of the relational completeness. We can regard a query language as a *level-1 fuzzy relationally complete* language if it can express all operators of FRA-1.

3. Fuzzy Constructs in Fuzzy Relational Query Languages

FRA-1 and FRC-1 are fundamental query languages of the proposed level-1 fuzzy relational data model. Since they are straightforward extensions to the counterparts in the conventional relational data model, we do not introduce any new syntactic constructs into them.

In order to introduce constructs expressing vagueness, the Fuzzy Selective Relational Algebra(FSRA) has been proposed in [LEE92]. In this section, we briefly describe FSRA and show that its expressive power is equivalent to those of FRA-1 and FRC-1.

3.1. The Fuzzy Seletive Relational Algebra

Because the vagueness in user's data requests are mostly expressed through selection predicates, the selection operator, i.e. σ, plays a major role in fuzzy query formulations. We introduce fuzzy constants and fuzzy comparators into the selection operator to facilitate expression of vagueness.

In contrast to the conventional (crisp) constant, a fuzzy constant is defined as a fuzzy set. Examples of the fuzzy constants are "tall", "small" and "about-5". While conventional comparators are used to represent crisp comparisons, the fuzzy comparators, ≈, !≈, are used to represent similarity-based comparisons.

DEFINITION 5

As in FRA-1, the *Fuzzy Selective Relational Algebra(FSRA)* has six basic operators i.e. σ*, Π, ∪, ∩, ×, −. Only selection operator is further extended to express fuzzy constants and fuzzy comparators. The other operators are all the same as those of FRA-1.

Selection operator of FSRA is defined as

$$\sigma^*_{X \Theta Y}(R),$$

where X is an attribute name , Θ is a comparator among =, ≠, ≤, ≥, >, <, ≈, !≈ and Y is either an attribute name or a constant. Here the constant is either a crisp constant or a fuzzy constant.

By using FSRA, we can express a vague query such as "Find part whose weight is heavy and color is similar to red". "Heavy" and "similar to" are fuzzy terms. Fuzzy constants and fuzzy comparators are used to express those fuzzy terms as follows.

$$\sigma^*_{weight = heavy}(\sigma^*_{color \approx "red"}(PART)),$$

where PART is a fuzzy relation whose tuples are descriptions of parts. Since conventional relations can be considered as fuzzy relations whose tuples belong to the relations at degree 1, FSRA can also be used on conventional databases.

To store semantics of the fuzzy constants and fuzzy comparators, we need special kinds of relations. We call them *semantic relations*, which can be classified into three categories.

	fuzzy constant	fuzzy comparator
continuous domain	(1)	
scattered domain	(2)	(3)

Figure 1. Classification of semantic relations

The classification is based on the domains and structures of the stored informations. Because a relation can hold only discrete data, we need an approximation to store information on continuous domain. But in the case of scattered domain, we do not need such an approximation.

A fuzzy constant is expressed as a fuzzy set(unary fuzzy relation), but a fuzzy comparator is expressed as a binary fuzzy relation. A fuzzy comparison on continuous domain can be substituted by a fuzzy predicate using a fuzzy constant on continuous domain. Let's see an example. The fuzzy comparison such that " X is similar to 5.0" can be substituted by the fuzzy predicate such that " X is about-5.0". So we exclude the case of fuzzy comparators on continuous domains.

We present the schema of each semantic relation.

(1) Fuzzy Constant on Continuous domain

{ (t, μ(t)) , t = < lower-value , upper-value >, 0 < μ(t) ≤ 1 }

where μ(t) denotes the degree to which the values in [lower-value, upper-value] conforms to the fuzzy concept of this semantic relation. An example semantic relation of this type is shown in Figure 2.

Domain of Height = [0, 200]

High	LowerValue	UpperValue	μ
	0	15	0.0
	15	50	0.0
	50	85	0.1
	85	125	0.3
	125	160	0.5
	160	185	0.7
	185	200	1.0

graphical representation

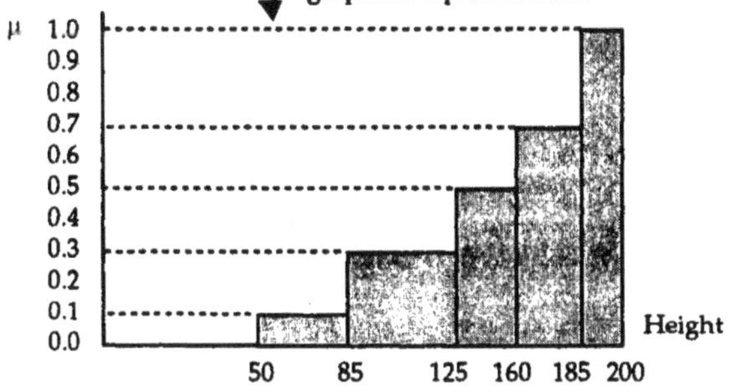

Figure 2. An example of the semantic relation.

(2) Fuzzy Constant on Scattered domain

{ (t, μ(t)) , t = < value >, 0 < μ(t) ≤ 1 }

where μ(t) denotes the degree to which "value" conforms to the fuzzy concept of this semantic relation.

(3) Fuzzy Comparator on Scattered domain

{ (t, μ(t)) , t = < A-value , B-value >, 0 < μ(t) ≤ 1 }

where μ(t) denotes the degree to which "A-value" is similar to "B-value".

3.2. Relationships among FSRA, FRA-1 and FRC-1

We have defined FRA-1, FRC-1 and FSRA. The relationships among those three query languages are shown in Figure 3.

Since we have shown that FRA-1 and FRC-1 have the same expressive powers in Corollary 1, the proof that the expressive power of FSRA is equal to FRA-1 implies that all three query languages have the same expressive powers. Clearly, th expressive power of FSRA is greater than or equal to that of FRA-1 because FSRA is a strict extension of FRA-1. If we show that the expressive power of FRA-1 is greater than or equal to that of FSRA, we can conclude that the two languages have the same expressive powers. Note that FSRA ia a level-1 fuzzy relationally complete language.

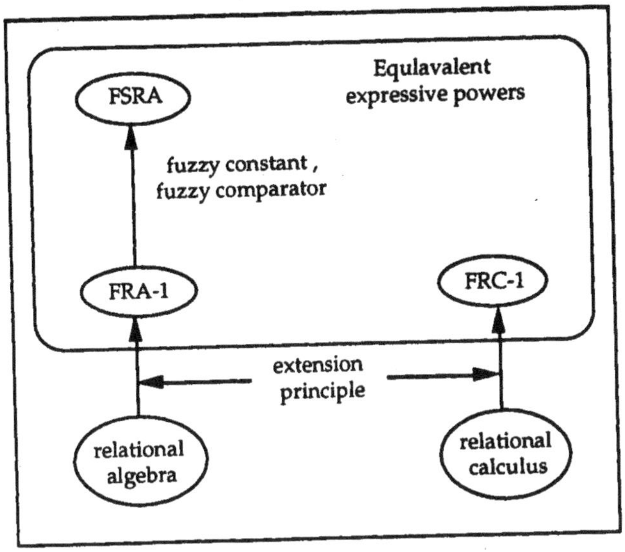

Figure 3. Relationships among FRA-1, FRC-1 and FSRA

THEOREM 3

Every query expressible in FSRA is expressible in FRA-1.

Proof:

We only extend the selection condition of FRA-1 to define FSRA. If we can transform any query in FSRA to that of FRA-1, the proof is completed. The following investigate each case of the extended features.

Case 1: Fuzzy Constant on Continuous Domain

$\sigma_{X_i = fuzzy\_term}(R)$

$= \Pi_{X_1,\dots,X_k}(\sigma_{X_i \geq LowerValue}(\sigma_{X_i < UpperValue}(R \times SR_{fuzzy\_term})))$

$\sigma_{X_i \neq fuzzy\_term}(R)$

$= \Pi_{X_1,\dots,X_k}(\sigma_{X_i \geq LowerValue}(\sigma_{X_i < UpperValue}(R \times \overline{SR}_{fuzzy\_term})))$

where SR_{fuzzy_term} is a semantic relation containing the information of fuzzy term and $\overline{SR}_{fuzzy\_term}$ is the complement of it.

Case 2: Fuzzy Constant on Scattered Domain

$\sigma_{X_i = fuzzy\_term}(R) = \Pi_{X_1,\dots,X_k}(\sigma_{X_i = Value}(R \times SR_{fuzzy\_term}))$

$\sigma_{X_i \neq fuzzy\_term}(R) = \Pi_{X_1,\dots,X_k}(\sigma_{X_i = Value}(R \times \overline{SR}_{fuzzy\_term}))$

where SR_{fuzzy_term} is a semantic relation containing the information of fuzzy term and $\overline{SR}_{fuzzy\_term}$ is the complement of it.

Case 3: Fuzzy Comparator on Continuous Domain

$\sigma_{X = Y}(R) = \Pi_{A_1,\dots,A_k}(\sigma_{A\text{-}Value = X}(\sigma_{B\text{-}Value = Y}(R \times SR_{SIM})))$

$\sigma_{X \neq Y}(R) = \Pi_{A_1,\dots,A_k}(\sigma_{A\text{-}Value = X}(\sigma_{B\text{-}Value = Y}(R \times \overline{SR}_{SIM})))$

where SR_{SIM} is a semantic relation containing the similarity between two values.

COROLLARY 2

FRA-1, FRC-1 and FSRA have the same expressive powers.

Proof:

From Corollary 1 and Theorem 3, the collorary immediately follows. Q.E.D.

4. Analysis of the Level-1 Fuzzy Relational Model

In section 2 and section 3, we have proposed a fuzzy relational model by defining fuzzy relations and fuzzy query languages to accomodate vagueness. This section analyses various aspects of the proposed model and also describes important functional advantages over the conventional relational model.

Effective retrieval for a vague query

Requests for data can be classified into specific requests and vague requests. Vague requests include fuzzy qualifications. While specific requests can be processed effectively in the conventional query systems, vague requests are not. To process vague requests in conventional query systems, users must retry specific queries repeatedly with minor modifications until they match satisfactory data.

As an example, suppose that a user issue a data request such as " Find heavy and long parts" on the database in Figure 5.

PART

No.	Name	Col	Wgt	Hgt	μ
001	nut	red	12.8	160.7	1.0
002	bolt	green	17.2	200.8	1.0
003	screw	blue	17.2	1000.9	1.0
004	screw	red	14.1	1100.9	1.0

Figure 5. An example database

First, the user may formulate a query using the relational algebra such as,

$$\sigma_{Wgt>500}\,(\sigma_{Len>1000}\,(PART)).$$

Because there is no tuple satisfying the above qualification, the result relation is null. Then he may modify the query to relax some constraints as follows.

$$\sigma_{\underline{Wgt>50}}\,(\sigma_{Len>1000}\,(PART))$$

Still, the result relation is null. So he may modify the query again such as,

$$\sigma_{\underline{Wgt>15}}\,(\sigma_{Len>1000}\,(PART))$$

Now, a tuple < 003, screw, blue, 17.2, 1000.9 > is retreived. If he becomes tired due to repeated trials of similar queries, he may be satisfied with this result, which we think is not satisfactory.

On the other hand, the proposed FSRA comes up with a solution effectively. To process queries in FSRA, we need semantic relations. Suppose we have semantic relations having semantics of "heavy" and "long" as in Figure 6.

We can express the afore-mentioned data request by using the FSRA as follows

$$\sigma^*_{Wgt=heavy}\,(\sigma^*_{Len=long}\,(PART))$$

It is transformed to a FRA-1 query as follows. For simplicity, we divide the transformed query into two subqueries.

HEAVY

LowerValue	UpperValue	μ
10	11.5	0.0
11.5	14	0.1
14	16	0.5
16	18.5	0.8
18.5	20	1.0

LONG

LowerValue	UpperValue	μ
100	500	0.0
500	800	0.1
800	1000	0.5
1000	1200	0.8
1200	1300	1.0

Figure 6. Sematic relations "HEAVY" and "LONG"

TEMP

$$= \Pi_{No, Name, Col, Wgt, Len}\,(\sigma_{Len \geq LowVal}\,(\sigma_{Len < UpVal}\,(PART \times LONG)))$$

RESULT

$$= \Pi_{No, Name, Col, Wgt, Len}\,(\sigma_{Wgt \geq LowVal}\,(\sigma_{Wgt < UpVal}\,(TEMP \times HEAVY)))$$

After processing the above queries, we have the result as in Figure 7.

No.	Name	Col	Wgt	Hgt	μ
001	nut	red	12.8	160.7	0.0
002	bolt	green	17.2	200.8	0.0
003	screw	blue	17.2	1000.9	0.8
004	screw	red	14.1	1100.9	0.5

Figure 7. Result of a FSRA query

As shown in Figure 7, we get the degree of query conformity for each tuple at one time. Clearly, FSRA is much more effective and flexible in processing vagueness than the conventional relational queries.

Ranking capability

In the case of a specific query, every tuple in the database either conforms to the query completely or does not conform to the query at all, i.e, query conformity is either 1 or 0. However, in the case of a vague query, the query conformity is a matter of degree. Let's suppose that an employer wants to find young employees in his company. Is an employee of 28 years, Tom fit for the employer's demand? How about the other employee of 30 years, John? Though Tom is better fit for the employer's demand, John is also fit for it to some extent. So we must rank the tuples in the answer according to their query conformities. Because the values in the μ attribute represent the query conformities in the proposed model, ranking the tuples according to the conformities to the given query can be easily achieved.

Compatibility with the conventional relational database

To be accepted by most database users, fuzzy database systems should have sufficient compatibilities with conventional database systems[MOT90]. FRA-1 and FRC-1 are strict extensions to the relational algebra and the relational calculus, respectively. The fuzzy relation is also a strict extension to the conventional relation. Thus, the proposed model is a strict extension to the relational data model and well compatible with the conventional database systems. When we restrict values in μ attributes to be either 0 or 1, the proposed model is reduced to the conventional relational model.

Individual qualifications

As a vague linguistic term may have different meanings to different users, fuzzy query systems must interprete the vague queries with individual qualifications. While one think that 1.000 dollars are big money, the other may think that they are not. Fuzzy query systems must support such kinds of individual differences. In FSRA, the meanings of vague terms, i.e. fuzzy constants and fuzzy comparators, are stored in the forms of semantic relations. As semantic relations are handled in the same manner as data relations, by using normal database operations, users can easiliy adjust semantics by modifying the contents of semantic relations. Because mappings from vague terms to the corresponding semantic relations reflect the individual qualifications, users can easily make the query system interprete the vague terms by using their own semantics.

Measure of expressive powers

There have been many efforts to accomodate vagueness in the relational data model. Some of them can handle a large variety of vagueness while the others concentrated on the specific vagueness. The proposed model provides a notion of *level-1 fuzzy relational completeness*. As in the relational data model, we can regard a query language as a level-1 fuzzy relationally complete language if it can express all operations in FRA-1.

5. Concluding Remarks

In this paper we have proposed a fuzzy relational data model. We have presented two fundamental query languages FRA-1 and FRC-1, and have presented a derived query language FSRA to express fuzzy constants and fuzzy comparators. Fuzzy constants and fuzzy comparators in FSRA are effective constructs to deal with vagueness in data retrieval requests. We have shown that FRA-1, FRC-1 and FSRA have the same expressive powers.

Unlikely to query systems accepting specific qualifications, the proposed fuzzy query systems have efficient ranking capabilities. Because the proposed fundamental query languages are strict extensions to the counterparts of the relational data model, they can be directly applicable to conventional relational databases with only additional semantic relations. In other words, the proposed model is well compatible with the conventional relational database systems. As semantic relations are handled in the same manner as data relations, the proposed model effectively support individual qualifications in query interpretations. We have mentioned the notion of level-1 fuzzy relational completeness, which is a fuzzified version of the conventional one. The notion of level-1 fuzzy relational completeness can be used as a theoretical measure of expressive powers of various fuzzy query languages.

We can extend the level-1 fuzzy relation to level-N fuzzy relation, which is a subset of cartesian product of level-N fuzzy sets[KLI88]. Such extensions need to be investigated to manage more fuzziness in the database.

References

[BUC82A] B. Buckles, E. Petry, "Fuzzy Databases and their Applications", *Fuzzy Information and Decision Processes*, M. Gupta, E. Sanchez, Eds., North-Holland., pp. 361-371, 1982

[BUC82B] B. Buckles, E. Petry, "A Fuzzy Representation of Data for Relational Databases", *Fuzzy Sets and Systems*, Vol. 7, pp.213-226, 1982

[COD70] E.F. Codd, "A Relational Model of Data for Large Shared Data Banks", *Comm. ACM*, Vol. 13, No. 6, pp. 377-387, 1970

[LEE92] D.H. Lee, H. Lee-Kwang, M.H. Kim, "A Study on the Fuzzy Selective Relational Algebra", *Proc. Int'l Conf. on Fuzzy Logic and Neural Network*, , pp. 353-356, 1992

[ICH86] T. Ichikawa, "ARES: A Relational Database with the Capability of Performing Flexible Interpretation of Queries", *IEEE Trans. Software Engineering*, Vol. 12, No. 5, 1986

[KAC86] J.Kacprzyk, A. Ziolkowski, "Database Queries with Fuzzy Linguistic Quantifiers", *IEEE Trans. SMC*, Vol. 16, No. 3, pp. 474-478, 1986

[KLI88] G.J. Klir, T.A. Folger, *Fuzzy Sets, Uncertainty, and Information*, Prentice-Hall International, Inc., pp.260-265, 1988

[MOT90] A. Motro, "Accomodating Imprecision in Database Systems: Issues and Solutions", *Data Engineering*, Vol. 13, No. 4, pp. 29-34, 1990

[MOT88] A. Motro, "VAGUE: A User Interface to Relational Databases that permit vague queries", *ACM Trans. on Office Information Systems*, Vol. 6, No. 3, pp. 187-214, 1988

[PRA84] H.Prade, C. Testemale, "Generalization Database Relational Algebra for the Treatment of Incomplete or Uncertain Information and Vague Queries", *Information Science*, Vol 34, pp. 115-143, 1984

[UMA91] M. Umano, Y. Ezawa, "Implementation of SQL-type Data Manipulation Language for Fuzzy Relational Databases", *IFSA Brussels.*, 1991

[WON90] M.H.Wong, K.S.Leung, "A Fuzzy Database-Query Language", *Information Systems*, Vol. 15, No. 5, pp. 583-590, 1990

[ZEM85] M. Zemankova, A. Kandel, "Implementing Imprecision in Information Systems", *Information Sciences*, Vol. 37, pp. 107-141, 1985

[ZEM89] M. ZemanKova, "FIIS: A Fuzzy Intelligent Information System", *Data Engineering*, Vol. 12, No. 2, pp. 11-20, 1989

Enhancing the Fuzzy Set Model with Positively Compensatory Operators

Joon Ho Lee, Won Yong Kim, Myoung Ho Kim and Yoon Joon Lee

Department of Computer Science
Korea Advanced Institute of Science and Technology
373-1, Kusung-dong, Yusung-gu, Taejon, 305-701, Korea

Abstract

The conventional fuzzy set model uses the MIN and MAX operators for the evaluation of boolean operators AND and OR, respectively. It has been criticized to generate incorrect ranked output in many cases. This is because the MIN and MAX operators do not well correspond with human behavior for document ranking. There are a variety of fuzzy operators to replace the MIN and MAX operators. In this paper we first investigate the behavioral aspects of the fuzzy operators and address important issues to affect retrieval effectiveness. We then present the enhanced fuzzy set model based on positively compensatory operators, which are suitable for achieving high retrieval effectiveness. It is also shown through experiments that the enhanced fuzzy set model provides similar retrieval effectiveness and higher retrieval efficiency in comparison with the extended boolean model.

1. Introduction

The research area called Information Retrieval (IR) was established in the early 1960s to develop computer-aided effective processes of searching and extracting specific information. An major role of IR systems helps determine which documents are most likely to be relevant to the given requirements. IR systems should rank documents in decreasing order of query-document similarity, and present a sequence of documents to users.

Boolean retrieval systems have been most widely used among commercially available IR systems. This is because high performance is achievable and users are able to express their information need conveniently by using a boolean query formulation. In conventional boolean retrieval systems, however, document ranking is not supported and similarity coefficients cannot be computed between queries and documents.

The fuzzy set model based on the MIN and MAX operators has been proposed in the past to support the ranking facility for boolean retrieval systems [Book80, Book81, Buel81a, Buel81b, Rade79, Sach76, Taha76, Wall79]. It uses document term weights reflecting the importance of individual terms to the document. Formally, an IR system based on the fuzzy set model is defined by the quadruple <T, Q, D, F>, where

(1) T is a set of index terms which are used to represent queries and documents.
(2) Q is a set of queries that can be recognized by the system. Each query $q \in Q$ is a legitimate boolean expression composed of index terms and the logical operators AND, OR and NOT.
(3) D is a set of documents. Each document $d \in D$ is represented by $\{(t_1, w_1), ..., (t_n, w_n)\}$ where w_i designates the weight of term t_i in d and w_i may take any value between zero and one, i.e., $0 \le w_i \le 1$.
(4) F is a retrieval function

$$F: D \times Q \rightarrow [0, 1]$$

which assigns to each pair (d, q) a number in the closed interval [0, 1]. This number is a measure of similarity between the document d and the query q, and is called the *document value* for document d with respect to query q.

The retrieval function F(d, q) is defined as follows:

i) For each term t_i in a query, the function F(d, t_i) is defined as the weight of t_i in document d, i.e., w_i.
ii) Logical operators, i.e., AND, OR and NOT are then evaluated by applying the rules given in Figure 1. For boolean queries containing more than one logical operator, the evaluation proceeds recursively from the innermost clause.

Boolean Formulation	Evaluation Formula
F(d, t_1 AND t_2)	MIN (F(d, t_1), F(d, t_2))
F(d, t_1 OR t_2)	MAX (F(d, t_1), F(d, t_2))
F(d, NOT t_1)	1 - F(d, t_1)

Figure 1. Similarity evaluation rules in the conventional fuzzy set model

The fuzzy set model is considered as an extension of the boolean retrieval system because it reduces to the boolean model when document term weights are restricted to zero or one. Though the fuzzy set model is an elegant approach, the MIN and MAX operators have properties adverse to retrieval effectiveness [Book80, Lee92, Robe78]. Since the first introduction of fuzzy set theory [Zade65], a variety of fuzzy operators have been proposed for the intersection (i.e., AND) and union (i.e., OR) of fuzzy sets. These fuzzy operators are classified into three groups such as averaging operators, Triangular norms (T-norms) and Triangular conorms (T-conorms) depending on their operational characteristics [Zimm91]. Since there can be a variety of fuzzy set models using different fuzzy operators, the fuzzy set model using the MIN and MAX operators will be called the conventional fuzzy set model.

In this paper we present that problems of the conventional fuzzy set model cannot be overcome even though any types of T-operators, i.e., T-norms and T-conorms are adopted to evaluate boolean operators. We then propose the enhanced fuzzy set model to use positively compensatory operators which belong to averaging operators. Various operational characteristics of positively compensatory operators are presented which are suitable for achieving high retrieval effectiveness. We also show through experiments that the proposed fuzzy set model provides similar retrieval effectiveness and higher retrieval efficiency in comparison with Salton's extended boolean model [Salt83, Salt85, Salt89].

The remainder of this paper is organized as follows. Section 2 gives classification of fuzzy operators. In section 3 we investigate the effect of various fuzzy operators on retrieval effectiveness by using operator graphs, and propose a new formulation of the fuzzy set model based on positively compensatory operators. In section 4 retrieval effectiveness and efficiency of the proposed fuzzy set model are compared with those of the extended boolean model. Finally concluding remarks are given in section 5.

2. Classification of Fuzzy Operators

The development of fuzzy set theory has allowed researchers to apply set theoretic concepts to sets of objects whose membership values vary in the interval [0, 1]. This applicability has been achieved by defining new operators for classical set theory operators. Often there is more than one fuzzy operator corresponding to a given classical operator, and the different operators have different properties.

After the first introduction of fuzzy set theory [Zade65], a variety of fuzzy operators have been developed for the AND and OR operations. They are classified into three groups such as averaging operators, T-norms and T-conorms [Zimm91], which will be denoted by A, T and T^c, respectively, for simplicity. Figure 2 shows the relationships between the three classes of fuzzy operators. Suppose F(k, S1) is equal to α and F(k, S2) is equal to β for an object k in two fuzzy sets S1 and

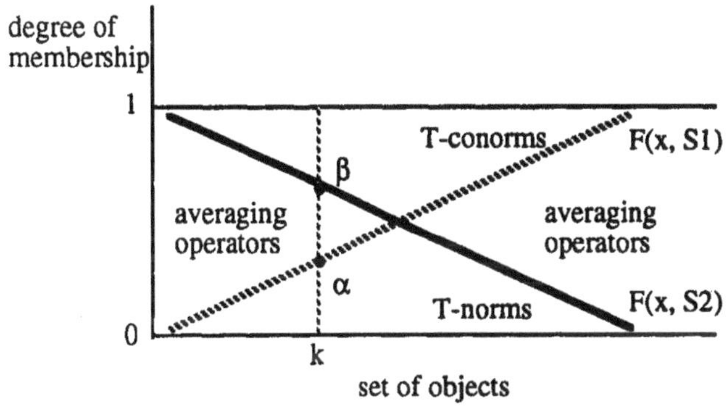

Figure 2. Mapping of averaging operators, T-norms and T-conorms

S2. When aggregating S1 and S2, the following conditions are satisfied.

$$\alpha \leq A\,(F(k, S1), F(k, S2)) \leq \beta$$
$$0 \leq T\,(F(k, S1), F(k, S2)) \leq \alpha$$
$$\beta \leq T^c\,(F(k, S1), F(k, S2)) \leq 1$$

2.1 The T-Operators

The T-operators, namely T-norms and T-conorms originated from the studies of probabilistic metric spaces. Later, it was proposed that T-norms and T-conorms could be used for the AND and OR operations, respectively, in the fuzzy set theory. The MIN operator belongs to T-norms and the MAX operator belongs to T-conorms. Figure 3 shows some T-operators and their operator graphs. (For more T-operators, see [Gupt91].) The operator graph is one way of representing the characteristics of an operator [Lee92]. We use operator graphs to analyze the behavioral properties of fuzzy operators. The operator graph is constructed for the given two operand graphs. The operator and operand graphs are represented by lines and dotted lines, respectively. The vertical coordinate in the graphs denotes the degree of membership. The operator graph is a set of points which are computed by applying the operator to two values from operand graphs.

	T(x, y)	$T^c(x, y)$
1	$x \bullet y$	$x + y - xy$
2	$MAX(x + y - 1, 0)$	$MIN(x + y, 1)$
3	$\dfrac{xy}{x + y - xy}$	$\dfrac{x + y - 2xy}{1 - xy}$
4	$\begin{cases} x & \text{if } y = 1 \\ y & \text{if } x = 1 \\ 0 & \text{otherwise} \end{cases}$	$\begin{cases} x & \text{if } y = 0 \\ y & \text{if } x = 0 \\ 1 & \text{otherwise} \end{cases}$

(a) The T-operators

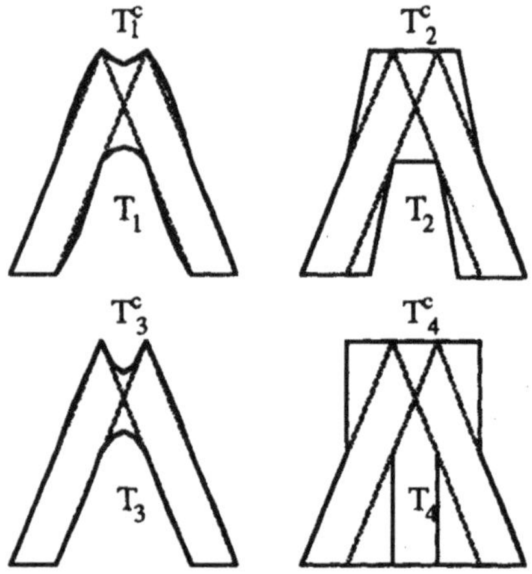

(b) The operator graphs for the T-operators

Figure 3. The T-operators and their operator graphs

2.2 The Averaging Operators

In fuzzy decision theory the "decision" has been viewed as the intersection or the union of fuzzy sets, and T-norms and T-conorms have been used to model human decisions in many cases. However, it has been noted that neither T-norms nor T-conorms are appropriate to model "managerial decisions". Averaging operators have been developed to overcome this problem [Thol79, Wern88, Zimm80, Zimm83]. In averaging operators the resulting value is controlled by a parameter γ. In Figure 4 three general operators, i.e., A_1-A_3 and a pair of operators distinguishing the AND operator, i.e., $A_{4.AND}$ and the OR operator, i.e., $A_{4.OR}$ are shown with the corresponding operator graphs.

(A_1) $\quad (x + y - x \bullet y)^{\gamma}\,(x \bullet y)^{(1-\gamma)}, \quad 0 \leq \gamma \leq 1$

(A_2) $\quad \gamma \bullet MAX(x, y) + (1-\gamma) \bullet MIN(x, y), \quad 0 \leq \gamma \leq 1$

(A_3) $\quad \gamma \bullet (x + y - x \bullet y) + (1-\gamma) \bullet (x \bullet y), \quad 0 \leq \gamma \leq 1$

$(A_{4.AND})$ $\quad \gamma \bullet MIN(x,y) + \dfrac{(1-\gamma)\,(x + y)}{2}, \quad 0 \leq \gamma \leq 1$

$(A_{4.OR})$ $\quad \gamma \bullet MAX(x,y) + \dfrac{(1-\gamma)\,(x + y)}{2}, \quad 0 \leq \gamma \leq 1$

(a) The averaging operators

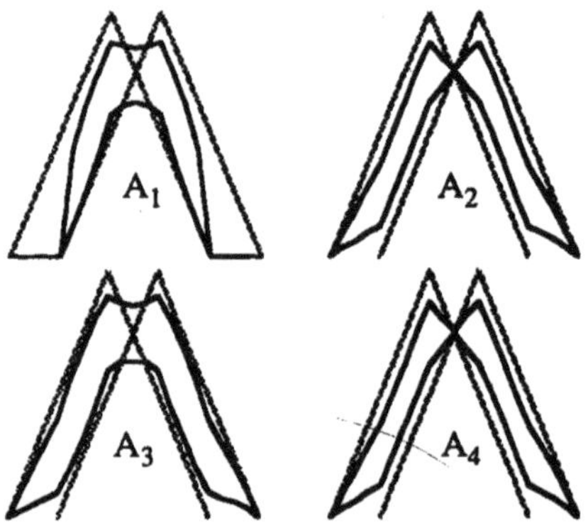

(b) The operator graphs for the averaging operators

Figure 4. The averaging operators and their operator graphs

3. Analyses of Fuzzy Operators for High Retrieval Effectiveness

3.1 Problems of the MIN and MAX Operators

The conventional fuzzy set model has been proposed to support the document ranking facility for boolean retrieval systems which suffer from an inability to rank the retrieved documents. It, however, has been criticized to be inappropriate as a model of IR systems [Book80, Robe78]. This is because the MIN and MAX operators do not well correspond with human behavior for document ranking. The rest of this section illustrates the problems. Although we explain only problems incurred by the AND operator, it should be noted that the use of the OR operator causes similar problems.

Example 1: Suppose that we have two documents d_1 and d_2 shown below. The documents are represented by two pairs of an index term and its weight.

d_1 = { (Thesaurus, 0.40), (Clustering, 0.40) }
d_2 = { (Thesaurus, 0.99), (Clustering, 0.39) }
q_1 = Thesaurus AND Clustering

When the MIN operator is used for the AND operation, the document values of d_1 and d_2 for the query q_1 are evaluated as 0.40 and 0.39, respectively. Hence, d_1 is retrieved with a higher rank than d_2. Most people, however, will obviously decide that d_2 rather than d_1 is more similar to q_1.

Example 2: Suppose that we have two documents d_3 and d_4 and a query q_2 as follows:

$d_3 = \{ (t_1, 0), (t_2, 1), (t_3, 1), \ldots, (t_{100}, 1) \}$
$d_4 = \{ (t_1, 0), (t_2, 0), (t_3, 0), \ldots, (t_{100}, 0) \}$
$q_2 = t_1$ AND t_2 AND ... AND t_{100}

Here, the conventional fuzzy set model using the MIN operator decides that document values of d_3 and d_4 for the query q_2 are the same, i.e., zero. Furthermore, the document value of d_3 is zero even though ninety nine terms of d_3 satisfy the query terms specified in the given query q_2.

The problems of the conventional fuzzy set model described in Example 1 and 2 are due to the fact that the MIN and MAX operators generate the resulting value which depends on only one operand without considering the other. In other words, the problems stem from the single operand dependency of the MIN and MAX operators.

3.2 Problems in T-Operators

The T-operators except for the MIN and MAX operators have the common properties as follows [Zimm91]: First, when the value of one operand is zero or one, the resulting value is equal to one of two operands. Second, they allow some compensation between the values of two operands in other cases, and the resulting value is less than the lower value or greater than the higher value. The aforementioned operational properties can be easily understood from Figure 3-(b).

Using other types of T-operators in the fuzzy set model can alleviate the problem given in Example 1 due to the second common property, i.e., compensatory effect, while the first common property still causes the same problem shown in Example 2. For example, when the product operator, i.e., $T_1(x, y)$ is used instead of the MIN operator in Example 1, the document values of d_1 and d_2 for the query q_1 are evaluated as 0.16 and 0.39 respectively, and hence d_2 is retrieved with a higher rank than d_1. A document value, however, is less than the lower value of two operand values or greater than the higher value. Since this property causes document values to depend heavily on the number of query terms, it can result in the additional problem illustrated in the next example.

Example 3: Suppose a document d_5 and two queries q_1 and q_3 are given as follows:

d_5 = {(Thesaurus,0.70),(Clustering,0.70),(System,0.70)}
q_1 = Thesaurus AND Clustering
q_3 = System

Using other types of T-operators except for the MIN and MAX operators will decide that d_5 is more similar to q_3 than q_1. For instance, if the product operator, i.e., T_1 is applied, the document value of d_5 is 0.49 for q_1 and 0.70 for q_2. Note that the similarity between q_1 and d_5 is less than that between q_3 and d_5, which clearly does not agree with most people's decision.

We have described that the T-operators do not well model human behavior for document ranking. We close this section with the following summarized statements. First, it is not desirable that document values depend on a single operand. This *single operand dependency* problem has been described in Example 1 and 2. Second, the compensated value, which is less than the lower value or greater than the higher value, has a negative effect on retrieval effectiveness. This *negative compensation* problem has been described in Example 3.

3.3 The Enhanced Fuzzy Set Model

Four averaging operators have been described in section 2.2. In this section we investigate the behavioral properties of the averaging operators, and propose the enhanced fuzzy set model based on averaging operators A_2 and A_4. We first indicate that the averaging operators A_2 and A_4 are mathematically equivalent though they are independently developed by different researchers at different time. The distinction of the AND and OR operators separates the averaging operator A_2 into two parts as follows:

$$(A_{2.AND}) \quad \gamma \bullet MAX(x, y) + (1-\gamma) \bullet MIN(x, y), \quad 0 \le \gamma \le 0.5$$

$$(A_{2.OR}) \quad \gamma \bullet MAX(x, y) + (1-\gamma) \bullet MIN(x, y), \quad 0.5 \le \gamma \le 1$$

In order to coincide the value range of the parameter of $A_{2.AND}$ with that of the parameter of $A_{2.OR}$, we change the operator $A_{2.AND}$ to a different form having the same value. By replacing γ with $1-\gamma$, we obtain the following expression.

$$(A_{2.AND}) \quad \gamma \bullet MIN(x, y) + (1-\gamma) \bullet MAX(x, y), \quad 0.5 \le \gamma \le 1$$

Then we can transform $A_{2.AND}$ and $A_{2.OR}$ into $A_{4.AND}$ and $A_{4.OR}$, respectively, by replacing γ with $(\gamma+1)/2$. In the remainder of this paper, we consider only the A_4 operator.

From Figure 4-(b) we can easily see that A_1 and A_3 allow negative compensation in some value ranges and A_1 always gives zero regardless of the other operand when one of operands is zero. Hence, the fuzzy set model based on A_1 does not avoid the single operand dependency and negative compensation problems, and the fuzzy set model based on A_3 causes the negative compensation problem.

The operator graph of $A_{4.AND}$ and $A_{4.OR}$ shows that the resulting value is always greater than the lower value of two operand values and less than the higher value with the exception that the values of both operands are equivalent. The operators having the aforementioned properties will be called *positively compensatory* operators because their compensatory effects overcome the problems described in Example 1, 2 and 3.

Consequently, we propose to use the positively compensatory operators as evaluation formulas of the fuzzy set model. This new formulation of the fuzzy set model can overcome all the problems described in Example 1, 2 and 3. The proposed fuzzy set model also provides higher retrieval effectiveness, which is shown in the next section.

4. Performance Evaluation

The Extended Boolean Model (EBM) has been proposed to overcome the problems of the conventional fuzzy set model, and shown to be an effective IR model in the literature [Salt83, Salt85, Salt89]. It represents a unifying retrieval model in which the conventional fuzzy set model and the vector space model are special cases. The query-document similarity in the extended boolean model is based on L_p vector norm computations, and is controlled by a parameter p, $1 \le p \le \infty$, providing a special interpretation for the boolean operators.

In the extended boolean model, the similarity between a query and a document is calculated by the two-step procedure as in the fuzzy set model. The only difference between the two retrieval models is similarity evaluation formulas computing query-document similarity. The formulas are defined as:

$$(E_{AND}) \quad F(d, t_1 \text{ AND } t_2) = 1 - \left[\frac{(1-F(d, t_1))^p + (1-F(d, t_2))^p}{2} \right]^{1/p}$$

$$(E_{OR}) \quad F(d, t_1 \text{ OR } t_2) = \left[\frac{F(d, t_1)^p + F(d, t_2)^p}{2} \right]^{1/p}$$

We have proposed the enhanced fuzzy set model based on the A_4 operator, which will be denoted by FSM_{A4}. In the remainder of this section we evaluate and compare retrieval effectiveness and efficiency of FSM_{A4} and EBM.

4.1 Experimental Collections

We use two different document collections covering items in library science and computer science [Salt83]. The library science items, designated as ISI 1460, cover highly cited items extracted from the Social Science Citation Index. The CACM 3204 collection covers articles published between 1959 and 1979 in the Communications of the ACM. Queries were formulated first in natural language for each of these collections, and later in boolean form by graduate students and staff of Cornell University. The ISI collection consists of 1460 documents and 35 queries. The CACM collection consists of 3204 documents and 52 queries, and we used only the 50 queries which do not request documents by particular authors. Both collections also contain relevance assessment of each document with respect to each query.

The fuzzy set model and the extended boolean model exploit document term weights to rank documents. The ISI and CACM collections do not have specific information about the actual importance of the terms. In this case, the weights of document terms can be derived from their occurrence frequency such as Inverse Document Frequency (IDF) and Term Frequency (TF) [Salt89]. If N is the number of documents in a collection and n_k is the number of documents in which term k occurs, then the inverse document frequency of term k, IDF_k, is defined as $\log N / n_k$. The term frequency TF_{ik} means the frequency of occurrence of term k in document i. The weight w_{ik} of term k in document i can be defined as $IDF_k \bullet TF_{ik}$. Since document term weights in the fuzzy set model and the extended boolean model must be in the interval [0, 1], the weight w_{ik} is normalized as follows:

$$\text{normalized } w_{ik} = \frac{TF_{ik}}{\text{maximum TF in document i}} \bullet \frac{IDF_k}{\text{maximum IDF in document i}}$$

4.2 Experimental Results

To evaluate the effectiveness of an IR system, it is customary to compute values of the recall and precision defined as

$$\text{Recall} = \frac{\text{Number of relevant items retrieved}}{\text{Total number of relevant items in collection}}$$

$$\text{Precision} = \frac{\text{Number of relevant items retrieved}}{\text{Total number of items retrieved}}$$

In general, users want to retrieve most everything relevant and to reject most everything extraneous - to get high recall and high precision.

The fuzzy set model and the extended boolean model rank documents in decreasing order of query-document similarity, that is, the most important items are obtained first. The ranked output then makes it possible to compute a recall and a precision value after the retrieval of each item. By interpolation the precision values can be calculated for fixed values of the recall, e.g., 0.1, 0.2 and so on up to 1.0.

Figure 5-(a) and -(b) shows retrieval effectiveness of FSM_{A4} and EBM for the experimental collections ISI and CACM, respectively. The horizontal coordinate denotes the value range of the associated parameter, and the vertical coordinate denotes the precision. A single precision value, which represents the average precision at three typical recall levels (0.25, 0.50, 0.75), was calculated for each parameter value. Figure 5 shows that retrieval effectiveness of FSM_{A4} almost coincides with that of EBM.

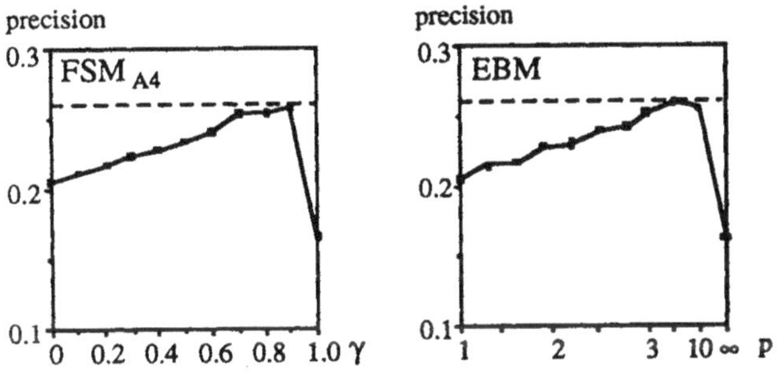

(a) The CACM 3204 collection

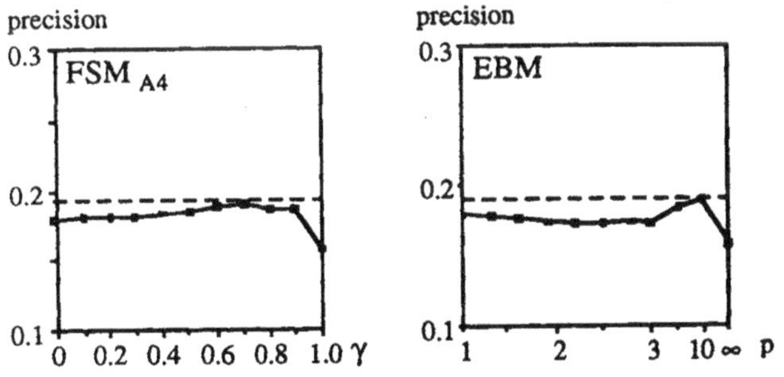

(b) The ISI 1460 collection

Figure 5. Retrieval effectiveness of the FSM_{A4} and EBM

To compare retrieval efficiency of FSM_{A4} and EBM, we measured computation time spent in evaluating "t_1 AND t_2"

and "t_1 OR t_2" 10,000 times. It took 0.04 and 1.54 seconds for FSM_{A4} and EBM, respectively. FSM_{A4} is much more efficient than EBM. It was indicated in the original proposal of the extended boolean model that the complexity of the E_{AND} and E_{OR} operators is a serious problem. In particular, recursive application of these operators produces complicated expressions for boolean queries with a large number of boolean operators. FSM_{A4} overcomes the computational inefficiency problem successfully.

5. Concluding Remarks

IR systems should be designed to aid users in determining which documents of those retrieved are most likely to be relevant to the given queries. Boolean retrieval systems have been most widely used among commercially available IR systems. Although conventional boolean retrieval systems accomplish efficient document retrievals, they suffer from an inability to rank the retrieved documents. The fuzzy set model and the extended boolean model, which are logical extensions of the conventional boolean model, have been proposed in the past to provide the document ranking facility.

It has been argued that the conventional fuzzy set model based on the MIN and MAX operators is not appropriate as a model for IR systems. This is because the MIN and MAX operators have properties adverse to effective document ranking. In recent years a variety of fuzzy operators have been developed which are classified into T-operators and averaging operators. We have presented the behavioral characteristics of the operators. We have shown that the problems of the conventional fuzzy set model are not overcome with any types of T-operators. We have then proposed the enhanced fuzzy set model based on positively compensatory operators, which are suitable for achieving high retrieval effectiveness and efficiency. The behavior of the enhanced fuzzy set model has been compared with that of the extended boolean model through experiments. The enhanced fuzzy set model provides similar retrieval effectiveness and higher retrieval efficiency.

References

[Book 80] A. Bookstein, "Fuzzy Requests: An Approach to Weighted Boolean Searches," Journal of the American Society for Information Science, Vol. 31, No. 4, pp. 240-247, 1980.

[Book 81] A. Bookstein, "A Comparison of Two Weighting Schemes for Boolean Retrieval," Journal of the American Society for Information Science, Vol. 32, No. 4, pp. 275-279, 1981.

[Buel 81a] D.A. Buell, "A General Model of Query Processing in Information Retrieval System," Information Processing & Management, Vol. 17, No. 5, pp. 249-262, 1981.

[Buel 81b] D.A. Buell and D.H. Kraft, "Threshold Values and Boolean Retrieval System," Information Processing and Management, Vol. 17, No. 3, pp. 127-136, 1981.

[Gupt 91] M.M. Gupta and J. Oi, "Theory of T-Norms and Fuzzy Inference Methods," Fuzzy Sets and Systems, Vol. 40, No. 3, pp. 431-450, 1991.

[Lee 92] J.H. Lee, M.H. Kim and Y.J. Lee, "Enhancing the Fuzzy Set Model for High Quality Document Rankings," Proceedings of the 19th Euromicro Conference, Paris, France, 337-344, 1992.

[Rade 79] T. Radecki, "Fuzzy Set Theoretical Approach to Document Retrieval," Information Processing & Management, Vol. 15, No. 5, pp. 247-259, 1979.

[Robe 78] S.E. Robertson, "On the Nature of Fuzz: A Diatribe," Journal of the American Society for Information Science, Vol. 29, No. 6, pp. 304-307, 1978.

[Sach 76] W.M. Sachs, "An Approach to Associative Retrieval through the Theory of Fuzzy Sets," Journal of the American Society for Information Science, Vol. 27, pp. 85-87, 1976.

[Salt 83] G. Salton, E.A. Fox, and H. Wu, "Extended Boolean Information Retrieval," Communications of the ACM, Vol. 26, No. 11, pp. 1022-1036, 1983.

[Salt 85] G. Salton, E.A. Fox, and E. Voorhees, "Advanced Feedback Methods in Information Retrieval," Journal of the American Society for Information Science, Vol. 36, No. 3, pp. 200-210, 1985.

[Salt 89] G. Salton, "Automatic Text Processing: The Transformation, Analysis, and Retrieval of Information by Computer," Addison Wesley, 1989.

[Taha 76] V. Tahani, "A Fuzzy Model of Document Retrieval Systems," Information Processing & Management, Vol. 12, No. 3, pp. 177-188, 1976.

[Thol 79] U. Thole, H.J. Zimmermann, and P. Zysno, "On the Suitability of Minimum and Product Operators for the Intersection of Fuzzy Sets," Fuzzy Sets and Systems, Vol. 2, No. 2, pp. 167-180, 1979.

[Wall 79] W.G. Waller and D.H. Kraft, "A Mathematical Model of a Weighted Boolean Retrieval System," Information Processing & Management, Vol. 15, pp. 235-245, 1979.

[Wern 88] B. Werners, "Aggregation Models in Mathematical Programming," in Mathematical Models for Decision Support, G. Mitra ed., pp. 295-319, 1988.

[Zade 65] L.A. Zadeh, "Fuzzy Sets," Information and Control, Vol. 8, pp. 338-353, 1965.

[Zimm 80] H.J. Zimmermann and P. Zysno, "Latent Connectives in Human Decision Making," Fuzzy Sets and Systems, Vol. 4, No. 1, pp. 37-51, 1980.

[Zimm 83] H.J. Zimmermann and P. Zysno, "Decisions and Evaluations by Hierarchical Aggregation of Information," Fuzzy Sets and Systems, Vol. 10, No. 3, pp. 243-260, 1983.

[Zimm 91] H.J. Zimmermann, "Fuzzy Set Theory and Its Applications," 2nd ed., Kluwer Academic Publishers, 1991.

CONCURRENCY CONTROL AND IO SCHEDULINGS

A PESSIMISTIC CONCURRENCY CONTROL ALGORITHM IN MULTIDATABASE SYSTEMS

Hyunyoon Yun and Buhyun Hwang

Department of Computer Science
Chonnam National University
300, Yongbong-dong, Bukgu
Kwangju 500-757, Republic of Korea
Fax; +82-62-520-6800

ABSTRACT

Global serializability and local autonomy are important issues in the multidatabase system (MDBS). This paper proposes the transaction processing model for an MDBS and a new concurrency control algorithm, called **Pessimistic Timestamp Method** (PTM), to ensure the global serializability of global transactions in the presence of local transactions. In PTM, global transactions are scheduled so that any execution of operations of the scheduled global transactions does not cause the violation of global serializability and a global deadlock. So, PTM dose not abort global transactions being executed due to the violation of global serializability or the occurrence of global deadlock, except for transaction failures and site failures. Also, PTM dose not confine local concurrency control (LCC) algorithms used at each LDBS.

Keywords : *multidatabase, global serializability, local autonomy*

1. INTRODUCTION

A multidatabase system (MDBS) is a distributed database system in which a number of different local database systems (LDBSs) are interconnected to facilitate the accesses of data across local database systems.[12)] The local database management systems (LDBMSs) may differ in data model, data definition and manipulation languages, transaction management policies, and internal data structures.[10)] The MDBS architecture allows local transactions and global transactions to coexist. To create the illusion of logical database integration without requiring physical database integration, the MDBS must cope with the problems: heterogeneity and autonomy of the participating LDBSs and the efficient transaction management.

Now our concern is the issue of the transaction management for MDBS. The objectives of multidatabase transaction management are to avoid inconsistent retrieval and to preserve the global consistency in the presence of local transactions. The global consistency can be guaranteed by atomicity and serializability of global transactions. In order to ensure the atomicity of global transactions, the two-phase commit protocol (2PC) is used. Also, serializability of global transactions is achieved by a concurrency control algorithm.

Local concurrency control (LCC) algorithms used at each LDBS can be grouped into two classes by their property: LCC algorithm is static or non-static. If LCC algorithm is static, for example, 2PL, Timestamp ordering, Optimistic concurrency control algorithm and Value date, the serialization point of a transaction is the same as its serialization order. If LCC algorithm is non-static, for example, Serialization graph testing, the serialization orders of two non-conflicting transactions will not be determined until a third transaction introduces an indirect conflict between them.[11)]

To integrate heterogeneous LCC algorithms, in the transaction management algorithm for MDBS, we have to consider the following two problems.

1. How can we process a global transaction when it violates global serializability or has the possibility of violation of global serializability. Briefly, this is referred to the processing problem.
2. How can we manage an indirect conflict introduced by a local transaction. Shortly, this is referred to the indirect conflict problem.

The traditional approaches to integrate heterogeneous concurrency control algorithms can be classified into two groups: bottom-up approach [7, 8, 9, 13, 14)] and top-down approach [1, 2, 3, 4, 5, 6, 11)].

The bottom-up approach collects local information from each LDBMS at the global level and thereafter checks global serializability. This approach is optimistic and requires considerable time and cost for the modification of each LDBMS to integrate LDBMSs. So, one problem of this approach is the destruction of local autonomy due to the modification of each LDBMS. The other problem is the abortion of the executed global transactions due to the violation of the global serializability. Consequently, a cascading abort can be happened by the aborted global transactions.

The top-down approach maintains a global serialization order, at local sites, which has been determined already at the global level. It is pessimistic and does not require the modifications of any LDBMS at all. In this respect, the top-down approach completely ensures the local autonomy. To determine the serialization order of the global transactions at each LDBS, the MDBS must deal not only with direct conflicts that may exist between the subtransactions of global transactions but also with the indirect conflicts that may be caused by the local transactions. But in this approach, the indirect conflicts among global transactions via local transactions can not be considered at the global level. Some of the indirect conflicts may cause the discrepancy between the Execution Order of global transactions in a history ($EO(H_i)$) and their Serialization Order ($SO(H_i)$). Consequently, it may destroy the global serializability like in Example 1.1. Several solutions have been proposed in the literature to deal with an indirect conflict problem, however, most of them are not satisfactory.[9]

Example 1.1: The discrepancy between $EO(H_i)$ and $SO(H_i)$

Let sites S_1 and S_2 contain data items {a} and {b,c}, respectively. Let R and W stand for a read operation and a write operation, respectively. The subscript used for R and W denotes a transaction identifier. Suppose that global transactions, G_1 and G_2, a global schedule of them, GS and a local transaction, L_1, are as follows:

G_1: $Wg_1(a)\ Rg_1(b)$
G_2: $Rg_2(a)\ Wg_2(c)$
GS: $Wg_1(a)\ Rg_1(b)\ Rg_2(a)\ Wg_2(c)$
L_1: $Wl_1(b)\ Rl_1(c)$

Let H_1 and H_2 be histories at S_1 and S_2, respectively:

H_1: $Wg_1(a)\ Rg_2(a)$
H_2: $Wl_1(b)\ Rg_1(b)\ Wg_2(c)\ Rl_1(c)$

Let "$\rightarrow^d$ " and "$\rightarrow^i$" denote a direct conflict and an indirect conflict, respectively. There are a direct conflict such as $G_1 \rightarrow^d G_2$ in H_1 and an indirect conflict such as $G_2 \rightarrow^i G_1$ in H_2 because of $L_1 \rightarrow^d G_1$ and $G_2 \rightarrow^d L_1$. $EO(H_1)$ and $EO(H_2)$ are both G_1G_2. But, an indirect conflict between G_1 and G_2 via L_1 is produced in H_2. Thus, $EO(H_2)$ (i.e., G_1G_2) becomes different from $SO(H_2)$ (i.e., G_2G_1) in H_2. A global history GH={H_1, H_2} is nonserializable because $SO(H_1)$ is G_1G_2 and $SO(H_2)$ is G_2G_1. □

The works of (3, 4, 5) have provided a formal framework for the research of top-down approach as well as addressing the concurrency control of global transactions. Let consider that LCC algorithms are non-static. Algorithms proposed in (3, 4, 5) may produce this discrepancy between $EO(H_i)$ and $SO(H_i)$ if the committed global transactions are removed from its Site Graph or Transaction Graph as soon as they are committed. Transaction Graph algorithm has no way of determining when it is safe to remove the edges of a committed global transaction. So, the method may work correctly if the removal of edges corresponding to committed transaction is delayed. Thus, the degree of concurrency will be scarified.[9] Also, an algorithm proposed in (2) may produce this discrepancy.

In another view, above two approaches can be specialized as the following three subapproaches.

Subapproach 1: If the execution of an operation of the active global transaction can violate global serializability, the active global transaction is aborted. [3,4,5]

Subapproach 2: The global scheduler does not schedule any operation of the global transaction which has the possibility of violation of global serializability. [1,2,6,11]

Subapproach 3: If a global transaction is to be completed and it violates global serializability, the global transaction is aborted. [9,13]

Subapproaches 1 and 2 are the top-down approach and Subapproach 3 is the bottom-up approach.

To work out the problems of transaction management, i.e., processing problem and indirect conflict problem, while preserving global serializability and local autonomy, in this paper we propose a new concurrency control algorithm, called **Pessimistic Timestamp Method** (PTM) which chooses Subapproach 2. First, in order to resolve the processing problem, PTM schedules the global transactions so that the serialization order of global transactions is the same as their execution order at all participating LDBSs. Also, PTM disallows the abort of a global transaction that is being executed due to the violation of global serializability or the occurrence of global deadlock except for transaction failures and site failures. Second, in order to resolve the indirect conflict problem, PTM introduces the concept of Timestamp(Ts). Ts is assigned to a local transaction (or a global subtransaction) when it is scheduled (or the subtransaction becomes prepare-to-commit state). The timestamp of each transaction is used to resolve the discrepancy between $EO(H_i)$ and $SO(H_i)$.

The remainder of this paper is organized as follows. Section 2 describes the our transaction processing model and data structures. In Section 3, we present a new concurrency control algorithms, called

PTM. The correctness of PTM is discussed in Section 4. Section 5 concludes the paper and outlines our on-going research.

2. TRANSACTION PROCESSING MODEL

Transaction processing model consists of three major components like in Figure 2.1: a global module, a local execution monitor (LEM), and a local module.

For our transaction processing model and its concurrency control algorithm, we have assumed that (1) each local concurrency control algorithm produces a serializable and recoverable history, (2) local transactions may write only non-replicated data items, (3) a global transaction manager knows whether the property of LCC algorithms used at each LDBS is static or not, (4) LDBMSs are not aware of each other and cannot exchange their concurrency control information, (5) the structure of the transactions which are processed in our transaction processing model is flat, i.e., the transactions have single level structure.

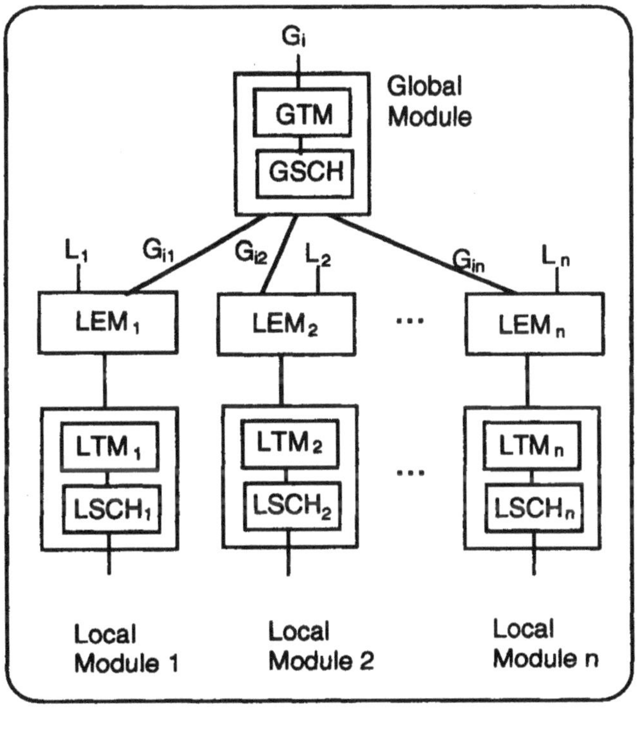

GTM: Global Transaction Manager
LEM: Local Execution Manager
LTM: Local Transaction Manager
$G_{i1},...,G_{in}$: Subtransaction of G_i
GSCH: Global Scheduler
LSCH: Local Scheduler
G_i: Global transaction $_i$
$L_1,...,L_n$: Local transaction

Figure 2.1 Transaction Processing Model

Definition 2.1: Site Reference Graph (SRG)
Graph SRG=(V,E) is an undirected graph, where V consists of transaction nodes and site nodes that the transaction references, and E is a set of edges, where each edge is formed between a site node and a transaction node. SRG(G) is a subgraph of SRG that consists of one transaction node G and site nodes that G references.

Definition 2.2: Execution Order Graph (EOG)
Graph EOG=(V,E), where V is a set of subtransactions and E is a set of directed edges that represent an execution order between two subtransactions. An edge, G_a -> G_b, represents that G_a must be executed before G_b.

In this section, we define the role and data structures of each module.

Global Module: The global module consists of a global transaction manager (GTM) and a global scheduler (GSCH). The role of a GTM is as follows.

1. Decomposition a global transaction into subtransactions.
2. Computation of dependency between subtransactions of a global transaction.
3. Management of global transactions until they have been aborted or committed.
4. Maintenance of SRG and EOG for each site.
5. A coordinator of the protocol to remove a committed transaction from SRG and 2PC protocol to commit a completed global transaction.
6. Maintenance of Data structure for Remove Protocol (DRP) and Data structure for Commit Protocol (DCP). DRP and DCP for each global transaction are a record which is composed of pairs of a site field and a mark field.

The role of GSCH is to have global transactions schedulable and to schedule each operation of a schedulable global transaction.

LEM : The role of LEM is as follows.

1. An interface of local transactions and subtransactions.
2. Making the information that is used to decide whether GSCH submits a subtransaction to LEM or not. This information is the unique timestamp Ts to be allocated to each transaction.
3. A participant of the protocol to remove a committed global transaction from SRG and 2PC protocol.

Therefore, LEM has to maintain the following data structures.

(1) STL : a Ts of the local transaction that has the Smallest Ts among the uncommitted Local transactions, i.e., Smallest {Ts(L) | L in ULTs}, where ULTs is a set of uncommitted local transactions.

(2) LIST_$G_{pc/c}$: a list of the global transactions of which state is prepare-to-commit state or commit state at the corresponding site. It is a list that is sorted in order of Ts.

Local module : Each local module consists of a local transaction manager (LTM) and a local scheduler (LSCH). It is identical to a conventional LDBMS.

3. PESSIMISTIC TIMESTAMP METHOD

In this section, we propose a method for scheduling of global transactions, called **Pessimistic Timestamp Method** (PTM), which guarantees global serializability and supports the parallel processing of subtransactions of a global transaction, and does not produce a global deadlock. It is necessary to define the concept of a Timestamp (Ts). Ts is a sequence number which is generated and maintained by LEM at each site independently. It is assigned to a local transaction (or a global subtransaction) when the local transaction is scheduled (or the subtransaction becomes PC state). Ts is used to remove a committed global transactions from SRG without the violation of global serializability and to resolve the indirect conflict problem.

In PTM, GSCH uses the SRG as a scheduling strategy. We can assume that if a graph SRG has a cycle then there is a possibility of interdependency among global transactions. So, If GSCH finds a cycle in SRG, it must create the EOG that represents the execution order between the scheduled subtransaction and the subtransaction to be scheduled. If a subtransaction which has no in-edge in EOG has not been scheduled then it can be scheduled immediately.

PTM is made of the following three algorithms based on the Ts.

A1 : Algorithm for scheduling of global transactions.
A2 : Algorithm for ensuring transaction atomicity.
A3 : Algorithm for removing a committed global transaction from SRG.

In the following discussion, we do not consider the site failures and the transaction failures.

3.1 The Scheduling of Global Transactions

After a global transaction is in a schedulable state, the operations of the global transaction can be scheduled to its corresponding site. A schedulable state means that each operation of a global transaction can be scheduled without checking a cycle in SRG.

The following abbreviations are used for convenience.

① G : a global transaction is to be scheduled
② SITE(G) : a set of sites that G wants to reference
③ SGTIC(G) : a set of global transactions that are included in cycles which contain G in SRG
④ SGT(S_i) : a set of global transactions that reference site S_i
⑤ G_{pc} : G is in PC (Prepare-to-Commit) state
⑥ G_{rm} : G is in RM (ReMove) state
⑦ Ts(G) : a timestamp of G

Algorithm for scheduling of global transactions makes a new global transaction schedulable by the use of SRG similar to Transaction Graph proposed in (5). SRG may have more than one cycle, but Transaction graph cannot have any cycle. When G is in a cycle of SRG, if global transactions, in the cycle, which reference sites to which G accesses are executed earlier than G, then global serializability is not destroyed even though there are more than one cycle in SRG.

Algorithm for scheduling of a global transaction

```
BEGIN
  Input an operation of G;
  IF an operation of G is one of  new arrived global
     transaction
  THEN BEGIN
          Create SRG(G) using SITE(G);
          Add SRG(G) to SRG;
       END;
       IF G is not in a cycle in SRG
       THEN BEGIN
              G is marked with "NC" (not in cycle);
              submit each operations of G to its
              corresponding site;
            END;
       ELSE BEGIN
              G is marked with "C" (in cycle);
              FOR Gx in SGT(Sx) ∩ SGTIC(G),
                  where  Sx in SITE(G)
              IF the property of LCC algorithm of
                 Sx is static
              THEN IF Gx has been marked with
                      "PC"
                   THEN no add an edge,
                          Gx -> G, to EOG for Sx
                   ELSE add an edge,
                          Gx -> G, to EOG for Sx;
              ELSE IF Gx has been marked with
                      "RM"
                   THEN no add an edge,
                          Gx -> G, to EOG for Sx
                   ELSE add an edge,
                          Gx -> G, to EOG for Sx;
            END;
  ELSE BEGIN
         IF G is included in EOG for its
            corresponding site
         THEN IF G in EOG has no in-edge
              THEN operations of G are scheduled
              ELSE operations of G have to be
                      delayed;
         ELSE operations of G are scheduled;
       END;
END.
```

In Algorithm for scheduling of a global transaction, since any execution of G marked with "NC" does not destroy global serializability, each operation of G can be submitted at any time to its site. If G has no in-edge in EOG for any site, it can be executed at that site even though G has been marked with "C". It is because the preceding subtransactions in EOG have been all executed at its site.

3.2 Ensuring Transaction Atomicity

In order to ensure the atomicity of a global transaction in MDBS, the semantically well-defined two-phase commit (2PC) protocol is generally used. We propose asynchronous 2PC protocol to control the execution of subtransactions between the individual LEM and GTM. "Asynchronous" at 2PC protocol means that PC message is sent to the corresponding participant as soon as the last operation of a subtransaction is submitted to its site and a global decision (COMMIT or ABORT) is sent to all its participants as soon as all of them have sent the acknowledgment for PC message. In PTM, as soon as the last operation of a subtransaction is submitted to LEM, GTM sends PC message to the corresponding LEM. If PC message is received from GTM, the LEM will respond with YES or NO which means whether the subtransaction is in PC state or not, when the execution of the subtransaction is over. And then LEM will wait for a COMMIT or ABORT message from GTM. If GTM is received YES from all sites that participate in the execution of a global transaction, it sends a COMMIT message to its all corresponding LEMs. If a COMMIT message is received, each LEM can commit the corresponding subtransaction. Otherwise, the subtransaction is aborted.

Algorithm for a participant of 2PC

```
BEGIN
  IF "PC" message is received from GTM
  THEN IF recognize that G is in PC state
       THEN BEGIN
               mark G with "PC";
               assign Timestamp to G_pc;
               send "YES" to GTM;
               Insert G_pc into List_G_pc/c
            END;
       ELSE send "NO" to GTM;
  IF the response from GTM is "COMMIT" message
  THEN send "COMMIT" message to LTM
  ELSE send "ABORT" message to LTM;
END.
```

PTM supports two cases to decide the time for removing subtransaction from EOG. First case, if LCC algorithm used at each LDBS is static, a coordinator of 2PC protocol removes the global transactions marked with PC from EOG to increase a degree of concurrency. Second case, if LCC algorithm used at each LDBS is non-static, a coordinator of REMOVE protocol, as described in the next section, removes the global transactions marked with RM from EOG.

Algorithm for a coordinator of 2PC

```
BEGIN
  After the last operation of each subtransaction is
  executed,
  GTM send "PC" message to the site which
  participate in the execution of the subtransaction of
  G.
  IF the response is "YES" from each participant site
  THEN BEGIN
          the mark field for the participant in
          DCP(G) is marked with "PC";
          IF the property of LCC algorithm of the
             participant is static
          THEN G_pc is removed from its
               corresponding EOG;
          IF every field of DCP(G) has been marked
             with "PC"
          THEN send "COMMIT" message to all
               participant LEMs;
       END;
  ELSE BEGIN
          send "ABORT" message to all participant
          sites;
          DCP(G) and DRG(G) are removed;
          G is removed from each EOG and SRG;
       END;
END.
```

3.3 Protocol for Removing a Committed Global Transaction from SRG

In this section, we describe the REMOVE protocol determining the safe time to remove a committed global transaction from SRG. In order to resolve the problem of an indirect conflict, we introduced the concept of Ts. Each LEM maintains the list of global transactions in PC or committed state. In the list, the global transactions are sorted in order of their Ts. Whenever a local transaction is submitted to LTM (or a subtransaction becomes PC state), LEM assigns unique Ts to the local transaction (or the subtransaction) and keeps STL at each site. If Ts of a global transaction G_x in the list of PC or committed global transactions is smaller than STL, LEM as a participant of REMOVE protocol sends "REMOVE" message which means to be able to remove G_x from SRG to GTM. If "REMOVE" message is received from all site in SITE(G_x), GTM as a coordinator of REMOVE protocol can remove G_x from SRG according to the algorithm for removing a committed global transaction.

Theorem 3.1 : Let G_{pc} be a subtransaction in PC state at one site. For any uncommitted local transaction L, if $Ts(G_{pc}) < Ts(L)$, the Execution Order (EO) of global transactions is the same as their Serialization Order (SO) at least at this site even if G is removed from SRG.

Proof : Let "$->^{d}$" denote a direct conflict. $Ts(G_{pc})$ is the Timestamp of G_{pc} when G becomes PC state at site S_i. Ts(L) is the Timestamp of a local transaction L when L is sent to LTM at S_i. If $Ts(G_{pc}) < Ts(L)$, L is scheduled after all operations of G_{pc} have been executed. For any active global transaction G_x, $G_{pc} ->^{d} L ->^{d} G_x$ can be created, but $L ->^{d} G_{pc}$ $G_x ->^{d} L$ cannot be created because any operation of G_{pc} has been executed before the execution the first operation of L. Since an indirect conflict between G_x and G_{pc} such as $L ->^{d} G_{pc}$ $G_x ->^{d} L$ through L is not produced, the EO of global transactions is the same as their SO. □

Definition 3.1 : Dependency relation
Let O_i and O_j be the operation of T_i and T_j, respectively. If O_i and O_j be conflict operations and O_i precede O_j in a history then we say that T_j is dependent on T_i. The dependency relation is denoted by "$T_i ->^{dp} T_j$".

Definition 3.2 : Cyclic dependency
Let $G_a ->^{dp} G_b$ denote that G_b is dependent on G_a. If there are dependency relations such as $G_a ->^{dp} G_1$, $G_1 ->^{dp} G_2$, ... , $G_n ->^{dp} G_a$, then we can say that a cyclic dependency exists among G_a, G_1, G_2,..., and G_n.

Algorithm for removing a committed global transaction from SRG

```
BEGIN
  IF all global transactions of a CCG in SRG have
      been marked with "RM"
  THEN the CCG is removed from SRG;
  IF all global transactions and sites in a CCG are
      included in a cycle
  THEN a global transaction marked with "RM" is
         removed from the CCG;
   FOR any global transaction G_x in any site in
         SITE(G_rm)
     IF G_x has been marked with "RM"
     THEN G_rm is removed from the CCG;
END.
```

Definition 3.3 : Connected Component Graph (CCG)
Let a graph G=(V,E), where V is a set of vertices and E is a set of edges. An undirected graph is called "connected" if for every pair of vertices there exists a path between them. A subgraph of a graph G is G'=(V',E'), where V' is a subset of V and E' is a subset of edges of E which connect vertices in V'. A subgraph G'=(V',E') is connected and there exists no other subgraph G"=(V",E") of G which is also connected and either V" ⊃ V' or E" ⊃ E'. We say that the subgraph G' is a Connected Component Graph (CCG).

Algorithm for a participant of REMOVE protocol

```
BEGIN
  IF STL is updated when a local transaction is
      scheduled or committed
  THEN FOR each G_pc/c in LIST_G_pc/c
           IF Ts (G_pc/c) < STL
           THEN BEGIN
                    G_pc/c is marked with "RM";
                    G_rm is sent to GTM;
                    G_rm is removed from LIST_G_pc/c
                END;
END.
```

If an LCC algorithm is non-static, a global transaction is removed from its EOG when its state becomes RM. It is the reason that a global transaction marked with "RM" has not an effect on having EO differ from SO.

Algorithm for a coordinator of REMOVE protocol

```
BEGIN
  IF "REMOVE" message of G is received from LEM
  THEN BEGIN
           update DRP(G_rm);
           IF the property of LCC algorithm of the
               participant is non-static
           THEN G_rm is removed from its EOG;
       END;
  IF every field of DRP(G) has been marked with "RM"
  THEN BEGIN
          G is marked with "RM" in SRG;
          Call for Algorithm for removing a
          committed global transaction from SRG;
       END;
END.
```

The following Example 3.1 shows how the global transactions are scheduled by PTM.

Example 3.1 : The scheduling of a global transaction and the removing of a committed global transaction

Case 1. The scheduling of a global transaction

Consider that G_1 and G_2 access both site S_1 and S_2. Suppose that G_1 has been scheduled, but not committed. When the global scheduler schedules G_2, it finds a cycle in SRG like in Figure 3-(a). So, in order to make G schedulable, it adds an edge such as $G_1 \rightarrow G_2$ to EOG for S_1 and EOG for S_2, respectively, which is maintained by global module, like in Figure 3-(b). By PTM, operations of G_2 can be scheduled after G_1 has been finished and removed from EOG for the site to be accessed by operations of G_2.

Let L be a local transaction at site which G_1 is removed from EOG. Since G_1 is removed from its EOG when for any L, $Ts(G_1) < Ts(L)$, the execution order of G_1 and G_2 does not become different from their serialization order by local transactions. Therefore, in this case, a cyclic dependency is not created even if SRG has a cycle.

Case 2. The removing of a committed global transaction

Assume that SRG is like in Fig. 3-(c) and G_1 has been marked with "RM". When a subtransaction of G_1 at S_1 and a subtransaction of G_1 at S_2 are all marked with "RM", G_1 in SRG is marked with "RM". Each subtransaction can be marked with "RM" if its Ts is less than STL of its site. Thus, there is not such conflict relations, $L \rightarrow^{d} G_1$ and $G_x \rightarrow^{d} L$, at each site, where L is a local transaction and G_x is a global transaction scheduled after G_1 is marked with "RM". Therefore, global serializability is not destroyed even if G_1 is removed from SRG. □

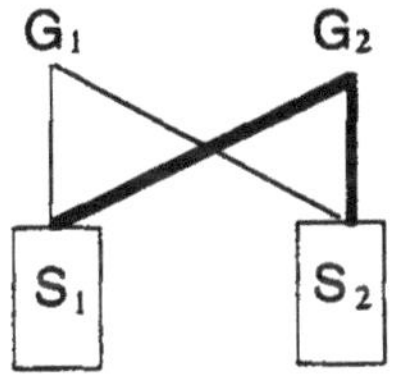

Figure 3-(a)

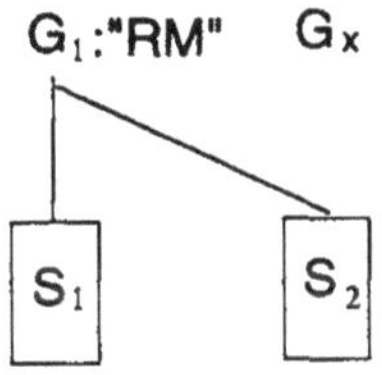

Figure 3-(c)

$G_1 \longrightarrow G_2$: EOG for S_1

$G_1 \longrightarrow G_2$: EOG for S_2

Figure 3-(b)

4. CORRECTNESS OF PTM

In most MDBSs, global serializability is used as the correctness criterion for a global concurrency control algorithm. Since PTM does not impose any restriction on LCC algorithm used at each LDBS, we have to concern about two classes of LCC algorithms, as mentioned above, in order to prove the correctness of PTM.

Theorem 4.1 : PTM always guarantees global serializability without any restriction of LCC algorithm used at each LDBS.

Proof : We have to consider the following two cases to prove the correctness of PTM. First case, suppose that SRG contains no cycle. In this case, global transactions can be executed in any order since a relative serialization order of global transactions is the same at all sites. So, global serializability is guaranteed. Second case, suppose that SRG contains a cycle. It implies that the possibility of cyclic dependency exists among the global transactions. Let G be a global transaction to be scheduled. Suppose that G is in a cycle of SRG. When G is in a cycle of SRG, PTM schedules G so that G is executed at each site after the execution of other global transactions in the cycle which access sites that G accesses. Also, PTM schedules global transactions so that the execution order and the serialization order are always identical at all sites by the use of Timestamp and EOG at each site. Thus the cyclic dependency among global transactions in the cycle is not created by G.

Let SGTIC(G) denote a set of global transactions in a cycle which contain G. Assume that a cyclic dependency among global transactions in the cycle is created by G. For a cyclic dependency to exist, there must be at least two dependency relations, $G_x \rightarrow^{dp} G$ and $G \rightarrow^{dp} G_y$ where G_x and G_y are in SGTIC(G) and G_x can be identical to G_y. But, if a dependency relation $G \rightarrow^{dp} G_y$ exists, PTM would have executed G_y after G was executed. This violates the scheduling principle of PTM. Therefore, the cyclic dependency among global transactions in the cycle is not created by G.

In conclusion, PTM always guarantees global serializability regardless of property of LCC algorithms used at each LDBS. □

5. CONCLUSIONS

We have presented a transaction processing model and its concurrency control algorithm PTM to achieve global serializability, local autonomy, a high degree of concurrency, and deadlock freedom in the presence of local transactions in MDBS. Since PTM schedules global transactions so that the serialization order of global transactions is the same as their execution order in all participating LDBSs, it does not confine LCC algorithm used at each LDBS at all. PTM does not abort global transactions being executed due to the violation of global serializability or the occurrence of global deadlock. Also PTM concurrently processes the subtransactions of a global transaction according to the dependency among them. Thus, a high degree of concurrency can be obtained. Especially, PTM completely guarantees local autonomy since it never requires the modification of an LCC algorithm.

The time overhead for cycle detection would be high and the storage space to keep the information needed for GTM and LEM is also overhead.

PTM must be advanced for the increase of performance. Also, the performance analysis for our algorithm through simulation is required to compare with other algorithms.

Now, recovery management algorithm for an MDBS is being developed based on PTM.

REFERENCE

1) Alonso Rafael, Garcia-Molina Hector, and Salem Kenneth, "Concurrency Control and Recovery for Global Procedures in Federated Database Systems," IEEE Data Engineering, pages 5 - 11, Vol. 10, No. 3, Sep. 1987.
2) Barker Ken and Ozsu M. Tamer, "Concurrent Transaction Execution in Multidatabase Systems," The Fourteenth Annual International Computer Software & Applications Conference, pages 282 - 288, Oct. 29 - Nov.2, 1990.
3) Breitbart Yuri, Silberschatz Avi, and Thompson Glenn, "An Update Mechanism for Multidatabase Systems," IEEE Database Engineering Bulletin, pages 12 - 18, 1987.
4) Breitbart Yuri and Silberschatz Avi, "Multidatabase Update Issues," Proceedings of SIGMOD, pages 135 - 142, 1988.
5) Breitbart Yuri, Silberschatz Avi, and Thompson Glenn, "Transaction Management in a Multidatabase Environment," Integration of Information Systems: Bridging Heterogeneous Databases, ed. A. Gupta, IEEE Press, 1989.
6) Du Weimin, Elmagarmid Ahmed K., and Kim Won, "Maintaining Quasi Serializability in Multidatabase Systems," Proceedings Seventh International Conference on Data Engineering, pages 360 - 367, April 1991.
7) Elmagarmid Ahmed K. and Leu Yungho, "An Optimistic Concurrency Control Algorithm for Heterogeneous Distributed Database Systems," IEEE Data Engineering, pages 26 - 32, 1987.
8) Elmagarmid Ahmed K. and Helal A. A., "Supporting Updates in Heterogeneous Distributed Database Systems," Fourth International Conference on Data Engineering, pages 564 - 569, Feb. 1988.
9) Geogakopoulos Dimitrios, Rusinkiewicz Marek, and Sheth Amit, "On Serializability of Multidatabase Transactions Through Forced Local Conflicts, Proceedings Seventh International Conference on Data Engineering, pages 314 - 324, April 1991
10) Gligor A. and Popescu-Zeletin R., "Transaction Management in Distributed Heterogeneous Database Management Systems," Information Systems, 11(4), pages 287 - 297, 1986.
11) Leu Yungho and Ahmed Elmagarmid K., "A Hierarchical Approach to Concurrency Control for Multidatabases," Proceedings of Second International Symposium on Databases in Parallel and Distributed Systems, pages 202 - 210, July 2-4, 1990.
12) Moon Songchun and Lim Jong T., "A Checkpointing Scheme for Heterogeneous Database Systems," 11th International Conference on Distributed Computing Systems, Arlington, Texas, U. S. A., pages 608 - 615, May 1991.
13) Pu Calton, "Superdatabases for Composition of Heterogeneous Databases," IEEE Data Engineering Conference, pages 548 - 555, 1988.
14) Sugihara Kazuo , "Concurrency Control Based on Cycle Detection," Proceedings of the International Conference on Data Engineering, pages 267 - 274, 1987.

AN OPTIMISTIC CONCURRENCY CONTROL PROTOCOL FOR REAL-TIME DATABASE SYSTEMS

Juhnyoung Lee and Sang H. Son

Department of Computer Science, University of Virginia, Charlottesville, VA 22903, U.S.A.

ABSTRACT

Transactions in real-time database systems are associated with certain timing constraints derived either from temporal consistency requirements of data or from requirements imposed on system reaction time. Fundamental requirements of real-time database systems are *timeliness*, i.e., the ability to produce expected transaction results early or at the right time, and *predictability*, i.e., the ability to function as deterministic as necessary to satisfy system specifications including timing constraints. There are a number of issues that have to be addressed in processing real-time transactions. To achieve the fundamental requirements, not only conventional transaction processing mechanisms have to be tailored to take timing constraints into consideration, but also new mechanisms that have not been required in conventional transaction processing need to be designed and added. In this paper, we focus on the problem of concurrency control for processing real-time transactions, and propose an optimistic concurrency control protocol. The proposed protocol employs *priority-based conflict resolution* schemes developed on *forward validation*. In addition, it utilizes the notion of *lazy serialization* implemented using dynamic timestamp allocation and dynamic adjustment of timestamp intervals. With these features, the proposed protocol is expected to produce transaction results in a timely manner.

1. INTRODUCTION

Real-time database systems are vital to a wide range of operations. As computers have been faster and more powerful, and their use more widespread, real-time database systems have grown larger and become more critical. For example, they are used in program stock trading, telephone switching systems, network management, automated factory management, and command and control systems. More specifically, in the program stock market application, we need to monitor the state of the stock market and update the database with new information. If the database is to contain an accurate representation of the current market, then this monitoring and updating process must meet certain timing constraints. Also, in this system, we need to satisfy certain real-time constraints in reading and analyzing information in database in order to respond to a user query or to initiate a trade in the stock market. For other examples given above, we can consider similar operations with timing constraints.

This work was supported in part by ONR, by DOE, by IBM, and by CIT.

All of these real-time database operations are characterized by (1) their time constrained access to data and (2) access to data that has temporal validity. They involve gathering data from the environment, processing of gathered information in the context of information acquired in the past, and providing timely response. They also involve processing not only archival data but also *temporal data* which loses its validity after a certain time interval. Both of the temporal nature of the data and the response time requirements imposed by the environment make transactions possess timing constraints in the form of either periods or deadlines. Therefore, the correctness of real-time database operation depends not only on the logical computations carried out but also on the time at which the results are delivered. The goal of real-time database systems is to meet timing constraints of transactions.

One key point to note here is that real-time computing does not imply fast computing. Rather than being fast, more important properties of real-time (database) systems should be *timeliness*, i.e., the ability to produce expected results early or at the right time, and *predictability*, i.e., the ability to function as deterministic as necessary to satisfy system specifications including timing constraints [Stan90]. Fast computing which is busy doing the wrong activity at the wrong time is not helpful for real-time computing. While the objective of real-time computing is to meet the individual timing constraint of each activity, the objective of fast computing is to minimize the average response time of a given set of activities. Fast computing is helpful in meeting stringent timing constraints, but fast computing alone does not guarantee timeliness and predictability. In order to guarantee timeliness and predictability, we need to handle explicit timing constraints, and to use time-cognizant techniques to meet deadlines or periodicity associated with activities.

There are a number of issues that have to be addressed in processing real-time transactions. To achieve the fundamental requirements, i.e., timeliness and predictability, not only conventional transaction processing mechanisms have to be tailored to take timing constraints into consideration, but also new mechanisms that have not been required in conventional transaction processing need to be designed and added. In this paper, we focus on the problem of concurrency control for processing real-time transactions

2. RELATED WORK

Most work on real-time concurrency control uses the notion of serializability as the correctness criteria [Abbo88, Abbo89, Buch89, Hari90, Hari90b, Huan89, Huan91, Lin90,

Sha88, Stan88], while some consider relaxation of consistency requirements based on the argument that it is desirable to trade off timeliness with data consistency [Lin89, Liu88, Son88]. In enforcing serializability, conventional concurrency control methods such as two-phase locking (2PL), timestamp ordering (TO), and optimistic concurrency control (OCC) have been used as the basis of real-time concurrency control. Most current work combines the conventional concurrency control schemes with priority-based conflict resolution methods such as *priority abort* [Abbo88, Huan91], *priority inheritance* [Sha88], *priority ceiling* [Sha88], *priority wait* [Huan91], and *serialization order adjustment* [Lin90].

Most of the initial work on real-time concurrency control has been conducted on utilizing 2PL [Abbo88, Abb89, Huan89, Sha88, Stan88]. This is not surprising because 2PL has been well studied in traditional database systems and is being widely used in commercial database systems. Besides, recovery mechanisms for use with 2PL are well understood. 2PL uses pure blocking for conflict resolution. The beneficial effect of blocking is conservation of resources, which makes 2PL advantageous particularly under resource-limited situations. However, blocking results in prevention of the progress of transaction execution. Subsequently, a low degree of concurrency is resulted, and conflict ratio is increased rapidly. Moreover, 2PL has inherent problems such as possibility of deadlocks and unpredictable blocking duration, which become even more serious for real-time transaction processing.

OCC scheduler [Kung81, Haer84] uses abort and restart to serialize concurrent data operations, thereby avoids blocking. Thus, OCC is free from deadlock. In addition, it has a potential for high degree of parallelism. These features of OCC make it promising particularly for real-time transaction processing. However, the abort-based conflict resolution of OCC has the problem of wasted resources and time, which becomes more serious for real-time transaction scheduling.

In OCC protocols that perform *backward validation*, the validating transaction either commits or aborts depending on whether it has conflicts with transactions that have already committed. Thus, this validation scheme does not allow us to take transaction characteristics into account. In *forward validation* [Haer84], however, either the validating transaction or conflicting ongoing transactions can be aborted to resolve conflicts. This validation scheme is advantageous in real-time database systems, because it may be preferable not to commit the validating transaction, depending on the timing characteristics of the validating transaction and the conflicting ongoing transactions. A number of real-time concurrency control methods based on OCC using forward validation scheme have been studied [Hari90, Hari90b, Huan91].

The rationale for OCC is based on an "optimistic" assumption regarding run-time conflicts: if only few run-time conflicts are expected, we can assume that most execution is serializable [Bern87]. Therefore OCC simultaneously avoids blocking and restarts in the optimistic situations. Unfortunately, however, this optimistic assumption on transaction behavior may not always be true in real world situations. In a database system where run-time conflicts are not rare, OCC depends on transaction restarts to eliminate nonserializable executions.

The adverse effect of transaction restarts for serialization is that resource and time are wasted. Especially in OCC, because data conflicts are detected and resolved only during the validation phase, a transaction can end up aborting after having used resources and time for most of the transaction's execution. When the transaction is restarted, previously performed work has to be redone. This problem of *time and resource waste* becomes even more serious in real-time transaction scheduling, because it reduces the chances of meeting the deadlines of transactions.

Another problem of OCC is *unnecessary aborts*. This problem is often caused by imperfect validation tests used in OCC protocols. Many validation test schemes are based on intersection of the read sets and write sets of transactions rather than on the actual execution order of transactions, since in general it is difficult to record and use entire execution history efficiently. Hence sometimes a validation process using read sets and write sets erroneously concludes that a nonserializable execution has occurred when it has not in actual execution. We call such a conflict virtual. A *virtual conflict* leads to one or more unnecessary transaction aborts. This problem of unnecessary aborts also results in waste of resource and time, and is serious in real-time transaction processing.

The concurrency control protocol proposed in this paper is based on OCC scheme using forward validation [Haer84, Robi82], which was also used as the basis for OCC-based real-time concurrency control schemes proposed in [Hari90b, Huan91]. Its goal is to overcome those two problems of basic OCC scheme described above to process efficiently transactions in a real-time database system. The proposed protocol employs forward validation and priority-based conflict resolution schemes developed for forward validation. In addition, it utilizes the notion of lazy serialization implemented using dynamic timestamp allocation [Baye82] and dynamic adjustment of timestamp intervals [Boks87]. With these features, the proposed scheme can reduce resource and time waste, avoid unnecessary aborts, and hence produce transaction results in a timely manner. Before we provide a procedural description of the protocol, we briefly explain the idea of its components.

3. ELEMENTS OF THE PROPOSED PROTOCOL

3.1. Forward Validation

In real-time database systems, forward validation scheme is preferable to backward validation, because it provides flexibility for conflict resolution in that a transaction is validated against active transactions in their read phase instead of committed ones, i.e., either the validating transactions or the conflicting active transactions can be aborted to resolve conflicts. A number of conflict resolution policies that are based on forward validation have been proposed. Some of the examples are *priority abort, priority sacrifice*, and *priority wait* [Hari90b, Huan91], which we will explain in Section 7. Aborting active transactions in their read phase instead of validating transaction that has finished its execution to eliminate nonserializable executions means that conflicts are detected and resolved earlier than in backward validation. Thus, forward validation scheme reduces the waste of resource and time.

3.2. Conflict Classification

Since the forward validation test is conducted against active transactions, when a test is performed for a transaction, say T_i, active transactions in the system are classified into sets according to their execution history (with respect to that of T_i). First, the set of the active transactions are grouped into two sets; a *conflicting set*, that contains transactions in conflict with T_i, and a *nonconflicting set*, that contains transactions not in conflict with T_i. The conflicting set is further divided into two sets; a *Reconcilably Conflicting (RC) set* and an *Irreconcilably Conflicting (IC) set*. Transactions in the RC set are in conflict with T_i, but the conflicts are reconcilable, i.e., serializable. However, transactions in the IC set are in conflict with T_i, and the conflicts are irreconcilable, i.e., nonserializable. Details about each of the transaction sets will be given later in this paper. The RC transactions do not have to be aborted for serialization, but are required only to adjust their execution histories with respect to the validating transaction, T_i, using the timestamp interval facility of this protocol. However, the IC transactions should be handled with priority-based real-time conflict resolution schemes such as priority abort, priority sacrifice, and priority wait.

3.3. Dynamic Timestamp Assignment

Another important aspect of this protocol is that it combines timestamp ordering flavor with OCC using dynamic timestamp allocation. Most timestamp-based concurrency control protocols use a static timestamp allocation method, i.e., each transaction is assigned a timestamp value at its startup time, and a total ordering among transactions in the system is built up. The static timestamp allocation is based on the notion of *eager serialization*, which is considered harmful. First, the total ordering built by the eager serialization scheme does not reflect any actual conflict. Hence, it is possible that a transaction is aborted even when it requests its first data access [Baye82]. Second, the total ordering of all transactions is too restrictive, and degrades the degree of concurrency considerably. The dynamic timestamp allocation method is based on the notion of *lazy serialization* that builds only a partial ordering among transactions on demand to reflect actual execution history. This dynamic timestamp allocation scheme is possible in this protocol due to the OCC's phase-dependent structure of transaction execution, which allows the determination of the final serialization order to be delayed until the final phase of transaction execution. During the read phase, a transaction gradually builds its temporary serialization order with respect to committed transactions on demand whenever a conflict with such transactions occurs. Only when the transaction commits (after passing its validation test), is its permanent timestamp order, i.e., the final serialization order, determined.

3.4. Dynamic Adjustment of Serialization Order

The dynamic timestamp allocation scheme implementing lazy serialization is elaborated with a timestamp interval facility [Boks87] that keeps track of temporary serialization order and allows serialization order to be dynamically adjusted. In this scheme, a timestamp interval (initially, the entire range of the timestamp space) is assigned to each transaction instead of a single value timestamp. The timestamp intervals of active transactions preserve the partial ordering constructed by serializable execution. The timestamp interval of a transaction is adjusted (shrunk) whenever the transaction reads or writes a data object to preserve the serialization order induced by committed transactions. When the timestamp interval of a transaction shuts out, it means the transaction has been involved in a nonserializable execution, and the transaction should be restarted. Thus, this facility provides another means to detect and resolve nonserializable execution early in read phase.

When a transaction, T_i, commits after its validation phase, the timestamp intervals of those active transactions categorized as reconcilably conflicting with respect to T_i are adjusted, i.e., the serialization order between the validating transaction T_i and its RC transactions are determined. The permanent serialization order, i.e., final timestamp of these active transactions is not determined, but the partial ordering between T_i and these active transactions is determined by adjusting their timestamp intervals. Therefore these transactions do not have to be aborted even though they are in conflict with the committed transaction, i.e., unnecessary aborts are avoided.

4. PROCEDURAL DESCRIPTION

In this section, we provide a more detailed procedural description of the proposed protocol. To execute the proposed protocol, the system maintains a *transaction table* and an *object table*. The transaction table maintains the following information on each ongoing transaction:

- *RS(i)*: read set of transaction T_i;
- *WS(i)*: write set of transaction T_i; and
- *TI(i)*: timestamp interval of transaction T_i.

The object table keeps a read timestamp and a write timestamp of each data object in the database, that are determined as follows;

- *RTS(p)*: the largest timestamp of committed transactions that have read data object D_p; and
- *WTS(p)*: the largest timestamp of committed transactions that have written data object D_p.

The timestamp interval assigned to each active transaction is used to record temporary serialization order induced during the read phase of the transaction. In addition to the timestamp interval, a final timestamp, denoted as *TS(i)*, is assigned to each transaction, say T_i, when it has successfully passed its validation test, and is guaranteed to commit. The final timestamps of committed transactions are not kept in the transaction table. However, the final timestamp of a committed transaction is used to update the read and write timestamps of the data objects it has accessed, that are recorded in the object table.

Figure 1 shows a procedural description of the read, validation and write phase of a transaction, say T_i, executed with the proposed protocol. At the start of the execution of a transaction, say T_i, its timestamp interval *TI(i)* is initialized as

[0, ∞), i.e., the entire range of timestamp space. For each read or write operation made by T_i, *TI(i)* is adjusted to represent the dependencies, i.e., serialization order induced by the operation. The adjustment of *TI(i)* preserves the order induced by the timestamps of all committed transactions which have accessed that data object.

This adjustment is accomplished using different set intersection operations for read and write operations. When T_i reads a data object, the order of the read operation is adjusted to place after all the write operations made by committed transactions. Thus, after the read operation, *TI(i)* is adjusted to include only the intersection portion of the current *TI(i)* and the timestamp space following the write timestamp of the data object, which is by definition the largest timestamp among the committed transaction that have written the data object. When T_i writes a data object, the order of the write operation is adjusted to place after all the read as well as write operations made by committed transactions. Thus *TI(i)* is updated to include only the intersection of the current *TI(i)* and the timestamp space determined by the read as well as write timestamp of the data object. In the given procedure, we assume timestamp intervals contain only integers. In the read phase, any operation of an active transaction, T_i, which

Read Phase

```
for every Dp in RS(i) do
    read(Dp);
    TI(i) := TI(i) ∩ [WTS(p) + 1, ∞);
    if TI(i) = Ø
    then restart(i);
    endif;
enddo;

for every Dq in WS(i) do
    write(Dq);
    TI(i) := TI(i) ∩ [WTS(q) + 1, ∞)
                   ∩ [RTS(q) + 1, ∞);
    if TI(i) = Ø
    then restart(i);
    endif;
enddo;
```

Validation and Write Phase

```
determine RC_set(i) and IC_set(i);
if IC_set(i) ≠ Ø
then conflict_resolution(IC_set(i));
endif;
if not ABORTED(i)
then select TS(i) from TI(i);
     update RTS(p) for every Dp in RS(i);
     update WTS(q) for every Dq in WS(i);
     adjustment(RC_set(i));
     execute write_phase(i);
endif;
```

Figure 1 The Proposed Protocol

introduces a nonserializable execution results in *TI(i)* to be Ø. A transaction T_i must be restarted if *TI(i)* becomes Ø.

When a transaction T_i finishes the read phase and enters the validation phase, first, its RC set, i.e., the set of active transactions reconcilably conflicting with T_i, and its IC set, i.e., set of active transactions irreconcilably conflicting with T_i are determined. To determine these sets, the protocol uses the read and write sets of active validating transaction and active transactions, recorded in the transaction table. The categorization procedure will be discussed in detail in the next section. If there is one or more IC transactions in the system, the protocol invokes a priority-based conflict resolution scheme such as priority abort, priority sacrifice, and priority wait, to resolve the conflict between T_i and the irreconcilably conflicting transactions. Depending on the priorities of the conflicting transactions and the chosen conflict resolution scheme, either the validating transaction or the conflicting active transactions are aborted, as we will explain in Section 7.

If T_i has not been aborted during the priority-based conflict resolution (if any), then it can be committed now. The committing process consists of the following actions. First, the final timestamp, *TS(i)*, of T_i is determined so that the order induced by the final timestamp should not destroy the serialization order constructed by the already committed transactions. In fact, any timestamp in the range of *TI(i)* satisfies this condition, because *TI(i)* preserves the order induced by all committed transactions. Thus, any timestamp from *TI(i)* can be chosen for the final timestamp. Second, the read and write timestamps of the data objects T_i has accessed should be updated, if necessary, to reflect the final timestamp of T_i. Finally, the timestamp intervals of all the RC transactions should be adjusted to reflect the final serialization order between T_i and them. This adjustment of the timestamp intervals of RC transactions is similar to the timestamp interval adjustment of an active transaction in the read phase in that it is done with set intersection operations and is based on the same reasons to determine serialization order. This adjustment procedure will be given in detail in Section 6.

One important point to note related with the validation process is that the final timestamp *TS(i)* from timestamp interval *TI(i)* can be chosen in favor of high priority transactions, though any timestamp from *TI(i)* is eligible. When choosing the final timestamp for a committing transaction, the protocol can check the priority of its reconcilably conflicting transactions, and decide the timestamp in such a way that higher priority transactions are left with larger timestamp intervals. Because a larger timestamp interval means less possibility of restarting the transaction in some sense, a transaction with higher priority needs to have a larger timestamp interval than a transaction with lower priority. Another point to note here is that the final timestamp itself does not have to be a specific number. The entire timestamp interval can be the final timestamp of a committed transaction. Accordingly, read and write timestamps of data objects can also be intervals of timestamps, instead of being a specific value. This extension of the final timestamp may provide more flexibility for adjustment of serialization order, and is to be examined in our experiment.

5. CONFLICT CLASSIFICATION

Suppose T_i is a committing transaction and T_j ($j = 1, 2, \ldots,$

$n, j \neq i$) are transactions in their read phase. Then, the occurrence of conflicts between T_i and T_j, and the types of the conflicts are detected by looking at intersections of read sets and write sets of T_i and T_j as follows:

(c_1) $RS(j) \cap WS(i) \neq \emptyset$ $\Rightarrow$ read-write conflict;
(c_2) $WS(j) \cap WS(i) \neq \emptyset$ $\Rightarrow$ write-write conflict;
(c_3) $WS(j) \cap RS(i) \neq \emptyset$ $\Rightarrow$ write-read conflict.

Before discussing the categorization of conflicting transactions, we first explain how to identify the state of an active transaction using these three conditions. For notational convenience, we introduce a simple notation as follows. We use a triple (c_1, c_2, c_3) to express the state of an active transaction. Each element of the triple indicates whether the corresponding conflict condition is satisfied or not. When a conflict condition, c_i, is satisfied, it is denoted simply as c_i. However, if a condition, c_i, is not satisfied by the transaction, it is denoted as $\sim c_i$. For example, if a transaction satisfies c_1 and c_3, but does not satisfy c_2, i.e., it has both read-write and write-read conflicts with the validating transaction, but no write-write conflict, then it is denoted as $(c_1, \sim c_2, c_3)$.

Using this notation and Venn diagrams, Figure 2 shows the six possible states of active transactions under the assumption that the write set of a transaction is a subset of its read set. There are two Venn diagrams of the triple $(\sim c_1, \sim c_2, \sim c_3)$ in (a) and (b). They indicate (a) no access to common data objects at all and (b) only read operations on common data objects, respectively. Both cases do not produce any conflict between T_j and T_i. The triple $(c_1, \sim c_2, \sim c_3)$ in (c) means that there is only read-write conflict, but neither write-write nor write-read conflict between T_j and T_i. The triple $(\sim c_1, \sim c_2, c_3)$ in (d) indicates the case when there is only write-read conflict between T_j and T_i. The triple $(c_1, \sim c_2, c_3)$ in (e) indicates the case when there are read-write conflict and write-read conflict, but no write-write conflict between T_j and T_i. Finally, the triple (c_1, c_2, c_3) in (f) means that between T_j and T_i, all the three possible conflicts, i.e., read-write, write-write, and write-read conflicts exist. Besides these combinations of conflict conditions, there are three more combinations, $(\sim c_1, c_2, \sim c_3)$, $(c_1, c_2, \sim c_3)$, and $(\sim c_1, c_2, c_3)$ which are unable to occur under the given assumption that the write set of a transaction is a subset of its read set, and hence they are not included in the figure.

We can categorize the active transactions according to their states. First, the transactions are classified into two groups;

- nonconflicting transactions, and
- conflicting transactions.

Obviously, transactions whose state satisfies the conflict conditions, $(\sim c_1, \sim c_2, \sim c_3)$ belong to the first set. The latter contains the rest of the conditions, $(c_1, \sim c_2, \sim c_3)$, $(\sim c_1, \sim c_2, c_3)$, $(c_1, \sim c_2, c_3)$ and (c_1, c_2, c_3).

Second, the set of conflicting transactions are further divided into two group;

- Reconcilably Conflicting transactions (*RC*), and
- Irreconcilably Conflicting transactions (*IC*).

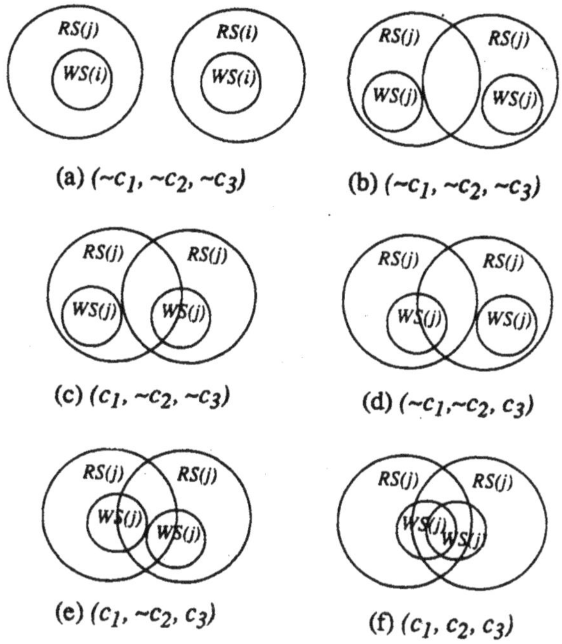

Figure 2 States of Active Transactions

Reconcilably conflicting transactions are ones which have only conflicts that can be serialized without aborting using the dynamic serialization order adjustment mechanism in this protocol, while irreconcilably conflicting transactions are ones that are involved in nonserializable execution which leads to aborting of either the validating transaction or active IC transactions.

6. SERIALIZATION ORDER ADJUSTMENT

To understand how to distinguish RC transactions and IC transactions, let us first consider the ways to resolve each conflict type by adjustment of serialization order.

(1) $RS(j) \cap WS(i) \neq \emptyset$ (read-write conflict)

The read-write conflict between the committing transaction, T_i, and the active transaction, T_j, can be serialized by the following timestamp interval adjustment of T_j;

$$TI(j) := TI(j) \cap [0, TS(i) - 1].$$

This adjustment of $TI(j)$ makes a partial ordering between T_i and T_j as $T_j \rightarrow T_i$, and is called *backward adjustment*. The meaning of this adjustment operation is that the read of T_j precedes the write of T_i on the same data object, i.e., the data read by T_j have not been written by T_i.

(2) $WS(j) \cap WS(i) \neq \emptyset$ (write-write conflict)

The write-write conflict between T_i and T_j can be serialized by the following operation:

$$TI(j) := TI(j) \cap [TS(i) + 1, \infty).$$

This adjustment operation makes a partial ordering between T_i and T_j as $T_i \rightarrow T_j$, and is called *forward adjustment*. This operation implies that the write of T_i precedes the write of T_j on the same data object, i.e., the write of T_j is not overwritten by T_i.

(3) $WS(j) \cap WS(i) \neq \emptyset$ (write-read conflict)

The write-read conflict between T_i and T_j can be serialized by

$$TI(j) := TI(j) \cap [TS(i) + 1, \infty).$$

Similarly, this adjustment of $TI(j)$ is a forward adjustment, and makes a partial ordering $T_i \rightarrow T_j$. The implication of this operation is that the data object read by T_i has not been written T_j.

From this discussion of dynamic adjustment of serialization order method, we can define a reconcilably conflicting transactions as ones all of whose conflicts with the validating transaction can be serialized by either forward adjustments only or backward adjustments only, but not both. That is, transactions whose state is either $(c_1, \sim c_2, \sim c_3)$ or $(\sim c_1, \sim c_2, c_3)$ among other possible states, belong to the set of RC transactions.

Now we give a pseudo code for the adjustment procedure. Suppose T_i is the validating transaction, and T_j ($j = 1, 2,..., n, j \neq i$) are reconcilably conflicting transactions.

```
adjustment(RC_set(i));
{
   for every Dp in RS(i)do
     for every Tj writing Dp do
        TI(j) := TI(j) ∩ [TS(i) + 1, ∞);
        if TI(j) = Ø
        then restart(j);
        endif;
     enddo;
  enddo;

  for every Dq in WS(i)do
     for every Tj reading Dq do
        TI(j) := TI(j) ∩ [0, TS(i) - 1];
        if TI(j) = Ø
        then restart(j);
        endif;
     enddo;

     for every Tj writing Dq do
        TI(j) := TI(j) ∩ [TS(i) + 1, ∞ );
        if TI(j) = Ø
        then restart(j);
        endif;
     enddo;
  enddo;
}
```

Figure 3 Serialization Order Adjustment

7. PRIORITY-BASED CONFLICT RESOLUTION

Finally, we are left only with the set of IC transactions. Transactions involved in conflicts that cannot be serialized by either forward adjustment only or backward adjustment only belong to IC transaction set. Obviously, a need of both forward and backward adjustment of timestamp interval for serialization results in the timestamp interval shut out. The transactions belonging to IC set are involved in nonserializable execution with the validating transaction. Transactions whose state is either $(c_1, \sim c_2, c_3)$ or (c_1, c_2, c_3) among other possible states, belong to the set of IC transactions.

As we mentioned in the previous section, we use priority-based conflict resolution schemes to resolve these irreconcilable conflicts. For the priority-based conflict resolution, it is useful to divide the IC set into two groups;

- Conflicting transactions with Higher Priority (*CHP*), and
- Conflicting transactions with Lower Priority (*CLP*).

CHP group contains transactions that belong to the IC set and have higher priorities than the validating transaction. In contrast, CLP group contains transactions that are in the IC set and have lower priorities than the validating transaction.

Now we summarize priority-based conflict resolution schemes proposed in [Hari90b, Huan91]. Suppose T_i is the validating transaction, and T_j ($j = 1, 2,..., n, j \neq i$) are irreconcilably conflicting transactions. Also, suppose l is the number of CHP transactions, and m is the number of CLP transactions ($n = l + m$).

(1) Priority abort

In this scheme [Huan91], when a transaction reaches its validation phase, it is aborted if its priority is less than that of all the conflicting transactions, i.e., all the IC transactions are with higher priority; otherwise, it commits and all the conflicting transactions are restarted. It can be described in a pseudo code as follows:

```
if (m = 0)
then restart(i);
else restart(j), j = 1, 2,..., n;
endif;
```

(2) Priority sacrifice

In this scheme [Hari90b], when a transaction reaches its validation phase, it is aborted if there exist one or more CHP transactions; otherwise it commits and all the irreconcilably conflicting transactions are restarted. Its pseudo code is given as follows:

```
if (l ≠ 0)
then restart(i);
else restart(j), j = 1, 2,..., n;
endif;
```

(3) Priority wait

In this scheme [Hari90b], when a transaction reaches its validation phase, if there exist one or more CHP transactions, it waits for CHP transactions to complete. Its pseudo code is given as follows:

```
while (l ≠ 0) do
   wait;
endwhile;
restart(j), j = 1, 2,..., n;
```

(4) Wait-50

In this scheme [Hari90b], a validating transaction is made to wait as long as more than half the IC transactions have higher priorities; otherwise it commits and all the IC transactions are restarted. The basic idea of this scheme is to maximize the beneficial effects of blocking, while reducing the effects of its drawbacks. It can be described in a pseudo code as follows:

```
while ((l ≠ 0) and (l > m)) do
    wait;
endwhile;
restart(j), j = 1, 2,..., n;
```

8. CONCLUDING REMARKS

In this paper, we have presented a new concurrency control protocol based on OCC. The goal of the protocol is to remedy the problem of wasted resource of conventional OCC protocols, and the problem of unnecessary aborts caused by incomplete validation tests. To achieve this goal, our scheme depends on early detection and resolution of conflicts using forward validation and timestamps, classification on conflicting transactions according to the types of conflicts and their priorities, and dynamic adjustment of serialization order using timestamp intervals.

Although we have argued that the proposed scheme has properties to produce results in a timely manner as well as to maintain data consistency, we need more concrete work on the performance of the scheme to support the argument. Through a simulation study using a fairly complete model of real-time database system [Lee92], we are currently evaluating the proposed scheme both in a deadline-driven scheduling environment and in a value-based scheduling environment. One of our goals in this performance evaluation study is to investigate if the complexity of the proposed scheme resulted from the dynamic management of timestamp interval is cost effective.

Also, we are considering several ways to improve the performance of the proposed protocol. In Section 4, without providing details, we have argued that the proposed scheme can be further optimized by using some strategies for choosing final timestamps of transactions, and using timestamp intervals for final timestamps. This argument will be verified by performing sensitivity tests in our simulation system. If the result shows that performance of the scheme is sensitive to those strategies, then we will develope appropriate mechanisms.

Finally, we will extend the proposed protocol so that it can be used in distributed real-time database systems. One advantage of OCC over 2PL is that the performance of OCC protocols does not suffer a significant degradation in distributed systems unlike 2PL protocols. Moreover, distribution of data is not only essential feature, but indeed is the key to the success of most practical real-time systems [Rodd89]. The proposed concurrency control scheme has a potential for good performance in a distributed real-time database systems.

Reference

[Abbo88] Abbott, R. and H. Garcia-Molina, "Scheduling Real-Time Transactions: A Performance Evaluation", *Proceedings of the 14th VLDB Conference*, August 1988.

[Abbo89] Abbott, R. and H. Garcia-Molina, "Scheduling Real-Time Transactions with Disk Resident Data", *Proceedings of the 15th VLDB Conference*, August 1989.

[Baye82] Bayer, R., K. Elhardt, J. Heigert and A. Reiser, "Dynamic Timestamp Allocation for Transactions in Database Systems", *Proceedings of the 2nd Int. Symposium on Distributed Data Bases*, September 1982, pp 9-20.

[Bern87] Bernstein, P. A., V. Hadzilacos, and N. Goodman, *Concurrency Control and Recovery in Database Systems*, Addison-Wesley, Reading, MA, 1987.

[Boks87] Boksenbaum, C., M. Cart, J. Ferrie, and J. Pons, "Concurrent Certifications by Intervals of Timestamps in Distributed Database Systems", *IEEE Transactions on Software Engineering*, Vol. SE-13, No. 4, April 1987.

[Buch89] Buchmann, A., D. R. McCarthy, M. Hsu, and U. Dayal, "Time-Critical Database Scheduling: A Framework for Integrating Real-Time Scheduling and Concurrency Control", *Proceedings of the 5th Data Engineering Conference*, February 1989.

[Care87] Carey, M. J., "Improving the Performance of an Optimistic Concurrency Control Algorithm Through Timestamps and Versions", *IEEE Transactions on Software Engineering*, Vol. SE-13, No. 6, June 1987, pp. 746 - 751.

[Haer84] Haerder, T., "Observations on Optimistic Concurrency Control Schemes", *Information Systems*, 9(2), 1984.

[Hari90] Haritsa, J. R., M. J. Carey, and M. Livny, "On Being Optimistic about Real-Time Constraints", *Proceedings of the 1990 ACM SIGACT-SIGART-SIGMOD Symposium on Principles of Database Systems (PODS)*, 1990.

[Hari90b] Haritsa, J. R., M. J. Carey, and M. Livny, "Dynamic Real-Time Optimistic Concurrency Control", *Proceedings of the IEEE Real-Time Systems Symposium*, Orlando, Florida, December 1990.

[Huan89] Huang, J., J. A. Stankovic, D. Towsley and K. Ramamritham, "Experimental Evaluation of Real-Time Transaction Processing", *Proceedings of the IEEE Real-Time Systems Symposium*, December 1989.

[Huan91] Huang, J., J. A. Stankovic, K. Ramamritham, and D. Towsley, "Experimental Evaluation of Real-Time Optimistic Concurrency Control Schemes", *Proceedings of the Conference on Very Large Data Bases*, September 1991.

[Kung81] Kung H. T., and J. T. Robinson, "On Optimistic Methods for Concurrency Control", *ACM Transactions on Database Systems*, 6(2): 213-226, June 1981.

[Lee92] Lee, J., "Scheduling Transactions in Real-Time Database Systems", *Ph.D. Dissertation Proposal*, Department of Computer Science, University of Virginia, September, 1992.

[Lin89] Lin, K., "Consistency Issues in Real-Time Database Systems", *Proceedings of the 22nd Hawaii International Conference on System Science*, January 1989.

[Lin90] Lin Y., and S. H. Son, "Concurrency Control in Real-Time Database Systems by Dynamic Adjustment of Serialization Order," *Proceedings of the 11th IEEE Real-Time Systems Symposium*, Orlando, Florida, December 1990.

[Liu88] Liu, J., K. Lin, and X. Song, "Scheduling Hard Real-Time Transactions", *The 5th IEEE Workshop on Real-Time Operating Systems and Software*, May 1988.

[Robi82] Robinson, J. T., "Design of Concurrency Controls for Transaction Processing Systems", *Ph.D. Thesis*, Technical Report CMU-CS-82-114, Carnegie-Mellon University, 1982.

[Rodd89] Rodd, M. G., "Real-Time Issues in Distributed Data Bases for Real-Time Control", *IFAC Distributed Databases in Real-Time Control*, Budapest, Hungary, 1989, pp. 1-7.

[Sha88] Sha, L., R. Rajkumar and J. P. Lehoczky, "Concurrency Control for Distributed Real-Time Databases", *ACM SIGMOD Record*, March 1988.

[Son88] Son, S. H., "Semantic Information and Consistency in Distributed Real-Time Systems", *Information and Software Technology*, Vol. 30, September 1988.

[Stan88] Stankovic, J. A., and W. Zhao, "On Real-Time Transactions", *ACM SIGMOD Record*, March 1988.

[Stan90] Stankovic, J. A., and K. Ramamritham, "What is Predictability for Real-Time System?", *Real-Time Systems*, 2: 247-254, Kluwer Academic Publishers, 1990.

New Disk Scheduling Algorithms for Reduced Rotational Latency

Kitae Hwang and Heonshik Shin

Department of Computer Engineering
Seoul National University
Kwanakgu, Seoul 151-742, Korea
E-mail : shinhs@erccw1.snu.ac.kr
Fax : +82-2-886-7589

ABSTRACT

Disk arm scheduling algorithms have been studied for many years to increase disk I/O performance. Most of the disks by the early 1980's are characterized as a linear seek time and their seek time is responsible for the most time of disk access. So, the existing disk scheduling algorithms have focused on the reduction of the average seek distance. Seek time has improved greatly and today's disks usually have nonlinear seek time characteristics, whereas the rotation speed has been steady at the 3600 RPM. So, it is of value to reduce average rotational latency.

In this paper we propose two disk scheduling algorithms, i.e. **Shortest Rotational Latency First(SRLF) and Shortest Access Time First(SATF)** for reduced rotational latency. SRLF services first a request with the shortest expected rotational latency and SATF services first a request with the shortest expected access time. We analyze the expected access time of the request serviced first by each of SSTF and SRLF under the uniform cylinder access. We evaluated the response time of SSTF, SRLF, and SATF through the simulations under the uniform and localized cylinder access. The results of the analysis and simulations show that the algorithms proposed in this paper are more efficient than SSTF which is known for the fastest response time.

1. INTRODUCTION

Disk arm scheduling algorithms have been studied for many years to increase disk I/O performance[2,3,4,5,7]. Most disks by the early 1980's had been made of simple stepper motors which have a linear seek time characteristic[3]. Since the seek time is responsible for the most time of disk access, most studies on the disk scheduling have focused on the reduction of the average seek distance or the number of cylinders from the current head position to the requested cylinder to improve the response time. SCAN and Shortest Seek Time First(SSTF) are the representative disk scheduling algorithms[4]. SCAN algorithm moves a disk head from the innermost cylinder to the outmost cylinder, or conversely. Then it services first a request closest on the moving direction of the disk head. SSTF services first a request closest to the disk head position. SSTF has been credited with the fastest mean response time among the existing disk scheduling algorithms[4].

Nowadays disk manufacturing technology based on a voice coil actuator is available for disk drives which show the nonlinear seek time characteristics as follows:

$$a + b\sqrt{n}, \qquad n > 0$$

where a is the settling time, b is the acceleration factor, and n is the seek distance[1,5]. In the case of a disk with a voice coil actuator, the reduction of the seek distance makes less contribution to the reduction of the seek time than in the case of a disk with linear seek time characteristics. With the exisiting disk arm scheduling algorithms a request spends rotational latency of a half revolution on the average, which is 8.35ms at 3600 RPM. Actually this time is never small in comparison with the seek time of a disk with a voice coil actuator. When b=0.5ms, the mean rotational time(8.35ms) is approximately equal to the difference between the seek time of 100 cylinders and the seek time of 712 cylinders for a voice coil actuator, i.e., $a+0.5\sqrt{712}$ - $(a+0.5\sqrt{100})$ = 8.34. In addition, the seek time has greatly improved with the nominal seek time of about 15ms, whereas rotation speed has been steady at 3600 RPM for a decade[8]. These facts motivate us to propose new disk scheduling algorithms based on the reduction of rotational latency.

In this paper we present two new disk scheduling algorithms for reduced rotational latency: Shortest Rotational Latency First(SRLF) and Shortest Access Time First(SATF). SRLF first services a request with the shortest rotational latency and SATF services first a request with the smallest sum of seek and rotational latency. It will be shown that the proposed algorithms achieve shorter disk access time than SSTF using analytic and simulation methods.

The remainder of this paper proceeds as follows: In

Section 2 disk access time model is described. New disk scheduling algorithms proposed in this paper are introduced and their expected access time is analyzed in comparison with that of SSTF in Section 3 and estimated through simulation in Section 4. Conclusions are drawn in Section 5.

2. ACCESS TIME MODEL

As shown in Fig. 1, the disk access time is defined as the sum of seek time, rotational latency, and transfer time and the disk access time. The queueing delay increases more rapidly as the mean disk access time becomes larger for a fixed arrival rate.

The transfer time is in proportion to block size, rotational speed, recording density of a track, and speed of the electronics connecting a disk to a computer. Transfer rates in 1990 are typically 1 to 4MB/sec[9]; so, the transfer time is relatively very small compared with the seek time and rotational latency

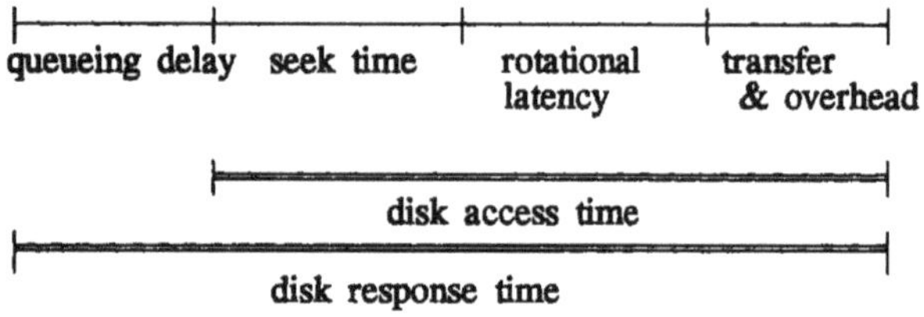

Figure 1 Time components of disk I/O

2.1 Rotational Latency

The rotational latency is defined as the time for a requested sector to rotate under the disk head. The average rotational latency to the desired sector is halfway around the disk. Currently it is approximately 8.3ms at the rotational speed of 3600 RPM. Although some manufacturers plan to go for 5400 RPM in the early 1990's, many difficulties exist in reducing rotational latency by increasing RPM[8].

2.2 Seek Time

The seek time is a function of seek distance. Nominal seek time is defined as the average time required for the disk head to move from any random cylinder to any other random cylinder. This factor has been the most important subject of research effort for the reduction of the response time. In the early days of disk design, the nominal seek time is one or two orders of magnitude larger than all the other components[8,10]: Now the nominal seek time for IBM 3380 disk is reduced to around 16ms.

A disk with a simple stepper motor actuator has a linear seek time characteristic:

$$\text{seek}(n) = \begin{cases} 0 & n = 0 \\ a + bn & n > 0 \end{cases} \qquad (1)$$

where n is the seek distance, a is the mechanical settling time, and b is the acceleration factor. For example, the values of a and b are 10ms and 0.1ms, respectively. For a disk with the linear seek time, the nominal seek time is simply the time required for a seek of the average seek distance, N/3, where N is the total number of cylinders.

But nominal seek time varies with the various actuator models. Disks with high performance voice coil actuators such as IBM 3380, have nonlinear seek time characteristics[1]:

$$\text{seek}(n) = \begin{cases} 0 & n = 0 \\ a + b\sqrt{n} & n > 0 \end{cases} \qquad (2)$$

Scranton et. al showed that the nominal seek time for a voice coil actuator is the time required for a seek of approximately 0.284N cylinders[1]. In the case of a disk with a voice coil actuator, therefore, the seek distance makes less contribution to the seek time than in the case of a disk with a simple stepper motor actuator. Meanwhile the rotational latency remains the same regardless of the seek time characteristics. This fact makes it worthwhile to attempt to reduce the rotational latency for shorter response time.

3. DISK SCHEDULING FOR REDUCED ROTATIONAL LATENCY

3.1 SRLF(Shortest Rotational Latency First)

We now describe a new disk scheduling algorithm, SRLF. While the existing disk scheduling algorithms, such as SSTF and variations of SCAN, are based on the seek distances of requests in a disk queue, the SRLF scheduling makes use of the rotational latencies of requests in the queue. SRLF services first a request with the shortest rotational latency.

In our research the disk subsystem is based on a simple model consisting of a single disk, a disk queue, and a scheduling program module as depicted in Fig. 2. For simplicity, it is assumed that the disk has one track per cylinder and that the drive has a single arm and a voice coil actuator; so, the seek time is characterized by the nonlinear seek time model of Eq.(2). The disk is assumed to have the circuitry to sense the rotational position in terms of the sector number that rotates under the disk head. This circuitry can be implemented easily by modifying the circuitry to sense the index point which is the starting point of track. The IBM 3380 disk subsystem also has the circuitry to sense the rotational position[9].

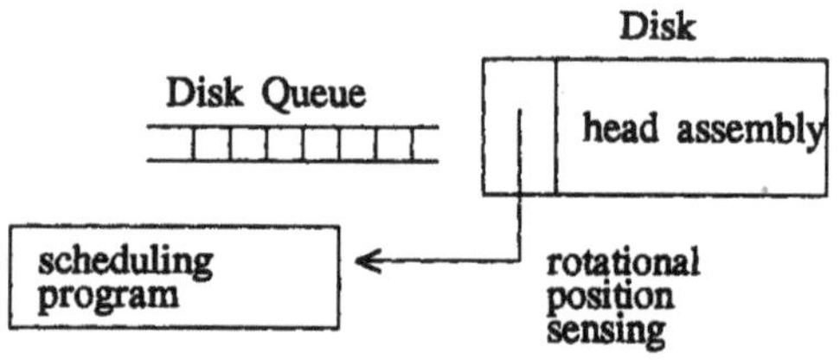

Figure 2 A disk model

We now introduce two basic terms to delineate the disk behavior: the **Expected Rotational Position(ERP)** and **Expected Rotational Distance(ERD)**. ERP is defined as the rotational position located at the end of seek activity resulting from a request in service, and ERD is defined as the rotational distance of a request in service. The expected rotational latency is equal to the multiplication of ERD and the rotational time per sector. The SRLF algorithm calculates ERP and ERD of each request in the disk queue and selects a request with the shortest ERD. The following symbols will be used throughout to describe the SRLF method formally.

r_i = i-th request in the queue
h = the head position(the cylinder number) at the scheduling instant
RP = the rotational position at the scheduling instant
R = one revolution time of a disk
M = the number of sectors in one track
N = the number of total cylinders
SR = R/M, the rotational time per sector
T = transfer time
c_i = the cylinder number of r_i.(ranges from 1 to N)
s_i = the sector number of r_i.(ranges from 0 to M-1)
$TSEEK_i$ = the seek time of r_i,

Let ERP and ERD of $r_i(i=1,2,..,k$ where k is the queue length) denote ERP_i and ERD_i, respectively. For the seek distance between the disk head and r_i or $|c_i-h|$, $TSEEK_i$, ERP_i, and ERD_i can be calculated to be as follows:

$$TSEEK_i = a + b\sqrt{|c_i-h|}$$
$$ERP_i = (RP + TSEEK_i/SR) \bmod M$$
$$ERD_i = \begin{cases} M+s_i-ERP_i, & \text{if } s_i - ERP_i < 0 \\ s_i-ERP_i, & \text{otherwise} \end{cases} \quad (3)$$
(unit: the number of sectors)

If there is any r_i whose seek distance $|c_i-h| = 0$, that is, whose cylinder number is equal to the head position, SRLF services it first. Otherwise, upon the calculation of $ERD_i(i=1,...,k)$ for all i, SRLF chooses a request with the smallest ERD_i among k requests for immediate service.

3.2 Performance Analysis

For the analysis of the expected access times the following assumptions are made: Each request arrives with a cylinder number randomly distributed within total data band width. The sector number of each request is distributed randomly within the range of [0,M-1]. The cylinder number and the sector number of a request are independent of each other. In reality, however, successive seeks are not independent. They show the localized access pattern such that the cylinder of next request is more likely the same as that of the last request. Nevertheless, it is difficult to analyze the average access time for localized access pattern. The assumption of the uniform disk access provides a good approximation of seek time and most disk scheduling algorithms aim at minimizing the expected access time computed under this assumption[6]. In this paper, SSTF is selected as the base algorithm for performace comparison with SRLF and SATF because it is known for the fastest mean response time[4]. The response time for localized access will be evaluated through the simulations in Section 4.

The performance of SSTF and SRLF is evaluated in terms of **Expected Shortest Seek Distance(ESSD)** and **Expected Shortest Rotational Latency(ESRL)**: ESSD and ESRL are defined as the average of the shortest seek distance and that of the shortest rotational latency, respectively, among requests in the disk queue.

3.2.1 Expected Shortest Seek Distance(ESSD)

Assuming that there exist k requests in the disk queue, let $X_i(i=1,2,..,k)$ be the random variables for the seek distance from the disk head position to the cylinder of r_i. These random variables are assumed to have identical distributions. The shortest seek distance for k random requests is the random variable X_s defined to be

$$X_s = \min(X_1,X_2,...X_k)$$

Thus,

$$ESSD = E[X_s]$$

Since the property of uniform access accounts for the fact that the X_i are independent, the seek distances of requests in the disk queue can be modeled as independent random variables. On the other hand, there are N^2 unique seeks: N seeks of length zero and 2(N-i) different seeks of length i, for i=1,2,...,N-1. Hence each of the $X_j(j=1,2,...,k)$ has the following distribution:

$$P(X=i) = 2(N-i)/N^2$$

or

$$P(X\geq i) = (2/N^2)\sum_{j=i}^{N-1}(N-j)$$
$$= (N-i)(N-i+1)/N^2$$

Thus

$$P[\min(X_1,X_2,...,X_k)\geq i)]$$
$$= P(X_1\geq i)\cdot P(X_1\geq i)\cdot\cdot\cdot P(X_k\geq i)$$

$$E[X_s] = \sum_{i=1}^{N-1} P[\min(X_1,X_2,...,X_k) \geq i)]$$

According to the result of Bitton[6], the equation becomes

$$E[X_s] \fallingdotseq N/(2k + 1) \quad (4)$$

For a disk with a linear seek time model and k requests in the disk queue, the expected disk access time of the request serviced first by SSTF is presented by

$$ACC_{SSTF(linear)} = a + bN/(2k+1) + R/2 + T$$

since the mean rotational latency of SSTF is R/2. For a disk with a voice coil actuator, however,

$$ACC_{SSTF} \fallingdotseq a + b\sqrt{N/(2k+1)} + R/2 + T$$

Using the simulation method(see Appendix) we have found the expected shortest seek time as a function of the seek distance for a voice coil actuator:

$$ACC_{SSTF(nonlinear)} = a + b\sqrt{SD_k N} + R/2 + T \quad (5)$$

where SD_k is defined in Appendix.

3.2.2 Expected Shortest Rotational Latency(ESRL)

Let X_1, X_2,..., X_k be the random variables uniformly distributed between 0 and R where subscript k denotes the number of requests in the disk queue. Then, X_i represents the rotational latency of r_i. Thus a random variable X_r or the shortest rotational latency becomes

$$X_r = \min(X_1, X_2, \ldots, X_k)$$

Since X_i is distributed within [0,R], the distribution of X_i is

$$P(X_i < \alpha) = \alpha/R$$

Then the distribution function of X_r is obtained as follows:

$$\begin{aligned} F_{X_r}(x) &= P(X_r < \alpha) \\ &= P(X_1 < \alpha \text{ or } X_2 < \alpha \text{ or } \cdots X_k < \alpha) \\ &= 1 - P(X_1 \geq \alpha \text{ and } X_2 \geq \alpha \cdots X_k \geq \alpha) \\ &= 1 - P(X_1 \geq \alpha)P(X_2 \geq \alpha) \cdots P(X_k \geq \alpha) \\ &= 1 - (1 - \frac{\alpha}{R})^k \end{aligned}$$

Then the density function of X_r is

$$f_{X_r}(\alpha) = F'_{X_r}(\alpha) = \frac{k}{R}(1 - \frac{\alpha}{R})^{k-1}$$

Therefore,

$$\begin{aligned} ESRL = E[X_r] &= \int_0^R \alpha f_{X_r}(\alpha) d\alpha \\ &= \frac{k}{R} \int_0^R \alpha (1 - \frac{\alpha}{R})^{k-1} d\alpha \\ &= \frac{R}{k+1} \end{aligned} \quad (6)$$

Thus, if k=1, then $E[X_r] = R/2$. The distribution of the cylinder numbers of requests serviced by SRLF is random because SRLF services requests considering rotational latency which is related with only sector number but independent of the cylinder number. Then the nominal seek time is equal to $a + b\sqrt{(0.284N)}$ and the expected access time of the request serviced first by SRLF is

$$ACC_{SRLF} = a + b\sqrt{(0.284N)} + R/(k+1) + T \quad (7)$$

3.2.3 Comparison of the expected access time

For the comparison of access times, ACC_{SSTF} and ACC_{SRLF}, their difference can be calculated as follows:

For the disk queue length of k,

$$\begin{aligned} ACC_{SSTF} - ACC_{SRLF} &= a + b\sqrt{SD_k N} + R/2 + T \\ &\quad - (a + b\sqrt{(0.284N)} + R/(k+1) + T) \\ &= b\sqrt{N}(\sqrt{SD_k} - \sqrt{0.284}) + R(\frac{1}{2} - \frac{1}{k+1}) \end{aligned} \quad (8)$$

The difference in the expected access time is determined by three constants *b*, N, and R as shown in Eq.(8) where the first and second multiplication terms are the differences in the seek time and the rotational latency, respectively. For k larger than 1, the first multiplication term becomes negative and the second multiplication term becomes positive. If k=1, Eq.(8) is 0 because the disk access time is the same irrespective of disk scheduling algorithms when there is only one request in the disk queue.

Eq.(8) is plotted for different values of *b* and R in Fig. 3, where the x-axis represents the number of requests at the scheduling instant. Under the current disk technology, R, N, and *b* are approximately 16.7ms, 1000, and 0.5ms, respectively. For these values, Eq.(8) is positive for all k as shown in Fig. 3. At present, therefore, we can conclude that SRLF achieves the shorter average access time than SSTF under the current disk technology.

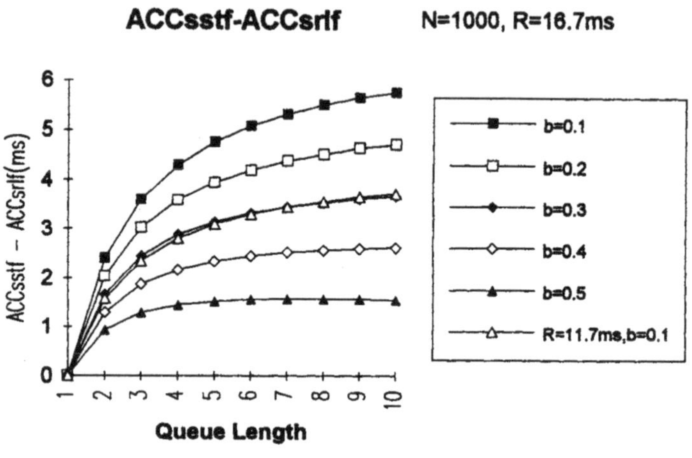

Figure 3(a) ACC_{SSTF} - ACC_{SRLF} with varing b

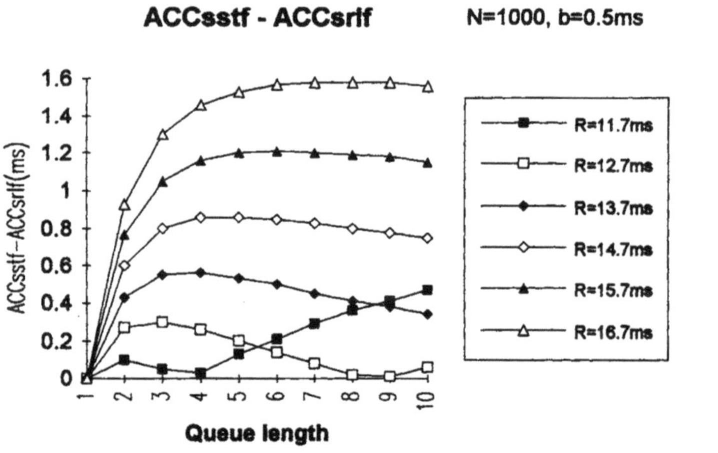

Figure 3(b) ACC_{SSTF} - ACC_{SRLF} with varing R

Which of the two algorithms will achieve the better performance in the future in terms of seek time and rotational speed? Recently, many efforts are being invested in speeding up disk rotation in spite of many difficulties. The seek time of a disk with a voice coil actuator can be improved by making the time factor a and b smaller[1]. Fig. 3a and 3b show some of the results from Eq.(8) for b and R in the range of [0.1ms,0.5ms] and [11.7ms 16.7ms], respectively. (We do not refer to a because a is not related with the Eq.(8)). For all these ranges, Eq. (8) turns out to be positive. As a result, SRLF services requests faster than SSTF. This makes the average response time of SRLF shorter than SSTF. So, we can claim that SRLF is superior to SSTF under the current and future technology.

3.3 SATF(Shortest Access Time First)

In addition to SRLF, we present another efficient disk scheduling algorithm, Shortest Access Time First(SATF). It takes both seek and rotational latency into consideration. For each request in the disk queue, SATF calculates the Expected Access Time(EAT) which is defined as the expected sum of the seek and rotational latency. If there are k requests in the disk queue, EAT of r_i or EAT_i can be derived as follows:

$$TSEEK_i = a + b\sqrt{|c_i - h|}$$

$$ERP_i = (RP + TSEEK_i/SR) \bmod M$$

$$ERD_i = \begin{cases} M + s_i - ERP_i, & \text{if } s_i - ERP_i < 0 \\ s_i - ERP_i, & \text{otherwise} \end{cases}$$

$$EAT_i = TSEEK_i + ERD_i \times SR \qquad (9)$$

SATF first services a request with the smallest EAT. In doing so, SATF achieves the shorter expected access time than SSTF and SRLF. Performance analysis in comparison with other algorithms will be shown in Section 4 through simulations.

3.4 Algorithm Overhead

The time complexity of SSTF is O(n), where n is the number of requests in the disk queue. Time complexities of SRLF and SATF are also O(n) because they search the disk queue just once. However, SRLF and SATF have some computational overhead because ERD and EAT must be calculated, respectively. Since these calculations are very simple as shown above, this overhead should not influence their performance too much.

4. PERFORMANCE EVALUATION

4.1 Simulation

We implemented a simulator using SLAM II[11] to evaluate the response time of the three algorithms of SSTF, SRLF, and SATF. The disk parameters used in the simulation is shown in Table 2.

Table 2 Disk parameters

Parameter	meaning	base value
N	Number of total cylinders	1000
a	Mechanical settling time	6ms
b	Acceleration factor	0.5ms
R	Full rotation time	16.7ms
T	Transfer rate	1Mbytes/sec
S	Bytes per sector	512
M	Sector per cylinder	40

The event flow of the simulator and it's description are given in Fig. 4 and Table 3, respectively, in which MAIN and DISKSCHDL are not an event but a program module. MAIN routine initializes SLAM variables and starts simulations by calling event 1 and event 6. The three algorithms are implemented in DISKSCHDL. The results of each experiment are averaged over 20 runs, each of which has executed 4000 disk I/O requests.

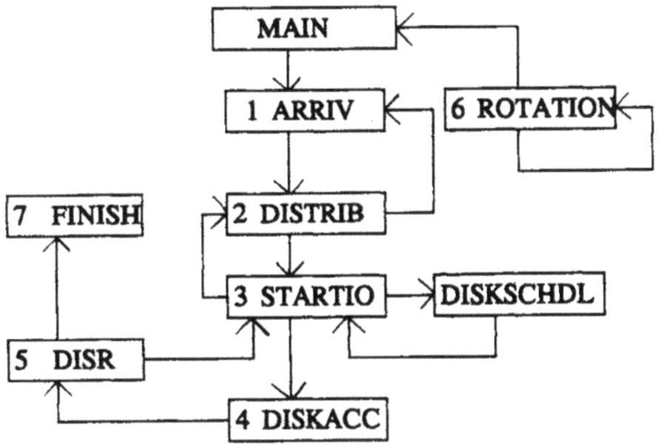

Figure 4 Event flow of simulator

Table 3 Event table

ARRIV	Simulates the request arrival and calls DISTRIB event.
DISTRIB	Inserts the arriving request in a disk queue and calls STARTIO. At the same time, it calls ARRIV for the arrival of next request.
STARTIO	Returns immediately if the disk is busy. If the disk is idle, it calls the scheduler DISK SCHDL which is the disk scheduler to choose a request, changes status of the disk to idle,and calls DISKACC.
DISK-ACC	Simulates physical disk I/O and calls DISR on completion of a disk I/O and calculates disk access time.
DISR	Simulates the disk interrupt service routine. It changes status of the disk to idle and calls FINISH. It also calls STARTIO to service arequest waiting in the queue.
ROTA-TION	Manages the rotational position and keeps up it. DISKACC and DISKSCHDL use this information to know the current rotational position
FINISH	Enumerates the simulation results

4.2 Workload

Requests arrive with arrival time exponentially distributed with mean of MeanArrivalRate. MeanArrivalRate which is defined as the number of disk I/O requests per second varies from 20 to 40. The distribution of requested sectors is assumed to be uniform within the range of 0 to M-1, and the requested size is assumed to be 4 sectors. We evaluate the response time for two cylinder access distributions. One is the uniform cylinder access such that requested cylinder numbers are distributed randomly within the range of 1 to N. The other is the localized cylinder access for more realistic case. Arriving requests are assumed to have the following localized property defined by Hofri[3]. Let p_{ij} be the probability of a request addressing cylinder j, given that the previous one was destined for cylinder i.

$$p_{ij} = \begin{cases} \alpha + \dfrac{1}{N} & i = j \\ \dfrac{1 - (\alpha + 1/N)}{(N-1)} & i \neq j \end{cases} \qquad 0 \leq \alpha < 1$$

where α reflects the degree of locality. $\alpha=0$ means uniform cylinder access and high values of α reflect strong locality.

4.3 Results

4.3.1 Experiment 1 : Uniform cylinder access ($\alpha=0$)

Fig. 5 shows the response time of three algorithms for base values of disk parameters. It turns out that both algorithms, SRLF and SATF considering rotational latency have the shorter response time than SSTF.

Table 4 shows the average seek distance, average seek time, and average rotational latency for base values of disk parameters. As listed in Table 4, among the three algorithms, the average seek distance of SSTF is the smallest while that of SRLF is the largest. Average rotational latency of SRLF is the smallest. SRLF tries to reduce rotational latency at the expense of seek time and achieves the smaller sum of rotational latency and seek time than SSTF. Of course, SATF is the best because it services first a request with the smallest sum of rotational time and seek time.

4.3.2 Experiment 2 : Localized cylinder access

Fig. 6 shows the response time of the three algorithms for α(α = 0.3, 0.5, 0.7, 0.9) using the base values of disk parameters. For all ranges of arrival rate, SATF shows the best performance among the three algorithms and the second is SRLF. As the locality becomes larger, it is natural that the average seek distance of SSTF become smaller. It may be asserted that SSTF should be better than SRLF at a high locality. As the locality increases, however, the average seek distance of SRLF is no longer the nominal seek distance(=N/3). Rather, it decreases. This is because SRLF services it first if there is any request whose cylinder is equal to the head position,.

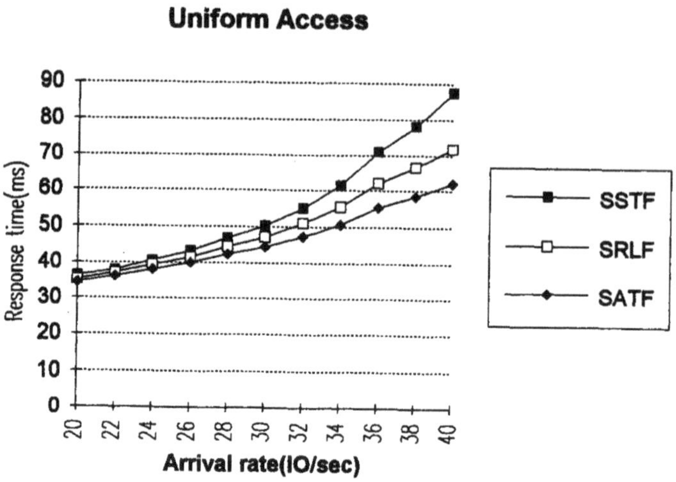

Figure 5 Response time under the uniform access

Table 4 The results of simulations for the uniform cylinder access

(a) Average seek distance

Arrival rate	20	24	28	32	36	40
SSTF	309	297	280	260	225	196
SRLF	333	333	332	333	333	333
SATF	320	313	304	296	280	268

(b) Average seek time(ms)

Arrival rate	20	24	28	32	36	40
SSTF	14.0	13.8	13.5	13.2	12.6	12.1
SRLF	14.4	14.4	14.4	14.4	14.4	14.4
SATF	14.2	14.1	14.0	13.8	13.6	13.4

(c) Average rotational latency(ms)

Arrival rate	20	24	28	32	36	40
SSTF	8.33	8.34	8.32	8.33	8.34	8.35
SRLF	7.86	7.56	7.16	6.98	6.05	5.52
SATF	7.89	7.62	7.29	7.15	6.47	6.11

At a high locality, SATF is more efficient than the other two algorithms as shown in Fig. 6. Fig 7 shows the average seek distances and the average rotational latencies for arrival rate of 26 IOs/sec. At the locality greater than 0.5, the seek distances of the three algorithms are almost the same as shown in Fig. 7a. At the locality of 0, SRLF has the smallest average rotational latency among the three algorithms. However, at the locality greater than about 0.2, SATF has the smallest average rotational latency. This result can be explained as follows: As the locality increases, more requests addressing the same cylinder arrive at the disk device and there may exist more requests whose seek distances are 0 in the disk queue. Thus a request with the shortest expected rotational latency may be serviced first by SATF because the expected access time of the request may be the smallest. This possibility becomes higher as the locality increases. If all requests address the same cylinder, the requests may be serviced in the order of rotation by SATF. The results of these simulations allow us to claim that the two proposed algorithms which consider the rotational latency are superior to SSTF which considers only seek time for a disk with a voice coil actuator.

5. CONCLUSION

So far, we have presented two disk scheduling algorithms of Shortest Rotational Latency First(SRLF) and Shortest Access Time First(SATF). SRLF services first a request whose cylinder is equal to the disk head position; if there is no such a request, it services first a request with the shorest expected rotational latency. SATF services first a request with the shortest expected disk access time.

We found out the seek distance which produced the average shotest seek time for a disk with a voice coil actuator for the disk queue length of k using the simulation. We analyzed the expected access time of the request serviced first by each of SSTF and SRLF, for a disk queue length of k, under the asssumption of the uniform cylinder access. The result of the analysis shows that SRLF has the shorter expected access time than SSTF under the current disk technology, i.e. N=1000, R=16.7ms, and *b*=0.5ms, and under the future disk technology supporting faster R and shorter *b*.

Recent studies show that the locality is an important property in accessing disk cylinders. In this study experiments have been conducted to find out the response time of SSTF, SRLF, and SATF through simulations with varing the degree of locality. For all ranges of workload settings, the results show that SATF has the best of the three algorithms and the second is SRLF. For the localities greater than 0.5, seek distances of the three algorithms are almost the same. However, the two algorithms proposed in this paper have the shorter average rotational latency. Especially, SATF is more efficient than the other two algorithms at the higher locality because it first services a request with the shorter rotational latency among the requests addressing the same cylinder. Consequently, the two disk schduling algorithms of SRLF and SATF for reduced rotational latency are more efficient than the existing algorithms.

< Appendix : Simulation results for $ACC_{SSTF(nonlinear)}$ >

Simulations were performed as follows:

a, *b*, and N are assumed to be 6ms, 0.5ms, and 1000, respectively. The following Step 1 to Step 5 are repeated for 10 values of k (k=1,2,...,10).

1. Generate the random head position and k independent random requests in a disk queue for 1000 cylinders.
2. Calculate the shortest seek time.
3. Repeat Step 1 and 2 100,000 times and average the shortest seek time.
4. Calculate the seek distance, SeekDist, which produces the average shortest seek time, AveShort which is the result of Step 3.

$$\text{SeekDist} = \left[\frac{(\text{AveShort} - a)}{b} \right]^2 = \left[\frac{(\text{AveShort} - 6)}{0.5} \right]^2$$

5. Calculate SD_k defined as SeekDist divided by 1000.

$$SD_k = \text{SeekDist}/1000$$

Table 1 shows SD_k: For k=1, the result(0.284) is in accord with the seek distance for the nominal access time derived by Scranton and Thompson[1]. Also for k=2, the result is approximately consistent with the seek distance (0.16N) obtained by Bitton and Gray to produce the expected seek time for mirrored disk[6]. Then, if there exist k random requests in a disk queue, the expected shortest seek time is expressed as

$$a + b\sqrt{SD_k N}$$

Hence, ACC_{SSTF} for a voice coil actuators can be expressed as

$$ACC_{SSTF(nonlinear)} = a + b\sqrt{SD_k N} + R/2 + T$$

Table 1 Seek distance for the expected shortest seek time for a voice coil actuator.

queue length k	1	2	3	4	5
SD_k	0.284	0.170	0.121	0.093	0.075
queue length k	6	7	8	9	10
SD_k	0.063	0.0544	0.0477	0.0427	0.0835

REFERENCE

[1] R. A. Scranton and D. A. Thompson, "The access time myth," IBM Res. Rep., Nov. 1983.
[2] Neil C. Wilhelm, "An abnomaly scheduling: A comparison of FCFS and SSTF seek scheduling using an empirical model for disk accesses," Comm. of ACM, Vol. 19, No. 1, Jan. 1976.
[3] Micha Hofri, "Disk scheduling : FCFS vs. SSTF revisited," Comm. of ACM, Vol. 23, No. 11, Nov. 1980.
[4] R. Geist and S. Daniel, "A continuum of disk scheduling algorithms," ACM Trans. on Computer Systems, Vol. 5, No. 1, Feb. 1987.
[5] Dina Bitton, "Arm scheduling in shadowed disks," Spring. COMPCON89, 1989, pp. 132-136.
[6] Dina Bitton and Jim Gray, "Disk shadowing," Proc. of the 14th VLDB Conf., 1988.
[7] Richard P. King, "Disk arm movement in anticipation of future requests," ACM Trans. on Compter Systems, Vol. 8, No. 3, 1990, pp. 214-229,
[8] S. W. Ng, "Improving disk performance via latency reduction," IEEE Trans. on Computers, Vol. 40, No. 1, Jan. 1991, pp. 22-30
[9] J. Hennessy and D. A. Patterson, Computer Architecture : A Quantitative Approach, Morgan Kaufmann Pub. INC., 1990.
[10] R. H. Katz, G. A. Gibson, and D. A. Patterson, "Disk system architectures for high performance computing," Proceedings of the IEEE, Vol. 77, No. 12, Dec. 1989.
[11] A. Alan B. Pritsker, Introduction to Simulation and SLAM II, John Wiley & Sons, New York, 1986.

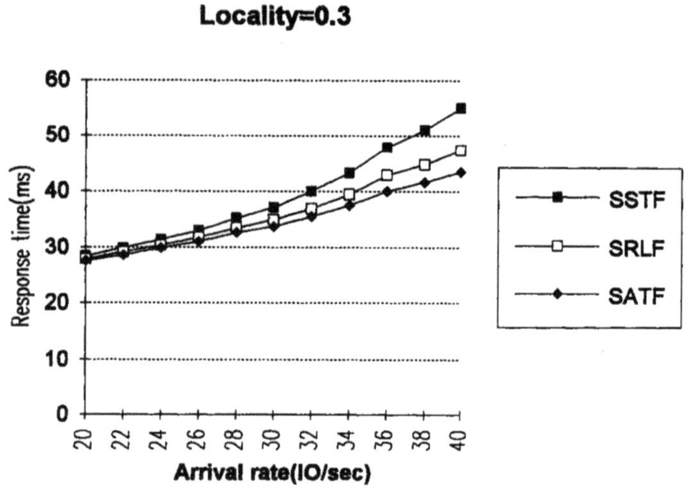

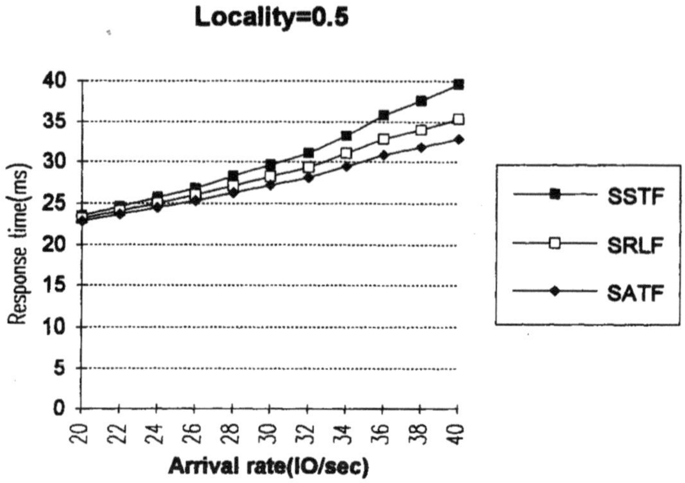

Figure 6(a) Response time for the locality of 0.3

Figure 6(b) Response time for the locality of 0.5

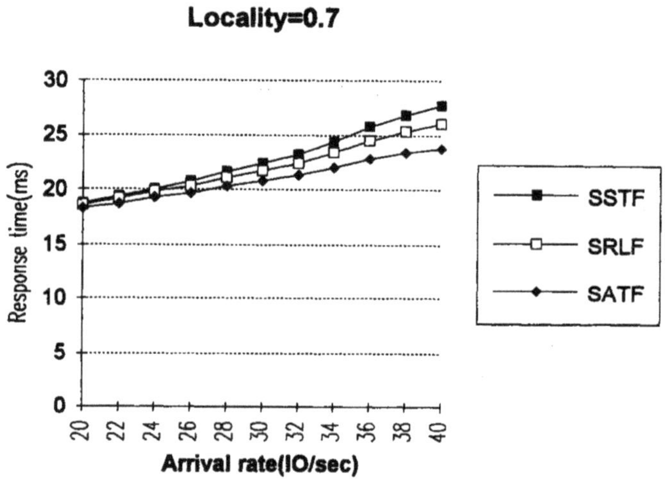

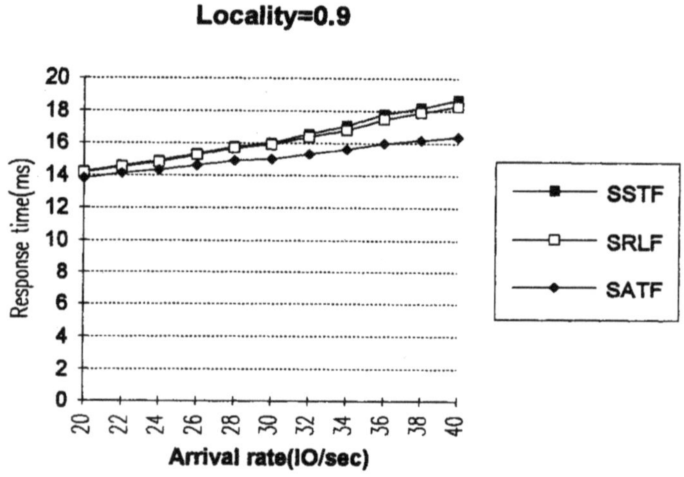

Figure 6(c) Response time for the locality of 0.7

Figure 6(d) Response time for the locality of 0.9

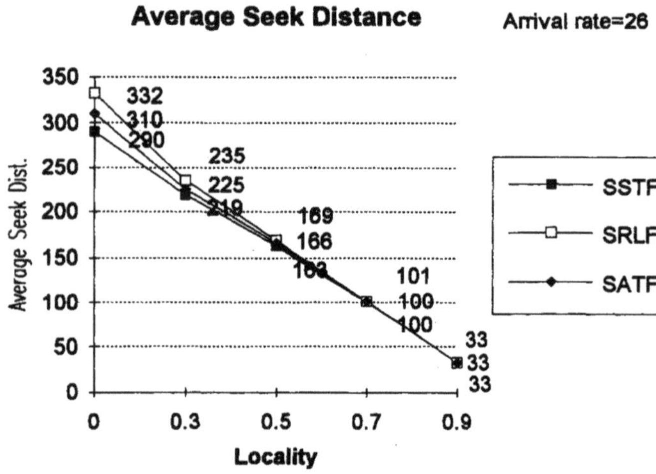

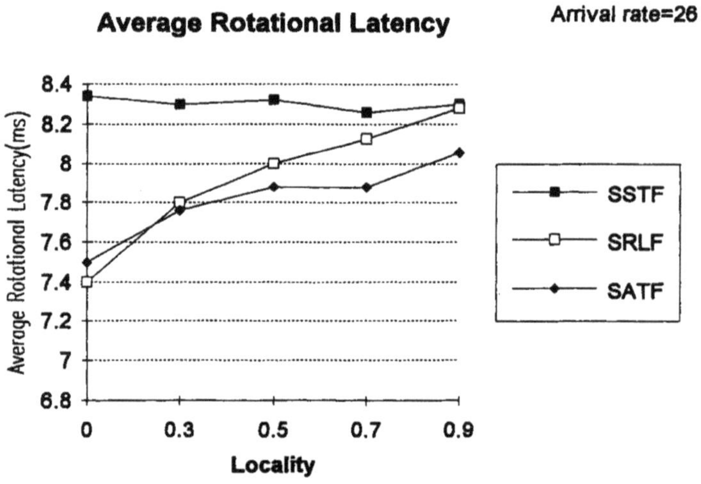

Figure 7(a) Average seek distance according to locality

Figure 7(b) Average rotational latency according to locality

QUERY PROCESSING (II)

APPLYING INTENSIONAL QUERY PROCESSING TECHNIQUES TO OBJECT-ORIENTED DATABASE SYSTEMS

Yang Hee Kim
Department of Computer Science, Suwon Industrial College

Hyoung-Joo Kim
Department of Computer Engineering, Seoul National University

ABSTRACT

Conventional database systems generate a set of facts (extensional answers) as an answer for a given query. This also applies to object-oriented databases where a set of objects will be returned.

However, deductive database systems give an opportunity to obtain the answer of a query as a set of formulas (intensional answers). Intensional answers provide users additional insight to the nature of extensional answers and can be computed only using the rules without accessing the database. So, they can be computed much faster and more cheaply than extensional answers.

In this paper, by introducing rules for abstract expression in the object-oriented database systems and by applying the intensional query processing techniques of deductive database systems to the object-oriented database systems, we make it possible not only to answer incomplete queries which are not able to be answered in conventional object-oriented database systems, but also to express the answer-set abstractly as the names of classes.

1 INTRODUCTION

Conventionally, a query to an object-oriented database (OODB) system is answered only by the set of objects that satisfy a given query [1] [7]. These objects may belong to different classes within a class hierarchy or they may be different complex objects somehow related to each other.

A deductive database is composed of extensional predicates (facts) and intensional predicates (rules). The extensional predicates contain objects of base relations while the intensional predicates contain deduction rules and conditions.

An intensional answer is a formula that states a condition to be satisfied by objects of the extensional answer. Thus, intensional answers are independent of a particular state in the database. Moreover, intentional answers can be computed much faster and more cheaply than extensional answers since in most of the time extensional answers are much larger than intensional answers. Intensional answers also represent the answer to the given query in a more compact way and extensional answers usually change more often than intensional answers. So, intensional answers provide a more stable answer to a query than the extensional answer. Furthermore, since the intensional answer is similar to a query, it can be evaluated like a query and returns a set of objects which are partial extensional answers. For a detailed description of the intensional query processing, we refer to [13].

In this paper, we introduce rules into OODB systems and apply the intentional query processing (IQP) techniques to OODB systems. Then, it becomes possible to answer incomplete queries by representing OODB schema in terms of rules. So far, all the query languages in OODB systems known to us are not able to give answers to incomplete queries. An incomplete query is a query on the attribute which belongs to a subclass but not the base class. Conventionally, the answer-set of a query in OODB is represented as a set of objects. But, the presence of semantics in OODB schema and IQP methodologies enable us to express the answer-set abstractly as names of classes. In this paper, we present an algorithm to obtain abstract representation of a given answer-set.

Rules which represent OODB schema in this paper consist of structural rules and subclassing rules. The structural rules in turn consist of "IS_A"-relation representing the class hierarchy. The subclassing rules represent characteristic properties of subclasses. We then transform all the rules to non-recursive Horn clauses and get an intensional answer by using SLD-resolution.

We provide some sample queries to show the advantages of an intensional answer to a given query in an OODB system over conventional answers.

We organize this paper as follows. In section 2, we discuss several researches which has been done in the IQP. In section 3, we look at the "IS_A"-relationship in OODB systems and the rules in OODB systems which are necessary in order to use the IQP. In section 4, we briefly review the definition of intensional answers, formalize methods to derive intensional answers for a class hierarchy model and give a detailed example. In the last section, we give conclusions and some remarks for possible extensions of the method in this paper.

2 RESEARCHES ON INTENSIONAL ANSWERS

There has been done a lot of researches in this area for last several years. While their approaches are different, all have the common goal which is to answer queries with a set of first-order logic formulas rather than a set of facts. But research which integrates this area and OODB was started only recently.

Cholvy and Demolombe [5] are the first who have considered the problem of providing answers to queries which are independent of a particular set of facts, that is, answers which are valid in all the states associated to these sets of facts. In this case, the answer is a set of first-order logic formulas, defining the rules that a given object should satisfy to belong to the answer. They make the hypothesis that the rule base is not recursive, but their algorithm accepts any form of clauses. In their work, a method is based on Resolution Inference Rules.

Based on the research presented by Cholvy and Demolombe [5], Pascual and Cholvy [10] restrict types of rules in intentional database (IDB) to Horn clauses, because Horn clauses have a lot of advantages. But, they do not give the algorithm to remove redundant resolution step and meaningless intensional answers. Song [13] and Song and Dubin [14] use only Horn-clauses for intensional databases and they give the detailed SLD-resolution steps to avoid generating meaningless intensional answers.

Imielinski [6], Pirotte and Roelants [11], Motro [9] and Motro and Yuan [8] use different approaches. Imielinski [6] introduces the type of answers which mix both atomic facts and general rules from projection, selection and join. So he tries to incorporate intensional predicates as a part of answers. Pirotte and Roelants [11] show how intensional answers can be generated from the query and how integrity constraints can filter out inadequate answers and produce simpler and more informatic answers.

Motro [9] describe a method that applies database constraints to generate intensional answers and Motro and Yuan [8] provide a simple query language incorporating intensional queries.

Vadaparty and Badrinath [16] develop a formalism to represent answers abstractly in OODB. They use the classes in the taxonomy to express the answer-set abstractly and obtain a unique optimal abstract representation.

3 LOGICAL REPRESENTATION OF OBJECT-ORIENTED DATA MODELS

3.1 Class Hierarchy

We look at a class hierarchy, representing "IS_A"-relationships between the different classes. We assume the following query syntax in our context :

SELECT ⟨ attribute of target record type ⟩
FROM ⟨ object variables ⟩
WHERE ⟨ predicate ⟩

The class hierarchy represented in the following Figure will be our object-oriented example database.

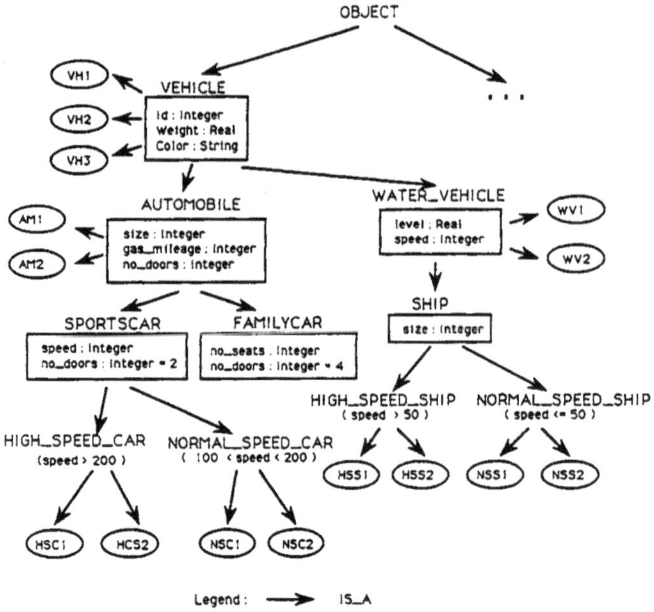

Figure 1. Class Hierarchy

A typical incomplete query for the class hierarchy in Figure 1 is the following:

SELECT VEHICLE.id
WHERE speed > 50

According to query languages in OODB systems known to us, the above query is incorrect. But by integrating intensional query processing into OODB systems, we can answer such a query.

In a conventional OODB we get back a set of vehicle ids where the speed of the vehicle is greater than 50 miles per hour. According to our sample database in Figure 1, we get back the following set:

{ HSC1, HSC2, ⋯, NSC1, NSC2,⋯, HSS1, HSS2,⋯ }.

All these objects belong to different subclasses of the base class object. In order to find all the applying objects, the database must provide a technique to search through all the subclasses of vehicle. But this is not the common "State of the Art" in OODB systems right now. There do not exist good query languages for OODB systems which are simple to use but at the same time powerful enough to use to fully account the advantages of an object-oriented system.

By using semantics in OODB schema and intensional query processing methodologies, the answer-set of a query is given by not a set of objects but names of classes to which answer objects belong. Since these abstract representation of the answer set is more concise, it provides us better understanding of the answer set.

In our example there are the following intensional answers :

- intensional-answer1 = all high_speed_cars
- intensional-answer2 = all normal_speed_cars
- intensional-answer3 = all high_speed_ships

In the next section of this paper, we will look at a way to automatically access the desired subclasses without being aware of the exact structure of the class hierarchy.

3.2 Rules for abstract expression

By introducing the notion of rules we can distinguish between different kinds of rules:

- integrity constraints
- "usual" rules
- structural rules
- subclassing rules

First, an OODB may have integrity constraints expressed as rules. These are not unique for object-oriented systems, but can be found in any database system. So, we are not interested in them here.

The second sort of rules are the "usual" rules that any deductive database can contain. Also these rules can be used the same way in an OODB system with rules as in deductive database systems.

More important rules we have to be concerned about are the rules that has to be established in order to complete an intensional query successfully within an OODB system. These rules come out of the class hierarchy of the objects and the information which is stored in the database schema. The rules concerning the class hierarchy are the structural rules and rules concerning the structual information of the subclassing schema are the subclassing rules.

The structural rules and subclassing rules in Figure 1 are the followings :

- structural rules
  - "IS_A"-rules

    IS_A(automobile, vehicle)
    IS_A(watervehicle, vehicle)
    IS_A(sportscar, automobile)
    IS_A(family_car, automobile)
    IS_A(ship, watervehicle)
    IS_A(high_speed_car, sportscar)
    IS_A(normal_speed_car, sportscar)
    IS_A(high_speed_ship, ship)
    IS_A(normal_speed_ship, ship)

- subclassing rules
  - high_speed_car(X) ← sportscar(X) ∧ speed(X,Y) ∧ greater(Y,200)
  - normal_speed_car(X) ← sportscar(X) ∧ speed(X,Y) ∧ greater(Y,100) ∧ less(Y,200)
  - sportscar(X) ← automobile(X) ∧ no_doors(X,Y) ∧ equal(Y,2)
  - family_car(X) ← automobile(X) ∧ no_doors(X,Y) ∧ equal(Y,4)
  - high_speed_ship(X) ← ship(X) ∧ speed(X,Y) ∧ greater(Y,50)
  - normal_speed_ship(X) ← ship(X) ∧ speed(X,Y) ∧ lesseq(Y,50)

4 FORMALIZATION OF INTENSIONAL QUERY PROCESSING IN OBJECT-ORIENTED DATABASE SYSTEMS

4.1 Definition of Intensional Answers

First of all, we briefly review the definition of intensional answers given in [5]. Define T as the database theory consisting of a set of facts and rules and let $Q(X)$ be a query where X is a tuple of free variables. Then, we want to find all the formulas $ans(X)$, such that

$$T \vdash \forall X(ans(X) \rightarrow Q(X))$$

i.e., $\forall X(ans(X) \rightarrow Q(X))$ is a theorem of T. So, the intensional answer $ANS(Q)$ to the query $Q(X)$ is defined by the set of formulas :

$$ANS(Q) = \{ans(X) : T \vdash \forall X(ans(X) \rightarrow Q(X))\}$$

where $ans(X)$ is a literal.

However, we want to restrict the answers within a defined domain of interest. Let $DP = \{P_1, ..., P_n\}$ be a set of predicate symbols either of the IDB or the extentional database (EDB). And let $L(DP)$ be the first order language whose predicate symbols are $P_1, ..., P_n$. Then define an intensional answer $ANS(Q, DP)$ to a query $Q(X)$ by :

$$\begin{aligned} ANS(Q,DP) = \; & \{ans(X) : ans(X) \in L(DP) \text{ and} \\ & T \vdash \forall X(ans(X) \rightarrow Q(X)) \text{ and} \\ & (ans(X) \text{ is not the negation of a tautology}) \text{ and} \\ & (\text{each } ans(X) \text{ is not redundant})\} \end{aligned}$$

To derive an intensional answer, the resolution will be applied to the database theory T and the negation of the theorem $\forall X(ans(X) \rightarrow Q(X))$. But the negation of the thorems is

$$\text{not } (\forall X(ans(X) \rightarrow Q(X)))$$

which is equal to

$$\exists X(ans(X) \wedge not(Q(X)))$$

That leads to the standard form

$$\{ans(X_0), \neg(Q(X_0))\}$$

where X_0 is a tuple of Skolem constants. So, the clause form for the resolution becomes

$$S \cup \{ans(X_0), \neg(Q(X_0))\}$$

where S is a set of clauses transformed from T. Since $ans(X_0)$ is not known at the beginning of the resolution process, we will start with $S \cup \{\neg Q(X_0)\}$. Resolving $S \cup \{\neg Q(X_0)\}$ will result in a resolvent $R(X_0)$ and then resolving $R(X_0)$ together with $ans(X_0)$ will result in the empty clause. That means that $ans(X_0)$ must equal to $\neg R(X_0)$.

In the following sections, we outline an algorithm deriving intensional answers for a class hierarchy model consisting of non-recursive Horn clauses. By limiting non-recursive clauses the algorithm can be terminated, and by Horn clauses efficient algorithm can be used.

4.2 Processing comparison literals

To compute intensional answers efficiently, subclassing rules should be represented in a proper form. Since testing satisfiability in first-order logic formula is undecidable, adopting first-order logic formula for managing subclassing rules is not desirable. Therefore, we need a subset of first order logic expressions which is powerful enough for expressing subclassing rules and in which the satisfiability problem can be processed efficiently.

Subclassing rules can be represented with the "simple predicates" [7]. The BNF of simple predicates abbreviated by SP is as follows.

⟨SP⟩ ::= ⟨SP⟩ ∧ ⟨SP⟩ | ⟨SP⟩ ∨ ⟨SP⟩ | ¬⟨SP⟩ | ⟨predicates⟩
⟨predicates⟩ ::= ⟨comparison operator⟩ (⟨variable name⟩, ⟨constant⟩)
| ⟨comparison operator⟩ (⟨variable name⟩, ⟨variable name⟩)
| ⟨comparison operator⟩ (⟨variable name⟩, ⟨variable name⟩ + ⟨ constant⟩)
⟨comparison operator⟩ ::= equal | not_equal | greater | greater_eq | less | less_eq

Rosencrantz and Hunt showed that the satisfiability problem of the set of simple predicate is NP-hard [12]. But they showed that conjunctive not_equal free predicates (simple predicates that do not contain not_equal and ∨) can be solved in polynomial time. We can represent a large class of subclassing rules with conjunctive not_equal free predicates.

The following algorithm changes a conjunctive not_equal free predicate to a weighted directed graph [12] [7].

Algorithm 1

Input : A conjunctive not_equal free predicate P.
Output : A weighted directed graph.

(v_1 and v_2 stand for variables and c stands for a constant)

1. Convert P into an equivalent predicate P′ containing only less_eq comparison literal as follows :

   1.1 Replace $v_1 = v_2$ with $(v_1 \leq v_2 + 0) \wedge (v_2 \leq v_1 + 0)$.
   1.2 Replace $v_1 < v_2$ with $v_1 \leq v_2 + (-1)$.
   1.3 Replace $v_1 \leq v_2$ with $v_1 \leq v_2 + 0$.
   1.4 Replace $v_1 > v_2$ with $v_2 \leq v_1 + (-1)$.
   1.5 Replace $v_1 \geq v_2$ with $v_2 \leq v_1 + 0$.
   1.6 Replace $v_1 = c$ with $(v_1 \leq 0 + c) \wedge (0 \leq v_1 + (-c))$.
   1.7 Replace $v_1 < c$ with $v_1 \leq 0 + (c - 1)$.
   1.8 Replace $v_1 \leq c$ with $v_1 \leq 0 + c$.
   1.9 Replace $v_1 > c$ with $0 \leq v_1 + (-c - 1)$.
   1.10 Replace $v_1 \geq c$ with $0 \leq v_1 + (-c)$.
   1.11 Replace $v_1 = v_2 + c$ with $(v_1 \leq v_2 + c) \wedge (v_2 \leq v_1 + (-c))$.
   1.12 Replace $v_1 < v_2 + c$ with $v_1 \leq v_2 + (c - 1)$.
   1.13 Replace $v_1 \leq v_2 + c$ with $v_1 \leq v_2 + c$.
   1.14 Replace $v_1 > v_2 + c$ with $v_2 \leq v_1 + (-c - 1)$.
   1.15 Replace $v_1 \geq v_2 + c$ with $v_2 \leq v_1 + (-c)$.

2. Convert P′ into a weighted directed graph. The graph has a node for each variable and a node for a constant zero. Conversion is as follows:

   2.1 $v_1 \leq v_2 + c$ corresponds to an edge from node v_1 to node v_2 with edge weight c.
   2.2 $v_1 \leq 0 + c$ corresponds to an edge from node v_1 to zero node with edge weight c.
   2.3 $0 \leq v_1 + c$ corresponds to an edge from zero node to node v_1 with edge weight $-c$.

There are two restrictions in the above algorithm. The one is that each variable should be integer valued. The other is that predicates can not have not_equal operators. Fortunately, many of subclassing rules involve integer valued domains such as engine size, price, number of doors, etc. And in this paper, we will deal with not_equal free predicates.

The next algorithm will change a weighted directed graph G with no multiple edges to a conjuntive less_eq predicate (not_equal free predicate that contains only less_eq)

Algorithm 2

Input : A weighted directed graph G with no multiple edges.
Output : A conjuntive less_eq predicate.

(v_1 and v_2 stand for variables and c stands for a constant)

1. An edge from node v_1 to node v_2 with edge weight c corresponds to $v_1 \leq v_2 + c$.
2. An edge from node v_1 to zero node with edge weight c corresponds to $v_1 \leq 0 + c$.
3. An edge from zero node to node v_1 with edge weight $-c$ corresponds to $0 \leq v_1 + c$.

The next algorithm will test comparison literals using a weighted directed graph and return a truth constant or a simplified predicate.

Algorithm 3

Input: A predicate consisting of the conjuction of an old comparision predicate (predicate in resolvent before resolution) and a new comparison predicate (predicate in resolvent after resolution)

Output: Truth constant (TRUE or FALSE) or simplified predicate

1. Apply algorithm 1 to the conjunction of old and new comparison predicate. And then we get a weighted directed graph G.

2. If G has a negative cycle then

    return FALSE.

   else

    If there is more than one edge from node v_1 to node v_2 then

      begin

      retain the minimum weight edge and discard the others

      apply algorithm 2 to G and we get a conjective less_eq predicate P

      change new comparison predicate to less_eq predicate using step1 of algorithm 1

      if P is the same as new comparison predicate then

        return TRUE

      else

        return P

      end

    else

      return old comparison predicate ∧ new comparison predicate

We can use Floyd's all shortest path algorithm to see if the graph has a negative weight cycles. In algorithm 3, the step 1 can be processed in a linear time, if-part of the step 2 (Floyd's all shortest paths algorithm) takes $O(k^3)$ and else-part of the step 3 can be processed in a linear time where k is a number of nodes in G.

4.3 An algorithm for Intensional Answers

In Section 3.2, we proposed structural rules and subclassing rules for class hierarchy. Before we get the intensional answers, first of all some rule transformations should be done in order to get unique intensional literals, secondly recursion in subcalssing rules should be removed, and "IS_A"-rules to the first order logic should be changed.

Unique intensional literals are literals that are either extensionally or intensionally defined but not both. So if we have literal p which is both EDB-defined and IDB-defined, then rename the extensional literal p* and introduce a new rule p ← p* in the IDB. In doing so, we can handle complete queries as well as incomplete queries for the intensional query processing.

Since structural rules and subclassing rules are conjuction in IDB, we can remove recursion in subclassing rules.

Finally we can change "IS_A"-rules to the first-order logic since the semantic of "IS_A" is implication. For example, IS_A(X,Y) can be changed Y ← X. Now, IDB corresponds to a set of non-recursive Horn clauses.

The following algorithm will compute intensional answers from a set of non-recursive Horn clauses consisting of EDB ∪ IDB and a query Q(X).

Algorithm 4

Input: A set of non-recursive Horn clauses consisting of EDB ∪ IDB and a query Q(X) where X is a tuple of free variables

Output: A set of $ANS_I(X)$ of intensional answers

1. Negate the query and convert it into the clause form

2. Repeat for all branches of a resolution tree

   2.1 Perform resolution using subclassing rules, structural rules or new rules

   2.2 If resolvent contains extensional literal p*

      If base literal is not in the attributes of p* then

        current branch is fail branch and return

      else

        current branch is success branch and return

   else /* if resolvent does not contain extensional literal */

      If resolvent contains at least two base literals then

      If factoring is impossible among base literals then

        current branch is fail branch and return

      else

          begin

          Perform the algorithm 3

          If result is FALSE then

            current branch is fail branch and return

          else if result is TRUE then

            current branch is success branch and return $ANS_I(X)$ = selected predicate

          else

            current branch is success branch and return $ANS_I(X)$ = selected predicate ∧ simplified predicate

          end

   Until it cannot be futher resolved

3. If all success branches contain extensional answers then

    begin

    choose the highest success branch

    generate the intensional answers by negating resolvent

    end

   else

    begin

    ignore success branch containing extensional answers and

    return intensional answers $ANS_I(X)$

    end

4.4 example

To show the application of the algorithm introduced in the above section, we will use our example database given in Fiqure 1.

EDB and IDB schema looks as follows :

<u>EDB</u>

vehicle(id, weight, color)

automobile(id, weight, color, size, gas_mileage, no_doors)

family_car(id, weight, color, size, gas_mileage, no_doors, no_seats)

sportscar(id, weight, color, size, gas_mileage, no_doors, speed)

high_speed_car(id, weight, color, size, gas_mileage, no_doors, speed)

normal_speed_car(id, weight, color, size, gas_mileage, no_doors, speed)

water_vehicle(id, weight, color, level, speed)

ship(id, weight, color, level, speed, size)

high_speed_ship(id, weight, color, level, speed, size)

normal_speed_ship(id, weight, color, level, speed, size)

<u>IDB</u>

"IS_A"-rules

subclassing rules

First we rename the extensional literal, add new rules in the IDB, remove recursion, and change "IS_A"-rules to the first order logic.

<u>EDB</u>

vehicle*(id, weight, color)

automobile*(id, weight, color, size, gas_mileage, no_doors)

family_car*(id, weight, color, size, gas_mileage, no_doors, no_seats)

sportscar*(id, weight, color, size, gas_mileage, no_doors, speed)

high_speed_car*(id, weight, color, size, gas_mileage, no_doors, speed)

normal_speed_car*(id, weight, color, size, gas_mileage, no_doors, speed)

water_vehicle*(id, weight, color, level, speed)

ship*(id, weight, color, level, speed, size)

high_speed_ship*(id, weight, color, level, speed, size)

normal_speed_ship*(id, weight, color, level, speed, size)

<u>IDB</u>

- "IS_A"-rules

  vehicle(X) ← automobile(X)
  vehicle(X) ← watervehicle(X)
  automobile(X) ← sportscar(X)
  automobile(X) ← family_car(X)
  watervehicle(X) ← ship(X)
  sportscar(X) ← high_speed_car(X)
  sportscar(X) ← normal_speed_car(X)
  ship(X) ← high_speed_ship(X)
  ship(X) ← normal_speed_ship(X)

- subclassing rules

  high_speed_car(X) ← speed(X,Y) ∧ greater(Y,200)

  normal_speed_car(X) ← speed(X,Y) ∧ greater(Y,100) ∧ less(Y,200)

  sportscar(X) ← no_doors(X,Y) ∧ equal(Y,2)

  family_car(X) ← no_doors(X,Y) ∧ equal(Y,4)

  high_speed_ship(X) ← speed(X,Y) ∧ greater(Y,50)

  normal_speed_ship(X) ← speed(X,Y) ∧ lesseq(Y,50)

- New rules

  vehicle(X) ← vehicle*(X)
  automobile(X) ← automobile*(X)
  family_car(X) ← family_car*(X)
  sportscar(X) ← sportscar*(X)
  high_speed_car(X) ← high_speed_car*(X)
  normal_speed_car(X) ← normal_speed_car*(X)

Now let us consider the query "Find a set of vehicle ids where the speed of the vehicle is greater than 50 miles per hour". The query can be written as

Q(X) = vehicle(X) ∧ speed(X,Y) ∧ greater(Y,50).

Thus the goal clause is

← vehicle(X), speed(X,Y), greater(Y,50)

Now the resolution tree is as follows.

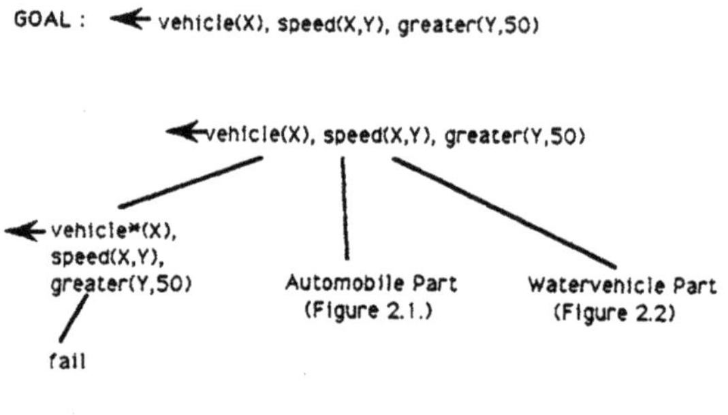

Figure 2. Resolution Tree

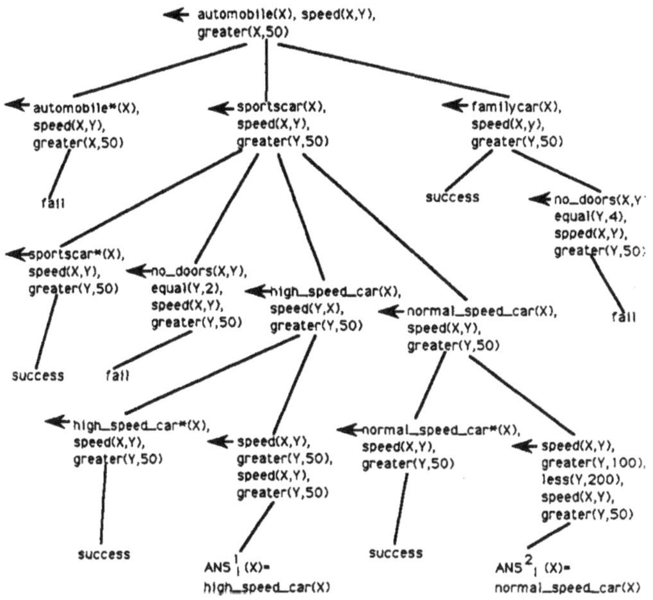

Figure 2.1. Automobile Part

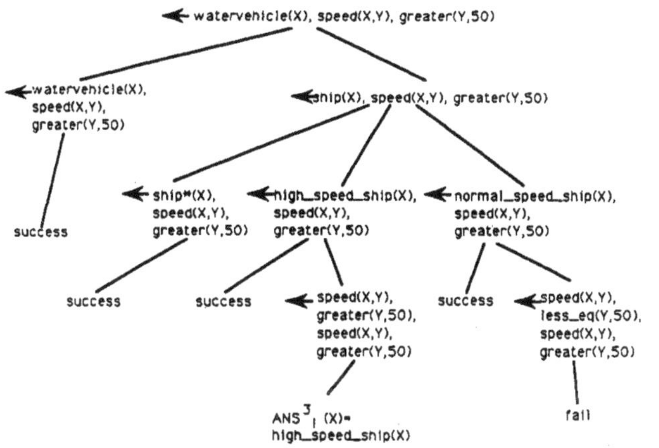

Figure 2.2. Watervehicle Part

Since there are three branches that have intensional answers, we have following intensional answers:

- $ANS^1_I(X)$ = high_speed_car(X)
- $ANS^2_I(X)$ = normal_speed_car(X)
- $ANS^3_I(X)$ = high_speed_ship(X)

5 CONCLUSIONS AND REMARKS

In this paper, we developed a formalism to obtain intensional answers for a class hierarchy model. By introducing rules into the OODB systems and applying the IQP techniques to the OODB systems, we are able to use the advantages of the semantics of OODB schema.

By using rules derived from the schema information, we are able not only to answer incomplete queries without knowing the exact structure of the database but also to express the answer-set abstractly as the names of classes. It provides us better understanding of the answer.

However, the method in this paper also has a disadvantage. For complete queries, the algorithm in this paper is less efficient than current query languages since our method answers a query only after it generates the complete resolution tree by using structural rules, subclassing rules, and new rules.

In this paper, we only obtain intensional answers for a class hierarchy model but not for a class-composition hierarchy. Our method does not seem to be powerful enough to represent a complex object hierarchy. It is probable that we need more powerful logic for reasoning intensional answers on complex objects.

References

[1] F. Bancilon, *Object-Oriented Database Systems*, in Proceedings of Seventh ACM SIGACT-SIGMOD-SIGART Symposium on Principles of Database Systems, pp. 152-162, Austin, Texas, March 21-23 1988.

[2] J. Banerjee, et al., *Data Model Issues on Object-Oriented Applications*, in ACM Transactions on Office Information Systems, Vol.5, No.1, March, 1987.

[3] S. Böttcher, M. Jarke and W. Schmidt, *Adaptive Predicate Management in Database Systems*, in Proceedings of 12th VLDB Conference, 1986.

[4] C. Chang and R. Lee, Symbolic Logic and Mechanical Theorem Proving, Academic Press, New York and London, 1973.

[5] L. Cholvy and R. Demolombe, *Querying a RuleBase*, in Proceedings of the first int'l conference on Expert Database Systems, ed.Kerschberg, L., pp. 365-371, Charleston, South Carolina, April 1-4, 1986.

[6] T. Imielinski, *Intelligent Query Answering in Rule Based Systems*, J. of Logic Programming, vol 4, no. 3, pp. 229-258, September, 1987. Also appeared as *Transforming Logical Rules by Relational Algebra*, in Proceedings of Foundations of Deductive Database Systems and Logic Programming, ed. Minker, J., pp. 338-377, Washington DC, August 8-12, 1986.

[7] H. J. Kim, *Logic Design of Object-Oriented Database Schema*, Technical Report : GIT-ICS-89/06, January, 1989.

[8] A. Motro and Q. Yuan, *Querying DataBase Knowledge*, Proceedings of ACM SIGMOD, Atlantic City, New Jersey, May 23-25, 1990, pp. 173-183.

[9] A. Motro, *Using Integrity Constraints to Provide Intensional Answers to Relational Queries*, in Proceedings of 15th VLDB Conference, 1989.

[10] E. Pascual and L. Cholvy, *Answering Queries Addressed to the Rulebase of a Deductive Database*, in Proceedings of 2nd Int'l Conference on Information Processing and Management of Uncertainty in Knowledgebased Systems, pp. 138-145, Urbino, Italy, July 1988, Springer-Verlag, Lecture Notes in Computer Sciences 313.

[11] A. Pirotte and D. Roelants, *Constraints for Improving the Generation of Intensional Answers in a Deductive Databases*, 1989 Int'l Conference on Data Engineering, pp. 652-659.

[12] D. J. Rosenkrantz and M. B. Hunt, *Processing conjunctive predicates and queries*, in Proceedings of the Sixth International Conference on VLDB, pp. 64-74, Montreal, 1980.

[13] Song, I-Y., Intensional Query Processing in Deductive Database Systems, Ph.D Dissertation, Louisiana State University, August 1988.

[14] I-Y. Song and D.Dubin, *IQPS:Implementation of an Intensional Query Processing Shell*, submitted for publication.

[15] I-Y. Song, H-J. Kim and P. Geutner, *Intensional Query Processing : A three step Approach* , in Proceedings of 1990 International Conference on Database and Expert Systems Application, pp. 542-549, Vienna, Austria, Aug.29-31, 1990.

[16] K. Vadaparty and B. R. Badrinath, *User-controlled Abstract Answers in Object-Orieneted Systems*, Technical Report : LCSR-TR-164, Department of Computer Science, Rutgers University, Department of Computer Science, Rutgers University, New Brunswick, NJ 08903, April, 1991.

HETEROGENEOUS QUERY OPTIMIZATION USING MAXIMAL SUB-QUERIES

A HH Ngu LL Yan * LS Wong†

School of Computer Science & Engineering
University of New South Wales
P.O.Box 1, Kensington 2033
NSW, Australia
email:anne@cs.unsw.oz.au

ABSTRACT: We propose a query optimization strategy in a loosely coupled multidatabase environment. The goal of our query optimization is to exploit both the global and the local levels of optimization to reduce the overall cost of evaluating a query. This requires finding a way to decompose a global query in the best possible way. We argue that finding maximal sub-queries in a global query is a way of ensuring that sub-queries sent to the local DBMS are in a form which can take advantage of local query optimization as well as reducing the number of queries required to be sent. This reduces the processing cost in a multidatabase system because sub-queries that are sent to the local databases have to be converted. The lesser number of sub-queries implies less conversion cost.

1 INTRODUCTION

Advances in networking and database technology during the past decade make it possible to process information from heterogeneous database systems which may be dispersed over a number of sites and are autonomous. Query issued at a local database system may require the access of databases of other components. Thus, there is a general consensus that query processing techniques from Distributed DataBase Management Systems (DDBMS) research can be adopted for multidatabase systems. However, unlike in DDBMS, underlying database components are not homogeneous and there is limited access to the statistical information about each of the local DBMS. In a loosely coupled multidatabase environment, the autonomy of each component DBMS has to be respected, moreover the local DBMS might not be able to provide the needed statistics because they do not have them. The problem is further aggravated by the fact that different local DBMS may differ in their abilities to process a query. For example, some DBMSs might not support semijoin operator.

Work on query processing and optimization on *tightly* coupled multidatabases has been researched since the early 80's. In [9], three approaches are summarized. The first approach is to have a simple global query processor which decomposes a query at the federated level into the elementary sub-queries which can be answered by a single database. The query translator receives these sub-queries in the global query language and translate them into queries of the relevant local DBMS. All the intermediate results that are generated by these sub-queries are assembled and the result presented to the user. There is no inter-site optimization of joins at the global query processor level.

The second approach is to have a very complex global query processor which has a dynamic planner. Optimization is performed at each step of the execution of a query. At every step, the global plan describes how to synchronize execution of local queries, merge partial results from the local DBMSs, exchange data between different local DBMS etc. This approach is excellent if the global planner can estimate the costs of executing each local query accurately. In a loosely coupled multidatabase systems, because of the autonomy of each component DBMS, there aren't any easy way to estimate the cost of local processing. Although in the context of the Pegasus project, a way to approximate the local processing cost is proposed [2], however, the cost of conversion and communication are not taken into account. Furthermore, sub-queries sent to the local DBMS are expected to be in the smallest unit, thus there is limited scope for local query optimization.

The third approach is a mixture of the above two. Here, a medium complex global optimizer is required and the power of the local DBMS optimizer is exploited when necessary. It is expected that the global optimizer will be able to transform a global query into a set of the largest possible sub-queries. This reduces the communication workload on the global query processor and at the same time it is able to make use of the local query optimizers.

In this paper, we describe a simple method of decomposing a global query which resulted in sub-queries that can exploit the local query optimizers. We assume that queries submitted by users are non-procedural, allowing a great degree of query optimization. The novelty of our approach is in the design of a simple query decomposition procedure which involves finding maximal sub-queries for

*Institute of Systems Science, Singapore
†On leave of absence from ISS. Now at the University of Pennsylvania.

a particular DBMS.

The paper is organized as follows. We first present the previous approaches to heterogeneous query optimization. In section 3, we present our query processing strategy and algorithm for finding the maximal sub-queries. In section 4, we give a discussion and an analysis of our algorithm. Finally in section 5, we conclude with a list of advantages of maximal sub-queries and suggestions for the future work.

2 OTHER APPROACHES

2.1 Mermaid

In the Mermaid system, now marketed as Interviso [10, 11], users formulate requests to the federated database using SQL. The SQL request is parsed and transformed to the internal command language called the Distributed Intermediate Language (DIL). A valid DIL parse tree is passed to the query optimizer. The query optimizer uses a dynamic planner for the efficient processing of the query. This implies that the later stage of execution of the query is determined by the result of the execution at the earlier stage. The optimizer also uses heuristics based on types of relation distribution, i.e. whether a relation is replicated, is at a single site, or is fragmented for decomposing the query. For example, if the relation is replicated in many sites, then the query can be sent to the site which can process it optimally.

Each sub-query is passed to the relevant component Database Interface (DBI). The DBI is responsible for translating decomposed DIL requests into the component query language, dispatching the query, getting the data from the local databases, and moving the temporary relations created to another site if required.

Mermaid adopts the optimization strategy that attempts to minimize the amount of data transferred between component DBMS. The federated database in Mermaid does not allow specification of inter-site joins. So the optimization problem is greatly simplified.

2.2 Multidatabases(MRDSM)

The system MRDSM [5, 7] is a loosely coupled multidatabase system. The fact that it is loosely coupled means that there is no assumption of a global integrated schema. This system provides a multidatabase language called MSQL [6] for formulating queries and manipulating the schemas. The same language is also used for the specification of federated schemas or views over multiple export schemas. The language extends SQL to cover features for naming conflict, type/scale differences and multiple semantics over the same data.

MSQL gives the user a lot of freedom as to how information in a multidatabase environment can be queried and manipulated. In Mermaid, users have to go through a tedious process to set up the federated schema and it is not possible to query anything which has not been set up or preintegrated. By using MSQL, any integration of semantics or schemas can be done incrementally as and when the users perceive it as necessary. Another significant advantage of providing the multidatabase language is that it can cater to the different needs of the federation users which cannot be anticipated by the federation DBA ahead of time. The disadvantage of using MSQL is that it expects a more knowledgeable user to use it effectively.

The multidatabase query language gives a lot of flexibility to the users in formulating the queries. It is very useful in an environment where it is important to run ad-hoc multidatabase queries. It is also very necessary for a multidatabase environment where databases join and leave the federation dynamically. The shortfall for such kind of system is that it is hard to optimize the global query. The emphasis on the autonomy of the component DBMS means information on location, replication and distribution is not available. In order to make it possible for the databases to join and leave the federation without much effect on the existing systems, each component DBMS is not required to give any information about its statistics to the federated level. In such an environment, we have to assume that each local database's optimizer will be fully exploited. The role of the global query processor here is passive, its major task is to merge the results from subqueries and present them to the user. There is no attempt for inter-sites query optimization.

2.3 Multibase

The system Multibase [11, 1] is a tightly coupled federated database system. Daplex is chosen as the canonical model for the federated schema. Database integration is achieved by defining a global view using the Daplex query language. The view definition incorporates rules for resolving schematic and semantics differences between the local databases.

Access to the federated schema is through Daplex queries. Query processing begins with the modification of the global Daplex query into equivalent queries over the local schemas of the existing databases. A global execution plan is constructed for the modified query. A decomposer is then employed to generate sequences of Daplex single-site queries. A decomposed query is filtered by removing operations from them that are not supported by the corresponding component DBMS (note: unlike in Mermaid, here the federated system cannot afford not to have the query processing power. It must have the ability to process those operations not supported by any of the component databases). A monitor is used to coordinate the execution of all the single site queries. These single site queries are translated into equivalent local queries and are subjected to local access path optimization.

The approach of query optimization in Multibase emphasizes generating the global query plan. The construction of such a plan requires a global view definition and the introduction of new operators such as moving the data to other sites, postprocessing and merging of the results. The `semiouterjoin` operator, which has the potential to reduce query processing cost when the query is on overlapping subtypes, is specially proposed in this context.

In Multibase, there is a strong emphasis on optimizing the global plan without restricting the number of subqueries that need to be sent to the component databases. This results in a very heavy workload for the global query processor since it has to deal with merging and postprocessing of more intermediate results. Furthermore, this approach is only for a tightly coupled federated database system where enough local DBMS statistics is known for estimating the local processing cost.

3 MOTIVATIONS & GOALS

The above three approaches provide the basic techniques for query processing in a multidatabase system. However, they either do not fully exploit the local optimizers or they are overly dependent on a global plan which does not has access to local DBMS statistics. For example, in Multibase, the construction of a global plan is good, but there is no provision to restrict the large number of sub-queries generated. In Mermaid, the dynamic planner follows the techniques used in the distributed systems. But without allowing inter-sites `join`, the query mechanism is too restrictive.

Althought the component DBMSs are autonomous and most of the query processing are performed at the component DBMS, global query optimization is still very important for reducing the total cost of processing. As a first step to improve the optimization proposed in the above three systems, we focus essentially on the decomposition of heterogeneous query to reduce the total cost of query processing.

Our goal is to show that the heuristic such as sending the biggest sub-queries to the component databases is very simple to implement and yet a useful step in optimization of the heterogeneous query. We propose an abstract representation of the multidatabase query where the operators can be treated as functional terms. This has the advantage of being easy to manipulate and avoids being tied to any specific kind of algebra.

The architecture of the query processor of our loosely coupled multidatabase system is shown in figure 1.

3.1 Query Processing and Optimization

In our architecture, users submit O2/SQL queries to the federated database which can be running at a special site or together with one of the local databases. The global query processor performs the following steps:

- **Query Modification/Translation:** Given a Query Q, rewrite it to an equivalent query Q' such that Q' refers to classes and relationships that exist in the conceptual schemas of the component DBMS, i.e. Q' is a query over all the local schemas from different DBMS that are involved in the query. A query tree as described in [4] can be used to represent Q'. Apart from the distributed and heterogeneous source

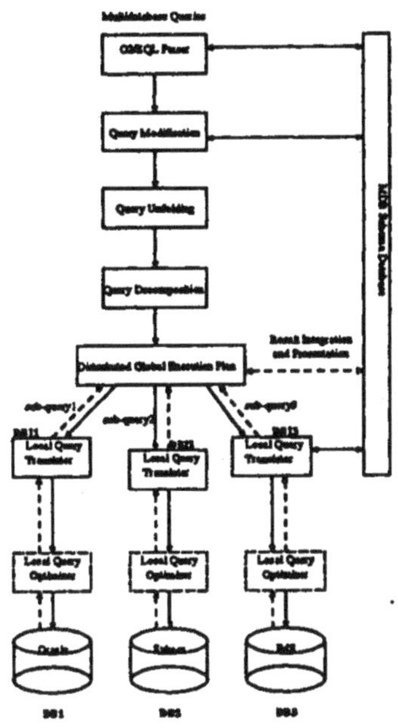

Figure 1: The Architecture of MDB Query Processor

of entities/relations, this problem is the same as for queries submitted against views [1].

- **Unfold the Query:** The idea of unfolding the query tree is to reduce the query tree to its lowest level of operation (i.e. those that are recognized by the optimizer). It can also be viewed as the process of compiling the query tree Q into an internal language. The internal language is similar to the Processing Tree (PT) as described in [3].

  The leaf nodes of an unfolded tree are entities of the physical schemas (as contrasted to the conceptual schemas before unfolding) in the local DBMSs and each non-leaf node represents an operation to be performed on the operand nodes resulting in a temporary file. An example is shown in figure 2 in section 3.2.

  We don't limit the possible operators set. However, the following are selected because they are common operations: Join, Selection, Projection and Union.

  The unfolded tree can be represented by a multiway tree rooted at node N. Each of the descendent nodes of N and N itself can either be:

  - an unary operator node - Projection or Selection
  - a binary operator node - Join, Union, Difference, Intersection
  - a leaf node - an atomic entity of the physical schema or a temporary file.

  The advantage of representing the query tree internally using an unfolded tree is that this is a very generalized representation not tied to any specific object oriented algebra. This is very important since formalization of object oriented algebra is still under intense research. Here we avoid discussing the issue of why a specific object oriented algebra is chosen. New algebraic operators can be accomodated easily when needed, because they will just be treated as new functions. Finally, the transformation rules as described in [4] for object oriented queries is applied to obtain a more favourable query tree before decomposing the tree. This has the advantage that no of joins, columns and rows might be reduced.

- **Query Decomposition:** The unfolded tree models the global query execution plan. Query decomposition is the process of finding the maximal sub-queries in the unfolded tree. This is comparable to the process of finding the best possible grouping of sub-queries. The output from this step is a list of maximal sub-queries and a new distributed execution plan consisting of instructions for processing the query and combining the partial results from the sub-queries.

  Note that we perform the traditional transformation/optimization on the query tree first before decomposing it. This separation is advantages because it simplies both steps. It does not make sense to decompose the query tree first and then apply the algebraic transformations. The transformation might render the decompositions useless and thus cannot exploit the local optimizers fully.

- **Query dispatching and translation:** Each maximal sub-query represented in the functional form is sent to its DBI where the query translator will use the mapping information between a local schema and the canonical schema to translate the query into the language of the local DBMS.

3.2 Query Decomposition

In this section we describe in detail our algorithm for query decomposition. In distributed relational database systems, query decomposition is a well known technique used to group a query into simpler components to reduce the complexity of optimization. Also the sub-queries that are produced will require less expensive operations, such as replacing `joins` by `semijoins`, and have a more efficient access path. Usually the algorithm works by partitioning the predicates in the `where` clause into several groups and for each group creating a subquery.

In our approach, the emphasis on query decomposition consists of generating the heterogeneous global query plan in such a way that there will be least number of sub-queries created. We call this process the finding of the maximal (biggest) sub-query that is executable at a single component DBMS.

The following example is used to illustrate the concept of maximal sub-queries. Suppose db1 has relations `a`, `b`, `c` and db2 has relations `e`, `f`, `g`. A query:

```
join(a, (project(union(b,c)))
```

is maximal because the entire query can be performed in db1. A query:

```
join(join(a,b), union(e, join(f,g)))
```

is not maximal because it needs both db1 and db2. The subexpression `join(f,g)` is not maximal despite being completely executable in db2, the maximal expression here is `union(e,join(f,g))`. Thus a sub-query is maximal in a query tree if:

- it is on a single database,
- no other query node can be added without violating the previous condition

The purpose of query decomposition is to find a way to label the query tree where all the sub-queries are maximal. This does not mean that all the sub-queries are independent. The result of one maximal sub-query can be used in another maximal sub-query.

Figure 2 shows how the query `join(a, join(b, union(e, join(f, g))))` is labelled (the twig is the label for the sub-query):

```
     join twig(q2,db1)
     /  \
    a   join
        /  \
       b   union twig(q1,db2)
            /  \
           e   join
               /  \
              f    g
```

Figure 2: An Unfolded Tree

The algorithm for query decomposition consists of taking the unfolded query tree as input and produces an output which is a pair consisting of a list of maximal sub-queries (i.e. those branches labeled as twig(..)) and a new plan which shows the instructions for combining the results of maximal subqueries. The sub-query and the new global plan from the above example are:

q1 =(union(e, join(f, g)), db2).
The new plan = twig(q2, db1) is the same as (join(a, join(b, q1)), db1)

The abstract form of the algorithm and its data structures are presented below:

```
type tree = record
    table:table_infor;
    BinaryOp: string;
    left, right: ↑tree;
    end
```

The structure *tree* is used to represent the input which is the unfolded tree. The `table` contains information such as in which database the entity resides, the type of the entity, the selection conditions, and the projection attributes. The BinaryOp represents the operation (e.g joint) applied to the left and right tree. The output is represented by the two structures, max_subq and otree.

```
type max_subq = record
   label:tuple(tag:string,db:string)
   sub_query:↑tree;
   next: ↑max_subq
   end;

type otree = record
   twig:tuple(tag:string,db:string);
   /*label for subquery*/
   MBop:string; /*MDB operators*/
   left, right: ↑otree;
   end
```

max_subq is a linked list consisting of all the maximal sub-queries identifiable in a global query. The label identifies each sub-query executable in a particular named database db. The sub-query is represented by the sub_query which is an unfolded tree.

otree is the structure of the output tree or the new global execution plan. The twig has the pair (tag,db) for identifying the sub-queries that need to be substituted. The MBop is the algebraic operator or name of a function applicable to the left and right operands of the tree.

```
Procedure find-max(Q:tree,var S:max_subq,var T:otree)
begin
   if (Q↑left = nil) and (Q↑right = nil) then
   begin
      create a max_subq S where
         sub_query = table_infor;
         label.tag = new tag,
         label.db = DB from the table;
      create a new otree T = twig(tag, db);
      return(S, T)
   end
   else
   begin
      find-max(Q↑left, S1, O1);
      find-max(Q↑right,S2, O2);
      if O1.twig.db = O2.twig.db
         /*merge them into a maximal sub-query*/
         begin
         create a new tag q;
         create a new max_subq= (q, O1.twig.db,
         sub_query=(Q.BOp,sub(O1,S1),sub(O2,S2));
         create a new otree T=twig(q,db);
         /* add the new sub-queries to the list */
         return((S1 union S2 union max_subq), T)
         end
      else
         create an otree T with O1 & O2
         as branches & Q.BOp as the opr;
         return(S1 union S2, T)
   end
end
```

If the input is just the table information (i.e. left and right branch of the tree is nil), then return the pair (S,T) where S is the maximal subquery. T is the output tree with the label twig(tag, db) where tag is a new tag and db is the name of the database where the table information resides.

If the input is a binary tree, then apply find-max recursively to the left and right branch of the tree which generate the pairs (S1,O1), (S2,O2) respectively. Then, we have to decide how to combine the pairs. If O1 is twig(A,c) and O2 is twig(B,d); to combine them, all we need is to check whether the two twigs are to be executed on the same database. If they are, we merge them into a single maximal query by returning the pair (S',T'). S' is the new maximal query and T' is the new twig. The maximal subquery S' is created by sub(O1,S1) and sub(O2,S2). This means apply the substitution in S_i to O_i, i.e. replaces every twig(tag,db) in O_i by the corresponding query in S_i.

If the two twigs cannot be executed on the same database, we return the pair (S',T') where S' is the two old maximal queries and T' (BinaryOp, O1,O2), is the new node in the output tree.

4 IMPROVEMENTS

The above algorithm does not take into account the semantics (properties) of the operators. It makes no effort in reconfiguring the query tree. It is a generic algorithm designed to illustrate the identification of maximal sub-queries. The output tree does not show the order of execution of the sub-queries. In fact, it just follows a bottom-up execution plan, where the operator is applied to the left and right operands. The execution ends at the root node, which corresponds to the answer of the query.

The problem of not making use of the semantics of the operator is that if the input data interact in a very convoluted way, for example in (a,b,c is in db1 and e,f,g is in db2):

join(a, join(e, join(b, join(f, join(c, g))))))

then we have no choice, but to load everything, because it is not possible to find any maximal sub-query here.

The first step in improving the algorithm is to make use of the properties of the operators to reconfigure the tree so that we can find better maximal sub-queries. The associative and commutative properties of the Join operator are such examples. The commutative law stated that (E_i is the entity):

$$E_1 \text{ join } E_2 = E_2 \text{ join } E_1$$

In certain situations, such as natural joins, an associative law states that:

$$(E_1 \text{ join } E_2) \text{ join } E_3 = E_1 \text{ join } (E_2 \text{ join } E_3)$$

Using the two laws, figure 3 can be reconfigured to figure 4 (a(1) is the short notation for stating that the physical entity a resides in db1),

```
          Join
         /    \
      a(1)    Join
              /  \
           b(1)  Join
                 /  \
              c(2)  Join
                    /  \
                 d(1) e(2)
```

Figure 3: Before Transformation

```
          Join
          /  \
      Join    Join
      /  \     / \
  a(1) b(1) d(1) Join
                 /  \
              c(2) e(2)
```

Figure 4: After Transformation

Notice that the above transformation are only beneficial if the join conditions can be ignored. That is they are all natural joins. The associative rule cannot be used if we introduce join conditions as in figure 5. Let us assume that the entities a, b and c are: a(a1,a2), b(b1, b2), c(c1, c2) respectively.

```
      Join  F2: a2=b1 & a1=c2
      /  \
  a(2)  Join F1: b2=c1
        /  \
     b(1) c(2)
```

Figure 5: Query Tree with Conditions

Since a and c are both entities from db2, swapping a(2) with b(1) will result in a more efficient sub-query. However, we cannot push a(2) down the tree by using the associative rule directly. It is necessary to know how to reshuffle the conditions when we swap the node positions of the query. To do that, we introduce the following transformation rule to reconfigure the tree (X stands for the cartesian product, F_i is the condition).

(E_1 Join $_{F1}$ E_2) Join $_{F2}$ E_3 = Select(F1 & F2) (E_1 X E_2 X E_3)

Application of the above rule transforms the tree in 5 to the one in figure 6 which is expressed using cartesian product and selection with the conditions F3 at the root node.

From this tree we group the entities residing in the same db together. We obtain an intermediate tree as in figure 7 after the grouping.

$F3 = F_1$ & F_2 ...F_m

```
        select F3: a2=b1 & a1=c2 & b2=c1
        |
        X
      / | \
  b(1) a(2) c(2)
```

Figure 6: A Flattened Tree

```
          select F3: a2=b1 & a1=c2 & b2=c1
          |
          X
        /   \
  db1 X       X db2
      |      / \
    b(1)  a(2) c(2)
```

Figure 7: An Intermediate Tree

Denote $IDB(F_i)$ = {db id | db is involved in F_i}

The next step is to rewrite F3 into conjunctive normal form and sort F3 according to the size of $IDB(F_i)$ in ascending order. For each node in the tree we define:

$IDB(N_i)$ = {db id | db is involved in the tree rooted at node N_i}

Now all that is required is to loop over the sorted F_1 & F_2 ...F_m and push the relevant conditions to the appropriate nodes. We briefly sketch the algorithm for pushing down the conditions.

Procedure **Push Down**
begin
  loop over sorted F_1 & F_2 ...F_m
  For each F_i
    look at all the children of rootnode N_1,...N_k
    if $\exists N_j$, $IDB(N_j) \supseteq IDB(F_i)$
      push F_i to the node N_j
    else choose the minimum $N'_1,...,N'_s$
      such that $\cup_{t=1,s} IDB(N'_t) \supseteq IDB(F_i)$
    Merge the nodes N'_1,..N'_s into a new
    node N' as the direct child of the rootnode
    with $IDB(N') = \cup_{t=1,s} IDB(N'_t)$
end

The successful application of the Push Down algorithm will produce the tree in figure 8 for the example shown in figure 5. Here the entities from the same DB are grouped together.

```
      Join F2': b2=c1 & a2=c1
      /  \
  b(1) Join F1': a1=c2
       /  \
    a(2) c(2)
```

Figure 8: A Reconfigured Query Tree

In summary, the chances of finding the maximal subqueries is increased by exchanging the nodes positions and the Push Down procedure. In cases when no conditions can be pushed down, we have to go back to the original tree. Since the new tree will involve cartesian product. Of course, in this case, we will end up with a query tree where most sub-queries are atomic (not maximal). When only some conditions can be pushed down, we end up getting a partially transformed tree, i.e. some sub-queries are maximal and some are not. It is necessary to compute the cost of executing this partially transformed tree verses the original tree to determine which tree should be used. Further research is necessary to resolve this issue.

4.1 Analysis

The major different between the cost of executing a query in heterogeneous DBMS system verses distributed DBMS system is that, data conversion and data transmission cost cannot be ignored.

We briefly sketch the cost model for heterogeneous query which is proposed by [8]. The parameters used in the cost model are:

- S_Startup_Cost = Local DBMS start up cost
- T_Startup_Cost = Transmission start up cost
- $S_{foreign}$ = The data imported from other DBMS for query reduction or query evaluation
- S_{local} = The total size of local relations
- S_{result} = The partial result of the query

Local_Query_Cost = S_Startup_Cost +
Local_Processing_Cost($S_{foreign} + S_{local}$)+
Transmission_Cost($S_{foreign}$) + Storage_Cost($S_{foreign}$)
+ Conversion_Cost($S_{foreign}$)
Transmission_Cost(S_{result}) = T_Startup_Cost +
Data_Transmission_Cost(S_{result})
Query_Cost = $\sum_{allqueries}$ Local_Query_Cost(Q)

In the above cost formula, the transmission cost of data to the current DBMS is treated as part of the local query cost because the data are imported to reduce the processing cost of the local query. One observation that can be drawn from the above cost model is that the cost of moving data around is significant. This encompasses the conversion cost, the transmission cost and the storage cost. These costs are linearly proportional to the size of the data. We believe that maximal sub-queries will reduce the transmission and conversion cost. The local processing cost might be increased, but so long as we can avoid cartesian product in any of the maximal sub-query, the increase will not be significant. It should not make much different to the local optimizer in executing three joins verses five joins.

We will provide an analysis on the following queries based on the above cost model. We assume that the local optimizers will on average execute the sub-query in near optimal way. A cost factor of 1 is assigned to each transmission and conversion cost.

Given the query in figure 9: The cost of processing calculated using the above cost criteria is (assuming random processing site is chosen based on the sizes of the partial result and the relation. Suppose relation a smaller than

```
          join
          /  \
       join  c(4)
       /  \
    join  e(1)
    /  \
 a(1)   b(4)
```

Figure 9: An Unlabelled Tree

b, STC is the storage cost, LPC is the Local Processing Cost):

a join b =
transmission_cost(a) + conversion_cost(a) + STC(a)
+ LPC(a join b) in db4
temp join e =
transmission_cost(e) + conversion_cost(e) + STC(e)
+ LPC(temp join e) in db4
temp2 join c = LPC(temp2 join c)
Total transmission and conversion cost = 4

This will also be the cost of executing the query in Multibase system where there is no restriction on the number of sub-queries being generated.

In Mermaid, the site for processing the operation is determined by using the semijoin. The cost of processing the query in figure 9 is calculated as:

a join b =
transmission_cost(b) + conversion_cost(b) +
STC(b) + LPC(a join b) in db1
temp join e = LPC(temp join e) in db1
temp2 join c =
transmission_cost(temp2) + conversion_cost(temp2) +
STC(temp2) + LPC(temp2 join c)
Total transmission and conversion cost = 4

With our approach, after grouping the query into maximal sub-queries as in figure 10: The cost of processing

```
                  join twig(q2,db4)
                  /  \
               join  c(4)
               /  \
twig(q1,db1) join  b(4)
             /  \
          a(1)   e(1)
```

Figure 10: A labelled Tree

is:

a join e = LPC(a join e) in db1
temp join b =
transmission_cost(temp) +
Conversion_cost(temp) + STC(temp)
temp join b join c =
LPC (temp join b join c) in db4
Total transmission cost and conversion cost = 2

This short analysis shows that finding maximal sub-queries will reduce the transmission and conversion cost in the multidatabase environment. It might increase the cost to the local processing component. But we believe that if maximal sub-queries do not have any cartesian product, the increase will not be significant. This is yet to be verified by actual simulation.

5 CONCLUSIONS

In a loosely coupled multidatabase environment, the need to preserve the autonomy of local databases means that there are few opportunities to do accurate cost-based optimization. We propose a framework which has the scope for global optimization and also can exploit the local processing power fully. The finding of maximal sub-queries is investigated as a potential global query optimization strategy. By taking into account the semantics of the operators, we can increase the chances of finding the maximal sub-queries.

The advantages of finding maximal sub-queries can be summarized as:

- It promotes local optimization especially for cyclic queries. It implies less data being returned because of the processing of a maximal query.
- It generates less temporary entities. One temporary relation is generated for each sub-query instead of each atomic operation.
- It reduces the transmission and conversion cost in processing the query.
- It can be coupled with other optimization strategies in distributed database systems. For example, semi-join can be applied when choosing the site for the execution of the sub-query.
- It provides an opportunity to build an execution plan which shows dependencies between sub-queries. This increases the chances for parallel execution.

Finding maximal sub-queries is a useful step in optimizing query in a loosely coupled multidatabase system. So far the analysis is based on our intuitive observations. Actual experimentation is needed to prove our point. Our future works include the coupling of this strategy with other heuristics. For example, experiments must be carried out to see the effect on the cost of executing the global query with finding maximal sub-queries followed by semi-joins. Also the conversion cost and transmission cost have to be estimated so that the advantage of the maximal sub-queries can be proven.

References

1) Dayal U. "Query processing in a multidatabase system." In W. Kim, David S. Reiner, Don S. Batory, editors, Query Processing in Database Systems, pages 82–108. Springer-Verlag, New York, 1983.

2) Du W., Krishnamurthy R., and Shan M.C. "Query optimization in heterogeneous dbms". In Proceedings of the 18th VLDB Conference, Vancouver, Canada, August 1992.

3) Krishnamurthy R., Boral H., and Zaniolo C. "Optimization of nonrecursive queries". In W. Chu, G. Gardarin, S. Ohsuga, and Y. Kambayashi, editors, Proceedings of the 12th VLDB Conference, pages 128–137, Kyoto, Japan, August 1986.

4) Lanzelotte R.S.G. , Valduriez P., Ziane M., and Cheiney J.P. "Optimization of nonrecursive queries in oodb". In C. Delobel, M.Kifer, and Y. Masunaga, editors, Proceedings of the 2nd DOOD Conference, pages 1–20, Munich, Germany, December 1991.

5) Litwin W., Abdellatif A. "Multidatabase interoperability". IEEE Computer, 19(12):10–18, December 1986.

6) Litwin W., Abdellatif A., Nicolas B., Vigier P., and Zeroual A. "MSQL: A multidatabse language". Technical Report 695, INRIA-Rocquencourt, B.P.105, 78153 LeChesnay Cedex, France, June 1987.

7) Litwin W., Mark L., and Roussopoulos N. "Interoperability of multiple autonomous databases". ACM Computing Surveys, 22(3):267–293, September 1990.

8) Ooi B.C., Chan C.Y., and Lu H. "Query processing in multidatabase systems". Technical report, Department of Information Systems and Computer Science, National University of Singapore, Kent Ridge, Singapore, May 1992.

9) Sheth A.P., Larson J.A. "Federated database systems for managing distributed, heterogeneous, and autonomous databases". ACM Computing Surveys, 22(3):183–236, September 1990.

10) Templeton M. et. al. "Interviso DD/D Builder's guide". Technical Report DILVO01-02, Data Integration, Inc., 3233 Federal Avenue, Los Angeles, LA, California 90066, January 1992.

11) Thomas G. et. al. "Heterogeneous distributed database systems for production use". ACM Computing Survey, 22(3):238–266, September 1990.

Temporal Query Processing for Scene Retrieval in Motion Image Databases

Junichi Takahashi

IBM Research, Tokyo Research Laboratory
5-19, Sanbancho, Chiyoda-ku, Tokyo 102, JAPAN

Abstract

This paper describes a temporal query processing algorithm for efficient scene retrieval in motion image databases. A motion image logically consists of sequential frames, and a scene, defined as an arbitrary portion of the frame sequence, is identified by a pair of numbers representing the initial and final frames of the scene. When the frame numbers are mapped onto a time-axis, a scene object can be represented as a record that has two time attributes for identifying the time interval of the scene object, as well as other attributes for describing scene properties. The proposed query processing method is intended to allow efficient processing of n-way temporal join in searching for overlaps and extensions of multiple intervals by comparison of time attributes for the join. Experiments show that the processing cost of our method increases linearly with respect to the number of compared records, whereas that of the conventional two-way nested-loop method increases exponentially.

1 Introduction

Motion pictures have penetrated widely and deeply into our societies owing to the recent popularization of audio and video equipment and the rapid development of multi-media and interactive technologies [8, 9]. The huge volume of collections of motion pictures makes it impossible to access motion pictures simply by depending on human memory, or on visual scanning of entire collections. The importance of motion image databases for retrieving target scenes of interest rapidly and with minimum effort is definitely recognized in museums, media organizations such as broadcasting centers, and private homes [12]. Because of the temporal properties of continuous media such as motion pictures, motion image databases are an important application of temporal databases, and there has been much recent discussion of technical issues related to motion image databases in the context of temporal databases [13].

A motion image logically consists of sequential frames, each of which is a two-dimensional still image. A scene, defined as an arbitrary portion of a frame sequence, is identified by a pair of numbers representing the initial and final frames of the scene. When the frame number of a motion image is mapped onto a time-axis, a scene object can be represented as a record that has two time attributes as well as other properties for describing the contents of scenes, such as characters and objects appearing in the scenes, or events and background details. When a user wants to retrieve scenes of interest quickly and randomly by specifying the conditions of these scene properties, searching for overlaps and extensions of multiple intervals in an image database are important operations.

So far, research on temporal databases has mostly addressed temporal representations of the time properties of real-world objects that have time-varying properties, as well as issues related to versions [15], operations on the objects [4, 5, 21, 23], temporal query languages [1, 10, 17, 19, 22, 24], and physical file organization [2, 16]. Access methods for temporal databases [6], and temporal query processing [14, 20] have been less frequently addressed, especially for n-way temporal join [11].

Temporal operations on time intervals must include evaluation of temporal relationships among the intervals [3], such as *before*, *after*, *overlapping*, and *included*. The crucial problem in temporal join processing in motion image databases is that a join is likely to be processed by using a two-way nested-loop algorithm, because both the initial and final frame numbers of different scenes should be compared simultaneously to evaluate the temporal relationships of two intervals. This is why efficient query processing is required for temporal operations such as comparison of temporal attributes.

The query processing method proposed in this paper is intended to allow efficient processing of n-way temporal join. The algorithm is described in the context of the relational representation of temporal objects, but it can also be applied to other temporal models, such as temporal ER databases [7] and temporal object-oriented databases [18].

2 Temporal representation of motion image databases

We can allocate a sequential frame number to each frame of a motion image. As the example in Figure 1 shows, a scene, *A* for instance, is an arbitrary portion of a motion image, and consists of a sequence of frames. A scene can be expressed as a pair consisting of the initial frame number and the final frame number. Different scenes may share frames, as scenes *A* and *C* do in this example. Processing for scene retrieval requires a pair of initial and final frame numbers to be found.

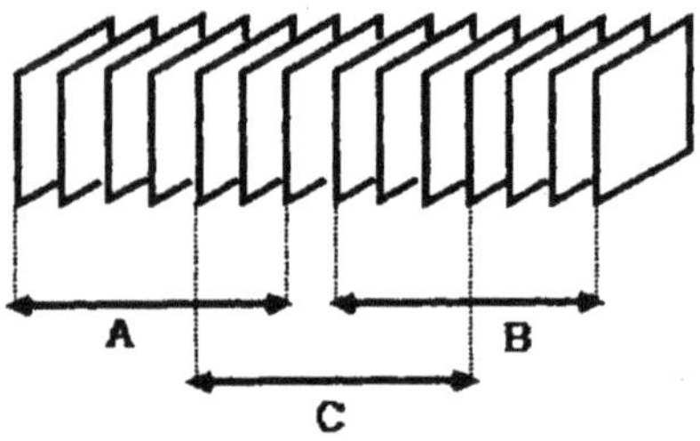

Figure 1. Scene objects in a motion image

Scene retrieval methods can be divided into two categories according to whether or not they use structural models. Higher efficiency in the management and retrieval of motion image databases is expected to result from the use of structural models [12], as the example in Figure 2 shows. A motion picture can be logically segmented into shorter scenes whose shortest scenes are called *cuts*, according to criteria such as physical correlations and/or changes in semantics. Each scene has one or more still frames, called *representative frames* or *RFs*, which typically represent the entire frame sequence.

The structural models can be grouped into two types with respect to time sequential and hierarchical models. The latter type describes the hierarchical structures of scenes in terms of the story, or scenario, of the motion image. In a scene hierarchy, a scene is represented as a set of nodes each of which stores the properties of the scene, and a set of links each of which represents a parent-child relationship between two scenes. On the other hand, the time sequential model [12] provide users with a flexible and easy-to-understand query specification of scene retrieval, in the sense that a scene structure can be regarded in terms of temporal relationships of pairs of intervals on a time-axis, such as *before*, *after*, *overlapping*, and *extension*.

Omoto et al. model a motion image as a set of semantic scene objects in an object-oriented database, with a pair of numbers representing the initial and final frames of each scene, as well as other scene properties allocated by a user [18].

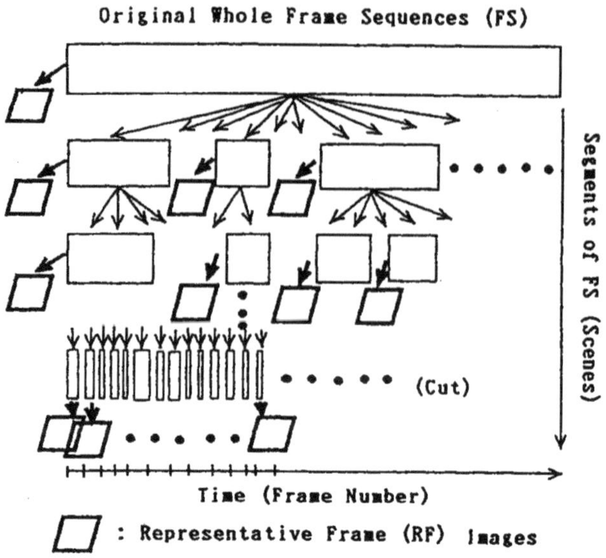

Figure 2. Example of a structural model of a motion image

Though their model of a motion image is very natural and useful as a mean for retrieving scenes of interest by matching scene properties, it can only be used to search for scenes that have been selected from a collection of pre-defined scene objects. In their model, it is inconvenient to add or modify scene properties to or from an arbitrary portion of a motion image, because all of the scene objects must be redefined each time update operations are performed. For example, if there is a scene $S_1 = [100,300]$ with the property K_1, and the user wants to add the property K_2 to scene $S_2 = [200,400]$, he has to redefine the following scenes: $S_1' = [100,200]$ with K_1, $S_{12} = [200,300]$ with K_1 and K_2, and $S_2' = [300,400]$ with K_2.

In this paper, we assume a time-sequential representation of scene properties for flexible indexing of arbitrary portions of motion images [12]. Figure 3 is a sample of a time chart showing the periods of allocation of properties to scenes. A Boolean query can be specified by using an arbitrary number of properties with any combinations of the logical operators AND, OR, and NOT. For example, target scenes that have both properties K_1 and K_2 can be retrieved by searching for the overlapping intervals of K_1 and K_2 in this time chart.

For the time-sequential representation of scene properties, we store a set of an initial frame number F_i and a final frame number F_f and a property K_i in a record $R = [F_i, F_f, K_i]$ $(F_i < F_f, 0 < i \leq m)$. A temporal table *D(start, end, property)* is a collection of these records, each of which has two temporal attributes for the initial and final frame numbers. Figure 4 shows a sample of table *D*.

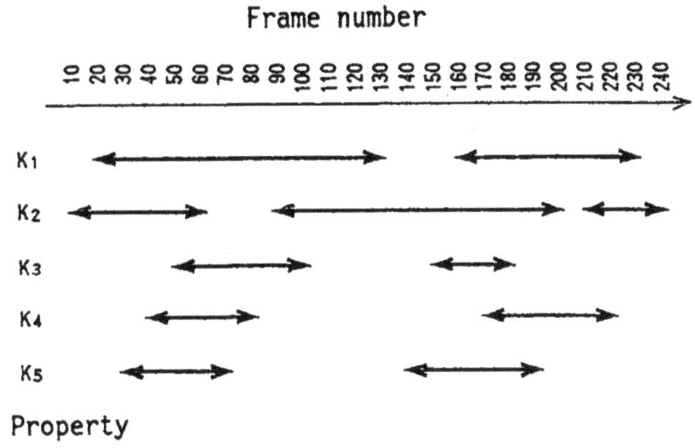

Figure 3. Time chart for representing scene properties

In this representation of scene properties, operations for adding and updating properties of scenes can be performed flexibly, because each scene property is described in a unique record, and modification of a property of a particular scene does not affect the allocation of other properties to the scene, or that of any properties of other scenes.

3 Problems in temporal query processing

Snodgrass proposed a method of searching for overlaps and extensions of intervals, based on temporal join, in the context of temporal databases [22]. The join operator is translated into some conventional join conditions that compare both the initial and final numbers of two intervals at a time. For the table shown in Figure 4, a query retrieving overlaps between intervals with property K_1 and those with property K_2 can be processed by translating the query into the following self-join SQL statement:

```
select d2.start, d1.end
from   D d1, D d2
where  d1.property in (K1,K2)
and    d2.property in (K1,K2)
and    d1.property¬=d2.property
and    d1.start<d2.start
and    d1.end>d2.start
and    d1.end<d2.end

union

select d2.start, d2.end
from   D d1, D d2
where  d1.property in (K1,K2)
and    d2.property in (K1,K2)
and    d1.property¬=d2.propeery
and   ((d1.start<d2.start and d1.end>=d2.end)
       or
      (d1.start=d2.start and d1.end>d2.end)
       or
      (d1.start=d2.start and d1.end=d2.end and
       d1.property<d2.property))
```

This query includes disjunctive temporal conditions, because there are three types of

Table *D*:

start	end	property
20	130	K_1
160	230	K_1
10	60	K_2
90	200	K_2
210	240	K_2
50	100	K_3
150	180	K_3
40	80	K_4
170	220	K_4
30	70	K_5
140	190	K_5

Figure 4. Example of a temporal database

overlapping between two intervals: (a) *intersect*, (b) *contains* or *contained*, and (c) *same*, as the example in Figure 5 shows. The first select clause in the above statement includes a condition on the time attributes *start* and *end* for intersecting intervals:

```
d1.start<d2.start and
d1.end>d2.start   and
d1.end<d2.end
```

In the same way, the second select clause includes three disjunctive conditions for containing, contained, and same intervals, respectively. In this case, a merge-sort or hash-join method cannot be applied effectively for processing the temporal join conditions. Because the two time attributes *start* and *end* are compared simultaneously, these conditions should be evaluated on the basis of a nested-loop algorithm that requires n^2 record comparisons, where n is the number of records in the table to be joined. The problem is that the search cost increases exponentially relative to the number of compared records.

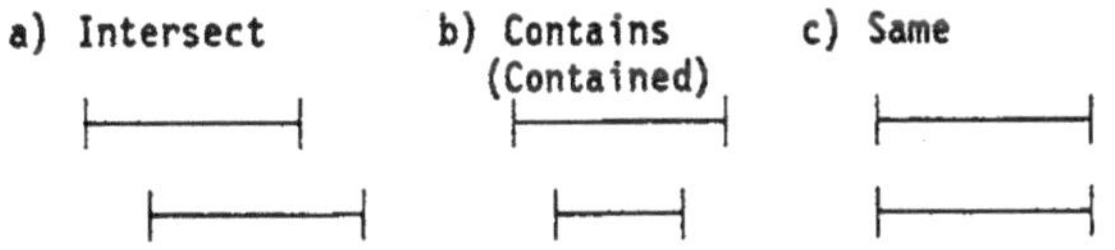

Figure 5. Types of interval overlapping

Elmasri proposed a time index access method that can be used to improve the performance of temporal selection, temporal projection, aggregate functions, and temporal join [6]. Because query processing with this index access method is two-way for temporal join operations, it requires iteration of the two-way processing to implement the n-way join for processing Boolean queries in a scene retrieval described such as that in the previous section.

Gunadhi et al. proposed a temporal query processing algorithm that is more efficient than the nested-loop based algorithm [11]. In their method,

Table D':

start	end	property
20	130	K_1
160	230	K_1
50	100	K_3
150	180	K_3
40	80	K_4
170	220	K_4

Figure 6. Intermediate table

two sets of records are separately sorted in ascending order of the starting numbers of intervals. These sorted records are sequentially accessed in order to match temporal attributes without duplicate access to the same records. The drawback of this algorithm is that it is intended for two-way join, and only for queries in which exactly two properties are specified for the search condition.

4 Temporal query processing

4.1 Outline of query processing

An outline of the query processing procedure is given here, using the example of the table shown in Figure 4. Assume that we want to retrieve intervals that have all the properties K_1, K_3, and K_4. Query condition Q is expressed in terms of a Boolean expression: $Q = K_1$ AND K_3 AND K_4. First, the records in table D are restricted to those that have been allocated one of the properties K_1, K_3, or K_4. An intermediate table D', shown in Figure 6, is created, which gives a set A including six intervals:

$$A = \{[20,130],[40,80],[50,100],[150,180],$$
$$[160,230],[170,220]\}.$$

If the whole interval Z is [0,300] in this example, we obtain candidate intervals $I(i)$ for evaluating the query condition Q:

$$I(i) = [L(i), L(i+1)] \quad (1 \leq i \leq |A| \times 2 + 1),$$

where $L(i)$ is the ith element of the list composed of the following $|A| \times 2 + 2$ elements of the initial or final number of intervals in set $A \cup Z$:

0, 20, 40, 50, 80, 100, 130, 150, 160, 170, 180,

220, 230, 300.

Note that the starting number $L(i)$ of the ith interval $I(i)$ is incremented by 1 if $L(i)$ is derived from the final number of any interval in list A, and that the final number $L(i+1)$ is decremented by 1 if $L(i+1)$ is derived from the starting number of any interval in list A. In this case, we get the following 13 candidate intervals:

[0,19],[20, 39],[40, 49],[50, 80],[81, 100],

[101, 130],[131,149],[150, 159],[160, 169],

[170, 180],[181, 220],[221,230],[231, 300].

Now, a truth table, shown in Figure 7, is created to evaluate whether each property specified in the query is allocated to each of these candidate intervals. The resultant intervals, [50, 80] and [170, 180] in this example, are given if the truth value of Q is TRUE for any of the candidate intervals in this truth table.

Interval	[0,19]	[20,39]	[40,49]	[50,80]
K_1	F	T	T	T
K_3	F	F	F	T
K_4	F	F	T	T
Q	F	F	F	T

[81,100]	[101,130]	[131,149]	[150,159]	[160,169]
T	T	F	F	T
T	F	F	T	T
F	F	F	F	F
F	F	F	F	F

[170,180]	[181,220]	[221,230]	[231,300]
T	T	T	F
T	F	F	F
T	T	F	F
T	F	F	F

Figure 7. Truth table for candidate intervals

4.2 Query processing procedure

This procedure assumes that the temporal table D has two temporal attributes for the initial and final number of intervals, and an attribute for the property of the intervals. The input of this procedure is a Boolean query Q composed of m properties of target intervals. The output of the procedure consists of intervals that satisfy the query condition. In the query results, if the final number of an interval is adjacent to the final number of another interval, those two intervals are merged into the shortest interval that includes both the intervals. The following is a description of the query processing procedure:

Step 1. Create a logical formula $P(P_1, P_2, \ldots, P_m)$ by replacing property K_i in query Q with logical variable P_i.

Step 2. Search records in table D that have one of the properties specified in query Q, and store the records in an intermediate table D' after sorting them according to the initial number F_i.

Step 3. Prepare the following work areas in main memory, and initialize them:

a) Target interval buffer: $S_t := [F_{it}, F_{ft}]$

b) Candidate interval buffer: $S_c := [F_{ic}, F_{fc}]$ where the initial values are $F_{ic} = F_{fc} = (F_i \text{ of } R_1) - 1$

c) Current interval buffer: $S_{ri} := [F_{iri}, F_{fri}]$ $(0 < i \leq m)$

d) Input buffer: $B := [F_{ib}, F_{fb}, K_b]$

e) Record buffer: $B' := [F_{ib}', F_{fb}', K_b']$

Step 4. If record buffer B' is empty, read a record into input buffer B from intermediate table D'. If there is no record to read, raise an EOF flag. If record buffer B' is not empty, copy B' to input buffer B, and clear B'.

Step 5. Find the number i such that $K_i = K_b$, and compare the final number of the intervals of the candidate interval and the current interval for i.

if $F_{fc} \geq F_{fri}$

then begin $F_{iri} := F_{ib}$; $F_{fri} := F_{fb}$; *end*;

else $B' := B$;

Step 6. Update the candidate interval buffer S_c as follows. Set the next number of the current final number of S_c to the new initial number of S_c. Set the minimum initial or final number among the current intervals that is larger than the final frame number to the new final number.

$F_{ic} := F_{fc} + 1$

$F_{fc} := \min\{F_{irj} - 1, F_{frk}\}$

where $F_{irj} > F_{fc}, F_{frk} > F_{fc}$

Step 7. Set the logical variables P_i by checking inclusion between the candidate interval and the current interval for i.

if $F_iC \geq F_{fri}$ AND $F_{fc} \leq F_{iri}$

then $P_i :=$ TRUE;

else $P_i :=$ FALSE;

Step 8. Evaluate the logical formula P by using values of P_i. If the logical formula P is TRUE, write the target interval S_t after checking the connection between the candidate interval and the target interval, which is found in the previous loop.

if $F_{ic} = F_{ft} + 1$

then $F_{ft} := F_{fc}$;

else $S_t := S_c$;

Step 9. If the EOF flag is not raised, go to step 4.

In the above procedure, steps 4 to 9 are iterated for each candidate interval. Because the intermediate table is sorted in ascending order of the initial number of intervals in step 2, it is possible to evaluate the truth value for the candidate intervals by making one sequential search of the intermediate table.

5 Experimental results

The search cost in the proposed temporal query processing method with respect to disk pages accessed includes: (1) the number of pages occupied by temporal table D, (2) the number of pages occupied by intermediate table D', and (3) the sorting cost for the intermediate table. Figure 8 shows a comparison of the response time in our method and that in the conventional two-way method, which utilizes nested-loop join processing. The search cost in our method is proportional to the number of records in the intermediate table D', because the target intervals are found by accessing the intermediate table only once. If the intermediate table is small enough to be accommodated in main memory rather than secondary storage, costs (2) and (3) can be ignored. It is possible to improve cost (1) by using a B^+-tree index on the property attribute of the temporal table D in restricting the records on the attribute.

In the conventional method, the records in the temporal table can be restricted to same records that appear in the intermediate table in our method with the properties specified in a query. But the search cost still increases exponentially rather than linearly with respect to the number of those records, because they are accessed repeatedly in each loop of the nested processing of time attribute comparison. Moreover, a query condition consisting of three or more properties must be processed by iterating the algorithm for two-way join sub-query as many times as the number of properties in the query, so the search time also

Table size in records (Intermediate table size)	Proposed method	Two-way method
Query: $Q_1 = K_1$ AND K_2		
472 (218)	7	10
944 (436)	14	29
1888 (872)	27	99
Query: $Q_2 = K_1$ OR K_2		
472 (218)	7	12
944 (436)	14	37
1888 (872)	27	137
Query: $Q_3 = K_1$ AND K_2 AND K_3		
472 (218)	7	N/A
944 (436)	14	N/A
1888 (872)	27	N/A

Response time in seconds
on an IBM 3081-KX3 running VM/SP

Figure 8. Search cost comparison

increases in proportion to the number of properties in the original query.

6 Conclusion

We proposed a temporal query processing algorithm for n-way temporal join in temporal databases, which can be applied to motion image databases for flexible and random search of scenes of interest. The algorithm is superior to the conventional two-way nested-loop method in terms of memory cost, flexibility, and performance. We also confirmed the performance of our query processing method when we built a prototype of a motion image database system [12]. We plan to make feasibility studies of the motion image database system for practical applications in a museum, in which our temporal query processing is used for flexible and efficient scene retrieval.

References

[1] Tansel. A., "A Historical Query Language," *Information Science*, vol. 53, pp. 101-133, 1991.

[2] Ahn, I. and Snodgrass, R., "Performance Analysis of Temporal Queries," *Information Science*, vol. 49, pp. 103-146, 1989.

[3] Allen, J., "Maintaining Knowledge about Temporal Intervals," *Communications of the ACM*, vol. 26, no. 11, pp. 832-843, 1983.

[4] Ariav, G., "A Temporally Oriented Data Model," *ACM Trans. on Database Systems*, vol. 11, no. 4, pp. 490-527, 1986.

[5] Clifford, J. and Warren, D., "Formal Semantics for Time in Databases," *ACM Trans. on Database Systems*, vol. 8, no. 2, pp. 214-254, 1983.

[6] Elmasri, R. et al., "The Time Index: An Access Structure for Temporal Data," *Proc. of 16th Int'l Conf. on Very Large Databases*, pp. 1-12, 1990.

[7] Elmasri, R. and Wuu, G., "A Temporal Model and Query Language for ER Databases," *Proc. of 6th Int'l Conf. on Data Engineering*, pp. 76-83, 1990.

[8] Fox, E. A. (ed.), "Interactive Technologies," *Communications of the ACM*, vol. 32, no. 6, 1989.

[9] Fox, E. A. (ed.), "Digital Multimedia Systems," *Communications of the ACM*, vol. 34, no. 4, 1991.

[10] Gadia, S., "A Homogeneous Relational Model and Query Language for Temporal Databases," *ACM Trans. on Database Systems*, vol. 13, no. 4, pp. 418-448, 1988.

[11] Gunadhi, H. and Segev, A., "Query Processing Algorithms for Temporal Intersection Joins," *Proc. of 7th Int'l Conf. on Data Engineering*, pp. 336-344, 1991.

[12] Hong, J-K., Tahahashi, J, and Kusaba, M., "A Motion Picture Archiving Technique, and Its Application in an Ethnology Museum," *Proc. of 3rd Int'l Conf. on Database and Expert Systems Applications*, pp. 209-214, 1992.

[13] Kawagoe, K., "Continuous Media Data Management," *ACM SIGMOD Record*, vol. 20, no. 3, pp. 74-75, 1991.

[14] Leung, T. and Muntz, R., "Query Processing for Temporal Databases," *Proc. of 6th Int'l Conf. on Data Engineering*, pp. 200-208, 1990.

[15] Lomet, D. and Salzberg B., "Access Methods for Multiversion Data," *Proc. of ACM SIGMOD*, pp. 315-324, 1989.

[16] Lum, V. et al., "Designing DBMS Support for the Temporal Dimension," *Proc. of ACM SIGMOD*, pp. 115-130, 1984.

[17] Navathe, S. and Ahmed, R., "A Temporal Relational Model and a Query Language," *Information Science*, vol. 49, pp. 147-175, 1989.

[18] Oomoto, E. et al., "Conceptual Model and Visual Interface for Video Databases," *IEICE Tech. Report DE89-50*, pp. 17-24, 1990.

[19] Sarda, N., "Algebra and Query Language for A Historical Data Model," *The Computer Journal*, vol. 33, no. 1, pp. 11-18, 1990.

[20] Segev, A and Gunadhi, H., "Event-Join Optimization in Temporal Relational Databases," *Proc. of 15th Int'l Conf. on Very Large Databases*, pp. 205-215, 1989.

[21] Segev, A. and Shoshani, A., "Logical Modeling of Temporal Data," *Proc. of ACM SIGMOD*, pp. 454-466, 1987.

[22] Snodgrass, R., "The Temporal Query Language TQuel," *ACM Trans. on Database Systems*, vol. 12, no. 2, pp. 247-298, 1987.

[23] Snodgrass, R., "Temporal Databases: Status and Research Directions," *ACM SIGMOD Records*, vol. 19, no. 4, pp. 83-89, 1990.

[24] Tuzhilin, A and Clifford, J., "A Temporal Relational Algebra as a Basis for Temporal Relational Completeness," *Proc. of 16th Int'l Conf. on Very Large Databases*, pp. 13-23, 1990.

Efficient Processing of Time-Joins in Temporal Data Bases

Satyendra P. Rana
Farshad Fotouhi
Department of Computer Science
Wayne State University
Detroit, MI 48202, U.S.A

ABSTRACT

We present several new algorithms for time-join in temporal data bases. The presented algorithms exploit inherent characteristics of temporal relations and thus are efficient than existing algorithms in the literature.. The focus of this paper is on minimizing wasteful tuple comparisons, which in turn has a bearing on buffer space requirements and disk I/O, during time-join processing.

1. INTRODUCTION

There are many application domains where one needs to capture time dependent information. Temporal database systems provide logical modeling of temporal data and the capability for handling complex temporal queries. One way to handle temporal data is to extend the relational model, as proposed by several authors[2,3,9,11]. Some researchers have also focussed on defining temporal extensions to conceptual data models and query languages [12]. There has also been parallel research in the area of defining efficient storage structures and access paths for temporal data[1,6,7,8,10].

In this paper, we focus on time-join processing in temporal databases. We assume the operand relations to be in first temporal normal form. All algorithms presented by us are refinements of the basic nested-loop approach. Our algorithms are more efficient than the existing algorithms in terms of wasteful tuple comparisons. Most of the presented algorithms also need comparatively lesser buffer space and are optimal in terms of disk I/O.

The organization of the paper is as follows. In section 2, we introduce temporal data model. The basic approach to time-join processing is described in section 3. In section 4, we present several new algorithms for time-join. The discussion of their comparative performance appears in the last section.

2. TEMPORAL DATA MODEL

We consider time as a sequence of discrete time instants where consecutive time instants differ exactly by one unit. Time unit is assumed to be same everywhere - it's further specification is immaterial for our purpose.

The temporal data model considered by us is same as in[5]. A tuple in a temporal relation has time attributes T_S (start time) and T_E (end time) in addition to a surrogate, time-varying attributes, and non-time varying attributes. The time interval $[T_S, T_E]$; $T_E \geq T_S$, semantically represents the lifespan or validity of the tuple in question. We assume all relations to be in the first temporal normal form [13]. That is, for a given surrogate instance in a relation, all tuples have non-intersecting lifespans.

Figure 1 shows two temporal relations in first temporal normal form. E# and D# represent surrogate attributes in relations EMP_DEPT and DEPT_MANAGER respectively.

EMP_DEPT

E#	D#	T_S	T_E
E1	D1	5	10
E2	D1	6	12
E1	D2	11	18
E2	D3	13	20
E1	D4	19	20

DEPT_MANAGER

D#	M#	T_S	T_E
D1	M2	1	4
D2	M1	2	9
D3	M3	3	5
D4	M5	3	7
D1	M4	5	12
D3	M6	6	10
D4	M7	8	12
D2	M8	10	15
D1	M9	13	17

Figure 1. Two temporal relations in their first temporal normal form

3. PROCESSING OF TIME-JOIN

Many temporal comparison operators have been defined in the literature. In computing time-join, we need the *'intersects'* operator. Given tuples x and y, x *intersects* y is true iff $T_S(x) \leq T_E(y)$ and $T_E(x) \geq T_S(y)$.

Consider two temporal relations r_1 and r_2. Let x and y denote arbitrary tuples of r_1 and r_2, respectively. A time-join (T-join) of r_1 and r_2 concatenates respective tuples x and y if and only if x *intersects* y is true. The start and end times of the resulting tuple, say z, are computed as follows:

$$T_S(z) = \max(T_S(x), T_S(y));$$
$$T_E(z) = \min(T_E(x), T_E(y)).$$

In a T-join, a tuple in r_1 may have one or more intersecting tuples in r_2; we cannot determine a priori how many result tuples will be produced. Thus, if conventional join processing methods are used, we would need to apply the nested-loop algorithm to compare each tuple in the outer relation with each tuple in the inner relation.

In this paper, we discuss only the class of algorithms which scan the relations sequentially and do not rely on any pre-existing index. Henceforth, we take r_1 as the outer relation and r_2 to be the inner relation. First, we describe the basic nested-loop algorithm and point out its inefficiency. In the next section, we present several refinements over the basic scheme.

Following notation is used in all algorithms:

SP (StartPointer): starting position in inner relation for next iteration,

OP (OuterloopPointer): . current position in outer relation,
IP (InnerloopPointer): current position in inner relation,
Read(r, Pointer): returns the tuple in r pointed by Pointer and Pointer is incremented to point to the next tuple in r. If the tuple in question is in buffer, a reference to that is provided directly, otherwise the tuple is read into buffer from disk.
EOR(r): pointer to the end of relation r.

Algorithm 1
(The basic nested-loop approach)

Input: temporal relations r_1 and r_2.
Output: Time-join of r_1 and r_2.

Method:

```
1.      SP := pointer to first tuple in r2;
        OP := pointer to first tuple in r1;
2.      while ( OP ≠ EOR(r1))
        {       x := Read(r1, OP);
                IP := SP;
                while (IP ≠ EOR(r2))
                {  y := Read(r2, IP);
                   if (x intersects y)
                          output T-join result of x, y;
                }
        }
```

The basic nested-loop approach is quite inefficient. The number of tuple comparisons is always the maximum possible (product of operand relations sizes). When the selectivity factor is not high, a relatively small fraction of these comparisons will generate tuples for the result relation. Thus, many unnecessary tuple comparisons are performed which may potentially be avoided.

In the basic nested-loop approach, each loop iteration scans the inner relation completely. In algorithms presented in the next section, the inner loop scans only an appropriate part of the inner relation., thereby reducing unnecessary tuple comparisons. This optimization is achieved at the cost of sorting relations in desired orders and/or by maintaining additional pointers during scan.

4. EFFICIENT TIME-JOIN ALGORITHMS

As mentioned earlier, the algorithms presented in this section are optimal in disk I/O as each tuple is read at most once. All algorithms are stated as if tuples are read one at a time but it would make no difference in tuple comparisons if block I/O is used instead. There will however be an impact on buffer space requirement and total disk I/O. For simplicity of presentation, we assume the availability of sufficient buffer space. In section 5, we discuss the buffer requirements of presented algorithms and the impact of limited buffer space. Our immediate objective is to minimize the number of tuple comparisons in time-join operation.

Following is an explanation of the terms used:
SCANNED(x, r_2): number of tuples of r_2 compared with x during computation of time-join; x ε r_1; INTERSECT(x, r_2): number of tuples of r_2 which intersect with x;
Therefore the number of wasteful comparisons in the entire join operation is

$$\sum_{x \varepsilon r1} \text{SCANNED}(x, r_2) - \text{INTERSECT}(x, r_2);$$

FIRST(x, r_2): the first tuple in r_2 intersecting with x;
LAST(x, r_2): the last tuple in r_2 intersecting with x;
SPREAD(x,r_2): number of tuples in r_2 from FIRST(x, r_2) to LAST(x, r_2);
PRE(x, r_2): number of tuples in SCANNED(x, r_2) which precede FIRST(x, r_2);
POST(x, r_2):number of tuples in SCANNED(x, r_2) which follow LAST(x, r_2);
IN(x, r_2) :: number of tuples in SPREAD(x, r_2) which do not intersect with x.
For a given x, the number of wasteful comparisons is given by:

$$\text{SCANNED}(x, r_2) - \text{INTERSECT}(x, r_2) = \text{PRE}(x, r_2) + \text{IN}(x, r_2) + \text{POST}(x, r_2).$$

Now we can try and reduce PRE, IN, and POST comparisons individually to reduce the overall wasteful comparisons.

• Minimizing POST comparisons

To minimize POST(x, r_2), we need a criterion to terminate join loop for x as early as possible. To stop scanning, we must infer that the remaining tuples of r_2 will not intersect with x. If tuples in r_2 are in random order, no such inference can be drawn during a sequential scan.

Let r_2 be sorted in the ascending order of T_S. Consider a tuple y in r_2 such that $T_S(y) > T_E(x)$, then it is obvious that no tuple preceding y in r_2 will intersect with x. We can state the termination condition for join loop for x as: " Stop when encounter first y in r_2 such that $T_S(y) > T_E(x)$ or EOR(r_2)". If this criterion is employed during scan, POST(x, r_2) turns out to be at most 1.

• Minimizing IN comparisons

The IN comparisons can be reduced by sorting the inner relation r_2, on T_S and T_E as illustrated by the following example:

$T_S(x) = 16$, $T_E(x) = 25$

Relation r_2 unsorted

	T_S	T_E
y_1	10	20
y_2	2	8
y_3	10	13
y_4	12	14
y_5	15	26

Relation r_2 sorted

	T_S	T_E
y_2	2	8
y_3	10	13
y_1	10	20
y_4	12	14
y_5	15	26

Relation	Tuples in SPREAD(x, r_2)	Tuples in IN(x, r_2)
r_2	{y_1, y_2, y_3, y_4, y_5}	{y_2, y_3, y_4 }
r_2 sorted on T_S	{y_1, y_3, y_4, y_5}	{y_3, y_4}
r_2 sorted onT_S &T_E	{y_1, y_4, y_5}	{y_4}

There are two points to be noted here: first, sorting on T_s would in general reduce IN comparisons but will not in general eliminate these completely; and second, further sorting on T_E would have a minimal impact (even though it is not obvious from the example above). Also, the ordering of r_1 has no impact on IN.

• Minimizing PRE comparisons

PRE comparisons can be avoided if we can directly jump to FIRST(x, r_2) when the join loop is initiated for any x ε r_1. In the absence of any indexing information, the pointer to FIRST(x, r_2) can only be obtained by drawing some inference from the previous join loops. As earlier, such an inference can be drawn only if tuples in r_1 are sorted in some order.

If r_1 is sorted in the ascending order of T_S, then the join loop for a tuple immediately after x, need not start before FIRST(x,r_2). Thus, by sorting r_1 on T_S and maintaining a pointer for FIRST() we can reduce PRE substantially. Note that ordering of r_1 on T_E does not contribute to the reduction of PRE.

Till this point we have categorized the potentially wasteful comparisons into PRE, IN, and POST comparisons and looked into how each of these can be reduced. To sum up the ideas from the above discussion we need r_1 and r_2 sorted on T_S, r_2 sorted on T_E, and a pointer for FIRST().

• Discarding tuples from buffer

Before we state the next algorithm based on these ideas there is one more thing we can do to optimize the join viz., discard tuples which may no longer be required. When both relations are sorted in the ascending order of start times, then during the join loop for a tuple x in r_1, the tuples preceding FIRST(x, r_2) can be safely discarded from the buffer since none of these could intersect with tuples succeding x. We incorporate an extra feature in the following algorithms to discard tuples from the buffer.

Now, we are ready to present algorithm 2 which incorporates all of the above ideas. As stated earlier, SP keeps track of where to start an iteration whereas OP and IP control processing of loops. Algorithm 2 is essentially the same as TJ-1 algorithm of Gunadhi & Segev[5], except that in their version outer relation is assumed to be further sorted on T_E as a secondary key.

Algorithm 2

```
Input:   temporal relations r1 and r2;
         r1 sorted in ascending order of Ts;
         r2 sorted in ascending order of both Ts (primary key) and
         TE (secondary key).
Output: Time-join of r1 and r2.
Method:
1.       SP := pointer to first tuple in r2;
         OP := pointer to first tuple in r1;
2.       while( OP ≠ EOR(r1))
         {      x := Read(r1, OP);
                IP := SP;
                flag := false;
                while( IP ≠ EOR(r2))
                {  y := Read(r2, IP);
                   if (TE(x) ≤ Ts(y)) exit inner while loop;
                   if (TE(y) ≤ Ts(x)
                      { if (flag = false)
                          {discard y from buffer;
                           SP = IP; }
                      }
                   else /* x intersects y */
                      { output T-join result of x ,y ;
                        flag := true; }

                }
                if ( SP = EOR(r2) ) END;
         }.
```

Consider the example shown in figure 1. Let EMP_DEPT be the outer relation and DEPT_MANAGER be the inner relation. Their time-join as processed by algorithm 2 is shown in the appendix. Algorithm 2 incurs a total of 15 wasteful comparisons, in contrast to algorithm 1 where 27 wasteful comparisons will be incurred. We notice that PRE is still a major contributor (9 in the example) to wasteful comparisons.

In algorithm 2, we reduce PRE by using ordering on T_S; viz., $T_S(x_1) \le T_S(x_2)$; for any x_2 in r_1 succeeding x_1 in r_1. However there is some additional information at our disposal which we can to further reduce tuple comparisons.

Recall that we assumed relations to be in the first temporal normal form i.e., the life span of any two tuples with same surrogate value do not overlap. We will refer to the collection of all tuples with identical surrogate value. as an SV chain. In case of EMP_DEPT relation in the example we have two SV chains -one for E1 and second for E2 (see, figure 2 below). A relation is then simply a merge of SV chains. In addition, if the T_S of each subsequent tuple within an SV chain is exactly one instance after T_E of the preceding tuple then we call an SV chain *continuous*.

E#	D#	T_S	T_E
E1	D1	5	10
E1	D2	11	18
E1	D4	19	20

E#	D#	T_S	T_E
E2	D1	6	12
E2	D3	13	20

Figure 2. Decomposition of EMP_DEPT relation into SV chains

Let r_1 and r_2 be sorted in the ascending order of T_S and are both comprised of single SV chains. Let x_1 and x_2 be two tuples in r_1 such that x_2 appears immediately after x_1. Let y be a tuple in r_2 that intersects with x_1. We make the following observations:

(i) If $T_E(y) \ge T_E(x_1)$ then y = LAST(x_1, r_2);
(ii) x_2 will not intersect with any tuple before LAST(x_1, r_2);
(iii) If r_1 and r_2 have both continuous chains, then
  (a) if T_E(LAST(x_1, r_2)) > $T_E(x_1)$
    then FIRST(x_2, r_2) = LAST(x_1, r_2)
  (b) if T_E(LAST(x_1, r_2)) = $T_E(x_1)$
    then FIRST(x_2, r_2) is the tuple next to LAST(x_1, r_2).

Above observations follow from the fact that the relations are in the first temporal normal form and imply that instead of starting join loop for x_2 from FIRST(x_1, r_2), as would be the case in algorithm 2, we must start it either from LAST(x_1, r_2) or the tuple next to it. This would reduce PRE comparisons further.

The above observations are directly useful when performing time-join of two SV chains. In a general case we can extend the same idea by maintaining separate pointers for each SV chain. Then we can employ the above scheme of starting comparisons for subsequent tuples within each SV chain. This certainly means more overhead and if the SV chains are too small compared to the size of the relations, the overhead of maintaining pointers will offset the gains of this scheme. In practice it is expected that the numbers of SV chains in the given relations will be much smaller than the sizes of the relations.

We now present several new algorithms exploiting the above ideas. The algorithms differ in respect of the arrangement of SV chains in the relations. In algorithm 3, SV chains in both relations are intermixed arbitrarily. We employ a list of pointers SP with pointers corresponding to SV chains. To simplify the exposition, the algorithms are described as if all distinct surrogate values are known a priori. These algorithms can be easily modified to deal with when SV chains are identified on the fly.

In algorithm 3, we maintain the list of pointers SP, with an entry for each SV chain of outer relation. These pointers help reduce PRE as well as to discard tuples from buffer. GlobalSP is a pointer before which the tuples in inner relation could be discarded from buffer.

Algorithm 3

Input: temporal relations r_1 and r_2;
r_1 and r_2 both sorted in the ascending order of T_S;

Output: Time-join of r_1 and r_2.

Method:

```
1.    For each SV chain S in r1
              set SP[S] to first tuple in r2;
      OP := pointer to first tuple in r1;
      GlobalSP := pointer to first tuple in r2;
2.    while (OP ≠ EOR(r1))
      {       x := Read(r1, OP);
              SP[Sx] := max( SP[Sx] , GlobalSP);
              IP := SP[Sx];
              flag := false;
              flag1 := false;
              while (IP ≠ EOR(r2))
              {       y := Read(r2, IP);
                      if (TE(x) ≤ TS(y)) exit inner while loop;
                      if (TE(y) ≤ TS(x))
                        { if (flag = false)
                            {discard y from buffer;
                             GlobalSP := IP; }
                        }
                      else /* x intersects y */
                        { output T-join result of x ,y ;
                          flag := true;
                          if (flag1 = false and TE(y) >TE(x))
                              {flag1 = true;
                               SP[Sx] := pointer to y; }
                        }
              }
              if ( flag1 = false) SP[Sx] := EOR(r2);
              if ( SP = EOR(r2)) END;
      }
```

The execution trace of algorithm 3 is given in appendix for the same example considered earlier. In comparison to 14 wasteful comparisons in algorithm 2, only 6 are incurred now and PRE is merely 1.

Algorithms 2 and 3 offer a substantial improvement over the basic nested loop algorithm but still incur non-zero wasteful comparisons. In algorithm 3, PRE is zero except possibly for first tuple of each chain in r_1.. Note that algorithm 3 has an overhead of maintaining additional pointers and further, an iteration in algorithm 3 has slightly more computational overhead than algorithm 2. However, relatively fewer iterations in algorithm should offset the overheads mentioned above. Algorithms presented next further reduce wasteful comparisons but with lesser overhead than that in algorithm 3. To be specific, these:

- reduce IN to zero,
- reduce POST to zero if chains in inner relation are continuous,
- reduce PRE to zero if the first tuple in each chain of outer relation intersects with the first tuple in each chain of inner relation.

Consider a tuple x in r_1 and let y = FIRST(x, r_2) and r_2 is sorted in the ascending order of T_S (primary key) and T_E (secondary key). A tuple, say z in r_2, after y will contribute toward IN only if $T_E(z) < T_E(y)$. This cannot be true, if z and y have the same surrogate value.

Consider two arbitrary tuples y_1 and y_2 in an SV chain such that y_1 immediately precedes y_2. Further, let y_1 intersects with x. POST can only be reduced to zero, if examination of y_1 allows us to conclude whether y_2 will intersect with x or not. Since y_1 and y_2 are on an SV chain, we have $T_E(y_1) < T_S(y_2)$. If $T_E(x) \le T_E(y_1)$, then obviously y_2 will not intersect with x. Let us assume that $T_E(x) > T_E(y_1)$. In this case, y_2 may or may not intersect with x. But if the SV chain is continuous, y_2 will intersect with x. The above observation allows us to reduce POSTto zero for an inner relation with continuous SV chains.

The above properties are not exploited by algorithm 3 because of the intermixing of SV chains in inner relation. Separation of SV chains will eliminate IN and reduce PRE and POST, but we will have to manage buffers separately for each SV chain.

We first present algorithm 4 where the inner relation r_2 is assumed to be a single SV chain. We then employ algorithm 4 to derive an algorithm for the general case when the inner relation comprises of multiple SV chains.

Algorithm 4

Input: temporal relations r_1 and r_2;
r_1 sorted in ascending order of T_S;
r_2 consists of a single SV chain (sorted in the ascending order of T_S).

Output: Time-join of r_1 and r_2.

Method:

```
1.    For each SV chain S in r1,
              set SP[S] to first tuple of r2;
      GlobalSP := pointer to first tuple of r2;
      OP := pointer to first tuple in r1;

2.    while (OP ≠ EOR(r1))
        { x := Read(r1, OP);
          SP[Sx] := max (GlobalSP, SP[Sx]);
          IP := SP[Sx];
          while (IP ≠ EOR(r2))
              { y := Read(r2, IP);
                if (TE(x) ≤ TS(y)) exit inner while loop;
                if (TE(y) ≤ TS(x))
                    {discard y from buffer;
                     GlobalSP := IP; }
                else
                    /* x intersects y */
                     output T-join result of x, y;
              }
          if (TE(x) = TS(y))
                SP[Sx] := pointer to y;
          else
                SP[Sx] := pointer to tuple preceding y, if any,
                          otherwise to y;
          if ( GlobalSP = EOR(r2) ) END;
        }.
```

When the inner relation comprises of multiple SV chains, the first step is to seperate out the chains thereby reducing the relation to a sequence of SV chains. Each chain is sorted in the ascending order of T_S but the chains themselves may appear in any sequence. Several algorithms may be derived now using algorithm 4 as a step. Given below is one such algorithm where we compute, using algorithm 4, the time-join of outer-relation seperately with each chain of the inner relation. An alternative strategy is to read a tuple of outer -relation and compute its join with all chains before going to the next tuple of outer-relation.

Algorithm 5

Input: temporal relations r_1 and r_2;
r_1 sorted in ascending order of T_S;
r_2 consists of a sequence of SV chains (each chain sorted in the ascending order of T_S).

Output: Time-join of r_1 and r_2.

Method:

```
1.    For each SV chain S in r2,
              perform time-join of r1 with S using algorithm 4.
```

In algorithm 6 below, we assume both relations to be single SV chains and then further employ it to derive algorithm 7 for the general case.

Algorithm 6

Input: temporal relations r_1 and r_2;
r_1 and r_2 both consisting of single SV chains
(each chain sorted in the ascending order of T_S.)
Output: Time-join of r_1 and r_2.
Method:

```
1.    OP := pointer to first tuple in r1;
      IP := pointer to first tuple in r2;

2.    while ( OP ≠ EOR(r1))
       { x := Read(r1, OP);
         while (IP ≠ EOR(r2))
             { y := Read(r2, IP);
               if (TE(x) ≤ TS(y)) exit innerwhileloop;
               if (TE(y) >TS(x))
                    output T-join result of x, y;
             }
         if (IP = EOR(r1)) END;
         if (TE(x) = TS(y)) IP := pointer to y
         else IP := pointer to tuple prceding y, if any, otherwise to y;
       }
```

Algorithm 7

Input: temporal relations r_1 and r_2;
r_1 and r_2 both sequences of SV chains
(each chain sorted in the ascending order of T_S.)
Output: Time-join of r_1 and r_2.
Method:

For each pair of SV chains S^1 in r_1 ans S^2 in r_2,
perform time-join of S^1 and S^2 using algorithm 5.

5. DISCUSSION

Temporal joins can be optimized by using special properties of the temporal data. In this paper, we presented several algorithms which are more efficient than the ones available in the literature so far. Existing algorithms in the literature also adopt the similar approach where relations are assumed to be pre-sorted in orders of start and end times. Our algorithms require somewhat weaker ordering but still perform better. This improvement is possible because of our exploitation of the first temporal normal form property of the relations. We now discuss some of the performance aspects of the presented algorithms. A detailed analysis of the relative performance of these is currently being pursued by the authors.

An iteration of the basic nested-loop algorithm is computationally least demanding and the minimum buffer size required to work is also least. If join selectively factor is very high, the basic nested loop algorithm will perform very well. We observe that the join selectivity in the case of temporal relation is expected to be much smaller, especially if the number of SV chains are less than the relation sizes. Algorithms 2 and 3 outperform the basic nested loop approach by cutting down on wasteful comparisons by smartly initiating and terminating iterations of the inner loop but require sorting of operand relations. Algorithms 4-7 present further improvements by exploiting the first temporal normal form property of relations. Algorithms 5 and 7 are especially attractive when relations are originally maintained as collection of ordered SV chains. Since temporal data is naturally generated and inserted in the chronological order in the database, what we need at join time is simply to extract individual SV chains from the relations. This can be performed by either a sequential scan of the relations prior to join or on the fly during join itself. Our future research will include detailed performance analysis of the presented algorithms by simulation experiments and extending our approach to other temporal intersection joins.

REFERENCES

1) Ahn, I., "Towards an Implementation of Database Management Systems with Temporal Support", in Proceedings of the Int. Conf. on Data Engineering, February 1986, pp. 374-381.

2) Clifford, J., Croker, A., "The Historical Relational Data Model (HRDM) And Algebra based on Lifespans", Proceedings of the Int. Conf. on Data Engineering, Feb. 1987, pp. 528-537.

3) Gadia S. K., "A Homogeneous Relational Model and Query Languages for Temporal Databases",ACM Trans. on Database Systems, Vol. 13, No. 4, pp.418-448 (198).

4) Gunadhi, H., Segev, A., "A framework for Query Optimization in Temporal Databases", Lecture Notes in Computer Science, vol.420. Z. Michalewitz (ed.), (Springer-Verlag.), Apr. 1990, pp. 131-147.

5) Gunadhi, H. and Segev, A., "Query Processing Algorithms for Temporal Intersection Joins", Proc. of the International Conference on Data Engineering, 1991, pp.336-344.

6) Kolovson, C., Stonebraker, M., "Indexing for Historical Databases", Proc. of the Int. Conf. on Data Engineering, 1989, pp. 127-139.

7) Lum V., et. al. "Designing DBMS support for the Temporal Dimension",Proceedings of the ACM SIGMOD Int. Conf. on Management of Data, June 1984, pp.150-180.

8) Rotem, D., Segev, A., "Physical Organization of Temporal Data", Proc. of the Int. Conf. on Data Engineering, 1987, pp. 547-553.

9) Snodgrass, R., Ahn, I., "A taxonomy of Time in Databases", Proceedings of ACM SIGMOD, May 1985, pp. 236-246.

10) Segev, A., Gunadhi, H., "Event-Join Optimization in Temporal Relational Databases", Proc. of the International Conf. on Very Large Databases, Aug.1989, pp. 205-215.

11) Snodgrass, R., "The Temporal Query Language TQuel", ACM Transactions on Database Systems, June 1987, pp 247-298.

12) Segev, A., Shoshani, A., "Logical Modelling of Temporal Databases", Proc. of the ACM SIGMOD International Conference on Management of Data, May 1987, pp. 454-466.

13) Segev, A., Shoshani, A., "The Representation of a Temporal Data Model in the Relational Environment ", Lecture Notes in Computer Science, Vol 339, M. Raffanelli, J.C. Klensin, and P. Svensson (eds.), (Springer-Verlag), 1988. pp. 39-61.

APPENDIX

Execution trace of Algorithm 2

<u>Join-loop for tuple (E1, D1, 5, 10)</u>
StartPointer ---> (D1, M2, 1,4)
Tuples of r_2 scanned: (D1, M2, 1, 4) * DISCARD
StartPointer ---> (D2, M1, 2, 9) FIRST
(D3, M3, 3, 5) *
(D4, M5, 3, 7)
(D1, M4, 5, 12)
(D3, M6, 6, 10)
(D4, M7, 8, 12) LAST
(D2, M8, 10, 15) *
PRE= 1, IN = 1, POST = 1 Tuples in Buffer = 7
* (non-intersecting tuple)

<u>Join-loop for tuple (E2, D1, 6, 12)</u>
StartPointer ---> (D2, M1, 2, 9)
Tuples of r_2 scanned: StartPointer ---> (D2, M1, 2, 9) FIRST
(D3, M3, 3, 5) *
(D4, M5, 3, 7)
(D1, M4, 5, 12)
(D3, M6, 6, 10)
(D4, M7, 8, 12)
(D2, M8, 10, 15) LAST
(D1, M9, 13, 17) *
PRE = 0, IN = 1, POST = 1 Tuples in Buffer = 8

<u>Join-loop for tuple (E1, D2, 11, 18)</u>
StartPointer ---> (D2, M1, 2, 9)
Tuples of r_2 scanned (D2, M1, 2, 9) * DISCARD
(D3, M3, 3, 5) * DISCARD
(D4, M5, 3, 7) * DISCARD
StartPointer ---> (D1, M4, 5, 12) FIRST
(D3, M6, 6, 10) *
(D4, M7, 8, 12)
(D2, M8, 10, 15)
(D1, M9, 13, 17) LAST
PRE= 3, IN = 1, POST= 0 Tuples in Buffer = 5

<u>Join-loop for tuple (E2, D3, 13, 20)</u>
StartPointer ---> (D1, M4, 5, 12)
Tuples of r_2 scanned (D1, M4, 5, 12) DISCARD
StartPointer ---> (D3, M6, 6, 10) FIRST
(D4, M7, 8, 12) *
(D2, M8, 10, 15)
(D1, M9, 13, 17) LAST
PRE = 1, IN = 1, POST = 0 Tuples in Buffer = 4

<u>Join-loop for tuple (E1, D4, 19, 20)</u>
StartPointer ---> (D3, M6, 6, 10)
Tuples of r_2 scanned (D3, M6, 6, 10) *DISCARD
(D4, M7, 8, 12) *DISCARD
(D2, M8, 10, 15) *DISCARD
(D1, M9, 13, 17) *DISCARD
PRE = 4, IN = 0, POST = 0 Tuples in Buffer = 0

Thus, we have a total of 15 wasteful comparisons (PRE = 9, IN =4, POST =2). The maximum buffer size needed to hold tuples of inner relation is 8.

Execution trace of Algorithm 3

<u>Join-loop for tuple (E1, D1, 5, 10)</u>
StartPointer[E1] ---> (D1, M2, 1, 4)
Tuples of r_2 scanned: (D1, M2, 1, 4) *DISCARD
StartPointer[E2] -->(D2, M1, 2, 9) FIRST
(D3, M3, 3, 5) *
(D4, M5, 3, 7)
StartPointer[E1] -->(D1, M4, 5, 12)
(D3, M6, 6, 10)
(D4, M7, 8, 12) LAST
(D2, M8, 10, 15) *
PRE = 1, IN = 1, POST = 1 Tuples in Buffer = 7

<u>Join-loop for tuple (E2, D1, 6, 12)</u>
StartPointer [E2] ---> (D2, M1, 2, 9)
Tuples of r_2 scanned (D2, M1, 2, 9) FIRST, DISCARD
(D3, M3, 3, 5) *DISCARD
(D4, M5, 3, 7) DISCARD
StartPointer[E1] -->(D1, M4, 5, 12)
(D3, M6, 6, 10)
(D4, M7, 8, 12) LAST
StartPointer[E2] -->(D2, M8, 10, 15) *
PRE = 0, IN = 1, POST= 1 Tuples in Buffer = 4

<u>Join-loop for tuple (E1, D2, 11, 18)</u>
StartPointer[E1} --> (D1, M4, 5, 12)
Tuples of r_2 scanned (D1, M4, 5, 12) FIRST, DISCARD
(D3, M6, 6, 10) *DISCARD
(D4, M7, 8, 12) DISCARD
StartPointer[E2] -->(D2, M8, 10, 15)
(D1, M9, 13, 17) LAST
StartPointer[E1] --> END
PRE = 0, IN = 1, POST = 0 Tuples in Buffer = 2

<u>Join-loop for tuple (E2, D3, 13, 20)</u>
StartPointer[E2] ---> (D2, M8, 10, 15)
Tuples of r_2 scanned (D2, M8, 10, 15) FIRST, DISCARD
(D1, M9, 13, 17) LAST,DISCARD
StartPointer[E2] --> END
PRE = 0, IN = 0, POST = 0 Tuples in Buffer = 0

<u>Join-loop for tuple (E1, D4, 19, 20)</u>
StartPointer[E1] ---> EOF
Tuples of r_2 scanned NONE
PRE = 0, IN = 0, POST = 0

We have a total of 6 wasteful comparisons (PRE = 1, IN = 3, POST = 2).. Maximum buffer size needed to hold tuples of inner relation is 7.

INTELLIGENT USER INTERFACE

QUALITATIVE BEHAVIOR MODELING OF INFORMATION PROCESSING COMPONENTS

Sang Hun Oh

Industrial Electronics R&D Center
Hyundai Electronics Industries Co., Ltd.
San 136-1, Ami-ri, Bubal-eub, Ichon-kun
Kyoungki-do, 467-860, KOREA

Yoon Joon Lee and Myoung Ho Kim

Department of Computer Science
Korea Advanced Institute of Science and Technology
373-1, KuSung-dong, YuSung-gu
Taejon, 305-701, KOREA
E-mail: mhkim@cs.kaist.ac.kr; Fax: +82-42-869-3510

ABSTRACT

This paper presents qualitative behavior modeling of Information Processing Components(IPCs), which are domain-specific software components for modeling reusable functions in database management systems(DBMSs). After introducing a detailed formal syntax of IPCs, we propose their modular, qualitative behavior generation mechanism. The proposed mechanism is based on qualitative modeling and simulation, thus produces a sequence of temporal state transitions of modeled IPCs. The proposed modeling mechanism aims to facilitate the scientific measurement of DBMSs.

1. Introduction

Besides the scientific measurement environment, it is also important to make use of systems domain knowledge when measuring software systems[2, 4, 10]. Software Quality Manager, which was proposed in [6], is a knowledge-based software metrics management system that provide software engineers with collective and comprehensive measurement environment that provides software engineers with domain knowledge about application systems and software measurement in an engineering way.

In the Software Quality Manager, Information Processing Components(IPCs) were designed to support both testing and measurement of DBMSs simultaneously through systematic management of the ever-increasing amount of knowledge about their software products[7]. As the IPCs were developed according to domain analysis technique[9], They can also aid in the construction activity by providing designers with development knowledge in the reusable forms. They can support testing job by generating their temporal behavior from the information about their interconnection with other components and their operational characteristics.

In this paper, a qualitative behavior modeling method of IPCs is proposed. The proposed method is based on qualitative modeling and simulation[3], thus produces a sequence of temporal state transitions of modeled IPCs, as a behavior of modeled DBMSs. As the complexity of software systems is so high that there must be a way to reduce the complexity in a modular way. To deal with such a high complexity, the proposed method also adopts software component concept, which is realized by IPCs. This paper describes how to generate the behavior of IPCs, especially on the qualitative modeling aspect. The proposed method aims to facilitate the scientific measurement of DBMSs. The produced behavioral information can be used by those who perform software measurement.

This paper is organized as follows. Section 2 presents the formal structure of IPCs. Then behavior generation method of DBMSs using IPCs is proposed in section 3. The application areas of the generated behavior include both assessment and measurement activities. Finally, concluding remarks are presented in section 4.

2. Design of Information Processing Components

2.1 Support of behavior analysis of designed DBMSs

Functional prototyping and simulation can reduce the difficulty of dynamic analysis of software systems being developed[2, 8]. To support the testing, we aim at utilizing the functional knowledge about DBMSs for the qualitative simulation of the dynamic behavior of designed DBMSs. If the functional knowledge is represented in independent objects, it is rather simple to generate the behavior of designed DBMSs. As a result, IPCs are determined to organize the functional knowledge of DBMSs in a object-oriented fashion. The reason of adapting object-oriented concept is that objects' external behavior is represented explicitly by their message transmission, and their internal behavior is hidden from other objects. Such operational characteristics make it simple to observe their interactions at the component and the system level.

We also must adopt the finite state machine as a behavior generation mechanism of IPCs. In finite state machine paradigm, a behavior of IPCs is represented by a sequence of temporal state changes. Thus, IPCs must be equipped with their primitive operations and their causality information, together with their meaningful sates. As IPCs are also based on the concept of objects, message passing mechanism can be used to represent the interaction between IPCs. The behavior generation of IPCs can contribute to the human beings' enhanced understanding of the functional analysis of the system being developed. This is because the execution history of DBMSs can become visible forms.

2.2 Support of DBMS measurement

The generated behavior of IPCs is represented by a sequence of state transition operations. If we can incorporate duration information into those operations in the sequence, it is possible to estimate total execution time of designed DBMSs. Such a work corresponds to a performance evaluation task. As the functions in IPCs are becoming stabilized, approximate performance parameters can be stored somewhere in it. Besides performance metrics, other software metrics can be measured from the generated behavior of IPCs[8]. This idea needs more work, but we argue that it is possible when DBMSs are developed with IPCs.

2.3 Formal specification of IPCs

2.3.1 The name part

The name of a reusable function is stored in the name part of the generic structure. The name stored in the name part play the role of identifier of IPCs so that the corresponding IPC is uniquely identifiable in a full collection of information processing components. If there are many variants of an IPC, the name of individual variants is described by appending sequence number into the name of the IPC.

Another important factor, besides construction of reusable software components, to the success of software reuse is how to manage a collection of reusable software components and how efficiently the retrieval of them is performed. These factors are greatly influenced by the classification scheme of a library of reusable software components[1, 5]. The classification scheme amounts to abstraction of the library.

When IPC constructors determine that a certain function X has high reusability, the name of the function, X, is stored in the name part of corresponding IPC construct. The syntax of the name part is shown in Figure 1(b), which defines that the name of reusable functions consists of alphanumeric characters. Names of meaningful entities such as buffer, memory, storage structure, query processor and disks and of their related operations are candidates of possible IPCs.

The examples of the names of buffer_management IPC include buffer_management, buffer_initialization, buffer_dump, buffer_allocation, buffer_discard, buffer_get, buffer_flush, buffer_finalization, buffer_invalidate, buffer_read, buffer_write and so on. These IPCs can be grouped with respect to the characteristics of their operation. As shown in Figure 2, the grouping is based on the phase when each IPC can be able to be executed during the entire life cycle of buffer. Such a grouping is helpful to find out the causality between IPCs and to generate meaningful sequence of IPC invocations. That can also contribute to the placement of IPCs in the library. That is, the grouping criterion is a classification scheme of a library of IPCs.

```
<IPC>    ::=   IPC  <ipc_name>
                  TELEOLOGY   <teleology_part>
                  STRUCTURE   <structure_part>
                  CAUSALITY   <causality_part>
                  BEHAVIOR   <behavior_part>
               END_OF_IPC   <ipc_name>
```

(a) Syntax of information processing components

```
<ipc_name>   ::= <name>
<name>       ::= <characters> { a meaningful list of characters }
<characters> ::= A| B| C |..| Y| Z | 1 | 2 | 3 |..| 9 | 0 | a | b | c |..| y | z
```

(b) Syntax of the name part

<Figure 1 The syntax of IPCs and the name part>

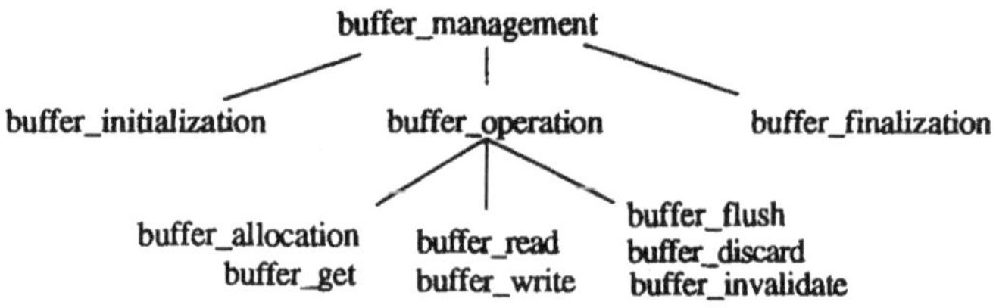

<Figure 2 Hierarchy of IPCs of buffer management>

2.3.2 The teleology part

The teleology part contains the purpose of an IPC. The purpose describes developer's decisions and intention such as why this IPC is selected, i.e., the selection conditions. The teleology part can be said an abstracted description of the name part. Thus, it is possible to understand or estimate the functional details and objectives of an IPC. The purpose of an entire system can also be understood or estimated from the collection of the teleology parts of selected IPCs. This part is an accomplishment of the design principle that IPCs should be equipped with abstract symbols.

As developers generally describe their intention in a narrative form, it is very difficult to represent it systematically. The optimal approach to modeling of developers' intentions is for them to describe it concisely. Owing to the narrativeness, Estimation the behavior of an IPC from the teleology part is now not automatically performed.

<teleology_part> ::= {a description of purpose of an IPC }

Some examples of the teleology part are as follows.

1. buffer_read - read a page from disk to buffer.
2. buffer_flush - write all pages in buffer pool to disk.
3. buffer_allocation - allocate a buffer to a page in a file
4. buffer_discard - discard a page stored in a buffer

2.3.3 The structure part

The structure part represents the interaction, inner structural and operational information of a function stored in an IPC. Input/output interface description and private data structure of an IPC is stored in this part. The input/output interface is described by generic parameterization technique. DBMSs engineers can predict more correct behavior of the IPC by examining the structure part and the teleology part, but they cannot judge whether the predicted behavior is correct and complete. Other information stored in causality and behavior parts is essential to extract correct behavior of an IPC.

The structure part, which is divided into IMPORT, EXPORT and CONSIST_OF sub-parts, describes the information about interactions between an IPC and its environments. As it is simple and better to simplify the interaction complexity, we adopt import/export mechanism as paths to and from its environments. The IMPORT sub-part represents other IPCs referenced by the IPC. In specific, as functions and data structures can become IPCs, we divided the imported IPCs into FUNCTION and DATA STRUCTURE types. The FUNCTION type includes IPCs which contain reusable functions; whereas DATA STRUCTURE type contains IPCs for meaningful, important abstract data types. Whereas, the EXPORT sub-part indicates IPCs provided by the IPC. The refined syntax of EXPORT sub-part is identical to those of IMPORT sub-part. The CONSIST_OF sub-part is to represent the interconnection information about sub-IPCs located in an IPC. It is a frequent case that a complex IPC is composed by several simpler IPCs. In this case, it is necessary to represent them and the relationships among sub-IPCs. Value NONE is specified in the <import_list> and <export_list> if no IPC is related.

If all of the sub-IPCs are stored in the IPC, that may be so complex that developers cannot understand the upper-level IPC. To avoid this problem, we determine a policy that no IPC can have detailed information about their sub-IPCs. In other words, the representation of sub-IPCs are stored in other independent IPCs and the upper-level IPC only references the sub-IPCs by holding their relationships in the CONSIST_OF and CAUSALITY part. Their CONSIST_OF part contains only the names of the related sub-IPCs; and their CAUSALITY part stores the interconnection information. Examples of the structure part for buffer_read is shown in Figure 3. Formal syntax of the structure part is depicted in Figure 4.

```
IPC buffer_read
   TELEOLOGY read a page from disk to buffer.
   STRUCTURE
      IMPORT FUNCTION
      IMPORT DATA STRUCTURE  disk, bufferpool, page
      EXPORT FUNCTION buffer_read
      EXPORT DATA STRUCTURE  NONE
      CONSIST_OF  disk_interface, page_reader
      . . .
END_OF_IPC buffer_read
```

<Figure 3 Example of structure part for buffer_read IPC>

2.3.4 The causality part

The objectives of the causality part are two-folded. First, as DBMSs have a layered hierarchical architecture, it is not unusual that complex functions are composed of more than one IPCs. For the purpose of representational homogeneity between a DBMS being constructed and its selected IPCs, the DBMS should be regarded as a complex IPC. Thus, we must provide a mechanism to represent the nesting of IPCs in a uniform way.

Another purpose of IPCs is to generate information about the dynamic part of DBMSs. To this end, we must provide a mechanism to represent temporal execution sequence among IPCs in order to describe the behavior of DBMSs and IPCs. Such sequence information is stored in the causality part. The behavior generation mechanism is also useful to their scientific measurement. If the timing information of operations, which is modeled as a time interval in a certain state, can be added to the sequence information, it is possible to estimate the performance metrics of DBMSs.

An IPC needs scheduling mechanism of the invocation sequence of sub-IPCs, in order to perform its function correctly. The causality part contains such scheduling information so that developers can describe it conveniently

```
<structure_part> ::= IMPORT  <import_list>
                     EXPORT  <export_list>
                     CONSIST_OF   <consist_of_list>
<import_list>     ::= FUNCTION <import_function_list>
                     DATA STRUCTURE <import_adt_list>
<import_function_list> ::= <function_list>
                     | <function_name> <function_list>
<function_list>   ::= <function_name>
                     | <function_name> <function_list>
                     | NONE
<function_name> ::= <name>
<import_adt_list> ::= <adt_list> | <adt_name> <adt_list>
<adt_list>        ::= <adt_name>
                     | <adt_name> <adt_list>
                     | NONE
<adt_name>        ::= <name>
<export_list>     ::= FUNCTION   <export_function_list>
                     DATA STRUCTURE   <export_adt_list>
<export_function_list> ::= <function_list>
                     | <function_name> <function_list>
<export_adt_list> ::= <adt_list> | <adt_name> <adt_list>
<consist_of_list> ::= <sub_ipc_list> | NONE
<sub_ipc_list>    ::= <ipc_list> | <ipc_name> <ipc_list>
<ipc_list>        ::= <ipc_name>
                     | <ipc_name> <ipc_list>
                     | NONE
```

<Figure 4 Syntax of the structure part>

and that testing of their correctness and completeness can be performed in a modular fashion.

First, it is necessary to identify the temporal operators for modeling the precedence condition between two sub-IPCs. For example, if sub-IPC A must be executed before sub-IPC B, then the sequence information is represented as "sub-IPC A precedes sub-IPC B," or "sub-IPC B follows sub-IPC A." Furthermore, we provide more semantically temporal operators to perform more deep semantic analysis on IPCs. These include ACCESSES, MODIFIES, NEEDS_VALUE_OF, SENDS_INFORMATION_TO, CREATES and ACTIVATES. As the meaning of each operator can be identified easily, we omit their more detailed explanation. If other semantic operators are identified, they can be added for more rich analysis and testing of IPCs. Syntax of the causality part of IPCs is in Figure 5.

```
<causality_part> ::= <uni_temporal_operator>
                    | <causality> <causality_list>
<causality_list> ::= <causality>
                    | <causality> <causality_list>
<causality>      ::= <ipc_name> <bi_temporal_operator> <ipc_name>
<bi_temporal_operator> ::= PRECEDES | FOLLOWS
                    | ACCESSES | MODIFIES
                    | NEEDS_VALUE_OF
                    | SENDS_INFORMATION_TO
                    | CREATES
                    | ACTIVATES
                    | . . .
```

<Figure 5 Syntax of the causality part>

Suppose that buffer_read IPC consists of two sub-IPCs named disk_interface, page_reader. And disk_interface sub-IPC performs interactions between buffer and disk; page_reader moves one page from disk to buffer. Then the causality in these two sub-IPCs can be represented as 'disk_interface

SENDS_INFORMATION_TO page_reader'., or 'disk_interface ACTIVATES page_reader.' As in the representations of the causality, there is vagueness in the interpretation of these temporal operators. Correct definitions of these operators must be done.

2.3.5 The behavior part

The behavior part represents functional and implementation details of the function stored in an IPC. Examples are algorithms, pre- and post-conditions of the function. As there can exist many variant algorithms to implement a function, the behavior part may store more than one algorithms. The behavior part is correspondent to methods of object-oriented concept. Formal specification language such as Z must be used to represent algorithms, in order to minimize ambiguity or misunderstanding and to maximize the automation of dynamic analysis of IPCs. This part can also be filled up by using functional modeling techniques. As IPCs aim to convey development knowledge to human beings as much as possible, the behavior part must have high readability and comprehensiveness.

The behavior part of IPCs explains how the function stored can be accomplished. Note that the objectives of IPCs is not to produce executable program codes, but to supply reusable functional information about DBMSs and other information useful for behavior simulation, dynamic analysis and semantic checking. Thus the behavior part needs to store abstracted information about a function, instead of program codes.

Design principles of IPCs include behavior analysis and measurement of DBMSs under design, as introduced in section 3. As the fundamental mechanism of behavior simulation is finite state machine, we model the behavior part to be able to produce state changes. Thus the behavior part consists of three sub-parts: PRE_CONDITION, POST_CONDITION and a formal description of the function of the IPC. The PRE_CONDITION and POST_CONDITION sub-parts are adapted from the well-known approach to verifying the consistency of a function[4, 10]. When generating a behavior of an IPC according to the input stimuli, it is necessary to check whether the input is valid, if the enabling condition of the IPC is satisfied and if the resulting state is correct. The PRE_CONDITION can check the validity of input condition and the enabling condition. The POST_CONDITION can test the correctness of the output state. During execution of the IPC, its execution history must be generated and recorded. As the behavior specification language is not yet completed, a semi-formal syntax of the behavior part and an example of buffer_read is shown in Figure 6 and 7, respectively.

In particular, the PRE_CONDITION and POST_CONDITION parts are strengthened to check the valid state of the IPCs, besides checking ordinary boolean expressions. The checkable states includes TRANSACTION_BEGIN, TRANSACTION_ABORT, DATABASE_OPENED, DATABASE_CLOSED and so on. Other meaningful states can be added to the list of IPCs' states as the development of DBMSs is performed further.

It is possible to check the validity of the states of IPCs, because the meaning of these states comes from the domain knowledge of DBMSs. Behavior analysis and measurement of DBMSs can be done by simulating and analyzing the behavior of IPCs with respect to the intended behavior. The two behaviors are represented as a sequence of these state changes.

```
<behavior_part>   ::=
                      PRE_CONDITION <condition>
                        POST_CONDITION <condition>
                        FUNCTION [{a formal description of
                        the function of the ipc }]
<condition>       ::= <boolean_expressions>
                        | <temporal_operator>
                        | <ipc_name>'S STATE_IN <states>
                        | NONE
<boolean_expressions> ::= {a set of ordinary boolean
                        expressions }
<temporal_operator> ::= ALWAYS
                        | AFTER | BEFORE | WHENEVER
<states>          ::= {a set of user-defined states meaningful
                        to the ipc. Examples are
                        SYSTEM_RUNNING,
                        SYSTEM_DOWN,
                        TRANSACTION_BEGIN,
                        TRANSACTION_ABORT,
                        TABLE_INITIALIZED,
                        TABLE_CLEARED,
                        DATABASE_OPENED,
                        DATABASE_CLOSED,
                        FILE_CREATED, FILE_OPENED,
                        FILE_CLOSED, etc. }
```

<Figure 6 Formal syntax of the behavior part>

```
IPC buffer_read
  TELEOLOGYread a page from disk to buffer.
  STRUCTURE\
    IMPORT FUNCTION
    IMPORT DATA STRUCTURE disk, bufferpool, page
    EXPORT FUNCTION buffer_read
    EXPORT DATA STRUCTURE NONE
    CONSIST_OF disk_interface, page_reader
    CAUSALIT
      disk_interface SENDS_INFORMATION_TO page_reader
      disk_interface ACTIVATES page_reader
  BEHAVIOR
    PRE_CONDITION
      disk'S STATE_IN DATABASE_OPENED & FILE_OPENED
      page'S STATE_IN BUFFER_ALLOCATED
    POST_CONDITION bufferpool'S STATE_IN PAGE_VALID
    FUNCTIO
      check(page number is valid)
      if not(page in bufferpool) disk_interface(move, page_number)
      fill(moved_page, bufferpool)
END_OF_IPC buffer_read
```

<Figure 7 Example IPC: buffer_read>

3. Qualitative Behavior Modeling of IPCs

Qualitative modeling of physical systems can be characterized as representation of their behavior through differential equations for describing the physical structure of a physical system. Thus, qualitative modeling of the systems can be performed conveniently by transforming the differential equations into qualitative constraints. As a result, it is essential to provide abstraction constructs for representing the structure of a software system, such as the differential equations, before its qualitative modeling.

This section investigates the abstraction methods and various definitions for qualitative modeling of software systems. The nature of physical and software systems seems very different, but they are both a realization of mechanism in the real world. The mechanisms are such things as laws describing physical processes or local components that can be described as operating according to such laws.

Important constructs for qualitative modeling of physical and electrical systems considered in this paper are lumped models of primitive components, parameters (variables) of systems, structural equations, causality and behavior definitions. What is qualitatively modeled in qualitative physics is domain knowledge about physics. We choose database management systems, as a domain knowledge for software systems, whose reusable software components are proposed in section 2.

3.1 Parameters of information processing components

The parameters of qualitative modeling and simulation are structural ones that must be able to characterize the states, or the interactions of systems. For instance, the parameters for electrical systems is represented as voltage and current quantities. Thus, domain-specific knowledge for analyzing electrical networks can be represented in a unified way. The domain knowledge for the analysis is divided into two parts: network laws and device models. The network laws describe how current and voltage quantities of connected components interact, while the device models describe the behavior of a component via the voltage and currents associated with its terminals. Current is measured going into a component's terminals and voltage is measured between network nodes.

If there are notions such as voltage and current, it is possible to model the parameters in a unified way. Currently, the state of a software system is represented by the states of its variable. Thus, the parameters of information processing components are determined to be represented by a set of the states of their sub-IPCs, which includes important data structures and other information processing components.

The example parameters of buffer_read IPC shown in Figure 7 are {disk, file, bufferpool, page, disk_interface, page_reader }. Other set of parameters of buffer_read are also possible according to the degree of detailed design. That is, the dynamics of buffer_read IPC is represented the behaviors of the six IPCs.

Each parameter must be represented qualitatively in terms of the reasonable function f: $[a, b] \rightarrow \mathbf{R}^*$. As the states of software systems is discrete, rather than continuous, we assume that the parameters have such reasonable functions whose range is discrete, which are named discrete reasonable functions. As only interested in the discrete state transitions, such notions as 'continuity' and 'continuously differentiable' are meaningless in the discrete reasonable functions. Thus, the discrete reasonable functions is defined as definition 1.

Definition 1. For $[a, b] \in \mathbf{R}$, define f: $[a, b] \rightarrow \mathbf{R}^*$ to be a reasonable function if
(1) f is continuous on [a, b],
(2) f has only finitely many critical points in any bounded interval.
(3) $\mathbf{R}^*$ is a set of meaningful states.

3.2 Lumped models of IPCs

Lumped models play the role of abstracting the mechanisms in a modular way. Electrical systems employ primitive components such as resistors, condensers and coils to describe their operations. A good explanation about lumped models is presented in [11]. The explanation is as follows.

> "An integrated circuit is implemented as a semiconductor wafer with different ions diffused or implanted into its surface. The equations necessary to describe a complex circuit at the device physics level are not easily solvable and, more importantly, would not provide the designer with much insight into the overall circuit behavior.
>
> In circuit theory, the complexity of these equations is reduced by modeling a region of space with a uniform electrical behavior as a single lumped element (e.g., a resistor, capacitor or mosfet). Each element has a set of terminals which allows it to interact with other elements. The electrical behavior of an element is described by a set of constitutive relations between state variables associated with the element's terminals."

Note that information processing components have been proposed as primitive constructs of database management systems. They can be defined as the results of functional modularization of database management systems. This definition means that the region of uniform operational behavior can be identified and represented into information processing components. Thus, lumped models for information processing components must model the uniform operational behavior in an abstracted form.

As the functions stored in information processing components correspond to mechanisms, the lumped models are determined to represent the laws related to the functions. Instead of finding out the laws whose shape is similar to that of physics or electronics, it seems reasonable to render new forms of the laws in software systems. As a basis of constructing lumped models of information processing components, it is necessary to identify the parameters characterizing the behavior of the lumped models, their landmark values and their qualitative state. The three items are argued to be sufficient to perform qualitative modeling and simulation of database management systems.

3.3 Identification of meaningful landmark values

All of the states of information processing components are candidates of the landmark values of the lumped models. Their full set of possible landmark values can be represented as a Cartesian products of their states and negated states of imported and exported functions and data structures. Among them, the meaningful landmark values are those that transform the state of an information processing component into a new states. For example, buffer_read IPC has three input data structures including disk, bufferpool and page. Thus the possible landmark values of the buffer_read IPC can be described in 4-tuple <disk, file, page, bufferpool>.

It is assumed that the possible states of bufferpool are {BUFFERPOOL_EMPTY, BUFFERPOOL_FULL}; the possible states of disk are {DATABASE_CLOSED, DATABASE_OPENED}; the possible states of file are {FILE_CLOSED, FILE_OPENED}; the possible states of page is {BUFFER_ALLOCATED, PAGE_VALID}. Thuen the number of possible landmark values of the buffer_read IPC is 25 Some of the possible states of buffer_read IPC is shown in Figure 8.

The identification of meaningful landmark values is assisted by its pre-conditions and post-conditions, because of temporal qualitative modeling of information processing components. The idea is that all of state combinations not satisfying pre-condition cannot affect the starting of the performance of IPCs. And all of state combinations not satisfying post-condition cannot affect the ending of the performance of IPCs.

The set of possible landmark values =
{<DATABASE_CLOSED, FILE_CLOSED, BUFFER_ALLOCATED, BUFFERPOOL_EMPTY>,
<*NOT* DATABASE_CLOSED, FILE_CLOSED, BUFFER_ALLOCATED, BUFFERPOOL_EMPTY>,
<DATABASE_OPENED, FILE_CLOSED, BUFFER_ALLOCATED, BUFFERPOOL_EMPTY>,
<*NOT* DATABASE_OPENED, FILE_CLOSED, BUFFER_ALLOCATED, BUFFERPOOL_EMPTY>,
<DATABASE_CLOSED, FILE_CLOSED, *NOT* BUFFER_ALLOCATED, BUFFERPOOL_EMPTY),
<*NOT* DATABASE_CLOSED, FILE_CLOSED, *NOT* BUFFER_ALLOCATED, BUFFERPOOL_EMPTY>,
<DATABASE_CLOSED, *NOT* FILE_CLOSED, BUFFER_ALLOCATED, BUFFERPOOL_EMPTY>,
<*NOT* DATABASE_CLOSED, *NOT* FILE_CLOSED, BUFFER_ALLOCATED, BUFFERPOOL_EMPTY>,
<DATABASE_OPENED, *NOT* FILE_CLOSED, BUFFER_ALLOCATED, BUFFERPOOL_EMPTY>,
. . . }

<Figure 8 The possible landmark values of the buffer_read>

As shown in Figure 8, its pre-conditions are "disk'S STATE_IN DATABASE_OPENED", "file'S STATE_IN FILE_OPENED" and "page'S STATE_IN BUFFER_ALLOCATED." And its post-conditions are "file'S STATE_IN FILE_CLOSED" and "bufferpool'S STATE_IN PAGE_VALID." That is, it is feasible to classify the possible landmark values according to the status of IPCs, as shown in Figure 9. Then the number of meaningful landmark values of buffer_read IPC can be reduced to six types. The set of meaningful landmark values is shown in Figure 10. The heuristic for defining meaningful landmark values of information processing components is as Figure 11.

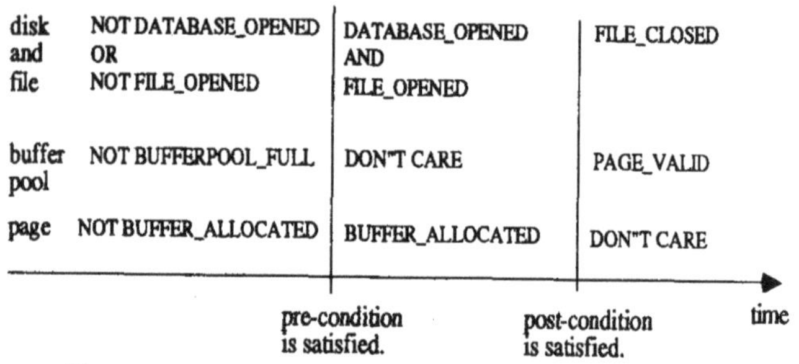

<Figure 9 Meaningful landmark values of buffer_read>

3.4 Qualitative states of IPCs

The qualitative state in the qualitative simulation are a pair <qval, qdir>, where qval is landmark value and qdir is the direction of changes. As the semantics of qdir in physical and software systems are different, the qualitative states is defined as definition 2.

In the temporal qualitative modeling of software systems, it is more important to represent the state changes of a module, together with the information about the moment when the module is called. Thus, the semantics of qdir is changed to {before, during, after} of the execution time interval of information processing components. The semantics of landmark values is changed to represented the changes of states of information processing components.

Definition 2 Let $l_1 < \ldots < l_k$ be the meaningful landmark values of an parameter of an information processing component whose discrete reasonable function is f: $[a, b] \rightarrow \mathbb{R}^*$. For any $t \in [a, b]$, QS(f, t), the qualitative state of f at time t, is a pair <qval, qdir>, defined as follows:

(1)

$$qval = \begin{cases} l_j & \text{if } f(t) = l_j \text{, a landmark va} \\ (l_j,\ l_{j+1}) & \text{if } f(t) \in (l_j,\ l_{j+1}) \end{cases}$$

(2)

$$qdir = \begin{cases} \text{before,} & \text{if qval =} \\ \text{during,} & \text{if qval =} \\ \text{after,} & \text{if qval =} \end{cases}$$

A system is a set $F = \{f_1, \ldots, f_m\}$ of discrete reasonable functions f: $[a, b] \rightarrow \mathbb{R}^*$, each with its own set of landmarks and distinguished time-points. The qualitative state of a system F of m functions is the m-tuple of individual qualitative states:

$$QS(F, t_i) = QS(<f_1, \ldots, f_m>, t_i)$$

1. Define the components of possible landmark values. The name of IPCs appearing in the pre-condition and post-condition become the components.
2. Identify the set of states each component can have.
3. The set of possible landmark values is the Cartesian products of the states of the components.
4. Among the set of possible landmark values, divide the set of landmark values according to the landmark value satisfying pre- and post-conditions. The other possible landmark values are divided again into the following groups.
1) Possible landmark values satisfying only the set of the components in pre-condition
2) Possible landmark values satisfying only the set of the components in post-condition
3) Possible landmark values satisfying the components varied during its operation
4) Possible landmark values satisfying any of the components before pre-condition
5) Possible landmark values satisfying any of the components after post-condition
6) Possible landmark values satisfying none of the components.

<Figure 10 Heuristics for meaningful landmark values>

The set of meaningful landmark values =
{ < DATABASE_OPENED, FILE_OPENED, BUFFER_ALLOCATED, *NOT* BUFFERPOOL_FULL> (by 1) in Figure 5),
< *, FILE_CLOSED, PAGE_VALID, *> (by 2) in Figure 5),
< DATABASE_OPENED, FILE_OPENED, BUFFER_ALLOCATED, *NOT* BUFFERPOOL_FULL>
< DATABASE_OPENED, FILE_OPENED, PAGE_VALID, *NOT* BUFFERPOOL_FULL>
< DATABASE_OPENED, FILE_CLOSED, BUFFER_ALLOCATED, *NOT* BUFFERPOOL_FULL>
< DATABASE_OPENED, FILE_CLOSED, PAGE_VALID, *NOT* BUFFERPOOL_FULL> (by 3) in Figure 5),
< DATABASE_OPENED, *, *, *>
<*, FILE_OPENED, *, *>
{*, *, BUFFER_ALLOCATED, *>
<*, *, *, *NOT* BUFFERPOOL_FULL>, (by 4) in Figure 5),
<*, FILE_CLOSED, *, *>
<*, *, PAGE_VALID, *> (by 5) in Figure 5),
< Others > (by 6) in Figure 5),
}

<Figure 11 The meaningful landmark values of the buffer_read IPC>

$$QS(F, t_i, t_{i+1}) = [QS(<f_1, \ldots, f_m, t_i>, t_{i+1})].$$

The qualitative behavior of F is the sequence of qualitative states of F:

$$QS(F, t_0), QS(F, t_0, t_1), QS(F, t_1), \ldots, QS(F, t_n).$$

For example, the buffer_read IPC has six parameters such as {disk, file, bufferpool, page }. Then the system F of buffer_read IPC is $\{f_{disk}, f_{file}, f_{bufferpool}, f_{page}\}$. The reason of integrating the qualitative states of individual discrete meaningful functions into a tuple is that no state change can be occurred unless all of parameters meet the pre- or post-conditions.

3.5 Qualitative constraints of information processing component

The purpose of qualitative constraints is modeling of the structure of a system. The structure of database management systems can be modeled as a collection of information processing components interconnected one another. Thus, there are two types of qualitative constraints: inter-components constraints and intra-components constraints. The interconnections among information processing components are modeled by inter-components constraints, while intra-component constraints describe the organization of sub-IPCs in an information processing components. A constraints can be modeled as inter- or intra-components constraints depending on the viewpoints of analyzers.

When the viewpoint of analyzer is focused on the internal behavior of one information processing components, the interior structure of the IPC is modeled as internal constraints. As there is no interconnections from/to its outside environment, the internal constraints can describe the structure only in a general way. The internal qualitative constraints are equivalent to device models of electrical components such as resistor and condenser.

In case of qualitative modeling based on differential equations, the qualitative constraints such as ADD, MULTI, MINUS and DERIV are sufficient to simulate the behavior of the qualitatively modeled systems. But, for the qualitative modeling based on finite state machines, another qualitative constraint for representing the state transitions between landmark values. We propose a new qualitative constraint called CHANGES. The formal definition of CHANGES is as follows:

Definition 3 CHANGES(f, g) is a two-place predicate on discrete reasonable functions f, g: $[a, b] \rightarrow \mathbf{R}^*$ which holds iff f(t) changes landmark of g(t) for any $t \in [a, b]$.

4. Conclusion

SQM is a knowledge-based software metrics management system that makes use of application domain in order to establish consistent software measurement environment. In [7], IPCs was proposed as software components for the SQM. In this paper, design principles and a formal structure, which consists of name, teleology, structure, behavior and causality parts, of IPCs have been introduced. The proposed generic structure has been refined and formally represented in BNF syntax.

As one of the application area of IPCs, we have proposed their their modular, qualitative behavior generation mechanism. The proposed mechanism is based on qualitative modeling and simulation, thus produces a sequence of temporal state transitions of modeled IPCs. The proposed modeling mechanism aims to facilitate the scientific measurement of DBMSs. Further works include implementation and evaluation of the proposed qualitative behavior generation mechanism.

References

1. T. J. Biggerstaff and A. J. Perlis, Software Reusability, Volume 1 Concepts and Models, ACM Press, 1990.
2. N. Fenton, Software Metrics, A Rigorous Approach,. Chapman & Hall, 1991.
3. B. J. Kuipers, Qualitative Simulation," Artificial Intelligence, Vol. 29, No. 3, September 1986, pp. 289-338.
4. S. Lee and S. Sluizer, "An Executable language for Modeling Simple Behavior," IEEE Transactions on Software Engineering, Vol. 17, No.6, 1991, pp. 527-543.
5. J. Neighbors, Software Construction using Components, Technical Report # 160, University of California, Irvine, 1980.
6. S. H. Oh, Y. J. Lee and M. H. Kim, "A Management Discipline of Software Metrics and the Software Quality Manager," International Journal of Software Engineering and Knowledge Engineering,Vol.2, No.3, 1992.
7. S. H. Oh, Y. J. Lee and M. H. Kim, "Design of Information Processing Components in the Data Management Domain," Proceedings of 1st International Conference on Information and Knowledge Management, Baltimore, USA, November 1992.
8. S. H. Oh, Y. J. Lee and M. H. Kim, "A Qualitative Quality Evaluation Scheme of Information Systems," Proceedings of 3rd European Conference on Software Quality, Madrid, Spain, November, 1992.
9. R. Prieto-Diaz, "Domain Analysis for Reusability," Proceedings of IEEE COMPSAC, 1987.
10. H. Weber and H. Ehrig, "Specification of Modular Systems," IEEE Transactions on Software Engineering, Vol.SE-12, No.7, July 1986, pp.784-798.
11. B. C. Williams, "Qalitative Analysis of MOS circuits," Artificial Intelligence, Vol.24, 1984, pp.281-346.

A MULTIMEDIA DATABASE
FOR AN ADVANCED TELESHOPPING APPLICATION

D. Maino[1], F. Mercalli[1], R. Negrini[2]

1 - Centro di Cultura Scientifica "Alessandro Volta" - Villa Olmo, Como - Italy
2 - Politecnico di Milano - p.za Leonardo Da Vinci 32, Milano - Italy

ABSTRACT

This paper illustrates some issues arising when designing an advanced teleshopping system based on a multimedia database. In particular, it is focused on a conceptual model (MMAIN) able to support the multimedia database. The studies here reported are part of the RACE Project ESSAI, whose goal is to implement by the end of 1994 a prototype teleshopping system based on advanced multimedia technologies. A large multimedia catalogue of products to be sold is to be implemented as part of the system. The high quality of multimedia data and the high flexibility of the data model required by such a system make the ESSAI multimedia database a rather advanced prototype.

1. INTRODUCTION

Multimedia technology opens the road to completely new ways to conceive computer applications. As a consequence, completely new ways of defining and manipulating data managed by those applications are needed.

The ESSAI Project, sponsored by the Commission of the European Communities under the RACE II Programme, is not an exception: it aims at implementing a teleshopping system prototype - made possible by the development of new hardware technologies - whose data management requirements are not adequately covered by traditional database management techniques.

For this reason, research activities have been started in the frame of the project in order to first define the peculiar requirements, in terms of data management, of this kind of application and secondly to design a feasible solution.

Various databases are present in ESSAI; in this paper we will concentrate on the most innovative one, i.e., the multimedia database containing information about products to be sold through the system.

At present, the requirement analysis has been completed and a conceptual model for the data has been sketched.

The goal of this paper is to outline these main conclusions, on which the implementation of the ESSAI prototype will be based.

In section 2 an overview of the whole ESSAI system is given, in order to better focus the problem. In section 3 the basic requirements for multimedia data management are listed. In section 4 a conceptual model capable to support the ESSAI multimedia database, called MMAIN, is discussed. In section 5 a logical architecture for a system supporting MMAIN is presented. In section 6 some conclusion remarks are reported. In Appendix A a summary of MMAIN concepts is presented.

2. THE ESSAI SYSTEM

The aim of the RACE II Project ESSAI is to implement by the end of 1994 a prototype teleshopping application based on an Integrated Broadband Communication network (IBC network).

The fundamental idea underlying the ESSAI Project is to show that, as the communication networks will offer more and more bandwidth at lower prices, the implementation of a teleshopping system based on many low cost *vending terminals* connected to a unique *control center*, in which almost all the processing power needed by the system is located, becomes achievable.

This will allow the installation of many terminals in a large number of sites where the setting up of a traditional shop is not practicable, greatly extending the market of the companies that will exploit the system.

The vending terminal should offer to the end-user a nice multimedia interface, in order to persuade her/him to buy the offered products.

If all the computing power is to be located in the control center, a large amount of information of disparate kinds should flow between the control center and the vending terminals: this justifies the need for an IBC network.

The overall architecture of the system, stemming from these preliminary considerations, is illustrated in figure 1.

Three main actor types are involved in the architecture of figure 1: the *service provider*, which is the company that will offer and manage the teleshopping system, the *good suppliers*, which are the companies that will exploit the teleshopping service in order to sell goods to their customers, and the *end-users*, which are the customers that buy goods through the vending terminals.

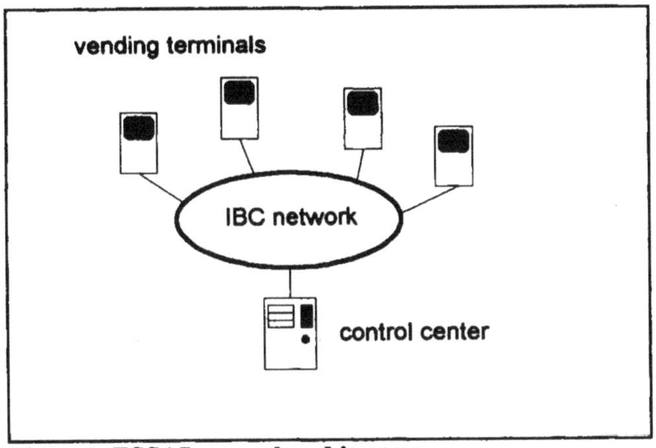

Figure1. ESSAI general architecture.

The vending terminal is the most important component in determining the success of the system on the end-user side. It is important to design a man-machine interface able to *attract* end-users. This means not only that a multimedia user interface is needed, but also that the quality of media data should be as high as possible.
A high resolution graphic display and a hi-fi reproduction system will be used for the output of data. For data input, it has been decided to make extensive use of a touch screen device, since it represents the most intuitive form of data input available on the market.
Besides the multimedia user interface above sketched, the terminal should feature a payment system, based on some sort of electronic payment form, such as a credit or debit card, in order to make it possible for the end-user to pay the goods she/he chooses.
This involves two more types of actor, a *payment authorization center* and a *bank*, that will interact with the teleshopping system through the service provider.
For what concerns goods delivery, immaterial goods, such as for instance cinema movies, may be directly delivered by the vending terminal through ticket printing, while material goods, as for instance a photo camera, may be indirectly delivered by mail; in this later case the terminal will hand out to the end-user a voucher, proving the purchase of the good.
In the control center three main components are present: the *payment system*, the *availability database* and the *catalogue database*.
The payment system is in charge to obtain from the terminal the payment data relative to the end-user, for instance data read from the credit card, and to ask the necessary payment authorization.

The availability database is the database containing information concerning the availability of the goods to be sold.
This is substantially derived from the stock databases of the good suppliers.
The catalogue database is the system in charge to manage all information about the products offered by good suppliers; it is, in a sense, the ESSAI electronic form of the usual paper catalogues that a supplier prepares for his customers. The catalogue database should show in the most comprehensive way the supplier offer.
The catalogue database is the most innovative kind of database present in the ESSAI teleshopping system since it must store and control a large amount of multimedia information, which is peculiar also in the requirements it imposes on the system in charge to manage it.

3. BASIC REQUIREMENTS

The catalogue database of ESSAI is the multimedia database management system (MMDB), which is in charge to manage data presenting the products available for sale through the teleshopping application.
These are mainly advertisement data and, as such, they are the product of the creative mind of an artist. This is a very important consideration, since it means that the MMDB cannot be based on a very rigid data model: it would be impossible to ask an artist to work following a predefined rigid scheme because her/his work has to be included in a computer system. Moreover, as opposed to usual data management environments, the external appearance of the data becomes as important as its content.
For this reason, we need a data model allowing extreme flexibility not just in defining how data are structured but also in defining how data are to be presented to the end-user.
In order to cope with this important requirement, information stored in the MMDB should include two different types of data: *content data* and *layout data*.
Content data is data as usually conceived: in the case of ESSAI it will be text, image, sound etc. to be shown or played at the teleshopping terminal.
Layout data - which is not considered in traditional database management systems - carries the information concerning how content data is to be externally organized and represented. This idea is not a new one: it has been included in ODA standard [2)] and it has been recognized as fundamental in many works [3)] [4)] but it becomes vital for the presentation of information to the end-user of a teleshopping application.
From the end-user point of view, it is clear that a teleshopping system will be accepted only if it will be able to simulate in the closest way the real selling world. End-users should be faced only with the buying activity, which they execute everyday and for which no training is needed.

This implies a couple of important consequences on the MMDB component of ESSAI.

A first requirement is to support *multimedia queries*. If the usual way to sell goods is to be simulated as close as possible, besides the traditional hierarchical catalogue search and the traditional queries based on alphanumeric data, multimedia queries should also be considered. In other words, multimedia data such as images and sound should not be simply attached to the traditional textual information, but should play a significant role as *active components*, that is, components that can be involved directly in query formulation.

For example, when a customer asks a shop assistant to show her all hats of a given style she is formulating a query on an image - the image of the hat - and the shop assistant answers with a collection of hats - similar to each other - much in the way a usual DBMS answers to a query with a collection of records having some properties in common.

In order to accomplish this task, an appropriate access method for multimedia data must be provided. As actually happens in traditional Information Retrieval Systems for textual information, indexes must be derived from multimedia data too. Indexes in this case take the more general name of *access structures*. A query involving multimedia data will determine a search into these access structures.

The current state-of-the-art in the image and sound processing fields seems not to allow the automatic generation of the access structures. Though this may be further investigated, it seems more reasonable to study methodologies and/or tools to support the manual generation of them.

A query language able to express multimedia queries should define, in addition to the usual operators, those ones needed to specify conditions on multimedia data.

It should be possible, for instance, to apply on image data CONTAINS, SIMILAR and ATTRIBUTE operators. The operator CONTAINS means "search for images containing a particular subimage"; SIMILAR means "search for images similar to a specified image"; ATTRIBUTE means "search for images with a particular attribute (color, brightness, etc.)".

A second requirement is the use of the hypermedia paradigm when organizing information. Consider, for instance, a person entering a shop to buy a camera. He initially looks at a rack full of cameras, which may be regarded as a first hypermedia node. Then he chooses a camera and asks the shop clerk to show it, getting a more detailed view corresponding to a second hypermedia node. Then, for instance, he asks the price, getting a third hypermedia node, which in this case is not an image but a sound item: the voice of the clerk answering the question.

It is worth to stress that customers are not tied to a predefined path to get information. Different customers may choose to "read" different "nodes" and to read them in different orders. This implies that the traditional way to linearly organize the information is impracticable. Hypermedia is a must. The MMDB component of ESSAI should thus be provided with functionalities to support hypermedia technology.

A last important requirement is the ability to manage multilanguage information. In fact, among the most appropriate sites to install ESSAI vending terminals there are airports and railway stations, where a lot of people speaking many different languages are likely to be attracted by the teleshopping application. A way to easily manage the representation of printed and spoken information in different languages is to be found.

4. DISCUSSION OF THE MMAIN MODEL

Taking into account the basic requirements illustrated in section 3, a conceptual model for the multimedia catalogue database of the ESSAI system called *MMAIN* (*M*odel for *M*ultimedia *A*dvertisement *IN*terfaces) is discussed in this section.

From the technical point of view, the main characteristic of advertisement data is its loose structuring. This is in contrast with traditional computer application areas, as for example office automation, where generally data possess, or should possess, a well defined structure.

Moreover, a large number of different media data should be supported at best.

According to these concepts, we devised a paradigm, to support the ESSAI catalogue database, derived from the one used in making movies. It uses fundamentally the notion of *scene*, composed by a set of *multimedia items*.

These are two well-known concepts for movie directors, who create movies by grouping together different scenes, each scene being in turn constructed by means of several items, at least an image sequence and a sound track.

In the ESSAI teleshopping application, in addition, it will be possible to have concurrently on the terminal screen still pictures, graphic animations, moving video, text and, most important, it will be possible for the end-user to interact with all these items through, for instance, screen buttons, joysticks, speech recognition.

In MMAIN, a scene is a set of text, sound, images (still or moving), etc. to be presented in the same interval of time, according to a well-defined layout structure. It can be thought as the unit of presentation on the teleshopping terminal, much in the same way a transparency is the unit of presentation in a conference speech.

A scene can also be viewed as a sort of container for multimedia data. You can imagine it as an interval on a temporal axis with a starting point and a ending point. Between these two points different *multimedia items* rise, live and die.

In figure 2 the scene concept is graphically represented.

The multimedia items composing a scene are of different types - images, audio, text etc. - and for this reason they exist in fundamentally different ways. Nevertheless they all have in common three attributes that clearly locate and characterize them within a scene: a *start time* - relative to the beginning of the scene - a *duration* and a *content*.

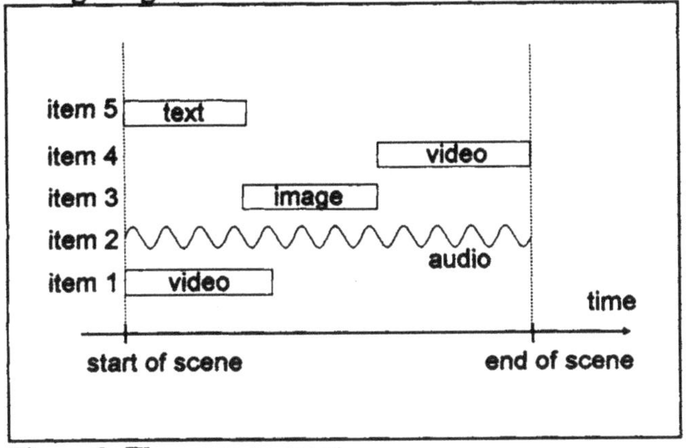

Figure 2. The scene concept

This is modeled introducing the type *MMItem*, representing the general case of multimedia item, featuring the attributes *StartTime*, *Duration* and *Content*.
The StartTime and the Duration attributes are the first components of the layout data mentioned in section 3. The underlying assumption here is that a generic multimedia item has its own, limited life.
Within the scene context an item may start at a generic point in time, not necessarily corresponding to the scene beginning, specified by the value of StartTime.
The Duration attribute represents the amount of time the item stands on the scene. The duration is limited to a maximum corresponding to the total scene duration.
The Content attribute represents the content data mentioned in section 3. In the most general case the Content attribute consists of a *BLOB* (*B*inary *L*arge *OB*ject), since for a generic MMItem the structure of the contained information is unspecified.
Further attributes forming layout data of a multimedia item depend on the particular type of the item itself.
For example, to model items that can appear on the screen - such as images, video sequences or text - a more specific type *VisualItem* is derived from MMItem. Besides inheriting the three MMItem attributes, VisualItem objects have additional attributes referring to their spatial representation: *XPosition*, *YPosition*, *ScaleFactor* and *RotationAngle*. Moreover, two attributes related to the temporal behavior of a generic VisualItem have been introduced: *RiseTime* and *FallTime*. They can be used to specify cross-fading effects.
An *AudioItem*, on the other hand, will have the additional attributes *Volume* and *Tone*.
These observations lead to the definition of a type hierarchy for multimedia items, which is depicted in figure 3. In this figure three further items are derived from VisualItem: *ImageItem* representing still pictures, *VideoItem* for full motion video and *TextItem* for the usual text.

As above mentioned, one can imagine the activity of creating a scene like as the making of a scene by a movie director. Continuing with this parallel, when a set of good scenes has been collected, the director proceeds in the editing of the movie, following her/his own favorite, well-defined, order. This means that, in MMAIN, a way should be also provided for the definition of a structure that plays

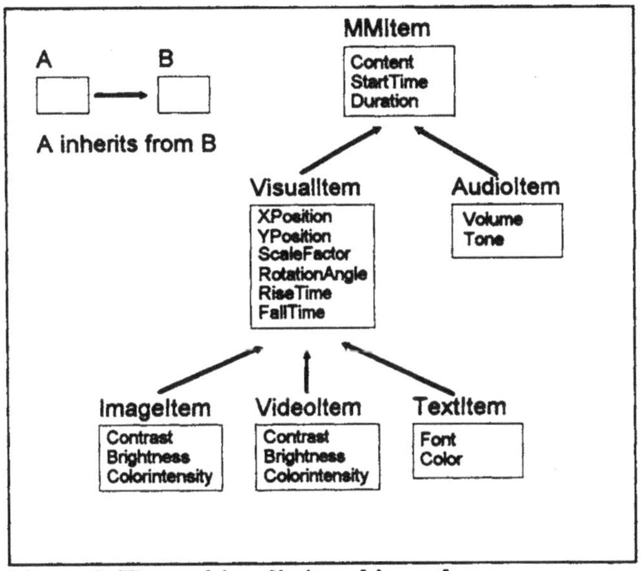

Figure 3. The multimedia item hierarchy

the role of the movie itself, that is a sort of container for scenes. This structure is called *presentation*.
Like a movie, a presentation is a set of related scenes, but with a major difference: the movie is an ordered sequence of scenes, an the order is defined by the director once and for all. This means, as everyone knows, that no interaction is possible between the audience and the movie.
On the contrary, in the MMAIN presentation an user should be allowed to interact with the system to change the order of scenes displaying.
Consider for instance a presentation for a car: there will be scenes regarding engine features, internal look, general performances and so on. An user should be allowed to jump with very few constraints from a scene to another, in order to examine those details in which she/he is particularly interested.
In figure 4 the presentation and movie parallel is shown.
It is clear that a non-trivial way to bind scenes in a presentation must be provided. The better solution is to exploit the hypermedia paradigm. In this paradigm information is organized in a non linear way by subdividing it into chunks, called *nodes*, and providing connections among them, called *links* 1).
In the ESSAI case, nodes correspond to scenes, and links may be used to connect related scenes, as above mentioned.
Links between scenes are activated through *anchors*, which are special items attached to the scene whose selection

allows to walk along the corresponding link. The main type of anchor in ESSAI will be a button on the touch screen of the selling terminal, but other solutions as for instance "audio buttons" activated through speech recognition, or physical input devices activated by some sort of mechanical action, are possible.

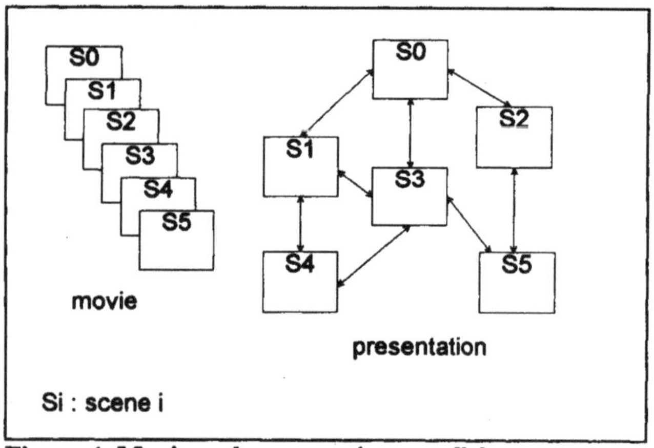

Figure 4. Movie and presentation parallel

Two more concepts complete the definition of MMAIN: the concept of *perspective* and the concept of *synchronization* of MMItem objects inside a scene.

The basic idea underlying the perspective concept is that information is an abstract entity that, in order to be communicated to a human being, must take one of many possible concrete representations. We say that a given information may be presented from different *perspectives*[1)].

The notion of perspective may be useful in many different cases. For example, it can be used in solving the multilanguage problem mentioned in section 3. We can imagine, for instance, an advertisement regarding a car: generally a good mixture of images, sound and text will be useful for explaining all the features of the car. But text and speech items should be displayed or played in the language of the end-user. So information that is to be displayed as text or played as speech may have different perspectives, each perspective corresponding to its translation in a given language.

The perspective concept may be useful in many other cases. For example, since sound items result completely unuseful for deaf people, information represented by default as voice explanations can have other perspectives associated, representing it as a text.

The concept of *synchronization* among multimedia items is needed to better control item behavior within a scene in time domain.

In fact, items in a scene are frequently related to each other in the temporal axis and cannot begin and display freely.

In normal situations the *StartTime* and the *Duration* attribute above defined may suffice to define these temporal relationships but in abnormal cases more specific information is needed.

Think, for instance, to the most simple case of synchronized items: a video sequence and its sound track. If no problems occur, it may be enough to specify the same start time and duration for both items, in order to get things work fine. But if the video sequence is delayed for some reason, the system should also postpone the start time of the sound track in order to still have audio and video synchronized. Problems like these are likely to occur in the ESSAI environment, since, as explained in section 2, multimedia data items travel through a network and thus may suffer random delays.

To deal with this problem, in MMAIN two main abstractions have been introduced: *sequential rendering* and *simultaneous rendering*.

Two items are sequentially rendered if the start time of the first plus its duration must be equal to the start time of the second.

Two items are simultaneously rendered if their start time must be equal.

In Appendix A a more formal definition of MMAIN is given. This is a not a complete result since research activities are still ongoing, but it can be nevertheless useful to better fix the ideas discussed in this section.

5. LOGICAL ARCHITECTURE

In figure 5, the logical architecture of a system supporting MMAIN, is illustrated.

At the top level it is composed of three major blocks.

The first block contains the *MultiMedia Storage Subsystem*, which provides storage containers for multimedia data and maintains information for retrieving these data (the *access structures*). The MultiMedia Storage Subsystem has to take care of data retrieval and, if necessary, of short term recovery. It is the real database engine for MMAIN.

A second block is composed by the *Data Analyzer* and *Data Formatter* modules; the first module should be able to analyze multimedia data (image, sound, text etc.), in order to construct for each of them the appropriate access structures to be stored in a portion of the database. The second module should be able to format (compress) data in order to store them in a convenient way. The operations performed by this block may be carried out off-line.

A third block is responsible for the interaction with the teleshopping application and is composed by the following parts. The *Query Composer* is the module that interacts with the application in order to get queries formulated by the user.

Queries may be specified in an implicit and non-precise way, for instance touching an object on the screen, and asking to get information on all objects similar to it. The Query Composer should be able to compose a precise query expressed in a formal query language, possibly starting from an unprecise one. The *Query Processor* should analyze the query elaborated by the Query Composer and, after having performed some checks on it, should decompose, optimize and send it to the MultiMedia Storage Subsystem. The *Hypermedia Browser* is in charge to manage the navigation among nodes, through anchors and links. Finally, The *Scene Builder* should provide the application with the retrieved data and manage all the directives useful for their presentation to the end-user.

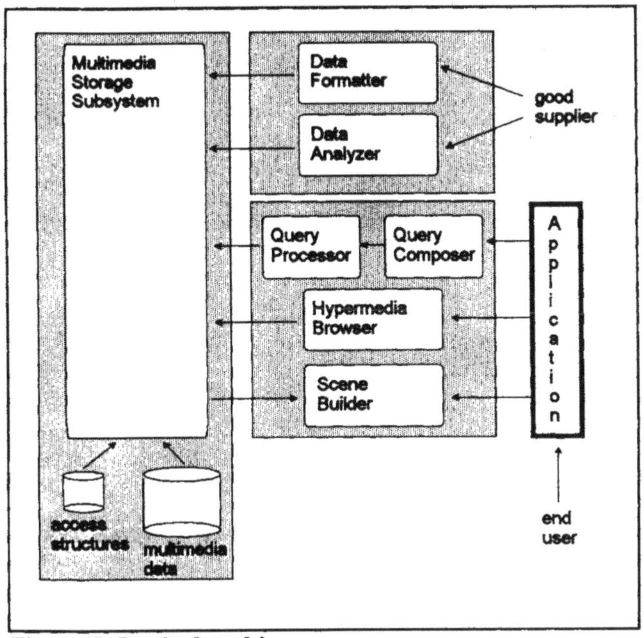

Figure 5. Logical architecture.

6. CONCLUSIONS

In this paper, the requirements in terms of data management needed by an advanced teleshopping system, being developed in the frame of the RACE II ESSAI Project, have been analyzed. The most important of them are: extreme flexibility, non-linear browsing of information and multiple language management.
A conceptual model satisfying those requirements, called MMAIN, has been proposed.
The MMAIN model solves the problem of flexibility by defining data through an inheritance hierarchy that can be specialized as needed and by introducing the concept of *layout data*.
The problem of non-linear browsing has been solved including the hypermedia paradigm, while multiple languages are managed through the *perspective* concept.
A logical architecture for a system to support MMAIN has also been presented. Future work will be directed to the implementation of such a system.
The step we are at present undertaking in ESSAI is to evaluate if, among existing multimedia authoring toolkits, there are systems that possess enough functionalities to be extended so as to include all MMAIN concepts. If this will reveal impossible, an ad-hoc system will be developed inside ESSAI.

7. ACKNOWLEDGEMENTS

The authors would like to acknowledge the other companies involved in the ESSAI Project Consortium that made possible the work reported in this paper.
These companies are: COSI (I), ASCOM AUTELCA (CH), SEVA (I), THOMSON-CSF L.E.R. (F), SYSECA (F), OST (F), STZ (D), ELEKTRONIK CENTRALEN (DK), ASCOM TECH (CH), ETH Zurich (CH), SNV (D).

APPENDIX A

Based on the discussion presented in section 4, in this appendix we try to give a more precise definition of the MMAIN model, in terms of data types and operations, using an object-oriented-like notation.

```
class DataBase {
        DBPresentations : setof (Presentation);
operations:
        GetPresentation(Name : String):Presentation;
        SendQuery(Query:String):setof(Presentation);
}

class Presentation {
        Name : String;
        Scenes : setof (SID) ;
        HyperMediaLinks : setof (Link);
operations:
        StartScene() : SID;
                // get first scene to be played
        FollowLink(Source : SID, Anchor : AID) : SID;
                // follow link activated by Anchor
}

class Scene {
        Identifier : SID;
        MultimediaItems : setof(MMID);
        Anchors : setof(AID);
operations:
        GetSimultaneous(Item : MMID) : setof(MMID);
                // Get MMItems to be simultaneously
                // rendered with Item
        GetSequential(Item : MMID) : setof(MMID);
                // Get MMItems to be sequentially
                // rendered with Item
}

class Link {
        SourceScene : SID;
        SourceAnchor : AID;
        DestinationScene : SID;
}
```

```
class MMItem {
        Identifier : MMID;
        Content : BLOB;
        StartTime : Time;
        Duration : Time;
}

class VisualItem is_a MMItem {
        XPosition : Integer;
        YPosition : Integer;
        ScaleFactor : Real;
        RotationAngle : Real;
        RiseTime : Time;
        FallTime : Time;
}

class AudioItem is_a MMItem {
        Volume : Integer;
        Tone : Integer;
}

class ImageItem is_a VisualItem {
        Contrast : Integer;
        Brightness : Integer;
        ColorIntensity : Integer;
}

class VideoItem is_a VisualItem {
        Contrast : Integer;
        Brightness : Integer;
        ColorIntensity : Integer;
}

class TextItem is_a VisualItem {
        Font : FontType;
        Color : RGB;
}

class MMAnchor {
        Identifier : AID;
        // ... to be further investigated;
}
```

SID, MMID and AID are object identifier internally generated and managed by the system.

REFERENCES

1) F. Garzotto, P. Paolini, D. Schwabe, "Authoring-in-the-large: Software Engineering Techniques for Hypertext Application Design", in Proceedings of the Sixth International Workshop on Software Specification and Design, Como, 1991, pp. 193-201.

2) ISO, Information Processing: Text and Office Systems: Office Document Architecture (ODA) and Interchange Formats, (ISO 8613, 1989), Parts 1-8.

3) Magda M. Mourad, "Object Representation for Multimedia Document Interchange", presented at the Conference ICC 1991;

4) C. Thanos, Multimedia Office Filing, (North-Holland, 1990, Amsterdam), Ch. 3 pp. 17-52.

AUTHOR INDEX

www.ingramcontent.com/pod-product-compliance
Lightning Source LLC
LaVergne TN
LVHW070142271026
850861LV00064B/68
9789810213800